# THE VIETNAM WAR
# AND INTERNATIONAL LAW

Volume 4

# The Vietnam War and International Law

*The Concluding Phase*

## AMERICAN SOCIETY OF INTERNATIONAL LAW

EDITED BY

RICHARD A. FALK

Volume 4

Princeton University Press

Princeton, New Jersey

1976

Printed in the United States of America

by Princeton University Press

To the Memory
of
Wolfgang Friedmann
Jurist and Gentleman
*par excellence*

# Note of Acknowledgments

THE PUBLICATION of this fourth and final volume was facilitated by the help and cooperation of many persons. I am particularly grateful to authors and publishers for granting us permission to reprint material. Detailed permissions appear in the back of the volume.

I would also like to thank members of the Civil War Panel of the American Society of International Law for their continuing interest and participation in this editorial venture, undertaken to assemble the critical materials bearing on legal aspects of the American involvement in the Vietnam War.

Once again, also, Princeton University Press has made it possible for us to bring this project to a natural conclusion. Sanford Thatcher of the Press has been helpful at every stage.

Andrea Praeger bore the main burden of detail in assembling the volume and Janet Lowenthal devoted some energy to preparing the final version of the manuscript for the publisher. It is a pleasure to thank both of these talented, vivacious research assistants of mine for so graciously coping with the frustrations of this kind of task, where for every detail dealt with three more emerge in its place. June Traube, as my secretary, contributed her multiple skills, also most graciously, to this endeavor. The work was rendered more pleasant and efficient by being carried out under the auspices of the Center of International Studies at Princeton University.

RICHARD A. FALK

# Contents

# THE VIETNAM WAR
# AND INTERNATIONAL LAW

## Volume 4

# Introduction*

OVER THE past several years the Civil War Panel of the American Society of International Law has devoted considerable attention to the legal issues presented by the Vietnam War. Because of the complex and controversial character of these legal issues, the Panel has emphasized the educational importance of a balanced presentation of conflicting interpretations by competent scholars and public officials. To this end the Panel has sponsored a series of volumes published under the general title *The Vietnam War and International Law*. This fourth volume brings the series, but not necessarily the work of the Panel, to a close. The Panel is also sponsoring a parallel set of volumes on *The Arab-Israeli Conflict* under the editorship of John Norton Moore. The first three of these volumes will be published by Princeton University Press in 1975, and a subsequent fourth volume is under active consideration.

As with earlier volumes the Panel has selected those writings on legal questions that are of high intellectual quality and that seem representative of the main positions in controversy. We have sought a balanced presentation of controversial material to the extent that the published literature allows it. In addition, we have solicited some new contributions for this final volume to achieve balance and to fill some gaps; but as is common in such a venture, not everything solicited was provided, even after written contributions had been promised. To some degree, imbalances in prior volumes are offset by opposite imbalances in this.

Section I contains five selections, two of which have not been previously published, that touch on general aspects of the relevance of international law to the Vietnam War. The initial selection by John Norton Moore, an active member of the Panel, seeks to assess the overall relevance of international law perspectives to the formation of national security policy; its approach clearly reflects the author's sense of the Vietnam experience. Edwin Brown Firmage, also a member of the Panel, has contributed a piece that explores the interplay of domestic and global legal perspectives vis-à-vis the sort of war/peace issues raised by the Vietnam War. Perry L. Pickert's study of "American Attitudes Toward International Law as Reflected in 'The Pentagon Papers' " is the first serious attempt to reconsider the international

* This Introduction was prepared for the Panel by the Editor of the volume.

law debate of the late 1960's in light of the new documentary material made available through the publication of the Pentagon Papers. Two further selections examine whether or not the United Nations system could play a more effective role in Vietnam-type conflicts.

Section II extends the consideration given in volumes 2 and 3 to special questions arising from interpretations of the laws of war. Some of these questions were provoked by specialized contexts, such as the use of herbicides and unofficial repatriation of prisoners of war; others involve perennial questions of the laws of war, such as treatment of prisoners of war or the law of air warfare, as reconsidered in the Vietnam context. Controversies over observation and violation of the laws of war are important concerns for the international lawyer. Monitoring the adequacy of these laws and interpreting the attitudes of governments toward compliance is especially necessary under modern conditions in which the technology and doctrines of warfare are undergoing such rapid and profound change. Internal warfare of the sort that took place in South Vietnam during the past decade presents a series of vital questions as to the adequacy and limits of international law under a variety of battlefield situations. Certainly, one impulse toward the modernization of the law of war, much of which dates back to the pre-World War I period, stems from perceived inadequacy in Vietnam-type settings.

Inquiry into the laws of war is intimately linked to the focus in Section III on issues of individual responsibility arising from their violation. A combat soldier is generally held criminally responsible for violations of the laws of war, and service field manuals confirm this responsibility. However, there is widespread disagreement on the corpus of applicable international law and on the extent to which legal responsibility should be imposed higher in the chain of civilian and military command. On the surface, this disagreement involves determining whether alleged violations of the laws of war are systematic and deliberate expressions of official policy. Underneath these arguments about facts and intentions are some elaborate juridical controversies that relate to the legal status and relevance of the Nuremberg experience, and to the assessment of individual responsibility of national leaders. In this context the Nuremberg experience refers both to the war-crimes trials held after World War II and to the International Law Commission's 1950 formulation of Principles embodied in the Nuremberg Judgment.

Section IV considers the legal issues surrounding the settlement of the Vietnam War. There are important theoretical questions bearing on how wars end when neither side achieves a military victory, but the selections in Section IV are more closely focused upon the negotiations of the settlement, the documents of settlement, and the disappointing record of implementation. Given the background, which centrally includes the so-called Second Indochina War spawned by the insufficiency of the Geneva Accords of 1954, there is an understandable anxiety that failures to implement the 1973 Paris Agreement may generate yet another Indochina War. All parties to the Paris Agreement allege that their adversaries have acted in substantial and persistent violation of the obligations assumed. On the accuracy of this accusation, and on this alone, can one find unanimous agreement among the four original Paris signatories. Impartial observers also share the view that the bargain which took several years, considerable drama, and much anguish to negotiate in Paris has not been implemented. At the same time, the Paris Agreement was successful in bringing home American POW's and provisionally ending the direct combat role of the United States.

The debate of a decade over the legal propriety of the war provoked a major domestic reappraisal of the American constitutional system. Earlier in the war the controversy centered on the intentions of the framers, especially with respect to the role of Congress in authorizing hostilities. A major feature of the debate centered on whether the Gulf of Tonkin Resolution of 1964 satisfied the constitutional requirements or whether a formal Declaration of War was required after Vietnam hostilities expanded into full-scale warfare early in 1965. Had the President exceeded his powers under the Constitution? Had Congress been tricked? Had Congressional votes on appropriations for the war amounted to an endorsement of Presidential claims? What role, if any, should the courts play in fixing the relative war-related roles of the Presidency and the Congress and in determining which acts (e.g., appropriations) amounted to a fulfillment of these roles? In a sense, these grand constitutional issues have been left unresolved; academic controversy continues to flourish, as is evident in the various lines of interpretation offered in Section V.

The controversy took a new turn as the war itself began to wind down. The focus shifted from the constitutional system to legislative efforts by Congress to develop more precise allocation of responsibility and authority for war-making and to put rather clear limits on Presidential discretion. The result of this new emphasis was the War Powers Act, a compromise enactment which won a large measure of mainstream support but which dissatisfied both those who supported the President's handling of the Vietnam War (see, for example, Eugene Rostow's article) and those who thought the war was waged in an unconstitutional manner. It is a peculiar kind of situation in which "the hawks" regard the War Powers Act as a shackle and "the doves" view it as an open-ended hunting license. Perhaps practical experience with the legislation will resolve the debate by generating some authoritative precedents. Much depends on the nature of future Presidential claims to use force abroad without benefit of either a Declaration of War or an authorization from the United Nations. Much will also depend on how Congress and the public react to these claims.

This volume concludes with a documentary appendix that presents the main materials related to the "settlement" of the Vietnam War, as well as the cognate efforts in Laos and Cambodia. Students of international law will probably devote considerable attention in the years ahead to an interpretation of these settlement materials. A second appendix provides a sampling of judicial decisions in cases arising out of the war; in addition, a text of the War Powers Act and President Nixon's veto message are included.

Just as the conflict in Vietnam (and in the whole of Indochina) persists, so the legal debates spawned by the war remain unresolved. In all probability, these debates have helped to sharpen an appreciation of what the international legal order will require in the future. Many of the selections in Volume 4 highlight shortcomings of the existing international legal order when it comes to war prevention or to the moderation and effective termination of warfare. These shortcomings are evident in any war setting, but become more salient as a consequence of the controversy generated by the American involvement in the Vietnam War. It should be noted that this controversy took place mainly within the United States, a tribute to the capacity of the society to tolerate dissent and engage in debate even while a major war was in progress. Such a domestic brake on national sovereignty is itself a significant factor, but unfortunately it is not generally present throughout world society.

Can the laws of war be revised? Can international procedures for peaceful settlement be strengthened? Can the motivation for large-scale involvement in foreign wars be diminished or even eliminated? Virtually every international lawyer shares these concerns, regardless of his or her individual position on the arguments raised by U.S. involvement in the Vietnam War. From the beginning it has been these shared concerns which have encouraged the Civil War Panel to sustain its internal dialogue and to carry on with its work despite the difficulties.

This volume, you will note, is dedicated to Wolfgang Friedmann, a leading participant on the Civil War Panel since its inception and Chairman of the Panel at the time that Volume 3 in this series was published. Professor Friedmann's violent death on the streets of New York is a tragedy of great magnitude and one that deserves to be linked in the political imagination of our time with the more general tragedy that has befallen Vietnam.

Richard J. Barnet
Thomas Ehrlich
Tom J. Farer
Edwin Brown Firmage
G. W. Haight
Eliot D. Hawkins
Brunson MacChesney
Myres S. McDougal

John Norton Moore
Stephen M. Schwebel
Louis B. Sohn
John R. Stevenson
Howard J. Taubenfeld
Burns H. Weston
Richard A. Falk, Chairman

# I. ROLE OF INTERNATIONAL LAW
# AND ORGANIZATION

# Law and National Security

## JOHN NORTON MOORE

THE role of law in the management of national security has been debated throughout American history. Traces of the debate may be found as long ago as 1793 in the exchange between Hamilton and Jefferson about the relative importance of "interests" and "morality" in deciding whether the United States should support France in the war with England. Jefferson found an obligation to support France under the 1778 treaty of alliance and urged that the treaty obligation was binding on the nation. Hamilton countered that there was no obligation but even if there were it did not require the United States to jeopardize its "essential interests."

At the turn of the century the debate achieved clearer focus in the writings of Alfred Thayer Mahan, the great sea power strategist, and Elihu Root, Secretary of State and a distinguished American jurist. The core of this second round was the importance of arbitration and other third-party machinery for the settlement of international disputes. Root and other jurists urged greater resort to international arbitration. Mahan countered that law, while sometimes useful, was incapable of dealing with questions of national expediency such as the Monroe Doctrine.

In the aftermath of World War II the debate was resumed more sharply and with a broader focus. On one side were international relations theorists such as Hans J. Morgenthau and George F. Kennan, who saw only a small role for international law and who opposed their "realist" position to what they believed were dangers of a "legalistic-moralistic" approach in dealing with national security issues. On the other side were jurists such as Hardy C. Dillard and Myres S. McDougal, who warned that the realists had an incomplete understanding of the role of international law and that their view, if influential, could be costly for American foreign policy.

The realists have, throughout the debate, had an important message. Over-reliance on international law can be a prescription for disaster in a loosely organized and intensely competitive international system. If the disappointments with arbitration treaties and universal disarmament schemes during the interwar years did not drive this home, the advent of the cold war cer-

tainly did. All this, however, has led to an overly broad indictment of the legal tradition. For while we have been preoccupied
with the dangers—some very real—of a "legalistic-moralistic"
strain in American foreign policy, we have failed to see the
cost resulting from the slender capacity of our national security
process to take an international legal perspective into account.

## II

National security decisions must consider a range of component
issues. At a first stage these include: What are the national goals?
Are they realizable in the context in which they must be pursued? If so, are they realizable at a cost-benefit ratio which
makes their pursuit in the national interest? Are preferable alternatives available which will achieve the goals at a more favorable ratio? And how can policies, once chosen, be most effectively
implemented and justified?

Legal considerations, like political, military and economic considerations, are relevant to each of these issues. Yet there are no
international legal specialists on the increasingly important
staff of the National Security Council even though that staff
now comprises over 50 substantive officers. Similarly, there is
virtually no reference in the Pentagon Papers to the legal dimensions of policy in the Vietnam War. These examples illustrate a structural weakness in the national security process which
impedes the consideration of international—and sometimes constitutional—legal components of policy.

There are, of course, showcase examples of national security
decisions in which legal considerations have played a constructive role. Chief among them are the Berlin crisis of 1948 and the
Cuban missile crisis of 1962. The "Forrestal Diaries" indicate
that Forrestal and President Truman discussed "the controlling
legal rights and undertakings" as a starting point for policy in
the Berlin crisis. The United Nations was also used extensively
and helpfully during the crisis. Similarly, because of early involvement of the State Department's Legal Adviser's Office, international legal considerations played a significant role in
shaping U.S. policy during the missile crisis. Legal initiatives included designation of the action as a quarantine—since a blockade might have been construed as an act of war—and collective
authorization by the Organization of American States (OAS).

Much more abundant examples can be found of insensitivity

to international legal considerations. In order to justify the initiation of bombing of North Vietnam in February 1965, for instance, the raids were announced as reprisals for Vietcong attacks on the U.S. military advisers' compound at Pleiku. A case can be made that this bombing of the North, like U.S. participation in the War, was a lawful defensive response against a prior intervention by North Vietnam amounting to an armed attack under Article 51 of the U.N. Charter. But there is overwhelming authority that reprisal, which is a technical legal term for minor coercion in response to a breach of an international legal obligation not amounting to an armed attack, is barred by the Charter. By their unawareness of the relevant legal considerations or their unwillingness to take them into account, American policy-makers had chosen a public justification blatantly in violation of international law.

The April 1965 intervention in the Dominican Republic provides another example of insensitivity to legal considerations. The announced purpose of the first phase of the U.S. action in landing 400 marines was to protect U.S. nationals, a purpose which if carefully implemented would be lawful. But the action was neither implemented nor justified with the legal basis for such action in mind. And the second phase of the action, which committed more than 21,000 U.S. forces to an effort to end the Dominican civil strife, was undercut from the beginning by the failure to initiate the action under Article 6 of the Rio Treaty and by the overly broad rhetoric of President Johnson in proclaiming the inadmissibility of another Communist government anywhere in the hemisphere, a reason for the action which would make it in violation of Article 2(4) of the U.N. Charter. These failures subsequently obscured the real differences between the U.S. action in the Dominican Republic and the Soviet action in Czechoslovakia.

Still another, and poignant, example is the lack of vigorous effort in the Indochina War, at least during the early years, to implement the laws of war. The United States is party to a variety of treaties relating to the conduct of warfare, including the Fourth Hague Convention of 1907 Respecting the Laws and Customs of War on Land and the four Geneva Conventions of 1949. It also recognizes a substantial body of customary international law setting minimum humanitarian standards for the conduct of warfare.

As the Son My tragedy amply confirms, violation of these standards may undermine the national effort as well as offend moral sensibilities. But the Son My tragedy also raises broader problems concerning the present status and effectiveness of the laws of war, problems which have been insufficiently considered by U.S. policy-makers. First, officially defined restrictions on combat too frequently have not been understood or implemented in the field. For example, there seems to have been wide disparity in understanding among regional commands in Vietnam that the "body count" was to include prisoners of war as well as enemy casualties and that "specified strike zones" did not override the laws of war which hold that attacks on noncombatants are not permissible. Second, the manifest ambiguities and deficiencies of the law, in face of the complexities of a counterintervention-ary setting and newer military technology, have largely gone un-attended. For instance, the principal legal analysis for the mas-sive use of chemical herbicides in Vietnam seems to have been a memorandum prepared in March 1945 by Major-General Myron C. Cramer, then Judge Advocate General, concerning the possible use of chemical anti-crop agents against pockets of Japanese on the Pacific islands. This example is symptomatic of a lack of adequate legal review of newer weapons and tactics.

Most important, adequate national and international machin-ery that can deal with the full sweep of these problems has been lacking. Though army regulations require compliance with the laws of war and many military and other government advisers made significant individual efforts to ensure compliance in the field, the chances for a more vigorous and imaginative implemen-tation would have been improved if an international legal per-spective sensitive to the issues had been systematically structured into higher levels of the national security process. This might have been supplied by an interdepartmental group charged with responsibility for oversight and development of the laws of war.

A fourth example of insensitivity to legal considerations is in the recurring failure to prepare an adequate constitutional basis for major military actions abroad. The failure of President Truman to secure explicit congressional authorization for the Korean War was followed by President Johnson's unnecessary reliance on an ambiguous series of attacks on American ships in the Gulf of Tonkin as the occasion for obtaining congressional authorization for the Indochina War. In both cases the failure to allow more adequately for the constitutional legal dimensions proved to be major weaknesses of policy.

The Cambodian incursion of April 30, 1970 provides a fifth example. There were at least three ways that more adequate consideration of international legal factors might have strengthened the U.S. response in the crisis.

First, North Vietnamese attacks on Cambodia might have been protested by the United States in the Security Council much as the Soviet actions in curtailing access to Berlin were taken to the Security Council to lay the groundwork for subsequent Allied action to reopen the city. The Cambodian complaint to the Security Council on April 22 would have seemed an opportune time to press such a complaint in the Council. And at a minimum, the incursion should have been immediately reported to the Security Council pursuant to the obligation under Article 51 of the U.N. Charter.

Second, the principal legal basis for the Cambodian incursion was that a belligerent state may take action to end serious violations of neutral territory by an opposing belligerent. Yet the important presidential address explaining the action to the nation did not mention the principle. This and other public pronouncements might have been more focused and carried greater weight had they emphasized the substantial international legal authority for the action.

Third, and most important, a prior understanding with Cambodia might have been obtained for public release at the time of the operation. In view of the requirement of Article IV, paragraph 3, of the SEATO Treaty, which provides that no action on the territory of a protocol state such as Cambodia "shall be taken except at the invitation or with the consent of the government concerned," such an advance agreement would have seemed particularly advisable.

Finally, and most recently, there is the example of the U.S. response to the Pakistan-Bangladesh-India war. Perhaps the lack of clarity in the U.S. position was attributable to the complexity of the situation. It is, after all, difficult to distinguish the damsel from the dragon when one side is engaged in mass murder of noncombatants and the other intervenes in a war of secession against a traditional rival. Nevertheless, America might have been more persuasive in focusing on the shortcomings of both sides if she had taken account of the legal aspects of the conflict.

Initially, the United States should have vigorously urged Pakistan to live up to the provisions of Article 3 of the Geneva Convention of 1949 Relative to the Protection of Civilian Persons in Time of War. Article 3 sets out a series of minimum standards for the protection of noncombatants "in the case of armed conflict not of an international character occurring in the territory" of a party to the Convention. In fact, the United States had an obligation under Article 1 of the Convention to undertake "to ensure respect for the . . . Convention in all circumstances."

With respect to the Indian action, the United States might have pointed out more specifically that the intervention violated a series of recent General Assembly Resolutions, including the 1960 Declaration on the Granting of Independence to Colonial Countries and Peoples and the 1965 Declaration on Inadmissibility of Intervention. The 1960 Declaration was particularly on point. Section 6 declares: "Any attempt aimed at the partial or total disruption of the national unity and the territorial integrity of a country is incompatible with the purposes and principles of the Charter of the United Nations."

The point is that the actions of both sides had their warts and that legal analysis could have helped to isolate the virus and prescribe the treatment.

The memoranda of the meetings of the Washington Special Action Group, made public by Jack Anderson, confirm that greater sensitivity to legal considerations was called for in the India-Pakistan crisis. These sources demonstrate that the National Security Council understood the advantages of utilizing the United Nations, a use which was helpful. But they evidence little awareness of international legal norms as a basis for appraisal of the Indian and Pakistani actions or for support of U.S. policy. For example, there was no mention of the General Assembly Resolutions condemning intervention in a war of secession—Resolutions which strongly supported U.S. opposition to the Indian intervention. Similarly, no mention was made of the 1949 Geneva Convention Relative to the Protection of Civilian Persons, despite a discussion of how best to ensure the safety of the Biharis in East Pakistan and the Bengalis in West Pakistan. More dramatically, although Henry Kissinger posed a question concerning the legal basis for the Indian naval blockade, there was no legal specialist present to answer it. The resulting discussion too easily suggested that there was no legal basis for an Indian blockade and failed to consider whether incidents involving American ships subsumed violations of international law even if the Indian blockade were legal.

The legal tradition is important in making policy as well as for its implementation and justification. The 1960 Bay of Pigs invasion illustrates the cost of failing to take an international legal perspective into account in planning for U.S. action. There is no evidence that the U.S. planners weighed the effects of supplying illegal assistance to the insurgents. It should have been evident that the effort—successful or unsuccessful—would establish a precedent for external assistance to exile insurgents which would work strongly against the national interest when transferred to Indochina or the Middle East. The effort was also likely to contribute to a loss of national influence as a result of the associated violations of the charters of the Organization of American States and of the United Nations. It would probably overstate the case to say that the abortive invasion would not have taken place if the legal tradition had been adequately considered, but it might have been less likely had there been full and candid presentation of the international legal costs of the action.

Quite apart from the utility of an international legal perspective in crisis management there is also a need for more systematic representation of the legal tradition in formulating a coherent and intellectually powerful foreign policy. Under the pressures of the cold war the nation has drifted away from a consistent vision of world order. Yet a foreign policy which focuses on the importance of the stability of the system and coöperative solution of global problems seems strongly in the national interest.

Internationally, such a foreign policy may be the best strategy for the United States to recoup its leadership; and nationally it may be a prerequisite to adequate domestic support of foreign policy. The present neo-isolationist tendencies within the United States are qualitatively different from the isolationism of the "America first" movement preceding World War II. Then the predominant strain was to avoid involvement in the affairs of Europe, whatever the moral cost. In contrast, the predominant strain in the present movement seems to be a pronounced— though sometimes misplaced—concern for the moral dimensions of American foreign policy. If such concern can be channeled into a coherent vision of world order, it may revive domestic support for the more active international policy which the nation must undertake in order to deal effectively with the myriad of problems in security, development and environment which lie ahead. The legal tradition has no monopoly of vision on world order; it does have a special contribution to make to the normative aspects of state conduct as well as global organization for solution of social problems.

III

The realist-jurist debate has done little to dispel widespread misperceptions about the value of the legal tradition in the management of national security. At least three such misperceptions continue to obscure its importance.

First, international law is thought of as saying what cannot be done, solely as a system for restraining and controlling national actions. No one proposes to exclude military or political considerations from planning simply because they do not always determine policy. Yet because of a misleading image of law as a system of negative restraint, we make such a judgment when it comes to law. In fact, the legal tradition can play a variety of important roles in planning and implementing national security decisions. These include, among others, focus on the long-run stability and quality of the international milieu; calculation of the costs and benefits resulting from violation of the law or compliance with it; focus on a range of international legal options for conflict management; concern with appraising and justifying national actions by reference to shared global interests; and supervision of the national interest in domestic operations that involve U.S. adherence to international agreements.

Law is also useful for solving social problems and communicating intentions. Examples include the 1967 Treaty for the Prohibition of Nuclear Weapons in Latin America, the recently signed Draft Convention on the Prohibition of the Development, Production, and Stockpiling of Bacteriological (Biological) and Toxin Weapons, and the ongoing efforts to reach agreement on an international régime for the resources of the deep seabeds. To focus exclusively on the difficulties of international law in constraining international behavior is to miss the creative opportunities which the law provides.

There are, of course, dangers in simplistic legal approaches to national security issues. These include, among others, equating general goals with specific policies without assessing the effectiveness of those policies, as for example, to urge that since we wish a warless world we should unilaterally disarm; pursuit of policies which are unrealistic in the present international system, as for example, to advocate submitting the Arab-Israeli or Indochina conflicts to the International Court of Justice; and over-reliance on the deterrent effect of international law or on formal legal arrangements divorced from power realities, as, for example, to rely solely on international law for the protection of the *Pueblo* despite the demonstrated willingness of North Korea to violate international law.

Though these dangers are real, none of them is inherent in a sophisticated legal approach. More important, the legal tradition complements the realist approach precisely where that approach is weakest, that is, in preoccupation with short-run goals at the expense of long-run interests in a healthy world order.

A second misperception is that a concern for international law is opposed to a concern for the national interest. But the "national interest" is not a self-defining concept. As it is understood by most theorists, it would include a strong interest in the stability and quality of the international system. Thus Raymond Aron says: ". . . the West must stand for an idea of an international order. The national interest of the United States, or even the collective interest of the Anglo-Saxon minority, will not win over any country nor will it cause any loyalties if it does not appear to be tied to an international order—the order of power as well as the order of law."[1]

International law may also help to elaborate the national interest in a variety of operational settings. For example, international law has distilled from centuries of experience a substantial body of norms for the conduct of hostilities. Not to comply with these is to risk breakdowns in military discipline, brutalization of participants with resultant social costs on return to civilian life, unnecessary escalation or continuation of conflict, reciprocal mistreatment of nationals, domestic loss of support and unnecessary destruction of human and material resources.

The real conflict between law and the national interest, when it arises, occurs in terms of the costs and benefits to the nation of pursuing a policy which is illegal. When the conflict arises,

[1] Raymond Aron, "The Quest for a Philosophy of Foreign Affairs," in Stanley Hoffmann, ed., "Contemporary Theory in International Relations." New York: Prentice-Hall, 1960.

too often the legal costs are not adequately appreciated. In the case of the Bay of Pigs invasion, for example, the probable benefits to the nation deriving from a successful action should have been weighed against the short-run cost in loss of U.S. influence resulting from a blatantly illegal policy and the long-run cost of undermining legal constraints contributing to the stability of the international system.

A third misperception comes in judging the utility of the legal tradition on an oversimplified model of law. A common error in this regard is to underestimate the importance of community perceptions of legality as a base for increase or decrease in national power. International law, particularly on issues of war and peace, does not always manifestly control the behavior of states. But it is not as widely perceived that even when international law does not control behavior, there are international norms—community expectations about the authority of national action which may in a variety of ways translate into power realties. For example, an action such as the Korean War, in which perceptions as to lawfulness are high, is likely to produce more allies than actions which are controversial such as the Indochina War or widely regarded as unlawful such as the British and French invasion of Suez.

If beliefs about the illegality of a nation's actions are intense and widespread there may be a generalized loss of national influence. The Soviet Union seems to have paid such a cost in the invasion of Czechoslovakia, as indicated by the disaffection of Soviet-oriented Communist parties and front organizations throughout the world. Perceptions about legality may also influence votes within international organizations such as the United Nations, the OAS Council of Ministers or even the International Committee of the Red Cross.

Another error resulting from an oversimplified model of law is the tendency to overestimate the indeterminacy of international legal norms. The lack of centralized legislative and adjudicative competence in the international system is a real factor contributing to gaps and tears in the legal fabric. But it is wrong to conclude that all international law is amorphous. International law has areas of clarity as well as of uncertainty and in this respect is not as qualitatively different from national law as one who has never suffered through the confusion of first-year law school might suspect. It is virtually undisputed among international lawyers that the U.S. role in the Bay of Pigs invasion, the Soviet role in the invasion of Czechoslovakia, and the British and French Suez intervention violated Article 2(4) of the U.N. Charter which proscribes "the threat or use of force against the territorial integrity or political independence of any state. . . ." It is also widely accepted that the allied intervention in the Korean conflict was a lawful exercise of collective defense under Article 51 of the Charter, that the Son My tragedy was in violation of Hague and Geneva rules and that the North Vietnamese mistreatment of allied prisoners is in violation of the Geneva Conventions. Many other examples of reasonably definite legal conclusions about war and peace issues could be given.

## IV

One important reason for the failure to take legal perspectives into consideration in the management of national security is that the machinery, as presently structured, is inadequate to the task.

The principal international legal adviser to the government is the Legal Adviser of the Department of State. In addition, there are many other offices engaged to some extent in the process, including, among others, the Office of General Counsel of the Department of Defense, the General Counsel of the Arms Control and Disarmament Agency and the Office of Legal Counsel of the Department of Justice.

There are a number of structural problems which prevent full utilization of this plethora of legal offices. The most important is that there is little legal advice used by the important National Security Council and NSC staff portions of the security process. Since its creation in 1947, the NSC and its staff have played an increasing role in the management of national security. There are persuasive reasons for dividing the national security process between State and the NSC-White House. Unfortunately, a consequence of this division has been to minimize concern for international legal considerations since there are no international legal specialists on either the White House or NSC staffs.

A second structural problem is the lack of centralized responsibility for the general development and supervision of the international legal aspects of national security decisions. The press of day-to-day business within each legal office and the lack of clear lines of responsibility between offices have hindered vigorous efforts to strengthen and develop international law.

Although not to overemphasize the importance of structural change as such, certain changes might improve the present inadequate consideration of the legal component of policy:

First, make the Legal Adviser of the Department of State a regular member of the National Security Council. This would have the advantage of introducing international legal considerations into crisis management where they are most needed. It would also give the Legal Adviser, who is called upon to justify policy, a better opportunity to influence the making and implementation of policy. In his new capacity, the Legal Adviser would be available to advise the President as well as the Secretary of State. An obvious parallel to this dual advisory role is the dual role of the Chairman of the Joint Chiefs of Staff who advises both the President and the Secretary of Defense. As a corollary to this change the Legal Adviser might also be made a member of any NSC group dealing with security crises, such as the Washington Special Action Group.

Second, add a new position, which might be called Counselor on National Security Law, to the staff of the National Security Council. One of the important mechanisms for coördinated foreign policy planning is the National Security Study Memorandum supervised by the NSC staff. Of 138 such memoranda prepared from 1969 through October 2, 1971, some 20 to 30 have a significant legal component. These include memoranda on Indochina, Cyprus, the Middle East, southern Africa, the nonproliferation treaty, the Nuclear Test-Ban Treaty, tariff preferences, chemical-biological agents, toxins, the seabed treaty and U.N. China admission. Though legal considerations are undoubtedly present in many of these memoranda as a result of interdepartmental consideration, an in-house legal expert within the NSC staff could assist in recognizing and coördinating the legal components of such planning. The Counselor and his staff would also be available to the President to provide advice on the legal dimensions of national security issues when, for reasons of speed or secrecy, the President chose not to utilize the formal machinery of the National Security Council. Finally, the Counselor could serve as a liaison with other government legal advisers, particularly the Legal Adviser of the Department of State and the General Counsel of the Department of Defense. Indeed, the coördinating function might extend to many hitherto-domestic agencies. The U.N. Conference on the Human En-

vironment and the upcoming conference on the law of the sea
are illustrative of a new global consciousness that promises both
a multiplication of national obligations and an increase in the
impact of international law on national life. In this respect, the
creation of a Counselor on National Security Law would parallel the recent addition of an Assistant to the President for
International Economic Affairs.

Third, create a permanent Interdepartmental Group on International Legal Affairs chaired by the Legal Adviser of the Department of State. Its purpose would be to coördinate and initiate
government programs for the implementation and development
of international law. More specifically, the Group would coördinate the executive position on issues with a substantial international legal component, for example the position on ratification
of the 1925 Geneva Protocol on Gas and Bacteriological Warfare. It would also identify international legal problems in current U.S. foreign policy and prepare position papers for consideration by the National Security Council. An example would
be the U.S. obligation under Article 25 of the Charter to accept
and carry out the U.N. sanctions against Southern Rhodesia—
sanctions which the United States supported and could have
vetoed—by refusing to import Rhodesian chrome once such
sanctions had been decided by the Security Council.

The Group would also have responsibility for assessing any
government action against the legal obligations binding on the
United States. This would include, for example, continuing
appraisal of compliance with the laws of war during the course
of hostilities. Another recent and practical example is the case
of the Lithuanian defector, Simas Kudirka, who was hastily
returned to Soviet custody on November 23, 1970, from the U.S.
Coast Guard cutter *Vigilant* in violation of the U.N. Protocol
Relating to the Status of Refugees. The incident might have been
prevented if the Protocol had been previously incorporated in
Coast Guard regulations (as it has been subsequently) by prohibiting the immediate return of defectors pending subsequent
determination of status as required under the 1951 Convention
Relating to the Status of Refugees.

Finally, the Group would have responsibility for promoting
the progressive development of international law by the United
States. In this capacity the Group might identify and promote
areas in which U.S. leadership could strengthen international

law. It might also encourage greater training in international law for government officials, for example, by enlarging the programs in international law offered by the Foreign Service Institute, the National War College and the Naval War College or by instituting such programs elsewhere. Similarly, it might identify and sponsor research in areas of international law which are unclear and which are of potential concern.

In its composition, the new Interdepartmental Group would be chaired by the Legal Adviser of the Department of State and would include the General Counsel of the Department of Defense and (if the position of Counselor on National Security Law were created) the newly created Counselor as well. In addition, the Group would include any government legal counsel deemed important for its effective functioning. In some respects, it might be modeled after the highly successful Interagency Task Force on the Law of the Sea which is chaired by the State Department Legal Adviser and responsible to the National Security Council. It would, however, be structured as a permanent interdepartmental group.

Finally, consultants on international law should be added to the Senate Foreign Relations and House Foreign Affairs Committees. The simplest and most effective way of doing so is to regularize the consideration of international legal factors in the day-to-day work of the principal congressional committees dealing with national security issues.

In the consideration of these proposals it should be remembered that the question is not whether international law will be controlling but the more modest one of whether it will be taken into account. As Stanley Hoffmann observes, "a comprehensive analysis of world politics and foreign policy cannot afford to neglect the law, both because of its *actual* importance and because of its *potential* importance for a better order. . . ."[2] By strengthening the national security machinery to take law more systematically into account America could lead in promoting the development of international law as well as in implementing President Nixon's statement in his 1970 World Law Day message that it "is not enough that we merely defend the law as we have known it in the past: we must also work to . . . extend its influence in international affairs as well as in our national life."

[2] Stanley Hoffmann, "Henkin and Falk: Mild Reformist and Mild Revolutionary," *Journal of International Affair:*, v. 24, 1970.

# Law and the Indochina War:
# A Retrospective View

## EDWIN BROWN FIRMAGE

We are mad, not only individually, but nationally. We check manslaughter and isolated murders; but what of war and the much vaunted
crime of slaughtering whole peoples?

Seneca: Ad Lucilim XCV.

How small, of all that human hearts endure,
That part which laws or Kings can cause or cure.

Oliver Goldsmith: The Traveller

## I. INTRODUCTION

This century, from the Hague Conferences through the Vietnam War,
has seen a profound change in attitudes toward the role of law as a constraint upon foreign policy. The Hague Conferences [1] represented at once
an attempt, however feeble, by men of mixed motives to emplace fledgling
prophylactic legal institutions upon the tendencies of the nation-states to
resolve disputes by war, and at the same time to limit war's destructive-
ness if prevention failed. World War I destroyed not only most of this
superstructure, but also massive portions of the more fundamental institutions of the dynastic state system of the time. When European balance
of power politics failed to maintain peace and preserve social order, the
ad hoc systems of the Hague Conventions were replaced by the League of
Nations, which provided a weak form of collective security and a standing conference system of dispute resolution.

The controversy in this country over our participation in the League
of Nations was not merely a debate between advocates of the geopolitics
of power and proponents of a stronger role for legal institutions in international relations. Both proponents and opponents of the League recognized the need for development of dispute resolution institutions to displace balance of power politics in the maintenance of peace. Woodrow
Wilson favored the League for precisely the same reason that Philander

---

[1] *See* Firmage, *Fact-Finding in the Resolution of International Disputes — From
the Hague Peace Conference to the United Nations,* 1971 UTAH L. REV. 421 (an
analysis of the evolution of fact-finding, peace-keeping, and dispute resolution techniques through the media of the Hague Conference, the League of Nations, the Bryan
treaties, and the United Nations).

Knox, Senator Borah, and J. Reuben Clark, Jr.,[2] opposed it; all were reacting against European balance of power politics. Wilson viewed the League system as the way to conduct foreign policy on a foundation of collective security, if not parliamentary politics. Knox, Clark, and others saw the League — inextricably tied to the Versailles settlement as the price Wilson paid for the world body — simply as an institutional means by which France and Britain might maintain a dominant position over Germany. In their view, the League amounted to European power politics in institutional disguise. Clark, far from opposing the concept of a standing conference system as a means of dispute resolution, proposed such a plan of his own.[3] The arbitration treaties of William Jennings Bryan, our participation in the Permanent Court of International Justice supported by Harding, the Kellogg-Briand Pact (defended by proponents and opponents of the League), the reliance upon arbitration as a means of dispute resolution by Elihu Root, Charles Evans Hughes, and J. Reuben Clark, Jr., and the disarmament conferences (sustained by leading proponents and opponents of the League) represent some degree of support for a legal or institutional approach to foreign policy — an approach excoriated by Acheson,[4] Kennan, and others after World War II.

Kennan's book, consisting of lectures delivered at the University of Chicago in 1951, became one of the most popular and influential writings on foreign policy. His criticism of excessive legalism in foreign policy was based upon his examination of American foreign policy from the Civil War to World War II:

> . . . I see the most serious fault of our past policy formulation to lie in something that I might call the legalistic-moralistic approach to international problems. . . .
>
> It is the belief that it should be possible to suppress the chaotic and dangerous aspirations of governments in the international field by the acceptance of some system of legal rules and restraints. This belief undoubtedly represents in part an attempt to transpose the Anglo-Saxon concept of individual law into the international field

---

[2] *See* Firmage & Blakesley, *J. Reuben Clark, Jr.: Law and International Order,* in J. REUBEN CLARK, JR. — DIPLOMAT AND STATESMAN 43, 54 *et seq.* (R. Hillam ed. 1973).

[3] *See id.* at 61–62 & n.46, *citing* Clark, *System of Pacific Settlement of International Disputes: A Program,* UNITY (Oct. 4, 1923). Clark proposed that there be created a world judiciary and world deliberative body, with quasi-legislative functions, which he called a "World Congress." *Id.* at 61.

[4] Mr. George Kennan complains, I think justly, of the disservice which lawyer secretaries of state did to American foreign policy during the years when they directed most of our effort to the negotiation of nearly a hundred treaties of arbitration, only two of which were ever invoked. He is, of course, quite right that all this misguided effort sprang from a complete failure to see the enormous threat to world stability which the Germans were so soon to carry into action. Even after the First World War, the realities of power were still obscured to us by our peculiar American belief that salvation lies in institutional mechanisms.

D. ACHESON, MORNING AND NOON 147 (1965). *See also* Acheson, *The Arrogance of International Lawyers,* 2 INT'L LAWYER 591 (1968); McDougal & Reisman, *Rhodesia and the United Nations: The Lawfulness of International Concern,* 62 AM. J. INT'L L. 1 (1968).

and to make it applicable to governments as it is applicable . . . to individuals.[5]

Elaborating upon these early observations, Kennan in his memoirs described our foreign policy between 1865 and 1939 as "utopian in its expectations, legalistic in its concept of methodology, moralistic in the demands it seemed to place on others, and self-righteous in the degree of high-mindedness and rectitude it imputed to ourselves." [6] He also criticized our

> inordinate preoccupation with arbitration treaties, the efforts towards world disarmament, the attempt to outlaw war by the simple verbiage of the Kellogg Pact, and illusions about the possibilities of achieving a peaceful world through international organization and multilateral diplomacy, as illustrated in the hopes addressed to the League of Nations and the United Nations.[7]

Kennan's penetrating criticism of our legalistic, institutional approach to foreign policy during the century preceding World War II was far more than a simple commentary on the limitations of one trained in the law to serve as Secretary of State. Rather, Kennan indicated an entire approach to foreign policy,[8] an approach shared not only by lawyers, but also by political scientists and historians, presidents and their advisors, and proponents and opponents of the League. To Kennan, this approach ignored the inevitable role of power in politics.

> The conception of law in international life should certainly receive every support and encouragement that our country can give it. But it cannot yet replace power as the vital force for a large part of the world. And the realities of power will soon seep into any legalistic structure which we erect to govern international life. They will permeate it. They will become the content of it; and the structure will

---

[5] G. KENNAN, AMERICAN DIPLOMACY 1900–1950, at 95–96 (1951).

[6] G. KENNAN, MEMOIRS: 1950–1963, at 71 (1972).

[7] *Id.*

[8] Kennan recorded in 1944 his reaction to the press reports of the Dumbarton Oaks discussions:

> Underlying the whole conception of an organization for international security is the simple reasoning that if only the status quo could be rigidly preserved, there could be no further wars in Europe, and the European problem, as far as our country is concerned, would be solved. This reasoning, which mistakes the symptoms for the disease, is not new. It underlay the Holy Alliance, the League of Nations, and numerous other political structures set up by nations which were, for the moment, satisfied with the international setup and did not wish to see it changed. These structures have always served the purpose for which they were designed just so long as the interests of the great powers gave substance and reality to their existence. The moment this situation changed, the moment it became in the interests of one or the other of the great powers to alter the status quo, none of these treaty structures ever stood in the way of such alteration.
>
> International political life is something organic, not something mechanical. Its essence is change; and the only systems for the regulation of international life which can be effective over long periods of time are ones sufficiently subtle, sufficiently pliable, to adjust themselves to constant change in the interests and power of the various countries involved.

G. KENNAN, MEMOIRS: 1925–1950, at 218 (1967).

remain only the form. International security will depend on *them*: on the realities of power — not on the structure in which they are clothed. We are being almost criminally negligent of the interests of our people if we allow our plans for an international organization to be an excuse for failing to occupy ourselves seriously and minutely with the sheer power relationships of the European peoples.[9]

The League's ultimate failure [10] to meet the challenge of the aggressor states in the 1930's, although in part due to its inherent institutional weakness, was more basically due to the failure of traditional balance of power diplomacy. The seeds of World War II were clearly sown at Versailles; the blame for the inability of the League to prevent the harvest must also be borne by those European states that refused to support the League at critical points and by the United States, which refused to participate. Basic power remained within the states, and they continued to make fundamental decisions that were translated by traditional means into action within the international sphere. In other words, the debacle of World War II represents not only a failure of legal institutions, but also the more basic failure of traditional balance of power diplomacy.

The United Nations and the League are alike in that both have had impressive success in preventing certain types of violence and in restoring and maintaining at least a short lived peace between belligerents, while both have had very little success in resolving the underlying causes of such violence.[11] Senator Fulbright, however, argues that the United Nations has not failed, because it has never been tried.[12] Certainly we retreated with undue and perhaps tragic haste from initial attempts to use this institution in the place of traditional alliance diplomacy.[13] Nevertheless,

---

[9] *Id.* at 218–19.

[10] Critics of the League of Nations often overlook its substantial achievements in maintaining the peace for over a decade after World War I, during which time the European map was redrawn. On at least one occasion, the League performed a crucial role in preventing a Balkan conflagration that could well have resulted in a European or world-wide war. *See* Firmage, *supra* note 1.

> The dispute of Albania against Yugoslavia and Greece in 1921 might well have resulted in substantial territorial losses, if not the disappearance of Albania, but for the actions of the Council of the League and its commission of inquiry which helped to establish the Albanian government and to settle that state's frontiers. Again, the Demir-Kapu frontier dispute between Greece and Bulgaria in 1925 might well have resulted in another Balkan war but for the forceful demands of Aristide Briand, President of the Council of the League. Greece, prepared to invade Bulgarian territory, pulled back after reception of Briand's telegram demanding that neither side resort to war. A commission of inquiry sponsored by the Council was later instrumental in settling the dispute. The eventual failure of the League has made it all too possible to forget its impressive successes in dealing with disputes of lesser magnitude than Manchuria or Spain, but still quite sufficient to have resulted in war in the absence of effective regimes of settlement.

Firmage, Book Review, 1972 AM. POL. SCI. REV. 1088.

[11] For analysis of fact-finding and peace-keeping efforts by the United Nations see Firmage, *supra* note 1, at 432 *et seq.*

[12] Address by William Fulbright before the Pacem in Terris III Conference, Oct. 8, 1973, in 119 CONG. REC. 18,830 (daily ed. Oct. 9, 1973).

[13] It is interesting to note that the current revisionist writing on the origins of the Cold War, coming in part from the New Left, was preceded by twenty years not only by the Old Left, epitomized by Henry Wallace, but also by the Old Right. J. Reuben

it is begging the question to assert that the United Nations — and the entire institutional approach to foreign policy that it represents — has not failed because it has never been used. Such an assertion must be followed by an inquiry into the reasons why the powerful nations have not used the United Nations as the primary vehicle for accomplishing their goals.

Beginning with the Cold War and the creation of NATO, and continuing in some degree until late 1972, when the United States ended its participation in the Vietnam War, the world has been gripped by an ideological struggle, the ferocity of which has not been matched since the Wars of Religion. This struggle has frozen international politics into a bipolar structure that has prevented the application of either traditional balance of power diplomacy or its more sophisticated alternative, legal institutionalism. The watershed years in international relations, beginning in the late sixties and extending to the present, have brought the opportunity for another beginning. As in 1815, 1918, and 1945, we now must reexamine the international community and the means by which its roots may be deepened. This Article will focus on the contributions that law — both municipal and international — can realistically make toward attaining the goal of a world community governed more by law and less by force.

## II. LEGAL OBLIGATION AND COMMUNITY

In evaluating the role of law in foreign affairs, a critical examination of Kennan's indictment of excessive legalism may be appropriate. Kennan perceived a relationship between a community and its institutions that determines the effectiveness of legal obligation. He therefore distrusted attempts by institutionalists to transplant the legal structure of a hierarchically ordered municipal system based upon a mature and somewhat homogeneous community into the highly decentralized and heterogeneous international community.

Kennan's criticism, however, ignored the mutual cause and effect relationship between a community and its institutions. That is, although a

Clark, Jr., a conservative Republican who served as Solicitor of the Department of State under Hoover and who adamantly opposed our participation in both the League and the United Nations, also opposed the creation of NATO and the polarization of the world into opposing armed camps which it represented:

"It would hardly do to form an open alliance against Russia; and both Britain and ourselves should be wary of an alliance with her. So the device is conceived as a 'union' of states, which, however, would tie the nations together more securely than an alliance and be a greater threat to Russia.

"But such an alliance would lead, and such a 'union' will lead, sooner or later, to a counter-alliance by the other nations that would challenge the power of such a 'union,' so meaning either constant war for supremacy or a war of absolute conquest by the one or the other and a consequent enslavement of the conquered. Peace without liberty spells a stalemate in civilization and spiritual development. 'Union now' has far more ill than good in it. Nor must America ever become a party to an attempted military domination of the world."

Quoted in Firmage & Blakesley, *supra* note 2, at 56.

certain critical mass of "community-ness" must exist before a legal structure will naturally emerge and be accepted as obligatory, legal institution may profoundly change and deepen community ties through its accommodation of successful experiences. The lesson then is not that we draft a utopian world constitution and invite the world to ratify and accede, but rather that we perceive embryonic legal institutions within the international system as possible contributors to the development of an emerging international community.

Ascertaining the relationship between power, morality, law, and community begins with an analysis of the nature of legal obligation. Proponents of Natural Law maintain that legal obligation can be objectively derived from the principles of justice; in contrast, Positivists focus on the role of the sovereign state, rather than the principles of justice, in formulating legal obligation. Our recent preoccupation with institutional systems and disregard of moral principles as constraints on sovereign authority reflect a theoretical dependence upon the tenets of Positivism. Although Natural Law is theoretically deficient because it fails properly to consider the role of power in developing legal obligation, Positivism is equally deficient because it is excessively preoccupied with the same. Accordingly, a return to Naturalist considerations, tempered by Positivist realism, may contribute substantially to the effectiveness of law in accomplishing international peace.

John Rawls recently stated in a neo-Naturalist thesis [14] that legal obligation first arises from a disposition to support efforts to improve social interaction through fair laws and fair institutional procedures.[15] Thus, although institutions might reinforce legal obligations and even create legal duties pursuant to fair procedures, the content of the law would forever remain the primary source of obligation. According to Naturalist theory, one may be obligated conscientiously to object to or civilly disobey laws dictated by the formal institutions, where such laws violate the primary principles of justice or are enacted in violation of fair procedures.[16] Thus, the Naturalist conception of law as voluntarily obligatory lends itself well to the international sphere, since institutional systems are often incapable of enforcing legal rules without voluntary compliance.

Positivists, in contrast, reject any objective constraints, such as principles of fairness, upon the sovereign's authority to make law. Although the sovereign may consent to being obligated — both internally by constitutional constraints and externally by treaties and voluntary participation in international institutions — such obligation, being self-imposed, need not be based on any principles of justice or fairness. Thus, Positivists contend that adherence to law in the international sphere is discretionary with the sovereign. Their reliance in foreign affairs on power politics,

---

[14] J. RAWLS, A THEORY OF JUSTICE (1971).

[15] *Id.* at 11–17.

[16] *Id.* at 371–82.

rather than objective legal norms, grows out of this contention. Legal realists in this country, including the McDougal school of thought, urge that legal institutions should be manipulatively used to promote national interests in international affairs. So interpreted, law is mere superstructure controlled by the power forces of the state. Thus, where states are ideologically opposed, law can provide at best a temporary truce, but it cannot establish ultimate peace.

Although adherence to either the Naturalist or the Positivist theory of obligation can assist in achieving international order, reliance on either theory in isolation may ultimately be reactionary. For example, the Positivists' excessive reliance on institutions partially justified a reversion to power politics when the institutions seemingly failed. Had the Positivists better understood the limited role that formal structure plays in the development of legal obligation, then the partial success of the institutions could have been appreciated and their ultimate inadequacy anticipated.

Thus, our earlier mistake was optimistically to assume that a complex superstructure sitting uncomfortably atop an embryonic community could resolve fundamental intracommunity conflicts. But Kennan's blanket indictment of the institutional approach to foreign policy, based on the weaknesses inherent in the early development of international institutions, also missed the mark. The problem was not that legal institutions were wholly ineffective, but only that they were not totally adequate. Further, nascent existence and use of legal institutions, even at first limited to peripheral international problems, would have been helpful in developing a community of greater depth, which might in turn have supported yet stronger institutions.

An institutional approach to foreign policy must begin with a proper assessment of the level of community that exists within the international system and the corresponding capacity of community members voluntarily to accept as obligatory rules emanating from community institutions. Stated differently, experience suggests that legal institutions absent the requisite foundation of community cannot yield world peace.

Yet there is nothing inherent in man's nature, nor in his cultural or national divisions, that precludes the development of a communal base sufficient to support a legitimate normative order. It is suggested that there exist as innate propensities within man a sense of fairness and a sense of community, which in combination provide a base sufficient to support a universal normative structure. Further, if law is to be obligatory, it is suggested that *any* legal system must accommodate this normative structure, at least to a minimal extent; thus, this normative structure would perform a critical role in maintaining both internal and external peace among sovereign states. This theory is impliedly supported by recent research in language learning by Noam Chomsky, by studies of moral development by psychologists Lawrence Kohlberg and June Tapp, and by research in comparative law by Rudolph Schlesinger.

Chomsky's research in language learning suggests that there exists in man an unconscious knowledge of innate principles of universal grammar. This innate mental structure allows successful experience to confirm a prior disposition "that there is a primitive, neurologically given analytic system which may degenerate if not stimulated at an appropriate critical period, but which otherwise provides a specific interpretation of experience . . . ." [17]

Thus, contrary to radical empiricism, which rejects the theory of innate forms of knowledge, Chomsky theorizes a system of belief not entirely dependent on environmental circumstances, but instead erected upon innate principles of mind: "A system of knowledge and belief results from the interplay of innate mechanisms, genetically determined maturational processes, and interaction with the social and physical environment." [18] Extrapolated to a theory of law, Chomsky's theory suggests that legal rules are possibly constructed on the basis of distinct innate schemata, or a universal normative structure, much like the universal structure of language. [19] Indeed, both the uniformity of legal principles and the regularity with which people accept rules of social interaction as obligatory are inconsistent with the empiricist's view that obligation arises from experience. Thus, abstract normative principles may be inherent in human nature and may impose limits on what the mind will accept as legally obligatory.

The notion that there may be innate principles of mind that determine a universal normative structure should be no surprise to students of comparative law. The concept of Jus Gentium — principles of law common to all nations by virtue of their being intrinsically consonant with right reason — existed historically under Roman law and survives today in article 38(1)(c) of the statute of the International Court of Justice. "These 'general principles of law' are not . . . peculiar to any legal system but are inherent in, and common to, them all. They constitute the common foundation of every system of law." [20]

Rudolph Schlesinger, in the Cornell Project, [21] recently attempted to define the "common core" of legal principles. Although the scope of

---

[17] N. CHOMSKY, PROBLEMS OF KNOWLEDGE AND FREEDOM: THE RUSSELL LECTURES 13 (1971).

[18] *Id.* at 21.

[19] Although Chomsky's investigation is presently limited to language, he suggests an investigation of other systems of belief as a natural further step: "I see no reason why other domains of human intelligence might not be amenable to such investigation. Perhaps, in this way, we can characterize the structure of various systems of human knowledge and belief, various systems of performance and interaction." *Id.* at 47.

[20] Jalet, *The Quest for the General Principles of Law Recognized by Civilized Nations — A Study,* 10 U.C.L.A.L. REV. 1041 (1963), *quoting* Cheng, *The Meaning and Scope of Article 38(1)(c) of the Statute of the International Court of Justice,* in 38 GROTIUS SOCIETY: TRANSACTIONS FOR THE YEAR 1952, at 125, 129 (1953).

[21] Financed by a grant from the Ford Foundation, the purpose of the Project as initially formulated was to determine "whether there are, in fact, any basic 'core' legal principles of private law generally recognized by civilized nations." Davis, *Comparative Law Contributions to the International Legal Order: Common Core Research,* 37 GEO. WASH. L. REV. 615, 616 (1969).

research was limited to contract law, the noticeable uniformity of contract principles discovered by the research supports the theory of a universal normative structure. Although legal realists have criticized the theory of common core research, their criticism has focused on the alleged pointlessness of discovering common core principles, not upon the fact of their existence.[22]

Further support for a universal normative structure theory is found in recent research by psychologists Kohlberg and Tapp. Their national, cross-national, and cross-cultural studies of the effects of moral and legal attitudes on behavior suggest that moral and legal development toward order and justice follows a universal sequence of distinct stages.[23] Kohlberg's research indicates that "[t]he development of moral thought follows a universal sequence of distinct stages." [24] Similarly, Tapp's research relates legal concepts to Kohlberg's moral levels.

Kohlberg's studies identify three general levels of moral judgment and two intermediate stages within each level. At level I, the "Preconventional Level," man interprets moral labels in terms of physical consequences. At the "Physical Power" stage of level I, superior power or prestige determines morality in terms of physical consequences. At the "Instrumental Relativism" stage of level I, moral acts are hedonistically characterized in terms of satisfying one's own needs; equitable considerations are present, but they are interpreted pragmatically. At level II, the "Conventional Level," morality is characterized by active support of the status quo. At the "Interpersonal Concordance" stage of level II, conformity to majority behavior determines morality. At the "Law and Order" stage of level II, one's moral duty is to obey fixed rules to maintain the given social order. Level III, the "Post Conventional" level, is marked by the appearance of autonomous moral principles. At the "Social Contract" stage of level III, morality is determined in terms of individual rights agreed upon by the society in the form of a hypothetical constitution. In this stage, procedural rules for reaching consensus opinions are critical, and possibility of social change is determined by social utility. The "Universal Ethic" stage of level III is characterized by universal, consistent,

---

[22] Even if comprehensive impressions of commonly accepted positive legal principles, attitudes and consistencies of decision making were somehow reduced to a manageable common denominator of core premises arguably constituting an extranational common law of mankind, the fabric of this law is so easily rent or so clearly vulnerable to unretributable alteration, change or even obliteration by those exercising raw political power within the territories of national enclaves that such a comprehensive project would be manifestly pointless.
*Id.* at 626.

[23] Kohlberg & Tapp, *Developing Senses of Law and Legal Justice*, 27 J. Soc. Issues at 89 (1971). The theoretical bases for Kohlberg's model are represented by John Dewey's genetic, experiential, and purposive reasoning (1910, 1916, and 1930), Jean Piaget's structural approach to moral development and cognitive thought (1928, 1929, and 1932), and Immanuel Kant's ethical analysis (1849). *Id.* at 67.

[24] *Id.* at 67.

and comprehensive moral decisions. Individual ethical principles prevail.[25]

Tapp's levels of legal development, which correspond to Kohlberg's levels of moral development, progress from prohibitive laws supported by threat of punishment, to prescriptive or neutral regulatory laws supported by vested interests, to rationally, beneficial laws supported by principled obedience.[26]

The implications of the Tapp and Kohlberg studies are that a universal normative structure exists and that movement toward full realization of that structure contributes to peace and justice within the community. Movement between stages, however, follows an incremental pattern requiring stimulation and assimilation, and the absence of either element tends to retard or even arrest community development to higher levels. To facilitate growth, therefore, the stimulator must encourage "[e]xperience-based activity involving conflict resolution, problem solving and participation in decision making," all of which promote voluntary compliance through perfecting a sense of responsibility, obligation, and justice. Tapp and Kohlberg observe:

> The match problem for affecting change in legal development is one of presenting stimuli sufficiently incongruous to stimulate conflict in the individual's cognitive schema, and sufficiently congruous to be assimilated with some accommodative effort.[27]

The relevance to the international sphere of data relating to the normative development of the individual obviously raises complex questions; nevertheless, several hypotheses will be suggested. The first hypothesis is that the individuals who ultimately are affected and bound by decisions, including the decision-makers themselves, must be willing to live with the results; this is not to say that the individuals who participate in the decision-making process can develop a corporate legal conscience through corporate experiences in conflict resolution. Rather, the degree to which the individuals have developed their legal consciousness bears directly on what decisions they will accept as obligatory. The second hypothesis is that the level of legal consciousness which the individual decision-makers have accommodated will necessarily limit the alternatives for decision available to them. Furthermore, the bounds of the alternatives certainly must be circumscribed by the limits that the participants are willing to accept. It follows that institutional structures and individual legal consciousness can reinforce each other in the accomplishment of peace.

The interplay between institutional structures and individual legal consciousness can contribute to international peace and justice in at least four areas. First, the degree to which a government conforms to its own legal constraints, constitutional or otherwise, bears directly on international

---

[25] *Id.* at 73–77.

[26] *Id.* at 84.

[27] *Id.* at 87.

peace. Second, the degree to which the government's decisional processes conform to international legal constraints also affects international order. Third, the extent to which a government promotes and sustains international institutions contributes to international order. Fourth, the level of legal consciousness attained by the world public actually constrains governments that would otherwise act contrary to international order.

A government's strict compliance with its own laws contributes to international order in several ways: (1) A government that has incorporated international law into its own civil or common law is obligated to international order by its own legal structure, apart from international constraints. (2) A state must habitually obey its domestic legal constraints before it can successfully accommodate international legal principles. A government, for example, that disregards its own legal procedures will likely act similarly in its relations with other states. Accordingly, strict compliance with domestic constitutional procedures benefits not only domestic order, but also international order, and vice versa. A comparison of our government's conduct in the Watergate affair and its unconstitutional acts in Indochina supports this proposition.[28]

This concept should not be viewed solely through the glasses of Western liberal thought. It is not asserted that progressive democratic societies will be peaceful and totalitarian states will be war-like; rather, it is asserted that states, regardless of their ideology, that adhere to internal legal constraints and abide their own rules of municipal order are less likely to violate international norms; conversely, violation of international norms may similarly predispose a government to violate municipal law.

The extent to which a government's formal decision-making machinery operates under international legal constraints necessarily affects international order. For example, efforts in establishing treaties and regulating conflicts between international actors substantially aid in preserving international order, notwithstanding the rationalist power politics theory to the contrary. Abram Chayes recognizes this view in an analysis of the working of arms control agreements.[29] Chayes asserts that the bureaucratic inertia of perpetuating and maintaining "organizational health . . . in terms of bodies assigned and dollars appropriated" [30] can be channelled in a normative direction by the processes of treaty negotiation and ratification.[31]

---

[28] Our participation in the Vietnam War was initiated and later maintained in violation of both constitutional and international law. In turn, later violations of municipal and constitutional law, known generically as Watergate, were in part caused by factors stemming from our involvement in Vietnam.

[29] Chayes, *An Inquiry into the Workings of Arms Control Agreements*, 85 HARV. L. REV. 905 (1972).

[30] *Id.* at 916, *quoting* G. ALLISON, ESSENCE OF DECISION: EXPLAINING THE CUBAN MISSILE CRISIS 82 (1971).

[31] [T]his very process of negotiation and ratification tends to generate powerful pressures for compliance, if and when the treaty is adopted. At least three interrelated phenomena contribute to these pressures: (1) by the time the treaty is adopted, a broad consensus within governmental and political circles

International institutions may substantially contribute to international order both by successfully resolving conflicts and by stimulating international community growth. Although Kennan's criticism of excessive institutionalism possesses penetrating insight, the growth of supernational entities has rendered his criticism increasingly less valid and more reactionary. Institutional structure, however, cannot replace a lack of consensus on critical issues. Obligations arising out of supra-national institutions will be binding only insofar as they comport with the level of legal development achieved by the participating states.

Finally, the growing consciousness of the universality of human experience contributes to the development of law and peace:

> There is a new realism emerging out of the need to adapt the state system to the multiple challenges of war, population pressure, global pollution, resource depletion, and human alienation. It is this new political consciousness that insists upon regarding America's involvement in the Indochina War as illegal and immoral *from the beginning* . . . .[32]

Our involvement in the Vietnam War offers an excellent vehicle for a detailed analysis of the significance to international peace and justice of governmental adherence to constitutional and international laws.

### A. Vietnam and Constitutionalism

This country, along with other states, can influence the growth of legal consciousness by force of example; a particularly potent example would be a return to the basic precepts of our own charter, thereby fostering an understanding of constitutionalism. Those exercising sovereign prerogatives are considered to be circumscribed by *leges imperii* — the laws of government. These laws normally antedate the exercise of sovereign power and determine the identity and the limits of persons that exercise such power. Contrary to those who perceive from the Vietnam experience a failure of our constitutional structure and the accompanying need for a convention to produce a new constitutional document,[33] it would seem at once more sound and more attainable to return to the basic prescriptions of the Constitution. Detailed analyses of the constitutional implications of our Vietnam involvement have been accomplished [34] and will not be re-

---

will be arrayed in support of the decision; (2) meanwhile, principal centers of potential continuing opposition will have been neutralized or assuaged, though often by means of concessions that significantly modify the substance of the policy; and (3) many officials, leaders of the administration or regime and opponents as well, will have been personally and publicly committed to the treaty, creating a kind of political imperative for the success of the policy.
*Id.* at 920.

[32] Falk, *Nuremberg: Past, Present, and Future,* 80 YALE L.J. 1501, 1510–11 (1971) • (footnote omitted).

[33] R. TUGWELL, A MODEL CONSTITUTION FOR A UNITED REPUBLICS OF AMERICA (1970).

[34] Berger, *War-Making by the President,* 121 U. PA. L. REV. 29 (1972); Fulbright, *Congress, The President and the War Power,* 25 ARK. L. REV. 71 (1971); Goldwater,

peated here; rather, only conclusions of law will be advanced. As will be seen, obedience to these most basic constitutional principles would at once restrain our own predilections toward the unlawful use of force, and would serve as an example to be followed by other states.

First, it is apparent that the war powers, although divided between the executive and the legislative branches, were deposited dominantly within the latter branch.[35] The deliberative branch was purposely given preponderant power as a check upon the impulsive use of military force. The logic of James Madison is as compelling now as it was during the battle over the ratification of the Constitution:

> Those who are to *conduct a war* cannot in the nature of things, be proper or safe judges, whether *a war ought to be commenced, continued or concluded*. They are barred from the latter function by a great principle in free government, analogous to that which separates the sword from the purse, or the power of executing from the power of enacting laws.[36]

Madison further noted the axiom that "the executive is the department of power most distinguished by its propensity to war: hence it is the practice of all states, in proportion as they are free, to disarm this propensity of its influence." [37]

Thomas Jefferson also indicated his pleasure in the decision to endow the Congress rather than the President with the war power; he wrote to Madison: "We have already given . . . one effectual check to the Dog of war by transferring the power of letting him loose from the Executive to the Legislative body, from those who are to spend to those who are to pay." [38]

---

*The President's Constitutional Primacy in Foreign Relations and National Defense,* 13 VA. J. INT'L. L. 463 (1973); Lofgren, *War-Making Under the Constitution: The Original Understanding,* 81 YALE L.J. 672 (1972); Rostow, *Great Cases Make Bad Law: The War Powers Act,* 50 TEX. L. REV. 833 (1972); Van Alstyne, *Congress, The President, and the Power to Declare War: A Requiem for Vietnam,* 121 U. PA. L. REV. 1 (1972); Wormuth, *The Nixon Theory of the War Power: A Critique,* 60 CALIF. L. REV. 623 (1972).

[35] Lofgren, *supra* note 34, at 688. Lofgren has carefully analysed the Convention, state ratification debates, trends in theory, and English influence. He concludes that the men of the day probably conceived of the President's war-making role in exceptionally narrow terms.

James Wilson, perhaps the leading legal theoretician of the Convention, said:
> The power of declaring war, and the other powers naturally connected with it, are vested in Congress. To provide and maintain a navy — to make rules for its government — to grant letters of marque and reprisal — to make rules concerning captures — to raise and support armies — to establish rules for their regulation — to provide for organizing . . . the militia, and for calling them forth in the service of the Union — all these are powers naturally connected with the power of declaring war. All these powers, therefore, are vested in Congress.

1 J. WILSON, WORKS 433 (R. McCloskey ed. 1967).

[36] Berger, *supra* note 34, at 39, *quoting* J. MADISON, *Letters of Helvidius,* in WRITINGS 148 (G. Hunt ed. 1906).

[37] *Id.* at 38, *quoting* 6 J. MADISON, *Letters of Helvidius,* in WRITINGS 138, 174 (G. Hunt ed. 1906).

[38] Fulbright, *supra* note 34, at 74, *quoting* 15 THE PAPERS OF THOMAS JEFFERSON 397 (J. Boyd ed. 1955).

Congress's powers to "provide for the common defence," [39] to "raise and support armies," [40] "to provide and maintain a navy," [41] "to regulate commerce with foreign nations," [42] "to define and punish piracies and felonies committed on the high seas, and offences against the law of nations,"[43] to "grant letters of marque and reprisal," [44] to "make rules concerning captures on land and water," [45] "to make rules for the government and regulation of land and naval forces," [46] "to provide for calling forth the militia to execute the laws of the union," [47] to "suppress insurrections and repel invasions," [48] "to provide for organizing, arming, and disciplining the militia, and for governing such part of them as may be employed in the service of the United States," [49] "to make all laws which shall be necessary and proper for carrying into execution the foregoing powers," [50] and, most importantly, "to declare war," [51] clearly leave the Executive only ministerial war power prerogatives, and these he may exercise only within parameters determined largely by Congress.

Congress's textual grant of power to "declare war" provides, with only one qualification, the exclusive power to initiate war,[52] whether declared or undeclared.[53] The sole qualification upon Congress's exclusive power

---

James Wilson, recognized as a proponent of a "strong Executive," referred to the "declare war" provision in ratification debates in Pennsylvania:
> This system will not hurry us into war; it is calculated to guard against it. It will not be in the power of a single man . . . to involve us in such distress; for the important power of declaring war is vested in the legislature at large . . . from this circumstance we may draw a certain conclusion that nothing but our national interest can draw us into a war.

2 J. ELLIOT, THE DEBATES IN THE SEVERAL STATE CONVENTIONS ON THE ADOPTION OF THE FEDERAL CONSTITUTION 528 (1937).

[39] U.S. CONST. art. I, § 8, cl. 1.

[40] *Id.* cl. 12.

[41] *Id.* cl. 13.

[42] *Id.* cl. 3.

[43] *Id.* cl. 10.

[44] *Id.* cl. 11.

[45] *Id.*

[46] *Id.* cl. 14.

[47] *Id.* cl. 15.

[48] *Id.*

[49] *Id.* cl. 16.

[50] *Id.* cl. 18.

[51] *Id.* cl. 11.

[52] See Wilson's statement in 2 J. ELLIOT, *supra* note 38. Secretary of State Daniel Webster said (in 1851):
> . . . I have to say that the war-making power in this Government rests entirely with Congress; and that the President can authorize belligerent operations only in the cases expressly provided for by the Constitution and the laws. By these no power is given to the Executive to oppose an attack by one independent nation on the possessions of another. . . . [I]f this interference be an act of hostile force, it is not within the constitutional power of the President . . . .

Quoted in Van Alstyne, *Congress, The President, and the Power to Declare War: A Requiem for Vietnam,* 121 U. PA. L. REV. 1, 11 (1972), *quoting* 7 DIGEST OF INTERNATIONAL LAW 163–64 (J. Moore ed. 1906).

[53] The Congress possesses all war-making powers of the United States. Those powers not specifically falling within the "declare war" provision most assuredly were residual in the "grant letters of marque and reprisal" clause. U.S. CONST. art. I, § 8, cl. 11.

to initiate war is the presidential prerogative to use military force to repel sudden attack upon the United States [54] and, after the War Powers Amendment, upon its forces.[55] James Madison and Elbridge Gerry made joint motion to change Congress's power from *make* war (the original wording of the clause as proposed by the Committee on Detail) to *declare* war, for the purpose as recorded by the notes of the convention kept by Madison, of "leaving to the Executive the power to repel sudden attacks." [56] Congress's war powers also extend to the circumstances of war's termination.[57]

As Commander-in-Chief, the President has substantial though not unlimited power to direct a war once it has been initiated by Congress. Hamilton, the powerful advocate of presidential prerogatives, outlined the limits of the President's power as Commander-in-Chief in *The Federalist Papers*:

> The President is to be commander-in-chief of the army and navy of the United States. In this respect his authority would be nominally the same with that of the king of Great Britain, but in substance much inferior to it. It would amount to nothing more than the supreme command and direction of the military and naval forces, as first General and admiral of the Confederacy; while that of the British king extends

---

*See* Lofgren, *War-Making Under the Constitution: The Original Understanding*, 81 YALE L.J. 672, 696 (1972).

Thomas Jefferson, as Secretary of State, analyzed the "undeclared war" element of reprisal:

> [A] reprisal on a nation is a very serious thing. . . . [W]hen reprisal follows, it is considered an act of war, and never failed to produce it in the case of a nation able to make war; besides, if the case were important and ripe for that step, *Congress must be called upon to take it;* the right of reprisal being expressly lodged with them by the Constitution, *and not with the Executive.*

Quoted in 7 INTERNATIONAL LAW DIGEST § 1095, at 123 (J. Moore ed. 1906) (emphasis added).

Pierce Butler, a Convention delegate from South Carolina, stated:

> It is improbable that a single member of the Convention have signed his name to the Constitution if he had supposed that the instrument might be construed as authorizing the President to initiate a war, either general or partial, without the express authorization of Congress.

Quoted in Fulbright, *Congress, the President and the War Power*, 25 ARK. L. REV. 71, 74 (1971). Early cases decided by the Supreme Court also left little doubt about the power of Congress over both "declared" and "undeclared" wars. The word "war" was not confined to mean only general ("declared") war. The Supreme Court furthermore found that the President must abide by the limitations set by Congress. Little v. Barreme, 6 U.S. (2 Cranch.) 170 (1804); Talbot v. Seeman, 5 U.S. (1 Cranch.) 1 (1801); Bas v. Tingy, 4 U.S. (4 Dall.) 36 (1800).

[54] The records of the constitutional convention leave little doubt that it was the intent of the Framers to provide an exception to the congressional war powers enabling the President to repel sudden attacks upon the United States. "Mr. MADISON and Mr. GERRY moved to insert *'declare,'* striking out *'make'* war; leaving to the Executive the power to repel sudden attacks." Van Alstyne, *supra* note 34, at 6, *quoting* 2 RECORDS OF THE FEDERAL CONVENTION OF 1789, at 318–19 (M. Farrand ed. 1911).

[55] S. 440, 93d Cong., 1st Sess. § 3 (1973), provides:

> To repel an armed attack against the Armed Forces of the United States located outside of the United States, its territories and possessions, and to forestall the direct and imminent threat of such an attack.

*See* 50 U.S.C.A. §§ 1541–48 (Supp. 1974).

[56] Van Alstyne, *supra* note 34, at 6, *quoting* 2 RECORDS OF THE FEDERAL CONVENTION OF 1789 (M. Farrand ed. 1911).

[57] Woods v. Cloyd W. Miller Co., 333 U.S. 138 (1948).

to the *declaring* of war and to the *raising* and *regulating* of fleets and armies, — all which, by the Constitution under consideration, would appertain to the legislature.[58]

The President, possessing no power to initiate or wage executive war other than the power to repel sudden attacks, has been further limited by Congress in his exercise of the powers of Commander-in-Chief.[59] Congress has statutorily circumscribed presidential prerogatives to use troops for particular purposes and in certain areas of the world.[60] He may not raise armies without congressional authorization,[61] nor may he violate the Laws of War as determined by Congress.[62] Congress's power to issue letters of marque and reprisal, coupled with the original understanding of congressional power to declare war, should mean that Congress has complete power over the commencement of war, whether declared or undeclared ("imperfect").[63] The vast majority of Executive wars cited [64] as precedents for the legality of the Executive origin of the Vietnam War based upon Commander-in-Chief powers of the President are distinguishable on their face as minor events, often involving the landing of troops to protect American civilians abroad.[65] The only valid precedent for the constitutional prerogative of the President to initiate war, though clearly distin-

---

[58] THE FEDERALIST No. 69, at 448 (Modern Library ed. 1937) (A. Hamilton).

[59] *See* Wormuth, *supra* note 34, at 652 *et seq.*

[60] *Id.* at 639–40. Congressional acts have regulated or forbidden the use of troops to accomplish the return of fugitive slaves and have forbidden the use of troops at polling places and as posse comitatus, or marines on shore. Other acts have provided for selective service and training limitations, and termination of activities in Indochina.

[61] *Id.* at 642. For example, Abraham Lincoln's use of volunteers at the beginning of the Civil War was dependent upon subsequent congressional legislation. United States v. Hosmer, 76 U.S. (9 Wall.) 432 (1870).

[62] Wormuth, *supra* note 34, at 645.

[63] Lofgren, *supra* note 34, at 699–700. Lofgren concludes:
Since the old Congress held blanket power to "determine" on war, and since undeclared war was hardly unknown in fact and theory in the late eighteenth century, it therefore seems a reasonable conclusion that the new Congress' power "to declare War" was not understood in a narrow technical sense but rather as meaning the power to commence war, whether declared or not. To the extent that the power was more narrowly interpreted, however, the new Congress' control over letters of marque and reprisal must have suggested to contemporaries that it would still control "imperfect" — that is, undeclared — war.
*Id.*

[64] 117 CONG. REC. 11,913–24 (1971) (remarks of Senator Goldwater); Goldwater, *The President's Constitutional Primacy in Foreign Relations and National Defense,* 13 VA. J. INT'L L. 463 (1973); Rostow, *Great Cases Make Bad Law: The War Powers Act,* 50 TEX L. REV. 833 (1972).

[65] Of the 137 cases of Executive action claimed by the State Department, forty-eight had clear congressional authorization, one was in self-defense, six were mere demonstrations, some others were trespass or spontaneous, unsanctioned acts by lower commanders, and several were clearly unconstitutional acts by the President. Wormuth, *supra* note 34, at 660 *et. seq.* "Even were these incidents to be regarded as equivalent to executive waging of war, the last precedent would stand no better than the first; illegality is not legitimized by repetition." Berger, *War-Making by the President,* 121 U. PA. L. REV. 29, 60 (1972).

guishable in terms of international law,[66] is the Korean War. In that regard, it must simply be affirmed that violation by a President of a clear and exclusive textual grant of authority to Congress must not be taken to legitimate similar subsequent violations.[67]

The Tonkin Gulf Resolution, though not a congressional authorization for war,[68] may reasonably be interpreted as an attempt by Congress to delegate its war powers to the President[69] and directly to authorize his acts in the nature of reprisals.[70] Even though the Supreme Court has not stricken a delegation of congressional powers to the Executive since the 1930's,[71] the specificity of the textual grant of the war power to Congress, together with its profound impact upon the entire conception of separation of powers, suggests that delegation of such powers should not be tolerated. In any event, whatever authority the President derived from the Tonkin Gulf Resolution was terminated with its repeal in 1971. At least after that time, the United States fought an unconstitutional war in Southeast Asia.

It seems clear that the war powers cannot be delegated by treaty, specifically by the provisions of the Southeast Asian Treaty,[72] without participa-

[66] Within the context of international law, two highly significant factors distinguish our participation in the Korean War from our role in Vietnam. First, the United Nations by Security Council resolution had determined the existence of an armed attack by the forces of North Korea upon South Korea. The resolution called upon all member states to provide military forces under a unified United Nations command to repel the attack. 5 U.N. SCOR, 476th meeting 5, U.N. Doc S/1588 (1950). Second, the massive, completely unambiguous nature of the armed attack verified by United Nations fact-finding at the time of the assault, contrasts sharply with the indirect aggression that characterized the early years of the Vietnam War. *See* Firmage, *Fact-Finding in the Resolution of International Disputes — From the Hague Peace Conference to the United Nations,* 1971 UTAH L. REV. 421, 445–46.

[67] Many writers who are critical of the several lists of "Executive wars" because of the insignificance of the examples set forth find little problem in accepting the Korean conflict and the Vietnam action as examples of "Executive wars." The Senate Foreign Relations Committee has issued a statement that "only since 1950 have Presidents regarded themselves as having authority to commit the armed forces to full scale and sustained warfare." S. REP. No. 707, 90th Cong., 1st Sess. 24 (1967).

President Johnson, in much the same way as President Truman handled the Security Council resolution, did not place primary legal reliance upon the Tonkin Gulf Resolution. Instead, he repeatedly asserted a constitutional, presidential power to conduct war in Southeast-Asia.

[68] Wormuth finds four differences between the Tonkin Gulf Resolution and initiation of war by Congress: (1) The Resolution did not initiate hostilities, but only authorized the President to do so; (2) The Resolution did not define our legal status, *i.e.,* general or limited war; (3) The Resolution defined no adversary state; and (4) No treaty of peace requiring Senate concurrence was demanded; accordingly, the President could freely conclude a peace as well as authorize a war. Wormuth concludes that since the Tonkin Gulf Resolution performed none of the functions of a declared war, it could not operate as a declaration of war. It was an outright presentation of the war power to the President and, as such, was an unconstitutional delegation of congressional power. Wormuth, *supra* note 34, at 691–92. *See also* Van Alstyne, *supra* note 34, at 20.

[69] Wormuth, *supra* note 34, at 692.

[70] See Tonkin Gulf Resolution, H.R.J. Res. 1145, 88th Cong., 2d Sess., 78 Stat. 384 (1964), wherein the President is authorized to repel an attack against United States forces and to "prevent further aggression."

[71] Schechter Poultry Corp. v. United States, 295 U.S. 495 (1935); Panama Refining Co. v. Ryan, 292 U.S. 388 (1935).

[72] *See* Firmage, *International Law and the Response of the United States to "Internal War,"* in 2 THE VIETNAM WAR AND INTERNATIONAL LAW 89, 116–17 (R. Falk ed. 1969). Article four, paragraph one, of the Southeast Asia Collective defense Treaty (SEATO) states:

tion by the House of Representatives in the treaty-making process.[73] SEATO requires that its member states act only "in accordance with [their] constitutional process." [74] The President must not be allowed the ultimate bootstrap of initiating an international agreement (SEATO), claiming the constitutional mandate to see "that the laws be faithfully executed," [75] and then waging a war — otherwise proscribed by the Constitution — upon the argument that it is required by the international agreement. Neither presidential power to initiate war nor congressional authority to delegate its war powers can be accomplished by international agreement contrary to constitutional restraints. In *Reid v. Covert*, the Supreme Court stated that

> no agreement with a foreign nation can confer power on Congress, or on any other branch of Government, which is free from the restraints of the Constitution.
> . . . It would be manifestly contrary to the objectives of those who created the Constitution [and] alien to our entire constitutional history and tradition . . . to construe Article VI as permitting the United States to exercise power under an international agreement without observing constitutional prohibitions.[76]

*Covert* mercifully lays to rest the question whether the power to make international agreements somehow releases the federal government from constitutional constraints, a question raised in part by a broad reading of *Missouri v. Holland* [77] and in part by Mr. Justice Sutherland's tortured history of the origin of national power to conduct foreign policy.[78]

---

Each party recognizes that aggression by means of armed attack in the treaty area against any of the parties or against any state or territory which the parties by unanimous agreement may hereafter designate, would endanger its own peace and safety, and agrees that it will in that event act to meet the common danger (1955) *in accordance with its constitutional processes.*
6 U.S.T. 81, T.I.A.S. No. 3170, *reprinted in* 60 AM. J. INT'L L. 647 (1966) (emphasis added).
[T]he treaty commitment, rather than empowering the President to undertake the use of military force, sets an international contractual obligation — obliging Congress to make the declaration of war if it intends to fulfill the treaty commitment.
Van Alstyne, *supra* note 34, at 14.

[73] The Constitution vests the war powers in both Houses of Congress, and not in the President and the Senate, as with the treaty power. The alternative — granting to the President the power to initiate war with Senate concurrence — was specifically considered and rejected at the Convention. *See* 1 RECORDS OF THE FEDERAL CONVENTION OF 1787, at 292, 300 (M. Farrand ed. 1911).

[74] SEATO Treaty, art. 4, ¶ 4, 6 U.S.T. 81, T.I.A.S. No. 3170, *reprinted in* 60 AM. J. INT'L L. 647 (1966).

[75] U.S. CONST. art. II, § 3.

[76] Reid v. Covert, 354 U.S. 1, 16–17 (1957).

[77] 252 U.S. 416 (1920).

[78] United States v. Curtiss-Wright Export Corp., 299 U.S. 304 (1936). According to Mr. Justice Sutherland, power to conduct foreign policy was somehow transferred directly from the Crown to the federal government and does not inhere to the federal government through grant from the Constitutional Convention. Justice Sutherland wrote for the Court: "As a result of the separation from Great Britain by the colonies acting as a unit, the powers of external sovereignty passed from the Crown not to the colonies severally, but to the colonies in their collective and corporate capacity as the

The constitutional mandate that the "executive power shall be vested" [79] in the President is not a grant of inherent power, much less an executive authorization to do all things "necessary and proper" to accomplish delegated prerogatives. Rather, it is simply the power ministerially to execute laws enacted by Congress. The President's constitutional mandate to execute the laws in no way authorizes the President to perform the legislative task of creating the laws to be executed. When considered in the context of the war power, the President's executive power does not in any way increase his enumerated power as "Commander-in-Chief." This is the meaning of the *Steel Seizure* and *New York Times* cases.[80] An acknowledgment of inherent presidential power would constitute a giant stride toward eliminating the distinction between republican government and imperial presidency.

Finally, it is quite proper that foreign affairs remain dominantly the domain of the political branches of government. Foreign affairs has constituted the "hard core" of the political question doctrine from the beginning. Even so, the courts have often spoken on vital issues of foreign policy.[81] As the communal roots of a society deepen and the community matures, it would seem reasonable that decisions could increasingly be made more in accordance with rules of law and somewhat less by political accommodation. Accordingly, one might expect to see a gradual but steady constriction of the scope of the political question doctrine. But where the Constitution accomplishes a clear textual grant of power to one political branch, it would seem entirely proper for the Court to reject the political question argument and reach the merits of a controversy. Under *Baker v. Carr*,[82] a "textually demonstrable constitutional commitment of the issue to a coordinate political department" qualifies as a political question. However, the branch to which such power has been granted must stay within its constitutional mandate; whether a branch exceeds such mandate is justiciable, according to *Powell v. McCormack*.[83] Whether we should be at war at a given time, with whom, and for what reason are political questions rightly reserved to the political branches. But the issue

---

United States of America." *Id.* at 316; *see* Lofgren, *United States v. Curtiss-Wright Export Corporation: An Historical Reassessment,* 83 YALE L.J. 1 (1973); Wormuth, *supra* note 34, at 694.

[79] U.S. CONST. art. II, § 1, cl. 1.

[80] *See* New York Times Co. v. United States, 403 U.S. 713 (1971); Youngstown Sheet & Tube Co. v. Sawyer, 343 U.S. 579 (1952).

[81] In keeping with the intentions of the framers, the Court has held that the President may repel a sudden attack, whether by invasion or by insurrection, that Congress may institute either general or limited war, and that the President in waging war may not exceed his statutory authority. The rank, status, duties, and discipline of members of the armed forces are fixed by Congress. The recruitment of the armed forces, the draft, the confiscation of enemy property, the appropriation of factories, the suspension of the writ of habeas corpus — all these and other topics have been adjudicated and held to belong to Congress.

Wormuth, *supra* note 34, at 678–79 (footnotes omitted).

[82] 369 U.S. 186 (1962).

[83] 396 U.S. 486, 514 (1969). *See also* Bond v. Floyd, 385 U.S. 116 (1966).

whether war was initiated in accordance with the Constitution's clear textual mandate to Congress is justiciable and should be decided by the Court.[84]

The concept of separated powers, properly checked and balanced, has too long been allowed to atrophy because of a tilt toward the Executive branch. This trend, too frequently advanced by Executive action during times of war, must be reversed, and a condition of equilibrium reestablished. Perhaps the causally related shocks of Vietnam and Watergate will generate currents of opinion sufficiently strong and enduring to facilitate institutional reform capable of returning us to old moorings.[85]

In addition to the constitutional constraints upon Executive action, extra-constitutional constraints must be preserved and in some cases revitalized. Although these concepts cannot be developed here, such constraints upon arbitrary presidential action include a strong political party structure to which the President would in some degree be accountable; a White House staff with seniors committed to republican government and the rule of law and juniors sufficiently beyond identity crises to avoid seduction; a Cabinet composed of members of sufficient independent political or professional base to allow private if not public dissent from presidential policies; and a presidential schedule that would allow leading politicians of both parties access to the presidential ear. Finally, a free press, though not formally a part of the system of checks

---

[84] In 1821, Chief Justice Marshall, in Cohens v. Virginia, 19 U.S. (6 Wheat) 264 (1821), stated:

> It is most true, that this court will not take jurisdiction if it should not: but it is equally true, that it must take jurisdiction, if it should. The judiciary cannot, as the legislature may, avoid a measure, because it approaches the confines of the constitution. . . . With whatever doubts, with whatever difficulties, a case may be attended, we must decide it, if it be brought before us. We have no more right to decline the exercise of jurisdiction which is given, than to usurp that which is not given. The one or the other would be treason to the constitution.

*Id.* at 404.

The abstention and political question doctrines are exceptions to Marshall's dictum, and perhaps rightly so. But the goal recognized in the statement remains valid, particularly as it relates to the question of a clear textual grant of power to one branch of government that is usurped by another without the necessity of a struggle.

*See also* Massachusetts v. Laird, 400 U.S. 886 (1970) (Harlan & Stewart, J.J., dissenting); Hart v. United States, 391 U.S. 956 (1968) (Douglas, J., dissenting); Holmes v. United States, 391 U.S. 936 (1968) (Douglas, J., dissenting); Mora v. McNamara, 389 U.S. 934 (1967) (Stewart & Douglas, J.J., dissenting); Orlando v. Laird, 443 F.2d 1039 (2d Cir.), *cert. denied,* 404 U.S. 869 (1971) (court found a justiciable question and reached the merits of the case concerning United States military activity in Vietnam).

[85] George Washington said:

> The necessity of reciprocal checks of political power . . . has been evinced. . . . To preserve them must be as necessary as to institute them. If in the opinion of the people, the distribution or modification of the Constitutional powers be in any particular wrong, let it be corrected by an amendment in the way in which the Constitution designates. But let there be no change by usurpation; for though this, in one instance, may be the instrument of good, it is the customary weapon by which free governments are destroyed. The precedent must always greatly overbalance in permanent evil any partial or transient benefit which the use can at any time yield.

35 G. WASHINGTON, WRITINGS 228–29 (Fitzpatrick ed. 1940).

and balances, provides the life fluid — from a position shielded by the first amendment — without which the entire constitutional structure would be impotent. A conditional privilege for newsmen's sources of information is essential.

## B. International Law and Vietnam

The existence of nuclear weapons has made massive warfare between nuclear-weapon states highly unlikely and has also precipitated increasingly strong customary legal constraints upon such forms of warfare. Similarly, the trauma of the Vietnam War, by force of its ghastly impact upon all participants, may affect certain international rules of behavior. The norms most likely to be affected are those governing the conditions under which nations go to war and the means by which war is fought.

Within the traditional norm [86] governing third party participation in civil strife, third parties could aid the incumbent government at least initially, they could not aid the insurgent faction at least until a status of belligerency was attained, and they were required to be neutral after such status was attained; this norm has been seriously undercut. A fundamental justification for a rule favoring the incumbent has been the accuracy of perceiving the valued roles performed by the incumbent in society. Thus, a legal presumption favoring the incumbent was defensible because its very existence strongly suggested its legitimacy. The term "legitimacy" is not used here in the legalistic sense of the acquisition of power by formally orthodox or proper means; rather, it is used, as the political scientist or sociologist would use it, to connote a sufficient affinity between the people and the institutions of government, based upon the preexistence of a cultural harmony between them, that allegiance naturally results without coercion.[87] Because of this affinity between the people and their government, the government could perform essential functions such as the maintenance of order, the collection of taxes, and the performance of other basic tasks. In those parts of the so-called Third World that have experienced colonial rule, the emergence of governing elites possessing the characteristics of political legitimacy has not occurred immediately, nor has it always taken the direction preferred by the former colonial ruler. Often, several factions have contended for dominance, or former colonial rulers have attempted to impose their choice for native leadership upon the society.

The result has been a blurred distinction between incumbent and insurgent. Most incumbents have lacked many if not all of the traditional characteristics of incumbency. In such a situation the underpinnings of the

---

[86] *See* Firmage, *Summary and Interpretation,* in THE INTERNATIONAL LAW OF CIVIL WAR 405 (R. Falk ed. 1970).

[87] *See* Firmage, *The War of National Liberation and the Third World,* in LAW AND CIVIL WAR IN THE MODERN WORLD (Moore ed. 1974). Lipset has defined legitimacy as the capacity of a political system to advance and maintain the belief that existing political institutions were the most appropriate for the community. Lipset, *Some Social Requisites of Democracy: Economic Development and Political Legitimacy* 53 AM. POL. SCI. REV. 69 (1959).

traditional rule, with its presumption of incumbent legitimacy, have been largely destroyed. The traditional rule cannot survive in those areas with a colonial past, at least until traditional elites emerge possessing sufficient legitimacy to govern.

It follows that a new norm governing third party involvement will develop; that rule will either allow unrestricted military aid to both incumbent and insurgent without distinction, or it will proscribe military assistance to any faction in a state experiencing civil strife, or it will allow some forms of aid under restrictions falling somewhere between the two pole positions. The first possibility would permit unrestrained intervention and is best described as the absence of a norm rather than the creation of a new one. The second possibility, proscribing any form of third party military aid, would probably be at once the most desirable and the least likely of accomplishment. Modified versions of this norm, sufficiently realistic to be acceptable to most powerful states, have been suggested and analyzed by Farer and Moore.[88] Our experience in Vietnam clearly demonstrates the illegality, the immorality, and the hopelessness of intervention in support of an incumbent regime that lacks sufficient legitimacy to govern without outside assistance.

World-wide offense at American participation in the Vietnam War stemmed not only from the perceived illegitimacy of our intervention, but also from the strategy and the weaponry employed. A clear absence of proportionality existed from the beginning; it was made apparent to the world because of television, and it was made more damning upon release of the Pentagon Papers, which revealed no serious debate on the moral and legal questions involved in waging modern war against a native society. A strategy necessitating free-fire zones, forced depopulation of major areas, carpet bombing, bombing of major urban areas, and use of the most sophisticated weaponry with massive firepower obliterates any distinction between combatant and non-combatant. The moral and legal consequences resulting from the needless deaths of hundreds of thousands of people should be enough to deter other states from similar conduct. But if this is not enough, the spectacle of our political fabric being more seriously rent by our involvement in Vietnam (followed both chronologically and causally by Watergate) than by any other event since the Civil War should give pause to states considering similar policies of intervention into post-colonial wars of separation and revolution.

## III. Conclusion

The end of American participation in the Vietnamese war, rapprochement with the Soviet Union, and normalization of relations with China effectively conclude the ideological binge that the world has enjoyed since

---

[88] Farer, *Harnessing Rogue Elephants: A Short Discourse on Intervention in Civil Strife*, in 2 THE VIETNAM WAR AND INTERNATIONAL LAW 1089 (R. Falk ed. 1969); Moore, *The Control of Foreign Intervention in International Conflict*, 9 VA. J. INT'L L. 205 (1969).

the political fossilization of the military conclusion of World War II. Traditional balance of power politics can now be indulged with more actors than two. This condition represents a giant step forward from that of the Cold War. In many respects, however, this places us back on square one — circa 1918 or perhaps 1945 — with the alternative of attempting in perpetuity a balance of power sufficient to ensure the peace or, in recognition of the inherent instability of such a system, attempting a deepened international community sufficient to support legitimate institutions for cooperation and dispute resolution. Law can contribute to the deepening of international community to the extent that it is acknowledged to be more than the superstructure of community and actually part of its warp and woof.

Reactionary foreign policy could result from two conditions. First, an attempt to return simply to the politics of classic balance of power, without recognizing the need for an increased role for institutions of law, would represent a tragic waste of this foreign policy watershed. Kissinger and Kennan can no more hope to control perpetually the multiple variables in such a system of inherent instability than could Metternich and Bismark. Second, premature or unjustified reliance upon legal institutions could result in a disillusioned reaction against them and could cause total reliance upon geopolitics and force.

To reiterate, international order can be furthered by introjecting legal constraints on decisional processes in four suggested areas. First, the degree to which a government adheres to its own legal constraints, constitutional or otherwise, bears directly on international peace. Second, the degree to which a government's decisional processes adhere to international legal constraints also affects international order. Third, the extent to which a government promotes and sustains international institutions contributes to international order. And fourth, the level of legal consciousness that the world public has realized acts as a real constraint on governments that would otherwise act in disruption of international order.

In earlier times, when men were perhaps closer to the truth than later generations may care to admit, sovereign discretion was considered to be limited by four levels of law: the laws of God; the laws of nature; *leges imperii*, or the laws of government — in our day, constitutional law; and finally, laws common to all nations, or international law. Today we accomplish the first by a well publicized prayer breakfast, deny the existence of the second, ravage the third by claiming our own past violations as precedent for continued violations, and use the fourth to rationalize a course of conduct determined largely by other motives. The first contribution of law to the accomplishment of peace might well consist of an attempt to control our own illegal predilections toward violence, recognizing that in recent years we have been among the major contributors to a violent world. An "Athenian stranger" observed hundreds of years ago that "the state in which the law is above the rulers, and the rulers are the inferiors of the law, has salvation, and every blessing which the gods can confer." [89] If we were to achieve that happy condition, we would at once eliminate much violence now caused by our own illegal acts, and perhaps we would then be in the position to deserve and receive the emulation of others.

---

[89] PLATO, LAWS BK. III (J.M. Dent Trans. 1934).

# American Attitudes Toward International Law as Reflected in "The Pentagon Papers"

PERRY L. PICKERT

THE LEGALITY of American intervention in Vietnam has been a key issue for both supporters and opponents of governmental policy. The government itself has used the SEATO Pact, the Geneva Accords, and claims of North Vietnamese aggression as justification for bombing North Vietnam and for introducing American combat troops into South Vietnam. Yet with all the debate over the legality of the war, little has been settled. The reason for the confusion is that there are few undisputed facts and the pertinent legal documents are flawed or ambiguous. None of the parties to the dispute can boast clean hands. All have participated in unspeakable violence while claiming rights under the law and moral sanction for their actions. The uncertainty of the law and the facts of the Vietnam case make both the assertion of a legal argument and its refutation easy matters. Each side has violated the law, so all justifications are attackable. Since it is doubtful that the relative merits and claims of the parties will be settled authoritatively by any independent tribunal, the legality of American intervention will remain a matter of opinion. Some opinions are better than others, but no simple answer will be forthcoming.

While it is impossible to give a simple and authoritative answer to the question of legality, the publication of "The Pentagon Papers"[1] does afford a more complicated view of the attitudes of American decision-makers toward international law. The purpose of this paper is to use the documents of "The Pentagon Papers" to reflect American assumptions about international law and the use of law, legal arguments, and legal techniques in the conduct of foreign policy.[2] In order

[1] The three texts used in this study are, in order of publication: Sheehan, N., Smith, H., Kenworthy, E. W., and Butterfield F., *The Pentagon Papers* (New York: Bantam Books, Inc., 1971), hereafter cited NYT plus page number; Senator Gravel Edition, *The Pentagon Papers: The Defense Department History of the United States Decision-making on Vietnam* (Boston: The Beacon Press, 1971), hereafter cited G. plus volume number and page number, e.g., G. II, p. 50; U.S. Department of Defense, *United States-Vietnam Relations 1945-1967* (Washington: U.S. Government Printing Office, 1971), hereafter cited GPO plus book number, volume number, and page number, e.g., GPO 1, III, p. A-15).

[2] At this point a few comments are necessary with regard to the use of "The Pentagon Papers." Although the Defense Department had many Presidential and State Department documents in its files, the Defense Department historians did not have access to the com-

to reveal in concrete contexts American use of international law, two case studies will be considered. The first concerns American attitudes toward the Geneva Accords. "The Pentagon Papers" illustrate the American policy dilemma which led to participation in the conference at Geneva. They further reveal the intricacies of the negotiations themselves and the subsequent role of the Accords in the conduct of American policy. The second case study concerns the use of the traditional concept of reprisal to initiate and pursue the bombing of North Vietnam.

## The Path to Geneva

It would be difficult to invent a set of legal relationships as complicated and confusing as the Geneva Accords. The combination of French logic and panic, two factions of Vietnamese, Russian deviousness, Chinese fear of Russian deviousness, British reserve, and American ingenuity produced what one might expect—a mess. It is not within the scope of this paper to analyze in detail the content of the Geneva Accords. Such a task would be a project in itself.[3] This paper is con-

---

plete documentation. They were also unable to do extensive interviewing of the principals. Thus Leslie H. Gelb, Chairman of the Office of the Secretary of Defense Task Force, which prepared the study concluded:

> The result was not so much a documentary history, as a history based solely on documents—checked and rechecked with ant-like diligence. Pieces of paper, formidable and suggestive by themselves, could have meant much or nothing. Perhaps this document was never sent anywhere, and perhaps that one, though commented upon, was irrelevant. (G. I, p. xv)

Therefore the documents cannot be considered as telling the complete inside story of decision-making. Each cable or memorandum must be weighed on its own and in terms of the context in which it was drafted. Beyond the problem of each particular document itself, we must also be aware that the documents presented in "The Pentagon Papers" have been selected for us by the Defense Department historians. This selection process rests on criteria which are not stated explicitly. The relative importance of a document and its selection for incorporation into the study depended upon the story the historians were trying to tell. It is conceivable that an equal number of conflicting documents remain classified. Although the quality of the Defense Department study is high and the narrative is generally consistent with the known facts, the conclusions of this paper rest on the three versions of "The Pentagon Papers" and nothing more.

[3] A complete and able treatment of the Geneva negotiations is available in Robert F. Randle, *Geneva 1954: The Settlement of the Indochinese War* (Princeton, New Jersey: Princeton University Press, 1969). Professor Randle analyzes the Geneva negotiations from both legal and political points of view. He concludes:

> The Geneva Agreements (the cease-fire agreements, the Final Declaration, and the unilateral declarations) were vaguely worded at crucial points. Indeed, they were incomplete and legally defective in various essentials. Thus in most instances it is meaningless to

cerned rather with the American role in the negotiation of the Accords and the subsequent role of the Accords in American relations with Vietnam.

The Geneva Accords themselves[4] consist of: (1) the Agreement between the Commander-in-Chief of the French Union Forces in Indo-China and the Commander-in-Chief of the People's Army of Vietnam on the Cessation of Hostilities in Vietnam; (2) the Agreement on the Cessation of Hostilities in Cambodia; (3) the Agreement on the Cessation of Hostilities in Laos; (4) the Final Declaration of the Geneva Conference on the problem of restoring peace in Indo-China; and (5) declarations by the Government of the French Republic, the Government of the United States of America, the Royal Government of Cambodia, and the Royal Government of Laos.[5]

As they concern Vietnam, these documents in the main represent French capitulation to the Viet Minh and the division of Vietnam into two temporary military zones, one for the communists in the north and one for the French Union Forces in the south. The agreement between the Commanders-in-Chief of the French Union and the People's Armies set up a Joint Commission (an equal number of representatives of the commanders of the two parties) and an International Commission for Supervision and Control in Vietnam (Canada, India, and Poland) to "be responsible for supervising the proper execution by the parties of the provisions of the Agreement."[6] The agreement between the Commanders-in-Chief also provided eventual elections to reunify the country, but stated that "the conduct of civil administration in each regrouping zone shall be in the hands of the party whose forces are to be regrouped there in virtue of the present Agreement."[7] In Article 14 (d), provisions were made to require that "any civilians residing in a district controlled by one party who may wish to go and live in the

---

speak glibly of this or that state violating the "Geneva Accords." (p. x).

Yet the publication of "The Pentagon Papers" removes the need to resort to inference in discerning American intent. The documents also allow scrutiny of the government's secret attitudes towards the Accords once they were made.

[4] For the remainder of this paper the term "Geneva Accords" will be used to denote the general political and legal settlement made in Geneva in 1954. Where it is possible to discern the particular agreement or declaration being referred to by the term "Geneva Accords," the more exact designation will be used.

[5] See Randle, op. cit., pp. 569ff., and Richard A. Falk, *The Vietnam War and International Law* (Princeton, New Jersey: Princeton University Press, 1968), pp. 543ff.

[6] Falk, op. cit., p. 554.                    [7] Ibid., p. 546.

zone assigned to the other party shall be permitted and helped to do so
by the authorities in that district."[8] The practical result of the work of
the Conference was the disengagement of France and the partition of
Vietnam into the Republic of Vietnam in the south and the Democratic
Republic of Vietnam in the north.

The history of American involvement in Vietnam can be traced to
the helter-skelter environment of the settlement of the extant problems
following the defeat of Japan and the beginning of the Cold War.
Americans found that the policies of anti-colonialism and anti-communism were somewhat contradictory. Even before the communist
threat emerged, America was caught on the horns of a dilemma:
self-determination versus allied solidarity. Both the British and the
French did not appreciate American anti-colonialism. Just as in the
settlement after the First World War, Americans proposed the concept
of a trusteeship. President Roosevelt expressed the feelings of many
with regard to the settlement of the colonial problem:

> . . . I had, for over a year, expressed the opinion that Indo-China
> should not go back to France but that it should be administered by an
> international trusteeship. . . .
>
> Each case must, of course, stand on its own feet, but the case of
> Indo-China is perfectly clear. France has milked it for one hundred
> years. The people of Indo-China are entitled to something better
> than that.[9]

Yet there was another side to the coin. American policy was primarily
concerned with the rebuilding of Europe through the Marshall Plan.
Since cooperation in war and peace with the British and the French
was the cornerstone of American foreign policy, the concept of trusteeship was not pressed too hard. During the course of World War II the
President was unwilling to disturb the vital alliance. While Roosevelt
was informed that it would be difficult to deny French participation in
the liberation of Indo-China, his response in January 1945 was, "I still
do not want to get mixed up in any Indo-China decision. It is a matter
for postwar."[10]

But the decision not to decide left the matter to the military. Since
the United States was concentrating its efforts on the Japanese home

8 Ibid., p. 547.
9 G. I, p. 10. Roosevelt's reply to a memorandum from Cordell Hull, 24 January 1944.
10 G. I, p. 11. Roosevelt to Stettinius, 1 January 1945.

islands, the command of Southeast Asia was divided between Chiang Kai-Shek to the north and British Admiral Lord Mountbatten to the south of latitude 16° North. Although the British did land a small detachment in Saigon, their policy deferred to the French from the outset.[11] Thus by default Vietnam was returned to French control and the Indochina War began. Even at the very beginning of the struggle, logical inconsistencies in American policy emerged. The need for alliances was not consistent with the policy of self-determination for all peoples. In spite of the fact that Britain and France were allies, there were fundamental differences on the issue of colonialism. The characteristic American response to this contradiction was legalism: the concept of trusteeship. The term contained an essential ambiguity. Just as in the days of the League of Nations, a trusteeship could be used both as "disguised annexation" and also as proof that American policy had secured significant movement in the direction of self-government. The American policy dilemma was resolved by achieving ambiguous acceptance of American principles in law while stopping short of taking positive action to control events. The United States would use pressure to gain legal acceptance of an ambiguously worded principle,[12] knowing full well that her ally was contemplating violating that very principle. Then, she would look the other way while her ally performed an ugly deed. American policy would be not to aid or condone the act. Afterward, America would chastise her ally for violating the principle she had forced her to accept.

This pattern can clearly be seen in the reestablishment of French control over Indo-China. Although she questioned the French claim of the support of the people and clearly stated that it was not American policy to "assist the French to reestablish their control over Indo-China,"[13] and although she continually chastised the French for not giving independence to the Vietnamese, the United States looked the other way as the Marshall Plan and military aid to France was channeled to Vietnam to execute policies which were publicly opposed. There are two ways to view this American tactic, both of which contain an element of truth. The first is to argue that the pressure used to gain acceptance of principles is not wasted because it gives the government

[11] G. I, p. 16.
[12] In this case Article 73 of the U.N. Charter, the Declaration Regarding Non-Self-Governing Territories.
[13] G. I, p. 17.

some leverage in trying to make progress toward the principles. In most cases the ally would act regardless of what Americans said or did. By getting the ally to accept the principles, the United States can at least keep the pressure on and push for policies consistent with her principles. On the other hand, the tactic may be seen as a cynical mechanism of rationalization both in terms of domestic politics and individual psychology. The rhetoric of principle can be used to obscure a policy of expediency. Success in achieving acceptance of ambiguous principles produces the impression of an aggressive moral thrust to American policy while expediency dictates the actual execution of policy. Thus we can see a vigorous international effort to establish the principles of independence and self-government for the colonial world while quietly returning command of these areas to the military control of the old colonial power.

In the period from 1945 to 1950, American policy rested on the tension between solidarity with France and constant pressure on the French to grant true independence to Vietnam. Americans felt the difficulties in the area were simply the result of the French failure to follow American advice and grant independence to Vietnam. Although there was considerable revolutionary activity in Vietnam by the Viet Minh, Southeast Asia was not considered a critical area. But in Eastern Europe the Cold War had begun in earnest, and by 1950 the events in Vietnam became irrevocably linked to the global struggle against communism. American neutrality in the Franco-Viet Minh War, 1946-1949, was to undergo an abrupt change. The ugly turn of events in Europe, Greece, Turkey, and China plus Soviet and Communist Chinese recognition of Ho Chi Minh's government prompted Secretary of State Acheson to make the following public statement on February 1, 1950:

> The recognition by the Kremlin of Ho Chi Minh's communist movement in Indochina comes as a surprise. The Soviet acknowledgment of this movement should remove any illusions as to the "nationalist" nature of Ho Chi Minh's aims and reveals Ho in his true colors as the mortal enemy of native independence in Indochina.[14]

Overnight, American policy toward Vietnam was shifted from a reserved policy toward Ho and pressure on France to a willingness to accept any French rationalization with a promise to get on with the war against the

14 G. I, p. 41.

communists.[15] France's "Bao Dai experiment" to give Vietnam the appearance of independence and nationalist leadership was accepted. Following the Elysée Agreement,[16] the United States began its shift of position. On May 10, 1949, the American Consul in Saigon was notified:

> At the proper time and under the proper circumstances, the Department will be prepared to do its part by extending recognition to the Bao Dai government and by expressing the possibility of complying with any request by such a government for U.S. arms and economic assistance.[17]

On February 4, 1950, President Truman approved U. S. recognition of the Bao Dai Government.[18] By May, the Department of State was working on plans to implement a program of $60 million in aid for Southeast Asia under the Mutual Defense Assistance Program for the general area of China.[19] By the end of the year the United States had signed the Pentalateral Protocol of 1950 with France, Bao Dai, Laos, and Cambodia, which provided for American advisors.[20] Although total United States assistance to the French reached only $10 million in the first year, 1950, by fiscal year 1954 the total was $1,063 million accounting for 78 percent of the French war costs.[21] On February 27, 1950, the National Security Council issued a report entitled "The Position of the United States with Respect to Indo-China." The conclusions of the report set out the basic policy of the United States which has never changed:

> It is important to United States security interests that all practicable measures be taken to prevent further communist expansion in Southeast Asia. Indo-China is a key area of Southeast Asia and is under immediate threat. . . .
>
> The neighboring countries of Thailand and Burma could be expected to fall under Communist domination if Indo-China were controlled by a Communist-dominated government. The balance of Southeast Asia would then be in grave hazard.

15 G. I, p. 34.
16 Formally an exchange of notes between Bao Dai and Auriol, signed on 8 March 1949. The French agreed to turn over the internal administration of Vietnam to the Vietnamese within the French Union. France retained control of the armed forces. (GPO 1, I, p. A-40, also GPO 1, II, p. A-7)
17 G. I, p. 33.          18 G. I, p. 41.          19 G. I, p. 42.
20 G. II, p. 288, and 3 United States Treaties and other International Agreements 2756.
21 G. I, p. 77.

Accordingly, the Departments of State and Defence should prepare as a matter of priority a program of all practicable measures designed to protect United States security interests in Indo-China.[22]

The terminology and assumptions of this National Security Council report are significant in three respects. In the first place, Vietnam is linked to the security interests of the United States. Secondly, this link is made on the basis of the "domino theory." The third important element of the National Security Council report was the assertion that "all practicable measures be taken to prevent further communist expansion in Southeast Asia." This means that the "domino theory" was taken for granted and that from February 27, 1950, onward, the problems with respect to Southeast Asia were merely a matter of means.

From the bureaucratic as well as logical points of view, the elevation of Vietnam to the highest level of security assumption had profound effects. It gave sanction to the development of a program with a specific objective: preventing a communist takeover of Vietnam. Furthermore, it recognized Vietnam as policy of the highest priority which could compete on an equal basis for American resources. Therefore, American "commitments and strategic priorities" were to be reassessed in terms of this new assumption.[23] Values considered below the level of national security interests would have to be sacrificed. For example, the first casualty to this elevation of the importance of Vietnam was the reluctance to help the colonial French. On the basis of the National Security Council Report, the Joint Chiefs of Staff, though "recogniz(ing) the political implications involved in military aid to Indo-China," recommended in view of the "unstable" political situation to drop "insistence upon independence for Vietnam and a phased French withdrawal" and to introduce "a small military assistance group to work with both the Vietnamese and French to stop the communists."[24] From this point onward, policies toward Vietnam are selected on the basis of "practicality" or expediency. In the hierarchy of policy arguments, national security is supreme. Propositions or policies of a lower level are used or cast aside depending on their usefulness in serving the highest principle. Once

22 G. I, p. 362.

23 G. I, p. 363. Memo from Deputy Under-Secretary of State Dean Rusk to Major General James H. Burns of the Office of the Secretary of Defense, 7 March 1950.

24 G. I, p. 365. Memorandum for the Secretary of Defense by Omar N. Bradley, Chairman for the Joint Chiefs of Staff.

the basic policy was established, it was merely a matter of selecting the available means to achieve the objective.

The events from 1950 to 1954 both reinforced and weakened Vietnam's claim as a pillar of American security. The loss of China to communism and actual engagement of American troops in Korea seemed to substantiate the assumptions of the "domino theory." On the other hand, Vietnam had to compete with the hot war in Korea for American military resources. An Army position paper concluded that since "The equivalent of 12 U.S. divisions would be required to win a victory in Indo-China, if the French withdraw and the Chinese Communists intervene" and "a victory . . . cannot be assured by U.S. intervention with air and naval forces alone . . . U.S. intervention with combat forces in Indo-China is not militarily desirable."[25]

But even in the desperate hours of Dien Bien Phu, the French declined American proposals for united action. The French were unwilling to grant American demands for Vietnamese independence as the price of American intervention. The French were also afraid the United States would assume the control of the operations. French General Paul Ely explained to Admiral Arthur Radford of the Joint Chiefs of Staff that "Americans acted as if the United States sought to control and operate everything of importance . . . the United States appears to have an invading nature as they undertake everything in such great numbers of people . . . (and that) U.S. administrative procedures are enormously wasteful, irritating, and paper heavy."[26] But beyond the military hesitance to deploy troops to another front in Asia and French reluctance to let Americans run the show, there was further the domestic political situation within the United States. The stalemated Korean War had dampened public support for land wars in Asia, and the Eisenhower Administration had just parried the attempt to curb Presidential authority in the form of the Bricker Amendment.

This situation prompted President Eisenhower, after a meeting of Admiral Radford, Secretary Dulles, and Congressional leaders on April 3, 1954, to reject unilateral intervention and to indicate that any United States military involvement in Indo-China would depend on

25 G. I, p. 471. Army Position on National Security Action No. 1074-A, 5 April 1954. Also see Secretary of the Army Stevens' memo of 9 May 1954, GPO 9, p. 475.

26 G. I, p. 457. Memorandum for the President's Special Committee on Indochina, 29 March 1954.

(1) formation of alliance for united action; (2) a declaration of French willingness to accelerate independence for Vietnam; (3) Congressional approval of United States involvement.[27] The experience of the Truman Administration of getting involved in the Korean War without a formal Congressional resolution was obviously on the President's mind. Therefore on the eve of the Geneva Conference of 1954, American decision-makers found themselves in a rather helpless position. The French Government was in a precarious political position at home, and the United States was trying to muster French support for the proposed European Defense Community. Both Vietnam and the Defense Community were highly volatile political issues in France, so little real pressure could be exerted there. The American public and Congress had tired of Asian wars and the British were not interested in further adventure in Asia. It is important to recall that American policy had not changed, but the means of achieving a non-communist government in Vietnam were scarce. The military situation was so bad that even Secretary Dulles questioned the feasibility of intervention. The French wanted American commitments to bolster their bargaining position, but Washington was in no mood to write a *carte blanche* for the French. The U.S. was willing to intervene for victory but not to facilitate a French capitulation. Dulles wrote to Geneva:

> They want, and in effect have, an option on our intervention, but they do not want to exercise it and the date of expiry of our option is fast running out.[28]

The real American desire was for the French to fight on to victory. Even through the first half of June, the Administration tried to keep the united-action option open, dependent on a series of French concessions, such as formal requests for aid from France and the Associated States (Vietnam, Laos, Cambodia), a French guarantee of independence for Vietnam with an unqualified option to withdraw from the French Union at any time, and a new military command structure. President Eisenhower was prepared to seek Congressional approval for such an effort.[29] The French were given the unpalatable choice of internationalizing the war or surrendering to the Viet Minh. The decision-makers in Washington were willing to take drastic action but felt limited by the

27 G. I, p. 94.
28 G. I, p. 523. Dulles to Smith, 14 June 1954.
29 G. I, p. 101.

domestic political requirements of some sort of united action and independence for Vietnam. Both of these prerequisites were steps France adamantly refused to take. Washington would take "all practicable measures," but the combination of domestic expectations and French recalcitrance cut the available means.

It must be pointed out at this stage, however, that both of the limitations posed by American domestic political considerations were connected to problems of legality. President Eisenhower was highly sensitive to the Constitutional requirement for Congressional approval for war. He knew meaningful American intervention meant war and possibly even a war with China. Further, the necessary Congressional approval was seen to rest on independence for Vietnam and some sort of united action. The united action should include the military participation of Britain and a regional group of interested Asian states and bringing the matter to the United Nations.[30] All of these measures implied an attempt to clothe American action with both domestic and international legality. Washington's struggle to attain French acquiescence to American domestic political demands produced a resolve to formalize a regional defense pact. Secretary Dulles was convinced of the need for a pact including Western and Asian allies by his experience in trying to persuade a bipartisan group of Congressional leaders to work for a resolution authorizing the President to use U.S. air-naval power to aid the French at Dien Bien Phu. The State Department Summary of Secretary Dulles's meeting concluded:

> It was the sense of the meeting that the U.S. should not intervene alone, but should attempt to secure the cooperation of other free nations concerned in Southeast Asia, and that if such cooperation could be assured, it was probable that the U.S. Congress would authorize U.S. participation in such "United Action."[31]

Of course it is impossible to distinguish exactly the role law plays in such a political argument. Perhaps the Congress wanted no part of any kind of intervention and simply phrased its displeasure in terms of legal requirements. But the formal legal requirements of a Congressional resolution, independence for Vietnam, and collective sanctions for intervention indicated a search for legitimacy in which legal forms play a part. Both President Eisenhower and Secretary Dulles felt

[30] G. I, p. 124.
[31] G. I, p. 101. Meeting of 3 April 1954.

the need of satisfying formal legal requirements prior to intervention. Just one week after his unsuccessful confrontation with Congressional leaders, Secretary Dulles journeyed to London and Paris trying to elicit support for united action.[32] By May, the National Security Council had established a planning board to work on possible groupings for regional organization.[33] Thus American decision-makers felt restricted in the execution of policy by the lack of at least the appearance of a formal legal obligation to intervene. In both the American position at the Geneva Conference and in the formation of the SEATO Pact, Americans sought to remove this handicap.

## The Geneva Negotiations

Since intervention was ruled out by French intransigence and the internal French political situation seemed to demand French withdrawal, Americans simply had to face the undesirable prospect of a French deal with the communists at Geneva. For both the Russians and the Chinese, American participation was required. They felt ridding Vietnam of the French would be meaningless if the agreement did not at least decrease the likelihood of American unilateral or multilateral intervention.[34] Mendes-France expressed the view that without a "clearcut U.S. guarantee that would protect Associated States in the event that the Communists did not honor the spirit of any agreement . . . a settlement would not be worth the paper it was written on."[35] Beyond that, the French wanted to use a threat of U. S. intervention to strengthen their position in negotiations. Although on the surface the British mouthed the hard line of Washington, it was well known that they were never convinced that Indochina's security was inextricably linked to the security of all Asia.[36] Therefore in terms of Vietnam, Washington had two conflicting policies: on the one hand was the desire to help the French get the best possible terms, including some specific American proposals; and on the other hand was the avoidance of becoming legally bound by unsatisfactory provisions of an agreement. Yet Washington also feared that if the U.S. was forced by an unacceptable settlement to disassociate itself, what Dulles characterized as "irreparable injury to Franco-American relations" might occur.[37]

---

[32] G. I, p. 101.        [33] G. I, p. 143.        [34] G. I, p. 167.

[35] G. I, p. 553. Dillon to State recording a conversation with Mendes-France on 11 July 1954.

[36] G. I, p. 142.

[37] G. I, p. 548. Dulles to Dillon, 8 July 1954.

Dulles's tactic was to first make it perfectly clear to the French that the U.S. was "not prepared at the present time to give any commitments that it will intervene in the war if the Geneva Conference fails."[38] Then he instructed Undersecretary Smith to adopt a stance of "an interested nation which, however, is neither a belligerent nor a principal in the negotiations."[39] Beyond this, the government agreed with the British to a list of seven principles of "an acceptable agreement."[40] Dulles' plan was to inform both the French and the communists that the U.S. would withdraw from the Conference if its seven principles were not met.[41] Since Secretary Dulles had categorically stated that "The United States will not, however, become cosignatory with the Communists in any Declaration,"[42] there was no question of the United States becoming a party to either the military agreement or the declaration of the Conference. The United States would make a unilateral declaration of its position. Dulles hoped to use the tension between "respect" and "disassociation" to prod the French to make a satisfactory settlement while at the same time keeping freedom of action by avoiding any commitments or obligations under the Geneva Accords. By "respect" Dulles meant that the U.S. "would not seek directly or indirectly to upset settlement by force."[43] But even "respect" was dependent on the inclusion of the seven American principles. Finally, to insure the maxi-

[38] G. I, p. 153.

[39] G. I, p. 507. Dulles to Smith, 12 May 1954.

[40] The seven US-UK requirements for an acceptable agreement were:

(1) Preservation of the integrity and independence of Laos and Cambodia, and assurances of Viet Minh withdrawal from those countries.

(2) Preservation of at least the southern half of Vietnam, and if possible an enclave in the Delta, with the line of demarcation no further south than one running generally west from Dong Hoi.

(3) No restrictions on Laos, Cambodia or retained Vietnam "materially impairing their capacity to maintain stable non-Communist regimes; and especially restrictions impairing their right to maintain adequate forces for internal security, to import arms and to employ foreign advisers."

(4) No "political provisions which would risk loss of the retained area to Communist control."

(5) No provision that would "exclude the possibility of the ultimate reunification of Vietnam by peaceful means."

(6) Provision for "the peaceful and humane transfer, under international supervision, of those people desiring to be moved from one zone to another of Vietnam."

(7) Provision for "effective machinery for international supervision of the agreement." G. I, p. 143.

[41] G. I, p. 543. Dulles to Dillon, 3 July 1954.

[42] G. I, p. 152.

[43] G. I, p. 146. Dulles to Smith, 24 June 1954.

mum flexibility in the final hours of a settlement, Secretary Dulles empowered General Smith to act on his own if time were short.

> If in your judgement continued participation in the Indochina phase of the Conference appears likely to involve the United States in a result inconsistent with its policy, as stated above, you should immediately so inform your Government, recommending either a withdrawal or the limitation of the U.S. role to that of an observer. If the situation develops such that, in your opinion, either of such actions is essential under the circumstances and time is lacking for consultation with Washington, you may act in your discretion.[44]

Secretary Dulles's fear was that the United States might seem to have become involved in "a multilateral engagement with Communists which would be inconsistent with our basic approach and which subsequently might enable Communist China to charge us with alleged violations of agreement to which it might claim both governments became parties."[45] The United States shared the Vietnamese view that the Geneva settlement would amount to nothing more than a pause in the fighting so that the United States did not want to be legally bound in any way. Among the seven principles the US-UK agreement required of a settlement was the insistence that there be "no political provisions which would risk loss of the retained area to communist control."[46] The election provisions of the military agreement and the Final Declaration of the conference were what Dulles had in mind. This was the only serious departure from the US-UK terms. Dulles expressed his objection,

> since it is undoubtedly true that elections might eventually mean unification of Vietnam under Ho Chi Minh this makes it all the more important they should be only held as long after ceasefire agreement as possible and in conditions free from intimidation to give democratic elements best chance. We believe important that no date should be set now and especially that no conditions should be accepted by French which would have direct or indirect effect of preventing effective international supervision of agreement ensuring political as well as military guarantees.[47]

[44] G. I, p. 507. Dulles to Smith, 12 May 1954.
[45] G. I, p. 569. Dulles to Smith, 19 July 1954.
[46] G. I, p. 144. See *supra* note 40, requirement 4.
[47] G. I, p. 546. Dulles to Dillon, 7 July 1954.

Thus the basic position of the United States in relation to the Geneva Conference can be seen. If left to its own devices, the United States would have simply not returned to the second phase of the talks, thereby leaving itself completely free.[48] But the French response was so strong that such a position might have seriously endangered Franco-American relations. The formula of a unilateral declaration taking note of the military agreements for Cambodia, Laos, and Vietnam and the Final Declaration of the conference were made to give at least the appearance of an American guarantee. The declaration asserted that the United States would "refrain from the threat or the use of force to disturb them" and also "would view any renewal of the aggression in violation of the aforesaid agreements with grave concern and as seriously threatening international peace and security."[49] Thus the American intent was to provide an optional guarantee, that is, a guarantee which carried no obligation or duty on the part of the United States but merely the option to act if the aggression was resumed. It was simply a threat. Also, the pledge not to use force to disturb the Accords was linked to Article 2 (4) of the Charter of the United Nations, so that it could be argued that no new obligations were undertaken. But more important is what was left unsaid. The United States gave no promise to uphold the Geneva Accords and also left open use of any means other than force to disturb the Accords. The third important element of the unilateral declaration was a clear statement opposing the provisions for elections on the basis of the Accords and substituting truly "free" elections supervised by the United Nations. Washington was clearly anticipating having to balk at the election provisions as established in the Accords. By proposing U.N. supervision, Washington was proposing a condition which communist countries had consistently rejected and yet a provision which seemed reasonable to American domestic opinion. The fourth element of the declaration gives some solace to the "representative of the State of Viet-Nam" in that the "United States reiterates its traditional position that peoples are entitled to determine their own future and that it will not join in an arrangement which would hinder this."[50] Since South Vietnam had announced it would not be a party to agreement and did not consider itself bound by the Accords, this meant self-determination for South Vietnam despite any provisions of the Geneva Accords.

[48] G. I, p. 548. Dulles to Dillon, Aldrich, and Johnson, 8 July 1954.
[49] Falk, *op. cit.*, p. 559.  [50] *Ibid.*

Therefore Washington established early the position that South Vietnam had the right of self-determination and thereby threw into question the "provisional" nature of the military demarcation lines. It must be noted, however, that the implications of the unilateral declaration seem obvious at first reading. Yet when these provisions are read in the full knowledge that Secretary Dulles had carefully developed a position which avoided any "multilateral engagement with Communists . . . which might enable Communist China to charge us with alleged violations of agreement to which it might claim both governments became parties,"[51] it can be seen that the unilateral declaration served its purpose well. To drive home the point that the United States would not become a party in any obligations or arrangements with communists, the American declaration took note of only the first twelve paragraphs of Final Declaration. The thirteenth paragraph was an agreement of the members of the conference to consult with one another on requests that might be referred to them by the International Supervisory Commission to study measures which might be necessary to ensure respect for the Accords. Secretary Dulles would have none of that. Dulles had used the tension between "disassociation" and "respect" to milk the best possible terms from the French and the communists. He had preserved the Franco-American alliance while avoiding any new international commitments. He encouraged the South Vietnamese to exercise their right of self-determination while making no concrete commitments. Most ironic was America's stance as protector of the Geneva Accords. By virtue of taking note of the Accords with major reservations as to elections and self-determination for South Vietnam, the United States selected the part of the Geneva Accords which suited its purposes and protected those elements, while casting aside the other provisions. When asserting rights or powers, the United States would recall its participation in deliberations at Geneva but when obligations, liabilities, or duties were mentioned, the United States would refer to the unilateral declaration.

## The Role of the Geneva Accords in American Policy

Since the question as to which party violated the Geneva Accords can only be debated without authoritative resolution, an interesting question which can be dealt with on firmer ground since the publication of "The Pentagon Papers" is: what were American attitudes toward

51 G. I, p. 569. Dulles to Smith, 19 July 1954.

the Geneva Accords, and in what sense did Americans feel bound by their provisions?

The simplest answer to a question about American attitudes toward the Geneva Accords would be to say that the United States cynically set out to subvert the agreement from the drafting stage onward. Unfortunately the reality is not that simple. While the Americans' carefully drafted unilateral declaration was intended to absolve the United States of any legal obligations, from 1954 onward American policy assumed the binding force of the Geneva Accords. Americans were sensitive to the kinds of activities and agreements which would retain the appearance of legality. The distinction between what was to be done in a covert versus an overt manner was made on the basis of the legal requirements of the Geneva Accords. At the critical stage of the elections to unify Vietnam, the United States was careful not to disturb the provisions of the Accords herself but rather left this to the Government of Vietnam. In the end, in 1961, when the United States found it necessary to disregard fundamental provisions of the military agreement, the Final Declaration of the conference and its own unilateral declaration, the decision-makers had both a rationalization for their own psyche and a cover for the action for public consumption. What is more, throughout the period, the Americans called the other side to task for so-called violations of the Geneva Accords.

A broader view of American attitudes toward the Geneva Accords shows ambivalence. On the one hand, the United States accepted the loss of North Vietnam and took no positive steps to recapture the North. On the other hand, the United States regarded the provisional demarcation lines as establishing a permanent international frontier. The United States would regard any attempt to disturb the provisional lines as aggression. In other words, the United States needed the Geneva Accords for the obligations they placed on the communists. In spite of the fact that America had carefully prepared a legal case for not being bound by the Accords, at least the appearance of compliance was necessary in order to give standing to complaints of communist abuses. Thus, from the American point of view, the situation was ideal. The United States could make a plausible case that it was not bound at all by the Geneva Accords. This argument would be reserved for the last ditch defense to preserve America's moral position of not breaking the law. At the second defensive line the United States would use its declaration as the ground for complaints of communist violations. On this level, the

United States would pick and choose the provisions of the Accords which bound the communists. Any U.S. or South Vietnamese violations would be excused on the grounds of self-determination for South Vietnam and the refusal of the South Vietnamese to become party to the Accords. The first line of defense was simply to treat South Vietnam as another state with which the United States had programs for aid and support. This view treated economic and military aid as a normal state of affairs having no bearing on the subversion of international agreements. The American attitude toward the Geneva Accords was therefore to accept the benefits of the agreement while rejecting its liabilities. But the more specific character of American ambivalence can be seen in the perceived implications of the Accords for American action in Vietnam.

Oddly enough the first real evidence that the United States felt bound by the provisions of the Geneva Accords was provided by Americans who planned to conduct the covert war against the communists. Early in 1954, while the French were still holding out at Dien Bien Phu, the Saigon Military Mission headed by Colonel Edward G. Lansdale, USAF, was created and authorized to go to Vietnam to "undertake paramilitary operations against the enemy and to wage political-psychological warfare."[52] At Geneva, agreement was reached that the "personnel ceiling of U.S. military personnel with MAAG (Military Assistance Advisory Group) would be frozen at the number present in Vietnam [on Aug. 1]."[53] Colonel Lansdale was faced with having only two officers in the whole of Vietnam. Consequently "a call for help went out. Ten officers in Korea, Japan, and Okinawa were selected and were rushed to Vietnam."[54] Working during the hectic period of the flux of refugees between zones, the Lansdale-group report pointed with pride to its accomplishments:

Haiphong was taken over by the Vietminh on 16 May. Our Binh and northern Hao teams were in place, completely equipped. It had been hard work to beat the Geneva deadline, to locate, select, exfiltrate, train, infiltrate, equip the men of these two teams and have them in place, ready for actions required against the enemy. It would be a hard task to do openly, but this had to be kept secret from the Vietminh, the International Commission with its suspicious French and Poles and Indians, and even friendly Vietnamese.[55]

[52] G. I, p. 574. Landale Team's Report on Covert Saigon Mission in 1954 and 1955.
[53] G. I, p. 576.          [54] Ibid.          [55] G. I, p. 583.

Although the American covert operations in North and South Vietnam were contrary to the spirit of the Geneva Accords, and the letter of both international and domestic law, the American attitude toward these activities was interesting. Americans went to ridiculous extremes to comply with the letter of the Geneva Accords. Formal compliance was important. While the military, in this case General O'Daniel, was willing to look the other way while Colonel Lansdale got away with a little hanky-panky, there is no question but that the military felt bound to uphold the letter of the law. To bend the law here and there was acceptable, but they were careful not to act so as to allow their being charged with a clear violation. A cynical lawbreaker would never be troubled about the timing of the arrival of covert operators. It is only a mind which sees itself as upholder of the law which is driven to such contradictions.

Throughout the 1954 to 1961 period, the Joint Chiefs of Staff were very specific in their attitude in regard to the introduction of American military personnel. Although they were willing to fudge a number here and there, the distinction between action under the Accords and a formal breach of the Accords was kept clear. The military was unwilling to get involved in piecemeal action which would surely lead to failure. The Geneva Accord guideline of mere replacement was used by the Joint Chiefs to make their point, so that both on the level of covert operations and planning for overt military action, the American activities presumed the binding force of the Geneva Accords.[56]

On the diplomatic level, Americans responded to the Geneva Accords with the formation of the SEATO Pact. General Smith's statement, "We must get that Pact!"[57] was part of an American diplomatic initiative which led to Manila in September 1954. In spite of the fact that both the United States and South Vietnam had not signed the Geneva Accords, the membership of Britain and France necessitated the use of a protocol to make the provisions of SEATO applicable to South Vietnam. Since the Accords had forbidden military alliances, Britain and France were bound not to form alliances with Vietnam. While on the one hand Secretary Dulles initiated the pact to put the communists on notice that aggression would be opposed, the United States, on the other hand, was not willing to undertake any firm commitments. The Joint Chiefs of Staff were opposed to any unilateral commitment which would restrict American freedom of action.[58] The result was Article IV

[56] G. II, p. 408.     [57] G. I, p. 212.     [58] Ibid.

of the treaty which was anything but a pledge to automatically respond with force to communist aggression. The article provides that the parties recognize armed attack in the treaty area would endanger their own peace and safety and that each party agrees "that it will in that event act to meet the common danger in accordance with its constitutional processes."[59] In the preliminary discussions with the French concerning an overall security umbrella for Indochina, the French used the word "Locarno," which the United States found to be an unfortunate choice of terms.[60] Obviously just as in the case of the Geneva Accords themselves, the United States wanted power to provide an optional guarantee. The SEATO Treaty was designed not to commit the United States to action but rather to give the appearance of a promise which would deter the communists and provide a sanction for executive action in the domestic American political context.

To a large extent, the SEATO Treaty was the result of President Eisenhower's and Secretary Dulles's confrontation with Congress which resulted in rejection of intervention in Vietnam at the time of Dien Bien Phu. The paper work was being prepared for a future crisis in Asia. The next time the Administration would have a solemn treaty commitment to honor. Secretary Dulles argued that Article IV constituted "a clear and definite agreement on the part of the signatories, including the United States, to come to the aid of any member of the Pact who under the terms of this treaty is subjected to aggression."[61] The difficulty with this argument is that neither the United States nor any of the other parties made such a commitment. The terms of the treaty give the option of unilateral intervention with the mere appearance of a multi-national commitment. Therefore, the SEATO Pact was constructed to meet the Congressional requirement of multilateral sanction for American intervention. Within the domestic arena the package was sold as total American commitment to defend Asia against communist aggression. Yet on the international level it would be hard to imagine using the language of the SEATO Treaty to induce an unwilling state to act to meet some alleged aggression. French and British reluctance to become involved in Vietnam demonstrates the weakness of the SEATO arrangement. The continual use of the treaty in political arguments within the United States testifies to its durability and power in fulfilling its major purpose. Thus the collective defense arrangement attempts to give the added weight of a pseudo-

[59] Falk, *op. cit.*, p. 562.    [60] G. I, p. 143.    [61] G. I, p. 212.

international legal obligation to policy decisions of the American executive. The SEATO Treaty itself was a response to the Administration's frustration in connection with the Geneva settlement. Since such treaties are drafted to have maximum domestic political effect and no international legal effect whatsoever, in order to keep American options open, American treaty commitments rest on the credulity of the audience rather than any legal obligations. On this level Americans use international legal forms without any real substantive content to make debating points in policy decisions in the domestic forum.

While the United States worked to beat the deadline of the military agreement for Vietnam and the diplomats prepared SEATO, a more specific stand was required as the deadline for elections approached. With respect to the Geneva Accords themselves, and the International Control Commission, Secretary Dulles held the view; "while we should certainly take no positive step to speed up present process of decay of Geneva Accords, neither should we make the slightest effort to infuse life into them."[62] But rigor mortis had set into the Geneva Accords even before they had supposedly come to life July 21, 1954. The French had prepared a legal trick to cloud the status of South Vietnam under the Accords. On June 4, 1954, nearly six weeks before signature of the Accords, the Laniel Government had recognized "Vietnam as a fully independent state in possession of all qualifications and powers known in international law,"[63] and Mendes-France promised to uphold the agreement. Thus, although the Geneva Accords bound France and her successors, it can hardly be argued that South Vietnam was a successor to France with respect to the Geneva Accords since Vietnam was granted its independence before the Accords were signed.

The point came clearly into focus as the last date for consultations to prepare for elections drew near (July 20, 1955). In a draft policy paper prepared in May, the United States suggested that Vietnam accept the elections with the provision of a secret ballot and strict supervision by the United Nations. This policy was consistent with the groundwork laid by the unilateral declaration of the United States and was safe, the Americans argued, since the communists in Germany and Korea had refused these conditions.[64] Vietnam could appear to uphold the Accords while insuring that no election would be held. The studied ambiguity of such a position shifted the onus of rejecting the Accords

---

[62] G. I, p. 241.
[63] G. I, p. 210. 4 June 1954.                    [64] G. I, p. 239.

to the communists without any risk of entanglement for the United States. However, there was a risk for the South Vietnamese. By proposing such conditions, the South Vietnamese would tacitly accept the binding force of the Accords and also stand the risk that the North Vietnamese would accept the conditions and demand the elections. The Vietnamese, however, were not interested in the American tactic which minimized American risks while maximizing the risks for the Vietnamese. Consequently, Diem settled the matter with an unequivocal statement:

> We did not sign the Geneva Agreements. We are not bound in any way by these Agreements, signed against the will of the Vietnamese people. . . . We shall not miss an opportunity which would permit the unification of our homeland in freedom, but it is out of the question for us to consider any proposal from the Viet Minh if proof is not given that they put the superior interests of the national community above those of communism.[65]

Diem refused even to meet the Viet Minh to discuss the election. The American role in the decision was not to press Diem. No positive action was necessary since he would not even talk to the communists. American policy from 1954 onward assumed that elections would be held. This assumption was based on the American estimate that France would remain in Vietnam.[66] The French were bound by the Geneva Accords. In fact there was considerable French pressure on Diem to hold the elections. There was pressure from French public opinion to hold the elections to avoid giving Hanoi a pretext for renewing the fighting while the French Expeditionary Corps remained in South Vietnam.[67] By the time the deadline for consultations rolled around, the French were gone. Diem was asserting his independence from the French and would no longer respond to French pressure. After all, he had the Americans. The situation prompted the French Foreign Minister to comment:

> We are not entirely masters of the situation. . . . The position in principle is clear: France is the guarantor of the Geneva Accords. . . . But we do not have the means alone of making them respected.[68]

Since the United States feared an election would result in a victory for Ho Chi Minh, the United States merely stopped talking about free

[65] G. I, p. 287.        [66] Ibid.        [67] G. I, p. 239.        [68] G. I, p. 286.

elections and supported Diem in his refusal to enter into pre-election consultations. A State Department historical study noted the shift from nominal acceptance of elections with a variety of conditions, to the position that "The whole subject of consultations and elections in Viet-Nam should be left up to the Vietnamese themselves and not dictated by external arrangements."[69] The fact that the United States was willing to disregard provisions of the military agreement was made clear when in unusually frank and unequivocal language Secretary Dulles publically stated:

> Neither the United States Government nor the Government of Viet-Nam is, of course, a party to the Geneva armistice agreement. We did not sign them, and the Government of Viet-Nam did not sign them and, indeed, protested against them. On the other hand, the United States believes, broadly speaking, in the unification of countries which have a historic unity, where the people are akin. We also believe that, if there are conditions of really free elections, there is no risk that the Communists would win."[70]

Even rejecting elections, Dulles does not reject elections. It is obvious that the concept of free election meant elections which the Free World would win. In the election crisis the Secretary was rather bold in stating that the United States and South Vietnam were not parties to the Geneva Accords. But it was not long before America and South Vietnam were to notice infiltration from the north which constituted aggression. Of course aggression across the DMZ was a violation of the Geneva Accords. With the exception of the Dulles outburst on the occasions of subverting the election provision of the Geneva Accords, the United States kept a low profile in South Vietnam. The French were gone and to borrow General Ely's phrase, the invading, enormously wasteful and paper heavy Americans had arrived. Diem had established a semblance of order unfortunately followed by the gradual degeneracy of his family and government. An insurgency movement gathered momentum while, at least by 1959, a significant increase of infiltration was observed coming from the north.[71] But until 1961 the United States could claim with at least a measure of truth that it had not disturbed the Geneva Accords by force. The Military Assistance Advisory Group had kept its personnel approximately within the replacement guideline. American aid, mostly police or military equipment, was given as economic assistance and was

69 G. I, p. 245.                    70 Ibid.                    71 G. I, p. 266.

not of a magnitude which would encourage Diem to move outside of South Vietnam. Direct violation of the Final Declaration of the Geneva Conference and the military agreement was avoided by the use of a protocol to give the Vietnamese the protection of SEATO without becoming a party to the treaty, and the United States signed no bilateral treaty with Diem. Although the United States was engaged in a variety of covert operations, they were well within the rules of the game and constituted no real threat to North Vietnam. Even the subversion of the elections could be blamed on Diem; the United States simply looked the other way. There were no foreign bases on Vietnamese soil. However, this state of affairs was disturbed in 1961 when the United States again discovered that Vietnam was about to fall to communism if heroic action was not taken. Thus for the first time since Geneva, the United States was forced to return to the 1950 National Security Council dictim and use "all practicable measures . . . to prevent further communist expansion in Southeast Asia."[72]

On April 29, 1961, President Kennedy approved an additional 100 men for assignment to the Military Assistance Advisory Group.[73] Although the numbers do not appear significant, the decision itself represented the first formal American breach of the military agreement and its own unilateral declaration. This act had both symbolic and practical importance. The decision was made in full consciousness by the decision-makers that the United States would no longer be bound by the provisions of the Geneva Accords. In preparation for the decision, Colonel E. F. Black's position paper had argued that the increase in personnel and the new types of weapons would require that the President decide the United States would no longer be bound by the Geneva Accords.[74] At the time, the crises in both Vietnam and Laos were acute and the President had ordered a 5,000 man force to be prepared to land near Hue (Tourane) and also in Udorn, Thailand. A cable from the Joint Chiefs, also on April 29, 1961, alerted the commander of American forces in the Pacific:

> 1. Request you prepare plans to move brigade size forces of approximately 5,000 each into Udorn or vicinity and into Tourane or vicinity. Forces should include all arms and appropriate air elements. Plans should be based solely on US forces at this time.

72 G. I, p. 362.
73 G. II, p. 38.                    74 G. II, p. 40.

2. Decision to make these deployments not firm. It is expected that the decision as to Thailand will be made at meeting tentatively scheduled here on Monday. Decision regarding Vietnam will be even later due to consideration of Geneva Accords.

3. It is hoped that these movements can be given SEATO cover but such possibility must be explored before becoming a firm element of your planning. State is taking action to explore this aspect.[75]

Although it was unnecessary to deploy these troops because the crisis in Laos subsided, the level of contemplated action was obviously greater than the hundred men actually deployed. From the spring to the fall of 1961, the military and civilian leadership were actively engaged in the choice of means to preserve a non-communist South Vietnam. The National Security Council policy of 1950 was to be put to a new test. The situation in Vietnam was perceived as so desperate that all the means contemplated for solution would require obvious violations of the Geneva Accords. The question was not whether to violate the Accords but rather how to violate them. The debate turned to numbers: 10,000, 25,000, or 40,000 American advisors. As in the cable above, the principals were perfectly aware that action would have legal consequences. In a paper entitled "Concept of Intervention in Vietnam," by U. Alexis Johnson, the various measures were weighed in terms of pros and cons. The working paper discussed the plan: "It breaks the Geneva Accords and puts responsibility on the U.S. for rationalizing the action before the U.N. and the world."[76] How, then, did the United States fulfill its responsibility?

The process of rationalization was a carefully orchestrated public relations offensive. In a joint memorandum to the President, Secretaries Rusk and McNamara recommended the deployment of "a significant number of United States forces" (8,000 possibly growing to 40,000) to Vietnam linked with a specific diplomatic initiative.[77] The plan included using SEATO "cover," an exchange of letters between President Kennedy and Diem, the issuing of the "Jordan Report" (which catalogued North Vietnamese infiltration), and the introduction of United States forces under the cover of a "humanitarian" flood relief effort in the Mekong Delta. On the need for multilateral action, the memo noted, "from the political point of view, both domestic and inter-

[75] G. II, p. 41.  [76] G. II, p. 76.
[77] G. II, p. 110, 11 November 1961.

national, it would seem important to involve forces from other nations. . . . It should be difficult to explain to our own people why no effort had been made to invoke SEATO. . . ."[78] The memo also noted that deployment should "not be contingent upon unanimous SEATO agreement."[79] The next stage was for Ambassador Nolting to approach Diem and get his cooperation in implementing the plan. Then:

> Very shortly before the arrival in South Viet-Nam of the first increments of United States military personnel and equipment proposed under 3., above, that would exceed the Geneva Accord ceilings, publish the "Jordan report" as a United States "white paper," transmitting it as simultaneously as possible to the Governments of all countries with which we have diplomatic relations, including the Communist states.

> Simultaneous with the publication of the "Jordan report" release an exchange of letters between Diem and the President.

> (a) Diem's letter would include reference to the Democratic Republic of [North] Vietnam violations of Geneva Accords as set forth in the October 24 Government of [South] Vietnam letter to the International Control Commission and other documents; pertinent references to Government of [South] Vietnam statements with respect to its intent to observe the Geneva Accords; reference to its need for flood relief and rehabilitation; reference to previous United States aid and the compliance hitherto by both countries with the Geneva Accords; reference to the United States Government statement at the time the Geneva Accords were signed; the necessity now of exceeding some provisions of the Accords in view of the DRV violations thereof; the lack of aggressive intent with respect to the Democratic Republic of [North] Vietnam; Government of [South] Vietnam intent to return to strict compliance with the Geneva Accords as soon as the Democratic Republic of [North] Vietnam violations ceased; and request for additional United States assistance in framework foregoing policy. The letter should also set forth in appropriate general terms steps Diem has taken and is taking to reform Governmental structure.

> (b) The President's reply would be responsive to Diem's request for additional assistance and acknowledge and agree to Diem's statements

---

[78] G. II, p. 113.                    [79] Ibid.

on the intent promptly to return to strict compliance with the Geneva Accords as soon as DRV violations have ceased.[80]

One important change in this strategy was revealed in a cable to Ambassador Nolting guiding him in the execution of the Rusk/McNamara plan. The Ambassador was instructed that Diem's letter to Kennedy "need not confirm to the world and Communists that Geneva Accords are being violated by our increased aid. Need not accuse ourselves publicly, make Communists' job easier."[81]

Although American official communications such as President Kennedy's letter to Diem retained an ambiguous stance towards the Accords, i.e., not being a party ourselves but holding the communists to their violations, on the secret level Americans felt they were about to breach an international obligation.[82] The private and public rationalization for this course was the violations of the Accords by the North Vietnamese. But an argument of non-compliance by the other side presumes the legally binding force of the arrangement. It also presumes compliance on the part of the complaining party. If the United States was not bound by the Accords and neither were the South Vietnamese, why all the fuss? The simple reason is that American action was taken to thwart communist aggression. South Vietnam was attacked, from within and without, and the United States was aiding in Vietnam's defense. Unfortunately, if there were no DMZ under the Accords and no obligation on the part of the Viet Minh, there could be no aggression. The whole of Vietnam would have been in a state of civil war from 1954 to the present. The core of the American justification for intervention rested on the concept of aggression in violation of the law. There is no aggression between two sides of an ongoing civil war. There is just fighting. The continuing civil war theory would require the complete victory of one faction over another, and this would imply, from the American point of view, the conquest of the North by the South with American aid. The United States, because of the lesson of Korea, was unwilling to risk the intervention of Russia and China which this course would involve. Thus Americans spoke with certain fondness of a return to the Geneva Accords. By this they meant not the formal documents of the Geneva Conference but rather the partition of Vietnam with a pro-Western south. Thus when Americans speak of the "Geneva Accords," they mean the part of the arrangement which coincides with

[80] G. II, p. 115.        [81] G. II, p. 119.        [82] G. II, p. 805.

American policy. Whenever the United States takes some action which appears to violate a provision of the Accords, the action is taken under cover. If discovered, it is argued that the action was taken in the spirit of the "Geneva Accords." But if the question persists, of course, the United States did not sign the Geneva Accords anyway, so what is all the fuss about?

The difficulty is that the United States wanted that portion of the Geneva Accords which brought a cease-fire, a demilitarized zone, and a non-communist government for South Vietnam. This was the portion of the agreement which the United States agreed to respect and perhaps guarantee. That no one else agreed to Washington's declaration is taken to be irrelevant. The years of nominal compliance and even the use of the "humanitarian" flood cover for the first significant increment of American forces was necessary to cast the United States in the role of guarantor of the Geneva Accords. The orchestrated duet of Kennedy and Diem was designed to cast American actions in the light of lawful responses to communist violations of the Accords. The reason for all this is that the United States set as its goal a return to that part of the Geneva Agreement which coincided with its policy: the limited goal of a non-communist government in the South. This goal would be achieved if the communists fulfilled their obligations under the Geneva Accords. The goal could only be achieved if the election provisions were disregarded. While the Viet Minh considered the election provision as an essential element of the Accords, the Americans were not greatly concerned. "Free" elections could be held at any time if only the North Vietnamese would hold up their side of the agreement. Since the Viet Minh had clearly undertaken to refrain from infiltration in the Geneva Accords, and this was the activity which Washington wanted to stop, it chose to articulate its demands in terms of communist obligations under the Accords. Washington wanted it both ways. It wanted to hold the Viet Minh to their side of the bargain without accepting any obligations itself.

The problem with the American legal policy was that it wanted too much. American decision-makers needed legal obligations and legal rights to defend their policies in the domestic political arena. However, they were unwilling to enter into any arrangements which would create clear duties. This would restrict freedom of action. Therefore, in the case of the Geneva Accords, the United States entered into no legal relationships. On the other hand, the government wanted to hold the

Viet Minh to account for any violations of it. The government mimicked observance of the Geneva Accords even to the extent of sending 8,000 men to Vietnam under the guise of humanitarian relief. The only possible explanation of this charade was to keep the appearance of legality for the benefit of American and world public opinion. The concept of SEATO "cover" is used in the same way. The communists have hardly been fooled. The British and French have shown little enthusiasm. Since the American people are the target of American international law, they are also its victims.

## Reprisal

In spite of the rather panicked atmosphere of Vietnam in 1961, things settled down again and many American advisors were even withdrawn. But by late 1963, gloom had returned. Diem fell and large portions of South Vietnam came under Viet Cong control. This time the crisis was viewed as so acute that American troops were required to fill a combat role and American bombing of North Vietnam was needed to preserve a non-communist government in the South. Again, the American people had to be prepared for intervention, but this time the numbers game was in the hundreds of thousands of men. Rather than using communist violations of the DMZ as a reason for non-compliance of the United States to the provisions of the Geneva Accords with respect to advisors, violations of the Accords were used to justify the bombing of North Vietnam.

In this context the concept of reprisal was used to prepare the American people for an undeclared war. Well before the Gulf of Tonkin incident, American decision-makers had decided that United States troops and bombing of the North were required to salvage the situation in South Vietnam. In January, 1964, a Joint Chiefs of Staff memorandum indicated that to insure victory, the "United States must make ready to conduct increasingly bolder actions in Southeast Asia." Among the measures recommended were bombing "key North Vietnamese targets, support for large-scale U.S. commando raids against critical targets in North Vietnam . . . committing additional U.S. forces, as necessary, in support of the combat action within South Vietnam," and "committing U.S. forces as necessary in direct action against North Vietnam."[83] In addition to the perceived need for large scale United States participation, a program of covert operations was

[83] G. III, p. 498.

initiated in February. First seriously discussed at the Honolulu conference of November 20, 1963, OPLAN 34A was reviewed by an interdepartmental group headed by Major General Krulak, USMC, and was approved by President Johnson on January 16, 1964.[84] The program was to include such activities as U-2 overflights, South Vietnamese bombing in Laos and North Vietnam, intelligence gathering and psychological operations in North Vietnam, commando raids along the coast, and hit-and-run raids into Laos.[85] The program was divided into four-month sections with each segment composed of the same types of activities but ever increasing in magnitude and tempo. The covert operations were "designed to result in substantial destruction, economic loss, and harassment."[86] The purpose of the pressure against North Vietnam was to punish the North for infiltrating the South.

The logic of reprisal was present in Vietnam well before the decision to bomb the North. Americans and South Vietnamese felt at a considerable disadvantage because they were forced into a defensive position and could not attack the source of the problem. Ambassador Taylor phrased the dilemma as early as November 1961 in the context of the decision to embark on a massive influx of American advisors:

> Can we admit the establishment of the common law that the party attacked and his friends are denied the right to strike the source of aggression, after the fact of external aggression is clearly established? . . . it is clear to me that the time may come in our relations to Southeast Asia when we must declare our intention to attack the source of guerrilla aggression in North Vietnam and impose on the Hanoi Government a price for participating in the current war which is commensurate with the damage being inflicted on its neighbor to the south.[87]

In terms of the policy debate of 1964, the principle of reciprocity was phrased as the Rostow thesis, namely, "covert aggression justifies and must be fought by attacks on the source of aggression."[88] As abstract propositions, the Taylor and Rostow formulations have considerable merit. It would be difficult to argue that a state or group of states would not have the right to defend themselves from covert attacks. The problem, however, is complicated by the prohibition of the use of force in international relations. War and the traditional techniques for the use

---

[84] G. III, p. 151.  [85] G. III, p. 150.  [86] *Ibid.*
[87] G. II, p. 97.  [88] G. III, p. 200.

of force to settle disputes have for the most part been made unlawful while no workable system has been substituted. The facts of the Vietnam War also reinforce the conclusion that some sort of action against the north was justified. From 1954 onward, there was certainly some relationship between the Viet Cong and Hanoi and after 1959, there was considerable movement of North Vietnamese regular troops into South Vietnam. By 1965 North Vietnamese units were operating at regimental strength below the DMZ. If such a situation occurred across most of the borders of the world, there would be little question as to the right of retaliation. But the Vietnam case is not so clear. First, there is the problem of the civil war in the whole of Vietnam. If it is a civil war, such action would not constitute aggression. The second problem is the timing and the extent of the infiltration. It is difficult to determine when and where the aggression started, or which side was at fault. Thirdly, there is the problem of the relative amounts of intervention. The rules of the game are not clear. While some covert activity is expected and tolerated, the level of activity deemed to have international significance is not settled. Finally, there is the question of the Geneva Accords. Did the failure of the South to hold the elections give the North the right to achieve results by force? All of these questions cloud the application of abstractions to the Vietnam case.

The complexity of the legal and moral issues were resolved into the simplicity of a desperate tactical situation and a need for strong measures. In this context, the concept of reprisal was used to justify American intervention. The concept of reprisal was used ambiguously before the Gulf of Tonkin incident. On the one hand, it was behind the logic of the covert operations. The whole OPLAN 34A was considered a signal to cease and desist. On June 18, and August 15, 1964, Canadian International Control Commissioner Seaborn met with Premier Phan Van Dong of North Vietnam to convey the meaning of the covert operations and the greater threat they implied.[89] But Hanoi was unmoved and the intensity of the covert operations increased according to plan. On the other hand, the concepts of reprisal and reciprocity were used in preparing the American people for large scale American intervention. In this context, William P. Bundy prepared, on May 23, 1964, a secret 30-day scenario of coordinated political and military action which would: (1) warn the North; (2) gain a Joint

[89] G. III, p. 292.

Resolution of the American Congress; (3) publish the "Jordan Report" documenting North Vietnamese atrocities and infiltration; (4) order the North to cease and desist; (5) conclude that the North had rejected all reasonable offers; and finally, (6) begin bombing the North. At first this would be done with South Vietnamese aircraft, but there would be a gradual transfer to American bombing to include the destruction of the North's ability to support the war in the South.[90] The planned Congressional Resolution accused the communists of violating the Geneva Accords and resolved:

> That the United States regards the preservation of the independence and integrity of the nations of South Vietnam and Laos as vital to its national interest and to world peace;
>
> To this end, if the President determines the necessity thereof, the United States is prepared, upon the request of the Government of South Viet Nam or the Government of Laos, to use all measures, including the commitment of armed forces to assist that government in the defense of its independence and territorial integrity against aggression or subversion supported, controlled or directed from any Communist country.[91]

The military planners had a dual problem. While the bombing of the north might be justified as a reprisal, the introduction of large numbers of American troops would have to be justified on the basis of reciprocity. However, this distinction was not made because the bombing itself would begin the escalation scenario. The problem was to have a credible justification for the first bloodletting. As early as March 16, 1964, Secretary McNamara recommended to the President that the military "prepare immediately to be in a position" on thirty days notice to initiate the program of Graduated Overt Military Pressure against North Vietnam.[92] In the context of this memo "Retaliatory Actions" meant bombing strikes and commando raids on a tit-for-tat basis, aerial mining, and reconnaissance flights using South Vietnamese with American assistance and support. "Graduated Overt Pressure" meant using both United States and South Vietnamese resources to attack military and possibly industrial targets. This memo was approved by the President and the order to begin planning was sent by the Joint Chiefs of Staff to the Commander-in-Chief, Pacific, on March 18, 1964. McNamara's

---

[90] G. III, p. 167.          [91] NYT, p. 286.          [92] G. III, p. 509.

recommendation was made with the full knowledge that "there would be the problem of marshalling the case to justify such action, the problem of communist escalation, and the problem of dealing with the pressure by premature or 'stacked' negotiations." Although the problems were seen as "extremely delicate,"[93] planning was begun.[94]

At this juncture, however, it must be recalled that the summer and fall of 1964 was also the time for Presidential politics in the United States, so there was considerable restraint on the aggressiveness of American action. Since President Johnson was running as a "dove" against "hawkish" Barry Goldwater, aggressive overt military action was out of the question. Yet both the planning for overt operations and the continuation of covert activity marked this period. From early spring on, there was little question in any of the decision-makers' minds that drastic action had to be taken. It was only a matter of how and when such coercion should begin. The concept of reprisal was still used on two distinct levels. On the first level, covert operations and the secret diplomatic moves were underway. On the second level, bombing was being considered as a reprisal for the ongoing activity of the North Vietnamese in South Vietnam. This use of the concept was only in the planning stage, and it joined military activity with diplomatic activity in an orchestrated program to gain support of American public opinion. But the fall of 1964 was not the time for William P. Bundy's 30-day scenario. On the 31st day, President Johnson might have been out of office.

On July 17 and 31, 1964, the U.S.S. *Maddox* was engaged in the so-called DE SOTO patrols off North Vietnam.[95] Her orders were to conduct various intelligence tasks such as "sampling electronic environmental radars and navagation aides" and to find the "location and identification of all radar transmitters."[96] The *Maddox* was to cruise no closer than eight nautical miles off North Vietnam. These missions were to include the triggering of North Vietnamese radar to determine their capabilities. As part of OPLAN 34A, the South Vietnamese, on July 30, made commando raids on Hon Me and Hon Nieu Islands which are North Vietnamese territory. At the time of these raids, the *Maddox* was heading into the waters off North Vietnam. Exactly what happened in the Gulf of Tonkin on August 2 and 4 will probably never be known with certainty, but it seems the North Vietnamese responded

93 G. III, p. 503.  94 G. III, p. 504.  95 G. III, p. 182.
96 G. III, p. 183.

to the American and South Vietnamese covert operations with an overt response.[97] On August 5, the United States conducted air strikes against the torpedo boat bases in North Vietnam, and on August 6, the United States Congress passed the Gulf of Tonkin Resolution which authorized the President "to take all necessary steps, including the use of armed force."[98] Thus, the North Vietnamese had taken steps which joined the two concepts of reprisal into one program of action. The planning of early summer fell into place; the reprisal was conducted, and the Joint Resolution was achieved. The information in the Pentagon Papers does not indicate that the Gulf of Tonkin incident was a staged event. Before August, the two concepts of reprisal were parallel and distinct. The covert operations were distinct from the 30-day scenario and reprisal planning. For the Washington decision-makers, the spectacular success of the Gulf of Tonkin incident was stimulating. Although no program of action or graduated pressure was initiated immediately, since August was too close to November, the planners in State and Defense saw considerable future for the Tonkin precedent.

On August 11, 1964, William P. Bundy circulated a memo entitled "Next Courses of Action in Southeast Asia," which was to begin the process of a policy of reprisal. Bundy argued for overtly stepping up the OPLAN 34A operation, cross-border operations, renewed DESOTO patrols, and tit-for-tat reprisal actions for North Vietnamese and Viet Cong activities. The program was designed "to maintain the initiative and morale of the GVN [Government of (South) Vietnam] and Khanh, but that would not involve major risks of escalation. Such actions could be such as to foreshadow stronger measures to come, though they would not in themselves go so far to change Hanoi's basic actions."[99]

Considerable subtlety was added to the concept of reprisal by Assistant Secretary of Defense John T. McNaughton in his development of William P. Bundy's plan in a memo of September 3, 1964, entitled "Plan of Action for South Vietnam." He saw no reason for shifting American and South Vietnamese action from the covert to the overt level. The Gulf of Tonkin incident was all the more effective because most of the world did not know that the patrols of the *Maddox* were part of a program of covert activities.

97 It must be noted that portions of the treatment of the Gulf of Tonkin incident are deleted from the published versions of "The Pentagon Papers."

98 Falk, *op. cit.*, p. 579.

99 NYT, p. 296.

*Actions.* The actions, in addition to present continuing "extra-territorial" actions (U.S. U-2 recce[100] of DRV, U.S. jet recce of Laos, T-28 activity in Laos), would be by way of an orchestration of three classes of actions, all designed to meet these five desiderata—(1) from the U.S., GVN and hopefully allied points of view, they should be legitimate things to do under the circumstances, (2) they should cause apprehension, ideally increasing apprehension, in the DRV, (3) they should be likely at some point to provoke a military DRV response, (4) the provoked response should be likely to provide good grounds for us to escalate if we wished, and (5) the timing and crescendo should be under our control, with the scenario capable of being turned off at any time. . . .[101]

The various "targets" of American action are clearly outlined in the McNaughton memo along with the delicate nature of the election problem within the U.S.

*Special considerations during next two months.* The relevant "audiences" of U.S. actions are the Communists (who must feel strong pressures), the South Vietnamese (whose morale must be buoyed), our allies (who must trust us as "underwriters"), and the U.S. public (which must support our risk-taking with U.S. lives and prestige). During the next two months, because of the lack of "rebuttal time" before election to justify particular actions which may be distorted to the U.S. public, we must act with special care—signalling to the DRV that initiatives are being taken, to the GVN that we are behaving energetically despite the restraints of our political season, and to the U.S. public that we are behaving with good purpose and restraint.[102]

In a meeting of Taylor, Rusk, McNamara, and General Wheeler on September 7, 1964, the Joint Chiefs of Staff advocated the idea of deliberately provoking North Vietnam into actions which could be made the excuse for reprisals.[103] While the group advocated renewing the covert operations, they recognized the sensitivity of the problem. The consensus as reported by William P. Bundy was:

---

[100] "Recce" means armed reconnaissance flights with authority to return and suppress fire.

[101] NYT, p. 356.  [102] NYT, p. 357.

[103] G. III, p. 110.

The main further question is the extent to which we should add elements to the above actions that would tend deliberately to provoke a DRV (North Vietnamese) reaction, and consequently retaliation by us. Example of actions to be considered would be running US naval patrols increasingly close to the North Vietnamese coast and/or associating them with 34A operations (South Vietnamese commando raids). We believe such deliberately provocative elements should not be added in the immediate future while the GVN (South Vietnamese Government) is still struggling to its feet. By early October, however, we may recommend such actions depending on GVN progress and Communist reaction in the meantime, especially to US naval patrols.[104]

On September 10, 1964, the President issued a National Security Action Memorandum approving the resumption of DESOTO patrols and OPLAN 34A commando raids. He indicated that "We should be prepared to respond as appropriate against the DRV in the event of any attack on US units or any special DRV/VC action against SVN (South Vietnam)."[105] Although the President rejected 34A covert air strikes "for the present," he indicated strengthening the Government of South Vietnam was the most important item at the moment and "such action should precede larger decisions. If such larger decisions are required at any time by a change in the situation, they will be taken."[106] It was also recognized that the North Vietnamese would publicize the nature of the South Vietnamese commando raids and that these operations might have to be made overt and justified by the South Vietnamese on the basis of infiltration from the North. The President also indicated that the destroyer patrols should be "well beyond the 12-mile limit and be clearly dissociated from 34A maritime operation."[107] Therefore, by keeping the nature of the destroyer patrols secret and postponing the American role in air strikes against the North, the President retained the "covert" nature of American participation in the pressure against the North. While the leadership, planning, and material for these activities was strictly American, the United States would retain a covert stance. Vietnamese cover would allow the United States to

104 G. III, p. 562. Courses of Action for South Vietnam, 8 September 1964.

105 G. III, p. 565. National Security Action Memorandum.

106 G. III, p. 566. The difficulty was not with the tactic of provocation, but merely a matter of the timing.

107 G. III, p. 565. National Security Action Memorandum No. 314, 10 September 1964.

adopt a policy of reprisal for allegedly illegal and unprovoked attacks when the communists responded. Although the rationale for postponing the provocative actions was the weakness of the South Vietnamese Government, the real reason was the political situation in the United States. This is clearly shown by the American response to the Viet Cong attack on the Ben Hoa American air base, killing five Americans and wounding seventy-six on November 1, 1964.[108] The Joint Chiefs of Staff responded by recommending B-52 strikes against the Phuc Yen airfield near Hanoi and against other airfields and petroleum storage areas throughout North Vietnam.[109] That President Johnson did not approve such a request on the eve of election is hardly surprising since he had campaigned as a "dove." However, there was certainly a feeling of a missed opportunity. Another indication that the American public was the primary audience of American reprisal plans was the Viet Cong bombing of the United States officer's billet in Saigon on December 24, 1964, killing several Americans. Although this would have been a perfect incident for a reprisal, the time was obviously not ideal as far as American politics was concerned.[110] President Johnson did not want to give the American people a war for Christmas.

After President Johnson's election, however, plans firmed up. William P. Bundy again prepared a scenario of military and public relations activity. Although he concluded that the problem was a "real jigsaw puzzle in which you have to weigh at every point the viewpoints of: (a) The American Congress and public, (b) Saigon, (c) Hanoi and Peiping, (d) key interested nations," he recommended the following series of actions and statements:[111]

CHECKLIST FOR SCENARIO ACTIONS

I. *U.S. Public Actions*
   A. White House statement following Tuesday meeting.
   B. Background briefing on infiltration in both Saigon and Washington
   C. Congressional Consultation
   D. Major speech
   E. Jordan Report (documenting N. Vietnamese infiltration)

108 G. III, p. 288.
109 G. III, p. 289.
110 G. III, p. 14.
111 The order of these priorities is quite revealing.

II. *GVN*
    A. Consultation with GVN  (S. Vietnamese Government)
    B. GVN statement

III. *Key Allies*
    A. Consultation with RLG  (Royal Laotian Government)
    B. Consultation with Thai
    C. Consultation with UK, Australia, New Zealand, and Philip
       pines
    D. SEATO Council statement  (?)

IV. *Communist Nations*
    A. Signals and messages to Hanoi and Peiping
    B. What to say to Soviets  (and Poles?)

V. *Other Nations*
    A. Canada, India, and France
    B. UN is required

VI. *Existing Categories of Military Actions*
    A. US Laos reconnaissance
    B. RLAF attacks in Laos  (Royal Laotian Air Force)
    C. GEN MAROPS  (Coastal commando raids)
    D. US high-level reconnaissance of DRV  (N. Vietnam)

VII. *Reprisal Actions*
    A. Renewed DESOTO patrol
    B. Another Bien Hoa or other spectacular

VIII. *Added Military or Other Actions*
    A. Stopping flow of dependents
    B. YT strikes in Laos: infiltration areas, Route 7  (U.S.A.F. in
       Laos)
    C. US low-level reconnaissance over DRV
    D. Strikes across the border into DRV: GVN and US roles[112]

At 2:00 A.M. on February 7, 1965, the Viet Cong carried out a well-coordinated attack against the American air base at Pleiku killing nine Americans. Fourteen hours later forty U.S. Navy jets from the USS *Coral Sea* and USS *Hancock* hit North Vietnamese barracks at Dong Hoi. On the same day, McGeorge Bundy presented a memo en-

112 G. III, p. 676, 28 November 1964.

titled, "A Policy of Sustained Reprisal" to the President. The memo stated: "We believe that the best available way of increasing our chances of success in Vietnam is the development and execution of a policy of *sustained reprisal* against North Vietnam—a policy in which air and naval action against the North is justified and related to the whole Viet Cong campaign of violence and terror in the South."[113] In the following weeks, the air war against the North shifted from the tit-for-tat reprisals conducted by joint American and South Vietnamese operations under the concept of FLAMING DART, approved by the President in late January 1965, to American operations titled ROLLING THUNDER, which commenced in March.[114] The logic of an ever-escalating crescendo which reflected the Bundy scenarios was carried into operation plans. By March 29, when Viet Cong terrorists bombed the United States Embassy in Saigon, the President made no special spectacular reprisal attack on the North.[115] The concept of reprisal was dropped and the air action was just another aspect of the war. Within a day the President decided to commit United States troops to a ground combat role in South Vietnam.[116] After the attack on the Embassy, the justification for the air war against the North was shifted to the "interdiction" of men and supplies into the South. By the beginning of May, plans were made for the first bombing pause. Given the code name MAYFLOWER, the pause was, in the President's words, "to clear a path either toward restoration of peace or toward increased military action, depending on the reaction of the Communists."[117] Since the communists refused to capitulate after five days, the air war began again in earnest.

The American reprisal policy can be seen to fill two distinct roles, one international and the second domestic. On the international level, the reprisal was used in a rather traditional manner. The covert coercion linked with the warnings of Blair Seaborn of the ICC, represented the classic use of reprisal. The Americans asserted that the Northern support of the Viet Cong was illegal and began a graduated series of coercive acts to prompt the North to cease and desist. It may be argued whether or not the American view was correct, but granting American assumptions, the coercion was proportional and it must be admitted that South Vietnam had grounds for complaint. On the level of do-

---

[113] G. III, p. 687.　　　　[114] G. III, p. 272.

[115] G. III, p. 348.　　　　[116] G. III, p. 348. 1 April 1965.

[117] G. III, p. 366. 10 May 1965, FLASH message from President Johnson to Ambassador Taylor.

mestic politics, there is also some justification for the policy. The Americans felt that the traditional rules of international law did not take into account the gradual escalation of infiltration which was conducted against South Vietnam. There was no clear moment of armed attack. Consequently, the just response to aggression could not be argued in traditional language. American action was required to save Vietnam, and the only question was how to get the American people behind what the government felt to be action in the national interest as well as morally justifiable. To do this the government felt that it was necessary to "prepare" the American people. Thus, the covert American activities were designed to provoke overt attacks on Americans which could be responded to under the concept of reprisal.

The whole American charade was based upon the need for moral and legal justification of American action to the American public. The decision-makers used the highly moralist and legalist rhetoric of American policy debate to create a consensus in favor of the action deemed necessary. The Gulf of Tonkin and the Pleiku incidents were characterized as breaches of the law for which just punishment was due. The difficulty was that the American case was in reality quite weak. The United States could not claim clean hands. American forces in Vietnam were hardly disinterested spectators. The charge of aggression rested on the validity of the Geneva Accords, which the United States had not signed, and the election provisions, which had not been upheld. As for the violations of international law, the activity of the American destroyers in the Gulf of Tonkin was hardly pacific. From the beginning of 1954 at least, Americans had participated in the violence and illegality of the Vietnam War. Of course Americans were not alone in this ugly mess. The North and South Vietnamese, the French, the Russians, and the Chinese all shared in the guilt.

What is perhaps most tragic even beyond the lying, the hypocrisy, and the bloodshed of the reprisal policy was its failure. The pieces of William P. Bundy's jig-saw puzzle did not fit together in a coherent manner. It is impossible to use a single policy for conveying messages to our allies and enemies, and for simultaneously justifying a particular course of conduct to the American people. During the summer of 1964, the problem was complicated further by Presidential politics. How could Hanoi interpret covert reprisals in conjunction with Johnson's "dove-like" coos? The American policy was caught somewhere between using reprisal as a technique in international relations and using it as an argument in domestic politics. The use of the instrument in one or the other context is possible, but to use it in both simultaneously is impossible. To use reprisal as pretext implies that the decision for war has already been made. To use reprisal as a means short of war requires decisive enough action to secure the desired concession. Unfortunately the United States conducted both policies simultaneously. The graduated intensity of covert activity indicated that Washington wanted to hide from its own people the fact that it wanted to enter the war. The covert nature of the operation indicated that the reprisal argument was to be used as a pretext. Yet many of the American decision-makers felt once Hanoi was convinced of American purpose, the issue would be solved and Hanoi would realize the folly of persistence. The covert and uncommitting nature of American action was counterproductive. Hanoi concluded that the American Government was hesitant because it did not have the support of the people. This was not the real reason for the hesitancy. The President, following the American tradition of keeping options open, had not made a decision. Both the Vietnamese and the American situations were fluid. American commitment to a government about to collapse would be stupid. So he waited for the decision while preparing the groundwork for various options. The dual use of reprisal and particularly the covert operations carried a momentum of their own. In spite of the fact that the President was able to keep the Gulf of Tonkin incident as a discrete incident, it merely whetted the appetite of those who wanted wider action. By the time the "larger decisions" were made, the situation in Vietnam was so desperate that even the policy of "sustained reprisal" offered no hope for success. Thus the American decision-makers tricked not only the American people but themselves as well. By using covert means, they subverted the traditional utility of reprisal; and by tricking the American people, they cheapened their word. Like the little boy who called "wolf," one day they would pay.

From the point of view of law, the American use of reprisal was also tragic. In classic international law, a reprisal was used to coerce small states to follow the will of powerful states. A cruiser would fire a few rounds at the presidential palace or the marines would land and a week later the affair would be settled. A few lives would regrettably be lost, but real violence was avoided. However, the sensibilities of great democracies and the pride of nationalism, coupled with the identity of morality and international law, have turned the reprisal into an instrument of escalating violence. It was American restraint and legal sensibility which dictated the policy of covert reprisal. It was the American notion that the uses of power must have a lily-white morality that drove Americans to trick the American people. These sensibilities and Vietnamese pride unleashed terrible forces of violence. In terms of law, the technique of reprisal was distorted into a grotesque; rather than minimize the violence, it helped to maximize it. Thus, in addition to cheapening its word, the government cheapened the law.

## Conclusion

American assumptions about the international legal order reflect a certain ambivalence. With respect to enemies, allies, and domestic public opinion, the United States steadfastly proclaims the legal and moral basis of American foreign policy. The law and moral principles are held in sacred regard. But the ritual of reverence which demands a lily-white appearance is seen by the practitioners of foreign policy as a severe limitation to practical and reasonable action. This is particularly true in crisis situations in which the United States faces ruthless adversaries. The moral and legal rhetoric of American policy asserts the validity and effectiveness of the law of cooperation, coexistence, and restraint, while the practitioners really believe that the law is only workable in situations of coexistence and cooperation.[118] This situation has resulted in a rhetorical use of international law and the practice of what is called the "rules of the game." While in principle legal norms exist in the law of restraint, such as the Charter of the United Nations, these rules are ambiguously worded and provide for no certain remedial procedures or measures. While the use of force is technically unlawful, there is no established and compulsory means for the settlement of disputes. The provisions of the law of restraint are vague or ambiguous, and the states have been careful to retain the right of auto-interpretation.[119]

118 See Leo Gross, "International Law and Peace," *The Japanese Annual of International Law* 11 (1967), pp. 1-14. In brief the law of coexistence consists of the rules which are necessary for international relations to exist at all. These rules are rarely violated. Diplomatic immunity is an example. The law of cooperation consists of law designed to help states work toward common objectives. The river commissions provide a good example. Finally the law of restraint refers to the twentieth-century attempt to use law to control the use of force between states. The Kellogg-Briand Pact, by attempting to outlaw war as an instrument of national policy, moved into the law of restraint.

119 This is the undisputed right of a state, in the absence of an agreement to the contrary, to interpret international agreements for itself at its own risk. See Leo Gross, "States

Thus while the law establishes the principles and provides the language of crisis discourse, auto-interpretation and the authority of national leadership render the law of restraint a pliant servant of policy. In fact the law itself is drafted in such a way as to admit of these uses. The use of the Geneva Accords in the two decades of the Vietnam crisis provides an excellent example of the tragic weakness of the law of restraint. The State Department concluded in 1961 that "the Geneva Accords have been totally inadequate in protecting South Vietnam against Communist infiltration and insurgency."[120] The problem was, as everyone at the Conference knew, there was no real agreement. The document had only the appearance of legal relationships. Yet for twenty years the various parties utilizing auto-interpretation and the spreading of half-truths claimed rights and protested violations of the Geneva Accords. The function of the Accords was not to define the legal relationships of the North and South Vietnamese. They knew perfectly well that they were at war. The function of the Accords was to give the French a little something to toss to public opinion in return for saving a lot of Viet Minh lives. The American participation in this process produced a document which the United States would continually use to justify its intervention. All this was possible only because no truly legal settlement or authoritative interpretation of the Accords was ever considered. The development of the SEATO Treaty is another example. The function of the Treaty is not to define international legal relationships. It was carefully drafted to include no obligations. Yet the Treaty was interpreted by the American government for the American people as a sacred commitment. Its use was to gain support for governmental policy.

The extension of law as rhetoric has also distorted the principles and techniques of customary international law. The limited use of force in reprisal is highly questionable under the law of the Charter. Yet states still feel the need to use coercion. The American use of the technique of covert reprisal reflects the need for a traditional technique and sensitivity to its current disrepute. Since the use of force and war itself now have connotations of illegality, the great powers and their clients have

---

as Organs of International Law and the Problem of Autointerpretation," in Lipsky, G., *Law and Politics in the World Community* (Berkeley: University of California Press, 1954), pp. 59-88.

[120] G. II, p. 45.

had to resort to a charade called "the rules of the game."[121] The problem is that no one knows for sure the content of these rules or how they are to be interpreted. The use of reprisal in Vietnam is a good example. The one thing that is clear from the whole mess is that both North Vietnam and Moscow have failed to get the message. The escalation scenarios were so subtle and sophisticated that no one understood them. The escalation ladder seems to maximize rather than minimize the violence. Traditional international law offered a similar pattern of increasing force as "the rules of the game," but the signals were clear, the language was universal. "The rules of the game" is a shoddy plastic substitute which disintegrates under pressure. The constant misreading of intentions and objectives which characterize the Vietnam escalation should be ample proof of the weakness of these rules if they exist. The game goes on and everybody loses. The extension of rhetorical international law to the traditional techniques of the use of force short of war has resulted in the distortion of the technique into an unclear and garbled message. The so-called "rules of the game" offers not more but less clarity.

In both the drafting of the law of restraint and the use of customary law, the rhetoric of legalism beyond the point to which states are willing to go in terms of real law has been unsuccessful in practice. Rhetoric is no substitute for law, and law which is nothing more than rhetoric provides no protection. The serious problem is not the failure of the law as law to achieve results and aid in the solution of the Vietnam dilemma. It is rather the ostensive success of the rhetorical law of restraint as practiced on the American people that is the real danger. The Geneva Accords, the SEATO Treaty, the covert operations, the policy of sustained reprisal, and the invocation of sacred commitments have worked. In spite of widespread opposition, the government has in fact been able to keep alive the policy that it is a matter of American national interest to preserve a non-communist government in South Vietnam. The purpose of this paper is not to analyze this assumption or even the policy itself. It cannot be denied that the vast majority of elected officials and their advisors either shared this view or did not feel the need to reject it. Even granting this assumption, the American use

121 See Richard A. Falk, "International Jurisdiction: Horizontal and Vertical Conceptions of Legal Order," *Temple Law Quarterly* 32 (Spring 1959), pp. 295-320; and Edward T. McWhinney, "Soviet and Western International Law and the Cold War in the Era of Bipolarity," *Canadian Yearbook of International Law* 1 (1963), pp. 63-81.

of law and legal argument is self-defeating. The short-run successes cheapen the law and the word of the government. The policy should be able to stand on its own feet. Using auto-interpretation and the authority of government, Americans have used legal arguments to trick the American people. The law which is drafted to serve this purpose is not law at all. Its role is not to define legal relationships between states, but rather to serve the government in bringing its case to the people.

That Americans feel "bound" by international law can hardly be questioned. The use of covert operations, SEATO, and "humanitarian" cover; the use of reprisal as a pretext for action; and the great care Americans took in the drafting of such documents as the unilateral declaration at Geneva in 1954 show that Americans take legal obligations seriously. In fact they take legal obligations so seriously that they draft documents in such a way that it can be plausibly argued that no legal obligation exists at all. American participation in the Geneva Accords and the drafting of SEATO are prime examples of this. Secretary Dulles insured that he made no agreements with the communists, and the Joint Chiefs of Staff were careful to make sure SEATO would not limit American flexibility. The problem with this stance is that American agreements are worth nothing. They carry the type of optional guarantee that the Wall Street lawyers have drafted for auto manufacturers. If the company wants out, there is an escape clause in the fine print of the first footnote. The result is not a matter of law but of power. The tragedy is that some day the United States will want to make an agreement which constitutes real law in the area of restraint. It will want to change from a rhetorical use of law to its proper legal use. But the habits of mind, the cheapening of legal language and legal technique, and disreputable reputation developed through years of the rhetorical use of the law will make such an agreement difficult. No state would consider a contract with such slippery foxes as the Americans. In terms of its own people, the government will have invoked international law and international agreements in vain so many times that in real crises the people will shrug their shoulders and turn the other way.

# United Nations Peacekeeping:
## An Alternative for Future Vietnams*

### DONALD W. McNEMAR

IN THE AFTERMATH of the United States disengagement from Vietnam, American society faces the question: were there any alternatives to such massive unilateral intervention by the United States? Discussions on this point usually focus on past actions such as troop commitments, bombing halts, military tactics, and peace overtures, but the question can also be fruitfully examined from a broader perspective: would a multilateral, rather than a unilateral, response have been more appropriate? In short, can United Nations peacekeeping be viewed as an alternative to "future Vietnams?"

The actual role played in the Vietnam situation by the United Nations was minimal and peripheral.[1] The war was frequently discussed in speeches made during the general debate of the General Assembly, but such comments and exhortations did not lead to involvement of the Organization in the conflict. The United States did take the initiative in proposing a Security Council resolution and succeeded in having the Vietnam question placed on the Council agenda on February 2, 1966. However, the proposed resolution was clearly unacceptable to other permanent members of the Council, and on February 26, 1966, it was reported that after informal discussions, the Council would not hold further debate on the topic at that time. The U.S. effort in the Council was generally viewed more as a propaganda effort than as a serious attempt to pursue peace through United Nations channels.

The Secretary-General took initiatives throughout the war in attempting to facilitate and encourage peace negotiations. U Thant criticized members, calling the intervention in Vietnam an example of the failure of U.N. members to observe the "fundamental injunction to refrain in their international relations from the threat or use of force

* An earlier version of this paper was presented at the American Political Science Convention, September 1973.

1 For general discussion of the role of the United Nations in the Vietnam war, see: Max Gordon, "Vietnam, the United States, and the United Nations," in *The Vietnam War and International Law*, Vol. 2, ed: Richard A. Falk (Princeton: Princeton University Press, 1969), pp. 321-57; and Lincoln P. Bloomfield, *The U.N. and Vietnam* (New York: Carnegie Endowment for International Peace, 1968).

against the territorial integrity or political independence of any state,"[2] and urging peace negotiations. Waldheim continued attempts to bring the prestige and influence of the Secretary-General's position as a world spokesman to bear on the pursuit of peace. Waldheim's presence at the international conference on Vietnam in Paris, without any substantive function in the negotiations, symbolized the role that the United Nations had played throughout the conflict as an organization which produced vigorous demands for peace but which had no effective means to carry them out.

Why did the United Nations play such a marginal role in the most disruptive and violent conflict since World War II? A variety of specific reasons for the restricted role can be suggested. Only one party to the fighting was a member of the Organization. Hanoi, France, and the Soviet Union viewed a resumed Geneva Conference, rather than the U.N., as the appropriate international forum. The U.S. saw little chance that the U.N. would support its position. Member states feared the Organization would be severely damaged either if the U.N. were caught in the midst of a struggle between the superpowers, or if the Organization went too far in endorsing the position of either power. These reasons all support the general proposition that once a great power has undertaken a major role in a conflict, the capacity of the United Nations for peacekeeping is extremely circumscribed.

This inability of the U.N. to act in the face of great power opposition was built into the original Charter concept of the Organization. The Charter envisioned allied action by the five great powers to guard the peace. The plan for a standing military force to carry out Security Council decisions and the granting of the veto to the five major powers recognized that collective security was to be based on a concerted effort by the great powers. When allied cooperation ended with the cold war, the U.N. was left with a peacekeeping potential that was based on voluntary contributions, host consent, and support of all veto powers. This shift insured that the U.N. was unable to act in a conflict involving a major power.[3] Inaction by the U.N. in the face of superpower moves

[2] U Thant, "The United Nations and the Human Factor," U.N. Press Release, SG/SM/ 782 (U. N. Office of Public Information, July 28, 1967).

[3] The assumption that the U.N. is not in a position to challenge action of a great power in the peace and security field is discussed in: Inis L. Claude, Jr., *Power and International Relations* (New York: Random House, 1962), pp. 155-204; and Oran R. Young, *The Intermediaries: Third Parties in International Crises* (Princeton: Princeton University Press, 1967).

was illustrated in Hungary, Czechoslovakia, and the Dominican Republic. The U.N. presence in the Suez was possible only because the superpowers overrode the great powers. In the case of Vietnam, once the United States became deeply involved there was no room for a United Nations presence.

The incompatibility between a unilateral intervention by a major power and a U.N. peacekeeping effort means that, if the U.N. is to be involved in such struggles, the multilateral option must be exercised either at the very outset of the conflict or at a decision point at which the great power has determined to change the nature of its involvement. Once the United States had defined the Vietnam situation as one of communist aggression against a free government, the U.S. demanded great freedom in responding to the problem. Although this definition of the nature of the conflict was contested by U Thant in his statement that the war was being fought by the Vietnamese, "not as a war of Communist aggression, but as a war of national independence,"[4] the American leaders remained committed to the proposition that Vietnam was a war between communist and democratic forces. Given this perception of the issue and the accompanying desire to bring to bear the full weight of American power and influence, there was no possibility of a U.N. peacekeeping operation in Vietnam.[5] The diplomatic efforts the U.S. did undertake at the U.N. came too late for there to be any substantive role for the Organization. Bloomfield notes that "by the time the U.S. did turn to the UN, the problem had in many ways become quite inappropriate for UN handling."[6] To the very end the United States insisted on as wide a latitude as possible in its actions, and rejected any meaningful role for the Organization.

Does the Vietnam lesson suggest that United Nations peacekeeping is totally irrelevant to wars limited to a single country or region? No, but it does make clear that the use of a multilateral option necessitates a different pattern of response by the superpowers in the future. Given the inordinate costs of the Vietnam operation in terms of human life, money, and domestic unrest, and the meager accomplishments of the American effort, foreign policy makers may indeed be willing to perceive differently the issues of the struggle and the aims of American

---

[4] Thant, "The United Nations and the Human Factor."

[5] The central importance of perception in defining the nature of a conflict is argued in: Ralph K. White, *Nobody Wanted War* (Garden City, N.Y.: Doubleday, 1968).

[6] Bloomfield, *The U.N. and Vietnam*, p. 10.

strategy in future contexts. Therefore, a multilateral involvement may become an attractive alternative despite the attendant loss of national control on the outcome and the tendency for such operations to be holding actions rather than leading to a clear resolution of the issues. United Nations action cannot be taken in competition with or as retaliation against the unilateral intervention of a major power, but U.N. peacekeeping may serve as a substitute for national action in the repertoire of great power foreign policy strategies.

Against the background of the U.S. actions in Vietnam and the United Nations deployment of peacekeeping forces in the Middle East, the Congo, and Cyprus, the precedents and experiences with unilateral and multilateral interventions can be developed into models for control of limited wars. The past record of United Nations action in this field does permit some generalizations about the nature of such efforts and the conditions under which a multilateral response may be desirable and effective.

## Models for Control of Limited Wars

Given the potential for limited wars such as Vietnam to escalate into major international wars, the control of limited wars has become an important task of contemporary statesmen. The concept of control is used here to refer to the decoupling of the struggle from the rest of the international system so that the conflict does not produce a major international disruption.[7] The concept is *not* used to refer to either the total prevention of such wars or the manipulation of the internal outcome of the violence. The emphasis in these models is on methods of insulating limited wars, so that the external involvement in such struggles does not lead to a widespread international war.

Three distinct models for controlling limited wars can be suggested on the basis of historical experiences and past reactions of potential intervenors in such conflicts. These primary models for controlling internal wars are: nonintervention, recognized intervenor, and collective intervention.

[7] Bloomfield and Leiss use the concept of control in a much broader sense to refer to a strategy which would "be neither to win nor to guide local conflicts; it would be to prevent, contain, or terminate them." Bloomfield and Leiss do not use control to include a strategy of manipulation, but they do emphasize the prevention and elimination of such local conflicts. In this study, the assumption is made that the conflicts will occur, and the emphasis is placed on insulating them from the rest of the international system. Lincoln P. Bloomfield and Amelia C. Leiss, *Controlling Small Wars: A Strategy for the 1970's* (New York: Alfred A. Knopf, 1969), p. xii.

The *nonintervention* model operates on the strict principle that no country will become involved in the internal conflicts of any other state. Under the rules of this system, all states follow a strict "hands-off" policy toward violence occurring within other countries. By not intervening, states isolate the society undergoing turmoil and allow the civil strife to run its course. If all states refuse to participate in any form, there is no longer danger that the internal war will be transformed into an international one. The model is successful only as long as all states adhere to the rule of nonparticipation. Once any country attempts to cheat on the system with the exception of gaining through intervention while the rest of the states refrain from intervention, the model breaks down. The basic requirement for this model is a system in which states are willing to accept any outcome of an internal dispute. By following a policy of noninterference, outside states are giving up any role that they might play in determining the results of civil strife; thus they must be prepared to accept any outcome of the struggle.

Historically, the nonintervention model operated in the European system prior to the French Revolution and from approximately 1850 to World War I. During these periods intervention was at a minimum as states pursued a policy of nonintervention with regard to civil wars. Many of the current international laws relating to restrictions on aid and to the rights and duties of neutrals in relation to civil wars are carry-overs from the European-centered system of the last half of the nineteenth century when the nonintervention model was in effect.

In the twentieth century the conditions supporting a widespread application of the nonintervention system have eroded, as illustrated by the Spanish civil war.[8] In this war states frequently demanded non-intervention and even established institutions to police outside par-

---

[8] For a description of the events in the Spanish civil war, see: Hugh Thomas, *The Spanish Civil War* (London: Eyre & Spottiswoode, 1961).

The international law questions relating to the Spanish civil war are considered in: James W. Garner, "Questions of International Law in the Spanish Civil War," *American Journal of International Law* 31 (1937), 66-73; Philip C. Jessup, "The Spanish Rebellion and International Law," *Foreign Affairs* 15 (1937), 260-79; and Arnold D. McNair, "The Law Relating to the Civil War in Spain," *Law Quarterly Review* 53 (1937), 471-500.

Operation of the Non-Intervention Agreements is specifically discussed in: Ann Van Wynen Thomas and A. J. Thomas, Jr., "The Civil War in Spain," in *The International Law of Civil War*, ed.: Richard A. Falk (Baltimore: Johns Hopkins Press, 1971), pp. 166-78; Dante A. Puzzo, *Spain and the Great Powers: 1936-1941* (New York: Columbia University Press, 1962), pp. 75-167; and Norman J. Padelford, *International Law and Diplomacy in the Spanish Civil War* (New York: Macmillan Company, 1969), pp. 53-120.

ticipation. However, the rise of communism and fascism meant that outside states were no longer indifferent about the outcome of such wars. States wanted to aid their ideological allies, and as a result, the outside participation in the Spanish civil war was extensive, despite the rhetoric of nonintervention.

The cold war greatly restricted the applicability of the model. Today the nonintervention model operates in those situations in which the struggle is of limited interest to the great powers. The civil wars in the Sudan and in Nigeria were characterized by considerable restraint on the part of outside powers, so that they qualify as contemporary examples of the nonintervention model. With the end of the cold war and the coming of detente, the class of limited wars in which the major powers are willing to refrain from active involvement and accept any outcome may expand greatly. Therefore, the nonintervention model may become increasingly important as a means of controlling limited wars.

The second model, the *recognized intervenor*, operates when one state is recognized by all others as the single intervenor in a given setting. The recognized intervenor may hold this position either out of an unquestionable power superiority, which leaves it unchallenged, or through the acceptance of its legitimacy by other states. The effectiveness of the model depends on the recognition by other states that one actor monopolizes intervention, thus eliminating the danger of competitive intervention.[9]

In the past this model has worked in such cases as the Roman Empire and Napoleonic France. The recognized intervenor model operates best in unipolar situations when one actor controls the decision of whether or not to intervene. This particular model currently operates in cases of strife within the sphere of influence of a major power.[10] In these instances the superpower assumes the role of recognized intervenor and handles the conflict with no potential challenge to its role and no danger of escalation. The Hungarian situation of 1956, the Dominican Repub-

[9] For comments on such competitive intervention in the past, see: Oran R. Young, "Intervention and International Systems," *Journal of International Affairs* 22 (1968), 183-84.

[10] For development of the theoretical concept of spheres of influence as a geopolitical area in the current world and of the nature of superpower hegemony in these areas, see: Richard A. Falk, "Zone II as a World Order Construct," in *The Analysis of International Politics*, eds.: James N. Rosenau, Vincent Davis, and Maurice A. East (New York: Free Press, 1972), pp. 187-208.

lic hostilities of 1965, and the Czech action in 1968 all represent cases of this model at work. Although spheres of influence have not disappeared, the results of the Vietnam conflict and efforts at detente may well lead to attempts to restrict use of the recognized intervenor model and to a greater willingness by the superpowers to pursue the nonintervention strategy.

A third means of controlling limited wars is through *collective intervention*, the most common example of which is the United Nations action. This model provides for the involvement of a group of states in the strife to prevent the extensive participation of a state on a unilateral basis. By collectivizing outside participation, the risks of competitive intervention resulting from the involvement of individual states can be overcome. This model has been applied in the past in such instances as the Holy Alliance's intervention in Naples and in Spain. Today this model may operate at the regional level with involvement of the OAS or OAU.[11] Action by regional organizations has been hindered by the dominance of single states, sharp divisions within groups, and restricted resources. The primary collective action to date has been undertaken by the United Nations in such cases as the Middle East, the Congo, and Cyprus, where U.N. peacekeeping forces were established to prevent the escalation of the conflict into a major international war.

When violent conflict occurs, then, states which are not themselves parties to the conflict have three basic options. The first is extremely limited participation or noninvolvement, a choice which, if all states pursued it, would produce control through the nonintervention model. The second alternative is unilateral intervention. This option results in controlling the conflict only in cases where one state is accepted as the recognized intervenor. However, if this role is disputed and more than one major power becomes seriously involved in the struggle, the prospects for general war through competitive intervention are great. The third strategy is to support some form of participation by a regional or international organization.[12] One result of the Vietnam war has been

[11] For discussion of those regional efforts which have been undertaken, see: Linda B. Miller, "Regional Organization and the Regulation of Internal Conflict," *World Politics* 19 (1967), 582-600.

[12] A case for the involvement of the U.N. in civil strife is made in: Richard A. Falk and Saul H. Mendlovitz, "Toward a Warless World: One Legal Formula to Achieve Transition," *Yale Law Journal* 73 (1964), 399-424. Evaluations of such a move are considered by the following: Oscar Schachter, "Preventing the Internationalization of Internal Conflict," *Proceedings of the American Society of International Law* (1963), 216-24; Louis

a questioning of the effectiveness of unilateral intervention, and a willingness to reexamine multilateral steps toward control of limited conflicts. Therefore, the operation and impact of the United Nations model must be assessed as a means for limiting violence and resolving conflicts in future Vietnam-type struggles.

## Operation of the United Nations Model

The United Nations model operates to minimize the disruptive effects of limited wars on the rest of the international system. Secretary-General Dag Hammarskjöld suggested that the U.N. perform this function of preventive diplomacy by participating in struggles outside the primary areas of the cold war in order to forestall competitive intervention by the superpowers.[13]

The potential and effectiveness of the U.N. model can be illustrated by presenting the situation in a grossly simplified form as a prisoner's dilemma situation involving two great powers.[14] Once a limited war has begun, the basic choice before the major actors is whether or not to intervene with military forces. A desirable outcome for any great power would be that it intervened while other powers refrained from intervention. However, the least desirable situation would be for more than one of the powers to make the decision to intervene, as this might result in international war. Considering the great powers as two players in a prisoner's dilemma situation, each with the choices of intervention or nonintervention, the following outcomes might result. If no state intervenes, the outcome is that a local government is engaged in a conflict over which no outside power has direct influence; thus, a neutral result for outsiders. However, if one state intervenes while the other does not, the assumed result is a government favorable to one side in a great power contest. This is credited as a significant gain for one power and as an equivalent loss for the other. If two great powers

B. Sohn, "The Role of the United Nations in Civil Wars," *Proceedings of the American Society of International Law* (1963), 208-15; and Richard A. Falk, "The International Regulation of Internal Violence in the Developing Countries," *Proceedings of the American Society of International Law* (1966), 58-67.

13 *Introduction to the Annual Report of the Secretary-General on the Work of the Organization*, 16 June 1959-15 June 1960, General Assembly Official Records, 15th Session, Supplement No. 1A (A/4390/Add. 1).

14 For discussion of such game situations, see: Anatol Rapoport and Albert M. Chammah, *Prisoner's Dilemma: A Study in Conflict and Cooperation* (Ann Arbor: University of Michigan Press, 1965).

intervene in the conflict, a major war—even a nuclear one—may result with a major loss to all parties.

The collective interest of the two states dictates that they both pursue a policy of nonintervention which results in no loss to either side. The question, therefore, becomes: how can outside powers "agree" to pursue a policy of nonintervention? Foreign states may be willing to refrain from intervention, *if*, and this is a very important if, they can be assured that the opponent will not make a gain at their expense. Much of the interest in intervening can be attributed to a desire to prevent adversaries from making an advance in that particular situation. If the United States were positive that the outcome of an internal war would be in no way a "victory for communism," nor would greatly extend Soviet or Chinese influence in developing areas, its interest in civil strife around the would would decrease considerably. When all great powers are given some assurance that none of their counterparts will gain from a given situation, then all are likely to show an increased willingness to refrain from intervention.

It is precisely by reassuring the major powers that other states will not make a gain in an internal war that the United Nations involvement can have an important effect on controlling limited wars. One result of U.N. involvement can be to fill the vacuum created by the internal breakdown into which great powers are tempted to move. Another result is the improvement of information available, since U.N. observers can report any efforts by outside states to move into the conflict. By using the U.N., great powers can move toward the cooperative solution of their prisoner's dilemma. Since many nations are concerned primarily with preventing gains by other actors, this end may be achieved more effectively by promoting a U.N. involvement than by sending national contingents.

Once the U.N. does become involved in such a conflict because states are willing to "let the U.N. do it" rather than intervene themselves, the Organization fulfills the role of recognized intervenor and encourages nonintervention. Part of the U.N.'s function is to observe and determine any actions which encroach on its monopoly. The U.N. can develop rules and procedures for other states in relation to the conflict, as a means of reinforcing the nonintervention stance of outside states. If foreign countries do violate the rules of nonintervention, the U.N. presence can quickly bring the facts to international attention. Thus, once nations have authorized U.N. involvement, the Organization becomes the only outside body directly involved, and the nonintervention system is reinforced.

## Components of the U.N. Model

The United Nations model consists of two components. The first is the U.N. field operation which is inserted into the conflict, and the second includes the norms which are developed concerning the participation of outside states in the conflict.

The United Nations peacekeeping forces which have been deployed in the Middle East, the Congo, and Cyprus provide the basis for characterizing and evaluating the U.N. field operations. These field operations to date have been composed of a collection of national forces seconded to the U.N. for use in particular instances of strife.[15] The forces have been under international command, but the troops remain national units raised on an *ad hoc* basis. Such forces have been mandated to do everything from observing to policing borders to preventing civil war. In the cases of major field operations, the U.N. presence has been introduced with the consent of the countries involved. Such consent has in the past solved the question of domestic jurisdiction, since the force was invited by the local government; in the future, host-consent may be forthcoming, or the U.N. may determine that the situation involves a threat to international peace and is, therefore, no longer essentially within domestic jurisdiction. The key to the Organization's initial involvement is strong support from the great powers plus a large majority of the U.N. membership.

Once the U.N. field operation is established, the troops are restricted to using force only for purposes of self-defense. While such orders may in certain instances result in fighting, as in the Katanga situation, the primary function of the force is to be visibly present, observing and reporting, rather than fighting in the struggle. The strict limits on the

---

15 A survey of local disorders in which the U.N. has become involved has been written by Linda B. Miller. She examines twelve cases under the categories of colonial wars, conflicts involving a breakdown of law and order, and proxy wars. Linda B. Miller, *World Order and Local Disorder: The United Nations and Internal Conflicts* (Princeton: Princeton University Press, 1967).

For discussion of the principles governing such U.N. forces, see: D. W. Bowett, *United Nations Forces: A Legal Study* (New York: Frederick A. Praeger, 1964), pp. 196-224; E. M. Miller (Oscar Schachter), "Legal Aspects of United Nations Action in the Congo," *American Journal of International Law* 55 (1961), 9-20; and Nathaniel L. Nathanson, "Constitutional Crisis at the United Nations: The Price of Peace Keeping, II," *University of Chicago Law Review* 33 (1966), 249-313.

U.N.'s use of force may contribute to general restraint throughout the conflict. While it is conceivable that the U.N. would authorize an enforcement action in a case such as southern Africa, experience to date has not been with fighting forces but rather with U.N. contingents designed primarily to limit the violence more through their presence than through their potential use of force. Emphasis on these strict restraints may be expected to characterize peacekeeping forces used to control future international violence.

While the U.N. force is not to become involved in internal issues, it must be acknowledged that the presence of a force of 20,000 men, as in the Congo, inevitably has certain effects on the outcome of the domestic issues. Noninterference in the internal questions must continue to be a goal of such U.N. operations, since the U.N. is in a peculiarly weak position to attempt to manipulate forces within a domestic crisis. While recognizing that its actions will have internal implications, the U.N.'s efforts at noninterference are necessary in order to maintain a certain neutrality which will permit it to act in future crises.

Accompanying the deployment of U.N. forces in the field has been the development of norms regarding the acceptability of intervention by outside states.[16] These expectations are developed through the resolutions of the Security Council and General Assembly, the actions of the Secretary-General, and the behavior of member nations. Once they have become general expectations among the member states, they have the impact of further restricting unilateral intervention by suggesting what is acceptable and what is unacceptable behavior. The norms do not take the form of absolute restrictions for all conflicts, but rather are contextually based and tend to be thresholds of unilateral action which are not to be crossed by states once the U.N. force has become involved in the conflict.[17] In the Congo case the threshold for unilateral military action was a prohibition on all forms of military supplies including equipment, advisors, and troops. In the Cyprus case, the restriction was

[16] For a more detailed discussion of the norms relating to the U.N. model which were applied in the Congo, see: Donald W. McNemar, "The Postindependence War in the Congo," in The International Law of Civil War, ed.: Richard A. Falk (Baltimore: Johns Hopkins Press, 1971), pp. 244-302. Hammarskjöld's own view of these actions is discussed in Brian Urquhart, Hammarskjöld (New York: Alfred A. Knopf, 1972), pp. 389-456.

[17] The threshold concept as a means of regulating civil war is discussed in: Richard A. Falk, ed., The International Law of Civil War (Baltimore: Johns Hopkins Press, 1971), pp. 23-24; and Tom J. Farer, "Harnessing Rogue Elephants: A Short Discourse on Intervention in Civil Strife," Harvard Law Review 82 (1969), 511-41.

on the provisions of troops and bombing support. In the UNEF involvement in the Middle East in 1973, the superpowers actively provided advanced military equipment, but the threshold, which was reinforced by the U.N. presence, was against the use of great power troops or the introduction of nuclear weapons.

These thresholds for unilateral intervention are worked out in the process of the conflict, and the presence of the U.N. force helps to reinforce them and to restrict the unilateral commitments to a level which does not tend to escalate the hostilities. The evolution of the expectation that a U.N. presence can lead to a prohibition on types of aid above the established threshold, despite the general rule that states are free to grant unilateral military aid or to enter into bilateral agreements with other states, can be observed in the reaction to Russian aid in the Congo case.

When Lumumba became disenchanted with the Secretary-General because the U.N. had not succeeded in halting the secession of Katanga, Lumumba turned to the Russians for assistance in mounting his own attack on Katanga. The Soviet Union provided Lumumba with 100 trucks for transporting his troops, fourteen Ilyushin transport planes, and two hundred technicians to fly the planes and repair the trucks.[18] The Secretary-General immediately took the position that such aid was contrary to the Council resolutions, stating:

The internal conflicts, which have become increasingly grave in the last few weeks and even days, have taken on a particularly serious aspect due to the fact that parties have relied on and obtained certain assistance from the outside contrary to the spirit of the Security Council resolutions and tending to reintroduce elements of the very kind which the Security Council wished to eliminate when it requested the immediate withdrawal of Belgian troops.[19]

[18] The precise amount of Soviet military assistance cannot be determined, but it was on the order suggested here. Hammarskjöld notes that "a certain number of planes, type IL-14, have been put directly at the disposal of the Government of the Republic of the Congo by the Government of the USSR, presumably with crews, technicians, ground personnel, etc." and asks about the 100 Soviet trucks promised to the United Nations but never delivered. U.N. Document S/4503, September 11, 1960, pp. 154-55. Colin Legum reports that "the Russians delivered 100 military trucks and 29 Ilyushin transport planes, together with 200 technicians." Colin Legum, *Congo Disaster* (Baltimore: Penguin Books, 1961), p. 141. The figures cited in the text are given in: Carl von Horn, *Soldiering for Peace* (New York: David McKay Company, 1966), p. 202.

[19] U.N. Document S/4482, September 7, 1960.

The Soviet Union maintained its right to grant military assistance at Lumumba's request, setting the stage for consideration of this issue in the U.N.

The right to grant assistance at the request of a recognized government is generally accepted in the international community, but other states determined that this right was restricted, in the case of the Congo, by the prior involvement of the United Nations. Ceylon and Tunisia proposed a resolution in the Security Council which asked that no military assistance "be sent to the Congo except as part of the United Nations action."[20] The Soviet Union then exercised its veto power to defeat this resolution, marking the first use of a Council veto on the Congo question and producing a split between the Soviet Union and the African states.[21] The General Assembly immediately was called under the "Uniting for Peace" resolution and an Assembly resolution on this subject was passed with seventy favorable votes and eleven abstentions—including the communist countries, France, and the Union of South Africa. This resolution called upon:

> all States to refrain from the direct and indirect provision of arms or other materials of war and military personnel and other assistance for military purposes in the Congo during the temporary period of military assistance through the United Nations, except upon the request of the United Nations through the Secretary-General for carrying out the purposes of this resolution and of the resolutions of 14 and 22 July and 9 August 1960 of the Security Council.[22]

Throughout the Congo case the U.N. resolutions, the positions of the Secretary-General, the efforts to secure removal of the Belgian paratroopers, the ending of Soviet assistance, and the removal of mercenaries from Katanga, all supported the prohibition against unilateral military involvement.

Likewise in Cyprus there were restrictions on unilateral military involvement.[23] When Turkish Air Force jets undertook air strikes against the Greek Cypriots in August 1964, the Turks claimed that these missions were in retaliation for Greek Cypriot attacks and were

20 U.N. Document S/4523, September 16, 1960.

21 Eight Council members voted for the resolution, but the Soviet Union and Poland voted against it and France abstained. The Soviet vote constituted a veto.

22 U.N. Document A/4510, September 20, 1960.

23 For analysis of the Cyprus case, see: James A. Stegenga, *The United Nations Force in Cyprus* (Columbus: Ohio State University Press, 1968).

permissible under Article IV of the Treaty of Guarantee, which gave the guaranteeing powers the right to intervene. This interpretation was rejected by other states and a Security Council resolution called upon all countries to "refrain from any action that might exacerbate the situation or contribute to the broadening of hostilities."[24]

In the 1973 Middle East crisis the threshold was drawn at a different point, but there was a clear understanding that the U.N. presence restricted the right of the two superpowers unilaterally to send troop contingents into the conflict. UNEF II was established amidst threats of Soviet and American interventions with their own troops, so that the insertion of the U.N. force between the belligerents was coupled with the expectation that no foreign military personnel would unilaterally be sent into the dispute.

If the U.N. model is to be effective in controlling internal wars, it is essential to minimize the likelihood of escalation through the involvement of outside states. The development of thresholds for acceptable bilateral military assistance in cases of multilateral action served to limit the escalation potential of the wars in the Congo, Cyprus, and the Middle East.

## Functions of the U.N. in Limited Wars

United Nations involvement in a limited war can fulfill an assortment of functions which contribute to the control of the situation. Naturally the particular conflict and political context affect the roles which will be played by the Organization, but it is possible to categorize broad areas of U.N. action. These functions can be generalized both from the nature of the international Organization itself and from its past experiences. The various functions of a U.N. force help to explain the total effect of the U.N. on minimizing violence in limited wars.[25]

The first function the U.N. serves in an internal war is to *centralize authoritative decision-making* with regard to the situation. The Organization provides a forum in the Security Council or in the General Assembly where states can hammer out agreements concerning the status of the conflict and the rules governing the participation of outside states. Since the international system is highly decentralized, the formulation of collective actions through the U.N. is a significant develop-

24 U.N. Document S/5868, August 9, 1964.

25 For a discussion of the functioning of the United Nations as a third party to conflicts, see: Young, *The Intermediaries: Third Parties in International Crises*, pp. 9-49.

ment. Inis L. Claude has described the process by which individual nations seek the Organization's approval for their actions, and Claude suggests that collective legitimization has become one of the most important political functions of the Organization.[26] The passage of U.N. resolutions bestows a certain international legitimacy on the policies of the Organization or the actions of individual states. In the absence of U.N. concern, states remain free to characterize the situation and pursue policies on a unilateral basis. But when the U.N. becomes involved in a limited war, decisions regarding the struggle are considered within a collective framework.[27]

*Observation and reporting* is a second task of a U.N. operation. The presence of a U.N. unit of even a few observers may prove to be a crucial source of information regarding developments in internal conflicts or limited wars. U.N. forces are constantly reporting to the Secretary-General and the other U.N. organs, providing them with vast supplies of information from an international perspective. In the Middle East the U.N. Truce Supervision Organization has been especially important in providing an impartial perspective on border attacks. Coming from an international source, such information concerning the action in a limited war may also undercut propagandistic reports of the situation by states hoping to influence the outcome of the conflict. Reporting can also mobilize public opinion regarding the situation. One of the sanctions available to the U.N. is public outrage, and the provision of information is an important part of this reaction. The injection of a U.N. force into a limited war produces a flow of observations and reports which insures an international window on the conflict and wide dispersal of information about the war.

A third role which a U.N. force can play is the *administration of territory*. An internal war may be accompanied by a complete breakdown of the national government's operations. While the U.N. is not equipped to take over states, it can provide important governmental services in situations of distress. In West Irian, the United Nations Temporary Executive Authority assumed full authority to administer the territory during the transfer of the area from the Netherlands to

---

[26] Inis L. Claude, Jr., "Collective Legitimization as a Political Function of the United Nations," *International Organization* 20 (1966), 367-79.

[27] An argument in support of U.N. intervention as a broadbased collective decision is found in: Richard A. Falk, *Legal Order in a Violent World* (Princeton: Princeton University Press, 1968), pp. 336-53.

Indonesia. Similarly, in the Congo the U.N. civilian operation assumed responsibility for operating ports and airfields, providing teachers, doctors, and lawyers, and assisting in the economic programs of the country.[28] The U.N., with the help of specialized agencies, can provide many of the governmental services needed in a state, and the administration of territory may be an important aspect of a U.N. force's involvement.

Another area of possible U.N. action is *facilitating mediation*. Since an internal war might be prevented or ended through mediation of the issues among the opposing parties, the U.N.'s capacity for assisting in this process may contribute importantly to minimizing violence. The Organization's experience has produced a variety of instruments for this task of peacemaking, including the single mediator employed in Cyprus; the Good Offices Committee employed in Indonesia, composed of Council members selected by the parties; and the Conciliation Commission used in the Congo, made up of representatives of governments providing troops for ONUC. The role played by these peacemaking bodies has varied from merely establishing procedures for negotiations, to making recommendations and exerting influence. The U.N. possesses particular assets for the peacemaking role, since the Organization is perceived as a relatively impartial third party which can, therefore, propose face-saving solutions. Furthermore, the weight of world opinion can be marshalled to support the Organization's proposals. Given these assets for peacemaking, facilitating mediation becomes an important part of any U.N. involvement.

A particularly critical U.N. function with regard to limited wars is the *policing of participation* by outside states. A U.N. force may perform this function either by specifically patrolling a border or by being dispersed throughout the country. UNEF assumed control of the border between Israel and Egypt and thereby prevented infiltration. ONUC was scattered throughout the Congo, and was able to report on the arrival of Russian military equipment and on the number of mercenaries fighting in Katanga. In some instances the U.N. may be able to physically prevent border crossings, but even where this proves infeasible the presence of international units can contribute to policing of intervention through observation and reporting on actions within a conflict. Since foreign states are particularly concerned about inter-

28 Harold Karan Jacobson, "ONUC's Civilian Operations: State-Preserving and State-Building," *World Politics* 17 (1964), 75-107.

vention in internal wars, the ability of the U.N. to control outside participation is integral to the U.N. model.

Another function which a U.N. force may perform is the *maintenance of order* within a state. Through patrols within the state and control of transportation and communication points, the presence of an international operation can contribute to the re-establishment of order in the society. In the Congo, the U.N. action included this as an important part of its function, and ONUC was fairly successful in protecting civilians and quelling violence which erupted from tribal fighting and mutiny in the army. The U.N. was engaged in similar efforts to maintain order in Cyprus. Since civil strife includes a tendency for violence to spread among the members of the society, the stabilizing effect of an international force may contribute to a return to normal conditions.

In addition it is conceivable that United Nations troops could function as an *enforcement force* in some future war. If a U.N. contingent were sent into a civil war for the purpose of enforcing a Council decision, it could well find itself asked to use military force to impose the decision. Using a U.N. force in southern Africa in support of demands of the liberation movements, as some have proposed, would exemplify this type of action. So far the Council has restricted its action to economic sanctions, but it is certainly a reasonable possibility that an international force could be called upon to enforce future Security Council decisions.

In summary, the insertion of a U.N. presence into a civil war can fulfill a wide range of functions. Not all are employed in every situation, but it is important to realize that the U.N. involvement can affect the struggle in numerous ways. Peacekeeping is frequently considered only from the perspective of preventing fighting, but the role of the Organization is much more varied. The potential of the U.N. for regulating international violence can be assessed by looking at its role in centralizing decisions, reporting on events, administering territory, facilitating mediation, policing intervention, maintaining order, or even enforcing a U.N. policy.

### Conditions for Operation of the U.N. Model

In determining whether or not the U.N. model will be applied to future Vietnams, the primary consideration is the attitude adopted by member states toward the involvement of the U.N.[29] The following list

---

[29] For another listing of conditions for U.N. action, see: United Nations Association of

suggests conditions which are necessary to permit operation of the U.N. model.

*1. Danger of conflict escalation*: The call for a U.N. "presence" increases when it appears likely that outside involvement in an internal war might lead to a direct confrontation between major powers. The establishment of UNEF II, in the face of not only a Soviet threat to send troops to the aid of the Egyptian army but also the American military alert, certainly illustrates this point.

*2. Limitation of great power influence*: Any case in which the U.N. becomes involved necessarily reduces the influence of other potential intervenors. In order for the U.N. to be effective, these other parties must be prepared to accept a diminution of their influence over the course of events. As a rule, the lower the ideological component or strategic importance of the conflict, the greater the likelihood that states will accept U.N. involvement. Because the ideological nature of the Vietnam war was stressed, the United States was not willing to accept the loss of control over the course of the war which U.N. involvement would have implied, whereas both the United States and the Soviet Union supported U.N. participation in the Congo.

*3. Change in the nature of the conflict*: As long as the U.N. continues to make host consent a prerequisite for action, the parties themselves must have some interest in shifting the struggle from the military plane to negotiations and in finding a non-military way to solve the crisis. In the case of UNEF II its establishment was possible only after the Egyptian interest had shifted from a desire to continue the war on the Sinai battlefield, to a wish to stop the fighting and begin negotiations.

*4. Consensus for U.N. involvement*: Because United Nations action is contingent upon the supply of troops, equipment, and finances by the member states, and requires the votes of a majority of members in order to continue, a broad consensus supporting U.N. involvement is essential. It is especially important for the great powers and the nations

---

the United States of America, *Controlling Conflicts in the 1970's*, A Report of a National Policy Panel established by the United Nations Association of the United States of America, 1969.

The interaction between general international conditions and the operation of the Organization is analyzed in: Oran R. Young, "The United Nations and the International System," in *The United Nations in International Politics*, ed.: Leon Gordenker (Princeton: Princeton University Press, 1971), pp. 10-59.

of the region in which the conflict is occurring to give continuing support to the U.N. operation. In the Nigerian civil war the OAU opposed U.N. involvement and thus the U.N. played no role in the dispute. In contrast, NATO supported a U.N. role in Cyprus and the U.N. was able to play an effective role with broad membership support and the voluntary provision of adequate troops and contributions.

### Future Applicability of the U.N. Model

The use of United Nations peacekeeping as an alternative to unilateral intervention in future limited wars depends on the extent to which the above conditions are met. With the reassessment of American foreign policy after Vietnam, the emergence of detente, and a new emphasis on the five power world, the attitudes toward future limited wars will be quite different from the approach to Vietnam in the 1960's. There will be increased willingness to revert to the nonintervention model as a means of controlling such conflicts, and more and more internal wars may simply be considered too unimportant to raise the danger of great power intervention; such was the international view of the intermittent civil war in the Sudan. However, the continued interest of powerful states in influencing other societies provides an incentive for them to become involved in certain conflicts. Therefore the risk of competitive intervention and escalation has not entirely disappeared, as was seen so dramatically in the United States-Soviet confrontation in the Middle East during the fall of 1973.

Given their desire to avoid such risks and to encourage the strategy of detente, the major powers may be more disposed to sacrifice unilateral influence over the course of events—a condition essential to permitting a multilateral response to limited wars. In the past the superpowers were very reluctant to sacrifice any power which might be considered a gain for the ideological enemy. However, one reaction to the American experience in Vietnam may be an increased understanding that struggles within developing countries may represent nationalist political goals or modernizing efforts rather than hostile communist actions aimed directly at U.S. security interests. This shift in outlook may induce a new willingness to accept some loss of influence in situations where the alternative is a lengthy involvement in a complex, essentially domestic struggle. This change in attitude would reduce the frequency of unilateral intervention, and greatly increase the instances of nonintervention and the number of cases involving a U.N. peace-keeping force.

In 1973, the rapid deployment of a U.N. force between the fighting armies of Israel and Egypt, and Israel and Syria demonstrated the Organization's continuing ability to quickly establish a U.N. force on an *ad hoc* basis. The support both of the parties to the war and of the member nations was readily forthcoming. Egypt, Syria, Israel, and their allies reached a point in the war where they were prepared to shift the conflict to the negotiating table. The U.N. members were willing to provide votes to support the operation, troops and equipment for the force, and finances to underwrite the U.N. action. When the United States and the Soviet Union confronted each other directly with threats to send troops into the Middle East war, an impartial collective force was essential if the threat of international war was to be avoided; the U.N. provided that peacekeeping force with the support of the great powers, the U.N. membership, and the warring parties.

The United Nations model will not be applicable to all future conflicts, but U.N. peacekeeping provides an important alternative to unilateral intervention in limited wars. With mounting costs of unilateral action, the attractiveness of collective involvement increases. As states, particularly the United States, reassess their foreign policies in the post-Vietnam era, the capacity of the United Nations to control limited wars through the application of some form of U.N. model may prove an important means of regulating future international violence.

# The United Nations and the Conflict in Vietnam

## M. S. RAJAN AND T. ISRAEL

The war in Vietnam, which has now happily ended, is undoubtedly the greatest tragedy that has overtaken the society of nations and the United Nations since the end of the Second World War: neither of these was able to do much to end the conflict. It has been a greater tragedy for the United Nations than for the society of nations in view of its avowed objectives: "to save succeeding generations from the scourge of war" and "to maintain international peace and security".

There is, however, a widespread impression that the United Nations had little or nothing to do with the peaceful settlement of the conflict in Vietnam and that, indeed, it was quite unconcerned with the conflict. From this certain conclusions are drawn, as much by the uninformed as by the informed, on the relevance or usefulness of the United Nations generally and in the resolution of international conflicts in particular. This article seeks to place in its proper perspective the rôle (however, marginal) of the United Nations in respect of the question and to assess whether or not, and to what extent, the widespread impression as to the relevance or usefulness of the United Nations in world affairs is valid.

Two preliminary general points need to be made. Quite naturally, the post-war period's largest and cruellest war received much wider and more sustained publicity in the world's Press and diplomatic relations than what the United Nations could, or did, do in respect of the conflict. The concern felt (as distinguished from the actions taken) by UN Members, UN organs, and the UN Secretary-General in respect of the Vietnam conflict received even less publicity. It is, therefore, necessary to narrate briefly the facts of UN actions and concern from the time of the Geneva Conference in 1954 till the end of the conflict early in 1973.

Secondly, it is a well-established fact that generally the failures of the United Nations are better publicized than its successes, partly because the former have been conspicuous and the latter modest. Furthermore, there is a natural tendency, as much among Governments as among individuals, to pin the failures on the Organization and not (more legitimately) on individual Members or groups of Members. This is due as much to the exaggerated expectations of what the United Nations can do as to the ignorance of the nature of the United Nations or the limitations under which it functions—both in terms of the UN Charter and in terms of the framework of world politics in which it unavoidably operates.

## GENEVA CONFERENCE

On the eve of the Geneva Conference on Indo-China (April-July 1954, Prime Minister Jawaharlal Nehru made a six-point proposal for the peaceful settlement of the Indo-China conflict.[1] The proposal included a suggestion that the decisions of the ensuing conference should be reported to the United Nations. He also made the suggestion that the United Nations should be asked to formulate a convention on non-intervention in Indo-China (including provision for enforcement under UN auspices), that other states should be invited to adhere to the convention, and that the good offices of the United Nations should be sought for purposes of conciliation.

In the Geneva Conference itself, the French proposals called for international commissions (presumably, outside the United Nations) to supervise the execution of the agreements reached in the conference. Likewise, the North Vietnamese asked for joint committees of beliigerents to supervise the implementation of agreements. The South Vietnamese delegation did mention the United Nations, but only in connexion with the question of providing economic assistance in the rehabilitation of Vietnam. However, the Cambodian proposal mentioned that "International supervision by neutral countries or a system of supervision by the United Nations should be established to supervise the execution of the above agreements". The People's Republic of China, which had been kept out of the United Nations, naturally avoided bringing in the UN for any purpose. At the most, it was willing to consider international supervision by a neutral nations' commission.

[1] For documents of the Geneva Conference, see *Documents on International Affairs, 1954* (London, 1957), pp. 121-42.

At the end of the conference, the Governments of Cambodia and Laos made it clear that they would not join any agreement with other states if it included the obligation to participate in a military alliance "not in conformity with the Charter of the United Nations".

On 21 July 1954, the US Government, which had not signed the Geneva agreements, made, outside the conference, a unilateral declaration which took note of the agreements, and said that "it will refrain from the threat or use of force to disturb them in accordance with Article 2(4) of the Charter of the United Nations dealing with the obligation of the members to refrain in their international relations from the threat or use of force". The declaration also cited a view that the United States had expressed earlier, on 21 June 1954, in Washington, D.C.: "In the case of nations now divided against their will, we shall continue to seek to achieve unity through free elections, supervised by the United Nations to ensure that they are conducted fairly."

It is clear that all the participants in the Geneva Conference—including France, which was a Member of the United Nations—deliberately kept the United Nations from involving itself in the implementation of the Geneva agreements. This was no doubt because China and the North Vietnamese régime were not Members of the United Nations. China had been kept out of the United Nations by the manoeuvres of the US Government: it had, therefore, good reason to suspect any involvement on the part of the United Nations.

The elections that were planned to be held in Vietnam were, of course, never held, owing to the attitude of the Ngo Dinh Diem régime of South Vietnam (which had not signed the agreements, France having done so on its behalf). Nor was the supervision of the implementation of the agreements by the three-member International Commission for Supervision and Control smooth or satisfactory, for reasons which are outside the scope of this study. Nearly a decade after the Geneva Conference, the Vietnam situation, in its different aspects, started figuring, off and on, before the different organs of the United Nations.[2]

---

[2] However, in September 1959, the Government of Laos complained to the UN Secretary-General that foreign troops had been crossing the north-eastern border of Laos, and identified these elements as belonging to the Hanoi régime. It asked for UN assistance, including dispatch of an emergency force, to halt the "aggression" and prevent it from spreading. The Security Council considered the matter and decided to send (over the objection of the Soviet Union) a four-nation sub-committee to investigate and report the facts of the case. This committee reported in November (after visiting Laos) that the

In May-April 1964, the Government of Cambodia made a complaint to the Security Council against certain alleged acts of aggression by US and South Vietnamese forces. It asked for a UN commission of inquiry to investigate the complaint. The United States and the régime in South Vietnam denied the charge, and suggested that the non-demarcation of the boundary between Cambodia and South Vietnam might be a possible reason for the complaint. They also alleged that the Vietcong rebels were freely crossing and re-crossing the boundary and were perhaps pursued by their (i.e. US/ South Vietnamese) forces. The US representative suggested a rôle for the United Nations in observing and enforcing respect for the common boundary with the help of UN observers or a UN force. The United States was willing, he said, to contribute towards the establishment of such a force. The Soviet delegate condemned the military activities of the United States and South Vietnam, which, he said, violated the Geneva agreements. He wanted the Security Council to condemn the United States and South Vietnam and take steps to protect the integrity of Cambodia.

The representative of South Vietnam (who had been invited to participate in the discussions), like the US representative, was quite willing to involve the United Nations by the establishment of a UN commission of experts to mark the boundary and the institution of joint patrols from both countries. Both the United States and South Vietnam apparently wanted the United Nations to involve itself in the Vietnam situation and intervene in the Vietnamese civil war, which was now going against the South Vietnamese régime.

The Security Council sent a three-member mission to South Vietnam which, on its return, recommended that the Council should send a group of UN observers to Cambodia to enforce respect for the borders. However, because of Cambodia's opposition to the recommendation, the United Nations took no further action. Cambodia continued to repeat the charge it had made earlier, and the United States and the South Vietnamese régime continued to deny it.

---

facts, as ascertained by it, did not establish the charge that there had been crossing of the frontiers of Laos by the troops of the Hanoi régime.

Three years later, in September 1963, a fourteen-nation group brought before the eighteenth session of the UN General Assembly (1963) an item entitled "Violation of Human Rights in South Vietnam" in respect of the people of the Buddhist faith who formed over 70 per cent of the population. A seven-nation UN mission visited South Vietnam and submitted a report on the facts of the complaint. However, the General Assembly, at the request of the sponsors of the item themselves, stopped further consideration of the complaint.

Later, in August 1964, the US Government desired the Security Council "to consider the serious situation created by the deliberate attack of the Hanoi regime on US naval vessels in international waters" (in the Gulf of Tonkin).   The Soviet representative described the US complaint as a "one-sided" affair and submitted a draft resolution whereby the Security Council would request the Hanoi régime (DRVN) to supply its version of the facts and also invite a representative of that régime to take part in the Council's meetings.   The Security Council accepted the Soviet suggestion to invite the Hanoi régime to present its case, but that régime declined the invitation. Some time later, the views of the Hanoi régime were presented to the Security Council by way of documents transmitted by the Soviet Union.[3]   The Hanoi régime called for respect for, and strict implementation of, the Geneva agreements, and declared that only the two Co-Chairmen (the Soviet Union and the United Kingdom) and participants in the Geneva Conference were competent to examine the problem and study measures to ensure that the agreements were respected.   It, thus, categorically rejected the US complaint, and declared solemnly that consideration of the problem did not lie with the Security Council, but with the members of the 1954 Geneva Conference. Also, it said that it would consider null and void any decision that the Council might take on the basis of the US complaint.

On the other hand, the régime in South Vietnam offered its full co-operation to the Council by saying that it would be ready to supply any information that the Council might require.   It charged the Hanoi régime with pursuing an aggressive policy against it for years, and alleged that Hanoi's refusal to appear before the Security Council implied that Hanoi's conditions were unacceptable.   The Saigon régime also took the stand that it was futile to convene a new Geneva Conference and that the futility of such a conference was demonstrated by repeated violations by the Vietcong of the 1954 agreements, as reportedly testified to in the special report submitted by the International Control Commission on 2 June 1972.

In view of these divergent views of the two groups, the Security Council was unable to take any further action on the US complaint.

In his "Introduction" to the *Annual Report* presented by him to the General Assembly at its twentieth session (1965),[4] the Secretary-General reviewed the work done by the Organization between June 1964 and June 1965, and remarked that the escalation of the conflict in Vietnam was perhaps

[3] UN Doc. S/5888, 12 August 1964.
[4] UN Doc. A/6001, pp. 38-40.

the most important development on the international scene which had repercussions on the functioning of the United Nations. However, the problem was one in regard to which the United Nations had not been able to take any constructive action, as was to some extent understandable, since the settlements reached in the Geneva Conference of 1954 had prescribed no rôle for the United Nations. He also noted that neither of the two Vietnams was a Member of the United Nations and that the parties directly interested in the conflict had openly voiced the view that the United Nations as such had no place in the search for a solution to the problem. He pointed out, however, that this could not by itself prevent the United Nations from discussing the problem, though it did militate against the Organization's ability to play a constructive rôle "at the present stage". He remarked, further, that because of the profound effects of the Vietnam situation on global and regional problems, he had made considerable personal efforts, through quiet diplomacy, to get the parties concerned to stop fighting and begin discussions, which alone, in his view, could lead to a solution. He could not emphasize too strongly "the profound and dangerous effect" which the situation in Vietnam was having on the atmosphere in the United Nations, as well as on the relations between East and West. According to him, not only was the conflict in Vietnam a gradual setback to the trends towards a thaw in international relations, but it also served to revive, intensify, and even extend some of the old attitudes of the Cold War. The conflict threatened to affect the peace of the world and the fate of mankind.

In the course of 1965, the conflict in Vietnam was not discussed formally as a separate item in any UN organ. However, during the year, a number of communications relating to various aspects of that situation were brought to the notice of the Security Council. In February, the United States complained against Vietcong attacks on bases and installations in South Vietnam. In February and March, some members of the Socialist bloc complained to the President of the Security Council of "United States armed aggression against the national liberation movements of the peoples of South-East Asia by stepping up its military action in South Vietnam and expanding its aggression in the Indo-China peninsula, particularly its armed provocations against the Democratic Republic of Vietnam". They charged that these US actions violated not only the Geneva agreements but also the UN Charter. In their view, the only way to restore peace in South-East Asia was through observance of the Geneva agreements, cessation of "aggression" by the United States, withdrawal of foreign troops from South Vietnam, and a peaceful settlement of the problem in accordance with the sovereign rights of the Vietnamese people. In July, the US representative informed the Security Council that the US President had decided to lend further "assistance" to the Saigon régime in "resisting foreign aggression", but that at the same time, he had reaffirmed to the Secretary-General the willingness of the United States to enter into negotiations without conditions for a peaceful settlement. The US representative emphasized that the United States stood ready to collaborate unconditionally with members of the Security Council in the search for an acceptable formula to restore peace and security in Indo-China.

In a New Year (1966) message (issued on 22 December 1965), the UN Secretary-General noted that the year (1965) was ending with the war in Vietnam, "a war more violent, more cruel, and more damaging to human life and property, more harmful to relations among the Great Powers, and more perilous to the whole world than at any other time in the conflict in Vietnam. That war must be stopped."[5] At a Press conference on 20 January 1966, he claimed that he had been doing his utmost for the past two-and-a-half years to bring about a peaceful settlement and was still continuing his efforts. "All now agreed that [the re-convening of the] Geneva [Conference] appeared the most appropriate framework for discussions, that any lasting settlement must have the unanimous support of all the Great Powers, including the People's Republic of China."[6] The Secretary-General felt that at least at this stage the United Nations could not be involved in the Vietnam conflict because, of all participants in the conflict, only the United States was a Member of the United Nations. He did not believe that any useful purpose would be served by an open debate in the Security Council. Some months later (on 6 April), the Secretary-General amplified his views by stating that he had been consistently opposed to any UN involvement in the conflict. He pointed out that just as the parties to the conflict had decided in 1954 to negotiate the end of the war at Geneva outside the framework of the United Nations (because France alone was then a Member of the United Nations), the conflict could not be settled at present under the auspices of the United Nations, because only the United States, of all the parties to the conflict, was a Member of the United Nations.[7]

The Secretary-General said that the first prerequisite to Security Council

[5] United Nations, Office of Public Information, *Yearbook of the United Nations, 1966* (New York, N. Y., 1968), p. 146. Cited hereinafter as *UN Yearbook, 1966.*
[6] Ibid.
[7] Ibid., p. 147.

action on any dispute was that the Council should be in a position to hear both sides of the question. However, there was then no prospect of the Peking or Hanoi régime's coming to the Security Council. Besides, according to the Secretary-General, Hanoi was afraid that the Geneva agreements of 1954 might be diluted if the question were brought before the Council. Peking also felt—rightly or wrongly—that in the Security Council, there was a usurper (i.e. Nationalist China) and that if it were asked to appear in the Council, it would face a party inimical to its interests.

On another occasion (12 May), the Secretary-General maintained that in saying for the past three years that the United Nations could not, and should not, involve itself in peace-keeping operations of any character in Vietnam, he was reflecting not only the views of the Big Powers—at least two of which were opposed to any such involvement (perhaps the Soviet Union and France) —but also those of the vast majority of the Members.[8]

On 31 January 1966, while resuming the bombing of North Vietnam, the United States requested an urgent meeting of the Security Council to consider the situation in Vietnam and submitted a draft resolution under which, *inter alia*, the Council would call for immediate discussions, without pre-conditions, among interested Governments with a view to arranging for a conference for the implementation of the Geneva accords of 1954 (and also of 1962, concerning Laos). In the preliminary discussions on the inclusion of the question in the agenda of the Council on 1 and 2 February, the US representative told the Security Council that the US approach to the United Nations arose from the urgency of finding a way to end the fighting in Vietnam, the failure of every effort made till then to bring about negotiations, and the primacy of the Security Council's responsibility for maintaining international peace and security. He said: "We have made repeated appeals for whatever help the United Nations, collectively or individually, through any of its organs, including the Secretary-General, might be able to provide in bringing about unconditional discussions and negotiations for an acceptable formula to restore peace in Vietnam. . . ." He added that previously the United States had heeded advice to the effect that to bring this question before the Council would interfere with peace initiatives. However, President Ho Chi Minh having closed the door to one avenue (according to him) and the door to another Geneva conference being closed for the time being (presumably because of the opposition of one or both the Chairmen, the Soviet Union and the United Kingdom), the United States had come to

[8] Ibid.

explore yet another-—the principal organ of the world body charged with the task of maintenance of international peace.[9]

The Soviet representative objected both to the convening of the Security Council and to the inclusion of the Vietnam question in the provisional agenda since, according to him, the question should be settled within the framework of the Geneva agreements. He also pointed out that by raising the question in the Council simultaneously with the resumption of its "barbaric" air raids on the DRVN, the United States was not aiming at a genuine settlement of the question. It was only using a diversionary tactic to cover the expansion of its aggressive war in Vietnam and to stage a propagandist show. The Soviet representative insisted that the problem of Vietnam should be resolved within the framework of the Geneva accords. He also cited a message from the National Liberation Front to the effect that the Security Council had no right to take any decision on questions involving South Vietnam.[10]

The representative of France (a signatory to the Geneva accords, both on its own behalf and on behalf of Vietnam, over which it then exercised authority) too opposed the inclusion of the question in the agenda. In his view, the United Nations, where only one of the principal parties concerned, the United States, was represented, was not the proper forum for hammering out a peaceful solution. Even if the other parties were invited, discussions could not be held on an equal footing. Moreover, UN intervention would only add to the existing confusion, as all parties to the conflict constantly referred to the need to respect the principles of the Geneva agreements.[11]

Many other members (including especially the United Kingdom, a Co-Chairman of the Geneva Conference) favoured consideration of the problem by the Security Council, on the ground that it had been entrusted by the Charter with the primary responsibility for the maintenance of international peace and security. The representative of the Netherlands considered that it would constitute a serious precedent if the Security Council refused to discuss such a dangerous threat to international peace as in Vietnam. In his view, the usual objection—namely, that not all countries concerned were Members of the United Nations—could not be decisive. Legally, under

[9] *Official Records of the Security Council of the United Nations (SCOR)*, yr 21, mtg 1271, p. 9. According to an informed American commentator, the United States made this move for psychological, rather than practical, reasons. Richard P. Stebbins, ed., *United States in World Affairs, 1966* (New York, N. Y., 1967), p. 37.

[10] *SCOR*, yr 21, mtg 1273, p. 3.

[11] Ibid., mtg 1271, p. 14.

Article 2(6) of the Charter, the Organization was to ensure that non-Members respected the principles of the Charter regarding the maintenance of international peace. For practical reasons, the countries concerned—notably North and South Vietnam and the People's Republic of China—should be invited to participate in the discussions of the Council. The representative of the Netherlands also maintained that the objection that the problem should be solved within the framework, not of the United Nations, but of the Geneva agreements of 1954, was not justified, since the purpose of the discussions in the Council was only to arrange for a conference to consider the application of the Geneva agreements.

Two of the members (Mali and Nigeria) took the middle path of upholding the right of any Member state to bring such a question as Vietnam to the Council, and at the same time of asserting that a discussion of the question was inopportune "in the present context". With the exception of the United States, all parties concerned were not only not Members of the Organization, but had explicitly expressed their opposition to any discussion in the United Nations. On the contrary, they had stated that they wanted the discussions to take place within the framework of the Geneva agreements. They had also underlined the fact that the resumption of bombing by the United States and the simultaneous convening of the Security Council did not constitute the best means of finding a lasting solution of the Vietnam problem.[12]

After some other members also had spoken for or against the inclusion of the item in the agenda of the Security Council, the Council decided in favour of inclusion, by nine votes to two, with four abstentions. At the suggestion of the President (Akira Matsui of Japan) it also decided that informal and private consultations should be held to decide on the most appropriate way of continuing the debate.

Subsequently, on 26 February, the President of the Security Council informed the members that some members (in conformity with the positions they had taken during the debate) had not participated in the envisaged consultations. Serious differences remained unresolved, he said, especially on the wisdom of the Council considering the problem "under the present circumstances". The general feeling was that a report in the form of a letter would be better than a formal Council meeting. The President of the Council also found a certain degree of common ground among many members of the Council over certain aspects of the problem. There was, for instance, concern and growing anxiety over the continuance of hostilities in Vietnam and a

[12] Ibid., pp. 16-21.

strong desire for their early cessation and for a peaceful settlement of the Vietnam problem.    There was also a feeling that a termination of the conflict should be sought through negotiations in an appropriate forum in order to secure implementation of the Geneva accords.    Meanwhile, the President of the Council added somewhat meekly, the Council would remain seized of the Vietnam problem.[13]    In effect, therefore, the Security Council failed to discuss the substance of the question.[14]

Presumably because of this impasse, the Secretary-General reiterated at a Press conference on 20 June 1966 the three steps which he had been presenting for some time to some of the parties principally concerned and which alone, according to him, could create conditions conducive to negotiations that might facilitate a return to the Geneva agreements of 1954 and a peaceful settlement of the Vietnam problem.    These three steps had been outlined on behalf of the Secretary-General by a spokesman at UN headquarters for the first time on 17 February 1966.    The three steps, which later came to be known as the three-point proposal, were:    (1) cessation of the bombing of North Vietnam by the United States; (2) scaling down of military activities in South Vietnam, which alone could lead to a cease-fire; and (3) the willingness of all sides to enter into discussions with those who were actually fighting.[15]

Some months later, on 1 September, in a letter to all the Permanent Representatives of the Member states of the Organization, the Secretary-General observed that the cruelty of the war in Vietnam and the suffering it had caused to the people of Vietnam were a constant reproach to the conscience of humanity.    He stated that peace in the area could be secured only through respect for the principles agreed upon at Geneva in 1954 and for the principles contained in the Charter of the United Nations.[16]

[13] UN Doc. S/7168, 26 February 1966.

[14] In identical letters on 11 July, the permanent missions of Byelo-Russia, the Soviet Union, and the Ukraine accused the United States of using the United Nations "as a cloak for expanding aggression".    In July-August, the representatives of Bulgaria, Czecho-Slovakia, Hungary, Mongolia, Poland, and Romania expressed similar views in their communications to the United Nations.

[15] On 19 October, in a message to the British Council of Peace in Vietnam, the Secretary-General amplified the three steps by stating that if the bombing was to cease, there should be no conditions and no time-limit.    He stated that the scaling down of all military activities by all parties was a preparatory measure towards a gradual restoration of the problem to its true national framework.    As to the third step, the Secretary-General said that it should not be construed as pre-judging in any way the substance of a final settlement.    See *UN Yearbook, 1966,* n. 5, p. 152.

[16] UN Doc. A/6400, 1 September 1966.

In his "Introduction" to the *Annual Report* presented by him to the General Assembly at its twenty-first session (1966),[17] the Secretary-General said that the chances of fruitful involvement by the United Nations in many issues crucial to it had been seriously impaired by a situation over which it had been unable to exercise any effective control. That situation, he pointed out, was the deepening crisis in Vietnam, where, in his view, the dangerous escalation of the fighting had been accompanied by an increasing intransigence and distrust among Governments and peoples. He had tried to assist in halting any further escalation of the conflict and in persuading the parties concerned to seek a solution at the conference table. He had been distressed to observe that such discussions as had been held were dominated largely by power politics. He remained convinced that the basic problem in Vietnam was not one of ideology, but one of national identity and survival.[18]

So grave was the situation in Vietnam at this time that although it was not on the agenda of the twenty-first session of the General Assembly at all, 107 of the 110 persons who spoke in the general debate of the session referred to it.[19] As one representative put it, the discussion turned into a veritable poll of international public opinion. All of them recognized the conflict in Vietnam as a serious threat to international peace and security. According to some of them, the conflict in Vietnam was the most dangerous of the problems then confronting the world, for it contained within itself the potentialities of a general conflagration which might go beyond the frontiers of South-East Asia and perhaps even unleash a third world war. Some others felt that the conflict in Vietnam had brought about a revival of international tensions, damaged the prestige of the United Nations, and frustrated the efforts to make the Organization truly universal in its membership.

Some of the speakers unequivocally endorsed the Secretary-General's proposal for ending the conflict in Vietnam. Others were only generally

---

[17] UN Doc. A/6301/Add. 1, 15 September 1966.

[18] Earlier, in a speech on 24 May, the Secretary-General had declared that the efforts to justify the worsening war in terms of a confrontation of ideologies were becoming more misleading. "Twenty years of outside intervention had so profoundly affected Vietnamese political life that it seemed illusory to represent it as a mere contest between communism and liberal democracy. That intervention had tended to alienate the people of Vietnam from their own destiny. Recent events had shown that the passion for national identity, perhaps one should say national survival, was the only ideology that might be left to a growing number of Vietnamese. What was really at stake, unless an early end to hostilities was brought about, was the independence, the identity, and the survival of the country itself." See *UN Yearbook, 1966*, n. 5, p. 152.

[19] *Official Records of the General Assembly of the United Nations (GAOR)*, session 21, plen. mtgs, mtgs 1411-14, 1416, 1418, 1420-4, 1426, 1428, 1430, 1432, 1434-8, 1440-7, and 1501.

sympathetic to the proposal. A majority of the speakers praised the Secretary-General for his efforts towards bringing about a peaceful settlement and encouraged him to continue those efforts. A number of representatives appealed to the Great Powers involved in the conflict to give all necessary support to the Secretary-General.[20]

The representative of the United Kingdom said that the ICSC, strengthened by the addition of representatives of other Powers, should be made responsible for supervision and control of the execution of the proposals made by the Secretary-General. It should have at its disposal a peace-keeping force similar to the UN Emergency Force in Egypt or the UN Peace-keeping Force in Cyprus.

Although a number of representatives favoured some kind of a rôle for the United Nations, the majority still appeared to share the Secretary-General's view that UN involvement was undesirable. For example, he representative of New Zealand was among those who said that the Organization might not be the appropriate forum for solving the problem, but the insisted at the same time that it was a fit place, indeed the only place, for all Members to voice their concern over the situation and their common desire to see negotiations begin. The French representative put the position pithily. According to him, the limit of the Assembly's capabilities was the weight of the expression of its collective sentiments.[21] The Canadian representative felt that continued efforts should be made through whatever openings might be available to Members individually or collectively to secure a reversal of the present course of events in Vietnam. A majority of representatives appeared to take the view that negotiations should take place under the auspices of either the re-convened old Geneva Conference or another Geneva-type conference outside the framework of the United Nations.

Outside the general debate also, many representatives referred to the situation in Vietnam while discussing a variety of other items on the agenda.

On 2 December, while accepting a second term, the Secretary-General, U Thant, told the Assembly that a threat to peace in Vietnam was a continuing source of anxiety, even anguish, to him. He said that he would regard it as his duty to make every effort possible on a personal basis to bring about

---

[20] Numerous representatives noted that the serious situation in Vietnam had affected the decision of the Secretary-General not to seek a second term. Some suggested that an immediate halt to the US bombing of North Vietnam and the withdrawal of US troops from South Vietnam might make it possible for the Secretary-General to reconsider his decision.

[21] *GAOR*, session 21, plen. mtgs, mtg 1420, p. 8.

a solution which would bring peace and justice to the people of Vietnam[22]

In his closing speech to the General Assembly, the President of the Assembly, Abdul Rahman Pazhwak of Afghanistan, echoed the views of the majority of the Members when he said that it was obvious that the United Nations could not intervene in any way in the war in Vietnam and that the Governments represented in the United Nations could not also remain aloof when questions of war and peace were at stake. Expressing appreciation of the personal rôle played by the Secretary-General, the President declared that there was universal agreement that a peaceful solution through negotiations was the only desirable solution.[23]

In March 1967, Secretary-General U Thant revealed at a Press conference that he had sent an *aide-mémoire* to all the participants in the conflict, outlining some steps for the ending of the conflict which represented a revision of his 1966 proposals. These steps were: (a) A general stand-still truce; (b) preliminary talks; and (c) reconvening of the Geneva Conference.[24] He emphasized that the United States should stop bombing North Vietnam. That would be the essential preliminary step. The US Government accepted the three steps, without, however, mentioning the essential pre-condition.

In reply to a letter from the US representative, the Secretary-General, in a letter on 30 December 1966, expressed appreciation of the assurance that the US Government would co-operate fully in the proposed discussions. He reiterated his three-point proposal, especially the importance of stopping the bombing of North Vietnam as the first and essential step.[25]

During the years 1967 and 1968, Cambodia made a number of complaints (more than 40 in 1967 and more than 60 in 1968) to the President of the UN Security Council against violations of its territory, air space, and territoral waters by US and South Vietnamese forces. The régime in South Vietnam and the United States denied the Cambodian allegation and made the counter-charge that Cambodia had permitted its territory to be used by North Vietnamese and Vietcong forces to attack South Vietnam. Cambodia in

---

[22] Ibid., mtg 1483, p. 4.

[23] Ibid., mtg 1501, pp. 14-15. During the Assembly session, the representative of Thailand transmitted to the Secretary-General a letter addressed to the latter by the Prime Minister of the Republic of Vietnam, saying that his Government stood ready to consider any effort by the Secretary-General, or by any organ of the United Nations, or by any of the Members of the Organization to secure a settlement of the conflict that would preserve the independence of the Republic of Vietnam and the right of its people to choose their own way of life. See UN Doc. S/7535, 6 October 1966.

[24] *UN Monthly Chronicle* (New York, N.Y.), vol. 4, April 1967, p. 69.

[25] UN Doc. S/7658, 30 December 1966.

its turn denied this charge.

Again, in the course of 1969 and 1970, Cambodia brought repeated complaints to the United Nations against the violation of its frontiers by the forces of the United States, by the Vietcong, and by North Vietnamese forces. It also deplored the strange indifference of the Security Council to these events. Various other countries too, including the United States and the Soviet Union, sent similar communications to the United Nations. The most significant of these was the one sent by Indonesia: it was a letter from the Mission of the Special Representatives of Foreign Ministers of Indonesia, Japan, and Malaysia—the three-nation team appointed by the conference of Foreign Ministers of eleven South-East Asian and East Asian countries held in Djakarta from 16 May to 17 May 1970 to discuss the critical situation arising from the events in Cambodia. This letter emphasized the dangerous and unpredictable consequences for peace and stability in South-East Asia of the developments in Cambodia.[26] Early in February 1971, the Secretary-General expressed a similar anxiety about the incursions of South Vietnamese forces (supported by the US Air Force) into Laos.

In his "Introduction" to the *Annual Report* presented by him to the General Assembly at its twenty-fifth session (1970), the Secretary-General once again claimed that for almost the entire duration of his mandate, he had been deeply preoccupied with the situation in Indo-China.[27] He forthrightly asserted that the conflict constituted a direct challenge to the principles and authority of the United Nations. It diverted the energies and technical and financial resources of some of the most powerful nations in the world "towards the barren task of advancing and consolidating the so-called zones of influence". The fact that the People's Republic of China and the two Vietnams were not represented in the United Nations had deprived the parties concerned of the UN channels of communication. It had, further, deprived the world community of the means of playing a mediatory rôle. Nevertheless he had himself made it clear time and again to the parties involved that the Organization and the Secretary-General were ready to make such efforts as they could in the service of peace in the area. On several occasions, he had lent his good offices, though with very limited success. He deplored the violation by all sides of the most basic human rights and of respect for human life and dignity. He noted, however, that in the midst of the tragic situations obtaining in all the three countries of Indo-China, the United Nations had

26 UN Doc. S/9843, 19 June 1970.
27 UN Doc. A/8401/Add. 1, 17 September 1971.

made a positive contribution through the work of the Economic Commission for Asia and the Far East and the Mekong Committee for the Indo-Chinese peoples. He hoped that even if, for various reasons, the United Nations did not succeed in playing a rôle in the settlement of the conflict, it would at least be able to contribute to the tremendous efforts for relief and reconstruction that would be needed after the end of the devastating conflict.

Likewise, in his "Introduction" to the following year's *Annual Report* (1971-72) also, the Secretary-General referred to the situation in Vietnam.[28] He said that he had once again offered his good offices to the parties involved, but in vain. In May 1972, when the situation in Vietnam became especially grave, he had addressed a memorandum to the President of the Security Council, and had also informally consulted the members of that body, although no action resulted therefrom. The Secretary-General recalled that he had indicated in that memorandum, *inter alia*, how he had been feeling "deeply concerned" that the United Nations, an organization created in the aftermath of a world war on purpose to safeguard international peace and security, should have been found to have no relevance to the grim situation in Vietnam, and how this attitude of indifference, if not contempt, towards the Organization could, if allowed to persist, "all too easily lead to the wholesale disaster which the United Nations was set up to prevent". He also noted, as strange, the fact that at a time when the United Nations and its main executive organ for international peace and security—the Security Council—were becoming more representative of the power realities in the world (he was referring to the likely representation of the People's Republic of China in the United Nations in the coming weeks), "there is a certain unwillingness to involve the United Nations in the reconciliation of some conflicts".

Early in May 1972, the United States notified the United Nations of the blockade of North Vietnamese ports it had put up and of certain "additional measures" it had taken, ostensibly under Article 51 of the Charter, by way of collective defence measures. Both the Soviet Union and the People's Republic of China (which had by now occupied the Chinese seat in the United Nations) strongly denounced these US actions. They declared that the new measures "constitute a further expansion of the war of aggression against Vietnam", that these actions were impermissible under international law and the UN Charter, and that the United States had no right to invoke Article 51

[28] UN Doc. A/8701/Add. 1, 9 August 1972.

of the Charter.   The Vietnam question "had nothing to do with the United Nations in the first place: the United Nations has never meddled in the Vietnam question since the Geneva Conference was held in 1954".[29]

When, in January 1973, the United States announced that it had stopped its bombing of North Vietnam, the Secretary-General expressed his happiness, as well as the hope that a formal cease-fire agreement would be signed without any delay.   "I know that I speak not only for the United Nations, but for all mankind, when I express the fervent hope that the peace settlement will be permanent and that the peoples of Vietnam and Indo-China will be able to finally begin the tremendous task of reconciliation and reconstruction. In these efforts, the United Nations stands ready to play any rôle which may be required of it."[30]   On 26 January, while welcoming the end of the Vietnam conflict, the representative of Indonesia, who was then Chairman of the Security Council, expressed the hope that at some stage the Security Council would be in a position to play a part in bringing lasting peace to Vietnam and South-East Asia in execution of the task assigned to it by the Charter.[31]

Subsequently, at the invitation of the United States and North Vietnam, the Secretary-General attended the international conference on Vietnam held in Paris in February 1973—a rather unflattering and belated recognition of the concern of the United Nations for a peaceful settlement of the Vietnam conflict.   The purpose of the conference was to acknowledge and guarantee the agreements previously arrived at by the parties to the conflict.   In the course of the conference, the Secretary-General repeated the old stand that the United Nations stood ready to assume its responsibilities whenever and wherever it was called upon to do so and to offer useful and realistic assistance (one form of which being relief and rehabilitation).   Should the Governments of the area so desire, he said, the United Nations and its family of organizations could play a significant rôle in receiving, co-ordinating, and channelling international relief and rehabilitation assistance to the Governments and peoples of the area.   There was some irony in the Secretary-General's statement that the success of the conference could be a major contribution to the fulfilment of the central task of the United Nations, namely maintenance of international peace and security.[32]

[29] UN Doc. S/10638, 11 May 1972.
[30] *UN Monthly Chronicle*, vol. 10, February 1973, p. 29.
[31] UN Doc. S/PV. 1686, 26 January 1973.
[32] *UN Monthly Chronicle*, vol. 10, March 1973, p. 30.

## Rôle of the United Nations

The above survey makes it clear that the involvement of the United Nations in the ending of the conflict in Vietnam, which began early in 1954, was intermittent and marginal. The record also underlines the fact that throughout this period, Members of the United Nations, both aligned and non-aligned, were deeply concerned over the gravity of the conflict, and hoped that the parties would settle it peacefully. Some Members—notably the United States—sent to the United Nations numerous communications during the period. The US representative repeatedly sought (in the later years of the conflict) to bring the question before the Security Council, though in vain. Above all, the UN Secretary-General, through his quiet diplomacy, encouraged and helped the parties concerned in seeking mutual accommodation and offered his own good offices and, if necessary, the good offices of the United Nations, for the purpose. He supplemented this quiet diplomacy by the forthright public expressions of his concern and anxiety for ending the conflict, though he was opposed to the idea of the United Nations getting involved in the conflict. On one occasion, he publicly expressed his sorrow that such a grave violation of peace as the war in Vietnam should be allowed to continue and that the United Nations should be unable to put an end to it.

Why was not the United Nations involved in the solution of this prolonged and grave conflict?[33] Before one goes into the reasons, one must concede that the fact that the United Nations was not substantially involved in the efforts to solve the gravest and longest violation of international peace and security—whatever the reasons and explanations therefor, and they were weighty—is a grave indictment of the Organization and of the society of nations. The reasons *for* UN involvement in the peaceful solution of the question were no less weighty.[34] What little the United Nations has achieved during the last three decades in maintaining or restoring international peace and security—in Korea, in the Middle East, in the Congo, in Cyprus, on the Indian subcontinent, and elsewhere—seems in retrospect of even less significance than before, because of the enormity of its default in the solution of the Vietnam conflict. No amount of reasons and explanations can justify the Organization's taking up essentially the rôle of a mere onlooker in

---

[33] Technically, the Vietnam question is still on the agenda of the Security Council.

[34] For a well-argued case for an active rôle by the United Natians, see Ranko Petkovic, "United Nations and Vietnam", *Review of International Affairs* (Belgrade), 5 May 1965, pp. 20-21.

respect of the conflict.

There were, of course, reasons for the United Nations opting for non-involvement. The stated reasons are that peace came to Indo-China as a result of the Geneva Conference of 1954 held outside the framework of the United Nations and that the agreements resulting therefrom provided for no rôle for the United Nations in respect of their implementation. Since the conflict arose from the non-implementation of the agreements, only the parties to the conference could deal with it. Besides, the two Co-Chairmen (the Soviet Union and the United Kingdom) were never agreed as to the origin of the conflict and the nature of its solution, so that the conference could not be re-convened.

Secondly, except the United States, none of the parties to the conflict—North Vietnam, South Vietnam, and the PRG of South Vietnam—were Members of the United Nations. Besides, North Vietnam and the PRG of South Vietnam were deeply suspicious of the United Nations, for they believed that it was an organization dominated and manipulated by the United States. What is of even greater significance, the two chief supporters of North Vietnam—China and the Soviet Union—were both angry and suspicious of the United Nations, because the United States had for many years manoeuvred to keep the People's Republic of China out of the United Nations. The *Peking Review* once remarked: "The United Nations is manipulated and controlled by the United States; it has degenerated into a US tool for aggression and has done many evil things."[35] Whether or not this charge was wholly true, is not quite the point. China even questioned the bona fides and integrity of Secretary-General U Thant in wanting to visit Peking and Hanoi to explore the possibility of a negotiated settlement. Even the South Vietnamese régime was not consistently in favour of the United Nations dealing with the Vietnam question.

For all these reasons, it is not surprising that none of these countries desired to make use of the UN forum to secure a peaceful settlement of the conflict. Jawaharlal Nehru once remarked that the Korean War would not have taken place if only the Peking régime had been represented in the United Nations.[36] With equal justification, one may say that if only the Peking régime had been represented in the United Nations, perhaps the Vietnam conflict would not have originated at all. Even if it had somehow originated, it would most certainly not have been so prolonged.

[35] *Peking Review*, 16 April 1965, pp. 15-16.
[36] Jawaharlal Nehru, *India's Foreign Policy* (Delhi, 1964), p. 280.

## POSITION OF NON-MEMBERS

It can, of course, be argued that since the UN Charter does make provision for the participation of non-Members in UN affairs, this cannot be taken as an adequate explanation for the failure of the United Nations to involve itself in the search for a peaceful solution of the Vietnam question.    Article 2(6) of the UN Charter lays down that "the Organization shall ensure that States which are not members of the United Nations act in accordance with these principles, so far as may be necessary for the maintenance of international peace and security".    But the Charter does not say how this can be achieved.    Nor does it create an effective mechanism to enforce the provisions of either Article 2(3) (which states that Members "shall settle their international disputes by peaceful means in such a manner that international peace and security and justice are not endangered") or Article 2(4) ( which states that Members "shall refrain in their international relations from the threat or use of force against the territorial integrity and political  independence of any State").    According to Article 11(2), the General Assembly may discuss  any question relating to the maintenance of international peace  and security brought before it by any non-Member under Article 35(2) and make a recommendation to the state/states or the Security Council or both.    Article 35(2) provides that a state which is not a Member of the United Nations "may bring to the attention of the Security Council or of the General Assembly any dispute to which it is a party if it accepts in advance, for the purposes of the dispute, the obligations of pacific settlement provided in the UN Charter".    Article 32 also provides that any state which is not a Member of the United Nations, if it is a party to a dispute under consideration by the Security Council, shall be invited to participate without vote in the discussions relating to the dispute.    The Article adds that the Council shall lay down such conditions as it deems just for the participation of a state which is not a Member of the United Nations.

All this assumes that non-Members would have sufficient respect for, or confidence in, the Organization to want to make use of it.    This, of course, was not the case with the states concerned in the Vietnam conflict.    The former US Secretary of State, Dean Rusk, once argued that the United Nations should act regardless of the participation or non-participation of any of the parties concerned in the deliberations of the Organization.    The fact that one or two parties "refused to accept the jurisdiction of the United Nations has nothing to do with the world responsibilities of the U.N. under its own Charter".[37]    This view  obviously assumes that  the  United Nations could take coercive or punitive action against non-Members under Article 2(6).  Though such an interpretation is plausible under the terms of the Charter, it is worth noting that the General Assembly and the Security Council have avoided expressly referring to Article 2(6) of the Charter in resolutions directed against non-Members, individually or generally.  In the case of Vietnam an overwhelming majority of Members would have resisted any such action by the United Nations.  Furthermore, when the most-powerful-ever nation in the world, the United States, could not coerce by means of arms two very small Powers—North Vietnam and the PRG of South Vietnam —how did the US Secretary of State expect  the  United  Nations to  be able to do so?   If he merely meant that the United Nations could and should find a peaceful solution by seeking the co-operation of non-Members, then, obviously, the fact that these non-Members did not accept or respect the jurisdiction of the United Nations mattered everything.  It is both improper and infructuous for UN organs to take action in respect of an issue without discussion and consultations with one of the parties, and in the face of that party's rejection of the jurisdiction of the United Nations to deal with it.

Furthermore, the experience of the United Nations in the matter of getting  non-Members to conform to the provisions of  Article  2(6)  has not been encouraging.  For instance, Franco's Spain, which was barred in 1946 from the membership of the United Nations (on the ground that it was a threat to peace) was admitted to the Organization some years later.  The People's Republic of China, which was branded an aggressor by the Security Council in 1950, was allowed to occupy the Chinese seat in the United Nations late in 1971 without any revocation of the earlier condemnation—the gravest that one could make under the Charter.  There is even a view that Article 2(6) (compared to Article 17 of the League Covenant) is so worded as not to impose any legal obligation on non-Member states, even with respect to international peace and security.[38]

## ATTITUDE OF PERMANENT MEMBERS

Besides the Soviet Union, France, a signatory to the Geneva agreements, was consistently opposed to the United Nations dealing with this question.

---

[37] *Department of State Bulletin* (Washington, D.C.), vol. 57, no. 1474, 25 September 1967, p. 384.

[38] *Repertory of United Nations Practice* (New York, N.Y., 1955), vol. 1 (Articles 1-22 of the Charter), p. 52.

This made it just impossible for members of the Security Council to get the United Nations involved in the Vietnam conflict; for they could hardly afford to ignore the attitude of two of the permanent members of the Council. Even the United Kingdom, a Co-Chairman of the Geneva Conference, was, for many years, opposed to UN involvement. Partly for this reason, it would have been impossible even for the General Assembly to pass any resolution requiring a two-thirds majority.

In the later years of the Vietnam conflict, the United States made persistent efforts to involve the United Nations in the settlement of the Vietnam conflict. When it found that a majority of the Members of the Organization and two permanent members of the Security Council (and, later, a third one too, viz. the People's Republic of China, which gained representation in the United Nations at the end of 1971) were opposed to the move, its spokesmen sought to deplore the attitude of the Organization and to pretend that the United States was more devoted to the United Nations than those who opposed the Organization's playing a rôle in the ending of the conflict. The truth was exactly the opposite. "The fact is", says a competent American critic, "that anything resembling a serious focus on the United Nations for Vietnam diplomacy came late in American policy in the fourteen-year history of progressive, expanding, unilateral American commitments."[39] Not only that. The United States started seeing virtue in finding a peaceful settlement of the Vietnam conflict only after it had found that a military solution was unrealizable in the foreseeable future. It went to the United Nations only when it desperately needed some face-saving procedure that might enable it to withdraw itself from its unilateral involvement and commitment in the conflict. For several years, many American private groups, the US Congress, and even official spokesmen had "called for UN action as a way to take the US off the hook by internationalizing the problem".[40] However, unfortunately for the United States, by the time it turned to the United Nations for a solution—partly from a desire to save its own face and partly from a newly developed conviction that to seek the help of the United Nations was the right way of solving the problem—the Vietnam conflict had become much too complicated for the United Nations to solve it, so that one may justifiably say that the United States itself was largely responsible for the failure of the United Nations to respond to the appeals made to it to work

[39] Lincoln P. Bloomfield, "The U. N. and Vietnam", in Richard A. Falk, ed., *The Vietnam War and International Law* (Princeton, N.J., 1969), vol. 2, p. 285.
[40] Ibid., p. 281.

out a peaceful solution under its auspices.   More than anything else, the success of the US manoeuvres to keep the People's Republic of China out of the United Nations for over twenty years just emasculated the United Nations as a forum for the peaceful settlement of the Vietnam problem, as of many other vital problems needing the co-operation of many Members.   It demonstrated the dominance and the influence that the United States exercised over the vast majority of the Members of the Organization to the detriment of the Organization and to the detriment of the credibility of the Organization among Members and non-Members alike.   The United States could not obviously have had it both ways: it could not throttle the Organization by its dominating influence and at the same time expect the Organization and a majority of the Members of the Organization to oblige it by getting it off the hook in the Vietnam War.   If any one country and its policies are to blame for the non-involvement of the United Nations in the Vietnam conflict, it is the United States and the policies it pursued till 1966.   The stubborn refusal of the Security Council even to discuss the substance of the question was indeed a kind of revenge that the Organization and its Members took against the American tactics of using the Organization as a slot-machine—of ignoring it when it did not suit its convenience, and of seeking to use it when it suited its own purposes.   And the United States never dared to take the question to the General Assembly, possibly for fear that it might have to encounter widespread criticism of its rôle in the Vietnam conflict, and equally lest it should fail to get through the Assembly any resolution that was acceptable to it.   Indeed, the US Government might have also feared the possibility of the Assembly passing a resolution, over its objections, condemning the US rôle in the Vietnam conflict.   How could the United States have honestly expected any help from the United Nations in getting it off the hook in Vietnam when it treated the Organization "as a receiver in bankruptcy"?

It can, of course, be argued that when, in February 1965, the US Government fulfilled, though belatedly, the requirement of Article 51 of the Charter and reported to the UN Security Council the measures it had taken in exercise of its right of self-defence, it transferred to the world body the responsibility of working out a peaceful solution and that the failure of the Organization to play any meaningful part in the resolution of the conflict thereafter entitled the United States (by virtue of the residual discretion of a sovereign state) to continue to take all actions, including armed action, in self-defence.   The argument can be easily, and effectively, answered.

The United States conformed to the requirement of Article 51, not only belatedly but also *pro forma*, and not in terms of the spirit of the Charter. It had made no attempt before 1965-66 to settle the dispute by peaceful means, in accordance with Article 33 of the Charter. This clearly exposes the *pro forma* nature of its report to the UN Security Council in January 1965. "As long as military victory was expected, the United States resented any attempt to question its discretion to use force or to share its responsibility for obtaining settlement. American recourse to procedures for peaceful settlement came as a last, rather than a first, resort."[41]   Furthermore, "during the entire war in Vietnam, the United States has shown no significant disposition to limit discretionary control over its national military power by making constructive use of collective procedures of peaceful settlement".[42] As for the failure of the United Nations to discharge its responsibility after receiving a report from the United States under Article 51, the inability or unwillingness of the UN Security Council to endorse the American claim of having acted in Vietnam in self-defence was indication enough of UN disapproval of the US claim. Few will dispute that the attitude of the United Nations in this case was a fair reflection of the attitude of the vast majority of the members of the society of nations in so far as the right of a state in customary international law to use force in self-defence was concerned. "Therefore, if the burden of justification for recourse to self-defence is upon the claimant, inaction by the United Nations provides no legal comfort on the substantive issue."[43]   The failure of the United Nations to act does not, automatically and once for all, relieve a Member state of its duty to submit its claims of self-defence to continuing review by the organized international community.   Article 51 of the UN Charter explicitly affirms that the report to the Security Council of the measures taken by Members in the exercise of the right of self-defence "shall not in any way affect the authority and responsibility of the Security Council . . . to take *at any time* such action as it deems necessary".[44]   Equally, when the United Nations refrains from passing judgement on the claims of a Member state to use force in self-defence, it does not mean that that state enjoys absolute discretion, without any limitations of customary international law, to settle a dispute by any means whatsoever.

As we have already pointed out, the fact that, barring the United States

[41] Richard A. Falk, "International Law and the United States Role in the Vietnam War", in Falk, n. 39, p. 382.

[42] Ibid., p. 383.

[43] Ibid., p. 381.

[44] Emphasis added.

with its chameleon-like attitude, none of the participants in the conflict was a Member of the United Nations made it difficult for the United Nations to play a constructive rôle in the resolution of the Vietnam conflict. There were also other difficulties. For instance, the parties involved in the conflict struck rigid and uncompromising attitudes, and that in public, to suit their own exclusive and contradictory objectives. It is, of course, possible to argue that the United Nations was ever a forum for working out a compromise or for securing adjustment of conflicting aims of nations—"a centre for harmonizing the actions of nations", as Article 1(4) of the UN Charter puts it. The trouble about this argument is that it stands on the large assumption —an assumption which cannot be made in respect of the participants of the Vietnam conflict—that all nations, whether Members or otherwise, have adequate faith in, and respect for, the United Nations. The only country among the participants to boast membership of the Organization was a late convert (and perhaps not a full convert) to a belief in the utility of the United Nations in securing an equitable adjustment of the differences and disputes arising among nations. And the others—all non-Members—had little reason to repose their trust in what they believed to be a US-dominated organization. For this situation of poor credibility of the United Nations—as much among Members as among non-Members—the United States must take a major share of responsibility. Lack of trust apart, quite probably, elements of Great-Power pressure and fear of Great-Power displeasure smothered any idea or possibility of the medium-ranking or small Powers bringing up the question before any organ of the United Nations.

### . . . And the Secretary-General

Why could not the Secretary-General take some step formally under Article 99? As mentioned above, he did repeatedly express his concern over the Vietnam conflict and offer his own good offices and the good offices of the Organization to the parties. He even proposed a concrete basis for negotiations—but only "acting within the limits of his good offices purely in his private capacity".[45] In May 1972, he submitted a memorandum to the President of the Security Council on the gravity of the situation resulting from the US blockade of North Vietnamese ports and the intensive bombing of Hanoi. It is difficult to see what he could have done beyond this in respect of an issue where the permanent members were divided in their attitudes

[45] UN Press release, SG/SM/683, 28 March 1967.

and the two Super Powers had ranged themselves on opposite sides. Even the few little initiatives he took and the views he expressed provoked the anger and criticism of one or the other Super Power. The US Government openly snubbed Secretary-General U Thant (as well as his successor, Kurt Waldheim, late in 1972) for his criticism of the US bombing of North Vietnam. This undermined the public standing of the Secretary-General and made it impossible for him to make any formal moves under Article 99. And undoubtedly he would not have exactly endeared himself to the Soviet Union or the People's Republic of China either by any such initiative.

China, North Vietnam, the PRG of South Vietnam, and South Vietnam so distrusted the United Nations and the Secretary-General that when they met for the Paris Conference of 1973, the utmost they were willing to do was to invite the Secretary-General to attend that conference, so that he might just witness the guaranteeing of the new agreements by other Powers, agreements which did not assign any rôle to the United Nations in their implementation and which did not even ask for a UN "presence". There has been no suggestion so far from either side that the United Nations and its family of organizations should have a rôle of some kind or other in the economic reconstruction and rehabilitation of the two Vietnams, a rôle repeatedly mentioned by the UN Secretary-General as especially suitable for the world body to play.

## PROSPECTS

What are the lessons that one may draw from the experience of the United Nations in respect of the Vietnam conflict?

Whatever the reasons therefor, there is no question that the non-involvement of the United Nations in the peaceful settlement of a grave and prolonged internal conflict like the conflict in Vietnam is both a failure of the main purpose of the Charter and a blow to the prestige of the world body. It is essential that the Organization should involve itself, and at an early stage, in all future conflicts. Of course, this depends partly—only partly—on the participants, whether Members or not. It is for the other Members and the Secretary-General to ensure that the United Nations serves both as a forum for hammering out peaceful solutions and as an instrument for implementing them. In regard to the conflict in Vietnam, the failure to bring the question before the United Nations is as much a failure of the vast majority of the Members of the Organization as that of the participants in the conflict.    Such a failure, one hopes, will not recur.

It is possible that the United Nations would still come into the picture in Vietnam; for, while the conflict has formally ended, and the United States has withdrawn its forces from Vietnam, peace is still not in sight.    Perhaps, if the United Nations had been involved in the implementation of the Paris agreements, even to the limited extent of being asked to maintain its presence, the repeated cease-fire violations now taking place in South Vietnam would never have occurred.    The four-Power International Commission of Control and Supervision created under the Paris agreements of 1973 does not appear to be functioning as effectively as an independent and neutral UN machinery would have been able to function.

The Paris agreements also provide (under Article 9) that the South Vietnamese people shall decide for themselves the political future of South Vietnam through "genuinely free and democratic elections under international supervision".    However, in view of the bitterness that has marked the conflict in Vietnam and the deep suspicions that the parties concerned still entertain of each other, one wonders if, when the general elections take place, any "international supervision" of them by an agency other than one functioning under the auspices of the United Nations can at all be effective or trustworthy.    One hopes that the two régimes in South Vietnam would even now agree to UN-supervised elections, so that the question of the  unification of Vietnam may be settled once for all.

Since the Paris agreements were signed, some statements have been made on behalf of the United States about possible US assistance for the economic reconstruction of Indo-China.    There have also been bilateral discussions between US and North Vietnamese official representatives. Without prejudice to these efforts, one might suggest that the economic reconstruction of Indo-China is a field where the United Nations can still be helpful, as the Secretary-General reiterated in his speech to the international conference on Vietnam. If bilateral US assistance fails to come off (as seems likely from recent Press reports), there will be no alternative but to provide multilateral assistance through the United Nations.

One lasting lesson of the Vietnam conflict is that the United Nations should be made truly universal in its membership.    Indeed, universality of membership is not just a desirable ideal or a distant goal to be accepted in principle, but a compelling necessity if the world body is to discharge its duties and fulfil the objectives for which it has been founded.    Had the Peking régime at least been admitted to the membership of the Organization in 1950, perhaps the Vietnam conflict (like the Korean War) would never have started. If both Vietnams had been admitted as suggested by the Soviet Union in 1957, the conflict might never have escalated as it did. The two régimes might have been able to compose their differences and disagreements peacefully within the framework of the United Nations instead of wearing each other out in a protracted, violent, and barren war. The fact that the Peking régime was kept out of the United Nations until the end of 1971 has done untold damage to the United Nations. Membership should no longer be treated as a favour conferred on a state (or any régime which maintains for a considerable period physical control over a territory), but an international obligation that the United Nations should not permit any state or régime from avoiding. This lesson seems to have already sunk into the minds of statesmen— even American statesmen—so that there is already some healthy talk of the possibility of giving representation in the United Nations to the three divided nations of the world—starting with the admission of the two Germanys.[46] Universality of membership is not only a virtue in itself but also a pragmatic necessity in the interest of the effectiveness of the United Nations, which is the most comprehensive and the most representative organ of the international community today.

There is an additional reason why a régime which exercises physical control over a territory for a reasonably long period should not be excluded from representation in some form (such as provisional membership) in international forums. As already indicated, it is difficult for the United Nations to enforce on non-Members the obligations specified under Article 2(6) of the Charter. It is equally true that Members could *use* non-Members to promote their own national purposes even as the United States used South Vietnam to promote what it believed (wrongly, in our view) to be its own national purposes and objectives, and pretended that it had gone to the support of South Vietnam under Article 51 of the Charter and that South Vietnam, a non-Member, was as much entitled as a Member to the benefits of that Article. That régime had not cared to fulfil the obligations specified in that Article; nor had the US Government, except in the formal, ritualistic sense. "The decision to exercise self-defence is a preliminary decision for which the state bears full responsibility, and it cannot be maintained that

---

[46] South Korea, South Vietnam, and West Germany have been represented in the United Nations for many years by observers. North Vietnam applied for UN membership as long ago as 1948 and has not so far withdrawn its application. South Vietnam applied for membership in 1951.

its own judgement is conclusive on the question of the respective rights of the parties concerned.   No one state can arrogate to itself the final right to determine unilaterally the question whether another state is in breach of established duties."[47]

To criticize the United Nations for its failure to involve itself in the search for a peaceful solution of the Vietnam question is one thing, but to say that on account of this failure the United Nations has become irrelevant in international affairs is altogether a different proposition.   For one thing, the United Nations is only a mirror of the outlook, wishes, and aspirations of its Members.   It is not, therefore, right to blame the Organization entirely for the shortcomings and failures of its Members.   The ineffectiveness of the United Nations in respect of the ending of the conflict in Vietnam is only the latest illustration of the deplorable gap, the contradiction, between the pursuit of ideals and of national interest by Members of the United Nations.

Secondly, it would be good to recall that the United Nations was established on the assumption of continuing Great-Power understanding.   In a general way, it is the failure of this assumption that has been responsible for the limited success of the United Nations, especially in the field of maintenance of peace and security.   There is no doubt that the conflict in Vietnam and the absence of UN involvement there in the search for a peaceful solution are due to the acute divisions that have plagued the mutual relations of the permanent members, especially the two Super Powers, and the exclusion of a potential permanent member, the People's Republic of China, from membership of the United Nations for more than two decades.   It is also a good illustration of what was well anticipated in the San Francisco Conference (1945)—the likely impotence of the United Nations in the face of conflicts between, or aggression by, either the Great Powers themselves or their client states. The correct conclusion to be drawn, therefore, is not that the conflict in Vietnam has shown the United Nations to be irrelevant, but that the United Nations can work only in accordance with the fundamental assumption on which it stands, and not otherwise.   There is, however, a paradox in the fact that the *détente* that came about in the mutual relations between the two Super Powers during the last decade (and which seems now to be maturing into an *entente*) has not helped the United Nations significantly, either in functioning smoothly or in making itself more effective than it was during the years of the Cold War.

[47] D. W. Bowett, *Self-defence in International Law* (London, 1958), p. 262.

Thirdly, the fact that the conflict in Vietnam occurred in spite of the existence of the United Nations does not prove that the Organization has become irrelevant: it merely underlines once more the double truth about the United Nations (of which public opinion often needs to be reminded) that the UN Charter confers but limited powers and resources on the Organization, even in respect of its basic purpose of maintaining and promoting international peace and security; and that the effectiveness of the United Nations depends much more on the context and background of international politics than on the terms of the Charter as such.

Lastly, those who ask whether the United Nations has not shown itself to have become irrelevant in world affairs by its failure in Vietnam are clearly asking the wrong question. The right question to ask is whether any state can do without the United Nations today. Indeed, international relations are inconceivable today without the Organization. It is not for nothing that membership of the Organization is the most-keenly-sought-after badge of sovereignty of any territory and people who claim to be a state. The fact that the United Nations is not, in practice, being used as it should be ideally, and in terms of the UN Charter, does not make it dispensable. It only signifies that at the present stage of development of the international society, international organization is yet to achieve the authority and status—and the indispensability—of a national government.

*July* 1973

# II. LAWS OF WAR

# Aftermath of Vietnam: War Law and the Soldier

## L. C. GREEN

ACCORDING TO the criminal law of most countries, the ordinary citizen is presumed to know the law and ignorance provides no defense. To some extent, in the Anglo-American system at least, a somewhat similar approach is adopted even where the civil law is concerned, for so much of civil liability depends upon the views of that imaginary—and perhaps imaginative—person: the ordinary reasonable man, the man on the Clapham omnibus. This robot who serves as a standard of behavior has made his appearance in every country to which the common law has been exported, although in some areas local magistrates have realized how unreal such a *tertiis comparationis* is.[1] To some extent it would seem that a similar assumption of knowledge is placed upon the ordinary soldier in so far as the law of war is concerned.[2]

The conference on the law of the sea held at Caracas in 1974, together with the failure of the two earlier Geneva Conferences to decide upon the width of the territorial sea; the endeavors of the International Law Commission to codify a variety of rules of international law; the impossibility of drawing up an effective convention on the suppression of international terrorism and the punishment of terrorists; the inability to settle upon a really satisfactory definition of aggression; conflicts as to the rules concerning state succession as well as expropriation of private alien property and compensation therefor; the statement of the Prime Minister of Canada when amending the Canadian declaration accepting the compulsory jurisdiction of the World Court that the law was unclear and insufficient;[3] controversies as to the use of deleterious gases for controlling riots, even when directed towards achieving national liberation, and as to the meaning of wars of national liberation; and incessant debates as to the true meaning of self-determination, all indicate how complex international law is and how difficult it would be today for anyone dogmatically to state that he knows the law or that

---

[1] See, e.g., Hookey, "The 'Clapham Omnibus' in New Guinea," in Brown, *Fashion of Law in New Guinea* (1969), pp. 117ff.; judgment of Bright J. in *R.* v. *Gibson*, S. Australia Judgment No. 1810, 12 Nov. 1973.

[2] See, e.g., Green, "Superior Orders and the Reasonable Man," 8 *Can. Y.B. Int. Law*, 61 (1970).

[3] Prime Minister Trudeau, Press Conf., 8 Apr. 1970, 9 *International Legal Materials* 600 (1970).

the ordinary man could be presumed to know it. In so far as the law of war is concerned, the situation is still not so very different from what it was in 1908 when Holland wrote:[4]

> The conduct of warfare is governed by certain rules, commonly spoken of as "the laws of war," which are recognized as binding by all civilized nations. These rules, which derive their origin partly from sentiments of humanity, partly from the dictates of honourable feeling, and partly from considerations of general convenience, have grown up gradually, and are still in process of development. They have existed, till comparatively recent times, only as a body of custom, preserved by military tradition, and in the works of international jurists. Their authority has been derived from the unwritten consent of nations, as evidenced by their practice.
>
> On many points, the rules of international law which relate to war on land have still to be gathered from unwritten custom and tradition; but, within the last forty years, attempts of two kinds have been made to deal with the topic in a more authoritative manner.
>
> In the first place, many nations, following the example set by the United States in 1863, have issued instructions to their respective armies, in accordance with what have been supposed by the several Governments to be the rules in question. These instructions are, of course, authoritative only for the troops of the nation by which they are issued, and differ considerably one from another.
>
> But something more was long felt to be desirable. In the second place, therefore, attempts were made, with varying success, to systematize the laws of war by international discussion, and to procure the general acceptance of a uniform code of those laws by international agreement. Thus it has come to pass that the greater bulk of the rules applicable to this topic, as newly defined and amplified by conferences of delegates duly accredited by the various Powers, have now been expressed in diplomatic Acts, which have received the formal assent of so large a number of States recognized as members of the Family of Nations, as to constitute, beyond question, a body of written International Law, of general obligation, except on a few points, as against a few dissentient Powers.

[4] Holland, *The Laws of War on Land* (1908), 1-2.

Holland was much impressed by the achievements of the Hague Conferences of 1899 and 1907, especially by Hague Convention IV and the Regulations attached thereto, and one might assume that when he was writing, so soon after the conference, there was some basis for his reliance upon the provisions for enforcement. Although Article 1 lays a duty upon the contracting parties to "issue instructions to their armed land forces which shall be in conformity with the Regulations respecting the laws and customs of war on land," the convention does not impose any personal liability on the individual member of the armed forces. Instead, Article 3 stipulates that "a belligerent party which violates the provisions of the said Regulations shall, if the case demands, be liable to pay compensation. It shall be responsible for all acts committed by persons forming part of its armed forces." It would appear from this that it was for each belligerent to lay down the manner in which individual members of the forces infringing the Regulations were to be punished as a matter of military discipline or national criminal law. On the other hand, it is provided in the Preamble that:

Until a more complete code of the laws of war has been issued, the High Contracting Parties deem it expedient to declare that, in cases not included in the Regulations adopted by them, the inhabitants and the belligerents remain under the protection and the rule of the principles of the law of nations, as they result from the usages established among civilized peoples, from the laws of humanity, and the dictates of the public conscience.

This broad guiding principle seems to underlie the attitude of military tribunals when faced with persons accused of having committed war crimes by breaching the rules of law, and international and national tribunals alike have not hesitated to try such persons on the basis of international law. Such an assumption of jurisdiction is, of course, easy when the accused is a member of the armed forces of the nation whose courts are involved. Then it is possible to try him in accordance with military law or the ordinary criminal law, for most countries operate on the basis that while their armed forces may be under special laws relating to the armed forces, they nevertheless remain subject to the ordinary criminal law as well, even though the trial may be conducted by a special tribunal. As regards those accused of war crimes who belong to allied or enemy forces, the only basis of jurisdiction in the absence of specific treaties is that stemming from the general duty and interest to uphold the rule of law, resulting "from the usages established among civilized peoples, from the laws of humanity, and the dictates of the public conscience."

It is one thing to make broad statements of this kind, but they leave open complex issues as to the definition of civilized peoples. This problem is not as futile as may appear. After all, among the "sources" of international law listed by Article 38 of the Statute of the World Court are the "general principles of law recognized by civilized nations." In the first place, while much has been written on the matter,[5] it would be difficult to decide what are general principles of law. The present writer has the impression that all that can reasonably be said, allowing for varying environments, ideologies, and ways of life, is that it is a general principle of law that unlawful homicide constitutes a criminal offense. It is even more difficult to define civilization and civilized conduct. It is an accepted rule of the international law of war that poison is a forbidden weapon and that its use constitutes a war crime. Does this mean that the aborigine who uses a poison-tipped dart and blow-pipe, and who kills the enemy at whom he fires, is less civilized and more of a criminal, than those who poison the atmosphere by releasing high explosive or nuclear bombs over a crowded city, when their only victims are likely to be civilians, for their enemies, at least the political leaders among them, are probably safe from harm in deep bomb-proof shelters? In this connection reference should be made to the United States Naval and Army Field Manuals. A note appended to Section 600 of the Naval Manual expressly states:[6]

> Unless restricted by customary or conventional international law, belligerents legally are permitted to use any means in conducting hostilities. Article 22 of the Regulations annexed to Hague Convention No. IV (1907), Respecting the Laws and Customs of War on Land, states: "The right of belligerents to adopt means of injuring the enemy is not unlimited." This article, which refers to weapons

5 E.g., Cheng, *General Principles of Law as applied by International Courts and Tribunals*, 1953; Friedmann, "The Use of 'General Principles' in the Development of International Law," 57 *American Journal of International Law* 279 (1963); Green, "Comparative Law as a 'Source' of International Law," 42 *Tulane Law Review* 52 (1967); Herczegh, *General Principles of Law and the International Legal Order*, 1969.

6 U.S. Dept. of the Navy, NWIP 10-2, *Law of Naval Warfare* (1955, amended 1959); see also, U.S. *Army Field Manual on Law of Land Warfare*, FM 27-10 (1956), paras. 33, 34.

and means of warfare, is merely an affirmation that the means of warfare are restricted by conventional (treaty) and customary international law. Although immediately directed to the conduct of land warfare, the principle embodied in Article 22 of the Hague Regulations is applicable equally to the conduct of naval warfare.

Commenting upon this, Tucker has said:[7]

. . . The guiding principle in a consideration of the rules governing the weapons and methods of naval warfare is that in the absence of restrictions imposed either by custom or by convention, belligerents are permitted in their mutual relations to use any means in the conduct of hostilities. . . . Historically, it is true that in the development of the means of waging hostilities it has been frequently asserted—both by governments and by writers on the law of war—that the introduction of a novel weapon or method must be regarded as unlawful until such time as expressly permitted by a specific rule of custom or convention. To the extent that such assertions have been based upon the alleged principle that what is not expressly permitted in war is thereby prohibited, they must be regarded as unfounded. It is not uncommon, however, that claims as to the illegality of a novel weapon or method of war have been based upon the quite different premise that the method or weapon in question violates some general principle of the customary law of war; that although not expressly forbidden by a specific rule of custom or convention, the disputed means nevertheless falls within the purview of the prohibitions contained in one or more of these general principles. The validity of this latter claim has occasionally been obscured by its identification with the unwarranted assertion that what is not expressly permitted in war is thereby prohibited. In fact, what ought to be contended is that the lawfulness of the weapons and methods of war must be determined not only by the express prohibitions contained in specific rules of custom and convention but also by those prohibitions laid down in the general principles of the law of war. . . .

. . . Recent experience has made it quite clear that the general principles of the law of war depend for their application upon standards which are themselves neither self-evident nor immutable. Hence, it is not merely the application of general principles to varying circum-

[7] *The Law of War and Neutrality at Sea* (1957), pp. 45-6, 48.

stances that is in question but the very meaning of the principles that are to be applied. It will be apparent, for example, that the scope of the immunity to be granted non-combatants must depend very largely upon the meaning given to the concept of military objective. But the concept of a military objective will necessarily vary as the character of war varies.[8] And even if it were possible today to enumerate with precision those targets that could be regarded as constituting legitimate military objectives, there could still remain the problem of determining the limits of the "incidental" or "indirect" injury that admittedly may be inflicted upon the civilian population in the course of attacking military objectives. The answer to this latter problem may largely depend, in turn, upon the kinds of weapons that are used to attack military objectives, including weapons whose legal status is itself a matter for determination in accordance with these same general principles.

This statement acquires fuller meaning in the light of some of the provisions in the Army Field Manual on the Law of Land Warfare:

35. Atomic Weapons.
The use of explosive "atomic weapons," whether by air, sea or land forces, cannot as such be regarded as violative of international law in the absence of any customary rule of international law or international convention restricting their employment.

The British Manual of Military Law[9] says that the use of such weapons is governed by "general principles," including "dictates of humanity, morality, civilization and chivalry":

36. Weapons Employing Fire.
The use of weapons which employ fire, such as tracer ammunition, flamethrowers, napalm, and other incendiary agents, against targets requiring their use is not violative of international law. They should not, however, be employed in such a way as to cause unnecessary suffering to individuals.

The British Manual states that, in the light of the practice of the belligerents during the Second World War, "the use of tracer and incendiary ammunition . . . must be considered to be lawful provided

8 See, e.g., comments by Smith on "War in Three Dimensions," *The Crisis in the Law of Nations* (1947), 67 *et seq.*

9 Part III, *The Law of War on Land* (1958), paras. 113-117.

that it is directed solely against inanimate military targets (including aircraft [—unmanned and on the ground only?]). The use of such ammunition is illegal if directed solely against combatant personnel."[10]

38. Gases, Chemicals, and Bacteriological Warfare.

The United States is not a party to any treaty, now in force, that prohibits or restricts the use in warfare of toxic or nontoxic gases, of smoke or incendiary materials, or of bacteriological warfare. . . . [While the] Geneval Protocol "for the prohibition of the use in war of asphyxiating, poisonous or other gases, and of bacteriological methods of warfare". . . has been ratified or adhered to by and is now effective between a considerable number of States . . . , the United States Senate has refrained from giving its advice and consent to the ratification of the Protocol by the United States, and it is accordingly not binding on this country.

Although this was the United States view, the British Manual implied[11] on the basis of the ban on poison, as well as on the Geneva Protocol, that such weapons are illegal, and in addition considered them unlawful on the basis that they cause "unnecessary suffering." But the U. S. Field Manual is important as illustrating the typical attitude of a country which did not consider the Geneva Protocol to be declaratory of customary law, and is by no means unique.[12] The American approach to poison is further illustrated by the comment to paragraph 37 of the Manual concerning the ban on poison in the Hague Regulations:

The foregoing rule does not prohibit measures being taken to dry up springs, to divert rivers from their courses, or to destroy, through chemical or bacterial agents harmless to man, crops intended solely for consumption by the armed forces (if that fact can be determined).

In this connection, the position of the Department of Defense with regard to the destruction of crops through chemical agents may be mentioned, as reported to the Senate Committee on Foreign Relations,[13] which was considering ratification of the Geneva Protocol in 1971. According to the General Counsel of the Department of Defense:

10 Para. 109.
11 Para. 111.
12 See Stein, "Legal Restraints in Modern Arms Control Agreements," 66 *American Journal of International Law* (1972), 255, 281.
13 10 *International Legal Materials* (1971), 1300.

It is our opinion and that of the Judge Advocate Generals of the Army, Navy and Air Force that neither the Hague Regulations nor the rules of customary international law applicable to the conduct of war and to the weapons of war prohibit the use of antiplant chemicals for defoliation or the destruction of crops, provided that their use against crops does not cause such crops as food to be poisoned [—it would be interesting to know how this is to be avoided other than by complete destruction of the crop in question—] nor cause human beings to be poisoned by direct contact, and such use must not cause unnecessary destruction of enemy property.

The standards of lawfulness, with respect to the use of this agent either as a defoliant or as a means to destroy crops, under the laws of war, is the same standard which is applied to other conventional means of waging war. . . . Hence, in order to be unlawful, the use of a weapon in the conduct of war must either be prohibited by a specifically agreed-upon rule, or its use must be such as would offend the general principle of humanitarianism, that is to say, such as would cause unnecessary destruction of property or unnecessary human suffering [—many would now include long-term ecological damage].
. . .

The discussion in paragraph 37 of the Manual [relating to the Hague Regulation banning poison and poisoned weapons] is based on the standard set forth above to the effect that the prohibition against the use of one type of weapon, i.e. poison or poisoned weapons, does not affect any prohibition on the use of other weapons and, in particular, it does not prohibit the use of chemical herbicides for depriving the enemy of food and water. This discussion does not regard chemical herbicides, harmless to man, as poison or poisoned weapons, for if they had been so considered, their use against crops intended solely for the consumption by the enemy's armed forces would clearly have been prohibited by Article 23 (a) of the 1907 Hague Regulations on Land Warfare. As the discussion points out, such a use does not fall within the prohibition [—and since we say it does not, *ergo* it does not].

We therefore believe that the correct interpretation of paragraph 37 (b) is that the use of chemical herbicides, harmless to man, to destroy crops intended solely for consumption by the enemy's armed forces (if that fact can be determined) is not prohibited by Article 23 (a) or any other rule of international law. It involves an attack by unprohibited means against legitimate military objectives. But an attack *by any means* [*sic*] against crops intended solely for consumption by noncombatants not contributing to the enemy's war effort would be unlawful for such would not be an attack upon a legitimate military objective.

Before continuing to cite from this opinion, it might be as well to mention the view of Major General Cramer, Judge Advocate General, in 1945 in a memorandum on destruction of crops by chemicals:[14]

> ... the use of chemical agents, whether in the form of a spray, powder, dust or smoke, to destroy cultivations or retard their growth, would not violate any rule of international law prohibiting poison gas; upon condition, however, that such chemicals do not produce poisonous effects upon enemy personnel, either from direct contact, or indirectly from ingestion of plants and vegetables which have been exposed thereto. . . .

> The proposed target of destruction, enemy crop cultivations, is a legitimate one, inasmuch as a belligerent is entitled to deprive the enemy of food and water, and to destroy his sources of supply whether in depots, in transit on land, or growing in his fields. . . .

> Such is my conclusion, reached after considerable research, and I believe it to be sound. However, I believe I should point out the possibility that the Japanese may come to or pretend to come to an opposite conclusion and invoke such use of these chemical agents as an excuse for retaliatory measures.

To return to the 1971 Statement by the General Counsel:

> Where it cannot be determined whether crops were intended solely for consumption by the enemy's armed forces, crop destruction would be lawful if a reasonable inquiry indicated that the intended destruction is justified by military necessity under the principles of Hague Regulation 23 (g) [—the destruction must be "imperatively demanded by the necessities of war"—], and that the devastation occasioned is not disproportionate to the military advantages gained. . . .
> The Geneva Protocol of 1925 adds no prohibitions relating to either

14 *Ibid.*, 1304.

the use of chemical herbicides or to crop destruction. . . . [A]ny attempt by the United States to include such agents within the Protocol would be the result of its own policy determination, amounting to a self-denial of the use of the weapons. Such a determination is not compelled by the 1907 Hague Regulations, the Geneva Protocol of 1925 or the rules of customary international law.

It is universally recognized that the laws of war leave much to the discretion of the military commander. They reflect the principles discussed in this opinion. But in reflecting their application, the rules themselves have gained their content and origin in the practices of States engaged in war, and, in particular, have arisen out of their reciprocal tolerance of what conduct was considered legitimate and what was not.

The extracts quoted above clearly indicate how subjective some of the relevant decisions are and leave the way open for divergences among states, whether belligerent or not. In view of the comment that the rules of war "have arisen out of their reciprocal tolerance," it raises the problem whether the potential divergences of behavior by the United States indicate that the country is not civilized, assuming that the rest of the world adopts a different standpoint, or whether, since the United States is civilized, any rule regarding the use of poison or chemical destruction of crops is clearly not a general principle of law, for if it were, the United States, as a civilized country, would recognize it. It would appear, therefore, that the most that can be said of general principles of law recognized by civilized nations is that this concept merely refers to those principles of law which are generally recognized by ourselves and those whom we regard as civilized. From the point of view of the member of the armed forces the situation is serious, for he may well find himself acting, either in the ordinary course of battle when he acts on his initiative, or in compliance with an order, in a way which is regarded by his own state as fully in accordance with the rules of international law concerning war. However, the same conduct might well be considered illegal by the enemy, and if he were to fall into the latter's hands he might well face a trial for war crimes arising out of that conduct.

Since it is often alleged that the members of one's own armed forces are never tried for war crimes, it is relevant from our point of view to mention the position expressed by international and municipal war crimes tribunals, as well as by courts martial faced with members of their own forces charged with offenses which if committed by the enemy would have been treated as war crimes. One of the problems that arises in connection with the duty of a soldier to comply with the law flows from the conflict between the demands of the law and the obligation upon him to obey the orders of his superiors. The position under the common law is made clear by such cases as *Axtell*,[15] tried for his part as one of the sentries on duty at the execution of Charles I. He

> justified that all he did was as a soldier, by the command of his superior officer, whom he must obey or die. It was resolved that was no excuse, for his superior was a traitor, and all that joined with him in that act were traitors, and did by that approve the treason; and where the command is traitorous, there the obedience to that command is also traitorous.

A somewhat similar decision was rendered much more recently by the Federal Supreme Court of the Federal Republic of Germany. Despite its name, the *War Crimes (Preventive Murder) (Germany) Case* [16] was a trial for murder under German law, although questions of international law were discussed, and had the accused been an alien the charge would have been for war crimes. The appellant contended that the lower court

> did not sufficiently ascertain the facts as to whether the divisional commander knew he was giving an order to commit a crime, and as to whether the accused was aware of the *mens rea* of the divisional commander, [but this argument] is irrelevant. . . . Such ignorance of the law as a military superior may be guilty of does not free the person who has received the order from individual responsibility if he carries out an order which he himself knows to be criminal. This applies all the more where, as here, the divisional commander was an engineer and the accused a lawyer.

On the other hand, one does not expect soldiers in the field to carry a law library around with them, and it is probably doubtful that active units would even have access to any basic textbook in international law or for that matter the Hague Regulations. However, courts have a tendency to assume a certain amount of knowledge as to what is right and what is wrong even in these circumstances. Thus, in *Chief Military*

15 Kelyng (1661), 13.                16 32 I.L.R. (1960), 563, 565.

*Prosecutor v. Melinki*[17] the Israeli tribunal pointed out that while a soldier can be held responsible for any breach of the criminal law, "you cannot demand from a soldier to clarify for himself, as soon as he gets a command from his commander and just on receiving it, whether the command is legal from all points of view. . . . The discipline of the army and the supremacy of the law balance each other and also complement one another. There is no contradiction between them, and each has to be kept intact without detracting from the other." The subordinate soldier must seek

> to interpret the feeling of law which is part of every man's conscience because he is a human being, although he is not familiar with a book of law. . . . Because of the special circumstances in which a man, who should obey the orders given to him by a superior authority, finds himself, the lawgiver excuses him of not knowing the command is illegal, only if the illegality does not reach the state of "manifestly illegal." . . . An average soldier could detect a clearly illegal order without asking a legal advisor or without looking at a book of law. These requirements of the law impose moral and legal responsibility on every soldier regardless of rank. . . . It is the duty of each soldier to examine, according to his conscience, the legality of the commands given to him. . . .

> In order to deprive a defendant of the plea of "justification," there is no need to prove that while obeying the order it was clear and obvious to the defendant that it was illegal, but the court has to be convinced that the order as given was clearly and obviously illegal for every man of average common sense. . . . If the defendant believed that the order was clearly lawful, it will not help him if the order was not reasonable, which means justified from an objective point of view. . . .

> The legal issue is whether from the point of view of the defendant, which is entirely personal and different for each one, the illegality of the given order was clear and obvious, not from the point of view of a "soldier of average common sense" in the position of the defendant. . . .

> The distinguishing mark of a "manifestly unlawful order" should fly like a black flag above the order given, as a warning saying "Pro-

---

[17] 1958/9, Pesakim (D), vol. 17, 90 (S), vol. 44, 362—extracts from the decision are to be found in the *Eichmann* judgments (36 I.L.R. 5).

hibited." Not formal unlawfulness, hidden or half-hidden, nor unlawfulness discernible only by the eyes of legal experts, is important here, but a flagrant and manifest breach of the law, definite and unnecessary unlawfulness appearing on the face of the order itself, the clearly criminal character of the acts ordered to be done, unlawfulness piercing the eye and revolting the heart, be the eye not blind nor the heart stony and corrupt—that is the measure of "manifest unlawfulness" required to release a soldier from the duty of obedience upon him and make him criminally responsible for his acts.

This judgment and these comments were approved in the *Eichmann* case and it is clear that the Israeli judges are convinced that certain acts are so clearly unlawful that the subordinate is obliged to disobey any order to commit them and that he needs no law book to help him in deciding on the lawfulness of the order and presumably of the consequential actions.

American jurisprudence, too, presents instances illustrative of the issues under discussion, with most of the cases revolving around the legality of orders received. As long ago as 1867 in *McCall v. McDowell*[18] D. J. Deady pointed out that:

The first duty of a soldier is obedience, and without this there can be neither discipline nor efficiency in an army. If every subordinate officer and soldier were at liberty to question the legality of the order of the commander, and obey them or not as they may consider them valid or invalid, the camp would be turned into a debating school, where the precious moment for action would be wasted in wordy conflicts between the advocates of conflicting opinions. . . . As a matter of abstract law, it may be admitted that ultimately the law will justify a refusal to obey an illegal order. But this involves litigation and controversy alike injurious to the best interests of the inferior, and the efficiency of the public service. . . . True, cases can be imagined, where the order is so palpably atrocious as well as illegal, that one must instinctively feel that it ought not to be obeyed, by whomever given. . . .

There is no need to loiter over the series of United States decisions which have been concerned with compliance with orders which were manifestly unlawful,[19] but instead to consider some of the decisions

---

[18] 15 Fed. Cas. 1235, 1240.
[19] For some of these, see Green, *loc. cit.*, n. 2 above.

arising from United States military operations in Korea and Vietnam. *U.S. v. Kinder*[20] involved a charge of homicide arising from the killing of a civilian prisoner, who was neither resisting or violent, nor attempting to escape or commit any offense. Apparently the order was given to discourage other local civilians from entering the prohibited area in which the deceased was killed and to boost troop morale. The Board of Review considered that:

> the superior officer issuing the order was fully aware of its illegality . . . and maliciously and corruptly issued the unlawful order. . . . [No justification will lie if the homicide is the result of an order] manifestly beyond the scope of the superior officer's authority and . . . so obviously and palpably unlawful as to admit of no reasonable doubt on the part of a man of ordinary sense and understanding. . . . [T]he accused was aware of the criminal nature of the order, not only from the palpably illegal nature of the order itself, but from the surreptitious circumstances in which it was necessary to execute it. . . . Of controlling significance . . . is the manifest and unmistakable illegality of the order. . . . Human life being regarded as sacred, moral, religious and civil law proscriptions against its taking existing throughout our society, we view the order as commandng an act so obviously beyond the scope of authority of the superior officer and so palpably illegal on its face as to admit of no doubt of its unlawfulness to a man of ordinary sense and understanding. . . . In our view no rational being of the accused's age [20], formal education [grade 11], and military experience [two years] could have . . . considered the order lawful. Where one obeys an order to kill . . . for the apparent reason of making [the] death an example to others, the evidence must be strong indeed to raise a doubt that the slayer was not aware of the illegality of the order. . . . The inference of fact is compelling . . . that the accused complied with the palpably unlawful order fully aware of its unlawful character. . . . [As to the defense argument] that the accused was mistaken in law as to the legality of the order of his superior officer, the defense fails for a prerequisite of such defense is that the mistake of law was an honest and reasonable one and . . . the evidence . . . justifies the inference that the accused was aware of the illegality.

[20] 14 C.M.R. (1954), 742, 770, 773-5, 776.

The war crimes court which heard the *Einsatzgruppen* case[21] had held that soldiers were not automata but reasoning agents, and the Review Board adopted this view:

> . . . a soldier or airman is not an automaton but a "reasoning agent" who is under the duty to exercise judgment in obeying the orders of a superior officer to the extent, that where such orders are manifestly beyond the scope of the issuing officer's authority and are so palpably illegal on their face that a man of ordinary sense and understanding would know them to be illegal, then the fact of obedience to the order of a superior officer will not protect a soldier for acts committed pursuant to such illegal orders. . . .

Even before the My Lai incident drew attention to some of the infractions of the laws of war that were being committed by American forces—and probably not by them alone—in Vietnam, other Vietnam incidents had resulted in courts martial of United States military personnel. In *U. S. v. Keenan*[22] it was held that not even the fact that the actions involved were in keeping with the training received by the accused would excuse obedience to an order palpably illegal on its face. It was reiterated in *U.S. v. Griffen*[23] that "the killing of a docile prisoner taken during military operations is not justifiable homicide," for an order to kill such a person is "so palpably illegal on its face as to admit of no doubt of its unlawfulness to a man of ordinary sense and understanding."

The first of the My Lai trials was that of Sergeant Hutto who was acquitted, but the statement of law in the Instructions given by the presiding Military Judge to the court members is of interest:[24]

> . . . under the facts standing before this court, that order . . . was *unlawful*. . . . Determination . . . that that order was illegal, does not resolve the issue . . . whether or not the accused was justified in his actions because he acted in obedience to orders. You must resolve from the evidence and the law whether or not the order . . . was mani-

21 *In re Ohlendorf* (1948), 4 *Nuremberg Mil. Tribs.* 470.
22 39 C.M.R. (1969), 109, 117.
23 *Ibid.* (1968), 586.
24 *U.S. v. Hutto* (1970/1)—a copy of these Instructions was made available by the librarian of the U.S. Judge Advocate General's School of Law (italics in original). The relevant section of the Instructions is reproduced in Norene, *Obedience to Orders as a Defense to a Criminal Act* (1971—unpublished JAG School thesis), 68-77.

festly illegal on its face, or if you are not satisfied beyond a reasonable doubt that the order was manifestly illegal on its face, whether or not the order, even though illegal . . . was known to the accused to be illegal or that by carrying out the alleged order [he] knew he was committing an illegal and criminal act.

. . . [A] member of the United States Army is not and may not be considered, short of insanity, an automaton, but may be inferred to be a reasoning agent who is under a duty to exercise moral judgment in obeying the orders of a superior officer.

. . . [A]n order . . . is unlawful if it directs the commission of a crime under United States law or under the law of war. . . .

. . . Acts of a subordinate in compliance with his supposed duty or orders are justifiable or excusable and impose no criminal liability, unless the superior's order is manifestly unlawful or unless the accused knew the order to be unlawful or that by carrying out the order the accused knew he was committing an illegal act.

. . . [A]n order is "manifestly unlawful," if under the same or similar circumstances, a person of ordinary sense and understanding would know it to be unlawful. . . . [U]nless you find beyond a reasonable doubt that the order given to the accused . . . was manifestly unlawful . . . , you must acquit the accused unless you find beyond a reasonable doubt that the accused had actual knowledge that the order was unlawful or that obedience to that order would result in the commission of an illegal and criminal act.

The fact that the law of war has been violated pursuant to an order of a superior authority, does not deprive the act in question of its character as a war crime, nor does it constitute a defense in the trial of an accused individual, unless he did not know and could not have been expected to know that the act ordered was unlawful.

. . . [O]bedience to *lawful* military orders is the sworn duty of every member of the armed forces; the soldier cannot be expected in conditions of war discipline to weigh scrupulously the legal merits of the orders received and certain rules of warfare may be controversial. Thus a subordinate is not criminally liable for acts done in obedience of an unlawful order which is not manifestly unlawful on its face, unless the subordinate has actual knowledge of the unlawfulness of the order or the unlawfulness of its demands. In the absence of such knowledge the subordinate must be considered duty bound to obey the order and he cannot properly be held criminally accountable for acts done in obedience to what he supposed was a lawful order.

... Knowledge on the part of the accused ... may be proved by circumstantial evidence. ... The tactical situation and pressures upon the soldiers of C Company prior to and during the incident ... are significant in a consideration of the knowledge of the accused as to the legality of the order only insofar as you are satisfied that he was aware of these facts, a determination you should make based upon your own training, experience and common sense. ... [T]he accused characterized this shooting by stating 'It was murder.' ... [H]e didn't agree with all the killing but he was doing it because he was told to do it; while he didn't approve all the killings, he did it because he was ordered to do it. ...

Sergeant Hutto was acquitted, but at a later date Colonel Howard, the presiding Military Judge, stated[25] that:

while he had ruled that the order in question was illegal, he had after labored consideration, stopped short of ruling that it was *manifestly* so, even though it was his opinion that such an extreme ruling as to the latter point would have been supportable at the appellate level.

This confirms how subjective may be the ultimate decision as to whether an unlawful act is "manifestly" so, while the evidence as to the facts including the accused's own opinion as to the nature of the killings; and the refusal of some of his comrades to participate indicate the difficulty involved in assessing any particular accused's knowledge of what is in fact illegal.

The most notorious of the My Lai cases was that of Lieutenant Calley, charged with acts arising out of the same sequence of events and based upon the same orders and, unlike Hutto, found guilty. The presiding Military Judge at the original trial was Colonel Kennedy, who said:[26]

The conduct of warfare is not wholly unregulated by law. Nations have agreed to treaties limiting warfare; and customary practices

---

25 Norene, *op. cit.*, 78 (italics in original).

26 *U.S. v. Calley* (1969/71, 1973)—the texts here used were made available by the Librarian, U.S. Judge Advocate General's School of Law.

governing warfare have, over a period of time, become recognized by law as binding on the conduct of warfare. Some of these deal with the propriety of killing during war. . . . The law attempts to protect those persons not actually engaged in warfare, and limits the circumstances under which their lives may be taken.

. . . Summary execution of detainees or prisoners is forbidden by law. . . . I instruct you as a matter of law, that if unresisting human beings were killed at My Lai (4)* while within the effective custody and control of our military forces, their deaths cannot be considered justified, and any order to kill such people would be, as a matter of law, an illegal order. Thus if you find that Lt. Calley received an order directing him to kill unresisting Vietnamese within his control or within the control of his troops, that order would be an illegal order.

The question does not rest there, however. A determination that an order is illegal does not, of itself, assign criminal responsibility to the person following the order for acts done in compliance with it. Soldiers are taught to follow orders, and special attention is given to obedience of orders on the battlefield. Military effectiveness depends upon obedience to orders. On the other hand, the obedience of a soldier is not the obedience of an automaton. A soldier is a reasoning agent, obliged to respond, not as a machine, but as a person. The law takes these factors into account in assessing criminal responsibility for acts done in compliance with illegal orders.

The acts of a subordinate done in compliance with an unlawful order given him by his superior are excused and impose no criminal liability unless the superior's order is one which a man of ordinary sense and understanding would, under the circumstances, know to be unlawful, or if the order in question is actually known to the accused to be unlawful. . . .

. . . Knowledge on the part of any accused . . . may be proved by circumstantial evidence, that is by evidence of facts from which it may be inferred that Lt. Calley had knowledge of the unlawfulness of the order which he has testified he followed. . . . If you find beyond reasonable doubt . . . that Lt. Calley actually knew the order under

---

* There were several villages at My Lai; the incident where Lt. Calley was involved occurred in the village designated My Lai (4).

which he operated was unlawful, the fact that the order was given operates as no defense.

Unless you find beyond reasonable doubt that the accused acted with knowledge that the order was unlawful, you must proceed to determine whether, under the circumstances, a man of ordinary sense and understanding would have known the order was unlawful. Your deliberations on this question do not focus solely on Lt. Calley and the manner in which he perceived the legality of the order found to have been given him. The standard is that of a man of ordinary sense and understanding under the circumstances.

. . . Unless you are satisfied from the evidence, beyond reasonable doubt, that a man of ordinary sense and understanding would have known the order to be unlawful, you must acquit Lt. Calley for committing acts done in accordance with the order.

The most marked characteristic of this Instruction is the absence of any reference to "manifest" unlawfulness, which was so basic a feature of the *Hutto* Instruction and was so fundamental to the reasoning of the Israeli tribunal in the *Melinki* case. On this occasion it would seem that the presiding judge merely considered it necessary for the accused, as a man of ordinary sense and understanding, to know that in the circumstances in which he was placed the order was in fact illegal. The verdict of guilt indicates that the court accepted this view, unless they considered Calley's subjective knowledge of the illegality to have existed beyond any reasonable doubt. The finding was confirmed by the Court of Military Review:

Judge Kennedy's instructions were sound and the members' findings correct. An order of the type appellant says he received is illegal. Its illegality is apparent upon even cursory evaluation by a man of ordinary sense and understanding. A finding that it is not exonerating should not be disturbed. . . . Appellant . . . argues that [*Keenan, Griffen* and *Kinder*] are all wrongly decided insofar as they import the objective standard of an order's illegality as would have been known by a man of ordinary sense and understanding. The argument is essentially that obedience to orders is a defense which strikes at *mens rea*; therefore in logic an obedient subordinate should be acquitted so long as he did not personally know of the order's illegality. Precedent aside, we would not agree with the argument. Heed must be given not only to subjective innocence-through-ignorance in the soldier, but to the consequences for his victims. Also, barbarism tends to invite reprisal to the detriment of our own force or disrepute which interferes with the achievement of war aims, even though the barbaric acts were preceded by orders for their commission. . . .

Once again there is no reference to "manifest" unlawfulness, but merely to such "illegality as is apparent upon even cursory evaluation by a man of ordinary sense and understanding," which is perhaps a somewhat wider concept and one that appears to be less technical and perhaps more readily understood by the ordinary soldier.

In earlier cases, as in some of the war crimes trials held after the Second World War,[27] there was a tendency to point out that a serviceman cannot be expected to carry Oppenheim, the Manual or other legal texts around with him, but it was nevertheless assumed that any ordinary and reasonable man, even including a soldier, would—or should—know automatically when an order was "manifestly" unlawful. However, the difficulties illustrated by the contradictory findings in *Hutto* and *Calley* suggest that not only is "manifestly" a controversial term, but the construction of the same facts by different tribunals may well lead to contrary results as a result of the use of such limiting terms. Perhaps it is time to abandon not only the word "manifest," but also "unlawfulness" or "illegality." These words are in themselves somewhat vague and open to varying interpretations. The "man of ordinary sense and understanding" is presumed by the law to know the law and, even though he is not expected to carry copies of the Criminal Code or of leading textbooks, interpretations and glosses around with him, he is adjudged liable for acts which are criminal since, as a citizen, he must have known that he was breaking the criminal law. It is doubtlessly necessary for the ordinary soldier to have some guide to enable him to decide which of the orders directed to him by his superiors are such that they are not to be obeyed and would result in punishment were he to comply with them. Since the standard is that of the ordinary man, it may be proper for the ordinary man's concept of criminality to be applied. In other words, it is suggested that the test of lawfulness of an order should be measured by whether the act consequent upon such order is one which would involve the doing of something which is

[27] *Loc. cit.*, n. 2 above.

"clearly criminal." It would appear[28] that this is in fact the line along which the Judge Advocate General's Department of the United States armed forces is at present moving, even though the 1969 edition of the Manual for Courts Martial provides[29]

An act performed manifestly beyond the scope of authority or pursuant to an order that a man of ordinary sense and understanding would know to be illegal or in a wanton manner in the discharge of a lawful matter, is not excusable,

while the suggested model instructions prepared by U.S. Army Judiciary, Office of the Judge Advocate General, with the assistance of the Judge Advocate General's School of Law,[30] still refer constantly to orders which are " 'plainly unlawful' if, under the same or similar circumstances, a person of ordinary sense and understanding would know it to be unlawful . . . [and] the burden is on the prosecution to establish the guilt of the accused by legal and competent evidence beyond a reasonable doubt that the order given to the accused . . . was plainly unlawful, as I have defined the term. . . ."

This requirement of "manifest unlawfulness" is to be found in a series of war crimes trials starting with the *Llandovery Castle* after the First World War and culminating in Nuremberg and the trials held by a variety of countries after 1945, as is to be seen by reference to any of the leading collections of war crimes trials reports. But the comments that have been made above with regard to the trials conducted by United States military tribunals of members of the United States armed forces are typical and of particular significance as national applications of the same principles. The problems confronting a soldier in deciding whether his action is criminal and may result in this trial are equally difficult whatever his nationality. The attitude of any tribunal that may try him is as subjective and likely to be as "unique" as were those which tried Hutto and Calley after My Lai. These facts merely emphasize the need to seek some common form of rules of war that may be generally if not universally acceptable and which may be imparted to the ordinary soldier for his guidance. In fact, as a result of the My Lai experience the United States has sought to introduce model courses on

---

28 Information given to the writer when visiting the JAG School of Law, Virginia.
29 Para. 216d.
30 Norene, *op. cit.*, 66-68.

the international law of war and has prepared an outline[31] for the guidance of those instructors whose task it is "to familiarize military personnel with their rights, duties and obligations under the Hague Conventions of 1907, the Geneva Conventions of 1949, and the customary law of war . . . [explaining] the obligation not to commit war crimes [and] to report all violations of the law of war." In addition to drawing attention to some typical acts which would amount to war crimes, such as desecration of the dead, including the taking of ears to substantiate a body count, from the point of view of our discussion perhaps the most important part of the document is that relating to obedience to superior orders:

> The legal responsibility for the commission of war crimes frequently can be placed on the military commander as well as his subordinates who may have committed the crime. Since a commander is responsible for the actions of those he commands, he can be held as a guilty party if his troops commit crimes pursuant to his command, or if he knew the acts were going to be committed even though he did not order them. . . .

> *Illegal Orders and Individual Responsibility.* In all cases, the person who actually commits a crime is subject to punishment, even if he acted pursuant to the orders of a superior. . . . Acting under superior orders is no defense to criminal charges when the order is clearly illegal as is [for example] an order to kill a prisoner of war. While an American soldier must obey promptly all legal orders, he also must disobey an order which requires him to commit a criminal act in violation of the law of war. An order to commit a criminal act is illegal.

It would appear from this statement that the United States military authorities, while accepting the principle that orders involving the commission of a war crime, or for that matter any other crime, should not be obeyed, have adopted the same approach as one finds in national criminal law, namely that members of the armed forces like other United States citizens know what the criminal law is, and should therefore know when an order would entail the commission of a criminal act.

[31] "The Geneva Conventions of 1949 and Hague Convention IV of 1907," Department of the Army, ASubjScd 27-1, 8 Oct. 1970.

The "Lesson Plan," reflecting the experience of Vietnam, gives examples of the type of order that should be disobeyed:

An order to execute a prisoner or detainee is clearly illegal. An order to torture or abuse a prisoner to get him to talk is clearly illegal. An order to torture anyone is obviously illegal. These are orders whose illegality is very clear [—although reports of what happened during the Vietnamese hostilities would suggest that the "clarity" and "obviousness" of the illegality of these orders are perhaps matters of somewhat recent enlightenment]. Is an order to dump a dead body into a well also illegal? Yes. The order is illegal for two reasons. A dead body in a well poisons the water and the poisoning of wells and streams is a war crime. Also it is mistreatment of a body, which is a war crime. What about an order to cut the ears off the enemy dead to prove a body count? This order is illegal, too. As we have seen, the mutilation of bodies is a war crime, and an order to cut off ears would therefore be illegal. Equally illegal would be permission to take as souvenirs valuables from dead bodies or from any prisoner. The law of war requires that valuables of dead soldiers be collected, safeguarded, and forwarded to the Central Prisoners of War Agency. If you steal watches or money off the dead and keep them, you are violating this law; and no order or permission can make your action lawful. There is always the question of what to do if it seems to be a situation of "my life or his." For example, you are on patrol with six men and capture an enemy soldier. It's burdensome to take him with you. To turn him loose would jeopardize the lives of the patrol. Your patrol leader orders you to execute him. Do you do it? [A number of alternative modes of actions are suggested ranging from taking him with you, evacuating by air, leaving him tied and gagged to be found by his own forces, and even] if the prisoner is willing, he can be given the job of carrying medical or food supplies, or assisting your own wounded. . . .

. . . The decision to execute, to murder the prisoner is an easy one. It is the wrong decision. It is also a war crime and a violation of the Uniform Code of Military Justice and under no circumstances will such an act be tolerated. Even carrying out an order is not a defense to a charge of murder. If you murder a prisoner you can be tried and executed. There are always, in actual combat, effective alternatives, which are legal, humane and which fit the military situation.

The alternatives to murder are limited only by our imagination and generally will be a better aid in accomplishing your mission. Any prisoner is important for intelligence purposes. . . . So far we discussed orders which could never be justified. They would always be illegal, and an American soldier should always disregard such orders. If you obey an illegal order you can be tried and punished.

In some cases, orders which could be legal in some situations may be illegal in others. The rules of engagement will guide your actions. These rules set out the targets which you may attack. By knowing these rules you will be able to act properly in different situations. If you disobey the rules of engagement, you can be tried and punished for disobedience of orders. The disobedience may also be a war crime for which you can be tried and punished. . . . An order to shell enemy soldiers located in a village is legal even though some civilians may be injured and their homes and livestock destroyed. Suppose, however, that we are conducting a cordon and search operation in the same village. Orders to burn down all the buildings in the village; to kill off all the livestock; to shoot everything that moves—are illegal orders. You must disregard such illegal orders [—shades of My Lai and Calley].

You should not presume that an order is illegal. If you think it is illegal, it is probably because the order is unclear. For example, while on patrol we capture a prisoner. On our return the patrol leader questions him. When the patrol leader finishes the questioning he tells you "get rid of that man." That order is not clear. The patrol leader undoubtedly [?] means to take the man to the Detainee Collection Point. Similarly, an order to clear an area of the enemy is not one to kill everything you see. Rather [?] it means to find the enemy soldier and destroy his ability and will to resist. Such an order obviously does not include looting a store, burning a farmer's house or murdering the women and children. Rather than presume that an unclear order directs you to commit a crime, ask your superior for clarification of the order. Above all, remember that if you are the leader, make your order clear and understandable. Don't put your subordinates in the position where they may think you are giving an illegal order.

But suppose you are given an illegal order: "Shoot every man, woman and child in sight." Obviously that is an illegal order. What do you do? First and most important you should try and get the order rescinded by informing the person who gave it that the order violates the law of war [—did the writer of this directive ever come into contact with a regular army sergeant?]. If he persists, you must disregard such an illegal order. This takes courage [!], but if you fail to do so you can be tried and punished for committing a criminal act in violation of the law of war. No one can force you to commit a crime, and you cannot be court-martialed or given any other form of punishment for your refusal to obey. The lack of courage to disregard an illegal order, or a mistaken fear that you could be court-martialed for disobedience of orders, is not a defense to a charge of murder, pillage or any other war crime. The Code of Conduct[32] states, "I am an American fighting man, responsible for my actions, and dedicated to the principles which made my country free." The American soldier who follows that Code should have no problem with illegal orders. Further, you have a second step to take if an illegal order results in a violation of the law of war. You must report such violation to the appropriate authorities. . . .

. . . Usually, the soldier will report any known or suspected violations of the law of war through his chain of command. . . . Most commanders have established reporting procedures by local regulations and directives which require prompt, initial reports through the chain of command. Failure to comply with these regulations and directives may subject you to prosecution under the UCMJ. While a soldier should normally report through his chain of command, you may hesitate to do so if someone in the chain above you was involved in the alleged crime, or if for some other reason you feel that such channels would not be effective. At such times, there are other officers to whom you can report or with whom you may properly discuss any possible violations of the laws of war. . . . You may also discuss the problem with a Judge Advocate, a military lawyer who knows the law of war and how it applies. Many soldiers prefer to discuss problems with the Chaplain, and this is an accepted way to report violations of the law of war. . . .

32 Dept. of the Army, AR 350-30.

These directives may sound perfectly reasonable outside the heat of battle and particularly to those who will not have to carry the brunt of actual fighting. The procedures for protest and report are, however, hardly practicable outside base camp, and suggest that the entire document was drawn up by personnel aware of what happened in Vietnam and anxious to avoid a repetition; but the directive has a ring of what one might expect from a civilian employed by the armed forces or of a civilian in uniform who remains secure in the safety of his office. There is no doubt that it is a good thing that troops should be instructed in the rudiments of war law and reminded that there are restrictions on their freedom of action; they should also be enjoined to bear in mind that they are rational beings, and not automata, and as such, not merely entitled but required to refuse to obey illegal orders (that is to say, orders which entail the commission of criminal acts). However, these guidelines, at least in their details, are frequently hardly practicable. Unfortunately, soldiers remain human beings susceptible to normal human emotions and ideological reactions. Further, the document ignores the fact that modern warfare is no longer what it was at the time of the Hague Conference. In 1907, it was still possible to recognize the enemy by the uniform or other identifying marks he wore. Already during the second world war, with the participation of partisan units and such bodies as the French Forces of the Interior, it frequently became difficult to distinguish fighting men from ordinary civilians. One of the problems of post-1945 hostilities centers on just this fact. It is easy to instruct men that they are only permitted to search out and destroy the fighting capacity of enemy troops, and must not take any action which would directly cause the death of women and children. But there is no attempt to tell the soldier how he is to distinguish the non-combatant child from a boy soldier, the civilian from an infiltrator or a saboteur, and the ordinary village population from guerrilla units, when the latter are dressed in exactly the same clothing as the former, as appears to have been the case in Vietnam. Moreover, ordinary soldiers under the strains and stresses of modern warfare can hardly be expected to bear all these injunctions in mind when the enemy with whom they are faced has been denigrated by their high command, their political leaders and the media to the level of uncivilized sub-humans.

Most systems of municipal criminal law reject the idea that an accused can avoid liability by pleading ignorance of the law or that he was complying with the order of an hierarchic superior who, he had presumed, knew what the law is. In the same way, most military systems take the same approach, and one might refer in this connection to the summing up of the 1970 Conference of the Société Internationale de Droit Militaire et de Droit de la Guerre. The Rapporteur pointed out:[33]

> For an order to contain in itself a feature that eliminates its unlawful character it must in the first place be legal both in form and content; an order which runs counter to the law, or which is unlawful as such, cannot be converted into an act possessing lawful character by reason of the commission of an act in furtherance of its execution. . . .

> Certain legislations recognize that in the exercise of this power and duty of verification [of the legality of the order] the subordinate may place an erroneous construction on the situation; in such case the position is governed by the rules relating to mistake as to subject matter.

> If the subordinate does not even entertain any doubt as to the incompetence of his superior or the unlawful character of the order if this mistake can be regarded as justified, i.e. if incompetence or illegality are not manifest, execution does not lead to liability because the subordinate can always raise the lawfulness of an order received.

> If on the other hand the subordinate does have doubts on these points, he must express these doubts to his superior. This may be done in various ways, but it is recognized that a subordinate must bring his doubts to the notice of his superior before carrying out an order he regards as unlawful if the order has not been cancelled. The mistake of the subordinate as to the unlawful character of the order will do away with criminal intent and prevent the subordinate from being punished.

> Lastly, if the unlawful character of the order is obvious, the subordinate must not and may not obey such an order and it is no longer open to him to raise the plea of mistake; when the purpose of the order is to cause an offence to be committed and when its unlawful character is obvious, the mistake of the subordinate—if it is a mistake—is henceforward a mistake of law that can exculpate no one; a subordinate, like all citizens and persons submitted to legisla-

---

[33] *Recueils de la Société de Droit Pénal et de Droit de la Guerre,* Ve Congrés International, Vol. 1, 1971, 371, 373.

tion, is presumed to know the law and he must know that no one, not even his superiors, is entitled by issuing orders to abrogate a provision of the law.

Once again we are presented with a presumption of knowledge of the law, including the international law of war. But no suggestion is put forward to indicate how the soldier should be informed of the content of that law or what his position is likely to be if the action he is about to take is considered compatible with that system by his own country, although rejected by other belligerents. However, since there are parallels in many of the municipal systems of criminal and military law, perhaps it may be possible to find a formulation that may be generally applied, at least among those countries which possess a similar understanding and approach to the principles of criminal justice and of the law in general. Moreover, in view of the growing frequency of multinational military exercises; of training maneuvres held on friendly soil; of the secondment of personnel, particularly officers, of one nationality for duty with the forces of another nation; and of the employment of national units in operations under the umbrella of the United Nations, perhaps one might hope that such a general formulation might prove more readily acceptable than might have been thought likely shortly after the termination of the second world war. The fact that some countries, for example, Germany, Israel, and the United States, have already applied the general principles of international law in this field against their own nationals lends some support to this hope.

Since most countries, and certainly those within the western alliance system, generally accept the maxim *ignorantia juris quod quisque tenetur scire, neminem excusat,* it is suggested that these countries be encouraged to replace the concept of "manifest illegality or unlawfulness," which is not readily understood by the ordinary man, by that of "obvious criminality," which is more likely to be appreciated and places the international law of war on the same level as ordinary criminal law. This would also encourage the soldier to regard international law as having equal authority and being equally binding as his own system of national law, so that ignorance of the one would, in his eyes, be no more a defense than is ignorance of the other. But this means that steps must be taken to make the armed forces aware of what the law of war is, and the American directive is an indication, however primitive, of what can be done along these lines. At the same time, there must be an abandonment of "the reasonable man of ordinary understanding." This individual is a man of peace living the ordinary life of a citizen in an urban conurbation or a rural environment. He must be replaced, as he has been in so many non-English environments; the man on the Clapham omnibus must give way, and the soldier must be measured by the standards of the reasonable soldier in similar circumstances to the accused. This may require military manuals and directives to be revised in the light of the experiences of serving officers, with constant updatings to recognize the changes that take place in warfare and to ensure that what appear as guidelines for the soldier do in fact reflect what he is likely to find in reality.

# Ratification of the Geneva Protocol on Gas and Bacterial Warfare: A Legal and Political Analysis

## JOHN NORTON MOORE[*]

### INTRODUCTION

ON November 25, 1969, President Nixon announced the initial results of a sweeping review of United States policy on chemical and biological warfare.[1] He reaffirmed the nation's traditional policy of no-first-use of lethal chemical weapons and extended the policy to incapacitating chemicals. He also renounced the use under any circumstances of biological weapons and methods of warfare, and declared that the United States will confine its biological research to defensive measures and dispose of existing stocks of bacteriological weapons not required for defensive research. Finally, he indicated that the Administration would ask the Senate to advise and consent to the ratification of the Protocol for the Prohibition of the Use in War of Asphyxiating, Poisonous or Other Gases, and of Bacteriological Methods of Warfare, signed at Geneva on June 17, 1925.[2]

The most important operative provisions of the Protocol provide:

> The Undersigned Plenipotentiaries, in the name of their respective Governments:
>
> Whereas the use in war of asphyxiating, poisonous or other gases, and of all analogous liquids, materials or devices, has been justly condemned by the general opinion of the civilised world; and
>
> Whereas the prohibition of such use has been declared in Treaties to which the majority of Powers of the world are Parties; and

* Professor of law and Director of the Graduate Program, The University of Virginia School of Law.

I am indebted to Archibald S. Alexander, Harry H. Almond, Jr., Richard R. Baxter, Thomas Buergenthal, George Bunn, Howard S. Levie, Taylor Reveley III, William D. Rogers, Peter Trooboff, and Hamilton DeSaussure for their many helpful suggestions. I would also like to thank Dorothy Herbert, who assisted in providing congressional materials, Frederick S. Tipson, who assisted with research, and Carl B. Nelson, who assisted with footnote revision. The views expressed and any errors and infelicities are my own.

[1] 61 DEP'T STATE BULL. 541 (1969).

[2] 94 L.N.T.S. 65.

To the end that this prohibition shall be universally accepted as a part of International Law, binding alike the conscience and the practice of nations;

Declare:

That the High Contracting Parties, so far as they are not already Parties to Treaties prohibiting such use, accept this prohibition, agree to extend this prohibition to the use of bacteriological methods of warfare and agree to be bound as between themselves according to the terms of this declaration. . . .[3]

At the Geneva Conference of 1925 the United States delegation took the lead in proposing the Protocol and subsequently signed it as did twenty-nine of the other delegations participating in the Conference. Because of inadequate coordination with the Senate, however, the United States ratification of the Protocol died eighteen months later without coming to a vote on the Senate floor.[4] At the present time approximately ninety-eight states are party to the Protocol, including all of the major military and industrial powers of the World, all of our NATO allies, the Soviet Union and all but one of its Warsaw Pact allies, and the People's Republic of China. There is also a substantial momentum toward increased participation. Since January 1970 some fourteen countries, including Brazil and Japan, have become parties. With the recent accession by Japan, the United States remains the only major military or industrial power not a party to the Protocol.[5]

Subsequent to President Nixon's announcement and prior to consideration of the Geneva Protocol by the Senate, a variety of other policy pronouncements indicated the momentum within the Administration on chemical and biological warfare (CBW) issues. Thus, on February 14, 1970, the President announced that the ban on biological weapons and methods of warfare would also apply to toxins—biologically produced chemical poisons.[6] On January 27, 1971, the President announced that the biological facilities at Pine Bluff Arsenal would

---

[3] The Protocol also creates a duty to "exert every effort to induce other States to accede to the . . . Protocol . . . ." *Id.* at 69.

[4] The Protocol was transmitted to the Senate for advice and consent to ratification on January 12, 1926, and because of the unexpected opposition which developed on the floor was referred back to the Senate Foreign Relations Committee on December 13, 1926. *See* 68 CONG. REC. 368 (1926).

[5] Testimony of Secretary of State William P. Rogers before the Senate Foreign Relations Committee, March 5, 1971.

[6] *See U.S. Renounces Use of Toxins as a Method of Warfare*, 62 DEP'T STATE BULL. 226 (1970); N.Y. Times, Feb. 15, 1970, at 1, col. 8.

be turned over to the Food and Drug Administration to investigate the health effects of chemical substances such as food additives and pesticides; and on October 18, 1971, he announced that the former Army Biological Defense Research Center at Fort Detrick, Maryland would be converted into a center for cancer research.[7] Related decisions include United States support for a draft arms-control convention that would ban the development, production and stockpiling of biological agents and toxins,[8] continuation of efforts to obtain international agreement on the control of development, production and stockpiling of chemical weapons, initiation of a review of the use of riot-control agents and herbicides in the Vietnam War, termination of the use of chemical herbicides for crop-destruction in Vietnam, and a gradual phase-out of the use of chemical herbicides for defoliation in Vietnam.[9]

On August 19, 1970, President Nixon transmitted the Geneva Protocol to the Senate for advice and consent to ratification. In his letter of transmittal the President said, "I consider it essential that the United States now become a party to this Protocol, and urge the Senate to give its advice and consent to ratification with the reservation set forth in the Secretary's report."[10] The accompanying report of Secretary of State Rogers proposed that the Senate give its consent to ratification subject to a single reservation:

> That the said Protocol shall cease to be binding on the Government of the United States with respect to the use in war of asphyxiating, poisonous or other gases, and of all analogous liquids, materials, or devices, in regard to an enemy State if such State or any of its allies fails to respect the prohibitions laid down in the Protocol.[11]

[7] Testimony of Secretary of State William P. Rogers before the Senate Foreign Relations Committee, March 5, 1971 (Pine Bluff Arsenal); Bush, *U.N. Commends Biological Weapons Convention and Requests Continued Negotiations on Prohibition of Chemical Weapons*, 66 DEP'T STATE BULL. 102, 104 (1972) (Ft. Detrick).

[8] *See* statement by Ambassador Leonard, "Geneva Disarmament Conference Agrees on Draft Text of Bacteriological Weapons Convention," in 65 DEP'T STATE BULL. 504 (1971).

[9] Testimony of Secretary of State William P. Rogers before the Senate Foreign Relations Committee, March 5, 1971.

[10] Letter of transmittal from President Richard Nixon to the Senate of the United States, Aug. 19, 1970, in SENATE FOREIGN RELATIONS COMM., 91ST CONG., 2D SESS., MESSAGE FROM THE PRESIDENT OF THE UNITED STATES TRANSMITTING THE PROTOCOL FOR THE PROHIBITION OF THE USE IN WAR OF ASPHYXIATING, POISONOUS, OR OTHER GASES, AND OF BACTERIOLOGICAL METHODS OF WARFARE, SIGNED AT GENEVA, JUNE 17, 1925, iii (1970) [hereinafter MESSAGE FROM THE PRESIDENT].

[11] Letter of submittal from Secretary of State William P. Rogers to the President, Aug. 11, 1970, *id*. at v.

This reservation parallels similar no-first-use reservations by France, the United Kingdom, the Soviet Union, the People's Republic of China and some thirty other countries. But with the exception of the Netherlands, all of these countries have more sweeping no-first-use reservations. Only the Netherlands reservation and the proposed United States reservation do not reserve the right to retaliate with biological weapons. Thus, the proposed United States reservation is consistent with President Nixon's renunciation of the use in all circumstances of biological and toxin weapons and methods of warfare. Secretary Rogers' report also indicates that the United States will not, by reservation, limit its obligations under the Protocol to the parties,[12] as have many other states. But by way of limitation, Secretary Rogers' report goes on to say, "It is the United States understanding of the Protocol that it does not prohibit the use in war of riot-control agents and chemical herbicides."[13] The Administration does not intend this informal understanding to be part of the instrument of ratification or otherwise formally conveyed to the parties to the Protocol.

During March of 1971 the Senate Committee on Foreign Relations held hearings on the Protocol. All of the distinguished witnesses, governmental and non-governmental, strongly supported ratification of the Protocol. Administration spokesmen particularly stressed the importance of ratification of the Protocol in promoting further international agreement on more comprehensive measures for controlling chemical and biological warfare. The principal policy issue which emerged during the hearings was the wisdom of the understanding that the Protocol does not include riot-control agents and chemical herbicides. A number of non-governmental witnesses—including McGeorge Bundy, Dr. Matthew Meselson, and Professor Thomas Buergenthal—pointed out that since many states interpret the Protocol to ban chemical riot-control agents and herbicides, the Administration's proposed understanding might undermine the effectiveness of United States ratification. A number of senators, both members and non-members of the Foreign Relations Committee subsequently echoed this point.[14] In view of the

---

12 *Id.* at vi.

13 *Id.*

14 The wide variety of witnesses testifying before the Senate Foreign Relations Committee included, among others, Secretary of State William P. Rogers, Philip J. Farley, the Deputy Director of the Arms Control and Disarmament Agency; G. Warren Nutter, the Assistant Secretary of Defense for International Security Affairs; McGeorge Bundy, President of the Ford Foundation; George Bunn, Professor of Law at the University of Wisconsin; Thomas Buergenthal, Professor of Law at the State Univer-

evident disagreement between some senators and the Administration concerning the proposed understanding with respect to riot-control agents and chemical herbicides, Senator Fulbright, as Chairman of the Senate Foreign Relations Committee, sent a letter to the President supporting ratification but asking

> that the question of the interpretation of the Protocol be reexamined considering whether the need to hold open the option to use tear gas and herbicides is indeed so great that it outweighs the long-term advantages to the United States of strengthening existing barriers against chemical warfare by means of ratification of the Protocol without restrictive interpretations.[15]

Following Senator Fulbright's letter to the President, the Administration and the Senate Foreign Relations Committee have been locked in an impasse: the Secretary of State has suggested that rejection of the Administration's understanding on riot-control agents and herbicides might result in loss of Administration support, while Senator Fulbright has expressed doubt that the Senate will consent to the understanding.[16] The Administration is presently reviewing the issue in the light of recently completed studies on the use of riot-control agents and chemical herbicides in Vietnam and the implications of that experience for future use by the United States of such agents in war. On the Senate side, importance continues to be attached by some senators to a broader interpretation of the Protocol. Senator Hubert Humphrey, for example, introduced a resolution which would express the Senate's support of

> a broad interpretation of the Geneva Protocol. In so doing [the Senate] recommends that the United States be willing, on the basis of reci-

---

sity of New York; Senator Gaylord Nelson; Representative Richard D. McCarthy; Mrs. Donald Clusen of the League of Women Voters; and Dr. Matthew Meselson, Professor of Biology at Harvard.

For remarks made by Senators not testifying, *see, e.g.,* the remarks of Senator Gravel on Mar. 30, 1971, calling for submission of the Protocol to the International Court of Justice for an interpretation as to whether it includes riot-control agents and herbicides, 117 Cong. Rec. E2481-82 (daily ed. Mar. 30, 1971).

15 117 Cong. Rec. S12189 (daily ed. July 27, 1971). Senator Fulbright continued: "If the Administration were to take the longer and broader view of our own interests, I cannot imagine any serious opposition to that decision either here at home or abroad." *Id.*

16 *See* the testimony of McGeorge Bundy before the Senate Foreign Relations Committee on March 19, 1971.

procity, to refrain from the use in war of all toxic chemical weapons whether directed against man, animals, or plants.[17]

Senator Humphrey's draft resolution roughly parallels Resolution 2603A, adopted by the United Nations General Assembly on December 16, 1969.[18] That Resolution interpreted the Geneva Protocol broadly as prohibiting the use in international armed conflicts of "[a]ny chemical agents of warfare—chemical substances, whether gaseous, liquid or solid—which might be employed because of their direct toxic effects on man, animals or plants." [19] Resolution 2603B, adopted by the General Assembly on the same day, called "anew for strict observance by all States of the principles and objectives of the Protocol," and invited "all States which have not yet done so to accede to or ratify the . . . Protocol." [20]

Although the House of Representatives is not a formal participant in the process of ratification, the Subcommittee on National Security Policy and Scientific Developments of the House issued, on May 16, 1970, an important report, *Chemical-Biological Warfare: U. S. Policies and International Effects*, which grew out of extensive hearings held by the Subcommittee in November and December of 1969.[21] The Committee concluded that

---

[17] S. Res. 154, 92d Cong. 1st Sess. (1971), *reprinted in* 117 Cong. Rec. S11920 (daily ed. Jul. 23, 1971). *See also* the resolution introduced by Senator Brooke, S. Res. 158, 92d Cong. 1st Sess. (1971), *reprinted in* 117 Cong. Rec. S12187 (daily ed. Jul. 27, 1971).

[18] G.A. Res. 2603A, 24 U.N. GAOR Supp. 30, at 16, U.N. Doc. A/7630 (1969).

[19] More completely, G.A. Res. 2603A recognized
   that the Geneva Protocol embodies the generally recognized rules of international law prohibiting the use in international armed conflicts of all biological and chemical methods of warfare, regardless of any technical developments . . . .
and declared
   as contrary to the generally recognized rules of international law, as embodied in the Protocol for the Prohibition of the Use in War of Asphyxiating, Poisonous or Other Gases, and of Bacteriological Methods of Warfare, signed at Geneva on 17 June 1925, the use in international armed conflicts of:
   (a) Any chemical agents of warfare—chemical substances, whether gaseous, liquid or solid—which might be employed because of their direct toxic effects on man, animals or plants;
   (b) Any biological agents of warfare—living organisms, whatever their nature, or infective material derived from them—which are intended to cause disease or death in man, animals or plants, and which depend for their effects on their ability to multiply in the person, animal or plant attacked.
*Id.*

[20] G.A. Res. 2603B, 24 U.N. GAOR Supp. 30, at 16-17, U.N. Doc. A/7630 (1969). *See also* G.A. Res. 2662, 25 U.N. GAOR Supp. 28, at 14, U.N. Doc. ——— (1970).

[21] Subcommittee on National Security Policy and Scientific Developments of the Committee on Foreign Affairs of the House of Representatives, 91st Cong., 1st

because of the obvious dangers to America's strategic position in the proliferation of biological and chemical weapons, it is in the national interest of the United States to adhere to existing international agreements aimed at CBW control and to seek new multilateral pacts which would ban the development, production and stockpiling of CB agents. Moreover, to the extent that such weapons, particularly those employing biologicals, threaten the existence of human life on earth or raise fears of extinction, our Nation has a duty to mankind to help obtain their effective prohibition.[22]

Accordingly,

[T]he Senate should speedily approve the protocol and the single reservation proposed by the President, thereby giving congressional endorsement to the unilateral and complete renunciation of biological warfare by the United States.

The question of the use of tear gas and herbicides in warfare should be left open in any formal or informal interpretation of the protocol made by the executive branch or the Senate, and once the United States becomes a party to the treaty it should seek agreement with the other parties on a uniform interpretation of the scope of the protocol, either through a special international conference among the parties or through established international juridical procedures.[23]

United States consideration of ratification of the Geneva Protocol is taking place against the broader and potentially more important background of international efforts for comprehensive control of development, production, stockpiling and all use in war of chemical and biological weapons. Pursuant to these efforts the Soviet Union and its allies submitted to the General Assembly a draft convention prohibiting the development, production, stockpiling, and destruction of chemical and bacteriological (biological) weapons; and the United Kingdom submitted to the Geneva Conference of the Committee on Disarmament a draft convention for the prohibition of biological methods of warfare.[24] On December 16, 1969,[25] and again on December 22, 1970,[26] the United

SESS., REPORT WITH AN APPENDED STUDY ON THE USE OF TEAR GAS IN WAR: A SURVEY OF INTERNATIONAL NEGOTIATIONS AND U.S. POLICY AND PRACTICES, CHEMICAL-BIOLOGICAL WARFARE: U.S. POLICIES AND INTERNATIONAL EFFECTS (Comm. Print. 1970).

22 Id. at 8-9.

23 Id. at 10.

24 See 10 INT'L LEG. MAT. 633-45 (1971).

25 See G.A. Res. 2603B, 24 U.N. GAOR SUPP. 30, at 16-17, U.N. Doc. A/7630 (1969).

26 G.A. Res. 2662, 25 U.N. GAOR SUPP. 28, at 14, U.N. Doc. ——— (1970).

Nations General Assembly requested the Geneva Conference of the United Nations Committee on Disarmament to give urgent consideration to reaching agreement on the prohibitions contained in these draft conventions. Subsequently, the United States, the United Kingdom, the Soviet Union and nine other states reached agreement within the framework of the Conference of the Committee on Disarmament on a "Draft Convention on the Prohibition of the Development, Production and Stockpiling of Bacteriological (Biological) and Toxin Weapons and on Their Destruction." [27] And on December 16, 1971, the United Nations General Assembly by a vote of 110 to zero, with only France abstaining, commended the Convention and expressed "hope for the widest possible adherence to the Convention." [28] The Convention was opened for signature simultaneously at Washington, London, and Moscow during April of 1972. Its most important operative provisions provide as follows:

### Article I

Each State Party to this Convention undertakes never in any circumstances to develop, produce, stockpile or otherwise acquire or retain:

(1) Microbial or other biological agents, or toxins whatever their origin or method of production, of types and in quantities that have no justification for prophylactic, protective or other peaceful purposes;

(2) Weapons, equipment or means of delivery designed to use such agents or toxins for hostile purposes or in armed conflict.

### Article II

Each State Party to this Convention undertakes to destroy, or to divert to peaceful purposes, as soon as possible but not later than nine months after the entry into force of the Convention all agents, toxins, weapons, equipment and means of delivery specified in Article I of the Convention, which are in its possession or under its jurisdiction or control. In implementing the provisions of this Article all necessary safety precautions shall be observed to protect populations and the environment.

---

[27] See Resolutions of the General Assembly at Its Twenty-Sixth Regular Session 21 September-22 December 1971, U.N. Press Release GA/4548, at Part II, 26-33 (Dec. 28, 1971), reprinted in 65 DEP'T STATE BULL. 508-10 (1971).

[28] G.A. Res. 2826, Resolutions of the General Assembly at Its Twenty-Sixth Regular Session 21 September-22 December 1971, U.N. Press Release GA/4548, at Part II, 26-33 (Dec. 28, 1971). See also Bush, supra note 7.

*Article III*

Each State Party to this Convention undertakes not to transfer to any recipient whatsoever, directly or indirectly and not in any way to assist, encourage, or induce any State, group of States or international organizations to manufacture or otherwise acquire any of the agents, toxins, weapons, equipment or means of delivery specified in Article I of the Convention. . . .[29]

In another resolution adopted on December 16 by the same large margin the General Assembly requested

the Conference of the Committee on Disarmament to continue, as a high priority item, negotiations with a view to reaching early agreement on effective measures for the prohibition of the development, production and stockpiling of chemical weapons and for their elimination from the arsenals of all States . . . .[30]

Because of the difficult issues of verification raised by a ban on chemical weapons, it is unlikely that agreement on a similar chemical ban will be reached as easily or as quickly.

The broadest context of relevant negotiations would also include the United States-Soviet Strategic Arms Limitation Talks (SALT), underway since November 1968, involving limitations of both offensive and defensive strategic weapons, and the second meeting of the Conference of Government Experts on the International Humanitarian Law Applicable in Armed Conflicts scheduled for May of 1972. Although not immediately linked with the Geneva Protocol, these negotiations are part of a pattern of arms limitation and law-of-war efforts which might

---

[29] DEP'T STATE BULL. 508, 508-09 (1971). On March 28, 1972 the Soviet Union presented a draft chemical convention roughly paralleling this draft biological convention. N.Y. Times, Mar. 29, 1972, at 3, col. 1.

[30] G.A. Res. 2827A, Resolutions of the General Assembly at Its Twenty-Sixth Regular Session 21 September-22 December 1971, U.N. Press Release GA/4548, at Part II, 34-37 (Dec. 28, 1971). A slightly more controversial resolution adopted the same day by a vote of 101 in favor, none against and ten abstentions urged

all States to undertake, pending agreement on the complete prohibition of the development, production and stockpiling of chemical weapons and their destruction, to refrain from any further development, production or stockpiling of those chemical agents for weapons purposes which because of their degree of toxicity have the highest lethal effects and are not usable for peaceful purposes.

G.A. Res. 2827B, Resolutions of the General Assembly at Its Twenty-Sixth Regular Session 21 September-22 December 1971, U.N. Press Release GA/4548, at Part II, 37 (Dec. 28, 1971).

be generally influenced by United States actions with respect to the Protocol.

Against the background of these efforts at more comprehensive control of CB and other arms, United States ratification of the Geneva Protocol assumes added importance. The Protocol is one of the most significant international limitations on the use of chemical and biological weapons, and its importance is recognized in the recent draft biological-weapons convention.[31] Furthermore, at least six General Assembly resolutions adopted since 1966 have urged universal adherence to the Protocol or called for strict observance of its principles.[32] If the United States continues as the only major power not a party to the Protocol, the leadership and influence that it can exert in these and perhaps other important arms limitation efforts may be affected adversely. Moreover, early ratification might give renewed impetus to the present momentum for improved control of CBW. In turn, early ratification depends in large measure on the position that the Administration and the Senate adopt regarding riot-control agents and chemical herbicides.[33] In light

---

[31] The Draft Biological Weapons Convention provides with respect to the Protocol:
The States Parties to this Convention, . . .
Recognizing the important significance of the Geneva Protocol of 17 June 1925 for the Prohibition of the Use in War of Asphyxiating, Poisonous or Other Gases, and of Bacteriological Methods of Warfare, and conscious also of the contributions which the said Protocol has already made, and continues to make, to mitigating the horrors of war,
Reaffirming their adherence to the principles and objectives of that Protocol and calling upon all States to comply strictly with them,
Recalling that the General Assembly of the United Nations has repeatedly condemned all actions contrary to the principles and objectives of the Geneva Protocol of 17 June 1925, . . . .
Have agreed as follows: . . . .
Nothing in this Convention shall be interpreted as in any way limiting or detracting from the obligations assumed by any State under the Geneva Protocol of 17 June 1925 by the Prohibition of the Use in War of Asphyxiating, Poisonous or Other Gases, and of Bacteriological Methods of Warfare.
65 DEP'T STATE BULL. 508, 508-09 (1971).

[32] See G.A. Res. 2162B (XXI) (Dec. 5, 1966); G.A. Res. 2454A (XXIII) (Dec. 20, 1968); G.A. Res. 2603 A & B (XXIV) (Dec. 16, 1969); G.A. Res. 2662 (XXV) (Dec. 7, 1970); G.A. Res. 2826 (XXVI) (Dec. 16, 1971); G.A. Res. 2927A (XXVI) (Dec. 16, 1971).

[33] For general background on CBW and United States policy, see F. BROWN, CHEMICAL WARFARE: A STUDY IN RESTRAINTS, (1968); WHEN BATTLE RAGES, HOW CAN LAW PROTECT? Proceedings of the Fourteenth Hammarskjöld Forum, J. Carey ed. (1971); CARNEGIE ENDOWMENT FOR INTERNATIONAL PEACE, THE CONTROL OF CHEMICAL AND BIOLOGICAL WEAPONS (1971); J. COOKSON & J. NOTTINGHAM, A SURVEY OF CHEMICAL AND BIOLOGICAL WARFARE (1969); S. HERSH, CHEMICAL AND BIOLOGICAL WARFARE: AMERICA'S HIDDEN ARSENAL (1968); R. McCARTHY, THE ULTIMATE FOLLY (1969); M. McDOUGAL & F. FELICIANO, LAW AND MINIMUM WORLD PUBLIC ORDER 632-40, 662,

of these current issues this Article will explore the background of United States CBW policy with special emphasis on the legal and political costs and benefits of ratification of the Protocol and of the associated options concerning riot-control agents and chemical herbicides.

## A Brief History of United States CBW Policy

### World War I and the Inter-War Years

During World War I both sides made steady use of various lachrymatory (tear), chlorine, phosgene and mustard gases. United States forces, which entered the War relatively late, were attacked on February 25, 1918, by Germans using phosgene shells. In turn, the United States used gas offensively beginning in June 1918. Apparently, the United States used only about 1,100 tons of the total 58,000 tons of gas fired by the allies in the War and did not use tear gas or other riot-control agents.[34]

The widespread use of gas in World War I, causing possibly 1.3 million casualties and 100,000 deaths, engendered almost universal abhorrence for gas warfare.[35] In the years following World War I the United States participated actively in the international efforts to control

---

664 (1961); H. Meyrowitz, Les Armes Biologiques et le Droit International (1968); CBW: Chemical and Biological Warfare (S. Rose ed. 1969); A. Thomas & A. Thomas, Legal Limits on the Use of Chemical and Biological Weapons (1970); Tucker, *The Law of War and Neutrality at Sea*, 50 Naval War College International Law Studies (1955); Baxter & Buergenthal, *Legal Aspects of the Geneva Protocol of 1925*, 64 A.J.I.L. 853 (1970); Bunn, *Banning Poison Gas and Germ Warfare: Should the United States Agree?*, 1969 Wisc. L. Rev. 375; Johnstone, *Ecocide and the Geneva Protocol*, 49 Foreign Affairs 711 (1971); Kelly, *Gas Warfare in International Law*, 9 Military L. Rev. 1 (1960); O'Brien, *Biological/Chemical Warfare and the International Law of War*, 51 Geo. L.J. 1 (1962); *Hearings on Chemical and Biological Warfare Before the Committee on Foreign Relations of the United States Senate*, 91st Cong., 1st Sess. (1969); *Hearings on Chemical-Biological Warfare: U.S. Policies and International Effects Before the Subcommittee on National Security Policy and Scientific Developments of the Committee on Foreign Affairs of the House of Representatives*, 91st Cong., 1st Sess. (1970); Report of the Subcommittee on National Security Policy and Scientific Developments, *supra* note 21; *Report of the Secretary-General on Chemical and Bacteriological (Biological) Weapons and the Effects of Their Possible Use*, U.N. Doc. A/7575; A/7575/Rev. 1 (1969); *Health Effects of Possible Use of Chemical and Biological Weapons—Report of a WHO Group of Consultants*, reprinted in *Hearings on Chemical-Biological Warfare: U.S. Policies and International Effects Before the Subcommittee on National Security Policy, supra* at 443.

34 S. Hersh, Chemical and Biological Warfare: America's Hidden Arsenal 4-5 (1968).

35 R. McCarthy, The Ultimate Folly 5 (1969). Seymour Hersh gives a figure of 91,000 deaths attributable to gas warfare in World War I. *See* S. Hersh, *supra* note 34, at 5.

chemical and biological warfare. Thus, the United States participated in negotiations leading to the Versailles Treaty of 1918, which, in Article 171, provided: "the use of asphyxiating, poisonous, or other gases and all analogous liquids, materials or devices being prohibited, their manufacture and importation are strictly forbidden in Germany." [36] Primarily because of the refusal of the Senate to consent to the provisions concerning United States membership in the League of Nations, the United States did not become a party to the Versailles Treaty. But Article 171 of the Treaty was incorporated by reference (along with the entire section of the Versailles Treaty of which Article 171 is a part) in the Treaty Restoring Friendly Relations between the United States and Germany of August 25, 1921.[37] Similar articles appeared in the United States peace treaties with Hungary and Austria.[38] Charles Cheney Hyde notes that because of this incorporation of Article 171 of the Treaty of Versailles in the peace treaties with the Central powers, the United States might be considered a party to a treaty outlawing gas warfare,[39] contrary to the language of *Army Field Manual 27-10*.[40] It is generally agreed, however, that the restriction on gas warfare incorporated into these peace agreements was a disarmament measure intended to be binding on the Central powers and not the United States.[41]

In another post-war initiative, Secretary of State Charles Evans Hughes led a United States delegation to the Washington Arms Conference, which drafted the Treaty on the Use of Submarines and Noxious Gases

---

[36] Treaty of Peace between the Principal Allied and Associated Powers and Germany, signed at Versailles, Jun. 28, 1919, [1919] GT. BRIT. T.S. No. 4, 2 TREATIES AND OTHER INT'L AGREEMENTS OF THE U.S., 1776-1949 119 (Bevans ed. 1969).

[37] 42 Stat. 1939, 1943 (1921), 8 TREATIES AND OTHER INT'L AGREEMENTS, *supra* note 36, at 145.

[38] 42 Stat. 1946 (1921), 5 TREATIES AND OTHER INT'L AGREEMENTS, *supra* note 36, at 215, 217-18 (Article II(1) of the Treaty of Peace with Austria); 42 Stat. 1951 (1921), 8 TREATIES AND OTHER INT'L AGREEMENTS, *supra* note 36, at 982, 985 (Article II(1) of the Treaty of Peace with Hungary).

[39] 3 C. HYDE, INTERNATIONAL LAW 1821 (2d ed. 1947).

[40] DEP'T OF THE ARMY FIELD MANUAL FM 27-10, THE LAW OF LAND WARFARE (1956). Paragraph 38 of the field manual provides with respect to "Gases, Chemicals, and Bacteriological Warfare":
> The United States is not a party to any treaty, now in force, that prohibits or restricts the use in warfare of toxic or non-toxic gases, of smoke or incendiary materials, or of bacteriological warfare.

*Id.* at 18.

[41] *See, e.g.,* A. THOMAS & A. THOMAS, LEGAL LIMITS ON THE USE OF CHEMICAL AND BIOLOGICAL WEAPONS 58-62 (1970); Bunn, *Banning Poison Gas and Germ Warfare: Should the United States Agree?,* 1969 WISC. L. REV. 375 at 376.

in Warfare (The Treaty of Washington).[42] The Treaty was signed in 1922 by France, Great Britain, Italy, Japan and the United States. Article Five of the Treaty, which was introduced by Senator Elihu Root, a member of the American delegation, included a broad ban against gas warfare. It provided as follows:

> The use in war of asphyxiating, poisonous or other gases, and all analogous liquids, materials or devices, having been justly condemned by the general opinion of the civilized world and a prohibition of such use having been declared in treaties to which a majority of the civilized Powers are parties,
>
> The Signatory Powers, to the end that this prohibition shall be universally accepted as a part of international law binding alike the conscience and practice of nations, declare their assent to such prohibition, agree to be bound thereby as between themselves and invite all other civilized nations to adhere thereto.[43]

There is evidence that the United States delegation sought to promote a comprehensive ban that would prohibit all use of gas, including tear gas, in war. A report prepared by the Advisory Committee of the United States Delegation urged that "chemical warfare, including the use of gases, whether toxic or nontoxic, should be prohibited by international agreement." [44] And a memorandum prepared by the General Board of the Navy, after weighing the humane uses of tear gas against the difficulty of demarcation between those gases which cause unnecessary suffering and those such as tear gas which need not, concluded that it is "sound policy to prohibit gas warfare in every form and against every objective, and [The General Board] so recommends." [45] But after presenting these Reports to the Conference Committee on Limitation of Armaments, Secretary of State Hughes, perhaps advertently, perhaps not, stated the recommendation of the American delegation more restrictively:

> [T]he American delegation, in the light of the advice of its advisory committee and the concurrence in that advice of General Pershing . . .

---

42 Treaty Relative to the Protection of the Lives of Neutrals and Noncombatants at Sea in Time of War and to Prevent the Use in War of Noxious Gases and Chemicals, Feb. 6, 1922, 3 TREATIES CONVENTIONS, INT'L ACTS, PROTOCOLS AND AGREEMENTS 3116 (Redmond ed. 1923).

43 *Id.* at 3118.

44 Conference on the Limitation of Armament, S. Doc. No. 126, 67th Cong., 2d Sess. 386 (1922).

45 *Id.* at 387.

and of the specific recommendation of the General Board of the Navy, felt that it should present the recommendation that the use of asphyxiating or poison gas be absolutely prohibited.[46]

The Senate consented to the Treaty of Washington without a dissenting vote but also without focused discussion on whether it prohibited the use of tear gas in war. Apparently the principal issue in the 1922 Senate debate was whether gas warfare in general was a relatively humane form of warfare and not whether riot-control agents should be a specially permitted form of gas warfare.[47] Ultimately, the Treaty of Washington did not enter into force because France refused to ratify it. France's refusal related to the provisions restricting submarine warfare rather than disagreement with the provisions restricting the use of gas in war.

Three years later an initiative of the United States Delegation to the Geneva Conference for the Supervision of the International Trade in Arms and Ammunition and in Implements of War led to the adoption by the Conference of the Geneva Protocol of 1925, which followed the language of Article Five of the ill-fated Treaty of Washington.[48] There was little discussion at the Geneva Conference of the scope of the prohibitory language of the Protocol, and none regarding whether it included riot-control agents or chemical herbicides.[49] The report of the United States Senate Foreign Relations Committee, which recommended approval of the Protocol, however, contained a statement by Theodore E. Burton, the representative of the United States at Geneva and a signatory of the Protocol for the United States, that the Protocol was "in accordance with our settled policy." He also recalled the broad definition of prohibited gases urged by the United States Advisory

---

[46] Id. at 387-88.

[47] See 62 CONG. REC. 4723-30 (1922). Professors Richard R. Baxter and Thomas Buergenthal observe that the failure of any Senator to inquire "whether Article 5 prohibited the use of tear gas or any other irritant chemical . . . [was] particularly noteworthy because the documents of the conference at which the treaty was drafted, and which were before the Senate, . . . [indicated] that this question had been considered but had not been unequivocally resolved." Baxter and Buergenthal, *Legal Aspects of the Geneva Protocol of 1925*, 64 A.J.I.L. 853, 859 (1970).

[48] For the background of the United States proposals and the adoption of the Treaty of Washington formula, see Baxter & Buergenthal, *supra* note 47, at 860-61.

[49] According to George Bunn "[t]here is no recorded discussion of tear gases by the delegates." Bunn, *supra* note 41, at 402. And Professors Baxter and Buergenthal write that "[n]o attempt was made at the Geneva Conference to discuss the scope of this prohibition and no reference to tear gas or other irritant chemicals appears in the records of the Conference." Baxter & Buergenthal, *supra* note 47, at 861.

Committee at the Washington Arms Conference which included the phrase *whether toxic or nontoxic*, and he cited the 1922 report of the Navy General Board, which had recommended the prohibition of gas warfare *in every form*.[50] Moreover, one of the arguments against the Protocol made by Senator David A. Reed during the Senate debate was that it would prohibit tear gas which "has been adopted by every intelligent police force in the United States . . . ."[51] Although Senator William E. Borah's rather cryptic reply indicated that the Protocol would not prevent the domestic use of tear gas, he seemed not to dispute Senator Reed's contention that the Protocol would prohibit the use of tear gas in war. The Protocol breezed through the Senate Foreign Relations Committee by a vote of eight to one, but it failed to come to a vote after it was reported out.[52] Apparently, it was defeated by a combination of the Administration's complacency induced by the approval of the Washington Treaty three years earlier and vigorous lobbying against it by the chemical industry, the Army Chemical Corps, and other groups.[53] The Protocol remained on the docket of the Senate Foreign Relations Committee until withdrawn by President Truman in 1947 as part of a general housekeeping effort to update the docket of the Foreign Relations Committee, a housekeeping effort initiated by the new chairman of the committee, Senator Arthur H. Vandenberg.[54]

In 1930, some doubt arose at the meeting of the Preparatory Commission for the League of Nations Disarmament Conference whether the Geneva Protocol of 1925 included lachrymatory gases. The British and French governments issued statements indicating that lachrymatory gases were included and ten of the remaining sixteen states present and party to the Protocol associated themselves with the British and French

[50] *See* Gellner & Wu, *The Use of Tear Gas In War: A Survey of International Negotiations and of U.S. Policy and Practice*, in Subcommittee on National Security and Scientific Developments, Report, *supra* note 21, at 11, 32.

[51] *See* 68 Cong. Rec. 150 (1926).

[52] *See* R. McCarthy, *supra* note 35, at 7.

[53] George Bunn says of the Senate failure to advise and consent to the Protocol:
> [p]robably because of the ease with which the Washington Treaty had sailed through the Senate, Secretary of State Kellogg did not make the effort to gain support for the Geneva Protocol that Secretary Hughes had made earlier for the Washington Treaty. Although Congressman Burton was the head of the United States delegation, no Senator was included. No advisory committee was enlisted. The Army's Chemical Warfare Service was not prevented from mobilizing opposition to the protocol. It enlisted the American Legion, the Veterans of Foreign Wars, the American Chemical Society, and the chemical industry.

Bunn, *supra* note 41, at 378.

[54] *See* 16 Dep't State Bull. 726 (1947).

statements. The remaining six states did not respond to the invitation to register their views.[55] Although the United States was not a party to the Protocol, Hugh Gibson, the United States Representative to the Preparatory Commission, took the occasion to indicate that the draft convention to be prepared by the Disarmament Conference should not ban lachrymatory gases. He said:

> I think there would be considerable hesitation on the part of many Governments to bind themselves to refrain from the use in war, against an enemy, of agencies which they have adopted for peace-time use against their own population, agencies adopted on the ground that, while causing temporary inconvenience, they cause no real suffering or permanent disability, and are thereby more clearly humane than the use of weapons to which they were formerly obliged to resort to in times of emergency.[56]

At the Disarmament Conference itself the Conference adopted a broadly worded ban that prohibited "the use, by any method whatsoever, for the purpose of injuring an adversary, of any natural or synthetic substance harmful to the human or animal organism, whether solid, liquid or gaseous, such as toxic, asphyxiating, lachrymatory, irritant or vesicant substances."[57] The United States representatives agreed to this proposal but the draft convention never went into force.

It seems fair to conclude that prior to World War II the policy of the United States Executive was to work to prohibit the use of all chemical and biological weapons, though there was some vacillation regarding the propriety of prohibiting lachrymatory gases. During this period the question whether to prohibit tear gases received little attention in comparison with the efforts to ban gas warfare in general; and the question whether to prohibit chemical herbicides, not yet developed, was not even raised. Evidence concerning the United States interpretation of the Geneva Protocol during this period is particularly sketchy.

---

55 LEAGUE OF NATIONS, DOCUMENTS OF THE PREPARATORY COMMISSION FOR THE DISARMAMENT CONFERENCE (SERIES X): MINUTES OF THE SIXTH SESSION (SECOND PART) 311-14 (1931).

56 Id. at 312.

57 2 LEAGUE OF NATIONS, CONFERENCE FOR THE REDUCTION AND LIMITATION OF ARMAMENTS: CONFERENCE DOCUMENTS 476, at 488 (1935). For a discussion of the general position of the United States at the Conference see J. WHEELER-BENNETT, THE PIPE DREAM OF PEACE 17-18 (1971).

## World War II and the Korean War

During World War II the United States did not use gas weapons, despite recommendations from several military sources in May and June of 1945 that favored the use of gas in the Pacific theatre.[58] Prior to the War President Roosevelt had said in general terms, "It has been and is the policy of this Government to do everything in its power to outlaw the use of chemicals in warfare. Such use is inhuman and contrary to what modern civilization should stand for." [59] An exchange of pledges to observe the Protocol had been made between the British, French, Italian and German governments at the outbreak of the War.[60] But reports during the War that the Germans might use gas weapons prompted Roosevelt to declare more specifically in 1943,

> From time to time since the present war began there have been reports that one or more of the Axis Powers were seriously contemplating use of poisonous or noxious gases or other inhumane devices of warfare. . . .
> Use of such weapons has been outlawed by the general opinion of civilized mankind. This country has not used them, and I hope that we never will be compelled to use them. I state categorically that we shall under no circumstances resort to the use of such weapons unless they are first used by our enemies.[61]

It is unclear whether Roosevelt meant to include riot-control agents or chemical herbicides, but no such weapons were used in combat during World War II.[62] That at least the decision to avoid use of gas was not made by default is suggested by Admiral Chester W. Nimitz's statement that one of his toughest decisions during the War occurred "when the War Department suggested the use of poison gas during the invasion of Iwo Jima." He went on to say, "I decided the United States should not be the first to violate the Geneva Convention." [63] Admiral Nimitz, of course, was speaking generally when he spoke of

---

[58] Gellner & Wu, *supra* note 50, at 26-27.

[59] L. BROPHY & G. FISHER, THE CHEMICAL WARFARE SERVICE: ORGANIZING FOR WAR 22 (1959).

[60] *See* Bunn, *supra* note 41, at 381-82.

[61] 8 DEP'T STATE BULL. 507 (1943).

[62] Brophy and Fisher limit Roosevelt's declaration to "poisonous or noxious gases," classifications which could be taken to exclude tear gas. *See* BROPHY & FISHER, *supra* note 59, at 88.

[63] *See* S. HERSH, *supra* note 34, at 25-26 n.xx.

"violating" the Geneva Convention, as the United States was not a party to the Protocol.

In March of 1945 Major General Myron C. Cramer, the Judge Advocate General of the Army, prepared a memorandum for the Secretary of War concerning the legality of the destruction of crops by chemicals. He concluded that no rule prohibited the use of chemical agents for the destruction of crops, provided "that such chemicals do not produce poisonous effects upon enemy personnel, either from direct contact, or indirectly from ingestion of plants and vegetables which have been exposed thereto." [64] There is, however, no indication that any such chemicals were subsequently used during World War II. Interestingly, the Cramer memorandum seems to have provided the principal legal basis relied on by the Department of Defense for the large scale use of herbicides in Vietnam some twenty years later.[65]

During the Korean War the United States again refrained from using chemical weapons in combat situations, though field commanders are reported to have requested permission to use gas, including tear and vomiting gases, to attack deeply entrenched enemy fortifications in order to break the deadlock in the latter stages of the war.[66] Since the United States was better prepared to use chemical weapons than the North Koreans and Communist Chinese, such use might have been militarily advantageous to the United States. United States military authorities did use tear and vomiting gases to quell rioting Communist prisoners of war on the theory that use in a POW camp is not a use "in war." [67]

The United States seems never to have used biological agents in war, but during the Korean War, Peking repeatedly alleged that the United States was engaged in germ warfare. A United States request in 1952 that the International Committee of the Red Cross (ICRC) undertake an investigation of the charges was blocked by North Korean and Communist Chinese refusal to cooperate with the ICRC. Several months later a United States sponsored resolution in the United Nations Security Council requesting that the ICRC investigate the Chinese allegations was vetoed by the Soviet Union; and in April 1953 a General As-

---

64 The Memorandum is reprinted in 10 INT'L LEG. MAT. 1304-06 (1971).

65 See the letter from J. Fred Buzhardt, General Counsel of the Department of Defense, to Senator J. W. Fulbright, *reprinted in* 10 INT'L LEG. MAT. 1303-04 (1971).

66 See Gellner & Wu, *supra* note 50, at 27.

67 See Gellner & Wu, *supra* note 50, at 27; A. THOMAS & A. THOMAS, *supra* note 41, at 148.

sembly Resolution proposing a five-state commission to investigate the charges was also blocked by North Korean and Chinese Communist refusal to cooperate.[68]

Summarizing United States policy with respect to chemical and biological warfare during World War II and the Korean War, the United States seemed to follow a no-first-use policy similar to that which emerged under the Geneva Protocol. The policy did not expressly prohibit use of riot-control agents, but, in fact, it consciously precluded the use of such agents in combat situations. The principal reasons for the adoption of the no-first-use policy seem to have been fear of retaliation in kind, concern for escalation to inhumane chemical or biological weapons, concern for possible adverse international political reactions from first use, and, during the Korean War, a consciousness that decisions on weapons would be particularly subject to international scrutiny. Though chemical herbicides were not used in World War II or the Korean War the issue had not really become focused.

In the years following the Korean War, the United States seems to have reassessed its CBW policy.[69] The outlines of the reassessment were by no means clear, but they suggested some relaxation of controls. The 1956 edition of the *Army Field Manual 27-10*, still the current field manual,[70] provides: "The United States is not a party to any treaty, now in force, that prohibits or restricts the use in warfare of toxic or non-toxic gases, of smoke or incendiary materials, or of bacteriological warfare." [71] The *Field Manual* expressed no opinion on a no-first-use limitation or on the extent of the customary international legal obligation which might be binding on the United States. Evidence of a possible relaxation in the United States no-first-use policy during

---

[68] *See* 10 M. WHITEMAN, DIGEST OF INTERNATIONAL LAW 461-66 (1968); S. HERSH, *supra* note 34, at 18-21; A. THOMAS & A. THOMAS, *supra* note 41, at 156; Fuller, *The Application of International Law to Chemical and Biological Warfare*, 10 ORBIS 247 (1966).

[69] *See* S. HERSH, *supra* note 34, at 22-33; Gellner & Wu, *supra* note 50, at 33-34.

[70] Although Seymour Hersh writes of a shift in CBW policy evidenced by differences between the 1954 and 1956 editions of DEP'T OF THE ARMY FIELD MANUAL FM 27-10, *supra* note 40, Professor Howard S. Levie has indicated to the author that there is no 1954 edition of the *Field Manual*. Apparently Hersh may have relied on an unofficial mimeograph draft prepared in 1954 which indicates on the cover sheet that the document was not approved either by the Judge Advocate General or by the Department of the Army. Needless to say, the differences between such a draft and the approved *Field Manual* are poor evidence of a shift in United States policy. *See* S. HERSH, *supra* note 34, at 23-24.

[71] THE LAW OF LAND WARFARE, *supra* note 40, at 18.

this period is provided by the Defense and State Department reactions to a resolution introduced in 1959 by Congressman Robert Kastenmeier. As a result of what he perceived to be an increased interest in CBW and a possible change in United States policy, Congressman Kastenmeier introduced a resolution affirming "the longstanding policy of the United States that in the event of war the United States shall under no circumstances resort to the use of biological weapons or the use of poisonous or obnoxious [sic] gases unless they are first used by our enemies." [72] When President Eisenhower was asked at a press conference in January 1960 about the possibility of a change in policy he said, "no such official suggestion has been made to me and so far as my own instinct is concerned, is to not start such a thing as that first." [73] Nevertheless, both the State and Defense Departments opposed the Kastenmeier resolution, stressing the need for presidential discretion.[74] It is unclear whether the discretion sought to be retained during this period related to first use of lethal CB or only to the use of incapacitating, riot-control, or anti-plant agents; but the breadth of the debate suggests that the issue may again have been the propriety of using chemical and biological weapons generally rather than the wisdom of imposing less restrictive controls on the use of riot-control or anti-plant agents.

## The Indo-China War

Breaking with the World War II and Korean War traditions, the United States has used both riot-control agents and chemical herbicides in the Indo-China War. Beginning in about 1962 chemical agents were supplied to South Vietnamese forces and, according to the *New York Times*, "no provision was made for special authorization to use them . . . and it was assumed that South Vietnamese commanders would use them as they saw fit." [75] Rear Admiral Lemos stated in testimony before a House Subcommittee in 1969 that "[t]he Department of Defense with the concurrence of the Department of State obtained Presi-

---

[72] See H.R. Res. 433, 86th Cong. 1st Sess. (1959), *reprinted in* 105 CONG. REC. 10824 (1959); SUBCOMMITTEE ON DISARMAMENT OF THE SENATE COMMITTEE ON FOREIGN RELATIONS, 86TH CONG., 2D SESS., CHEMICAL, BIOLOGICAL, RADIOLOGICAL (CBR) WARFARE AND ITS DISARMAMENT ASPECTS 20 (1960).

[73] PUBLIC PAPERS OF THE PRESIDENTS, DWIGHT D. EISENHOWER 1960-61 29 (1961).

[74] See A. THOMAS & A. THOMAS, *supra* note 41, at 167-68; Gellner & Wu, *supra* note 50, at 34.

[75] N.Y. Times, Mar. 24, 1965, at 7, col. 1.

dential approval in November 1965 for the use of CS and CN in Vietnam." [76] The United States has relied primarily on CS (ortho-chlorobenzylidenemalonoitrile) in Vietnam but has also used CN (w-chlorocetophenone) and initially provided DM (diphenylaminechloroarsine or adamasite) to South Vietnamese forces.[77] CS, CN and DM are, in the terms of the 1969 *Report of the United Nations Secretary-General*, "tear and harassing gases." [78] According to the Report, "tear and harassing gases rapidly produce irritation, smarting and tears. These symptoms disappear quickly after exposure ceases";[79] however, the Report further noted, "[d]eaths have been reported in three cases after extraordinary exposure to . . . (CN) in a confined space." [80] Thus, in military concentrations and with prolonged exposure any of these gases may be lethal, but deaths would be rare, particularly from CS.[81] Interestingly, CS popularly called "super" tear gas, is both the most irritating and least toxic of the three common harassing agents.[82] According to the *Army Field Manual* on such weapons (*FM 3-10*), DM can be lethal and its use is not approved "in any operation where deaths are not acceptable." [83] Apparently for this reason DM is no longer part of the United States arsenal.[84]

---

[76] Statement of Rear Am. William E. Lemos, Director of Policy Plans and National Security Council Affairs, Office, Assistant Secretary of Defense for International Security Affairs [hereinafter cited as Statement of Rear Adm. Lemos], in *Hearings on Chemical-Biological Warfare: U.S. Policies and International Effects Before the Subcommittee on National Security Policy and Scientific Developments of the Committee on Foreign Affairs of the House of Representatives* 91st Cong., 1st Sess. (1970) 223, 224-25.

[77] *See* Gellner & Wu, *supra* note 50, at 28-29.

[78] *Report of the Secretary-General on Chemical and Bacteriological (Biological) Weapons and the Effects of Their Possible Use*, U.N. Doc. A/7575; A/7575/Rev. 1 (1969), at 45.

[79] *Id.*

[80] *Id.*

[81] The testimony of Dr. Matthew S. Meselson before the Senate Foreign Relations Committee on April 30, 1969, mentions "claims by unofficial observers" of "a few deaths from CS in Vietnam." *See Hearings on Chemical and Biological Warfare Before the Committee on Foreign Relations of the United States Senate*, 91st Cong., 1st Sess. 7 (1970).

[82] *See Report of the Secretary-General*, *supra* note 78, at 45. As Professor Howard S. Levie has pointed out, contrary to Seymour Hersh the "S" in "CS" does not stand for "super" but is derived from the codevelopers of the gas. *See* S. HERSH, *supra* note 34, at 60, and Levie, The Impact of New Weapons and Technology in the Indo-China Conflict, unpublished paper delivered at a meeting of the American Society of International Law in Washington, D. C., 1971.

[83] DEP'T OF THE ARMY FIELD MANUAL FM 3-10, EMPLOYMENT OF CHEMICAL AND BIOLOGICAL AGENTS para. 11 at 7 (1966).

[84] *See* statement of Rear Adm. Lemos, *supra* note 76, at 241.

A statement by Secretary of State Dean Rusk in 1965 suggested that tear gas would be used in Vietnam only for humanitarian purposes, such as separating combatants and non-combatants:

> We do not expect that gas will be used in ordinary military operations. Police-type weapons were used in riot control in South Viet-Nam— as in many other countries over the past 20 years—and in situations analogous to riot control, where the Viet Cong, for example, were using civilians as screens for their own operations.[85]

Subsequently tear gas was authorized for use in normal combat operations, though, according to the testimony of Rear Admiral Lemos, such use for humane purposes where combatants and non-combatants are intermingled is a recommended use.[86] Evidently, however, tear gas has been used predominantly in normal combat operations to support attacks on occupied positions, defend positions, clear tunnels, break contact with the enemy, and aid in rescuing downed airmen.[87] In recent years, as the direct involvement of United States ground combat forces has been winding down, the use of tear gas has been substantially curtailed.[88]

Since about 1962 chemical herbicides have been used in Vietnam, first experimentally, and then extensively.[89] Principal uses have included improving visibility by defoliating jungle areas concealing enemy supply bases and trails, defoliating allied base perimeters, and defoliating dense growth along roads and waterways which might harbor an ambush.[90] At one time herbicides were also used in a controlled program to destroy crops reputedly intended for Vietcong forces.[91] According to Defense Department figures, as of July 1969, the United

---

[85] 52 DEP'T STATE BULL. 529 (1965). The evolution of United States policy in the use of riot-control agents in Vietnam provides an example of the difficulty in proposing a particular use restriction as a firebreak for weapons control.

[86] See statement of Rear Adm. Lemos, supra note 76, at 237.

[87] See, e.g., id. at 225-28.

[88] See the Department of Defense data, "Procurement of CS, CS1, and CS2 For Southeast Asia," set out in a statement by Senator Humphrey on the Geneva Protocol, 117 CONG. REC. S11920, S11921 (daily ed. Jul. 23, 1971).

[89] See generally on the use of herbicides in Vietnam S. HERSH, supra note 34, at 144-67.

[90] See statement of Rear Adm. Lemos, supra note 76, at 229.

[91] See id. at 230.

> Crops in areas remote from the friendly population and known to belong to the enemy and which cannot be captured by ground operations are sometimes sprayed. Such targets are carefully selected so as to attack only those crops to be grown by or for the VC or NVA.

States had sprayed approximately 5,070,800 acres in South Vietnam with herbicides, a figure equivalent to more than ten percent of the land area of the country.[92] Initially, herbicides were believed to be neither harmful to man nor permanently damaging to plants. Subsequent evidence indicates that intensive exposure to some agents may be harmful both to man and the natural environment through a variety of both direct and more subtle synergistic effects.[93] Recently President Nixon ordered the termination of crop destruction by chemical herbicides, and began a phase-out of the use of chemical herbicides for defoliation.[94] According to the testimony of Secretary of State Rogers before the Senate Foreign Relations Committee on March 5, 1971,

> During the phase out, our herbicide operations will be limited to defoliation operations in remote, unpopulated areas or to the perimeter defense of fire bases and installations in a manner currently authorized in the United States and which does not involve the use of fixed-wing aircraft.[95]

Secretary Rogers also disclosed plans for disposing of "the stocks of agent 'Orange' presently in Viet-Nam." [96] Agent Orange is a 50-50 mixture of two commonly used defoliants, 2,4-D and 2,4,5-T, both of which may have adverse effects on the environment and human health.[97]

---

[92] SUBCOMMITTEE ON NATIONAL SECURITY POLICY AND SCIENTIFIC DEVELOPMENTS, REPORT, *supra* note 21, at 5.

[93] *See generally* Galston, *Defoliants,* in CBW: CHEMICAL AND BIOLOGICAL WARFARE 62-75 (S. Rose ed. 1969); R. McCARTHY, *supra* note 35, at 74-98.

[94] *See* the testimony of Secretary of State William P. Rogers before the Senate Foreign Relations Committee, March 5, 1971.

[95] *Id.* at 3.

[96] *Id.*

[97] *See* R. McCARTHY, *supra* note 35, at 76, 74-98. L. Craig Johnstone, the former chief of the Pacification Studies Group of the Military Assistance Command in Vietnam, writes in FOREIGN AFFAIRS:

Many scientists have expressed concern over the possible effects of herbicides on humans. The principal military herbicide, Agent Orange, was banned from further use in 1970 due to preliminary evidence of the possibility that it produced birth defects after it had been used extensively in Vietnam. Of the two remaining agents used there today, neither is allowed for general agricultural use in the United States because of possible environmental and toxic effects.

Johnstone, *Ecocide and the Geneva Protocol,* 49 FOREIGN AFFAIRS 711, 718 (1971).

On Nov. 4, 1971, an order of the United States Environmental Protection Agency upheld a previous determination cancelling certain registered uses of the herbicide 2,4,5-T. The Administrator indicated that the previous action was mandated by the following facts:

1. A contaminant of 2,4,5-T—tetrachlorodibenzoparadioxin (TCDD, or dioxin)— is one of the most teratogenic chemicals known. The registrants have not estab-

With respect to the legal issues involved in use of herbicides, a letter from J. Fred Buzhardt, the General Counsel of the Department of Defense, to Senator Fulbright on April 5, 1971, conveys the opinion of the General Counsel and that of the Judge Advocate Generals of the Army, Navy and Air Force:

[N]either the Hague Regulations nor the rules of customary international law applicable to the conduct of war and to the weapons of war prohibit the use of anti-plant chemicals for defoliation or the destruction of crops, provided that their use against crops does not cause such crops as food to be poisoned nor cause human beings to be poisoned by direct contact, and such use must not cause unnecessary destruction of enemy property. . . .

The Geneva Protocol of 1925 adds no prohibitions relating to either the use of chemical herbicides or to crop destruction to those de-

---

lished that 1 part per million of this contaminant—or even 0.1 ppm—in 2,4,5-T does not pose a danger to the public health and safety.

2. There is a substantial possibility that even "pure" 2,4,5-T is itself a hazard to man and the environment.

3. The dose-response curves for 2,4,5-T and dioxin have not been determined, and the possibility of "no effect" levels for these chemicals is only a matter of conjecture at this time.

4. As with another well-known teratogen, thalidomide, the possibility exists that dioxin may be many times more potent in humans than in test animals (thalidomide was 60 times more dangerous to humans than to mice, and 700 times more dangerous than to hamsters; the usual margin of safety for humans is set at one-tenth the teratogenic level in test animals).

5. The registrants have not established that the dioxin and 2,4,5-T do not accumulate in body tissues. If one or both does accumulate, even small doses could build up to dangerous levels within man and animals, and possibly in the food chain as well.

6. The question of whether there are other sources of dioxin in the environment has not been fully explored. Such other sources, when added to the amount of dioxin from 2,4,5-T, could result in a substantial total body burden for certain segments of the population.

7. The registrants have not established that there is no danger from dioxins other than TCDD, such as the hexa- and heptadioxin isomers, which also can be present in 2,4,5-T, and which are known to be teratogenic.

8. There is evidence that the polychlorophenols in 2,4,5-T may decompose into dioxin when exposed to high temperatures, such as might occur with incineration or even in the cooking of food.

9. Studies of medical records in Vietnam hospitals and clinics below the district capital level suggest a correlation between the spraying of 2,4,5-T defoliant and the incidence of birth defects.

10. The registrants have not established the need for 2,4,5-T in light of the above-mentioned risks. Benefits from 2,4,5-T should be determined at a public hearing, but tentative studies by this agency have shown little necessity for those uses of 2,4,5-T which are now at issues. . . .

In Re Hercules, Inc. and Dow Chemical Co., Order of the Administrator of the Environmental Protection Agency (I.R.&F. Docket Nos. 42 & 44, Nov. 4, 1971), at 4-5.

scribed above. Its preamble declares that its prohibition shall extend to "the use in war of asphyxiating, poisonous or other gases, and of all analogous liquids, materials or devices." Bearing in view that neither the legislative history nor the practices of States indicate that the Protocol draws chemical herbicides within its prohibitions, any attempt by the United States to include such agents within the Protocol would be the result of its own policy determination, amounting to a self-denial of the use of the weapons. Such a determination is not compelled by the 1907 Hague Regulations, the Geneva Protocol of 1925 or the rules of customary international law.[98]

Consistent with its use of riot-control agents and chemical herbicides in Vietnam, the United States has maintained in United Nations discussions of the use of these chemicals that their use is lawful and is not prohibited by the Geneva Protocol of 1925. In 1965 the Soviet representative to the United Nations attacked the United States for using tear gas and herbicides in Vietnam; and on November 7, 1966, Hungary introduced a draft resolution calling for strict compliance by all states with the principles of the Geneva Protocol of 1925.[99] In sponsoring the resolution Hungary intended to censure the United States for using tear gas and herbicides in Vietnam. The United States supported the final resolution which, with the benefit of western amendments, merely "calls for strict observance by all States of the principles and objectives of the Geneva Protocol," condemns "all actions contrary to those objectives," and invites all states to accede to the Protocol.[100] In explaining its vote for the resolution and in responding to Soviet and Hungarian charges that the use by the United States of chemicals in Vietnam violated the principles of the Geneva Protocol, Ambassador Nabrit, the Deputy United States Representative, said:

> The Geneva Protocol of 1925 prohibits the use in war of asphyxiating and poisonous gas and other similar gases and liquids with equally deadly effects. It was framed to meet the horrors of poison gas warfare in the First World War and was intended to reduce suffering by prohibiting the use of poisonous gases such as mustard gas and phosgene. It does not apply to all gases. It would be unreasonable to contend that any rule of international law prohibits the use in combat against an enemy, for humanitarian purposes, of agents that Governments around the world commonly use to control riots by their own

[98] 10 Int' Leg. Mat. 1300, 1302-03 (1971).

[99] A/C.1/L.374, reprinted in Documents on Disarmament 694 (1966).

[100] G.A. Res. 2162B, 21 U.N. GAOR Supp. 16, at 11, U.N. Doc. A/6316 (1966).

people. Similarly, the Protocol does not apply to herbicides, which involve the same chemicals and have the same effects as those used domestically in the United States, the Soviet Union and many other countries to control weeds and other unwanted vegetation.[101]

On December 16, 1969, the General Assembly adopted a resolution submitted by Sweden that was intended to construe the Geneva Protocol to embody a rule of customary international law binding on all states, and to ban the use of tear gas and herbicides. The resolution recited "that the Geneva Protocol embodies the generally recognized rules of international law prohibiting the use in international armed conflicts of all biological and chemical methods of warfare, regardless of any technical developments. . . ."[102] It was adopted by a vote of eighty-to-three with thirty-six abstentions.[103] The United States voted against the resolution, along with Australia and Portugal, explaining its opposition on the dual grounds that a General Assembly resolution was not a proper vehicle for interpreting a multilateral treaty and that the conclusion in the resolution regarding what is prohibited under generally recognized rules of international law was erroneous in several respects. Specifically, Ambassador James F. Leonard, the United States Representative to the Conference of the Committee on Disarmament, objected to the inclusion of riot-control agents and chemical herbicides within the ban, the suggestion that the Protocol was a no-use rather than a no-first-use ban, and the shift from the Protocol language "in war" to the broader phrase "in international armed conflicts."[104]

The most recent and important pronouncement of United States CBW policy was President Nixon's declaration of November 25, 1969. As indicated previously, the President declared that the United States will not initiate the first use of lethal or incapacitating chemicals and will make no use of biological weapons or methods of warfare. Subsequently, he extended the biological ban to include toxins and referred the Geneva Protocol of 1925 to the Senate for advice and consent with the understanding that "it does not prohibit the use in war of riot-control agents and chemical herbicides."[105]

---

[101] Statement of United States Representative Nabrit to the U.N. General Assembly, Dec. 5, 1966, 21 U.N. GAOR A/P.V. 1484 U.N. Doc. —— (1966), *reprinted in* DOCUMENTS ON DISARMAMENT 800, 801 (1966).

[102] G.A. Res. 2603A, 24 U.N. GAOR SUPP. 30, at 16, U.N. Doc. A/7630 (1969).

[103] U.N. GAOR ——, U.N. Doc. —— ( ).

[104] 65 DEP'T STATE BULL. 505 (1971).

[105] For references *see* notes 1, 6 & 13 *supra*.

In testimony before the House Subcommittee on National Security Policy, Thomas R. Pickering, the Deputy Director of the State Department Bureau of Politico-Military Affairs, defined "riot control agents" as understood by the United States to be "those (*a*) producing transient effects—such as lachrymation, etc.—that disappear within minutes of removal from exposure and (*b*) are widely used by governments for domestic law enforcement purposes." [106] At least in their effects, such agents resemble "harassing agents," as defined by a World Health Organization (WHO) report. According to the WHO report, "[a] *harassing agent* (or short-term incapacitant) is one capable of causing a rapid disablement that lasts for little longer than the period of exposure." [107] The United States definition of "riot control agents" is more restrictive than the WHO definition of "harassing agents," since riot-control agents must be "widely used by governments for domestic law enforcement purposes." At the present time the only militarily significant agents in this category are CN and CS gas. Similarly, Mr. Pickering restricted the definition of "chemical herbicides" to "those chemical compounds which are (*a*) designed to be plant growth regulators, defoliants and desiccants, and (*b*) are used domestically within the United States in agriculture, weed control, and similar purposes." [108] This definition seems to preclude future use in war of those chemical herbicides, such as "Agent Orange," which are banned for domestic use within the United States.

The Vietnam experience has caused the United States to refine its earlier, more general, no-first-use policy, modifying it selectively to permit first use of some agents, and to prohibit any use of other agents. Under current policy the United States may not use biological weapons even to retaliate in kind, yet riot-control agents and chemical herbicides may be used on a first-use basis, so long as their use is otherwise consistent with the laws of war. From a legal perspective, at least the Executive seems to take the view that riot-control agents and chemical herbicides are permitted both by the Geneva Protocol and by customary

---

[106] Statement of Thomas R. Pickering, Deputy Director, Bureau of Politico-Military Affairs, Department of State, December 18, 1969, *Hearings on Chemical-Biological Warfare, supra* note 76, at 173, 177. Mr. Pickering defined incapacitating agents "as those producing symptoms—such as nausea, incoordination and general disorientation, etc.—that persist for hours or days after exposure to the agents has ceased." *Id.*

[107] *Health Effects of Possible Use of Chemical and Biological Weapons—Report of a WHO Group of Consultants, reprinted in Hearings On Chemical-Biological Warfare, supra* note 76, at 443, 445.

[108] Statement of Thomas R. Pickering, *supra* note 106, at 177.

international law.[109] Although not completely clear, it seems a reasonable inference from a variety of policy pronouncements that the United States views the first use of any other chemical or biological weapon as a violation of both the Protocol and customary international law.[110]

## AN EXAMINATION OF THE LEGAL EFFECTS OF THE GENEVA PROTOCOL

### Legal Restraints Binding on Non-Parties

A variety of legal restraints, stemming from both convention and customary international law, place restrictions on the use of CBW by non-parties to the Geneva Protocol. Though the United States is not a party and in fact opposed its adoption, the Hague Gas Declaration of 1899 prohibited "the use of projectiles the sole object of which is the diffusion of asphyxiating or deleterious gases." [111] The Hague Declaration proved largely ineffective during World War I, in part because projectiles were designed to spread shrapnel as well as gas, because gas was released from cylinders rather than "projectiles," and because the French claimed that the lachrymatory (tear) gas they used was not an "asphyxiating or deleterious" gas.[112] An example of the breakdown of

---

109 *See, e.g.,* Statement of John B. Rhinelander, Deputy Legal Adviser, Department of State, in *Hearings on Chemical-Biological Warfare, supra* note 76, at 200.

110 Policy pronouncements concerning a policy of no-first-use of lethal agents are not necessarily equivalent to statements of legal position, but when taken with the consistent *lack* of statements concerning lawfulness of first use of such agents they suggest that the United States views the first use of lethal agents as unlawful under both customary international law and the Protocol.

One specific pronouncement on the illegality of the use of lethal agents was made by Ambassador Goldberg in a letter dated Jul. 24, 1967, concerning charges that the United Arab Republic used poison gas in Yemen. Ambassador Goldberg said:

> The United States position on this matter is quite clear. . . . The use of poison gases is clearly contrary to international law and we would hope the authorities concerned in Yemen heed the request of the ICRC not to resort in any circumstances whatsoever to their use.

M. WHITEMAN, *supra* note 68 at 476. Ambassador Goldberg did not clarify whether this requirement was one of no use or no-*first*-use or was rooted in the Protocol or customary international law.

There is more doubt whether the United States takes the position that the first use of incapacitating agents would be a violation of customary international law. It seems a reasonable inference from the Administration's focus on the chemical riot-control and herbicide exceptions and the recent extension of the no-first-use policy to incapacitating agents that it is now the United States view that the first use of incapacitating agents would violate customary international law as well as the Protocol.

111 Declaration (IV 2) Concerning Asphyxiating Gases, *reprinted in* J. SCOTT, THE HAGUE CONVENTIONS AND DECLARATIONS OF 1899 AND 1907, 225-26 (3d ed. 1918).

112 *See* Bunn, *supra* note 41, at 375, 376.

the Hague Declaration occurred on April 22, 1915, during the second battle of Ypres when the Germans used cylinders rather than projectiles to release chlorine against the Allied lines in the first major gas attack of the War.[113]

Of greater contemporary importance than the Hague Gas Declaration are a variety of restrictions on the conduct of warfare embodied in the Hague Regulations of 1907,[114] which are equally applicable to some uses of CB agents. These restrictions include, among others, the Article 23 prohibitions against using "poison or poisoned weapons," killing or wounding "treacherously," and using "arms, projectiles, or material calculated to cause unnecessary suffering." Article 25 prohibits "the attack or bombardment, by whatever means, of towns, villages, dwellings, or buildings which are undefended." The Geneva Conventions of 1949[115] are also relevant to some possible uses; for example, Article 13 of the Convention Relative to the Treatment of Prisoners of War prohibits "[m]easures of reprisal against prisoners of war." [116] Although the Article 23 proscriptions may apply to some gases as weapons they probably do not prohibit the use of tear gas per se apart from individual uses which may cause unnecessary suffering or are otherwise prohibited.[117] Similarly, the Hague Article 25 prohibition and the Geneva proscrip-

---

[113] See S. HERSH, supra note 34, at 5-6.

[114] Convention Respecting the Laws and Customs of War on Land, Hague Convention No. IV and Annex, Oct. 18, 1907, in 2 TREATIES, CONVENTIONS, INT'L ACTS, PROTOCOLS AND AGREEMENTS BETWEEN THE UNITED STATES OF AMERICA AND OTHER POWERS, 1776-1909, 2269, 2285 (Malloy ed. 1910).

[115] The Geneva Convention for the Amelioration of the Wounded and the Sick in the Armed Forces in the Field, T.I.A.S. No. 3362 (1949); The Geneva Convention for the Amelioration of the Condition of Wounded, Sick, and Shipwrecked Members of Armed Forces at Sea, T.I.A.S. No. 3363 (1949); The Geneva Convention Relative to the Treatment of Prisoners of War, T.I.A.S. No. 3364 (1949); The Geneva Convention Relative to the Protection of Civilian Persons in Time of War, T.I.A.S. No. 3365 (1949).

[116] Similarly, Article 33 of the Geneva Civilian Convention prohibits "[r]eprisals against protected persons and their property."

[117] Scholars are divided on the question whether the Hague proscription of "poison or poisoned weapons" extends to modern CBW in general and if so to what agents. For a discussion of the literature see A. THOMAS & A. THOMAS, supra note 41, at 49-57. In an analysis which seems illustrative of the majority view Professor Erik Castrén indicates that the Hague prohibition of "poison or poisoned weapons" is rooted in "the idea that treacherous forms of warfare are unlawful." Accordingly he views "odorless and invisible poisonous gases" as unlawful but indicates that "the prohibition against poison does not extend to asphyxiating gases." E. CASTRÉN, THE PRESENT LAW OF WAR AND NEUTRALITY 194 (1954). The weight of authority would seem to be that at least CS and CN are not prohibited per se by the Hague Regulations.

tions against taking reprisals on civilians and prisoners of war are specific use restrictions rather than prohibitions against all uses of chemical or biological weapons. These Hague and Geneva rules are binding on the United States as a signatory, and at least the Hague rules have become, for the most part, customary international law.

The principal restrictions on the use per se of CBW by non-parties to the Geneva Protocol are those of customary international law. Though there is some scholarly opinion to the contrary, the weight of opinion seems to support the view that customary international law prohibits at least the first use of lethal chemical agents in war.[118] Thus, the recent use of lethal gases, including mustard and possibly nerve gas, by the United Arab Republic against Royalist villages in the Yemen Civil War was condemned by a number of spokesmen as a violation of international law and was supported by no one. Egypt simply denied any such use and invited an investigation.[119] It also seems reasonably clear that customary international law prohibits the first use of lethal biological agents in war, though this may not have been as clear before the recent 1966 and 1969 United Nations resolutions.[120] A good case

---

[118] *See, e.g.,* Baxter & Buergenthal, *supra* note 47, at 853. Professors Baxter and Buergenthal do not qualify their statement by a first-use restriction. Their view is: "[t]he weight of opinion appears today to favor the view that customary international law proscribes the use in war of lethal chemical and biological weapons." *Id.* at 853. In view of the widespread no-first-use reservation to the Protocol, the principal evidence of the scope of the customary prohibition, it seems clear only that the first use of such lethal chemicals is prohibited. *See,* Bunn, *supra* note 41, at 388.

Some scholars indicate in general terms that the Geneva Protocol is so universally recognized that it "must be regarded as binding the community of nations independently of treaty obligation." *See, e.g.,* M. GREENSPAN, THE MODERN LAW OF LAND WARFARE 354 (1959). This view, though a majority view, offers little assistance in precisely delineating the scope of the customary law prohibition.

Some scholars, however, such as Professor Howard S. Levie, have taken the position that there is no accepted rule of customary international law which prohibits the use of chemical weapons. Letter from Professor Howard S. Levie to Professor John Norton Moore, Feb. 28, 1972.

[119] See the discussion of the use of gas warfare in the Yemen Civil War in A. THOMAS & A. THOMAS, *supra* note 41, at 151-53. *See also* Levie, *Some Major Inadequacies in the Existing Law Relating to the Protection of Individuals During Armed Conflict,* in WHEN BATTLE RAGES, HOW CAN LAW PROTECT? (Working Paper and Proceedings of the Fourteenth Hammarskjöld Forum, J. Carey ed. 1971) 1, 17.

Italy used gas against Ethiopia during the 1930's. In League debates Italy admitted the use and claimed that it was a lawful reprisal for earlier violations of the law of war by Ethiopia. *See* A. THOMAS & A. THOMAS, *supra* note 41, at 141-43.

[120] *See, e.g.,* Baxter & Buergenthal, *supra* note 47, at 853; Bunn, *supra* note 41, at 388. Writing in 1962 Professor William O'Brien concluded that customary international law prohibits "the first use of chemical weapons" but not "biological warfare." O'Brien,

can also be made that the customary international norm is evolving to prohibit the first use of incapacitating chemicals in war and all use of biological agents in war.[121] It is unclear whether the customary rule prohibits all use in war of lethal or incapacitating chemical agents, but the customary rule probably does not prohibit all use in war of riot-control agents or chemical herbicides. Though the 1969 General Assembly Resolution suggests that all of these categories are prohibited, such a broad prohibition is questionable both in view of state practice and the terms of the Geneva Protocol as evidence of customary international law.

Most statements of the customary law norm, such as that in the 1969 General Assembly Resolution, purport broadly to prohibit "the use" of CBW. But the Geneva Protocol itself, which is evidence of the customary law norm, has been qualified by a common reservation in effect limiting the Protocol to a no-first-use convention for most treaty relations. Since reprisals in kind are still permitted for prior violation of the laws of war, possibly the principal difference between a customary law of no use and a customary law of no-*first*-use is merely whether the requirements of reprisal law (such as prior diplomatic protest and proportionality of response) must be followed before retaliating with otherwise prohibited CB agents, or whether prior violation permits unrestricted retaliation with CB agents other than as prohibited by specific use restrictions.[122]

---

*Biological/Chemical Warfare and the International Law of War*, 51 Geo. L.J. 1, 59 (1962). See generally the discussion of the authorities in Bunn, *supra* note 41, at 386 n.57.

[121] With respect to the use of biological weapons, Professor Castrén, for example, urges that "[g]eneral opinion seems to condemn bacteriological warfare even more severely than the use of gas." E Castrén, *supra* note 117, at 195. See also M. Greenspan, *supra* note 118, at 358. The Draft Convention on the Prohibition of Biological and Toxin Weapons would, of course, prohibit the development, production and stockpiling of biological and toxin weapons. This is some additional evidence that a customary norm is developing which would also prohibit any use in war of biological or biologically derived toxin weapons.

[122] George Bunn suggests that the customary law requirements of a lawful reprisal must still be followed "even if the obligations of the protocol are suspended by the terms of paragraph two [the no-first-use reservation]." Bunn, *supra* note 41, at 393 n.82. *But see* Baxter & Buergenthal, *supra* note 47, at 872-73. It would seem equally plausible that the specific reservation would govern rather than the more generalized customary law of reprisals in cases where the contending belligerents are both parties to the Protocol. Possibly the applicability of the law of reprisal depends on whether the use is prohibited by customary international law as well as by the Protocol and, if so, on the scope of the customary norm.

The position of the United States is that riot-control agents and chemical herbicides are not prohibited by any rule of customary international law. Judging by their vote with the United States against General Assembly Resolution 2603A, Australia and Portugal seem to support this position.[123] Moreover, both Japan—in ratifying the Geneva Protocol with an informal understanding that it does not ban use of riot-control agents[124]—and Great Britain—in announcing the understanding of the British government that the use of CS "smoke" is not prohibited by the Geneva Protocol[125]—seem *a fortiori* to have adopted the view that no rule of customary international law prohibits the use of riot-control agents (in Britain's case, CS gas) per se. On the other hand, Resolution 2603A—which uses deliberately broad language both to include tear gas and herbicides and to declare that such coverage constitutes "generally recognized rules of international law . . ." and which was adopted by an overwhelming vote of eighty to three, with thirty-six abstentions—provides some evidence that the customary rule is a broad one. But since almost one third of the states that voted either voted against the resolution or abstained, the vote is perhaps another indication that the customary law concerning tear gas and herbicides is unclear. Moreover, the states dissenting or abstaining included most of the NATO members and many major or significant military powers, such as the United States, France, Great Britain, Italy, Japan, Belgium, Canada and Nationalist China, whose views would be particularly important in shaping a norm of customary international law. Since the Geneva Protocol of 1925 is to some extent a law-creating (or recognizing) convention, the interpretation given the Protocol and the number and identity of the parties to the Protocol will also have a significant effect on the scope and strength of the customary international law rule. The scope and strength of the Protocol regime is not, however, automatically transferable to the customary norm. This caveat applies to reliance on any multilateral treaty to infer customary international law, but it is particularly applicable when the treaty contains a common reservation expressly limiting its binding legal effect to relations between the parties to the treaty, as does the Protocol.

---

[123] 24 U.N. GAOR ——, U.N. Doc. —— (    ).

[124] *See* the testimony of Secretary of State William P. Rogers before the Senate Foreign Relations Committee, March 5, 1971.

[125] 795 Parl. Deb. (Hansard), H.C. No. 50, at 18 (Written Answers to Questions, 1970). For a fuller version of Mr. Stewart's statement, see text at note 173 *infra*. *See also* Carlton & Sims, *The CS Gas Controversy: Great Britain and the Geneva Protocol of 1925*, 13 SURVIVAL 333 (1971).

## Further Legal Restraints Binding on Parties

The Geneva Protocol binds parties "as between themselves" not to "use in war . . . asphyxiating, poisonous or other gases, and . . . all analogous liquids, materials or devices," and not to use "bacteriological methods of warfare." Though by its terms it purports to prohibit any use in war of the agents within its scope, at least thirty-eight states have entered a reservation that the Protocol shall cease to be binding with respect to any enemy state that violates the Protocol or whose allies violate the Protocol.[126] Thus, at least in situations in which at least one of the actors has entered such a reservation, the Protocol is in effect a no-first-use ban. If none of the actors has entered such a reservation, the general treaty rule permitting parties specially affected by a material breach to suspend the operation of the treaty in whole or in part against the defaulting state might sometimes allow roughly the same result.[127] In any event, the Protocol clearly does not prohibit the development, testing, manufacturing or stockpiling of gas and biological weapons but only their use. In fact, it has been widely suggested that one of the chief sanctions that prevented the use of chemical, and possibly biological, warfare in World War II, and which supports the efficacy of the Protocol regime in general, is the availability of a retaliatory capability.

## Reservations to the Protocol

At least thirty-eight states have entered one or both of two general reservations to the Protocol. These reservations seem to be modelled on the French reservations, France being the first state to ratify the Protocol.[128] The French reservations are:

> 1. The said protocol shall be binding on the Government of the French Republic only with respect to the States which have signed and ratified it or which have acceded to it;

---

[126] See the Reservations to the Protocol collected in MESSAGE FROM THE PRESIDENT, supra note 10, at 5-8.

[127] As evidence of this general rule, see Convention on the Law of Treaties, opened for signature at Vienna, May 23, 1969, Art. 60, par. 2(b), U.N.Doc. A/CONF. 39/27 (1969) [hereinafter the Vienna Convention]. Professors Baxter and Buergenthal discuss a variety of ways in which the no-first-use reservation might permit greater latitude in response to a first use than would the general treaty rule. See also the Vienna Convention, Art. 60 pars. 2(c), and 5.

[128] See Bunn, supra note 41, at 389.

2. The said protocol shall automatically cease to be binding on the Government of the French Republic with respect to any enemy State whose armed forces or whose allies fail to respect the interdictions which form the subject of this protocol.[129]

There are a variety of minor variations on both themes, none of which seems particularly desirable, or in most circumstances even meaningful. For example, Great Britain substitutes for the first reservation: "The said protocol shall be binding on His Britannic Majesty only with respect to the Powers and States which have signed and ratified it or which have acceded to it permanently." [130] The modification, "acceded to it *permanently*," rather than the simpler "acceded to it" of the French formula, would be significant only in the as yet non-existent circumstance of a temporarily qualified accession or a notification of future withdrawal. Canada adopts the "acceded to it permanently" language of the British change and adds the words "de jure" or "de facto" to qualify "allies" in the second reservation.[131] Since "allies" would without qualification seem to include both de jure and de facto allies this Canadian modification also seems otiose. And Spain and the People's Republic of China use the language "subject to reciprocity." [132]

One important exception is the more limited reservation of the Netherlands which reserves the right to retaliate only with chemical, not biological, weapons in case of prior violation by an enemy state or its allies.[133] And one special reservation of regional importance is that of Syria, which has entered a reservation declaring:

> The accession of the Syrian Arab Republic to this protocol and its ratification by its Government shall in no case signify recognition of Israel and could not lead to establishing relations with the latter concerning the provisions prescribed by this protocol.[134]

Since the Protocol contains the language, "the High Contracting Parties . . . agree to be bound as between themselves," and "each Power will be bound as regards other Powers," the first common reservation seems redundant except, perhaps, as emphasis to negate any possible

---

[129] The French reservation is reprinted in MESSAGE FROM THE PRESIDENT, *supra* note 10, at 6.

[130] *Id*. at 5.

[131] *Id*. at 6.

[132] *Id*. at 6, 7.

[133] *Id*. at 6.

[134] *Id*. at 7.

inference that non-parties may benefit from the Protocol regime. Perhaps without this first reservation, the Protocol would have had a greater effect in bringing about, or at least evidencing, a customary international prohibition; but this difference seems minimal, and even if the parties had omitted the first reservation, the differential impact on the development of customary international law would have depended more on the intention of the parties in not filing the reservation.

The second common reservation may be of major importance in making clear that the treaty imposes a no-first-use obligation, rather than a no-use obligation, and in allowing retaliation for a violation by an ally of an enemy state as well as by the enemy state itself. Since, at least by the terms of the French model of the second reservation, prior violation causes the Protocol to "automatically cease to be binding" on the reserving state, it is not clear that retaliation must be either in kind or proportional to the initial violation. This point can be enormously significant when a state erroneously assesses the scope of prohibited agents, or uses an agent in good faith which it, but not the opposing belligerent, interprets the Protocol to permit.[135]

### The Scope of the Protocol: Riot-Control Agents

The principal uncertainties in the scope of the Protocol are whether its prohibition extends to riot-control agents (agents commonly in use by domestic police forces for riot-control purposes) and chemical herbicides (plant growth regulators, defoliants, and desiccants). There is also a significant grouping of issues concerning the threshold of applicability of the Protocol "in war." Occasionally a question is raised concerning the inclusion of weapons employing fire and smoke. Interpretation of the Protocol on each of these issues may easily be confused with the related task of interpreting the scope of the customary international law prohibition. But whereas the customary rule is evidenced by the practice and *opinio juris* of all states, both parties and non-parties to the Protocol, the scope of the Protocol is evidenced by the terms of the Protocol, and if the terms are unclear, by the preparatory work, the context of its conclusion, and the subsequent practice of the parties.[136]

---

135 See note 122 *supra*.

136 *See* the Vienna Convention, *supra* note 127, Art. 31, par. 1, Art. 31, par. 3(b), and Art. 32. For a broader analysis of the problem of treaty interpretation, see M. McDougal, H. Lasswell & J. Miller, The Interpretation of Agreements and World Public Order (1967).

Considering first the interpretation of the Protocol with respect to riot-control agents, the English language version of the Protocol prohibits "the use in war of asphyxiating, poisonous or other gases, and of all analogous liquids, materials or devices." The language "or other gases" seems broad enough to prohibit an harassing agent, such as tear gas, which is admittedly not an "asphyxiating" or "poisonous" gas. But it may be urged in favor of a restrictive interpretation that by the principle of *ejusdem generis* "other gases" should be similar to those enumerated, *i.e.* similarly deleterious as "asphyxiating" or "poisonous" gas, and that the relatively mild riot-control agents are thus not included. It may also be urged in favor of a restrictive interpretation that the purpose of the Protocol is to eliminate weapons which cause unnecessary suffering and that the retention rather than the prohibition of tear gas would best serve this purpose. Finally, it may be noted that the equally authentic French text prohibits the use in war of *gaz asphyxiantes, toxiques ou similaires*. That is, *similaires* must mean gas with an effect on man similar to that of toxic or asphyxiating gas and thus could not include tear gas which is much less deleterious.[137]

The principle of *ejusdem generis* would certainly suggest that "other gases" should be interpreted to permit the use in war of helium for barrage balloons. But it is unclear under the principle whether the kind of similarity required would be a seriously deleterious effect on man, as the argument to exclude riot-control agents requires, or any toxic effect on man, an interpretation which would still include such agents. And in response to the argument based on the French text, it has been said: "Those who espouse this argument overlook the fact that the phrase '*gaz toxiques*' includes, as a matter of French usage, all chemical weapons that are employed for their toxic effect on living organisms. It thus applies to such irritant chemicals as tear gas." [138] One difficulty with this latter interpretation is that if *gaz toxiques* was meant initially to be an all inclusive category, the specific companion prohibitions of *gaz asphyxiantes . . . ou similaires* would seem superfluous. Another interpretation that could reconcile the French and English texts yet still support a broad interpretation banning tear gas is that the term "*similaires*" might have been meant to qualify the broad prohibition against the use of all gas "in war" to prohibit only the use of gas in any form as a weapon against man (and possibly the use against plants as well)

---

137 *See generally* Bunn, *supra* note 41, at 394-99.

138 Baxter & Buergenthal, *supra* note 47, at 856 n.16.

but not to prohibit other uses of gas "in war" such as the use of helium in barrage balloons.

On balance, neither the textual arguments supporting a restrictive interpretation that would permit riot-control agents, nor a broad interpretation that would prohibit such agents seems wholly persuasive, and the answer, if any, must lie in the history of the Protocol and the subsequent practice and interpretation of the parties.

Lachrymatory gases were well known to the draftsmen of the Protocol. It has been estimated that 12,000 tons of lachrymators were used in World War I, and by 1925 tear gas was also being used by domestic police agencies.[139] A League of Nations report on the effects of chemical and biological weapons prepared by a group of experts in 1924 divided the known chemical agents used in war into three classes—toxic agents, suffocating or asphyxiating agents, and irritant agents, which category was said to include lachrymatory, sneeze-producing, and blistering agents.[140] It should also be recalled that the Hague Gas Declaration of 1899 prohibited "the use of projectiles the sole object of which is the diffusion of *asphyxiating or deleterious gases*," and that this vague language gave rise during World War I to a debate concerning whether tear gas was included. The British and French both contended that it was not. Some German writers, on the other hand, urged that the French had violated the Hague Declaration in World War I by first employing tear gas projectiles and that this justified the subsequent German chlorine attack at Ypres.[141]

In light of the then existing knowledge of tear gas and the World War I debate about the scope of the Hague Gas Declaration, the drafting history of the Protocol is remarkably unclear with respect to the inclusion of tear gas. There seems to be no record of a discussion of tear gas by the delegates at the 1925 Geneva Conference.[142] Congressman Theodore F. Burton, the American representative, did express "the very earnest desire of the Government and people of the United States that

---

139 *See* Baxter & Buergenthal, *supra* note 47, at 857; Bunn, *supra* note 41, at 397.

140 *See* LEAGUE OF NATIONS OFF. J., Spec. Supp. 26, at 122-24 (1924).

141 For an analysis of the German case, see A. THOMAS & A. THOMAS, *supra* note 41, at 140-41.

142 *See* Baxter & Buergenthal, *supra* note 47, at 861; Bunn, *supra* note 41, at 402. Professor Bunn urges,

> If [the delegates] . . . had been determined to prohibit gases the experts had said were in use by police departments to prevent loss of life, they might have been expected to do so more explicitly, or at least to have discussed the point.

*Id.* at 402.

some provision be inserted in this Convention relating to the use of asphyxiating, poisonous, and deleterious gases," [143] a possibly non-restrictive but nevertheless vague formula, mildly reminiscent of the Hague Gas Declaration. Moreover, the report of the legal committee used the language "asphyxiating, poisonous or other similar gases," [144] and another committee described the prohibited class as "asphyxiating, poisonous and other deleterious gases." [145] These latter formulations also mildly suggest a non-restrictive interpretation that would permit tear gas, but they are hardly conclusive. This evidence of a non-restrictive interpretation is somewhat offset by the apparent assumption during the United States Senate debate on ratification that the Protocol banned the use of tear gas.[146] Since the final language of the Protocol was taken from that used in the Treaty of Versailles and subsequently adopted in Article Five of the 1922 Treaty of Washington, an analysis of the negotiating history of these treaties may be suggestive (but again hardly conclusive) of the interpretation attached to this language by the draftsmen at the Geneva Conference.[147]

Article 171 of the Treaty of Versailles provided that "the use of asphyxiating, poisonous or other gases and all analogous liquids, materials or devices being prohibited, their manufacture and importation are strictly forbidden in Germany." An earlier draft, which had been approved in principle by the foreign ministers and heads of government, used the language "Production or use of asphyxiating, poisonous or similar gases . . . are forbidden." [148] There is no record of a discussion of tear gas at the Conference or evidence that the change to arguably more restrictive language was felt to be significant.[149] It has been argued in favor of a permissive interpretation, moreover, that the gases prohibited against "manufacture and importation" in Germany were, by the language of the Treaty, already "prohibited" and that since the use of tear gas per se was neither prohibited by the Hague

---

[143] LEAGUE OF NATIONS, PROCEEDINGS OF THE CONFERENCE FOR THE SUPERVISION OF THE INTERNATIONAL TRADE IN ARMS AND AMMUNITION AND IN THE IMPLEMENTS OF WAR 155 (1925).

[144] *Id.* at 745.

[145] *Id.* at 596.

[146] 68 CONG. REC. 150 (1926).

[147] On the background of the Protocol language, see generally Baxter & Buergenthal, *supra* note 47, at 860-61.

[148] 4 FOREIGN RELATIONS OF THE UNITED STATES, THE PARIS PEACE CONFERENCE 1919 232 (1943).

[149] Bunn, *supra* note 41, at 398.

Gas Declaration of 1899 nor by the Hague Regulations of 1907, the treaty did not prohibit all use of tear gas by Germany.[150] This argument, though carrying some weight, may prove too much. At least certain uses of any gas, including tear gas (such as the use in projectiles or a use in any manner to cause unnecessary suffering) were prohibited by the time of Versailles; yet the somewhat mysterious declaration in the Versailles Treaty did not explain why any chemical agents were already prohibited apart from such uses. Another argument for an intepretation of the Versailles language which would permit the use of riot-control agents points out that the French text of Article 171 uses the word *similaires* for *other*, as does the French text of the 1922 Washington Treaty and the Geneva Protocol. But as the loose translation into French of Article 172 of the Treaty suggests, it would be a mistake to place great weight on the discrepancy between the English and French texts.[151]

To summarize the evidence bearing on interpretation of the Geneva Protocol from the language and history of the Versailles Treaty, it seems most accurate to say that the draftsmen of the Versailles Treaty did not specifically advert to the problem whether tear gas was to be included and that the language is inconclusive. Even if the draftsmen at Versailles had shared one or another interpretation, it by no means follows that the draftsmen at Geneva would have been aware of that interpretation when they adopted the then widely accepted language of the Versailles and Washington Treaties. This conclusion seems particularly true in view of the nuance relied upon by contemporary advocates of one or another interpretation.

Though there was no specific discussion of tear gas at Versailles or Geneva, the issue was raised during the drafting of the 1922 Washington Treaty. Again the Conference adopted the Versailles formula and the issue was not explicitly resolved, though several pertinent reports were available to the Conference. One report from the technical experts of the negotiating countries, which included the input of a United States

---

150 *See* Bunn, *supra* note 41, at 398-99.

151 Developing this argument, Professors Baxter and Buergenthal indicate
[t]hat little significance can be attached to the slight divergency between the English and French texts of Article 171 is apparent, moreover, from the language of Article 172 of the treaty. It required Germany to disclose to the Allies "the nature and make of all explosives, toxic substances or other *like* chemical preparations used by them in the war. . . ." The French text of Article 172 renders the more restrictive "or other like chemical preparations" simply as "ou *autres* preparations chemiques."
Baxter & Buergenthal, *supra* note 47, at 858.

expert, concluded, as a compromise between those experts who favored gas weapons and those who did not, that the only "practicable" limitation was to "prohibit the use of gases against cities and other large bodies of noncombatants . . . ." [152] But the reports of the Advisory Committee to the American Delegation and of the Navy General Board not only urged a broader use prohibition on gas warfare, but also specifically concluded that tear gas should be banned because of the difficulty in distinguishing between categories of gases. The Advisory Committee recommended that "chemical warfare, including the use of gases, whether toxic or non toxic, should be prohibited by international agreement." [153] And the Report of the Navy General Board concluded, "[t]he General Board believes it to be sound policy to prohibit gas warfare in every form and against every objective, and so recommends." [154] Despite these recommendations that tear gas be included in any ban, the resolution actually offered by the United States and adopted by the Conference used the Versailles formula; and the remarks of Secretary of State Hughes and Senator Elihu Root in offering the resolution did not make it clear whether it was intended to include tear gas.[155] Scholars suggesting an interpretation of the Treaty of Washington that would have permitted the use of tear gas have relied on a restrictively worded statement by Secretary of State Hughes that the American delegation "felt that it should present the recommendation that the use of asphyxiating or poison gas be absolutely prohibited." They have also relied on an understanding by Senator Root that the Versailles Treaty, which was adopted as the model for the resolution, was a restatement of the ban on poison gases "which had been adopted during the course of the Hague Conferences." [156] On the other hand, scholars suggesting a broad interpretation that would have prohibited tear gas have noted the two reports specifically contending that tear gas should be banned and have urged that in view of Secretary Hughes' presenting these reports to the Conference, it would be "most unlikely that a government which believed that Article 5 did not outlaw all forms of chemical warfare would have failed to states its views to the Conference." [157]

---

152 CONFERENCE ON THE LIMITATION OF ARMAMENT, *supra* note 44, at 384-85.

153 *Id*. at 386.

154 *Id*. at 387.

155 *Id*. at 387-88.

156 *See* Bunn, *supra* note 41, at 400. Professor Bunn adds: "these [the Hague rules] probably were never intended to apply to tear gases." *Id*. at 400.

157 Baxter & Buergenthal, *supra* note 47, at 860.

On balance, it seems that the principal issue at the 1922 Conference was whether chemical weapons in general were worse than other categories of weapons and should thus be banned. Once this issue was decided affirmatively the delegates as a whole were insufficiently concerned with whether tear gas should be included in the ban to make the record clear. In any event, the sketchy record of the discussion at the 1922 Conference seems a flimsy reed upon which to base either a permissive or a restrictive interpretation of the Geneva Protocol, which was adopted at a subsequent Conference.

If the negotiating history of the Protocol is inconclusive on whether the Protocol prohibits the use of riot-control agents, subsequent interpretations by the parties reveal both a continuing dispute on whether tear gas is prohibited and that today more parties support an interpretation prohibiting riot-control agents than support an interpretation permitting such agents. During its 1930 meetings, the Preparatory Commission for the League of Nations Disarmament Conference considered a draft disarmament provision that would have prohibited the "use in war of asphyxiating, poisonous or similar gases." The substitution of "similar," apparently derived from the French text of the Geneva Protocol, for "other," which was the English version, engendered some concern that the draft was not intended to outlaw irritant or tear gases. In response to this concern the British delegation declared:

> Basing itself on this English text [of the Geneva Protocol], the British Government have taken the view that the use in war of "other" gases, including lachrymatory gases, was prohibited. They also considered that the intention was to incorporate the same prohibition in the present Convention.[158]

And in response to a British request for opinions of the other powers on the subject the French Delegation agreed:

> All the texts at present in force or proposed in regard to the prohibition of the use in war of asphyxiating, poisonous or similar gases are identical. In the French delegation's opinion, they apply to all gases employed with a view to toxic action on the human organism, whether the effects of such action are more or less temporary irritation of certain mucuous membranes or whether they cause serious or fatal lesions. . . .

[158] LEAGUE OF NATIONS, DOCUMENTS OF THE PREPARATORY COMMISSION FOR THE DISARMAMENT CONFERENCE (SERIES X): MINUTES OF THE SIXTH SESSION (SECOND PART) 311 (1931).

The French Government therefore considers that the use of lachrymatory gases is covered by the prohibition arising out of the Geneva Protocol. . . .[159]

Delegations from Canada, China, Czechoslovakia, Italy, Japan, Romania, Spain, Turkey, Yugoslavia, and the USSR also agreed with the British interpretation, and at the time eight of these states were parties to the Protocol.[160] Czechoslovakia subsequently became a party in 1938 and Japan became a party in 1970, though with an informal understanding that the Protocol did not prohibit the use of tear gas. The remaining six states that were both party to the Protocol and members of the Preparatory Commission did not respond to the British request for an opinion.[161] Although as has been pointed out, Hugh Gibson, the United States representative to the Preparatory Commission, took issue with the Franco-British interpretation, the United States was not a party to the Protocol and Mr. Gibson's remarks seemed addressed more to the coverage of the proposed new draft than to an interpretation of the Protocol. In any event, the exchange of views provided an opportunity for ten of the twenty-eight states then party to the Protocol to indicate their support for a broad interpretation prohibiting lachrymatory gases. Furthermore, no party to the Protocol had publicly adopted an interpretation permitting such gases. The Preparatory Commission, however, reported in 1931 that "it was unable to express a definite opinion on this question of interpretation." [162]

The subsequent Disarmament Conference accepted the broad ban suggested by the Special Committee appointed to consider CBW. The ban included

all natural or synthetic noxious substances, whatever their state, whether solid, liquid or gaseous, whether toxic, asphyxiating, lachrymatory, irritant, vesicant, or capable in any way of producing harmful effects on the human or animal organism, whatever the method of their use.[163]

---

[159] *Id.*

[160] *Id.* at 311-14.

[161] *Id.*

[162] DEP'T STATE, REPORT OF THE PREPARATORY COMMISSION FOR THE DISARMAMENT CONFERENCE 45 (1931). The Commission went on to say: "[v]ery many delegations, however, stated that they were prepared to approve the interpretation suggested in the British Government's memorandum." *Id.*

[163] I LEAGUE OF NATIONS, CONFERENCE FOR THE REDUCTION AND LIMITATION OF ARMAMENTS: CONFERENCE DOCUMENTS 210, 214 (1932).

The United States representative to the Conference agreed to this broad ban, which was apparently adopted because of the concern over the difficulty of differentiating chemical agents on the basis of their relative harmfulness.[164] Although the Disarmament Commission ultimately failed to reach agreement on general disarmament, and although the Commission was not interpreting the Geneva Protocol, the apparent consensus within the Special Committee that tear gas should be banned is another indication of the willingness of at least some of the parties to the Protocol to prohibit the use of tear gas in war. The failure of any of the parties to the Protocol to use tear gas in combat situations during World War II or the Korean War may lend further support to an interpretation that the Protocol prohibits the use of tear gas as well as other chemical agents.

The use by the United States of riot-control agents and chemical herbicides in the Indo-China War precipitated a new round of debates concerning the correct interpretation of the Protocol even though neither the United States nor (unless bound by the French ratification of May 9, 1926) North Vietnam, South Vietnam, Laos and Cambodia are party to the Protocol. Thus, in November 1966 Hungary, which has been a party to the Protocol since 1952, introduced a draft resolution in the First Committee of the United Nations General Assembly calling for compliance by all states with the principles of the Geneva Protocol. In explaining its resolution Hungary made clear its view that the gases and herbicides used by the United States in Vietnam were prohibited by the Protocol.[165] During the course of debate the initial Hungarian draft—which declared that the Protocol "prohibits the use of chemical and bacteriological weapons"[166]—was altered to render ambiguous the scope of the Protocol ban.[167] George Bunn has written of these and subsequent United Nations debates during 1966, 1967, and 1968:

> In the 1966, 1967, and 1968 debates in the United Nations General Assembly and the Geneva Disarmament Conference, only the Soviet Union and its allies actively opposed the United States position that tear gases in war did not violate the protocol. Belgium agreed with the American view. The French, without mentioning tear gases, hinted that they no longer believed in giving the protocol the broad interpre-

---

164 *See* the references cited in Baxter & Buergenthal, *supra* note 47, at 864 n.56.

165 21 U.N. GAOR A/C.1/1451, U.N. Doc. —— (    ).

166 DOCUMENTS ON DISARMAMENT 694, 695 (1966).

167 G.A. Res. 2162B, 21 U.N. GAOR SUPP. 16, at 11, U.N. Doc. A/6316 (1966).

tion they had given it in the 1930's. The United Kingdom and Kenya referred to the opposing views on tear gas without taking sides. Most countries, however, remained silent.[168]

Australia, which has been a party to the Protocol since 1930, and which has used tear gas in Vietnam, also supported the American position that "the use of . . . riot control agents, herbicides and defoliants does not contravene the Geneva Protocol nor customary international law."[169] But if "only the Soviet Union and its allies actively opposed the United States position," the lack of active support from more than one or two states for the United States interpretation did not on balance strengthen the case for permissive interpretation.

That the tide was running against the permissive interpretation was even more evident in 1969 when the United Nations General Assembly adopted a resolution sponsored by Sweden and eleven other states (ten of the twelve sponsors being parties to the Protocol) which was clearly intended to interpret the Protocol to prohibit tear gas and anti-plant chemicals. The resolution declared

> contrary to the generally recognized rules of international law, as embodied in the [Geneva] Protocol . . . the use in international armed conflicts of:
> (a) Any chemical agents of warfare—chemical substances, whether gaseous, liquid or solid—which might be employed because of their direct toxic effects on man, animals or plants . . . .[170]

The resolution was adopted by a vote of eighty-to-three with thirty-six abstentions. Australia, Portugal and the United States cast the three opposing votes. Portugal, like Australia, has been a party to the Protocol since 1930. Of the states that supported the Swedish resolution forty-one are party to the Protocol, and among those abstaining on the vote thirty-three are party to the Protocol. Since less than half of the states presently party to the Protocol expressed by their vote approval of a broad interpretation prohibiting tear gas and herbicides, and since more than one-third of the parties to the Protocol abstained, the resolution should not be deemed a conclusive interpretation of the Protocol.[171]

---

168 Bunn, *supra* note 41, at 404-05.

169 *See* 24 U.N. GAOR A/C.1/1716 at 82, 87, U.N. Doc. ——— (Provisional 1969).

170 G.A. Res. 2603A, 24 U.N. GAOR SUPP. 30, at 16, U.N. Doc. A/7630 (1969).

171 Abstaining countries included such militarily and industrially significant countries as Britain, France, Canada, Japan and many NATO members. France and perhaps

The interpretive effect of such a vote is further obfuscated by the nature of votes on General Assembly resolutions: such votes need express neither an instructed opinion on all of the included issues nor a position intended to be legally binding on the voting state. Nevertheless, comparing the forty-one parties voting in favor with the two parties voting against indicates that a broad interpretation prohibiting tear gas and herbicides has substantially greater support among the parties than does a restrictive interpretation.

Though not nearly as relevant in interpreting the Protocol as the subsequent interpretations of the parties, it is by no means politically irrelevant that thirty-nine non-parties to the Protocol also voted in favor of a broad interpretation while only one non-party voted against it. Moreover, in his preface to the 1969 *United Nations Report on Chemical and Biological Weapons*, United Nations Secretary-General U Thant urged United Nations members

> [t]o make a clear affirmation that the prohibition contained in the Geneva Protocol applies to the use in war of all chemical, bacteriological and biological agents (including tear gas and other harassing agents), which now exist or which may be developed in the future.[172]

Two recent interpretations suggest, however, that despite the 1969 General Assembly resolution and the invitation of the Secretary-General, the dispute about the scope of the Geneva Protocol is still alive. On February 2, 1970, Michael Stewart, the British Secretary of State for Foreign and Commonwealth Affairs, announced to Parliament that although the British government had not changed its position that tear gases are prohibited by the Protocol, it did not interpret this ban as extending to CS—the principal tear gas relied on by the United States in Vietnam and by Great Britain in Northern Ireland. By way of explanation Mr. Stewart said:

> [M]odern technology has developed CS smoke which, unlike the tear gas available in 1930, is considered to be not significantly harmful to man in other than wholly exceptional circumstances; and we regard

---

other states in this group apparently agreed with the purpose of the resolution but disagreed with its legality as a method of interpreting the Protocol. *See generally* Gellner & Wu, *supra* note 50, at 24-26.

172 *Report of the Secretary-General on Chemical and Bacteriological (Biological) Weapons and the Effects of Their Possible Use*, U.N. Doc. A/7575; A/7575/Rev. 1 (1969), at xii.

CS and other such gases accordingly as being outside the scope of the Geneva Protocol. CS is in fact less toxic than the screening smokes which the 1930 statement specifically excluded.[173]

Mr. Stewart's attempt to demonstrate that the British position has not changed is painfully tortured, but the shift by an important party to the Protocol away from a position staunchly supporting a broad interpretation demonstrates that the issue is not yet resolved.

The second such recent interpretation was that of the Japanese government in ratifying the Protocol in May, 1970. In the debates in the Diet the Japanese government indicated that Japan interpreted the Protocol to permit the use in war of riot-control agents.[174]

To summarize the legal effect of the Geneva Protocol with respect to riot control agents, the text and negotiating history of the Protocol are inconclusive. Subsequent interpretations of the Protocol by the parties indicate that the question whether these agents are included is still open, but that substantially greater support exists for a broad interpretation prohibiting such agents than for a restrictive interpretation permitting such agents.

### The Scope of the Protocol: Chemical Herbicides

A second question regarding the scope of the Protocol is whether chemical herbicides are included. Chemical herbicides, such as those used by the United States in the Indo-China War, were developed toward the end of World War II. Not surprisingly, a 1924 study initiated by the League of Nations indicates that experts were not then aware of any chemical agents harmful to plants, even though there was some concern about possible biological agents harmful to crops.[175] Many of these chemicals, developed during World War II, are now used domestically in small quantities to control unwanted vegetation. Their use by the United States in Vietnam is their first and only use in war to date. Initially such chemicals were assumed to be harmless to man and the environment. Evidence available within the last few years indicates that many such chemicals may have direct and more subtle synergistic

---

173 795 Parl. Deb. (Hansard), H.C. No. 50, at 18 (Written Answers to Questions 1970). *See also* Meselson & Baxter, *Use of Tear Gas in War: An American View,* The Times (London), Feb. 12, 1970, at 11, col. 3 (letter to the editor).

174 Testimony of Secretary of State William P. Rogers before the Senate Foreign Relations Committee, March 5, 1971.

175 LEAGUE OF NATIONS OFF. J., Spec. Supp. 26, at 121, 124, 126 (1924).

effects harmful to man and that at least in quantities and combinations used in war they may produce long lasting adverse ecological effects.[176] Both the late development of such chemicals and the recent realization of their potentially harmful effects make an analysis of the scope of the Protocol with respect to such chemicals more uncertain than with respect to riot-control agents.

The language of the Protocol that prohibits the use in war not only "of asphyxiating, poisonous or other gases," but also of "all analogous liquids, materials or devices" is arguably broad enough to include herbicides. Moreover, it is not decisive that chemical anti-plant agents were not known at the time the Protocol was concluded in 1925. The principal issues are whether the parties intended to extend the scope of the Protocol to agents harmful to plants, and if the parties did not advert to this question in 1925, whether the Protocol has been subsequently supplemented by an interpretation of the parties extending the Protocol to such agents.

There is no record of any discussion of anti-plant weapons at either the 1919 Versailles or 1922 Washington Conferences. At the 1925 Geneva Conference, however, the Polish delegate expressed concern about possible bacteriological warfare against crops as well as bacteriological antipersonnel weapons.[177] And as has been discussed, the 1924 report of the League experts also adverted to the possibility of bacteriological warfare against crops, although most experts felt that no existing bacteriological substances were "capable of destroying a country's . . . crops." [178]

In support of an interpretation of the Protocol that would permit use of chemical anti-plant agents, it may be urged that the principal thrust of the Protocol was to prohibit inhumane antipersonnel weapons and that chemical anti-plant agents were neither known nor mentioned at the Geneva Conference or any of the Conferences leading up to Geneva. It has also been noted that the French response in 1930 to a question raised by the British concerning the inclusion of lachrymatory

---

176 *See, e.g.*, Galston, *Defoliants, supra* note 93, at 62-75; Statement of Dr. Arthur W. Galston, Professor of Biology and Lecturer in Forestry, Yale University, *Hearings on Chemical-Biological Warfare, supra* note 76, at 107.

177 LEAGUE OF NATIONS PROCEEDINGS, *supra* note 143, at 340. The Polish delegate said: "Bacteriological warfare can also be waged against the vegetable world, and not only may corn, fruit and vegetables suffer, but also vineyards, orchards and fields." *Id.*

178 7 LEAGUE OF NATIONS OFF. J., Spec. Supp. 26, at 126 (1924).

gases emphasized "gases employed with a view to toxic action on the human organism . . ." This interpretation should not receive undue weight, as the context related to lachrymatory gases and not anti-plant chemicals. It is perhaps more significant that the Disarmament Conference of 1933, which otherwise accepted a broad CBW ban, spoke only in terms of "harmful effects on the human or animal organism." Lastly, it might be urged in support of a permissive interpretation that the Geneva Protocol was modeled on the Versailles Treaty, which by its language regulated chemicals already prohibited (probably by the Hague Gas Declaration of 1899 and the Hague Regulations of 1907). Since no existing law prohibited anti-plant chemicals per se, such agents remained lawful apart from particular uses which might violate the Hague Regulation ban against employing poison or "material calculated to cause unnecessary suffering," or other ban on particular use.

On the other hand, no evidence indicates that the draftsmen sought deliberately to exclude anti-plant chemicals from the broad wording of the Protocol. Moreover, the expression of concern about the possible destruction of crops through use of the only anti-crop agents then known suggests that the draftsmen intended to prohibit at least anti-crop weapons as well as antipersonnel weapons. As Professors Richard R. Baxter and Thomas Buergenthal have written,

> There is no evidence in the negotiating history of the Protocol to indicate that its draftsmen intended to *exclude* from its reach the use in war of plant-destroying chemical agents. There is, on the other hand, considerable evidence to justify the belief that the Protocol sought to outlaw chemical and biological warfare in general irrespective of whether it was directed against human beings, animals, or plants.[179]

On balance, the negotiating history concerning chemical herbicides is not very helpful. It demonstrates only that the draftsmen, unaware of such yet-to-be-developed chemicals, did not specifically consider whether they should be prohibited or permitted. The negotiating history also demonstrates that the draftsmen were aware of the possibility of anti-crop agents and probably intended to prohibit biological anti-crop agents, the only such agents then known.

Whether or not the Protocol was initially intended to prohibit chemical herbicides, the 1969 General Assembly vote on Resolution 2603A, which specifically interprets the Protocol to prohibit the use in war of

---

179 Baxter & Buergenthal, *supra* note 47, at 853, 867.

chemical and biological agents directed against "man, animals or plants," demonstrates substantial support among parties to the Protocol for a broad interpretation prohibiting such chemicals. The only parties to the Protocol which seem to have taken the unequivocal position that herbicides are not included within the Protocol are Australia and Portugal. Arrayed against these two parties to the Protocol and the United States, a non-party, are some forty-one parties to the Protocol and thirty-nine non-parties which voted for the resolution. The legal significance of this resolution for interpreting the Protocol, of course, is subject to the same qualifications discussed with respect to its significance concerning riot-control agents. These include a failure by more than half of the present parties to the Protocol to take an unequivocal stand on chemical herbicides, and the inherent ambiguity in translating a political vote on a General Assembly resolution into a legally binding interpretation.[180]

### The Scope of the Protocol: Weapons Employing Fire and Smoke

An occasional authority has urged that the Geneva Protocol bans fire weapons such as white phosphorus, flamethrowers, or napalm as "analogous liquids, materials or devices."[181] The principal argument that napalm is covered is that it may cause death by carbon monoxide poisoning or oxygen deprivation. By the overwhelming weight of authority, however, such weapons are not prohibited by the Protocol.[182] A recent statement by Professor Ian Brownlie is representative:

---

[180] During the First Committee debates prior to the adoption by the General Assembly of G.A. Res. 2603 (XXIV), only a handful of states specifically adverted to and took the position that the use of riot-control agents and chemical herbicides was banned by the Geneva Protocol. See the documents at 24 U.N. GAOR A/C.1/X, U.N. Doc. ——— (Provisional 1969), reporting the First Committee debates during November and December, 1969.

[181] For example, some experts at the 1969 International Conference of the Red Cross in Istanbul expressed the opinion that napalm falls within the Protocol. The weight of opinion at the Conference was that it does not. See INTERNATIONAL COMMITTEE OF THE RED CROSS, REAFFIRMATION AND DEVELOPMENT OF THE LAWS AND CUSTOMS APPLICABLE IN ARMED CONFLICT 61-63 (Report submitted to the XXIst International Conference of the Red Cross, held in Istanbul in September, 1969).

[182] Professors Thomas and Thomas conclude after an extensive analysis of the literature that

> the conclusion can be reached that no matter what might have been the thought prior to World War II, the use of incendiary weapons is now considered legitimate subject only to whatever effect the restraints of proportionality in the unnecessary suffering principle as well as the noncombatant and other principles might have.

A. Thomas & A. Thomas, supra note 41, at 240. See also Brownlie, Legal Aspects, in

Neither the legal definition nor, it seems fairly clear, the scientists include fuels and incendiary weapons in the category of chemical weapons. As Dr. Sidel points out in his paper on napalm, explosives and incendiary weapons are 'physical' weapons, producing their effects by blast and heat. As a class it is doubtful if such weapons are prohibited since they do not appear to fall within the terms of the Geneva Protocol.[183]

This conclusion is supported by the absence of any discussion of such weapons as chemical weapons at the Versailles, Washington, and Geneva Conferences. Even more significant are the opinions of a majority of the delegates at the 1969 Conference of Government Experts sponsored by the International Committee of the Red Cross that napalm was not banned by the Protocol,[184] and the absence of any intent evident during the recent General Assembly debates on the scope of the Protocol to include such weapons. It is also significant that the 1969 *Report on Chemical and Biological Weapons* by United Nations consultant experts specifically excludes incendiary weapons employing fire and smoke from the category of "chemical and bacteriological (biological) weapons." The consultant experts conclude,

> We also recognize there is a dividing line between chemical agents of warfare in the sense we use the terms, and incendiary substances such as napalm and smoke, which exercise their effects through fire, temporary deprivation of air or reduced visibility. We regard the latter as weapons which are better classified with high explosives than with the substances with which we are concerned. They are therefore not dealt with further in this report.[185]

The conclusion that incendiary fire and smoke weapons are not banned by the Protocol is further supported by a recent General Assembly Resolution, approved on December 20, 1971, which calls for a separate study "on napalm and other incendiary weapons and all aspects of their possible use."[186] Secretary of State Rogers' letter submitting the Pro-

---

CBW: CHEMICAL AND BIOLOGICAL WARFARE 141-54 (S. Rose ed. 1969); N. SINGH, NUCLEAR WEAPONS AND INTERNATIONAL LAW 151 (1959); and Levie, *supra* note 82.

183 Brownlie, *supra* note 182, at 150.

184 *See* International Committee of the Red Cross, supra note 181, at 61-63.

185 *Report of the Secretary-General, supra* note 172, at 7.

186 G.A. Res. 2852, Resolutions of the General Assembly at Its Twenty-Sixth Regular Session 21 September-22 December 1971, U.N. Press Release GA/4548, Part V at 58, 61 (Dec. 20, 1971).

tocol to the President for transmission to the Senate indicates that the United States understands that the Protocol does not prohibit "[s]moke, flame, and napalm." [187]

It should be emphasized that weapons employing fire and smoke, though not prohibited by the Geneva Protocol, are nevertheless subject to the general laws of war, both customary and conventional. Thus, Department of the Army *Field Manual 27-10* says with regard to weapons employing fire:

> The use of weapons which employ fire, such as tracer ammunition, flamethrowers, napalm and other incendiary agents, against targets requiring their use is not violative of international law. They should not, however, be employed in such a way as to cause unnecessary suffering to individuals.[188]

It is generally agreed that even though no rule of international law prohibits napalm and other incendiary weapons per se, the use of such weapons against other than hardened targets—for example, a bunker or tank—would generally violate the unnecessary suffering principle.[189]

*Threshold of Applicability of the Protocol: The "Use in War" and "Methods of Warfare"*

By its title, the Geneva Protocol is concerned with "the Prohibition of the Use in War." Similarly, the preamble on chemical agents speaks of "the use in war," and the operative paragraph on bacteriological agents speaks of "methods of warfare." Several problems are presented by this language. First, what is "war" within the meaning of the Protocol? And second, are there any uses "during" war which are not uses "in" war or "methods of warfare"?

The Protocol does not define what is meant by "war." By analogy to the threshold of applicability of the laws of war in general, and the Geneva Conventions of 1949 in particular,[190] the Protocol would apply to any armed conflict between two or more parties to the Protocol, whether or not formally declared or otherwise recognized by one or

---

[187] Letter of submittal from Secretary of State William P. Rogers to the President, August 11, 1970, in MESSAGE FROM THE PRESIDENT *supra* note 10, at vi.

[188] THE LAW OF LAND WARFARE, *supra* note 40, at § 36, 18.

[189] Professor Greenspan writes: "it would appear that fire should not be employed as an antipersonnel weapon, although it may lawfully be used against other material objectives." M. GREENSPAN, *supra* note 118, at 362. *See also* the authorities collected in A. THOMAS & A. THOMAS, *supra* note 41, at 238-40.

[190] *See* Article 2 common to the four Geneva Conventions of 1949, *supra* note 115.

both parties. It is the factual state of international armed conflict between parties to the Protocol rather than conclusory legal formalities which determines applicability.[191] This conclusion seems supported by General Assembly Resolution 2603A of December 16, 1969, which uses as the operable threshold language "the use in international armed conflicts." Apparently this language was, for at least forty-one parties to the Protocol, synonymous with the Protocol phrase "the use in war." Thus, the principal threshold problem in defining "war" or "international armed conflict" within the meaning of the Protocol is to determine, regardless of legal formalities, whether a conflict amounts to an "international" armed conflict rather than mere "civil strife" or "internal conflict." In terms of applicability of the laws of war in general this determination presents either of two issues: whether there is a sufficiently high level of external intervention to justify application of the international laws of war, or whether there is a sufficiently intense level of internal conflict, as for example in a war of secession such as the Nigeria-Biafra Civil War or the Pakistan-Bangla Desh Civil War, to justify application of the international laws of war. The first facet of this problem, though drawing increasing attention in recent years, has not been satisfactorily resolved. And although the second facet of the problem has long been recognized as a problem in the law of war, no satisfactory test has yet been widely accepted. It should be noted that both questions are common to all customary and conventional laws of war including the Protocol; but the specifics of a particular convention may answer one or both.

With respect to interpretation of the Protocol's applicability in interventionary settings (the type I problem), a mixed civil-international conflict of the magnitude of the Indo-China War, if it involved parties to the Protocol as opposing belligerents, would certainly trigger applicability. A good case can also be made that the Protocol prohibits any use of a prohibited agent by one party or its allies against another or its allies, regardless of the magnitude of the conflict. Such a case might be based either on a determination that any conflict involving two or more parties to the Protocol is automatically an international armed conflict, or that by its terms the Protocol applies "as regards other Powers" party to the Protocol. Regardless of the formalistic basis, this conclusion seems strongly supported by the arms control and law of war *raison d' etres* underlying the Protocol.

---

191 *See* Baxter & Buergenthal, *supra* note 47, at 868-69.

With respect to applicability in purely internal conflicts (the type II problem), the Protocol applies "as regards other Powers" party to the Protocol. Thus, despite its humanitarian basis, the Protocol does not apply to an internal conflict not involving two or more parties to the Protocol.

Once insurgents are recognized as "belligerents" (a form of recognition largely out of fashion), the customary international law of war would apply in the relations between the belligerents.[192] And today customary law might apply even below this belligerency threshold. As has been seen, once applicable, customary international law would include most, if not all, of the Protocol restrictions. In addition, some conflicts not of an international nature may also be governed by the protection accorded noncombatants under Article 3 of the 1949 Geneva Conventions, although the threshold applicability of Article 3 presents a formidable problem of its own.[193]

There is general agreement that the laws of war, and a fortiori the Protocol, do not apply to purely internal low level violence—including sporadic rioting. This agreement is paralleled by the general understanding, evident throughout the negotiating history, that the Protocol does not prohibit the domestic use of tear gas. Beyond situations of relatively low level and sporadic violence, it would seem useful to encourage wide application of the humanitarian provisions of the Protocol in civil conflicts or interventionary settings, whether or not involving parties to the Protocol. A low threshold for applicability of the customary laws of war would probably be the most effective way to accomplish this objective, since applying the customary laws of war would bring to bear most of the Protocol proscriptions.

The second general threshold problem of applicability concerns the uses "during" war that may not be uses "in war" or "methods of warfare" within the meaning of the Protocol. The principal problem which seems to have been raised in this respect is whether the Protocol would prohibit the use of riot-control agents in a prisoner of war camp against rioting prisoners. Though not a party to the Protocol, the United States used tear gas to subdue rioting North Korean and Chinese prisoners during the Korean War. At least one commentator,

---

[192] See, e.g., THE LAW OF LAND WARFARE, supra note 40, at § 11(a), 9.

[193] See, e.g., Farer, The Humanitarian Laws of War in Civil Strife: Towards a Definition of International Armed Conflict, VII REVUE BELGE DE DROIT INTERNATIONAL 20 (1971).

Congressman Richard D. McCarthy, who is generally critical of CBW, has taken the position that such use is permissible:

> Tear gas was used by American soldiers to subdue rioting North Korean and Chinese P.O.W.s. But this was clearly the way to handle a situation where rifles would otherwise have had to have been turned on unarmed prisoners.[194]

On the other hand, legal commentators seem split on whether such use would be permissible under the Protocol. Professors Thomas and Thomas have taken the position that such use is permissible:

> Cognizance should be taken of the use of riot control, incapacitating tear, and vomiting agents by United States military forces to control North Korean prisoners of war in prison camps. Since they were not used in war itself, they could be excluded from a rule prohibiting the use of gas in war.[195]

And Professors Baxter and Buergenthal have taken the position that such use would be prohibited:

> Does the use of gas against unruly prisoners of war constitute a use in "war"? It appears that it does, since prisoners of war rioting against the forces of the Detaining Power have in fact resumed hostilities against the Detaining Power and are engaged in "warfare" with it. It would be strange indeed if gas could not be used against enemy soldiers in combat but could be freely employed against them once they were taken prisoner. The very use of gas against prisoners awakens memories of the use of gas in the concentration camps of the Second World War.[196]

From an analytic perspective, a threshold question is whether the Protocol prohibts the use of tear gas at all. If it does, the question becomes whether *all* of the restrictions of the Protocol apply to riots in POW camps or whether *none* of them apply. Since the language "use in war" is not self-defining and since the negotiating history provides no definition, the issue should be resolved in the light of the purposes of the Protocol.

---

194 R. McCarthy, *supra* note 35, at 45.

195 A. Thomas & A. Thomas, *supra* note 41, at 148.

196 Baxter & Buergenthal, *supra* note 47, at 869.

In support of a broad interpretation some urge, as have Professors Baxter and Buergenthal, that rioting prisoners have resumed "warfare" against the detaining power. Moreover, to erase all per se restrictions on the use of chemical and biological agents to subdue rioting in a POW camp might lead to significant abuse of helpless prisoners.

In support of an interpretation permitting the use of tear gas against rioting POW's, even if tear gas is otherwise prohibited by the Protocol, it may be urged that the principal thrust of the Protocol is the normal combat situation and not the riot in the POW camp. Moreover, permitting use only in POW camps provides a fairly clear line not likely to result in escalation, since the battlefield pressures to resort to lethal weapons or to use gas to increase the lethality of other weapons are absent. Indeed, because use of lethal weapons against unarmed prisoners would clearly be unacceptable, the situation more closely resembles the permitted use in a domestic disturbance. Also, the alternatives to tear gas as a non-lethal weapon may be less effective than the alternatives to gas as a lethal weapon. Finally, the customary law of war, the Hague Regulations of 1907, and the Geneva Conventions of 1929 and 1949 Relative to the Treatment of Prisoners of War impose a more stringent standard of "humane treatment" for the treatment of prisoners rather than the less restrictive "unnecessary suffering" standard applicable on the battlefield.[197] And Article 42 of the 1949 Geneva Convention provides even more specifically,

> The use of weapons against prisoners of war, especially against those who are escaping or attempting to escape, shall constitute an extreme measure, which shall always be preceded by warnings appropriate to the circumstances.[198]

---

[197] See, e.g., Article IV of the Annex to the 1907 Hague Convention No. IV, 2 TREATIES, CONVENTIONS, INT'L ACTS, PROTOCOLS AND AGREEMENTS 2281, 2282 (Malloy ed. 1910); Article 2 of the 1929 Geneva Convention Relative to the Treatment of Prisoners of War, 47 Stat. 2021 (1932), 2 TREATIES AND OTHER INT'L AGREEMENTS, *supra* note 36, at 932, 938; *and* Article 13 of the 1949 Geneva Convention Relative to the Treatment of Prisoners of War, T.I.A.S. No. 3364 at 14 (1949).

[198] Article 42 of the 1940 Geneva Convention Relative to the Treatment of Prisoners of War, T.I.A.S. No. 3364 at 36 (1949).

Pictet supports the position that the use of tear gas in POW camps as a minimum force weapon to subdue rioting is permitted—indeed preferred—under Article 42.

> The use of force by guards may also be justified in the case of rebellion, and the remarks already made above concerning attempts to escape are applicable here also. The analogy is not absolute, however, and in the event of mutiny there may be other possibilities as regards the weapons to be used. Before resorting to

Thus, the riot in the POW camp is unlike other "warfare" situations in that these international proscriptions prevent the detaining power from freely using conventional firepower to subdue the "warfare."

There is no authoritative answer to the question whether the Geneva Protocol applies to rioting in prisoner of war camps. If the Protocol applies, no prohibited agents may be used against prisoners; but if the Protocol does not apply, the use of chemical and biological agents in prisoner of war camps is governed solely by the special regimes for the protection of prisoners. Either interpretation would seem reasonable, but the latter interpretation seems more compatible with the purposes of the Protocol as well as preferable policy. Moreover, the use of tear gas against rioting prisoners seems far more humane than firearms, which would presumably be a permitted "extreme measure" under Article 42 of the Geneva Convention. But if a permissive interpretation is adopted, it should be recognized that conflicting interpretations may provide an excuse for opposing belligerents to allege first use under the Protocol and thereby to escalate to otherwise forbidden chemical or biological agents. Thus, if the Protocol bans the use of tear gas generally, it might be dangerous to use it to subdue rioting prisoners of war in conflicts to which the Protocol otherwise applies even though a strong case can be made that it is a permitted use. Specific agreement on the use of tear gas against prisoners would obviate this problem and it would be useful to attempt to promote such agreement.

In addition to the use of tear gas against rioting prisoners of war, there may be other situations in which a use "during" war is not necessarily a use "in war" within the meaning of the Protocol. For example, the use of tear gas by domestic police forces to control disturbances by the civilian population during a mixed civil-international conflict is not necessarily a use "in war" within the meaning of the Protocol. Thus, the Saigon police might legally use tear gas during the Vietnam War to quell an unruly demonstration for increased veterans disability benefits, even if the Protocol were applicable to the conflict. Similarly, the use of herbicides to increase civilian agricultural production rather than as a weapon against opposing belligerent forces or their crops would not seem to be a use "in war" or "method of warfare" within the meaning of the Protocol.

---

weapons of war, sentries can use others which do not cause fatal injury and may even be considered as warnings—tear-gas, truncheons, etc.
THE GENEVA CONVENTIONS OF 12 AUGUST 1949, COMMENTARY III, GENERAL CONVENTION RELATIVE TO THE TREATMENT OF PRISONERS OF WAR (J. Pictet ed. 1960), at 247.

One area of potentially dangerous ambiguity is whether the use of herbicides for military objectives on one's own territory or the territory of one's allies and resulting in the destruction of the property of the using state and its nationals—or its co-belligerents and their nationals—rather than the property of the enemy would be a use "in war." Particular United States and South Vietnamese uses of herbicides on territory in South Vietnam under government control and resulting in the destruction of South Vietnamese forests and plantations rather than Vietcong crops would be an example. The use of herbicides to clear the perimeters of United States or South Vietnamese bases would be another example. On the one hand, law-of-war prohibitions usually exist for the protection of opposing combatants, nationals of an opposing power, or civilians in occupied territory.[199] On the other hand, the case for applicability is strengthened by the military purpose of such use, by the uncertain allegiance of much of the civil population in mixed civil-international conflicts, and by the uncertain toxic and ecological effects of the widespread use of some such agents even on one's own territory.

On balance, any use directed against enemy crops, bases, or territory would probably be a use in war within the meaning of the Protocol. Beyond that it is unclear whether uses not immediately directed against the enemy, such as the clearing of allied base perimeters or highway rights-of-way, would be a use in war. Because of the difficulty in drawing lines which will be viable in the field, it might be preferable to interpret "use in war" to include any use of herbicides for military purposes in a conflict involving two or more parties to the Protocol. But pending greater international agreement on the meaning of "use in war" and a full appraisal of the environmental impact of alternatives to chemical herbicides, it seems preferable to preserve some flexibility in borderline uses. The real focus should be to prohibit the massive and repeated applications of chemical herbicides over large areas, on crops, and in populated regions.[200]

---

[199] For example, Article 23(g) of the Hague Rules regulates destruction or seizure of "the enemy's property." 36 Stat. 2277 (1909), 2 Treaties, Conventions, Int'l Acts, Protocols and Agreements, *supra* note 197, at 2285.

[200] These uncertainties in interpreting "use in war" within the meaning of the Protocol indicate the existence of important uncertainties other than the inclusion of riot-control agents and herbicides. The United States should carefully consider a modality of ratification capable of dealing with the full range of these uncertainties in interpretation. The complexity of the issues also suggests a flexible modality for resolving the issues, preferably a forum which is both expert and non-politicized. For example, how should the question of use of chemical herbicides for the clearing of base perimeters be

### THE GENEVA PROTOCOL AND THE USE OF RIOT-CONTROL AGENTS AND CHEMICAL HERBICIDES IN THE INDO-CHINA WAR

The use by the United States of riot-control agents and herbicides in the Indo-China War is widely perceived as an important factor in United States ratification of the Geneva Protocol. It may be helpful to examine briefly both the legal regime presently applicable to such use and the regime that would apply following ratification.

At the present time the United States is bound by the customary international norms concerning the legality of chemical and biological weapons per se and the laws of war, both customary and conventional, concerning particular uses of any such generally permissible weapons. It is widely assumed that whatever the theoretical threshold for applicability to internal conflicts and interventionary settings, the customary laws of war apply fully to conflicts of the magnitude of the mixed civil-international conflict in Indo-China. But no rule of customary international law prohibits the use of riot-control agents or chemical herbicides per se, although in view of the large vote in favor of General Assembly Resolution 2603A such a rule has significant support. At least for the present, tear gas and herbicides may lawfully be used in the Indo-China War to the extent that specific uses do not contravene particular prohibitions on the conduct of warfare. For example, it would be illegal to use tear gas in any way to cause unnecessary suffering, to kill persons rendered *hors de combat* by tear gas when the means is available to take them prisoner, to use herbicides against crops for their poisonous effect on belligerents expected to consume the crops, or to destroy crops which were known to be or reasonably should have been known to be intended for civilian use.[201] These same legal

---

resolved even if herbicides are otherwise prohibited? Adequate consideration of this question requires expert opinion on whether alternative techniques of clearing, such as the use of the "Rome plow" or high explosives, might not be more damaging to regional ecology than the use of herbicides. Another relevant consideration of mixed fact and law is the weight to be accorded a "no herbicide" line as an aid to verification and prevention of CB escalation. The range, importance, and complexity of these issues suggests the utility of a conference approach.

201 The crop destruction program in Vietnam, which has been discontinued by the Nixon Administration, may have sometimes exceeded the limits imposed by customary international law in inadequately differentiating in the field between crops intended for civilian and those intended for military use. Although the scope of the customary international law rule concerning crop destruction is uncertain, at a minimum it prohibits destruction of crops intended solely for consumption by noncombatants and it may prohibit destruction unless the crops are intended solely for combatant use. *See* authorities cited in note 223 *infra*. Moreover, the burden of demonstrating sub-

restrictions would apply to the occasional uses of tear gas by the North Vietnamese and Vietcong as well as by allied forces.

In the event of ratification, the United States would, at least in the eyes of many states accepting a broad interpretation of the Protocol, assume an additional obligation not to use tear gas or herbicides "in" the war against other parties "which have already deposited their ratifications." There would also be a substantial question of which uses of tear gas and herbicides "during" the war were uses "in" war within the meaning of the Protocol. North Vietnam, South Vietnam, Laos, and Cambodia have not ratified, acceded to, concluded a succession agreement, or notified the Secretary-General of the United Nations that they are bound by the Geneva Protocol. Unless they can be said to be bound by the French ratification of May 9, 1926, which was "applicable to all French territories"—an obligation which these states have apparently not recognized—ratification of the Protocol would not impose additional legal obligations on the United States in the Indo-China War.[202]

## A COST-BENEFIT ANALYSIS OF UNITED STATES OPTIONS

In analyzing whether and how the United States should adhere to the Geneva Protocol, one should keep in mind that the issue is neither solely interpretation of the Protocol and customary international law nor the desirability of banning the use in war of particular chemical and biological weapons. United States options are constrained by a customary international regime applicable to the use of chemical and biological weapons; an existing Protocol with a substantial legislative history; the necessity of interacting with the other parties to the Protocol, many of whom have interests differing from those of the United States; a long history of United States policy with respect to CBW and CB arms control measures; and domestic politics. In this milieu United States decision-makers must consider the art of the possible as well as what is ideally desirable from the perspective of national or international policy. It may seem anomalous, at least in terms of the principles underlying the laws of war, that the lawfulness of the use of tear gas in war

stantial military necessity [*i.e.* that crops are intended for military consumption] should rest on the state employing crop destruction.

202 One caveat to this conclusion should be noted: it might be urged that the Soviet Union, the People's Republic of China and other states providing military assistance to North Vietnam, even though taking no active part in the hostilities, are belligerents, and that as such the Protocol would apply in the relationship between the United States and North Vietnam, their ally. Such an interpretation would be strained on both counts.

is controversial while only minimal legal constraints apply to aerial bombardment of major population centers or the use of napalm. But in the context in which the issue arises, it is not at all anomalous to pursue reasonable agreement on CBW when, for whatever reason, such agreement may be obtained. Other problems can be dealt with when the opportunity arises, though the anomaly does suggest that opportunities to deal with these other problems should be sought vigorously.

In analyzing the costs and benefits of ratification of the Protocol this section will first examine the substantive issues (issues of content) concerning the desirability of ratification of the Protocol, the desirability of ratification with a no-first-use or reciprocity reservation, and the desirability of ratification with some form of riot-control and herbicide understanding or reservation. Discussion will then turn to the issues bearing on selection of a specific modality of ratification (issues of procedure). Possible modalities include ratification with an informal understanding, an understanding formally communicated to the depository power, an express reservation, submission to the International Court of Justice, an effort to obtain international agreement to an annex interpreting the Protocol, and delay in ratification pending an international agreement or authoritative pronouncement on interpretation.

## Issues of Content

### Ratification in General

No fundamental changes in the international rights, privileges, powers and immunities of the United States or third parties would result from United States ratification of the Geneva Protocol. The weight of opinion is that all states are presently bound by a customary international law rule prohibiting at least the first use of lethal chemical and biological agents in war. Nevertheless, ratification by the United States would have significant legal effects. The principal effects would be to reinforce these customary legal relations with a conventional law source; to strengthen the customary law by United States adherence to the Protocol; possibly (depending on the scope of the present customary norm of international law) to extend the United States CBW obligation to prohibit a first use of incapacitating chemicals; probably (depending on the scope of the present customary norm and the extent of the United States reservation) to extend the United States CBW obligation to prohibit any use of biological methods of warfare; perhaps (depending on the scope of the present customary norm) to broaden the concept of a use-permitting-violation to include a first use by any of the allies of an opposing belligerent and vice-versa; and (as the Protocol is interpreted by many parties and in the absence of a formal reservation, understanding, or annex accepted by these other parties) to cast doubt on the lawfulness of the first use by the United States against other parties to the Protocol of riot-control agents and chemical herbicides. The United States has already extended the no-first-use restraint to incapacitating chemicals, has unilaterally renounced the production, stockpiling, and all use of biological weapons and has signed an international convention to this effect. Ratification would cost little and would generate substantial national and international benefits. The costs of ratification measured in terms of reduced freedom of action, *i.e.*, not necessarily real costs, may be summarized as follows:

[1] The United States would assume a conventional obligation not to use lethal or incapacitating chemical or biological methods of warfare except in retaliation for first use. This obligation largely parallels that already binding on the United States by customary international law.

[2] If the United States limits its no-first-use reservation to chemical weapons, it would assume a conventional obligation not to make any use of biological methods of warfare against parties to the Protocol not having a broader no-first-use reservation. This obligation would stop short of the present unilaterally adopted national policy which, though not yet legally binding, ends United States manufacture, stockpiling, and use of such weapons.

[3] Absent acceptance by most of the parties to the Protocol of a reservation, understanding, or annex to the contrary, the United States might lose some of its present freedom with respect to the first use in war of riot-control agents and chemical herbicides. The degree of loss, if any, would ultimately depend upon whether a broad or restrictive interpretation of the Protocol becomes generally accepted and how customary international law evolves with respect to such agents.

The benefits of ratification may be summarized as follows:

[1] Ratification would strengthen the national security by reinforcing the customary and conventional legal norms prohibiting at least the first use in war of lethal or incapacitating chemical and biological agents and by adding a conventional legal right against some ninety-

eight states with respect to the first use against the United States or any of its allies. In addition, if the United States files the presently contemplated no-first-use reservation limited to chemical weapons, *all use* of biological weapons against the United States would be prohibited in relations with accepting parties who have not filed a no-first-use reservation or who like the Netherlands have a similarly limited no-first-use reservation.

[2] Ratification would contribute to the present momentum toward more comprehensive measures for the control of chemical and biological warfare.

[3] Ratification would enhance United States influence with respect to current CB and other arms control negotiations and efforts to strengthen the legal regime governing the laws of war.

[4] Ratification would constitute a direct response to the recent resolutions of the United Nations General Assembly inviting "all States which have not yet done so to accede to or ratify the Geneva Protocol," and the appeal of the United Nations Secretary-General to the same effect.[203]

On balance, the national interest of the United States, as well as the global interest of the world community, strongly support United States ratification of the Protocol. Not surprisingly, almost all individuals and organizations that have recently studied the issues—including the President, the Secretary of State, the Senate Foreign Relations Committee, the House Subcommittee on National Security Policy and Scientific Developments, the American Chemical Society, the American Society of Microbiology and the Council of the Federation of American Scientists—have urged ratification.[204]

## Reciprocity and No-First-Use

Of the two common reservations to the Protocol, there seems little reason for or against adopting the "reservation" that "[t]he . . . protocol shall be binding . . . only with respect to the States . . . [which are parties]." The principle that a treaty is binding only between parties is implicit in the law of multilateral treaties. Since the principle is also

---

203 In his foreword to the July 1969 *Report of the Secretary-General on Chemical and Biological Weapons*, Secretary-General U Thant appealed "to all States to accede to the Geneva Protocol of 1925." *Report of the Secretary-General, supra* note 172, at xii.

204 *See* James M. McCullough, *Chemical and Biological Warfare: Issues and Developments During 1970*, CONGRESSIONAL RESEARCH SERVICE OF THE LIBRARY OF CONGRESS (UG 447, 71-37 SP, Jan. 18, 1971), at 7.

explicit in the Protocol itself, it seems simpler to ratify without such a reservation. Ratification without the reservation might also set a mood more conducive to rapid extension of the customary legal regime to that of the Protocol, thus more completely binding non-adhering states. It should be made clear that the United States' reasons for not depositing such a reservation are that such a reservation would be redundant and that the United States seeks to encourage more rapid extension of the customary norm to that of the Protocol. Failure to deposit such a reservation should not be based on an assumption that the treaty regime and the customary international legal obligation are today necessarily congruent. The recommendation of the Secretary of State to the Senate is consistent with omitting this reciprocity "reservation." [205]

The second common reservation, the no-first-use reservation, provides that "[t]he . . . protocol shall automatically cease to be binding . . . with respect to any enemy State whose armed forces or whose allies fail to respect the interdictions which form the subject of this protocol." Some thirty-eight states out of the eighty-five states that were parties to the Protocol in June 1970 had deposited roughly similar reservations. One additional state, the Netherlands, limits the no-first-use reservation to chemical agents.[206] Unlike the first common reservation, this reservation may change the legal meaning of the Protocol in several material respects and probably should be entered. First, it makes clear that the Protocol is a no-first-use prohibition rather than a no-use prohibition. Without such a reservation the legal right of retaliation for prior violation will depend upon the treaty rules concerning excuse of performance for material breach, or possibly on the customary international law of reprisals for violation of the laws of war, both of which may be more restrictive than the reservation.[207] Second, at least a common form of such reservation may broaden the right of retaliation from a right only

---

[205] See the letter of submittal from Secretary of State William P. Rogers to the President, August 11, 1970, MESSAGE TO THE PRESIDENT, supra note 10, at vi. "Unlike France, the Union of Soviet Socialist Republics, the United Kingdom, and most other reserving States the United States would not assert by reservation a limitation of its obligations under the Protocol to the Parties thereto." Id.

[206] The Netherlands reservation is as follows:

This protocol as regards the use in war of asphyxiating, poisonous, or other gases, and any similar liquids, materials, or processes, shall automatically cease to be binding on the Royal Government of the Netherlands with respect to any enemy State whose armed forces or whose allies fail to respect the interdictions which form the subject of this protocol.

MESSAGE FROM THE PRESIDENT, supra note 10, at 6.

[207] See the discussion in notes 122 & 127 supra.

against a violating belligerent to a right against all belligerents allied with a belligerent first violating the Protocol. The advantage of clearly establishing such a broad right of retaliation for prior violation of the Protocol is that since the Protocol is not a true arms-control measure, it may be largely enforced by a right of retaliation for first use. The Protocol regime will be most effective if that retaliatory right is clearly established not only with respect to a violating enemy state, but also with respect to its allies as well. On the other hand, such a reservation may also increase the risk of escalation when prohibited weapons are used.

Secretary Rogers has proposed that the United States ratify with a no-first-use reservation limited, as is that of the Netherlands, to a right of retaliation only with chemical weapons. In the context of the recently announced United States policy not to develop, manufacture, stockpile or use biological weapons or toxins for offensive purposes in war, this limitation of the no-first-use reservation makes excellent sense. If the principal purpose of this reservation is to preserve a clear right of retaliation as a substitute for a more complete arms-control measure, there is little point in reserving rights with respect to weapons that according to national policy, should not be developed or used in any circumstances. Moreover, if the United States limits its reservation to retaliation by chemical weapons, only chemical weapons could be used in retaliation against the United States if the United States reservation were in turn invoked against the United States by a party without a broader no-first-use reservation.[208] The limitation, of course, would also make ratification consistent with the spirit of United States support for the recently concluded Draft Convention on the Prohibition of the

---

208 Conversely, the United States or any other state with a narrower reservation might still be legally entitled reciprocally to invoke the broader reservation in a dispute with a state which has filed such a reservation. See, e.g., the Vienna Convention, Art. 21, para. 1(b); L. McNair, The Law of Treaties 573 (1961). This leaves a significant loophole in the Protocol regime with respect to the use of biologicals. The need effectively to plug this loophole against any use of biologicals is an additional argument suggesting the need for more comprehensive agreement on interpretation of the Protocol and strengthening of the Protocol regime. It should also be noted that although the preamble of the Draft Convention on the Prohibition of Biological and Toxin Weapons speaks of excluding "completely the possibility of bacteriological (biological) agents and toxins being used as weapons," the agreement itself contains no use restriction other than the Protocol restriction incorporated by reference. A more complete regime for the elimination of biological and toxin weapons should make clear that the use of such weapons is prohibited in all circumstances, including retaliation in kind under the Protocol and reprisal under customary international law.

Development, Production and Stockpiling of Bacteriological (Biological) and Toxin Weapons and on their Destruction.

## Chemical Riot-Control Agents

The principal arguments for the United States to reserve through some modality, the right to use chemical riot-control agents are as follows:

> [1] Such agents per se do not violate the principles of the laws of war prohibiting weapons causing unnecessary suffering or indiscriminate effects on non-combatants.
>
> [2] Such agents can in some combat circumstances provide a more humane option, thus promoting the principles of the laws of war.
>
> [3] Such agents may be militarily advantageous.

The principal arguments against reserving the right to use chemical riot-control agents are as follows:

> [1] Because the Geneva Protocol is interpreted by many, if not most, parties to prohibit the use of riot-control agents, there is a danger that the use by the United States of such agents in war may be interpreted as a first use justifying retaliation by any opposing belligerent not agreeing with the permissive interpretation. [It should be noted that this danger would be minimized or avoided if the United States could obtain widespread international agreement permitting the use of riot-control agents.].
>
> [2] Prohibiting riot-control agents would promote the effectiveness of the Protocol in controlling lethal and incapacitating CB agents.
>
> [3] Prohibiting riot-control agents might enhance the chances for more complete arms-control agreement on CB and increase United States influence on arms-control negotiations.
>
> [4] The use of riot-control agents in war may be politically costly, as the United States' experience with their use in Indo-China suggests.

It may be helpful briefly to develop each of these arguments for and against reserving the right to use chemical riot-control agents.

First, chemical riot-control agents per se do not violate the principles of the laws of war. The major principles of the laws of war concerning the prohibition of weapons per se, as opposed to particular use restrictions, focus on the propensity of the weapon to cause unnecessary suffering and the difficulty of using the weapon in a manner which discriminates between combatants and non-combatants.[209] Nothing inherent in the nature of CS or CN gas violates these principles, although they may be used in a manner that would be violative. In fact, the use of such agents may allow greater discrimination between combatants and non-combatants, when, for example, an opposing force is using civilians or prisoners as a shield against hostile fire. Since the use of these agents per se does not violate the principles of the laws of war, it is unpersuasive to urge as an argument against them that they are typically employed in combat to cause enemy casualties rather than solely to reduce casualties.[210] The issue is not whether a particular weapons system causes combatant casualties—a characteristic shared in common by all weapons—but whether, considering all uses, on balance it is consistent with the principles of the laws of war. Neither riot-control agents nor any other weapon may be used to enhance casualties when the agent alone would place enemy troops *hors de combat* and enable capture or when its use would increase the seriousness of the injuries which enemy troops would otherwise suffer.

Second, the use of chemical riot-control agents can in some circumstances reduce combatant or non-combatant suffering and casualties. Although this potential for humane use provided the initial rationale for the use of such agents in Vietnam, and such uses have been recorded, some evidence indicates that opportunities for humane use may be relatively infrequent on the battlefield. Rear Admiral William E. Lemos, the Director of Policy Plans and National Security Council Affairs of the Office of the Assistant Secretary of Defense for International Security Affairs, testified before the House Subcommittee on National

---

[209] *See generally* M. McDougal & F. Feliciano, Law and Minimum World Public Order 46, 77 (1961); J. Pictet, The Principles of International Humanitarian Laws (1966); Farer, *The Laws of War 25 Years After Nuremburg*, Int'l Conciliation 14-17 (No. 583, May 1971).

[210] *See, e.g.*, Foreword by Professor George Wald to the Ballantine edition of the Secretary-General's Report on Chemical and Bacteriological (Biological) Weapons and the Effects of Their Possible Use xiii, xv (1970).

> The distinction between lethal and incapacitating gases, however, fails entirely under combat conditions. Under combat conditions the tear gases, for example, are used to drive the enemy out from under cover and render him helpless so that he can be destroyed by other means. In Vietnam the tear gases have been used routinely to drive the enemy into the open before bombing and artillery attacks, or before an infantry assault. Under combat condition, tear gas is part of a thoroughly lethal operation; and the fact that in Vietnam this operation has involved many noncombatants in its sweep hardly helps our case.

*Id.* Implicit in this argument, of course, is a firebreak argument based on an arms control rationale rather than a law of war rationale. The firebreak argument is certainly one of the more serious objections to the use of riot-control agents.

Security Policy that the United States has used riot-control agents in Vietnam principally in conjunction with attacks on occupied positions, in defense of position, in tunnel clearing, in breaking contact with the enemy, in defense against ambush, and in rescuing downed airmen.[211] In most of these cases CS is used for its military effectiveness rather than its effectiveness in preventing unnecessary suffering or in allowing greater discrimination between combatants and noncombatants. Some evidence also indicates that riot-control agents tend to be stronger when adapted for military use and that their injurious effects, such as blistering of the skin, may be greater than agents in domestic use.[212] In fact, some scholars have suggested that a humanitarian case might be made *against* the use of riot-control agents. Thus, Professor Tom Farer writes,

> As in the case of any means, assessment of the humanitarian characteristics of gas without reference to specific tactical and strategic contexts—without reference, that is, to the way in which the military has found its employment to be economic—can be dangerously naive. The military setting of gas use is fundamentally different from the civilian, because in the former gas is merely a prelude to engaging an armed and organized adversary.
>
> What is the humanitarian case against gas? Certainly an important negative feature is the possibility, cited above, that gas may flush out and herd together belligerents and civilians who will form a single target for the attacker's fire. Secondly, it is by no means certain that the now most commonly employed gas, CS, does not have permanent harmful effects. An investigating team appointed by the British government following use of CS in Northern Ireland to quell sectarian violence, found no evidence of lasting illness among previously healthy persons. But it concluded that further study was necessary, with particular reference to the effects of the gas on the young, the aged, and those with impaired health.[213]

---

211 Statement of Rear Adm. Lemos, *supra* note 76, at 223, 225-28.

212 When used with proper precautions, CS is a relatively safe agent for riot-control because there is a large difference between the amount needed to cause brief incapacitation and the amount that causes serious injury or death. When used in combat, where many of the currently employed CS weapons contain much more of the agent than do police-type munitions, CS can cause severe blisters and skin burns that take one or two weeks to heal. Although extreme exposures in some combat situations may exceed the human lethal dosage, the primary effect of CS is not to kill but to incapacitate.
Statement of Dr. Matthew Meselson before the Senate Committee on Foreign Relations, Mar. 26, 1971.

213 Farer, *supra* note 209, at 19.

Determination of the humaneness of riot-control agents should be based on the total context of their actual and potential military use. Evidence of individual instances of humane use does not, by itself, justify a decision to permit such agents; conversely, neither do the possible harmful effects of such agents justify prohibiting them without also considering the harmful effects of the alternatives which might otherwise be used and the possibility of effective use restrictions for situations of potential abuse.

There has been little experience with efforts to promote use of riot-control agents to increase the ability to discriminate between combatants and non-combatants or to reduce total casualties. Even though some humane uses have been made in Vietnam, the potential for such use may be substantially greater than the Vietnam experience would suggest. Thus if there had been a vigorous national policy to isolate and operationalize potential humane uses of riot-control agents, the evidence of humane use might be far more impressive. Despite the dangers in the use of riot-control agents pointed out by Professor Farer and others, such agents may have a significant potential for promoting human rights which it would be shortsighted to neglect.

Third, riot-control agents may reduce allied casualties relative to enemy casualties or otherwise enable more efficient completion of a military mission. Assessment of the military effectiveness of riot-control agents depends on informed military judgment, and until the present Defense Department studies on their use in Vietnam are released, little hard evidence is available. But at least some experts who have studied the effectiveness of chemical riot-control agents in Vietnam are skeptical of their utility.[214] They indicate that the enemy soon adapts defensively by supplying gas masks to its forces and that in any event the military uses of riot-control agents are marginal. Other experts, such as Admiral Lemos in his testimony before the House Subcommittee on National Security Policy, urge that the use of CS gas in Vietnam has been militarily effective in a variety of operational settings. In summarizing

---

[214] *See, e.g.,* statement of Dr. Matthew Meselson before the Senate Committee on Foreign Relations, Mar. 26, 1971:

> To summarize, CS seems to have been a useful auxiliary weapon in certain situations when it was first introduced. However its use and its utility have greatly declined, because the enemy has learned to cope with it, especially by equipping his troops with gas masks. Indeed, on numerous occasions he has used CS on a limited scale against us.

*See also* Johnstone, *supra* note 97.

his testimony with respect to the use of riot-control agents Admiral Lemos said:

> The riot control agent, CS, has become a lifesaving part of military operations in Vietnam. CN, the older agent, because of its relative ineffectiveness, is now seldom used. The use of CS in combat operations clearly reduces casualties among friendly troops, permits extraction of civilians who may be under enemy control often without casualties, and frequently allows the enemy the option of capture rather than casualties. Perhaps the most valid indication of the effectiveness of CS in combat operations is that U.S. personnel continue to carry CS grenades to the field in lieu of some of their normal high explosive ammunition, and ground commanders often call for CS rather than high explosives. Riot-control agents are a valuable aid in accomplishing our mission and in protecting our forces.[215]

Turning to the arguments on the other side, there are four principal arguments against reserving the right to use riot-control agents. First, since the Protocol is interpreted by many, if not most, parties to prohibit riot-control agents, the use by the United States of such agents may be interpreted as a first use justifying suspension of the Protocol. In considering whether riot-control agents should be included in the United States ratification of the Protocol it is important to keep in mind that the issue is not simply whether from a law-of-war or arms-control perspective such agents *should* be permitted. Many, if not most, parties to the Protocol interpret it as prohibiting riot-control agents. Unless the United States enters an understanding or reservation permitting such agents that is accepted by the other parties to the Protocol, or obtains international agreement permitting such use, any use of such agents by the United States, or possibly by any of its allies, might be interpreted as a first use justifying the use of lethal or incapacitating chemical or biological weapons against the United States and its allies. It is probably true that the legal restraint provided by the Protocol is a less effective check against escalation of CBW than the threat of retaliation in kind or the prohibition of the development, manufacture and stockpiling of CB agents. Nevertheless, if the Protocol is worth ratifying at all, it should not be undermined with an ambiguity that could lead to a colorably lawful use of lethal and incapacitating CB against United States forces.[216] It is perhaps instructive to remember that one German justi-

---

215 Statement of Rear Am. Lemos, *supra* note 76, at 223, 228.
216 This argument rests on an interaction between the principles of content and

fication for the use of lethal gases in World War I was that such use was in reprisal against a prior illegal French use of tear gas.

A second argument for not reserving the right to use riot-control agents is that prohibiting such agents would promote the effectiveness of the Protocol in controlling lethal and incapacitating CB agents. The Geneva Protocol is to some extent an agreement based on a law-of-war rationale that prevents the use of weapons which cause unnecessary suffering; but it is probably even more a product of an arms-control rationale (though it is not a comprehensive arms-control agreement). Thus, a principal reason for ratification is to promote the national security by strengthening international legal barriers against the use of lethal and incapacitating chemical and biological agents against the United States or its forces in the field. The recent Secretary-General's report describes vividly the enormous increase in firepower provided by such weapons and their potentially devastating effect on population centers. In comparison with the importance of prohibiting lethal and incapacitating CBW, the importance of retaining the right to use riot-control agents is relatively minor. If abandoning the right to use riot-control agents would materially strengthen controls on major CB agents, abandonment might well be advisable.

A variety of reasons lend at least some support to the conclusion that prohibiting chemical riot-control agents may strengthen control of lethal and seriously incapacitating CB agents. Whether rational or irrational, prohibition of the use of "any gas" in warfare is a widely shared international standard for controlling CBW. Moreover, because of the difficulty of distinguishing precisely the effects of different gases and the possibility of the development of militarily significant new gases, a simple standard prohibiting all use of gas in warfare is less likely to

---

procedure concerning United States policy choices in relation to the Protocol and the use of riot-control agents and herbicides. Since it seems of major inportance it is emphasized here as a principle of content. In general, the argument has been missed or underrated as scholars have focused on analysis either of principles of content or of principles of procedure without considering the dynamic interrelation between them. Professors Baxter and Buergenthal have pointedly indicated the problem:

> If an enemy state should construe the Protocol as prohibiting the use of tear gas and the United States should nevertheless use that weapon, the enemy state might then tax the United States with the first violation of the agreement and use other forms of chemical and bacteriological warfare under claim of right. It would be easy to cast off the restraints of the Protocol in an argument about how far it carries. Thus the continued use of tear gas by the United States could lead to retaliatory use of far more devastating chemicals by a state claiming that it is acting in full conformity with the law.

Baxter & Buergenthal, *supra* note 47, at 876.

lead to uncertainty and escalation. There are also real problems in verification, particularly as new additives or more effective forms of tear
gas are developed. In general, those arms-control agreements which use
relatively simple and unambiguous standards are likely to fare better
than those which rely on vaguer criteria for applicability. As Thomas
Schelling has said with respect to the non-use of gas weapons in World
War II:

> "Some gas" raises complicated questions of how much, where, under
> what circumstances; "no gas" is simple and unambiguous. Gas only
> on military personnel; gas used only by defending forces; gas only
> when carried by projectile; no gas without warning—a variety of
> limits is conceivable. Some might have made sense, and many might
> have been more impartial to the outcome of the war. But there is a
> simplicity to "no gas" that makes it almost uniquely a focus for agree-
> ment when each side can only conjecture at what alternative rules the
> other side would propose and when failure at coordination on the first
> try may spoil the chances for acquiescence in any limits at all.[217]

Possibly a rule permitting the use only of chemical riot-control agents
would provide a viable line; in this respect the British designation of
CS is even clearer. But given the present international disagreement
about the status of such agents, a "no gas" line seems more reliable. There
is perhaps also some truth in the argument that the use of any gas in
war will breed familiarity with gas warfare, create vested interests
groups in favor of chemical warfare, result in development of general
gas weapons technology and manufacturing capability, and in these and
other ways break down internal restraints against escalation to more
lethal agents. This argument has less weight for an arms-use prohibition
than for a more comprehensive ban on development, manufacturing and
stockpiling; but it may nevertheless indicate an added source of pressure
for escalation under any type of limitation agreement.[218]

---

217 T. SCHELLING, ARMS AND INFLUENCE 131 (1966).

218 These "firebreak" arguments are among the most serious against the use of riot-
control agents. For example, Professor John Edsall points out:

> By using gas, even riot-control agents, we are encouraging escalation in the use
> of more deadly gases by other nations. The danger of such escalation is surely
> a greater threat to the future security of the United States than any short term
> gains from the use of gas by us in war can justify.

*Proceedings of the Conference on Chemical and Biological Warfare, Sponsored by the
American Academy of Arts and Sciences and the Salk Institute, July 25, 1969, reprinted
in* HEARINGS ON CHEMICAL-BIOLOGICAL WARFARE, *supra* note 76, at 451, 487. *See also*
the remarks of Dr. Matthew Meselson, *id.* at 487-88.

A third argument for not reserving the right to use riot-control agents is that prohibiting them might enhance the chances for more complete arms-control agreement on CW, and increase United States influence in arms-control negotiations. A comprehensive agreement on CW, comparable to the Draft Convention on Biological and Toxic Weapons, depends in large part on reaching agreement on principles for verifying compliance. Nevertheless, agreement may also be influenced by the disagreement concerning chemical riot-control agents and herbicides. If the United States were to adopt an interpretation of the Protocol that riot-control agents are included, or renounce the first use of such agents against parties to the Protocol in the absence of an international agreement or authoritative pronouncement permitting their use, such a policy might increase the chances for comprehensive agreement on CW. The demonstration of continued momentum and flexibility on CBW issues might also increase United States influence in other arms-control and law-of-war negotiations.

The fourth argument suggesting that the United States should ratify the Protocol without reserving the right to use riot-control agents is that past use has incurred significant political costs. Internationally, the initial use of tear gas in Vietnam met with vocal outcry and a Soviet sponsored campaign within the United Nations against the use.[219] The uproar was sufficient to prompt the United States Information Agency to protest the use.[220] And nationally, when the use of tear gas in Vietnam was first brought to public attention in the spring of 1965, the news triggered a negative public reaction.[221] According to Seymour Hersh and Congressman Richard McCarthy, these negative international and national political reactions caused the Administration to halt the use of tear gas in Vietnam, a decision which proved only temporary.[222]

In weighing these competing considerations, it is difficult to arrive at an informed conclusion in the absence of more information about the actual and potential humanitarian and military uses of chemical riot-control agents. Nevertheless, the humanitarian potential of such agents suggests a modest initial presumption in their favor if international agreement can be reached permitting them and they are narrowly and precisely defined. It should be noted that all of the arguments against reserving the right to use riot-control agents lose much of their force if in-

---

[219] See S. HERSH, supra note 34 at 168-70.
[220] Id. at 171.
[221] R. McCARTHY, supra note 35 at 45-46.
[222] S. HERSH, supra note 34, at 173; R. McCARTHY, supra note 35, at 46.

ternational agreement can be reached permitting such agents. In the absence of international agreement or an authoritative determination permitting the use of riot-control agents, the balance would seem to favor a policy that they will not be used by the United States against another party to the Protocol. In striking this balance, the danger of a United States use of riot-control agents legitimating enemy use of lethal or incapacitating chemicals under the common no-first-use reservation is a particularly important consideration.

## Chemical Herbicides

The principal arguments for reserving, through some modality, the right to use chemical herbicides are as follows:

[1] Such chemicals per se do not violate the principles of the laws of war prohibiting weapons causing unnecessary suffering or indiscriminate effects on noncombatants.
[2] Such chemicals may be militarily advantageous.

The principal arguments against reserving the right to use chemical herbicides are as follows:

[1] Because the Geneva Protocol is interpreted by many, if not most, parties to prohibit the use of chemical herbicides, there is a danger that the use by the United States of such chemicals in war may be interpreted as a first use justifying retaliation by any opposing belligerent not agreeing with the permissive interpretation.
[2] The use of chemical herbicides may endanger man and the environment in ways that at present are insufficiently understood.
[3] The use of chemical herbicides in war may be politically costly, as the United States' experience with their use in Indo-China suggests.
[4] Prohibiting chemical herbicides would promote the effectiveness of the Geneva Protocol in controlling lethal and incapacitating CB agents.
[5] Prohibiting chemical herbicides might enhance the chances for more complete arms-control agreement on CW and increase United States influence in arms-control negotiations.

The first argument for reserving the right to use chemical herbicides is that such chemicals per se do not violate the principles of the laws of war, since not all, or even most, uses cause either unnecessary suffering or indiscriminate effects on civilians. The use of chemical herbicides against crops which are or reasonably should be known to be intended for civilian use probably would be a violation of the laws of war whether or not such chemicals are prohibited per se.[223] The differential impact on civilians of anti-crop programs carried out by any means suggests that such programs should be a prohibited use, unless it is certain that crops are intended solely for consumption by the armed forces.[224] But the moderate use of herbicides, for example, to defoliate an allied base perimeter or an enemy base camp, does not necessarily cause unnecessary suffering or indiscriminate effects on civilians.

Second, chemical herbicides may be militarily advantageous. The testimony of Rear Admiral Lemos indicates a variety of ways in which herbicides have been used to military advantage in Vietnam. These include defoliation of base perimeters, lines of communication, infiltration routes, and enemy base camps. Herbicides have been used to a lesser extent for destruction of crops "in areas remote from the friendly population and known to belong to the enemy and which cannot be captured by ground operations." [225] This crop destruction program seems

---

[223] The precise scope of this rule is uncertain. A recent Defense Department pronouncement says

> [A]n attack *by any means* against crops intended solely for consumption by noncombatants not contributing to the enemy's war effort would be unlawful for such would not be an attack upon a legitimate military objective.
>
> Where it cannot be determined whether crops were intended solely for consumption by the enemy's armed forces, crop destruction would be lawful if a reasonable inquiry indicated that the intended destruction is justified by military necessity under the principles of Hague Regulation Article 23(g) and that the devasation occasioned is not disproportionate to the military advantage gained.

Letter from J. Fred Buzhardt, General Counsel of the Department of Defense, to Senator J. W. Fulbright, Apr. 5, 1971, in 10 INT'L LEG. MAT. 1300, 1302 (1971). This seems a looser standard from that in DEP'T OF THE ARMY FIELD MANUAL FM 27-10, *supra* note 40, which states only that the rule "does not prohibit measures being taken to . . . destroy, through chemical or bacterial agents harmless to man, crops intended solely for consumption by the armed forces (if that fact can be determined)." *Id.* at 18. The matter is one of emphasis, however, and the two statements are not inconsistent. *See generally* the excellent unpublished paper by Professor George Bunn delivered at the 1970 Annual Meeting of the American Academy for the Advancement of Science, entitled "Herbicides and International Law."

[224] L. Craig Johnstone points out:

> In the course of investigations of the program in Saigon and in the provinces of Vietnam, I found that the program was having much more profound effects on civilian noncombatants than on the enemy. Evaluations sponsored by a number of official and unofficial agencies have all concluded that a very high percentage of all the food destroyed under the crop destruction program had been destined for civilian, not military use.

Johnstone, *supra* note 97, at 719.

[225] Statement of Rear Adm. Lemos, *supra* note 76, at 223, 230.

suspect since it is difficult to find and isolate crops intended solely or even primarily for combatant use. Some military uses, particularly against crops, may also be politically counter-productive, as, for example, when crops of uncommitted civilians are destroyed. And with respect to some uses of herbicides, for example clearing base perimeters, alternatives such as the "Rome plow" might be available if the use of herbicides were prohibited. One consideration in determining whether some uses of herbicides should be permitted is simply whether these alternatives to herbicides could be more destructive of regional ecology than the limited use of herbicides. Quite possibly "Rome plows" or high explosives would be more destructive. To summarize, present evidence indicates that some uses of chemical herbicides can be militarily advantageous but that associated costs can also be high. A more complete assessment of the military effectiveness of herbicides may be provided when Defense Department studies on the use and effects of the herbicide program in Vietnam are released.

There are four principal arguments against reserving the right to use chemical herbicides. First, since many, if not most, parties interpret the Protocol to prohibit the use of chemical herbicides, the use by the United States of such chemicals might be interpreted as a first use justifying retaliation. By retaining the right to use a marginally important weapon, the United States might precipitate lawful, or at least colorably lawful, retaliation with lethal and incapacitating CB agents against United States forces.

Second, the use of chemical herbicides may endanger man and the environment in ways that at present are insufficiently understood. The massive and widespread use of herbicides in Vietnam is the first time such chemicals have been used in war. During the last few years concern has grown within the scientific community, both in the United States and abroad, that some herbicides may be harmful to humans and, if used massively and repeatedly, may injure regional ecology.[226] Some

---

226 *See, e.g.,* Galston, *supra* note 93, at 62-75; R. McCarthy, *supra* note 35, at 74-98; Statement of Dr. Arthur W. Galston, Professor of Biology and Lecturer in Forestry, Yale University, in Hearings on Chemical-Biological Warfare, *supra note* 76, at 107; *In Re* Hercules, Inc. and Dow Chemical Co., Order of the Administrator of the Environmental Protection Agency (I.R.&F. Docket Nos. 42 & 44, Nov. 4, 1971), at 4-5.
One of the most thoughtful analyses of the costs and benefits of the military use of herbicides is D. Brown, *The Use of Herbicides in War: A Political/Military Analysis,* in Carnegie Endowment for International Peace, The Control of Chemical and Biological Weapons 39 (1971). Brown concludes after a careful assessment of the

evidence suggests that some commonly used chemical herbicides and their contaminants may be potent teratogenic agents, that is, chemicals such as thalidomide, capable of producing birth defects in humans. Such agents may have their principal effects on a future generation. Similarly, harmful ecological effects may be long hidden and may affect future generations years after the termination of the conflict. As A. W. Galston has written:

> To damage or kill a plant may appear so small a thing in comparison to the human slaughter every war entails as to be of little concern. But when we intervene in the ecology of a region on a massive scale we may set in motion an irreversible chain of events which could continue to affect both the agriculture and the wildlife of the area—and therefore the people—long after the war is over.[227]

Such long term effects would make the use of chemical anti-plant agents quite indiscriminate in their effects on non-combatants. They would also render such weapons questionable from the standpoint of environmental protection, a concern which must be added to the traditional policies of the law of war in future decisions to legitimize a particular weapons system.

Third, the use of chemical herbicides in war may be politically costly. The United States' use of herbicides in Vietnam has produced adverse political reaction within South Vietnam, within the United States, and within the United Nations. The overwhelming vote for the adoption of General Assembly Resolution 2603A in 1969, which declares the use of anti-plant agents in international armed conflicts "contrary to the generally recognized rules of international law," provides some evidence of the strong international political opposition to such use. And if contemporary opposition is any guide, the international community will probably refuse to accept the legitimacy of chemical herbicides in the future. Only the United States and Portugal seem to have urged permitting such agents.

Fourth, prohibiting chemical herbicides would promote the effectiveness of the Protocol in controlling lethal and incapacitating CB agents. The need for clear lines in arms-control measures suggests the utility

---

United States experience with herbicides in Vietnam that "[r]eview of the U.S. experience in Vietnam suggests that herbicide operations have been at cross-purposes with the political/psychological aims of 'unconventional warfare.'" *Id.* at 59.

[227] Galston, *supra* note 93, at 62.

of prohibiting the use in war of "all chemicals" as well as "all gas." For example, the use of chemicals against plants, particularly crops, could present difficult problems in determining and verifying whether particular agents were herbicides directed against plants, poisons directed against enemy combatants, or herbicides directed against plants but inadvertently poisonous to enemy combatants and noncombatants.

Lastly, prohibiting chemical herbicides might enhance the chances for more complete arms-control agreement on CW, and increase United States influence in arms-control negotiations. Supporting reasons parallel those discussed earlier in considering this argument as an argument for not reserving the right to use riot-control agents.

On balance, the dangers of anti-crop uses, the uncertainty surrounding the effects of anti-plant chemicals on man and his environment, the strong international opinion against the use of such chemicals, and the danger that the use of herbicides will trigger retaliation with lethal CB agents, strongly suggest that the national interest would be best served by not reserving the right to use chemical herbicides "in war." And unlike the balance on riot-control agents, if the United States seeks an international agreement interpreting the Protocol, it should seek an agreement that chemical herbicides are included.

### Issues of Procedure

A variety of issues concerning the best modality for United States ratification of the Geneva Protocol should be considered.[228] The principal modalities of ratification are as follows:

[1] ratification preceded by a unilateral declaration of interpretation (an informal understanding);

[2] ratification with an understanding formally communicated to France as the depositary power;

[3] ratification with an express reservation;

[4] ratification followed by an effort to obtain an interpretation by the International Court of Justice;

[5] ratification followed by an effort to obtain international agreement to an annex interpreting the Protocol;

[6] delay in ratification pending an international agreement or authoritative pronouncement on interpretation.

Each of these options has advantages and disadvantages. None offers a completely satisfactory resolution of the issues.

---

[228] This analysis draws heavily on the work of Professors Richard R. Baxter and Thomas Buergenthal. *See* Baxter & Buergenthal, *supra* note 47, at 873-79.

*An Informal Understanding*

Ratification preceded by a unilateral declaration of interpretation—an informal understanding—is the path of least resistance. Such a tack would minimize the immediate international political response and, at least in the short run, bypass the necessity for reaching international agreement on interpretation. An informal understanding announced by the Executive or the Senate in the course of United States consideration of the Protocol would not legally bind other parties. Thus, they need not formally respond to the United States interpretation. Such an understanding would have legal effect only as evidence of the subsequent interpretation of one party to the Protocol and perhaps also as some evidence of the *opinio juris* concerning the customary international norm.

The strength of this first option is also its weakness. By avoiding the necessity of international agreement, an informal understanding would contribute to the existing uncertainty about interpretation of the Protocol. Continuation of this uncertainty after ratification has at least three major disadvantages.

First, given the present ambiguity in interpretation, other states which have not taken a position would retain relative freedom in interpreting the Protocol, even though the United States would, by announcing an interpretation, lose much of its flexibility. Thus, even if the United States interprets the Protocol to prohibit riot-control agents or herbicides, it will not thereby preclude other parties from urging that these agents are permitted. In this respect, the General Assembly debate on Resolution 2603 (A) indicates that few states have taken a specific stand with respect to their own interpretation concerning riot-control agents and chemical herbicides, despite the one-sided vote on the Resolution.[229] And at least four states in addition to the United States have interpreted the Protocol to permit the use of at least some riot-control or anti-plant chemicals.[230]

Second, and even more important, an informal understanding concealing a lack of international agreement may increase the risk of CB escalation. The danger would still exist that a controverted use would be interpreted as a first use removing all legal restraints imposed by the Protocol. In this regard, there is ample uncertainty concerning both the applicability of the Protocol prohibition to riot-control agents and

[229] See note 180 *supra*.
[230] Australia, Japan, Portugal and the United Kingdom.

chemical herbicides, and the scope of the use "in war" limitations on prohibited chemical and biological agents. The force of this argument is not as strong as it might first appear, since the legal restraint is not the only, or even the principal, restraint on escalation. The fear of retaliation and escalation, and the new draft agreement prohibiting the development, manufacture, and stockpiling of biological agents are more important factors. Nevertheless, if a principal purpose of ratification is to strengthen the legal restraints against CB use, then modalities of ratification which undermine that restraint are surely costly.

In general, it is important that arms-control agreements be as simple and unambiguous as possible. This principle is even more apt when the agreement subsumes, as does the Geneva Protocol, a no-first-use reservation arguably permitting the removal of all Protocol restraints in response to prior violation. Even if the United States expressed an informal understanding that the Protocol prohibits riot-control agents and chemical herbicides, some ambiguity would continue in relations with parties that have not expressed an understanding or between parties that have expressed contrary understandings.

Third and last, an informal understanding that the Protocol does not prohibit riot-control agents or chemical herbicides would provide no real legal protection against a charge of violation of the Protocol. Since a United States understanding would have only the weak legal effect of evidencing a subsequent interpretation of one party to the Protocol, if a majority of parties disagreed, the United States would have little defense against a charge of law violation. It is questionable whether retention of a right which, if exercised, might be widely regarded as a law violation would be desirable. If, of course, the United States were to adopt an interpretation that riot-control agents and chemical herbicides were prohibited by the Protocol, this objection to an informal understanding would lose most of its force, though it would still apply to other disputed issues of interpretation.

In summary, an informal understanding has the advantages of minimizing potential political opposition to the United States interpretation of the Protocol and avoiding the difficulties and trade-offs in reaching international agreement on interpretation. In the short run it probably maximizes United States flexibility in pursuing preferred policy. On the other hand, an informal understanding provides no real legal protection; may by increasing the uncertainty regarding coverage augment the risk of escalation; and does not commit all parties to a definite interpretation of the Protocol.[231] These objections would be lessened, but not completely avoided, if the United States adopted an informal understanding that riot-control agents and chemical herbicides were included in the Protocol.

## A Formal Understanding

As a second modality, the United States could ratify the Protocol with an understanding formally communicated to France as the depositary power. Such an understanding might be conveyed in the instrument of ratification or separately and might invite a response by other parties to the Protocol. According to the *Restatement Second of the Foreign Relations Law of the United States,* "A party may make a declaration which indicates the meaning that it attaches to a provision of an agreement but which it does not regard as changing the legal effect of the provision." [232] A formally communicated understanding in any form probably would result in more vocal political opposition than an informal understanding, particularly if the United States' understanding interprets the Protocol not to prohibit riot-control agents and chemical herbicides. Moreover, if the understanding were communicated in the instrument of ratification, France would probably officially notify the other parties of the understanding, thereby exacerbating international reaction.[233] Such an understanding might also be treated as a reservation subjecting the United States ratification to possible rejection by a non-accepting state or to ambiguous acceptance limited to

---

[231] One strategy for committing other nations without the necessity of a new conference might be to announce a statement for signature concerning an interpretation on riot-control agents and herbicides and perhaps even on no use of biological agents or the meaning of "use in war." Apparently, Sweden has raised a similar proposal in the discussions of the Eighteen Nation Disarmament Commission. The disadvantages of this approach are that it has only a minimal legal effect and is more inflexible than a conference in offering opportunities for agreement.

See generally on the comparative advantages and disadvantages of a procedure for registration of national interpretations Archibald S. Alexander, *Limitations on Chemical and Biological Warfare Going Beyond Those of the Geneva Protocol,* in CARNEGIE ENDOWMENT FOR INTERNATIONAL PEACE, THE CONTROL OF CHEMICAL AND BIOLOGICAL WEAPONS 94, 99-108 (1971).

[232] RESTATEMENT (SECOND) OF THE FOREIGN RELATIONS LAW OF THE UNITED STATES § 124, comment *c* at 391 (1965).

[233] The Protocol provides: "The ratifications of the present Protocol shall be addressed to the Government of the French Republic, which will at once notify the deposit of such ratification to each of the signatory and acceding Powers." 94 L.N.T.S. 65 at 69.

areas other than those to which the reservation relates.[234] In addition, unlike an express reservation, a formally communicated understanding would increase only marginally the legal protection of the United States, is unlikely to reduce materially the uncertainties surrounding interpretation of the Protocol, and would not necessarily commit other parties to a definite interpretation. In short, this second option would substantially increase legal and political risks, while generating few, if any, benefits over other options. If, however, the United States wishes to announce an interpretation that riot-control agents and chemical herbicides are covered by the Protocol, a formal understanding might increase the momentum for this interpretation more than an informal understanding. In view of the present political lineup on the issues of riot-control agents and chemical herbicides, such an interpretation would involve little risk of rejection of treaty relations.

### An Express Reservation

As a third possibility the United States might ratify the Protocol with an express reservation. The legal effect of a reservation is similar to that of a counter-offer and would present the other parties to the Protocol with several choices. They could accept the reservation, thus according full legal protection to both the United States and the accepting state. Or they could object that the reservation "is incompatible with the

---

[234] *See* the Vienna Convention, *supra* note 127, Art. 19; Art. 20, para. 4(b); Art. 21, para. 3.
Article 19 of the Vienna Convention provides:

*Formulations of reservations*

A State may, when signing, ratifying, accepting, approving or acceding to a treaty, formulate a reservation unless:

(a) the reservation is prohibited by the the treaty;
(b) the treaty provides that only specified reservations, which do not include the reservation in question, may be made; or
(c) in cases not falling under the sub-paragraphs (a) and (b), the reservation is incompatible with the object and purpose of the treaty.

*Id.*

Art. 20, para. 4(b) provides:

an objection by another contracting State to a reservation does not preclude the entry into force of the treaty as between the objecting and reserving States unless a contrary intention is definitely expressed by the objecting State.

*Id.*

And Art. 21, para. 3 provides:

When a State objecting to a reservation has not opposed the entry into force of the treaty between itself and the reserving State, the provisions to which the reservation relates do not apply as between the two States to the extent of the reservation.

*Id.*

object and purpose" of the Protocol, thus either totally denying legal relations with the United States under the Protocol or, if they prefer, partially denying legal relations with the United States to the extent of "the provisions to which the reservation relates." [235] This latter option would, in the context of a reservation concerning the use of riot-control agents and chemical herbicides, create uncertainty concerning which provisions would be in force. Since a reservation is equivalent to a counter-offer, the United States would obtain full legal protection in its interpretation with respect to all accepting states regardless of the interpretation given to the Protocol among other parties.

The advantages of an express reservation would be considerable if it were widely accepted. A reservation would provide full legal protection, would, at least vis-à-vis the United States and each accepting party, commit both parties to a definite position with respect to the subject of the reservation, and would reduce the range of ambiguity likely to lead to escalation under the no-first-use provision.

The disadvantages of an express reservation would also be considerable. The risk is substantial that many states would reject the United States ratification in whole or in part, thus undercutting the advantages of ratification. In view of the widespread political opposition to the use of riot-control agents and chemical herbicides, this risk would be acute if the United States reserved the right to use such agents. And if the United States does not reserve such a right, an express reservation seems pointless. The desirability of obtaining a conventional restraint on United States use of lethal and incapacitating CB might prove sufficient to elicit at least some acceptances from states which are opposed to the use of riot-control agents and herbicides. Nevertheless, the risk of widespread rejection of treaty relations would remain acute, particularly with those parties with whom we most need relations under the Protocol. A second limitation of an express reservation is that even if the United States obtains bilateral acceptance of its reservation, uncertainties would remain between other parties to the Protocol. Such an approach is also not as flexible as a conference approach in dealing with the full range of ambiguities in interpretation of the Protocol.

## An Advisory Opinion From the International Court of Justice

A fourth possibility is for the United States to ratify the Protocol and then to seek an advisory opinion from the International Court of Justice

---

[235] *Id.*

interpreting the Protocol. The United States might informally indicate prior to ratification that the use of riot-control agents and chemical herbicides is unclear under the Protocol, or that in the absence of an authoritative determination the United States interprets one or both as permitted or prohibited, but that in view of the varying interpretations of the parties, the United States thinks it wise to seek a decision of the International Court of Justice. The most convenient jurisdictional basis for an opinion of the Court would probably be to sponsor a General Assembly or Security Council resolution requesting an advisory opinion from the Court pursuant to Article 96 of the Charter.[236] Advantages of such a policy would be the obvious fairness of submitting the question of interpretation to the Court and the strong impetus toward a uniform interpretation of the Protocol.

The plan, however, is not without disadvantages. The General Assembly and Security Council could prevent the plan by opposing a resolution seeking an advisory opinion or could even refuse to accept the opinion of the Court when rendered. More importantly, an advisory opinion would not be legally binding on parties to the Protocol (though it would be an influential authoritative pronouncement) and could further fragment and entrench individual interpretations of the Protocol. Furthermore the plan would not provide an opportunity to exert diplomatic influence to reach a preferred solution. Though the problem can be couched wholly as a question of legal interpretation of the Protocol, there are in reality several issues, one of which is what chemical agents, if any, should be internationally permitted quite apart from the Protocol. To confine the issue solely to interpretation of the Protocol is to forego this question on the shaky basis that it has already received adequate treatment by the framers of the Protocol. And on the question of whether riot-control, and chemical herbicides should be permitted, the Court would probably not be as useful a decision-maker as, for example, an international conference of government experts. Finally, there is also some risk that such a strategy would create pressure amounting in effect to advance acceptance by the United States of an interpretation that may not command widespread acceptance.[237]

---

[236] Art. 96 para. 1. Some of the specialized agencies, such as the World Health Organization, also have been authorized by the General Assembly to seek an advisory opinion from the International Court of Justice pursuant to Article 96 paragraph 2 of the Charter. For a recent list of United Nations organs and specialized agencies authorized to request advisory opinions see [1970-71] I.C.J.Y.B. 35-36.

[237] There may also be some risk that a United Nations debate or International Court

In a context in which a uniform interpretation is itself an important policy goal, even apart from what that interpretation is, an advisory opinion of the International Court of Justice should be considered a serious option despite its disadvantages. If the judgment of the Court were that riot-control agents and chemical herbicides are included in the Protocol, the strong impetus toward uniform interpretation would be a substantial gain. On the other hand, if the judgment were that riot-control agents and chemical herbicides were not included, the decision would probably serve as a major impetus to a conference solution which would permit a freer policy appraisal of the issues.

## An Annex to the Protocol

As a fifth possibility the United States might follow ratification of the Protocol with an effort to obtain international agreement to an annex interpreting the Protocol. The recommendations of the House Subcommittee on National Security Policy and Scientific Developments suggest this possibility[238] and its advantages would be considerable if it were possible to obtain widespread agreement. An annex would afford full legal protection to the acceding parties among themselves, would reduce ambiguities in interpretation and thus the danger of escalating use, and would commit all acceding parties to a definite interpretation of the Protocol. If a large number of parties signed an annex, it would also constitute strong evidence of the subsequent practice and interpretation of the parties which would legally influence the freedom of interpretation of non-signers of the annex.

A major advantage in seeking an annex to the Protocol is that initial agreement could be hammered out by government experts, thus affording greater flexibility than other options. An exchange among government experts, either at a conference or otherwise, would not be restricted entirely to an interpretive function, but could attack ambiguities by seeking compromise on the full range of issues. For example, a conference of government experts could resolve the threshold question of use "in war"; could determine the propriety of using riot-control agents in POW camps; and could decide whether the use of herbicides around one's own base perimeter is a use "in war." Furthermore, such a con-

proceeding would provide the occasion for a propaganda attack on the United States use of riot-control agents and chemical herbicides in Vietnam.

238 REPORT OF THE SUBCOMMITTEE ON NATIONAL SECURITY POLICY AND SCIENTIFIC DEVELOPMENTS, *supra* note 21, at 10. They also support the possibility of obtaining an interpretation from the International Court of Justice.

ference might also decide that the use of herbicides should be broadly prohibited but that riot-control agents, if carefully defined, should be permitted. If the conference determined that riot-control agents should not be totally prohibited, it could carefully define the acceptable agent or agents. Such a conference might also recommend a supplemental agreement prohibiting all use, rather than just first use, of biological and toxin weapons, and would provide an opportunity to commit other states to an interpretation of the Protocol with respect to incapacitating gases. In short, a conference approach would offer greater flexibility and might serve to depoliticize the issues, both internationally and nationally.

A final advantage of seeking an annex is that such a tack would give the United States considerable freedom in attempting to influence substantive results. Such freedom would not exist if the issues were submitted for judicial determination.

Unfortunately, an annex or conference approach, like other options, is not without substantial disadvantages. The principal disadvantage is the political difficulty of obtaining widespread agreement on an annex or even attracting a significant gathering of states to a conference to discuss the issues. The temptation of many states, whether for political reasons or otherwise, would be to decline such a conference with an indication that the Protocol is clear and needs no interpretation. Moreover, it would be particularly difficult to attract representatives of all camps to such a conference while the Indo-China War continues.

A second disadvantage is that such an annex might complicate rather than clarify the issues in interpretation of the Protocol. If some but not all parties to the Protocol signed such an annex, a complex pattern of relationships might emerge between those signing the annex and those not signing the annex, between those with and without reservations to the annex, etc. Though this danger is real, confusion already exists because of the Protocol's ambiguities. The real issue is whether a conference approach is a helpful way to confront and narrow these ambiguities or whether a conference would magnify existing disagreement.

Since a conference approach maximizes the possibility of a meaningful policy appraisal, a preliminary effort to ascertain which states would be willing to attend seems worthwhile.[239] A recent British article evalu-

---

[239] Judging from their present positions, a conference might receive the active support of Australia, Great Britain and Japan as well as the United States. Possibly France, Canada, Belgium and the Netherlands might also support such a conference. On the other hand, it might be difficult for the Soviet Union and its allies to support

ating the alternatives available to Great Britain in clarifying whether CS gas is included in the Protocol dealt with multilateral approaches as among the more attractive options.[240]

## A Delay in Ratification

Finally, the United States could delay ratification pending an international agreement or authoritative pronouncement on interpretation. Normally, it is preferable to know the legal effect of a treaty prior to ratification. Also, a delay in ratification might give the United States greater bargaining power in obtaining an acceptable interpretation. On the other hand, delay might reduce United States influence in interpretation since the United States position would have legal significance for interpreting the Protocol only if the United States were a party.

In any event, delay in ratification has at least two serious disadvantages which strongly suggest that the Protocol should be ratified as soon as possible regardless of resolution of the issues concerning riot-control agents and chemical herbicides. First, to delay ratification because of uncertainty about the coverage of riot-control agents and chemical herbicides is to put the cart before the horse. The principal reason for ratification is to strengthen the barriers against use of lethal chemical and biological weapons, and the United States interest in strengthening such barriers far exceeds any interest in retaining the right to use riot-control agents and chemical herbicides. Regardless of the interpretation which ultimately prevails on riot-control agents and chemical herbicides it is in the national interest to strengthen the barriers against chemical and biological warfare. It should be remembered that some scholars assert that no presently accepted customary international law prohibits the use in war of chemical agents and that ratification of the Protocol would clarify the prohibition against the first use of lethal agents against the United States. Moreover, the new draft biological weapons convention has no use restriction and in that respect is dependent on the Protocol.

Second, there is presently a strong trend toward increased participation in the Protocol. United States ratification would have a major influence in maintaining or increasing this momentum and would greatly

such a conference, particularly in view of their criticism of the United States use of riot-control agents and chemical herbicides in Vietnam. A conference convened by the International Committee of the Red Cross might provide a less politicized and more expert forum for careful policy appraisal than one sponsored by individual states.

[240] See Carlton & Sims, supra note 125, at 338.

strengthen the Protocol regime. Ratification might also increase United States influence in a variety of arms control and law of war negotiations. Continued delay in ratification could be costly in reducing both opportunities for influence.

Since the Protocol would not be applicable to the Indo-China War even if the United States were a party, there seems little reason to delay ratification pending an end to the war. It may be true that a conference to interpret the Protocol would be less likely and more politicized while the use of riot-control agents and chemical herbicides continues in Vietnam. But the possibilities of a conference might also recede as the issues lose visibility. On balance, it would seem wise to ratify the Protocol as soon as possible.

## CONCLUSION

The United States took the lead in proposing the Geneva Protocol and should have ratified it in 1926. The case for ratification is much stronger today. Ratification would strengthen the international restraints against the use of modern CB agents, an arsenal second only to nuclear weapons in potential for devastation. Ratification would also contribute to the present momentum for more comprehensive CB arms control measures and would increase United States influence in arms control negotiations. In view of this momentum and the importance of strengthened legal controls on lethal CB agents, prompt ratification is desirable regardless of the outcome of the dispute concerning the use of riot-control agents and chemical herbicides. In ratifying, the United States should enter a no-first-use reservation limited to lethal and incapacitating chemicals, as suggested by President Nixon in his letter of transmittal to the Senate. This limitation would reenforce President Nixon's pledge that the United States will not use biological weapons under any circumstances.

United States policy concerning riot-control agents and chemical herbicides is neither a purely legal question nor a purely political one. More parties interpret the Protocol to ban riot-control agents and chemical herbicides than interpret the Protocol to permit them. Nevertheless, there is no definitive legal interpretation on these or a number of other important issues which may arise under the Protocol. The issues are in flux and the United States position will affect their resolution. Because of this dynamic interrelation between legal interpretation and policy appraisal, it is important to take the full legal and political context into account. It is wrong to emphasize the humane uses of riot-control agents, while neglecting the danger of escalation resulting from ambiguous resolution of the lawfulness of such agents. It is equally wrong to try to resolve the issues by legal interpretation without considering whether the humane potential of such agents merits an attempt at agreement permitting them. The United States should also consider the procedural constraints on operationalizing policy under the Protocol regime. In fact, adequate appraisal involves a complex matrix of political and legal factors crosscut by considerations of both content and procedure.

The principal interests of the United States, shared in common with all nations, are to obtain uniform resolution of the issues concerning riot-control agents and chemical herbicides and an international on-the-merits appraisal of the desirability of permitting the use of such agents. If the potential exists for international agreement permitting the carefully circumscribed use of riot-control agents to promote human rights in armed conflict, it would be tragic to lose the opportunity because of an ossified interpretation of a Protocol drafted with only episodic consideration of the issues.

In the full context of national constraints and opportunities, it seems preferable to support an interpretation that the Protocol prohibits the use of chemical herbicides "in war." Reasons supporting this conclusion include the strong international consensus against the use of such chemicals, the widely shared interpretation that the Protocol prohibits their use, the dangers to noncombatants of anti-crop programs, the insufficiently understood long run consequences for man and his environment from the use of such chemicals, and the political costs associated with their use. Finally, massive use of chemical herbicides may have such an indiscriminate impact on noncombatants and their progeny as to warrant per se prohibition.

Regarding the meaning of use "in war," there is little international consensus on, or indeed recognition of, the issues raised by the use of chemical herbicides. Probably any use directed against enemy crops, bases, or territory would be a use "in war" within the meaning of the Protocol. Beyond these prohibitions it is unclear whether uses not immediately directed against the enemy, such as the clearing of allied base perimeters, would be a use "in war." Pending greater international agreement on the meaning of this phrase and appraisal of the environmental impact of alternatives to chemical herbicides, it seems preferable to preserve some flexibility in such uses.

Because of their potential for humane use, a decision on riot-control agents is more difficult than that on chemical herbicides. The potential humane uses of such agents warrant a careful international appraisal of their permissibility. If widespread international agreement permitting such agents can be reached, and if the permitted agents are narrowly and precisely defined to guard against escalation (for example, limited to a chemically defined form of CS), such an agreement may well be desirable. But if most states continue to oppose the use of such agents, and particularly if they interpret the Protocol to prohibit such agents, an opposite unilateral interpretation by the United States would contribute to undermining the effectiveness of the Protocol as a legal restraint—a cost that would outweigh any benefits of reserving the right to use such agents.

In interpreting the meaning of "in war," it is unclear whether the Protocol would apply to the use of riot-control agents against rioting prisoners of war, even if such agents are otherwise included in the Protocol. The strong humanitarian case for the use of riot-control agents as a minimum force alternative to more lethal weapons and the minimal dangers of using such agents in POW camps strongly suggest that such use should be permitted. The uncertainty concerning the permissibility of such use, however, suggests the wisdom of promoting an international understanding that such use is permitted.

The full context of constraints and opportunities also suggests that the United States should support an international conference of government experts (or consideration of the issues at an ICRC conference) for the purpose of promoting uniform agreement on interpretation of the Protocol and careful appraisal of related policy issues. Such a conference might prepare an annex to the Protocol or recommend an alternative procedure for agreeing on uniform interpretation. A conference approach offers a number of advantages. These include full legal protection without the risk of rejection of treaty relations, legal commitment of a maximum number of parties, opportunity for multilateral agreement to minimize the risk of escalation to lethal CB agents, opportunity to resolve the full range of ambiguities in interpretation (and to reach further agreement on, for example, no use of biological and toxin agents), and finally, some degree of de-politicization of the issues.

In view of the position of many parties that the Protocol prohibits riot-control agents and chemical herbicides, it is quite possible that too few states would support a conference to make such an approach feasible. In that event, the United States should consider as an alternative an advisory opinion from the International Court of Justice on whether the Protocol extends to riot-control agents and chemical herbicides. Though submission to the International Court of Justice has a number of disadvantages—including the non-binding effect of an advisory opinion and limitation of the issue to interpretation of the Protocol—it has real merit in offering fair resolution of the dispute and a chance to promote widespread agreement on interpretation.

It is important for the Executive and the Senate to reach agreement on a policy for riot-control agents and chemical herbicides as soon as possible. As a starting point both might candidly admit that there is no authoritative interpretation on whether riot-control agents and chemical herbicides are included in the Protocol. A reasonable compromise might then be that the United States should promote an interpretation that prohibits the use of chemical herbicides "in war" but that permits the use of riot-control agents if carefully delimited to promote human rights in armed conflict. Both the Administration and the Senate might also agree that in view of the importance of promoting widespread international agreement on interpretation of the Protocol, the United States will support international consideration of the issues, preferably through an international conference but if that proves impractical, through submission to the International Court of Justice. Pending international agreement or an authoritative pronouncement confirming or negating its interpretation, the United States could provisionally maintain that riot-control agents are permitted, but should do so cognizant of the inadvisability of using riot-control agents against another party to the Protocol until the issues are resolved.

The really interesting questions are those that have no good solution. By this standard the issues concerning the use of riot-control agents and chemical herbicides are signally fascinating. Paradoxically, the complexity of these questions suggests a variety of solutions, since trade-offs in costs and benefits make a number of them roughly equivalent. The real danger is not making a mistake on riot-control agents and chemical herbicides, but that the search for a perfect solution will distract from the more important goal of strengthening the barriers against use of an increasingly sophisticated CB technology. Prompt United States ratification of the Geneva Protocol would close a major breach in the most important of these barriers and would be truly a giant step for mankind.

# Weapons Potentially Inhumane:
# The Case of Cluster Bombs

## MICHAEL KREPON

THE speaker is a retired colonel in the American army. He has seen three wars at close hand and still limps as the result of an encounter with a German land mine. When he talks about antipersonnel weapons, and about fighting a war in which civilians may be in the line of fire, he can still do so with complete authority and without reservations: "I'd just as soon see a dozen civilians go before one soldier."

The field commander's concern on behalf of his men—a concern shared in armies throughout history—has been transformed into a particularly cruel reality by the nature of modern war. In the Vietnam War, it has been estimated by the Senate Judiciary Subcommittee on Refugees and Escapees that as many as 425,000 civilians lost their lives in South Vietnam alone between 1965 and 1973. Other wars have seen as great a proportionate toll on civilians, but largely because of hardship and deprivation or individual acts of massive destruction. While the final grim bombing of Hanoi reminds us that the Vietnam War was not free of such events, the great bulk of civilian casualties came in the day-to-day conduct of a war from which they could not escape.

No side had a monopoly on generating such massive human suffering. The Vietcong and North Vietnamese certainly were not lacking in the will or ingenuity to cause pain. But they were no match for the Americans in terms of the hardware to do it.

One particular kind of hardware employed in Vietnam is now receiving increasing attention, as it will play an even more important role in future police actions and wars, both conventional and guerrilla. "Area weapons" are so named because of their dispersion characteristics. By virtue of the enormous territory they can cover, such weapons present a strong potential danger to noncombatants. An additional element of controversy stems from their classification as "antipersonnel weapons"—munitions that are effective primarily or solely against human beings.

Both in design and in its practical deployment, the most indiscriminate antipersonnel weapon used in the Vietnam War was almost certainly the so-called Cluster Bomb Unit (CBU). The CBU story is worth looking into, because it shows the way weap-

ons move from research and development to deployment and use
—and how the bureaucratic world of memoranda and deference
relates to the world of fire and iron on the battlefield. Moreover,
the story can lead as well as any to the basic questions—whether
any form of international control of such weapons is possible and
whether there are procedures by which the United States, even
acting alone, might take proper account of the political and
humanitarian considerations that surround this type of weapon.[1]

## II

In a cluster bomb unit, hundreds of bomblets, each slightly
larger than a baseball, are lodged within a hollow dispenser.
Dropped from fighter or bomber aircraft, the dispenser splits
apart, releasing its contents. The small bomblets, known as bomb
live units (BLUs), are grooved in such a way as to fragment
before, during or after impact, depending on the fuse employed;
in addition, the casing itself is designed to fragment into small
particles. Upon detonation, each dispenser can blanket an oval,
linear or figure-eight patterned area on the ground. The shower
of fragmentation can be effective against light military targets,
but for the most part the CBU is effective only against human
beings. Because of the high velocity of the fragments and the
uniformity of their dispersion, it is a virtual certainty that any

---

[1] This article is based on research for a broader study on area weapons undertaken
by the Student Advisory Committee on International Affairs. Lee Kimball, School of
Advanced International Studies, Johns Hopkins University, assisted in the research and
interviews, and Gary Gilbert, University of Maryland, assisted in the research. All
statements quoted directly or in substance have been checked with the sources interviewed.

There are three major information centers on area weapons in the United States, although information in all three is quite spotty. The American Friends Service Committee's
research arm, NARMIC (112 South 16th Street, Philadelphia 19102) has extensive files
and clippings that are open to the public. They have published *The Simple Art of Murder, Antipersonnel Weapons and Their Developers*. The Indochina Resource Center
(1322 18th Street, N.W., Washington, D.C. 20036) also has extensive files open to the
public. On the west coast, NACLA (Box 226, Berkeley 94701) has investigated the subject.

Abroad, the subject has received much wider public attention. Substantial evidence is
contained in John Duffett, ed., *Against the Crime of Silence: Proceedings of the Russell
International War Crimes Tribunal*, Flanders, N.J.: O'Hare Books, 1968. Recently, the
International Committee of the Red Cross has published the most judicious overview of
the subject, *Weapons That May Cause Unnecessary Suffering or Have Indiscriminate
Effects*, Geneva (7 Rue de la Paix), 1973. An offshoot of the Red Cross study is the
Swedish working group study by Torgil Wulff, *et al.*, entitled: *Conventional Weapons:
Their Deployment and Effects From a Humanitarian Aspect*, Stockholm: The Royal
Swedish Ministry for Foreign Affairs, 1973 (available from the Swedish Embassy, 600
New Hampshire Avenue, N.W., Washington, D.C. 20037). The Stockholm International
Peace Research Institute (SIPRI, Sveavagen 166, S-113 46, Stockholm) has published
five volumes on chemical and biological warfare and one on incendiaries; one is soon to
be published on area weapons.

person located within the pattern area will be killed or wounded.

The use of fragmentation to cripple an enemy is not a new concept. The hand grenade is perhaps the simplest example of the principle at work. Even conventional blast bombs employ the fragmentation principle to a limited extent. But the ability to control a fragmentation pattern and to disperse it over a wide area for tactical uses is strictly an outgrowth of the war in Indochina.

Munitions designers developed fragmentation bombs during World War II, but the results showed more promise than sophistication. The major development in fragmentation during the Korean War was the Claymore mine. Later versions which projected steel balls rather than a fragmented metal plate were used in Vietnam. The real breakthrough in controlled fragmentation, however, happened after the Korean War ended. Working at the Development Center at China Lake, California, and at Eglin Air Force Base, Florida, the Navy and the Air Force designed a bomb live unit with fragmentation characteristics far superior to anything previously used by U.S. armed forces. Later versions of this BLU, nicknamed "pineapples" by the North Vietnamese, were the first to be used in the theater. But the overall weapons system, designated the CBU-2 series, still had kinks. Pilots had to fly low and level to make the system work; otherwise, bomblets would not eject from the dispenser. CBU-2s were in the inventory before a single plane sortied over Vietnam. Limited numbers were deployed on aircraft carriers off the coast of Vietnam, and some were no doubt used in combat. But there was no ground swell of support for their use, primarily because of the low and level tactic required to deliver them.

Sometime prior to 1963, work began within the Air Force research and development (R-and-D) shop at Eglin to modify the dispensing system. Field reports called for a dive-release mechanism so that CBUs could be dropped in a way that did not invite antiaircraft fire. Eventually, this work produced so-called second generation CBUs—the CBU-20 series—which not only included the dive-release mechanism, but also delivered far more destructive bomblets.

CBU-24s—their bomblets nicknamed "guavas" by the North Vietnamese—were the most widely used cluster bombs of the war. They contained far more fragments than any previous weapon of this kind and, above all, were able to cover a much wider area. The exact range of destruction of the CBU-24 remains a classified military secret not publicly disclosed by the Pentagon. However, a Japanese team of experts traveling in North Vietnam and observing the effects has estimated that a single CBU dropped in a linear pattern and detonated at an altitude of 600 feet was able to disperse its fragments so as to kill or wound people at an effective range of 300 meters by 1,000 meters.[2] A report by the International Committee of the Red Cross places the correct figure at 300 by 900 meters.[3] A Swedish team of experts agrees with the Red Cross figures, estimating further that a single fighter aircraft carrying CBUs could cover an area anywhere from one to 15 square kilometers.[4] While these figures are generally halved by American experts (noting the possible bias of the sources), the area coverage remains extraordinary, bearing in mind that the ordnance package for a single F4 Phantom can include eight CBUs or, with special racks, as many as 15 to 20.

Operational tests in April 1966 proved beyond a shadow of a doubt the flak suppression possibilities of the new weapon. Soviet antiaircraft units used by the North Vietnamese were only about ten to 12 feet across, an extremely difficult target to knock out even though only a small amount of damage could render them inoperative. CBUs, by literally pockmarking an entire area, could either knock out the antiaircraft weapon or prevent it from firing, thus providing the maximum amount of cover for U.S. aircraft, surpassing even napalm in effectiveness. It did not take a great deal of imagination to envision other tactical uses for CBUs unrelated to flak suppression.

Almost overnight, the new CBUs became the compleat weapon for area denial. Vice Admiral Lloyd M. Mustin, in his capacity as Director of Operations for the Joint Chiefs of Staff, became involved. "Once we tested them," he said in an interview, "the immediate question became 'How many can we make?' " In the light of the immediate favorable military judgment, the decision to deploy followed rapidly, and by the summer of 1966 the new CBUs were in use against targets in North Vietnam.

Thus, the debate on deployment and use was not prolonged. The participants agree that most of it took place in military

[2] Duffett, op. cit., p. 260.
[3] ICRC, op. cit., p. 44.
[4] Wulff, et al., op. cit., p. 122.

circles, and that the principal question was whether the extraordinary military usefulness of the new weapon outweighed the risk of the revelation of its nature to enemies present and future. For the weapon did embody significant advances; the technology of controlled fragmentation had advanced to such a degree that the CBU-20 series represented one of the infrequent advances below the nuclear threshold acceptable for use on the battlefield. "We thought," said a current high-ranking military officer, "these weapons could give us a quantum leap on the enemy, but not break the unwritten rules."

Some Pentagon officials were reluctant to show an ace card—which could then be duplicated by the Soviets and Chinese. It appears that this question arose again and again, as successive advances further refined the CBU design. Some models, indeed, were never deployed, and retain today their status as "classified munitions"—to be kept under wraps in order to shield their production techniques or their battlefield applications.

However, the CBU-24 was apparently never designated as a classified munition, and the debate on protecting its techniques was quickly resolved. The problem of flak suppression was becoming progressively more acute as the weight of bombing in the North was steadily stepped up throughout 1966, and the CBU-24 would presumably complicate the enemy's task of rebuilding lines of communication and strike a blow at his morale. Potential enemies, it was argued, would develop CBUs soon enough, if they did not already possess them.

By not designating the CBU-24 as classified its proponents sidestepped a number of questions. To have done so would almost automatically have brought in a wider array of civilians and compelled some discussion of the political consequences of deploying a weapon that was not only far more effective than any previous one, but also far more likely to cause civilian casualties. It appears that in this and other respects the military promoters of the weapon went to considerable lengths not to raise the broader questions.

Here it is also relevant to note (and several participants do so) that the decision to use the CBU-24 followed a drawn-out bureaucratic debate over the use of another flak suppression weapon—napalm. When air operations began over Southeast Asia, and especially after U.S. forces became directly engaged (in mid-1964 in Laos, and then over North Vietnam in early

1965), the Joint Chiefs argued strongly that napalm should be authorized for substantial use—on the ground that it had become an accepted conventional instrument of war, and that it would be highly effective. Civilians in the Defense and State Departments, under the leadership of Assistant Secretary of Defense John McNaughton, countered not by arguing the inhumanity of the weapon per se, but how its use would be regarded by "world opinion." This political argument was extremely frustrating to the Joint Chiefs, who managed to make only slight dents in the napalm prohibition. Through 1961–64, napalm was authorized only for search and rescue operations, for Vietnamese forces flying under American tutelage, and for specified operations in Laos. Finally, in the spring of 1965, the United States began combat air operations in earnest, and the question of napalm use took on greater urgency. Only after direct representations to the President by the Chiefs was the napalm restriction lifted, on March 9, 1965, to permit use in any combat situation.[5] And so when CBUs were ready for operational use a year later, the Chiefs were in no mood to engage in another debate over ordnance selection.

According to Mustin, no formal request was ever made by the Joint Chiefs to any political authority to use CBUs. "In our view, they were a purely conventional weapon, and we regarded them as available, and the less said, the better. Somebody somewhere would want to raise the argument, 'Well, do we or don't we want to authorize the use of this weapon?'. . . . We in J-3 [Directorate for Operations] had ways of exchanging information with our subordinate echelons all the way out to pilots on the line, and we just said, 'As far as we know, that's authorized to you, you've got 'em, use 'em when you want, and keep your mouth shut, or somebody will tell you that you can't.' "

It is a fair conclusion that military officers in the Pentagon downplayed the question of CBUs to deflect political channels from making an issue of their use, as they had done with napalm. CBUs were categorized and explained as a standard weapon, to be taken off the shelf—"conventional iron-mongery," in Mustin's words. Then again, since CBUs were described as flak suppression ordnance, demonstrably effective in protecting the lives of

[5] *The Pentagon Papers: The Defense Department History of United States Decision-Making on Vietnam,* the Senator Gravel edition, Boston: Beacon Press, 1971–72, v. III, p. 278.

U.S. pilots, how could civilian channels argue against them? Finally, CBUs were never a headline-type weapon, either in the research-and-development stage or after deployment. Civilian assistant secretaries for R-and-D in the Navy and the Air Force had more pressing problems to consider. CBUs did not run into engineering problems; on the contrary, they were developed without major cost overruns or defects. Controlled fragmentation, from an R-and-D standpoint, was purely a technical matter. A former participant in the review process says with some disdain, "They made decisions on a cost-effective basis. They compared CBUs to blast bombs for cost and weight of effort." Because no political questions were raised, civilian heads of R-and-D programs turned their attention elsewhere. "We knew they were being developed," said another former official, "but they weren't a high profile item."

The Joint Chiefs, then, were only continuing the low profile inherited from the R-and-D community. The Chiefs did not believe they were being deceptive in their presentations to political channels; the top military men merely didn't volunteer anything about possible political repercussions. And since they were never quizzed about them with any severity from political channels, there the matter rested. Representations were, of course, made to the Secretary of Defense, but within the context of use and resupply of conventional ordnance needed to cut aircraft losses. At least one senior civilian official had the impression that the weapon was merely a more decisive way to use fragmentation—with no idea of the very wide effective range involved.

Once deployed, the major political question arose over inadequate resupply. CBUs may have been cost-effective, but they were still costly. In the military's estimation, the United States never achieved a manufacturing capability to meet demand adequately—and not because the Joint Chiefs never pressed the point. In some circles, Secretary of Defense Robert McNamara's reluctance in approving new production facilities was scandalous. In interviews with military and civilian officials, two schools of thought on his motivation for limiting CBU production emerge. The first argues economics. McNamara was determined not to end this war, so the theory goes, with huge surpluses of military equipment, as had happened during previous wars. Furthermore, he was suspicious of bloated and vague requirements brought to him by the Joint Chiefs. So it was natural that his practice of cutting requests for matériel by the Chiefs would carry over to the CBUs. The second argument, less popular than the first, hints that McNamara used the resupply power to place restrictions on CBUs in the theater. This argument is weakened somewhat by McNamara's choice of the CBU-24 as the kill weapon for his scheme to build an infiltration barrier to protect South Vietnam.[6] Once the Secretary of Defense committed his prestige to the barrier, he had to make sure there were enough CBU-24s for that purpose.

For whatever reasons, the resupply problem was a real one. Demand was so great that there were regular airlifts of CBUs from one base to another to share limited supplies. Although no formal rules of engagement were placed on where, when and how CBUs were to be used, Mustin assumes there were oral instructions "of the most stringent variety" from field commanders to pilots not to use them "unless you've got a flak target." In addition, Mustin believes there were instructions to bring unexpended munitions back to base, instead of dropping them in designated areas, as was the case for standard blast bombs. Other military officials support this view. But the extent to which individual pilots exercised such restraint necessarily varied, given assertions by the press and foreign observers of their use in built-up areas, notably in North Vietnam but also on occasion in South Vietnam. Lack of supply proved to be the most effective political check on indiscriminate use, because once they were operational, civilian officials had little to say about CBUs.

Thus, political involvement at the State Department and in the Office of the Secretary of Defense was throughout of the shallowest kind. They, too, viewed these munitions in conventional terms. Moreover, many of the political officials were as hardline about tactics as their colleagues in uniform. The question of CBUs arose after significant numbers of U.S. troops had already been committed to the struggle, when political judgments were at a clear disadvantage in relation to military imperatives. CBU deployment took place after a series of protracted bureaucratic debates over military tactics, including decisions to use herbicides and napalm, when the political side was depleted from successive losses. Finally, political officials could not argue from a budgetary angle, as CBUs were undeniably cost-effective. Consequently, civilian input on CBUs related mostly to the question

---

[6] *Pentagon Papers, op. cit.,* v. IV, pp. 121–22.

of revealing or not revealing the weapons in question. There was virtually no debate at technical or policy-making levels about the indiscriminate nature of the munition and mechanics for monitoring its use.

## III

So the CBUs went into extensive use by the U.S. Air Force, becoming, in the words of a high Pentagon official of the period, "the darling of the aviators." They were employed primarily in North Vietnam and against the trail complex in eastern Laos. The most common targets were antiaircraft installations (flak suppression) and truck parks. They also appear to have been employed in connection with B-52 raids, primarily in key supply areas in Laos and the southern part of North Vietnam, and in connection with the final B-52 raids against the Hanoi area in December 1972 and early January 1973.

So far as the South was concerned, the restraints appear to have been more severe and the employment more limited. Perhaps the most hard-hit province was Quang Tri (adjacent to the border with the North), where an observation team led by the staff of the Senate Judiciary Subcommittee on Refugees and Escapees obtained considerable testimony on their use during the Communist Easter Offensive of 1972. Within the past year, news reports have indicated that in some areas unexploded CBU bomblets form a significant part of the vast problem created by unexploded weapons littering the countryside.[7]

No knowledge is available on whether CBUs caused extensive civilian casualties in the trail areas of Laos; although no special restraints were apparently applied to their use in these areas, the general ground rules required that targets be at a significant distance from known villages.

In North Vietnam, however, extensive evidence exists. "Guavas" became a prime exhibit of the North Vietnamese to visitors, and the best descriptions of the range of CBU effectiveness have come, as already noted, from foreign observers who were given the opportunity to examine its effects extensively—in a situation where these could be readily separated from the very different impact of other types of bombs. The North Vietnamese would routinely take visitors to see traces of cluster bombing in

---

[7] Thus, *The Washington Post* reported on July 8, 1973, that undetonated "guavas" were acting like miniature land mines in the effort to reclaim fields for farming.

Quang Binh and Phu Tho provinces, while reports of cluster bombing drops against six North Vietnamese cities—Hanoi, Haiphong, Nam Dinh, Thai Binh, Vinh, and especially Viet Tri —filtered out in various media during the course of the war.[8] Given this wide area of use, one can say with assurance that a weapon with a damage radius of several square kilometers must have caused extensive civilian casualties, and in a high ratio to the military damage it unquestionably inflicted on its intended targets.

In the South, CBUs were much less extensively employed in proportion to other munitions; by and large, North Vietnamese antiaircraft in the South was mostly in direct connection with substantial military units and used at some distance from populated areas. On the other hand, in a few cases at the high point of the fighting, North Vietnamese units were active in areas largely under enemy control, and these included some of the highly populated provinces along the border and central coast. In general, efforts to separate out what proportion of civilian casualties was due to action by the Vietcong and North Vietnamese rather than to action by American, South Vietnamese and allied forces have been able to produce only the roughest sort of estimates.[9]

What is certain is that the CBU established itself during the Vietnam War as a highly effective weapon. Although the models used were not able to destroy well-placed guns or missiles, their total effect within the designated area did succeed in silencing the weapons and doubtless inflicting substantial casualties on their crews. Accordingly, from a military standpoint the CBU is now an established weapon in the U.S. Air Force. It is estimated that 29 percent of the Air Force's ordnance procurement budget for fiscal 1973 went to purchase controlled fragmentation munitions of the CBU type, and the U.S. inventory currently contains 30 varieties of CBUs, including some with incendiary loadings.[10]

Moreover, since the Vietnam experience is widely known, it appears certain that controlled fragmentation weapons of the

[8] The most detailed and comprehensive account of this evidence of CBU use is in Duffett, *op. cit.,* pp. 147–270.

[9] The Senate Judiciary Subcommittee study mission estimates that "well over 50 percent of civilian casualties were attributed to GVN and U.S. firepower." *Hearing on the Relief and Rehabilitation of War Victims in Indochina,* Washington: G.P.O., 1973, part IV. p. 9.

[10] In the FY 1973 ordnance appropriation of $666.3 million, the following appropriations were itemized: $37.5m for CBU-25; $9.3m for CBU-55; $44.2m for CBU-58; $96m for MK-20 (Rockeye); $8.5m for BLU-32; figures from The Center for Defense Information, Washington, D.C.

CBU type will become a staple in arsenals at all points on the ideological spectrum. In recent months it has been reported that CBU stocks were rushed to Israel during the Yom Kippur War to combat Soviet-supplied SAM missile sites.[11] How far this might go is suggested by reports that the Portuguese, recalling their part in helping the United States supply Israel during the same war, have let it be known that they require sophisticated weapons to deal with guerrilla antiaircraft activity in their African territories.[12] Nor is it likely that the CBU technique has been neglected by the Soviet Union and its associates.

## IV

As the CBU story shows, powerful forces are at work to diminish the humanitarian perspective in policy-making. Policy assumptions, bureaucratic behavior, and political imperatives all work to dehumanize in the abstract; when placed in the context of weapons development and use during wartime, they become brutally real. This is especially true when area weapons are billed as life-savers to American infantrymen and pilots. The nature of the bureaucratic war machine does the rest—it minimizes responsibility while maximizing the possibilities of wide-scale damage to save American lives.

It is fatuous to believe that these dehumanizing forces can be swept aside, regardless of the indiscriminate characteristics of conventional weapons. The rules of international law are far too fragile and hazy to protect civilians from the devastation generated by controlled fragmentation munitions. The Fourth Hague Convention of 1907 (concerning the laws and customs of war on land) is considered a landmark in this field. The often-quoted provisions state, "The right of belligerents to adopt means of injuring the enemy is not unlimited," and "it is especially forbidden . . . to employ arms, projectiles, or material calculated to cause unnecessary suffering." International law has moved precious little from these strictures to the Geneva Convention of 1949, the last attempt by the international community to deal with the rules of warfare.

The Vietnam War has now underlined the urgent need to update the rules of warfare for the modern-day arsenal. Recently, a Swedish working group has attempted to devise guidelines for

[11] *The Washington Post,* November 10, 1973, p. A16.
[12] *The Washington Post,* November 14, 1973.

limiting the abuse of CBUs. Among their recommendations are limiting the size of the individual CBU fragments and fragment velocity; limiting the weight of the CBU canister; and limiting the use of CBUs to "well localized, military targets."[13]

Others have directed their attention to drafting additional protocols to the Geneva Convention. Under the prodding of the International Committee of the Red Cross, a governmental conference was convened in Geneva in February of this year to discuss draft protocols for international and non-international armed conflicts. Each protocol has extensive provisions relating to civilian populations. Articles 46 and 26 of the international and non-international draft protocols, for example, state in part:

The employment of means of combat, and any methods which strike or affect indiscriminately the civilian population and combatants, or civilian and military objectives, are prohibited. In particular it is forbidden:
(a) to attack without distinction, as one single objective, by bombardment or any other method, a zone containing several military objectives, which are situated in populated areas, and are at some distance from each other;
(b) to launch attacks which may be expected to entail incidental losses among the civilian population and cause the destruction of civilian objects to an extent disproportionate to the direct and substantial military advantage anticipated.

After the opening round of the Geneva Conference, American officials will participate this summer in interim talks related to conventional weapons. In February 1975, the Conference will reconvene, with the goal of producing protocols for ratification. Whether or not the above draft Articles and many others relating to civilian populations emerge unscathed is, at this point, a matter of conjecture. As expected, there are reports of considerable dissatisfaction on the part of the U.S. delegation with the draft proposals. The official American position is classified.

V

Whatever the possibilities of effective international agreement—and one must admit that they do not seem great—it is possible for the United States to take its own measures to meet the questions raised by area weapons. Would the CBU record have been the same if decision-makers had clearly faced the human-cost consequences of their actions? Can we not at least design the decision-making mechanism so that such questions cannot be set aside as easily as they appear to have been in the CBU case? And

[13] Wulff et al., op. cit., pp. 164-7.

must we not reckon that both present weapons and others not yet fully developed will raise on a continuing basis not only questions of political damage to America's reputation but the most fundamental issues of humane behavior?

In the very narrow realm of developing and using instruments of war, the United States could make four procedural changes that would make embarrassing questions more difficult to avoid, and sharpen the focus on the human costs of policy decisions. These would be:

*1. Get political input on weapons development from the start.*

At present there is virtually no input from the Department of State or the White House during the early phases of weapons development. Yet this is precisely where it should be done, because once area weapons are operational, checks on them become more difficult to enforce. Despite this, politico-military affairs personnel at State receive only occasional summaries of R-and-D projects, and these relate almost exclusively to the field of strategic weapons. The White House has recently abolished the Office of Science and Technology, which could have played a useful monitoring role. The Congress has the power of review via the appropriations process, but this procedure is notoriously weak. The newly created Office of Test and Evaluation in the Pentagon can be a useful place to start. Still this checkpoint, like all others at present, effectively lies within the R-and-D community. But weapons developers are asked very specific questions about their work, and they are trained to give very specific answers. "My job," in the words of a current R-and-D official, "is to hear what the brass wants, to say whether it's possible with the financial restraints and the state of the art, and then to deliver as much as I can."

As we have seen from the CBU study, political input generally comes in only at the last moment and at the highest levels. Obviously, the President and his top advisers have limited expertise to weigh the operational consequences of their decisions when working in a crisis atmosphere. They must rely heavily on the opinions of the Joint Chiefs, but this is not enough.

One way to develop political expertise on individual weapons is to ask political questions at the outset of weapons development. In an interview, Dr. Eugene G. Fubini, former Deputy Director of Defense Research and Engineering, suggests a "four-sided table" approach to each R-and-D project. Around the table would sit one intelligence analyst who discusses what kind of threat exists; one operations expert who says what operation he needs and can carry on provided he has been given the tools; one matériel analyst who discusses what actually can be developed given current technology; and one cost analyst who determines how many weapons could be available and at what cost. Fubini calls for a person-to-person discussion that will: (a) force a realistic evaluation of the threat; (b) emphasize "force" performance rather than weapons performance as the basic problem; (c) tie performance to an acceptable operational concept. In an informal sense, such a table already exists; operations, intelligence, cost, and matériel analysts communicate with one another but their discussions are all too often devoid of the political analysis Fubini and others call for.

A way to insure political analysis is to add a fifth corner to the negotiating table (appropriate enough in the Pentagon) and add a political analyst who will evaluate the political implications of the weapon. As there is no way of judging which R-and-D projects eventually bear fruit (defoliants were a low priority item before Vietnam), political officers should be assigned to every development project. In addition to participating in the Defense Systems Review Council which evaluates R-and-D projects, political officers should be familiar with the operations of R-and-D field units, matériel and systems commands of the various services, and R-and-D efforts farmed out to private firms by the Defense Department.

This procedure in no way ensures a "humane" political input to R-and-D decisions. But the effort can certainly be no worse than current practice, and has the potential of being much better.

*2. Evaluate collateral damage possibilities of weapons as they are developed.*

"Weapons are somewhat like drugs," notes Dr. Alexander Flax, former Assistant Secretary of Air Force Research and Development. "You buy them for their positive results, and you don't always recognize their side effects." Weapons developers need to be asked about the side effects of their products. Providing the best weapons that technology can produce can be disastrous, so that categorization of weapons effects in all imaginable situations before they are deployed is imperative. Decisionmakers will need this information if they are to reduce collateral damage as they go about the business of prosecuting a war.

There are many ways to generate proper testing and data for collateral damage. The Weapons Systems Evaluation Group (WSEG), has been in the business of evaluating weapons' capabilities since it was organized in 1949. The jargon at WSEG may be the thickest in the entire Pentagon, perhaps because of its work with computers evaluating the damage characteristics of nuclear weapons. WSEG can also simulate the collateral damage for antipersonnel weapons, based on the weapons' specifications, location of noncombatants, and delivery accuracy. At each stage of the R-and-D process (basic research, exploratory development, engineering development, and production), WSEG or some other agency of government should evaluate collateral damage. With chemical weapons, environmental and teratogenic assessments should be required as well.

*3. Prepare guidelines for antipersonnel weapons' use prior to engagement.*

No one can predict with any certainty the dynamics of warfare. And no country will be bound by strict rules of engagement or ordnance selection drawn up in a vacuum. These caveats aside, it is still necessary to formulate a framework in these areas within which the armed forces of this country will operate. The most frustrating aspect of the Vietnam War from a military perspective was that an overreaching strategy never was formulated, and that the North Vietnamese, Vietcong, Soviets and Chinese did the designing for us. If contingency guidelines on ordnance selection and rules of engagement are drawn up far in advance, they will force a pointed discussion on subjects that were never raised in any systematic fashion during the Vietnam War. Hawks and doves, whether in uniform or out, chafed against the ground rules as they evolved, but few public servants on either side resigned, fearing that their replacements would be even less effective in the bargaining process. If guidelines were drawn at the outset, individuals would have to face up to their responsibilities more candidly. This procedure is also fairer to the military, who should know what they're getting into and under what ground rules. Finally, establishing ground rules at the outset can be more effective in holding the line against the expanding threshold for collateral damage which marked the Vietnam War. Baselines can be used to evaluate how far from the ground rules field operations have strayed, and to analyze operations in view of concrete policy objectives.

*4. Conduct field checks once weapons are operational.*

Once the decision to go to war has been made, pressures to increase collateral damage and to loosen checks on military commanders will be enormous. Once weapons are introduced onto the battlefield, their uses seem to multiply.

An organization in charge of a military operation can be required to deliver collateral damage assessments, and encouraged to be candid about them. But there is still no substitute for an independent evaluation by some body that does not have its reputation at stake in the proceedings.

Analysis of weapons' performance should not be left exclusively to the military. Technicians, civilian intelligence analysts, and laymen all have a constructive role to play here. Robert Komer, former chief pacification adviser in Vietnam, argues for a greater role by technicians. "Scientists designed the weapons," says Komer, "and they know best what they can do." Another top-ranking official at the State and Defense Departments during the war years suggests a review board including distinguished technical experts to monitor the research, development, and operational phases of weaponry.

Military operations analysts can still play a useful role. They have been used in the past to evaluate major engagements. Although they would be less than welcome by field commanders on counterinsurgency operations, they are nonetheless needed. In equipping police or allied forces, the United States uses as a rule of thumb the principle that our military friends should have roughly the same kind of equipment as their enemies. This principle prevents our allies from fighting the wrong kind of war, and relying on equipment rather than motivation. The same principle does not hold true for U.S. troops. "The last thing a professional military man wants is a fair fight," says Major General Daniel S. Campbell, U.S.A. (Ret.), former Joint Chiefs of Staff liaison to the National Security Council. "He wants a preponderance of strength on his side." The firepower at the disposal of U.S. forces is unmatched anywhere. Quite aside from the consequences of this fact for winning guerrilla wars, the consequences for generating collateral damage are unmistakable. Operations analysts can be one mechanism for limiting battlefield abuses, if they are specifically asked to comment on damage and weapons' effects.

Other kinds of checks can be applied as well. During the Vietnam War, officials at the State Department tended to dwell on the question of target selection, even though ordnance selection resulted in far greater human costs. In the future, the State Department's Bureau of Intelligence and Research (INR) should initiate research memoranda on the political repercussions of ordnance selection.

More simply put, what these recommendations are directed toward is opening up the decision-making process. The consequences of excessive secrecy have been more recently under fire domestically, but the results are the same: a filtering process which eliminates all nonsupportive information and fosters self-justification through abdication of responsibility. Greater participation by sensitive political officials would sustain a healthy adversary process at every stage of decisions to develop and use weapons.

## VI

When all is said and done, however, there is no amount of procedural tinkering that can effectively substitute for intelligent and humane political leadership at the highest levels.

Military officials believe it is their job to protect the interests of the United States, as defined by political authorities. Political officials believe it is their job to define those interests, but they are reluctant to oversee the way the military goes about performing its task. The one instance where political input is expected and given to military commanders relates to nuclear weapons. Everyone concedes that there must be political oversight of these indiscriminate and lethal weapons. With the Vietnam War, we have perfected another kind of ordnance—CBUs—which result in a different kind of indiscriminate destruction. The issues raised by area weapons must be faced squarely. The consequences of not doing so will weigh heavily on our nation's reputation and conscience. The former field commander I quoted at the start of this article has had the opportunity to evaluate antipersonnel weaponry, and he has no hesitation about using it in the future. But at least he realizes the costs when he says, "God help the civilians in the next war."

# Proscription of Ecocide:
# Arms Control and the Environment

## ARTHUR H. WESTING

*"This article directs attention to the largely unrecognized ecological impact of the techniques likely to be employed in the many small wars we can look forward to in the years to come. The Indochina war provides an example of what can be expected when a major nation becomes involved in a counterinsurgency war on foreign shores. . . . I am convinced that what is urgently required at this time is the establishment of the concept that widespread and serious ecological debilitation—so-called ecocide—cannot be condoned."*

*Arthur H. Westing, a professional forester, is professor of botany at Windham College, Putney, Vt. This article is based in part on material presented to the 1972 International Non-Governmental Organizations (NGO) Conference on Disarmament in Geneva.*

It is axiomatic that warfare is detrimental to the environment. To begin with, the preparation for war is detrimental in several ways. It consumes scarce and nonrenewable resources, usually on a priority basis. It also generates a variety of pollutants during the manufacture and testing of the war matériel, thereby having an adverse effect on still other natural resources. The present arms race is particularly wasteful of our global resources [1]. Second, the practice of war is detrimental to the environment. Military action consumes nonrenewable resources, often at a lavish rate. And, of course, the battles debilitate the theater of war itself, the concern of this paper.

It may at first appear extraneous or trivial to voice concern over the ecological disruptiveness of warfare. On the one hand, the justification (valid or presumed) for such a grave action as war might readily be assumed to outweigh any possible ecological concerns. On the other, the human agony inexorably involved in any armed conflict would tend to relegate ecological concerns to the background.

There are, however, a number of reasons for examining the ecological dimensions of warfare in some detail. First, the subject has been almost universally ignored in the past, precluding a rigorous assessment of its importance. Second, world environmental problems appear to have reached the point where any substantial regional perturbation of the physical environment becomes a matter of international concern. Third, certain methods of warfare likely to be practiced in the future with increasing regularity are particularly destructive of the environment.

Wars can be divided conveniently into large wars —world wars, general wars—and small wars—local wars, limited wars. The latter can be either international or intranational; they include the civil wars, counterinsurgency wars, and wars of national liberation.

The worldwide trend is clearly in the direction of local wars fought largely within the bounds of one nation (although, of course, often with outside participation). Of the 24 wars recorded by Wright [2] between 1900 and the beginning of World War II, only 21 per cent were classified as being intranational. In contrast, of the 97 wars recorded by Kende [3] since World War II, 84 per cent were classified as intranational. (The number of wars one comes up with for any particular time period depends, of course, on the criteria one establishes for a war [4].) Moreover, Kende's analysis [3] shows that South and Southeast Asia, Africa, and Latin America are increasingly becoming the scenes of local war. And it seems that the factors leading to such wars are intensifying rather than diminishing.

In the unlikely event of a future world war, one can be reasonably certain that its environmental impact would be profound. The ecologically devastating potential of the nuclear, biological and particularly horrible chemical weapons found in the major arsenals of the world is already recognized [5]. Fortunately, the necessity for proscribing these weapons and for avoiding world war is also recognized.

## Lesson of Indochina War

In its long and frustrating attempt to crush an elusive enemy during the Indochina war, the United States continually made lavish use of technologically sophisticated and expensive weaponry. This capital-intensive approach appears to have been an attempt to trade off matériel for men, that is, high monetary expenditures for low troop commitments, and thus for a low casualty rate.

Although the United States seems to have made

every effort to control as large a proportion of the Indochinese population as it could (i.e., to win as many hearts and minds as possible), at no time during the war did it ever attempt to physically control more than a minute fraction of the land area of Indochina. In fact, despite occasional U.S. infantry operations, the so-called search-and-destroy operations, essentially no real estate changed hands during the entire war.

What was carried on over the years with a remarkable amount of vigor was the attempt by the United States to make a major fraction of Indochina's land surface continuously inhospitable to its enemy. This had the dual purpose of driving the indigenous rural peoples into the U.S.-controlled population centers and of depriving the enemy combatants of local support (willing or otherwise). One might add that it had the additional effect of making these displaced persons dependent upon U.S. largesse. This strategy of counterinsurgency warfare has been referred to as "forced-draft urbanization" [6].

### Saturation Bombing

The United States carried out its grand strategy of widespread area denial in a number of suitably grand and innovative fashions. These need only to be mentioned here since they and their devastating ecological impact have been described adequately elsewhere. Perhaps the most bizarre means of denying forest cover and sanctuary to the enemy was via the aerial spraying of vast areas with plant-killing poisons or herbicides[7]. However, forested regions that were particularly troublesome from a military standpoint were destroyed with even greater finality, if less finesse, simply by being scraped away by companies of massed giant tractors (Rome plows) [8]. But the most devastating and least appreciated approach to area denial on a continuing basis was the program of pattern or saturation bombing, truly awe-inspiring in its magnitude [9]. Among the other counterinsurgency activities by the United States in Indochina of potential ecological significance were the weather modification [10] and the forest fire (fire storm) programs [11].

The precise over-all extent of ecological damage to Indochina may never be known. (Sen. Gaylord Nelson introduced a bill, S. 3084, that would provide for an assessment of the ecological damage brought about by the Indochina war. The bill died in committee in the 92nd Congress and, having been reintroduced (S. 365), is well on its way to doing the same in the 93rd.) It is clear, however, that in the process of attempting to deny its enemy freedom of movement and local support in the rural and wild reaches of Indochina, the United States has significantly debilitated the forests, the wildlife, the soils and the very ecosystems via its lavish employment of area denial weaponry. Such widespread ecological debilitation becomes particularly serious to a largely agrarian society that must depend to a great extent on an adequate natural resource base for its well-being. Indeed, one of the saddest results of the war has been the separation of a peasant people from its land.

It can be seen that the Indochina war has demonstrated the strategic attractiveness and efficiency to the military of ecologically destructive techniques. It has thereby imposed upon us the necessity for examining the traditional approaches to disarmament and arms control in this special context.

### Traditional Approaches

The simplest and most straightforward means of avoiding ecological damage through military activities is to prevent warfare itself. I sympathize with the minority that rejects armed conflict as a legitimate human activity and presses for general and complete disarmament [12]. I recognize, however, that the prevailing view has always been to consider war to be justified under a variety of more-or-less extraordinary sets of circumstances. Indeed, throughout the history of mankind there appears to have been no significant period of peace on Earth [2].

If general and complete disarmament seems too utopian an approach to avoiding ecological warfare, to what extent would the traditional approaches to making war more palatable be applicable? Traditionally, arms control has been approached from one of three directions: the focus has been on man, certain geographical regions, or particular weapons.

With respect to man, codes have been established relating to the protection of enmeshed civilians, of sick, wounded, and shipwrecked combatants, of medical personnel and chaplains, and of prisoners of war. There is an amalgam of so-called rules of war based upon the Hague and Geneva Conventions, the Nuremberg Principles, U.N. General Assembly resolutions, etc. The widely recognized 1949 U.N. Convention on Genocide is another important case in point. The modern concept of war crimes and crimes against humanity is an outgrowth of these rules of war, all apparently related to man per se [13, 14]. It can be seen that this whole category of arms control—as important as it is in humanizing warfare—does not provide a direct approach to controlling ecological warfare. On the other hand, keeping the focus on man may help to gain the acceptance of some ecologically advantageous proposals. For example, the pillaging of Polish forests by the Germans during World War II was classed as a war crime at Nuremberg [15].

With respect to regional controls, the following agreements exist: the Antarctic Treaty of 1959; the Outer Space Treaty of 1967; the Treaty (of Tlatelolco) for the Prohibition of Nuclear Weapons in Latin America of 1967, and the Sea-Bed Treaty of 1971. Whatever their basic individual objectives, such international agreements are, of course, ecologically valuable. They provide, albeit fortuitously, for the protection of a region in the same sense that a wildlife refuge or sanctuary does. Not only is protection provided for the involved ecosystems with their living and non-living components, but also perhaps for some crucial link in the greater cycles of nature that serve to maintain the biosphere, our worldwide ecosystem. Regional arms limitations are thus to be encouraged both for humanitarian and ecological reasons.

With respect to weapons, there is a long history of more-or-less successful attempts at limitation. Among the early proscriptions of particularly odious weapons are the St. Petersburg Declaration of 1868, prohibiting the use of exploding bullets, and The Hague Declaration of 1899, doing the same for soft-nosed, expanding bullets. Perhaps the most important example of this approach to arms control is the Geneva Protocol of 1925 which prohibits the use of chemical and bacteriological agents in war. In this area, one also must mention the Biological Warfare Convention of 1972. Furthermore, there are continuing efforts to prohibit or at least limit nuclear weapons, such as the U.N. General Assembly Resolution of 1961, the Partial Test Ban Treaty of 1963, the Non-Proliferation Treaty of 1968, the Nuclear Accidents Agreement of 1971 and the SALT Agreements of 1972.

The weapons limitation approach has important applications with respect to ecological warfare. For example, some of the most widespread and long-lasting ecological damage to South Vietnam was caused by chemical weapons. Strict adherence by the United States to the Geneva Protocol of 1925 would have precluded this form of attack [16]. It is important to add here parenthetically that weapons limitation agreements should include a prohibition not only of use but also of manufacture and possession as well as procedures for inspection.

Consideration of the several traditional approaches to arms control as outlined above suggests that they are adequate to cope with some of the ramifications of ecological warfare. A new conceptual approach thus appears necessary.

## Legal Proscription of Ecocide

I am convinced that what is urgently required at this time is the establishment of the concept that widespread and serious ecological debilitation —so-called ecocide—cannot be condoned. I would first limit it to ecocide caused by military activities, although it might well be argued that such a limitation is shortsighted. On the other hand, I would not restrict the concept to intentional military ecocide. Intent may be not only impossible to establish without admission but, I believe, it is essentially irrelevant.

The underlying philosophical justification for establishing the notion that ecocide is an unacceptable human activity may well differ among peoples. It could range from an ill-defined reverence or respect for nature (of which man is but one small part) to the more anthropocentric consideration that the biosphere provides man with his life-support system. As an extension of this ambivalence

it becomes a little difficult to decide upon the precise limits of ecocide. At what point does ecology in the strictest sense merge into human ecology and this in turn into anthropology or sociology?

Be that as it may, Falk [17] provides us with a proposed Convention on the Crime of Ecocide which would serve to establish ecocide as a crime in international law. A convention of this sort should be designed to complement the Genocide Convention of 1949. Indeed, in some instances it would be difficult to decide which is the more appropriate convention to invoke, as for example in the case of widespread chemical destruction of the agricultural lands of entire primitive cultural groups [18].

What is next required is legal instruments whose focus is the category of military activity and/or the nature of the target. One pioneering effort in this direction is the draft treaty on geophysical warfare prepared by Sen. Claiborne Pell, which was overwhelmingly affirmed by the U.S. Senate as S.R. 71, 93rd Congress. (The House, however, has been more recalcitrant, despite the efforts of Rep. Donald M. Fraser—H.C.R. 659, 92nd Congress; H.R. 329, 93rd Congress.) The Pell treaty would prohibit any military weather modification activities such as manipulating precipitation or lightning, or directing or diverting storm systems; it would prohibit the instigation of earthquakes; and it would prohibit any ocean modification such as changing ocean currents or creating tidal waves. Falk [17] has also drafted a treaty which would prohibit environmental warfare, stressing the specific ecocidal techniques employed by the United States in Indochina.

It appears to me that one of the most useful approaches to preventing future military ecocide is to focus on the target rather than, or in addition to, particular weapons and techniques. Thus I would urge a proscription of any weapon or technique on the basis of whether it devastates a wide area. It is a strategy of area denial—no matter what the method employed—that is likely to be a particular threat to the regional ecology. Moreover, it seems to me that such military activity can be rather clearly and simply defined (an important consideration in the drafting of an appropriate legal instrument) and infractions readily recognized. It is also useful to add here that area denial techniques cannot discriminate well between military and non-military targets or between combatants and non-combatants—further compelling reasons for their prohibition. Indeed, on the basis of the Indochina experience, the major brunt of any environmental warfare is far more likely to be absorbed by the civilian sector of the recipient nation than the military sector.

My plea for a straightforward proscription of military ecocide may seem too restrictive to some. In that case, one might at least hope that ecocide be recognized now as the rural counterpart of the infamous obliteration of the ancient city of Carthage by the Romans 21 centuries ago. Farer [14] points out that the prohibition of a "Carthaginian peace" can be considered the master principle underlying the rules of war. As such the wrongfulness of ecocide demands at least to be taken into account when alternative strategies are being considered.

Once the formidable problems associated with the formulation of legal instruments aimed at preventing ecological warfare are overcome, the task would still remain of having them accepted by the major governments of the world—unilaterally, bilaterally and multilaterally. The problem is that when a government reaches the point of pursuing its aims through warfare, the tendency is for it to employ the most powerful and tactically efficient weapons at its disposal. One crucial restraint on such a tendency, it seems to me, is provided by public opinion; weapons generally considered to be abhorrent are less apt to be employed. A realization of the close interdependence of man and nature is only just beginning to emerge as a result of the increasing stress man is imposing on this relationship. Thus, in the last analysis, I believe that only by arousing world opinion to recognize the abhorrence of any major ecological destruction that we will be able to achieve international acceptance of a proscription of ecocide.

## REFERENCES

1. M. E. Chacko, et al., "Economic and Social Consequences of Arms Race and of Military Expenditures" (New York: United Nations, 1972).

2. Q. Wright, Study of War: With a Commentary on War Since 1942 (2d ed.; Chicago: University of Chicago Press, 1965).

3. I. Kende, "Twenty-five Years of Local Wars," Jour. Peace Research, 8:1 (1971), 5.

4. F. Blackaby, et al., SIPRI Yearbook of World Armaments and Disarmament, 1968/69 (Stockholm: Almqvist & Wiksell, 1970), 359-373.

5. U Thant, et al., "Effects of the Possible Use of Nuclear Weapons and the Security and Economic Implications for States of the Acquisition and Further Development of these Weapons" (New York: United Nations, 1968); U Thant, et al., "Chemical and Bacteriological (Biological) Weapons and the Effects of Their Possible Use" (New York: United Nations, 1969); and "Health Aspects of Chemical and Biological Weapons" (Geneva: WHO, 1970).

6. S. P. Huntington, "Bases of Accommodation," Foreign Affairs, 46 (1967-68), 642.

7. A. H. Westing, "Herbicides in War: Current Status and Future Doubt," Biological Conservation 4 (1971-72), 322.

8. A. H. Westing, "Leveling the Jungle," Environment 13:9 (1971), 8; and S. E. Draper, "Land Clearing in the Delta, Vietnam," Military Engineer, 63 (1971), 257.

9. A. H. Westing and E. W. Pfeiffer, "Cratering of Indochina," Scientific American, 226 (May 1972), 20; errata, 226 (June 1972), 7; and R. Littauer and N. Uphoff, eds., Air War in Indochina (rev. ed.; Boston: Beacon, 1972).

10. D. S. Greenberg, "Vietnam Rainmaking: A Chronicle of DOD's Snowjob," Science & Govt. Rept. 2:5 (1972), 1; S. M. Hersh, "Rainmaking Is Used as Weapon by U.S.," N.Y. Times, July 3, 1972, July 4, 1972, July 9, 1972; and D. Shapley, "Rainmaking: Rumored Use Over Laos Alarms Arms Experts, Scientists," Science 176 (1972), 1216.

11. R. Reinhold, "U.S. Attempted to Ignite Vietnam Forests in '66-67," N.Y. Times, July 21, 1972, July 22, 1972, July 23, 1972; and D. Shapley, "Technology in Vietnam: Fire Storm Project Fizzled Out," Science 177 (1972), 239; "Shrinking Sanctuary," Time 91:17 (1968) 28.

12. J. E. Bristol, et al., In Place of War: An Inquiry into Nonviolent National Defense (New York: Grossman, 1967).

13. T. Taylor, Nuremberg and Vietnam: An American Tragedy (Chicago: Quadrangle Books, 1970).

14. T. J. Farer, "Laws of War 25 Years After Nuremberg, Intl. Conciliation, No. 583 (1971).

15. U.N. War Crimes Commission, History of the United Nations War Crimes Commission and the Development of the Laws of War (London: His Majesty's Stationery Office, 1948), 496.

16. A. H. Westing, "Herbicides as Agents of Chemical Warfare: Their Impact in Relation to the Geneva Protocol of 1925," Environmental Affairs 1 (1971-72), 578.

17. R. A. Falk, "Environmental Warfare and Ecocide," Bull. Peace Proposals 4 (1973), 1.

18. A. H. Westing, "U.S. Food Destruction Program in South Vietnam," in Wasted Nations, edited by F. Browning and D. Forman (New York: Harper & Row, 1972), 21-25.

# Environmental Warfare and Ecocide

RICHARD A. FALK*

Princeton University

## I

In Indochina during the past decade we have the first modern instance in which the environment has been selected as a 'military' target appropriate for comprehensive and systematic destruction. Such an occurrence does not merely reflect the depravity of the high-technology sensibilities of the war-planners. It carries out the demonic logic of counterinsurgency warfare, especially when the insurgent threat is both formidable and set in a tropical locale. Recourse to deliberate forms of environmental warfare is part of the wider military conviction that the only way to defeat the insurgent is to deny him the cover, the food, and the life-support of the countryside. Under such conditions, bombers and artillery seek to disrupt all activity, and insurgent forces find it more difficult to mass for effective attack. Such policies have led in Indochina to the destruction of vast tracts of forest land and to so-called 'crop-denial programs'. The US Government has altered tactics in recent years, shifting from chemical herbicides to Rome Plows as the principal means to strip away the protective cover of the natural landscape, but the basic rationale of separating the people from their land and its life-support characteristics persists. Such policies must be coupled with the more familiar tenets of counterinsurgency doctrine which seek to dry up the sea of civilians in which the insurgent fish attempt to swim. This drying up process is translated militarily into making the countryside unfit for civilian habitation. To turn Indochina into a sea of fire and compel peasants

to flee their ancestral homes was consciously embodied in a series of war policies including 'free-fire zones', 'search and destroy' operations, and the various efforts to move villagers forcibly into secure areas. Therefore, it is important to understand the extent to which environmental warfare is linked to the overall tactics of high-technology counterinsurgency warfare, and extends the indiscriminateness of warfare carried out against people to the land itself. Just as counterinsurgency warfare tends toward genocide with respect to the people, so it tends toward ecocide with respect to the environment.

It may be more than coincidental that at the historical moment when we are in the process of discovering the extent to which man's *normal* activities are destroying the ecological basis of life on the planet, we should also be confronted by this extraordinary enterprise of deliberate environmental destruction in Indochina. These conscious and unconscious tendencies need to be linked in any adequate formulation of the world order challenge confronting mankind. It is also worth noting that so far, at least, the target area of environmental warfare is the Third World– a sector of world society that has largely disavowed the relevance of the ecological agenda to its scheldule of priorities. Environmental warfare is a dramatic reminder of the extent to which the planet as a whole must mobilize a response to the ecological challenge to sustain life on earth and beat back reversions to barbarism emanating from the 'advanced' regions and applied to those that are relatively 'backward'. It is a form of dangerous provincialism for the countries of Asia and Africa to call for 'benign neglect' when it comes to this subject-matter; perhaps the relevance of ecological issues can be grasped more clearly by Third World leaders and peoples in relation to environmental warfare.

* Richard A. Falk is Professor of International Law and Practice, Princeton University. He is the author and editor of a number of books on international law, including *Legal Order in a Violent World*, *The Vietnam War and International Law*, and *The Status of Law in International Society*.

## II

On a more technical level, several issues of related concern need to be considered. First of all, it seems important to assess the extent to which patterns of environmental warfare violate existing criteria of legal judgment. Secondly, there is a need to promote the development of new law that captures the uniqueness of recent developments and anticipates future dangers; in particular, the search for clear standards of legal prohibition directed explicitly toward environmental warfare might help shape future conduct. Many governments, reluctant to protest against what the United States has been doing in Indochina, have avoided a concern with environmental warfare. At this stage it is possible to formulate, at least, a series of public demands around which popular support needs to be rallied if governments and world institutions are to join in the movement for rectifying action.

## III

In considering the relevance of international law I wish to make several preliminary points that bear on more specific assessments:

1) The connection between treaties and customary international law;

2) The role of world community consensus in interpreting the requirements of international law;

3) The importance of principles of customary international law for the interpretation of legal status of disputed tactics of warfare;

4) The importance of moral considerations in judging what is permissible behavior of governments and their officials;

5) The significant distinction between the *illegality* of governmental conduct and the *criminality* of individual conduct (whether or not in the line of official duty).

1) *The connection between treaties and customary international law.* There has been a tendency by governments to confine the scope of the law of war to treaty law. Such confinement is improper. Even the US Army Field Manual 27-10 acknowledges that customary international law complements treaty rules. It is important to understand that customary norms exist and apply because of the degree to which modern weaponry and battlefield tactics have evolved since the time when the basic treaties were formulated at the turn of the century. The broad lawmaking treaties in 1907 bearing on the law of war were themselves specific embodiments of general principles of belligerent restraint as they related to war technology and tactics existing at that time. These customary principles, more than the treaty rules they gave rise to, remain the primary basis for giving legal substance to the law of war in the face of a drastically altered technological and military environment. New treaties would be desirable, because of their capacity to generate agreed interpretations of the specific implications of new weaponry and tactics in relation to the customary principles underlying the law of war. Such treaties could provide authoritative reading of limits on state behavior; they would also be more likely to engender respect, as contemporary government officials would have taken part in the reformulation process and renewed their commitments by participating in the treaty-making rituals of solemnity.[1] But in the absence of a a new round of Hague-type conferences, the best ground that exists for legal judgment is to examine contested belligerent practices in light of the more general policies to which they gave expression. Customary principles of international law [see section 3 below] are of great importance in understanding the legal status of the various dimensions of environmental warfare.

2) *The role of community consensus in interpreting the requirements of international law.* The increasing number of actors, their diversity, and the complexity of international life make it more difficult to rely upon procedures based on *governmental consent* to develop either binding new interpretations of old rules or generation of new rules of international law. In such a context a *consensus* of governments acting within the *scope* of *formal procedures* is increasingly viewed as capable of generating

authoritative interpretations and standards. The most significant arena wherein these newer procedures of law-creation have been used is the General Assembly of the United Nations. The status of these resolutions remains controversial, especially among the more sovereignty-oriented governments, but I think the record of reliance on such resolutions in areas of arms control, space, and human rights creates a body of practice in support of the contention that these resolutions can, where intended by a large majority of governments, declare and create law. True, the *degree* of authoritativeness and effectiveness of such law-making activity will depend on such factors as the strength and quality of consensus, the strength and quality of dissent, the specificity of demand, the willingness to implement conformity with prior legal and moral expectations. The basic point is that the General Assembly now possesses a quasi-legislative competence that needs to be seriously considered whenever it is relevant, especially when it sets forth a prevailing interpretation of the content of a previously agreed upon legal rule.

3) *The importance of principles of customary international law for the interpretation of disputed tactics of warfare.* Four principles of customary international law provide guidelines for the interpretation of any belligerent conduct not specifically covered by valid treaty rule:

– *Principle of necessity.* No tactic or weapon may be employed in war that inflicts superfluous suffering on its victims, even if used in the pursuit of an otherwise military objective;

– *Principle of humanity.* No tactic or weapon may be employed in war that is inherently cruel and offends minimum and wisely shared moral sensibilities;

–*Principle of proportionality.* No weapon or tactic may be employed in war that inflicts death, injury, and destruction disproportionate to its contribution to the pursuit of lawful military objectives;

– *Principle of discrimination.* No weapon or tactic may be employed in war that fails to discriminate between military and non-military targets and that is either inherently or in practice incapable of discriminating between combatants and noncombatants.

These four principles are general and are admittedly difficult to apply to the complexities of the battlefield. However, a rule of reason can be used to identify patterns (as distinct from instances) of clear violation, where the weapons and tactics are used in such a way as cannot be reasonably constructed as compatible with these principles of overriding constraint. Such principles also reflect a minimum moral content that underlies the whole enterprise of a law of war, admitting its inevitable horror, but still striving for a mitigating framework of restraint.

Customary principles of international law are especially important in relation to the law of war because of its dynamic character. The underlying commitment of governments to restraint depends upon the interplay between good faith adherence to these four principles and the actualities of war. The famous De Martens clause inserted in the Hague Conventions acknowledged this importance:

Until a more complete code of the laws of war has been issued, the high contracting Parties deem it expedient to declare that, in cases not included in the Regulations adopted by them, the inhabitants and belligerents remain under the protection and the rule of the principles of the law of nations, as they result from the usages established among civilized peoples, from the laws of humanity, and the dictates of public conscience.

Widely ratified treaties such as the 1925 Geneva Protocol on Gas, Chemical, and Bacteriological Warfare may also attain the status of customary international law by virtue of a consensus among governments active in the world community – even if the consensus falls short of unanimity – and thereby bind non-parties. The reasoning here is analogous to that used in section 2 to discuss the potentially authoritative status of General Assembly Resolutions purporting to interpret a treaty. G.A. Resolution 2603A (XXIV), which extends the coverage of the Geneva Protocol to tear gas and herbicides, illustrates both an effort to make a binding interpretation of a treaty rule and to extend the coverage of the treaty to the entire community including non-parties. In the text of G.A. Resolution 2603A 'the General Assembly... called for the strict observance by all States of the principles and objectives of the Geneva Protocol' and 'Declares as contrary to the generally recognized rules of international law as embodied in the Geneva Protocol' the use of tear gas and chemical herbicides. The point here, which will be discussed later, is that the United States is bound by 'the principles and objectives' of the Geneva Protocol, including the interpretation of its scope even though it has not ratified the treaty. In essence, such a conclusion reflects the view that an impartial third party – for instance, the International Court of Justice – would find that the United States is bound by the Geneva Protocol and by the interpretation of its scope affirmed by the overwhelming majority of governments. Such a prediction may be made either because the Resolution is itself law-proclaiming and authoritative, or because it is indeed an accurate declaration of the proper meaning of the Geneva Protocol (and parallel norm in customary international law).

As a practical matter, US ratification may still be important because much of the international law of war depends for effective application upon self-enforcement, especially when the actor is a major state not in conflict (and hence not deterred by) another major state. The United States would be much more likely to respect the Geneva Protocol, as generally, if it explicitly ratified the treaty, even though the case remains that it is bound by its terms even prior to ratification.

A final point has to do with the common contention that governments have generally used whatever weapons and tactics seemed to confer upon them a military advantage without according much heed to restraining prin-

ciples of customary international law, or for that matter, of treaty law. There is even a common misunderstanding that a claim of military necessity overrides legal restraints. The agreed understanding of governments embodied in the law of war is that legal restraints have been formulated with due regard for military necessity, and that any further unilateral abridgements are violations. To say that the law of war is frequently violated is merely to affirm that governments are not very law-abiding in this area, and are indeed criminally disposed, especially where their vital interests are at stake. Such a conclusion argues more for a different system of law enforcement – perhaps spearheaded by a law-minded citizenry – than for a suspension or negation of these international rules. Also, there is evidence, even bearing directly on the use of gas in war, to suggest that legal restraints were respected including by the United States, despite the fact that it has not been a party to the Geneva Protocol, and despite the prospect of some military advantage resulting from the use of gas in the Pacific island warfare against the Japanese during World War II.

4) *The importance of moral factors in judging what is permissible behavior of governments and their officials.* The law of war attempts to reconcile minimum morality with the practical realities of war. This reconciliation is best summarized in the four principles of customary international law. The moral sense of the community provides a legislative direction for the growth and understanding of international law. In no area is it as appropriate as in relation to war to contend that 'the law' does and should reflect that which ought to have been done or not done by governments and their representatives. Morality, in this sense, attempts to fill the legislative vacuum created by the institutional deficiencies of international society and adapt law to some extent to the rapidly changing realities of war. In this sense the growth of the international law of war may contain a greater element of retroactivity than in the more developed constitutional systems of do-

mestic society, but the retroactivity exists only on a legalistic plane. The Nuremberg initiative provides our most dramatic illustration of a legislative spasm in international law that rested on the firmest grounds of shared morality, but aroused criticism from legalistically inclined observers.[3] The Indochina context, given the public outrage over the desecration of the land at a time of rising environmental consciousness, creates a target of opportunity comparable to Nuremberg. Surely it is no exaggeration to consider the forests and plantations treated by Agent Orange as an Auschwitz for environmental values, certainly not from the perspective of such a distinct environmental species as the mangrove tree or nipa palm. And just as the Genocide Convention came along to formalize part of what had already been condemned and punished at Nuremberg, so an Ecocide Convention could help carry forward into the future a legal condemnation of environmental warfare in Indochina.

5) *The significant distinction between the illegality of governmental conduct and the criminality of individual conduct.* International law is most characteristically concerned with regulating the behavior of governments. The laws of war are binding of governments, although national legal systems generally make the laws of war binding on combat personnel and provide criminal sanctions applicable in the event of violations.[4] As well, the Nuremberg approach makes individuals criminally liable for violations of the laws of war even if the violations were committed in the line of duty and in deference to orders issued by bureaucratic or military superiors. That is, international law directs that individual conformity will the laws of war take precedence over normal obligations to domestic law or military and civilian lines of command. The practical consequences of such a directive have engendered many difficulties during the Indochina War for conscientious Americans. The Nuremberg obligation may be taken more seriously in the United States than elsewhere because of a tradition of respect for individual conscience and because the war crimes trials

after World War II were so greatly a reflection of US initiative. Daniel Ellsberg and Anthony Russo, draft and tax resisters, and an expanding national movement of civil disobedience all draw support from the wider logic of Nuremberg which not only implies a citizen's duty to refuse participation in illegal war policies or an illegal war, but also creates a legal basis for individual action to prevent governmental crimes of war.

IV

.It is now possible to assess the legality of the main components of environmental warfare as it has been waged in Indochina. It is important legally to distinguish between weapons and tactics that are designed to damage the environment and those that, like bombs, are designed to strike human or societal targets but which may also, as a side effect, damage the environment. It is also important to distinguish between specific occasions of environmental warfare and persistent patterns of warfare that produce cumulative effects on ecosystems that can be properly called 'ecocide' or policies that can be designated as 'ecocidal'. And finally, it is necessary to decide whether the scope of environmental warfare includes the human effects of these weapons. The issue on one level is whether man is to be conceived, for this purpose, as an integral element of 'the environment'; at a more practical level the issue is whether human side effects of chemical weapons like 2, 4, 5–T are to be included in a discussion of environmental warfare. The problem with the more expansive definition is that all forms of warfare are detrimental to man and his artifacts, and in this sense all warfare could be conceived to be environmental (or ecological) warfare – thereby missing the distinctive feature of US warfare in Indochina and the specific dangers of ecosystem destruction that are posed by high-technology counterinsurgency warfare, especially if carried on in tropical settings. At the same time it is artificial to ignore altogether our own human concerns; and an orientation toward the subject based on a conception of human ecology seems appropriate, wherein bonds between man and nature provide an essential focus for inquiry. Therefore we define environmental warfare as including all those weapons and tactics which either intend to destroy the environment *per se* or disrupt normal relationships between man and nature on a sustained basis. The focus is on environmental warfare as practiced by the United States in Indochina, rather than on the full gamut of weaponry detrimental to environmental values, which would certainly include biological, radiological, and nuclear weapons as well as those discussed here.

We will consider the legal status of the following weapons and tactics used in Indochina from this perspective:

1) The use of herbicides;
2) The use of Rome Plows to achieve deforestation;
3) Bombardment and artillery fire;
4) Reported reliance on weather modification techniques.

1) *The use of herbicides.* There is extensive information available on the use of herbicides in the Indochina War, principally in South Vietnam.[5] The major chemicals used as military herbicides were Agent Orange (a mixture of 2,4–D and 2, 4, 5–T) used against forest vegetation; Agent White (a mixture of 2,4–D and Picloram) also used mainly against forest vegetation; Agent Blue (Cacodylic Acid) used against rice and other crops. US Defense Department figures disclose a steady escalation in the use of chemical herbicides from 1962 up through the early months of 1968, with a slight tapering off up through the middle of 1969 when the last figures were released. In this period, 4,560,600 acres of forest land and 505,000 acres of crop land were sprayed, the total amounting to 5,065,600 acres, or more than 10 % of the entire area of South Vietnam (see evidence on Cambodia). The rate of application has been roughly thirteen times the dose recommended for domestic use by the US Drug Administration.

President Richard Nixon reportedly terminated the use of herbicides for crop destruction and announced a phase-out of the defoliation efforts in 1970. Defoliation has not been halted by Nixon, but rather the task has been shifted from chemicals to plows, which from an ecological point of view achieve even more disastrous results.

The environmental damage caused by defoliants can still not be fully assessed. However, there is strong evidence to suggest that some varieties of trees in South Vietnam, particularly nipa palms and mangroves, have been destroyed, not merely defoliated, by a single application; multiple applications kill other trees. The AAAS–HAC study concluded that half of the hardwood trees north and west of Saigon have been damaged. Westing estimated that by December 1970, 35 % of South Vietnam's dense forests had been sprayed; 25 % once, 10 % more than once. Madame Nguyen Thi Binh, speaking in Paris on behalf of the Provisional Revolutionary Government of South Vietnam, alleged that between 1961 and 1969 43 % of arable land and 44 % of forest land had been sprayed at least once and in many cases two, three, or more times. In this process over 1,293,000 persons were 'directly contaminated.'[6] John Lewallen concludes: 'The forests of South Vietnam have not been merely damaged for decades or centuries to come. Nor have they simply been deprived of rare tree species. It is probable that many areas will experience an ecosystem succession under which forest will be replaced by savanna.'7. Often elephant grass overwhelms a forest area that has been defoliated to such an extent as to prevent reforestation altogether.

There is ample evidence, then, that military herbicides have been extensively used throughout South Vietnam, especially heavily along rivers, estuaries, on village and base perimeters, and in relation to suspected base areas and supply trails. Defoliants were generally sprayed from the air in specially fitted C-123 cargo planes, often near populated areas and with their dispersal significantly spread beyond intended areas by wind factors. As a consequence, the herbicides contaminated crops, either leading to their destruction or, as the evidence suggests, to teratogenic effects on unborn children. There have been numerous authenticated reports of human and animal poisoning throughout the course of the war.

*Military rationale.* The basic military justification for the massive defoliation program was to deny the NLF protective cover, thereby guarding defensive positions against ambush and surprise attack and enabling improved target identificaton for offensive operations. The destruction of crops was justified as an effort to deny food to NLF forces in areas under their control.

*Legal rationale.* The legal rationale of the US Government has been well stated by J. Fred Buzhardt, General Counsel to the Department of Defense, in a letter to Senator J. William Fulbright, dated April 5, 1971:

[N]either the Hague Regulations nor the rules of customary international law applicable to the conduct of war prohibit the use of anti-plant chemicals for defoliation or destruction of crops, provided that their use against the crops does not cause such crops as food to be poisoned by direct contact, and such use must not cause unnecessary destruction of enemy property.

The Geneva Protocol of 1925 adds no prohibitions relating either the use of chemical or to crop destruction to those above. Bearing in view that neither the legislative nor the practice of States draw chemical herbicides within its prohibitions, any attempt by the United States to include such agents within the Protocol would be the result of its own policy determination, amounting to a self-denial of the use of weapons. Such a determination is not compelled by the 1907 Hague Regulations, the Geneva Protocol of 1925, or the rules of customary international law.[7]

In essence, the US Government claims that no existing rules of international law prohibit the military use of herbicides.

*Legal appraisal.* It seems clear that an overwhelming majority of governments regards (1) the Geneva Protocol as binding on non-parties, and (2) as extending its prohibition to cover military herbicides. The protocol is binding because it enjoys the status of customary international law, a status that the United States has not seriously challenged. Indeed, the US Government has argued its adherence to the terms of the Protocol, contending only that its prohibition does not extend to military herbicides (or riot control gasses). In submitting the Protocol to the Senate Foreign Relations Committee for ratification, Secretary of State William Rogers provided an accompanying statement which said: 'It is the United States understanding of the protocol that it does not prohibit the use in war of riot-control agents and chemical herbicides.'[8]

Such an understanding of the scope of the Protocol is not shared by the international community as a whole. UN General Assembly Resolution 2603A (XXIV) supported by a majority of 80–3 (with 36 absentions) indicated its express intention to dispel 'any uncertainty' as to the scope of the Protocol and contained following operative paragraph:

*Declares* as contrary to the generally recognized rules of international law as embodied in the Geneva Protocol the use in international armed conflicts of any chemical agents of warfare: chemical substances, whether gaseous, liquid, or solid, which might be employed because of their toxic effects of man, animals, or plants.

This paragraph puts forward a dual basis for disregarding the more restrictive understanding of the Protocol put forward by the American government. First of all, G.A. Resolution 2603A constitutes evidence of what most governments regard the scope of the prohibition to be. Secondly, 2603A is itself supported by a consensus of such character as to give its law-declaring claims an authoritative status by virtue of the quasi-legislative competence enjoyed by the General Assembly.

This view of the scope of the Geneva Protocol derived from positive international law also accords with the emerging moral consensus and community expectations relating to environmental quality. Hence, when in doubt as to the scope of a treaty rule it seems desirable to seek a determination that accords with unfolding community sentiments. On the level of customary international law, the broad principles of discrimination and proportionality seem at odds with the novel claim to attack vast areas of forest land so as to deprive an adversary of natural cover. It is questionable whether high-technology counterinsurgency warfare waged against a low-technology opponent can ever be reconciled in its basic character with the framework of restraint provided by the four principles of customary international law. In this sense the problems raised by claims to use military herbicides are but part of a larger set of legal concerns.

On balance, it seems possible to conclude that the US use of military herbicides in Indochina violated the Geneva Protocol, which is both a treaty and a standard of prohibition that enjoys the status of customary international law. This assessment of existing law could be confirmed by seeking an Advisory Opinion on the status and scope of the Geneva Protocol from the International Court of Justice. Such an Advisory Opinion is not really necessary, but if, as expected, it confirmed the interpretation of the Protocol embodied in 2603A then it would lay the US contention to rest once and for all.

When it comes to crop destruction the prohibition on military herbicides stands on even stronger legal ground. As Tom Farer points out, such tactics are 'at best indiscriminate, and they may in fact discriminate against civilians because, even if the food supply which survives defoliation was distributed evenly, in absolute terms civilians would suffer disproportionately in that there are more of them and many civilians, the young, for instance, have particularly intense needs for certain foods'.[9] Government studies have indeed convincingly shown that crop destruction as an international military tactic had the principal effect of reducing the food available to civilians; NLF food requirements were given priority in areas under their control and were small enough in relation to available food to be satisfied. A former high official in the so-called pacification program in Vietnam, L. Craig John-

stone, put the effects of crop destruction as follows: 'In the course of investigations of the program in Saigon and in the provinces of Vietnam, I found that the program was having much more profound effects on civilian noncombatants than on the enemy. Evaluations sponsored by a number of official and unofficial agencies have all concluded that a very high percentage of all the food destroyed under the crop destruction program had been destined for civilian, not military use. The program had its greatest effect on the enemy-controlled civilian populations of central and northern South Vietnam. In Vietnam the crop destruction program created widespread misery and many refugees.'[10] Such effects on the civilian population are evidently a central ingredient of counterinsurgent strategy vis-à-vis the countryside, and so crop destruction is fully consistent with such war policies aimed at refugee generation and pacification as 'free-fire zones', 'harassment and interdiction' artillery fire, forcible removal of refugees, and 'search and destroy' missions. The use of chemical herbicides to destroy crops destined for civilian consumption is one of the points where the allegations of ecocide merge with allegations of genocide.

2) *Use of Rome Plows and bulldozing equipment.* A second major form of warfare waged directly against the environment has been to clear the land of vegetation by means of systematic plowing. According to Paul R. Ehrlich and John P. Holdren:

Perhaps the crudest tool the United States is using to destroy the ecology in Indochina is the 'Rome plow'. This is a heavily armored caterpillar bulldozer with a 2.5 ton blade. The Rome Plow can cut a swath through the heaviest forest. It has been used to clear several hundred yards on each side of all main roads in South Vietnam. In mid-1971 five land clearing companies were at work, each with some thirty plows, mowing down Vietnamese forests. By then some 800,000 acres had been cleared and the clearing was continuing at a rate of about 2,000 acres (3 square miles) daily.[11]

Pfeiffer and Westing conclude that by 1971, Rome plowing 'had apparently replaced the use of herbicides to deny forest cover and sanctuary to the other side'. They conclude the Rome plowing is more effective than chemicals and 'is probably more destructive of the environment.' This tactic has been used to 'scrape clean the remaining few areas of the Boi Loi Woods northwest of Saigon'. Pfeiffer and Westing visited an area of forest that had been plowed several years previously; it was covered with cogon grass which, according to these experts, makes 'further successional stages to the original hardwood forest very unlikely.'[12] Such plowing inflicts ecological damage that may last very long, perhaps permanently.

*Legal rationale.* As far as I am aware, no attempt has been made to defend Rome plowing as a legitimate tactic of war. A defense of this practice, if attempted, would have to rest on the argument that it is a legitimate military objective to deny the enemy protective cover and that, in any event, no rules of prohibition can be discovered in either Treaty or customary international law.

*Legal appraisal.* All of the law of war was drafted and evolved in a pre-ecological frame of mind. There are no standards or rules that contemplated a military strategy that sought to destroy the environment as such. Article 22 of the Annex to the Hague Convention on Land Warfare could be relevant in interpreting present content: 'the right of belligerents to adopt means of injuring the enemy is not unlimited.' The US Supreme Court often interprets Constitutional norms as embracing conduct not contemplated at the time of ratification, but reflecting an evolving sense of limits within the world community.

Nevertheless, I think it is not easy to conclude that Rome plowing, however, much it offends ecological consciousness, constitutes a violation of existing standards of international law. This point up the need for the formulation of clear standards of prohibition, in a new Protocol on Environmental Warfare (Annex 2).

Finally, it is possible to view such environmental devastation as an instance of 'a crime against humanity' in the Nuremberg sense, suggesting again the quasi-legislative potentialities created in a situation of moral outrage. The link between environmental destruction of the Vietnamese forests and crimes against humanity is by way of 'human ecology'. the environment being interrelated in organic fashion with human existence.

Indeed there is some relatively hard evidence to support such an inference. In the official history of the UN War Crimes Commission there is the following report:

During the final months of its existence the Committee was asked in a Polish case (Commission No. 7150) to determine whether ten Germans, all of whom had been heads of various Departments in the Forestry Administration in Poland during the German occupation (1939–1944), could be listed *as war criminals on a charge of pillaging* Polish public property. It was alleged that the accused in their official capacities caused the wholesale cutting of Polish timber to an extent far in excess of what was necessary to preserve the timber resources of the country, with a loss to the Polish nation of the sum of 6,525,000,000 *zloty*. It was pointed out that the Germans, who had been among the first as a nation to foster scientific forestry, had entered Poland and wilfully felled the Polish forests *without the least regard to the basic principles of forestry.* The Polish representatives presented a copy of a circular signed by Goering under date of 25th January, 1940, in which were laid down principles for a policy of *ruthless exploitation of Polish forestry.* It was decided by the Committee that *prima facie* existence of a war crime had been shown and nine of the officials were listed as accused war criminals.[13]

3) *Bombardment and artillery fire.* Pfeiffer and Westing have usefully summarized the general information available:

In the seven years between 1965 and 1971 the U.S. military forces exploded 26 billion pounds (13 million tons) of munitions in Indochina, half from the air and half from weapons on the ground... For the people as a whole it represents an average of 142 pounds of explosive per acre of land and 584 pounds per person... most of the bombardment was concentrated in time (within the years from 1967 on) and in area. Of the 26 billion pounds, 21 billion were exploded within South Vietnam, one billion in North Vietnam, and 2.6 billion in Southern Laos.[14]

These awesome statistics will be further augmented by the escalation of bombing in 1972 to the highest levels of the war. Unlike category 1 and 2 practices, category 3 practices are not designed per se to destroy the environment. The element of intentionality is probably absent, although with the accumulation of experience the environmental consequence of bombing patterns becomes part of what is known by the war planners.

On the basis of the evidence available, several distinct patterns of ordinance use should be separately considered for purposes of legal analysis:

*Craterization.* Pfeiffer and Westing estimate 26 million craters, covering an area of 423,000 acres, and representing a displacement of about 3.4 billion cubic yards of earth. Much of the cratering has been caused by 500 pound bombs dropped from high altitude B-52 flights and from large artillery shells. Such a bomb typically produces a crater that is 30 to 40 feet wide and 5 to 20 feet deep (depending on topographical conditions), although larger craters have been reported. The effects of craters are numerous:

– arable and timber land are withdrawn from use virtually indefinitely;[15]
– unexploded bombs or fragments make neighboring land unsatisfactory for normal use and cause injury to man and animals;
– craters that penetrate the water table become breeding grounds for mosquitoes, increasing the incidence of malaria and dengue fever;

– craters displace soil, and especially in hilly areas accentuate soil runoff and erosion, causing laterization of the land in and around craters;
– bombardment of forest areas has harmed the timber industry by outright destruction; also, metal shards weaken trees and make them vulnerable to fungus infection.

*Legal rationale.* The bombardment involves legitimate bombardment of suspected concentrations of enemy troops or supplies. Environmental damage is an unintended side-effect not regulated in any way by existing international law. To the extent the bombing is indiscriminate then it is subject to independent attack. The demonstration of environmental damage adds little to the legal analysis of the status of Indochina bombing patterns.

*Legal appraisal.* No explicit rules of prohibition seem available to assess the legal status of craterization. However, the scale and magnitude of bombardment raises special issues under Article 22 of the Annex to the Hague Convention on Land Warfare and in relation to Crimes Against Humanity as specified at Nuremberg.

It does seem desirable, nevertheless, to seek new legal rules and principles that are explicitly concerned with the environmental side-effects of standard war policies. Also it is necessary in this context to regard belligerent action beyond the capacity of the environment to absorb and respond in a short period of time as involving the independent crime of ecocide.

Would a Nuremberg II tribunal convened to assess liability of US leaders for craterization in Indochina convict on this count? It is difficult to predict the outcome on this issue because the law is murky and because of an apparent absence of a direct intent to destroy the environment on the part of US civilian and military leaders.

*'Daisy-cutters.'* Gigantic bombs, weighing 15,000 pounds, were being dropped at an estimate rate of two per week since mid-1971 in South Vietnam to establish instant clearings for fire-base helicopter landing areas, and according to some accounts, on areas of sus-

pected troop concentrations. These bombs kill all animals and people who happen to be within a quarter-mile radius of the blast. The cleared area is completely deforested.

*Legal rationale.* Bombing and damage incidental to valid military purpose in a context where no rule of prohibition exists.

*Legal appraisal.* The specific action does not seem to violate positive norms of international law. Condemnation is partly an expression of outrage in relation to overall devastation of Indochina and partly an expression of an emerging ecological consciousness. Again, the legal retroactivity of prohibition in a Nuremberg II setting would be more than offset by a sense that such bombs are indiscriminate in effect and disrupt in fundamental fashion man's links to the environment.

*Electronic battlefield; systematic bombing; 'free-fire zones'.* In these settings bombing patterns are indiscriminate with respect to all that breathes and moves. The saturation bombing also devastates the land and tends to depopulate the area subject to attack. Fred Branfman has described in agonizing detail the total destruction of the idyllic and prosperous subsociety of 50,000 in the Plaine des Jarres in Laos.[16]

*Legal rationale.* There is none. The facts have been officially repressed or distorted by the US Government.

*Legal appraisal.* To the extent these war policies involve attacks on civilian targets, such as rural villages, they are clearly in violation of international law. To the extent that the separate acts of environmental destruction are considered the legal status is, at present, more problematic. To the extent that an inhabited ecosystem, such as the Plaine des Jarres, is devastated by direct action, then it seems to be a crime against humanity in the spirit of Nuremberg I.

4) *Weather modification.*[17] There is an increasing indication that the United States has seeded clouds over Laos in order to increase rainfall. The military rationale for such a tactic is to muddy or cause flooding in the vicinity of the network of roadways constituting the Ho Chi Minh trail. A cloud-seeding plane like a reconnaisance plane that drops flares could accomplish its mission by dropping 35 to 100 pounds of silver iodine over a six-hour period. The Defense Department has shrouded the subject in secrecy and has refused to make any statements of uneqivocal denial or confirmation. Nevertheless, a series of collateral accounts, including some references in the *Pentagon Papers* and some leaked information appearing on March 18, 1971 in a news column by Jack Anderson create a strong basis for believing that weather modification has been used in Indochina as a deliberate weapon of war.

Such tactics, because of their relative covertness and widespread potential for devastating impacts on a target area (and, perhaps, on global weather patterns as well) pose a great danger to the future of world order. It is vital to arouse public concern at this time and seek a clearcut prohibition on weather modification for military purposes.[18]

Because of the secrecy surrounding the activity and its novelty in the history of warfare, it is virtually impossible to carry legal analysis any further at this stage. Even more so than poison gas and bacteriological weapons, weather modification poses dangers of indiscriminate and uncontrollable damage, clearly a menacing genie that needs to be recaptured and confined for all time. It seems mandatory in such circumstances to seek an absolute legal prohibition on the practice of weather modification for military purposes.

## V

On the basis of this brief description of the legal status of the main elements of environmental warfare in Indochina it seems clear that there are two distinct sets of tasks:

1) To take steps to strengthen and clarify international law with respect to the prohibition of weapons and tactics that inflict environmental damage, and designate as a distinct crime those cumulative war effects that do not merely disrupt, but substantially or even irreversibly destroy a distinct ecosystem.

2) To take steps to stop and rectify the ecological devastation of Indochina, to censure the United States for these actions, to impose upon the United States a minimum burden of making available ample resources to permit ecological rehabilitation to the extent possible in the shortest time and in the most humane manner, and to assess fully the various ecological effects of the war upon Indochina.

To accomplish (1) we suggest the following action, illustrated by draft instruments:

– A Proposed International Convention on the Crime of Ecocide (Appendix I);

– A Draft Protocol on Environmental Warfare (Appendix II);

– A Draft Petition, to be signed by individuals and nongovernmental organizations, addressed to the Secretary General of the United Nations (Appendix III).

To deal with the more specific problems generated by the Indochina war we propose the following:

– A Draft Peoples Petition of Redress on Ecocide and Environmental Warfare addressed to governments and to the United Nations (Appendix IV).

## VI

Special difficulties pertain to taking appropriate legal action with respect to environmental devastation in Indochina. First of all, the United States as a preeminent state in the world system is able to block serious inquiry into this subject-matter. I believe this obstructive capability accounted for the failure to inscribe the issue of environmental warfare on the agenda of the UN Conference on the Human Environment. Secondly, and relatedly, the United Nations is not able to pursue effective initiatives without the assenting participation of its most powerful Members, especially the United States; the silence of the UN through a decade of warfare in Indochina is a shocking relevation of the extent to which the Charter is a dead letter whenever its violation is primarily attributable to one of the two superpowers. Thirdly, the United States has not lost the Indochina war in

the way in which Germany lost World War II- and as such, its leaders and policies are unlikely to be subjected to critical review by either an independent commission of inquiry or by an intergovernmental tribunal of judgment.

Given these realities, it is necessary to develop an action plan with some prospect for success. This plan will have to discount the possibilities of relying upon governments or on intergovernment organizations, although governments that are willing to formulate a critical response – as did Prime Minister Oluf Palme at the Stockholm Conference in June 1972 – help greatly to expose the failure of public institutions to protect public values. Similarly, the petitions seeking redress of grievances directed at those institutions entrusted with formal responsibility help to expose institutional responses that sustain or acquiesce in the practice of environmental warfare and ecocide. Such efforts to present petitions emphasize the need to stimulate a world populist movement, both nationally and internationally, as a way of eroding the power of governments over lives and ecological destinies.

The most important arenas of action may be nongovernmental in character. At some point it may be desirable to organize a peoples' commission of inquiry and redress that seeks to focus the facts of environmental devastation and ecocide on Indochina, and to formulate appropriate demands for censure and relief.

On a more fundamental level, the issues of environmental warfare are peculiarly resistant to inter-governmental collaboration because of their apparent link with counterinsurgency warfare. It is the counterinsurgent that tends to pursue the tactics and rely upon the weapons that do the most damage to the environment. That is, governments have a particular interest in being able to use their technological advantages to neutralize whatever advantages of dispersal and maneuverability are enjoyed by an insurgent. In Indochina this technological and tactical gap has led almost all of the serious environmental damage to have been inflicted by the forces aligned with the incumbent government. It can be argued, in addition, that without military herbicides, Rome plowing, and massive airpower, battlefield outcomes would have been decisively in favor of the insurgent forces. Therefore, it would seem that environmental devastation is a virtually inevitable byproduct of a sustained campaign of counterinsurgency, especially if carried out in the tropics against insurgent forces enjoying a strong base of populai support: in such circumstances not only must the sea be drained to imperil the fish, but its life-supporting ecology must be destroyed as well. Given the prospect of future insurgent challenges, it is unlikely that governments will be agreeable, at least not without a major populist campaign beforehand, to foreclose by assent to legal prohibitions their military options for counterinsurgent response.

This consideration suggests wider grounds for skepticism as to legal responses. Even in the Third World a large technological gap exists between the weaponry and tactics of the government and that of its internal challengers. Throughout the world most governments are confronted by insurgent challenges and seek to use all effective means to defeat them. The common governmental consensus is abetted by arms sales and transfers which make all governments increasingly dependent on high-technology military establishments. From this dependence, the willingness and capability to wage environmental warfare is almost certain to follow.

It needs to be understood that international law, and by and large, continues to reflect the perceived self-interest of governments. In terms of both formation and implementation, international law presupposes reciprocal interests in patterns of voluntary compliance. As such, international law is a consensual system. If these interests do not exist or are not perceived to exist, then it is difficult to generate new law or enforce old law in international affairs. This general comment is peculiarly true for the law of war which raises vital questions of governmental survival. Unlike interstate warfare, the insurgent actor is unrepresented in the international legal order, and the law is likely to be shaped to serve the

perceived military interests of governments (i.e. actual and potential counterinsurgents).

Such conclusions reinforce our view that the state system is *inherently incapable* of organizing the defense of the planet against ecological destruction.[19] The prospects for ecological protection are therefore intimately linked with the prospects of initiating a world populist movement that can incorporate the ecological imperative at the same time that it works to secure equity for all people on earth.

NOTES

1. Such an argument is convincingly set forth in Abram Chayer, 'An inquiry into the workings of arms control agreements', *Harvard Law Review*, Vol. 85 (March 1972), pp. 905–969.

2. Indeed, it could diminish the scope of its obligation by accompanying its ratification with either a reservation or a statement of understanding which maintained the option to use herbicides and riot control gasses.

3. For range of responses see William J. Bosch, *Judgment on Nuremberg: American attitudes toward the major German warcrime trials,* Chapel Hill, N.C., University of North Carolina Press, 1970.

4. The Geneva Conventions of 1949 even have a common provision obliging Parties to the treaties 'to enact any legislation necessary to provide effective penal sanctions' for persons committing or ordering 'grave breaches'.

5. See esp. J. B. Neilands, G. H. Orians, E. W. Pfeffer, Alje Vennemma, and Arthur H. Westing, *Harvest of death: chemical warfare in Vietnam and Cambodia,* New York, Free Press, 1972; John Lewallen, *Ecology of devastation: Indochina,* Baltimore, Md., Penguin, 1971; Thomas Whiteside, *The withering rain: America's herbicidal folly,* New York, Norton, 1971.

6. Madame Nguyen Thi Binh made this statement at the Paris Peace Conference, Feb. 19, 1970 (quoted in Barry Weissberg, ed., *Ecocide in Indochina,* San Francisco, Calif., Canfield Press, 1970, p. 19).

7. Lewallen, p. 80.

8. Mr. Rogers' testimony was on March 5, 1971.

9. Tom J. Farer, 'The laws of war 25 years after Nuremberg', *International Conciliation,* No. 583, May 1971, p. 20.

10. Johnstone, 'Ecocide and the Genova Protocol', *Foreign Affairs,* Vol. 49, pp. 711–720, at 719.

11. 'Ecocide in Indochina' (mimeo. paper), Dec. 1971, p. 2.

12. Arthur W. Westing and E. W. Pfeiffer, 'The cratering of Indochina', *Scientific American*, Vol. 226, May 1972, pp. 26–29, at 26–28.

13. *History of the UN War Crimes Comission and the development of the laws of war*, London, 1948, p. 496.

14. Westing and Pfeiffer, p. 21.

15. Same 24.

16. Fred Branfman, ed., *Voices from the Plain of Jars*, New York, Harper Colophon, 1972.

17. This section relies upon Deborah Shapley, 'Rainmaking: rumored use over Laos alarms arms experts, scientists', *Science*, Vol. 176, 16 June 1972, pp. 1216–1220.

18. Senator Claiborne Pell 'strongly believes' that clouds in North Vietnam have been seeded since 1966, and have caused thousands of deaths by provoking devastating floods. See *New York Times*, June 27, 1972, p. 12. Apprehension is increased by the connection between rainmaking and confirmed reports that dikes have been bombed.

19. This position is developed in my book *This endangered planet: prospects and proposals for human survival*, New York, Random House, 1971.

## APPENDIX I

*A Proposed International Convention on the Crime of Ecocide*

The Contracting Parties

acting on the belief that ecocide is a crime under international law, contrary to the spirit and aims of the United Nations, and condemned by peoples and governments of good will throughout the world;

recognizing that we are living in a period of increasing danger of ecological collapse;

acknowledging that man has consciously and unconsciously inflicted irreparable damage to the environment in times of war and peace;

being convinced that the pursuit of ecological quality requires international guidelines and procedures of cooperation and enforcement,

Hereby agree:

*Article I.* The Contracting Parties confirm that ecocide, whether committed in time of peace or in time of war, is a crime under international law which they undertake to prevent and to punish.

*Article II.* In the present Convention, ecocide means any of the following acts commited with intent to disrupt or destroy, in whole or in part, a human ecosystem:

(a) The use of weapons of mass destruction, whether nuclear, bacteriological, chemical, or other;

(b) The use of chemical herbicides to defoliate and deforest natural forests for military purposes;

(c) The use of bombs and artillery in such quantity, density, or size as to impair the quality of the soil or to enhance the prospect of diseases dangerous to human beings, animals, or crops;

(d) The use of bulldozing equipment to destroy large tracts of forest or cropland for military purposes;

(e) The use of techniques designed to increase or decrease rainfall or otherwise modify weather as a weapon of war;

(f) The forcible removal of human beings or animals from their habitual places of habitation to expedite the pursuit of military or industrial objectives.

*Article III.* The following acts shall be punishable:

(a) Ecocide;

(b) Conspiracy to commit ecocide;

(c) Direct and public incitement to ecocide;

(d) Attempt to commit ecocide;

(e) Complicity in ecocide.

*Article IV.* Persons committing ecocide as defined in Article II or any of the acts described in Article III shall be punished, at least to the extent of being removed for a period of years from any position of leadership or public trust. Constitutionally responsible rulers, public officials, military commanders, or private individuals may all be charged with and convicted of the crimes associated with ecocide as set forth in Article III.

*Article V.** The United Nations shall establish a Commission for the Investigation of Ecocide as soon as this Convention comes into force. This Commission shall be composed of fifteen experts on international law and assisted by a staff conversant with ecology. The principal tasks of the Commission shall be to investigate allegations of ecocide whenever made by governments of States, by the principal officer of any international institution whether or not part of the United Nations Organization, by resolution of the General Assembly or Security Council, or by petition signed by at least 1000 private persons. The Commission shall have power of subpoena and to take depositions; all hearings of the Commission shall be open and transcripts of proceedings shall be a matter of public record. If the Commission concludes by majority vote, after investigating the allegations that none of the acts described in Article III has been committed then it shall issue a dismissal of the complaint

* Article V may be the most controversial provision in this proposal, and could be either deleted altogether or appended as an optional protocol, to enhance the prospects for ratification of the basic Convention.

accompanied by a short statement of reasons. If the Commission concludes, by majority vote, after investigating the allegations that acts within the scope of Article III have been or are being committed then it shall issue a cease and desist order, a statement recommending prosecution or sanction of specific individuals or groups, and a statement of reasons supporting its decisions. The Commission shall also recommend whether prosecution proceeds under national, regional, international or ad hoc auspices. Regardless of decision minority members of the Commission may attach dissenting or concurring opinions to the majority decision. In the event of a tie vote in the Commission, the Chairman shall cast a second vote. The Commission shall have rule-making capacity to regulate fully its operations to assure full realization of the objectives of this Convention but with due regard for the human rights of individuals as embodied in the United Nations Declaration of Human Rights.

*Article VI.* The Contracting Parties undertake to enact, in accordance with their respective Constitutions, the necessary legislation to give effect to the provisions of the present Convention and, in particular, to provide effective penalties for persons guilty of ecocide or any of the other acts enumerated in Article III.

*Article VII.* Persons charged with ecocide or any of the other acts enumerated in Article III shall be tried by a competent tribunal of the State in the territory of which the act was committed, or by such international penal tribunal as may have jurisdiction with respect to those Contracting Parties which shall have accepted its jurisdiction.

*Article VIII.* Ecocide and the other acts enumerated in Article III shall not be considered as political crimes for the purpose of extradition.

The Contracting Parties pledge themselves in such cases to grant extradition in accordance with their laws and treaties in force.

*Article IX.* Any Contracting Party may call upon the competent organs of the United Nations to take such action under the Charter of the United Nations as they consider appropriate for the prevention and suppression of acts of ecocide or any of the other acts enumerated in Article III.

*Article X.* Disputes between the Contracting Parties relating to the interpretation, application or fulfillment of the present Convention, including those relating to the responsibility of a State for ecocide or any of the other acts enumerated in Article III, shall be submitted to the International Court of Justice at the request of any of the parties to the dispute.

*Article XI.* The present Convention, of which the Chinese, English, French, Russian and Spanish texts are equally authentic, shall bear the date of . . . .

*Article XII.* The present Convention shall be open until . . . for signature on behalf of any Member of the United Nations and of any non-member State to which an invitation to sign has been addressed by the General Assembly.

The present Convention shall be ratified, and the instruments of ratification shall be deposited with the Secretary-General of the United Nations.

After . . . the present Convention may be acceded to on behalf of any Member of the United Nations and of any non-member State which has received an invitation as aforesaid.

Instruments of accession shall be deposited with the Secretary-General of the United Nations.

*Article XIII.* Any Contracting Party may at any time, by notification addressed to the Secretary-General of the United Nations, extend the application of the present Convention to all or any of the territories for the conduct of whose foreign relations that Contracting Party is responsible.

*Article XIV.* On the day when the first twenty instruments of ratification or accession have been deposited, the Secretary-General shall draw up a *procès-verbal* and transmit a copy of it to each Member of the United Nations and to each of the non-member States contemplated in Article XII.

The present Convention shall come into force on the ninetieth day following the date of deposit of the twentieth instrument of ratification or accession.

Any ratification or accession effected subsequent to the latter date shall become effective on the ninetieth day following the deposit of the instrument of ratification or accession.

*Article XV.* The present Convention shall remain in effect for a period of ten years as from the date of its coming into force.

It shall thereafter remain in force for successive periods of five years for such Contracting Parties as have not denounced it at least six months before the expiration of the current period.

Denunciation shall be effected by a written notification addressed to the Secretary-General of the United Nations.

*Article XVI.* If, as a result of denunciations the number of Parties to the present Convention should become less than sixteen, the Convention shall cease to be in force as from the date on which the last of these denunciations shall become effective.

*Article XVII.* A request for the revision of the present Convention may be made at any time by any Contracting Party by means of a notification in writing addressed to the Secretary-General.

The General Assembly shall decide upon the steps, if any, to be taken in respect of such request.

*Article XVIII.* The Secretary-General of the United Nations shall notify all Members of the United Nations and the non-member States contemplated in Article XII of the following:

(a) Signatures, ratifications and accessions received in accordance with Article XII;

(b) Notifications received in accordance with Article XIII;

(c) The date upon which the present Convention comes into force in accordance with Article XIV;

(d) Denunciations received in accordance with Article XV;

(e) The abrogation of the Convention in accordance with Article XVI;

(f) Notifications received in accordance with Article XVII.

*Article XIX.* The original of the present Convention shall be deposited in the archives of the United Nations.

A certified copy of the Convention shall be transmitted to all Members of the United Nations and to the non-member States contemplated in Article XII.

*Article XX.* The present Convention shall be registered by the Secretary-General of the United Nations on the date of its coming into force.

*Resolution relating to the study by the International Law Commission of the question of an international criminal jurisdiction.*

The General Assembly,

Considering that the discussion of the Convention on the Prevention and Punishment of the Crime of Ecocide has raised the question of the desirability and possibility of having persons charged with ecocide tried by a competent international tribunal,

Considering that, in the course of development of the international community, there will be an increasing need of an international judicial organ for the trial of certain crimes under international law,

Invites the International Law Commission to study the desirability and possibility of establishing an international judicial organ for the trial of persons charged with ecocide or other crimes over which jurisdiction will be conferred upon that organ by international conventions;

Requests the International Law Commission in carrying out this task to pay attention to the possibility of establishing a Criminal Chamber of the International Court of Justice.

APPENDIX II

*Draft Protocol on Environmental Warfare*

Considering that environmental warfare has been condemned by public opinion throughout the world and that the deliberate destruction of the environment disrupts the ecological basis of life on earth;

Mindful of the extent to which the future of mankind is linked with the rapid development of protective attitudes toward environmental quality;

Conscious of the extent to which existing and prospective weapons and tactics of warfare, particularly counteringsurgency warfare or reliance on nuclear weapons, disrupt ecological patterns for long periods of time and destroy beneficial relationship between man and nature;

Recalling such prior expressions of collective concern with the general effects of war as expressed in General Assembly Resolutions 1653 (XVI) and 2603A (XXIV);

We, as representatives of governments and as citizens of the world community, do hereby commit ourselves as a matter of conscience and of law to refrain from the use of tactics and weapons of war that inflict irreparable harm to the environment or disrupt fundamental ecological relationships;

This Protocol prohibits in particular:

1. All efforts to defoliate or destroy forests or crops by means of chemicals or bulldozing;

2. Any pattern of bombardment that results in extensive craterization of the land or in deep craters that generate health hazards;

3. Any reliance on weapons of mass destruction of life or any weapons or tactics that are likely to kill or injure large numbers of animals.

We, as undersigned, will seek to gain as many individual and institutional accessions to this Protocol as possible;

The protocol shall come into effect after the first five signatures and is binding thereafter on all governments of the world because it is a declaration of restraints on warfare that already are embodied in the rules and principles of international law;

Violation of this Protocol shall be deemed an international crime of grave magnitude that can be charged and considered, by fair trial proceedings, wherever an alleged culprit can be charged and considered, by fair trial proceedings, wherever an alleged culprit can be apprehended; in cases of extreme necessity trials in absentia are authorized.

Done in Stockholm, Sweden, June 1972.

## APPENDIX III

*Draft Petition on Ecocide and Environmental Warfare*

The undersigned

*Mindful* of their concern with the ecological quality of this planet and with the purposes and principles of the Charter of the United Nations;

*Gravely concerned* by the evidence of ecological devastation in Indochina and by the spread of counterinsurgency weaponry and doctrine to governments throughout the world;

*Fearful* of the further willingness of governments to conduct their operations without due deference for the conditions of ecological welfare, especially during periods of armed conflict;

1. *Declare* that

(a) The commission of acts of ecocide is an international crime in violation of the spirit, letter, and aims of the United Nations and, as such, is a direct violation of the Charter of the United Nations and violates the sense of minimum moral obligation prevailing in the world community;

(b) The protection of man's relation to natural ecosystems is a legal, moral obligation deserving of the highest respect and directly related to the prospects for human survival and social development;

(c) Any government, organization, group, or individual that commits, plans, supports, or advocates ecocide shall be considered as committing an international crime of grave magnitude and as acting contrary to the laws of humanity and in violation of the ecological imperative;

2. *Request* the Secretary-General of the United Nations to take the following steps:

(a) Convene an emergency session of the Security Council to order the United States to cease and desist from all war policies responsible for the ecological devastation of Indochina;

(b) Compile a report on the ecological damage done to Indochina and urge the establishment of a commission of inquiry composed of experts that would submit periodic reports to the General Assembly of ecological effects of the war on Indochina and courses of action, together with funding, available to secure maximum rehabilitation of ecological quality;

(c) Request the International Law Commission to prepare an International Convention on Ecocide, a Protocol on Environmental Warfare.

and a Code on individual and collective responsibility relative to the crime of ecocide;

(d) Convene a conference of governments during 1974 to take appropriate legal steps to outlaw ecocide and to provide the legal framework needed to prohibit environmental warfare, including principles and procedures to assess responsibility and to enjoin activity destructive of environmental values.

## APPENDIX IV

*Peoples Petition of Redress on Ecocide and Environmental Warfare*

The Undersigned

Recognizing that modern weapons of mass destruction are capable of causing widespread and enduring devastation of the human environment;

Concerned by the evidence of long-term, extensive ecological damage caused in Indochina by a variety of weapons including bombs, napalm, herbicides, plows, and poisonous gases used principally and massively by the United States in the course of waging the Indochina war;

And further concerned by reports of the supply and sale of these means of waging war by the United States to other governments including the Saigon administration of South Vietnam and the government of Portugal;

Do hereby petition all governments to renounce weapons and tactics of war designed to inflict damage to the environment as such;

And call especially on the Government of the United States of America to immediately stop the destruction of the human environment in Indochina and to stop the sale and transfer of weaponry designed primarily to carry on environmental warfare;

And call upon the United Nations to take steps immediately to condemn reliance by the United States on environmental warfare in Indochina, to investigate and report the full extent of ecological damage resulting from the Indochina war; to consider and recommend steps that could be taken to restore the environment in Indochina as rapidly as possible; and to assess responsibility for ecological damage and to call for appropriate reparations from the government(s) responsible after the termination of hostilities;

We further appeal to the United Nations to convene promptly a world conference to draw up an international convention prohibiting recourse to weapons and military tactics designed primarily to destroy or modify the human environment and to prepare a draft Convention on Ecocide to parallel the Genocide Convention.

# The Laws of Air Warfare:
## Are There Any?†

## HAMILTON DESAUSSURE

Activity has increased within the United Nations recently to reexamine the laws of war, and to update them to meet the modern conditions of armed conflict. In a resolution adopted unanimously on 13 January 1969, UN Res 2444, the General Assembly emphasized the necessity for applying basic humanitarian principles to all armed conflicts and affirmed the three principles laid down by the International Committee of the Red Cross at their Vienna conference in 1965: First, that the rights of the parties to a conflict to adopt means of injuring the enemy are not unlimited; second, that the launching of attacks against the civilian populations *as such* is prohibited; and third, that "a distinction must be made between persons taking part in hostilities and the civilian population with the view of sparing the latter as much as possible."

The U.N. General Assembly Resolution then invited the Secretary General, in consultation with the International Committee of the Red Cross, to study how better to apply the existing laws of war for "the better protection of civilians, prisoners and combatants and for the further limitation on certain methods and means of warfare." All states were asked to ratify the Hague Laws of War Conventions of 1899 and 1907, the Geneva Gas Protocol of 1925, and the Geneva Conventions of 1949. Pursuant to that resolution, the Secretary General circulated for comment among member stated and international organizations, a report entitled "Respect for Human Rights in Armed Conflicts."[1] His report contains a historical sur-

†This article is based on an address by Colonel DeSaussure at the 1970 International Law Session of the Naval War College.

[1] Report of Secretary General, Respect for Human Rights in Armed Conflicts, A/7720, 20 November 1969.

vey of the existing international agreements pertaining to the laws of war, urging those stated which have appended reservations to withdraw them.

The Secretary General requested that "special emphasis be placed on the dissemination of the conventions to military personnel at all levels of authority, and on the instructions of such persons as to the IR principles and on the IR application." The observation was made that both juridical and military experts are needed to study this subject "to achieve, under the conditions of modern warfare, an adequate comprehension of the full range of technical and legal problems."

The Secretary General makes no specific plea for a convention regulating air warfare, but he does seem to indict "massive air bombing" by noting that, in some cases, this type of warfare has contributed to a very broad interpretation of what constitutes a permissible military objective. He states that strategic bombing has, in some instances, been used for intimidating, demoralizing and terrorizing civilians "by inflicting indiscriminate destruction upon densely populated areas." In the replies to the report, only Finland specifically adverted to the need for a codification of the laws of air warfare.

U.N. resolution 2444 was the result of a UNESCO Conference on Human Rights in Teheran in April of 1968. There, a resolution was adopted by the Conference with only one abstention and no votes against. It was couched in stronger terms than those later used in U.N. Resolution 2444, referring to the widespread violence and brutality of our times, including "massacres, summary executions, tortures, inhuman treatment of prisoners, killing of civilians in armed conflicts and the use of chemical and biological means of warfare including napalm bombing."[2]

With the background of U.N. Resolution 2444 and the Teheran declaration, the ICRC expanded its scope of studies to include the application of the laws of war to the conduct of hostilities. A committee of experts of the ICRC convened in February, 1969, and formulated a report entitled "Reaffirmation and Development of the Laws and Customs Applicable in Armed Conflicts."[3] It is the most authoritative treatment of the laws of war since World War II. It was the culmination of their observations made during the last 20 years of perennial armed conflicts, especially in Korea, the Middle East, Vietnam and the Yemen.

The tempo continues to increase for insuring respect for human rights in

---

[2]Final Act of the International Conference on Human Rights Resolution, XXIII, Teheran, April–May, 1968.

[3]International Committee of the Red Cross, Report of Experts, Prepared for Presentation to the 21st International Conference of the Red Cross at Istanbul, Turkey, in September, 1969.

armed conflicts. On September 18, 1970, the Secretary General issued a supplemental report on the subject.[4] Shortly thereafter, on December 9, 1970, the General Assembly overwhelmingly adopted UN Res 2675 entitled "Basic Principles for the Protection of Civilian Populations in Armed Conflicts."[5] Essentially, these basic principles were designed to separate out the civilian population from those "actively taking part in the hostilities" so that the former might be spared. Of particular interest were two fundamental principles which were specific in application. "Dwellings and other installations that are used only by civilian populations"; and "Places or areas designated for the sole protection of civilians, such as hospital zones or similar refuges" should not be "the object of military operations." The other six principles were more in the nature of general admonitions to spare the civilian populations as much as possible and to distinguish them from combatants.

This increased emphasis to the regulation of armed conflict by the ICRC as well as the U.N. General Assembly makes it imperative for air planners and flyers to know their rights and duties under the laws of war.

There is no dearth of opinion that in the matter of air warfare there are, in fact, no positive rules. Air Marshall Harris, the noted chief of the British Bomber Command in World War II, wrote shortly after its conclusion: "In the matter of the use of aircraft in war, there is, it so happens, no international law at all."[6] This view has been echoed in more recent times by well-known international lawyers who have specialized in studies on the laws of war. "In no sense but a rhetorical one," wrote Professor Stone in 1955, "can there still be said to have emerged a body of intelligible rules of air warfare comparable to the traditional rules of land and sea warfare."[7] Professor Levie labeled the nonexistence of a code governing the use of airpower in armed conflict one of the major inadequacies in the existing laws of war.[8] While the view of Air Marshall Harris reflects a certain hopeless attitude toward any attempt to regulate this important form of warfare, the views of Professors Stone and Levie reflect pleas to focus effort on its regulation and clarification.

In view of the very substantial role of air power in modern armed conflicts and the history of how this role has increased from World War I

---

[4]Supplemental Report of the Secretary General, Respect for Human Rights in Armed Conflicts A/8052, 18 September 1970.

[5]UN GA Res 2675 (XXV) 109 in favor, none against, 8 abstentions.

[6]Harris, *Bomber Offensive* 177 (1947).

[7]Stone, *Legal Controls of International Conflicts* 609 (1959).

[8]Levie, Report to the New York Bar Association, *Major Inadequacies in the Existing Laws of Armed Conflict* (1970).

to Vietnam, it is surprising to reflect that only three provisions of international legislation ever came into force with the specific view of regulating air operations in wartime. The first of these was the 1899 balloon declaration adopted in plenary session at the First Hague Peace Conference without debate. It provided simply that "The Contracting Powers agree to prohibit, for a term of five years, the launching of projectiles and explosives from balloons or by other new methods of a similar nature." The declaration was proposed by the Russian delegate and supported by a remarkably prescient Dutch delegate who stated that "the progress of science . . . has been such that things hitherto beyond belief are realized today. We can foresee the use of projectiles or other things filled with deleterious gases, soporific, which, dropped from balloons in the midst of troops, would at once put them out of commission."[9] The first balloon declaration expired by its terms in 1904, but at the Second Hague Peace Conference in 1907 the Russian delegation proposed its renewal. By this time, however, aircraft were looked upon no more as "too imperfect to be of any practical use in warfare"[10] and the adoption of the second balloon declaration was far from unanimous.[11] The 1907 balloon declaration was to remain in force until the close of the projected third Peace Conference, intended to be held in 1915, but yet to be called. Like the first declaration, the second was only in force in a war exclusively between contracting parties. Since France, Spain and Russia, among others, did not adopt it, and Germany only on condition all other parties to the Conference would sign, it obviously never fulfilled its intended legal effect.

The third provision of conventional law specifically framed to regulate air warfare, is article 25 of the 1907 Hague Convention respecting the laws and customs of war on land (H.C. IV). That article provides, "The attack or bombardment, *by whatever means,* of towns, villages, dwellings, or buildings which are undefended is prohibited." The negotiating record shows that the words, "by whatever means," were inserted specifically, to regulate bombing attacks by air. It has been frequently referred to as a basis for seeking to limit the air operations of belligerents, and for protesting the declared illegal air activity of an enemy. However, undefended cities, in the historic sense, meant only those in the immediate zone of ground operations which could be seized and occupied by advancing ground forces without the use of force. In this sense the concept of the undefended locality has proved as empty in air combat as the balloon

---

[9]Scott, *The Hague Peace Conferences,* vol. 1, p. 659–660.

[10]Lawrence, *Principles of International Law,* p. 527.

[11]29 States for (Germany on condition of unanimity); 6 against (France and Russia included); 10 States did not vote. Scott, *op. cit.,* vol. 1, p. 652.

declarations. These three provisions, so utterly ignored in the use of air-power by belligerents, are the total sum of formal rules ever agreed to by any states on the conduct of hostilities from the airspace.

One official and ambitious attempt was made to codify the laws of air warfare after World War I. At the Washington Conference on the Limitation of Armaments in 1921, a resolution was unanimously approved by the United States, the United Kingdom, France, Italy and Japan which called for a commission of jurists to convene at the Hague to study the subject. Legal experts from those countries and the Netherlands met there from December, 1922 to February, 1923, and framed an all-embracing codification of the subject intended to be a compromise between the "necessities of war and the requirements of the standards of civilization."[12] The Hague air rules were never ratified even by the parties to the Conference. They do reflect the only authoritative attempt to set down concisely the rules for air combat. Prior to World War II, certain nations did indicate their intent to adhere to these rules, notably Japan in 1938 in their China campaign, but by World War II their influence was minimal.

This paucity of conventional rules has left airmen stranded for authoritative and practical guidance. It is true that the airman is subject to the general laws of war to the same general extent as the sailor and the soldier, but where does he look for special rules governing his air activity? The British *Manual of Air Force Law* dispensed with any effort to formulate air warfare rules, by stating in a footnote that in the absence of general agreement, it was impossible to include in that manual a chapter on air warfare.[13] The authoritative *U.S. Army Field Manual* (FM 27-10, July 1956) on the law of land warfare, apart from references contained in the Geneva Conventions of 1949, respecting the status of aircrews as prisoners of war and medical aircraft, refers to air activities in time of armed conflict in only four instances, certainly a very meagre source of guidance for the inquiring airman when one notes the extensive scope of intended guidance of the draft Hague Air Rules of 1923. The latter embraces subjects as to the marking of aircraft, aerial bombardment, the use of incendiary explosive bullets, the status of neutral, and of enemy, civil aircraft and of combatant and civil air crews. Yet, today's U.S. Air Force crewman, about to enter a combat theater, is still referred officially to the *Army Field Manual* for official instruction. In a similar vein, the Swiss Army Manual provides that "Air warfare is not a special category; in so far

---

[12]From the Rappoteur's Summary, *International Law and Some Current Illusions* (J. P. Moore, Rep. 1924).
[13]British *Manual of Air Force Law* 2 (1944).

as aerial operations aim at terrestial objectives they are subject, in principle, to the rules of war on land, but only to the extent that the vector of the aerial weapons does not require special rules."[14]

The U.S. Air Force did undertake the task of drafting guidance on the subject of air warfare in 1956. After four years of research, a draft manual on the subject was finalized. However, the decision to release it for publication has never been made. The draft Air Force manual has been made available to the students of the Air Force Academy and the Air War College for research and discussion purposes. Because of its unofficial nature, however, it has not been available to aircrews and air planners. Its influence even within the U.S. Air Force is relatively slight.

As the world's greatest air power, as the most effective user of the airspace for combat operations, why has the United States held back in the promulgation of a complete set of rules regulating air warfare? Certainly it is not because of any incompatibility with the U.N. Charter. The Charter itself provides that "in order for the UN to take urgent military measures, Members shall hold immediately available national air force contingents for combined international enforcement action."[15] The Charter provides the Security Council with authority to take such action *by air,* as well as by land and sea forces, as necessary to maintain or restore the peace.[16] Obviously, any codification of the laws of air warfare are compatible with the provisions of the U.N. Charter as well as being extremely suited to the times when the Secretary General, the General Assembly, and the ICRC are seeking more effective means of protecting the civilian populations from the ravages of armed conflict. However, three fundamental dilemmas confront the effective codification of air rules, and may, in some degree, have influenced our own Air Force in refraining from taking the lead in this subject. The Air Force cannot, no more than could the Commission of Jurists at the Hague in 1923, fully lay down effective rules of air combat without a certain concordance among the major air powers as to how to resolve them. The first of these dilemmas is the permissible scope of the military objective. Inherent in this problem is whether, in air warfare, there is any realistic distinction to be made between combatants and noncombatants. Also, whether there is a middle category, the so-called quasi-combatant, which comprises either the industrial or auxiliary work force of the enemy within the permissible limits of the military objective. For example, is the Vietnamese hamlet, which bristles with the small and heavy armaments of the enemy, to be compared with the Abbey of Monte

---

[14]Manuel des lois et coôtumes de la guerre pour l'armée suisse (1963), para. 44.
[15]Article 45.
[16]Article 42.

Cassino in World War II? Is the village which feeds, supports and shelters the Viet Cong to be equated to the large industrial cities of the Ruhr Basin in World War II?

U.N. Resolution 2444 stated that the civilian population should not be the object of attack as such. But what constitutes the legitimate, immune part of that population remains ill defined. Further, are civilians the direct object of attack when vital industrial and strategic targets are in the immediate vicinity; and how much incidental bombing of civilians in industrial areas or Viet Cong strongholds transfer the true civilian segment from the indirect-object category to the direct-object one? The late Professor John Cobb Cooper, in a lecture to the Naval War College in 1948, termed the definition of the military objective and the bombing of the civilian population the most crucial issue confronting any attempt to regulate this subject. The Secretary General does recommend an alternative to arriving at an acceptable and agreed-upon definition of the military objective. This would be an enlargement of the concept of safety or protected zones to include specified areas where women, children, elderly, and sick could be located with immunity from air attack. Such areas would contain no objectives of military significance, nor be used for any military purpose. They would have to be marked specially and clearly to be visible from the air.[17]

To be effective, there would have to be an adequate system of control and verification of these zones. This verification would be carried out either by some independent agency as the ICRC or by one or more nonbelligerent nations acting in the capacity of a protecting power.[18] There is ample precedent[19] for the creation of such protected areas (in the 1949 Geneva Conventions). The sick and wounded, and the civilian Geneva Conventions contain as annexes, draft agreements, hopefully to be signed by potential belligerents before the outbreak of hostilities, which provide for their establishment. It is specified that such zones are to comprise only a small part of the belligerent's territory, that they be thinly populated, and that they be removed and free from all military objectives or large industrial or administrative establishments. They may not be defended by military means (which includes the use of antiaircraft weapons, tactical fighter aircraft or guided weapons).

It seems to the writer that a concept of protected zones, incorporating a broader category of the civilian population to be sheltered, is indeed an alternative to the concept of the undefended town or the open city which

---

[17] See paras. 45–87, Secy. Gen. Report A/8052, 18 Sept. 1970.

[18] A/7720, note 2, *supra* at 49, 50.

[19] Geneva Convention for the Amelioration of the Condition of the Wounded and Sick in the Field (TIAS 3362); and Geneva Convention for the Protection of Civilians (TIAS 3365).

has not found favor in actual practice.[20] There are some who do not believe the establishment of safety zones for potentially large segments of the civilian population is practicable. To be effective, it is thought that these zones would require thousands of square miles which would create insurmountable logistics problems and inevitably cause the areas to be used unlawfully for military advantages.[21]

However, the immunized areas need not be so broad. If one grants that the industrial work centre, for those actively engaged in work directly sustaining the war effort, or the village hamlet used as a military support base, really have no entitlement to immunity, the physical breadth of the protected areas visibly diminishes.[22] As a realistic alternative to the elusive and vague scope of the military objective, who can deny their greater aptitude for understandable delimitations to air combat?

The Hague commission of jurists' definition of the military objective is a case in point. Military forces; military works; military establishments or depots; factories engaged in the manufacture of arms, ammunition, or distinctively military supplies; lines of communication or transportation used for military purposes, *only,* could be bombed from the air under those Rules. This was hardly broad enough to cover the enemy's marshalling yards, his industrial centers, his shipping facilities and his means of communication. Moreover, air bombardment of cities, towns and villages *not in the immediate neighborhood of ground operations* was prohibited.[23] This proved too limited when such cities and towns, far removed from the ground action, were known to be vital to the enemy's war effort. The totality of World War II saw both the Allies and the Axis expand considerably on the military objective. The German Luftwaffe destroyed Warsaw, Rotterdam and Coventry by air very early in the war.

The first thousand-bomber raid of the war was launched by the British on Cologne the night of 30 May 1942, and destroyed 12 percent of the city's industrial and residential sections and caused 5,000 casualties.[24] It set the tone for the whole British night-bomber offensive against the Third Reich: the concept that area bombing of important industrial centers was best suited to bring Germany to her knees. U.S. forces, with their superior

---

[20]As to the inaptness of the term "undefended" to immunize towns, villages, dwellings from air attack, *see* Stone, *Legal Controls of Armed Conflict* (1959) 623. For a like view that an "open city" has little applicability in air warfare, *see* Jennings, *Open Towns* 22 BRIT. Y. B. INT'L. L. 258.

[21]*See* Levie, *op. cit. supra* note 8 at 45.

[22]Perhaps the *workers* in a large industrialized centre, do recapture their immunity temporarily when they disperse to residential suburbs; but the hamlet held by and supporting the enemy keeps the civilians living there ever exposed to attack.

[23]Hague Rules of Air Warfare Article 24(2) (1963).

[24]*See* 28 Air Force Magazine 34 (1945).

navigational aids, did seek to confine their targets to individually selected and identified factories, oil refineries, industrial plants, and shipyards in Europe; but in the Far East, Tokyo and Yokohama were saturated with explosive and fire bombs because of the Japanese shadow industries, the war production and parts-making conducted in the individual home.

The first night air raid by U.S. superfortresses in the Far East occurred on 9 March 1945 over Tokyo, and it is reported that 280 of these bombers destroyed several square miles of the center of the city. In the Korean conflict, precision bombing was again emphasized by the Air Forces (mostly U.S.) of the U.N. Command. The repair ships, dock yards, and military warehouses of North Korea were bombed without too much damage to the surrounding city. In the Vietnamese conflict, again, area or saturation bombing has been reintroduced, this time to penetrate the vast jungle canopy which serves as a protective layer of the network of Viet Cong and North Vietnamese storage areas, communication and transportation complexes and command posts. And in preselecting air targets, proximity to ground operations is not even remotely a factor.

The Secretary of Defense recently termed U.S. air strikes in the North "limited duration protective reaction air strikes" against North Vietnamese missile and antiaircraft gun positions "in response to attacks on our unarmed reconnaissance aircraft."[25] On the other hand, the North Vietnamese continue to charge that U.S. aircraft have been attacking densely populated areas of the North such as Haiphong, Quanh Ninh, Ha Tay, and Hoa Binh killing a considerable number of North Vietnamese civilians.[26] And a U.S. Congressman fresh from a tour of Southeast Asia reports his belief that a large number, "perhaps thousands," of villages may have been destroyed by American Air Power in 1968 and 1969.[27] It must be left to the historians, at a time when careful factual inquiry is possible, to record to what extent the civilian population and their hamlets and villages have been destroyed by spill-over air attacks, or because they harbored military objectives. The Defense position has been repeatedly and clearly stated that "No US aircraft have been ordered to strike any civilian targets in North Vietnam at any time. United States policy is to target military targets only. There has been no deviation from this policy. All reasonable care is taken to avoid civilian casualties . . . No dikes have been targeted in North Vietnam, in Nam Dinh or elsewhere and we have no knowledge that any pilot has disobeyed his orders."[28]

---

[25]Akron Beacon Journal 21 November 1970, page 1.

[26]*Id.*

[27]Akron Beacon Jouranl 19 April 1970, page 5.

[28]Report of Sec. McNamara to House Armed Services Committee Feb. 1966 reported in 10 Whiteman, Digest of International Law 428.

It is an inevitable outgrowth of U.S. air strikes, however, that comparisons are made in today's press between the My Lai incident, the trial and conviction of Lt. Calley for premeditated murder under Article 118 of the UCMJ, and the deaths and injuries which air bombing brings. One correspondent distinguished the area bombing of industrialized cities in an all-out confrontation, such as World War II, which *may* in his view be permissible, from a conflict in which a technologically advanced nation such as the U.S. becomes immersed in an armed conflict involving a fairly primitive, agricultural-based country. In the latter type of conflict, it is argued incidental casualties to civilians from the air is more akin to the charges directed at Lt. Calley and other ground troops similarly charged.[29]

Both the charter for the trial of major war criminals for Europe and for the Far East define the wanton destruction of cities, towns or villages, or devastation not justified by military necessity, as a war crime, and inhumane acts committed against the civilian population as a crime against humanity.[30] Several high German Air Force officers were indicted for war crimes, notably Field Marshall Goering, and Generals Milch and Speidel. However, none was tried for his part in air operations.[31] It has been argued ably that the situation existed because both sides had equally participated in such attacks from the air, and therefore trial of Axis and Japanese leaders on this charge was inappropriate.[32] But it must be conceded that failure to indict any officers for air campaigns reflected the fact there were no *clear cut* delimitations of the military objective on which to base a violation. As Professor Cooper observed, the concept was too vague.

The ICRC has drawn a distinction between occupation or tactical bombardments and strategic ones. In the former category are those air raids closely allied to ground fighting. The experts suggested the institution of open and immune localities for the protection of civilians. In strategic bombardments, the experts believed the military objective must be sufficiently identified by the attacking force, and that any loss of civilian life must be proportionate to the military advantage to be secured. Whenever the principle of proportionality might be violated, the combatant should refrain from attack.[33] The experts failed, however, adequately to define what constitutes a military objective, just as did the Hague Commission of Jurists.

---

[29]*See* Sheehan, *Should We have War Crimes Trials?*, Akron Beacon Journal March 13, 1971.

[30]Articles of the International Military Tribunal, Established by the London Agreement Article 6. A similar Tribunal was Established in the Far East.

[31]The Einsatz-Gruppen case, 15 Law Reports of the Minor War Crimes Tribunals 114, 115 (1947).

[32]Trial of the Major War Criminal Tribunals, 337 (1947).

[33]Report of the ICRC Experts, note 6, *supra*, at 44.

They do not consider strategic area bombing a premissible form of combat. They cite the proposition that to "attack without distinction, as a single objective, an area including several military objectives at a distance from one another is forbidden whenever elements of the civilian population or dwellings, are situated in between." In a similar vein, the Secretary General's supplemental report on respect for human rights in armed conflicts provides that "consideration might be given to the specific prohibition of the use of 'saturation' bombing as a means of intimidating, demoralizing and terrorizing civilians by inflicting indiscriminate destruction upon densely populated areas."[34]

While neither the Red Cross nor the Secretary General condones area bombing, belligerents are not likely to forego a valuable strategic option for air attacks which has proved so helpful in securing a more favorable and quicker termination of the conflict. Like the philosophy of defining the military objective exclusively, formulations which leave the military incapable of accomplishing its assignments are certain to be ignored. Hence, the wide divergence between the expression of hopes of experts and the actual practices of belligerents.

A more realistic and forceful distinction is made by Professor Telford Taylor in his recent book, *Nuremberg and Vietnam: An American Tragedy*. It is one thing, writes Professor Taylor, for the U.S. pilot to have bombed large industrialized areas in World War II to cripple the enemy's war-making capability. Although it was inevitable the civilian population would be harmed, the high-flying pilot could not distinguish within the industrialized centres between the war-making facilities and the civilian population therein. Quite another circumstance, writes the Professor, for the demarcation of large free strike (air) zones suspected of guerilla activity, where after the zone is cleared of friendly troops and civilians, tactical air strikes and "squirrel hunting" by small planes and helicopters is instituted. "This is using the aircraft for the same purpose that the infantryman uses his gun, and the pilot ought to be held to the same standards of distinguishing combatants from noncombatants."[35] It remains to be seen, however, whether even this logical delineation between the strategic and the tactical use of air power will stand up to the military necessities demanded by a belligerent whose air power constitutes her most effective deterrent to the infiltrations and jungle tactics of a powerful foe.

The Hague Convention for the Protection of Cultural Property does

---

[34]Para. 42, Report of the Secretary General A/8052, 18 September 1970.
[35]Taylor, *Nuremberg and Vietnam: An American Tragedy* (1970), p. 142 *et seq.*

provide a useful and *realistic* middle ground.[36] This convention is the product of an intergovernmental conference convened at the Hague in 1954. Whereas the Geneva Conventions of 1949 are for the protection of persons, the 1954 Hague Convention preserves cultural property. It is of special significance to airmen for several reasons. First, it equates "large industrial centers" to "military objectives," by providing that places of refuge for movable cultural property must be placed at an adequate distance from either. Second, it broadens the concept of the military objective by providing that this term includes, *by way of example,* airports, broadcasting stations, establishments engaged in work of national defense, ports, railway stations of relative importance, and main lines of communication. Third, it recognizes that the principle of imperative military necessity deprives cultural property of its protection. Finally, it stipulates that in no event shall property be the subject of reprisal raids.

All of these are important realistic principles fully applicable to air combat. The use of places of refuge, clearly marked and identified for the protection of cultural property, could be the beginning of a wedge to increase the number of objects and buildings to be immunized; just as the extension of hospital, safety or neutralized zones is the opening to increase the areas for the protection of civilians. Certainly the establishment of safety zones for property and people is compatible with area as well as precision bombing techniques. Neither concept requires the destruction of identified protected areas placed at an adequate distance from large industrial centers, places of military encampment and dangerous militarized areas as armed villages supporting the enemy.

The second dilemma inhibiting the development of the laws of air warfare centers around the choice of weapons which may be employed. The historic St. Petersburg Declaration of 1868 which prohibited the use of explosive, fulminating, or inflammable substances in bullets has no application to air warfare. The use of such bullets in air war is for the purpose[37] of destroying aircraft and the enemy's resources on the ground and in the air, not primarily for the purpose of injuring enemy personnel. For the same reason, the old Hague Declaration of 1899 prohibiting the use of expanding bullets has not been extended to air operations. There are, however, three general areas where the type of weapon employed has evoked particular controversy with respect to aircraft.

---

[36]*Convention of The Hague of The Protection of Cultural Property in Event of Armed Conflicts* (14 May 1954), reported in the ICRC Expert Report in Annex 5, at N16. At the time of this writing the United States is not a party, but it is expected that it will be.

[37]*But see* Spaight, *Air Power and War Rights* 198 (1947). The Declaration of St. Petersburg is reproduced in the ICRC Expert Report as Annex 1.

First, is the use of atomic weapons. There is substantial legal opinion that such weapons are unlawful. This view has been reflected by U.N. Resolution 1653 (XVI) which specifically provides that "Any state using nuclear and thermonuclear weapons is to be considered as violating the Charter of the United Nations, acting contrary to the laws of humanity and as committing a crime against mankind and civilization." The Secretary General notes, however, that the legal effect of this resolution is subject to question because of the divided vote, 55 for, 20 against, and 26 abstentions. The ICRC experts were divided on how best to handle the question of nuclear use.

They were unanimous that such weapons were incompatible with the expressed aim of the Hague Conventions to reduce unnecessary suffering. The present U.S. view as expressed in the *U.S. Army Field Manual* on the laws of war is clear. The use of "Explosive 'atomic weapons' whether by air, land, or sea" does not violate international law in the absence of any customary rule or international convention.[38] The Red Cross also gave tacit recognition to this viewpoint at Vienna in 1965, by providing that the "General principles of the laws of war apply to nuclear and similar weapons."[39]

It must not be forgotten, however, that there is strong legal authority denying the lawfulness of the atomic bomb. "While target-area bombing comes close to the border line of permissibility," wrote Spaight shortly after World War II, "atom bombing definitely oversteps it."[40] And in the only published case discussing its legality, that concerning the claim of five Japanese for injuries sustained at Hiroshima and Nagasaki, a Japanese District Court was of the view that such bombing violated both customary law, in that it was necessarily indiscriminate, and treaty law, in that its blast and radioactive effect violated the Hague Regulations of 1907 against the use of poisons and poisoned arms as well as the Geneva Protocol of 1925.[41]

The second general area arousing controversy relates to the use of fire weapons and specifically napalm. Again, the official U.S. position, as reflected in our Army Field Manual, is that their employment against targets requiring their use is not in violation of international law, with the

---

[38] *U.S. Army Field Manual* (FM 27-10) at 18.

[39] ICRC Resolution XXVIII, Vienna 1965, XXth Conference of ICRC.

[40] Spaight, *Air Power and War Rights* (3 ed., 1947) 276; *see also* Greenspan, *The Modern Law of Land Warfare* (1959) 368, and Stone, *Legal Controls of International Conflict* (1959) 342.

[41] The Shimoda Case, digested 58 AJIL 1016 and commented on 59 AJIL 759; *cf.* O'Brien, *Limited Nuclear Warfare*, 8 Military Law Review 162; Singh, *Nuclear Weapons and International Law* (1959).

caveat that they are not to be used in a way to cause unnecessary suffering to individuals.[42] This view is in opposition to the Teheran resolution of May, 1968 which expressly condemned napalm bombing. Some ICRC experts viewed the use of incendiaries as prohibited by the Geneva Protocol of 1925 because of its asphyxiating effects, while others considered it was the use to which incendiaries were put which determined its lawfulness.[43] U.N. Resolution 2444 does not specifically condemn the use of incendiaries, including napalm, but the Secretary General states that regulation of its use clearly needs an agreement. Certainly, the extensive resort to incendiaries in World War II, Korea and Vietnam has demonstrated the military efficacy of this weapon. It is reasonable to conclude that only by special international agreement will its use ever be regulated.

The third area of general uncertainty relates to the use of weapons calculated to affect the enemy through his senses (including his skin), the use of chemical and bacteriological weapons. Included in this category are the use of noninjurious agents such as tear gas and also the use of herbicides and defoliants. All of these possible means of warfare center around the Geneva Gas Protocol of 1925 and its precise compass. The Protocol prohibits the use in war of asphyxiating, poisonous or other gases and all analogous liquids, materials, or devices and, further, the use of bacteriological methods of warfare. More than 65 States are formally bound by this agreement.

In 1966 the U.N. General Assembly passed a resolution by 91 in favor, none against, and four abstentions, that called for the strict observance of the Protocol by all States and asked those members who had not done so to ratify it.[44] No one is against this Protocol, but its correct interpretation finds nations in disagreement. Some believe the use of incendiaries and napalm are prohibited under the Protocol, many believe that riot-control agents, such as tear gas, may not be employed, and there is a strong view that even herbicides fall within its purview. The U.S. position on these various views was stated by the President and the Secretary of State earlier last year. On 19 August the President, in submitting the Protocol to the U.S. Senate, stated that "The U.S. has renounced the first use of lethal and incapacitating chemical weapons and renounced any use of biological or toxic weapons."[45] The Secreatry of State noted that the Protocol had been

---

[42]U.S. Army Field Manual (FM 27-10) at 18.

[43]Geneva Protocol of June 17, 1925 for the Prohibition of the Use in War of Asphyxiating, Poisonous or other Gases and of Bacteriological Methods of Warfare, reprinted in the ICRC Expert Report as Annex 3.

[44]United Nations General Assembly Resolution 2163 (XXI), 5 Dec. 1966.

[45]President Nixon's Message in LXIII Dep't State Bull. 273, September, 1970.

observed in almost all armed conflicts since 1925, and that the United States' understanding was that the Protocol did not prohibit the use in war of riot-control agents and chemical herbicides; and further, that smoke, flame, and napalm are not covered by the Protocol's general prohibition.[46] The Senate Foreign Relations Committee is showing considerable reluctance to recommend ratification of the Pact with this interpretation. Senator Fulbright and others have stated that by insisting that herbicides and riot-control agents are not banned by the Protocol and would still be used in Vietnam, all the advantage of ratifying the Treaty would be lost. (Washington Post, March 23.) Unless the executive branch revises its understanding of the Geneva Protocol of 1925, to include herbicides and tear gas, it is doubtful the Senate will give advice and consent to the Protocol's ratification.

The third dilemma concerns the status of the aircrewman. Here is a problem of the enforcement of clearly defined rules rather than the development of new ones. The fallen airman poses problems of growing concern as he seems to be singled out for mistreatment or unauthorized public display with increasing frequency. Both the Hague Conventions of 1899 and 1907 respecting land warfare contained provisions that members of the armed forces were entitled to be treated as prisoners of war. Of course, this included all members, whether combatants on land, sea, or in the airspace.

Early in World War I there was some question as to the enemy airman's status, but no case appeared in which they were denied prisoner-of-war status. In World War II, however, the concept began to be advanced by some that airmen, unlike their brothers in arms on land and at sea, were not necessarily entitled to be treated humanely. In 1943, Himmler ordered all senior SS and police officers not to interfere between German civilians and English and United States flyers who bailed out of their aircraft. In 1944 Hitler ordered allied aircrews shot without trial whenever such aircrews had attacked German pilots of aircrews in distress, attacked railway trains or strafed individual civilians or vehicles. Goebbels referred to Allied airmen as murderers and stated that it was "hardly possible and tolerable to use German police and soldiers against the German people when the people treat murderers of children as they deserve."[47]

Although captured Allied airmen were largely accorded prisoners-of-war status by German authorities, there is enough evidence of mistreatment in the reports of the trials of the major and minor war criminals in Europe to

---

[46]*Id.*

[47]For the Views of the Axis Leaders on the status of downed Allied Airmen, *see* 26 Reports of the Trial of Major War Criminals 275; 27 *id.* at 246; and 38 *id.* at 314 (1949).

reflect the beginnings of what could be a disturbing precedent. In the Far East, Allied airmen also suffered from deprivation of their prisoner-of-war status.

Two of the U.S. aircrews which participated in the famous Doolittle air raids on Tokyo and Nagoya from the U.S. naval carrier *Hornet* were captured by Japanese troops when they made forced landings in mainland China. At the time of their capture, there was no Japanese law under which they could be punished. This was remedied four months after their capture by the passage of the Enemy Airmen's Act of Japan. This act made it a war crime to participate in an air attack upon civilians or private property, or conduct air operations in violation of the laws of war. The law was made retroactive to cover those U.S. airmen already in their hands. In October, 1942, two months after the passage of the Enemy Airmen's Act, three of the Doolittle raiders were sentenced and executed. The Judgment of the International Tribunal for the Far East reflects many instances thereafter in which captured Allied airmen were tortured, decapitated and even deliberately burned to death.[48]

The Charters of the Nuremberg and Tokyo International Military Tribunals expressly make it a war crime to murder or ill-treat prisoners-of-war. Both General Keitel of the German Army General Staff and Kaltenbrunner of the Gestapo were charged with, and convicted of mistreating POWs, in part, it appears, for their role in the mistreatment of captured Allied airmen.[49]

However, in the trial of Japanese judges, Japanese judicial and prison officials were convicted on a different basis. The thrust of the holdings of the War Crimes Commissions in these cases was that the U.S. airmen were deprived of a fair trial and not that U.S. airmen, as lawful combatants, were entitled to POW status. The 1949 Geneva Convention on POWs confirmed the entitlement of aircrew members to the benefits of that Convention including "civilian members of military-aircrews" and "crews of civil aircraft." Article 85 provides that prisoners-of-war prosecuted under the laws of the detaining power for acts committed prior to capture shall retain, even if convicted, the benefits of that Convention. Compliance with these provisions would prevent the denial of POW status to airmen, even those convicted during hostilities under such laws as the Japanese Enemy Airman Act.

Unfortunately, most of the Communist-bloc countries have entered

---

[48]See *Judgment of the International Military Tribunal for the Far East,* Chapter VIII, at 1025 (1948).
[49]Trial of the Major War Criminals 289–92.

reservations to article 85. The reservation of the North Korean Government is typical. They refused to be bound to provide POW status to individuals convicted under local law of war crimes based on the principles of Nuremberg and the Tokyo Far East International Military Tribunal. The Government of China and the North Vietnamese reservations are similar. There are many cases of mistreatment of U.S. airmen in the Korean conflict, and the extortion from U.S. airmen of false germ warfare confessions for propaganda purposes, and publicly parading them through the streets under humiliating circumstances, is well known. Although all captured U.N. Forces suffered to some extent under the fairly primitive conditions of confinement which existed, it was the airman who was singled out especially for public degradation, exposure to the press, and the forcing of confessions of illegal conduct.

The fate of all prisoners of war held by the North Vietnamese is of present great concern because of the refusal of that Government to consider the 1949 Geneva Convention applicable to that conflict. Of interest to this discussion, however, is the particular light in which they consider captured U.S. airmen. A Hanoi press release with a date line of 10 July 1966 could well be expected to reflect their official attitude on this issue. A North Vietnamese lawyer writes that U.S. pilots are not prisoners-of-war but criminals, that air raids on densely populated areas in South Vietnam and on pagodas and hospitals in both the South and the North were conducted by B-52 bombers, and are concrete war crimes under paragraph 6(b) of the Nuremberg War Crimes Charter. He also cites the bombing and strafing of the dike system and other irrigation works and densely populated cities such as Hanoi and Haiphong as war crimes. (There is a striking parallel between this reference to the dike systems and irrigation works and Article 17 of the ICRC Rules for the Protection of Civilians. Article 17 invites the States concerned to agree on the immunity from destruction "of engineering works or installations—such as hydroelectric dams, nuclear power stations or dikes" which might, if attacked, endanger the civilian population "through the releasing of natural or artificial forces."[50] This view apparently shared by the North Vietnamese lawyer and the drafters of the ICRC Rules is a substantial departure from practices in World War II where dikes and dams as well as bridges were attacked from the air.)

The North Vietnamese lawyer specifically refers to article 8 of the Nuremberg Charter and states that even though accused airmen have acted strictly on orders given by their government or superiors, they remain

---

[50]*See* Report of the XXIst Conference of the Red Cross, Reaffirmation of the Laws and Customs of Armed Conflict, Annex 1, p. 040.

individually responsible for the air attacks. The lawyer writes that the North Vietnamese Government "deliberately and clearsightedly ruled out (protection for) those prosecuted and accused of war crimes and crimes against mankind" in adhering to the Geneva Prisoner-of-War Convention. This is why, he concludes, U.S. pilots, whom he labels as pirates, saboteurs and criminals, can be tried, and presumably punished, under the North Vietnamese law of 20 January 1953, which he states relates to crimes against the security of North Vietnam.

It was the unanimous opinion of the Secretary General and the ICRC experts that even when airmen had committed acts justifying their treatment as war criminals, they should be treated as prisoners-of-war.[51] Both believed that an airman behind enemy lines, in distress, and not employing any weapon should be protected from the civilian population.[52] Neither, however, gave any significant attention to the relation of war crimes as defined at Nuremberg and Tokyo to the conduct of air operations. In view of the non-prosecution of any Axis airman or official for his part in air activities, strategic bombing which by its nature is bound to cause a great deal of suffering and devastation, must be judged on different grounds. Certainly the impermissibility of the defense of superior orders has very questionable application to air combat. The experts and the Secretary both raised this issue in their report by stating that when the attack of the military objective will cause serious loss to the civilian population, and is disproportionate to the military advantage, they must refrain from the attack. In recommending that the principles in U.N. Resolution 2444 be introduced into army military instruction, especially for air forces, the experts also state that this is "to remind all the members of the armed forces that it is sometimes their duty to give priority to the requirements of humanity, placing these before any contrary orders they might receive."

The airmen might properly ask how is he to know, flying off the wing of his flight leader at 30,000 feet, at night, or over a solid covering of clouds, whether the damage his bombs inflict will meet the test of proportionality or his bombing will be indiscriminate. Or if he does exercise his individual judgment on a particular raid, and refrains from the attack by leaving the formation, what proof can he give when a charge is brought by his own authorities for misbehavior before the enemy. It would seem that the prosecutors and judges who presided at the War Crimes Trials in World War II had such thoughts when they chose to refrain from the prosecution of Axis airmen or officials for their participation in the conduct of air campaigns.

---

[51]*See* Report of the ICRC Experts at 77.
[52]*Id.* at 78.

Admittedly, the pilot of a tactical fighter plane or a helicopter who performs his mission at low level and can identify clearly his individual target, is more akin to the infantry rifleman. Professor Taylor has written that the crews of helicopters and small reconnaissance planes who go "squirrel hunting" for individuals, using machine guns and "sniping with bombs," are "using the aircraft for the same purposes the infantryman uses his gun" and ought to be judged by the same standards.[53] Certainly, evidence that an airman deliberately singled out harmless non-combatants or individual dwellings (not concealing military targets) could constitute a war crime and result in a murder charge. Eight crewmen from two U.S. Army helicopter gunships were charged late last year, either as principals or accessories, to the deliberate killing or wounding of a number of Vietnamese civilians by firing grenades from their craft along a rice field where the Vietnamese were located.[54] Clearly, such conduct, if proved, falls squarely within the parameters of Professor Taylor's remarks.[55] However, the fundamental difference between the airman who is not charged with such conduct and does not purposely single out and attack individual civilians or defenseless homes, and the infantryman is clearly set forth in the only War Crimes Trial to rule precisely on the subject of aerial bombardment:

> A city is bombed for tactical purposes; communications are to be destroyed, railroads wrecked, factories razed, all for the purpose of impeding the military. It inevitably happens that nonmilitary persons are killed. This is an incident, a grave incident to be sure, but an unavoidable corollary of battle action. *The civilians are not individualized.* The pilots take their aim at the railroad yards, houses along the tracks are hit and many of the occupants are killed, but this is entirely different in law and in fact from an armed force marching up to these same railroad tracks, entering those houses abutting thereon, dragging out the men, women, and children, and shooting them.[56]

These then are the three central dilemmas that impede the development of the laws of air warfare. All past effort to define, by all-inclusive enumeration, those objectives which are proper military targets have failed. Either they have been too restrictive or too indefinite to have been accorded much respect in actual practice. General exhortations to refrain from terror bombing, indiscriminate bombing and morale bombing equally have a nebulous ring. There is no adequate standard to judge what constitutes this type of warfare, and no nation has considered that their

---

[53]Taylor, *Nuremberg and Vietnam: An American Tragedy* 147.

[54]Washington Post, May 3, 1971, p. 5.

[55]*Cf.* with report that in the Korean Conflict, UN Commanders authorized attack upon civilians who were used as grenade and ammo carriers for the North Koreans. 6 Karig, Battle Report (The War in Korea) (1952) p. 107.

[56]Einsatz-Gruppen Case 4 Tr. War Crim. Cases 446–467.

combatant air forces have ever resorted to the use of terror or indiscriminate attacks.

The 1954 Hague Convention for the protection of cultural property signals a milestone, by providing agreement for the refuge of certain types of objects and buildings. Perhaps this concept can be enlarged to immunize other clearly defined resources and facilities of a belligerent nation. Common consent for the extension of hospital and safety zones to cover larger segments of the civilian population, removed from vital target areas, also is a growing possibility.

The dilemma of the choice of weapon is created by the uncertain status of the use of nuclear force, the use of incendiaries, including napalm, in air operations, and the use of modern agents designed to control the movement of people without producing significant harm, and to destroy plants, trees and food resources by chemical means. The applicability of the Hague Regulations and the Geneva Gas Protocol to those forms of waging war is far from settled, and in the eyes of some taints the aircrewman who is detailed to employ them.

Finally, the status of the aircrewman, who all too frequently serves as the focal point of the opposing belligerent's indignation and charges that the laws of war have been violated, must be restated. It is the airman who is especially vulnerable to mistreatment and denial of his rights under the Geneva Convention of 1949, because of the tremendous destructive capacity within his control, and because he brings the misfortune of war to the enemy hinterland. Clarification of the Nuremberg principles as they apply to him, the airman, and withdrawal of reservations making possible his treatment as a war criminal are badly needed. His legitimate combatant status must be reaffirmed. That neither the weapons prescribed for his use, nor the targets pre-selected for his particular mission, operate to remove him from the ranks of lawful combatants must be recognized uniformly.

As difficult as these three central dilemmas make it to codify or formulate air law rules for armed conflict, the continued use of air power in armed conflicts in the Middle East and in Southeast Asia make imperative the issuance of concrete guidance for airmen of all armed forces. This writer recently queried a responsible, knowledgeable Air Force lawyer as to whether the time was not at last propitious to update and promulgate the Air Force rules of 1956–1960 which never left the drafting stage. His reply is worth quoting as a thoughtful argument against an Air Force sponsored publication:

> One of the real difficult problems in dealing with the laws of war is to take an objective, legalistic analysis of what the law is and apply it to circumstances of today's conflict, bearing in mind that to a large extent International

> Law in this area is made by customary practices. Since the United States is the one that is principally involved in the use of a wide variety of sophisticated weapons, to assert restraint on the use of weapons not required by the current status of the law, yet demanded by certain segments of the international community, is painful indeed. Such self-imposed restraint designed to accommodate moral sensitivities, develop a customary rule of law and yet win a war is an almost impossible task. I am almost of the view that for the United States to participate in or to play an active role in the development of the laws of war with respect to legality of weapons or tactics is an almost impossibility while we are presently engaged in armed conflict.[57]

Certainly, there is much merit in this viewpoint. The lack of any real, distinctive guidance for the airman in the British and Swiss Manuals on the laws of air warfare seems to support a view that codification of this subject is premature, absent greater development of customary law. On the other hand, neither the Secretariat of the United Nations, the General Assembly, nor the International Committee of the Red Cross have thus far been capable of working out a practical useful accommodation between operational (or military) necessity and the need for respect for human rights in armed conflict.

Understandably, the efforts of the UN and the ICRC are directed toward sparing the civilian population from the ravages of war. Humanitarian admonitions by these agencies to refrain from terror bombing, indiscriminate bombing, and the use of weapons which cause unnecessary suffering or mass destruction carry great optative value. However, the Air Force planner, the Wing Commander, his operations officer, and the crewmen themselves relate much more strongly to Air Force doctrine in the form of specific rules and regulations. Such rules and regulations become part of the overall functioning of the military effort, in war as well as in peace, and must be taken into account in mission counseling, briefing and general Air Force instruction to aircrews and ground support members alike. In contrast, it has to be admitted that such well intended efforts as the ICRC rules of 1956 for the Limitation of the Dangers to the civilian population can be of only peripheral significance to the airman and his superiors until they are translated into concrete and detailed instructions by Air Force or Defense publication.

In addition, the efforts of the ICRC and the UN Secretariat have a utopian ring when they seek to eliminate area bombing, require the airman to return with his bombs (presumably even in high level, all-weather bombardment) if the target cannot be "duly identified"; and to make a selective in-the-air choice as to the targets he will attack, based on the doctrine of

---

[57] Letter to the writer from an Air Force officer dated 13 April 1971.

proportionality. Far better would it be for the Air Force to set forth its position on these matters in specified, practical instructions in an Air Force manual, pamphlet or regulation.

While the UN and the ICRC are naturally and primarily occupied with the protection of the civilian population, the airman must be concerned with many, many other limitations on the use of his aircraft and accompanying weapons in armed conflict. Does the Hague Rule requiring that quarter be given to defenceless ground combatants, prohibit attacks on disabled enemy aircraft? Does the Hague Rule requiring combatants to wear "fixed distinctive emblem recognizable at a distance" and to "carry arms openly," have any applicability to the flying crewman? Is the descending enemy crewman subject to attack? Is the crewman who carries saboteurs and spies for air drop behind enemy lines tainted by this conduct if captured? What is his status if he falls into enemy hands while on a propaganda mission which has for its purpose the incitement of the enemy to desert? May he attack non-military public aircraft of the enemy, or civil enemy aircraft, and must his own aircraft bear national, belligerent markings, or may he adorn it with the markings of the enemy?

It is doubtful, indeed, that this and many other such important questions will have been considered by the conference of Government experts which is to convene at Geneva 24 May thru 12 June 1971, for the purpose of reaffirming and developing the international humanitarian laws applicable to armed conflicts. State and Defense representatives will have attended this conference for the U.S., but if the past efforts of the ICRC are a prelude to the future, this ICRC conference may not have solved the three basic dilemmas confronting the Air Force in today's conflict, nor will they have had the time needed to consider the many detailed, ancillary rules of air warfare which so urgently need articulation today.

# International Law Aspects of Repatriation of Prisoners of War During Hostilities

## RICHARD A. FALK

### I

On September 2, 1972, the North Vietnamese Foreign Ministry issued a statement announcing the release of three American pilots who were being held in detention since their capture by North Vietnam. The statement gave no particular reason for the release except to affirm North Vietnam's "lenient policy" and to indicate that the release was being made "on the occasion" of an annual independence day holiday called National Day. It was subsequently learned that the release was part of a wider amnesty, which included Vietnamese citizens who had been sent to jail for ordinary criminal activity.

The North Vietnamese statement also indicated that the pilots would be released "to a U.S. social organization animated with good will and a desire to bring about an early end to the U.S. war in Viet Nam and to help those released not to be used in activities against the Vietnamese people and the Government of the Democratic Republic of Vietnam." Through contact with the North Vietnamese delegation negotiating in Paris, it was learned that the Committee of Liaison with Families of Servicemen Detained in North Vietnam had been designated as "the social organization" entrusted with the task of escorting the released Americans back to the United States.[1] In addition, each family of a released man was invited to send a relative to Hanoi and to join in the repatriation process. Minnie Lee Gartley, mother of Navy Lt. JG Markham Gartley, and Olga Charles, wife of Navy Lt. JG Norris Alphonzo Charles, accepted the invitation. No relative of the third released pilot, Air Force Major Edward K. Elias, responded positively to the invitation. Initially, Major Elias' father accepted but later withdrew on advice from Pentagon officials.

In the release statement reference was made to earlier repatriations of a comparable kind that had taken place in 1968 and 1969. Three earlier releases had occurred, each involving three pilots and each involving an escort group comprised of well-known Americans who were actively

---

[1] A second anti-war organization in the United States—People's Coalition for Peace and Justice—was also designated by the North Vietnamese to receive the three pilots, but the planning and execution of the undertaking was carried out virtually exclusively under the auspices of the Committee of Liaison. The escort group consisted of the two co-chairmen of the Committee of Liaison, Cora Weiss and David Dellinger and of the Rev. William Sloan Coffin, Jr., the chaplain of Yale University, and the author of this article. Peter Arnett of Associated Press also traveled as a member of the escort group, but made the trip solely for journalistic purposes.

opposed to the Vietnam War and later became charter members of the Committee of Liaison. The statement issued in Hanoi charged that:

In 1969 the U.S. Government compelled the U.S. pilots released in July that year to put forward distortion [sic] about the humane treatment policy of the government of the DRV. At complete variance with their previous statements the U.S. Government has also used those released pilots in war activities against the Vietnamese people and other peoples of Indochina. It is for this reason that such releases have been temporarily suspended. . . .

The point was reiterated with reference to this news release as follows:

The government of the DRV draws particular attention of the U.S. government to this: in the interests of the families of the U.S. pilots captured in North Vietnam stop using the released pilots to slander the DRV and further the U.S. policy of aggression in North Vietnam.

In Hanoi officials of the North Vietnamese Government made it clear, furthermore, that the prospects for additional releases of this type would be diminished if there was any interference by the U.S. Government prior to entry into the territorial limits of the United States. And, indeed, there were no releases for three years after the 1969 experience. To make the prospect of such interference less likely the return trip was arranged via Peking, Moscow, and Copenhagen rather than by way of the normal and more direct route of Vientiane, Laos, and Bangkok.

The escort group together with Mrs. Gartley and Mrs. Charles arrived in Hanoi on September 16, 1973 and the three pilots were formally released to the custody of the escort group on the evening of September 17. The release ceremony consisted of a transfer of control from the North Vietnamese Army to a spokesman of an organization called The Committee of Solidarity, who in turn, transferred custody to the Committee of Liaison, the acceptance of which was effected by Cora Weiss on behalf of the escort group.

Between September 17 and 24 the three released pilots lived in the Hoa Binh Hotel in Hanoi with their relatives and the four escorts. An informal atmosphere prevailed and there were no guards present. The pilots were as free as the other American visitors to move about. Some social activities and visits to heavily bombed areas were organized by the Solidarity Committee during the week, but there was no obligation on the part of the pilots or others to take part.

Neither the relatives nor the pilots participated with the escort group in their various meetings with North Vietnamese high officials (including Pham Van Dong, the Prime Minister), or in discussions about conditions in the prison camps, or in a meeting on September 25 with seven other captured American pilots.

While in Hanoi the entire group discussed on several occasions the appropriate procedure for returning to the United States. The escort group did suggest that it had a series of responsibilities: to encourage civilian return for the sake of remaining pilots and their families and to secure as humane and orderly a process of return as possible for the sake of the three pilots and their accompanying relatives. Accordingly, on September 22, 1972 the following cablegram was sent to President Nixon from Hanoi by the escort group:

> We are happy to report that Navy Lt. Markham Gartley, Air Force Major Edward Elias, and Navy Lt. jg Norris Charles have been released to our custody so that we may escort them home to the United States.
>
> In accordance with the expressed expectations of the North Vietnamese Government, and in order not to jeopardize the possibility of future releases, we believe the repatriation of these men should be carried out in the following manner:
>
> (1) The men shall proceed home with us and representatives of their families in civilan aircraft.
>
> (2) The men, if they wish, shall be granted a 30 day furlough.
>
> (3) The men shall receive a complete medical checkup at the hospital of their choice, civilian or military.
>
> (4). The men shall do nothing further to promote the American war effort in Indochina.
>
> We believe that these terms are reasonable and humane and in the best interests of the remaining pilots and their families.

No response or acknowledgment was received directly or indirectly from the U.S. Government.

On the same day the pilots, on their own initiative, sent a second cablegram to President Nixon:

> In the best interests of all parties concerned we think we should be allowed to return to New York with the escort delegation and be allowed to spend a few days with our families, if so desired.

None of the cables sent by the released prisoners or the escort group elicited any official response. All of these cables were made available to the press at the time they were sent.

On September 25 in the late afternoon the group departed by plane from Hanoi and proceeded to Peking. On the morning of September 27 the group boarded the regularly scheduled flight to Moscow.

On arrival in Moscow the plane was met by several representatives of the United States Embassy, led by Mr. Adolph Dubs, the Chargé d'Affaires. The escort group explained to Mr. Dubs that it had no objection to his meeting with the pilots, but that it felt an obligation to provide them with civilian escort back to the United States and that any official attempt to order them to leave our escort might jeopardize the prospects for future releases. It was also made clear to Mr. Dubs that the escort believed that he had no authority to give orders of any kind to the men while outside Embassy premises in Moscow. Mr. Dubs "warmly recommended" that the pilots consider returning to the United States by means of a U.S. Medevac plane that could take them directly home from Moscow. The pilots thanked Mr. Dubs for his offer but indicated their preference, "for the sake of all concerned," to continue back to the United States under our escort. They affirmed their good health. Mr. Dubs offered the pilots and their relatives Embassy hospitality, including a place to sleep, food and drink, and phone calls to the United States. These offers were also declined.

The group left Moscow on the morning of September 27 and deplaned for a stopover and change of planes at Copenhagen. Once again the plane was met by Embassy representatives who once again offered the possibility of return by Medevac plane, which on this occasion was standing by the runway at the Copenhagen Airport. As in Moscow, the pilots declined all offers including offers of Embassy hospitality.

From Moscow onwards two members of the U.S. Embassy staff were on the plane. The three pilots accepted the suggestion of the Embassy officials that they change into military uniform shortly before deplaning in the United States.

On arrival at Kennedy Airport in New York early in the evening of September 28 the plane was cleared of passengers other than our group (4 escorts, 2 press, 2 relatives, and 3 pilots). U.S. Government representatives came on board, and the pilots were told that they would immediately be flown to the military hospital closest to their area of residence. Such an arrangement was acceptable to Major Elias, but it was not satisfactory to either Lt. Gartley or Lt. Charles who wanted to be with their families for several days before reporting for a checkup and debriefing at a military hospital. Both pilots had also hoped to meet with the press and to attend a private reception in the airport vicinity that had been planned by the Committee of Liaison for their relatives and for relatives of other POWs. There was considerable personal distress on the part of the two families when it was learned that all of the pilots were expected to depart immediately by plane for a military hospital. It is not altogether clear whether the pilots were given any orders to this effect or whether only a more informal kind of insistence was relied upon by government officials.

After returning to the United States the men were given medical checkups and debriefings at the three hospitals. All three of the pilots have been allowed to be with their families and to talk with the public, although the specific arrangements have varied to a certain degree. Finally, a representative of the Department of Defense gave assurances to the House Armed Forces Committee that none of these men would be reassigned to duty that related in any way to the Indochina War.[2]

## II

Several legal issues are presented by these facts. First of all, there is some question as to the relevance of the Geneva Convention relative to the Treatment of Prisoners of War. As has been discussed in the literature, North Vietnam claims that the Geneva Conventions do not apply because

[2] *See* New York Times, Oct. 11, 1972, at 9.

these captured men are "war criminals" under their reservation to Article 85 that was included, in common with other Socialist bloc countries, in their instrument of ratification.[3]    The United States has rejected this invocation of the Article 85 reservation, but even accepting this rejection, it remains unclear whether North Vietnam would be bound to treat the armed conflict as one of international character bringing the whole of the Convention into play or would be bound only to uphold the more general and limited mandate of Article 3.    North Vietnam on its side claims the right to determine treatment standards and provides only the assurance that it is pursuing a lenient policy that protects the humanitarian interests of the individuals concerned.[4]

Since the capture of the first American pilot by North Vietnam in August 1964, the U.S. Government has made a consistent demand that North Vietnam apply the Geneva Conventions, has asserted that the terms of the Convention are fully applicable to this war, and, by implication has indicated an acceptance of corresponding obligations toward enemy personnel.    No American official has claimed a right to disregard the Geneva Conventions because of North Vietnam's refusal to be bound in any strict sense.  It should be noted, of course, that the *formal* acceptance of the Geneva system does not assure *better* treatment of prisoners as a matter of actual fact.[5]  The escort group regarded the Geneva Prisoners of War

[3] For an intelligent appreciation of this issue *see* Note, *The Geneva Convention and the Treatment of Prisoners of War in Vietnam,"* 80 HARVARD L. REV. 851 (1967), reprinted in 2 FALK, ed., THE VIETNAM WAR AND INTERNATIONAL LAW, 397–415, at 405–15 (1969).

[4] There are a number of distinct treatment issues including frequency and transmittal of mail and packages, release of sick and wounded prisoners for treatment and confinement in a neutral country, failure of North Vietnam to provide all information at its disposal about men held captive, and allegations of various sorts of abuse. *See. Hanoi Refuses to Comply with the Terms of the Geneva Convention of 1949*, Dept. of State, Public Information Series, Oct. 5, 1972.    In addition to denying any wrongdoing, the North Vietnamese charge the U.S. Government with spreading false propaganda about prison conditions and with seeking to disrupt prison camp discipline by abusing mail privileges through the infiltration of forbidden items, especially to facilitate covert communication between prisoners and the Department of Defense.    Also, the Son Tay raid of Nov. 21, 1970 manifested a willingness by American military forces to disrupt normal security arrangements for POWs in North Vietnam.    Although the Son Tay camp was abandoned, Administration officials threatened to repeat such rescue efforts.    In view of this threat directed at North Vietnamese prison security it is not surprising that POWs were thereafter kept under greater confinement.    This tightening of prison discipline was confirmed by conversations with several present prisoners.

[5] Throughout the war there have been numerous reports of abuse of North Vietnamese and National Liberation Front prisoners by the United States and by the South Vietnamese Government, despite their acceptance of the Geneva system.    Perhaps the most serious kind of abuse was the widespread practice in certain theaters of ground combat of inflating "body count" totals by killing prisoners.    The most well-known disclosures surrounded the court martial proceedings of Lt. James Duffy.    Some material on this case, including Lt. Duffy's own statement, is found in FALK, KOLKO, and LIFTON, eds., CRIMES OF WAR 239–54 (1971).    There have also been numerous reports of battlefield reliance on "water torture" to secure information from captured enemy personnel or suspects.    In addition, the reliance by Saigon authorities on

Convention as a source of authoritative guidelines to the extent relevant to this type of repatriation.

The principal point of difficulty with this approach arises because repatriation to a belligerent power while hostilities are in progress is not covered in explicit terms by the Geneva Prisoners of War Convention. Part IV of the Convention, which deals with Termination of Captivity, is divided into three sections:

> Section I: Direct Repatriation and Accommodation in Neutral Countries [Articles 109–117]
>
> Section II: Release and Repatriation of Prisoners of War at the Close of Hostilities [Articles 118–119]
>
> Section III: Death of Prisoners of War [Articles 120–121]

It is readily apparent that Section I does not apply because these pilots were not sick or wounded, nor were they repatriated to a neutral country; that Section II does not apply because hostilities were continuing; and that Section III does not apply because the men were alive.

At the same time, the Geneva provisions on repatriation of the sick and wounded provide some guidelines that seem relevant to this situation. Article 117 is the most direct instance:

> No repatriated person may be employed on active military service.

Certainly, if such a restriction is applicable to sick or wounded men repatriated to a neutral country, then it is even more strongly relevant to repatriations that send healthy combat personnel back to a belligerent power while the war continues. The U.S. Government seems also to accept the relevance of Article 117, at least as it applies to this repatriation.[6] It is not clear whether activity by a repatriated prisoner to arouse public support for the war would violate Article 117. [The fourth guideline in the escort cable to President Nixon on September 22 proposed that "the men shall do nothing further to promote the American war effort in Indochina,"]which was intended to be wider than Article 117 and to take account of the past use of previously repatriated men from North Vietnam to engage in official or semiofficial pro-war propaganda.[7] The rationale for this wider prohibition is that it is inconsistent with the spirit of the release, as Hanoi made clear in its statement of September 2, for repatriated men to take even an indirect public role in relation to the war effort. The escort group believed that North Vietnam's position was reasonable on this point

---

torture in their prison system seems documented beyond reasonable doubt. One famous incident involved "the tiger cages" at Con Son prison which were unintentionally exposed to United States congressional visitors in July 1970. See "Statement on Con Son Prison" of Cong. Augustus F. Hawkins reprinted in same volume, at 258–60; see also Drinan, at 255–57 on American involvement.

[6] See supra note 2.

[7] See, e.g., Hearings on American Prisoners of War in Southeast Asia, 1971, Before the Subcommittee on National Security Policy and Scientific Developments of House Committee on Foreign Affairs, March 23–25, 30–31; April 1, 6, 20, 1971 (Cf. statements of Barnet, Meacham, and Weiss with those of Overly and Stockstill, at 2–24, 215–240, 359–406).

and that such propaganda activity would definitely discourage future releases.

Aside from Article 117, the Geneva Prisoners of War Convention does not give much guidance as to reasonable terms of repatriation. The September 22 escort cable sought to fill this vacuum by providing additional guidelines, formulated with a view to promoting the best interests of the three released men and of the remaining pilots and their families, in response to experience with earlier repatriations during the Vietnam War.

Guideline 1 affirmed the importance of a civilian escort back to the United States. Although the release was unconditional, the North Vietnamese officially indicated its preference for civilian return and declared that any interference would jeopardize further releases. The Defense Department, including the Secretary of Defense, advised the media that the pilots should present themselves to U.S. military jurisdiction at the earliest possible opportunity and intimated that they could be found absent without leave (AWOL) for their failure to do so. In this situation the pilots were caught in a crossfire between official directives by the United States and their sense of obligation to the remaining prisoners and their families. By rejecting U.S. Government initiatives in Moscow and Copenhagen, the pilots accepted the primacy of Guideline 1, and the government by its failure to issue orders while en route or to threaten any disciplinary action since return can be said to have substantially acquiesced, although Secretary Laird made some public statements about possible disciplinary actions that seemed calculated to have an intimidating impact.[8] Indeed, the U.S. Government representations in Moscow and Copenhagen can be regarded as nothing more than an effort to establish by independent means whether the released men did indeed wish to accept civilian escort back to the United States. Washington was clearly prepared to have the pilots leave civilian escort, "warmly recommending" that they do so, even though such a result could have jeopardized the prospect for future releases.

Guideline 2 involving a post-return option of a thirty-day furlough was designed to provide as humane a reentry into American life as possible and to take issue with the assumption of the Department of Defense that all repatriated prisoners of war would require prolonged medical detention. Warren G. Nutter, Assistant Secretary of Defense, had testified before a congressional committee as follows on May 11, 1972:

> We assume that all returnees will require medical attention, some much more than others. Certainly, all will require rest and time to readjust. Therefore, our policies require that all returnees be placed immediately under medical auspices for complete medical checkups.[9]

After being with these men and their relatives for a week after their release, it was clear to the escort group, as well as to the released pilots and their relatives, that there was no immediate need for medical sur-

[8] See N.Y. Times, Sept. 30, 1972, at 11 for indication of this shift in official policy as a consequence of a White House decision.

[9] Hearings on American Prisoners of War in Southeast Asia, 1972, same subcommittee at note 7, supra. Part 3, Feb. 3, March 16, 1972 (Mr. Nutter's statement begins at 25, the quoted passage appears at 31).

veillance. A discretionary period of leave seemed like a desirable option to include in this kind of repatriation. As a matter of formal position the government has not granted the returnees an option of immediate leave, but, in fact, the medical confinement has been so "open," at least as compared to what happened after prior repatriations, that a relaxed period of reunion with families has been possible. It may be that a preliminary medical examination, perhaps under neutral auspices if the returnee so wishes, could determine whether it is appropriate to grant a thirty-day furlough before checkup and debriefing.

Guideline 3 recognizes that a medical checkup is desirable but grants the repatriated man the option of choosing either a civilian or military hospital. This guideline was formulated on the basis of reported abuses in relation to prior treatment in military hospitals and to the government's professed intention to provide a returnee with "proper balance" on the war during the period of detention and debriefing.[10] It seemed objectionable to compel a prisoner released during a controversial war to undergo a process that would include his political reeducation, perhaps under circumstances that might be intimidating or even threatening.[11] In particular, the escort group was sensitive to recent disclosures that reveal Soviet reliance on medical and psychiatric detention to remove clinically normal, but politically dissident, voices from society.

In fact, the three pilots preferred, or at least were unwilling to contest, the government's insistence on a medical checkup under military auspices. To date, however, there have been no complaints or evidence of political pressures and reeducation such as accompanied prior releases, and therefore the publicity associated with the formulation of this guideline may have served a constructive purpose.

Perhaps, the guidelines set forth in the September 24 cable are drawn too specifically with the particular situation of this war and these men in mind to serve as a general precedent, but it does seem desirable for the International Committee of the Red Cross and others concerned with repatriation to a belligerent power during hostilities to consider proposing a new section in Part IV of the 1949 Convention. The United States Government has been reluctant to deal with or confer status upon the Committee of Liaison with Families of Servicemen Detained in North Vietnam. Since its inception in 1969 the Committee has attempted to facilitate the transmission of information and mail between the prison camps and prisoner families. Until the Paris accords of 1973, the North Vietnamese Government had refused to deal with the U.S. Government on prisoner issues; it was willing to deal with the Committee of Liaison.

No attempt has been made to account for the existence and role of the Committee of Liaison by reference to the Geneva Prisoners of War Convention, but it seems clearly possible to do so.

[10] See article by Everett R. Hollis, "U.S. Planned More Gradual Homecoming for P.O.W.'s," N.Y. Times, Sept. 30, 1972, at 10.

[11] On this see SMITH, P.O.W.: TWO YEARS WITH THE VIETCONG (1971), esp. epilogue by Donald Duncan on George Smith's treatment by U.S. medical authorities after his release from National Liberation Front captivity, at 285–94.

Article 9 of the Convention is as follows:

The provisions of the present Convention constitute no obstacle to the humanitarian activities which the International Committee of the Red Cross or *any other impartial humanitarian organization* may, subject to the consent of the Parties to the conflict concerned, undertake for the protection of prisoners of war and for their relief.

Article 10 reads:

The High Contracting Parties may at any time agree to entrust to an organization which offers all guarantees of impartiality and efficacy the duties incumbent on the Protecting Parties by virtue of the present Convention.

When prisoners of war do not benefit or cease to benefit, no matter for what reason, by the activities of a Protecting Power or of an organization provided for in the first paragraph above, the Detaining Power shall request a neutral State, or such an organization, to undertake the functions performed under the present Convention by a Protecting Power designated by the Parties to a conflict.

If protection cannot be arranged accordingly, *the Detaining Power shall request or shall accept, subject to the provisions of this Article, the offer of the services of a humanitarian organization, such as the International Committee of the Red Cross, to assume the humanitarian functions performed by Protecting Powers under the present Convention.*

Any neutral Power or any organization invited by the Power concerned or offering itself for these purposes, shall be required to act with a sense of responsibility towards the Party to the conflict on which persons protected by the present Convention depend, and shall be required to furnish sufficient assurances that it is in a position to undertake the appropriate functions and to discharge them impartially.

No derogation from the preceding provisions shall be made by special agreements between Powers one of which is restricted, even temporarily, in its freedom to negotiate with the other Power or its allies by reason of military events, more particularly where the whole, or a substantial part, of the territory of the said Power is occupied.

Whenever in the present Convention mention is made of a Protecting Power, such mention applies to substitute organizations in the sense of the present Article.[12]

There are several problems with conferring a formal status on the Committee of Liaison. First, was it designated by the Detaining Power? There was no formal designation, as such, but a series of dealings on prisoner matters between the North Vietnamese Government and the Committee amounted to such a designation. Clearly the Committee of Liaison by aiding the exchange of mail and information and by facilitating interim repatriation contributed toward the realization of the humanitarian objectives of the Convention.

Secondly, does the Committee of Liaison qualify as an "impartial" humanitarian organization? The Committee is exclusively composed of American citizens who have taken a public position against the U.S. role in Indochina. On the other hand, these individuals are American citizens con-

---

[12] 6 UST 3316; TIAS 3364; 75 UNTS 135; 47 AJIL Supp. 119 (1953). **Emphasis** added.

cerned with the welfare of their fellow American prisoners detained in North Vietnam. The Committee did not seek to do more in relation to prisoner issues than to serve its humanitarian purposes and to disseminate its views on the condition of camps and on how to secure the repatriation of other prisoners. Such views were at variance with the Administration position on these matters and with other private and nongovernmental groups that also proclaim their humanitarian purposes, despite their commitment to President Nixon's war policies.[13] As President Nixon and Secretary Laird have frequently observed "this is strictly a humanitarian issue." That is, Americans might disagree about the war, but no American questioned the propriety of helping the American prisoners secure better conditions and quicker release. In the circumstances of the war, the Committee of Liaison, precisely because its members opposed the war, were uniquely able to produce tangible benefits for the prisoners of war and their families.[14] Such tangible benefits seem to be just those humanitarian contributions that Articles 9 and 10 of the Geneva Convention have in mind.

Thirdly, does the Committee of Liaison require the consent of the U.S. Government before it can perform these humanitarian functions? The situation here is quite ambiguous. Although government officals have been critical of the Committee of Liaison, there was no effort to interfere with its activities. The government, indeed, did not oppose granting Mr. David Dellinger, who was at the time subject to court-imposed travel restrictions, permission to leave the United States on the escort mission even though the trip would involve travel to countries with whom there were no extradition arrangements and even though his alleged crimes could readily be viewed as nonextradictable "political" offenses. The point is that the government might have relied on a technical objection to Mr. Dellinger's inclusion in the escort group, but refrained from doing so.

The language of Articles 9 and 10 is also ambiguous with regard to whether the belligerent must agree to the designation of a humanitarian organization. I think it most reasonable, both in relation to treaty interpretation and policy rationale, to view the second paragraph of Article 10 as giving the Detaining Power, North Vietnam, the capacity to deal with an organization, like the Committee of Liaison for purposes of carrying out the basic substantive mandate of the Convention to promote the interests of prisoners of war.

There is also some support for this view derived from hearings before the Senate Foreign Relations Committee. The Department of State submitted a statement clarifying certain points on the Geneva Conventions which included a significant reference to the meaning of Article 10:

> Common Article 10 (Article 11 of the Civilian Convention) provides for substitutes for protecting powers when protected persons for any

---

[13] E.g., the initiatives associated with Ross Perot, the Texas millionaire, or the activities of the National League of Families of American Prisoners and Missing in Southeast Asia.

[14] As of November 1972 the Committee of Liaison has delivered 14,000 letters from and to prisoners detained in Vietnam and has also provided informational services for relatives of detained men.

reason do not benefit by the activities of such a power. In such an event, the detaining power is requied unilaterally to undertake the functions performed by a protecting power. If such protection cannot be arranged, the detaining power is obligated to request or accept the offer of the services of a humanitarian organization, such as the International Committee of the Red Cross, to assume the humanitarian functions performed by protecting powers.[15]

The statement notes its opposition to a Soviet bloc reservation to Article 10 because its effect is to "diminish the belligerent rights of the state on which the protected persons depend." These states made a reservation that they would not accept a designation "unless the consent of the government of the state of which the protected persons are nationals has been obtained."[16] Such a statement seems to confirm the United States view that the Detaining Power had the capacity, even the duty, to designate an impartial humanitarian organization and that such designation would be determinative at least in the absence of objection from the country whose men are detained that the organization is not "impartial" or not "humanitarian."[17]

It would seem clear, then, that the Committe of Liaison could be designated by North Vietnam to carry out humanitarian functions, including repatriation in accordance with Article 10. The failure of the U.S. Government to make an objection either to the Committee or to the repatriation procedures is a further indication of this propriety. Given such an Article 10 role, then it seems reasonable for the Committee of Liaison to have some authority to specify guidelines that cover the discharge of a humanitarian mission not dealt with in the Convention and hence unreasonable for the U.S. Government not to respond either by way of acceptance, reasoned rejection, or through the proffer of an alternative set of guidelines.

It should be reiterated here that the discussion of Article 10 does not imply a formal application of its procedure to this repatriation. Article 10 does cast rather authoritative light, however, on what the treaty-drafting governments, and particularly the U.S. Government, regarded as *reasonable*

[15] *Hearings on the Geneva Conventions for the Protection of War Victims, Before the Senate Foreign Relations Committee,* June 3, 1955, at 62.

[16] *Id.* North Vietnam has made a reservation to its adherence exempting itself from Article 10.

[17] *See also Hearings, supra* note 15 at 62, for a covering letter from John Foster Dulles, as Secretary of State, to Senator Walter F. George, Chairman of the Committee:

It is particularly recommended that this Government should not accept these reservations. The United States, should, however, express its intention to enter into treaty relations with the reserving states so that they will be bound toward the United States to carry out all the provisions of the conventions on which no reservations were specifically made. It should be clear that we hope that the reserving states will at some time elect to withdraw their reservations and if in the event of conflict reserving states seek to use their reservation in an unwarranted fashion so as to defeat the broad humanitarian purposes of the conventions, the United States would, of course, be in a position to consider that it was not required further to apply the conventions vis-à-vis such defaulting states. By acting as it has in relation to this September 1972 repatriation North Vietnam has, it would seem, made a proper use of Article 10 so as to promote the underlying objectives of the Prisoner of War Convention.

in a situation in which no governmental actor was available to carry out the humanitarian mandate of the Convention. Actions in this situation, then, can be assessed in terms of such standards of reasonableness.

Fourth, does not the U.S. Government have some protection against the use of the process of repatriation to disseminate hostile propaganda? Why should North Vietnam not be expected to deal with a "genuinely" neutral organization? Such issues are difficult to resolve. There is a deep disagreement as to what constitutes neutrality in the POW context. If the North Vietnamese Government can be faulted for its attitude of hostility toward the International Committee of the Red Cross, then the U.S. Government can be criticized on purely humanitarian grounds for its reliance on various pro-war groups interested in the POW issue. In such circumstances, the Detaining Power has to be able to make the designation in the first instance, and the impropriety of its action has to be assessed by reference to whether or not there has been substantial fulfillment of the humanitarian purposes underlying the Geneva Convention. In this instance there has been no indication or allegation that the Committee of Liaison did more than provide escort facilities under as pleasant conditions as possible and with due regard for the welfare of the returning men and the remaining pilots.

While in Hanoi the Committee of Liaison also delivered and received mail, forwarded specific inquiries regarding health of detained men, examined complaints about camp conditions, received evidence from North Vietnam as to American abuse of mail privileges by including improper materials in packages designed to aid clandestine communication and possible rescue operations, and met with seven additional POWs in a free exchange of views. The Committee of Liaison escorts also expressed their views on the civilian damage being done by the air war and on the proper way to end the war and bring home the other American POWs, but this was done in their individual capacity. No effort was made to associate the three released men with views. The men were allowed, at most, to have a forum for the expression of their views, an opportunity that was used only very sparingly. The situation would have been different, it seems, if these men had been "brainwashed" and were then given a wide public forum to denounce the war under the cover of their repatriation, but no one has made such charges. In their absence, these released men are citizens with constitutional rights of freedom of speech; as such, they are entitled to oppose (or favor) the war, as they may have before being shot down, and they are certainly not precluded from saying that they saw (or didn't see) hospitals and churches that had been destroyed by bombs. The range of reactions exhibited by these three men toward the war confirms the view that they were not brainwashed and that they were not released because it was expected that they would denounce the war or join the peace movement.[18]

[18] These three men were released without conditions and without any explanation of the basis on which they were chosen. Their behavior since the moment of release exhibits a sense of independence on the part of the three men.

In conclusion, then, the Committee of Liaison appears to have been an appropriate organization for North Vietnam to designate to carry out the humanitarian objectives of the Geneva Conventions under the special circumstances of this war. Furthermore, there is nothing in the Convention nor in the Committee's record of performance to indicate its unsuitability for such a role. And, finally, the U.S. Government itself has done nothing to repudiate this designation, and it is not clear that such a repudiation could be justified in relation to the facts or to the guidelines embodied in the Convention.

## III

It seems appropriate to make some wider observations about this minor event:

(1) The humanitarian objectives of the Convention may have to be realized in a flexible manner that is responsive to the characteristics of a particular armed conflict;

(2) A private organization of nationals of the "enemy" state may be more acceptable to the Detaining Power in certain situations than either the International Committee of the Red Cross or a neutral or even a friendly third power government;

(3) The Geneva system is comprehensive enough to provide general guidelines of relevance even in relation to a form of repatriation not specifically covered by the existing treaty;

(4) Treaty revision efforts should take explicit account of the possibility of repatriation of healthy prisoners to the enemy belligerent during the period of active hostilities;

(5) Repatriated prisoners should also be entitled to humanitarian protection once returned to their country of nationality and should be removed from any further relationship, direct or indirect, to an armed conflict in progress.

## IV

We are left, then, with the underlying policy issue: How do we interpret the release and repatriation of three prisoners out of a prisoner population in North Vietnam of several hundred? Why only three? Why these three? There is no way to resolve altogether this underlying set of doubts. We can, however, make an analysis of whether this release seemed generally reasonable in method and effect and therefore deserved implementation.

First of all, it was a consensual process. The North Vietnamese initiative was not repudiated, as such, by the U.S. Government or by the three men selected for release.

Secondly, there was some humanitarian benefit for the three families concerned and some degree of reassurance more generally felt, given their good health and positive reports of general camp conditions and morale.

Thirdly, there were no negative consequences to legitimate prisoner interests.

It can be argued, of course, that North Vietnam was motivated by a desire to make hostile propaganda in connection with the release. Why else did they release the men into the custody of anti-war leaders? Why else did they provide tours of the bombed areas and entertainment for the released men and their relatives? Why was it insisted that the released men be returned to the American people rather than the American Government? Why was a return route arranged that was indirect and proceeded as far as possible by way of countries opposed to American policy in Vietnam? Why was the release timed to coincide with a pre-election period in which the Administration's war and prisoner policy was under attack by the opposition candidate? On one level, North Vietnamese motivations are of no account. Their behavior seemed correct, their initiative promoted a humanitarian end, and no effort was made to impose conditions on the terms of release.

In retrospect, it seems important to understand several features of the context. First of all, a humane experience of repatriation was aided by the presence of an accompanying relative and that some unnecessary trauma was generated by the efforts of the government to obtain jurisdiction over the men prior to and immediately upon their return to the United States. Secondly, the situation as to the Vietnamese prisoners does not resemble the situation of the Korean prisoners and expectations about repatriation should be adjusted accordingly. Thirdly, a long war in which reasonable and loyal citizens reach opposite conclusions about the best interests of the country places particular burdens on combat personnel who are captured under these circumstances, especially in relation to compliance with the Code of Conduct.[19] Fourthly, in these circumstances humanitarian purposes in accordance with the Geneva system may be and have been, in fact, served by a link between the enemy government and a prisoner of war organization constituted by anti-war nationals.

It seems reasonable, on this basis, to regard the North Vietnamese National Day Release as creating a precedent with international law relevance. At least, in the absence of revision of the Geneva Prisoner of War Convention, this release provides guidelines and experience as to repatriation during hostilities to a belligerent power, and affirms the capacity of a nongovernmental organization of private citizens to play a direct role in this process.

[19] For a sensitive treatment of the dilemma confronting a prisoner of war *see* Michael Waltzer's essay *Prisoners of War: Does the Fight Continue After the Battle?* in WALZER, OBLIGATIONS: ESSAYS ON DISOBEDIENCE, WAR, AND CITIZENSHIP 146–166 (1970). The problems posed for a conscripted citizen-soldier of a democratic society who opposes a war policy before his capture is particularly acute. Government writing does not exhibit an awareness of these issues. *See* "POW—The Fight Continues After the Battle," Report of the Secretary of Defense's Advisory Committee on Prisoners of War, Aug. 1955, which heavily reflects an effort to establish POW guidelines that would be resistant to brainwashing tactics used so successfully by North Korea in the Korean War. *See also* Prugh, *The Code of Conduct for the Armed Forces,* 56 COLUMBIA L. REV. 678 (1956); Note, *Misconduct in the Prison Camp: A Survey of the Law and an Analysis of the Korean Cases, ibid.,* 709.

# International Law Aspects of Repatriation of Prisoners of War During Hostilities: A Reply

## HOWARD S. LEVIE

### I

In the July 1973 issue of the *Journal*,[1] there appeared an article with the above title written by Professor Richard Falk, in which he, in effect, advanced the thesis that the release of prisoners of war for repatriation during the course of hostilities in Vietnam to an *ad hoc* and self-styled "humanitarian organization" (which admittedly consisted solely of individuals who were vocal opponents of the United States participation in those hostilities) either constituted a valid and forward-looking interpretation of the provisions of the Geneva Convention of 1949 relative to the Treatment of Prisoners of War[2] (hereinafter referred to as "the 1949 Convention") or indicated the need for revision of that instrument. The subject appears to be one which calls for an analysis in considerably greater depth than the treatment provided in the article by Professor Falk.

In this article, I shall discuss, independently of the facts alleged and the arguments advanced in the article by Professor Falk, the legal aspects involved in (1) the release and repatriation during the course of hostilities of prisoners of war who do not come within the mandatory provisions of Article 109 *et seq.* of the 1949 Convention (in other words, those who are not so "seriously wounded" or so "seriously sick" as to be entitled to release and repatriation as a matter of right); and (2) the use of an "impartial humanitarian organization" to accomplish this purpose. Thereafter, I shall point out some of the areas in which I agree or disagree with the proponent of this procedure.

### II

Historically, there have been three major methods employed by Detaining Powers for the release and repatriation during the course of hostilities of able-bodied prisoners of war—ransom, exchange, and parole. The ransom of captured military personnel, which reached its peak in its application to chivalry in medieval times, had, for all practical purposes, disappeared by the end of the seventeenth century.[3] It was replaced by

---

[1] 66 AJIL 465 (1973) (hereinafter cited as Falk).

[2] 6 UST 3316; 75 UNTS 135; 47 AJIL Supp. 119 (1953).

[3] One author asserts that "[f]aint though unmistakeable traces of it [ransom] survive even into Napoleon's war, . . . ." Lewis, Napoleon and His British Captives 43 (1962). *See also*, Levie, *The Nature and Scope of the Armistice Agreement*, 50 AJIL 880, 897 (1956). Perhaps it may be said to have reappeared momentarily as a result of the sequel to the Bay of Pigs episode.

exchange when continental armies became national and professional and
when obtaining the release of captured military personnel became accepted
as the responsibility of the sovereign.  Exchange was man-for-man and
grade-for-grade (with tables of "equivalent values") so that, at least in
theory, it would not result in any change in the relative military strengths
of the two sides.[4]  Exchange still existed as late as the American Civil War,
but it ceased to be a really effective procedure during that conflict.[5]

Parole is the third method of effectuating the release and repatriation of
prisoners of war during the course of hostilities.  Under this procedure,
the prisoner of war agrees to certain conditions that will govern his conduct upon his release from a confined status.  It has proven relatively
unimportant as a method of procuring the release and repatriation of
prisoners of war during the course of a conflict.  Historically, it developed
primarily into a method of permitting the prisoner of war more freedom
within the territory of the Detaining Power, rather than of procuring his
release and repatriation.[6]  Moreover, Article 21(2) of the 1949 Convention,
like its predecessors, specifically contemplates that Powers of Origin may
prohibit their captured military personnel from giving or accepting parole;
a number of countries, including the United States, the United Kingdom,
and France, have traditionally restricted the right of their military personnel
to give or accept parole.[7]

Article 72 of the Geneva Convention of 1929 Relative to the Treatment
of Prisoners of War [8] (hereinafter referred to as "the 1929 Convention")
suggested the possibility of agreements between belligerents for the repatriation during hostilities of "able-bodied prisoners of war who have undergone a long period of captivity."  A similar but somewhat more extensive
provision was included in the 1949 Convention.  Article 109(2) provides
that the Parties may "conclude agreements with a view to the direct repatriation or internment in a neutral country of able-bodied prisoners of war who

[4] When, for some reason, a formal exchange could not be made, a prisoner of
war might be released and repatriated in a temporary parole status until his counterpart had been repatriated and the formal exchange had thus been completed.  Lewis,
*supra* note 3, at 45.

[5] The occasional procedure mentioned in the previous note was substantially the
system adopted as a general procedure in the rather ineffectual Dix-Hill Cartel during the American Civil War.  LEWIS & MEWHA, THE HISTORY OF PRISONER OF WAR
UTILIZATION BY THE UNITED STATES ARMY, 1776–1945, at 29–30 (1955); MURPHY,
PRISONERS OF WAR: REPATRIATION OR INTERNMENT IN WARTIME 2–3 (1971).

[6] The release and repatriation on temporary parole mentioned in note 4, *supra*,
was the exception rather than the rule; and the Dix-Hill Cartel, in attempting to
make it the rule, failed to accomplish the intended result to the satisfaction of either
side.

[7] *See*, for example, U.S. Army Field Manual 27-10, THE LAW OF LAND WARFARE,
para. 187a (1956); Article III, *Code of Conduct for Members of the Armed Forces*,
Exec. Order No. 10631, Aug. 18, 1955, 3 CFR, 1954–1958 Comp., at 266; United
Kingdom, THE LAW OF WAR ON LAND, BEING PART III OF THE MANUAL OF MILITARY
LAW, para. 246, n. 1 (1958); CODE DE JUSTICE MILITAIRE, ARMÉE DE TERRE, Art. 235
(Dalloz, 1963).

[8] 47 Stat. 2021; 2 Bevans 932; 27 AJIL SUPP. 59 (1933).

have undergone a long period of captivity." [9]   This provision may be considered as an attempt to encourage the belligerents to adopt one of these procedures (and to give neutral states and others a basis for proposing them), rather than as a legal authorization to do so, inasmuch as no such authorization was needed in order to enable belligerents lawfully to enter into such agreements. Article 6(1) of the 1949 Convention specifically contemplates the conclusion of special agreements by the Parties concerning prisoner-of-war matters, subject only to the limitations that any such agreement may not "adversely affect" the prisoners of war to whom it purports to apply and that it may not "restrict the rights" elsewhere conferred upon them by the Convention. Paragraph 2 of the same article contemplates that a Party may unilaterally give prisoners of war more favorable treatment than is required by the 1949 Convention itself. Certainly, an agreement for the repatriation of longtime, able-bodied prisoners of war during the course of hostilities would not fall within the ambit of either of the limitations mentioned above; [10] and it would in any event be more favorable treatment than required by the 1949 Convention. [11] Moreover, the Detaining Power could justifiably assert that individuals so repatriated would be barred from further participation in the hostilities against it. [12]

[9] On Dec. 9, 1970, the UN General Assembly adopted a Resolution in which it:
> Urges compliance with Article 109 of the Geneva Convention of 1949 . . . which provides for agreements with a view to the direct repatriation . . . of able-bodied prisoners of war who have undergone a long period of captivity. (A/RES/1676 (XXV) (1970)).

In Havens, Release and Repatriation of Vietnam Prisoners, 57 ABAJ 41, 44 (1971), the author argues that after 18 months as a prisoner of war an individual should be entitled to release and repatriation. However, he cites no authority for this interpretation of the provisions of the 1949 Convention.

[10] Article 109(3) prohibits the involuntary repatriation of sick and injured prisoners of war during the course of hostilities. Normal rules of treaty interpretation would seem to make this provision inapplicable to the repatriation during hostilities of able-bodied prisoners of war unless it can be said that as a result of the settlement reached in Korea in 1953, supported by a number of resolutions of the UN General Assembly, a norm of international law has evolved which prohibits the involuntary repatriation of prisoners of war under any circumstances.

[11] Although both the 1929 and the 1949 Conventions contemplate that such repatriations will be accomplished under agreements between the Parties, there is certainly no reason why one Party cannot elect to take such action unilaterally if it so desires. Article 6(2) of the 1949 Convention specifically mentions this possibility and Article 118(2) of that Convention, dealing with post-hostilities release and repatriation, specifically provides for, and even requires, unilateral action if no agreement covering the subject is reached by the belligerents. Pakistan initiated this unilateral action in November 1972 with respect to the Indian prisoners of war it then held. N.Y. Times, Nov. 28, 1972, at 1, c. 2.

[12] Article 117 of the 1949 Convention provides that "[n]o repatriated person may be employed on active military service." This provision is, of course, quite ambiguous. PICTET (ed.), COMMENTARY ON THE GENEVA CONVENTION RELATIVE TO THE TREATMENT OF PRISONERS OF WAR 538–39 (1960) (hereinafter cited as PICTET, COMMENTARY). U.S. military authorities have construed Article 117 as only prohibiting the repatriated serviceman from participating in combat against the former Detaining Power and not as requiring his complete separation from the military service.

Unfortunately, despite the fact that World War II saw many prisoners of war held in captivity for periods in excess of five years, apparently no belligerent sought to implement Article 72 of the 1929 Convention.[13] And in none of the many armed conflicts which have occurred since the end of World War II (and since the 1949 Convention became effective) has there been an agreement for the repatriation of able-bodied prisoners of war prior to the cessation of hostilities.[14] However, it is not really difficult to understand why neither of the substantially similar provisions of the two Prisoner-of-War Conventions has ever been implemented by belligerents. Any bilateral agreement providing for the repatriation during hostilities of able-bodied prisoners of war would merely be a new name for the old procedure of exchange, a procedure which fell into disuse because, despite its man-for-man and grade-for-grade aspects, it inevitably turned out to be more advantageous for one side than for the other.[15] Indeed, this same factor has even militated against the repatriation during the course of hostilities of seriously wounded or sick prisoners of war.[16]

It being accepted that releases and repatriations during the course of hostilities of longtime, able-bodied prisoners of war are within the contemplation of existing international law, despite the failure of any belligerent state to do so as a matter of practice, let us move to the next problem. What are the qualifications required of a body for it to fall within the category of organizations empowered to perform the humanitarian functions which the 1949 Convention authorizes for the benefit of prisoners of war?

Article 8 of the 1949 Convention is the basic article establishing the Protecting Power with its manifold humanitarian and other functions.[17] However, Article 9 of that Convention specifically provides that humanitarian activities for the benefit of prisoners of war may also be performed

American Prisoners of War in Southeast Asia, 1971, Hearings before the Subcomm. on National Security Policy and Scientific Developments of the House Comm. on Foreign Affairs, 92d Cong., 1st Sess., 350 (1971) (hereinafter cited as 1971 Hearings).

[13] Although the REPORT OF THE INTERNATIONAL COMMITTEE OF THE RED CROSS ON ITS ACTIVITIES DURING THE SECOND WORLD WAR (September 1, 1939–June 30, 1947) (1948) includes a 21-page discussion of the numerous repatriations of seriously wounded and seriously sick prisoners of war in Europe (Vol. I, at 373–93), it does not even mention any proposal by a belligerent or neutral state or a humanitarian organization to implement Article 72 of the 1929 Convention.

[14] Probably no armed conflict which has occurred since 1945 (except for those involving the French in Vietnam, Korea, and the later Vietnamese conflict) has really continued for a long enough time for any prisoner of war to be considered as having "undergone a long period of captivity."

[15] The Dix-Hill Cartel, supra notes 5 and 6, failed because in the early years of the American Civil War the equal exchange of able-bodied prisoners of war favored the Union, while later in the conflict it favored the Confederacy, LEWIS & MEWHA, supra note 5, at 30. Of course, this criticism is not true of internment in a neutral country, the alternative provided for in Article 109(2).

[16] See LINDSAY (ed.), SWISS INTERNMENT OF PRISONERS OF WAR 3 (1917):
The fear expressed by France [in February 1915] that under the system of exchange wounded soldiers would be returned to Germany who could still be of military service [an amputee could work in a depot, thus relieving an able-bodied solider], was common to other belligerents. . . .

[17] Levie, Prisoners of War and the Protecting Power, 55 AJIL 374 (1961).

by the International Committee of the Red Cross (the ICRC) or by "any other impartial humanitarian organization." The organization and operations of the ICRC are widely known and have received well-merited recognition throughout the 1949 Convention.[18] The precise nature of the organizations which fall within the meaning of the term "any other impartial humanitarian organization" is considerably less clear.

Article 88 of the 1929 Convention, which was the direct progenitor of Article 9 of the 1949 Convention, did not include the possibility of the intervention of any "humanitarian organization" other than the ICRC for the purpose of furnishing assistance to prisoners of war. That possibility received recognition for the first time in a proposal made by the Italian representative during a meeting of a committee of the Diplomatic Conference which drafted the 1949 Convention.[19] The Italian proposal to add the words "or any other impartial humanitarian body" after the reference to the ICRC in the original draft of the article received the strong support of the Director-General of the International Refugee Organization (IRO) who pointed out that, in view of the existing collaboration between governments and the IRO, "it would seem opportune to extend the provisions of Article 8 [now Article 9 of the 1949 Prisoner-of-War Convention], to enable governments to avail themselves of its services in case of necessity." [20] The proposal was adopted by the Joint Committee of the Diplomatic Conference after a debate in which the representative of the United States had supported the use for humanitarian purposes of "welfare organizations of a non-international character" and the Committee had rejected a Burmese proposal to narrow the Italian proposal to "any other *internationally recognized* impartial humanitarian body." [21] It was approved at a Plenary Meeting of the Diplomatic Conference without debate.[22]

The foregoing is the substance of the *travtaux préparatoires* concerning the addition of the words "or any other impartial humanitarian organization" to Article 9 of the 1949 Convention.[23] In attempting to elucidate the precise meaning of these words, it is therefore necessary to look elsewhere for help. The ICRC's discussion of the matter in a 1960 publication is extremely helpful.

> The humanitarian activities authorized must be undertaken by the International Committee of the Red Cross or by any other *impartial humanitarian* organization. The International Committee is mentioned in two capacities—firstly on its own account . . .; and secondly, as an example of what is meant by "impartial humanitarian organization. . . ."

[18] *Ibid.*, at 394–96. See also I ICRC REPORT, *supra* note 13, at 11–29.

[19] Fourth Meeting of the Joint Committee, FINAL RECORD OF THE DIPLOMATIC CONFERENCE OF GENEVA OF 1949, Vol. IIB, at 18, 21 (hereinafter cited as FINAL RECORD).

[20] Annex 24, FINAL RECORD, Vol. III, at 32.

[21] FINAL RECORD, Vol. IIB, at 60 (emphasis added).

[22] Article 7/8/8/8, *ibid.*, at 346.

[23] At some point in the deliberations the word "body" was changed to "organization" but this author was unable to pinpoint the event in the FINAL RECORD, a result not unique to this particular matter.

The organization must be *humanitarian;* in other words it must be concerned with the condition of man, considered solely as a human being, regardless of his value as a military, political, professional or other unit. It must also be *impartial.* Article 9 does not require it to be international. . . . Furthermore, the Convention does not require the organization to be neutral, but it is obvious that impartiality benefits greatly from neutrality.

In order to be authorized, the organization's activities must be purely humanitarian in character; that is to say they must be concerned with human beings as such, and must not be affected by any political or military consideration. Within those limits, any subsidiary activity which helps to implement the principles of the Convention is not only authorized but desirable under Article 9. . . .[24]

There are, then, three basic requirements for an organization's qualifying as "any other impartial humanitarian organization" within the meaning of Article 9 of the 1949 Convention: first, it must be *impartial* in its operations; second, it must be *humanitarian* in concept and function; and third, it must have some institutional, operational, and functional *resemblance to the ICRC.*[25] Negatively, it need not be international in creation and it need not be neutral in origin.

What is meant by "impartial"? An "impartial" organization is one which, as an institution, is unbiased and unprejudiced, fair and equitable to both sides in its operations, one which neither by act nor by statement gives any indication that it prefers one side over the other.[26] The mere fact of being established and based in a neutral country does not of itself make an organization "impartial."[27] Conversely, the mere fact of being estab-

---

[24] PICTET, COMMENTARY, 107–08.

[25] Both the phrasing of the provision of the 1949 Convention and the doctrine of *ejusdem generis* indicate the validity of the conclusion reached by the ICRC that it was to be considered "as an example of what is meant by 'impartial humanitarian organization'."

[26] No matter how politically remote its policymakers and other members may be from the cause of the war and from the belligerents, they will, of course, inevitably have individual prejudices with respect to any armed conflict that may be in progress. However, if the organization is to be able to maintain its aura of "impartiality," even these individual preferences must be both suppressed and concealed because of the human difficulty of ascribing "impartiality" to an organization whose policymakers and other members have publicly expressed individual preferences and prejudices.

[27] During the hostilities in Korea the Chinese charged, with the support of the USSR, and totally without justification and solely for political reasons, that the ICRC was a "capitalist spy organization." United Kingdom, Ministry of Defence, TREATMENT OF BRITISH PRISONERS OF WAR IN KOREA 33–34 (1955). The actions of the North Vietnamese during the hostilities in Vietnam would seem to indicate a similar attitude. Falk, *The American POWs; Pawns in Power Politics,* THE PROGRESSIVE, March 1971, at 13, 16. Under the circumstances, it is unexpected, indeed, to find the USSR communicating to the Secretary-General of the United Nations its belief in the need for the ICRC to undertake additional tasks relating to the protection of human rights in armed conflict and omitting any suggestion for the use of "other impartial humanitarian organizations" for this purpose. Report of the Secretary-General, *Respect for Human Rights in Armed Conflict,* UN Doc. A/8052, Sept. 18, 1970, at 119, 120.

lished and based in a belligerent country does not necessarily indicate a lack of "impartiality." While, as a practical matter, it will undoubtedly be most difficult to identify an organization which is not "neutral" in location but which is accepted as "impartial," this is neither a paradox nor an impossibility. Such an organization will usually be one which operates exclusively in the territory of its own nation, preparing material assistance for dispatch through neutral relief channels, such as the ICRC, to the prisoners of war of its own nationality held by the enemy; and, more relevantly, it will be one which is permitted to and does provide material assistance to enemy prisoners of war held in the territory of its own nation.[28] It is, however, almost inconceivable that an organization which is established and based in the territory of one belligerent will be permitted to function in the territory of an opposing belligerent, no matter how impartial and humanitarian its reputation and its operations.[29] Wartime public opinion alone would be a sufficiently powerful force to prevent an "enemy" organization from functioning freely in the territory of the other side—except under the most unusual circumstances.[30]

The meaning of the term "humanitarian" is considerably less controversial and its application presents far fewer problems. As stated by the ICRC in the excerpts quoted above, "humanitarian" denotes "concerned with the condition of man, considered solely as a human being." In the context of the prisoner of war, a "humanitarian organization" is one which has the objective of protecting and improving the welfare of the prisoner of war and the conditions under which he exists. Certainly, this is, and has long been, a major objective of the ICRC, and, as we have seen, the ICRC serves as a model for identifying the organizations which come within the meaning of Article 9 of the 1949 Convention.

[28] During World War II, the Young Men's Christian Association, the National Catholic Welfare Conference, and other similar organizations, were permitted, in varying degrees, to supplement the humanitarian work of the ICRC on behalf of enemy prisoners of war held in the United States. Rich (ed.), *A Brief History of the Office of the Provost Marshal General, World War II*, at 489–91 (mimeo., 1946). Some of these organizations might, upon investigation, qualify under Article 9. While their orientation was, for the most part, primarily religious, they normally offered humanitarian assistance to all enemy prisoners of war, without regard to their origin, nationality, or religion. Of course, religious supplies furnished by them were limited to those of their own denomination.

[29] When the representative of the United States at the 1949 Diplomatic Conference supported the proposed change in the draft of Article 9 and referred to "welfare organizations of a non-international character," he unquestionably had in mind the operation of such orgainzations in their own country, based upon the experience in the United States during World War II mentioned in the previous note.

[30] There could certainly be little dispute that, during World War II, it would have been impossible for the American Red Cross, or the YMCA, or the National Catholic Welfare Conference, all American-established and based humanitarian organizations, to have obtained permission to function in Germany or Japan, or for the German or Japanese Red Cross to have obtained permission to function in the United States. The same was indubitably true of the American Red Cross, the Red Cross of the Republic of Vietnam, and the Red Cross of the Democratic Republic of Vietnam (DRV) during the hostilities in Vietnam.

Finally, the entity seeking to bring itself within that provision—or which one of the belligerents seeks to bring within that provision—must be an "organization" and as such it must have some institutional, operational, and functional resemblance to the ICRC. An individual does not qualify.[31] A small, *ad hoc* loose-knit group consisting of individuals who have joined together for a specific and limited purpose and which is obviously destined to have a limited life span does not qualify. There must be some institutional basis, some operational experience and tradition, which clearly establishes it as an organization that is both impartial and humanitarian.[32] An established religious organization could probably qualify institutionally even though it had not been previously engaged in prisoner-of-war welfare activities. A national Red Cross Society could probably qualify institutionally as could an organization which has operated in the field of relief from natural disasters. An international organization, such as the United Nations or the Organization of American State,[33] or an agency thereof, such as the UN High Commissioner for Refugees or the OAS Council, could probably qualify institutionally. The possibilities are almost limitless.

One additional facet of the designation of "impartial humanitarian organizations" requires mention. Article 9 of the 1949 Convention makes the activities of the ICRC or of any other impartial humanitarian organization "subject to the consent of the Parties to the conflict concerned."[34] In the debate on the proposed amendment to the draft article which contemplated the activities of impartial humanitarian organizations other than the ICRC,[35] the representative of France pointed out that "the activities of humanitarian bodies were always subordinated to approval by Parties to the conflict."[36] The provision of the 1949 Convention has been interpreted, and properly so, as requiring the consent of all the Parties "upon which the possibility of carrying out the action contemplated depends."[37] This is why it is inconceivable that even a universally recognized humanitarian organization, if established and based in the territory of one belligerent, would be able to function in the territory of the other.[38]

---

[31] No matter how humanitarian may have been H. Ross Perot's motives, his misguided activities on behalf of the American prisoners of war then held in North Vietnam could not have been considered as falling within any provision of the 1949 Convention.

[32] The "institutional basis" and the "operational experience and tradition" need not necessarily have been prisoner-of-war oriented, or even war-oriented.

[33] Some official action previously taken by the international organization might have called in question its impartiality but it would not affect its "institutional" qualifications.

[34] It can be assumed that the People's Republic of Korea and the Democratic Republic of Vietnam would rely on this provision in justification of their right to refuse to allow the ICRC to perform its customary humanitarian functions within their territories. Whether they did indeed act on the basis of law is another question.

[35] *See* text in connection with notes 19–23, *supra*.

[36] FINAL RECORD, Vol. IIB, at 60.

[37] PICTET, COMMENTARY, 109.

[38] *Supra* note 30. If Switzerland were a belligerent, the ICRC would undoubtedly find itself refused permission to function in the territory of that country's enemy, despite the century-old tradition of impartial humanitarianism which the ICRC enjoys.

An organization obviously *cannot* function if it does not have the permission and approval of the sovereign of the territory in which it proposes to operate (normally, this would be the Detaining Power); it legally cannot, and certainly *should not*, function if it does not also have the permission and approval of the other sovereign concerned (normally, this would be the Power of Origin).[39]

To summarize:

(1.) An adequate legal basis exists in international law for the release and repatriation of longtime, able-bodied prisoners of war during the course of hostilities (Article 109(2)).

(2.) While the legal basis for such action contemplates a consensual arrangement, the 1949 Convention not only permits but encourages unilateral action which is more favorable to the prisoners of war than is required by the Convention itself (Article 6(2)).

(3.) Bilateral release and repatriation of longtime, able-bodied prisoners of war during the course of hostilities, as provided in the 1949 Convention (Article 109(2)), is actually a return to the historic procedure of exchange with the added limitation against the further use of the repatriated prisoners of war "on active military service" (Article 117).

(4.) Either the International Committee of the Red Cross or "any other impartial humanitarian organization" may perform humanitarian activities for the welfare of prisoners of war provided that the appropriate Parties to the conflict give their consent (Article 9).

(5.) An "impartial humanitarian organization" within the meaning of Article 9 of the 1949 Convention is one which is unbiased and unprejudiced, fair and equitable to both Parties concerned, one which neither by act nor by statement gives any indication that it prefers one side over the other; one which has the humanitarian objective of protecting and improving the welfare of the prisoners of war and the conditions under which they exist in their status as captives; and one which is truly an "organization," a status measured, in the final analysis, by its institutional, operational, and functional resemblance to the ICRC.

### III

From the foregoing general discussion of the legal aspects of the release and repartriation during hostilities of longtime, able-bodied prisoners of

---

It could, of course, continue to perform those humanitarian functions which might be performed in Switzerland.

[39] This is why the reservation made to Article 10 of the 1949 Convention by the USSR and the other Communist countries (including, subsequently, the DRV) and objected to by the Western countries, appears to have a valid basis. Levie, *supra* note 17, at 385, n. 32. That article provides that if there is no Protecting Power, and, for some reason, a new Protecting Power cannot be designated, the Detaining Power may request the services of a neutral state or of a humanitarian organization such as the ICRC to perform the functions of the Protecting Power. The Communist reservation properly makes the consent of the Power of Origin necessary for the designation of such a substitute. (For a more detailed discussion of the reservation to Article 10, *see* text at pp. 707–09.)

war through the intervention of humanitarian organizations, it is obvious that Professor Falk and I are in substantial agreement on the merit of such releases and repatriations from a humanitarian point of view. He suggests the need for "flexible" interpretation, or, alternatively, revision of the 1949 Convention in order to accomplish his basic purpose.[40] This is unnecessary because the provisions of Article 109(2) of the 1949 Convention specifically cover exactly the contingency with which he is concerned,[41] thereby making "flexible" interpretation or revision unnecessary.

We part company completely when he attempts to enlarge the scope of the term "impartial humanitarian organization" so as to bring within its ambit a group such as the self-styled "Committee of Liaison with Families of Servicemen Detained in North Vietnam" [42] (hereinafter referred to as the "Committee of Liaison") the members of which were far more concerned with anti-war propaganda than with the welfare of prisoners of war.[43] The Committee of Liaison was anything but "impartial"; it was more strongly motivated by political than by humanitarian considerations; and its existence as an "organization" within the meaning of the 1949 Convention was, at the very least, debatable.

To put the matter in proper perspective, it will be helpful to summarize briefly the events which are the basis for the legal thesis with which we are dealing. The process really began in October–November 1967 [44] when the Viet Cong released three captured American soldiers in Phnom Penh, Cambodia, to Thomas E. Hayden, an American identified by the press as being the representative of "anti-war groups" in the United States.[45] Then in February 1968 the Democratic Republic of Vietnam (DRV) released three American pilots in Hanoi to the Rev. Daniel Berrigan and Howard Zinn, also identified by the press as representatives of "anti-war groups." [46] Some months later, in July–August 1968, the

[40] "Observations" Nos. (1) and (4), Falk, at 477.

[41] *See* text at pp. 694–95 and note 9, *supra*.

[42] Mrs. Cora Weiss, co-chairman with David Dellinger of this Committee, testified as follows with respect to this group:

> The Committee of Liaison was established on January 15, 1970, after three women, including myself, of Women Strike for Peace, returned from a trip to North Vietnam. In our announcement of formation and purpose, we stated that the purposes of the committee were (1) to facilitate communication between prisoners and their families; and (2) to inquire on behalf of families regarding the status of their missing relatives.

1971 *Hearings* 230. An "Information Sheet" issued by the Committee of Liaison during the month of its inception stated that it had been established "at the request of the North Vietnamese." The Information Sheet goes on to give assurances that the Committee of Liaison "is not in any sense representing the government of North Vietnam." *Ibid.*, 532.

[43] Falk, 473–74.

[44] The significance of mentioning a time period instead of an exact date is discussed in note 86, *infra*.

[45] The men released were Sgt. Edward R. Johnson, Sgt. Daniel L. Pitzer, and Sgt. James E. Jackson. N.Y. Times, Nov. 13, 1967, at 2, c. 6. On three subsequent occasions the Viet Cong released a total of six additional American servicemen in the field, allowing them to return to U.S. military control without the benefit of an escort.

DRV released three more American pilots in Hanoi, this time to Mrs. Robert Scheer, Vernon Grizzard, and Stuart Meacham, once again identified by the press as representatives of "anti-war" groups.[47]  In August 1969 the DRV released three American servicemen in Hanoi, this time to Rennard C. Davis and David Dellinger, who were identified as representing the "National Mobilization Committee to End the War in Vietnam."[48] Finally, in September 1972, there occurred the release of three American pilots in Hanoi to Mrs. Cora Weiss, David Dellinger, Professor Falk et al.[49] Thus, the DRV made the first release of three captured American servicemen in February 1968; the second in August 1968; the third in August 1969; and the fourth and last in October 1972.  The first two of these releases were made to well-known anti-war individuals; the latter two were made to two different anti-war groups.  Each was attended with great publicity over an extended period of time.  Each involved the release of only a token number of prisoners of war.  Each involved prisoners of war who could only have been selected for release for reasons other than their physical condition or length of confinement, the grounds mentioned in the 1949 Convention for releases and repatriations during the course of hostilities.[50]

The cablegram sent by the "escort group" to the President of the United States from Hanoi [51] (which was, perhaps not unexpectedly, immediately broadcast by Hanoi radio) displayed either remarkable presumption, remarkable ignorance, or remarkable naiveté.[52]  The four "guidelines" laid

[46] The men released were Maj. Norris M. Overly, USAF, captured in Sept. 1967; and Capt. Jon D. Black, USAF, and Lt. (j.g.) David P. Matheny, USN, both captured in Oct. 1967.  N.Y. Times, Feb. 17, 1968, at 1, c. 8.

[47] The men released were Maj. James F. Low, USAF, captured in Dec. 1967; Capt. Joe V. Carpenter, USAF, captured in Feb. 1968; and Maj. Fred N. Thompson, USAF, captured in March 1968.  N.Y. Times, Aug. 5, 1968, at 15, c. 1.

[48] The men released were Lt. Robert F. Frishman, USN, captured in Oct. 1967; Seaman Douglas B. Hegdahl, captured in April 1967; and Capt. Wesley L. Rumble, USAF, captured in April 1968.  N.Y. Times, Aug. 5, 1969, at 1, c. 2.

[49] Lt. (j.g.) Markham L. Gartley, USN, had been captured in Aug. 1968; Lt. (j.g.) Morris A. Charles, USN, had been captured in Dec. 1971; and Maj. Edward K. Elias, USAF, had been captured in April 1972.  David Dellinger was once again one of the emissaries selected by the DRV to receive the release of the three prisoners of war, but this time it was not in his capacity as a member of the "National Mobilization Committee," but in his parallel capacity as a member of the Committee of Liaison. N.Y. Times, Sept. 17, 1972, at 3, c.4.

[50] Only Frishman could be said to have had a physical condition which might have warranted his release and repatriation on medical grounds.  Gartley, who had been a prisoner of war for more than four years, certainly qualified as a "longtime" prisoner of war.  Hegdahl had been a prisoner of war for 28 months, Frishman for 22 months, and Rumble for 16 months.  All of the other men released and repatriated by the DRV had been prisoners of war for less than one year (actually, for periods of between 4 and 9 months).

[51] Falk, 467, 471–72.  Falk seems to have been surprised that no answer was received from the U.S. Government by the Committee of Liaison to this and other messages sent from Hanoi.  Ibid., 467.  It is difficult to believe that he really expected answers.

[52] While the cablegram does state that the conditions it contained were "[i]n ac-

down for the benefit of the U. S. Government by the Committee of Liaison warrant individual comment, particularly in the light of the claim being advanced that the Committee of Liaison was an "impartial humanitarian organization."

The first paragraph of the cablegram demanded that the three prisoners of war released by the DRV to the Committee of Liaison for repatriation to the United States "shall proceed home with us and representatives of their families in civilian aircraft." The DRV could have made a case for insisting upon the use of civilian aircraft up to the territorial limits of the United States; but that it would omit such a major requirement from its public statement, and then privately so advise the members of the escort groups seems, to say the least, rather odd.[53] On the other hand, if the use of civil aircrft and the designation of authorized fellow passengers was a condition asserted on the initiative of the escort group, the group demonstrated that it, and the Committee of Liaison which it represented, were anything but "impartial." Moreover, despite the obvious mental reservations displayed by members of the escort group,[54] it is a universal rule of military law that upon his departure from the territory and control of the enemy (whether by release, escape, or any other method), a prisoner of war has the duty to report at once to the first available authorities of his country. Members of anti-war groups frequently display a singular inability to recognize that the relationship between a member of the military service and the military authorities has evolved over the centuries as a result of the dictates of necessity and differs considerably from the relationship between a civilian and the civilian authorities.

The second paragraph of the cablegram called for the granting of a 30-day "furlough" to the three prisoners of war being released and repatriated.[55] How such a completely internal, administrative matter could possibly have been deemed to be within the purview of either the DRV or of an "impartial humaniatrian organization" is exceedingly difficult to perceive.[56] It was just about as much the business of either the DRV or the Committee of Liaison as it would have been to lay down a condition that the men were to receive automatic promotions or to be entitled to

---

cordance with the expressed expectations of the North Vietnamese Government," Falk indicates clearly that its contents were developed by the "escort group" as an outgrowth of internal discussions which took place in Hanoi with respect to the group's "responsibilities" (*ibid.,* 466–67) and that the releases by the DRV were, in fact, unconditional. *Ibid.,* 471.

[53] It is, of course, possible that the desire of the Committee of Liaison to retain "custody" of the three men and to travel by civilian, rather than military, aircraft, could have been motivated by the publicity anticipated from a press conference and reception planned for their arrival at Kennedy Airport. *Ibid.,* 468.

[54] *Ibid.,* 471.

[55] The use of the term "furlough" shows a practical ignorance of contemporary military vocabulary. It was never applicable to officers and disappeared from the military lexicon shortly after World War II. Only a certain antiquarian interest would have prompted the three officers to request a "furlough."

[56] Was the granting of 30-day "furloughs" one of the "expressed expectations of the North Vietnamese Government"? *See* note, 52, *supra.*

additional pay for the period during which they had been prisoners of war. The members of the escort group seem to have labored under the impression that their first contact (except for Dellinger) with the problem of returned prisoners of war offered a subtle occasion to educate the military services about the process of repatriation. They were apparently unmindful of the fact that thousands of prisoners of war had been repatriated by the armed forces after World War II and the Korean War.[57]

The third paragraph of the cablegram demanded a "complete medical checkup at the hospital of their choice, civilian or military." Once again the Committee of Liaison pronounced itself on an internal, administrative matter in an area in which the military services have had far more experience than the members of the escort group. The members of the Committee again demonstrated an unwillingness to accept the fact that the three prisoners of war continued to be members of the military service, subject to military control and discipline, and were not just civilian members of the general public and "protegés" of the Committee of Liaison. Moreover, despite the demand for a medical checkup in a hospital made in the cablegram, the escort group later apparently realized that this would completely remove their "protegés" from their control and, as they approached the United States, their medical judgment changed. "[I]t was clear to the escort group . . . that there was no immediate need for medical surveillance." [58] However, once they were back in the United States they had to concede that "the pilots preferred, or at least were unwilling to contest, the Government's insistence on a medical checkup under military auspices." [59]

The fourth paragraph of the cablegram prescribed that the three men being repatriated "shall do nothing further to promote the American war effort in Indochina." As we have seen, Article 117 of the 1949 Convention contains an ambiguous prohibition against a repatriated prisoner of war's

[57] For example, after Korea some 4,400 prisoners of war were released and repatriated. Each was put through a processing which had been well organized beforehand and which included preliminary hospitalization and medical examination in Japan, return to the United States when medically approved, further hospitalization either in Hawaii or in the military hospital nearest to his home, complete medical examination and treatment, and extended leave as soon as medical clearance was granted.

[58] Falk, 471–72. Elsewhere reference is made to "reported *abuses* in relation to prior treatment" and the suggestion is advanced that there should be "a preliminary medical examination, perhaps *under neutral auspices*" (*ibid.*, 472, emphasis added). Incredible as it may seem, these two quotations refer to the treatment of repatriated prisoners of war in military hospitals in the United States!

[59] *Ibid.*, 472. Here and elsewhere throughout the article statements appear implying that anything done for the benefit of repatriated prisoners of war in the United States occurred solely because of public pressure by the escort group and in spite of strong governmental (or military service) predilections to the contrary. This, of course, disregards the fact that everything done for these men, as well as those who preceded and followed them, evolved from a refinement of the procedures for repatriated prisoners of war applied after World War II and Korea.

being "employed on active military service." [60] Like the United States, the ICRC interprets this to prohibit taking part "in armed operations against the former Detaining Power or its allies." [61] Certainly, any reasonable interpretation of Article 117 is far from the broad ban which the "impartial," anti-war Committee of Liaison sought to impose. [62]

The fact that the Committee of Liaison opposed U. S. participation in the hostilities in Vietnam is apparently considered one of the more decisive arguments in establishing both its "impartiality" and its "humanitarianism." [63] Conversely, it is at least implied that support of U. S. participation in the hostilities in Vietnam establishes a lack of "impartiality" and "humanitarianism." Thus, the "National League of Families of American Prisoners and Missing in Southeast Asia," an organization all of whose members were relatives of servicemen either known to be prisoners of war or missing in action and whose goal was "to achieve better treatment for Americans held captive and to learn the status of those missing in acion," [64] is dismissed as being one of the "groups that also proclaim their humanitarian purposes, despite their commitment to Mr. Nixon's war policies." [65] While there is merit to the conclusion that the "National League" did not qualify as an "impartial humanitarian organization" within the meaning of Article 9 of the 1949 Convention, this is not because of its failure to oppose U.S. participation in the Vietnamese conflict, but because, as in the case of the Committee of Liaison, there is no basis for concluding that it was the type of organization envisaged by the draftsmen of the 1949 Convention.

The failure of the U.S. Government to oppose Dellinger's application for leave to travel with the escort group when he was free on bail pending an appeal is construed as evidence of an implied consent by the United States to the activities of the Committee of Liaison. [66] The fact that the U.S. Government did not "interfere with its activities," [67] or "make an objection" to the Committee, [68] and that "the North Vietnamese initiative was not repudiated," [69] are also cited as evidence that the United States agreed to and concurred in the activities of the Committee of Liaison and that "it was a consensual process." [70] In other words, it is contended that the failure of the U.S. Government to interfere with and to prevent the repatriation in 1972, just as it had taken no action to interfere with or prevent the earlier repatriations, constituted a legal acceptance of the

[60] *Supra* note 12.

[61] PICTET, COMMENTARY, 539.

[62] If one of these men had resigned from the military service and had then gone on a speaking tour in support of U.S. participation in the hostilities in Vietnam, he clearly would not have violated Article 117 of the 1949 Convention; but he would have violated the broader prohibition of the fourth "guideline."

[63] Falk, 473–74.

[64] 1971 *Hearings* 25.

[65] Falk, 474 and n. 13. (In the cited note, the activities of the "National League of Families" are equated to the activities of H. Ross Perot.)

[66] *Ibid.*, 474.

[67] *Ibid.*

[68] *Ibid.*, 475.

[69] *Ibid.*, 477.

[70] *Ibid.*

Committee of Liaison as an "impartial humanitarian organization." [71]   That contention does not even appear to warrant discussion.

The argument advanced with respect to the proper interpretation of Articles 9 and 10 of the 1949 Convention is also without validity. Despite the fact that Article 9 is so specific in requiring the consent of both Parties to an armed conflict before the ICRC or an impartial humanitarian organization may undertake activities for the protection or relief of prisoners of war,[72] the argument is made that the language of both Articles 9 and 10 is "ambiguous with regard to whether the belligerent [belligerents?] must agree to the designation of a humanitarian organization"; [73] and the conclusion is reached that it is "most reasonable" to interpret Article 10(2) "as giving the Detaining Power, North Vietnam, the capacity to deal with an organization like the Committee of Liaison." [74]

The DRV is at least a de facto state and its "capacity to deal" with the Committee of Liaison, or any other group, cannot be doubted; but to use this circumstance to establish that the Committee of Liaison is, therefore, an "impartial humanitarian organization" which may be unilaterally designated by the DRV as a substitute for the Protecting Power is quite another matter.   The attempt to attain this result is, in effect, based upon the following reasoning: Article 10(2) of the 1949 Convention provides that if there is no Protecting Power and if no organization offering all guarantees of impartiality and efficacy to perform the duties of the Protecting Power has been designated to perform those duties under Article 10(1), "the Detaining Power shall request a neutral State, or such an organization, to undertake the functions" of the Protecting Power.   In acceding to the 1949 Convention, the DRV made a reservation to Article 10 stating that it would not "recognize as legal" such a request by the Detaining Power "unless the request has been approved by the State upon which the prisoners of war depend." [75]   A substantially similar reservation to Article 10 had been made by the USSR and the Soviet bloc countries upon signing the Convention in 1949 and in their subsequent ratifications.[76]   The reason given by the USSR for the reservation was the belief that "the Government of the country to which the protected persons belong [cannot be prevented] from taking part in the choice of the substitute for the Protecting Power." [77]   In recommending that the Senate give its advice and consent to the ratification of the 1949 Convention by the United States, the Department of State advised the Senate of its opposition to the USSR and similar reservations.[78]   This opposition, according to Falk,

[71] *Ibid.*
[73] Falk, 474.
[75] 274 UNTS 339.

[72] *See* text *supra* at pp. 700–01.
[74] *Ibid.*

[76] *See* note 39 *supra.* The USSR reservation provides for "the consent of the Government of the country of which the prisoners of war are nationals."   191 UNTS 367. Either wording refers, of course, to the Power of Origin.

[77] FINAL RECORD, Vol. IIB, at 347.

[78] *Geneva Conventions for the Protection of War Victims, Hearing before the Senate Comm. on Foreign Relations,* 84th Cong., 1st Sess., on Executives D, E, F, and G, 82d Cong., 1st Sess., at 62 (1955).

seems to confirm the United States view that the Detaining Power had the capacity, even the duty, to designate an impartial humanitarian organization and that such designation would be determinative at least in the absence of objection from the country whose men are detained that the organization is not "impartial" or not "humanitarian."[79]

Thus, based upon the DRV reservation to Article 10 of the 1949 Convention and the earlier stated objection of the Department of State to the DRV-type reservation to that article, the conclusion is reached that a Detaining Power may unilaterally designate an "impartial humanitarian organization" to perform functions with respect to prisoners of war.

In the first place, it must be borne in mind that Article 10 deals, not with the activities of the "impartial humanitarian organization" referred to in Article 9, but with the activities of Protecting Powers and of "substitutes" for Protecting Powers. It seems incredible that the contention would be made that the Committee of Liaison, a small group of completely inexperienced individuals, whose only common thread was opposition to U.S. participation in the hostilities in Vietnam, could possibly qualify as an organization "offering guarantees of impartiality and efficacy to perform the duties of the Protecting Power,"—which are the requirements set forth in Article 10(1) for an organization that may be designated under Article 10(2).

In the second place, the DRV, like the USSR and the Soviet bloc countries at the 1949 Diplomatic Conference, made its reservation to Article 10 because it considered that the article improperly reduced the right of the Power of Origin to participate in the selection of a substitute for the Protecting Power. Inasmuch as the DRV became a Party to the 1949 Convention only on the condition that no neutral state or humanitarian organization could be designated by a Detaining Power to act as a substitute for the Protecting Power without the consent of the Power of Origin, it is certainly inverse reasoning to claim that this established the right of the DRV, acting as a Detaining Power, unilaterally so to designate the Committee of Liaison,[80] without the consent of the United States, the Power of Origin.

In the third place, instead of referring to the suggestion made in a letter written by Secretary Dulles to the Senate Foreign Relations Committee concerning the attitude which the United States should take with respect to the Soviet bloc reservations,[81] it would have been more appropriate to refer to the position actually and officially taken by the United States in connection with ratification of the 1949 Convention:

> Rejecting the reservations which States have made with respect to the Geneva Convention relative to the treatment of prisoners of war, the United States accepts treaty relations with all parties to that Convention, except as to the changes proposed by such reservations.[82]

In other words, while the United States has treaty relations with any state

---

[79] Falk, 475.
[81] Ibid., n. 17.
[80] Ibid.
[82] 6 UST 3316, 3514; 213 UNTS 383.

which has ratified or acceded to the 1949 Convention with a reservation to Article 10, those treaty relations are subject to the changes made by the reservation, which means that *neither the United States nor the reserving state*, when acting as a Detaining Power, may designate a neutral Power or a humanitarian organization as a substitute for the Protecting Power without the approval of the Power of Origin.[83]

One basic question remains. Why did they do it? Why did the North Vietnamese unilaterally release these randomly-selected, token-size groups of prisoners of war for repatriation? Were the North Vietnamese more humanitarian-minded than the belligerents of World War I? Of World War II? Of Korea? Were they inspired to do what they did because of empathy for the men released and repatriated? All of these questions carry their own negative responses.[84]

The Vietnam War was unlike past conflicts. Previous wars had not seen the establishment and proliferation of anti-war groups which functioned openly, seeking publicity that was not always easy for them to obtain.[85] The release of token numbers of prisoners of war to these groups for repatriation at rather lengthy intervals served, on each occasion, as a major propaganda device, one which for a number of days gave the North Vietnamese and the particular anti-war group large-scale newspaper, television, and radio coverage.[86] Had the releases been purely humanitarian in nature, the prisoners of war selected for release would have been those who were the most seriously wounded or sick, or those who had been the longest in prisoner-of-war status; but neither of these valid criteria was used in the selection process.[87]

[83] PILLOUD, RESERVATIONS TO THE 1949 GENEVA CONVENTIONS 5 (1958).

[84] A number of questions, basically along this same line, appear in the Falk article, at 477 and 478. They are not answered except by the statement that "North Vietnamese motivations are of no account." *Ibid.*, 478.

[85] When the Viet Cong made the first prisoner-of-war release, in Nov. 1967, Nguyen Van Hieu, the VC representative in Phnom Penh, Cambodia, where it took place, was quoted as follows:

Mr. Hieu said that the soldiers were being released in cooperation with American opponents of the United States involvement in the Vietnam war in the expectation that they would be able to contribute usefully to the United States peace movement.

N.Y. Times, Nov. 13, 1967, at 2, c. 6. This revealing statement was not repeated on the occasion of the subsequent releases.

[86] Some evidence of this can found in the fact that with each release of prisoners of war there would be a great fanfare when the announcement of the proposed release was made, or when the ecort group set off for Hanoi, or when it arrived in Hanoi—and then there would be an unexplained delay of a number of days while the publicity, of course, continued. For example, in the second 1968 release the delay was "pretty close to three weeks" (1971 *Hearings* 222) and in the 1972 release of which Falk gives us a blow-by-blow description the unexplained delay was from Sept. 17 to 24 (Falk, 466). While it is true that a Gallup poll conducted in Feb. 1970 revealed that a majority of Americans did not believe the glowing statements made by the members of the escort groups upon their return to the United States, a surprising number of Americans apparently did believe them—and even if the number had been much smaller, the propaganda value to the DRV far outweighed the cost, which was negligible.

[87] Actually, it is probable that no criteria were used. *See* note 50 *supra*. In the

The significance for the future of what transpired in the concluding months of American participation in the war in Vietnam is not great. In an all-out armed conflict, one which is a "war" both under international law and in an American constitutional sense, private repatriations by civilians will probably not be practical, because the members of the anti-war group in any belligerent country participating in such an event would undoubtedly find themselves spending at least the balance of the period of hostilities in close confinement after having been tried and convicted of treason or of communicating with the enemy. Second, as a practical matter, with the limitations which would exist on wartime travel, particularly across international borders, it would probably be all but impossible for an "escort group" to accomplish its function. Third, and most important, with the close censorship of the news media which is maintained during wartime, there would be little or no propaganda value in releasing token-sized groups of prisoners of war for repatriation as the Power of Origin could completely control the amount of publicity, if any, which the event would be allowed within its territory, the place where the impact of the propaganda is actually desired. Without the publicity which releases and repatriations are designed to generate, the motive for such action by a belligerent withers on the vine.

In conclusion, while there are both legal and humanitarian bases for the release and repatriation, or internment in neutral countries, during the course of hostilities of longtime, able-bodied prisoners of war, this highly laudable purpose can best be accomplished through resort to the established and recognized facilities of the Protecting Power and the International Committee of the Red Cross, rather than through the use of partisan, *ad hoc* groups which have extremely limited public acceptance and recognition.

---

July–Aug. 1968 release the three pilots released had been prisoners of war for only four to seven months. Note 47 *supra.* Concerning the selection of these three individuals, one witness before the House Subcommittee testified:

> When Thompson, Low and Carpenter were brought together at the time of their release, they tried to figure out why they had been selected. They determined, as many others have since determined, that the obvious conclusion was that none of them had been held very long, all were in apparent good health, they were not debilitated or injured, nor had they been subjected to extremes of brutality. And, too, each had been penned up separately, in a solitary cell, barred from learning all they might otherwise have learned about the general condition of the prison camps or the general condition or treatment of other prisoners.

> As Major Thompson says, "We were safe bets to release. People would see us and say, 'Maybe they do take good care of their prisoners'."

1971 *Hearings* 387.

# Correspondence

## RICHARD A. FALK

To the Editor-in-Chief:

As I find Professor Levie's careful reply [1] to my article on repatriation of prisoners of war during hostilities [2] both predictable and unconvincing, it seems almost purposeless to continue the exchange. He would presumably find any further effort on my part equally predictable and unconvincing. We speak past one another, not because one of us is a "good" international lawyer and the other is not (although I allow him this interpretation if he wishes it), but because we approach this subject matter from decisively different political perspectives and from adverse jurisprudential traditions. These differences may be worth elucidating, and I shall try to do so briefly. It may be appropriate to point out that I write both as the author of the article Professor Levie attacked and as a member of the civilian escort group that carried out the prisoner repatriation in September 1972.

Much of Professor Levie's argument stems from his view that antiwar American citizens were incapable of constituting an "impartial humanitarian organization" within the meaning of the Geneva Convention relative to the Treatment of Prisoners of War. My view is that the Committee of Liaison was the *only* kind of organization that could have served as an effective instrument for POW repatriation given the peculiar circumstances of the Vietnam war. Furthermore, as discussed in my original article, the Committee possessed the experience, the resources, and the personnel to discharge this role in a responsible fashion. And, finally, I would argue that the actual repatriation was carried out in a manner that justifies this claim of competence. To deny the Committee, or its analogue in the future, status is either to render repatriation of this type impossible or to place it outside any boundaries of reciprocal responsibility in a situation where various sets of interests are at stake.

What is Professor Levie's evidence for his conclusion that the Committee "was more strongly motivated by political than by humanitarian considerations?" And by what criteria of "humanitarian?" Many of those Americans who were against America's involvement in the Vietnam war regarded themselves as primarily motivated by humanitarian considerations, including, incidentally, the most active participants in the Committee of Liaison. My main point here is that the Geneva Convention is vague and ambiguous on how to qualify an "impartial humanitarian organization" and that this flexibility is helpful, if our primary concern is to mitigate the hardships of war for individuals unfortunate enough to become prisoners of war.

[1] 67 AJIL 693 (1973).        [2] *Id.*, 465.

Professor Levie also writes that the Committee of Liaison "displayed either remarkable presumption, remarkable ignorance, or remarkable naiveté" by setting forth a series of guidelines to control the repatriation process in a cable to the President of the United States sent prior to the departure of the escort group from Hanoi. Professor Levie's attitude obviously stems from his deference to the government and confidence in its willingness to treat a situation of this kind in a sensitive and humane fashion. We did not regard deference as appropriate under the circumstances, nor did we have Professor Levie's confidence in the way in which the government would handle the situation. Our transmission of these guidelines to the President was designed to reduce uncertainty on both sides and to assure that crass politics would not overwhelm the humanitarian objective of the repatriation. The escort group, as well as the released prisoners and their accompanying relatives, shared the conviction that the prospect of additional prisoner releases were partly dependent on noninterference with the escort procedure by the U.S. Government until the released pilots reached U.S. territory. While we were in Hanoi there was every indication that the U.S. Government intended to make a major effort to remove the released men from our civilian escort at the first point of contact, then presumed to be Vientiane, Laos. We sought to convey our judgment as to the adverse consequences of such removal to the most responsible official in the U.S. Government. We were also convinced, on the basis of knowledge about prior repatriations, that the debriefing and medical detention process under military auspices could be painful and unfair, especially if the repatriated prisoner happened to have antiwar sentiments. The ordeal of George Smith in American military hospitals was probably worse than anything he endured while an NLF POW.[8] The Committee of Liaison had first hand information about a series of other confirming horror stories. In any event, the main point here is that the Committee felt it was reasonable in an atmosphere of tension and confusion to seek an understanding with the U.S. Government on guidelines that could make the repatriation process as humane as possible. We did not want the men under our escort to be abused, nor did we want their renewed availability to the U.S. Government to be used in furtherance of the Indochina war effort, nor did we want future releases of other POW's in North Vietnam to be jeopardized.

Our arrival in the United States at Kennedy Airport suggested that our anxieties were not entirely misplaced. I witnessed the abuse of Lt. Gartley and his mother by public officials who crassly denied the family a few days of privacy which they had previously requested for compelling personal reasons. Whether for reasons of bureaucratic inertia or because of political anxiety, the government insisted at the airport on asserting immediate military jurisdiction. It was an insensitive display of government power, hardly supportive of Professor Levie's general confidence in the

[8] *See* former Marine Sgt. Donald Duncan's epilogue to Smith's book POW: TWO YEARS WITH THE VIETCONG (1971).

government's commitment to a humanitarian (and nonpolitical) approach to the POW issue.

But more important than the immediate context is the lawmaking issue of principle involved. I believe that American citizens, acting as civilian escort on behalf of the Committee of Liaison on the basis of a prior arrangement with the Government of North Vietnam, had a right and obligation to fill the law vacuum within which they were operating. By sending the guidelines cable, the Committee was making a claim as to the proper norms that should govern their role in this sensitive transnational setting. There was no applicable legal framework in the Geneva rules or elsewhere in international law to guide the participants in this type of nongovernmental or private repatriation. As such, the action taken by the Committee of Liaison established, in my view, a precedent having international law relevance. This precedent could be invoked by participants in subsequent analogous circumstances to demonstrate the reasonableness of their behavior and claims in relation to receiving released prisoners for repatriation to their country of origin, or possibly to some other designated place. There is no scientific or normative reason to entrust governments with an exclusive lawmaking role in war/peace contexts, especially in a setting where individuals are principal victims and beneficiaries.

Professor Levie concludes his article by alleging that "the significance for the future of what transpired in the concluding months of American participation in the war in Vietnam is not great." Perhaps. However, the potential role of "private repatriations" seems considerable in a world beset by divided polities, inconclusive wars, and nongovernmental or private armies. One could imagine private repatriations in relation to the India-Pakistan war or the various categories of war prisoners held in the Middle East. A more explicit legal framework for private repatriations might make the process more regular and the option more plausible.

Such extensions of the practice of private repatriation to new contexts would admittedly be an unexpected sequel to the North Vietnamese policy of selective repatriation. We claim only that our experience with one instance of repatriation provides a useful starting point for an effort to place the private repatriation process within a legal framework. Furthermore, the mixed dealings of governments and nongovernmental groups in such a repatriation procedure is an unusual, but interesting, illustration of a new mode of lawmaking in international affairs that is worthy of attention by students of international law.

RICHARD A. FALK

# III. WAR CRIMES AND INDIVIDUAL RESPONSIBILITY

# VIETNAM AND THE NUREMBERG PRINCIPLES: A COLLOQUY ON WAR CRIMES

PRESENTED AT RUTGERS LAW SCHOOL
Newark, New Jersey
November 13, 1971

Sponsored By:

THE RUTGERS SOCIETY OF INTERNATIONAL LAW

Participants:

TOM J. FARER, Professor of Law
Rutgers Law School, Camden, New Jersey

ROBERT G. GARD, JR., Brigadier General, GS
United States Army

TELFORD TAYLOR, Professor of Law
Columbia Law School, New York, New York

edited by

Judith R. Hall

Marc R. Staenberg

and

Rutgers · Camden Law Journal Staff

## REMARKS OF TELFORD TAYLOR

The Chairman has been kind enough to mention the book[1] I've written which has the same subject as this afternoon's proceedings. That book was written a year ago; a good deal has happened in the intervening year, and I would like to concentrate on those happenings with special regard to the Calley and Medina trials and the Henderson trial now in progress. First, however, I think it would be helpful to the discussion and to my fellow panelists if I fill in some background material.

As those of you who have been working in this field are aware, there are two rather different dimensions to the problem. One has to do with the aggressive war concept which was first the subject of adjudication at Nuremberg: that is, whether it can be regarded as a crime in international law to wage an aggressive war. That has, of course, been the source of a great deal of controversy in a good many settings these last few years, as illustrated by the great division of public opinion over the Vietnam War. It has arisen in connection with the refusal to serve in the armed forces, with the refusal to be sent to Vietnam, with the refusal to pay income taxes, and in other contexts. On this aggressive war issue my opinion is that while it is a very important question, and while I do believe there is room for argument that our total involvement in Vietnam has been in violation of the aggressive war principle, I see no court or jurisdiction available to adjudicate the matter. Basically, I regard American involvement in Vietnam as having been the result of the political process. No matter how wrong one may think it to have been, it has come about through executive and congressional action reflecting at the time a substantial body of opinion. Our escape from what I regard as the very difficult and bad situation that we have gotten into should be, I believe, along political rather than judicial lines.

The other dimension of the problem concerns the conduct of the military. I would like at the outset to state that it is my belief that, whether one is a hawk or a dove, there *is* a value in trying to establish and observe some limitations on the way war is waged. I am aware, from having spoken in this general area to other university audiences, that this view is not universally shared, and the echo often comes back to me that war is intrinsically so bad that the idea of trying to limit it in any way is futile and self-contradictory. Maybe some of you feel

---

1. TELFORD TAYLOR, NUREMBERG AND VIETNAM: AN AMERICAN TRAGEDY (1970).

that way. It seems to me, however, that, regardless of one's attitude about war as a whole, the rules of war have both a practical and a humanitarian basis that is valuable. Despite all their shortcomings we are much better off with them than we would be without them, and I approve of efforts to articulate them and enforce them.

It is from that standpoint that I would now like to begin my more particular discussion. As you know, the laws of war are embodied in the Hague and Geneva Conventions, which were drafted over the period between the late 1890's and 1949, and are reflected in other treaties and other forms as well.[2] Their general contents have been embodied in the *Army Field Manual*[3] and the *Air Force Manual* and are substantially part of our military law. These are rules by which our armed forces are supposed to abide, inasmuch as we are Party to the 1949 Geneva Conventions which we ratified in 1956, thereby making them part of the supreme law of the land.[4] Clearly, we are required to enforce them. The Prisoner of War and Civilian Population Conventions of 1949 explicitly require every signatory to pass whatever legisla-

---

2. *See, e.g.,* Convention Relative to the Opening of Hostilities, *signed at The Hague* October 18, 1907, [1909] 36 Stat. 2259, T.S. No. 538, 1 BEVANS 619; Convention Respecting the Law and Customs of War on Land, with Annex of Regulations, *signed at The Hague* October 18, 1907, [1909] 36 Stat. 2277, T.S. No. 539, 1 BEVANS 631 [hereinafter cited as Hague—Laws and Customs of War on Land]; Convention Respecting the Rights and Duties of Neutral Powers and Persons in Case of War on Land, *signed at The Hague* October 18, 1907, [1909] 36 Stat. 2310, T.S. No. 540, 1 BEVANS 654; Convention Concerning Bombardment by Naval Forces in Time of War, *signed at The Hague* October 18, 1907, [1909] 36 Stat. 2351, T.S. No. 542, 1 BEVANS 681; Convention for the Adaptation to Maritime Warfare of the Principles of the Geneva Convention of July 6, 1907, *signed at The Hague* October 19, 1907, [1909] 36 Stat. 2371, T.S. No. 543, 1 BEVANS 711; Convention Relating to Prisoners of War, *signed at Geneva* July 27, 1929, [1932] 47 Stat. 2021, T.S. No. 846, 118 L.N.T.S. 343; Convention for the Amelioration of the Condition of the Wounded and the Sick of Armies in the Field, *signed at Geneva* July 27, 1929, [1932] 47 Stat. 2074, T.S. No. 847, 118 L.N.T.S. 303; Convention for the Amelioration of the Condition of the Wounded and Sick in Armed Forces in the Field, *dated at Geneva* August 12, 1949, [1955] 6 U.S.T. 3114, T.I.A.S. No. 3362, 75 U.N.T.S. 31 [hereinafter cited as Geneva-Wounded and Sick]; Convention for the Amelioration of the Condition of the Wounded, Sick and Shipwrecked Members of Armed Forces at Sea, *dated at Geneva* August 12, 1949, [1955] 6 U.S.T. 3217, T.I.A.S. No. 3363, 75 U.N.T.S. 85 [hereinafter cited as Geneva-Wounded and Sick (Sea)]; Convention Relative to the Treatment of Prisoners of War, *dated at Geneva* August 12, 1949, [1955] 6 U.S.T. 3316, T.I.A.S. No. 3364, 75 U.N.T.S. 135 [hereinafter cited as Geneva—Prisoners of War]; Convention Relative to the Protection of Civilian Persons in Time of War, *dated at Geneva* August 12, 1949, [1955] 6 U.S.T. 3516, T.I.A.S. No. 3365, 75 U.N.T.S. 287 [hereinafter cited as Geneva—Civilians].

3. U.S. DEPARTMENT OF THE ARMY, THE LAW OF LAND WARFARE (FIELD MANUAL No. 27-10) (1956) [hereinafter cited as ARMY FIELD MANUAL].

4. By virtue of U.S. CONST. art. VI, cl. 2, the provisions of ratified treaties become part of the supreme law of the United States.

tion and to take whatever steps are necessary for the enforcement of the rules of war, whether against their own forces, as happened in the Calley trial, or against enemy soldiers or others who may come into their hands by capture or otherwise.[5]  The obligation to provide the machinery, by court martial or by some other means, to apply these rules and enforce them against those accused of violations is an explicit treaty obligation which we have assumed.

The central thrust of my remarks will be to examine the extent to which we have fulfilled that obligation in connection with our own operations in Vietnam.  I regard this problem as very much deeper than simply a matter of the treaty, whether we have complied with it or not.  The United States was, more than any other country, responsible for the Nuremberg trials, for the application of these principles at Nuremberg, where heavy sentences, including a number of death penalties, were imposed on enemy civilians and military personnel for violations.  We sponsored the United Nations resolution[6] which approved the Nuremberg principles, and, under those circumstances, it seems to me we have both a moral and intellectual obligation to examine our own conduct in the light of the principles that were enunciated there.

I think in making any assessment of our conduct of operations in Vietnam, we have to begin by observing that there are two principal categories of acts which have been the focus of accusations of unlawful conduct by American forces in Vietnam.  The first category includes those sporadic departures from proper behavior not resulting from directives and regulations issued by the high command in Vietnam. This category is most sensationally and most tragically exemplified by the My Lai, or Son My, killings.  As I think General Gard may point out in more detail, it is not true that My Lai has been the only such episode that the army has recognized as involving transgressions of the laws of war; there have been numerous others.  But My Lai was in its scope very much larger than the others and, of course, attracted far more public attention and touched the public conscience very deeply.

Other breaches that would fall in the same category as the My Lai, or Son My, killings include the mistreatment upon some occasions of prisoners of war in the hands of our own troops.  For example, there was the *Lieutenant Duffy* case, which preceded My Lai. Lieutenant Duffy was tried for ordering the murder of a North Vietnam-

---

5.  Geneva—Wounded and Sick, art. 49; Geneva—Wounded and Sick (Sea), art. 50; Geneva—Prisoners of War, art. 129; Geneva—Civilians, art. 146.
6.  G.A. Res. 95, 1st Sess., at 188, U.N. Doc. A/64/Add. 1 (1946).

ese prisoner who'd been held overnight and was in safekeeping. He was simply killed in the morning—a direct violation of the laws of war[7] and a clear violation of the Army's governing directives and regulations.[8] According to the defendant's testimony, this killing resulted from a failure of discipline and leadership and from the belief in the importance of "body count" as it was put. "Body count," which was considered similar to notches on a gun, could be increased by killing prisoners instead of keeping them. I can only characterize such conduct as totally inexcusable, unlawful, and murderous.

As for the My Lai affair, I have never heard any substantial evidence or any substantial accusation that what happened there was in accordance with orders given at a high military level. It may or may not be true that Captain Medina ordered these things to happen. Many people testify that he did. He denied it, and the jury that tried him found in accordance with his testimony. The point is, however, that I know of nothing which suggests that My Lai and other comparable episodes are the consequence of orders issued at high levels directing that that sort of thing should happen. Indeed, such things are quite contrary to the Rules of Engagement and other regulations laid down by our high command in Vietnam for the conduct of operations there. Therefore, in examining responsibility for a tragedy like My Lai, I think we can well start out with the assumption that there must have been failures of training, indoctrination, discipline, and leadership, *i.e.* insufficient training and indoctrination of troops as to what was expected of them in Vietnam and what they should have expected to encounter, insufficient discipline in the enforcement of restrictions and observance of attitudes and policies, deficiencies in leadership and in imposing sanctions, and deficiencies in carrying through and in seeing that limitations were observed and that the attitude of the troops toward the civilian population remained a decent, humane, and courteous one in accordance with the whole purpose of our being in Vietnam. In the case of such failures, the responsibility for occurrences like My Lai rests not only on those who directly participated, but also on those who were responsible for the failures which, I think, essentially explain why aberrations have occurred.

The My Lai and Lieutenant Duffy incidents are examples of the first of the two main categories of improper military conduct that we are trying to assess here. The other category is quite different. It involves operational practices and tactics which *are* in accordance with

7. *See* Geneva—Prisoners of War, art. 13.
8. ARMY FIELD MANUAL, ¶ 85 at 35; ¶ 89 at 36.

directives laid down from the highest level and which are of dubious legality under the Hague and Geneva Conventions.  I should say by way of preface that all of these high command policies are in a sense debatable, either in fact or law, as to whether or not they have been unlawful.  But let me, without trying to take too fixed a position, describe the several areas in which the action of high level commanders is at least of questionable legality.  The first is in connection with the delivery of prisoners to the South Vietnamese.

The Hague and Geneva Conventions clearly state that one is not supposed to turn prisoners over to another country without reasonable basis for believing that they will be treated in accordance with the laws of war by the country to which one is delivering them.[9]  It seems to me that there has been an abundance of evidence, some of it from sources reliable enough to give one grave disquiet, that a great many prisoners have been turned over to the South Vietnamese with more than enough grounds for suspicion that they would not be treated in accordance with the Hague and Geneva rules once they were in South Vietnamese hands; that, on the contrary, they would be very badly mistreated in complete contravention of these rules.[10]

Another area which is debatable, although more in law than in fact, involves the extensive removal of South Vietnamese civilians from their homes, in numbers running well-nigh into the millions.  There is a great deal of controversy about this.  Much of the evacuation was done with the consent of the South Vietnamese Government.  The applicability of specific provisions of the Geneva Convention is questionable,[11] but the human consequences of this have been more than disquieting and have resulted in millions of people living in terrible circumstances.

Things that I myself regard as somewhat less important but still very much worth discussing include the use of weapons of dubious legality, such as tear gas.  Perhaps on the face of it this does not sound like the most serious of all problems.  However, the use of tear gas is probably unlawful under the Conventions relating to the use of gas, although that is open to some argument, too.[12]  Next, there is the problem of crop destruction.  The Geneva Conventions are quite clear that

---

9. Geneva—Prisoners of War, art. 12.

10. *See* IN THE NAME OF AMERICA 55-90 (S. Melman ed. 1968) [hereinafter cited as IN THE NAME OF AMERICA].

11. *See* Geneva—Civilians, art. 49.

12. *See Hearings on the Geneva Protocol of 1925 Before the Comm. on Foreign Relations,* 91st Cong., 2d Sess. (1971) (published 1972) for a compilation of these arguments.

crop destruction is justifiable when the crops are going to be consumed by enemy troops.   On the other hand, the Conventions are equally clear that destruction of crops to be used by the civilian population is unlawful.[13]   Here there is relatively little debate about the law and much more debate about the facts.   Have civilian food supplies been destroyed or haven't they?   I have an article by a former official of the Disarmament Commission, who was not, I think, predisposed to find unlawful behavior on our part, and he came to the conclusion that we had destroyed crops extensively in areas where they would have been consumed by the civilian population, thereby causing great distress. I cannot vouch for the facts one way or the other, but here again is one of those many circumstances where there is reliable information that should give one cause to inquire further.

There is yet a third category of questionable acts which partakes of both the first and second categories: conduct which is not in accordance with the directives laid down from above, but which nonetheless seems, from time to time, to take place with the approval or toleration of people at a high level.   I refer to the seemingly punitive use of air bombardment and artillery firepower against civilians who have harbored the Viet Cong or who are suspected of having harbored the Viet Cong, and the use of fire power and bombardment against areas from which sniper fire may have come—where the response has been out of all proportion to the hazard raised.   I say that this category partakes of both characteristics because if one examines our rules of engagement, one finds that they are virtually impeccable.   One rule—one of General Westmoreland's own rules—directs the troops to "use your firepower with care and discrimination, particularly in populated areas."[14]   The rules are explicit that civilians should not be regarded as hostile or subjected to punishment merely because they have harbored the Viet Cong, because, "that may well depend to a large extent upon factors and forces beyond [the civilian's] control."[15]   Viet Cong and North Vietnamese have used terror extensively to force the civilian population to harbor the Viet Cong, and thus it seems to me that the directive is a sensible and humane acknowledgment that such behavior should not necessarily give rise to retributive action.

But contrast this instruction in the Rules of Engagement with the language of a document that Jonathan Schell discovered.   It was a leaf-

---

13. *See* Geneva—Civilians, art. 55.

14. Westmoreland, General William C. (COMUSMACV), *Guidance for Commanders in Vietnam.*

15. *Id.*

let issued by the United States Marine Corps, entitled "Ultimatum to the Vietnamese People," informing them that, "The U.S. Marine Corps will not hesitate to destroy immediately any village or hamlet harboring the Viet Cong." Another Marine leaflet informed the inhabitants that their village was bombed "because you harbored the Viet Cong and will be bombed again if you harbor the Viet Cong in any way." I cannot testify from personal knowledge to the authenticity of these documents, but so far as I know they have gone unchallenged and are one of many indications which I think should long ago have been subjected to some kind of official inquiry or scrutiny.

Also indicative of the need for inquiry are the figures on the number of civilians killed, wounded, and homeless. Here, we have to rely largely on the reports of Senator Edward Kennedy's Refugee Committee,[16] because very little other official information has been forthcoming. The number of killed, wounded, and homeless reported by Kennedy's Committee is so large that the conclusion seems inescapable that, wherever the responsibility lies, firepower has been used in Vietnam in a manner that has caused very wide destruction and loss of life, disproportionate to the ends attainable, in a degree indefensible under the Geneva Conventions.

That is a brief rehearsal of the areas which seem to me to warrant scrutiny and, in judicial terms, commissions of inquiry. Let us consider what the official response to these acts has been. Focusing on the first category, we can examine the army's handling of the My Lai episode. The evidence brought out at the proceedings which were held suggests that the My Lai killings were chiefly the work of a platoon of infantrymen under Lieutenant Calley, who was in turn subordinate to Captain Medina, the company commander. There were other platoons involved in the same operation; there has been very little public disclosure of how the other two platoons behaved. I will have another word to say about that later. In any event, two or three of the enlisted men were put on trial for their participation in the massacre. They were acquitted, and, after the acquittal, the charges were dropped against all the others. Under a decision of the Supreme Court a number of years ago, an overseas serviceman who has left the service can no longer be tried by court-martial for something that he did while he was in service abroad.[17] And it is by no means clear that any ci-

---

16. STAFF OF SENATE COMM. ON THE JUDICIARY, REPORT ON CIVILIAN CASUALTY AND REFUGEE PROBLEMS IN SOUTH VIETNAM, 90th Cong., 2d Sess. (Comm. Print 1968).

17. United States *ex rel.* Toth v. Quarles, 350 U.S. 11 (1955).

vilian court has jurisdiction to try him either. Professor Bishop, at the Yale Law School, thinks there may be ways around this without passing new legislation. This is by no means certain, however, and the fact is that despite the time lapse since that decision by the Supreme Court, no legislative action has been taken to fill the gap. Thus, once the enlisted men have left the service, there is no way to try them at all. At the first of the two trials that were held, Private Meadlo, who had confessed on television with great publicity to his participation in the killings, appeared as a prosecution witness. And so the military juries were confronted with this spectacle of Private Meadlo, who was immune from prosecution, testifying against soldiers who were unlucky enough to be still in uniform and therefore susceptible to trial. I submit that this kind of iniquitous comparison was bound to cause the jury to feel that this was so grossly unfair that it became hard for them to convict the enlisted men at all.[18] Thus the failure to fill in a jurisdictional gap seems to me responsible for a large part of the failure to enforce the rules of law against the enlisted men involved in this tragedy.

I thought that an acquittal of Lieutenant Calley would have been monstrous and very harmful to the national interest. I also thought that the sentence imposed upon him was unduly severe; it was, of course, reduced from life to twenty years and my guess is that it will be further reduced before he sees the inside of a jail, if he ever does. However that may be, what happened to him must be weighed side by side with the outcome of the Medina trial. On this, I have some fairly sharp observations. Captain Medina, assuming that his testimony is true and that he himself did not order what happened at My Lai, was not very far away. He was within a few yards of what was going on. He had available constant radio communication with his platoon commanders. He denied at his trial that he actually knew that the killings were taking place until after they were finished and he was informed by Lieutenant Calley. The military judge advocate charged the jury that they could not find Captain Medina guilty unless they were satisfied beyond a reasonable doubt that he had actual knowledge of these killings. The consequence of this was that since he could not be found guilty unless he had actual knowledge, it also had to be established that the killings took place after the point in time when that knowledge came to him. Well, now, nobody was putting a stop watch on what was going on there, and to require the jury to find that certain killings, particular killings, took place after some hypothetical point when Me-

---

18. This reluctance was intensified, in my estimation, by the fact that it was quite plain that Lt. Calley was the source of the conduct. (Note by Professor Taylor).

dina's mind finally clicked, "Killings are going on," imposed, I think, an impossible task upon the jury and made an acquittal inevitable.

Unfortunately, the instructions were wholly wrong.[19]   The military manual tells us that command responsibility exists if the commader knew or *should have known* that his troops were engaged in unlawful conduct.[20]   The circumstances here are such that it is very difficult to come to the conclusion that he shouldn't have known.   But, in any event, the test given to the jury was completely wrong.   I'm not prepared to say that the charge itself was a violation of our obligation to enforce the laws of war, but certainly if that kind of misinterpretation of the *Uniform Code of Military Justice* persists, it will make it very difficult to hold officers of any rank responsible, unless we have things in writing the way the Germans used to do.   In practical effect if not in theory, this would appear to have been a default under our treaty obligations.

The other aspect of My Lai was the so-called cover-up.   Captain Medina fully confessed to this and admitted that he had not reported but had concealed what had taken place there.   That in itself is an offense against the laws of war[21] but one for which he was not charged. The Peers Commission recommended charges on this score against fourteen officers; in thirteen cases the charges were dismissed without ever being tried.   One trial, of Colonel Henderson, is still under way. And the morning paper a couple of days ago informed us that Captain Medina, who has now been discharged and is in the clear and who was never accused of covering up the massacre, will appear as a defense witness for Colonel Henderson.   No doubt he will testify that he, Captain Medina, covered it up so that Colonel Henderson never knew about it. As you can see, the pyramiding process here is quite fruitful.

As to the liability of those in authority for questionable practices which are the consequence of higher level directives, themselves of

---

19.  The instructions from the military judge to the members of the court trying Captain Medina appear in II THE LAW OF WAR—A DOCUMENTARY HISTORY 1729 (L. Friedman ed. 1972).  The portion of the charge referred to appears at 1732.

20.  ARMY FIELD MANUAL, ¶ 501 at 178.

21.  In the Geneva Conventions, "reporting" is treated as follows: "Each High Contracting Party shall be under the obligation to search for persons alleged to have committed, or to have ordered to be committed, such grave breaches, and shall bring such persons . . . before its own courts."   Geneva—Wounded and Sick, art. 49; Geneva—Prisoners of War, art. 129; Geneva—Civilians, art. 146.   The army has its own reporting requirement in MILITARY ASSISTANCE COMMAND FOR VIETNAM (MACV) DIRECTIVE 20-4.   Although this directive is limited to the Vietnam conflict, the army is currently preparing an AR (Army Regulation) to require investigation and reporting of violations of the laws of war under all circumstances.

dubious legality: this is an area that Professor Farer will address in some detail. And, therefore, I will simply state my own general position, which is that if the laws of war were subject to enforcement by an impartial international tribunal of general jurisdiction (that is, if Nuremberg had turned into a continuing process) available to any kind of engagement, it would seem to me that the Nuremberg principles ought to be enforced against those with high rank in our government, whether civilian or military, the way they were after World War II against the Germans. But that situation does not obtain, and usually principles must be mixed a bit with expediency in this less than perfect world. It seems to me, on the whole, that there are much greater public values to be achieved from a public confrontation. Some kind of a commission of inquiry with power to compel testimony so that we can discover the truth about our own conduct of operations in Vietnam will probably do us much more good than attempting one or two more courts-martial. I think that the informational and confrontational aspects of such an inquiry in terms of the public moral health are far more important than the results to be obtained from any further accusatory proceedings, especially since the outcome of the Medina trial has in many ways insulated those of higher rank against prosecution. Unhappily, I don't believe that even this is likely to be, politically speaking, very probable. But I think that if I were in a position of influence or authority, it would be in this direction that I would put my efforts and my influence.

## REMARKS OF TOM J. FARER

The calamitous impact of our Indochinese adventure on the people of that desperate land has left some of us in a state of disillusion limned by Ernest Hemingway's reflections on the First World War: "Abstract words such as glory, honor, courage or hallow were obscene beside the concrete names of villages, the number of roads, the names of rivers, the numbers of regiments, and the dates. Finally, only the names of places had dignity."[22]

In our war, there is one name and one place locked irretrievably into the mind, and that place is, of course, My Lai—a graveyard rescued from historical obscurity to allow the claim of war crimes into the respectable forums of our society. In a double sense, we owe this meeting today to the people of My Lai, deceased. Before My Lai, polite society was not prepared to contemplate the possibility that our engagement in Vietnam might be something more sinister than a blunder. It

---

22. E. HEMINGWAY, A FAREWELL TO ARMS 191 (1949).

was not ready, perhaps in part because too many of its leading figures were either still in Washington filling the offices to which they had
been called, presumably by virtue of birth or talent, or were uncomfortably recent emigrés.    One does not lightly refer to the president of
the World Bank or the Ford Foundation as a possible war criminal.    But
now that the issue has become unavoidable, every decent man is searching for answers to three questions.    First, to what extent have our
actions in Indochina violated the rules and principles which comprise
the laws of war?    Second, assuming that prohibited acts have occurred,
who if anyone can be held criminally responsible?—what I call the
*mens rea* problem.    Third, assuming that a *prima facie* case of criminal
responsibility can be established with respect to specific persons, will
the prospects for the avoidance of comparable behavior in the future
be enhanced by pressing for their characterization as war criminals?

Turning to the first question, in the light of my general agreement
with Professor Taylor's description of the applicable law and his conclusion that there have been widespread violations, it would be superfluous of me to essay a comprehensive answer.    There are, however, one
or two points which, particularly because of their intimate connection
with the second question, the question of culpability, I'd like to develop a little bit further.    In the debate swirling around question one—
that is, whether there have been violations of the laws of war—there
are, as Professor Taylor notes, essentially two types of controversy.
One dispute turns on whether acts conceded by all hands to violate
the laws of war occurred with notorious frequency.    The other turns
on the consistency of certain openly authorized activities with the rules
and principles of the laws of war.    The former dispute might be
characterized conventionally as one of fact, and the latter as one of
law or at least mixed fact and law.

In the dispute of fact category I place all acts of torture and execution: prisoners and civilian suspects flung from helicopters, tied to
vehicles and dragged across fields, or introduced through the medium of their testicles to the electrical stimulus of the field telephone.    In
the dispute of law category we would list the use of tear gas, high altitude saturation bombing of zones, and the forced migration of civilians to camps and the concomitant destruction of their villages, including the extermination of livestock and poisoning of wells.

Unfortunately, for purposes of easy normative classification,
there are activities which are both factually and legally problematical.
In the case of herbicides, for example, as Professor Taylor pointed out,
people debate: (a) whether their use is precluded under all circum-

stances; (b) assuming no flat preclusion, whether they may be used to starve civilians in order to compel their departure from rebel-held territory or to increase the administrative burdens of rebel government or for any other reason; and (c) the factual question of whether herbicides were employed in Vietnam against the civilian population.

Another set of activities marked by factual and legal uncertainty is the unannounced air and artillery assaults on villages. Under the laws of war, the assault is justified if the consequent destruction of the civilian population is not disproportionate to the anticipated military gain,[23] which, in the case of Vietnam, is measured in terms of American lives conserved and enemy soldiers rendered *hors de combat*. The issues are: what evidentiary standards were employed in determining the presence and size of the enemy force; were those standards sufficiently high to satisfy the criteria of the laws of war; what standards for calculating the proportionality of civilian damage were employed and were those standards acceptable?

In assessing questions of fact, private individuals obviously labor under a serious handicap in that they cannot compel the production of documents or the testimony of witnesses. Hence, we have had to rely on accounts of journalists and a limited number of former veterans.[24] This evidence is necessarily anecdotal. It would hardly suffice as a basis for conviction in a formal criminal trial. But conviction, of course, is not the issue. The real issue is whether sufficient evidence has been brought forward to justify each of us as judges deploying only the sanction of personal contempt to infer guilt in the absence of contrary proof which, if it exists, should be available to those who stand accused in the unofficial arenas of society. Considering that much of our evidence comes from eye witnesses—many of them trained observers and most, if not all of them, free from any obvious corrupting interest (indeed, some of our most damning evidence comes from journalists who at one time or another supported the war), I've reached the following tentative conclusions: first, that the torture of prisoners either by or under the direction of, or with the acquiescence of, Americans was commonplace;[25] second, that the so-called Phoenix Program to "root out" (not

---

23. *See* Farer, *The Laws of War 25 Years After Nuremberg*, 583 INTERNATIONAL CONCILIATION 1, 16-17 (1971).

24. Much of the eyewitness evidence is compiled in IN THE NAME OF AMERICA, note 10 *supra*.

25. *See* AGAINST THE CRIME OF SILENCE 405-513 (J. Duffett ed. 1970); IN THE NAME OF AMERICA, *supra* note 10, at 79-87. This conclusion is also supported by veterans at various hearings under the name of *Winter Soldier*, held by the Vietnam Veterans Against the War, and by a wide variety of newspaper articles and books.

my words) the Viet Cong infrastructure was in substantial part, if not primarily, an exercise in assassination which is clearly precluded by the laws of war;[26] and third, that the standards employed in targeting artillery and aircraft assault frequently manifested a large indifference to principles of proportionality and discrimination between civilians and noncombatants.[27]

With respect to questions of law, it is more difficult to conclude with quite the same measure of confidence that crimes have been committed. I would like to argue those questions in detail because I am prepared to defend the following propositions: first, that the use of nonlethal gas in Vietnam is illegal; second, that there are important limitations on aerial bombardment that have been exceeded in Vietnam; and third, that the forced migration of people and the permanent destruction of their homes violates the laws of war. However, because I want to concentrate on the second question, the question of culpability, I am not going to explore the basis for my conclusions now. I hope that I will have an opportunity to elaborate upon them later.

Turning now to the question of individual culpability, I want to begin with the group at the end of the decisional pipeline whose acts violated unequivocal prohibitions. I turn, in other words, to Lieutenant Calley and his friends. The principal defense of Calley has been premised on the alleged blurring of behavioral standards occasioned by the tactics and strategies authorized or tolerated or ineffectively restrained by our highest military and civilian officials. That is, the defense rests on the assumption that as a consequence of our methods of conducting the war, the distinction between bombs and shells, between napalm and bullets, between the very earth and the sky, had lost all meaning for Calley, however coherent the distinctions might remain for those who danced in the ballrooms of Washington.

Probably the most lucid exposition of this defense is contained in a paper presented recently by Professor Wasserstrom, the distinguished legal philosopher from U.C.L.A.[28] He contends that the failure of the laws of war to draw a categorical distinction between combatants and noncombatants, between soldiers and civilians, a distinction which

---

26. *See* Hague—Laws and Customs of War on Land, art. 23(b); ARMY FIELD MANUAL, ¶ 31 at 17.

27. *See* IN THE NAME OF AMERICA, *supra* note 10, at 159-268; AGAINST THE CRIME OF SILENCE, *supra* note 25, at 147-280; Gott, *Precision Bombing Not Very Precise*, in CRIMES OF WAR 397 (R. Falk, G. Kolko, R. Lifton ed. 1971); F. HARVEY, AIR WAR—VIETNAM (1967).

28. Wasserstrom, unpublished paper presented at symposium conducted in the Fall of 1971 by the American Society of International Law.

would preclude the bombing of military targets where major civilian damage is a necessary incident to the destruction of the military target, deprives them of moral coherence. They fail, in his opinion, to connect effectively with moral distinctions which enjoy paramount importance in domestic society, and, therefore, under the conditions which prevailed in Vietnam, including the pervasive decimation of civilians by all kinds of means, they were congenitally defective as guides for Calley. Rather than being reinforced by the conventional morality of domestic society, the laws of war were actually cutting right across it.

At the time Wasserstrom presented his paper, I responded along the following lines. The laws of war, I argued, may appear incoherent as a projection of the domestic value system, of the way we think people ought to be treated in our own society, but when perceived as the product of a difficult negotiation between values in severe competition, they are coherent. The laws of war do not draw an absolute distinction between combatants and noncombatants because the vast majority of people in each country are prepared in time of war to treat monolithically the loyal population of the enemy state, if that is deemed essential to the achievement of the objectives of the war. If one accepts what I call the uni-dimensional criterion of coherence offered by Professor Wasserstrom, it is doubtful that even domestic criminal law systems could pass the test of being morally coherent since they too are the visible products of mediation between divergent values. For example, the hustlers of Harlem end up in Attica, while those of Madison Avenue find dubious peace in a condominium on Fifth Avenue. Neither group is committed to the values of honesty; both respond to values such as aggressive acquisitiveness and individual assertion. Society draws lines which are clearly arbitrary when measured only against one of the competing values—honesty on the one hand, acquisitiveness and self-assertion on the other. Yet most people know what the lines are, and, despite the lack of pure moral coherence, we at least presume that people know or ought to know on which side of the line their behavior falls. And we punish them accordingly.

After further reflection, I still adhere to that view but perhaps with a little less sanctimonious self-assurance. For if torture, rape, and assassination *were* commonplace in Vietnam, then can't one argue that an obtuse, insecure, uneducated little man like Calley was simply incapacitated from questioning or doubting the order or the implication of the order that the village should be "wasted"—that is, utterly eliminated as a problem? On the other hand, it seems to me probable that a severe punishment for Calley would have had a powerful deterrent effect on the potential Calleys still out in the field or likely to be out in the field again in some future war. So, after weighing the general deterrent value of Calley's punishment against the circumstances which may have reduced his personal awareness of criminality, I still come down on the side of a far more severe sanction than Professor Taylor appears to deem appropriate. Professor Taylor's error, as I see it, is to emphasize the question of culpability without taking adequate account of the deterrence objective of the criminal law.

Let us now speak of men in high places. For openers, let's consider Townsend Hoopes's indignant rejection of the Nuremberg analogy as applied to our senior civilian and military figures,[29] an analogy which he attributed to "[s]ensitive clever children . . . [whose] judgments [are] unshaped by historical perspective and untempered by any first hand experience with the unruly forces at work in this near cyclonic century."[30]

The trouble, of course, is that a first hand experience of cyclones could make fools of us all. Why is Hoopes repulsed, I ask myself, by any suggestion that our leadership might be personally guilty? His answer is that "Lyndon Johnson, though disturbingly volatile, was not in his worst moments an evil man in the Hitlerian sense. And his principal advisors were, almost uniformly, those considered when they took office to be among the ablest, the best, the most humane and liberal men that could be found for public trust."[31] He goes on to say that, "[N]o one doubted their honest, high-minded pursuit of the best interests of their country, and indeed of the whole non-communist world, as they perceived those interests. Moreover, the war they waged was conducted entirely within the framework of the Constitution, with the express or tacit consent of the majority of the Congress and the country until at least the autumn of 1967. . . ."[32] And he concludes by saying that, "[S]et against these facts the easy designation of individuals as deliberate or imputed 'war criminals' is shockingly glib, even if one allows for the inexperience of the young."[33]

---

29. Hoopes, *The Nuremberg Suggestion,* in CRIMES OF WAR 233 (R. Falk, G. Kolko, R. Lifton ed. 1971).

30. *Id.* at 235.

31. *Id.* at 236.

32. *Id.*

33. *Id.*

The main difficulty I have with this bouillabaisse of exculpations is the capaciousness of the pot. Virtually every conceivable set of leaders in every conceivable historical circumstance might be able to climb inside and hide. If we look back on Roman history, for example, we find emperors and their aristocratic predecessors as well who no doubt thought of themselves as engaged in "the high-minded pursuit of the best interests of their country" and indeed of the whole Mediterranean world—as they perceived those interests. Was Cato a monster or an honest, high-minded man acting in his best lights to preserve legitimate Roman security interests, when he presided over the extirpation of the entire Carthaginian nation? His successors, when they demolished the Temple and dispersed the Jews into two millenia of exile, obviously acted in the name of peace and order.

Even Hitler, your prototypical monster, might find his way into Hoopes's exculpatory soup. For Hitler came to power, you will recall, by constitutional means and has it not for years been evident that, as long as he was successful, Hitler seemed to most Germans to be the ablest and the best man that could be found for public trust, a man engaged in the "honest high-minded pursuit of the best interests of his country"? The point was never better made than in Hannah Ahrendt's description of Eichmann. She wrote,

> [Eichmann's] conscience was indeed set at rest when he saw the zeal and eagerness with which 'good society' everywhere reacted as he did. He did not need to 'close his ears to the voice of conscience,' as the judgment has it, not because he had none, but because his conscience spoke with a 'respectable voice,' with the voice of respectable society around him.[34]

It seems fairly certain that unlike some of his more loathsome subordinates, Hitler did not seek personal gain of a mercenary sort. His concupiscence seems to have been quite unremarkable. Indeed, given his opportunities, he emerges as a patently respectable bourgeois sort of fellow, light years away from the sexual eccentricities of the Roehm clique. He was ambitious, but for Germany as well as himself, and, above all, he seems like Eichmann to have been an idealist, genuinely striving for a new order which would, he believed, bring unimaginable benefits not only to the average German but to other superior races as well.

A lack of respect for Hoopes's mishmash of distinctions hardly requires one, as a corollary, to embrace the view that there are no important distinctions between our leaders and the monsters of the Third

---

34. H. ARENDT, EICHMANN IN JERUSALEM 126 (Viking Press ed. 1969).

Reich, however.  America's war leaders during the middle 1960's were, it seems to me, largely insensitive to the possible criminality of their acts.  In this respect, they did differ significantly from the Nazis who consciously rejected traditional conceptions both of the acceptable ends of politics and the means for their achievement.  There is evidence of this in Hitler's denunciations of international society's existing order.  You have, moreover, the written instructions to the troops about to invade Russia demanding summary execution of all political commissars, directing that German soldiers not be prosecuted for offenses against Russian civilians unless it were necessary for the discipline and security of the army, and offering the comforting assurance that considerations of international law were out of place in dealing with Bolsheviks.  And nothing could be more revealing of the consciousness of the German leadership than Himmler's speech to the commanders of the higher S.S. and the police leaders.  He said,

> To have stuck it out and, apart from exceptions caused by human weakness, to have remained decent, that is what has made us hard.  This is a page of glory in our history which has never been written and is never to be written.  The order to solve the Jewish question, this was the most frightening order an organization could ever receive.  We realize that what we are expecting from you is 'superhuman'—to be 'superhumanly inhuman.'[35]

These, I would submit, are the words of outlaws seeking the total overthrow of an existing legal, cultural, and normative order, by all necessary means.

Is it any wonder, then, that America's leaders in the 1960's could not imagine themselves in the Nuremberg dock?  They seem reasonably decent men—even in comparison to Hitler's conservative opponents, the July 20th conspirators who failed in their attempt to assassinate the *Fuehrer*.  One can, I think, be fairly confident that if this latter group had survived, they would have been exonerated at Nuremberg; yet their leader, the former mayor of Leipzig, wrote in 1942 of the need for a "permanent solution that would save [all European Jews] from their unseemly position, as a more or less undesirable 'guest nation' in Europe."[36]  He favored their expulsion to an independent state in a colonial country.  Of such moral stuff was a good German made.

Nor, I would argue, did contemporary leaders of other nations offer a standard of decency which might reasonably have engendered a

---

35. *Quoted id.* at 105.
36. Carl Friedrich Goerdeler, *quoted id.* at 103.

sense of criminal responsibility in the White House and its precincts. The French? Hardly the French, who had suppressed a Madagascan bid for independence with a pitiless massacre, who had tortured in Algeria and fought a long, ravaging war in Indochina all for reasons not discernibly better and at least arguably more debased than those which were common currency in Washington. Third world leaders? In Nigeria and the Congo, blacks slaughtered blacks for the abstraction of nationhood and the gritty substance of power. Russia? Washington found the comparison altogether favorable. The rules of war had not, after all, saved Nagy's life when the Russians seized Hungary. And above all there was the perceived restraint of the Vietnamese operation itself. No mining of Haiphong, no blockade of Sihanoukville, no invasion of the North Vietnamese panhandle; in sum, a refusal (since reversed[37]) to appreciate the "wisdom" of General LeMay's view that the best way to solve the problem was to bomb them back to the Stone Age. The question really is not whether the self-congratulatory assumptions of people in Washington were true, but whether they in fact colored the perspectives of the men we are called on to judge.

The not-outrageous absence of the consciousness of criminality among our leaders in the mid 1960's does not, however, wholly exculpate them. Negligent homicide is not premeditated murder, but it *is* a serious crime.

If I'm right in believing that on the basis of the available evidence, they can be so charged, there remains the final question of whether pressing for recognition and acknowledgment of criminal culpability will help to prevent further Vietnams. After balancing the arguments—arguments too involved for summary explication at this time—I conclude that the answer is yes. I see few signs of contrition and abundant evidence that men still masticating the fruits of social power are writing off Vietnam as simply a case where the costs got out of hand. That perception, that evaluation of the Vietnamese experience, will not save people in other lands where the cost of intervention might appear more manageable. What is required is a fundamental shift in the mind set of our national decision-makers and the generations that will succeed them. I think that the allegation of criminal conduct can have the necessary shocking and educational effect.

* * *

*Professor Farer added the following interpolation in December 1972:*

---

37. *See* Professor Farer's EPILOGUE, *infra* at 57, referring to post-colloquy events.

What do I mean when I speak of a new mind set or political consciousness?   Perhaps it would be useful to begin by describing the prevailing one.   It was vividly evoked by Daniel Ellsberg when he wrote:

How many will die in Laos?

What is Richard Nixon's best estimate of the number of Laotian people—"enemy" and "non-enemy"—that US firepower will kill in the next twelve months?

*He does not have an estimate.*   He has not asked Henry Kissinger for one, and Kissinger has not asked the Pentagon; and none of these officials has ever seen an answer, to this or any comparable question on the expected impact of war policy on human life.   And none of them differs in this from his predecessors. (Systems analysts in the bureaucracy make estimates as best they can of factors judged pertinent to policy: "costs" or "benefits," "inputs" or "outputs."   The deaths of "non-combatant people" have never been regarded by officials as being relevant to any of these categories.)[38]

Ellsberg spoke, as I do, from personal knowledge, knowledge of his colleagues and himself.   In July 1962 when I journeyed to the Pentagon to serve as Special Assistant to the late John McNaughton, then General Counsel and already established as one of McNamara's inner circle, the human quality most admired among the Kennedy legions was "tough-mindedness" or its equivalent—"hard-nosed."   These appellations did not refer simply to the capacity for clear and comprehensive analysis, although to be fair that was a commendable feature of the ideal decision-maker.   But if that were all the freight these terms of fraternal endearment were designed to carry, other vehicles would have performed with more obvious efficiency.   No, they were signs of a good deal more than respect for a lucid intellect.   In part, the idea of "toughness" went to the very definition of lucidity, screening out analysis and conclusions which were not justified solely in terms of the economic achievement of policy objectives.   And except in the most general and hence effectively futile sense, it restricted objectives to those which aggrandized power—of individuals, of bureaucracies, and of the nation.

The idea of toughness referred also, of course, to a certain affective style for presenting or reacting to ideas—a style which in turn influenced the shape of the research, analysis, and recommendation that produced and elaborated these very ideas.   One strove for hard

---

38. Ellsberg, *Laos: What Nixon Is Up To*, N.Y. REV. OF BOOKS, Mar. 11, 1971, at 16.

images, aggressive metaphors, and, above all, either the elimination or the quantification of the ultimate unquantifiable. Those few men who referred occasionally to such abstractions as "world opinion" or displayed a purely humanitarian concern for, let us say, the plight of the Third World's masses were regarded with that subtly veiled revulsion normally reserved for persons suffering from a disfiguring disease. On the other hand, the man who could pronounce "megadeath" without flinching was a man who might be entrusted with a high responsibility.

\* \* \*

*End of Professor Farer's interpolation. General Gard commented, in June 1973:*

Professor Farer assisted Mr. McNaughton, when he was General Counsel, prior to our introduction of ground troops in Vietnam; I was Mr. McNaughton's Special Assistant for several months in 1966, when he was Assistant Secretary of Defense (International Security Affairs). Mr. Ellsberg had left Washington, and even the government service, well before the period in which he implies personal knowledge of what issues were *not* considered in reaching policy decisions concerning the war!

I can state from my experience both as Special Assistant to Mr. McNaughton and as one of the two Military Assistants to Mr. McNamara, then Secretary of Defense, that such questions as possible civilian casualties were given weight even in the selection of individual targets in North Vietnam. Professor Farer's personal impressions were formed during the early period of the Kennedy Administration when the Berlin and Cuban Missile crises created situations in which "toughness" appears to have been appropriate.

\* \* \*

*End of General Gard's comment. Professor Farer continued:*

I know there are no saints in the political game. Its tediousness, its frustrations, its risks, and its impulse towards the monopolization of players' lives all conspire against the entry of gentle people and modest egos. Accepting this, by reference to a change in their mind set, I do not imply the hope of substituting government by angels for that of men. Nor do I propose the total rejection of force in international relations any more than I would insist that a man assaulted on the streets rely on moral adjuration for his defense. But I think we can effect the radical devaluation of force as a technique for enhancing national, organizational, or personal power. And we can enhance respect for bleeding hearts, and compassion for the bleeding heads to which they respond, attitudes as traditionally remote from the study groups in the Council on Foreign Relations as My Lai is from Washington.

Regardless of the depressing historical evidence, I think we should try to produce leaders who could write a letter like the following with which I'd like to conclude. This was a letter written during the Biafran revolt by a professor at Yale Law School, Arthur Leff. He wrote to the *New York Times*:

> I don't know much about the relevant law; my colleagues here who do say there is no insurmountable hindrance. But I don't care much about international law, Biafra, or Nigeria, because babies are dying in Biafra. We still have food for export. Let's get it to them any way we can, dropping it from the skies, unloading it from armed ships, blasting it in with cannons if that will work. I can't believe there is much political cost in feeding babies, but if there is, let's pay it. Forget all that blather about international law, sovereignty, and self-determination, all that abstract garbage. Babies are starving to death.

I think the Nuremberg analogy may be one useful means to the end of bringing into the corridors of power that kind of humane passion.

## REMARKS OF ROBERT G. GARD, JR.

I'm speaking privately, as a student of politico-military affairs; my views do not represent those of the army or any other agency of the Government.

For a soldier, untrained in law, to appear here is rather presumptuous, and I find myself somewhat at a loss in discussing the law of war with a lawyer who finishes his talk saying, "Let's forget about international law." Nevertheless, I think I will try to discuss international law and the law of war—with the admission that there are also serious moral considerations involved which must be considered in any extensive study of what has happened in Vietnam.

The relationship of warfare to international law is very complex, but the term "war crimes" often is used popularly, and improperly, to convey moral outrage concerning our involvement in Vietnam. I think we have just heard very sincere and articulate evidence of precisely that. I don't want to dwell on legalisms, but I do think the point must be made: what is unwise and perhaps even unjust is not necessarily illegal. Also, I think it's useful to make a differentiation, probably well known to all of you here, between the law concerning the decision to employ force or to go to war—*jus ad bellum*, and the law involving the conduct of war itself—*jus in bello*.

First, the question of the decision to employ force. There is a long history of the concept of just wars deduced from natural law and not limited to the defense of one's own territory. The category of Crimes Against Peace, waging wars of aggression, was first considered an international crime at Nuremberg. A difficult aspect of the problem is defining aggression. Aggression, in fact, seems impossible to codify short of a situation as clearcut as the enunciation of territorial ambitions by Nazi Germany. I agree with what Professor Taylor has written in his book and has repeated to some extent here today—that Crimes Against Peace must be considered basically a political, not a legal, question that must be tried at the bar of political justice.

Also, I don't want you to leave with the impression that civilian governmental officials, for example the Secretary of Defense, weren't concerned in a moral sense by what was going on in Vietnam. Townsend Hoopes's arguments don't really apply, in my view. I agree with Professor Farer that whether or not the individuals involved are evil men, as Hitler was an evil man, is probably beside the point. But if one wants to apply the Nuremberg precedent to the current situation, I think it essential to refer to what was considered at that time to be a war of aggression, a Crime Against Peace. I wasn't there, as Professor Taylor was, but I did find an article published in 1949 by Associate Justice of the Supreme Court Robert Jackson,[39] who was Chief Prosecutor prior to Professor Taylor and who participated in the early formulations of what these crimes were considered to be, when we agreed in the London Charter to prosecute. It's very clearly stated several times in that article that the punishable case against the Germans was based on an ambition for territorial conquest.[40] The criteria established for those who should be charged were that they had been in high positions in government and had been privy to the plans formulated by the Chief of State. It would be my submission that if we're going to apply the Nuremberg principle of Crimes Against Peace to the current situation, we should use the same criterion of territorial conquest. Whether or not the present war resulted in unfavorable or even tragic consequences should not be controlling.

Now, *jus in bello*—the conduct of war itself. There are two sub-categories, if I read the law correctly. The first is Crimes Against Humanity. These were associated at Nuremberg with Nazi policies and programs concerning slave labor and the systematic and deliber-

---

39. Jackson, *Nuremberg in Retrospect: Legal Answer to International Lawlessness,* 35 A.B.A.J. 813 (1949).
40. *Id.* at 814, 882.

ate extermination of minorities—destruction of people because of what they were, Jews or Gypsies, for example. The other category of *jus in bello* is war crimes as such—incidents arising from the conduct of the war. These include violations of both customary and treaty law of war, principally the specific guidance and prohibitions in the Hague and Geneva Conventions. These are pragmatic and inductive. I certainly endorse Professor Taylor's view that it is highly desirable that we continue these prohibitions and enforce them.

Considering the framework of the law and the conduct of warfare, evil and nasty as it is, there are two inter-related governing principles: military necessity and proportionality. Military necessity permits measures reasonably necessary to accomplish the military mission of securing the complete submission of the enemy as soon as possible, but it requires limiting the use of violence to measures not forbidden by specific prohibition. Proportionality requires that the violence itself not be disproportionate to the military advantage gained. Now these precepts are very general with an admittedly wide range of interpretation. So we found at Nuremberg that to obtain a finding of guilty, the act in question had to be judged either willful or wanton. If you examine the *Rendulic* case,[41] which dealt with the widespread destruction of areas in the face of a Russian advance, you will find that this was in fact not a military necessity but, since Rendulic perceived it to be so at the time, he was found not guilty.

Finally, there are specifically prohibited acts. These are enumerated in the Geneva Conventions. Military necessity cannot excuse violations of these specific prohibitions.

Let me interject a point here. As Professor Farer implied, the application of military power in warfare cannot be regulated by the standards that obtain in domestic society. I therefore question the applicability of the analogy of negligent homicide. Also, even though it was suggested by such a distinguished and articulate lawyer, charging someone with criminal conduct for the purpose of shocking and educating the public seems to me to be rather poor law. It is indeed difficult, as Professor Farer stated, to comprehend the nature of a military conflict in the ballrooms of Washington; I might add that it is equally difficult in the lecture halls of Newark. It's even difficult to comprehend the nature of the war in Vietnam after having served in just one area of it for a year. Although the country looks small on

---

41. United States v. List (*The Hostage Case*), 11 TRIALS OF WAR CRIMINALS BEFORE THE NUERNBERG MILITARY TRIBUNALS 759, 1296 (U.S. Gov't Printing Office 1950).

the maps we use, it's relatively large.   The nature of warfare there was very different from area to area; so admittedly my own perspective is also limited.

Maybe it would be useful for me to spend a minute or two trying to give you some feel for what I think are problems within the military profession caused by the evolution of its role in our society.   I'll try to make it brief; but I think it is essential if we are to understand the employment of force in Vietnam.

We were, until recently, protected from foreign power centers by vast oceans, and we sought our security in what I would call a concept of "national defense."   We maintained a minuscule standing armed force which we expanded in time of war.   This concept was underpinned by a doctrine of what could be called "mutual exclusion" of civilian and military functions.   Civilians conducted diplomacy and politics without participation by the military; the military conducted wars to victory without civilian intrusion.   This was well-suited to the traditional American liberal ethic, still deeply set in the American consciousness, which opposed standing armies and the use of force, but sanctioned war to eliminate a threat to freedom.   Although unacceptable without a moral imprimatur of high order, once war was embraced as a crusade, it could become boundless in its prosecution.   This implied little or no restraint on violence to defeat an enemy.

Traditional military professionalism, which developed after the Civil War, reflected this concept of national defense and the doctrine of mutual exclusion.   Its expertise lay essentially in the ordered application of military force in combat operations.   Its simple, but not easy, criterion was the destruction of the enemy armed force with the fewest possible friendly casualties, a standard consistent with the societal approach to war.   This restricted concept of expertise was grounded on a transcendent sense of duty to the state through its lawfully constituted authority.   Policy was determined by political authority, not by those who executed it.   The military was an instrument of the state, and the soldier felt he would be committed to combat only for causes justifying the ravages of war.

I don't want to claim too much for this oversimplification, but I would contend that it was generally accepted both in our society and by the military until the Korean War.   Moreover, due at least in part to the doctrine of massive retaliation developed after the Korean War, I think a full understanding of the implications of the requirement to integrate military policy and operations with other instruments of statecraft was not comprehended fully until the early sixties, when the Kennedy doctrine of "flexible response" was put into effect. Vietnam came as a test case of a new concept which you might call "national security" policy and strategy, as opposed to "national defense," requiring the interweaving with the military of political, sociological, psychological, and economic considerations both in peace and war. When we became involved in military operations in Vietnam, we had made only the most preliminary adjustments to these new concepts, not only within the military establishment but also within other agencies of our government.

The conflict in Vietnam is highly complex; I think we all agree on that. It's a combination of an externally supported civil war and an invasion from the North. The complexities of the guerilla effort have proved particularly difficult. The enemy has employed terrorism, including assassination, kidnapping, and impressment of women and children into service in both military and quasi-military functions. Such measures as widespread assassination, extensive use of booby traps, and the deliberate rocketing of urban areas create an atmosphere of insecurity and uncertainty.

"Counter-insurgency" is itself a relatively new concept to the military. Its strategy is highly complicated, and techniques were not really understood by the military institution nor, I would argue, by civilian agencies or the informed public. The inclination was to stress the traditional mission of destroying the enemy force with the fewest possible friendly casualties. The mission, of course, is still applicable, but in a situation such as Vietnam, it certainly can no longer be exclusive or even paramount.

As a further complication, the military found itself engaged not only in military operations but, because of a shortage of personnel in civilian agencies, also involved directly in, or even managing the operations of, such other institutions as the Agency for International Development, the U.S. Information Agency, and the C.I.A. Some military personnel even served as part of the embassy staff. There are virtues in traditional military training, but the military orientation of "getting the job done" also encourages reduction of complex situations to simpler problems, and the "can-do" attitude leads to an emphasis on familiar tactics, not the development of new techniques.

Following the introduction of troops, our operations can be considered in three phases. In 1965, our forces went in as a kind of "fire brigade," moving to intercept the most serious enemy attacks and to prevent military victory by the North Vietnamese and Viet Cong regular forces. In the second phase, we took the offensive against these main force units to drive them away from population centers into sparsely settled hinterlands. At about the end of 1966, these two phases had been accomplished quite successfully, apparently with the support of the majority of the American public.

The third phase, which has proved the most difficult, includes elimination of main force units; although complicated by the situation in Vietnam, this is consistent with the traditional concept of the mission of the military profession. The other element, destruction of the guerilla force structure, is foreign to our modern experience and fraught with difficulty.

Prior to the introduction of U.S. ground combat troops, General Westmoreland commissioned a study on the applicability of the laws of war to Vietnam. He could have concluded quite properly that the Viet Cong did not so meet the criteria as to merit any protection whatever. Rather, he issued instructions providing protected status for people clearly excluded by the Geneva Conventions and issued orders on rules of engagement involving the application of force, especially firepower, which exceeded the requirements of the Geneva Conventions. Professor Taylor has called the instructions "virtually impeccable."[42] A delegate of the International Committee of the Red Cross said in 1966, when the directive was revised and reissued, that it

> is a brilliant expression of a liberal and realistic attitude. . . . This text could very well be a most important one in the history of humanitarian law, for it is the first time . . . that a government goes far beyond the requirements of the Geneva Convention in an official instruction to its armed forces . . . .[43]

It is perfectly true that publication of directives is not enough; observance and enforcement are essential. Moreover, there is a question of moral responsibility that transcends these instructions, as well as the issue of what acts are juridically legitimate under the terms of the Geneva Conventions. I would agree with Professor Taylor that in the early stages our training was probably deficient and that, in retrospect, some of our supervision undoubtedly was inadequate. And that while you can argue about the technical legality of the destruction of food crops, it was recognized eventually as being unwise and was discontinued. The "body count," which has received a great deal of adverse publicity, was not instituted by the military. Since the Office of the Secretary of Defense used casualty data as a basis of evaluation

---

42. *See* text accompanying note 14 *supra*; NUREMBERG AND VIETNAM, *supra* note 1, 168.

43. Haight, *Geneva Convention and the Shadow of War*, in NAVAL PROCEEDINGS 47 (1968).

and planning, there was a desire by that office to be certain that reports reflected actual enemy dead. The term "body count" became popular.

The turnover of prisoners we capture is a controversial matter. We obtained the agreement of the South Vietnamese Government to open every one of its P.O.W. camps to the inspection of the International Committee of the Red Cross, and that agreement has been honored. The highly publicized atrocious conditions at Con Son did not involve P.O.W.s, but rather criminals and other prisoners of the South Vietnamese Government.

The use of tear gas may be considered contrary to the 1925 convention on chemical warfare,[44] but we are not yet a party to that treaty. Our early uses of tear gas in Vietnam were in fact humanitarian in intent—for example, to flush non-combatants out of caves so that they would not be killed along with enemy soldiers. It is true that we tried to use it later for other purposes. These included trying to flush the Viet Cong out of bunkers so we could attack them more easily than by requiring our soldiers to assault fortified positions to force them out.

As to firepower, the rules of engagement do in fact restrict the use of firepower. The term "indiscriminate use of firepower" is employed frequently as a sweeping indictment. I concede that I may be sensitive on this point, since for nine months I commanded ninety-six cannons and the personnel who employed them. In fact, last spring I had an exchange with Neil Sheehan in the *New York Times* on the subject.[45] There is no question that there is a general inclination to use firepower to destroy enemy combatants when the only alternative is to risk the lives of our own troops. I don't think a soldier need apologize for that. No doubt there have been errors as well as unjustified, deliberate instances of misuse of firepower. These should not be condoned, and in my experience were not condoned. Yet, from the popular literature, one gets the impression that we bombed and shelled large areas indiscriminately; in fact, area bombing was done only with the authorization of South Vietnamese political and military officials, and it was applied only in places where prior warning had been given

---

44. Protocol for the Prohibition of the Use in War of Asphyxiating, Poisonous or Other Gases and of Bacteriological Methods of Warfare, *signed at Geneva* June 17, 1925, 94 L.N.T.S. 65.

45. The exchange of letters between Mr. Sheehan and General Gard appeared in N.Y. Times, May 16, 1971 § 7 (Book Review), at 10-12. The exchange was prompted by Mr. Sheehan's earlier review (Sheehan, *Should We Have War Crime Trials*, N.Y. Times, Mar. 28, 1971 § 7 (Book Review), at 1) of a number of books dealing with the subject of the United States' military involvement in Southeast Asia.

and from which civilians had been evacuated. Far from being "unrestricted," there were stringent limitations on the use of firepower. For example, not only were we precluded from firing on a village from which sniper fire was coming, but we didn't even return fire into a village from which our large airfield was being mortared, even though we were taking casualties and millions of dollars worth of equipment was being destroyed. As Sheehan put it in his response to me in the *Times*, returning such fire clearly would have been consistent with the Geneva Conventions.[46] The fact is that the restrictions did exist, they were explicit, and we did comply.

I was unaware of any leaflet threatening unannounced destruction of villages and hamlets harboring Viet Cong. Warning of impending attack on a village is both humanitarian and in accordance with the rules of engagement. If the actual policy of the Marine units in question, however, was to attack the village without such warning, it was clearly contrary to the rules of engagement and should have been punished accordingly.

Senator Kennedy's figures on the number of civilians killed, wounded, and homeless are not the only source for that data and seem to me questionable. I understand that he took official data and multiplied the figures for the early years by two. In the more recent years, he's been multiplying by four. The official figures are available, but I don't have them.

Concerning the evacuation of civilians, NVA and VC tactics attempt to exploit the civilian population in vulnerable areas. Incidentally, nowhere in the laws of war can one find precedents requiring protection for civilians caught in an engagement between military forces. This is a difficult dilemma in Vietnam, and evacuation of civilians in certain areas was judged to be the most humane policy. In the Geneva Conventions, the only prohibition on evacuation of civilians concerns the population of occupied territories.[47] Plainly, this prohibition was written to cover the case of Nazi deportations from one country to another for slave labor. Even if you argue, however, that what applies to *enemy* civilians must a fortiori be required as a minimum standard for treatment of *allied* civilians, the fact remains that the Convention says that, "The Occupying Power may undertake total or

---

46. "The incident of restraint that Colonel Gard cites is admirable—particularly since the laws of war would appear to have permitted his unit to return fire. It is a pity there was not more such restraint." Letter from Neil Sheehan in N.Y. Times, May 16, 1971, § 7 (Book Review), at 12.

47. Geneva—Civilians, art. 49.

partial evacuation of a given area if the security of the population or imperative military reasons so demand."[48]

But even though it may be technically legal, one can, of course, still question the *advisability* of requiring civilians to move from their homes. In this context, it should be noted that in 1956, the International Committee of the Red Cross in proposing rules for limiting the dangers to civilian populations in time of war, sought to require belligerents "to protect the civilian population subject to their authority from the dangers to which they would be exposed in an attack—in particular, by removing them from the vicinity of military objectives and threatened areas."[49]    The Secretary General of the United Nations, in a 1970 report to the General Assembly, said:

> The most effective way of minimizing or eliminating the risk to civilians would be to make systematic efforts to the effect that civilians do not remain in areas where dangers would be prevalent. The General Assembly . . . [should] consider the usefulness of an appropriate resolution—a call on all authorities involved in armed conflicts of all types to do their utmost to insure that civilians are removed from, or kept out of, areas where conditions would be likely to place them in jeopardy or expose them to the hazards of warfare.[50]

Certainly the judgments involved are open to question and review, but where the alternatives are having civilians caught in major engagements or placing them temporarily in camps—and it's the policy that their stay in camps should be *temporary*—then I think you must at least give the policy of evacuating them the benefit of the doubt. This is not to argue that adequate provision—a legitimate moral, if not a legal, imperative—has been made for these unfortunate victims of war.

Protection of prisoners of war and detainees is traditional and well understood by the military which has an obvious vested interest. Abusing P.O.W.s and detainees is a violation of the rules of war, the *Uniform Code of Military Justice*, and directives from the various headquarters in Vietnam.[51] The *Calley* case appears from the press to have been a clearcut instance of the murder of unarmed and unresisting de-

---

48. *Id.*

49. REPORT OF INTERNATIONAL COMMISSION OF THE RED CROSS FOR THE JANUARY, 1957 NEW DELHI CONFERENCE (Draft Rules), art. 1, at 11 (Geneva 1956).

50. Report of the Secretary General, *Respect for Human Rights in Armed Conflicts*, 25th Sess., U.N. Doc. A/8052 (1970).

51. *See* Geneva—Prisoners of War, arts. 3, 12, 13, 17, 130; Geneva—Wounded and Sick, art. 3; Hague—Laws and Customs of War on Land (Annex), arts. 4, 23; 10 U.S.C. §§ 893, 918 (1970); ARMY FIELD MANUAL, ¶ 9, at 84-92.

tainees. Calley allegedly even considered them to be prisoners of war. As Professor Taylor pointed out, this was by no means the first case in which soldiers were tried for killing or mistreating Vietnamese. Other are doubtless guilty, but that does not make Calley innocent. As to the severity of the sentence: if the jury returns a verdict of premeditated murder, the court is required to sentence the defendant to life imprisonment or death; it has no other choice.

The charge of the judge in the *Medina* case, which was quite rightly criticized by Professor Taylor,[52] was contrary to current regulations, although completely consistent with the Nuremberg precedent. At Nuremberg, the three civilian judges who presided at the High Command case wrote: "The Commander *must have knowledge* of these offenses and acquiesce or participate or criminally neglect to interfere in their commission, and the offenses must be patently criminal."[53] Now, of course, we have gone well beyond the standards of Nuremberg concerning the responsibility of the Commander. Our own *Field Manual* states that he is guilty "if he has actual knowledge or *should have had knowledge* . . . ."[54] The question of whether a commander should have had knowledge in a particular case is one of fact.

I didn't hear the evidence in the *Medina* case, although I am somewhat familiar with the press accounts. The question is whether or not at the time in question he should have been with that particular platoon. As Professor Taylor rightly says, there were two other platoons under Medina's command in the area, one of which was reportedly engaged in active operations. On the other hand, the cover-up by Medina is inexcusable. Oddly enough, that was a clear violation of the regulations of the Military Assistance Command in Vietnam,[55] but I can find nowhere in the Geneva Conventions that concealing a crime is itself a crime, though by pointing this out my intent is certainly not to condone the cover-up. Medina admitted that if he had reported the incident, he was going to cause considerable difficulty for himself and for his unit, and for that reason he decided to cover it up. This concealment wasn't included in the charges against Medina, on the theory that to add a charge of violating regulations to the charge of murder would be compounding unnecessarily the number of specifications, which is contrary to procedures involving the *Uniform Code*

---

52. *See* note 19 and accompanying text *supra*.

53. United States v. Von Leeb (*The High Command Case*), 11 TRIALS OF WAR CRIMINALS BEFORE THE NUERNBERG MILITARY TRIBUNALS 1, 545 (U.S. Gov't Printing Office 1951).

54. ARMY FIELD MANUAL, ¶ 501, at 178 (emphasis added).

55. *See* MACV Directive 20-4, *supra* note 21.

*of Military Justice.* I do not think, however, that this has insulated higher commanders from appropriate action. Lieutenant Colonel Barker, Medina's superior, is dead. Henderson is being tried. Generals Young and Koster have been punished by administrative action because the evidence was not considered sufficient to warrant a court martial.

It may be that Vietnam was a unique situation calling forth mistakes unlikely to be repeated. I feel, nevertheless, that an impartial study of the application of military force in pursuit of political objectives would be appropriate. Such a study would be important for the military, because of the effect of the Vietnam conflict on that profession, and would also shed light on the manner in which military operations should be integrated with other instruments of statecraft. The study would be important for American society as a whole, as well, because we are all concerned about the morality as well as the legality of our operations in Vietnam. We do have a moral responsibility to honor our legal commitments. And in a democratic society there is a moral responsibility to insure that military force is applied to serve the national interest in a manner consistent with societal values.

## COMMENTS AND REBUTTAL

### Telford Taylor

I would like to make just two observations. Since the sponsoring theme of this gathering is international law, and the host organization is the Rutgers Society of International Law, I will try to point out a couple of areas where it seems to me that further revision, clarification, and application of the law in international conferences or elsewhere would be very worthwhile.

General Gard differs with me on the debatability of whether or not the removal of refugees from their homes was a violation of the Convention. I well recognize that there are problems, but I do not at all agree with him that it is not debatable. I would like to point out one feature of the situation which explains much of the difficulty and confusion surrounding this matter: that is that no one quite knows what Vietnam is in terms of international law. It's not like Germans in Alsace-Lorraine or French in the Ruhr; it's not like a case where there is a clear national boundary with the forces of one nation occupying land in another nation where the classical rules for the protection of civilians in occupied territories apply. We haven't gone into North Vietnam where the rules applicable to the protection of civilians of occupied territory would plainly obtain.  Are we *occupying* South Vietnam?  It's hard to put it that way.  We are there presumably by invitation of the South Vietnamese Government; they are our allies. Therefore, one regards the inhabitants of South Vietnam not as the inhabitants of a hostile occupied land, but as if we were using France as a base for hostile operations against Germany.  The most recent parallel situation to this was in the Napoleonic Peninsular Wars nearly two centuries ago, when Napoleon was invited into Spain by the Royal Government.  The British then invaded Spain to fight against the French. At that time, the laws of war had not yet been articulated, but it did present a somewhat analogous situation.  Presently, we find that the laws of war have not addressed themselves with sufficient directness towards the kinds of problems the Vietnam context presents, and this is an area where I think international consideration of the problem could perhaps clarify and accomplish a great deal.

To bring the discussion back to a more dialectic zone, General Gard spoke of the treatment of refugees as being a moral problem. I would disagree that it is only that.  I think if one reads further than he apparently read in the Geneva Conventions, one would find that they *do* explicitly require that civilian populations shall not be removed unless adequate provision for their accommodation has been made.[56]  The obligation does transcend the moral one, and it is under the Conventions a legal one, and I submit that it has been violated.

## Tom J. Farer

The main point I want to make is to concede the nature of my own unease about the question of the applicability of the Nuremberg principles.  I think that General Gard's basic point is that here's a war fought by an army which has demonstrated, at least at the highest command levels, a greater sensitivity for the treatment of prisoners of war and the civilian population than other armies in more or less comparable positions either *have* demonstrated or are likely to demonstrate. People like myself and Professor Taylor, and those who have gone further than we, are essentially claiming that although the United States may have acted better than anyone else under comparable circumstances, or at least no worse (and I think General Gard would argue better), nevertheless we're claiming that they're criminals.

Now, what's the norm?  Is the norm some abstract ideal to which no one makes any more than formal gestures of adherence?  How can

---

56. Geneva—Civilians, art. 49.

you have a criminal norm which in fact has everybody on the criminal side? International law, General Gard is arguing, must be interpreted in terms of the average case, and, if the United States is behaving better than the average case, it becomes absurd to suggest that the United States is acting in a criminal way.

(Professor Farer then turned to General Gard and asked, "Do I capture some of your feeling about this?" General Gard replied, somewhat skeptically, "Some.")

I should think I capture all of it, because it seems to me easily the most plausible argument you can deploy. I find that it does cause me a good deal of unease because, as I've tried to point out in my own remarks, if you take the French who have been in somewhat similar circumstances, their behavior has been beastly. In Algeria, the torture was open, conceded, and systematic.

If I could just drop a footnote here, occasioned by reference to the French: I thought the statement that the South Vietnamese had accepted I.C.R.C. supervision of their camps was näive, to put the best face on it. The French also accepted considerable inspection of the camps. The trouble is that torture generally doesn't occur in the camp. It occurs immediately after capture, because most of the useful intelligence information has a very brief life span. "Where is your unit now? Where will it be tomorrow?" Once you've got that information the man is simply a sucked lemon. He is of no further use; you send him to a camp and forget about him. Thus, coercive forms of interrogation occur prior to the arrival of the prisoner at the camp. You throw the man out of the helicopter on the way *to* the camp. You can have all the inspection you want at the camp; reference to its existence is not responsive to the question of whether or not people are being tortured.

But I'll come back to my main point, the point that really troubles me. To what kind of a standard are we holding the U.S.? Let me try this distinction, although it's a distinction that raises problems. The laws of war really consist of two kinds of rules—rules that come into being in two different ways. There are the treaty rules, the rules codified in the Geneva and Hague Conventions, and then there are the customary rules which both fill in the interstices and lay down the principled foundation for those rules. To the extent that we have violated codified rules, it seems to me not irrelevant that others have done the same thing, but at least much less significant, particulary since most countries have not, after all, been involved in this particular context.

All we can say is that two or three other countries in a somewhat similar setting have done some of the same things. Where, however, we're talking about rules that have evolved through practice—and the only practice we have is the behavior of a few countries—then I have a little more difficulty in finding a U.S. violation. Now the distinction I draw is much too clear to comport with reality, because treaties are themselves clarified and modified by practice. Nevertheless, I think it may be a marginally helpful distinction.

\* \* \*

*The following was interpolated by Professor Farer in December, 1972:*

I am not sure, however, that the distinction will help General Gard very much. In the first place, behavior unaccompanied by claims of legal justification (or, a fortiori, inconsistent with one's stated legal position) does not tend to establish new law. We do not claim a right to torture. We do not claim a right to incinerate villages without warning because of a suspicion that a handful of enemy combatants may be resting in them. We do not claim a right to assassinate persons suspected of involvement in the N.L.F. We do not claim a right to destroy the economic fabric of civilian life in North Vietnam. We just do these things while denying that they are happening. Our denials witness the felt obligation to live by the principles of proportionality, humanity, and discrimination between combatants and non-combatants. They are the testament of our shame, not the measure of our duty.

In the second place, I do not believe that any state since World War II has been in a comparable situation. The means we have employed are unparalleled in their destructive effects. It certainly is possible that the French in Algeria and the British in Malaya would have behaved identically had they the means. Nevertheless, we indict people not for what they would like to have done but for what they did. The rest is speculation.

Finally, I question the accuracy of General Gard's description of U.S. behavior. It conflicts with accounts of journalists and soldiers who either had no vested interest in the substance of their reports or actually testified against their personal or professional interests. Whatever the formal rules of engagement, the pervasive reality of U.S. behavior in Indochina is the repeatedly indiscriminate, grossly disproportionate use of firepower on the ground and in the air, and the consequent devastation of the civilian population.

* * *

*End of Professor Farer's interpolation. General Gard commented, in June, 1973:*

Professor Farer appears to have engaged in the old debating technique of attributing to your opponent an argument he did not make and then devastating it! Certainly I did not claim justification for atrocious behavior simply because there have been violations or because other nations have, or might not have, set such a precedent.

My main point was that there was a deliberate effort to adapt both the treaty and conventional rules of warfare to the very difficult situation in Vietnam. The main disagreement is really the extent to which our general behavior conformed with our regulations. I question the objectivity of those who claim that we generally ignored the rules. I do know from my own admittedly limited experience and perspective that adherence to the guidelines was the norm and deviation from them the aberration, and I have confirmed that perception in conversations with large numbers of soldiers of all ranks.

* * *

*End of General Gard's comment. Professor Farer continued:*

Perhaps by insisting upon the existence of the rules and enforcement of these rules, at least in the personal character of conduct, we'll prevent other states in comparable contexts from engaging in this behavior. Or more likely, since it is exceedingly difficult to win a guerrilla war without engaging in violation of the traditional rules, we may deter future interventions by the United States or other states. That, too, is an interesting line of speculation.

### Robert G. Gard, Jr.

I told you at the beginning I'd be in hot water appearing on the platform with two such distinguished lawyers.

Let me clear up the easiest question first. My comment about the I.C.R.C. inspection in P.O.W. camps was not meant to answer Professor Farer's concern with their torture before they got there, but rather Professor Taylor's concern as to whether or not we should turn prisoners over to the Vietnamese. I should add that, in my opinion, the torture of prisoners was not so widespread as Professor Farer thinks it was. There were 269 convictions, before the *Calley* case, for such offenses as murder, rape, robbery, and assault, in which a large proportion of the victims were detainees and prisoners. This indicates that the command was willing to take steps to deter and punish this sort of action when a case could be made.

Secondly, while I've had no legal training and recognize that I am getting into difficult technical problems, I would like to re-emphasize Professor Taylor's remark that the Geneva Conventions weren't designed for the kind of conflict that we're having in Vietnam. I have the impression that under our legal system, if one is to be convicted of a crime, he must have violated some positive law. All I was trying to suggest in my brief review of the substantive law of war, is that I think we took a quite liberal interpretation, not only of the Geneva Conventions but of the Nuremberg principles, and made an attempt to apply them. On the other hand, I do object to accusing people of violations of the law because it would have a desirable shock effect.

One final point: I will agree with Professor Taylor that the displacement of civilians may be a debatable point. My argument is that Vietnam is not an occupied territory and that you cannot extrapolate from rules for regulating behavior in an occupied territory to the rules to be applied to allied territory. Moreover, even if it *were* an occupied territory, the Convention clearly allows displacing personnel for their safety.[57] In any event, there remains the question of whether we provided sufficient support for the evacuees. People in Vietnam in the Agency for International Development and elsewhere tell me that, given the standard of living in the country, what we did was not unreasonable. I suppose this is a way of saying we're not particularly proud of the conditions, but we don't think we're guilty of gross neglect.

### Question Period

*The first question concerned the source for the figures on civilian casualties.*

*General Gard replied:*

Senator Kennedy's figures up to about 1967 would have to be divided by two, and those after 1967 divided by four. My information is based on reports from the Agency for International Development, the Vietnamese, and the military hospitals. I can tell you that contrary to the accusations of genocide, the population of South Vietnam has increased by two million since the introduction of our troops. But I can't give you any better figures than the data that have been collected on the scene. Hospital admissions are in the public record but not in my memory.

*The questioner suggested that perhaps the figures were something we would rather not keep.*

---

57. *Id.*

Of course we keep them. In this war we've tried to measure every-thing that could be measured in an attempt to assess progress.

*The questioner then suggested that General Gard had an inter-est in concealing the figures.*

No, sir, I am not trying to cover them up. I am just telling you that I don't know what they are. Some comparisons have been made of civilian casualties in World War II with those that have occurred in Vietnam. Those in Vietnam have been proportionately far lower. This isn't to say that I'm insensitive to civilian casualities or that I don't deplore them. It isn't even to say that there shouldn't have been far fewer. I'm just telling you I can't give you numbers. I'm sorry.

*The next questioner was Professor Steven Cohen. He suggested that perhaps there was a point at which civilian casualties became so great that a war would then be criminal regardless of its ends.*

*General Gard commented:*

Well, to begin with, it depends on whether you think there is any-thing worth fighting a war for. That is, is there anything other than the defense of your own territory—which is an aim I assume you would endorse—about which you're willing to fight? One man's collective defense is another man's criminal behavior. I think we get right back to trying to decide what aggressive war is and what it is not.

*Professor Taylor added:*

I thought the question was a little more limited than the one you've answered. I didn't think he meant whether just taking hundreds of thousands of lives is criminal, but whether taking innocent civilians' lives in that amount is or is not criminal. I don't think that makes the answer necessarily any easier, but I think that's the question we've got to address. Now, if we regard it simply in terms of numbers, and if the answer to your question is yes, then anything which takes innocent civilians' lives in large quantity is criminal. We would then have to backtrack and declare that the whole business of strategic air warfare as it was waged in World War II was criminal. We'd have to go even further back, because naval blockades are directed at the civilian population and, if they're effective, will result in the starving of women, children, the elderly, and the sick. Thus to say that military operations are criminal whenever they result in extensive deaths of noncombatant civilians would, I think, require unwinding a great deal that has been wound. Perhaps that should be done, but you can-not derive any principle like that from Nuremberg. You've got to derive it from somewhere else, if at all. There was no such general rule as that laid down at Nuremberg, nor is it laid down in any of the Hague or Geneva Conventions. Indeed, this is the very basis upon which our mutual friend Professor Wasserstrom undertakes to say the rules of war don't really make enough difference.

*Professor Farer:*

I would like to expand on that a little. It might be nice if we could go back to the Eighteenth Century type of war where small professional armies fought in open fields, more or less removed from the civilian population. I presume that no one will attribute the relatively restrained nature of those conflicts to a more refined moral sense. Obviously, it was just a question of what made sense militarily in terms of the total structure of the societies concerned. Today, if you find yourself in a war where your advantage consists, for example, in the ability to engage in aerial bombardment and the other side has an advantage in ground combat, what do you do? Suppose the only way to stop the Germans from engaging in genocide from 1940-1945 was to subject every German city to firebomb attacks? Or suppose the Allies had had nothing but nuclear weapons? Should we have used them? What do you think?

*Professor Cohen hesitated, thinking the question rhetorical, then asked if an answer were expected.*

*Professor Farer:*

Yes. I'm asking you. You're confusing two bodies of law. One defines the occasions when it is permissible to use force. The other body of law—the one with which we are principally concerned—is indifferent to the question of who acted justly or unjustly in getting into war. It is concerned solely with the question of how it should be fought once it has begun. You are suggesting that the two may link up because if you have to use certain horrible means to win, then even if your cause is just, you ought not to fight. A just end is not sufficient, you would say, to determine the justness of a war. You are properly concerned about the impact of the war upon "innocents." But particularly in a democratic state, where he elects his government, can a civilian be deemed wholly innocent? Even in authoritarian states there are difficulties. We have ample evidence, I think, that the German population supported the government and worked hard to implement its policies.

Before retiring for a moment, I want to pursue a proposition launched earlier by General Gard. The proposition is that aggressive war is largely a political rather than a legal concept. I don't really think that is what Professor Taylor argues in his book. Of course, he is the expert about what he meant, but as I at any rate interpreted it, he was saying that, because of its complexities, *this particular conflict* does not lend itself to legal characterization. This is quite different from saying that no instance of recourse to force is susceptible to legal appraisal. There are hard cases; there are easy ones. As General Gard pointed out, the German case is the easy case. There the plan was to acquire territory—*lebensraum*. As far as I am concerned, the U.N. Charter is sufficiently explicit about a much larger group of cases.

We had a forum two weeks ago in Washington where Paul Warnke, the former Assistant Secretary of Defense, seemed to reject even the hard cases. He seemed to say the standard was: is it in the national interest? That is the antithesis of the U.N. Charter, which says that force can be used only in self-defense, either individual or collective. I think one of the reasons we've come around to this view—at least at the level of rhetoric—is a concern with the anti-humanitarian impact of war.

*General Gard:*

The concept of collective self-defense is critical to what Professor Cohen is saying. The Kellogg-Briand Pact[58] established that resort to force is a bad idea in principle, but it seems to me that if you limit your concern to immediate threats to the security of your own country, you may foreclose taking early action in what could later become a widespread conflict. For example, you can posit a not totally unlikely case of the Soviets giving overwhelming support to the Egyptians against Israel, and I'm sure that many people who are basically against the use of force would endorse assistance for Israel, even with our own troops.

*Professor Taylor:*

I don't agree with General Gard that aggressive warfare is essentially a political problem. My objection to trying to adjudicate the validity of the American war in Vietnam is that there is no tribunal with jurisdiction and facilities equipped to do that. I don't think the concept as we tried to administer it at Nuremberg is essentially a political concept. It certainly had strong political overtones and, as a result, some unfortunate features. For example, the Russians sat on the Tribunal, and there were many people who would have said that they should have been subjected to trial themselves for crimes against

---

58. Treaty for the Renunciation of War as an Instrument of National Policy, *signed at Paris* August 27, 1928, [1929] 46 Stat. 2343, 94 L.N.T.S. 57.

the peace against Finland. However, the jurisdiction of the Tribunal was limited, and that was one of the unfortunate features of it.

But it ought to be possible, it seems to me, at least in some circumstances, to determine whether a war is aggressive or not by some kind of general principles that we would describe as legal. I am not troubled the way General Gard is by the definitional problem here. It is quite true that it is difficult—impossible, I think—to sit down and write a self-administering definition of aggressive war, but this comes to me as nothing so shocking. I've taught criminal law from time to time and have tried to instruct students in the metes and bounds of self defense. How does one determine whether physical aggression in the scale of one, two, or three people is self-defense or not? It's very difficult if you come across a street brawl between two people. How do you know who was the aggressor? It is legally permissible to come to the aid of somebody who's been attacked, but it may be very difficult to figure out who in fact that was. And so it's even more difficult if we encounter these difficulties in the dimension of a three-way street scrap, and we've never been able to write a definition of self-defense that will adequately resolve the innumerable possible circumstances in which the law and the facts are very difficult to ascertain. I don't find it shocking that there are international situations—as in the Middle East today—where determining who was the aggressor might pose very great difficulties.

When one comes to the adjudication of the Vietnam situation, there is still another problem. At Nuremberg, as General Gard has pointed out, territorial aggrandizement was involved, and territorial aggrandizement, I might add, is also not a self-defining expression. However, that's not the only problem. The German government certainly could be described as monolithic. There was a single will at the core that was determining national behavior, and individuals who were party to his statements and intentions knew what was going to happen. All had basically the same motivations. Washington is not like that. It may have its faults, but it is a product of shifting aggregations of power, and people may come to the same conclusions for quite different reasons. They may have had quite different motivations for approving or disapproving of what went on in Vietnam. So the attribution of individual criminal responsibility is much more difficult than it was with a dictatorship.

There are any number of other differences, and I have tried to elaborate them in the book to explain why I think it's next to impossible for a domestic American court to adjudicate this question accurately. That doesn't mean that I accept the notion that the lack of definition is fatal to such adjudication or that it's basically a political question. It is rather that I don't think we have the jurisdiction or the tools at the moment to solve it juridically.

*General Gard:*

I'd like to add one more thing. If you are going to abandon a war solely on the ground that you're killing hundreds of thousands of noncombatants, what would you have done in World War II? If I remember correctly, in capturing Manila alone there were tens of thousands of civilian casualities. Compound that with a number of other cities that were recaptured, and perhaps you would have drawn the conclusion that we should have stopped fighting. I think you are trying to say that there may be a point where the casualties become disproportionate to *any* justifiable goal, but it seems to me that it would be almost impossible to develop any kind of standard that could be applied rationally.

*Professor Jose A. Cabranes, the Chairman of the Colloquy, then interjected a question of his own. He noted that a year previous to the Colloquy, at the American Bar Association meeting in St. Louis, a panelist in a discussion sponsored by the International and Comparative Law section, indicated his feeling that the people, regardless of how high a level they are—whether they are on a Cabinet level, on a staff, counsel, or presidential level—that those people have to be prosecuted one way or another. Professor Cabranes asked the panel to comment.*

*Professor Taylor:*

What is required for the success of that sort of prosecution is the development of the favorable set of circumstances which did obtain after World War II. Subject to its limitations and failings, I think Nuremberg was a response to those conditions. But recall that the Nuremberg prosecutions came about after a total victory over an enemy, with resulting virtually complete access to his files and documents. We don't have anything like that here. The Nuremberg prosecutions also came about at a moment when the movement toward international law was very strong. The circumstances of World War II had generated a great deal of worldwide support for such a movement. And Justice Jackson referred specifically to that immediate situation as requiring that we exploit it and do the best we could with opportunities that were unlikely to occur again. I don't see those circumstances as being likely to develop out of the Vietnamese situation, and I don't see an international temper today that would summon the same kind of support for an international tribunal as in 1945 and 1946. If such circumstances were generated, then there would be nothing to prevent—and it would seem to me highly desirable—our doing what we did before but with different people in different situations. We might then try to give some continuity and feeling of generality to the principles of law employed at Nuremberg.

*Professor Farer commented:*

In the aftermath of Nuremberg, there was an effort to establish an international criminal court. But as Julius Stone has noted, "Events quickly showed it to be not acceptable, at any rate to the major states, and at the decisive level of competence to which the advocates of such a court aspired."[59] Efforts within the U.N. structure to draft an acceptable charter for such a court were finally suspended in 1957 by a resolution of the General Assembly in which the Assembly "decide[d] to defer consideration of an International Criminal Jurisdiction until such time as the General Assembly takes up again the question of defining aggression and the question of a draft code of offenses against the peace and security of mankind."[60] Well, they have been laboring over the definition of aggression for about eighteen years—quite diligently I'm sure—and they're now closer to agreement than they ever have been before. So perhaps that barrier will be crossed in the near future.

At that time, governments will encounter a problem I faced recently when I joined a group of private citizens attempting to draft a charter for an international criminal court. The group tended immediately to divide in two. One faction thought it would be simply splendid to have an international criminal court to try hijackers, people who kidnap ambassadors, and other rebels against the established order. The other group was primarily eager to prosecute prime ministers, presidents, and generals. [Laughter] This did make for a fairly incongruous assortment of people. Indeed, it would be surprising to find this precise collection again in the same room [laughter] working on a common project. Finding yourself in a room with people who have a fundamentally different conception of justice and world order induces a kind of cultural shock. Despite that little difficulty, we did manage to adopt a draft which I think compares rather favorably with those which are immured at the U.N.

---

59. Stone, *Introduction* to TOWARD A FEASIBLE INTERNATIONAL CRIMINAL COURT xi (J. Stone & R. Woetzel ed. 1970).

60. G.A. Res. 1187, 12 U.N. GAOR Supp. 18, at 52, U.N. Doc. A/3805 (1957).

It seems to me not inconceivable that an international court will be established in the foreseeable future. If it is, I foresee that it will have jurisdiction only over crimes such as assaults against officials. Genocide and other crimes against humanity will be ignored. Or, the Convention creating the court might contain a list of crimes and allow each signatory to select those with respect to which it accepts the court's jurisdiction. How many are likely to accept the court's jurisdiction over its officials for crimes against humanity? Why, the U.S. Senate won't even accept the substantive provisions of the Genocide Convention.

*General Gard:*

I suppose if international society eventually becomes more of a community, it might be possible to develop that sort of tribunal; I don't see it as feasible in the near term. In the context of Professor Farer's proposal, I'm sure that many here would want the individual I'm about to quote brought before such a court. He said:

> I'm opposed to unconditional American withdrawal from South Vietnam because such action would betray our obligations to people we've promised to defend, because it would weaken and destroy the credibility of American guarantees to other countries, and because such a withdrawal would encourage the view in Peking and elsewhere that guerrilla wars supported from the outside are relatively safe and inexpensive ways of expanding Communist power.[61]

The man who said that sponsored the Tonkin Gulf Resolution;[62] his name is J. William Fulbright.

*Professor Farer interjected:*

You'd have to have a statute of limitations.  [Laughter]

*General Gard:*

Yes, but where does guilt stop?  You indicated that you wanted to try the people who got us into the war, and he obviously was in an important position of leadership.

*The next questioner identified himself as being a Vietnam veteran. He suggested that the occurrence of war crimes in Vietnam had largely to do with hatred generated by differences, particularly racial differences.*

*Professor Farer:*

One relevant response would be that some of the worst war crimes have been committed on one another by people of the same race.  In

---

61. Citation unavailable.
62. H.R.J. Res., 1145, 88th Cong., 2d Sess., 78 Stat. 3840 (1964).

Pakistan, where I think one can begin to talk, without abusing the term, about decimation of genocidal proportions, the color of the protagonists is roughly the same.

*The questioner protested:*

It's not just a question of color, it's long hair, it's the national guard. . . . It's not just a question of color. . . .

*Professor Farer:*

Right—but you are conceding that there are multiple criteria for which people will kill each other on a massive scale—hair, color, class. . . . And in Ireland—what is it there? Religion!

*General Gard:*

I would like to point out that there was a deliberate attempt in previous wars, certainly in World War II, to indict people because of their nationality or because of their race, as with the Japanese. In this country, there's a very unfortunate practice of calling people by such names as wops, kikes, niggers, slopes—a practice which I hope we'll abandon. At least in this war, there was no national propaganda effort against the North Vietnamese as people.

*The next questioner suggested that perhaps the military had a responsibility not to let itself get pushed into a situation in which it didn't know how to operate and, as a result, cause such actions as the evacuation of civilians.*

*General Gard:*

What is really relevant to me as a soldier relates to what I said about the military professional perceiving himself as the instrument of duly constituted political authority. I know you would join me in saying that one thing none of us wants is for our armed forces to decide, on some kind of organized basis, which policy decisions they will obey and which they will not.

So far as evacuating citizens is concerned, that was done to protect lives, and was done with the specific approval of the constituted government. The subsequent use of air power or artillery in the evacuated areas was likewise done with the approval of the constituted government.

*Professor Taylor:*

Of course, in discussing the whole question of the importance, if any, of the approval of the South Vietnamese Government, I think we ought not overlook the fact that there are a number of provisions in the 1949 Conventions that are generally applicable, particularly portions of Article 3.[63]    These have relevance regardless of the nature of the South Vietnamese Government and whether its consent is of any importance or not.    These provisions are not as detailed or as extensive as some of the others, but one can't escape international obligations by saying that such-and-such was done with the consent of the South Vietnamese Government.

*Professor Farer:*

The whole notion that you have the right to commit barbarous acts if you have the consent of the host government really goes back to the idealization of the scorched earth policies pursued by the Russians, both in the Napoleonic wars and in the Second World War.    There's been an extraordinary amount of näivete associated with the perception of those two conflicts.    Many people talk about it as if every Russian peasant grabbed a torch, ran to his farmhouse, and set it aflame rather than have those French or German pigs move into it. My guess is that most peasants, whether they are Russians, or Vietnamese, or anything else, are not so committed to the national war effort that they want to see themselves, their family, their homes, and their villages destroyed.    I think that until recently we've tended to assume there's something wonderfully valorous about the scorched earth policy.    In fact, the scorched earth policy is normally an effort by a small elite that runs a government to preserve itself by sacrificing a significant proportion of its population.

Now I want to return to the fundamental question Professor Cohen raised, the question of why in the end are we so bitterly opposed to the war.    Is it just a question of the means being too outrageous to bring about a magnanimous end?    I don't think so.    One reason many people are opposed to the Vietnam War is the whole question of the perceived illegitimacy of the Saigon government.    Why? Because so much turns on whether the Saigon Government is a genuinely autonomous entity.    By virtually all the formal indices of international law, it is a legitimate government.    It is, for instance, widely recognized.    Of course, it is a fact that fifty, sixty, or seventy countries' governments will recognize just about *anything* if they are told to by their respective super-power patrons.    But in this case recogni-

---

63. Article 3, common to all three Geneva Conventions (Geneva—Civilians, Geneva—Prisoners of War, Geneva—Wounded and Sick), provides (emphasis added):
> In the case of armed conflict *not of an international character* occurring in the territory of one of the High Contracting Parties, each Party to the conflict shall be bound to apply, as a minimum, the following provisions:
> (1) Persons taking no active part in the hostilities . . . shall in all circumstances be treated humanely . . . .

tion does rest upon some objective fact. First, Saigon does control a part of South Vietnam, even if the U.S. helps Saigon's shifting guard to remain in control. Secondly, the Saigon regime is accepted by many international organizations as the legitimate representative of the South Vietnamese people.

If, however, you look beneath the surface, this is really a colonial regime. It was created by the French, and we have maintained it since their departure. There was no true interregnum between the colonial period and the post-colonial period. But, that is equally true of a number of other states. At least several of the French West African territories, for example, are essentially dependencies of the French Government. So I recognize that, in questioning the legitimacy of our puppet (or, if you will, Frankenstein), I may appear to be challenging a central assumption about the international legal order. In any event, legitimacy in its legal sense is not an important issue for the anti-war movement. Rather, it is the cruelty and greed and corruption and ineptness which emanate from Saigon. We do not believe it can preside over a relatively decent modernization process.

*General Gard:*

There's one additional thing. We have an understandable inclination to apply our standards of political legitimacy to countries to which our standards may be very foreign. I do not want to comment on the National Government of South Vietnam, but I can tell you that I have personally observed local elections[64] which by our standards were perfectly legitimate—and, if I understand the Vietnamese circumstances correctly, the district and the village are about as far as the average person's political cognizance extends. Local officials serve with great courage because, of the some 120 Viet Cong assassinations per week, many of the victims are these very officials. Nonetheless, they continue to run for office.

*The next question was put by Mr. Harold Staenberg:*

I would like to ask a question of Professor Taylor. Going back to the My Lai situation and your indication that one of the problems was a failure of proper indoctrination, and, having been in the service and having been in World War II and having a feeling that over the years from that time to the present there has been a breakdown—a deterioration of the attitude of gentlemanliness—I feel that we are going to hear and see more and more of the My Lai situation. And are we not seeing more and more of the deterioration of gentlemanliness as long as the people of our country are constantly in the war situation?

---

64. Some, although not all, of which were later suspended (ed.'s note).

*Professor Taylor:*

You mean, I take it, that if things like Vietnam go on at length there will be an erosion and a deterioration of standards from long exposure to it. Well, that may be. I think, however, that we've got a slightly different problem in South Vietnam because, with the anomalous situation of the government there, it's very difficult to tell what South Vietnam is. Gentlemanly is really the wrong word to use. Controlled, disciplined behavior *vis-a-vis* the enemy is perhaps easier to achieve than the kind of thing one needs for South Vietnam. Certainly our objectives there, if properly understood at the beginning, must have been rather more political and social than military. If I'm rightly informed, the opposition within the Department of Defense—among those who, like General Gavin, were opposed to it from the beginning—was that *military* means weren't well adapted to the objectives we were trying to achieve in South Vietnam. Now, if we are going to use military means it seems to me that the degree of indoctrination, training, restraint, and general education required to operate effectively in Vietnam in pursuit of the political objectives was far greater than it was in World War II. In Vietnam, we are fighting in a country totally unfamiliar to most of our troops, with a racial problem injected immediately, with no front line, with all the difficulties General Gard has mentioned about identifying enemy and friend, and all of these things put a strain on troop conduct which I suspect was a good deal greater than most of what was encountered in World War II.[65]

Now, as to whether having World War II and then Korea and then South Vietnam is going to result in a further deterioration of standards, I really don't know how to answer that. I don't know whether we are really getting out of Vietnam or not, whether this is going to be a thing which will rapidly die off, or whether we're fooling ourselves, and we're still in there on a military basis for a long time to come. It also comes back, of course, to the point that Professor Farer was speaking to a while ago about the extent to which a Calley trial is a deterrent which powerfully influences behavior in the future. That, in turn, gets us back to the question of the general criminal law and what value there is in punishment—what deterrent effect it ever does have. If Calley's had not been an isolated conviction—if it were simply one of several systematic efforts to impose sanctions upon violations of the laws of war—I would agree that it served a purpose. But if we are

---

65. One can find, however, some very interesting parallels between the problems we have had in South Vietnam and what the Germans faced in the Balkans during World War II. (Note by Professor Taylor).

going to come out of this whole My Lai episode with a conviction of Lieutenant Calley and nobody else, and that seems to me where we're going to come out, then I think most of the deterrent value will be lost because everybody will say that it is absolutely absurd to try to place the whole criminal responsibility for a violation of this magnitude on one person, however blameworthy he may have been. It will be seen as an aberrant thing, rather than as a systematic sanction of the sort we expect in regular criminal law.

*General Gard commented on the same question:*

I'd like to add a comment concerning the thrust of the question. Maybe just the reverse is happening. World War II, for example, was virtually unlimited as to the application of force. Nobody worried very much about the fact that we killed thousands of noncombatants; it was just unfortunate. It was justified not only by saving the lives of our troops, but also by saving time. In Korea, there were certain limitations on the use of force, but very few on the bombing of North Korea, and little concern for resultant civilian casualties. But in the Vietnam case, there is a public outcry, and public trials during the war of our own troops for war crimes.[66] There is, I would contend, a considerable degree of concern in our society today for noncombatants, a genuine concern for their safety. It's been reflected here, in this room. You most certainly didn't hear anything like this after the Korean War. I do believe that our society and our military are far more concerned about these humanitarian considerations than ever before.

*Another questioner picked up the same issue and pressed it further:*

I think that in World War II we felt we were protecting ourselves as best we might. The difference is today, we are very much opposed to our involvement because we feel we may be criminals in just being there. I think the public itself has judged this to be wrong.

*General Gard:*

That's what I'm saying.

*The questioner persisted:*

But I think if we were attacked by another nation the day after tomorrow, public opinion would be just as it was in World War II. I don't think we would continue with this sense of guilt that we have

---

66. To be precise, of course, the soldiers being tried are specifically charged with violations of the UNIFORM CODE OF MILITARY JUSTICE, 10 U.S.C. § 801 *et. seq.* (1970).

about the fighting in Vietnam. However, the suggestion was that there is a deterioration of our own morals in this country because of the long stretch of military activity.

*General Gard:*

However inadequately, that's what I was trying to address. My argument is that it is a hopeful sign that we are concerned about such considerations as the proper conduct of a war while the war is going on. We really never have been before.

*Professor Charles Jones asked Professor Farer for clarification as to what charges he thought might be brought against the upper echelon people in the United States Government.*

*Professor Farer:*

I think we will all want to get in on this question.

At a minimum, I would charge them with acquiescence in certain kinds of behavior conceded to be illegal, such as torture and the summary execution of civilian suspects which appears to have characterized the Phoenix Program. I trust General Gard will have something to say about it.

For those unfamiliar with Phoenix, this was the name given to the program for getting at the Viet Cong infrastructure, as it's called— the Viet Cong civilian leadership in the villages. I talked to a fellow who was a lieutenant out in Vietnam doing intelligence work, and I asked him was it, or was it not, an assassination program. He said in large measure it was an assassination program. We trained people, generally the thuggish dregs of Vietnamese society, to go out and eliminate people we had identified to our satisfaction as being Viet Cong leaders. The laws of war make it quite clear that you have to try to capture suspects and then provide them with a fair trial. If they resist capture, and you have a fire fight, they may be killed, but you can't go out and execute them. That's black letter law.

Ambassador Komer, who ran the program, conceded in Congressional testimony that some people were killed. But, he said, it was at the beginning, and the trouble was that the Vietnamese didn't realize that this was a politically sophisticated program; before we kind of wised them up as to the way the program would work, a few of them ran wild. We finally harnessed them and things are going fine now. Maybe. But a recent *New York Times* report placed the number killed at somewhere around 20,000.[67] Were they all resisting arrest?

---

67. N.Y. Times, Oct. 4, 1972, at 3, col. 1, *citing* unpublished Report of House Foreign Operations and Government Information Subcommittee, put the number of sus-

A second set of charges might be made in cases where the facts are clear, but the law is unclear. Tear gas is one example. Most people don't take the tear gas argument seriously. They say, "Look, it's used in domestic society all the time, so how could there be a customary rule of law precluding its use in conflicts of an international character?" At first, that seems like a pretty telling rhetorical question, but in fact there are important distinctions between the use of tear gas in domestic society and in international wars. The most important distinction is that in domestic cases, it's usually used humanely as a substitute for bullets. In Vietnam, although initially it may have been used as a substitute, it eventually became a prelude. You got people out in the open, and then you cut them down with shrapnel and bullets. Necessarily you rooted out not only suspected Viet Cong in bunkers, but also the inhabitants of the village who all had their own little tunnels to protect them from U.S. bombing. They were rooted out by the gas and cut to pieces. That's one difference between the use of tear gas in domestic society and the use of tear gas in international society, and it's coupled with the fact that in domestic society you usually have forces of public opinion to restrain escalation in the use of gas. You don't have that force when you're dealing with the "enemy," so not only do you escalate in terms of using the gas as a prelude to bullets, but you also escalate by moving closer and closer in the kind of gas you use or the dosage you use to the lethal end of the effects continuum. When people say a gas is nonlethal, what they mean is that ordinary doses on ordinary people are not lethal. Use greater doses, slightly more lethal gas, and eventually it becomes lethal for a certain number of people. That's one problem. Another problem is that in a war zone, because of inadequate food and the breakdown of sanitary and medical services, most people are not "ordinary"—they're weak and sick and therefore more subject to serious injury or death from gas than people affected in a riot. For all these reasons, as well as the weight of practice and opinion, it is by no means nonsensical or absurd to argue that there is a customary rule against the use of gas—tear gas or any other kind—in international conflicts.

In addition to the various specific charges for which I believe there is a prima facie case of criminality, one might conclude that the pervasive tendency of our leaders to resolve questions of law in favor of

---

pected Viet Cong agents killed between 1968 and May of 1971 at 20,587. In an earlier report, the *Times* had put the number of Viet Cong "neutralized" (killed, captured, jailed or defected) for 1970 at 22,341. N.Y. Times, Aug. 2, 1971, at 2, col. 7.

use of force, in favor of injuring the population or sacrificing the population for alleged military objectives, suggests in its totality an indifference to the distinction between combatants and noncombatants, a distinction which is fundamental to the laws of war.

*General Gard:*

Well, I feel the way I did when I was a graduate student, and my professor startled me by saying, "Ja, ja, I agree with your reasons but not your conclusions." The more I hear Tom Farer talk, the more I agree with his reasons but not his conclusions.

First, let me say that, so far as tear gas is concerned, I have no problem in principle with outlawing something internationally even though we use it domestically. I personally think the advantage is probably on the side of eliminating the use of all gas in warfare, including tear gas. But that's not the position of our Government which, as you know, has included a reservation in its interpretation of the Convention involved. We want to be able to continue to apply herbicides and tear gas for certain limited purposes. As for "free fire zones," the words themselves imply that you could shoot anything that moved in the area. I would certainly concede that the term itself is unfortunate and should never have been used. Though it was changed in 1965, it seems to linger on because people tend to use familiar names from habit. "Free fire zone" really meant only that the military was excused from obtaining clearance from the political authority; all the other rules of engagement applied. These zones were located mainly in remote areas where, if there were any people left at all, they were very few and very scattered. What few there were, we tried to evacuate.

The phrase "saturation bombing" has practically become one word, in the same way that "unrestricted" always appears before the term "use of firepower." But I was just over in Vietnam and flew from Saigon down into the Delta. I flew over areas in which we'd fought relatively large actions, and it was very difficult to find even the scars of artillery rounds. Right now in Europe there's more devastation still perceivable from World War II than you'd be able to find in the populated areas of Vietnam. The phrase "saturation bombing" calls up a mental image of something that simply never occurred. So far as "the judgment was always made in favor of the use of force" is concerned, I can assure you that many requests for B-52 strikes in areas of the Delta were denied. In the whole area—I suppose I must have operated in about ten provinces—I saw two B-52 strikes in a year, and they were in remote areas with no inhabitants or cultivated fields.

I think that people have the impression that Vietnam probably looks something like Berlin after World War II. That's simply an erroneous image.

*Professor Taylor:*

As to the question of "free fire zone," I think another dimension ought to be put on it to round out the picture. I'm not contesting the factual observations of General Gard at all, but I do think there's more to be said. The change in name, I'm sure we agree, is not really germane to the issue here. It's not going to do anybody any good to call a thing by a nicer name and, indeed, the change in name perhaps indicates sensitivity on the point more than anything else.

I believe General Gard is quite right when he speaks about the directives here. Once again, to the best of my knowledge, the official directives on this did not mean that, once such a zone was declared, anybody who moved in there was fair game. The directives stipulated that "free fire zone" was simply a release from the necessity for obtaining political approval. Here again we come to the question of whether the practice at all corresponded to the directive, and General Gard's observations may or may not accord with those of others. As he said, Vietnam is not all alike, and the American units that operate there aren't all alike. The necessities and circumstances in one area may have been quite different from those in the Delta, and the training and practice of one air unit or artillery unit may have been quite different from those of another. This could account for a great deal of the variety of observation that we seem to encounter. Given the volume of civilian casualties (and even if we do cut Senator Kennedy's numbers in two, we're still left with a total which is sufficiently appalling), I'm bound to say that I don't think that we can solve this by saying that the directives were right or that things in the Delta didn't look too bad, because I think that still leaves a large area for inquiry. That's precisely why it seems to me that it would be best for the Army, best for the nation, best for everybody, if we could have a commission of inquiry with subpoena power that would illuminate some of these factual discrepancies. Otherwise, they will remain to prick the conscience and, perhaps, give rise to unfounded suspicions for years to come.

*General Gard:*

I don't disagree in principle. I admitted my perspective was limited. I do know that where I operated, the area into which I could *not* shoot was larger than that into which I could; I know also that units elsewhere in Vietnam were operating under the same set of rules.

Any time we scratched a Vietnamese civilian with fragmentation from the artillery or from the air there was a formal written investigation by someone not a member of the unit involved. While there is evidence that some military excesses occurred, I believe it should be noted that although all such instances are regrettable, civilian casualties in Vietnam do not appear to be disproportionately high compared to other wars in modern times, especially World War II and Korea.

I can address Phoenix if anyone is interested; otherwise, in response to the caveat on limited time available, perhaps Professor Farer and I can discuss it privately. Let me simply state that I was briefed by Mr. Komer in Vietnam as the prospective top American military officer on the program. Although I was not assigned to Phoenix, it was clear from the briefing that assassination was not the objective. Indeed, it would be counterproductive in "rooting out" the infrastructure.

*Mr. Richard Feldman, a student at Rutgers Law School, asked General Gard to elaborate on what he meant when he said traditional military professionalism and the laws of war did not apply in the guerilla situation and to the Viet Cong in particular. He also asked Professor Taylor and Professor Farer to comment on what we have learned from the Vietnam experience.*

*General Gard:*

What I tried to say in my opening remarks was that we had trouble adapting our traditional tactical concepts of military operations to a situation that was very different from a conventional war, and far more complex. That is why I said that, not just for moral, but also for purely professional reasons, I would like to see an unbiased examination of the application of the military instrument in pursuit of political objectives in Vietnam. The initial objectives were relatively simple for us: go in and defeat the main force units. We were trained for that; it was the kind of mission the American military received traditionally. The more difficult problem arose when we found ourselves in the guerrilla phase of the conflict, trying to defeat the enemy military force but having a great deal of difficulty locating it. In spite of the lack of precise applicability of the Nuremberg precedents and the Geneva Conventions, we did try to interpret them liberally and apply them in Vietnam.

*Professor Farer:*

On the question of what can be done, it may be useful at the outset to recall that the experience in Vietnam is not unique. The Germans engaged in considerable anti-guerrilla warfare in the Balkans and in Russia. Looking further back, there was virulent guerrilla warfare in Spain waged against the French during the Napoleonic period. There is no doubt, however, that guerrilla warfare is far more common today. Moreover, although it generally breaks out between factions within a country, there is almost invariably some degree of foreign involvement and concern. It is this latter feature, the intensity of international concern, which really seems to distinguish the present era.

During the "classical" period of international law, which I measure from the Treaty of Westphalia in 1648 to the middle decades of our own century, the international community was normally uninterested in what the government in power was doing to maintain itself. Now, even in purely civil conflicts there's a growing concern with the way the conflict is conducted, as is illustrated by the civil wars in Nigeria and Pakistan. The international community is beginning to assert a right of supervision. Thus in order to maximize their freedom to appropriate the most effective means for crushing rebellions, elites—particularly in the numerous states which always appear to be trembling on the edge of rebellion—tend to oppose increased specification of their humanitarian obligations. Just last June there was a conference of law-of-war experts in Geneva which was designed to lay the foundation for a subsequent diplomatic conference with a mandate for revision of the Geneva Conventions in the light of recent conflicts. Proposals for rather comprehensive extension of the Conventions to civil conflicts are reported to have received a fairly glacial reaction. And the glacial reaction doesn't come particularly from the major powers. It often comes from the governments of the developing states, who may not be pleased with U.S. policy in Vietnam, but who are absolutely determined to maintain themselves in power against their own potential rebels. It's extremely difficult to get governments to adopt, before the fact, a whole set of limitations on what they'd like to see as their discretion to deal with armed conflict as it arises.

But there remain some clear rules. Torture is *out*. Terror bombing—where you don't simply kill a lot of civilians in the process of destroying a military objective but actually go in and kill civilians in order to destroy morale—that's *out*. (You'll note that the Nigerian Federal Government during its civil war made very strenuous efforts to demonstrate that it was *not* engaged in that kind of behavior.) Summary execution of prisoners is also beyond the pale. The trouble is that there are an awful lot of things that are still in, and, as a consequence, a lot of people get killed.

Professor Richard A. Falk of Princeton has argued that an anti-guerrilla war by a high technology power like the United States has what he calls a genocidal momentum.[68]  He means that once the guerrillas have won the support of a substantial segment of the population, it becomes virtually impossible to separate the guerrilla from his popular base.  So, those who have the means simply begin to destroy everyone in "infested" areas.  The rules of war are kicked aside.

This is not inevitable in guerrilla conflict because in many instances the guerrillas are wiped out by superior technology before the necessary rapport with the population has been achieved.  All of the efforts to establish guerrilla enclaves in Latin America—Colombia, Venezuela, Bolivia, and so on—exemplify this failure.  The case of Vietnam is significantly affected by the fact that it is as much a colonial war as a kind of ideological insurgency.  The cadres of the N.L.F. and their northern patrons enjoy a special legitimacy earned during the colonial struggle.  Moreover, while defeating the French, they established relationships with large chunks of the Vietnamese population. When the Americans replaced the French and Diem's repression began, the rebellion did not start from scratch.

*Professor Taylor declined to comment further on Vietnam as a learning experience, feeling that he had already covered all he could on that point.  Professor Cabranes then referred the question to General Gard, asking him to focus particularly on whether his colleagues in the military establishment shared his desire for a full-scale, broad-based inquiry.*

*General Gard replied:*

Well, contrary to popular perception, we, in what's called the "military establishment," do hold different views.  I would like to see an inquiry, but not just from the standpoint of war crimes, because I think legal concepts are being used to voice moral outrage.  I would like to see such an inquiry done by a carefully constituted group of reasonably objective analysts.  There are numbers of people in uniform very troubled by questions concerning the application of military force in Vietnam, who I think would endorse what I'm saying.  There are others who feel that an objective analysis is not feasible, and still others who believe we shouldn't drag all this back out again for no really useful purpose.

Let me close with the statement that everyone I know in the mili-

---

68. Falk, unpublished paper presented at a symposium conducted in Fall 1971 by the American Society of International Law.

tary is in agreement that we do want prohibitory laws of war. We feel that they must remain in effect, and we do want them enforced.

## EPILOGUE

### Comment by Professor Farer

A year has passed since the colloquy recorded above. During that year the United States has cast off nearly all of the remaining tattered restraints which bound us to the shadow of humanity. In North Vietnam we have bombed hospitals and schools, while either denying the eyewitness accounts of neutral observers or claiming accident. We have openly destroyed factories and power plants—and in the process homes and people—without the slightest effort to demonstrate any significant relationship between the targets and the prosecution of the war in the South. And finally, we have moved agonizingly close to genocide by *any* definition as we have bombed the fragile system of dikes which represents the margin of life for ten million people. It has been done under cover of wildly conflicting claims: that no dikes have ever been bombed, that there may have been a few accidents, or that the dikes were only the incidental victims of strikes against "legitimate" targets such as roads or trucks which crossed them—as if the principle of proportionality did not exist.

In the South, and in Laos and Cambodia, we bomb everywhere. There have been B-52 saturation raids within thirty miles of Saigon. If we were to meet again today, I wonder whether General Gard would still imply that blind, indiscriminate bombing occurred only in virtually empty parts of Indochina. I wonder whether he would again tell us that the scars on the face of Indochina are no worse than the remnants of World War II in Europe.

We came to Indochina, we said, as nation-builders. And it is nations we have built, nations of widows and orphans, of amputees and refugees. We have built for the future. What we have done there will not soon be forgotten.

### Comment by General Gard

Now that six more months have passed, Professor Farer's epilogue can be placed in context. It was written at the time of the brief, but intensive, bombing campaign in North Vietnam leading to the agreement for withdrawal of all U.S. forces and return of our prisoners.

Professor Taylor, who opposed this bombing campaign in general and the use of B-52's in urban areas in particular, reported from his own eyewitness observations that despite accidental damage to a hospital, there was no evidence to indicate that civilian property was attacked intentionally.[69]    The total number of casualties, as reported by Hanoi, were fewer "than the number of civilians killed by the North Vietnamese in their artillery bombardment of An Loc in April, or the toll of refugees ambushed when trying to escape from Quang Tri at the beginning of May."[70]    It is now obvious that there was no attempt to create destruction by bombing dikes.    With only minimum effort, floods on the scale of those caused by heavy rainfall the year before would have been easy to induce, but there was no flooding.

If we were to meet again, I see no reason to change my position on the application of firepower.

---

69. Personal communication to General Gard by Professor Taylor.
70. *The Use of Air Power,* THE ECONOMIST, Jan. 13, 1973, at 15.

# A Response to Telford Taylor's "Nuremberg and Vietnam: An American Tragedy"[1]

## WALDEMAR A. SOLF[*]

UNDER THE headline "Military Made the Scapegoat for Vietnam," Charles G. Moskos, Jr., Chairman of the Department of Sociology, Northwestern University, examines (1) the attitudes and behavior of combat soldiers in Vietnam and (2) the reaction of elite groups in our society. Professor Moskos commented:

> It is a cruel irony that so many of our national leaders and opinion shapers who were silent or supported the original intervention during the Kennedy administration now adopt moralistic postures in the wake of the horrors of that war. There appears to be emerging a curious American inversion of the old "stab in the back" theory. Where the German general staff succeeded in placing the blame for the loss of World War I on the ensuing civilian leadership of the Weimar Republic, the liberal Establishment in America now seems to have embarked on placing the onus of the Vietnam adventure on the military.
>
> . . . [A] minor industry exists in the production of books and lectures castigating the military mind, the Pentagon, and GI butchers.
>
> . . . It would not be too far afield to say that antimilitarism has become the anti-Semitism of the intellectual community.[2]

Professor Telford Taylor,[3] who is best remembered as Justice Robert H. Jackson's successor as Chief of Counsel at Nuremberg after the War Crimes trial of the major war criminals, became an instant giant of the new industry by suggesting that if one were to apply to Dean Rusk, Robert McNamara, McGeorge Bundy, Walt Rostow and General William Westmoreland the same standards that were applied in the trial of General Tomoyuki Yamashita "there would be a very strong possibility that they

---

* Acting Chief, International Affairs Division, Office of The Judge Advocate General, Department of the Army. A.B., University of Chicago; J.D., University of Chicago Law School. The views herein are those of the author and do not necessarily constitute the views of the Judge Advocate General, Department of the Army or any other agency of the United States government.

1 T. TAYLOR, NUREMBERG AND VIETNAM: AN AMERICAN TRAGEDY. Random House, 1970. Pp. 224.

2 WAR CRIMES AND THE AMERICAN CONSCIENCE 175-181 (Knoll & McFadden eds. 1970).

3 Columbia University Law School. Professor Taylor teaches Constitutional Law.

would come to the same end as he did."[4] This suggestion by the person described on the dust jacket as "U.S. Chief Counsel at Nuremberg" inevitably elevates Professor Taylor to the status of a first magnitude star among the scapegoat makers.

Regretably, Professor Taylor produced a work replete with demonstrable errors of law and contradictions. He thereby forfeits the opportunity to assume a place among the very few who are qualified by experience and academic standing to produce "trustworthy evidence" of what international law really is.[5] There are, of course, too many who, without experience in the field, write at length about what it ought to be [6] and some who affirm that it is what it is not.[7]

## PROFESSOR TAYLOR'S CHARGES

Stated broadly, Taylor attributes to influential policy makers criminal culpability under three categories:

### 1. *Commander's Responsibility for Acts of Subordinates*

As the senior American commander in Vietnam, General Westmoreland is vicariously liable for failing to prevent atrocities committed by troops under his command. These include:

a. Slaughter of villagers.

b. Wanton destruction of property.

c. Complicity in the torture of prisoners by the South Vietnamese.

d. Murder of prisoners of war.

### 2. *Unnecessary Killing and Devastation resulting from Tactical Decisions*

The manner in which military operations were conducted occasioned loss of life and unnecessary suffering disproportionate to the military advantage gained. Under this charge, Taylor mentions the forced resettlement of rural families, the creation of "free-fire" zones, and devastation of large areas of the country in order to expose the insurgents.

---

[4] Interview with Professor Taylor on the Dick Cavett show on Jan. 8, 1971, as reported in the N.Y. Times, Jan. 9, 1971, at 3, col. 1.

[5] *See* Mr. Justice Gray's comments in *Pacquete Habana*, 175 U.S. 677, 700 (1900).

[6] Speculation as to the interpretation of treaties, or the practice of nations is a legitimate enterprise which may influence the development of international law.

[7] Altering the text of a multilateral treaty appears to be a brand new approach. Compare the text of the Annex to Hague Convention IV, *Regulations Respecting the Law and Customs of War on Land,* as published in 2 FALK, THE VIETNAM WAR AND INTERNATIONAL LAW, 500ff (1969), *with* the official text in 36 STAT. 2277; T.S. No. 539; II Malloy Treaties at 2269. One criticism levelled at law making treaties on the law of war is that they are hindsight oriented to the experience of the last war. But if the Falk text is correct, the 1907 Hague Regulations anticipated strategic bombing some eight or nine years before the first enterprising observation pilot thought it expedient to toss a grenade from the cockpit of his plane.

### 3. The Strategic Charge

The decision to use military rather than political means of aiding South Vietnam did not gain a military advantage and was therefor unnecessary. Unnecessary military violence is criminal.

These charges will be discussed in reverse order.

## THE STRATEGIC CHARGE

In discussing President Johnson's strategic decision of 1965, when confronted with a deteriorating situation, to deploy large mobile forces to Vietnam, Taylor implies that military success supplies its own justification of military necessity. Conversely, he implies that military failure is proof that no military advantage was to be gained by the course of action followed and that the resulting ravages of war are therefore unnecessary. He quotes with approval Colonel Corson's view [8] that:

> ". . . American judgment as to the effective prosecution of the war was faulty from beginning to end"; that we became "over-involved militarily in the armed forces of the present, under-involved politically in the human forces of the future"; and that in the upshot our political and military leaders alike lost sight of the old law of war that "it is a mistake, illegal and immoral, to kill people without clear military advantage in a war." [9]

Stating the objective of U.S. policy in Vietnam to be "to stop Communism at the 17th parallel," Taylor suggests that the strategy selected in 1965 involving the use of mobility and massive fire power by large military forces foreseeably resulted in high civilian casualties and property destruction. In his view this course of action was not successful in achieving the stated objective, and, therefore, the casualties and devastation could not be justified by military necessity.[10]

Taylor's view of how the Vietnam conflict should have been conducted is one which cannot be assessed conclusively except by the judgment of history. The concept that unsuccessful military operations are their own proof of unnecessary violence injects a new dimension — *res ipsa loquitur* — to the basic principle of military necessity as justification for the violence of war.

Military necessity was stated at Nuremberg as permitting:

> [A] belligerent, *subject to the laws of war*, to apply any amount and kind of force to compel the complete submission of the enemy with the least possible expenditure of time, life, and money. . . . It permits the destruction of life of armed enemies and other persons whose

---

[8] R. CORSON, THE CHANGING NATURE OF WAR (1970).

[9] TAYLOR, *supra* note 1, at 188.

[10] *Id.* at 189-192.

destruction is incidentally unavoidable by the armed conflict of the war; . . . but it does not permit the killing of innocent inhabitants for purposes of revenge or the satisfaction of a lust to kill. . . . It does not admit the wanton devastation of a district or the willful infliction of suffering for the sake of suffering alone.[11] (Emphasis added.)

The Nuremberg courts considered it to be their duty to consider the defense of military necessity in the light of the facts and circumstances as they appeared to a decision maker at the time he made his decision; not on the basis of hindsight. Some of these circumstances, omitted from Taylor's perspective, are:

By 1964 the Vietcong were preparing for the third or final phase of insurgency — the formation of conventional armed forces to destroy the Saigon Government — while simultaneously stepping up guerrilla and political warfare. A Vietcong division was formed for the final phase. In December 1964 it attacked the village of Binh Gia, 40 miles east of Saigon, and virtually annihilated two South Vietnamese battalions. At the same time, the first commitment of regular North Vietnamese Army regiments had taken place near Dak To in the Central Highlands.

Capitalizing on the political disorders which affected the Saigon government, upon the infirmity of government administration throughout the country, and the deteriorating morale of the Vietnamese armed forces, the North Vietnamese and the Vietcong were moving in for the kill. Additional North Vietnamese forces were on the move through Laos.

---

[11] United States v. List, XI TRIALS OF WAR CRIMINALS BEFORE THE NUREMBERG MILITARY TRIBUNALS U.S. GPO 1253-54 (1950-51). [Hereinafter cited as TRIALS OF WAR CRIMINALS.] One of the more interesting contradictions in Taylor's book is his apparent approval of the repudiated German doctrine of military necessity (*Kriegsraison*) which proclaimed that any action—whether or not prohibited by the law of war—may be taken if it is necessary for the purposes of war. (*See* United States v. Von Leeb, XI TRIALS OF WAR CRIMINALS, *supra* at 541 for the rejection of *Kriegsraison*.) He refers to the emphatic prohibitions of conventional and customary law of war against the killing of prisoners of war, and suggests that these absolute prohibitions may be disregarded under the "operation of military necessity." In a footnote he states that:

> The Lieber rules of 1863 recognized this necessity by providing that a commander may be permitted to direct his troops to give no quarters, in great straits, when his own salvation makes it *impossible* to cumber himself with prisoners. The . . . recent Army manuals contain no comparable provision.

TAYLOR, *supra* note 1, at 35-36. Indeed they do not. Paragraph 85 of the 1956 FIELD MANUAL, *The Law of Land Warfare*, provides:

> A commander may not put his prisoners to death because their presence retards his movements or diminishes his power of resistance. . . . It is likewise unlawful for a commander to kill his prisoners on grounds of self preservation, even in the case of airborne or commando operations . . . .

Military necessity cannot be used to justify acts forbidden by the law of war inasmuch as necessity was discounted in framing the prohibitory rule. A moment's reflection should show that it is never necessary to kill a disarmed prisoner. If the military mission is such that prisoners might "cumber" the unit, their weapons can be destroyed and the prisoner be bound where they can be later recovered by their friends.

The weakness of the government stemmed in part from the fact that since 1962 there had been over 6,000 assassinations and 30,000 kidnappings among the civilian population. 463 government officials had been assassinated and 1,113 had been kidnapped in 1964 alone.

By the late spring of 1965, the South Vietnamese Army was losing each week almost one infantry battalion to enemy action. Moreover, the enemy was gaining control of at least one district capital town each week.

Pacification programs and land reform could not continue in the face of the deteriorating security situation. The Government, unable to meet the crisis with its own resources, called for the support of U.S. ground forces.[12]

Bernard Fall's contemporary judgment of the 1965 decision to deploy ground forces to Vietnam is that:

> [It resulted in] the First Battle of the Marne of the Vietnamese war, . . . no turning point as yet, but a halt to the runaway disaster.
>
> In South Vietnam, after being stopped at Chu-Lai, Plei-Me and the Ia-Drang, the Communist regulars lost enough of their momentum for the time being not to be able to bring about the military and political collapse of the Saigon government late in 1965 — a situation which would have altogether closed out the American "option" of the conflict.[13]

Whatever may be the judgment of history as to whether President Johnson had any other alternative, hindsight is not one of the tools legitimately used by courts in assessing criminal liability for the use of unnecessary force. As early as 1851, in a case arising out of the war with Mexico, the Supreme Court had occasion to comment:

> In deciding upon . . . necessity, the state of the facts as they appeared to the officer at the time he acted, must govern the decision; for he must necessarily act upon information of others as well as his own observation. And if, with such information as he had a right to rely upon, there is reasonable grounds for believing that the peril is immediate and menacing, or the necessity urgent, he is justified upon it; and the discovery afterwards that it was false or erroneous will not make him a trespasser. . . ."[14]

Even more cogent is the judgment of the tribunal of which Professor Taylor was Chief of Counsel in the case of General Lothar Rendulic. In order to provide his forces with time in which to evade advancing Russian forces, General Rendulic adopted a scorched earth policy which devastated the Norwegian province of Finmark. The inhabitants were

---

[12] Westmoreland, Report on the War in Vietnam, U.S. GPO 197-198 (1968).
[13] B. FALL, LAST REFLECTION ON A WAR 172 (1967).
[14] Mitchell v. Harmony, 54 U.S. (13 How.) 420 (1851).

evacuated and all villages, housing, communications and transport facilities were completely destroyed. In retrospect, it appears that the devastation was not necessary. Rendulic was charged with wanton destruction not justified by military necessity. On these facts the court commented:

> We are not called upon to determine whether urgent military necessity for the devastation and destruction of Finmark actually existed. We are concerned with the question whether the defendant at the time of its occurrence acted within the limits of honest judgment on the basis of the conditions prevailing at the time. The course of a military operation by the enemy is loaded with uncertainties, such as the numerical strength of the enemy, the quality of his equipment, his fighting spirit, the efficiency and daring of his commanders, and the uncertainty of his intentions . . . . It is our considered opinion that the conditions, as they appeared to the defendant at the time were sufficient upon which he could honestly conclude that urgent military necessity warranted the decision made. This being true, the defendant may have erred in the exercise of his judgment but he was guilty of no criminal act. We find the defendant not guilty on this portion of the charge.[15]

Taylor was not oblivious to these principles. He searched for evidence that, by the exercise of reasonable diligence, it would have been foreseeable in 1965 that the strategy of mobility and firepower was not suitable to the attainment of the stated objective. The evidence he cited are expressions of German diplomats protesting that the massacre of Klissura and reprisal shootings of villagers ordered by Nazi commanders only served to strengthen guerrillas hiding in the woods and mountains of Greece and Yugoslavia.[16]

The relevance of massacres and atrocities in occupied areas to the strategic decision to deploy large forces to Vietnam is hard to follow unless Taylor means to imply that what happened to Son My was a planned part of that strategy.

## THE TACTICAL CHARGE

The law of war provides extensive protection to military personnel after they lay down their arms,[17] to the sick and wounded members of

---

[15] United States v. List, *supra* note 11, at 1296-97.

[16] TAYLOR, *supra* note 1, at 192-95.

[17] Geneva Convention Relative to the Treatment of Prisoners of War, Aug. 12, 1949, T.I.A.S. No. 3364.

armed forces,[18] and to civilians in territory actually and effectively occupied by a hostile force.[19]

The law as it really is, however, extends only rudimentary protection to civilians who get caught in the cross fire of military operations on the battle field. These protections for noncombatant civilians in the area of hostilities are derived from the principle of military necessity and its converse, the rule of proportionality which provides that loss of life and damage to property must not be out of proportion to the military advantage gained. From these principles certain minimal rules may be said to be derived under the customary law of war.

a. Noncombatant civilians must not be made the object of attack directed at them alone.[20]

b. Pillage and unnecessary destruction of property is forbidden.[21]

c. Civilians — like prisoners of war — in the hands of their enemy must be treated humanely and may not be murdered, tortured or mutilated or otherwise subjected to inhumane treatment.[22]

Taylor correctly points up the state of the law in this regard:

It is sad but true that the weak and helpless are not exempt from the scourge of war. Indeed, they are likely to be the first to succumb to the starvation and other deprivations that are the consequence and, indeed, the purpose of an economic blockade. In this day and age they are at least as often the victims of aerial bombardment as are

---

[18] Geneva Convention for the Amelioration of the Condition of the Wounded and Sick in Armed Forces in the Field, Aug. 12, 1949, T.I.A.S. No. 3362; Geneva Convention for the Amelioration of the Condition of the Wounded, Sick, and Shipwrecked Members of Armed Forces at Sea, Aug. 12, 1949, T.I.A.S. No. 3363.

[19] Geneva Convention Relative to the Protection of Civilian Persons in Time of War, Aug. 12, 1949, art. 47ff, T.I.A.S. No. 3365; Annex to Hague Convention IV, Regulations Respecting the Laws and Customs of War on Land, Oct. 18, 1907, art. 42-56, 36 Stat. 2277, T.S. No. 539.

[20] FIELD MANUAL 27-10. *Law of Land Warfare*, para. 3 (1956); although UN General Assembly resolutions are not law, it may be fair to state that Resolution 2444 (XXIII) Dec. 19, 1968, is a fair statement of the present law. There are, of course, several moves under way to improve the protection of civilians in armed conflict. These, however, are not the law today.

[21] *See* Hague Convention, *supra* note 19, at art. 23g. The Hague Regulations are generally considered as declaratory of customary law.

[22] Although not free from doubt, it is probable that Common Article 3 of each of the 1949 Conventions, expressly applicable in armed conflicts not of an international character, expresses the minimum standard applicable to all victims of war who do not, or are no longer actively engaged in hostilities. Article 3 does not preclude the detaining power from punishing insurgents after a fair trial. But minimum standards of humane treatment are required. In the words of the ICRC commentary on Article 3:

[The Article] ... merely demands respect for certain rules, which are already recognized as essential in all civilized countries. ... What Government would ... claim before the world, in case of civil disturbance which could justly be described as mere banditry, that, Article 3 not being applicable, it was entitled to leave wounded uncared for; to torture and mutilate prisoners, and to take hostages? (Pictet, Commentary, III Geneva Convention 36).

regular troops. The death of an infant in consequence of military operations, therefore, does not establish that a war crime has been committed.[23]

A close look at the Geneva Civilians' Convention will show that the conventional law of war distinguishes between the law applicable in occupied territory on the one hand, and the minimum protection to the population generally (including the battle area) on the other.[24] It distinguishes, moreover, between "protected persons" and others. Professor Taylor recognizes that the term "protected persons" (who are entitled to more extensive protection than other victims of war) does not include nationals of a co-belligerent state "while the state of which they are nationals has normal diplomatic representation in the State in whose hands they are."[25]

In considering Taylor's charges with respect to the tactics employed by U.S. forces a distinction must be drawn between the rules applicable to the conduct of hostilities — where the military objective is the defeat and destruction of the enemy and his war making potential — and the rules of belligerent occupation — where the military objective is the security of the area and the forces of the occupying belligerent.

How much, if any, part of South Vietnam could, in the 1965-1968 time frame, be considered to be occupied territory? Certainly the cities which had been spared devastation except from Viet Cong and North Vietnamese terror attack were not occupied by U.S. forces. Neither were rural areas firmly under Government control. The disputed areas were more likely to be classified as battle areas. Mere reconnaissance in force and hit and run forays into Viet Cong stronghold areas for the purpose of finding, fighting, fixing and destroying enemy forces, their secure bases, and their stockpiles of war supplies did not result in occupation.[26] Were the "free fire areas" and the forced resettlement of rural families — of which Taylor and other war critics complain, to be judged in the light of the rules applicable in occupied areas or in the light of those applicable in battle areas?

The fluid military situation that prevailed in 1965-1968 involved not only guerrilla warfare as described by Taylor, but also the employment of large division size units based in Cambodian and Laotian sanctuaries as well as in such Viet Cong strongholds as the Mekong Delta and War

---

[23] TAYLOR, *supra* note 1, at 134-35. *See also* Pictet, Commentary, IV Geneva Convention, ICRC 10 (1956).

[24] *Compare* Part II (Articles 13-26) *with* Articles 47-131, Geneva Civilians Convention, *supra* note 19.

[25] Geneva Civilians Convention, *supra* note 19, at Art. 4.

[26] Hague Regulation, *supra* note 7, Art. 43 provides: "Territory is considered occupied when it is actually placed under the authority of the hostile army. The occupation extends only where such authority has been established and can be exercised."

Zones C and D. These areas were honeycombed with underground bunker complexes. These large units were capable of fighting in conventional formations, as well as in smaller guerrilla bands. The military problem presented in disputed areas and the law applicable thereto is described by Taylor:

> . . . [I]n Vietnam the weaker inhabitants are not only victims, but often also participants. It is not necessary to be a male, or particularly strong, to make a booby-trap, plant a mine, or toss a hand grenade a few yards. American soldiers are often the losers in these lethal little games played by those who appear helpless and inoffensive. Furthermore, these actions are not occasional aberrations; on the contrary, they are basic features of Vietcong strategy. As the leading military figure of North Vietnam, General Vo Nguyen Giap, has put it:
>
>> The protracted popular war in Vietnam demanded . . . appropriate forms of combat: appropriate for the revolutionary nature of the war in relation to the balance of forces then showing a clear enemy superiority. . . . The form of combat adopted was guerrilla warfare . . . each inhabitant a soldier; each village a fortress. . . . The entire population participates in the armed struggle, fighting, according to the principles of guerrilla warfare, in small units. . . . This is the fundamental content of the war of people.
>
> Now, guerrilla warefare is not intrinsically unlawful, but as waged by the Vietcong it is undeniably in violation of the traditional laws of war and the Geneva Conventions, based as they are on the distinction between combatants and noncombatants. Combatants need not wear uniforms (which the North Vietnamese generally do) but must observe the conventional four requirements: to be commanded by a person responsible for his subordinates; to wear a fixed distinctive emblem recognizable at a distance; to carry arms openly; and to conduct their operations in accordance with the laws and customs of war. The Vietcong commonly disregard at least the second and third provisions, and in response to the Red Cross inquiry, declared that they were *not* bound by the Geneva Conventions, on the grounds that they were not signatories and that the conventions contained provisions unsuited to their action and their organization . . . of armed forces.
>
> Like a spy, a guerrilla may be a hero, but if he engages in combat without observing the requirements, he violates the laws of war and is subject to punishment, which may be the death penalty. Nor is there any special court for juveniles; the small boy who throws a grenade is as "guilty" as the able-bodied male of military age. This may seem a harsh rule, but it is certainly the law, and its continuing validity was reaffirmed in several of the Nuremberg trials.[27]

Taylor's statement of the law is correct, and if the letter of Article 4

---

[27] TAYLOR, *supra* note 1, at 135-136.

of the Geneva Prisoner of War Convention were followed, few Viet Cong would be entitled to prisoner of war status. The U.S. directives to field forces on prisoners of war, however, extend the status of privileged combatants to all persons captured while engaged in combat or committing other belligerent acts. It is also extended to irregulars and guerrillas who have engaged in combat. It excludes only terrorists, saboteurs, and spies.[28] Concerning this directive the International Committee of The Red Cross delegate to Saigon had occasion to say:

> The MACV instruction . . . is a brilliant expression of a liberal and realistic attitude. . . . This text could very well be a most important one in the history of the humanitarian law, for it is the first time . . . that a government goes far beyond the requirements of the Geneva Convention in an official instruction to its armed forces. The dreams of today are the realities of tomorrow, and the day those definitions or similar ones will become embodied in an international treaty . . . will be a great one for man concerned about the protection of men who cannot protect themselves. . . . May it then be remembered that this light first shone in the darkness of this tragic war of Vietnam.[29]

The laws of war are based on the past experience of the major powers. The drafters of the Hague Convention on the Laws of War of 1907 looked back to the wars of the nineteenth century; the Geneva Conventions For the Protection of War Victims of 1929 were considered in the context of World War I; and the Geneva Conventions For the Protection of War Victims of 1949 dealt with issues which arose in World War II. In most instances they envisioned relatively stable fronts, orderly lines of communication, and secure rear areas. The participation of guerrilla bands was recognized but only as a side issue.

The divergence between what the drafters of the rules of war envisioned and the situation in Vietnam required innovative application of the basic principles to the situation confronting the Free World forces. These innovations resulted in U.S. policies, directives and procedures which Taylor calls "virtually impeccable."[30]

Among the policies adopted to protect noncombatants was their evacuation from the battle area - the so called "forced resettlement of rural families". In this connection all that need be said is to cite the UN Secretary General's 1970 report to the General Assembly on *Respect for Human Rights in Armed Conflict:*

---

28 Military Assistance Command, Vietnam Directive 381-46, Annex A, 62 Am. J. Int'l L., 766 (1968).

29 Haight, *The Geneva Convention and the Shadow War,* U.S. Naval Institute Proceedings, 47 (1968).

30 TAYLOR, *supra* note 1, at 162; *See* Report of the Department of the Army Review of the Preliminary Investigation into the My-Lai Incident, ch. 9 (Mar. 1970). [Hereinafter referred to as the Peers Report].

... [T]he circumstances of modern warfare may render difficult an adequate protection of civilians in all situations. . . . It would seem, therefore, that, while military personnel should exercise caution and respect, to the limit of the possible, the relevant norms relating to the protection of civilians under any circumstances, the most effective way of minimizing or eliminating the risk to civilians would be to make systematic efforts to the effect that civilians do not remain in areas where dangers . . . would be prevalent.

The importance of such efforts bear emphasizing, and the cause of the protection might be enhanced if the General Assembly would consider the usefulness of including as part of an appropriate resolution a call on all authorities involved in armed conflicts of all types to do their utmost to ensure that civilians are removed from, or kept out of, areas where conditions would be likely to place them in jeopardy or to expose them to the hazards of warfare.[31]

Taylor's objection to the forced evacuation of rural families is that it is violative of Article 49 of the Geneva Civilians Convention. That article is to be found in the section dealing with Occupied Territory and was primarily intended to forbid the Nazi practice of the mass evacuations and deportations from occupied territory to provide slave labor for the German war industry.[32]

The technique to which Taylor objects is declaring an area from which civilians are evacuated as a "free fire zone" and then to attack the presumed enemy with artillery fire or air strike without prior clearance from the Vietnamese provincial authorities.[33]

The Peers report describes this policy:

In 1966, certain . . . areas were declared as cleared areas to all Free World Military Assistance forces by GVN and became known as "free fire zones." Simply stated, a free fire zone was a specifically delineated geographic area, that had been previously approved for use of all means of fire power and maneuver. Such an area was cleared for firepower unless notification to the contrary was given. In 1967 MACV replaced its use with the term "specified strike zone (SSZ)." An SSZ was defined as "those areas approved by a province chief where a strike may be conducted without additional political clearance."[34]

This fire control technique, used in areas where a maximum effort had been made to clear the civilian population from a planned battle area, is included within the Rules of Engagement which Taylor describes

---

31 UN Doc A/8052, at 15 (1970).
32 Pictet, *supra* note 23, at 277-280.
33 TAYLOR, *supra* note 1, at 145-46.
34 Peers Report, *supra* note 30, at 9-7.

as "virtually impeccable." Nevertheless, Taylor indicts the top leadership for conducting air strikes in such areas.

In contrast to his finding that "free fire zones" violate the law of war, Taylor gives the aerial bombardment of North Vietnam a legal clearance, "I can see no sufficient basis for war crimes charges based on the bombing of North Vietnam. Whatever the law of war *ought* to be, certainly Nuremberg furnishes no basis for the accusations."[35]

Taylor thus indicts the use of fire power and mobility to strike known enemy areas from which an effort had been made to remove non-combatants, while approving the use of air bombardment in North Vietnam where there was no means to clear the civilian population from the target area. His reasoning is hard to follow. Strategic bombardment of populated places was not considered a war crime at Nuremberg. Neither was the tactical use of fire power in battle areas against military targets notwithstanding that civilian casualties resulted incidentally from both. The United Nations War Crimes Commission, after analyzing the World War II war crimes cases found that the laws of war which relate to actual conduct of hostilities were seldom made the basis of war crimes prosecution.[36]

Unquestionably there have been cases when air power or artillery fire was deliberately misused. Such incidents inevitably occur in war. Whenever reasonable evidence of war crimes is presented to responsible commanders it results in investigation and, if substantiated, in trial by court-martial.[37]

After analyzing Henry Salsbury's report on air bombardment of North Vietnam and the statements made at the Bertrand Russell War Crimes trials, Taylor found them insufficient to substantiate allegations of intentional air attack against civilians as such.[38] But on the same type of secondary evidence—the works of journalists—he is willing to assume widespread reprisal attacks against innocent civilians in South Vietnam. One may wonder how frequently journalists who came upon the evidence of war crimes, reported them through appropriate military channels so that an appropriate investigation might be made before the loss of witnesses. How often did they save them up for publication in the new industry of the scapegoat makers?

---

35 TAYLOR, *supra* note 1, at 142.

36 U.N. War Crimes Commission, XV LAW REPORTS OF TRIALS OF WAR CRIMINALS, London H.M. Stationery Office 109 (1947-1949). [Hereinafter cited at XV LAW REPORTS].

37 TAYLOR, *supra* note 1, at 155.

38 *Id.* at 142.

## COMMANDER'S RESPONSIBILITY
## FOR ACTS OF HIS SUBORDINATES

The principle that a commander may be responsible for the acts of his subordinates is a traditional one. During the Black Hawk War of 1832, Abraham Lincoln, then a captain of militia, was convicted by a court-martial for failing to control his men who had opened the officers' supply of whiskey and partook thereof to the extent that some straggled on the march. He was sentenced to carry a wooden sword for two days.[39]

In preventing war crimes, however, Captain Lincoln's military record was somewhat better. It is recorded that an old Indian with a safe conduct rambled into the camp and the men rushed to kill him. Lincoln jumped to the side of the Indian and by effective command action prevented the atrocity.[40]

The principle of command responsibility is stated in the Army Field Manual:

In some cases, military commanders may be responsible for war crimes committed by subordinate members of the armed forces, or other persons subject to their control. Thus, for instance, when troops commit massacres and atrocities against the civilian population of occupied territory or against prisoners of war, the responsibility may rest not only with the actual perpetrators but also with the commander. Such a responsibility arises directly when the acts in question have been committed in pursuance of an order of the commander concerned. The commander is also responsible if he has actual knowledge, or should have knowledge, through reports received by him or through other means, that troops or other persons subject to his control are about to commit or have committed a war crime and he fails to take the necessary and reasonable steps to insure compliance with the law of war or to punish violators thereof.[41]

That principle was applied at "Nuremberg" which Professor Taylor defines as "both what actually happened there and what people think happened, and the second is more important than the first." [42] In particular he refers to the case of General Tomoyuki Yamashita which most vividly projects in the popular mind an image of absolute command responsibility.[43]

---

[39] SANDBURG, ABRAHAM LINCOLN 30 (one vol. 1954).

[40] Id.

[41] FIELD MANUAL 27-10, supra note 20, at para. 501.

[42] TAYLOR, supra note 1, at 13-14.

[43] Reel, Commentary on Taylor's charges, N.Y. Times, Jan. 19, 1971, at 36, col. 3 (Letters to the editor). A. Frank Reel, who had been one of General Yamashita's defense counsel, indicates that Yamashita was punished not for anything he had done, but because of the position he had held.

Professor Taylor asks the broad question:

... [A]re the people of the United States able to face the proposition that Jackson put forth in their name, and examine their own conduct under the same principle that they applied to the Germans and Japanese at the Nuremberg and other war crimes trials? [44]

Later, referring specifically to the Yamashita case he suggests:

... [T]he Son My courts-martial are shaping the question for us, and they cannot be fairly determined without full inquiry into higher responsibilities. Little as the leaders of the Army seem to realize it, this is the only road to the Army's salvation, for its moral health will not be recovered until its leaders are willing to scrutinize their own behavior by the same standards that their revered predecessors applied to Tomoyuki Yamashita 25 years ago.[45]

Appearing on the Dick Cavett television show of January 8, 1971, he stated more explicitly:

If you were to apply to [people like General Westmoreland] ... the same standards that were applied in the trial of General Yamashita there would be a strong possibility that they would come to the same end as he did.[46]

The scope of the ensuing discussion deals with two distinct "Nuremberg" standards:

a. The substantive standard: What level of omission is necessary to hold a commander vicariously liable for the offenses committed by his subordinates not ordered by him?

b. The procedural standard: By what standard should criminal charges against a commander be adjudicated?

## The Substantive Standard

The context in which Professor Taylor's implications are made requires a brief recital of the Yamashita case.

General Yamashita commanded the Fourteenth Army Group of the Japanese Army in the Philippine Islands during the last year of the Japanese occupation from October 9, 1944 until September 3, 1945 when he surrendered to American forces and became a prisoner of war. On September 25 he was charged with a violation of the law of war specifying that he "unlawfully disregarded and failed to discharge his duty to control the operations of the members of his command per-

---

[44] TAYLOR, *supra* note 1, at 13.

[45] *Id.* at 182.

[46] N.Y. Times, Jan. 9, 1971, at 3, Col. 1.

mitting them to commit brutal atrocities and other high crimes. . . ."[47]

The trial, which began on October 8, 1945 resulted in his conviction on December 7, 1945.

The proof adduced against General Yamashita showed that during his tenure in command a large number of Filipinos and Americans, including prisoners of war, guerrillas, and innocent civilians were brutally mistreated.

There was some testimony that certain offenses reflected official policy, and some occurred in the immediate vicinity of General Yamashita's headquarters. There was also some testimony indicating direct knowledge on the part of General Yamashita. The credibility and competence of much of this inculpatory evidence is discussed in the section dealing with the procedural standard. Suffice it to say that under the rules established for the commission it was received in evidence—over vigorous defense objection—and obviously considered by the members of the commission.[48] Moreover, even if the direct evidence of knowledge and complicity were excluded, the Government contended in the Supreme Court that the large number of atrocities shown offered circumstantial evidence of knowledge and a consistent policy of lawlessness.[49]

The theory of the defense was that because of the confusion attending the defeat of his forces, General Yamashita had no knowledge of any atrocity and that he did not have the capability to exercise the required command control.

The defense adduced no evidence of any command action to prevent atrocities; there was no evidence of any personal intervention on the part of the commander to require adherence to the law of war, nor was there any showing that the processes of Japanese military justice were invoked to punish any perpetrators of war crimes. Yamashita did testify that had he known of the atrocities he would not have condoned them.

It is in the context of the defense of ignorance of fact that Taylor contends that "in sharp contrast [to the circumstances] that confronted General Yamashita in 1944 and 1945, with his forces reeling back in disarray before the oncoming American military power house," American military commanders "were splendidly equipped with helicopters and other aircraft which endowed them with every opportunity to keep the course of fighting and its consequences under close and constant observation."[50]

---

[47] *In re* Yamashita, 327 U.S. 1, 5, 13-14 (1946). Bills of Particular alleged 123 gross atrocities committed by members of the forces under his command. *Id.* at 14.
[48] *See* note 77 *infra,* and LAW REPORTS, *supra* note 36, Vol. IV, at 18-23.
[49] Brief of Respondent 55-56.
[50] TAYLOR, *supra* note 1, at 181,

The relevance of this rhetoric is obscure. As far as can be determined, it has never been contended that American commanders were unaware that war crimes had been committed by Americans in Vietnam, nor does Taylor cite any such claim. He describes as "virtually impeccable" [51] the command directives issued by General Westmoreland in an effort to prevent war crimes,[52] to insure that known or suspected war crimes are promptly reported, investigated and processed to action.[53] He is aware that substantiated allegations of violations of the law of war have usually resulted in trials by court-martial.[54] He fails to record the manifestations of General Westmoreland's command emphasis, follow-up and personal concern in the prevention of war crimes as recorded in the Peers report.[55] If he considers that General Westmoreland knew of Son My before the belated letter of Mr. Ron Ridenhour, on March 1969,[56] he fails to make that allegation and offers no proof. He fails, moreover, to cite the detailed procedures on handling prisoners of war and civilian detainees which are available in the public domain, and which go far beyond the letter of the Geneva Prisoner of War Conventions in according prisoners of war protection to guerrillas who do not meet the Convention

---

[51] *Id.* at 168. "Impeccable" directives are usually issued in response to a problem which he caused concern to the commander.

[52] MACV Directive 27-5, Nov. 2, 1967, quoted in 62 AM. J. OF INT'L. L. 765 (1968); Peers Report, *supra* note 30, at 9-12.

[53] *Id.* MACV Directive 27-4; Peers Report, *supra* note 30, at 9-10 to 9-12.

[54] TAYLOR, *supra* note 1, at 55. *See* note 97, *infra* for an analysis of relevant court-martial statistics.

[55] At page 9-14, 9-15, the Peers Report, *supra* note 30, states:

> MACV published several other documents pertaining to U.S. policy with regard to ROE [Rules of Engagement], treatment of Vietnamese nationals, and the reporting of war crimes. Letters, memoranda, and messages emphasizing COMUSMACV's concern for these subjects, and reaffirmations of MACV policy were published on many occasions. In addition, the COMUSMACV command policy file emphasized these subjects. At his Commander's Conferences, COMUSMACV repeatedly discussed the necessity for proper treatment of Vietnamese nationals and proper control of firepower.
>
> On 3 December 1967, General Westmoreland closed his Commander's Conference by directing each commander to reduce firing accidents, report all accidents/incidents direct to MACV, and insure that all troops understand the "Nine Rules" that govern their conduct in RVN. Documentation of COMUS-MACV policy and interest in these areas was and is plentiful.
>
> The necessity for subordinate commanders to implement the MACV directives as well as the stated and implied policies was also emphasized. The chain of command within the MACV unified command afforded the means for the necessary delegation of authority to implement MACV policies. Within the chain of command, subordinate units usually published directives elaborating upon the regulations of the higher headquarters and insuring that at their lower level of command the specifically directed responsibilities assigned to them were further implemented. Another factor used by subordinate headquarters in determining applicability or the requirements to implement the directives of a higher headquarters was the mission assigned to the subordinate unit.

[56] Peers Report, *supra* note 30, at 1-7.

standard.[57] Nor does he acknowledge that the International Committee of the Red Cross had ready access to American prisoner of war collecting points and Vietnamese internment camps.

By his Yamashita analogy, Professor Taylor must be alluding to "what people think" is the Nuremberg standard, that a commander is per se criminally liable for the misconduct of his troops, but neither the *Yamashita* case[58] nor Nuremberg went that far.

The United States Supreme Court, which determined only the jurisdiction of the tribunal and whether the charge alleged an offense, stated the standard as follows:

> [The provisions of the Hague Conventions and the 1929 Geneva Convention] plainly impose on the petitioner . . . an affirmative duty to *take such measures as were within his power and appropriate in the circumstances* to protect prisoners of war and the civilian population.[59] (Emphasis added).

What actually happened at Nuremberg is more explicit. Professor Taylor, then the prosecutor in the High Command case, urged that under the Hague regulations a military commander is per se responsible for crimes committed within the area of his command. The tribunal rejected Professor Taylor's argument:

> Modern war . . . entails a large measure of decentralization. A high commander cannot keep completely informed of the details of military operations of subordinates and most assuredly not of administrative measures. He has a right to assume that details entrusted to responsible subordinates will be legally executed . . . . There must be personal dereliction. That can occur only where the act is directly traceable to him or where his failure to properly supervise his subordinates constitutes criminal negligence on his part. *In the latter case, it must be a personal neglect amounting to wanton, immoral disregard of the action of his subordinates amounting to acquiescence.*[60] (Emphasis added).

The degree of negligence defined as criminal by the Nuremberg Tribunal is in striking contrast to that which Professor Taylor describes. Referring to Colonel Corson's statement "that the atrocities, alleged or otherwise, are a result of bad judgment, not criminal behaviour," Taylor

---

[57] Annex A of MACV Directive 381-46 of Dec. 27, 1967, *Criteria for Classification and Disposition of Detainees;* MACV Directive 20-5 of Mar. 15, 1968, *Prisoners of War—Determination of Eligibility;* published in 62 Am. J. of Int'l. L. 765-775 (1968).

[58] The Commission believed that "the crimes were so extensive and widespread, that they must have either been wilfully permitted, or secretly ordered by the accused." *See* note 77 *infra.*

[59] *In re* Yamashita, 327 U.S. 1, 10 (1945).

[60] United States v. Von Leeb, XI Trials of War Criminals, *supra* note 11, at 534-44.

reverts to his role as prosecutor: "Colonel Corson overlooks, I fear, that negligent homicide is generally a crime of bad judgment rather than evil intent."[61]

I fear that Professor Taylor has overlooked the fact that negligent homicide is usually a misdemeanor of relatively recent origin found in motor vehicle codes. It is predicated on simple negligence in the operation of motor vehicles and was probably intended to provide a reasonable compromise verdict in involuntary manslaughter cases.[62] It has no relation to the international law of war, at least not with respect to grave breaches as defined in Article 130 of the Geneva Prisoners of War Convention or Article 147 of the Geneva Civilians Convention. These denounce the commission, or order to commit, against protected persons the following:

> *Willful* killing, torture or inhuman treatment . . . *willfully* causing great suffering or serious injury to body or health, *willfully* depriving a protected person of the rights of fair and regular trial prescribed in the . . . Convention; and extensive destruction and appropriation of property, not justified by military necessity and carried out unlawfully and wantonly. (Emphasis added).

There remains for consideration another relevant matter: a commander's authority over military justice.

The military commission which condemned General Yamashita delivered a brief explanation for its findings. In part, it stated:

> Clearly, assignment to command military troops is accompanied by broad authority and heavy responsibility . . . . It is for the purpose of maintaining discipline and control, among other reasons, that military commanders are given broad powers of administering military justice . . . .[63]

The commission consisted of five general officers who were unquestionably familiar with the authority commanders exercised during World War II in respect to the administration of military justice. It was the matter of command control over courts-martial which lead to the enactment of the Uniform Code of Military Justice, which forbids specifically

---

[61] TAYLOR, *supra* note 1, at 178, *cf.*, his view on bombing in North Vietnam at 140; *cf. also* United States v. List, *supra* note 11.

[62] PERKINS, CRIMINAL LAW 75-76 (2d ed. 1969). In military law negligent homicide is not limited to motor vehicle cases. The standard, however, is simple negligence. Manual for Courts-Martial, U.S., para. 213f (12) (rev. ed. 1969).

[63] Record of the trial before the Military Commission, convened by C. G. U.S. Army Force, Western Pacific, at 4061.

many of the practices prevelant when Professor Taylor was in uniform.[64] As a Unified Commander, General Westmoreland was not authorized to convene courts-martial. Except for the authority to refer reports of investigation to a subordinate for appropriate action, he could not influence the judicial discretion of any subordinate commander, much less that of a court-martial.[65] Even the appearance of command influence brings down the condemnation of the United States Court of Military Appeals,[66] and affords fuel for other segments of the new industry.[67]

Additional aspects of modern military justice will be considered in the discussion pertaining to procedural matters.

## The Procedural Standard

Professor Taylor's suggestion that the behaviour of the Army's leaders be scrutinized by the standards applied to General Tomoyuki Yamashita,[68] may imply that this scrutiny be conducted by the procedural standards under which General Yamashita was tried and condemned.

When he suggests that a special military commission — rather than an ordinary court-martial — is better suited to try the Son My cases,[69] he betrays a nostalgic preference for the Post World War II procedures. After all, an ordinary court-martial, like a jury, is hedged in with procedural limitations, exclusionary rules of evidence, and due process standards. These procedural safeguards were deliberately curtailed in the regulations established for war crimes military commissions during and after World War II.[70] In 1949, however, the procedural standards applied to General Yamashita were repudiated by the Geneva Conventions. It is noteworthy that less than four years after the Yamashita trial had begun, the principal Allies were willing to agree that the manner in which that

---

[64] See 10 U.S.C. §837, Art. 37 (1959), which prohibits any commander from censuring, reprimanding, or admonishing any member, military judge, or counsel with respect to findings, sentences, or any other function of the judicial proceeding. He is also forbidden from attempting to coerce or improperly influence the judicial functions of the court, or the judicial acts of any convening, approving or reviewing authority. The authority to conduct instruction in military justice is severly restricted to procedural and substantive law, thus excluding policy guidance. Moreover, performance in courts-martial may not form a basis for fitness reports.

[65] Manual for Courts-Martial, *supra* note 62, at para 5, 13.

[66] See United States v. Johnson, 14 U.S.C. M.A. 548 (1969).

[67] See SHERRILL, MILITARY JUSTICE IS TO JUSTICE AS MILITARY MUSIC IS TO MUSIC (1970).

[68] TAYLOR, *supra* note 1, at 182.

[69] *Id.* at 163.

[70] See *Ex parte* Quirin 317 U.S. 1 (1942); Mason, *Inter Arma Silent Leges*, 69 HARVARD LAW REVIEW, 806, 813-31 (1956); and Dissent by Mr. Justice Rutledge, *In re* Yamashita, 327 U.S. 1, 61-72; D'Amato, *War Crimes and Vietnam* 57 CALIF. L. REV. 1055, 1069-73 (1969).

case — and other World War II war crimes trials — had been conducted, would in the future constitute a grave breach of the law of war.[71]

When General Yamashita surrendered on September 3, 1945, he became a *prisoner of war* and was treated as such until charges were preferred against him on September 25.[72] Article 63 of the 1929 Geneva Convention Relative to the Treatment of Prisoners of War provided: "A sentence will only be pronounced on a prisoner of war by the same tribunal and in accordance with the same procedures as in the case of persons belonging to the armed forces of the Detaining Power." Under the Articles of War in effect during World War II, prisoners of war were expressly made subject to court-martial jurisdiction by the provision of Article of War 12.[73] Moreover, many of the procedural safeguards which had been incorporated into court-martial procedures in 1911, 1916, and 1921 had been made specifically applicable by the Articles of War to military commissions which exercised jurisdiction under the law of war.[74] Article of War 25 allowed the reading of depositions in evidence under prescribed conditions "before any military court or commission *in any case not capital.*" (Emphasis added). Depositions were allowed in capital cases only at the instance of the accused.

Nevertheless, the order establishing the military commission which tried Yamashita authorized the receipt of all evidence that would "have probative value in the minds of reasonable men" including reports of investigators, affidavits, depositions, statements, diaries, letters, and other documents deemed relevant to the charge.[75] Much of this evidence was not admissible either in a court-martial or a military commission under the Articles of War and the Manual for Courts-Martial.

At the trial, numerous affidavits, depositions, letters and newspaper articles, motion picture films with sound track added, were received over objection by the defense.[76] Most of these items tended to show the commission of widespread atrocities by Japanese forces in the Philippines. As there was some corroboration by witnesses, and the defense did not deny that troops under Yamashita's command had committed widespread atrocities, it is sometimes suggested that the otherwise incompetent evi-

---

71 "Grave Breaches . . . shall be those involving any of the following acts . . . .: willfully depriving a prisoner of war of the right of fair and regular trial prescribed in these Conventions." Art. 130, 1949 Geneva Prisoner of War Convention.

72 U.N. War Crimes Commission, IV LAW REPORTS OF TRIALS OF WAR CRIMINALS, 3 (1947-1949) [Hereinafter cited as IV LAW REPORTS].

73 41 Stat. 787 (1920).

74 *Id.* at 792-94, Articles of War 24, 25, 38. Traditionally military commissions had operated without statutory authorization as common law war courts not subject to the procedural rules applicable to courts-martial.

75 IV LAW REPORTS, *supra* note 72, at 57.

76 *Id.* at 23, 34, 57-58.

dence was harmless if it was an error. Some of the least trustworthy evidence, however, bore directly on the issue of lack of knowledge and some highly damaging second hand hearsay and rumor tended to show that Yamashita actually ordered a policy of atrocities.[77]

Because the commission made no explicit finding that the atrocities had been ordered by the accused, it was contended that, even if it had been an error to receive such hearsay, there had been no sufficient showing of prejudice because the tribunal had apparently given the evidence little weight.[78]

Yet there are indications in the judgment of the Commission that the hearsay evidence had its impact. In part, the Commission stated:

> The Prosecution presented evidence to show that the crimes were so extensive and widespread, that they must have either been *willfully permitted*, or *secretly ordered by the accused*.[79] (Emphasis added).

It is recognized that only the Anglo-American judicial system applies the exclusionary rules to evidence in criminal cases. There is little to fear from the consideration by Civil Law judges of any relevant evidence. Civil Law judges have a tradition of independence and extensive training and experience in the evaluation of evidence "which might have probative value to reasonable men." But the Commission that tried Yamashita was not composed of professional Civil Law judges. They were five general officers of the Army who were not lawyers. To the extent that they were familiar with military law, they had been exposed to the exclusionary rules which screened out rumor, incompetent hearsay, and other unreliable evidence. As members of the Commission, they were freed from the restraint of the exclusionary rules. To suggest that the rumors directly implicating Yamashita in the ordering of atrocities was harmless error is highly speculative. By today's standards such speculation would be intolerable. The burden is on the prosecution to show beyond a reasonable doubt that incompetent evidence did not contribute to the verdict obtained.[80] The present standard is in sharp contrast to the explanation offered by the UN War Crimes Commission that, "No trial has come to [their] notice in which an allegation based upon [the de-

---

[77] *Id.* at 19-20. Narciso Lapus, a collaborator was permitted to testify that his employer, the Philippine General Ricarte, had told the witness that General Yamashita had issued a general order to wipe out the whole Philippines if possible. The witness also stated that Yamashita subsequently rejected Ricarte's plea that he should withdraw the order. Filemon Castillejos, who operated a restaurant for the Japanese, testified that two Japanese officers and two soldiers had told him that a telegram ordering the killing of all Americans in the Philippines had been received from General Yamashita.

[78] *Id.* at 62.

[79] *Id.* at 34.

[80] Chapman v. California, 386 U.S. 10 (1967).

nial to a prisoner of war of Geneva Convention protection] led undisputably to a conviction." [81]

On appeal from the denial by the Philippine Supreme Court of Yamashita's petition for a writ of habeas corpus, the Supreme Court of the United States rejected the applicability of both the Articles of War and the Geneva Convention of 1929, holding that they were intended to apply only to offenses which were committed by prisoners of war *subsequent* to their capture.[82]

The rationale of the *Yamashita* case became a precedent for Nuremberg [83] and other war crimes tribunals. Pleas by the accused and requests by the International Committee of the Red Cross for compliance with the provisions of the 1929 Geneva Convention were rejected in most reported cases.[84] Generally this rejection rested on the assertion that under customary law those who violated the laws of war could not avail themselves of the protection which they afford and that the 1929 Convention, which made no mention of precapture offenses, was not intended to modify customary rules.[85] This is equivalent to the view that those who are charged with violations of the municipal criminal law may not avail themselves of the procedural safeguards which that law provides for the protection of defendants.

Article 85 of the 1949 Prisoner of War Convention works a deliberate repudiation of this practice. It provides, "[p]risoners of war, prosecuted under the laws of the Detaining Powers for acts committed prior to capture shall retain, even if convicted, the benefits of the present Convention."

Among these benefits is Article 102, which provides:

A prisoner of war can be validly sentenced only if the sentence had been pronounced by the same courts according to the same procedure as in the case of members of the armed forces of the Detaining Power, and if, furthermore, the provisions of the present chapter have been observed.

The proceedings of the Diplomatic Conference make it clear that a repudiation of the Yamashita rule was intended.[86] The delegates were unanimous in the view that prisoners of war tried for war crimes should have the benefits of the Convention until their guilt has been proven.

---

[81] XV LAW REPORTS, *supra* note 36, at 100.

[82] *In re* Yamashita, 327 U.S. 1 (1946).

[83] The Nuremberg Charter explicitly exempted the tribunal from "technical rules of evidence." I Trial Major War Criminals 15. For an illuminating discussion of the type of evidence received at Nuremberg see D'Amato, *supra* note 70.

[84] Pictet, Commentary III, *supra* note 22, at 413.

[85] *Id.* 414.

[86] 2A Final Record 389-90, 559; Pictet, Commentary III, *supra* note 22, at 413 n. 1.

The Soviet Bloc, however, objected to the entitlement of prisoners of war to these benefits after conviction and interposed reservations to that effect.[87] The North Vietnamese reservation to Article 85, on the other hand, excludes persons "prosecuted and convicted" of war crimes. Apparently, North Vietnam construes this as depriving one accused of war crimes of the benefits from the time of the accusation.[88] Thus, North Vietnam still claims to follow the rule of the Yamashita case.

The Convention not only precludes a Detaining Power from trying prisoners of war by special ad hoc national tribunals, but it also precludes, for all practical purposes, their trial by International Military Tribunals. The Grave Breaches Articles provide only for trials in national courts. As it is improbable that the military law of the Detaining Power will authorize foreign judges to sit in judgment of its own military personnel in any event, the creation of international tribunals of mixed composition will be next to impossible. Thus the International Military Tribunals of Nuremberg and Tokyo may represent an almost unique position in history.[89]

Insistance that these trials be held by the regular national courts or military tribunals provides a certain standard of justice and procedure and insures familiarity of the court with its well established tradition and procedures. This minimizes the danger that the courts will deprive the accused of rights because of ignorance.

Notwithstanding that international law now would forbid the trial of prisoners of war before an ad hoc special military commission, Taylor would have the Son My defendants — who are protected only by the

---

[87] Pictet, Commentary III, *supra* note 22, at 422-24. In response to a request for clarification of its reservation, the Soviet Union advised the Swiss Government that the reservation applies only after "the sentence becomes legally enforceable." After the sentence has been served, the benefits of the convention would be resumed.

[88] Pinto, Roger, Hanoi, *et. al.*, Convention de Geneva, Le Monde (Paris) 27 December 1969. *But see* Paul de la Pradelle, Le Nord — Vietnam et les Conventions Humanitaire de Geneve, Revue Generale de Droit International Public, (Paris: April-June 1971).

[89] As a precedent for International Military Tribunals Taylor cites the 1474 tyranny trial of the Burgundian Governor of Breisach, Peter Hagenbach, by the tribunal of judges from Alsace, Switzerland, and other member states of the Holy Roman Empire. Apparently so preoccupied with the World War II pattern of trial of the defeated by the victors, Taylor assumed that: ". . . after Charles' defeat and death Hagenbach was charged with conduct that trampled underfoot the laws of God and man. . . ." TAYLOR, *supra* note 1, at 81.

Superficial examination of his cited authorities [GEORGE SCHWARZENBERG, II, INTERNATIONAL LAW AS APPLIED BY INTERNATIONAL COURTS AND TRIBUNALS 462-3 (1968)] or the ENCYCLOPEDIA BRITANNICA would have revealed that Charles was alive, well, and still powerful in May 1474 at the time of the Breisach trial. (4 ENCYCLOPEDIA BRITANNICA 407 (1947 ed.), v. 5 at 288, v. 21 at 684). As a matter of historical conjecture, Swiss participation in that trial was probably one of the causes of the Swiss-Burgundian war which began in 1476 and led to Charles' ultimate defeat and death at Nancy on January 6, 1477.

Uniform Code of Military Justice and the Constitution — tried before such a tribunal.

> [T]here is much to be said for trying the Son My cases before a special military commission, to which able judges and lawyers, outside the military chain of command might be appointed. As has been seen, the defense of superior orders does not eliminate criminal responsibility, but rather shifts it upward, and that is the direction an ordinary court-martial will be least likely to look.[90]

One may wonder, if American constitutional due process is a consideration, why Taylor gives no thought to an ordinary jury trial.[91] Is it because a jury, like a court-martial will be instructed to consider only the issue before it . . . the guilt or innocence of the accused, . . . not to range up or down, to determine who else may share in the defendant's guilt, if he is guilty. These may be functions for a grand jury, but not of a trial jury. Both a jury and a court-martial may go to war with a rule of law if the rule offends its sense of justice,[92] but it will not convert a criminal trial into a political fishing expedition.

Taylor's preference for military commissions with procedural rules specially tailored to accomplish extraordinary functions is revealed in his discussion of the case of Lt. James Duffy who was convicted of the premeditated murder of a helpless prisoner. When the court was informed that the mandatory sentence was life imprisonment, the court revoked its findings and convicted Duffy of involuntary manslaughter.[93] Indignantly Taylor exclaims:

> What is one to make of all this? "Involuntary Manslaughter" denotes an unintentional negligent killing, and is a singularly inappropriate label for the conduct on which Duffy's conviction was based.
>
> . . . *If ever a case cried out for an explanatory opinion, it is this one, but opinions are not part of court-martial practice.*[94] (Emphasis added).

Is it part of the jury practice in New York for the jury to render an explanatory opinion?

---

[90] TAYLOR, *supra* note 1, at 163. Nuremberg established that a superior order is not a defense to an order which is plainly and obviously illegal. An order to kill helpless prisoners in one's custody is as plainly and obviously an illegal order as can be imagined.

[91] One of the virtues (or evils) of a military commission is that its composition and procedures are not prescribed by statute. The President is therefore free to establish it in any form or shape he desires. It may be set up under rules which curtail procedural rights as in the Quirin and Yamashita cases, or it may be composed as an exact replica of a Federal District Court with grand juries and petit juries, as are the U.S. Civil Administration Courts, Ryukyu Islands. *See* Rose v. McNamara, 375 F. 2d 924 (D.C. Cir. 1967), *cert. denied*, 389 U.S. 856 (1967).

[92] H. KALVEN & H. ZEISEL, THE AMERICAN JURY 495 (1966).

[93] TAYLOR, *supra* note 1, at 151, 161.

[94] TAYLOR, *supra* note 1, at 162.

Without benefit of explanatory opinion, Taylor then attributes the findings to what an anonymous officer calls the "mere gook rule." (A tendency toward leniency to Americans who kill Vietnamese civilians, because the Vietnamese were regarded as somehow second class human beings or "mere gooks.")

If animosity toward Viet Cong and Viet Cong sympathizers contributes to jury verdicts, Taylor has cited ample reasons for such animosity.[95] It is difficult to attribute such attitudes to leadership, however. I can recall no war in recent memory when there has been so little hate propaganda against the enemy from national or military leadership. In fact, the veneration of the Viet Cong by the peace movement at home, may contribute to some degree to the soldier's frustration and animosity toward suspected Viet Cong.[96]

Taylor cites only one verdict in support of the existence of a "mere gook rule" and here he generalizes from inadequate empirical data.

I have analyzed the results over a three-year period of court-martial trials for murder, rape, and manslaughter in which the victim was Vietnamese and I find that the acquittal rate is somewhat less than that found in various studies of American jury cases.[97] If courts-martial behave pretty much like American juries, it seems that the drafters of the Uniform Code of Military Justice have achieved at least one of their objectives. I find no corroboration for the existence of a "mere gook rule" in the performance of American courts-martial.

On at least one occasion, Taylor, a teacher of Constitutional Law, betrays his impatience with the Fifth Amendment. Referring to charges against 14 officers for failing to take appropriate action on Son My reports, Taylor states, "[t]he matter was then transferred to the jurisdiction

---

[95] *See supra* note 27.

[96] Moskos, *supra* text, at 1.

[97] The number of persons tried by court-martial convicted and acquitted for murder, manslaughter and rape — June 1965 through June 1968 (Vietnamese victims).

| Offense | Tried | Convicted | Acquitted | Lesser Offenses | Percent Acquitted |
|---------|-------|-----------|-----------|-----------------|-------------------|
| Murder | 31 | 16 | 7 | 8 | 23 |
| Rape | 17 | 13 | 4 | 0 | 23.5 |
| Manslaughter | 11 | 7 | 2 | 2 | 18 |

COMPARATIVE ACQUITTAL RATE

| | Court-Martial Vietnamese Victim | Kalven & Zeisel Sample Jury | 1945 Census |
|---------|---------------------------------|------------------------------|-------------|
| Murder | 23% | 19% | 32% |
| Rape | 23.5% | 40% | 38% |
| Manslaughter | 18% | 45% | 51% |

H. KALVEN & H. ZEISEL, *supra* note 92, at 42.

of Lieutenant General Mathew [*sic*] O. Seaman, . . . who shortly
announced dismissal for lack of evidence against seven of the officers."[98]
In a footnote to the passage, Taylor observes "One of the officers cleared
by General Seaman had invoked the privilege against self-incrimination
while testifying before the Hebert Committee." [99] Not even when Taylor
was in uniform was it possible in a court-martial, to prove guilt on the
basis of a claim of the privilege against self-incrimination. Now, it can't
even be done that way in California.[100]

If Taylor had in mind applying the procedural standards of the
*Yamashita* case to America's military leaders, his rhetorical question might
truly get an affirmative answer. Fortunately, for American Justice and
the integrity of the Constitutional standard of due process, those procedural standards are things of the past. Let them remain buried with
the thumb screw, the rack, and the third degree.

CONCLUSION

Professor Taylor states that one of the purposes of his book is to
examine this question: "What are the Nuremberg legal principles, and
what is their meaning as applied to American involvement in Vietnam?"[101]

He then affirms that in his discussion he will avoid assumptions and
preconceptions as to how these questions should be answered, "since . . .
they need to be considered quite as carefully and urgently by those who
execute or support our Vietnam policies as by those in opposition."

In a sense, he may have accomplished his purpose, for by a melange
of inaccuracies, half truths, and rhetorical implications, he offers something for all viewpoints. Every man, no matter what his views, can find
them corroborated at least by implication, somewhere in the 207 pages
of text. Taylor's style is facile and graceful. His style tends, on a first
reading, to conceal the multiple contradictions and inaccuracies. But the
book falls far short of fulfilling the promise of its stated purpose. His
factual passages are often based on the preconceptions and assumptions
of the careless secondary sources upon which he relies much too heavily.
His statements of law are selected to support the legal results which ought
to follow upon his view of the fact. Regretably, he failed to head the
principles he enunciated in his opening statement to the court that
tried the High Command case, "[T]he issues here are far too grave
to warrant any trick of advocacy: the evidence is quite compelling
enough to provide its own eloquence."[102]

---

98 TAYLOR, *supra* note 1, at 167.
99 TAYLOR, *supra* note 1, at 167.
100 Griffin v. California, 380 U.S. 609 (1965).
101 TAYLOR, *supra* note 1, at 12-13.
102 United States v. Von Leeb, X TRIALS OF WAR CRIMINALS, *supra* note 11, at 63.

# After My Lai: The Case for War Crimes Jurisdiction Over Civilians in Federal District Courts

## JORDAN J. PAUST*

*One official justification for failure to prosecute ex-soldiers accused of war crimes rests on uncertainty that any acceptable forum has jurisdiction to try former servicemen. Captain Paust argues that the federal district court may apply the international law of war under existing statutes to trials of civilians. Writing as an advocate, Captain Paust proposes innovative constitutional and statutory interpretations that may provide a practical solution for a national dilemma.*

In April 1971 the United States declared that it would not seek to prosecute United States ex-servicemen who have violated the international law of war in Vietnam. Only two justifications were given for the government's failure to engage in a war crimes prosecution program. First, a rather dubious excuse for law enforcement rests on "the view of some government legal experts" that "the issue is 'too hot' politically now."[1] Secondly, some legal experts within the government had expressed a doubt whether present federal law allows the trial of civilians for war crimes committed while in the military. Apparently this doubt has resulted in the termination of prosecution efforts altogether.[2] Although it is not the purpose of this article to question the administration's decision, it seems that refusal to attempt to prosecute ex-servicemen, and refusal thereby to let the courts resolve these legal issues that are said to form a basis for disagreement within executive circles, casts some doubt on the sincerity of the second justification. A lack of consensus within the administrative structure on the validity of a jurisdictional basis for enforcement of the law should not preclude all attempts to prosecute those who have violated widely accepted normative precepts. Moreover, a politically selective enforcement program, which would be tantamount to a rejection of international law[3] and to a rejection of general "law and order," should

---

* Captain, Judge Advocate General's Corps, U.S. Army; Faculty, The Judge Advocate General's School; Member, California Bar; A.B., UCLA, 1965; J.D., 1968; LL.M. program, University of Virginia. The opinions expressed herein are those of the author and do not necessarily represent the views of the Judge Advocate General's School or any other governmental agency.

1 Wash. Post, Apr. 13, 1971, § A, at 1; *see* Wash. Post, Apr. 4, 1971, § A, at 3.

2 The proviso has been added that the door is left open to prosecution in the future. Note 1 *supra*.

3 For the duty under the 1949 Geneva Conventions to prosecute or extradite all persons who have committed "grave breaches" of the Conventions and the general duty to prosecute violators of the international law of war see Paust, *My Lai and Vietnam:*

not be attributed to the present administration. We are left, then, with the question of whether the United States can prosecute ex-servicemen for violations of the law of war.

Three forum possibilities for the trial of ex-servicemen are trial in a general court-martial, trial in a specially created military commission with procedural guarantees implemented as part of its structure, and trial in a federal district court. The first two forum potentials have been ably discussed by other writers.[4] These possibilities were also considered within the government during recent efforts to adopt new legislation in connection with the prosecution of war criminals either in the federal courts or in special tribunals.[5] Some writers have suggested, however, that "[s]ole recourse to general courts-martial" for trial of violations of the international law of war "does not provide a complete solution or one which is entirely satisfactory" since the trial of civilians in a military tribunal could raise serious questions of constitutional dimensions and since there is no compelling reason why United States nationals, who are present within U.S. territory, "should not be accorded a trial before a federal court, including in-

---

*Norms, Myths, and Leader Responsibility* (1971) (not yet in print); Paust, *Legal Aspects of the My Lai Incident: A Response to Professor Rubin,* 50 ORE. L. REV. 138 (1971), in 3 THE VIETNAM WAR AND INTERNATIONAL LAW 359 (R. Falk ed. 1971). There can be no political excuse for failure to enforce the international Geneva law. *See also* THE GENEVA CONVENTIONS OF 12 AUGUST 1949, COMMENTARY IV, GENEVAL CONVENTIONS RELATIVE TO THE PROTECTION OF CIVILIAN PERSONS IN TIME OF WAR (J. Pictet ed. 1958) [hereinafter cited as THE GENEVA CONVENTIONS OF 12 AUGUST 1949, COMMENTARY IV]. Grave breaches will not remain unpunished. *Id.* at 587. "[A]ny person" who committed a grave breach shall be the subject of domestic legislation for prosecution purposes. *Id.* at 592. There is said to be a duty "to ensure that the person concerned is arrested and prosecuted with all speed." *Id.* at 593. The United States and other nations proposed to create an obligation to extradite or prosecute *"all* persons committing or ordering to be committed such grave breaches." III FINAL RECORD OF THE DIPLOMATIC CONFERENCE OF 1949, at 42 (1949) (emphasis added). For a U.S.S.R. proposal see *id.* at 44, and for the text adopted by the Special Committee of the Joint Committee see *id.* at 43. Each proposal and the final text referred to "all" persons. For further discussion see Esgain & Solf, *The 1949 Geneva Convention Relative to the Treatment of Prisoners of War: Its Principles, Innovations, and Deficiencies,* 41 N.C.L. REV. 537, 579 (1963).

4 Note, *Jurisdiction over Ex-servicemen for Crimes Committed Abroad: The Gap in the Law,* 22 CASE W. RES. L. REV. 279 (1971) (advocating future federal district court jurisdiction but failing to recognize the possibility of existing jurisdiction in the district courts); Note, *Jurisdictional Problems Related to the Prosecution of Former Servicemen for Violations of the Law of War,* 56 VA. L. REV. 947 (1970).

5 *See* 115 CONG. REC. 36154 (1969) (statement by Senator Ervin introducing bills S. 3188 and S. 3189, relating to the trial of certain former servicemen and certain other civilians for war crimes if they are no longer subject to trial by military courts-martial); N.Y. Times, July 15, 1970, at 17, col. 1 (concerning new legislation to confer federal court jurisdiction); McGaffin, *U.S. May Try 22 Ex-GI's for My Lai,* N.Y. Post, Mar. 11, 1970, at 4; Mackenzie, *Special War Crimes Panel Weighed to Try Ex-GI's,* Wash. Post, Nov. 27, 1969, at 1; U.S. NEWS & WORLD REPORT, Dec. 22, 1969, at 34; *see generally* N.Y. Times, July 15, 1970, at 17, col. 6; Green, *The Military Commission,* 42 AM. J. INT'L L. 832 (1948) (concerning the creation of a new military commission); Kaplan, *Constitutional Limitations on Trials by Military Commissions,* 92 U. PA. L. REV. 119 (1943); Shaneyfelt, *War Crimes and the Jurisdiction Maze,* 4 INT'L LAWYER 924 (1970).

dictment by grand jury, trial by jury, and trial before a judge with life tenure."[6]

Trial in a federal district court, replete with procedural safeguards, offers an attractive third forum that has received little discussion in recent publications. This article seeks to articulate an argument that jurisdiction presently exists in the federal district courts to entertain prosecutions against civilians for violations of the law of war. Perhaps as lawyers we are singularly inept in changing our historic viewpoints,[7] but it is the purpose of this article, at least in the context of the present topic, to provide the reader with an opportunity to consider a new approach that offers the nation a possibility of law enforcement that conforms to community expectations. Rather than focus on the duty of the United States to enforce the law of war, a topic that has been emphasized by the author in the past,[8] our inquiry will concern the nature of the applicable law within the domestic system, its applicability to civilians and ex-servicemen, the constitutional power of the federal judiciary relative to the prosecution of the law of war, congressional action in the area of law enforcement and forum creation, and some of the procedural aspects of district court trials, including jury trial, appellate review, and venue.

## I. ENACTMENT OF THE LAW OF WAR INTO DOMESTIC CRIMINAL LAW

The first inquiry into the question of jurisdiction in the federal district courts for the prosecution of violations of the law of war should concern the existence of jurisdiction in any domestic forum. Although the United States may well have an international duty to prosecute war criminals,[9] this international obligation cannot by itself constitu-

---

[6] Esgain & Solf, *supra* note 3, at 585-86.

[7] Much of the difficulty seems to stem from an inability of many lawyers writing in this area to perceive any of the present legal possibilities in the absence of an encumbering past experience. Perhaps also associated is a tendency in the legal profession to assign a quality of expertise to those practices or institutions with which most lawyers are unfamiliar. It is inherently dangerous for legalists to allow the tendency to continue because, despite the implications relevant to a legal system based on the experience of the common man (the jury system), the propensity carries with it the possibility of our creating a great number of experts in multiple areas of social concern who will be able to pursue their courses without the benefit of and unimpeded by legal input or inquiry. For a focus on lay expertise and its effect on the role of law and lawyers see Miller, *Drawing the Indictment, Symposium on Science, Technology and the Law*, SATURDAY REV., Aug. 3, 1968, at 39; Reich, *Toward the Humanistic Study of Law*, 74 YALE L.J. 1402 (1965).

[8] *See* note 3 *supra*; U.S. DEP'T OF ARMY, FIELD MANUAL NO. 27-10: THE LAW OF LAND WARFARE ¶¶ 506(b), 507(b) (1956) [hereinafter cited as ARMY FM 27-10]. *See also* U.S. DEP'T OF NAVY, LAW OF NAVAL WARFARE, ¶ 330(a) (1955, Supp. 1965).

[9] *See* note 8 *supra*. Note also that an international obligation is specifically created in the 1949 Geneva Conventions on signatories to prosecute anyone, even a national, who commits a grave breach of the Conventions. *See* Article 146, Geneva Convention Relative

tionally create jurisdiction in a United States forum, or even create domestic criminal law for the purpose of prosecution, since the power to define and punish offenses against the law of nations is one of the enumerated powers given to Congress under Article I, Section 8, of the Constitution.[10] This means the entire Congress has that power, and the obligations incurred by the President with the advice and consent of only the Senate cannot create federal criminal law, even though treaties become the supreme law of the land for other purposes.[11]

---

to the Protection of Civilian Persons in Time of War, Aug. 12, 1949, [1955] 3 U.S.T. 3616, T.I.A.S. No. 3365 (effective Feb. 2, 1956); Article 129, Geneva Convention Relative to the Treatment of Prisoners of War, Aug. 12, 1949, [1955] 3 U.S.T. 3418, T.I.A.S. No. 3364 (effective Feb. 2, 1956); Article 49, Geneva Convention for the Amelioration of the Condition of the Wounded and Sick in Armed Forces in the Field, Aug. 12, 1949, [1955] 3 U.S.T. 3146, T.I.A.S. No. 3362 (effective Feb. 2, 1956); THE GENEVA CONVENTIONS OF 12 AUGUST 1949, COMMENTARY IV, *supra* note 3, at 592-93 (concerning the international duty to prosecute one's own nationals, allies, and enemies). *See also* W. WINTHROP, MILITARY LAW AND PRECEDENTS 778 (2d ed. 1920) (stating that the trial of officers, soldiers, and civilians who have committed violations of the law of war is the duty of each billegerent under the general principles required by nineteenth century usage).

10 *See* The Over the Top, 5 F.2d 838, 845 (D. Conn. 1925) (treaties do not by themselves create federal criminal law); United States v. Ekenstam, 7 U.S.C.M.A. 168, 21 C.M.R. 294 (1956); *see also* Reid v. Covert, 354 U.S. 1 (1957) (rule that regardless of the sovereign power of other nations, the United States is a creature of the Constitution, and any power not contained therein remains in the people). *Contra*, Henfield's Case, 11 F. Cas. 1099, 1120 n.6 (No. 6360) (C.C.D. Pa. 1793) (stating "that though there has been no exercise of the power conferred upon congress by the constitution 'to define and punish offenses against the laws of nations,' the federal judiciary has jurisdiction of an offense against the laws of nations, and may proceed to punish the offender according to the forms of the common law". *See also* United States v. Smith, 27 F. Cas. 1147 (No. 16,323) (C.C.D. Mass. 1792); Morris v. United States, 161 F. 672, 675 (8th Cir. 1908) (dictum) (inferring an exception from the need for congressional implementation for treaties or international law).

It seems that the Supreme Court has not resolved this conflict and, indeed, may have supported the opinion in *Henfield's Case* by distinguishing it from the problem of prosecution of the common law in federal courts without any congressional implementation in that treaty violations have at least partial congressional support by the concurrence of the Senate. *See* United States v. Worrall, 2 U.S. (2 Dall.) 384, 391 (C.C.D. Pa. 1798) and The Three Friends, 166 U.S. 1, 53 (1897) (citing *Henfield's Case* but pointing out that Congress in that instance deemed it "advisable" to pass an implementing act); *see generally Ex parte* Grossman, 267 U.S. 87, 115 (1925) (pointing out that Justice Wilson, a member of the court in *Henfield's Case*, had been a member of the Constitutional Convention and Committee on Style). *Henfield's Case* is extremely interesting because it concerned the prosecution of a United States citizen for a violation of the law of nations, a special session of Congress called by General Washington, and a distinct explanation to the British government by Mr. Jefferson. We shall assume that *The Over the Top* represents the better view today, but shall find that even then we have no real difficulty in establishing the validity of a United States prosecution of the law of war. For a more detailed focus on the constitutional and historic bases of the congressional power to define and punish violations of the law of nations see Comment, *The Offenses Clause: Congress' International Penal Power*, 8 COLUM. J. TRANSNAT'L L. 279 (1969).

11 Reid v. Covert, 354 U.S. 1, 17 (1957); The Over the Top, 5 F.2d 838 (D. Conn. 1925). For the view that treaties, as well as customary international law, become the supreme law of the land, see The Paquete Habana, 175 U.S. 677 (1900). Note that the President may hold a related power to punish violations of the law of war under the separate war power; if this were true, he could impose disciplinary sanctions in certain circumstances against violators under the general power to wage war even though Congress had not acted to define and punish the offenses and thus create federal criminal law. *Cf. Ex parte* Quirin, 317 U.S. 1, 29 (1942). The Court in *Quirin* did not make a decision on the separate question of presidential power but found congressional action in the enactment of

It appears settled, however, that by the Articles of War[12] Congress enacted domestic criminal law to punish violators of the law of war.[13] In *Ex parte Quirin*[14] the Supreme Court stated that Congress had explicitly provided in the Articles of War that military tribunals have the power to try offenses against the law of war in appropriate cases. Traditionally, military law is said to derive its constitutional source from the enumerated power of Congress to make rules for the regulation of the armed forces. In *Ex parte Quirin*, however, the Supreme Court concluded that Congress had not only exercised this enumerated power in enacting the Articles of War but had also exercised the separate power to define and punish offenses against the law of nations.[15] The Court also made it clear that Congress could "define and punish" without specific codification:

> It is no objection that Congress in providing for the trial of such offenses has not itself undertaken to codify that branch of international law or to mark its precise boundaries, or to enumerate or define by statute all the acts which that law condemns.[16]

---

the 1916 Articles of War. The exercise of congressional power coupled with the President's power to execute that law was found to justify jurisdiction in a military commission for an offense against the law of war. *See In re* Yamashita, 327 U.S. 1, 7-8 (1946).

[12] Act of Aug. 29, 1916, ch. 418, § 3, 39 Stat. 650, 652-53 (Articles 12 and 15).

[13] *In re* Yamashita, 327 U.S. 1, 7-8 (1946); *Ex parte* Quirin, 317 U.S. 1, 28, 30 (1942); United States v. Schultz, 1 U.S.C.M.A. 512, 519, 4 C.M.R. 104, 111 (1952). Congress actually incorporated the law of war into United States law. *See* U.N. Doc. E/CN.4/927/Add. 1 (1967) (United States stated that the law of war is "incorporated into" United States law by Article 18 of the U.C.M.J.). Instead of creating a separate codification for the law of war, Congress chose to exercise its power to "define and punish" the law of war as "offenses" against United States law by merely "incorporating" (or "adopting") international law into domestic law. *In re* Yamashita, 327 U.S. 1, 7-8 (1946); *Ex parte* Quirin, 317 U.S. 1, 28, 30 (1942); United States v. Schultz, 1 U.S.C.M.A. 512, 4 C.M.R. 104, (1952). "Congress [has] incorporated by reference . . . all offenses which are defined as such by the law of war." *Id.* at 519, 4 C.M.R. at 111. It is apparently unimportant that Congress chose to exercise its constitutional power to "define and punish" the offenses against the law of war in Title 10 and the offenses of piracy and felonies committed on the high seas or on special federal territory in another title of the United States Code. The law of nations is much broader than the law of war, which is only part of the law of nations. Apparently Congress has not completely exercised its power to implement all of the law of nations by federal statute.

[14] 317 U.S. 1 (1942).

[15] The Court in *Ex parte* Quirin, 317 U.S. 1 (1942), constantly referred to the prosecution of "offenses" against the law of nations, stating that Congress has exercised its authority to define and punish offenses, has "incorporated by reference" all "offenses which are defined as such by the law of war," and has made a choice in "adopting the system of common law applied by military tribunals." *Id.* at 28, 30. A later statement of the Court indicates that the law of war was implemented into United States law: "[T]he Act of Congress, by incorporating the law of war, punishes." *Id.* at 38. These same phrases were repeated in *In re* Yamashita, 327 U.S. 1, 7-8 (1946).

[16] *Ex parte* Quirin, 317 U.S. 1, 29 (1942). The Court continues, "An act of Congress punishing 'the crime of piracy, as defined by the law of nations' is an appropriate exercise of its constitutional authority, Art. 1, § 8, cl. 10, 'to define and punish' the offense, since it has adopted by reference the sufficiently precise definition of international law," citing cases. *Id. See* United States v. Schultz, 1 U.S.C.M.A. 512, 522, 4 C.M.R. 104, 114 (1952)

Since the present Articles 18[17] and 21[18] of the Uniform Code of Military Justice (U.C.M.J.)[19] contain the same language found in Articles 12 and 15 of the old Articles of War, it seems safe to conclude that Congress reenacted the law of war as domestic criminal law[20] when it codified the Articles of War into the U.C.M.J. in 1950 and when it subsequently amended the U.C.M.J. in 1964. This is consistent with the rule that interpretations in force when a statute is reenacted are deemed to have tacit congressional approval. The cases of *Ex parte Quirin*[21] and *In re Yamashita*[22] had interpreted the language of Articles 12 and 15 to create domestic criminal law, and Congress chose not to modify this judicial interpretation when it subsequently reenacted these sections.

If this analysis is correct, then domestic criminal law does exist for the prosecution of violations of the law of war. Since the specific provisions of the U.C.M.J. that deal with the law of war have been held to create an offense against the laws of the United States,[23] enacted under the power of Congress to define and punish offenses against the law of nations, the status of the other provisions of the U.C.M.J. is irrelevant. The law of war, invoked by Articles 18 and 21, will thus

---

(stating that the law of war has its own common law, that it is nowhere precisely codified, and that "[b]y definition, the law of war must be a concept which changes with the practice of war and the customs of nations. It is neither formalized nor static."). A standard is thus provided in the form of international law, and apparently this decision precludes an attack on the ground that the applicable law might be void for vagueness. Furthermore, there being a limit to possible offenses in the international law of war, the existence of sufficient guides and restraints on the President should make Article 18 a proper standard and delegation of congressional power. *See In re* Yamashita, 327 U.S. 1, 17 (1946). *But see* W. WINTHROP, *supra* note 9, at 840 n.13. Winthrop gives examples of such inherently vague charges made in the 1860's as "[b]eing a bad and dangerous man."

[17] Article 18 provides:
> Subject to section 817 of this title (article 17), general courts-martial have jurisdiction to try persons subject to this chapter for any offense made punishable by this chapter and may, under such limitations as the President may prescribe, adjudge any punishment not forbidden by this chapter, including the penalty of death when specifically authorized by this chapter. General courts-martial also have jurisdiction to try any person who by the law of war is subject to trial by a military tribunal and may adjudge any punishment permitted by the law of war. . . .

10 U.S.C. § 818 (1970).

[18] Article 21 provides:
> The provisions of this chapter conferring jurisdiction upon courts-martial do not deprive military commissions, provost courts, or other military tribunals of concurrent jurisdiction with respect to offenders or offenses that by statute or by the law of war may be tried by military commissions, provost courts, or other military tribunals.

10 U.S.C. § 821 (1970).

[19] 10 U.S.C. §§ 801-940 (1970).

[20] *See* Reid v. Covert, 354 U.S. 1, 3 (1957) (referring to violations of the U.C.M.J. as "offenses against the United States."); *Ex parte* Quirin, 317 U.S. 1, 28 (1942).

[21] 317 U.S. 1, 28, 30 (1942).

[22] 327 U.S. 1, 7-8 (1946).

[23] *See* note 13 *supra*.

remain a part of the criminal law of the United States even if the general penal provisions[24] of the U.C.M.J. are interpreted to be mere regulations enacted under the power to regulate the armed forces.

Once it is established that the substantive provisions of the international law of war have been incorporated into domestic criminal law, two important issues remain. First, those who may be held accountable must be identified. The primary inquiry here deals with the amenability of civilians to the law of war. Secondly, the proper tribunals to apply the law of war must be determined.

## II. Applicability of the Law of War to Civilians

This criminal law as enacted by Congress is applicable by its terms to "any person who by the law of war is subject to trial by a military tribunal."[25] Apparently this allows prosecution of certain civilians as well as ex-soldiers and soldiers for violations of the law of war.[26] Although most of the penal provisions of the U.C.M.J. are only applicable to military persons[27] and although cases concerning the application of

---

24 10 U.S.C. §§ 877-940 (1970).

25 10 U.S.C. § 818 (1970). Furthermore, the crime is extraterritorial in nature. *Id.* § 805.

26 *See* United States v. Schultz, 1 U.S.C.M.A. 512, 519, 521, 4 C.M.R. 104, 111, 113 (1952); Yabusaki, 67 B.R. (Army) 265, 271 (1947) (C.M. 318,380). The language "any person" was not without precedent, since the word "whosoever" and the phrase "all persons" were interpreted early in our history to express congressional intent to confirm jurisdiction over civilians and all others. *See, e.g.,* Judge Advocate General of the Army, Digest Op. 132, 133-41, 138-39, 245-48 (1866). Further evidence of the trial of civilians for violations of the law of war by military commission or court-martial appears in W. Winthrop, *supra* note 9, at 778-79, 784 n.57, 787, 791-92, 796; Judge Advocate General of the Army, Digest Op. 1067 n.6, 1070-72 (1918); 11 Op. Att'y Gen. 297 (1865); 3 F. Wharton, Digest of the International Law of the United States 326-30 (1886) (concerning a famous court-martial in 1818); Judge Advocate General's School, Text No. 4, War Powers and Military Jurisdiction 29 (1943). "A military commission is a criminal war court used as an instrumentality for the more efficient execution of the war powers vested in Congress and the President. It is used primarily for the trial of *civilians* for offenses against the laws of war." *Id.* (emphasis supplied). Note that the "war powers" are not the sole basis for jurisdiction. *Cf.* 2 L. Oppenheim, International Law 582 (8th ed. 1958) (citing large numbers of civilians and ex-soldiers tried for war crimes in various national tribunals after World War II); The Geneva Conventions of 1949, Commentary IV, *supra* note 3 (application of the Geneva Conventions to "any person"); W. Winthrop, *supra* note 9, at 776, 778, 779, 831, 834 (prosecution of certain United States civilians other than ex-servicemen); Army FM 27-10, *supra* note 8, ¶ 499 (stating that a war crime is a violation of the law of war by any person, military or civilian); Green, *supra* note 5, at 844. *See also* G.A. Res. 95, U.N. Doc. A/64/Add. 1 (1946) (resolution affirming the principles of the Nuremburg Charter and Judgment); Int'l. L. Comm'n, Report, 5 U.N. GAOR, Supp. 12, U.N. Doc. A/1316 (1950).

27 10 U.S.C. §§ 877-934 (1970). Sections 904 and 906, which deal with the related subjects of treason, espionage, and aiding the enemy, are the only exceptions to the "persons subject to this Chapter" (under Articles 2 and 3 of the U.C.M.J.) language in these subchapter 10 penal articles.

The legislative history of the espionage article may be found in Warren, *Spies and the Power of Congress to Subject Certain Classes of Civilians to Trial by Court-Martial,* 53 Am. L. Rev. 195, 206 (1919), in which Warren states that the application of the espionage article was extended in 1862 from enemy aliens to "all persons" in order to include citizens of the United States, especially Confederate Army personnel and "civilians in sympathy therewith." *See* Act of Feb. 13, 1862, ch. 25, § 2, 12 Stat. 340.

military law seem to turn on a question of military status,[28] Congress apparently intended to apply certain provisions of the U.C.M.J. in Title 10 of the United States Code to civilians.[29] The Supreme Court has dramatically curtailed the power of courts-martial to try servicemen for offenses not related to military service.[30] This contraction of court-martial jurisdiction consequently restricts the application of the general provisions of the U.C.M.J. But it seems that the Supreme Court has cut back on the attempted application of the U.C.M.J. to civilians only in connection with laws based upon the congressional power to regulate the armed forces and on the general jurisdictional sections of the U.C.M.J.[31] The Court has not specifically excluded jurisdiction over civilians under Articles 18 and 21 of the Code,[32] and Article 18 concerns an entirely different body of law, based on an entirely different Congressional power.

It is important to emphasize that Article 18 creates a law not purely military and not purely civilian in nature, but a law designed to punish all offenses against the law of war. The international nature of this law and its corresponding obligations makes it a different creature from either domestic regulations for the government of troop conduct or traditional civilian criminal law. It is a body of international law developed by civilized nations of the world for the prosecution of any person who violates the commandments of the world community. The international scope of the law of war is not diminished by the requirement of our constitutional system that this law be implemented in the United States by congressional legislation. Furthermore, the law of war is implemented under the power to define and punish offenses against the law of nations and remains separate from enactments under the power to regulate the armed forces even though Congress

---

28 See, e.g., Kinsella v. United States ex rel. Singleton, 361 U.S. 234 (1960); McElroy v. Guagliardo, 361 U.S. 281 (1960); United States ex rel. Toth v. Quarles, 350 U.S. 11 (1955); cf. O'Callahan v. Parker, 395 U.S. 258 (1969).

29 See Kinsella v. United States ex rel. Singleton, 361 U.S. 234, 247-49 (1960); Toth v. Quarles, 350 U.S. 11, 14-16 (1955). The Court has prohibited the trial of civilians by courts-martial in peacetime. Reid v. Covert, 354 U.S. 1, 35 (1957). This prohibition, however, does not preclude the application of the law of war to civilians in forums other than courts-martial. See also United States v. Schultz, 1 U.S.C.M.A. 512, 519-20, 4 C.M.R. 104, 111-12 (1952).

30 See O'Callahan v. Parker, 395 U.S. 258 (1969).

31 Cases cited note 28 supra; Latney v. Ignatius, 416 F.2d 821 (D.C. Cir. 1969). The general jurisdictional sections are found in Articles 2 and 3 of the U.C.M.J.

32 Indeed, by citing Ex parte Quirin and In re Yamashita in Toth v. Quarles, 350 U.S. 1, 14 n.4 (1955), Justice Black apparently preserved the application of Article 18 of the U.C.M.J. to civilians. Cases before Toth had also taken the same view. United States v. Schultz, 1 U.S.C.M.A. 512, 519-21, 528; 4 C.M.R. 104, 111-13, 115 (1952); Yabusaki, 67 B.R. (Army) 265, 271 (1947) (C.M. 318,380) (dictum). But cf. Esgain & Solf, supra note 3, at 583 n.182. Esgain and Solf advance the theory that Toth and its progeny concern a separate line of cases from Ex parte Quirin and Yamashita.

has chosen to codify the law of war in the U.C.M.J., sandwiched between enactments of pure "military law." Recent proposals by Senator Ervin to reenact the law of war and to expressly extend federal court jurisdiction to civilians who commit war crimes would also be included in the U.C.M.J.[33]

The difference between the source of congressional power for enactments of pure "military law" and the source of power for violations of the law of war not only allows an important distinction to be made concerning the line of cases culminating in *O'Callahan v. Parker*,[34] but also allows a distinction to be made concerning cases indicating that courts-martial have exclusive jurisdiction over offenses under pure "military law."[35] *Toth v. Quarles* and *O'Callahan v. Parker* dealt with "military law" and the power to regulate the armed forces,[36] whereas *Ex parte Quirin* concerned the international law of war and the power to define and punish offenses against the law of nations.

Winthrop pointed out that the law of war authorizes the arrest, trial, and punishment of American citizens who violate the law of war.[37] A problem arose, however, from the historic statutory restriction of court-martial jurisdiction almost exclusively to members of the military force.[38] This restriction on the power of courts-martial to try civilians led to the creation of the military commission, a tribunal separate from the court-martial and endowed with different powers.

Today we find a similar exclusion by judicial decision of court-martial jurisdiction over civilians concerning "military law," but the exclusion thus far concerns only military law as opposed to court-martial jurisdiction over all persons who violate the law of war under Article 18 of the U.C.M.J. History would seem to show that if the

---

33 Note 5 *supra*. It is "unquestionably competent" for Congress to legislate over two powers in a single statute or article of a statute. United States v. Mackenzie, 30 F. Cas. 1160, 1165 (No. 18,313) (S.D.N.Y. 1846). *See* note 87 *infra*.

34 395 U.S. 258 (1962); cases cited note 28 *supra*.

35 Bell v. Clark, 308 F. Supp. 384, 388 (E.D. Va. 1970); United States v. Mackenzie, 30 F. Cas. 1160 (No. 18,313) (S.D.N.Y. 1846). *See* Burns v. Wilson, 346 U.S. 137, 147 (1953) (dicta in concurring opinion of Minton, J.). This opinion dealt only with the review of court-martial decisions rather than with initial jurisdiction in the federal district courts. *See also* Carter v. Roberts, 177 U.S. 496 (1900) (relevant only to review); *Ex parte* Potens, 63 F. Supp. 582, 586 (E.D. Wis. 1945); United States *ex rel.* Wessels v. McDonald, 265 F. 754, 760 (E.D.N.Y. 1920); *Ex parte* Foley, 243 F. 470, 474 (W.D. Ky. 1917); United States v. Keaton, 19 U.S.C.M.A. 64, 41 C.M.R. 64 (1969) (stating an unawareness of venue in the civilian courts); MANUAL FOR COURTS-MARTIAL, UNITED STATES ¶¶ 8, 12 (1969) [hereinafter cited as MCM] (stating that courts-martial have "exclusive jurisdiction of purely military offenses," but leaving open the question of jurisdiction over offenses against the law of war).

36 The Court was more concerned with jurisdiction of courts-martial than with the law itself. *See also* Reid v. Covert, 354 U.S. 1 (1957); W. WINTHROP, *supra* note 9, at 773.

37 W. WINTHROP, *supra* note 9, at 776, 778.

38 *Id.* at 831.

Supreme Court holds that a civilian may not be tried by court-martial or by military commission, the occasion would again arise for the trial of offenses against the law of war in a different tribunal. The substantive offense would remain, but a change of forum would be required.

Nevertheless, we have not yet reached that state, and Congress and the Supreme Court have left open the possibility of trial of civilians in a military commission. Furthermore, the law of war has been applied to civilians in the past,[39] and this occurred regardless of decisions to exclude civilians from military jurisdiction under "military law." A distinction based on the difference in the nature of the laws involved was implied by language in *Ex parte Mudd*,[40] by dictum in *Hammond v. Squier*,[41] by the Court's declaration in *Ex parte Quirin*,[42] and by the ruling in *Colepaugh v. Looney*.[43]

Of further interest is the fact that approximately 2000 cases were tried by military commission during the Civil War and Reconstruction.[44] In a sense these cases dealt with the trial of our own nationals. Some of these, as in the case of Dr. Mudd,[45] were civilians who were subject to military commission jurisdiction for violations of the law of war during that era.[46] Also of interest would be the trial of United States civilians by military tribunals overseas under the body of international law governing occupation of foreign territory,[47] since jurisdiction rested in Articles 12 and 15 of the old Articles of War.[48] The case of *Madsen v. Kinsella* is also important concerning the concurrent

---

[39] *See* authorities cited note 26 *supra*.

[40] 17 F. Cas. 954 (No. 9899) (S.D. Fla. 1868) (manuscript opinion). *See also* 11 Op. Att'y Gen. 297 (1865).

[41] 51 F. Supp. 227, 232 (W.D. Wash. 1943).

[42] 317 U.S. 1, 37 (1942). The Court declared that the petitioner's status as a United States citizen and civilian would not affect the military commission's jurisdiction to prosecute violations of the law of war.

[43] 235 F.2d 429 (10th Cir. 1956), *cert. denied*, 352 U.S. 1014 (1957). *See also* Reid v. Covert, 354 U.S. 1 (1957); Toth v. Quarles, 350 U.S. 11 (1955); United States v. Schultz, 1 U.S.C.M.A. 512, 519-23, 4 C.M.R. 104, 111-15 (1952); Shaneyfelt, *supra* note 5 (terse, conclusionary account of some of the jurisdictional problems); Note, *Jurisdictional Problems Related to the Prosecution of Former Servicemen for Violations of the Law of War*, 56 Va. L. Rev. 947 (1970) (discussing jurisdiction of a military commission over ex-servicemen but ignoring the possibility of prosecution under Articles 13 and 16 of the Geneva Convention Relative to the Protection of Civilian Persons in Time of War (1949)).

[44] W. Winthrop, *supra* note 9, at 831, 834.

[45] Dr. Mudd was tried for complicity in the assassination of President Lincoln. *See Ex parte* Mudd, 17 F. Cas. 954 (No. 9899) (S.D. Fla. 1868).

[46] *See* W. Winthrop, *supra* note 9, *passim*; United States v. Cashiel, 25 F. Cas. 318 (No. 14,744) (D. Md. 1863); authorities cited note 26 *supra*.

[47] *See, e.g.*, Madsen v. Kinsella, 343 U.S. 341, 358 n.23 (1952). The Court states that the occupation court in Germany tried some 1000 cases a month including twenty-five to thirty cases involving United States civilians. *See also* Rose v. McNamara, 375 F.2d 924 (D.C. Cir.), *cert. denied*, 389 U.S. 856 (1967).

[48] *See* text accompanying note 17 *supra*; United States v. Schultz, 1 U.S.C.M.A. 512, 522, 4 C.M.R. 104, 114 (1952).

jurisdiction of military commissions over violations of the law of war[49] in that the existence of concurrent jurisdiction over these offenses in forums other than courts-martial points to the inaccuracy of any statement that court-martial jurisdiction is exclusive. Furthermore, statements that court-martial jurisdiction is exclusive disregard the express conferral of concurrent jurisdiction in 10 U.S.C. § 821.[50]

The *Schultz*[51] case reaffirmed a statement in *Hammond v. Squier* that the law of war grants to military tribunals no power to try American nationals for "purely military offenses" when they are not subject to "military law."[52] The court went on to state, however, that nothing precludes a military tribunal from prosecuting a civilian for a violation of the law of war.[53] Furthermore, the court held that under Article 12 of the Articles of War general courts-martial have the same jurisdiction over violations of the law of war as other military tribunals, and that such jurisdiction extends to civilians who are subject to the law of war "without regard to whether they may also be subject to military law."[54]

Thus, both the Court of Military Appeals and the federal courts are in agreement that civilians are subject to prosecution in a military commission for violations of the law of war under language like that of the present Articles 18 and 21 of the U.C.M.J.; furthermore both are in agreement that violations of the law of war are not "purely military offenses" or "military law."

---

49 343 U.S. 341, 354-55 (1952).

50 Cases cited note 34 *supra*. Assertions that court-martial jurisdiction is exclusive appear only in cases applying pure "military law" as opposed to cases dealing with the international law of war implemented under Article 18 of the present U.C.M.J. *See also In re* Bush, 84 F. Supp. 873 (D.D.C. 1949) (writ of habeas corpus).

51 United States v. Schultz, 1 U.S.C.M.A. 512, 4 C.M.R. 104 (1952).

52 *Id.* at 522, 4 C.M.R. 104 at 114, *citing* Hammond v. Squier, 51 F. Supp. 227, 231 (W.D. Wash. 1943); *see also* 2 JUDGE ADVOCATE GENERAL OF THE ARMY, DIGEST OP. 939 (1953).

53 The same statement was made in Hammond v. Squier, 51 F. Supp. 227, 232 (W.D. Wash. 1943). But *compare* 24 OP. ATT'Y GEN. 570, 571 (1903) (executive opinion stated that a court-martial loses jurisdiction over a serviceman once he is discharged from the armed forces, and that a military commission loses jurisdiction upon the formal proclamation of peace), *with* Aikins and Severs, 5 B.R. (Army) 331, 360-61 (1949) (C.M. 337,089), *and* United States v. Fleming, 2 C.M.R. 312, 315, 318 (1951) (which allowed court-martial jurisdiction over law of war prosecutions on the basis of Articles 12 and 15 of the 1916 Articles of War and Articles 18 and 21 of the 1950 U.C.M.J. despite the fact that court-martial jurisdiction for regular "military offenses" had expired under old law due to a discharge from prior enlistment). This is logically a precedent for the trial of ex-servicemen in a general court-martial. Note that the "in time of war" problems connected with military commission jurisdiction over ex-servicemen seem to add to the desirability of the federal district court forum.

54 United States v. Schultz, 1 U.S.C.M.A. 512, 519, 4 C.M.R. 104, 111 (1952). Aikins and Severs, 5 B.R. (Army) 331 (1949) (C.M. 337,089) and United States v. Fleming, 2 C.M.R. 312 (1951), confirm the possible jurisdiction over war crimes prosecutions of persons not subject to normal "military law" jurisdiction for past conduct. The court in *Schultz* also declared, "If a specification states an offense in violation of the law of war, categorizing it as a violation of military law is not a fatal defect." United States v. Schultz, *supra* at 523-24, 4 C.M.R. at 115-16.

It seems reasonable to conclude, then, that we have a federal statute that creates federal criminal law to punish violations of the law of war, and that these offenses are also applicable to the prosecution of civilians or ex-servicemen. Another inquiry must be made, however, concerning prosecution under that law in the federal district courts.

### III. JURISDICTION IN THE FEDERAL DISTRICT COURTS

#### A. Concurrent Judicial Action under Constitutional Normative Requirements

Arguably, although Congress has the power to make rules for the regulation of the armed forces under Article I, Section 8, Clause 14, of the Constitution and although Congress may also create courts inferior to the Supreme Court under Article I, Section 8, Congress may not create a quasi-constitutional executive forum[55] with *exclusive* judicial powers concerning the enforcement of acts of Congress once it has also created a judicial forum.

Article III, Section 2, of the Constitution states that the *"judicial power shall extend to all Cases, in Law or Equity, arising under this Constitution, the Laws of the United States, and Treaties made . . ."* (emphasis supplied). Under Article III, Section 2, there exists a dual basis for arguing that the judicial power under Article III extends to the prosecution of offenses against the law of nations incorporated into domestic law: this prosecution involves cases arising under the laws of the United States and, in most instances, would also involve treaties made by the United States. The combination of Article III, Section 2 judicial power bases in the case of violation of the law of war is certainly more solid than in attempts to extend judicial power to "regulations" prescribed by Congress to govern our domestic armed forces—the pure "military law" of the U.C.M.J. It should be noted that federal courts had early declared that judicial power extends to violations of international law,[56] though there has been greater reluctance to extend into the realm of executive troop regulations or pure "military law."[57] Al-

---

[55] By "executive forum" the author means any military tribunal created by the President. This includes courts-martial, military commissions, and provost courts. Although these tribunals have historically been convened by the President pursuant to statutory authority given by Congress, arguably the President could create some of these tribunals without enabling legislation under his war powers as Commander-in-Chief.

[56] Henfield's Case, 11 F. Cas. 1099 (No. 6360) (C.C.D. Pa. 1793). *See* Respublica v. de Longchamps, 1 U.S. (1 Dall.) 111 (Pa. Ct. of Oyer & Terminer 1784); Morris v. United States, 161 F. 672 (8th Cir. 1908); United States v. Smith, 27 F. Cas. 1147 (No. 16,323) (C.C.D. Mass. 1792). For an historic sketch of judicial power function and involvement under the offenses clause see Comment, *supra* note 10, at 293-300.

[57] *See* United States v. Mackenzie, 30 F. Cas. 1160 (No. 18,313) (S.D.N.Y. 1846); *see also* Bell v. Clark, 308 F. Supp. 384 (E.D. Va. 1970), *aff'd*, 437 F.2d 200 (4th Cir. 1971).

though a careful balance is required between judicial and executive roles in the enforcement of general military law, in the area of war crimes prosecution not only is it politically feasible to have a judicial role, but the executive branch would welcome some concurrent judicial involvement. Furthermore, military interests can be completely served in the constitutional sense. If there is a sufficient military connection, the military has complete control in the prosecution of conduct as a violation of the military regulations or "pure" military law under the U.C.M.J. as has been the practice and policy.[58]

This does not necessarily mean that an executive forum cannot exist, nor that Congress cannot cut back the judicial power of particular inferior courts within the judicial system.[59] It seems, however, that when a matter involves the judicial power an executive forum cannot itself exercise "judicial power" functions to the exclusion of those forums in which the judicial power has been vested by reason of Article III, Section 1. In other words, Congress cannot constitutionally preclude all judicial action within Article III courts concerning the enforcement of the laws of the United States, since an attempted cutback of every judicial involvement in a "judicial power" function, when Congress also grants executive power to carry out similar functions, would in that total context constitute a direct interference with the judicial power. This is particularly true where criminal laws are concerned. It is too simplistic to argue that there is no interference with the judicial power when an executive forum has been granted the right to act by Congress and Congress can withdraw certain judicial powers. This is too simplistic because the argument ignores the problem posed by Article III, Section 2, when a judicial forum in fact exists.

Indeed, a judicial-power forum exists in the federal district courts, and Congress granted to the federal courts jurisdiction over "all offenses

---

[58] *See* ARMY FM 27-10, *supra* note 8, ¶ 507:

Violations of the law of war committed by persons subject to the military law of the United States will usually constitute violations of the Uniform Code of Military Justice and, if so, will be prosecuted under that Code.

This means "pure" military law. This military control of prosecution would probably also extend to the trial of civilians when in the field and in time of war. The remaining cases, trial of civilians at home, do not involve any interference with military power if prosecution exists in federal courts as much as an interference with judicial power if prosecution exists in military tribunals as far as functional power alignment is concerned under our constitutional normative values. Reid v. Covert, 354 U.S. 1 (1957) states:

Every extension of military jurisdiction is an encroachment on the jurisdiction of the civil courts, and, more important, acts as a deprivation of the right to jury trial and other assured constitutional protections.

*Id.* at 21.

[59] *See* Lockerty v. Phillips, 319 U.S. 182, 187 (1943). For a discussion of congressional control over federal court jurisdiction see C. WRIGHT, LAW OF FEDERAL COURTS § 10, at 22-26 (2d ed. 1970).

against the laws of the United States" in 18 U.S.C. § 3231. Judicial power extends to all cases arising under the laws of the United States, and therefore extends to "all offenses against the laws of the United States" as "cases arising under" those laws. Therefore, federal courts have the judicial power to prosecute all offenses against the laws of the United States. The only question seems to be whether Congress has cut back on this power and, if it has, whether it can do so constitutionally by exclusive executive jurisdiction. One argument made in *United States v. Mackenzie*[60] was that the fifth amendment modified some judicial requirements in cases arising under the armed forces, but the fifth amendment mentions only indictment by grand jury and does not seem to reduce the judicial power itself.

Apparently extending the judicial cutback is language in *Bell v. Clark*:[61]

> The civil courts do not have concurrent jurisdiction with military tribunals to try crimes arising under the Uniform Code of Military Justice. See 10 U.S.C. § 821.

That court went on to say that Congress has the power to extend the application of a criminal statute to extraterritorial acts of United States citizens[62] and has acted pursuant to that power to enact 18 U.S.C. § 3238 to provide a forum for the trial of offenses against the United States not committed within any state. The court, however, failed to recognize the possibility of prosecution of any U.C.M.J. offense in the federal district court. It should be noted, however, that the offense with which the court was concerned in *Bell v. Clark* was an offense of the pure "military law" type and not a violation of the law of war under Article 18 of the U.C.M.J.[63] The difference in the nature of the offenses and congressional powers involved may cause the same court to reach a different conclusion regarding an offense against the law of war. Later in this article we shall consider the accuracy of the court's reason-

---

60 30 F. Cas. 1160 (No. 18,313) (S.D.N.Y. 1846).

61 308 F. Supp. 384, 388-89 (E.D. Va. 1970), *aff'd*, 437 F.2d 200 (4th Cir. 1971). *See* cases cited note 34 *supra*; United States v. Mackenzie, 30 F. Cas. 1160 (No. 18,313) (S.D.N.Y. 1846). *Mackenzie* "is not an adjudicated case, but the report of the charge of Judge Betts to a grand jury." Neall v. United States, 118 F. 699, 703 (9th Cir. 1902).

62 308 F. Supp. 384, 388 (E.D. Va. 1970). The court cited United States v. Bowman, 260 U.S. 94 (1922) and Chandler v. United States, 171 F.2d 921 (1st Cir. 1948), *cert. denied*, 336 U.S. 918 (1949). Numerous sections of Title 18, U.S.C. (1970) have extraterritorial application, *e.g.*, § 471 (counterfeiting); § 1001 (fraud and false statements against United States); § 1111(B) (murder within special territorial and maritime jurisdiction); § 1952 (use of interstate and foreign commerce to aid racketeering); § 2073 (false entries and reports of monies and securities); § 2101 (riots); § 2381 (treason).

63 The offense was rape in violation of 10 U.S.C. § 920 (1970).

ing concerning its interpretation of Article 21 of the U.C.M.J.; it is sufficient to point out here that this court apparently would not grant concurrent jurisdiction in the federal courts, though the issue was not raised in that case as one involving a violation of the law of war by a civilian. Also of interest is *United States v. Keaton*,[64] in which the Court of Military Appeals declared that it was not aware of venue in the civil courts for those offenses prescribed in the Uniform Code which are not, at the same time, violations of the laws enacted under the authority of Article III, Section 2, of the Constitution. The court there dealt with a military offense, and not a law of war violation.

These cases do not preclude an assertion of *judicial* power by the Article III courts. In fact, *United States v. Keaton* indicates that the Court of Military Appeals is merely unaware of such an assertion; and *Bell v. Clark* represents the apparent intent of one district court not to assert this power. Courts-martial are not justified by the Executive branch as Article III courts and are said to have no part of the judicial power.[65] Assuming this to be correct, we need not analyze the power of Congress to limit Supreme Court review of criminal cases from an inferior court created with judicial power under Article III.[66] It is sufficient to point out that courts-martial could not exercise exclusive judicial powers since they possess no judicial power in the first place.

It follows that the federal courts, since they alone can contain the *judicial* power under Article III and the judicial power *extends* to all cases arising under the laws of the United States, have at least "concurrent" jurisdiction concerning enforcement of the laws of the United States. Therefore, it is not necessary for us to inquire into the growth of the constitutional grant of power of Congress to "make rules" into an ability to set up an executive system for judicial determinations relative to the penal or disciplinary enforcement of those rules once they are made. However suspect this growth and this attempted by-pass of the judicial power may be in the eyes of some,[67] it is sufficient here to consider the argument that Congress, the Executive, or any combina-

---

64 19 U.S.C.M.A. 64, 67, 41 C.M.R. 64, 67 (1969).

65 *See* O'Callahan v. Parker, 395 U.S. 258 (1969); Kinsella v. Krueger, 351 U.S. 470, 475 (1956); Toth v. Quarles, 350 U.S. 11, 17 (1955); Kurtz v. Moffitt, 115 U.S. 487, 500 (1885); Dynes v. Hoover, 61 U.S. (20 How.) 65 (1857); United States *ex rel.* Wessels v. McDonald, 265 F. 754 (E.D.N.Y. 1920); MCM, *supra* note 35, ¶ 8; DEPARTMENT OF THE ARMY, PAM. NO. 27-174, at 16 (1965); W. WINTHROP, *supra* note 9, at 49.

66 U.S. CONST. art. III, § 2. But 10 U.S.C. § 876 (1970) states that courts-martial decisions are final and binding. Apparently one can argue that Congress can limit appellate jurisdiction only from Article III courts and that 10 U.S.C. § 876 does not constitutionally bind the Supreme Court if courts-martial are not in fact Article III courts.

67 *See* cases cited note 28 *supra*; Reid v. Covert, 354 U.S. 1 (1957).

tion of the two cannot exercise judicial power in the area of criminal law to the exclusion of at least concurrent action in the judiciary.[68]

Furthermore, any expertise developed by the military in this area can be readily utilized by the federal courts through the calling of military personnel as expert witnesses. The Court in *Sterling v. Constantin*[69] was unwilling to defer to military expertise in an area concerning the limits of "military discretion, and whether or not they have been overstepped in a particular case" and declared that, when concerned with martial law as opposed to civilian law, such determinations are "judicial questions."

The long history of military court-martial or military commission action does not preclude concurrent judicial action. This history merely helps to establish congressional ability under Article I, Section 8, to create a forum for executive action in the exercise of the power to regulate the armed forces. Actually, the real growth of executive power to regulate the armed forces has only taken place in the latter half of our nation's history. Prior to 1863 Congress itself had not even authorized military jurisdiction over military persons who had committed civilian type offenses such as murder, rape or robbery—offenses now described by our courts as governed by "military law."[70] At common law soldiers were prosecuted for any offense in the civil courts except when "in time of war" and "in the field."[71] Even if it were argued that a long exercise of uninterrupted power has carved out exclusive jurisdiction in courts-martial, that historical development does not preclude a correction to conform to the overriding source of power in Article III of the Constitution.

We may also note that even during the historical development, general principles have emerged in the area of joint offenses. One of these principles is that jurisdiction of civil and military tribunals is

---

68 The Court has stated that "Constitutional prohibitions . . . cannot be nullified by the Executive or by the Executive and the Senate combined." Reid v. Covert, 354 U.S. 1, 17 (1957). Arguably, the two bodies cannot entirely exclude the judiciary from operating when a matter involves the judicial power under Article III, Section 2, of the Constitution. Since the judicial power exists in a judicial forum and has been extended to certain matters, it would be as constitutionally violative to deny judicial involvement as it was in the case of *Reid v. Covert* to deny due process rights to individuals. Each would entail a destruction of constitutional grants by the executive branch. Furthermore, the language quoted in the *Reid* case is in conformity with the principle enunciated in The Over the Top, 5 F.2d 838, 845 (D. Conn. 1925), which also supports the argument here that two governmental bodies cannot destroy or usurp the power granted to another body through the Constitution. *Contra,* United States v. Mackenzie, 30 F. Cas. 1160, 1166 (No. 18,313) (S.D.N.Y. 1846).

69 287 U.S. 378, 401 (1932).

70 Reid v. Covert, 354 U.S. 1, 23 n.42 (1957); 8 Op. Att'y Gen. 396 (1857).

71 354 U.S. at 24-25 n.44.

generally concurrent and not exclusive.[72] There seems no reason why this principle should not apply when concurrent jurisdiction is based upon an offense against the law of war as implemented under 10 U.S.C. § 818.[73]

It is clear today that in the area of dual offenses, courts-martial do not possess exclusive jurisdiction in cases in which an act is also prosecutable in the state courts,[74] or the federal district courts.[75] Conversely, that an act is also prosecutable in the district courts does not stop the military from exercising court-martial jurisdiction if some service connection exists.[76] Furthermore, it cannot be assumed that Congress ever intended, even in time of war, to deprive the Government of the United States of the right to try persons for crimes committed against it.[77] The problem is that it is not altogether clear in our law whether initial jurisdiction exists in the federal courts for the same offense as is prosecutable in military tribunals. Although Congress has never expressly limited the prosecution of crimes under Title 10 to a military forum, these crimes have thus far been prosecuted only in military courts.[78]

---

[72] United States v. Cashiel, 25 F. Cas. 318 (No. 14,744) (D. Md. 1863); *Ex parte* Koester, 56 Cal. App. 621, 206 P. 116 (1922); Application of Baer, 180 Misc. 330, 41 N.Y.S.2d 413 (1943); *Ex parte* Bright, 1 Utah 145 (1874). *Cf.* O'Callahan v. Parker, 395 U.S. 258, 268 (1969) (statement that a military trial of a soldier committing a civilian offense is suspect).

[73] *Contra,* Bell v. Clark, 308 F. Supp. 384 (E.D. Va. 1970). *But see* Henfield's Case, 11 F. Cas. 1099 (No. 6360) (C.C.D. Pa. 1793).

[74] "Undoubtedly the general rule is that the jurisdiction of civil courts is concurrent as to offenses triable before courts-martial." Franklin v. United States, 216 U.S. 559, 568 (1910). *See, e.g.,* Caldwell v. Parker, 252 U.S. 376 (1920); United States ex rel. Drury v. Lewis, 200 U.S. 1 (1906); Castle v. Lewis, 254 F. 917 (8th Cir. 1918); United States v. Matthews, 49 F. Supp. 203 (E.D. Ala. 1943); United States ex rel. Wessels v. McDonald, 265 F. 754, 760 (E.D.N.Y. 1920); Scott v. State, 247 Ala. 62, 22 So. 2d 529 (1945); People v. Denman, 179 Cal. 497, 177 P. 461 (1918); *Ex parte* Koester, 56 Cal. App. 621, 624, 206 P. 116, 118 (1922); State v. Inman, 224 N.C. 531, 31 S.E.2d 641 (1944), *cert. denied,* 323 U.S. 805 (1944); *Ex parte* Sumner, 143 Tex. Crim. 238, 158 S.W.2d 310 (1942); Funk v. State, 84 Tex. Crim. 402, 208 S.W. 509 (1919).

[75] *See, e.g.,* Schmitt v. United States, 413 F.2d 219 (5th Cir. 1969); Kennedy v. Sanford, 166 F.2d 568 (5th Cir. 1948); Canella v. United States, 157 F.2d 470 (9th Cir. 1946); United States v. Hirsch, 254 F. 109 (E.D.N.Y. 1918); United States v. Carr, 25 F. Cas. 306 (No. 14,732) (C.C.S.D. Ga. 1872); United States v. Cashiel, 25 F. Cas. 318 (No. 14,744) (D. Md. 1863); United States v. Cornell, 25 F. Cas. 646 (No. 14,866) (C.C.D.R.I. 1819).

[76] United States v. Daniels, 19 U.S.C.M.A. 529, 42 C.M.R. 131 (1970); United States v. Harris, 18 U.S.C.M.A. 596, 40 C.M.R. 308 (1969).

[77] United States v. Canella, 63 F. Supp. 377, 383 (S.D. Cal. 1945), *aff'd,* 157 F.2d 470 (9th Cir. 1946). Arguably, Congress could not have intended to prosecute the law of war and also to make military jurisdiction exclusive since this would deprive the United States of the ability to prosecute the law against civilians. Congress was aware of judicial restrictions on military jurisdiction over civilians because the most recent enactment of the U.C.M.J. followed *Toth* and the other cases that curtailed military jurisdiction over civilians for violations of "pure military law."

[78] *Contra,* Henfield's Case, 11 F. Cas. 1099 (No. 6360) (C.C.D. Pa. 1793). That case did not involve a pure military offense but a violation of international law.

## B.  Congressional Conferral of Federal Court Jurisdiction

Besides the argument that Congress could not preclude some sort of concurrent judicial action in this area, there exists an argument that Congress has conferred original jurisdiction over all offenses against the laws of the United States by 18 U.S.C. § 3231 (originally the Judicial Courts Act of Sept. 24, 1789)[79] in the federal district courts, and has never expressly declared that Title 10 offenses, which are offenses against the laws of the United States, are not prosecutable in federal courts. Furthermore, the specific grant of jurisdiction to the military forums, in Articles 18 and 21 of the U.C.M.J., neither impliedly deprives the civil courts of the concurrent jurisdiction they already possess nor makes military jurisdiction exclusive.[80]

One might still argue that the two congressional grants of jurisdiction, one to the federal courts and the other to the military, imply that each of the grants is exclusive. There are two problems with this argument, however. First, the grant to the federal district courts concerns jurisdiction over all offenses against the laws of the United States, which by plain language includes Title 10 offenses. One might still conjure that military jurisdiction was impliedly, and contrary to plain language, exclusive and not concurrent. If this is the ground, it would be well to point out that such is not a normal interpretation or

---

[79] 1 Stat. 73 (1789). Under the Judicial Courts Act the circuit courts shared "exclusive cognizance of *all crimes and offences cognizable under the authority of the United States,* (a) except as this act otherwise provides, or the laws of the United States shall otherwise direct" (emphasis added) under a system of district and circuit court jurisdiction. *Id.* at 76, 79. The current 18 U.S.C. § 3231 (1970) provides:

> The district courts of the United States shall have original jurisdiction, exclusive of the courts of the States, of all offenses against the laws of the United States.

> Nothing in this title shall be held to take away or impair the jurisdiction of the courts of the several States under the laws thereof.

[80] People v. Denman, 179 Cal. 497, 177 P. 461 (1918) (specifically referring to the same language as found in Articles 12 and 15 of the old Articles of War, Act of Aug. 29, 1916, ch. 418, 39 Stat. 650). *Accord,* United States v. State of California, 328 F.2d 729, 733 (9th Cir. 1964), *citing* Gittings v. Crawford, 10 F. Cas. 447, 450 (No. 5465) (C.C.D. Md. 1838), which was quoted in Börs v. Preston, 111 U.S. 252, 260 (1884); United States v. Bank of N.Y. & Trust Co., 296 U.S. 463, 477-78 (1935); *see* Neall v. United States, 118 F. 699, 705 (9th Cir. 1902); United States v. Hirsch, 254 F. 109, 112-13 (E.D.N.Y. 1918). *See also* Caldwell v. Parker, 252 U.S. 376, 388 (1920); Coleman v. Tennessee, 97 U.S. 509, 514 (1878).

In our history it seems that the federal courts had exclusive jurisdiction over all crimes and offenses cognizable under U.S. authority except where otherwise "direct[ed]" (i.e., by specific language), 1 Stat. 73, 79 (1789). The military (though experienced in prosecution since the Revolution) was later said to be "governed by the rules and articles of war," 1 Stat. 96 (1789); but nothing was stated to the effect that Congress thereby directed that military jurisdiction was to be exclusive in the governing of a soldier's conduct or that offenses cognizable under U.S. authority (as with implementation and prosecution of the law of war) could not fall within the ambit of federal jurisdiction. Indeed, it seems that on this point we are in the same position today.

inference. This should not be a permissible inference constitutionally since the judicial power should not be exclusive in an executive forum that possesses no judicial power in the first place.

One recent case apparently to the contrary is *Bell v. Clark*;[81] but

---

[81] 308 F. Supp. 384 (E.D. Va. 1970), *aff'd*, 437 F.2d 200 (4th Cir. 1971). The same conclusion is found in dictum by Justice Washington in Houston v. Moore, 18 U.S. (5 Wheat.) 1, 28-29 (1820), in which he states: "[M]ilitary offenses are not included in the act of Congress, conferring jurisdiction upon the Circuit and District Courts; no person has ever contended that such offenses are cognizable before the common law Courts . . . ." It is interesting to note that the same Justice said later in arguing another of his own views that "the mere assignment of jurisdiction to a particular Court, does not necessarily render it exclusive." In United States v. Mackenzie, 30 F. Cas. 1160, 1166 (No. 18,313) (S.D.N.Y. 1846) the court went further in stating that the military has exclusive jurisdiction over "the subject matter within their cognizance." The court stated that the Articles of War, 1 Stat. 96 (1789), were within the exclusive cognizance of courts-martial and that the Crimes Act of 1790, 1 Stat. 112, did not change that result and establish federal court jurisdiction over violations of military penal law. Even if we accept this interpretation, the problem remains concerning *violations of the law of war* which are not purely military penal law derived from the power of Congress to regulate the armed forces. If it is true, as stated in United States v. Mackenzie, *supra* at 1164, that the fifth amendment excepts from the Third Article of the Constitution the requirement of a jury trial in some cases arising in the armed forces, nothing is mentioned in the fifth amendment concerning violations of the law of nations. Furthermore, the court recognized that the offense there did not involve a violation of the law of nations but a violation of military law under the old Articles of War, and the history of the exercise of those two congressional powers is quite different. Presumably violations of international law at that time would fall under the Crimes Act of 1790 since they were not part of the Articles of War of 1789 and did not involve the same historic background.

It should be added that before the 1789 Articles of War or the 1790 Crimes Act the *states* were called upon to exercise jurisdiction over violations of the law of nations, and this fact adds to the arguments that there was a distinction between "military offenses" and violations of the international law of war, that a dual potential for prosecution existed in state courts and military tribunals, and that there had been a history of civil court jursidiction over law of war violations which should be of some import in our inquiry as to whether law of war prosecutions in 1790 and later could have properly fallen under the Articles of War or the Crimes Act or both. *See* J. KENT, COMMENTARY ON INTERNATIONAL LAW 427 (1866), citing 7 JOURNALS OF CONGRESS 181, which state that during the Revolutionary War the Congress determined to "maintain inviolate the obligations of the law of nations, and to have infractions of it punished in the only way that was then lawfule, by the exercise of the authority of the several states . . . ." *See* Wright, *The Law of the Nuremberg Trial*, 41 AM. J. INT'L L. 38 (1947) ("The Continental Congress of the United States in several resolutions adopted, from 1779 to 1781, called upon States to provide for punishment of 'offenses against the law of nations.'") An example of state court jurisdiction over violations of the law of nations is the case of Respublica v. de Longchamps, 1 U.S. (1 Dall.) 111 (Pa. Ct. of Oyer & Terminer 1784).

Even if the *Mackenzie* case is good law today, one could argue that courts-martial have exclusive jurisdiction over purely military offenses until further congressional action, but that it was *possible* to pursue federal court jurisdiction over violations of international law under the early Crimes Act, which punished offenses against the United States law. *But see* Henfield's Case, 11 F. Cas. 1099, 1120 (No. 6360) (C.C.D. Pa. 1793), stating that there had been no exercise of the power to define and punish violations of the law of nations by 1793 (apparently no express exercise of that power at least), although this lack of express congressional implementation did not stop that court from pursuing the prosecution of international law in a federal court. None of these cases directly limits prosecution of violations of the law of nations in the federal district courts today, although it is evident from a reading of the cases that different possibilities of interpretation exist, and it is not the intent of the author to ignore those different possibilities. However, the fact that two views are possible does not detract from the validity of the better view, if there be one, and the reader should note that the author retains almost tenaciously the right to argue what he considers to be the better view: that Congress has not restricted the right of the federal courts to prosecute violations of the law of nations known as the law of war.

the court gave no reason for its conclusion that civil courts do not have jurisdiction other than a mere citation of Article 21 of the U.C.M.J. The court's conclusion apparently disregards the interpretation by many courts over the years[82] that the language in Article 21 does not impliedly deprive the civil courts of the jurisdiction they already possess.

The implied conclusion in *Bell v. Clark* that Article 21 excludes civil court jurisdiction because of an implication through silence is not in conformity with the principle enunciated in *Reid v. Covert*[83] that, under the grand design of the Constitution, civil courts are the normal repositories of power to try persons charged with crimes against the United States. This principle, when connected with the ruling of the case itself, implies that no complete transfer of civil court jurisdiction to the military courts can ever be inferred and that an express congressional denial of civil court jurisdiction is necessary.[84] That *Reid v. Covert* implies that civil court jurisdiction continues unless expressly excluded is further supported by language in the *Reid* case stating that military jurisdiction is extraordinary and very limited. The Court in *Reid* also stated that military jurisdiction was "intended to be only a narrow exception to the normal and preferred method of trial in courts of law."[85]

In light of this opinion it would be unrealistic and simplistic to conclude that Congress by enacting this extraordinary and narrow exception excluded by implication and silence the normal, preferred method of trial. There is no evidence of congressional intent to derogate the jurisdiction that the civil courts already possess. To infer such an intent is contrary to the history of our system, the many relevant cases decided over the years, the principles which *Reid v. Covert* and *O'Callahan v. Parker* found fundamental to justice under the law, the mandate of Article III of the Constitution that judicial power be in the Article III courts, and the express grant of original jurisdiction to federal district courts over all offenses against the laws of the United States.[86]

---

82 *See* cases cited notes 69, 70 & 72 *supra.*

83 354 U.S. 1, 21-22 (1957). This case was cited in Bell v. Clark, 308 F. Supp. 384 (E.D. Va. 1970), but the court apparently did not conclude that the principles there enunciated could overcome an inference from silence in Article 21 of the U.C.M.J.

84 *See* Neall v. United States, 118 F. 699, 705 (9th Cir. 1902). *Contra,* United States v. Mackenzie, 30 F. Cas. 1160 (No. 18,313) (S.D.N.Y. 1846).

85 Reid v. Covert, 354 U.S. 1, 21 (1957).

86 18 U.S.C. § 3231 (1970). Furthermore, there is an actual implication to the contrary (i.e., that the statute did not intend to create exclusive military jurisdiction but only guarantee more clearly the concurrent jurisdiction of certain military tribunals). In *Yabusaki,* 67 B.R. (Army) 265, 270 (1947) (C.M. 318,380), General Crowder's quoted testimony

Furthermore, *Reid v. Covert*[87] stated that no statute can be framed to make civilians amenable to military jurisdiction in time of peace. It could be argued that Articles 18 and 21 of the U.C.M.J. cannot be interpreted to make civilians amenable to military jurisdiction; it could further be argued that, if Article 18 applies the law of war to civilians, necessarily Congress intended that the law be enacted in Article 18 but that prosecutions of civilians for violating that law in time of peace be tried in the federal courts under 18 U.S.C. § 3231 and not in military courts. This would merely require a court to conclude that Article 18 of the U.C.M.J. enacts the law, but that Article 21 impliedly recognizes the preexisting jurisdiction in the federal courts under 18 U.S.C. § 3231. In interpreting Article 21 of the U.C.M.J., a court might consider the following language from *Lewis v. United States*:[88]

> It would require plain language to justify courts to construe a statute to the effect that the courts are deprived of jurisdiction to try persons charged with commission of crimes and in effect proclaim a general pardon for criminals not yet tried. Clearly Congress did not intend such a disastrous result.

Even if the distinction between the law of war and "military law" is interpreted to allow trial of civilians in military tribunals for war crimes, the normative principle that Article III courts should be the repositories of judicial power still militates against a holding that military tribunals have exclusive jurisdiction to try civilians for violations of the law of war.

The following language of *Neall v. United States*[89] concerning joint offenses and the old federal court system also seems relevant to our present consideration:

> Forcible reasons may be suggested why courts-martial should be given exclusive jurisdiction of all offenses which are punishable under the articles of war, but we are not convinced that either in the constitution or in the acts of congress the intention has been expressed to except from the jurisdiction of the civil courts offenses committed by any persons or class

---

before the Senate Military Affairs Committee in 1916 concerning the old Article 15 (now Article 21, U.C.M.J.) reveals the congressional intent when he stated that the Article "just saves the war courts the jurisdiction they now have and makes concurrent a jurisdiction with courts-martial, so that the military commander in the field in time of war will be at liberty to employ either form of court that happens to be convenient . . . ." *See* S. REP. No. 130, 64th Cong., 1st Sess. 40 (1915).

[87] 354 U.S. 1, 35 (1957); *accord*, O'Callahan v. Parker, 395 U.S. 258 (1969).
[88] 14 F.2d 369, 371 (8th Cir. 1926).
[89] 118 F. 699, 705 (9th Cir. 1902).

of persons. . . . The judiciary act of September 24, 1789, gives
to the circuit courts "exclusive cognizance of all crimes and
offenses cognizable under the authority of the United States,
except where this act otherwise provides, or the laws of the
United States shall otherwise direct."

The court went on to say that the circuit courts may be given concurrent jurisdiction with other tribunals whenever the laws of the United
States shall so direct, and that it was so directed by the Act of April 30,
1790 concerning the Articles of War. The court then stated:

> There has been, and is, no express enactment that the jurisdic-
> tion of the military courts shall be exclusive, or that the
> general grant of jurisdiction to the circuit court shall in such
> cases be superseded. The intention to devest the civil courts
> of their regular jurisdiction will not be ascribed to congress in
> the absence of clear and direct language to that effect, in
> view of the "known hostility of the American people to any
> interference by the military with the regular administration of
> justice in the civil courts." Coleman v. Tennessee, 97 U.S.
> 509, 514, 24 L. Ed. 1118.[90]

Here it is argued that the federal district courts already possess jurisdiction to entertain prosecutions for violations of the law of war under
10 U.S.C. §§ 818 and 821 by reason of the jurisdiction conferred on the
district courts to entertain original jurisdiction over *all* offenses against
the laws of the United States under 18 U.S.C. § 3231. Congress did not
expressly exclude federal court jurisdiction in enacting the U.C.M.J. in
1950 and again in 1968. Express exclusion is necessary under 18 U.S.C.
§ 3231, and, therefore, the original jurisdiction of the civil courts to
prosecute all offenses against the laws of the United States continues to
exist. Since a violation of the law of war is an offense against the laws
of the United States, it can be prosecuted in the federal district courts,
which are the normal and preferred forums for all United States
prosecutions.[91]

---

90 *Id. See also* Reid v. Covert, 354 U.S. 1, 21 (1957). The language in *Neall* is directly
contrary to the argument made in United States v. Mackenzie, 30 F. Cas. 1160 (No. 18,313)
(S.D.N.Y. 1846).

91 Reid v. Covert, 354 U.S. 1 (1957). In note 76 *supra* it is pointed out that the first
Articles of War in 1789 did not contain violations of the law of nations and the language
of the first Crimes Act of 1790 conferred jurisdiction on the federal courts for violations
of all offenses against the laws of the United States or offenses cognizable under the authority of the United States except where prohibited. Apparently the 1790 Act put all
other offenses against the United States under federal court jurisdiction. Since congressional implementation of the law of war would constitute United States law, jurisdiction
would have been in the federal courts. It is not relevant then that specific implementation
of the law of war as United States law did not come until later and then under a different

It is not necessary to decide whether military jurisdiction is a form of executive or judicial power for the purpose of establishing concurrent jurisdiction in the federal courts, although the rule is that military forums possess no judicial power. Furthermore, nothing expressly or directly precludes the bringing of an action in the federal district court even after commencement of executive action in the military forum. Only two expressions stand in the way of such an action in the federal courts: first, the rule of *Ponzi v. Fessenden*,[92] which allows jurisdiction to proceed in the forum which first takes custody of the accused;[93] and secondly, 10 U.S.C. § 844(a) which prohibits a second trial for the same offense. However, 10 U.S.C. § 844(b) states:

> No proceeding in which the accused has been found guilty by a court-martial upon any charge or specification is a trial in the sense of this article until the finding of guilty has become final after review of the case has been completed.

This apparently leaves open the possibility of prosecutions in two different forums until one of them becomes final.

The author has contended thus far that the law of war has been enacted into domestic criminal law, that this domestic criminal law applies to civilians, and that the district courts have jurisdiction, derived either from the general conferral of jurisdiction to the district courts for crimes against the United States or from constitutional implications, to try civilians for offenses against the law of war.

If this is the state of existing law, the procedural complements of district court jurisdiction are well suited to the trial of these cases. If this is held not to be the state of existing law, procedural advantages to trial in the district court argue in favor of express congressional creation of jurisdiction in the district courts.

## IV. PROCEDURAL ASPECTS OF DISTRICT COURT TRIALS FOR WAR CRIMES

### A. Availability of Jury Trial

One argument in favor of district court jurisdiction over civilian violators of the law of war stems from the availability of jury trial in

---

statute. In United States v. Mackenzie, 30 F. Cas. 1160, 1165 (No. 18,313) (S.D.N.Y. 1846), the proposition is advanced that it is "unquestionably competent for congress to legislate over all those subjects [different powers] in a single statute or section . . . ."

[92] 258 U.S. 254 (1922); *accord*, United States v. Wells, 28 F. Cas. 522 (No. 16,665) (D. Minn. 1872).

[93] *Cf.* cases cited note 28 *supra*.

the district courts. Military tribunals have not traditionally utilized a citizen jury. The Court suggested in *Ex parte Quirin* that some violations of the law of war may require trial by jury:

> We may assume that there are . . . offenses against the law of war which would not be triable by military tribunal here . . . because they are of that class of offenses constitutionally triable only by jury.[94]

Although the language does not imply that violations of the law of war are triable in the federal district court, it certainly implies that some offenses may be "constitutionally triable only by a jury" and that a forum with a jury system would be required.[95] This statement does provide some guidance when coupled with the view that the Court must interpret congressional enactments concerning the creation of a quasi-constitutional forum in a manner that does not restrict jurisdiction of a constitutional forum unless expressly so restricted by Congress.

The argument could be made that since some of the offenses must be tried by a jury, Congress could not have impliedly precluded concurrent jurisdiction for the prosecution of such offenses in a jury system. The courts will not infer a congressional intent that would be contrary to an express purpose to prosecute violations of the law of war. The courts should not recognize an express congressional intent to enforce the law and then infer from silence an intent to limit the government in its ability to enforce the law. In fact, it could be argued that Congress, by expressing a purpose to enforce the law of war, has impliedly reserved concurrent jurisdiction in the proper forum for its enforcement—the federal district courts, at least for offenses that would only be constitutionally triable in a federal court or a similar system under the name of a military commission.

---

94 317 U.S. 1, 29 (1942).

95 Since the President may promulgate procedures for a military commission, the President could provide for a form of jury system within a military commission and make the military commission look so much like a federal district court that it should satisfy most objections on appeal. Yet there is an easier way—simply to use the federal district court in the first place.

Furthermore, there is a view that prosecutions for grave breaches of the 1949 Geneva Conventions must be made in the ordinary national courts and not in ad hoc military tribunals. G. DRAPER, THE RED CROSS CONVENTIONS 106-08 (1958). Professor Draper's view also seems consistent with recent trends in the area of human rights that seem to condemn use of ad hoc tribunals as being inconsistent with the right to trial by a "competent, independent and impartial tribunal established by law," and to a review by a higher tribunal according to law. International Covenant on Civil and Political Rights, article 14(1) and (5), G.A. Res. 220, 21 U.N. GAOR, Supp. 16, at 52-58, U.N. Doc. A/6316 (1966) (vote 106-0). This is an attempt to implement into treaty law the normative precepts in Article 10 of the 1948 Universal Declaration of Human Rights, G.A. Res. 217, 3 U.N. GAOR, U.N. Doc. A/810, at 71 (1948).

Indeed, with regard to the trial of civilians it can be argued that the courts have no alternative but to conclude that Congress reserved federal court jurisdiction and was unwilling to permit such a radical departure from our system as to allow the trial of civilians by military tribunal.[96] Necessarily Congress did not intend to derogate the express jurisdiction conferred on district courts for the prosecution of violations of all acts of Congress under 18 U.S.C. § 3231. Thus, it would be argued, concurrent jurisdiction remains in the federal district courts for the prosecution of violations of the law of war.

## B. Appellate Review

A completely separate problem, expressed in cases like *Burns v. Wilson*,[97] concerns the review of military decisions once they become final. Those cases that restrict civil court review of military decisions do not preclude the existence of a concurrent jurisdiction in the civil courts that can be competitive until the military decision becomes final and entitled to respect by virtue of 10 U.S.C. §§ 867(b) and 876. Indeed, *Burns v. Wilson* expressly left open the possibility of *de novo* "review" in the federal district courts in addition to the well-established, limited review by habeas corpus.[98]

Apparently some federal courts are not willing to take the initiative and entertain cases transferred from a military forum to the federal court. This does not impair the right of the federal courts to initiate trial in the first place, since transfer involves legal questions different from questions of initial prosecution in a forum with concurrent jurisdiction. Two recent cases in this area of collateral intervention by federal courts are *Torres v. Conner*[99] and *MacDonald v. Flanagan*.[100] In both, the attempts to gain federal court jurisdiction after commence-

---

[96] Reid v. Covert, 354 U.S. 1, 35, 40-41 (1957); Toth v. Quarles, 350 U.S. 11 (1955); Duncan v. Kahanamoku, 327 U.S. 304, 314 (1945). In *Reid* the Court stated that courts of law alone have power under the Constitution to try civilians for offenses against the United States. *But see Ex parte* Quirin, 317 U.S. 1, 37 (1942); Colepaugh v. Looney, 235 F.2d 429, 432 (10th Cir. 1956), *cert. denied*, 352 U.S. 1014 (1957); Hammond v. Squier, 51 F. Supp. 227 (W.D. Wash. 1943).

[97] 346 U.S. 137, 142 (1953). *See* Noyd v. Bond, 395 U.S. 683, 694 (1969) (discussing Supreme Court appellate jurisdiction after commencement of an action in the military courts); United States v. Augenblick, 393 U.S. 348 (1969) (indicating a possible ground for collateral attack if substantial rights are involved); Whelchel v. McDonald, 340 U.S. 122 (1950); Hiatt v. Brown, 339 U.S. 103 (1950); Grafton v. United States, 206 U.S. 333, 345, 348 (1907); *In re* Grimley, 137 U.S. 147, 150 (1890); *Ex parte* Vallandigham, 68 U.S. (1 Wall.) 243 (1863). *See also In re* Yamashita, 327 U.S. 1, 8 (1945) (review of military commission decisions); *Ex parte* Quirin, 317 U.S. 1, 24 (1942).

[98] 346 U.S. at 142-43. *See* United States v. Augenblick, 393 U.S. 348 (1969).

[99] Civ. No. 13,895 (N.D. Ga., July 2, 1970).

[100] Civ. No. 915 (E.D.N.C., July 17, 1970).

ment of military proceedings were unsuccessful; but they mark perhaps the beginning of more efforts to obtain collateral remedies in federal courts. The traditional principle seems to revolve around an exhaustion of available military remedies or a showing that this would be futile and would impair substantial constitutional rights.[101]

Due process problems may arise in the context of the review of decisions of a military commission. The appellate structure of a military commission is left to the discretion of the President. This ad hoc system of review may violate the international precepts of the Geneva Conventions.[102] Furthermore, with any system of military or Presidential review there exists the related problem of due process, embodied in the tradition of an independent judiciary with life tenure. Presumably, any appellate structure the President could create would lack judges with life tenure and would not be wholly independent. The use of the federal district courts, then, would have additional advantages since review would be within the stable and established system of the federal courts. Review in the federal circuit courts and in the Supreme Court would be vulnerable neither to due process attacks nor to criticism under the Geneva Conventions. Moreover, the argument expressed earlier that the executive cannot constitutionally foreclose judicial involvement may apply to review by courts invested with judicial power.

## C. Venue

Perhaps of interest is the problem of proper venue for district court prosecution. Under Article III, Section 2, Clause 3, of the Constitution the trial of all crimes except impeachment shall be held in the state where the crime was committed, "but when not committed within any State, the Trial shall be at such Place or Places as the Congress may by Law have directed."

Congress, it seems, has directed that offenses not committed within any state be tried in certain forums. In 18 U.S.C. § 3238 Congress directed that the trial of all offenses not committed in any district

---

101 Noyd v. Bond, 395 U.S. 683, 693-94 (1969), *citing* Gusik v. Schilder, 340 U.S. 128 (1950). *See* Baltimore Sun, Aug. 11, 1970, at 4. None of these cases dealt with civilians or the law of war per se, nor did they entail initial jurisdiction in the federal court. Rather these treated transfer or review once action has been commenced in the military forum with questions of adequacy of remedies in the military forum once it has proceeded.

102 *See* G. DRAPER, *supra* note 95.

*shall be in the district in which the offender,* or any one of two or more joint offenders, *is arrested or is first brought*; but if such offenders are not so arrested or brought into any district, an indictment or information may be filed in the district of the last known residence of the offender or of any one of two or more joint offenders, or if no such residence is known the indictment or information may be filed in the District of Columbia. (emphasis supplied)[103]

This congressional direction necessarily deviates from the normal rule provided by Rule 18 of the Federal Rules of Criminal Procedure, which sets venue in the district in which the offense was committed; but express provision in that Rule was made for exceptions that are "otherwise permitted by statute or by these rules." The predecessor to 18 U.S.C. § 3238 was Chapter 36, Section 8, of the Act of 1790, which declared that jurisdiction to try an offense existed in the district "where the offender is apprehended or into which he shall first be brought." Justice Story in *United States v. Thompson*[104] stated that "[t]he provision is in the alternative; and therefore the crime is cognizable in either district."

Concerning the trial of a civilian for violations of the law of war committed overseas, it seems that the government may bring an action in the district in which the offender is arrested or is "first brought."[105] Regarding a civilian presently within the United States it would appear that proper venue be initially where the person is arrested, subject to a change of venue under Rule 20 of the Federal Rules of Criminal Procedure.

Of further interest is the statement in the *Manual for Courts-Martial* that:

> The jurisdiction of courts-martial does not, in general, depend on where the offense was committed [Art. 5] . . . . Similarly, the jurisdiction of a court-martial with respect to offenses against military law is not affected by the place where the court sits.[106]

Article 5 of the Code, 10 U.S.C. § 805, states: "This chapter applies in all places."

---

[103] The language emphasized expresses a congressional intent to prosecute offenses committed in certain overseas areas and this general intent has existed since the very first Congress. *See* Reid v. Covert, 354 U.S. 1, 8 (1957).

[104] 28 F. Cas. 102 (No. 16,492) (C.C.D. Mass. 1832).

[105] An interesting recent application of this rule may soon be seen in the case of one Mario Escamilla. *See* N.Y. Times, July 31, 1970, § 1, at 1, col. 6. The case deals with an alleged murder on a floating iceberg and venue in the federal district court where the accused was first brought. For a discussion of this problem see 51 B.U.L. REV. 77 (1971).

[106] MCM, *supra* note 35, ¶ 8.

Since the law creating an offense against the law of war under Articles 18 and 21 is applicable in all places, and courts-martial have derived proper venue from Article 5 almost anywhere concerning almost all offenses, it would seem that proper venue for a federal court prosecuting under that same chapter of the Code could include equally wide possibilities. The federal court would be utilizing Title 10 to obtain numerous venue possibilities on the theory that this has been "directed" by Congress in accordance with Article III, Section 2, of the Constitution, and "otherwise permitted by statute" in accordance with Rule 18 of the Federal Rules of Criminal Procedure. Of course, the easier solution rests with an application of 18 U.S.C. § 3238.

Since most war crimes would occur overseas, and since military tribunals regularly function overseas, witnesses may be more readily available to a military tribunal than to a district court in the United States. This is probably a theoretical benefit only because it is very probable that trials for war crimes would be conducted in the United States even if a military forum were chosen.[107] This speculative complication is no reason to reject the usefulness of the district court in those cases that present no difficulty in obtaining witnesses or in those cases in which the difficulty would equal that experienced by a military tribunal.

## V. Conclusion

In summary, it can be argued that both civilians and soldiers can be tried in a federal district court for violations of the law of war under 10 U.S.C. §§ 818 and 821 and 18 U.S.C. § 3231. There is no need to initiate prosecutions of ex-soldiers in a military forum, which is suspect in the eyes of some members of the Supreme Court, and thereby chance the possibility of reversal on appeal with the resultant criticism of the administration for failure to faithfully prosecute offenses against the laws of the United States. Avoiding this result would seem particularly desirable in this time when much rhetoric has been generated concerning "law and order."

Indeed, it would be unforgivable to intentionally initiate prosecution likely to be overturned on appeal and thus shift to the Court any guilt resulting from failure of the United States to carry out its inter-

---

107 Fed. R. Crim. P. 17(e) allows service upon witnesses anywhere in the United States or on certain persons abroad in accordance with 28 U.S.C. § 1783 (1970). *See* Note, *Jurisdiction over Ex-servicemen for Crimes Committed Abroad: The Gap in the Law*, 22 Case W. Res. L. Rev. 279, 300 (1971).

national obligations and to execute the law. Law, order, and justice demand something more.

Although probably not satisfying to those whose views are securely contained in the conceptions of the past, yet not a complete existential leap into the unknown, a new focus on the district courts would provide the United States an alternative forum for the prosecution of war criminals. The United States, it seems, can readily fulfill its international obligations and the promises implicit in statements made to the United Nations concerning United States implementation and enforcement of the law of war. The executive department need not wait for Congress to provide new authorization. The government can initiate prosecution now in the federal district courts.

# IV. SETTLEMENT OF THE VIETNAM WAR

# The Justness of the Peace

## RICHARD A. FALK AND EUGENE V. ROSTOW

## JOINT LUNCHEON WITH THE INTERNATIONAL LAW SECTION OF THE AMERICAN BAR ASSOCIATION

The luncheon was presided over by Mr. Benjamin Busch, Chairman of the Section on International Law of the American Bar Association. The CHAIRMAN observed that the aim of this series of jointly sponsored luncheons was to join the halls of academia and the practitioners, since only through the study and wise application of international law would there be hope for peace and rule under law. In introducing the first speaker, he remarked that the Vietnam war must command our very serious and devoted attention. It has been the longest and most costly war in our history and has left us uncertain whether it began legally, whether it has ended honorably, or whether it will go on forever.

### THE JUSTNESS OF THE PEACE
#### REMARKS BY RICHARD A. FALK*

Let me start by relating two points I think most Americans are in agreement about at this time: the first is a widely shared sense of relief that includes both critics and supporters of our earlier policy that the

* Princeton University Center for International Studies.

direct American combat role in Vietnam at least is apparently over, and that American forces, both prisoners of war and ground troops, have been repatriated and withdrawn. It must be understood that this point of initial agreement is not so substantial if considered more closely.

Critics of American policy are concerned by the continuing and accelerated U.S. combat role in Cambodia. They are also concerned by reports of the transfer of American military and paramilitary roles in South Vietnam to American civilian personnel who will number close to 10,000. They are concerned about the continuation of an apparent American advisory and financial role in support of South Vietnam's cruel system of imprisonment that affects several hundred thousand people and by the persistence of the so-called Phoenix program, which engages in a large-scale civilian assassination operation. Critics, despite their sense of relief, are most of all anxious about the provisional character associated by American leaders with the ending of the combat role. The President has several times uttered warnings and threats of an American readiness to reintervene in Vietnam once again by means of a unilateral national decision made, perhaps, only in the White House. Therefore, because of the tenuous nature of our withdrawal, the effort of Congressman Jonathan Bingham to condition any sort of direct American reintervention in the Vietnam war on prior congressional authorization is extremely important in order to insure that the sense of relief that all of us presently feel endures. It is accurate to observe that this is the first spring in almost a decade that American soldiers are neither dying nor killing in Vietnam, and for this, as long as it lasts, let us be grateful. So that it may last longer, let us not forget that it is still necessary to act to maintain the present greatly diminished American involvement in the Indochina War.

The second point of general consensus, it seems to me, is the recognition that the relevant facts of political and military control in South Vietnam, the motivation of the various actors in the continuing struggle that is going on there, and the degree to which these actors support the various features of the Paris agreements is an extremely complicated matter. No one can have any very positive sense about it at this time. In my judgment there are no easy, one-sided answers, for instance, to the question of allocating responsibility for the violation of various central provisions of the Paris agreements.

The news reporting has been particularly inadequate because both sides have tried to keep media personnel from gaining access to areas in the field where combat is taking place. The North Vietnamese and Provisional Revolutionary Government people in the south were for a long time prevented from even talking to newspaper people.

As a further preliminary point, may I state that I see no useful function in further debating the various questions as to how the Paris agreements came about, whether they could have been negotiated years earlier, whether the Christmas bombing altered the terms in favor of the position of the United States and Saigon, and more generally, all those large questions bearing on the legality of American involvement over the years, although obviously one's attitude towards these issues influences one's approach to the present situation.

I think it is important to focus at the present time on the condition that now exists in Indochina, particularly in Vietnam. I would like to emphasize two features of this situation which I regard as most unfortunate. Despite all my disagreements with President Nixon's policies for ending the war over the past several years, I believe he obtained for himself in the Paris agreements of 1973 a great opportunity to promote prospects for peace in Vietnam and reconciliation at home. He has in fact chosen not to take advantage of this opportunity. Rather he has chosen to maintain the continuity of American policy by once again associating our national interest with the survival of the Thieu regime in South Vietnam, and he has so identified peace with honor exclusively with those who have supported the war that those who have opposed the war are deemed dishonorable.

First with respect to Vietnam itself, it seems to me that the U.S. Government could have and should have chosen to support evenhandedly the concepts embodied in the Paris agreements, rather than to continue its posture of unqualified commitment to the Thieu Administration. Our government could have shown an interest in the enforcement of the provisions in the Paris agreements against all parties. In particular those provisions anticipating negotiations on the release of political prisoners and the establishment of the conditions necessary for the dynamics of political self-determination to take place in South Vietnam should have been strongly backed by Washington. Most explicitly, the United States could have called for serious implementation of Article XI, especially Saigon's obligation therein assumed to allow freedom of movement for refugees and freedom of assembly for all Vietnamese. In such a context the dynamics of political opposition could take place more naturally; by securing compliance with the Paris agreements opponents of the Saigon regime would not be forced into a choice between acquiescence and the battlefield.

These political provisions were important because they sought to create a middle ground for anti-Saigon forces between the battlefield and acquiescence in which the unresolved struggle over the political control of South Vietnam could take place. As even Henry Kissinger acknowledged at his January 24 press conference, the questions of governmental legitimacy in South Vietnam have not yet been settled. There is no pretension that the Vietnam War is over in the sense that its main issue, that is, who is to control the political destinies of South Vietnam, has been settled by the Paris agreements. The only question is whether it might yet be possible to shift the conflict from the battlefield to the political process. That shift is the main open issue, and therefore when we charge the other side with violation of the infiltration provisions and with recourse to battlefield strategies, it has to be understood in relation to the refusal by President Nixon or Thieu's regime to do anything whatsoever to show that these political provisions in the agreements are taken seriously.

In this sense, the San Clemente communique of Nixon and Thieu issued on April 3 is an extremely significant document. It is President Nixon's formal acknowledgement of approval for the way in which Nguyen Van Thieu was carrying out the Paris agreements and governing South Vietnam. In this formal document our President associated himself fully with President Thieu; I quote from the communique: "President Thieu expressed his earnest desire for reconciliation among the South Vietnamese parties." To allow that kind of statement to be made by Thieu when he is keeping in jail between 40,000 and 250,000 noncommunist political opponents who are identified with moderation and neutralism—student leaders, Buddhist leaders, and so on—is utter hypocrisy. Then to say you are in favor of a policy of accomodation, and to associate the United States with that kind of interpretation of what reconciliation means, seems to me to undermine any prospect for upholding the basic bargain embodied in the Paris agreements. It indicates to me, and I think to the Vietnamese as well, that the American purpose in adhering to the Paris agreements was to reach a narrow tradeoff in which we would secure the return of our prisoners in exchange for the withdrawal of our ground troops, but would not alter our basic posture of alignment with the Saigon regime. Nixon has not acted as if it is in America's interest to implement the agreement as a whole, but only to use it as a tool to promote the survival of the Thieu government. The problem with our policies for years has been that we have associated our interests and our victory with the success of this regime.

I am suggesting that there was a viable alternative to pro-Saigon loyalism open to President Nixon after the Paris agreements and the agreement provided the framework in which to implement this alternative. It is true the civil war might have resumed in any event, whatever Mr. Nixon had done. But what I am suggesting is that the failure to seek an even-handed implementation of the Paris agreements and the failure to show any interest in the flagrant, persistent, and systematic violations of that agreement by the Saigon Administration, doomed that part of the agreement which looked toward the establishment of, or the move toward, peace and a political solution of the conflict. This made it impossible for the opponents of the Saigon Administration to place any reliance upon the dynamics of political self-determination. The reason that Thieu was the only opponent among the four negotiating parties of the Paris agreements (everybody else was happy about it, but Thieu had to be dragged into it) was that in truth he probably can't survive the dynamics of political self-determination. His opponents did have confidence in it, I am convinced, because the balance of political forces in South Vietnam is in their favor.

We become aware of a real issue for American policymakers: one has to be either prepared to sacrifice Thieu, or prepared indefinitely for reintervention in South Vietnam, and in Vietnam generally. There is no middle way. We have stuck to the same path that has been pursued throughout this decade. We have not disassociated ourselves from the old objectives, and we are as committed as we ever were to the frustration of self-determination for South Vietnam and to the indefinite maintenance in control of a Thieu-like regime. The United States does not insist on Thieu as the head of the government, but only the persistence of a Thieu-like regime. In my view that is the central failure of American statesmanship with respect to the agreement negotiated in Paris.

My second point, and a much briefer one, concerns the domestic implementation of the agreement; that is, failure by the Administration and by President Nixon to use the moment of the cease-fire and the repatriation of the prisoners and withdrawal of American forces as a moment for national reconciliation here at home. Instead he has used the occasion to deepen, if anything, the polarization that has been built up over the years around the issue of the war. I refer in particular to his speech before the South Carolina legislature, which is probably his fullest statement of what peace with honor means. In that speech he clearly identified the pro-war pilot POW's as exemplifying peace with honor and made no allowance for the fact that many conscientious Americans disagreed with this policy. Nixon would not have had to renounce his own support for the war policies. But he had a great opportunity as a statesman to say that there were many points of view in America about the war, that people reasonably disagree, and that various kinds of sacrifices were made by people who disagreed with the war policies. It is a sacrifice to go to jail; you do risk your career in going to Canada. It may not be the same thing as going into the armed forces, but in many ways I think it is a harder decision for the individual who makes it.

What I am suggesting is that Nixon had a great opportunity to achieve reconciliation by acknowledging the realities of the anti-war sentiment that had built up in the country and in Congress over the years. In the 1969–1971 period, 60 percent of Americans polled about the war thought it immoral for the United States to be involved in Indochina. 60 percent is a large segment of the society. It was not a deviant position to have acted in opposition to the war. Therefore, just as the returning POW's have been a symbolic issue for the Administration, so is the hardening of the position on amnesty a symbolic position for those of us who have opposed the war. Rather than moving toward reconciliation, the President has actually adopted a more rigid position on amnesty since the cease-fire. He has made people feel that in order to establish their own honor in relation to the society, they have to repudiate those who opposed the war. This kind of one-sided view of the war encourages a continuation of the destructive polarization in American society that was stimulated by our involvement.

In conclusion, I would say that as a consequence we have neither peace nor justice nor honor. We are still entangled inappropriately and ineffectually in the destinies of South Vietnam. And we still have a country that is deeply divided. A fair portion of America regards the government in Washington as lacking in sensitivity toward the claims of its citizens to have positions based on their conception of honor as associated with scruples about supporting America's involvement in the war.

The future of America's role in Vietnam remains in doubt. As of now we can only lament our continuing contribution to the torment of the Indochinese people. In particular, the U.S. Government has not demonstrated a commitment to the Paris agreements, and has rather expressed mainly its fidelity, no matter what, to the Saigon Administration despite its blatant repudiation of central provisions of the settlement bargain. Furthermore, the President has deprived Americans of an occasion for rejoicing about the cease-fire by his insistence in associating honor with pro-war Americans and dishonor with anti-war Americans.

## REMARKS BY EUGENE V. ROSTOW*

The topic assigned to us today is "The Justness of the Peace." I take it from what Mr. Falk has said that he thinks the peace is unjust because it involves support for the Thieu regime, which he regards as cruel and unjust. He discussed various shortcomings of that regime from the point of view of democratic theory without comparing it in these respects to its rival in North Vietnam.

I don't think that really is the issue which the Society asked us to discuss. At least it is not the issue that I have perceived, or can perceive. I don't think we were asked to consider which Vietnamese government is more democratic. And I do not understand how that can be an issue of international law. But I am not going to address the problem of "The Justness of the Peace" that was made in Paris for Vietnam from the point of view of my personal criteria about how South Vietnam and North Vietnam should be organized. What I shall try to do is to address the question in the perspective of the standards of justice embodied in international law. The Paris agreements were international agreements terminating an international conflict. The question I should like to pose is whether that peace arrangement meets the standards of justice of international law as embodied in the UN Charter and its development.

When we talk about the peace in Indochina, we are at a great disadvantage, of course, because we do not know how these various arrangements are going to work out. As Mr. Falk says, there are arguments, or at least there are conflicting statements, about who is violating the agreement, who is preventing the cease-fire. But there is no argument whatever about the fact that one of the most critical features of the settlement, namely, the evacuation of North Vietnamese forces from Laos and Cambodia, has not taken place although American forces have been withdrawn.

I can see no alternative today, therefore, to considering "the paper peace" as if it were, or would soon become, a reality in North and South Vietnam, Laos, and Cambodia. We should therefore examine the docu-

* Yale University Law School.

ments themselves as best we can understand them, the cease-fire settlement of January, as backed by the declaration of the states assembled in Paris early in March, the Act of Paris.

Save for a little blurring around the edges, the understanding reflected in these documents is the same as the armistice arrangements in Korea. It is the same as the Korean settlement because both episodes are dominated by exactly the same overriding considerations of international law, and of the international politics which lie behind international law. The agreements signed in Paris, like those which ended the war in Korea, rest on the principle that South Vietnam, like South Korea, is a separate state with the right to defend itself against attack from outside, whether that attack is conducted by organized armies, an invasion of guerrillas, or international assistance to internal insurrection; that the United States and other nations have the right recognized as just under international law to assist South Vietnam in that process of defense; and, correlatively, that North Vietnam should not interfere in the processes of self-determination within South Vietnam through force, through the infiltration of guerrillas, or through military assistance to insurrectionary forces within South Vietnam.

In other words, the peace of Paris rests on the premise that there are indeed two separate states in Vietnam (to borrow Chancellor Brandt's phrase about the situation in Germany, two states within a single nation, if you will) that those states can unite if they wish peacefully by political agreement, but that they cannot use force against each other.

Secondly, it rests on the related principle that every state is responsible for the use of force from its territory, from which it follows that North Vietnam cannot and must not use Laos and Cambodia as an infiltration route to attack South Vietnam. In this regard, the Paris settlement expressly reaffirms the 1962 Geneva agreements about Laos and Cambodia.

Let me be extremely clear. The agreements of Paris fully accept the official position of the United States throughout this long, bitter, and tragic affair. Since Truman's time, and most emphatically after the Geneva Conference, the United States has taken the view that two states emerged in Vietnam within the meaning of international law, two states exercising authority within their respective jurisdictions, and protected against external attack by the principles of the Charter, endowed, that is, with an inherent right of self-defense and a right to ask other states to assist them in the exercise of that right.

This was the premise of the SEATO Treaty, through which we sought to deter attack by announcing our state interest in the territorial integrity and political independence of South Vietnam. In this respect, both our posture and that of South Vietnam was entirely "just" according to the standards of international law. Article 51 of the Charter fully accepts both South Vietnam's inherent right to defend itself under the circumstances of recent history and the right of the United States and other nations to help South Vietnam if they wished to do so.

This position has been the premise of American policy as a matter of constitutional as well as international law. The United States has carried on the conflict both under the treaty itself, as President Truman did in Korea, and through congressional actions backing the President's interpretation and application of the treaty.

To this position three answers have been offered, notably by Mr. Falk. These answers are not always consistent, but they do constitute three fundamentally distinct legal theories. In the first place, it is contended, the war in Indochina is not an international war, but a civil war; North Vietnam and South Vietnam are part of a single state and not two separate states. This is an argument that the Soviet Union made against the action which we took in Korea in defending South Korea's right to protect itself against attack from North Korea. It is a fact confirmed by the experience of twenty long years that South Vietnam and North Vietnam are separate states within the meaning of international law. They function as separate states; they have been recognized by many nations; and they have exercised authority and participated in world affairs as separate states.

The second argument against the official United States position, and one which I believe is also contradicted (at least on paper) in the agreements reached in Paris, is that the failure to hold a referendum on reunification in 1956 justified North Vietnam's attack on South Vietnam. This argument, like the first, is without substance. There was no promise in the arrangements that emerged in Geneva in 1954 that there would be such a referendum. The statement on the subject was embodied in something called a "Declaration" issued at the end of the conference by the two co-chairmen, and supported, even nominally, by only four of the nine participants in the conference. In any event, even if there had been such an international promise, under the usages that have developed around Article 51 of the Charter the breach of a political promise does not justify the wronged party in using force. This was precisely the position taken at the time of Suez, where the British and the French claimed that the Egyptians had breached treaty agreements with them regarding the Canal, and that the breach of those treaty arrangements justified their intervention by force. The Security Council overruled the French and British position at Suez just as the Vietnam agreements of January and March reject the theory that North Vietnam was privileged to attack South Vietnam because no referendum was held. I think it is generally agreed both in usage and in the literature of international law that a breach of an agreement of that sort is not the kind of act which could be considered as justifying the use of force under Article 51.

The third argument advanced to attack the position of the United States in this regard is that Hanoi was justified in providing assistance to the insurgents in a civil war *within* South Vietnam. International assistance to revolutionaries, it is claimed, is permissible in order to uphold the right of self-determination of peoples.

It used to be considered orthodox black-letter doctrine that a state in a condition of civil war had a right to ask for help from friendly states, but that no state had a right under international law to assist the insurrectionaries. Now, we are told, international law has changed in this regard.

The orthodox position was taken by the United Nations as a matter of course in the late forties with respect to Greece. The insurrection within Greece was being helped from Yugoslavia, Albania, and Bulgaria. UN policy then was that the United States and Great Britain had a right to assist Greece, but that no other state had a right to assist the revolutionaries.

This was the basis for policy with regard to the Congo, when the Katanga secession occurred. It was the position taken by the international community in the Nigerian crisis during the Biafran secession. It was accepted as self-evident when the Soviet Union invaded Hungary in 1956 and Czechoslovakia in 1968. The objection on those occasions was not that the Soviet Union could not legally assist the Government of Hungary or the Government of Czechoslovakia in putting down an insurrection at their request, but that there were no such governments and therefore no such requests.

The claim that international law should recognize a right of states to assist revolutionary movements within another state, which has been asserted recently in the literature about Vietnam, is entirely without foundation either in state practice or in the nature of the UN Charter as a covenant among states. If accepted, it would be an extremely dangerous doctrine and one which would be completely incompatible with the notion of the Charter as a system of arrangements among states.

We have had some experience with this alleged doctrine. They are not happy precedents to recall. Before World War I, the Russian Government had a doctrine of assistance to Slav peoples, which helped to bring turmoil to the Balkans and led to World War I. The argument is made in behalf of the Palestinians today. And of course it was the argument of Hitler when he proposed liberating the Sudeten Germans from the yoke of Czechoslovakia. It is an argument I regard as entirely incompatible with the possibility of peace and also entirely incompatible with our notions of international law that under the Charter force can only be used under the authority of the United Nations itself or by unilateral decision only in self-defense or in assisting a nation exercising its right of self-defense.

Mr. Falk has proposed that in circumstances of civil war the international community should accept and sanctify another very dubious precedent, quite as dubious as the precedent of Sudetenland, that is the nonintervention policy adopted during the Spanish Civil War. On that occasion Britain and France declined to help the Government of Spain, while Germany and Italy helped the revolutionaries. Some writers now contend that in such situations states should be legally free to help the revolutionaries, which has always been regarded as illegal.

These are the only arguments that have been addressed to the official position of the United States and its allies in South Vietnam throughout the period of the war. On paper, at least, the peace arrangements reached in Paris in January and March completely repudiate these arguments and confirm the position of the United States. For that reason, I was surprised to hear Mr. Falk say that he approved the Paris agreements. To me, they deny everything he has written on the subject for eight or nine years.

The Paris agreements necessarily rest on the proposition that there are indeed two states in Vietnam; that North Vietnam has no right to invade South Vietnam or to seek to coerce a political solution in South Vietnam; that it must withdraw its forces from Laos and Cambodia; and that it must pursue the ultimate reunion of Vietnam as a single state, if all the parties wish to do so, exclusively by political means. The only rights of self-determination possessed by anyone in this situation, these agreements say, are the rights of the people and political factions of North Vietnam.

We were asked today to talk about "the justness" of the peace for Vietnam. This, I submit, is the answer to the question provided by the standards of international law. The Paris agreements fully conform to the accepted norms of international law and faithfully reflect them and thus authoritatively answer the arguments which have been advanced in behalf of the claim that North Vietnam has a right to intervene in South Vietnam.

Thus I conclude that the Paris arrangement is the only arrangement that is compatible not simply with the Charter and the precedents under the Charter but with the political necessities which the Charter represents. The political process through which we have been seeking to vindicate these Charter provisions in Greece, and Turkey, and Berlin, and Korea, and now Vietnam has been a trying and costly period of great national effort. In that tragic struggle, we and other nations have deemed the safest rule to be that of the Charter, to accept no unilateral change in the relationship between the Soviet Union and the United States achieved by force.

We are deeply troubled today because the consensus which lay behind the American response to Korea in 1950 no longer dominates the national mind. Men think and believe and feel there must be something wrong with the ideas of the Charter, if they lead to such ghastly results as those in Korea and in Vietnam.

Many have forgotten, and others are not old enough to remember, the episodes of the thirties which led to the articulation of those rules in the particular form achieved at San Francisco. The invasion of Ethiopia, the invasion of Manchuria, German and Italian assistance to General Franco's revolution in Spain, these were all violations of international law then and they are violations of international law now. The conviction of the men of 1945 was that peace can only be achieved if such violations are met, and met early, before the momentum of war becomes overpowering and sweeps all before it.   We are now reexamining those ideas, trying to discover whether there is an alternative.   Thus far, we have failed to produce one.

I submit to you that the agreements for Vietnam reached in Paris faithfully respect the concept of justice which underlies our international law.   This is a problem altogether distinct from the justice of the internal organization of South Vietnamese society, about which Mr. Falk spoke.   International law is largely concerned with the problem of maintaining the peace.   Without general international peace, which requires strict curbs on the international use of force, men will not be free to pursue the other goals of justice, internal democracy, and internal social development, to which Mr. Falk referred.

Let me say this in closing: a rule of international law that condoned the international use of force in the name of self-determination or wars of national liberation could only multiply the horror of the processes of anarchy we see throughout the world, as guerrilla warfare spreads through individual and small group acts of terror.   Such a rule would release international society from all the taboos and restraints which international law has so slowly and painfully built up since the 17th century to curb, limit, and ultimately abolish war.

In reply to criticisms from the floor, Mr. Rostow made the following remarks:

First let me make it clear at once that I am not speaking for the Administration.   I left the Government of the United States on January 20, 1969.

Secondly, I was asked to talk for not more than 20 minutes, and I did want to expound the difficult question of the justness of the peace from the point of view of the standards of justice embodied in international law.

Third, if you will look at the March issue of the Yale Law Journal,* you will see that I have recently published a lengthy examination of this entire literature.   I do not read the recent declaration adopted by the General Assembly as altering in any way, except conceivably for colonial regimes, the pre-existing international law under which it is perfectly legitimate to assist a state which is widely recognized and not legitimate at all to assist revolutionary forces within that state. Indeed, the declaration makes that point over and over again.

The reason I wanted to approach our topic in this way is very simple.   In the long and troubled years of debate about Vietnam in the United States, we have lost sight of the fundamental line of reasoning and the fundamental line of policy which led us into the quagmire of Indochina with the full support of public opinion.

The speaker has said she is tired of these points.   That is her right. But neither she, nor Mr. Falk, nor anyone else has shown why they are wrong.

---

* 82 YALE LAW JOURNAL 829 (1973).

I thought I had dealt with the points raised by Mr. Falk about the justness of the peace in my original presentation. Whether the President has served as an emollient or an irritant in our domestic affairs is an interesting question, about which I have ideas, but it does not seem to me to concern the question assigned us today.

I can add a word on the other issue raised, whether we are supporting peace or Thieu's regime. On the basis of long experience, I can tell you that that was never an issue. There was never an alternative to the policy that was pursued until October 1972, because the only issue ever presented, the only issue on which in 30 or 40 or 50 approaches we ever stuck, was that we would not accept the National Liberation Front as the sole legitimate representative of the South Vietnamese people. That was the sole issue all of those years and it is the issue now. When the North Vietnamese position changed on that subject in October 1972, an agreement became possible. That was the only issue, I can assure you, in all of the negotiations.

The CHAIRMAN called upon the speakers for their closing remarks.

Mr. FALK: With due deference to Mr. Rostow I was rather surprised for two reasons by the tenor and approach he has taken. Firstly he gave us a set of legal rationalizations on the underlying issue of American involvement in Vietnam vintage 1963 or so. This might be interesting for certain legal antiquarians, but it is not, I thought, the issue that we should have been discussing today.

Secondly, to associate his conception of international law with the text of the Paris agreements boggles my imagination. I defy him to reconcile his views of the settlement with several central provisions designed to alter the struggle within South Vietnam by specifying the sort of political competition that could serve as a non-violent alternative to the civil war that had been going on. Even Henry Kissinger is not such a loyalist as to argue Mr. Rostow's extreme position. In his January 24 press conference Kissinger said that the civil war in South Vietnam, not the civil war in *all* of Vietnam but the civil war in *South* Vietnam, is unresolved. Such a statement of fact has nothing to do with liking or disliking Thieu's regime. The agreement has certain provisions that do not allow Thieu to rule the way he has been ruling and, to the extent that he insists on continuing to keep political prisoners in jail and confines millions of refugees to the cities by not allowing them to go back to NLF-held territories, he is in flagrant violation of the agreement.

It should be noted, also, that Article 4 of the Paris agreement is a unilateral commitment by the United States not to intervene in South Vietnam. Interestingly there is no corresponding obligation on the part of North Vietnam contained in that article or elsewhere. Article 21 obliging the United States to contribute reconstruction aid is tantamount to a reparations obligation embodied in the main agreement. To analogize this settlement to the ending of the Korean War is so remote from anything contained in the Paris agreements or the situation which exists in real-world Vietnam, to borrow John Norton Moore's phrase, that

I find it difficult to respond. The issue in Korea was to recreate a solid line between the conventional armies of the two Koreas. The issue in Vietnam is to set up a political framework that can serve internal contending forces in South Vietnam as an alternative to battlefield civil war. The political alternative manifestly depends upon implementing those political provisions.

I have argued that President Nixon and the Administration could and should have taken an even-handed view of the agreement they negotiated. If we want to avoid the continuation of the war and avoid the necessity for reintervention, Washington has to take the *whole* agreement seriously, not just the provisions it likes. An opportunity for statesmanship in the cause of peace has been lost; it required taking the whole agreement seriously.

Therefore, I do find Mr. Rostow's entire approach disappointingly unresponsive to either the Paris agreements or the present situation in Vietnam.

MR. ROSTOW: It gains nothing to say that my arguments are vintage 1963. The problem is not to classify them or to apply adjectives about them. Approaches like that are usually an excuse for not facing the issue. The question is, wherein am I wrong? The arguments of 1963, of 1954, and so on, have often been discussed, but in my judgment, which in this case is based on a recent re-reading of the whole literature, they have never been met or answered in a coherent, convincing factual way. The pattern of development of international law simply does not support the theories which have been advanced to answer them.

I quite agree with Mr. Falk that the arrangements posited at Paris anticipate a political process within South Vietnam. But it is a political process of concern only to the South Vietnamese, not to the North Vietnamese. I analogized the arrangements for Vietnam to those that terminated open hostilities in Korea for one reason and one reason only. However much Mr. Falk may profess to be surprised by it, they do indeed require exactly the same pattern of conduct on the part of North Vietnam, with one conceivable exception, that was required of North Korea, that is to say, to stay out of political affairs within South Vietnam, and to get out of Laos and Cambodia. There could be no argument, I think, with the fact that they are not yet out of Laos and Cambodia.

There is of course no question but that the Paris agreements recognize a state of political dissension within the separate state of South Vietnam, quite apart from the requirements of conduct which it imposes on North Vietnam. It announces certain rules for political reconciliation and development within South Vietnam on the part of the two South Vietnamese factions. How that process is going to be carried out, and indeed whether it is going to be carried out, and the role we have in trying to see that it is carried out, depend upon one thing which both agreements make very clear: the faithful observance of the cease-fire by North Vietnam and the United States, and by the two parties within South Vietnam. So far we have not reached that step. What leverage we might have to interfere within South Vietnam if we ever reach that point, I don't know.  Of course I am in favor of the fulfillment of those obligations and deplore interferences with them from either side.  But I notice again that Mr. Falk is talking only about interferences from one side.  And I repeat that the political terms of the arrangement are for the South Vietnamese, not the North Vietnamese or the Americans.

The key point I am trying to make here today is that it is essential to focus on one question of primary importance to international law and to the possibility of peace in our bitter and dangerous world.  That is why I stressed the parallel between the Korean armistice and the Paris agreements for Vietnam.  If we want to achieve a reasonably stable general system of peace, is there any alternative but to insist on the principle which governs both the Korean settlement and the Paris agreements for Vietnam?

# Viet Nam 1974: A Revolution Unfulfilled

## TRAN VAN DINH

"I know the war will go on
and I will walk toward horizons lit with a million flames.
On this road there will be no more travelers
and at this ferry no one will wait to cross the river."

Lt. Col. Nguyen Van Duong
December 1973[1]

A grateful humankind tormented by the cruel war in Viet Nam breathed a sigh of relief at the signing of the Paris Agreement on January 27, 1973. In the ensuing months, Viet Nam became forgotten in a world beset by a bloody Middle East conflict, violences from Chile to Thailand, the American "Watergate Affair" and above all, the energy crisis.

But while the signing of the Paris Agreement brought peace of mind to the peoples outside, it did not bring peace to the Vietnamese people themselves. In the first nine months after the cease-fire, an estimated 50,000 Vietnamese were killed,[2] more than the total U.S. deaths in the preceding 10 years, and far more than the total casualties in the 1967 and 1973 Middle Eastern wars put together.

## II

One of the fundamental causes of this continuing sad state of affairs has been the ongoing American policy in Viet Nam. The United States first entered the Viet Nam scene in 1950, paying 80 per cent of the French costs between 1950 and 1954 during the First Indochina War (1945–1954). Its stated reason for doing so was to suppress a revolution whose success was seen as a serious threat to "freedom" and as the extension of the Chinese Communist "yellow peril." Despite the signing of the Paris Agreement and the U.S.-Chinese détente, nothing much changed in 1973 except in words: now the U.S. would continue to intervene in the name of "honor," a "generation of peace" and "national security." Through a 20,000

---

[1] From a poem by Lt. Col. Nguyen Van Duong, intelligence officer of the South Vietnamese (Saigon) 5th Infantry Division; translated by Le Kim Dinh; *The New York Times*, December 26, 1973.

[2] According to Saigon sources, 11,724 South Vietnamese (Saigon) soldiers and 1,991 civilians have been killed since the cease-fire. The same sources claimed that Saigon troops have killed 41,825 North Vietnamese and Viet Cong. (*Time* magazine, December 31, 1973)

man civilian operation[3] and through massive economic and military aid, the U.S. has acted contrary to Article 4, Chapter 2 of the Agreement which reads: "The United States will not continue its military involvement or interfere in the internal affairs of South Viet Nam."

The U.S. ability to continue intervening in Viet Nam after the Paris accord, despite widespread popular feeling in the United States against re-intervention was based on American ignorance of the Vietnamese revolution. Almost all of the tens of millions of words written about Viet Nam in the U.S. since 1954 have dealt with one aspect or another of U.S. policy and its results: financial aid, ground troops, pacification programs, bombings, orphans, refugees, political prisoners, the dead and the wounded at My Lai and countless other villages and towns. The "Viet Cong" remain faceless black-pajamaed mysteries to be pictured only as corpses or the shadowy embodiments of diabolical qualities nations at war always attributed to those they fight.

## III

In actual fact, anyone familiar with Viet Nam's past could easily see that Vietnamese—and particularly Vietnamese Marxists—are not "inscrutable orientals." For, just as American goals did not basically change in 1973, neither have those of the revolutionary Indochinese Communist Party (now the Lao Dong, Viet Nam Workers) since its founding in 1930 by Ho Chi Minh. The main objectives of the Vietnamese revolution remain essentially Vietnamese, representing a basic continuity in the history of the country. They are: Doc Lap (independence, to mean simply the absence of foreign troops and foreign interferences), Thong Nhat (national unity—both territory and people) and Cong Binh Xa Hoi (social justice for the masses). These three elements constitute the twentieth-century version of the Vietnamese traditional Chinh Nghia which is often translated with some inaccuracy as just cause.[4] Political legitimacy in Viet Nam has been always defined according to Chinh

---

[3] For details see "Vietnam Half War Half Peace for Americans Who Remain," in *The Baltimore Sun* by Matthew J. Seiden, November 28, 1973.

[4] Chinh means just. Nghia originally came from the Chinese Yi (儀) which Joseph Needham translated as justice (science and civilisation in China), H. G. Creel as right (Confucius and the Chinese way) and Fung Yu Lan as the oughtness of a situation (short history of Chinese philosophy). But like many words borrowed from the Chinese, the Vietnamese Nghia has significantly modified its meaning to meet with the particular conditions of Viet Nam. The most recent Vietnamese dictionary, the Tu Dien Tieng Viet (Vietnamese Dictionary, Hanoi, 1967) defines Nghia as follows:-what that conforms to reason; that which can be a model for human relationship; an act of compassion which

Nghia. Those who oppose it or do not uphold it are Nguy or illegitimate.

The 1954 Geneva Agreements which ended the First Indochina War recognized the independence and unity of Viet Nam and declared that the 17th parallel which temporarily divides Viet Nam into two "zones" is "provisional and should not in any way be interpreted as constituting a political or territorial boundary."[5]

Likewise, the 1973 Paris "Agreement on Ending the War and Restoring Peace" which ended the Second Indochina War (1960–1973) specifies in Article 1 that "the United States and other countries respect the independence, sovereignty, unity and territorial integrity of Vietnam as recognized by the 1954 Geneva Agreements on Vietnam." The present territorial division of Viet Nam is therefore provisional pending its reunification under one single government. Before this takes place, all régimes in "South Vietnam" are transitional and their legitimization would have to be arranged among contending parties.

For domestic reasons and to avoid being accused of having "sold out" the Saigon régime, the U.S. has tried, through verbal threats and B52 "carpet bombings," in vain to soften the impact of Article 1. Yet, on January 23, 1973, the day the Agreement was initialed in Paris, President Nixon, in Washington, in a televized address stated that "the United States will continue to recognize the government of Republic of Vietnam (Saigon) as the SOLE LEGITIMATE GOVERNMENT OF SOUTH VIETNAM" (emphasis added). But President Nixon himself was contradicted the next day, January 24, 1973, when Dr. Henry A. Kissinger during a press conference admitted that, in regard to the question of "who is the legitimate ruler of South Vietnam," the Agreement "leaves it open to negotiations among the parties the political evolution of South Vietnam and therefore the definition of WHAT ULTIMATELY WILL BE CONSIDERED BY ALL SOUTH VIETNAMESE THE LEGITIMATE RULE" (emphasis added). This meant, of course, that Saigon's claim to be the sole legal government of South Viet Nam is empty under the Agreement which made it clear that until the final settlement, there are two "administrations" (the Government, Republic of Viet Nam or GRVN and the Provisional Revolutionary Government of South Viet Nam or PRG) in South Viet Nam. Months later, Dr. Kissinger's own State Department

---

benefits the mass of people.
[5] Article 6 of the Final Declaration of the Geneva Agreements.

would ignore the Agreement's clear provision and supported Nixon's January 23 line. On September 10, 1973, in a diplomatic note protesting the building of 12 airfields in the PRG zone, Saigon asserted that the PRG could not receive civilian aircraft in its zone without prior consent of the GRVN. In a move obviously coordinated with Saigon, the U.S. Department of State, on the same day, sent a note to the Democratic Republic of Viet Nam (Hanoi) supporting the GRVN's position and arguing that the introduction of aircraft into any part of South Viet Nam without the GRVN's consent was "not authorized by the Agreement of January 27, or permitted by international law." The note threatened the "grave risks which the Democratic Republic of Vietnam would run by violating the airspace sovereignty of the Republic of Vietnam."[6] I am inclined to believe that the violation of the principle of unity and territorial integrity of Viet Nam, the non-recognition of the existence of the two "administrations" in the South will lead to a third Indochina war.

## IV

The 1973 Paris Agreement has thus fulfilled in principle and on paper the two main objectives of the Vietnamese revolution: independence and unity. The third objective: social justice for the masses should in principle be left to the Vietnamese to decide among themselves. And social justice cannot be carried out without the recognition of the existing political realities in South Viet Nam. While every Vietnamese at least publicly accepts the principle of national independence and national unity, there are those who may fear the establishment of a socialist system in the South.

One should not forget that the French colonial régime created an important bourgeois class: a "landed" bourgeoisie in the former Cochin-China, an "intellectual" bourgeoisie, and a "compradore" bourgeoisie (which lived off the presence of foreigners) in the cities. To protect their interests, these elements generally adopted and promoted the anti-communist, individualistic, materialistic ideology learned from the French and later from the Americans. Yet, these same people, because of the fact that they are Vietnamese cannot stand to see their country devastated and kept at war for the benefit of a foreign power and its small group of supporters.

In a broad, indirect sense, the 1973 Paris Agreement has dealt with this reality in its Article 12 which defines the formation of a

6 Department of State Press Release No. 325, September 11, 1973.

Council of National Reconciliation and Concord composed of three equal "segments" (the GRVN, the PRG and the South Vietnamese neutralists or the third force). The Council's task is to be "promoting the two South Vietnamese parties' implementation of the Agreement, achievement of national reconciliation and concord, and insurance of democratic liberties" as well as "organizing the free and democratic elections." Its acceptance demonstrated the lack of dogmatism on the part of the PRG. It is a major PRG concession, regardless of the fact that even such conservatives as Ambassador Henry Cabot Lodge,[7] Douglas Pike,[8] and former Vice President Vice Air Marshal Nguyen Cao Ky[9] all have admitted that the National Liberation Front (NLF), the political arm of the PRG, has been the closest to the Vietnamese masses.

It was only a realistic concession by the PRG. Unlike the First Indochina War, the Second Indochina War with its indiscriminate use of massive U.S. firepower and the influx of U.S. dollars has devastated the countryside, driven millions of peasants into the cities, angered intellectuals and students and generated a small class of war profiteers living, unwillingly in some cases, on artificial prosperity. All these diverse elements, whether or not they have supported the PRG in the past, are now primarily interested in the restoration of peace rather than in the victory of one side or the other. The Council of National Reconciliation and Concord, as its name indicates, is clearly the key to peace in Viet Nam.

## V

Like any agreement, the Paris Agreement was reached by compromises on both sides (the DRV and the U.S.) which for different reasons (strategic—international for the DRV; tactical—domestic for the U.S.) wished for a settlement of the war. The losing side was clearly Saigon. No longer does it have the visible manpower backing of over half a million U.S. soldiers (not counting the U.S. Seventh Fleet and the U.S. Air Force), the logistical support of the American armada, although Washington has massively introduced into South

[7] "For years, now in Southeast Asia, the only people who have been doing anything to the little man—to lift him up—have been the Communists." (*The New York Times* Feb. 27, 1966)

[8] "Aside from the NLF, there has never been a truly mass-based political party in South Vietnam." ("Viet Cong," MIT Press, 1966)

[9] "I perfectly agree with them (the Viet Cong) when they take the land of the rich and give it to the poor. I perfectly agree with them when they give a rifle to a peasant and say to him: 'Fight for a better life.' I personally agree with them when they abolish the privileged classes and when they say that the system of division of classes is wrong." (Interview with Orianna Fallaci, *The Washington Post,* April 7, 1968)

Viet Nam two months before the Agreement, in November and December 1972, armaments which boosted the Saigon air force to some 1,300 fixed-wing aircrafts and 800 helicopters. Moreover, Saigon has to contend with the presence of Hanoi troops besides those originating in the South. The acceptance by the U.S. of these Northern troops south of the 17th parallel evidenced the U.S. recognition that Viet Nam, territorially, is one country. The balance of forces is still impressive on the Saigon side. Its armed forces have a total of 1.1 million[10] out of a population of about 18 million. With a desertion rate officially admitted at 12,000 a month (in reality higher) the Saigon administration must dip into the reservoir of able-bodied Vietnamese to maintain its army at full strength, thus depriving the country of a large part of productive labor force.

Besides the army, the police force has grown quickly to become one of the most modernized security forces in the world. It was raised from 28,000 under the Diem régime in 1963 to the present level of 122,000.[11] These and the 278,000 civil servants (62,000 of them in Saigon) whom President Nguyen Van Thieu attempted to reorganize into "revolutionary" cadres constitute his official support. He has been organizing them into a political party, the Dan Chu (Democratic Party). But like the countless government-sponsored parties in South Viet Nam since 1954, the Dan Chu has no real political strength. On the eve of the November 1, 1963 coup d'etat, Ngo Dinh Nhu, the all-powerful brother and political adviser to President Ngo Dinh Diem told me confidently that "in case of crisis" (which he knew was at hand) he could "mobilize 1,500,000 Thanh Nien Cong Hoa (Republican Youth), his wife 1,000,000 Phu Nu Lien Doi (Women Solidarity) and his brother, the President, 3,000,000 members of the Phong Trao Cach Menh Quoc Gia (Movement for National Revolution). The next day, when Colonel Nguyen Van Thieu's division attacked the Presidential palace, Nhu and his brother fled to Cholon (Saigon's China town), took refuge at the home of a Chinese friend, only to be arrested and murdered by their own officers.

President Thieu's support, important as it is in number, is just as

10 434,000 in the infantry; 45,000 in the navy; 50,000 in the air force; 13,000 in the marines; 294,000 in the regional forces; 258,000 in the popular forces.

11 79,000 uniformed police; 22,300 in the special branch which guards against communist infiltration; 17,350 field police, a para-military police operating in the countryside; 2,750 marine police who patrol the nation's waterways. (*The U.S. News and World Report;* November 5, 1973). This number of course does not include thousands of full-time and part-time police informers.

illusory if not more so. Politics in Saigon, wrote Henry S. Bradsher of the conservative *Washington Star-News* (January 13, 1974) "has become largely a palace affair." He has not only organized his employees into a political party, he also tried to put up a façade of "democracy." He engineered and financed the formation of a legal opposition party, the Cong Hoa (Republican Party), the symbol of which is not the U.S. elephant (for that would be too obvious) but a Golden Lion. A recent visitor from Saigon described President Thieu's power base this way: "His régime is like a planet of 5 moons. He is of course the planet. Around him gravitate four moons, the commanders of the four military regions. The 5th moon is his nephew, Hoang Duc Nha." He added: "The planet gets its light from the sun which is Washington. As long as the sun gives its light, the planet and the moons will turn."

President Thieu's real support is therefore the United States which pays for his army, his police, his bureaucracy and finances his economy. In December 1973, the U.S. Congress passed a series of bills which gave him more than 1.5 billion dollars in direct military and economic aid. His government's budget amounts to $800 million less than 10 per cent of which is self-generated.

## VI

President Nguyen Van Thieu knows that the correct implementation of the 1973 Paris Agreement would bring about his downfall. He has made certain that the people under his control—and even his own bureaucracy—would not know the details of the accord. A Saigon official who visited Washington in late February 1973 was so happy when he could get hold of *The New York Times* issue of January 25, 1973, in which the full text of the Agreement was printed. President Thieu has no intention of retiring and is preparing to perpetuate his régime in the manner of General Park of South Korea and President Marcos of the Philippines. The Senate elections in August 1973 from which opposition slates were excluded gave him a two-thirds majority in both the House and the Senate. The Consitution is being amended to permit him to run for a third term in 1975.

Unlike the GRVN, the DRV and the PRG saw in the implementation of the Paris Agreement the fulfillment of the basic aims of their revolution. Immediately after the signing of the Agreement, the DRV and the PRG constantly broadcast the text, distributed it widely in printed forms, instructed their cadres to explain to the people the provisions of the Agreement.[12] A directive by the Central Committee of Hanoi's Lao Dong Party to its members in the South and reconstructed by the U.S. intelligence[13] ruled out against any offensive operation during the first 60 days of the cease-fire and cautioned against reprisals against Saigon officials. The PRG made a similar pledge through its Liberation Radio.[14] The DRV and PRG for their own interests decided to enter the phase of political and legal struggle, aiming at mobilizing public support at home and abroad for the Agreement and at converting their opponents to their side. Indeed, during the first few weeks following the cease-fire, fraternization between junior South Vietnamese (Saigon) officers and PRG officers took place. A high-ranking Saigon officer, Brigadier General Tran Van Cam, commander of the 23rd Division at Kontoum in the highlands admitted to American columnists Evan and Novak that such local accommodations were "chronic," and expressed "deep concern" about them.[15]

It is in this fraternization and the growing number of neutralists among Vietnamese at home and abroad that President Thieu sees the real threat to his régime. He reacted by closing all doors to the formation of the Council of National Reconciliation and Concord. On November 8, 1973, the Saigon spokesman, Bui Bao Truc, simply dismissed the existence of a third force (the neutralists). On December 21, 1973, Hoang Duc Nha, President Thieu's nephew and Director of Information, attacked the neutralists and reiterated that there is no third force in South Viet Nam. On December 29, 1973, President Thieu himself told a gathering at the National Political Training Center that there will be neither reconciliation nor general elections as defined in Article 12 of the Paris Agreement. He also attacked the third force.[16] For the same reason, he refuses to release political prisoners in defiance of Article 8 of the Agreement. Once released, the majority of them would swell the ranks of the third force or the PRG. President Thieu considers independent intellectuals as potential recruits for the third force too and has attempted to keep them under control. On November 21, 1973, 200 writers, journalists, and publishers, nearly all of them members of the Viet Nam Pen Club

---

12 According to The Liberation Press Agency of April 7, 1973, study sessions on the Agreement were organized the length and breadth of the liberated areas.

13 *The New York Times* News Service; *The Washington Star-News;* November 23, 1972.

14 Reported by the UPI from Saigon, October 29, 1972.

15 *The Washington Post,* May 18, 1973.

16 *The Washington Post,* December 30, 1973.

(an affiliate of the International Pen Club) met in Saigon to issue a statement on "the deep crisis affecting the present situation of the press and publishing." They unanimously voted to form a "committee to struggle for the rights of writings and publishing."

## VII

With all opposition, potential and real, silenced or bought off, President Thieu launched in October a campaign to accuse the DRV of massive infiltrations into the South and the PRG of numerous violations of the Paris Agreement. On January 4, 1974, President Thieu openly called on his armed forces to attack the PRG in their controlled areas. He said: "The Vietnam War has begun again."[17] His statement confirmed the attacks his armed forces have carried out since the beginning of the cease-fire against the PRG zones. In November 1973, Ed Bradley, the CBS correspondent in South Viet Nam, reported on CBS News in the U.S. on November 14 and 16 about the situation in the PRG areas which he visited: "During our two weeks with the Viet Cong, we saw planes on bombing runs or heard the shelling every day and on several occasions had to scramble into bunkers in the middle of the night." According to U.S. military sources quoted in the October 3, 1973 issue of *The New York Times,* during the first six months after the signing of the Paris Agreement, the U.S. provided the Saigon air force alone with 142,000 bombs, rockets and flares and 13.8 million rounds of small-arms ammunition. In clear violation of Article 7 of the Agreement, the Pentagon announced plans to replace Saigon's F-5A fighters with more advanced F-5E (*The Washington Star-News,* January 8, 1974). These are not to replace attrition or losses. They are to modernize the Saigon air force whose pilots are now trained at Williams Air Base in Arizona.

President Thieu's campaign was well orchestrated. Washington officials made statements combining threats with deliberate confusion of the situation in South Viet Nam and hints of big powers' behind-the-scene manipulations. Faced with this situation, the PRG's Foreign Ministry on November 2, 1973, issued a communiqué detailing Saigon's major offensives against its zones during the previous nine months and concluded: "The people's Liberation Armed Forces of South Vietnam, acting strictly on orders of their command in defence of the liberated zone, its population and the Paris agreement, will fight back firmly to give the kind of punishment they

[17] *The Washington Post,* January 4, 1974.

(Saigon forces) deserve."[18] The "nibbling war" was escalating rapidly.

As the Year of the Buffalo ended and the Year of the Tiger had begun (January 23, 1974) there were more than enough proofs that the 1973 Paris Agreement on" Ending the War and Restoring Peace in Vietnam" has neither ended the war nor restored peace. The only alternative to a bloodier third Indochina war lies not in more Kissinger-Tho meetings or secret big-power maneuvers which in the long run will not change the basic aims of the DRV and the PRG. It lies in the full and correct implementation of the 1973 Paris Agreement especially the implementation of Article 12 and the immediate formation of the Council for National Reconciliation and Concord. The Paris Agreement is the only instrument available that can satisfy the basic objectives of the Vietnamese revolution and the deep aspirations for peace, independence, unity and social justice of the long suffering Vietnamese people. In the meantime, it is not a bad idea to call for a moratorium on all kinds of aid by all foreign powers to all parties in Viet Nam, except perhaps aid from international, non-governmental humanitarian organizations.

18 The Foreign Broadcast Information Service, November 5, 1973.

# One Year of Implementation of the Paris Agreement on Viet Nam

A year ago, on January 27, 1973, the Agreement on Ending the War and Restoring Peace in Viet Nam was signed in Paris.

Under the Agreement, the United States undertakes to respect the independence, sovereignty, unity and territorial integrity of Viet Nam and the South Vietnamese people's right to self-determination, to stop all its military activities in both zones of Viet Nam, to withdraw from South Viet Nam all its troops, military personnel, armaments, and war material, not to continue its military involvement or intervene in the internal affairs of South Viet Nam, and to contribute to healing the wounds of war and to post-war reconstruction in the Democratic Republic of Viet Nam.

The Agreement recognizes the existence in South Viet Nam of two administrations—the Provisional Revolutionary Government of the Republic of South Viet Nam and the Government of the Republic of Viet Nam—two armies, two zones controlled by the two South Vietnamese parties, and three political forces, and provides for steps to carry into effect the South Vietnamese people's right to self-determination.

The Agreement stipulates that the reunification of Viet Nam shall be carried out step by step through peaceful means on the basis of discussions and agreements between North and South Viet Nam, without coercion or annexation by either party, and without foreign interference.

Together with the Vietnamese people, the whole of progressive mankind has warmly welcomed the Paris Agreement on Viet Nam, and has expressed the wish that it will be strictly implemented.

Now, one year after the signing of the Paris Agreement on Viet Nam, the South Vietnamese people should have been in a position to live in peace, national reconciliation and concord, with full democratic freedoms to decide themselves the political future of South Viet Nam. Yet, in South Viet Nam, guns have not yet been stilled, the bloodshed has continued, destructions are still a daily occurrence; hundreds of thousands of political prisoners continued to be detained by the Saigon Administration, and the democratic liberties of the people living in the Saigon-controlled zone continue to be trampled underfoot; the National Council of National Reconciliation and Concord has not been set up. The situation in South Viet Nam has been deteriorating.

What is the cause of the present situation in South Viet Nam? What is to be done to ensure a strict implementation of the Paris Agreement on Viet Nam?

It is precisely the purpose of this document to give an answer to these questions.

Part One

# TWO OPPOSING POLICIES IN THE IMPLEMENTATION OF THE PARIS AGREEMENT ON VIET NAM

The Paris Agreement on Viet Nam which has been solemnly acknowledged by the Act of the International Conference on Viet Nam, and given further precision by the June 13, 1973 Joint Communiqué of the four signatory parties, constitutes an embodiment of the great victory of the Vietnamese people in their patriotic struggle against U.S. aggression.

Its content meets the fundamental national interests of the Vietnamese people and conforms to the trend of our times. It is a solid political and legal basis for the Vietnamese people to carry on their revolutionary struggle in the new stage in order to maintain and consolidate peace and make it lasting, to step up the building of socialism in the North, to achieve independence and democracy in the South, and to carry out the peaceful reunification of their country, thereby contributing to peace in Indochina, South-East Asia and the world.

It is the unswerving policy of the Government of the Democratic Republic of Viet Nam as well as that of the Provisional Revolutionary Government of the Republic of South Viet Nam to scrupulously respect and implement the Paris Agreement on Viet Nam, and at the same time, to demand that the United States and the Saigon Administration do the same.

On September 1, 1973, Premier of the Democratic Republic of Viet Nam Pham Van Dong pointed out: "As for our people, the Government of the Democratic Republic of Viet Nam and the Provisional Revolutionary Government of the Republic of South Viet Nam, to strictly respect and scrupulously implement the Paris Agreement is not only an obligation incumbent on us as signatory parties, but also a great policy of ours."

The Paris Agreement constitutes a heavy blow dealt at the U.S. policy of aggression and the interests of the Saigon Administration, a hireling of the United States; it is a rejection of the "Nixon doctrine" in Viet Nam and Indochina. That is precisely the reason why the U.S. Government has always opposed the implementation of many essential provisions, and has, at the same time, tolerated and encouraged the violations of the Agreement by the Saigon Administration. Its purpose is to erase step by step the fact that there exist two administrations, two armies, two zones of control and three political forces in South Viet Nam, to impose U.S. neo-colonialism on South Viet Nam, and to perpetuate the partition of Viet Nam.

Part Two

# THE IMPLEMENTATION OF THE PARIS AGREEMENT ON VIET NAM OVER THE PAST YEAR

## I. PROVISIONS ALREADY IMPLEMENTED

Under Articles 2, 3 and 5 of the Agreement, the United States has ceased all its acts of war in South Viet Nam, stopped the bombing, ended the mining of the territorial waters, ports, harbours and waterways of the Democratic Republic of Viet Nam, deactivated or destroyed the mines it had laid along ten channels in the latter's territorial waters, and withdrawn from South Viet Nam its troops and those of the other foreign countries allied with it.

The return of the captured and detained military personnel and foreign civilians of the parties under Article 8(a) of the Agreement was carried out simultaneously with U.S. troop withdrawals. Pursuant to Article 8(a), the Government of the Democratic Republic of Viet Nam and the Provisional Revolutionary Government of the Republic of South Viet Nam returned to the United States all the U.S. military personnel and all foreign civilians captured in North and South Viet Nam, totalling 588 persons. During the same period, the Provisional Revolutionary Government of the Republic of South Viet Nam returned 5,016 captured and detained military personnel of the Saigon Administration. The U.S. and Saigon Administration side returned to the Provisional Revolutionary Government of the Republic of South Viet Nam 26,508 military personnel captured and detained by it, and is still detaining a number of prisoners.

The ending of the U.S. war of aggression against the Vietnamese people in both zones and the withdrawal of the U.S. expeditionary corps from South Viet Nam which put an end to a 115-year-long occupation of Vietnamese territory by foreign troops, constitutes a historic event of great political significance. This victory is inspiring the Vietnamese people in their persistent struggle to ensure respect for, and a scrupulous implementation of, all the provisions of the Paris Agreement, and to secure the Vietnamese people's fundamental national rights and the South Vietnamese people's right to self-determination.

## II. THE UNITED STATES AND THE SAIGON ADMINISTRATION HAVE BEEN SYSTEMATICALLY VIOLATING MANY ESSENTIAL PROVISIONS OF THE AGREEMENT

### THE CEASEFIRE IS NOT YET EFFECTIVE IN SOUTH VIET NAM

Article 2 of the Paris Agreement on Viet Nam clearly stipulates: A ceasefire shall be observed throughout South Viet Nam as of 24.00 hours GMT on January 27, 1973, and the complete cessation of hostilities shall be durable and without limit of time.

Article 3 of the Agreement stipulates: The Parties undertake to maintain the ceasefire and to ensure a lasting and stable peace. As soon as the ceasefire goes into effect, the armed forces of the two South Vietnamese parties shall remain in-place, stop all offensive activities against each other, and strictly abide by the following stipulations:

– All acts of force on the ground, in the air, and on the sea shall be prohibited.

– All hostile acts, terrorism and reprisals by both sides will be banned.

The Protocol concerning the Ceasefire has given further precision on the above provisions, and laid down concrete steps to maintain the ceasefire and ensure lasting peace in South Viet Nam; for instance, it prohibits armed patrols into areas controlled by opposing armed forces and flights by bomber and fighter aircraft of all types, armed attacks against any person either military or civilian, by any means whatsoever, all combat operations on the ground, on rivers, on the sea and in the air, all hostile acts, terrorism or reprisals, and all acts endangering lives or public or private property. The Protocol also makes clear that the above-mentioned prohibitions shall not hamper or restrict the civilian supply, freedom of movement, freedom to work, freedom of the people to engage in trade, and civilian communication and transportation between and among all areas in South Viet Nam.

On January 27, 1973, the Command of the South Viet Nam People's Liberation Armed Forces ordered all regular, regional and guerilla units to cease fire throughout South Viet Nam, to remain in-place and stop all offensive activities.

The military delegation of the Democratic Republic of Viet Nam and the military delegation of the Provisional Revolutionary Government in the Four-Party Joint Military Commission and subsequently, the military delegation of the Provisional Revolutionary Government in the Two-Party Joint Military Commission have made many proposals and put forward many steps for a strict implementation of the ceasefire, for instance, the three steps proposed on March 17, 1973 to end the hostilities, and the five points of May 11, 1973 for ending hostilities. On April 25, 1973, the delegation of the Provisional Revolutionary Government of the Republic of South Viet Nam to the Consultative Conference in La Celle Saint Cloud (Paris) made a proposal for immediate cessation of all hostilities, and strict observance of all the provisions concerning a ceasefire that is durable and without limit of time.

In contrast, the Saigon Administration has frenziedly sabotaged the ceasefire with U.S. encouragement and assistance. On January 28, 1973, one hour before the ceasefire went into effect, Nguyen Van Thieu, the chieftain of the Saigon Administration, bluntly declared that "the ceasefire does not mean the end of the war", that "the ceasefire does not mean real peace". At the same moment, great infantry forces of the Saigon Army with air, tank and artillery support, launched operations against areas under the control of the Provisional Revolutionary Government of the Republic of South Viet Nam.

As pointed out by *U.S. News and World Report* of January 29, 1973, the purpose of such operations was "to move into contested areas—even communist controlled regions—and reduce the number of people and territory dominated by Reds".

The Saigon Administration's sabotage of the ceasefire is part of an overall plan called "territory-invading plan" which includes four stages: preparations, pre-ceasefire actions, actions concomitant with the ceasefire, and post-ceasefire actions. Under this plan, the Saigon Administration's armed forces have been ordered:

– to expand military operations aimed at "securing control over 100 per cent of the population and territory" in the preparatory stage;

– to expand to a maximum the sphere of control and "launch simultaneous attacks against enemy units, inflict maximum losses on them or pin them down in remote places" before the ceasefire;

– to achieve increased "coordination among units while invading territory" as the ceasefire is ordered;

– "to secretly invade the territory or cut off the enemy-controlled area" after the ceasefire.

Since that time, the Saigon Administration has launched operation upon operation to grab lands in the area controlled by the Provisional Revolutionary Government of the Republic of South Viet Nam; at the same time, it has stepped up police and "pacification" operations in the area under its control. What is particularly serious, of late, the Saigon Administration has conducted large-scale operations in the provinces of Binh Dinh, Quang Ngai, Quang Duc, Kontum, Gia Lai, Tây Ninh, Chuong Thien, etc. It has also launched savage air strikes against many areas lying deep in the liberated zone, razing many villages, and committing countless crimes against the South Vietnamese people.

From January 28 to December 15, 1973, the Saigon Administration committed 301,097 violations, comprising:

   34,266  land-grabbing operations (including 37 division-size operations and 5,250 regiment-size ones);

   35,532  artillery shellings;

   14,749  aerial bombardments and reconnaissances;

216,550  police and "pacification" operations.

The Saigon Administration has killed or injured over 6,000 civilians.

In response to the profound aspirations of all social strata in South Viet Nam, on October 15, 1973, the Command of the South Viet Nam People's Liberation Armed Forces called on the Saigon Administration to strictly observe the ceasefire and to scrupulously implement the Paris Agreement, at the same time, it asserted the legitimate right of the Provisional Revolutionary Government of the Republic of South Viet Nam to take appropriate measures against the sabotage of the Agreement:

– to give resolute ripostes to the Saigon Administration war acts, to defend the liberated zone, protect the people's lives and property, to safeguard the Agreement

– to resolutely fight back at any place, with appropriate forms and forces so long as the Saigon Administration continues its war acts, to compel the other side to scrupulously and strictly implement the Paris Agreement on Viet Nam, and stop all its acts of violation and sabotage of the Agreement.

The implementation of the Paris Agreement must be coupled with the struggle against any U.S. and Saigon action in violation of the same, and with due punishment inflicted on the Saigon Administration's sabotage of the ceasefire.

# HUNDREDS OF THOUSANDS OF POLITICAL PRISONERS ARE STILL LANGUISHING IN PRISONS AND DETENTION CAMPS OF THE SAIGON ADMINISTRATION

Article 8(c) of the Paris Agreement on Viet Nam stipulates: The two South Vietnamese parties will do their utmost to resolve the question of the return of the Vietnamese civilian personnel captured and detained in South Viet Nam within ninety days after the ceasefire comes into effect.

The Protocol concerning the Return of Captured Military Personnel and Foreign Civilians and Captured and Detained Vietnamese Civilian Personnel stresses that each party shall return all captured persons without denying or delaying their return for any reason, and shall facilitate their return and reception. Pending their return, all Vietnamese civilian personnel captured and detained in South Viet Nam shall be treated humanely at all times, and in accordance with international practice . . .

Pursuant to Article 8 (c) of the Agreement, the military delegation of the Provisional Revolutionary Government of the Republic of South Viet Nam has repeatedly stated its willingness to return to the Saigon Administration all the Vietnamese civilian personnel captured and detained by the Provisional Revolutionary Government of the Republic of South Viet Nam, and to complete this operation within ninety days as provided for by the Paris Agreement on Viet Nam.

But, at U.S. instigation, the Saigon Administration has refused to return all political prisoners captured and detained by it. Although it is detaining over 200,000 Vietnamese civilian personnel belonging to the National Front for Liberation, the Provisional Revolutionary Government of the Republic of South Viet Nam, and various political and religious tendencies which do not side with either party in South Viet Nam, Nguyen Van Thieu has bluntly stated: "There are no political prisoners in South Viet Nam. There are only two kinds of prisoners: 21,000 common-law convicts and 5,081 communist prisoners." (Nguyen Van Thieu's letter to Pope Paul VI dated April 9, 1973)

Shortly before the ceasefire, the Saigon Administration already resorted to many perfidious tricks in an attempt to avoid the return of prisoners. For instance, it sent detainees from one prison to another, dispersed prisoners to various jails, registered political detainees as "common-law" convicts, compelled detainees to sign "release certificates", brought many prisoners to unknown destinations, or secretly killed them.

Speaking at the U.S. Senate, Senator E. Kennedy said: "The Thieu Government may choose any label it desires for civilians detained for political reasons, but by every international standard, what are commonly called 'political prisoners' exist in South Viet Nam today." (Congressional Record, Wash. June 4, 1973)

Public opinion in South Viet Nam, many national and international organizations, well-known personalities and Western press have exposed the cynical lies of Nguyen Van Thieu and his agents.

On February 21, 1973, 30 political organizations in Saigon urged the Nguyen Van Thieu Administration to release the 200,000 political prisoners still kept in custody. Father Chân Tin, a representative of the Committee to Reform the Prison System in South Viet Nam and deputy Ho Ngoc Nhuân denounced that Administration for its continued detention of 202,000 political prisoners.

The U.S. magazine *Newsweek* of Dec. 18, 1972, wrote: "Nearly 45,000 South Vietnamese have been tried, convicted and jailed for political offences, and up to 100,000 others have been arrested and thrown into prisons established everywhere, including Poulo Condor, without trial. They are men and women who are writhing and languishing in the prisons . . . for their political activities did not please Thieu."

After a trip to South Viet Nam, U.S. Bishop Thomas J. Gumbleton asserted: "I can state unequivocally that there are political prisoners in Saigon's jails and in jails throughout the provinces. They are in jail not for any crime, but simply because they are in political opposition to the present government. The proof is overwhelming, and it is clear that these prisoners are subjected to inhuman treatment, including deliberate and prolonged torture." (*National Catholic Reporter*, May 11, 1973)

Speaking before the U.S. Congress on September 18, 1973, Fred Branfman, Co-director of the Indochina Resources Center in Washington, said: "The Government of the Republic of Viet Nam is clearly attempting to avoid the release of the vast majority of its political prisoners, in clear violation of the Paris Accord . . . I was given a prison by prison breakdown totalling 202,000 political prisoners prepared by the Committee to Reform the Prison System . . ."

"The main device used by the Government of the Republic of Viet Nam to justify holding political prisoners has been reclassification. This has been an attempt to change their status to that of common-law criminals . . . The U.S. Embassy in Saigon confirmed this practice to Senator E. Kennedy in a letter dated April 3, 1973."

Even for the 5,081 Vietnamese civilian personnel whose detention has been admitted by it, the Saigon Administration has returned so far to the Provisional Revolutionary Government only over 1,500.

In the meantime, it has jailed tens of thousands of persons who desire peace and stand for national reconciliation and concord.

The civilian personnel kept by the Saigon Administration in "tiger cages" or other jails are living in inconceivable conditions. As the U.S. magazine *Time* of March 19, 1973, put it, "It is not really proper to call them men any more. 'Shapes' is a better word–grotesque sculptures of scarred flesh and gnarled limbs."

Former U.S. Senator George Murphy has said that the long story of the Saigon Administration's inhuman treatment of prisoners in South Viet Nam is well-known to broad segments of public opinion around the world (*Reuter*, June 7, 1973)

The 3rd International Conference of Catholics in Solidarity with the Peoples of Viet Nam, Laos and Cambodia held in Turin (Italy) from November 1 to 4, 1973 unanimously passed an appeal in which it condemned the policy of sabotage of the Paris Agreement pursued by the United States and the Nguyen Van Thieu Administration, exposed the regime of repression and terror imposed by Saigon which has turned the areas under its control into a huge prison, and denounced the continued detention of 200,000 political prisoners in South Viet Nam. (*AFP*, Turin, November 4, 1973)

Thus, a year after the signing of the Paris Agreement on Viet Nam, and at variance with its explicit provisions, hundreds of thousands of political prisoners are still languishing in prisons and detention camps of the Saigon Administration.

It is to be stressed that the United States is the builder of the police organization and the system of prisons and detention camps in South Viet Nam.

On April 30, 1971, U.S. Senator W. Anderson, speaking before the U.S. Congress, denounced that the United States had spent at least 266,000 dollars to build more "tiger cages" in Poulo Condor. On September 9, 1973, Senator E. Kennedy denounced the U.S. Government for violation of the Paris Agreement on Viet Nam by continued financial support for the police apparatus and prison system in South Viet Nam.

Heavy responsibility rests with the U.S. Government for the fate of the political prisoners now being detained by the Nguyen Van Thieu Administration.

# THE SOUTH VIETNAMESE PEOPLE'S DEMOCRATIC LIBERTIES CONTINUE TO BE TRAMPLED UPON

Article 11 of the Agreement stipulates: "Immediately after the ceasefire, the two South Vietnamese parties will:

– Achieve national reconciliation and concord, end hatred and enmity, prohibit all acts of reprisal and discrimination against individuals or organizations that have collaborated with one side or the other;

– Ensure the democratic liberties of the people: personal freedom, freedom of

speech, freedom of the press; freedom of meeting, freedom of organization, free-
dom of political activities, freedom of belief, freedom of movement, freedom of
residence, freedom of work, right to property ownership, and right to free enterprise."

In the Appeal of January 28, 1973, the Central Committee of the South Viet
Nam National Front for Liberation and the Provisional Revolutionary Government of the Republic of South Viet Nam stated that they would fully guarantee
the democratic liberties to the people, achieve national reconciliation and concord
so that all South Vietnamese people could end hatred and enmity, and jointly
shape a new life, and rebuild the country, and demanded that the Saigon Administration do the same. On June 28, 1973, the Delegation of the Provisional
Revolutionary Government of the Republic of South Viet Nam to the La Celle
Saint Cloud Conference proposed specific measures aimed at guaranteeing the
democratic liberties, and among other things, that the two parties "issue a decision to the effect that all persons belonging to all political tendencies or religious
beliefs will be allowed freedom of activities in both zones of the two South Vietnamese parties, and that newspapers belonging to all tendencies will be freely
circulated between the two zones". It was also proposed that the two parties
immediately enact laws to guarantee full democratic liberties to the people, as
a first step to speed up the settlement of the internal political questions of South
Viet Nam in a spirit of national reconciliation and concord.

At the same Conference, on July 18, 1973, the Delegation of the Provisional
Revolutionary Government of the Republic of South Viet Nam put forward a
proposal about "fundamental stipulations to guarantee democratic liberties to the
South Vietnamese people" for the two South Vietnamese parties to agree upon
and undertake to enact at once in the zone under their respective control.

With its extremely fascist and warlike nature, the Nguyen Van Thieu Administration has ignored these constructive proposals and continued to trample underfoot the people's democratic liberties as if it had not made any commitment in
Paris.

One day only after the signing of the Agreement, Nguyen Van Thieu bluntly
stated that "as for all our affairs, laws, administration, we'll do exactly as in the
past, nothing is changed . . . If Communists enter the village, they will be shot dead
on the spot."

One day only after the four parties signed the June 13, 1973 Joint Communiqué, the Saigon Administration's spokesman stated: "The Government of the
Republic of Viet Nam reserved its right to maintain restrictions to democratic
liberties."

On March 1, 1973, the *Washington Post* remarked that the Saigon Administra-

# SYSTEM OF U.S. CONSULATE GENERALS AND CONSULATES IN SOUTH VIETNAM

(In fact, American Military Command system in military zones and provinces in South Vietnam)

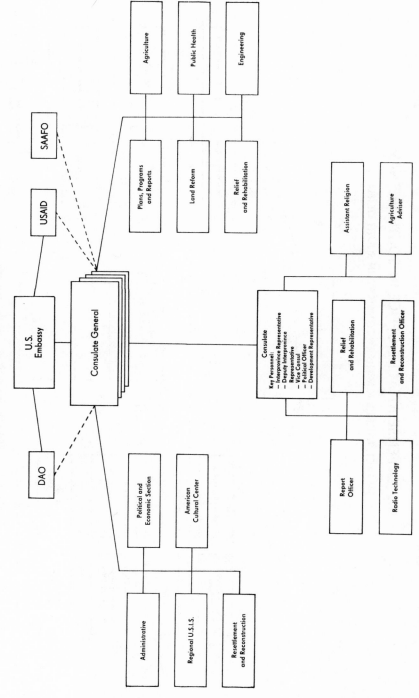

# U.S. DEFENSE ATTACHE OFFICE IN SOUTH VIETNAM

## (IN FACT, AMERICAN MILITARY COMMAND IN SOUTH VIETNAM)

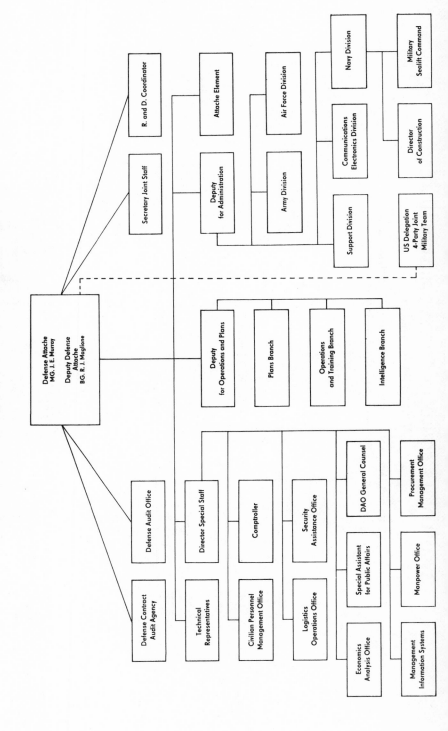

tion "had restricted democratic liberties more than it had done before the Agreement came into effect". That is a well-grounded remark in view of the fact that shortly before and after the signing of the Agreement, the Saigon Administration has enacted dozens of new "decrees" such as:

- The "decree on local security" banning all market strikes and demonstrations and allowing the police to open fire on the spot;
- The "new press decree" stifling freedom of the press, and resulting in dozens of newspapers being closed down;
- The "decree" abolishing village elections. All chiefs of province are to be appointed by Nguyen Van Thieu, the administrative apparatus at grassroots level is in the hands of officers loyal to Thieu;
- The "decree on the status of parties" aimed at eliminating 26 political parties in South Viet Nam, leaving in existence only the so-called "Democratic Party" and other organizations belonging to Thieu;
- The "decree" on the setting up of nine new criminal courts in Saigon and a number of provinces;
- The "decree N° 090" repressing anyone regarded as "dangerous" by the Saigon Administration.

Everything, from the tribunals to the press, is in the hands of Nguyen Van Thieu's army and police. Over 7,000 army and police officers of the Saigon Administration have been sent to various provinces to strengthen the apparatus of coercion and repression.

Hundreds of police operations are conducted each day with a view to purging, arresting or killing people, herding them into concentration camps, or preventing them from returning to their native villages. The "accelerated pacification" and "Phoenix" programmes which are carried on and expanded by the Saigon Administration in the areas under its control with a force of 125,000 policemen is merely a protracted campaign of white terror directed by the SAAFO which was formerly CORDS.[1]

Anyone suspected of communist or neutralist convictions or even of sympathy with neutralism, is considered "dangerous" and may be jailed or shot dead.

The so-called "crop-protecting plan" now being carried out by the Saigon Administration is merely a plan for plunder of rice, even in places recently devastated by typhoons and floods, and for economic blockade of the zone under the control of the Provisional Revolutionary Government of the Republic of South Viet Nam.

According to still incomplete figures, in nearly one year from the signing of the Paris Agreement on Viet Nam to December 15, 1973, the Saigon Administration

[1] Civil Operations and Rural Development Support.

conducted hundreds of thousands of police and "pacification" operations in the
course of which it "purged" over 3 million people, arrested and tortured over
36,000 persons, plundered hundreds of thousands of tons of rice, tens of thousands
of head of cattle, forcibly took away 145 billion South Vietnamese piastres, and
herded over 920,000 people into concentration camps.

It is clear that the purpose of the Saigon Administration is not to ensure democratic liberties and achieve national reconciliation and concord, but to make its
regime more fascist in crude violation of Article 11 of the Paris Agreement on
Viet Nam, thus turning the zone under its control into a huge concentration camp,
a hell on earth.

That is precisely the reason why the various social strata in Saigon and other
Saigon controlled areas have been intensifying further and further their struggle
for peace, democracy, a better life, and national reconciliation and concord.


## NO PROGRESS HAS BEEN RECORDED
## IN THE SETTLEMENT OF THE INTERNAL MATTERS
## OF SOUTH VIET NAM

Article 9 of the Agreement asserts that the South Vietnamese people's right to
self-determination is sacred, inalienable, and it stipulates that the South Vietnamese people shall decide themselves the political future of South Viet Nam
through genuinely free and democratic general elections under international
supervision.

Article 12 of the Agreement clearly points out that the two South Vietnamese
parties shall hold consultations in order to set up a National Council of National
Reconciliation and Concord of three equal segments. According to the fundamental spirit of these provisions, the two South Vietnamese parties shall jointly settle
the internal matters of South Viet Nam in a spirit of national reconciliation and
concord, mutual respect, without annexation of either side by the other, and
without foreign interference.

National reconciliation and concord are a deep aspiration of the South Vietnamese people, the realistic way to maintain lasting peace and to achieve the South
Vietnamese people's right to self-determination.

Proceeding from the policy of great national unity clearly expounded in its program of action and in the Political Program of the South Viet Nam National Front
for Liberation, the Provisional Revolutionary Government of the Republic of
South Viet Nam has repeatedly stated its willingness to cooperate with all people
—whatever their past—who stand now for peace, independence, democracy and

national concord, to end hatred and suspicion with a view to jointly building a life of love and happiness. It has called upon the Saigon Administration to place the interests of the Fatherland above all, to respond to the demands of people from all walks of life, to rapidly set up through sincere consultations the National Council of National Reconciliation and Concord of three equal segments, and to organize at an early date genuinely free and democratic general elections to allow the South Vietnamese people to freely decide their political regime.

On April 25 and June 28, 1973, at the La Celle Saint Cloud Conference, the Provisional Revolutionary Government of the Republic of South Viet Nam put forward reasonable and sensible proposals aimed at ensuring a total ceasefire and the return of all captured civilian personnel, guaranteeing the people's democratic liberties, setting up the National Council of National Reconciliation and Concord, holding genuinely free and democratic general elections in order to realize the South Vietnamese people's genuine right to self-determination, and resolving the question of the Vietnamese armed forces in South Viet Nam.

The Government of the Democratic Republic of Viet Nam has declared its full support to the policy and constructive proposals of the Provisional Revolutionary Government of the Republic of South Viet Nam.

The attitude of the U.S. Government and the Saigon Administration in this question is completely at variance with the spirit and letter of the Paris Agreement.

The Agreement clearly stipulates: "Foreign countries shall not impose any political tendency or personality on the South Vietnamese people." (Article 9c). However, U.S. President R. Nixon has openly declared to recognize the Nguyen Van Thieu Administration as the only legal administration in South Viet Nam. And as a matter of fact, the U.S. Government continues to maintain and strengthen this administration as an instrument of U.S. neo-colonialism in South Viet Nam.

As for the Saigon Administration, right from the beginning, it has not concealed its opposition to the Paris Agreement. It has evaded the most fundamental and urgent questions, namely to achieve a total ceasefire, to return all captured civilian personnel, and to ensure democratic liberties in order to create favourable conditions for resolving the internal matters of South Viet Nam as provided for in the Agreement: at the same time, it has sought every means to sabotage the achievement of national reconciliation and concord.

It has rehashed the unreasonable U.S. demand for the so-called "withdrawal of North Vietnamese troops" which has been rejected by the Paris Agreement and considered it a prerequisite for the settlement of the political questions in South Viet Nam.

With regard to the functions of the National Council of National Reconciliation and Concord, the Paris Agreement has explicitly stipulated: promoting the two South Vietnamese parties' implementation of the Agreement, achievement of national reconciliation and concord, ensurance of democratic liberties, and organization of the general elections. Yet the Saigon Administration wants to turn the National Council of National Reconciliation and Concord into a mere electoral commission in the framework of the so-called "Constitution" of the Thieu regime.

The Paris Agreement has explicitly stipulated that the National Council of National Reconciliation and Concord is composed of three equal segments. However, the Saigon Administration has tried hard to deny the existence of political and religious tendencies which stand on neither side in South Viet Nam, in an attempt to prevent these political forces from participating in the political life in South Viet Nam.

With a view to deceiving public opinion, the Saigon Administration has made a proposal concerning a specific date for the general elections, thus pretending to have at heart the implementation of the South Vietnamese people's right to self-determination. As is known, the shooting has not stopped in South Viet Nam, the people in the Saigon-controlled zone have continued to be denied all democratic liberties, hundreds of thousands of political prisoners belonging to various political and religious tendencies have remained in detention, opposition forces have continued to be subjected to repression and terror. General elections held in such conditions would be a mere farce as had been done in South Viet Nam, and which would result in giving a legal cover to Nguyen Van Thieu's dictatorial regime and eliminating the Provisional Revolutionary Government of the Republic of South Viet Nam. To hold such general elections is in fact to deny the South Vietnamese people's right to self-determination, and to act at variance with the Paris Agreement on Viet Nam.

In view of the aforesaid obstinate attitude of the Saigon Administration, no progress has been recorded as yet in the settlement of the internal matters of South Viet Nam.

# THE UNITED STATES IS NOT WILLING TO PUT A COMPLETE END TO ITS MILITARY INVOLVEMENT AND INTERFERENCE IN THE INTERNAL AFFAIRS OF SOUTH VIET NAM

The Paris Agreement clearly stipulates: The United States will stop all its military activities against the territory of the Democratic Republic of Viet Nam by ground, air and naval forces wherever they may be based . . . (Article 2); will not continue its military involvement or intervene in the internal affairs of South Viet Nam (Article 4); within sixty days of the signing of the Agreement, there will be a total withdrawal from South Viet Nam of troops, military advisers, and military personnel including technical military personnel and military personnel associated with the pacification program, advisers to all paramilitary organizations and the police force, armaments, munitions, and war material of the United States and those of the other foreign countries allied with it (Article 5).

The Agreement also explicitly stipulates that the dismantlement of all military bases in South Viet Nam of the United States and of the other foreign countries allied with it shall be completed within sixty days of the signing of the Agreement (Article 6), and the two South Vietnamese parties shall not accept the introduction of troops, military advisers, and military personnel including technical military personnel, armaments, munitions and war material into South Viet Nam (Article 7). The two South Vietnamese parties shall be permitted to make periodic replacements of armaments on the basis of piece-for-piece, of the same characteristics and properties, under the supervision of the Joint Military Commission of the two South Vietnamese parties and of the International Commission of Control and Supervision.

The United States has seriously violated all the above-mentioned provisions.

Before the signing of the Paris Agreement on Viet Nam, the United States had already evaded the Agreement by establishing the biggest airlift in the history of the wars in Indochina to urgently introduce into South Viet Nam hundreds of aircrafts, tanks, artillery pieces, and tens of thousands of tons of other armaments and munitions at the average rate of 700 tons a day.

The troops of the United States and of its allies withdrawing from South Viet Nam, did not bring away with them their armaments, munitions and war material. This amounts in fact to illegally introducing hundreds of thousands of tons of armaments and war material into South Viet Nam in violation of the provisions of Article 7. The United States has also failed to dismantle its military bases in South Viet Nam, as stipulated by Article 6 of the Agreement.

Over the past year, the United States has illegally brought on repeated occasions armaments, munitions, aircraft, tanks, and artillery pieces into South Viet Nam to lend a helping hand to the Saigon Administration in its sabotage of the ceasefire and of the Agreement. In the face of the condemnation by public opinion, it has claimed by way of excuse that its actions "are consistent with Article 7 of the Agreement". In fact, Article 7 prohibits the introduction of armaments, munitions and war material into South Viet Nam and allows the two South Vietnamese parties to make replacements of armaments only under the supervision of the Two-Party Joint Military Commission and of the International Commission. As long as the two South Vietnamese parties have not reached any agreement on the date of replacement of armaments, the kinds of armaments to be replaced, and the modalities of replacement and supervision, the United States is not permitted to bring into South Viet Nam any kinds of armaments, munitions and war material whatsoever.

What is particularly serious, the United States has left behind tens of thousands of military personnel disguised as civilians, and has not ceased to secretly bring thousands more into South Viet Nam. At present, there are already over 24,000 U.S. military personnel disguised as civilians working in the various services of the Defense Ministry, the various branches and services of the army, the police organizations, intelligence agencies and pacification services of the Saigon Administration.

To direct and manage this system of "advisers", the United States has disguised its former military organizations as "civilian" agencies. D.A.O.[1] is a variant of the former MACV[2]; S.A.A.F.O. (Special Assistant to the Ambassador for Field Operations) is as a matter of fact the former CORDS[3]–in a disguised form to assume continued direction of the "pacification" and "Phoenix" programs; U.S.A.I.D.[4] is nominally an economic agency, but has been for a long time now responsible for training, equipping, and giving advice to the police force of the Saigon Administration. As for the four U.S. "consulates general" in Da Nang, Nha Trang, Bien Hoa, and Can Tho, and the U.S. provincial "consulates" established since the signing of the Paris Agreement on Viet Nam, they are in fact U.S. commands in the various military regions and provinces of South Viet Nam.

With such an organization system, the United States is actually directing the war and repressive machine of the Nguyen Van Thieu Administration in the conduct of land-grabbing and "pacification" operations in South Viet Nam.

What is particularly significant, the U.S. military aid to the Saigon Administra-

---

[1] Defence Attaché Office.
[2] Military Assistance Command in Viet Nam.
[3] Civil Operations and Rural Development Support.
[4] United States Agency for International Development.

tion after the signing of the Paris Agreement is even bigger than in war-time. Elliot Richardson, former U.S. Defense Secretary, reported to the Defense Appropriations Committee of the U.S. House of Representatives that in the 1973–1974 fiscal year, the U.S. military aid to South-East Asia is not a mere 2.9 billion dollars, but actually 4.069 billion, surpassing by far the 2.735 billion dollars of military aid to South-East Asia in the 1972–1973 fiscal year. According to figures given in the Record of the U.S. Senate Armed Services Committee, out of this 4.069 billion dollars, the appropriations for "the use, maintenance, and purchase of arms" in South Viet Nam alone accounted for over 3 billion dollars. This does not include the military expenditures concealed under other headings, and the aid to the police organization and prisons in South Viet Nam.

It is clear that the United States, although compelled to withdraw its troops from South Viet Nam, is not willing to put a complete end to its military involvement and intervention in the internal affairs of South Viet Nam, and has not given up its design of strengthening and consolidating the Saigon Administration and army, and clinging to South Viet Nam through military aid and the system of disguised "military advisers".

With regard to the Democratic Republic of Viet Nam, in the carrying out of its obligations concerning the removal, permanent deactivation or destruction of mines in the territorial waters, ports, harbours, and waterways of North Viet Nam, the United States deliberately created delays and obstacles in an attempt to prolong in practice the blockade of the territorial waters of the Democratic Republic of Viet Nam. It failed to carry out its obligation of removing the deactivated mines and to provide all appropriate facilities for the removal of mines in the waterways of the Democratic Republic of Viet Nam.

On the other hand, the United States has not stopped its encroachments on the sovereignty, territory and security of the Democratic Republic of Viet Nam. From the signing of the Paris Agreement to December 15, 1973, it sent on 39 occasions aircraft to intrude into the airspace of the Democratic Republic of Viet Nam for espionage activities over many places in North Viet Nam such as Vinh Linh, Quang Binh, Ha Tinh, Nghe An, Thanh Hoa, Hoa Binh, Yen Bai, Vinh Phu, Ha Bac, Tuyen Quang, Lang Son, Son La, Quang Ninh, and even Ha Noi and Hai Phong. It has also repeatedly sent warships to waters adjacent to the Democratic Republic of Viet Nam.

In the meantime, in application of the so-called "strategy of deterrence", the United States maintains big air and naval forces in Thailand and South-East Asia in an attempt to intimidate the Vietnamese people and the other peoples of Indochina.

# THE UNITED STATES HAS DELAYED THE CARRYING OUT OF ITS OBLIGATION WITH REGARD TO THE HEALING OF THE WOUNDS OF WAR IN THE DEMOCRATIC REPUBLIC OF VIET NAM

Article 21 of the Paris Agreement on Viet Nam stipulates: The United States will contribute to healing the wounds of war and to postwar reconstruction of the Democratic Republic of Viet Nam and throughout Indochina.

The DRVN–U.S. Joint Economic Commission was formed on March 1, 1973, and held its first meeting on March 15, 1973. After over one month of discussions, on its own, the U.S. side suspended sine die on April 19, 1973, the work of the Commission and of the group of experts. Thus, it acted at variance with the agreement reached between the two sides to the effect that the Commission's work would be completed on April 30, 1973, that is 60 days after the formation of the Commission.

The firm struggle of the Democratic Republic of Viet Nam brought the United States back to the meetings of the Joint Economic Commission on June 18, 1973. This time, the United States agreed with the Democratic Republic of Viet Nam on the amount of the credit and its use for the five-year plan and the plan of the first year of the U.S. contribution to healing the wounds of war and to postwar reconstruction in the Democratic Republic of Viet Nam; however, it posed political conditions for the signing of the document on the agreed points in an attempt to delay it.

This is clearly an attempt to shirk its responsibility and obligation under Article 21 of the Paris Agreement.

As is well-known, in the criminal air and naval war of destruction it conducted against the Democratic Republic of Viet Nam, the United States destroyed virtually all towns and cities, devastated many villages, hospitals, schools, factories, state farms, and other economic installations. It is a matter of course that the United States is duty-bound to contribute to healing the wounds of war in the Democratic Republic of Viet Nam, and the United States itself has accepted this under Article 21 of the Agreement. The Vietnamese people, international law, the conscience of the world's peoples, and of the progressive people of the United States will not allow Washington to shirk this responsibility and obligation incumbent on it.

## REGARDING CAMBODIA AND LAOS

Article 20 of the Agreement on Ending the War and Restoring Peace in Viet Nam, acknowledged by Article 8 of the International Conference on Viet Nam, stipulates: The parties participating in the Paris Conference on Viet Nam shall strictly respect the fundamental national rights of the Cambodian and the Lao peoples, i.e., independence, sovereignty, unity, and territorial integrity, and shall respect the neutrality of Cambodia and Laos.

It is the unswerving policy of the Government of the Democratic Republic of Viet Nam as well as of the Provisional Revolutionary Government of the Republic of South Viet Nam to strictly respect the independence, sovereignty, unity, territorial integrity and neutrality of Cambodia and Laos in accordance with Article 20 of the Paris Agreement and Article 8 of the Act of the International Conference on Viet Nam. This policy strictly respects the national interests of the Cambodian and the Lao peoples and is consistent with the interests of peace in Indochina and South-East Asia. In consequence, it enjoys the approval and support of the socialist countries, the independent countries and peace-loving people around the world.

What is the attitude of the United States and the Saigon Administration regarding the problems of Cambodia and Laos?

In Cambodia, right after the conclusion of the Paris Agreement on Viet Nam, the United States mobilized B.52's and other kinds of aircraft to launch a 161-day bombing campaign with 35,000 sorties and 240,000 tons of bombs dropped (Cambodian Head of State Norodom Sihanouk's speech at the Algiers Conference, September 1973) in an attempt to destroy the liberated areas.

Besides, the United States has introduced many more U.S. military advisers and military personnel into Cambodia to directly take in hand the command of the Lon Nol puppet troops. D. Doolin, U.S. Assistant Secretary of Defense, has confirmed that all U.S. activities in Cambodia, including military activities, are directed by the U.S. Ambassador (AP, May 8, 1973). Many U.S. generals such as General F. Weyand, former Commander-in-chief of the U.S. Forces in South Viet Nam, Admiral N. Gayler, Commander of the U.S. Forces in the Pacific, and General J. Vogt, Commander of the 7th Air Force . . . have come to Phnom Penh to control and direct their agents.

After it was compelled to stop the bombing of Cambodia on August 15, 1973, the United States sent in big quantities of war material such as cargo planes, bombers, 155-mm guns, armoured vehicles and river patrol boats . . . On October 19, 1973, Nixon asked Congress to extend to the Lon Nol Administration an additional military aid of 200 million dollars in the 1973–1974 fiscal year.

To support Lon Nol troops, the United States has made an increased use of Khmer-stock mercenaries from South Viet Nam, and also of Saigon regular troops. Five Saigon Ranger battalions with tank and armoured support crossed the frontier in Châu Dôc between the 14th and the 17th of August 1973, and moved deep into Cambodian territory.

The United States has continued to use Thailand as an airbase, a training base and a logistic base in order to carry out its design of intervention and aggression in Cambodia. It maintains in that country 45,000 troops, over 600 aircraft of various types, including B.52's. On June 30, 1973, Thai Vice-Minister of Foreign Affairs Chatchai Chunhawan admitted that 10,000 Phnom Penh troops had completed a training program in Thailand. An airlift from Thailand to Cambodia has been established to supply fuel. According to the Thai newspaper Nation, the United States has shipped about 3,000 tons of munitions a month from Thailand to Cambodia.

In Laos, the United States has had to let the Lao parties sign the Agreement on Restoring Peace and Achieving National Concord, but right after this event, it sought every means to delay the signing of the Protocol to the Agreement. The most serious trick was the engineering of the military coup of August 20, 1973, in Laos through the extremist reactionary group in the country and the reactionaries in exile in Thailand, and with the direct assistance of the reactionary Thai authorities of Thanom Praphas.

The United States still conducts on a regular basis reconnaissance flights in the air space of Laos, numbering 1,500–2,500 sorties a month. It continues to supply by air the Vientiane army and the U.S.–set up Vang Pao Special Forces with arms and munitions. U.S. military advisers operating in all military regions of the Vientiane Government side have been ordered to stay in Laos for an indefinite period. The United States continues to finance the maintenance of more than 20 Thai regular battalions on Lao soil. In his report to the Foreign Relations Committee, Mc.Murtrie Godley, former U.S. Ambassador in Vientiane, admitted that 15,000 to 20,000 Thai troops–labelled "volunteers" of Thai nationality–are being stationed in Laos, and the United States has to spend 26 million dollars a year for this force (Voice of America, May 10, 1973).

The U.S. military and economic aid to Laos has remained high–over 350 million dollars a year.

Since the conclusion of the Vientiane Agreement, with the support of the United States and of the reactionary Thanom Praphas clique in Thailand, the Vientiane army has launched over 200 land-grabbing operations against the areas under the control of the Lao patriotic forces. In April 1973, the United States sent B.52's to support a big land-grabbing operation conducted by 16 battalions, including Vientiane mobile troops, Thai regular troops, and "Special Forces" units, against Tha Vieng, Tha Thom south-east of Xieng Khouang. The United States also took a direct part in more than 200 droppings of commandos and local bandits for reconnaissance and sabotage activities in the rear area of the Lao patriotic forces.

On May 7, 1973, the Xieng Khouang people and troops shot down a U.S. plane, and captured U.S. pilot Emmet Kay along with six Lao bandits.

The continued U.S. military involvement and intervention in Cambodia and Laos with a view to carrying into effect the "Nixon doctrine" and imposing neo-colonialism on those two countries constitutes a flagrant violation of Article 20 of the Paris Agreement on Viet Nam, and of Article 8 of the Act of the International Conference on Viet Nam.

## SLANDERS AND THREATS, FAMILIAR TRICKS OF AMERICAN IMPERIALISTS

While systematically violating many essential provisions of the Paris Agreement, the United States and the Saigon Administration has sought every means to hinder the normal activities of the military delegations of the Government of the Democratic Republic of Viet Nam and of the Provisional Revolutionary Government of the Republic of South Viet Nam to the Four-Party Joint Military Commission and to the Two-Party Joint Military Commission, with a view to having free hands for violating the Agreement.

On the other hand, they have unceasingly levelled against the Government of the Democratic Republic of Viet Nam and the Provisional Revolutionary Government of the Republic of South Viet Nam slanderous charges about so-called "violations" of the Agreement. For instance, they have claimed that North Viet Nam "has infiltrated men and weapons into South Viet Nam", that "it has built twelve airfields in South Viet Nam" . . . Now, they are circulating new allegations such as: "The Communists are preparing a major offensive in South Viet Nam", "North Viet Nam is plotting to kindle a new war in South Viet Nam", etc.

Along with slanders, the United States has uttered insolent threats against the Vietnamese people. On May 3, 1973, President R. Nixon said: "North Viet Nam is creating the danger of reviving the conflict with the United States." Key personalities in the Nixon Administration have repeatedly referred to the possibility of "a new intervention of the U.S. Air Force in Indochina". Recently, on November 30, 1973, U.S. Secretary of Defense J. Schlesinger bluntly stated: "President Nixon has the right to order a new bombing campaign in Indochina".

The purpose of the U.S. and Saigon slanders is to cover up their violations, to mislead public opinion, and at least to make it believe that "both sides have committed violations", at the same time, to prepare for new military adventures, and still cruder violations of the Agreement. But these odious allegations cannot easily deceive the American people and world public opinion. As is well-known, the so-called "Bac Bo Gulf incident" was brazenly engineered, and the whole U.S. war in Viet Nam is full of lies as the secret Pentagon Papers have shown.

The U.S. threats are aimed at compelling the Vietnamese people to fold their arms before the violations committed by the United States and the Saigon Administration, so that they can carry on the U.S. neocolonialist schemes in South Viet Nam. But facts have shown that the Vietnamese people will never submit before the insolent threats and brute force of the U.S. imperialists. The Vietnamese people are resolved to carry on their unyielding struggle to have the Paris Agreement on Viet Nam scrupulously implemented by the United States and the Saigon Administration.

Part Three

# THE URGENT PROBLEMS OF THE MOMENT
# TO MAINTAIN AND CONSOLIDATE LASTING PEACE
# IN VIET NAM

From the implementation of the Paris Agreement on Viet Nam over the past year, a number of conclusions may be drawn:

1) The Government of the Democratic Republic of Viet Nam as well as the Provisional Revolutionary Government of the Republic of South Viet Nam has always strictly respected and scrupulously implemented all provisions of the Agreement and firmly demanded that the other side do the same.

In contrast, the United States while compelled to implement a number of provisions, has ceaselessly committed crude violations of essential provisions of the Agreement. At the same time, it has encouraged and helped the Saigon Administration to sabotage the Agreement with a view to erasing the fact that there exist in South Viet Nam two administrations, two armed forces, two zones of control, and three political forces.

The Paris Agreement on Viet Nam is a juridical whole whose provisions are closely inter-related. Its purpose, as has been mentioned in the Preamble, is to "end the war and restore peace in Viet Nam on the basis of respect for the Vietnamese people's fundamental national rights and the South Vietnamese people's right to self-determination, and to contribute to the consolidation of peace in Asia and the world."

By systematically violating, in disregard of their pledge, essential provisions of the Paris Agreement on Viet Nam, especially those concerning the ceasefire, the Vietnamese people's fundamental national rights, and the South Vietnamese people's right to self-determination, the United States and the Saigon Administration have acted at variance with the purport of the Agreement.

The two diametrically opposed policies have clearly shown who is implementing and who is sabotaging the Paris Agreement on Viet Nam. Only the United States and the Saigon Administration have violated the Paris Agreement on Viet Nam. The allegation to the effect that "both sides have committed violations" cannot deceive public opinion.

2) The main and immediate cause of the present situation in South Viet Nam lies in the unwillingness of the United States to put a complete end to its military involvement and intervention in the internal affairs of South Viet Nam. The Nguyen Van Thieu Administration, which has frenziedly sabotaged the ceasefire and is hysterically embarking on a military escalation in South Viet Nam, is precisely the instrument of this U.S. policy. There is absolutely no question of "the United States having ended its military involvement" and "the present conflict in South Viet Nam being merely a civil war" as is being claimed by key personalities in the U.S. ruling circles. Full responsibility rests with the United States for the very serious situation now obtaining in South Viet Nam.

3) In order to maintain and consolidate lasting peace in Viet Nam and to contribute to the cause of peace in Indochina, South-East Asia and the world, the urgent question now is, the United States and the Saigon Administration must strictly respect and scrupulously implement the Paris Agreement on Viet Nam, the Act of the International Conference on Viet Nam, and the June 13, 1973 Joint Communiqué.

The United States must put a complete end to its military involvement and intervention in the internal affairs of South Viet Nam, seriously carry out its obligation regarding the healing of the wounds of war in the Democratic Republic of Viet Nam, and strictly respect the fundamental national rights of the peoples of Laos and Cambodia. Such a course would show that the United States has drawn practical lessons from an out-of-date policy which involved it in a very costly war in terms of lives and property, which has proved to be the longest and hardest one in American history, and it would bring about favourable conditions to progress to the normalization of the relations between the Democratic Republic of Viet Nam and the United States on the basis of respect for each other's independence and sovereignty, and non-interference in each other's internal affairs.

The Saigon Administration must strictly respect the ceasefire, put an immediate end to all land-grabbing operations against the zone under the control of the Provisional Revolutionary Government of the Republic of South Viet Nam, stop all police and "pacification" operations, return all Vietnamese civilian personnel captured and detained by it, put an immediate end to all acts of repression, coercion, and purge, and fully guarantee the people's democratic liberties, first of all, freedom of movement, and freedom of work. It must seriously respond to the six-point proposal put forward on April 25, 1973 by the Provisional Revolutionary Government of the Republic of South Viet Nam, and further clarified on June 28, 1973, so that an agreement on the internal matters of South Viet Nam could be reached rapidly.

In the interest of the nation and of world peace, the Government of the Democratic Republic of Viet Nam as well as the Provisional Revolutionary Government of the Republic of South Viet Nam is unswervingly resolved to scrupulously implement the Paris Agreement on Viet Nam, and demands that the United States and the Saigon Administration do the same. The Government of the Democratic Republic of Viet Nam fully supports all measures that the Provisional Revolutionary Government of the Republic of South Viet Nam considers necessary to punish the war acts of the Saigon Administration, to safeguard peace, and to preserve the Agreement.

Just as the Provisional Revolutionary Government of the Republic of South Viet Nam, the Government of the Democratic Republic of Viet Nam reaffirms its position, namely to strictly respect the independence, sovereignty, unity, territorial integrity, and neutrality of Laos and Cambodia as provided for by Article 20 of the Paris Agreement and Article 8 of the Act of the International Conference on Viet Nam. It resolutely supports the just struggle of the Lao people to build a peaceful, independent, neutral, democratic, unified and prosperous Laos. It resolutely supports the just struggle of the Cambodian people to build an independent, sovereign, neutral, democratic and prosperous Cambodia in her territorial integrity.

The Vietnamese people and the Government of the Democratic Republic of Viet Nam call on the governments and peoples of the socialist countries, the independent countries in Asia, Africa and Latin America, all peace and justice-loving countries, the international peace and democratic organizations, the peoples of the world, and the American people to extend increased support and assistance to the just cause of the Vietnamese people, and to firmly demand that the U.S. Government and the Saigon Administration strictly implement the Paris Agreement, the Act of the International Conference on Viet Nam, and the June 13, 1973 Joint Communiqué in order to ensure a stable peace in Viet Nam, and contribute to the preservation of peace in Indochina, South-East Asia and the world.

The Vietnamese people and the Government of the Democratic Republic of Viet Nam firmly believe that the struggle to ensure respect for, and implementation of, the Paris Agreement on Viet Nam will end in victory.

Ha Noi January, 1974.

# V. CONSTITUTIONAL STRUCTURE
## AND WAR-MAKING

# The Supreme Court and the Vietnamese War*

## PHILIPPA STRUM

ALMOST ALL the important political-economic-social conflicts arising throughout American history have been filtered through the Supreme Court, enabling it to perform two major functions within the American political process. Its primary function has been to place its legitimizing imprimatur upon resolutions originating with the "political" branches. Its second and related function, concentrated in the twentieth century, has been the self-appointed one of civil liberties ombudsman. Both roles were brought into question by the Vietnamese War.

United States involvement in Southeast Asia has been a key—if not *the* key—issue of American national politics in the 1960's and 1970's. Nevertheless, superficial examination of the role played by the Court in cases involving the constitutionality of American involvement would seem to indicate that the Court refused to play any role whatsoever. The Court denied certiorari not only to cases challenging the constitutionality of the war itself, but to related cases involving the issues of the right of the military to order servicemen to Vietnam and the right of the executive to draft civilians for service in Vietnam. Obviously, this raises the question of the Court's policy-making role in war-time. It is tempting but insufficient to postulate that the Court has no alternative other than to maintain a "hands-off" approach during war. Closer examination reveals that the Court's refusal to grant certiorari can be interpreted as an attempt to preserve lower court decisions that held the alleged unconstitutionality of a President-initiated war to be justiciable. A total of four justices voted to grant certiorari in the war cases, although at no time did all four vote to do so in the same case. The Court also played an extremely active role in considering the collateral questions of conscientious objector exemptions, the permissible limits of anti-war speech, and the right of the press to print information which the government deemed inimical to national security. Even in the latter areas, however, the Court's record is erratic. While it perverted the language of a statute in order to extend draft

* The author wishes to express gratitude for their gracious assistance to Burt Neuborne and Philip Ryan of the American Civil Liberties Union and to John D'Anton, formerly of the *Rutgers University Law Review*. They are in no way responsible for errors of fact or logic.

exemptions as far as possible, the Court stopped short of adopting the selective conscientious objector standard. It upheld the right of school children to protest the war symbolically but declined to recognize draft card burning as symbolic speech. While rejecting one instance of prior restraint, it accepted the theory of restraint before publication. The problem thus becomes twofold: was the Court following a consistent strategy in the war-related cases, and what might such a strategy indicate about the parameters of possible Court policy-making in time of war?

## I. *Challenges to the Constitutionality of the War*

The litigation engendered by challenges to the constitutionality of the war was initiated by draft-resisters,[1] reservists,[2] servicemen ordered to Vietnam,[3] taxpayers and citizens,[4] and a state acting on behalf of its citizens.[5] Whenever the plaintiffs, who invariably lost in the lower courts, asked the Supreme Court for certiorari, it was denied; where they appealed as a matter of right, the appeal was dismissed *per curiam*. The Court's refusal to consider the issue of constitutionality must be explained. First, however, it is necessary to consider whether there is any reason that the Court *should* have heard the cases. The answer lies in the two constitutional areas of separation of powers and civil liberties.

### A. *Separation of Powers*

The Constitution explicitly gives Congress the power to declare war.[6] The history of the Convention proves that the decision not to allow the President to declare a war was deliberate.[7] Clearly, military situations

---

[1] See, e.g., *United States v. Sisson, appeal dismissed*, 399 U.S. 267 (1970); *Ashton v. United States, cert. den.*, 394 U.S. 960 (1969); *United States v. Prince, cert. den.*, 393 U.S. 946 (1968); *Hart v. United States, cert. den.*, 391 U.S. 956 (1968); *Holmes v. United States, cert. den.*, 391 U.S. 936 (1968); *Mitchell v. United States, cert. den.*, 386 U.S. 972 (1967).

[2] See, e.g., *McArthur v. Clifford, cert. den.*, 393 U.S. 1002 (1968).

[3] See, e.g., *DaCosta v. Laird, cert. den.*, 405 U.S. 979 (1972); *Perkins v. Laird, cert. den.*, 405 U.S. 965 (1972); *Orlando v. Laird, cert. den.*, 404 U.S. 869 (1971); *Mora v. McNamara, cert. den.*, 389 U.S. 934 (1967).

[4] See, e.g., *Atlee v. Richardson*, judgment affirmed *per curiam*, 411 U.S. 911 (1973); *Sarnoff v. Shultz, cert. den.*, 409 U.S. 929 (1972); *Velvel v. Nixon, cert. den.*, 396 U.S. 1042 (1970); *Kalish v. United States, cert. den.*, 396 U.S. 835 (1969).

[5] *Massachusetts v. Laird*, motion to file bill of complaint denied, 400 U.S. 886 (1970).

[6] *United States Constitution*, Article I, Section 8, paragraph xi.

[7] See, e.g., Raoul Berger, "War Making by the President," 121 *University of Pennsylvania Law Review* 29 (1972); Francis L. Coolidge, Jr., and Joel David Sharrow, "Note: War-Making Powers," 50 *Boston University Law Review* 5 (1970); Charles A. Lofgren, "War-Making Under the Constitution: The Original Understanding," 81 *Yale Law Journal*

may arise which demand immediate reaction by the nation in the form of unilateral Presidential action. Just as clearly, pre-Vietnam Presidents who took such action accepted in both theory and practice the necessity for Congressional ratification and for Congressional permission at every further step taken.[8] The overwhelming difference between the past situations and that of Southeast Asia was the systematic attempt by the Executive in the latter instance to maintain maximum freedom of action by under-informing and deceiving both the American public and the Congress. Should there be any doubt that the deception was deliberate, a perusal of the Pentagon Papers[9] will dispel it. Thus in effect both Presidents Johnson and Nixon[10] asserted for themselves the unilateral right to identify enemies of the United States, to declare war against them, to wage the war that they themselves had declared, and to deny Congress and the electorate the information which would have allowed those bodies to reach a substantive judgment about the presidential action. The effect was to hold the Presidents unaccountable to any equal or higher authority for their actions. If the separation of powers can be understood as an attempt by the framers of the Constitution to ensure constant dialogue between the two branches and to preclude unilateral action by either one, then for all practical purposes there was no separation of powers on the issue of Vietnam. Emasculation of a basic constitutional doctrine is cause for general concern; whether such emasculation has in fact occurred is an appropriate concern of the judiciary. As Justice Stewart points out in his dissent from the Court's denial of certiorari in *Mora* v. *McNamara*,[11] there was not

---

672 (1972); William Van Alstyne, "Congress, the President, and the Power to Declare War: A Requiem for Vietnam," 212 *University of Pennsylvania Law Review* 1 (1972); Don Wallace, Jr., "The War-Making Powers: A Constitutional Flaw?", 57 *Cornell Law Review* 719 (1972); Francis D. Wormuth, "The Nixon Theory of the War Power: A Critique," 60 *California Law Review* 623 (1972).

[8] Berger, *id.*, at 58-66; Van Alstyne, *id.*, at 8-13; Wormuth, *id.*, at 629-635. Also see American Civil Liberties Union's *amicus* brief in *Orlando* v. *Laird*, reprinted in Leon Friedman and Burt Neuborne, *Unquestioning Obedience to the President* (New York: Norton, 1972), at 62-67.

[9] Neil Sheehan et al., *The Pentagon Papers* (New York: Bantam), 1971.

[10] President Nixon adopted the rationales asserted by the Johnson Administration, with the additional arguments that he had a right to keep troops in Southeast Asia as long as necessary to work out a "peace with honor" and to free American prisoners of war, and that he had a right to bomb Southeast Asia until peace had been brought to all of it. See, e.g., his message accompanying his veto of the 1973 supplemental appropriations bill. *New York Times*, June 28, 1973, p. 4, c. 4-8.

[11] 389 U.S. 934 (1967).

only the question of whether the action taken by the Executive in Vietnam constituted a war as referred to in Article I, Section 8, but also the question of whether such a war-like action might not be justified by the United States' treaty obligations or the Tonkin Gulf resolution or both.

Justice Stewart's queries raise the possibility both that certain lower-level military actions short of full-scale war could be taken by the President without Congressional approval and that Congressional actions short of explicit approval might be interpreted as fulfilling the requirement of Article I, Section 8. In either case, his opinion suggests the necessity for some kind of Congressional validation should a low-level military action escalate. Earlier Court cases indicate a clear belief that Congress has the sole power over even a limited war.[12] As the American Civil Liberties Union argued in its amicus brief in *Orlando* v. *Laird*,[13] prior Presidents had always sought explicit authorization from Congress both for major wars and for "secondary military commitments" along the lines of the naval "wars" against France in 1798-1801 and against Tripoli in 1802. All other military engagements not subject to Congressional approval were characterized by the "limited, short-term commitment of small numbers of men for short periods of time to achieve a definite objective invariably related to an attack upon American lives and property," as opposed to the large-scale action taken in Vietnam.[14]

The question of whether continued Congressional appropriations for the war could be construed as ratification was to become important in the litigation engendered by the war. It is possible that one of the reasons the Court has always insisted that Congressional motivation is not fit matter for judicial scrutiny is that it is usually difficult to determine. When over five hundred people have been involved in the vote for and against a statute, it is obviously risky to assume knowledge of what was going in the mind of each legislator. This is all the more so considering that different legislators are subject to a variety of different

12 Longren, *id.*, Wallace, *id.*

13 Reprinted in Friedman and Neuborne, *id.*

14 The appellant's brief in *Berk* v. *Laird* cites in an Appendix a host of "Presidential Statements Acknowledging Need for Explicit Congressional Exercise of the War Power." Reprinted in Friedman and Neuborne, *id.*, at 169-174. The opposite legal argument is made by former Secretary of State William P. Rogers in "Congress, the President, and the War Powers," 59 *California Law Review* 1194 (1971); he in turn is answered by Wormuth, *id.*

pressures and that there may be an infinite number of reasons for the seemingly simple vote of "yes" or "no." There is evidence that many Congresspersons were careful to disassociate a vote for appropriations from an expression of approval. A number specifically stated that they were voting not for an extension of hostilities but for the mechanism by which to end them.[15] There is also the problem of political pressure once hostilities have begun. Legislators who wish to vote against appropriations bills are placed in the politically impossible position of denying the equipment necessary to save the lives of "our boys overseas." The extent to which this preordains the Congressional vote and the implications for both the separation of powers and democracy have been suggested by Robert Bressler:

> The public, denied any role of significance, is used by the executive as a foil to weaken other political institutions. At the propitious moment of international crisis the Congress is inevitably circumvented and the public, then most vulnerable to demagoguery and deception, is confronted with a fireside chat, a special address, or a televised press conference. The result, as conservative James Burnham has pointed out, is Caesarism—the culmination of the executive state: "The mass of the people and the individual Caesar, with the insulation of the intermediary institutions removed, become like two electric poles. . . . The vote is reduced to the primitive Yes-No . . . and the assemblies become a sounding board for amplifying Caesar's voice."[16]

While this may appear to be political rather than legal argumentation, it raises the basic legal issue of whether Presidential actions which effectively circumvent the Congressional war power—whether those actions be the deployment of troops without prior authorization or the utilization of the media to negate the possibility of true Congressional choice—are also a violation of the constitutional doctrine of separation of powers. Two very specific constitutional questions immediately become apparent: Are there any limitations to the admitted Presidential power to respond to military actions deemed hostile to the United

---

[15] See Friedman and Neuborne, *id.* at 89-108. The opposing argument; i.e., that appropriations votes constituted specific endorsement, can be found in the brief submitted by the United States Attorney in *Berk* v. *Laird* and *Orlando* v. *Laird* before the Second Circuit Court of Appeals.

[16] Robert J. Bressler, "The Ideology of the Executive State: Legacy of Liberal Internationalism," 3 *Politics and Society* 245, 251 (1973).

States either because of direct attack on United States territory or because of attack on territory to the defense of which the United States is committed by treaty? Once troops have been deployed by the President and are actually engaged in battle, can continued Congressional appropriations be construed as ratification of Presidential action or must the Congressional authorization be specific and distinct from other legislation?[17] Corwin has noted:

> The war power of the United States . . . has undergone a threefold development. In the first place, its constitutional basis has been shifted from the doctrine of delegated powers to the doctrine of inherent powers. . . . In the second place, the President's power as Commander-in-Chief has been transformed from a simple power of military command to a vast reservoir of indeterminate powers in time of emergency. . . . In the third place, the indefinite legislative powers claimable by Congress in wartime in consequence of the development first mentioned may today be delegated by Congress to the President to any extent; that is to say, may be merged to any extent with the indefinite powers of the Commander-in-Chief.[18]

Was there, in fact, any such delegation by Congress in the instance of Vietnam? Granted the existence of inherent power, what are its limits? These questions, fit for judicial determination, present sufficient justification for intervention by the Supreme Court. The civil liberties issues involved were equally amenable to judicial action.

## B. *Civil Liberties*

> We have never ruled, I believe, that when the Federal Government takes a person by the neck and submits him to punishment, imprisonment, taxation, or submission to some ordeal, the complaining person may not be heard in court. The rationale in cases such as the present is that government cannot take life, liberty, or property of the individual and escape adjudication by the courts of the legality of its action.
>
> Mr. Justice Douglas, dissenting, *Massachusetts* v. *Laird*[19]

---

17 See Anthony A. D'Amato et al., "Brief for Constitutional Lawyers' Committee on Undeclared War as Amicus Curiae," 17 *Wayne Law Review* 67, 135 (1971).

18 Edward S. Corwin, *The President: Office and Powers*, 4th rev. ed. (New York: New York University Press, 1957), pp. 261-262.

19 400 U.S. 886, 898.

American military action in Southeast Asia raised many substantial civil liberties problems: was it a violation of civil liberties for a citizen to be sent to die in a war that had not been explicitly declared such by Congress? was it a violation for him to be drafted either to serve directly in such a war or to free another serviceman to do so? was it a violation for the government to put him in jail if he refused to serve? was it a violation for citizens not drafted to be taxed to support the war? was it a violation for monies already collected to be diverted from other government services to support of the war? was it a violation for the government to attempt to limit speech and press in the name of the "national security" off-shoots of the war?

Both the Warren and the Burger Courts might have been expected to grant certiorari to civil liberties cases, although the decisions of the two Courts might have differed. The Warren Court's extension of civil liberties requires no reiteration here. The Burger Court, although far less innovative and more conservative in its approach to traditional civil liberties, has occasionally expanded them when presented with a good argument for doing so.[20] *United States* v. *United States District Court*[21] involved issues both of civil liberties and of separation of powers, and the Burger Court's unanimous decision there struck down asserted Executive power. Thus both Courts refused to hear cases which raised two major constitutional issues at times when they had signalled interest in those issues elsewhere. At the very least, one can infer that the justices must have had substantial motivation for their choice. Perhaps the explanation lies in the political question doctrine.

## C. *The Constitutionality of the War as a Political Question*

The Court's most authoritative definition of a political question to date is to be found in Justice Brennan's opinion in *Baker* v. *Carr:*

> . . . Prominent on the surface of any case held to involve a political question is found a textually demonstrable constitutional commitment of the issue to a coordinate political department; or a lack of judicially discoverable and manageable standards for resolving it; or the impossibility of deciding without an initial policy determination

---

[20] See, e.g., *Keyes* v. *School District,* 413 U.S. 189 (1973); *Roe* v. *Wade,* 410 U.S. 113 (1973) and *Doe* v. *Bolton,* 410 U.S. 179 (1973); *Furman* v. *Georgia,* 408 U.S. 238 (1972); *United States* v. *United States District Court,* 407 U.S. 297 (1972); *Argresinger* v. *Hamlin,* 407 U.S. 25 (1972).

[21] 407 U.S. 297 (1972).

of a kind clearly for nonjudicial discretion; or the impossibility of a court's undertaking independent resolution without expressing lack of the respect due coordinate branches of government; or an unusual need for unquestioning adherence to a political decision already made; or the potentiality of embarrassment from multifarious pronouncements by various departments on one question.[22]

Earlier, Brennan simplified this by defining a political question as "essentially a function of the separation of powers."[23] It will be suggested later that this is judicial verbiage designed to obscure the true nature of the political question and that it actually defines nothing. Accepting the definition on its face for the moment, however, the question of whether the alleged unconstitutionality of the war was a political question remains. It is extraordinarily important to note that the Court never called the question a political one. It offered no explanation of its refusals to hear the cases. Thus there is no definitive answer.

Turning to the lower courts, one discovers disagreement. Some courts found the question to be political;[24] others did not.[25] Justice Douglas argued in his dissents from all of the refusals to hear the cases that the question was not political, and in *Massachusetts* v. *Laird* he utilized the six *Baker* criteria to refute one by one the contentions of lack of justiciability.[26] Justice Stewart's dissent in *Mora*[27] and *Atlee,*[28] Justices Stewart and Harlan's dissent in *Massachusetts* v. *Laird,*[29] and Justice Brennan's dissents in *DaCosta*[30] and *Atlee*[31] indicate that they felt the issue was at least arguable. As Justice Douglas pointed out in *DaCosta* v. *Laird,* the circuit courts were in conflict as to justiciability, and the Court was the only body capable of rendering a final decision.[32]

---

[22] 369 U.S. 186, 217 (1962).     [23] *Id.*

[24] See, e.g., *Drinan* v. *Nixon,* 364 F. Supp. 853 (1973); *Gravel* v. *Laird,* 347 F. Supp. 7 (D.D.C. 1972); *Head* v. *Nixon,* 342 F. Supp. 521 (5.D.La.), 468 F. 2d 951 (5th Cir. 1972); *Sarnoff* v. *Shultz,* 457 F. 2d 809 (9th Cir. 1971); *Massachusetts* v. *Laird,* 327 F. Supp. 378 (1971); *Davi* v. *Laird,* 318 F. Supp. 278 (W.D. Va. 1970); *Luftig* v. *McNamara,* 126 U.S. App. D.C. 4, 373 F. 2d 664 (D.C. Cir. 1967); *United States* v. *Mitchell,* 369 F. 2d 323 (2d Cir. 1966).

[25] See, e.g., *DaCosta* v. *Laird,* 448 F. 2d 1368 (2d Cir. 1971); *Orlando* v. *Laird,* 443 F. 2d 1039 (2d Cir. 1971; *Mottolla* v. *Nixon,* 318 F. Supp. 538 (N.D. Cal. 1970); *Berk* v. *Laird,* 317 F. Supp. 715 (E.D.N.Y. 1970), 429 F. 2d 303 (2d Cir. 1970).

[26] 400 U.S. 886, 898 (1970).     [27] 389 U.S. 934 (1967).

[28] 411 U.S. 911 (1973).     [29] 400 U.S. 886, 900 (1970).

[30] 405 U.S. 979, 981 (1972).     [31] 36 L. Ed. 2d 304 (1973).

[32] 405 U.S. 979, 980-981. See also Memorandum of Decision by District Judge Sweigert, calling for Supreme Court action because of the conflict between the circuits. *Campen* v. *Nixon,* 56 F.R.D. 404 (N.D. Cal. 1972).

The Court chose not to do so, thus leaving in doubt whether subsequent courts would exercise any restraint whatsoever on any Presidential commitment of troops to combat.

A great many law review articles argued that the question was justiciable.[33] In spite of such attempts at persuasion and the dissent of four of its own members, the Court chose not to decide the justiciability question. It will be argued below that the Court's refusal to end the confusion was deliberate. In order to illuminate the Court's attitude toward the "political thicket" created by the war, however, it is necessary to examine three categories of war-related cases in which the Court rendered substantive decisions.

## II. *Cases Decided by the Court: The Chequered Career of Conscientious Objectors, Dissenters, and the Press*

### A. *Conscientious Objectors*

The Court decided a series of cases brought by conscientious objectors who faced induction into the armed forces at the same time it refused to hear cases challenging the constitutionality of the war itself. The procedural decision made by the Court in each case it took was in favor of the kind of judicial review of Selective Service board decisions —and pre-induction review, at that—that the Court had previously eschewed.[34] Two questions present themselves: why did the Court reverse its earlier decisions not to involve itself in this area? why did it render specific substantive decisions?

The Court's involvement can be traced to the administrative chaos that reigned throughout the Selective Service System and its unwillingness to permit the System to operate under what the National Advisory Commission on Selective Service labelled an arbitrary "rule of discretion" rather than a "rule of Law."[35] Local draft boards, composed of citizens with little or no knowledge of law, were frequently not even informed by the Board of the current state of the law or of Court rulings affecting it, nor was any attempt made to insure compliance with

[33] See, e.g., D'Amato, *id*; Warren F. Schwartz and Wayne McCormack, "The Justiciability of Legal Objections to the American Military Effort in Vietnam," 46 *Texas Law Review* 1033 (1968); Lawrence R. Velvel, "The Constitution and the War: Some Major Issues," 49 *Journal of Urban Law* 231 (1971).

[34] See, e.g., *Falbo* v. *United States*, 320 U.S. 549 (1944); *Witmer* v. *United States*, 348 U.S. 375 (1955).

[35] National Advisory Commission on Selective Service, *In Pursuit of Equity: Who Serves When Not All Serve* (1967), p. 31.

it.[36] Even where the boards understood the law, they did not always feel themselves bound to follow it where it favored the claims made by putative conscientious objectors.[37] This was not too serious a problem until 1967. Prior to that time, the Selective Service Act permitted those whose applications for conscientious objector status were rejected by local boards to appeal to the Justice Department for a re-examination of eligibility.[38] In 1967, the Act was altered to eliminate Justice Department intervention,[39] in part because the number of appeals for exemption had resulted in a backlog of cases. At the same time, the increased manpower demands made by the war, combined with heightened opposition to the war and the resultant surge in applications for the exemption, resulted in chaos within the System.[40] Further anarchy was contributed by General Hershey, who apparently viewed the System as an appropriate mechanism for the imposition of his political views on dissenters, and who engaged in such flagrant misuses of the System as an attempt to invoke delinquency sanctions against anti-war activists.[41] His successor, no more fazed by legal considerations than Hershey, was quoted in the *New York Times* the day after the Court handed down its decision in *United States* v. *Welsh*[42] as construing it in such a way as to negate it completely.[43] From 1967, when the Justice Department was removed from the process, until 1971, when Congress rewrote the draft law to provide for adequate administrative machinery,[44] the Supreme Court and the lower federal courts found themselves acting as ombudsmen for the System.[45] The content of their decisions demon-

[36] See Kent Greenawalt, "All or Nothing At All: The Defeat of Selective Conscientious Objection," 1971 *Supreme Court Review* 31, 43-44 (1971); Robert L. Rabin, "Do You Believe in a Supreme Being—The Administration of the Conscientious Objector Exemption," 1961 *Wisconsin Law Review* 642, 657-671 (1967); Ralph Reisner, "Selective Service Appeal Boards and the Conscientious Objector Claimant: Congressional Standards and Administrative Behavior," 1971 *Wisconsin Law Review* 521, 545 (1971).

[37] Greenawalt, *id.*

[38] *Id.*

[39] 81 Stat. 104 (1967).

[40] Burt Neuborne, "Selective Service: Introduction," 39 *Brooklyn Law Review* 1249, 1251 (1973); Reisner, *id.*

[41] See his letter to local draft boards, quoted in *National Student Association* v. *Hershey*, 412 F. 2d 1103, 1105-06 (D.C. Cir. 1969).

[42] See below, p. 546.

[43] *New York Times*, June 17, 1970, p. 1, c. 1. reporting the news conference of Selective Service Director Curtis W. Tarr. See also his Local Board Memorandum No. 7, July 6, 1970.

[44] 50 U.S.C. App. § 471a (1970).

[45] See cases reported in *Selective Service Law Reporter, passim*, 1968-1971.

strates a desire to protect would-be c.o.'s, even if to do so entailed a deliberate misreading of statutes.

Much of the Supreme Court's statute-reading in this area concerned the "Supreme Being" clause of the Selective Service Act. In 1917, Congress exempted pacifists from the draft.[46] In 1940, the exemption was extended to members of non-pacifist religions whose individual opposition to all war was based on "religious training and belief."[47] Two court challenges claiming that exemption should be based on non-religious beliefs, although decided against the plaintiffs,[48] resulted in the 1948 alteration of the Act. The amendment read, "Religious training and belief in this connection means an individual's belief in a relation to a Supreme Being involving duties superior to those arising from any human relation, but does not include essentially political, sociological, or philosophical views or a merely personal moral code."[49]

In 1965, the Court was faced with the case of *United States* v. *Seeger*,[50] resulting from Seeger's claim that he merited the exemption on the grounds of his religious belief. Although he "preferred to leave the question as to his belief in a Supreme Being open,"[51] he admitted that "the cosmic order does, perhaps, suggest a creative intelligence."[52] The Court found Seeger entitled to his exemption, holding that Congress' use of the words "Supreme Being" rather than "God" indicated its intention that the application be judged by the test of "whether a given belief that is sincere and meaningful occupies a place in the life of its possessor parallel to that filled by the orthodox belief in God of one who clearly qualifies for the exemption."[53] Perhaps forecasting its later decisions, the Court cited a variety of theologians, including Paul Tillich to the effect that the word "God" referred to "the depths of your life, of the source of your being, or your ultimate concern, of what you take seriously without any reservation. Perhaps, in order to do so, you must forget everything traditional that you have learned about God. . . ."[54] Justice Douglas, in concurrence, refused to "assume" that Congress

[46] 40 Stat. 76, 78.

[47] 54 Stat. 885, Ch. 720.

[48] *United States* v. *Kauten*, 133 F. 2d 703 (CA 2d Cir. 1943); *Berman* v. *United States*, 156 F. 2d 377 (CA 9th Cir. 1946), *cert. den.*, 329 U.S. 795.

[49] 62 Stat. 604, Ch. 265, 50 U.S.C. App. § 456 (j).

[50] 380 U.S. 163 (1965).

[51] *Id.*, at 166. The words are those of the Court.

[52] *Id.*, at 187. The words are Seeger's, quoted by the Court.

[53] *Id.*, at 166.

[54] Tillich, *The Shaking of the Foundations* 57 (1948), quoted at 380 U.S. 187.

could have been "so parochial as to use the words (Supreme Being)" in a narrow sense, for he "would attribute tolerance and sophistication to the Congress, commensurate with the religious complexion of our communities."[55] Congress promptly demonstrated its tolerance and sophistication by deleting all reference to a "Supreme Being" from the Act while continuing to insist that "religious training and belief" did not include "essentially political, sociological, or philosophical views, or a merely personal moral code."[56] Nothing daunted, the Court proceeded to vote the new version out of existence.

In *Welsh* v. *United States*[57] the Court was faced with a would-be conscientious objector who, as the Court admitted, insistently and explicitly denied that his views were religious.[58] The Court circumvented this difficulty by refusing to take Welsh's denials seriously:

> We think this attempt to distinguish Seeger fails for the reason that it places undue emphasis on the registrant's interpretation of his own beliefs. The Court's statement in Seeger that a registrant's characterization of his own belief as "religious" should carry great weight . . . does not imply that his declaration that his views are nonreligious should be treated similarly. When a registrant states that his objections to war are "religious," that information is highly relevant to the question of the function his beliefs have in his life. But very few registrants are fully aware of the broad scope of the word "religious" as used in § 6 (j), and accordingly a registrant's statement that his beliefs are non-religious is a highly unreliable guide for those charged with administering the exemption.[59]

Thus if a registrant claimed religiosity, he was to be heeded; if he refused to claim religiosity, he was not. "Religion," which the Court in *Seeger* had suggested was to be defined by theologians, was now transfigured into a legal term definable only by lawyers and judges.

Law review commentaries on Justice Black's opinion for himself and Justices Douglas, Brennan, and Marshall bordered on the apoplectic.[60] Justice Harlan, concurring, was more restrained, but still found the

---

55 *Id.*, at 188, 192.
56 81 Stat. 104, 50 U.S.C. App. § 456 (j).     57 398 U.S. 333 (1970).
58 398 U.S. 341.                               59 *Id.*
60 Comment, "Constitutional Law—'Religious' Conscientious Objector," 16 *New York Law Forum* 968, 973 (1970); Note, "Right to Conscientious Objector Classification for Ethical Opposition to War," 84 *Harvard Law Review* 230, 233 (1970); Note, "Selective Service—Conscientious Objector," 39 *Fordham Law Review* 347, 355 (1970).

Court's construction of the statute understandable only in "an Alice-in-Wonderland world where words have no meaning. . . ."[61] Harlan nevertheless concurred on the grounds that, having chosen to create the category of conscientious objector, Congress could not "draw the line between theistic or nontheistic religious beliefs on the one hand and secular beliefs on the other hand" without violating the Establishment Clause of the First Amendment.[62] Thus Harlan would have invalidated the statute altogether, leaving it to Congress either to write a new one providing coverage for those who objected on moral or philosophical grounds or to eliminate the exemption entirely. Given the sequence of the Court's interpretation of "Supreme Being" in *Seeger* and Congress' subsequent deletion of the phrase from the Act, it may well be that the majority of the justices was unwilling to run the risk of the exemption's being dropped.[63]

Two years earlier, in *Oestereich* v. *Selective Service Board No. 11*,[64] the Court had refused to allow a draft board to revoke a divinity student's exemption for having returned his draft card to the Government as an expression of opposition to the war. In its decision, the Court interpreted the section of the draft law prohibiting pre-induction judicial review[65] as being inapplicable to the finding of delinquency on the basis of "activities or conduct not material to the grant or withdrawal of the exemption."[66] Similarly, in remanding the case of *Breen* v. *Selective Service Local Board*,[67] the Court extended preinduction judicial review to a student whose deferment was revoked after his draft board found the public surrender of his draft card at an anti-war meeting to constitute "delinquency" under the Act. The Court again relied on statutory construction to find that Congress had not intended the delinquency provision to be utilized as punishment for non-possession of a draft card.[68] Both *Oestereich* and *Breen* can be seen as the Court's reaction to the almost total lack of administrative standards within the System and to the utilization of the vacuum for punitive political purposes.

[61] 398 U.S. 344, 354.          [62] 398 U.S. 356.
[63] Justice White, with Chief Justice Burger and Justice Stewart joining in his opinion, dissented from both the Court's statutory construction and Harlan's finding of unconstitutionality. *Id.* at 367. Justice Blackmun did not participate in the case.
[64] 393 U.S. 233 (1968).
[65] Military Service Act of 1967, 81 Stat. 104, § 10 (b) (3).
[66] 393 U.S. 237.          [67] 396 U.S. 460 (1970).
[68] 396 U.S. 465.

In 1971, the Court signalled that it had reached the outer limits of its protection of conscientious objectors. More specifically, the Court declined to extend the exemption to selective c.o.'s.[69] One plaintiff had based his categorization of wars as just and unjust on "a humanist approach to religion"[70] which was "guided by fundamental principles of conscience and deeply held views about the purpose and obligation of human existence";[71] the other believed that as a devout Catholic he had a religious obligation not to participate in unjust wars. The Court concurred in the lower courts' findings that there was no doubt about "the sincerity or the religious character" of the two men's view.[72] Both thus came within the guidelines about religious belief laid down by the Court in *Welsh,* and the only question was whether honest and legally religious objections to some rather than all wars qualified one for the exemption. The Court found that § 6 (j) was not meant to include selective objectors, however religious their belief. It held that the provision was not an establishment of religion, since its purposes were "neutral and secular" and "valid neutral reasons exist for limiting the exemption to objectors to all war."[73] Further, the provision was not an interference with the free exercise of religion, since " (t)he incidental burdens felt by persons in petitioners' positions are stictly justified by substantial governmental interests that relate directly to the very impacts questioned."[74] Seven members of the Court subscribed to all three points.[75]

The reasons for the Court's decision would appear to be four-fold. First, there is Justice Marshall's observation that selective c.o. status presents practical problems:

> . . . opposition to a particular war may more likely be political and nonconscientious, than otherwise. . . . The difficulties of sorting the two, with a sure hand, are considerable. . . . Since objection may fasten on any of an enormous number of variables, the claim is ultimately subjective. . . . In short, it is not at all obvious in theory what sorts of objections should be deemed sufficient to excuse an objector, and there is considerable force in the Government's contention that

---

69 *Gillette* v. *United States, Negre* v. *Larsen,* 401 U.S. 437, *reh den* 402 U.S. 934.

70 Quoted at 401 U.S. 439.

71 Language of the Court, 401 U.S. 439.        72 401 U.S. 440.

73 *Id.,* at 454.        74 *Id.,* at 462.

75 Without explanation of his position, Justice Black subscribed to the first only. *Id.,* at 463. Justice Douglas dissented on First Amendment grounds. *Id.*

a program of excusing objectors to particular wars may be "impossible to conduct with any hope of reaching fair and consistent results...."[76]

Without denying that it might well be possible to construct an administrative scheme that would allow for selective conscientious objection, it is clear that the Court had no reason to believe either Congress or the Selective Service Board would agree to do so and that the Court itself was not about to begin writing an administrative manual. This meant that the Court could not find that Gillette and Negre were covered by § 6 (j), for at the very least, the lack of standards would have worsened the administrative chaos and arbitrariness that had originally led the Court to reconsider the question of pre-induction judicial review. Second, and following closely from the first point, the only alternative temporarily favorable to Gillette and Negre would have been to find that § 6 (j) did not include them and was therefore unconstitutional. This would have eliminated the conscientious objector exemption. Given the past history of the dance performed by the Court and Congress over the c.o. question, the popular distaste for "draft dodgers" that persisted in spite of increasing dissatisfaction with the war, and the inability of Congress to agree on any constructive measures vis-à-vis the war, there was good reason for the Court to believe that a Congress confronted with the choice of extending the exemption to selective objectors or eliminating it entirely would choose the latter course.[77] Third, the decreasing draft calls and the President's acceptance of the idea of an all-volunteer army for the near future[78] suggested that the problem was beginning to disappear. Finally, the much improved administrative machinery established by Congress and the new regulations promulgated by the Selective Service System must have suggested to the justices that they could begin to withdraw from the entire area of the draft.[79] Thus there was no good reason—beyond a

[76] Id., at 455-456.

[77] Cf. "Right to Conscientious Objector Classification for Opposition to a Particular War," 85 Harvard Law Review 179, 188 (1971); "Selective Service System—Scope of the Conscientious Objector Exemption After Gillette v. United States," 19 Kansas Law Review 475, 484 (1971).

[78] President Nixon had proclaimed an all-volunteer army to be a major 1972 budget goal. New York Times, July 30, 1970, p. 13, c. 3. He had then promised that the draft would end by mid-1973. New York Times, January 29, 1971, p. 1, c. 4.

[79] Cf. Neuborne, id., at 1254, to the effect that the Court did indeed withdraw after 1971.

short-lived moral victory—for extending temporary protection to selective objectors.

## B. *Symbolic Speech*

Dissenters punished by their draft boards found an ally in the Court, as discussed above. In three other cases heard by the Court in the period under consideration, dissenters punished by other civil and criminal authorities were given a mixed reception.

The draft-card-burning case[80] has been sufficiently commented upon[81] not to require extensive elaboration here. Briefly, O'Brien was convicted of burning his draft card; the appellate court found the amendment to the draft law[82] making draft-card burning a criminal offense to be unconstitutional but affirmed his conviction under the lesser included offense of non-possession. Both O'Brien and the Government filed for certiorari.

The Court divided seven to one in upholding the amendment and reinstating the judgment and sentence of the District Court. O'Brien had argued that draft-card burning constituted symbolic speech and that the amendment, added to a statute that previously made non-possession a crime, was designed only for the unconstitutional purpose of suppressing speech. Rejecting O'Brien's insistence that the Court consider the Congressional motivation behind the amendment,[83] the Court found four legitimate purposes served by possession of an unburnt draft card.[84] It proceeded to limit symbolic speech by proclaiming that "when 'speech' and 'nonspeech' elements are combined in the same course of conduct, a sufficiently important governmental interest in regulating the nonspeech element can justify incidental limitations on First Amendment freedoms."[85] Applying this balancing test, the Court accepted the amendment as valid.

The decision was a remarkable one to have emanated from the Warren Court. The majority opinion, written by the Chief Justice himself, utilized the "balancing test" in such a way as to make Warren

---

[80] *United States* v. *O'Brien*, 391 U.S. 367 (1968), *reh den* 393 U.S. 900.

[81] See, e.g., Louis Henkin, "The Supreme Court 1967 Term: Foreward," 82 *Harvard Law Review* 63 (1968); Michael Katz, " 'When a Nation is at War'—The Supreme Court in a Post-Utopian Era," 23 *Rutgers Law Review* 1 (1968); Lawrence R. Velvel, "Freedom of Speech and the Draft Card Burning Cases," 16 *Kansas Law Review* 149 (1968); 37 *George Washington Law Review* 596 (1969).

[82] Title 50, U.S.C. App., Section 462 (b) (3).

[83] *Id.*, at 376.          [84] 391 U.S. 378-380.          [85] *Id.*, at 376.

sound Frankfurterian and gave no clue to his acceptance of the First Amendment's special place in the Constitution. It is the contention of this writer that the amendment was indeed designed to curb speech and was clearly unconstitutional, and that the Court's decision can be attributed to a combination of the political circumstances and a failure on the part of O'Brien's attorneys.

Flimsy though legislative history may frequently be as a guide to Congressional motivation, the extraordinary legislative background of the amendment in question proves its purpose to be political and punitive. It was introduced by Representative Mendel Rivers on August 5, 1965, passed by the House on August 10, introduced in the Senate on August 10, and passed by that body on August 13.[86] Representative Rivers, one of only three speakers to "debate" the amendment, described it as "a straightforward clear answer to those who would make a mockery of our efforts in South Vietnam. . . . if it can be proved that a person knowingly destroyed or mutilated his draft card, then under the committee proposal, he can be sent to prison, where he belongs. This is the least we can do for our men in South Vietnam fighting to preserve freedom, while a vocal minority in this country thumb their noses at their own Government."[87] The bill passed 393 to 1.[88] Senator Strom Thurmond, introducing it in the Senate, spoke of "mass public burnings of draft registration cards. It is not fitting for our country to permit such conduct while our people are giving their lives in combat with the enemy."[89] Senator Thurmond was the sole Senator to speak about the proposal. At no point during the eight days from its introduction in the House to its passage by the Senate was it argued that the amendment was necessary for the continued efficient functioning of the Selective Service System or for any other valid legislative purpose. As one commentator noted:

> Use of draft card burning has proved to be one of the most successful means for dissenters to obtain the attention and command the space and time of our national news media. Indeed, its very effectiveness was the moving force in the enactment of the 1965 Amendment.

---

[86] Congressional Record-House, 89th Cong., 1st Sess., August 5, 1965, p. 19534; August 10, p. 19872; Congressional Record-Senate, 89th Cong., 1st Sess., August 10, 1965, p. 19746; August 13, p. 20433.

[87] Congressional Record-House, 89th Cong., 1st Sess., p. 19872.

[88] *Id.*

[89] Congressional Record-Senate, 89th Cong., 1st Sess., p. 20433.

In explaining the purpose of the legislation to the full House Armed Services Committee, the Committee's Chief Counsel stated, "Now this is the answer, of course, to this attempted mass destruction of draft cards. These bums that are going around the country burning draft cards while people are dying in South Vietnam have brought about this type of action on the part of the chairman. . . ."[90]

The Court was not anxious to hear the case. The conviction of David Miller on similar charges in the Second Circuit had been appealed to the Court, which had denied certiorari.[91] Now, with the First Circuit's declaration that the amendment was unconstitutional, the Court was faced with a conflict between the circuits and apparently felt constrained to exercise its jurisdiction. It heard oral argument on January 24, 1968, at a time when, however tired of the war the country may have become, it was in no mood to indulge draft-card burners—as indicated by President Nixon's election six months after the opinion was announced. The amendment had been passed by an all-but-unanimous Congress. There is always the possibility that legislators are counting on the Court to save them from the effects of their own politically necessary votes by striking down the legislation they have passed, but given the political climate in 1968, the Court may not have wished to take the chance of Congressional retaliation.

The most extraordinary feature of the decision is its total lack of reference to the actual necessity for the amendment. No one from the Selective Service System was quoted to the effect that the cards served the multiplicity of functions attributed to them by the Court. No evidence was cited that the Selective Service System wanted or had asked for the amendment. No evidence was considered as to whether the putative ends of the legislation were not in fact already being achieved before the legislation saw the light of day. Even had the Court wished to utilize the balancing test, it could not possibly have hoped to achieve a realistic balance while ignoring the weight of the arguments on one side of the scale. As Louis Henkin commented, in noting that O'Brien "deserved a better opinion":[92]

Also to be considered were the fact that the particular form of communication had become recognized as eloquent and effective;

90 37 *George Washington Law Review* 596, 600 n. 34 (1969). See also Velvel, *id.*, at 167-170; Brief for O'Brien before the Supreme Court, 16-21.

91 *Miller* v. *United States, cert. den.*, 386 U.S. 911 (1967).

92 Henkin, *id.*, at 80.

that for the persons concerned to express what O'Brien sought to express, there were few if any alternative forms of communication of comparable effectiveness; that, whatever its purposes, the Act of Congress would knowingly suppress these communications. One might also ask just how disruptive the burning of draft cards is and whether Congress had effective alternatives to safeguard the administration of the Selective Service program. Such questions are asked when the government regulates the proselytizings of religion, the persuasions of labor, the protests of Negroes or the legal proceedings of the poor. O'Brien was entitled to no less.[93]

It is quite possible that the Court gave short shrift to such considerations because they were not properly raised by counsel. The American Civil Liberties Union, which represented O'Brien before the Court, submitted an otherwise admirable brief which except for part of one page out of seventy-nine made no mention of the redundancy of the legislation. The ACLU argued that the amendment served no rational legislative purpose, but it did not show why the admittedly rational and acceptable purpose of an efficient Selective Service System was in no way accomplished by it. Since the Court usually refuses to examine Congressional motivation, the ACLU should have argued that no matter how legitimate or illegitimate the motivation, the amendment suffered from unnecessary overbreadth and its conflict with the First Amendment therefore rendered it unconstitutional. This lapse on the part of the organization that guided so much of the anti-war litigation through the courts with such expertise can only be attributed to an understandable inability even to imagine that the Court would not strike down the amendment. It gave the Court nothing to work with, however, and that along with the political climate resulted in the defeat for O'Brien.

In another decision defining symbolic speech, the Court found that three students' suspension from public high school and junior high school respectively for wearing black armbands as a protest against the war violated the First Amendment.[94] The Court had shied away from the possibility that O'Brien's protest was the kind of symbolic speech protected by the Amendment. In *Tinker*, however, it cited a host of precedents in support of its contention that the armband-wearing was not only symbolic speech but "closely akin to 'pure speech,' "[95] and

---

[93] *Id.*, at 81.
[95] *Id.*, at 505.
[94] *Tinker* v. *Des Moines*, 393 U.S. 503 (1969).

that it had nothing whatsoever to do with disruptive conduct.[96] The school authorities' fear of potential disruption, the Court maintained, was not sufficient grounds for banning armbands.[97] One factor which may have contributed to the Court's holding is reflected in Justice Fortas' observation that the schools had not found objectionable the wearing of political campaign buttons or "even . . . the Iron Cross, traditionally a symbol of Nazism."[98] In any event, the Court, which had extended its protection to anti-war protestors punished by the Selective Service System, now extended it to schoolchildren as well.[99]

The Court went even further in *Street* v. *New York*.[100] Street was convicted of malicious mischief under a New York statute making it a misdemeanor publicly to "mutilate, deface, defile, defy, trample upon, or cast contempt upon, either by words or act," an American flag.[101] Street, a black New Yorker, publicly burned an American flag and simultaneously protested aloud against the shooting of James Meredith by a Mississippi sniper. The Court found that it was unclear whether or not Street's words contributed to the trial judge's determination of his guilt, and since any punishment for such speech would have been unconstitutional, the conviction could not stand.[102] Chief Justice Warren's rather remarkable dissent[103] discusses the uncontested facts of the incident as they emerged at the trial, indicating that Street's act was not initially accompanied by any speech and that his oral protest was made only to the police officer who happened upon the scene.[104] As Warren pointed out, Street's counsel argued at the trial that flag-burning constituted speech, and that was the real issue raised by the case.[105] If Warren's recapitulation of the incident is correct, the five-judge majority engaged in a rather deft maneuver designed to avoid the issue of the constitutionality of flag-burning. The political atmosphere that resulted in the O'Brien case still existed when *Street* was argued before the Court (October 21, 1968). It was not the appropriate time for the Court to take a stand in support of the kind of "bums" who burned draft cards or American flags. The 1968 Court could hardly

---

96 *Id.*, at 505-506.          97 *Id.*, at 508.          98 *Id.*, at 510.

99 The case is also interesting because of Justice Black's long and rather pathetic dissent, in which he castigates the younger generation for its lack of discipline and respect for authority. *Id.*, at 515, 524-525.

100 394 U.S. 576 (1969).

101 New York Penal Law § 1425, subd. 16, par. d (1909).

102 394 U.S. 589-594.

103 *Id.*, at 594.          104 *Id.*, at 599.          105 *Id.*, at 596-598, 590.

have disagreed with Street's sentiments about the attack on Meredith; it utilized sufficient subterfuge to protect him without exposing its own political flank.

## C. The Pentagon Papers

The attempt of the government to prevent the New York Times and the Washington Post from continuing their publication of the Pentagon Papers became entangled in claims of national security, the need for a prompt judicial decision as opposed to the usual stately pace of matters judicial, and the doctrine of prior restraint. Although the Court's decision[106] technically upheld the right of publication by a six to three majority, the writing of a separate opinion by each member of the Court reflected a broader range of views than was implied by numbers alone. Justice Black maintained his absolutist interpretation of the First Amendment[107] and Justice Douglas concurred with the absolutist position in the case of the press.[108] They were the only two justices to condemn prior restraint under any circumstances. Justice Brennan, while castigating the restraint involved in the injunctions under discussion,[109] nevertheless accepted the propriety of restraint about military matters in wartime upon the presentation of "governmental . . . proof that publication must inevitably, directly, and immediately" result in overwhelming damage to the United States.[110] Justice Stewart argued that the Executive has the inherent power to determine when secrecy and prior restraint are necessary,[111] but that it cannot use the judiciary to implement that secrecy in the absence of proof that disclosures of the information would result in "direct, immediate, and irreparable damage to our Nation or its people."[112] Justice White agreed that the government's evidence was insufficient,[113] but maintained that the sole power to suppress material prior to publication lies with Congress and that Congress had not chosen to give that power to the Executive.[114] It had authorized post-publication criminal sanctions, however, and Justice White made no bones about the propriety of their use in this instance.[115] Justice Marshall emphasized the contention that final power lies with Congress and added that Congress had specifically refused to grant the power to the Executive.[116] Chief Justice

---

106 New York Times Company v. United States, 403 U.S. 713 (1971).
107 Id., at 714-720.
108 Id., at 720.  109 Id., at 725.  110 Id., at 726-727.
111 Id., at 728-730.  112 Id., at 730.  113 Id., at 731.
114 Id., at 732, 740.  115 Id., at 733-740.  116 Id., at 740-748.

Burger expressed his distress at the "frenetic haste"[117] with which the case had proceeded. He blamed the haste on the *Times*, which should have consulted with the Government during the months when it was readying the documents for publication.[118] He contested the absolutist interpretation of Black and Douglas;[119] protested the lack of evidence available to the Court;[120] and would have remanded the case to the District Court for a more leisurely perusal of the evidence, while permitting the injunctions to lie.[121] Justice Harlan, while also distressed at the "frenzied" pace of the litigation,[122] wrote the only dissent that does not itself sound frenzied. He listed the questions which he felt should have been raised prior to judgment[123] and concluded that since the time factor deprived the government of "adequate opportunity" to present its case, the proper course would have been to give it the benefit of the doubt and uphold its claim.[124] He added that the power to determine the necessity for secrecy rests with the President but is subject to a limited kind of judicial review.[125] Justice Blackmun reiterated the non-absolute nature of the First Amendment, the occasional permissibility of prior restraint, and distress at all the haste involved.[126]

Thus two justices (Black and Douglas) rejected prior restraint entirely; three (Brennan, Stewart, White) felt the government had not demonstrated adequate need for prior restraint here; three (Stewart, Harlan, Burger[127]) argued that the President's power to invoke secrecy is inherent but is subject to judicial review; two (White, Marshall) contended that the secrecy power lies with Congress.[128] As the decision was rendered *per curiam*, the only firm doctrine which emerges from the case is contained in the Court's citation of *Bantam Books, Inc.* v. *Sullivan*: "Any system of prior restraints of expression comes to this Court bearing a heavy presumption against its constitutional validity."[129] Nevertheless, one should not be misled by the plethora of opinions into assuming that the only result of the Court's decision was

---

[117] *Id.*, at 749.

[118] *Id.*, at 750-751. The Chief Justice does not appear to comprehend the assumption of the First Amendment that in a society that is to remain democratic the press must be the natural enemy of the government, as amply demonstrated by Watergate.

[119] *Id.*, at 749.    [120] *Id.*, at 748, 751.    [121] *Id.*, at 752.

[122] *Id.*, at 753.    [123] *Id.*, at 753-755.    [124] *Id.*, at 755-756.

[125] *Id.*, at 756-758.    [126] *Id.*, at 759-763.    [127] Cf. Burger, *id.*, at 752 n. 3.

[128] As six of the justices concurred in the opinions written by various of their brethren, it is possible to arrive at a different numerical breakdown. The numbers above reflect only the views of each justice as expressed in his own opinion.

[129] 372 U.S. 58, 70, quoted at 403 U.S. 714.

confusion. The primary results were the continued publication of the Pentagon Papers by the *Times* and the *Post*; the republication of them by a host of other newspapers around the country; the cursory summary of them by the television news programs, which nevertheless had the effect of bringing them to the attention of the American people; the issuing of the documents in paperback form; the successful demand of Congress that the Executive give it access to that which the newspapers already possessed; and, thus, the negation of the doctrine of an inherent unchecked Executive power of secrecy and the insistence that the American people had a right to information concerning the decisions being made about Vietnam in their name.

### III. *The Court's Pre*-Holtzman *Response to Anti-war Litigation*

The discussion above, while not including every case which could be considered to involve anti-war litigation, is sufficient to suggest a pattern. The Court did not hear the cases which charged that the war was unconstitutional, for reasons to be delineated below, and yet it responded positively to the claims of plaintiffs in corollary matters. In effect, the Court went as far as it could in defense of particular victims of the war while avoiding the primary question of the war's legality.

It is especially important to note that the Court did not declare the basic question to be non-justiciable. The reason for this emerges from an understanding that the war was in fact unconstitutional, that the Court could not safely say so, and that by refusing to say anything the Court held to a road that was at least not harmful and at best a prod for action by Congress.

The actions taken by Presidents Johnson and Nixon in Southeast Asia were a violation of the constitutional doctrine of separation of powers. Not only was no effort made to elicit a Congressional declaration of war, but both Presidents deliberately held back from the Congress and from the people the kind of information that would have been necessary if an intelligent decision was to be made about the war's relationship to the national interest. The withholding of information is itself proof that the Congressional role was deliberately negated. One might contend that the desire to avoid a single concentrated power was the major motivation behind the framework of the Constitution. If this is correct, the Presidents' actions made a mockery out of the entire constitutional system.

While a number of lower courts held that the cases were justiciable and that continued Congressional appropriations were sufficient evidence of Congressional ratification of the war effort, possibly because they did not know how else to dispose of the cases, a major 1973 decision suggested that the courts had finally begun to move in the direction of reality. Judge Charles E. Wyzanski, Jr., wrote the opinion for the United States Court of Appeals for the District of Columbia Circuit in the case of *Mitchell* v. *Laird*,[130] which involved a plea by thirteen members of the House for a declaration of the war's unconstitutionality and for an injunction against further unilateral Presidential action. The Court was unanimous in holding the case to be non-justiciable on the grounds that President Nixon, who found a war going on when he took office, had an obligation as Commander-in-Chief, "in good faith and to the best of his ability, to bring the war to an end as promptly as was consistent with the safety of those fighting and with a profound concern for the durable interests of the nation. . . ."[131] Whether or not he did so, the Court declared, was the kind of question not amenable to a judicial decision.[132] However, speaking for two of the three judges sitting in the case, Judge Wyzanski rejected the idea that Congressional appropriations could be construed as ratification:

> This court cannot be unmindful of what every schoolboy knows: that in voting to appropriate money or to draft men a Congressman is not necessarily approving of the continuation of a war no matter how specifically the appropriation or draft act refers to that war. A Congressman wholly opposed to the war's commencement and continuation might vote for the military appropriations and for the draft measures because he was unwilling to abandon without support men already fighting. An honorable, decent, compassionate act of aiding those already in peril is no proof of consent to the actions that placed and continued them in that dangerous posture. We should not construe votes cast in pity and piety as though they were votes freely given to express consent.[133]

Thus, as of March 1973, and in at least one circuit, appropriations no longer implied consent. The Tonkin Gulf Resolution, which had been cited earlier by the Executive branch as Congressional ratification, had been withdrawn. The argument made by the then Assistant Attorney-General Rehnquist, among others, that the President was en-

---

130 476 F. 2d 533 (D.C. Cir. March 20, 1973).
131 *Id.*, at 8.          132 *Id.*, at 8-9.          133 *Id.*, at 7-8.

titled to take whatever action was necessary to protect troops in the field and to reclaim prisoners of war,[134] was not applicable after withdrawal and repatriation were completed in April. Constitutional and statutory justifications for continued military involvement in Southeast Asia were suddenly in short supply. Precisely because the Court had not declared the question to be political, a number of legislators began seeking declaratory and injunctive relief on these grounds.[135]

Even before the District Court decision in *Mitchell*, the proponents of the war's constitutionality had at best relied on a flimsy argument. The remarks of legislators, voting for appropriations, specifically indicating that their votes were not meant to constitute a declaration of war;[136] the clear legislative history demonstrating that the Tonkin Gulf Resolution was designed to give the President only limited powers;[137] the section of the SEATO treaty absolving it of any attempt to nullify existing constitutional requirements;[138] the felt need of past Presidents to elicit a specific declaration of war from Congress—all indicate that the constitutionality of the war was highly questionable. In its amicus brief in *Massachusetts* v. *Laird*, the Constitutional Lawyers' Committee on Undeclared War declared:

The Vietnam war may very well have provided us with an example of a war in which the President could at no time have gotten a majority of Congress to authorize getting into the war, but once in, a majority of Congress (or two-thirds if necessary to override a Presidential veto) could not be amassed to get the nation out of the war.[139]

This is the very essense of unconstitutionality. To quote once again, this time a former President of the United States:

[134] William H. Rehnquist, "The Constitutional Issues—Administration Position," 45 *New York University Law Review* 628 (1970).

[135] See, e.g., *Holtzman* v. *Richardson*, D.C.E.D., N.Y., 73 C 537. As of July 1, 1973, similar cases were being prepared by the American Civil Liberties Union in Boston and San Francisco. The National Emergency Civil Liberties Committee was also filing suit in California.

[136] D'Amato, "Brief," *id.*, at 135.

[137] See Congressional Record-Senate, 88th Cong., 2d Sess., 18403-18430, August 6, 1964; 18442-18450, 18456-18459, 18461-18462, 18469-18470, August 7, 1964; Congressional Record-House, 88th Cong., 2d Sess., 18539-18554, August 7, 1964.

[138] SEATO Treaty Article IV, Paragraph 1: "Each Party . . . agrees that it will . . . act to meet the common danger in accordance with its constitutional processes." *Department of State: Treaties and Other International Acts Series*, no. 3170.

[139] D'Amato, *id.*, at 141. Also see Anthony Lewis in the *New York Times*, June 28, 1973, p. 47.

The provision of the Constitution giving the war-making power to Congress was dictated, as I understand it, by the following reasons: Kings had always been involving and impoverishing their people in wars, pretending generally, if not always, that the good of the people was the object. This our convention understood to be the most oppressive of all kingly oppressions, and they resolved to so frame the Constitution that no one man should hold the power of bringing this oppression upon us.[140]

At this point it is germane to consider the nature of the political question. As has been suggested elsewhere at great length,[141] the Court will find a domestic (as opposed to foreign) problem to be a political question when it is faced with a choice between two possible decisions, one of which would probably not be enforced and would become evidence of judicial impotence, and the second of which would be a denial of a basic principle of American law. It is fairly self-evident that the Court had reason to wonder whether any injunction it might issue would be honored by the Executive branch. The President's intention not to comply with such an injunction was made specific in the government's brief before the Court in *Massachusetts* v. *Laird*:

> Even assuming an injunctive remedy could be devised with sufficient flexibility to prevent military and political disaster, . . . this Court would face insurmountable enforcement difficulties. Judicial supervision of withdrawal from Vietnam would entail unthinkable complexities and a possible confrontation of massive scope. . . . One may readily suppose that Congress would continue to act in conjunction with the Executive. . . .[142]

It has been argued[143] that the Court could have issued a declaration of unconstitutionality, that Congress would have responded with a declaration of war, and that the Court would have retained its position as a neutral judicial body while substantially enhancing its prestige. This is second-guessing, and an institution protective of its prerogatives and

---

140 Abraham Lincoln, quoted in Anthony A. D'Amato, "Massachusetts in the Federal Courts: The Constitutionality of the Vietnam War," 4 *Journal of Law Reform* 11, 20 (1970).

141 Philippa Strum: *The Supreme Court and "Political Questions"* (University of Alabama Press, 1974).

142 Brief for defendant, 32-33.

143 Schwartz and McCormack, *id.*, at 1050.

power could not afford to take that kind of chance.[144] Given the attitude about the Executive's susceptibility to law that was embodied in the Watergate affair, it is questionable whether President Nixon would have taken more than cursory notice of any negative Court decision.[145] Thus the Court could not safely declare the war to be unconstitutional. The case would have presented a classic political question if the only alternative remaining to the Court was to declare the war constitutional in such a way as to imply that the President was above the law, that Article I, Section 8, does not mean what it says and that Congress does not have the sole power to declare war, and that the Constitution therefore really doesn't matter very much. It should be obvious that the Court would wish to declare no such thing. Logically, therefore, the Court should have said that the issue was a political question, and thrown responsibility for deciding whether or not there was to be a war back to Congress. Yet there was another option. The argument made by a number of lower courts that appropriations implied consent—or, alternatively, that the configuration of appropriations, the draft, the Tonkin Resolution, and treaty obligations gave the President the requisite power—could easily have been adopted by the Court. That, however, would have meant that any future President who managed to get troops into battle and who then dared Congress not to appropriate the funds necessary to save the troops' lives would effectively possess a unilateral war power. Clearly, that was a precedent the Court was not willing to set. The Court therefore did nothing, and rather cleverly so.

Theodore Sorenson probably summed up the Court's reason for doing nothing when he commented, in oral argument before the District Court in *Berk*:

---

[144] It might be remembered that even a President as concerned about constitutionality and retention of the constitutional system as Lincoln ignored the separation of powers when confronted with a war situation and demonstrated indifference to attempts by the Court and its members to curb him. See, e.g., *Ex parte Merryman*, 17 Fed. Cas. 144 (C. Ct. Md., 1861), no. 9487. Also note the Court's reluctance to hand down its decision in *Ex parte Milligan*, 71 U.S. (4 Wall.) 2 (1866), until the war was officially ended. Cf. Glendon A. Schubert, Jr., *The Presidency in the Courts* (Minneapolis: University of Minnesota Press, 1957), at 173-175, 185-189; Edward S. Corwin, *The President: Office and Powers*, 4th rev. ed. (New York: New York University Press, 1957), at 228-234.

[145] Even supporters of the war effort might have been reluctant to vote for a declaration of war, given the legal complications that would have ensued. The other signatories to SEATO would have had a legal obligation imposed upon them; the question of what should be done about or to nations aiding and abetting the enemy, specifically in the case of Russian ships supplying the North Vietnam, would have arisen, etc.

To say that this is a political issue—that it is not a justiciable case—
is to say that there is no such thing as an unconstitutional war; that
there is no restraint on the exercise of the power of the President
who wishes to send American forces into combat anywhere in the
world.[146]

So the Court could not declare the question to be political, assuming
that it cared about the maintenance of the constitutional system. Even
if it thought the war unconstitutional—and it is the strong suspicion
of this writer that it did—it was prevented by the enforcement problem
from so holding. That it did not choose the third alternative and find
sufficient Congressional ratification can be perceived as the Court's
disinclination to set a precedent for its future involvement in difficult
war-related questions. However, it can also be understood as the Court's
refusal to legitimize the action taken by the Executive here. As Michael
Katz has observed quite correctly, the judicial decision in *Korematsu*[147]
which sustained the detention of Japanese-Americans was "a far more
subtle blow to liberty than the promulgation of the order itself," because the judicial precedent had a longer-lasting effect than did the
military policy.[148] It was this kind of blow that the Court avoided in
eschewing the third alternative.

It is difficult to believe that a Court so concerned about the civil
liberties of men sent to fight a war in spite of their belief in the illegitimacy of all wars that it was willing to engage in the most blatant misreading of statutes and to appoint itself a super-administrator of the
Selective Service system was unaware of or unconcerned about the
larger civil liberties questions raised by the war itself. The Court, in
doing its best to protect conscientious objectors and dissenters, remained
extremely active on what might be considered the periphery of the war.
As its decisions ran as far against administration policy as was politically
feasible, one might reasonably speculate that the justices were not entirely comfortable with the war effort.

Be that as it may, and without suggesting a conspiracy on the part of
the justices or anything more than the gradual growth of policy on a
case-by-case basis, it seems clear that the Court's response to anti-war
litigation was as positive as possible. Both those lower court decisions

146 Quoted in Friedman and Neuborne, *id.*, at 35.
147 *Korematsu v. United States*, 323 U.S. 214 (1944).
148 Katz, *id.*, at 10 n. 28.

that the war issue was justiciable and those that it was not were allowed to stand, thus leaving the question open and avoiding a difficult decision. If the political situation altered to the point where the Court could safely hear a war case, it had established no precedent for not doing so. However, it was likely that the Congressional response to lower court decisions and to Supreme Court non-action would render a Court decision unnecessary. The Congress had reacted quickly and angrily to lower court interpretations of appropriations as ratification,[149] which would make it more difficult for future Presidents to justify appropriations requests as no more than support for troops already in battle. Congress had been put on notice that it could not appropriate monies for war without being held to have declared war, and yet the Court avoided establishing a binding precedent to that effect. At the same time, the judiciary's refusal to act as a limitation on the Presidential war-making power[150] helped spur Congress into assuming responsibility. Senator Javits' war-powers bill,[151] requiring the President to seek prompt Congressional approval of any commitment of troops to battle, had been introduced and was moving through the Congressional bureaucracy. It was both an example of the Congress' overdue assertion of responsibility and a potential basis for judicial decision in the case of future Vietnams.[152] So, of course, was the establishment of a cut-off date for the Cambodian bombing.[153] The cut-off, representing a compromise necessitated by the President's veto of an appropriations bill forbidding use of the funds for warfare in Cambodia, along with the President's promise to seek Congressional approval for any military

[149] See comments by legislators at 117 Cong. Rec.-Senate, 8322-23, June 4, 1971; 9685-9688, June 22, 1971. Legislative awareness of the implication to be derived from appropriations was much in evidence during the debate that led to a cut-off in appropriations for bombing. See 93rd Cong., 1st Sess.-Senate, 9831, 9840, 9843; 93rd Cong., 1st Sess.-House, 3557-3597. Also see the report of the Senate Foreign Relations Committee on the War Powers bill, discussed below, n. 151.

[150] It should be remembered that as of July 1973 no court whatsoever had found the war in Vietnam to be unconstitutional.

[151] S. 3964. The text and a discussion of the reasons for the bill can be found in Jacob K. Javits, "Congress and the President: A Modern Delineation of the War Powers," 35 *Albany Law Review* 632 (1971).

[152] One of the assumptions underlying the bill, of course, is that it alone will be sufficient to preclude the kind of Executive adventurism that would result in such a suit. It is not altogether impossible, in spite of recent precedent, that future Presidents will consider themselves bound by law.

[153] P. L. 92-52 (July 1, 1973).

action taken after the cut-off date, was agreed to by the President following Congressional threats to attach not-for-use-in-Indochina amendments onto all bills needed by the Administration.[154]

It began to appear that the war would end without the Court taking any action detrimental to itself and that the Court's tactic of non-involvement had succeeded. The Court had managed to render non-decisions that were similar to findings of a "political question" without setting the potentially destructive precedent of a political question; it retained its position as arbiter of First Amendment problems and protected the majority of dissenters appearing before it; it left the door open for future assertions of judicial power if the political climate permitted. Unfortunately for the Court, the *Holtzman* case was waiting in the wings.

## IV. *The Court and* Holtzman

On July 25, 1973, Judge Orin Judd of the United States District Court in Brooklyn (E.D.N.Y.) acceded to the plea of Congressperson Elizabeth Holtzman and four members of the Air Force that the bombing of Cambodia be declared unconstitutional and be enjoined.[155] Judge Judd interpreted Congess' repeated adoption of the Fulbright proviso, limiting military aid to Cambodia to activities necessary for withdrawal of American forces and repatriation of American prisoners, along with its repeated use of the Mansfield amendment in military appropriations acts, as indicating that Congress had authorized military action in Cambodia only until American forces and prisoners had left Vietnam.[156] He pointed to the debate over the August 15 cut-off date as evidence for his contention that the date was set to avoid a Presidential

---

[154] It was factors such as the changing political climate, the President's blatant contempt for Congress, and the lack of even superficially acceptable justifications for a military presence in Indochina following the signing of a peace agreement and the retrieval of American prisoners of war, rather than court decisions, that led to Congress' much overdue assertion of power. Nevertheless, some credit must be given to Congressional awareness of the way the courts were interpreting continued appropriations. Senate Majority Leader Mansfield was quoted by the *Times* to the effect that he would append bombing fund cut-off amendments to bills "again and again until the will of the people prevails"; the chairman of the House Appropriations Committee was unable to persuade House sponsors of the cut-off amendment not to follow suit. *New York Times*, June 28, 1973, p. 5, c. 1.

[155] *Holtzman* v. *Schlesinger*, 361 F. Supp. 553 (1973).

[156] *Id.*, at 555-557, 562-563.

veto rather than to indicate Congressional approval of bombing until August 15.[157] Holding that the bombing of Cambodia was not authorized by Congress and was therefore unconstitutional,[158] he thereby became the first (and sole) judge to find any aspect of the war illegal and to enjoin it. He stayed his injunction for two days in order to permit an appeal to be taken.[159]

It should be noted that Judge Judd's decision was limited, in the sense of finding only the Cambodian bombing illegal. He rendered no judgment about the legality of other facets of the Vietnamese war, indicating his acceptance of the *Orlando* rule that "the test of whether there were manageable standards for adjudication (is) 'whether there is any action by the Congress sufficient to authorize or ratify the military activity in question' " and that in the pre-truce period "there was evidence of 'an abundance of continuing mutual participation in the prosecution of the war.' "[160] He cited the statement in *DaCosta* that "we specifically do not pass on the point . . . whether a radical change in the character of war operations . . . might be sufficiently measurable judicially to warrant a court's consideration. . . ."[161] Thus his opinion can be read as accepting the constitutionality of earlier military actions in Vietnam because of implied Congressional approval of those actions, while holding that the Cambodian bombing represented a "radical change in the character of war operations"[162] unauthorized by Congress. We shall return to this point again in commenting upon later Supreme Court action.[163]

The government took its case to the Court of Appeals, which granted a stay of the injunction until argument could be heard on August 13 (later changed to August 8).[164] Holtzman et al. immediately appealed

[157] *Id.*, at 559-560, 564-566.
[158] *Id.*, at 566.          [159] *Id.*, at 566.
[160] *Id.*, at 562, citing *Orlando v. Laird*, 443 F. 2d 1039, 1042.
[161] *Id.*, at 562, citing *DaCosta v. Laird*, 471 F. 2d at 1151.
[162] *Id.*

[163] A hint about what Judge Judd's decision would be was included in his Memorandum and Order denying the government's motion for dismissal. There, he read the precedents to mean that "the question of the balance of constitutional authority to declare war, as between the executive and legislative branches, is not a political question." *Holtzman v. Richardson*, 361 F. Supp. 544, 551. He then distinguished *Atlee* as dealing "with a general challenge 'to the constitutionality of the war in South East Asia' " (*Id.*, at 551, citing 347 F. Supp. 689, 691) whereas *Holtzman*, "dealing with Cambodian combat operations, involves other issues. . . ." (*Id.*, at 551).

[164] *Schlesinger v. Holtzman*, 484 F. 2d 1307 (1973).

to Justice Thurgood Marshall, in his capacity as Circuit Justice for the Second Circuit, for a vacature of the stay. On August 1, he denied the motion on procedural grounds.[165] Finding that the suit involved complicated "questions of standing, judicial competence, and substantive constitutional law which go to the roots of the division of power in a constitutional democracy,"[166] Marshall held that "the complexity and importance of the issues involved and the absence of authoritative precedent" made it "inappropriate" for "a single Circuit Justice" to vacate the stay.[167] He noted that the Court of Appeals could hear the case on an accelerated schedule.[168]

Justice Marshall, however, left no doubt about his own view of the substantive claim. His *dicta* on the point include the following:

. . . petitioners forcefully contend that continued United States military activity in Cambodia is illegal.[169]

Some may greet with considerable skepticism the claim that vital security interests of our country rest on whether the Air Force is permitted to continue bombing for a few more days, particularly in light of respondents' failure to produce affidavits from any responsible government official asserting that such irreparable injury will occur.[170]

In my judgment, petitioners' contentions in this case are far from frivolous and may well ultimately prevail.[171]

A fair reading of Congress' actions concerning the war in Cambodia may well indicate that the legislature has authorized only "partial hostilities"—that it has never given its approval to the war except to the extent that it was necessary to extricate American troops and prisoners from Vietnam.[172]

. . . if the decision were mine alone, I might well conclude on the merits that continued American military operations in Cambodia are unconstitutional.[173]

When the final history of the Cambodian War is written, it is unlikely to make pleasant reading. The decision to send American troops "to distant lands to die of foreign fevers and foreign shot and

---

165 *Holtzman* v. *Schlesinger*, 414 U.S. 1304 (1973).
166 *Id.*, at 1314.           167 *Id.*, at 1305.           168 *Id.*, at 1305 n2, 1315.
169 *Id.*, at 1308.           170 *Id.*, at 1309.           171 *Id.*, at 1311.
172 *Id.*, at 1312.           173 *Id.*, at 1313.

shell". . . . may ultimately be adjudged to have not only been unwise but also unlawful.[174]

Given Justice Douglas' consistent dissents from the Court's refusal to grant such cases *certiorari*, along with Justice Stewart's dissents in *Mora, Atlee,* and *Massachusetts* v. *Laird,* and Justice Brennan's dissents in *DaCosta* and *Atlee,*[175] it now looked as if the Court had the four votes necessary to hear the case.

On August 2, intrepid ACLU lawyers tracked down Justice Douglas at his Goose Prairie, Washington, home (he has no telephone) and asked him to vacate the stay. Justice Douglas heard argument the following day and issued an order at 9:30 A.M. on August 4 granting the vacature.[176] He called the case, "in its stark realities" one which involved "the grim consequence of a capital case," because unless the bombing was halted immediately "we know that someone is about to die."[177] Pointing out that a stay in a capital case does not include a ruling on the merits but is granted when a due process question arises "because death is irrevocable,"[178] Douglas read the differing constructions of Congress' August 15 deadlines as constituting a "substantial" controversy necessitating vacature of the stay.[179] As did Judge Judd, Douglas differentiated the Cambodian question from the over-all problem of Vietnam, stating that "if the 'war' in Vietnam were assumed to be a constitutional one, the Cambodian bombing is quite a different affair."[180] Thus Douglas seemed to be inviting the Court to support him on the grounds that the larger war was no longer the issue.

No sooner had the Court issued Douglas' order than the Pentagon announced that it would not obey it.[181] The Justice Department asked Chief Justice Burger to reconvene the Court in special term. Instead, Justice Marshall polled his brethren by telephone and announced at 3:30 P.M. that seven of them concurred in his reinstatement of the stay.[182] Thus Justice Douglas' order remained in effect for only a few hours.

[174] *Id.,* at 1315, quoting concurring opinion of Justice Black in *New York Times* v. *United States,* 403 U.S. 713, 717.

[175] *Supra,* n. 27-31.

[176] *Holtzman* v. *Schlesinger,* 414 U.S. 1316 (1973).

[177] *Id.,* at 1317.

[178] *Id.,* at 1319.        [179] *Id.,* at 1319-1320.        [180] *Id.,* at 1319-1320.

[181] See statement of Assistant Secretary of Defense for Public Affairs Jerry W. Freidheim, *New York Times,* August 5, 1973. p. 3, c.1.

[182] *Schlesinger* v. *Holtzman,* 414 U.S. 1321, 1322 (1973). Justice Douglas protested in dissent that telephonic polling violated the Court's own rules. *Id.,* at 1323-1326.

On August 8, the Court of Appeals heard oral arguments. A few hours later, in a two to one decision, the Court reversed Judge Judd.[183] Reiterating the Court's *DaCosta* contention that the question was a political one, Judge Mulligan added,

> If we were incompetent to judge the significance of the mining and bombing of North Vietnam's harbors and territories, we fail to see our competence to determine that the bombing of Cambodia is a "basic change" in the situation and that it is not a "tactical decision" within the competence of the President.[184]

Although it eschewed substantive judgment, the court found room in its opinion to disagree with Judge Judd's reading of the significance of the August 15 deadline. It expressed itself as unable to "see how this provision does not support the proposition that the Congress has approved the Cambodian bombing,"[185] stated that the "resort to legislative history is unjustified,"[186] and then added that its own reading of the legislative history differed from that of Judge Judd.[187] Judge Oakes, in dissent, argued that even pre-truce appropriations for military action in Southeast Asia were voted when Congress was ignorant of the secret Cambodian bombings and therefore could not be taken as legal approval of the war efforts.[188] Holtzman's requests that Justice Burger convene an extraordinary session of the Court were denied, and a few days later, on August 15, the case became moot.[189]

The *Holtzman* case did little to enhance the Court's prestige. The public was treated to the sight of two justices tumbling over each other in their haste to undo each other's decisions while the Pentagon cavalierly proclaimed its power to pick the decision it would follow. The full Court foreswore its usual measured deliberations and its own rules in order to rush out a decision over telephone wires. At a time of national upheaval, a member of the Court let it be known that he considered the daily expenditure of lives to be illegal but that he could do nothing about it. All in all, it was far from the Court's finest hour.

183 *Holtzman* v. *Schlesinger*, 484, F. 2d 1307 (1973). On August 3, Holtzman had petitioned the Court of Appeals for an *en banc* hearing. The five judges of the court who could be reached unanimously denied the motion, on the grounds that convening the court *en banc* would have delayed a hearing. *Id.*, at 1308.

184 *Id.*, at 1310, citing *DaCosta* v. *Laird*, 471 F. 2d 1146.

185 *Id.*, at 1313.

186 *Id.*, at 1314.          187 *Id.*, at 1314.          188 *Id.*, at 1316-1317.

189 On April 15, 1974, the Supreme Court refused to grant Holtzman's plea for *certiorari*. The decision was unanimous and *per curiam*. *Holtzman* v. *Schlesinger*, 416 U.S. 936.

The question immediately arises of what else the Court might have done and why it chose not to do it. Upon examination, it appears that the institutional integrity preserved by the Court's insistent self-efface-ment in the war cases was not in danger here and that the Court could have decided *Holtzman* with impunity.

It has been suggested above that the Court might well have been concerned about the enforcement problem that would have resulted from calling the pre-truce war illegal. The President might have ignored the Court, limiting the possibilities of its future action (e.g., would a Court thus publicly slapped by the President have ventured to decide as the Court did in *United States* v. *United States District Court?*).[190] And in *Holtzman*, one might argue, the threat was demonstrated again by the Pentagon's immediate reaction to Douglas' order of vacature. Nevertheless, the circumstances surrounding *Holtzman* were unique. By early August, the Congress and the country had turned against the war. That is the clear meaning of the appropriations bill vetoed by the President and the August 15 deadline created to avoid a further veto. Legislators now felt that it was safe to vote against appropriations, the troops and prisoners having been repatriated. The Executive's accept-ance of the Congress' action was made obvious by the affidavit filed by Secretary of State William P. Rogers before the Court on August 4.[191] According to Rogers' memo, Cambodia had been informed that the United States intended to cease "all combat activities" by August 15, and the two countries had engaged in "intensive planning" to make that possible.[192] Since plans for withdrawal had already been made, would a President suffering the embarrassment of the televised Senate Water-gate committee proceedings not simply pledge to speed up implementa-tion as much as possible? Rogers had argued that "the absence of . . . air support prior to (August 15) would permit hostile military forces to disrupt those plans and would expose United States military and civilian personnel who are responsible for their implementation, to grave risk of personal injury or death,"[193] but Justice Marshall's skepti-cism about the extent of the national interest involved in the bomb-ing[194] might well have been shared by other members of the Court.

Even had the President insisted that it would take until August 15 to

[190] 407 U.S. 297 (1972).

[191] *New York Times*, August 6, 1973, p. 4, c. 3-8, included as a footnote to Court of Appeals decision, 484 F. 2d 1307, 1310-1311.

[192] *Id.*, at 1310.     [193] *Id.*, at 1310.     [194] *Supra*, p. 33.

complete withdrawal, the Court could only have gained by restoring the injunction. It is most unlikely that the President would have couched a declaration in tones of defiance; rather, the probability is that he would have issued a statement emphasizing his determination to uphold pledges made to the Cambodians and the need to maintain the international credibility of American promises. At most, since Rogers' statement constituted a public Administration promise to stop the bombing by August 15, the President would have been in defiance of the Court order for only a few days. And given the mood of the country, it is doubtful that a President already suspected of subversion of liberties and of participation in "dirty tricks" would have received the bulk of the electorate's support.

It must be reiterated here that there would have been no need for the Court to review the constitutionality of the entire war. Following Judge Judd's example and Justice Marshall's hints, the Court could have confined itself to the Cambodian bombing as a "radical change in the character of war" unauthorized by Congress. In the *Youngstown* decision,[195] the factor accorded greatest weight by most of the justices was earlier Congressional refusal to give the President the kind of power he exercised in seizing the steel mills. Congressional actions preceding the establishment of the August 15 cut-off date could easily have been interpreted as conclusive under the same kind of negative-action test.[196] Thus, with no danger to itself, and on a firm legal footing, the Court could finally have asserted its moral leadership and reminded both government and electorate that the Constitution was indeed the supreme law of the land.

In the absence of conclusive evidence from the justices themselves, the Court's decision not to do so is potentially attributable to a number of considerations. Justice Burger may have insistently denied tentative suggestions from other justices for a special session, especially as it is hardly far-fetched to speculate that he would not have wanted the Court to render a verdict of unconstitutionality. Members of the Court in favor of such a verdict may have felt that since the bombing was almost over, and since the Court would probably not be able to speak with an undivided voice, it was better to leave the issue alone. This view would have been strengthened by the realization that it would take some time for the Court to reassemble in Washington and that the ad-

---

[195] *Youngstown* v. *Sawyer*, 343 U.S. 579 (1952).
[196] Cf. *Little* v. *Barreme*, 2 Cr. 170 (1804).

ditional number of days consumed in hearing argument and writing opinions would result in the issuance of hurried opinions on a matter of great national consequence. Having done that once, in the Pentagon Papers case, the Court may well have chosen to avoid a repetition. The Court may have supported Justice Marshall's second edict on the grounds that to halt a war by telephone and without communal consideration of argument by both sides would have been unseemly. Finally, the Court may have felt that Justice Marshall's overruling of Justice Douglas represented enough embarrassment and that it would be best to let the war die its own imminent death. All these are sound reasons, especially since the justices may not have known which way a majority would have voted. To rush back to Washington, only to render a decision of constitutionality in a matter the justices had scrupulously avoided, would have been self-defeating. The justices who presumably would have voted for *certiorari* may well have preferred no decision to a possible decision upholding a Presidential war.

All this having been said, however, it is difficult not to mourn the Court's refusal to seize its opportunity and reassert the moral leadership so desperately needed by the country during the summer of 1974. Earlier supporters of the war were eagerly jumping off what suddenly appeared to be a sinking ship, and even the electorate had had enough. It is hard to believe that a majority of the justices considered the bombing constitutional. If, thinking it to be illegal, they refused to act when they could have done so with institutional impunity, one might well ask for what purpose they were husbanding their power. If the Court refuses to exercise judicial review in the face of flagrant violation of the Constitution, how legitimate a democratic institution can it be? And refusing to recognize its own political role, how potent a legal institution can it be?

Thus the Court, having steered its way dextrously through the dangerous waters churned up by most of the war cases, foundered on *Holtzman*. Its previous non-decisions had had the happy effect of leaving full responsibility for American actions in Southeast Asia with what the Court delights in calling the "political" branches of the federal government, and with the American people. Once the Congress and the people had finally spoken, however, the Court paid no heed. Thus there is still no definitive ruling that a Presidential war is unconstitutional or that, as Judge Judd indicated, it "cannot be the rule that the President needs a vote of only one-third plus one of either House in order to conduct a war."[197] As the law now stands, it is possible to argue that, in clear contradiction of Article I, Section 8, "Congress must override a Presidential veto in order to terminate hostilities which it has not authorized,"[198] and that the Court has tacitly concurred in Congress' loss of its monopoly over the power to declare war.

[197] *Holtzman* v. *Schlesinger*, 361 F. Supp. 553, 565.

[198] *Id.*, at 565.

# War-Making Under the Constitution: The Original Understanding

## CHARLES A. LOFGREN†

The first major public debate over the division of war-making power between Congress and the President occurred in mid-1793 following President Washington's proclamation of American neutrality[1] in the war which had broken out between England and France at the beginning of that year. Defending Washington's action in a series of newspaper articles under the disarming pseudonym of "Pacificus," Alexander Hamilton, a participant in the Constitutional Convention six years earlier, argued that since war-making was by nature an executive function, Congress could exercise only those aspects of it which the Constitution specifically grants the legislature. These grants, being exceptions to the general rule, must be narrowly construed.[2] James Madison, a principal framer of the Constitution and co-author with Hamilton and John Jay of *The Federalist Papers,* found the Constitution equally clear, but to the opposite effect. Writing as "Helvidius," Madison asserted that war-making was a legislative function and that any exceptions in favor of the executive must be strictly interpreted.[3]

The debate thus opened has continued sporadically to the present day. Most recently, limited wars in Korea and Indochina have occasioned renewed interest in the question of which branch of the federal government is constitutionally empowered to commence war.[4] In the

† Associate Professor of History, Claremont Men's College. B.A. 1961; M.A. 1962; Ph.D. 1966, Stanford University. The author is indebted to Professors Keith Berwick, Leonard Levy, and John Niven for comments on an earlier draft; to the staffs of the Henry E. Huntington and Los Angeles County Law Libraries for their assistance and kindnesses; and to the Faculty Research Committee of Claremont Men's College and the Relm Foundation for financial support.

1. Proclamation of April 22, 1793, 1 AMERICAN STATE PAPERS: FOREIGN RELATIONS 140 (W. Lawrie & M. Clark eds. 1833).

2. *See* 4 THE WORKS OF ALEXANDER HAMILTON 437-44 (H. Lodge ed. 1904). Specific exceptions to the President's war-making power, as listed by Hamilton, were "the right of the Legislature 'to declare war and grant letters of marque and reprisal'." *Id.* at 439. *See* U.S. CONST. art. I, § 8.

3. *See* 6 THE WRITINGS OF JAMES MADISON 138-88 *passim* (G. Hunt ed. 1906). Under Madison's interpretation, the key exception to the war-making power of Congress was the provision that the President was "Commander in Chief of the Army and Navy of the United States, and of the militia when called into the actual service of the United States." *Id.* at 148. *See* U.S. CONST. art. II, § 2.

4. The literature on this topic is enormous. Useful introductions may be found in *Hearings on War Powers Legislation Before the Subcomm. on National Security Policy and Scientific Developments of the House Comm. on Foreign Affairs,* 92d Cong., 1st Sess.

course of this debate, however, constitutional scholars have generally failed to examine thoroughly the problem of how Americans in 1787-88 understood the war-making clauses of the Constitution.[5] Such scholarly reticence[6] doubtless has some claim to prudence since Madison and Hamilton, who presumably knew something about the original intent, came to contradictory conclusions within a few years of the Constitutional Convention. But the fact that two of the framers were in disagreement is thin justification for according this significant issue inadequate treatment. Hence, by examining the debates and proceedings which accompanied the framing and ratification of the Constitution, and particularly by considering ideas prevalent among Americans of that day as they interpreted the clauses in question, I shall attempt in this article to throw light on two important questions: (1) What was the original understanding respecting the allocation between the President and Congress of the general power to commence war? And (2) was that power understood to include the commencement of *undeclared* war?

(1971); *Hearings on Congress, the President, and the War Powers Before the Subcomm. on National Security Policy and Scientific Developments of the House Comm. on Foreign Affairs*, 91st Cong., 2d Sess. (1970); M. PUSEY, THE WAY WE GO TO WAR (1969); Note, *Congress, the President, and the Power to Commit Forces to Combat*, 81 HARV. L. REV. 1771 (1968); E. CORWIN, THE PRESIDENT: OFFICE AND POWERS 1787-1957: HISTORY AND ANALYSIS OF PRACTICE AND OPINION (4th rev. ed. 1957); HOUSE COMM. ON FOREIGN AFFAIRS, BACKGROUND INFORMATION ON THE USE OF UNITED STATES ARMED FORCES IN FOREIGN COUNTRIES, H.R. REP. No. 127, 82d Cong., 1st Sess. (1951). For earlier studies, see J. ROGERS, WORLD POLICING AND THE CONSTITUTION: AN INQUIRY INTO THE POWERS OF THE PRESIDENT AND CONGRESS, NINE WARS AND A HUNDRED MILITARY OPERATIONS 1789-1945 (1945); C. BERDAHL, WAR POWERS OF THE EXECUTIVE IN THE UNITED STATES (1921).

5. The clauses of primary significance are art. I, § 8, empowering Congress "[t]o declare War [and] grant Letters of Marque and Reprisal . . . ," and art. II, § 2, making the President "Commander in Chief of the Army and Navy of the United States, and of the Militia of the several States, when called into the actual Service of the United States . . . ." Of lesser importance is the clause of art. I, § 10, providing that "[n]o State shall . . . engage in War, unless actually invaded, or in such imminent Danger as will not admit of delay." The clauses of art. I, § 8, dealing with the raising, support, government, and regulation of land and naval forces—that is, the war-supporting clauses—are outside the scope of the present study. For debate surrounding them, see Donahoe & Smelser, *The Congressional Power to Raise Armies: The Constitutional and Ratifying Conventions, 1787-1788*, 33 REV. OF POL. 202 (1971).

6. Recent commentators have discussed the original understanding, but, regardless of their positions on present-day issues, they have generally limited such discussions to an examination of the one debate in the Federal Convention on changing the wording of the clause giving Congress the power "to make war" so that it conferred power "to declare war." For this debate, see 2 THE RECORDS OF THE FEDERAL CONVENTION 318-19 (M. Farrand ed., rev. ed. 1937) [hereinafter cited as FARRAND, RECORDS]. *See, e.g., 1970 Hearings on Congress, The President, and the War Powers, supra* note 4, at 207, 211 (statements of J. Stevenson, Legal Advisor, Dep't of State, and W. Rehnquist, Ass't Att'y Gen.); Bickel *et al., Indochina: The Constitutional Crisis*, in 116 CONG. REC. 7117, 7122-23 (daily ed. May 13, 1970); PUSEY, *supra* note 4, at 44-47 (treating some other points, but only vaguely); Note, *Congress, the President, and the Power to Commit Forces to Combat, supra* note 4, at 1773 & nn.14, 16; Wormuth, *The Vietnam War: The President versus*

## I. Problems of Allocating Power: From the Articles of Confederation to the Constitution

Under the Articles of Confederation, Congress exercised both legislative and executive powers. Consequently, the Articles, in dealing with the war-making power, needed only to provide that the "United States in Congress assembled, shall have the sole and exclusive right and power of determining on peace and war." (An exception provided that individual states might engage in war if they were actually invaded or were threatened with imminent Indian attack.)[7] Like the Constitution, however, the Articles today appear somewhat ambiguous on their face as to whether a war conducted by the United States necessarily had to be a "declared" war. They conferred the "right and power of *determining* on . . . war," but also referred to certain acts the states might perform only after a congressional "declaration of war."[8] Thus, while contemplating that at least some wars would be "declared" in form, the document did not explicitly resolve the question of whether the nation might engage in other sorts of war.[9]

Whatever the case with the Confederation, in 1787 the Philadelphia Convention drafted a Constitution which provided for a federal government with distinct branches, thereby necessitating some attention to the allocation of the war-making power of the government. Yet, while the new Constitution increased the already severe limitations

---

the Constitution, in 2 THE VIETNAM WAR AND INTERNATIONAL LAW 710, 713-17 (R. Falk ed. 1969); R. HULL & J. NOVOGROD, LAW AND VIETNAM 170 (1968). *But see* Reveley, *Presidential War-Making: Constitutional Prerogative or Usurpation?*, 55 VA. L. REV. 1243, 1281-85 and accompanying notes (1969) (citing other evidence from the convention itself); R. Russell, The United States Congress and the Power to Use Military Force Abroad, April 15, 1967, at 1-65 (unpublished Ph.D. dissertation in the Fletcher School of Law and Diplomacy Library, Tufts University). While Russell neglects several points discussed in the present article, *see especially* pp. 680-83 & pp. 688-99 *infra*, and gives less attention to certain other items, *see especially* pp. 683-88 *infra*, his conclusions are generally consistent with mine. Deserving special mention is *Hearings on War Powers Legislation Before the Senate Comm. on Foreign Relations*, 92d Cong., 1st Sess. at 7-121 *passim* (1972) (statements and testimony of Professors H.S. Commager, R. Morris, and A. Kelly, Mar. 8-9, 1971), which I was able to examine only after the present article was written. This provides an excellent, albeit relatively brief, discussion of the original understanding of 1787-88 in the course of a broader review of the history of war-making in its constitutional dimensions.

7. ARTS. OF CONFED. arts. VI, IX. These provisions relating to war-making in the final Articles of Confederation were virtually unchanged from the first draft of the document in July 1776. *See* 5 JOURNALS OF THE CONTINENTAL CONGRESS 1774-1789, at 549-50 (1906).

8. ARTS. OF CONFED. arts. VI, IX (italics added).

9. Since the Articles did authorize the granting of letters of marque and reprisal, they tacitly suggest that other sorts of hostilities were contemplated. Much depends, however, on the types of situation to which letters of marque and reprisal were thought applicable, and on whether such situations were to be classified as war. The same ambiguity arises with respect to the Constitution and is discussed at pp. 692-96 *infra*.

which the Articles of Confederation had placed on state war-making,[10] similar explicitness did not mark the division of war-making power between Congress and the President. Nor have the records of the debates in the Federal Convention proved an adequate guide in resolving the ambiguities inherent in the "plain words" of the Constitution, principally because the question of the manner in which the nation should be committed to war was not one of the chief concerns of the delegates in Philadelphia. Criticism of the Confederation government for its inability to support federal objectives, both domestic and foreign, had not included the complaint that the Confederation was deficient in its ability to commit the nation to war.[11]

The main report of the one debate which explicitly considered allocation of the war-making power occupies little more than one page out of the 1,273 which contain the printed records of the Convention.[12] This debate occurred on August 17, 1787, while the Convention was considering the clause of the draft constitution reported by the Committee on Detail on August 6 which gave Congress the power "to make war."[13] Charles Pinckney of South Carolina opened the debate by arguing that the legislature as a whole was too cumbersome a body to exercise this power. He contended that it should be vested in the Senate, which was smaller and would be more knowledgeable in foreign affairs, and which by virtue of its treaty power[14] had the authority to make peace. Pierce Butler, from Pinckney's own state, carried the latter's argument a step further and called for vesting the power in the President, but his proposal received no recorded support. Madison and Elbridge Gerry of Massachusetts then "moved to insert 'declare'; striking out 'make' war; leaving the Executive the Power to repel sudden attacks."[15] This wording, from Madison's notes, suggests that the change from "make" to "declare" was intended in some fashion to broaden the executive's power in the war-making area.

The available record of the remainder of the debate indicates, how-

---

10. Under the Articles, states could grant letters of marque and reprisal after a congressional declaration of war, subject to congressional regulation, while under the Constitution they are absolutely forbidden to make such grants. *Compare* ARTS. OF CONFED. art. VI, *with* U.S. CONST. art. I, § 10.

11. *See* Farrand, *The Federal Convention and the Defects of the Confederation*, 2 AM. POL. SCI. REV. 532, 535-37 (1908).

12. *See* 2 FARRAND, RECORDS, *supra* note 6, at 318-19.

13. *Id.* at 181-82.

14. At this point in the Convention's proceedings, the Senate still had exclusive authority to make treaties, the President not yet having been given power to make treaties with the advice and consent of the Senate. *See id.* at 183, 392-94, 498, 538.

15. *Id.* at 318 (emphasis added).

ever, that the delegates may not have understood the change in such an unambiguous way, or indeed in any one way at all. For example, Roger Sherman of Connecticut protested that the clause as originally reported, that is, without the Madison-Gerry amendment, "stood very well. The Executive shd. be able to repel and not to commence war. 'Make' better than 'declare' the latter narrowing the power too much." It thus appears that Sherman believed that the original wording already left the executive free to repel sudden attacks and hence that in this respect the proposed change was nugatory. But he apparently thought that by narrowing the power of Congress, the alteration would unduly broaden the executive's power in some other ways. Oliver Ellsworth, also of Connecticut, at first concurred with Sherman in opposing the change. George Mason of Virginia, who "was against giving the power of war to the Executive, because [he was] not safely to be trusted with it; or to the Senate, because [it was] not so constructed to be entitled to it . . . and was for clogging rather than facilitating war," and who on that basis might well have agreed with Sherman and Ellsworth, instead supported the change. Madison's notes indicate that at this point a vote on the proposed change was taken, resulting in a tally of seven states to two in favor of the amendment. Then, in the face of an argument advanced by Rufus King of Massachusetts "that '*make*' war might be understood to 'conduct' it which was an Executive function," Ellsworth accepted the need for the alteration in wording and Connecticut switched its vote, making the poll eight to one in favor of the Madison-Gerry amendment.[16]

In editing the records of the Convention, Max Farrand concluded that the official journal of the Convention, as regards the votes taken, was at times unreliable, inconclusive, or both,[17] and for this reason Madison's figures are used here. If accurate, these figures indicate that King's argument had but a marginal effect on the fate of the Madison-Gerry amendment, since it would have passed without Connecticut's vote. But this is a case where the journal figures do not accord with Madison's. The journal indicates that the Madison-Gerry amendment initially *lost* by a vote of four states to five and that it was

16. *Id.* at 318-19. *See also* Note, *Congress, the President, and the Power to Commit Forces to Combat, supra* note 4, at 1773 n.16. Only nine states cast votes because Massachusetts abstained on the issue, New Jersey and New York were not represented at this point, and Rhode Island never attended the Convention.

17. 1 FARRAND, RECORDS, *supra* note 6, at xiii-xiv. Madison himself later "corrected" some of his information to bring it into conformity with the journal, but such emendations were not made in his notes of the debate under discussion.

only on the second vote that the amendment carried—by an eight to one margin.[18] *If* the journal is accurate in its voting figures and *if* King's argument was the key statement made between the two votes, then it had a far greater effect on the outcome than Madison's account would suggest.

The "ifs" must remain, for the record is unclear. The only certainty which emerges from the debate is that the wording was changed. What the various delegates thought the change accomplished can only be set forth in terms of possible interpretations: (1) the change broadened executive power by giving the executive the authority "to repel sudden attacks"; (2) the original wording already having given the executive that power, the alteration broadened his power in some more general fashion; (3) the modification lessened the chance for involvement in war; or (4) the new wording removed any suggestion that Congress would control the conduct of a war *after* it was begun. Of these possibilities, the first two suggest an intention to broaden the executive's power in *some* way. The third, and particularly the statement of Mason from which it is derived, does not bear clearly one way or the other on the question of executive-versus-legislative power. The fourth possibility suggests that the change referred to something other than the process of initially committing the nation to war. As if to reinforce the conclusion that the change meant different things to different delegates, Butler of South Carolina, after the new wording had been approved, "moved to give the Legislature [the] power of peace as they were to have that of war."[19] In his mind, it seems, the Madison-Gerry amendment had done little. The legislature still had the power "of war."

## II.   Indications of an Original Understanding

If the discussion and votes on August 17 were the only source of evidence revealing the original understanding of war-making under the Constitution, those eager for a definite conclusion would have due cause for despair. But the private intentions of the Convention's delegates in changing "make" to "declare," whatever they were, did

---

18.   2 *id.* at 313-14. Russell appears more convinced than I am that the journal's record of these votes is accurate, and he suggests that Madison may have mislabeled one of the vote counts. His position on the largely inconclusive meaning of the debate is, however, close to mine. *See* Russell, *supra* note 6, at 39-43.

19.   2 FARRAND, RECORDS, *supra* note 6, at 319.

not control the way Americans of that day generally understood the Constitution's war-making clauses. Fortunately, we can gain additional and more conclusive evidence from (a) other deliberations of the Federal Convention and the Constitution itself; (b) the state debates over the ratification of the Constitution; (c) some seventeenth and eighteenth century trends in the theory and practice of war and reprisal; and (d) a consideration of English influences.

## A.  The Convention and Its Product

In 1787 and 1788, Americans ratified the Constitution, not a set of proceedings in the Federal Convention.[20] In fact, the Convention's records remained largely secret for thirty years.[21] Still, the deliberations in Philadelphia are worth examining for clues as to how Americans of that day generally understood war-making in its constitutional dimensions. The Convention's members were, after all, members of and leaders in a broader community, so it is likely that their fundamental assumptions were shared by other Americans. In addition, the Constitution itself provides clues to how the delegates' contemporaries understood war-making under it.

The plan of government submitted by Edmund Randolph on behalf of Virginia became the focus of the Convention's first deliberations. It contained no specific reference, however, to the power of either the executive or the legislative branch to commit the nation to war,[22] but instead neatly side-stepped the question. Randolph recommended that the "National Legislature . . . ought to be impowered to enjoy [among other things] the Legislative Rights vested in Congress by the Confederation" and that the "National Executive . . . ought to enjoy the Executive rights vested in Congress by the Confederation."[23] The only recorded remarks bearing on how such criteria for division might affect the allocation of war-making power came on June 1, 1787. Charles Pinckney cautioned that the powers of war and peace might properly be classed as executive powers. James Wilson of Pennsylvania, although admitting his preference for "a single magistrate, as giving most energy dispatch and responsibility to the office [of National Executive]," took exception: "[h]e did not

---

20. *See, e.g.,* 1 J. STORY, COMMENTARIES ON THE CONSTITUTION OF THE UNITED STATES 388-90 (1833).
21. 1 FARRAND, RECORDS, *supra* note 6, at xi-xv.
22. *See id.* at 18-23.
23. *Id.* at 21.

consider the Prerogatives of the British Monarch [which included the power of making war] as a proper guide in defining the Executive Powers. Some of these prerogatives were of a Legislative nature. Among others that of war & peace &c." Madison agreed with Wilson,[24] but the resolutions which the Convention eventually passed and sent to the Committee on Detail on July 26 were no more explicit regarding the division of war-making power than Randolph's original plan had been. In a sense they were even less explicit because they did not contain the general proposition that the executive should enjoy the executive powers vested in the Confederation Congress.[25]

Despite the paucity of prior debate and the ambiguity of the resolutions sent to it, the Committee on Detail had little trouble in allocating the war-making power. Randolph and Wilson each prepared draft constitutions which assigned the power "to make war" to the legislature. The draft reported by the committee to the Convention on August 6 followed the same scheme. Clearly, as the committee sensed the will of the Convention on these points—points which, it must be remembered, had scarcely been debated—war-making fell almost automatically to Congress. At the same time, the committee made the executive, now denominated the President, the Commander in Chief of the armed forces. In view of the concurrent grant to Congress of the broad power "to make war," the Presidency did not carry with it any authority to initiate war, except perhaps the restricted power of repelling sudden attacks which Sherman was soon to attribute to it. After the committee reported, the Convention spent a month debating and sometimes modifying its recommendations, changing, *inter alia*, Congress' power "to make war" to a power "to declare war." The Commander-in-Chief clause, however, was passed unchanged and without recorded debate on August 27, 1787. This expeditious, unremarked assent again suggests a narrow, non-controversial conception of the clause.[26]

Charles Pinckney's recommendation that Congress be given the power to grant letters of marque and reprisal was approved on September 5. Perhaps, as Joseph Story later contended, the Convention

---

24. *Id.* at 64-65, 70.
25. *See* 2 *id.* at 129-34.
26. These developments can be traced in *id.* at 143, 145, 168, 172, 182, 185, 426-28; p. 676 *supra*. On the narrow view the Convention took of the President's role as Commander in Chief, see especially May, *"The President Shall Be Commander in Chief" (1787-1789)*, in THE ULTIMATE DECISION: THE PRESIDENT AS COMMANDER IN CHIEF 3-19 (E. May ed. 1960).

desired to remove any remaining doubt about the authority of Congress to authorize some form of undeclared hostilities.[27] At the least, it thus became possible for Americans in 1787-88 to draw such a conclusion, with their precise interpretation of the scope of the power depending on how they understood the purpose of letters of marque and reprisal.[28] The Convention's final product contained all three provisions: Congress received the power to declare war and to grant letters of marque and reprisal, and the President became Commander in Chief.[29]

The Convention also left several less direct clues to how the delegates and their contemporaries may have understood the Constitution's war-making provisions. One is found in the plan of government that Alexander Hamilton presented to the Convention on June 18. This discloses that Hamilton, despite his preference for a greatly strengthened executive, was inclined to limit severely the executive's role in initiating war. He would have given the Senate, not the President, "the sole power of declaring war." The President was instead "to have the direction of war *when authorized or begun.*"[30] His scheme also supports the conclusion that the delegates and their contemporaries in America did not understand the term "declare" in a narrow, technical sense. On Hamilton's theory the President could direct war only after it had been commenced. His sole reference to the commencement of war, however, was the grant empowering the Senate to declare it—yet not even in the eighteenth century were all wars technically "declared."[31]

27. *See* 2 FARRAND, RECORDS, *supra* note 6, at 326, 508-09; 3 STORY, *supra* note 20, at 63-64.
28. Despite Justice Story's comment, recent students of the war-making issue have generally neglected the significance of the power to grant letters of marque and reprisal, which is discussed at pp. 692-96 *infra.* For an example of the complete omission of this power from a list of "specific powers relevant to [the] discussion" of the original understanding, see Rogers, *Congress, the President, and the War Powers,* 59 CALIF. L. REV. 1194, 1195 (1971). Secretary of State Rogers' article appeared earlier as a prepared statement in *1971 Hearings on War Powers Legislation, supra* note 4, at 122.
29. U.S. CONST. art. I, § 8, art. II, § 2.
30. 1 FARRAND, RECORDS, *supra* note 6, at 292 (emphasis added). Notes on the plan Hamilton presented to the convention on June 18 are found in *id.* at 282-93. The version he presented in draft form to Madison late in the convention is in 3 *id.* at 617-30. On Hamilton generally during the Convention, see B. MITCHELL, ALEXANDER HAMILTON: YOUTH TO MATURITY 1755-1788, at 389-413 (1957); J. MILLER, ALEXANDER HAMILTON AND THE GROWTH OF THE NEW NATION 151-83 (1964).
31. During the debate of August 17, on the war-making clause, Elbridge Gerry (or perhaps Madison in recording Gerry's remarks) had used "declare" in a similarly loose sense. Pierce Butler proposed "vesting the power [*i.e.,* the power to *make* war, since the amendment to change the wording had not yet been proposed] in the President." Gerry, commenting after Madison's and his amendment to change the wording had been offered but before it had been voted on, and with evident reference to Butler's remark, soon objected that he "never expected to hear in a republic a motion to empower the Execu-

Another clue is provided by the placement within the Constitution of the restrictions on the power of the states to wage war independently of the central government. In Philadelphia, limitations even stricter than those which had been included in the Articles[32] emerged during the deliberations of the Committee on Detail and were included as separate coordinate articles in the draft reported by that committee to the Convention. The Committee on Style, however, placed the prohibitions in the *legislative* article, where they appear in the final Constitution.[33] If the Committee on Style decided on this arrangement by reasoning that any authority possessed by the states to make war would derogate from the power of the new Congress, the committee assumed something that the Convention had never explicitly resolved—namely, that commencing war is properly a legislative function. Like the earlier action by the Committee on Detail in assigning the power "to make war" to Congress, the Committee on Style's action suggests that there was no need for clarification by the Convention, since the notion was generally accepted.

Two points may detract from the soundness of this conclusion. First, the limitations on states placed in Article I included restrictions on the foreign relations power of the states.[34] This would imply, using a similar argument based on placement, that the delegates also viewed foreign relations as properly within the legislative sphere, despite the apparent fact that the President was given substantial power in the foreign relations area. Offsetting the contention that on this account the argument based on placement is unsound is the fact that the Convention did provide the Senate with a check on the President's treaty-making powers, a check that George Washington at first took especially seriously.[35] In addition, it gave Congress far

tive alone to *declare* war." 2 FARRAND, RECORDS, *supra* note 6, at 318 (emphasis added). Whether the precise wording in Madison's notes is an accurate rendition of Gerry's usage or whether it reflects Madison's imprint is immaterial. Either alternative supports the conclusion that "declare" did not have a very strict meaning in current American usage. This conclusion is elaborated at p. 685, pp. 693-96 *infra*.

32. *See* note 10 *supra*.

33. *See* 2 FARRAND, RECORDS, *supra* note 6, at 169, 187, 577, 597; U.S. CONST. art. I, § 10: "No State shall . . . grant letters of Marque and Reprisal . . . [nor,] without the Consent of Congress, . . . engage in War, unless actually invaded, or in such imminent Danger as will not admit of delay."

34. "No State shall enter into any Treaty, Alliance, or Confederation . . . [nor,] without the Consent of Congress, . . . enter into any Agreement or Compact with another State, or with a foreign Power . . . ." U.S. CONST. art. I, § 10. Neither here nor in the restrictions on state war-making did the final document contain any substantive changes from the report of the Committee on Style.

35. *See* R. HAYDEN, THE SENATE AND TREATIES 1789-1817, at 1-106 (1920). Hayden concludes that "Washington made treaties 'by and with the advice and consent' of the Senate in a sense and to an extent that no later President ever has." *Id.* at 103.

more power than the President in what contemporaries hoped and thought would be the dominant and proper form of America's relations with the world—commercial relations.[36] Similarly detracting from the force of the argument based on placement is the fact that we simply do not know much about the considerations which guided the Committee on Style.[37] It is quite possible that in placing the restrictions on state war-making, the committee and its chief draftsman, Gouveneur Morris of Pennsylvania, were not concerned with the implications just discussed. Yet the suspicion remains that something more than style prompted the committee's change, since the limitations could easily have been continued as one or more separate articles or else placed in Article IV, which contains other provisions relating to the states. In any event, placement of the state war-making restrictions may have contributed to a general impression that Congress was intended to be dominant in the field.

A final indirect clue to how Americans in the late 1780's understood war-making under the Constitution comes from the provision that states may not engage in war "unless actually invaded, or in such imminent Danger as will not admit of delay."[38] Although the Convention had given some attention to the issue of surprise attack during its one debate over the main war-making grant to Congress,[39] this is the only explicit reference to the matter in either the completed Constitution or the earlier drafts. While the provision may appear inconsequential to a late twentieth century observer, it undoubtedly had far more meaning in the 1780's when communications and transportation would not have allowed an immediate federal response to a truly surprise attack. In such a situation, the real problem would have been whether states might act prior to a national decision. The provision allowing state action may have seemed more consequential, too, both because state-versus-federal authority was a major issue in the general constitutional controversy of the day, and because the Constitution otherwise narrowed the sphere of permissible state activity in the war-making area. Yet the completed Constitution contained no indi-

36. *See, e.g.,* P. VARG, FOREIGN POLICIES OF THE FOUNDING FATHERS 1-69 (Penguin ed. 1970); G. STOURZH, BENJAMIN FRANKLIN AND AMERICAN FOREIGN POLICY 238-46 (2d ed. 1969); F. GILBERT, THE BEGINNINGS OF AMERICAN FOREIGN POLICY: TO THE FAREWELL ADDRESS *passim* (1965).

37. *See* Letter from James Madison to Jared Sparks, April 8, 1831, in 3 FARRAND, RECORDS, *supra* note 6, at 498, 499; C. ROSSITER, 1787: THE GRAND CONVENTION 224-30 (1966); M. FARRAND, THE FRAMING OF THE CONSTITUTION OF THE UNITED STATES 181-82 (1913).

38. U.S. CONST. art. I, § 10.

39. *See* pp. 675-77 *supra.*

cation that the states were to have exclusive responsibility to meet surprise attack.[40] In sum, the question of how an observer in the late 1780's would have interpreted the provision cannot be definitively answered, but its presence in the Constitution at least further suggests that Americans of that day need not have envisaged that the President as Commander in Chief would have an especially broad role in repelling sudden attack.

## B.  *The State Ratification Debates*

The state ratification debates, like the Philadelphia Convention, were little concerned with how the new government would initiate war. As an example, five of the eleven states which ratified the Constitution before the new government commenced operation offered amendments to it, but of the seventy-seven amendments thus proposed, only one—from New York—dealt with the power of Congress to declare war. Moreover, that proposal, to require a two-thirds vote in each house of Congress for a declaration of war, was designed to protect state or regional interests rather than to alter the balance of war-making power between Congress and the President. By contrast, twenty-eight of the proposed amendments concerned elections and procedures under the new government, fourteen dealt with individual rights and privileges, nine with taxation and finance, six with the raising and maintenance of armies and control of the militia (*i.e.,* the war-*supporting* function) and five each with commerce and the jurisdiction of courts.[41]

Contemporary newspaper, pamphlet, and state convention debates display a similar lack of attention to the allocation of the war-making power. Although, for example, the first North Carolina convention eventually found the Constitution objectionable enough not to ratify

---

40.  *See also* p. 687 *infra.*

41.  *See* Ames, *The Proposed Amendments to the Constitution of the United States During the First Century of Its History,* in 2 ANNUAL REPORT OF THE AMERICAN HISTORICAL ASSOCIATION FOR THE YEAR 1896, at 307-09 (1897). For the texts of the amendments, see 1 DEBATES IN THE SEVERAL STATE CONVENTIONS ON THE ADOPTION OF THE FEDERAL CONSTITUTION 322-31 (J. Elliot ed. 1888); 3 *id.* at 659-61 [hereinafter cited as ELLIOT, DEBATES]. The five states offering amendments in order of ratification, were Massachusetts, South Carolina, New Hampshire, Virginia, and New York. The amendments nearly proposed by Maryland, those declared by the first North Carolina convention to be necessary before that state ratified, and those proposed by Rhode Island in its tardy ratification also support the conclusions in the text. *See* Ames, *supra,* at 309-10; 1 ELLIOT, DEBATES 336-37; 2 *id.* at 550-53; 4 *id.* at 244-47. In several instances my classification of an amendment differs from that of Ames. In any event, only the New York amendment noted in the text and another New York amendment to prohibit the President as Commander in Chief from commanding the Armed Forces in person (both of which are in 1 *id.* at 330) bore on the external war-making powers of the proposed government.

it, the clause giving Congress the power "to declare War [and] grant Letters of Marque and Reprisal" was "read without any observation."[42] James Winthrop in Massachusetts and Richard Harry Lee in Virginia both objected to the increased centralization which characterized the proposed government, but both agreed that the power of war could, in Lee's words, "be lodged no where else, with any propriety, but in this [the central] government."[43] The explicit restrictions on state war-making in the Constitution received almost no attention, adverse or otherwise, in the state debates.[44] Though the authors of *The Federalist Papers* were not above beating a straw man in arguing their case,[45] in Number 41 Madison commented: "Is the power of declaring war necessary? No man will answer this question in the negative. It would be superfluous, therefore, to enter into a proof of the affirmative."[46] The existing Confederation government already held the power to make war. Its presence in the Constitution could hardly be a matter of controversy. In addition, the war-making power did not have the direct connection with such broader issues as state-versus-federal taxation and civilian-versus-military rule that the war-*supporting* powers had—the latter connection producing considerable debate.[47]

Yet, again like the Philadelphia Convention, the state debates offer revealing, albeit indirect and sometimes inferential, evidence about how contemporaries understood the Constitution's war-making clauses. Significantly, several comments strongly hint that Americans in 1787-88 thought the power to *declare* war assigned to the new Con-

---

42. 4 *id.* at 94.

43. ESSAYS ON THE CONSTITUTION OF THE UNITED STATES 1787-1788, at 98 (P. Ford ed. 1892) [hereinafter cited as FORD, ESSAYS]; PAMPHLETS ON THE CONSTITUTION OF THE UNITED STATES 1787-1788, at 300-01 (P. Ford ed. 1888) [hereinafter cited as FORD, PAMPHLETS].

44. "Almost," because Madison made cursory mention of them. *See* THE FEDERALIST No. 44 (J. Cooke ed. 1961) (except as noted, all citations herein to *The Federalist* are to the definitive Cooke edition).

45. Publius argued that opponents of the Constitution were proposing a series of regional confederations in place of a federal union, but the latest study of the ratification controversy in New York finds practically no talk of this sort among the state's antifederalists. *See* THE FEDERALIST Nos. 3, 5 (J. Jay), No. 13 (A. Hamilton); L. DEPAUW, THE ELEVENTH PILLAR: NEW YORK STATE AND THE FEDERAL CONSTITUTION 173 (1966).

46. THE FEDERALIST No. 41, at 269-70. I have sought to avoid over-reliance on *The Federalist* as a guide to the original understanding. As Professor McLaughlin remarked years ago, "[T]hese essays were probably of service in winning support of the Constitution; but the extent of that service we naturally cannot measure. For much immediate practical effect they were perhaps too learned, too free from passion. . . . *The Federalist* probably had more effect after the new government went into operation than in the days of uncertainty when the fate of the union seemed to hang in the balance . . . ." A. McLAUGHLIN, A CONSTITUTIONAL HISTORY OF THE UNITED STATES 208-09 (1935).

47. *See* Donahoe & Smelser, *supra* note 5, and the citations contained therein; A. EKIRCH, THE CIVILIAN AND THE MILITARY 27-31 (1956).

gress was practically identical with the old Congress' power of *determining on* war. After stating in *The Federalist Number 41* that it would be superfluous to examine whether the power of declaring war was necessary, Madison remarked: "The existing confederation establishes this power in the most ample form."[48] In the New York convention John Jay implicitly equated the power of the old Congress to determine on war with the power to declare war. Robert R. Livingston was more direct: "But, say the gentlemen, our present [Confederation] Congress have not the same powers [as the new Congress]. I answer, They have the very same . . . [including] the power of making war . . . ."[49] During the Pennsylvania convention James Wilson not only implicitly equated declaring war and entering war, but also explicitly foreclosed exercise of the power by the President acting alone:

> This [new] system will not hurry us into war; it is calculated to guard against it. It will not be in the power of a single man, or a single body of men, to involve us in such distress; for the important power of declaring war is vested in the legislature at large: this declaration must be made with the concurrence of the House of Representatives: from this circumstance we may draw a certain conclusion that nothing but our national interest can draw us into a war.[50]

Consistent with these comments indicating a broad view of the power of the new Congress, supporters of the Constitution described the position of the President as Commander in Chief in narrow terms. Most notably, Hamilton contended that the office involved only command in a military sense, with no policy role. The President's authority, he wrote,

> would be nominally the same with that of the King of Great Britain, but in substance much inferior to it. It would amount to nothing more than the supreme command and direction of the military and naval forces, as first general and admiral of the confederacy; while that of the British king extends to the *declaring* of war, and to the *raising* and *regulating* of fleets and armies; all which by the constitution under consideration would appertain to the Legislature.[51]

48.   THE FEDERALIST No. 41, at 270. Madison reiterated this view in the Virginia convention. *See* 3 ELLIOT, DEBATES, *supra* note 41, at 259.

49.   2 *id.* at 278, 284.

50.   *Id.* at 528.

51.   THE FEDERALIST No. 69, at 465.

James Iredell, who contended that "[o]ne of the great advantages attending a single Executive power is the degree of secrecy and dispatch with which on critical occasions such a power can act,"[52] nevertheless described the office of Commander in Chief in a constrained fashion strikingly similar to Hamilton's portrayal.[53]

In accordance with this view, the federalists ignored a clear opportunity to describe the office of Commander in Chief in broad terms. At issue was the fear harbored by contemporaries that joining the purse with the sword would promote tyranny. There was a check in this regard even in England, where, as Patrick Henry observed, "The King declares war; the House of Commons gives the means of carrying it on."[54] The Constitution, though, would join the two powers in the new central government or, according to a noteworthy variation of the argument, in Congress.[55] The antifederalists, of course, preferred to remedy the situation by giving the states greater control over taxation and the raising of armies—a solution obviously unacceptable to the Constitution's supporters, who, however, were not themselves united on the issue. Hamilton and Madison defended the proposed arrangements in part by claiming that the Constitution did separate the purse and the sword, with Congress holding the one and the President the other; but on balance they tended not to emphasize this division. Instead, to meet the antifederalist argument, Hamilton and Madison drew attention to the need for federal control of the purse and thereby avoided stressing a broad role for the President as Commander in Chief.[56] Other federalists, showing even more reluctance to take an expansive view of the executive's power in this area, produced a different and revealing defense. "Are the people of England more secure," asked John Marshall, "if the Commons have no voice in declaring war? or are we less secure by having the Senate [sic] joined with the President?"[57] Oliver Ellsworth posed a similar question:

> [D]oes it follow, because it is dangerous to give the power of the sword and purse to an hereditary prince, who is independent of the people, that therefore it is dangerous to give it to the Parlia-

52. FORD, PAMPHLETS, *supra* note 43, at 352.
53. *See* 4 ELLIOT, DEBATES, *supra* note 41, at 107-08. Iredell was not inconsistent in these two positions, for his quotation in this paragraph comes from a discussion of presidential conduct *during* war.
54. 3 *id.* at 172.
55. *See* 2 *id.* at 376-77; 3 *id.* at 172, 378-79. For the sources of the concern over the joining of purse and sword, see May, *supra* note 27; EKIRCH, *supra* note 47, at 3-24; L. SMITH, AMERICAN DEMOCRACY AND MILITARY POWER 20-24 (1951).
56. *See* 2 ELLIOT, DEBATES, *supra* note 41, at 348-51; 3 *id.* at 393-94.
57. *Id.* at 233.

ment—to Congress, which is your Parliament—to men appointed by yourselves, and dependent upon yourselves? This argument amounts to this: you must cut a man in two in the middle, to prevent his hurting himself.[58]

When judged against future developments, "Publius" may have been "understandably wrong . . . in giving a purely military cast to the President's authority as commander-in-chief,"[59] but the evidence indicates that his view in this respect accorded well with that of his contemporaries in the state debates.

Even so, federalist comments about the desirability of governmental energy, efficiency, and dispatch are sometimes taken to indicate a latitudinarian view of the executive war-making power.[60] Indeed, during the ratification controversy, the federalists contended that the proposed national government's enhanced ability to raise armies and build fleets would promote national security, in part by deterring surprise attack on the United States.[61] That this was a "winning issue" suggests contemporaries were probably not convinced that the constitutional provision allowing state response to surprise attack[62] was an adequate safeguard by itself, which in turn gives color to the conclusion that they looked to the President to act in cases of sudden attack. But during the ratification debates, the federalists never in fact defended the presidential office on grounds that its energy and dispatch were required in the *commencement* of war against a foreign enemy in emergency situations. What emerges instead is the conclusion that they were intent on defending the national government without regard to a particular branch.[63]

---

58. 2 *id.* at 195. *Cf.* comments of Edmund Randolph, who had refused to sign the Constitution in Philadelphia and eventually voted for ratification in Virginia only after considerable wavering. 3 *id.* at 201.

59. Rossiter, *Introduction* to THE FEDERALIST PAPERS xiii (C. Rossiter ed. 1961). *But cf.* C. ROSSITER, THE SUPREME COURT AND THE COMMANDER IN CHIEF 67 (1951).

60. *See, e.g.,* Rogers, *supra* note 28, at 1196 & n.10, in which, however, the key statement of the argument (the text associated with footnote 10) is simply not supported by a reading of the authorities cited in that footnote. On the discrepancy, *compare id., with* THE FEDERALIST Nos. 49 & 63 (both Madison, but misassigned by Rogers to Hamilton through use of a nineteenth century edition of *The Federalist*), Nos. 70-75 (Hamilton). Although certain of these numbers of *The Federalist* discuss the conduct and direction of war (Nos. 70, 72, 74) and the presence of secrecy and dispatch in the Constitution's treaty-making process (*i.e.,* including the Senate) (No. 75), none discusses the topics of the *commencement* of war or other hostilities against another nation, or the locus-of-power problem with respect to such commencement.

61. *See* Marks, *Foreign Affairs: A Winning Issue in the Campaign for Ratification of the United States Constitution,* 86 POL. SCI. Q. 444 (1971).

62. *See* pp. 682-83 *supra.*

63. *See* Marks, *supra* note 61, at 456-57, and the citations therein.

In a similar vein, although the federalists undoubtedly envisioned the Constitution as designed both to meet immediate problems and to comprehend future demands, they seem not to have discussed the allocation of power to commence war in the context of such a theory. Writing in *The Federalist Papers,* for example, Hamilton boldly noted, "The authorities essential to the care of the common defence . . . ought to exist without limitation: *Because it is impossible to foresee or define the extent and variety of national exigencies, or the correspondent extent & variety of the means which may be necessary to satisfy them."*[64] He subsequently reiterated the point: "There ought to be a capacity to provide for future contingencies, as they may happen; and as these are illimitable in their nature, so it is impossible safely to limit that capacity."[65] In the first instance, however, he was specifically concerned with the powers "to raise armies—to build and equip fleets—to prescribe rules for the government of both—to direct their operations—to provide for their support." In the second, he was considering the problem of providing an adequate revenue for the proposed government. In sum, although defending the notion of a flexible, expandable Constitution, these statements plainly refer to immediate problems other than that of commencing war. Moreover, Hamilton's broad purpose in both instances was to defend federal power, *once more without specification of branch,* against exceptions and reservations in favor of the states.[66]

Of course, their silence does not necessarily mean Americans in the late 1780's rejected the idea that the President had responsibility to respond to sudden attack. Particularly in view of the common expectation that George Washington would be the first President,[67] it is conceivable that they simply and tacitly assumed that there would be a presidential role in this regard. There was certainly sentiment present in the Federal Convention that "[t]he Executive shd. be able to repel . . . war" as Roger Sherman had explained.[68] What the preponderance of evidence suggests, however, is that *if* men of the day generally shared such an assumption, they still conceived of the President's war-making role in exceptionally narrow terms.

---

64. THE FEDERALIST No. 23, at 147.
65. *Id.* No. 34, at 211.
66. *See id.* Nos. 23, 34. *See generally id.,* Nos. 23-36 (A. Hamilton).
67. *See, e.g.,* 6 D. FREEMAN, GEORGE WASHINGTON: A BIOGRAPHY 117 & n.1 (1954).
68. *See* pp. 675-77 *supra.*

## C. The Theory and Practice of War and Reprisal

Americans of the revolutionary generation paid considerable attention to a broad range of European and especially English ideas and controversies involving law, government, and international affairs.[69] The works of Hugo Grotius,[70] Samuel Pufendorf,[71] Emmerich de Vattel,[72] and particularly Jean Jacques Burlamaqui[73] were widely read and quoted.[74] Books by Thomas Rutherforth[75] and Richard Lee[76] (whose work was largely a popularization of the views of Cornelius van Bynkershoek)[77] appear to have been less widely read but still received attention.[78] Many of the fairly well educated and cosmo-

---

69. See, e.g., B. BAILYN, THE IDEOLOGICAL ORIGINS OF THE AMERICAN REVOLUTION 22-54 (1967); 1 A. CHROUST, THE RISE OF THE LEGAL PROFESSION IN AMERICA: THE COLONIAL EXPERIENCE 33-37 (1965); T. COLBOURN, THE LAMP OF EXPERIENCE: WHIG HISTORY AND THE INTELLECTUAL ORIGINS OF THE AMERICAN REVOLUTION (1965); GILBERT, supra note 35; M. KRAUS, THE ATLANTIC CIVILIZATION: EIGHTEENTH CENTURY ORIGINS (1949); Bailyn, Political Experience and Enlightenment Ideas in Eighteenth-Century America, 67 AM. HIST. REV. 339 (1962).

70. H. GROTIUS, THE RIGHTS OF WAR AND PEACE (1625; J. Barbeyrac trans. 1738) (to facilitate reference, here and in the following notes I have indicated both an early edition and the edition I used) [hereinafter cited as GROTIUS].

71. S. PUFENDORF, ON THE LAW OF NATURE AND NATIONS (1688; C. & W. Oldfather transl. 1934) [hereinafter cited as PUFENDORF].

72. E. DE VATTEL, THE LAW OF NATIONS (1758; 2 vols. in 1, trans. from French 1759-60) [hereinafter cited as VATTEL].

73. J. BURLAMAQUI, THE PRINCIPLES OF NATURAL AND POLITIC LAW (2 vols., T. Nugent trans. 1752; 3rd ed. 1784) [hereinafter cited as BURLAMAQUI].

74. See BAILYN, supra note 69, at 27-29; P. HAMLIN, LEGAL EDUCATION IN COLONIAL NEW YORK 197-99 (1939); R. HARVEY, JEAN JACQUES BURLAMAQUI: A LIBERAL TRADITION IN AMERICAN CONSTITUTIONALISM 79-105 (1937); C. WARREN, A HISTORY OF THE AMERICAN BAR 163, 181-82 (1911); B. WRIGHT, AMERICAN INTERPRETATIONS OF NATURAL LAW 7-8, 44, 50-51, 58, 60, 67, 79, 89-90 (1931); Weinfeld, What Did the Framers of the Federal Constitution Mean by "Agreements and Compacts"?, 3 U. CHI. L. REV. 453, 458-59 (1936); cases cited in note 76 infra. BAILYN, supra, at 28, cautions, however, that the Americans' knowledge of these works was sometimes superficial; but this was probably less true of the lawyers who used them.

75. T. RUTHERFORTH, INSTITUTES OF NATURAL LAW (2 vols. 1754-56; Am. Ed. 1799) (also spelled Rutherford) [hereinafter cited as RUTHERFORTH].

76. R. LEE, A TREATISE OF CAPTURES IN WAR (1759) [hereinafter cited as LEE].

77. C. VAN BYNKERSHOEK, A TREATISE ON THE LAW OF WAR: BEING THE FIRST BOOK OF HIS QUAESTIONUM JURIS PUBLICI (1737; P. DuPonceau trans. 1810) [hereinafter cited as BYNKERSHOEK].

78. In November 1782 the Confederation Congress appointed a committee to compile a list of books to be purchased for its use. In January 1783 the committee reported a list of 309 books, only to have the budget-minded Congress decline to buy them. The list, which is indicative of recommended reading for the statesman of the 1780's and of which James Madison was probably the principal author, included not only Lee and Rutherforth but also Grotius, Pufendorf, Vattel, and Burlamaqui. Lee was in Thomas Jefferson's library for the period. Luther Martin read portions of Rutherforth to the Constitutional Convention (Farrand in the index to his RECORDS lists this as Samuel Rutherford, but Madison's and Yates' notes contain no indication of a first name, Thomas Rutherforth's name was spelled both Rutherford and Rutherforth, and the context would suggest it was Thomas Rutherforth's work which was being read); Hamilton quoted Rutherforth in Federalist 84; and James Wilson cited Rutherforth in his 1790-91 law lectures. Bynkershoek's Quaestionum appears to have been much less well-known, with the 1783 "statesman's" list merely giving the title of another book of his, followed by "with all his other

politan men to whom the deferential American society of that day looked for leadership[79] thus must have been familiar with these treatises. Among the topics the treatises considered were several which helped illuminate the war-making power of the new government being considered in 1787-88. Consequently, these works, in conjunction with historical trends visible in the late eighteenth century, offer further insight into the original understanding of war-making under the Constitution, and particularly the problem of undeclared war.

The writers in question discussed the necessity of declarations of war, but reached no consensus. Although none of them held a declaration necessary in a defensive war, Grotius, Pufendorf, and Vattel thought one required in a non-defensive war, if that war was to be legal with respect to the consequences attaching to it (for example, immunity from criminal prosecution for those waging it). Burlamaqui, however, was not entirely clear on the point. He stated that in a non-defensive war a declaration "ought" to be issued as a token of the respect which sovereigns should show each other, and so left unclear whether there was here a legal obligation or only some principle of comity. The remaining authors contended that a declaration was never legally necessary, but they agreed with Burlamaqui that it was desirable in that it put neutrals on notice to observe their obligations toward the belligerents and allowed the enemy one last chance to give satisfaction. Several of the writers stated that a declaration might be either absolute or conditional. The absolute declaration was a simple and unconditional announcement of war. The conditional declaration was essentially an ultimatum, that is, a demand that the enemy perform some act, coupled with a warning that otherwise war would follow as a matter of course with no further notice.[80]

---

works." Within several years of the Constitution's framing and ratification, Lee, Rutherforth, and Bynkershoek were all extensively cited by counsel in a number of prize cases heard by the U.S. Supreme Court. *See* L. Smith, The Library List of 1783, 1969, at 2-3, 123-25, 127, 129-30 (unpublished Ph.D. dissertation in the Honnold Library of the Claremont Colleges); 2 CATALOGUE OF THE LIBRARY OF THOMAS JEFFERSON 74 (E. Sowerby comp. 1953); 1 FARRAND, RECORDS, *supra* note 6, at 438, 440; 4 *id.* at 209; 1 THE WORKS OF JAMES WILSON 163, 192 (R. McCloskey ed. 1967); THE FEDERALIST No. 84; Glass v. The Sloop Betsey, 3 U.S. (3 Dall.) 6 (1794); Talbot v. Jansen, 3 U.S. (3 Dall.) 133 (1795); M'Donough v. Dannery and the Ship Mary Ford, 3 U.S. (3 Dall.) 188 (1796); Bas v. Tingy, 4 U.S. (4 Dall.) 37 (1800).

79. *See* Pole, *Historians and the Problem of Early American Democracy*, 67 AM. HIST. REV. 626 (1962). In saying that American society of the 1780's was deferential, I do not intend to become involved in the much-debated question of whether it was "democratic," politically or otherwise. Deference and democracy are not necessarily mutually exclusive.

80. *See* GROTIUS 57-58, 552-55; PUFENDORF 1294-95, 1307 (Pufendorf mainly refers his readers to Grotius on the subjects of declarations of war and reprisals); 2 VATTEL 3, 21-26; 2 BURLAMAQUI 269-72; BYNKERSHOEK 6-27; LEE 13-39; 1 RUTHERFORTH 451; 2 *id.* at 522-23, 549-53.

It must initially be recognized that when these authors spoke of declarations of war, they generally meant formal announcements to the enemy with proper ceremony, usually in his capital.[81] In point of fact, however, European states had not made such declarations for well over a century.[82] The common practice was to publish an announcement domestically and to inform the enemy, if at all, by means of a written communication such as a diplomatic note.[83] To cope with the disparity between theory and practice, Burlamaqui had sought to distinguish between a "declaration" and a "publication" of war.[84] But, with the possible exception of two American treaties concluded during the revolutionary and Confederation periods,[85] there appears to have been no acceptance of this distinction in the United States.[86] In view of these facts, it seems probable that a contemporary would have taken "declaration of war," as used in the treatises, to mean what nations had *customarily* done in "declaring" war during the preceding century or so.[87]

Once that equation was made, the treatises may well have affected the way those who debated the Constitution in 1787-88 understood the document. One intriguing possibility is that a person familiar with the literature on conditional declarations of war could easily have concluded that Congress might conditionally authorize the President

81.  *See* citations in note 80 *supra*.
82.  This may have been what Hamilton had in mind when he wrote that "the ceremony of a formal denunciation of war has of late fallen into disuse . . . ." THE FEDERALIST No. 25, at 161.
83.  *See* G. MARTENS, SUMMARY OF THE LAW OF NATIONS FOUNDED IN THE TREATIES AND CUSTOMS OF THE MODERN NATIONS OF EUROPE 274-75 (1788; W. Cobbett trans. 1795); 2 J. WESTLAKE, INTERNATIONAL LAW 20-21 (2d ed. 1913).
84.  2 BURLAMAQUI 272-73. Vattel hinted at the same distinction (*see* 2 VATTEL 25), but generally used "declaration" to include both formal denunciation to the enemy and publication.
85.  In their English (*i.e.*, American) texts, the Treaties of Amity and Commerce with France, Feb. 6, 1778, 8 Stat. 12 (1778), T.S. No. 83, and the Netherlands, Oct. 8, 1782, 8 Stat. 32 (1782), T.S. No. 249, used the phrase "proclamation of war" in articles (22 and 18, respectively) relating to the effects of an announcement of war *within* the announcing nation and used "declaration of war" elsewhere. The French and Dutch texts did not observe the distinction. *See* 8 Stat. 12, 32 (1778, 1782), 2 T.I.A.S., 2 TREATIES AND OTHER INTERNATIONAL ACTS OF THE UNITED STATES OF AMERICA 3, 59 (H. Miller ed. 1931). The original instructions of the Continental Congress regarding the French treaty (the so-called Treaty Plan of 1776) also included the distinction. *See* 5 JOURNALS OF THE CONTINENTAL CONGRESS 1774-1789, at 774 (1906). Other contemporary American treaties ignored it.
86.  *See, e.g.*, Treaty of Amity and Commerce with Sweden, April 3, 1783, 8 Stat. 60 (1783), T.S. No. 346, 2 TREATIES AND OTHER INTERNATIONAL ACTS, *supra* note 85, at 123; Convention of Peace, Commerce, and Navigation with France, Sept. 30, 1800, 8 Stat. 178 T.S. No. 85, 2 TREATIES AND OTHER INTERNATIONAL ACTS, *supra*, at 457. These used "declaration of war" in contexts similar to those in which the treaties cited in note 85 *supra* used "proclamation of war."
87.  That at least some writers in the general period did so is seen in J. KENT, DISSERTATIONS, BEING THE PRELIMINARY PART OF A COURSE OF LAW LECTURES 66 (1795); MARTENS, *supra* note 83, at 274-75.

to conduct a war if another nation refused to meet American demands.[88] More importantly, though, the treatise writers' contention that declarations were not needed in defensive wars raised the question of undeclared war, and this was a matter that the treatises considered at some length.

Grotius had argued that declared war was "perfect" war in the sense of being complete—that is, involving whole nations on each side. Accordingly, undeclared war was "imperfect." The latter occurred "where no perfect War is absolutely denounced; yet where a certain violent protection of our rights is necessary," with the violence consisting of state-authorized private reprisals directed at property held by the subjects of another nation.[89] The later commentators agreed that imperfect war and reprisals were closely related, if not identical, but they took a broader view of what constituted reprisals, holding that states using public forces might themselves make reprisals. Burlamaqui's view is representative:

> A perfect war is that which intirely interrupts the tranquillity of the state, and lays a foundation for all possible acts of hostility. An imperfect war, on the contrary, is that which does not intirely interrupt the peace, but only in certain particulars, the public tranquillity being in other respects undisturbed.
>
> . . . This last species of war is generally called reprisals, of the nature which we shall here give some account. By reprisals then we mean *that imperfect kind of war, or those acts of hostility which sovereigns exercise against each other, or, with their consent, their subjects, by seizing the persons or effects of the subjects of a foreign commonwealth, that refuseth to do us justice . . . .*[90]

---

88. It would probably be anachronistic to equate such a view with permissiveness toward *delegation of power* in the modern sense.

89. *See* GROTIUS 538-49 (the quotation is at 540). *See also id.* at 57-58.

90. 2 BURLAMAQUI 258. *See* LEE 20, 40-51; 2 RUTHERFORTH 485, 516, 522-23, 537-53; 1 VATTEL 249-51; 2 *id.* at 25-26 (but Vattel's equation of imperfect war with reprisals is less completely developed than that of the other writers) ; 1 M. HALE, HISTORIA PLACITORUM CORONAE: THE HISTORY OF THE PLEAS OF THE CROWN 162 (S. Emlyn ed. 1736). Hale's comments in this regard are particularly significant, because, compared with other English jurists prior to Blackstone, "Hale was a particularly well-known and attractive figure" to Americans. BAILYN, *supra* note 69, at 30 n.11. It is also noteworthy that language practically identical to that in the first paragraph of the quotation from Burlamaqui was included, but without citation in Miller v. The Ship Resolution, 2 U.S. (2 Dall.) 1, 21 (Ct. App. in Cases of Capture 1781). Suggestive of the broadened concept of reprisals is this comment from an American about twenty years after the framing and ratification of the Constitution:

Reprisals are either *general* or *special*.—They are *general* when a sovereign, who has or thinks that he has received an injury from another prince, issues orders to his military officers, and delivers commissions to his subjects to take the persons and property of the other nation, wherever the same may be found. It is, at present, the

There was consensus that imperfect war and state reprisals, commonly called general reprisals, could easily lead to perfect war.[91]

These opinions of the eighteenth century authors comported with two features of recent history, as seen in the late 1780's. First, hostilities without declarations of war were common during the period. Indeed, the undeclared hostilities in 1754-56 which marked the beginning of the Seven Years War between Britain and France, occurred mainly in America. During the War of the American Revolution, moreover, Britain and France never expressly declared war on each other, unless France's treaty with the United States may be so construed.[92] The second feature involved the practice of European states with respect to reprisals. From the twelfth through the seventeenth centuries, these states had regularized and legitimated private reprisals in time of peace by the sovereign's granting of letters of marque and reprisal to individuals who had specific claims against subjects of other states. Such letters authorized seizure of the property and sometimes the persons of the other state's subjects. When issued during war, the letters empowered individuals who were not members of public armed forces to take from the enemy and his subjects. Then, during the first half of the eighteenth century, the practice of granting letters of marque and reprisal for satisfaction of private claims during peace virtually disappeared. States, however, continued to make reprisals to press their own claims, using both public naval forces and private ships sailing under privateer commissions or letters of marque and reprisal. These state or general reprisals not uncommonly resulted in outright war. English history furnished several such examples which were undoubtedly familiar to those who debated the Constitution: the wars with the Netherlands in 1652 and 1664, with Spain in 1739, and with France in 1756 were all preceded by public naval reprisals.[93]

first step which is generally taken at the commencement of public war, and is considered as equivalent to a declaration of it.

*Special* reprisals are granted, in time of peace, to individuals who have suffered an injury from the subjects of another nation . . . .
BYNKERSHOEK 182 n. * (trans. note). *See generally* 7 J. MOORE, A DIGEST OF INTERNATIONAL LAW 119-30 (1906).

91. *See* 2 BURLAMAQUI 261; LEE 20, 45; 1 VATTEL 250. *See also* GROTIUS 57-60. While Rutherforth does not explicitly deal with the point, neither does he contradict the conclusions of the other writers on it.

92. *See* J. MAURICE, HOSTILITIES WITHOUT DECLARATION OF WAR 1700-1870, at 12-26 (1883); 3 R. PHILLIMORE, COMMENTARIES ON INTERNATIONAL LAW 110-15 (1857); 2 WESTLAKE, *supra* note 83, at 22-23. Phillimore contends (at 115) that France's announcement of her American treaties in 1778 had the effect of a declaration.

93. *See* A. HINDMARSH, FORCE IN PEACE: FORCE SHORT OF WAR IN INTERNATIONAL RELATIONS 43-56 (1933); 3 PHILLIMORE, *supra* note 92, at 108-09, 118; Maccoby, *Reprisals as a*

In sum, familiarity with Grotius and his successors and with then-recent history would have suggested to one in the late 1780's that undeclared war was no oddity and that the issuance of letters of marque and reprisal for satisfaction of private claims was outmoded. An American who was knowledgeable about these topics therefore faced the problem of explaining the Constitution's use of the wording "declare" and "letters of marque and reprisal." He might have done this in several ways, but certain interpretations would have made more sense to him than others.

In regard to the word "declare," he might have settled on any of a variety of possibilities:

(1) *America would restrict herself to fully declared wars.* However, this interpretation would have run counter to the prevalence of undeclared war in the eighteenth century, which would have been a matter of some importance to a generation that made a practice of deriving lessons from history.[94] In addition, it would have contradicted a goal of the new diplomacy with which Americans were so enamored, namely, that force should be restricted and the effects of war controlled.[95] Indeed, in 1785 provisions reflecting this goal had been included in the Treaty of Amity and Commerce between the United States and Prussia.[96] But fully declared wars were less likely to be limited in their material dimensions.

(2) *The provision giving Congress the power to declare war was merely a formality. In practice, America would avoid war by limiting her relations with the world to trade and commerce.*[97] Many Americans undoubtedly hoped the United States could remain aloof from war, but a generation which avidly followed European affairs, which had confronted European activities in America and Barbary depredations in the Mediterranean during the 1780's,[98] and which contained some

---

*Measure of Redress Short of War,* 2 CAMB. L.J. 60, 60-67 (1924); 1 LETTERS AND PAPERS RELATING TO THE FIRST DUTCH WAR 1651-54, at 301-02 (S. Gardiner ed. 1899); 2 THE ROYAL NAVY: A HISTORY 422-25 (W. Clowes ed. 1898); 3 *id.* at 51-52, 266-67; 1 J. CORBETT, ENGLAND IN THE SEVEN YEARS WAR 83 (2d ed. 1918).

94. *See* Adair, *"Experience Must Be Our Only Guide": History, Democratic Theory, and the United States Constitution* in THE REINTERPRETATION OF EARLY AMERICAN HISTORY 129 (R. Billington ed. 1966); COLBOURN, *supra* note 69 *passim* and especially 4-6, 185.

95. *See generally* works cited in note 36 *supra.*

96. Treaty of Amity and Commerce with Prussia, Sept. 10, 1785. 8 Stat. 84, 94-96, T.S. No. 292, 2 TREATIES AND OTHER INTERNATIONAL ACTS, *supra* note 85, at 162, 178-79. This provision followed the instructions of Congress. *See* 26 JOURNALS OF THE CONTINENTAL CONGRESS 1774-1789, at 358-59 (1928).

97. *See* T. PAINE, COMMON SENSE AND OTHER POLITICAL WRITINGS 22-23 (Liberal Arts Press ed. 1953). *See generally* the works cited in note 36 *supra.*

98. *See, e.g.,* T. BAILEY, A DIPLOMATIC HISTORY OF THE AMERICAN PEOPLE 52-65 (8th ed. 1969).

eminent realists[99] would hardly have counted on the complete disappearance of war.

(3) *Congress' power to declare war was to be interpreted strictly; as a result the Constitution left the waging of undeclared war unaccounted for. Authority over it must have been either unvested or perhaps somewhat deviously vested in the executive branch.* It seems unlikely, however, that an observer in 1787-88 would have concluded that the Constitution would leave such an important power unvested. Certainly no one commented on the omission. It also seems improbable that a contemporary would have accepted the alternative that the power was lodged with the executive. Contemporaries spoke and wrote in narrow terms of the President's sole martial role as Commander in Chief.[100]

(4) *As used in the Constitution, "declare" had a broader meaning than it did in the treatises and international practice. It meant "commence."* This interpretation, unlike the first three possibilities I have discussed, would probably have seemed plausible to someone in 1787-88, because contemporary statements suggested that the power of the new Congress to commence war would be at least as broad as that of the Confederation Congress.[101] This deviation from international usage would have seemed proper, as well, since the Constitution involved domestic arrangements.

(5) *Whatever the scope of the term "declare" as used in the Constitution, any war-commencing power not covered by it was vested in Congress by virtue of that body's control of reprisals.* This possibility, which is at once distinguishable from, yet compatible with interpretation (4), would also have seemed plausible because the treatises closely assimilated imperfect war and reprisals.

The last interpretation suggests the need for more detailed consideration of how an observer, acquainted with the treatises and the relevant history, would have interpreted the Constitution's grant to Congress of power to issue letters of marque and reprisal. Here, too, there are several possibilities:

(1) *The phrase "letters of marque and reprisal" was used in the Constitution in a technical sense and was intended to give Congress authority to grant such letters to private individuals in both peace and*

99. *See, e.g.,* R. HOFSTADTER, THE AMERICAN POLITICAL TRADITION AND THE MEN WHO MADE IT 3-17 (1954).

100. *See* pp. 679-80, 685-87 *supra.*

101. *See* p. 685 *supra.*

*war.* This interpretation, however, ignores the fact that special letters of marque and reprisal, for the peacetime satisfaction of private claims, had fallen into disuse and general reprisals had become the rule. As a necessary and proper concomitant of the powers to commence and conduct war, letters could be issued in war whether or not the Constitution mentioned them. In fact, if granted during a declared war as a military measure, there could be little objection to their being granted by the President, who, as Commander in Chief, was charged with the conduct of war. Under this interpretation, then, the phrase would have been archaic and redundant in intent.

(2) *The power was merely a careless and meaningless carry-over from the Articles of Confederation.*[102] A contemporary would have noted, though, that the Convention had given new attention to the problem of letters of marque and reprisal. The states, which could issue such letters in time of war under the Articles, were altogether prohibited from issuing them under the Constitution.[103] Thus it would have seemed unlikely that the retention of the power was meaningless.

(3) *The phrase most importantly conferred on Congress power over general reprisals outside the context of declared war.* While the wording in question admittedly spoke broadly of granting "letters of marque and reprisal," issuance of the *special* variety had passed out of fashion in peace time. The clause thus could easily have been interpreted as serving as a kind of shorthand for vesting in Congress the power of *general* reprisal outside the context of declared war.[104] For someone in the late 1780's, this interpretation, far more than the first two, would have given the phrase meaning and would have been consistent with history and the treatises. Once accepted, this

102. Of course, what we know about the history of the clause in the Philadelphia Convention (*see* p. 679 *supra*) was generally unknown in 1787-88.
103. ARTS. OF CONFED. art. VI; U.S. CONST. art. I, § 10.
104. The making [of] a reprisal on a nation is a very serious thing. Remonstrance and refusal of satisfaction ought to precede; and when reprisal follows, it is considered an act of war, and never failed to produce it in the case of a nation able to make war; besides, if the case were important and ripe for that step, Congress must be called upon to make it; *the right of reprisal being expressly lodged with them by the Constitution, and not with the Executive.* Opinion of Thomas Jefferson, Sec'y of State, May 16, 1793, *quoted in* 7 J. MOORE, INT'L LAW DIGEST 123 (1906) (emphasis added). On the matter of the wording regarding reprisals serving as shorthand, *cf.* L. LEVY, ORIGINS OF THE FIFTH AMENDMENT 430 (1968): "[C]onstitution-makers, in that day at least, did not regard themselves as framers of detailed codes. To them the statement of a bare principle was sufficient . . . ." The same point might also be made in connection with the equation of "to declare war" and "to commence war."

interpretation in turn would have given increased plausibility to the view that Congress possessed whatever war-commencing power was not covered by the phrase "to declare war."

In short, while one cannot pretend that the matter is beyond all doubt, it seems plain that knowledge of the theory and practice of war and reprisal would have helped convince a late-eighteenth century American that the Constitution vested Congress with control over the commencement of war, whether declared or undeclared.

## D.  *English Influences*

If, as the preceding discussion indicates, Americans in 1787-88 saw Congress as having the dominant voice in the commencement of war, they were breaking with English constitutional theory under which war-making was a Crown prerogative.[105] This is not surprising, for the scope of executive power in America narrowed considerably after independence. In the late 1780's, of course, the trend toward weaker executives was reversed. The reversal, however, resulted from domestic considerations—stronger and more independent leadership seemed necessary to insure liberty and stability *within* the country— and it had little or no connection with external problems of war-making.[106] Departure from English theory concerning the initiation of war was therefore consistent with broader developments in post-independence America.

Although the English theoretical model lost favor in America, prior English experience and thought were still quite relevant to the evolving American view of war-making. Even in England itself, practice did not coincide with theory. In the seventeenth century, Sir Matthew Hale had written: "The power of making war or peace . . . in England is lodged singly in the King, *tho it ever succeeds best when done by parliamentary advice.*"[107] In 1775 another student of the English constitution, Jean de Lolme, commented that the King

> has the prerogative of commanding armies, and equipping fleets —but without the concurrence of his Parliament he cannot maintain them . . . . He can declare war—but without his Parliament

---

105.  1 W. BLACKSTONE, COMMENTARIES *249-50.
106.  *See* G. WOOD, THE CREATION OF THE AMERICAN REPUBLIC 1776-1787 *passim* and especially at 393-564 (1969).
107.  1 HALE, *supra* note 90, at 159 (emphasis added).

it is impossible for him to carry it on. In a word, the Royal prerogative, destitute as it is of the power of imposing taxes, is like a vast body, which cannot of itself accomplish its motions . . . .[108]

Hale and de Lolme, of course, were not directly considering the theoretical locus of the war-making power in England. They asserted only that parliamentary control over the war-supporting function provided practical checks on the King's prerogative. On the basis of such analyses, however, the English system did not present a polar contrast to the evolving American notions of congressional control over warmaking. Rather, it contained elements which, on the one hand, were imitated in the American Constitution with its provisions for a clear legislative monopoly of the war-supporting function, and, on the other, suggested *tendencies* toward legislative control of the war-making function itself.[109]

Other English sources which Americans probably noted would have led them to similar conclusions about the desirability of a diminished executive role in war-making. The English commonwealthmen of the seventeenth and eighteenth centuries, whose views were especially appealing in America, admittedly did not emphasize the problem of warmaking as such. Their major concern regarding military matters was that standing armies posed a domestic threat. Their outlook nonetheless generally favored a diminished executive role.[110] The same was true of the broader group of Whig writers who proved so popular in revolutionary America.[111] In 1774, James Burgh went so far as to imply that Parliament should have a substantial and independent voice not only in the supporting of war, but also in its commencement, conduct,

108. J. DE LOLME, THE CONSTITUTION OF ENGLAND 48 (1775). *See generally id.* at 47-62.
109. Of course, the development of cabinet government in England blocked the growth of an independent parliamentary check on the executive. The cabinet, with or without the Crown's connivance, came both to exercise executive functions and to manage parliament. But to the extent that they were aware of these tendencies toward cabinet government, eighteenth century Americans deprecated them as manifestations of the corruption—that is, the improper use of influence—which they thought was so generally menacing to a proper balance in government and hence to liberty. *See* B. BAILYN, THE ORIGINS OF AMERICAN POLITICS 14-58 (1968); M. THOMSON, A CONSTITUTIONAL HISTORY OF ENGLAND 1642-1801, at 353-84 (1938).
110. *See* C. ROBBINS, THE EIGHTEENTH CENTURY COMMONWEALTHMAN (1959). But at least one of the commonwealthmen, Henry Neville (1620-1694), was explicit in his desire to "take from the king the power of making war and peace . . . ." *Id.* at 39. Far from a coherent group, the English Commonwealthmen or Real Whigs were intellectual descendants of the Puritan revolutionaries of the 1640's and 1650's. They had republican and non-conformist tendencies and were enamored of natural right theories, freedom of thought, limited government, and parliamentary reform. By the end of the eighteenth century, they had merged into the broader stream of English radicalism. *See id. passim.*
111. *See* COLBOURN, *supra* note 69, *passim.*

and conclusion.[112] John Locke, writing some ninety years earlier, had separated what he called the federative power, which included war-making, from the ordinary executive power. He saw the same authority as properly exercising both powers, but his separation of them for purposes of analysis may have aided in establishing a basis for their later actual separation.[113] At any rate, Thomas Rutherforth was explicit in his opinion in the 1750's that war-making was a legislative function because it had to rest on the "common understanding" of the nation.[114] All considered, it is not surprising to find that at the Philadelphia Convention James Madison and James Wilson characterized war-making as properly legislative.[115]

## III. Conclusion: The Original Understanding in Theory and Early Practice

Although the change from "make" to "declare" in the clause empowering Congress "to declare War" was open to several interpretations among the members of the Philadelphia Convention, there is enough evidence to allow some cautious generalization about the original understanding concerning war-making. The Confederation Congress exercised both legislative and executive functions; the new Congress would not. Nevertheless, specific remarks equating the war-making powers of the two Congresses, together with other comments about war-making being a legislative function, suggest that contemporaries thought the power of the proposed legislature to commence war would be as broad as that of the Confederation Congress. Since the old Congress held blanket power to "determine" on war, and since undeclared war was hardly unknown in fact and theory in the late eighteenth century, it therefore seems a reasonable conclusion that the new Congress' power "to declare War" was not understood in a narrow technical sense but rather as meaning the power to commence war, whether declared or not. To the extent that the power was more narrowly interpreted, however, the new Congress' control over letters

---

112. See 1 J. BURGH, POLITICAL DISQUISITIONS: OR AN ENQUIRY INTO PUBLIC ERRORS, DEFECTS, AND ABUSES . . . 371 (1774). See also id. at 193-95, 414-45.

113. See J. LOCKE, THE SECOND TREATISE OF GOVERNMENT 83-84 (Liberal Arts Press ed. 1952).

114. 2 RUTHERFORTH 64-67.

115. See p. 679 supra. See also 1 THE WORKS OF JAMES WILSON, supra note 78, at 433-34 (Wilson's 1790-91 law lectures).

of marque and reprisal must have suggested to contemporaries that it would still control "imperfect"—that is, undeclared—war. Otherwise, the provision involving such letters would have seemed practically meaningless in view of the status of reprisals by the late 1780's. Taken together, then, the grants to Congress of power over the declaration of war and issuance of letters of marque and reprisal likely convinced contemporaries even further that the new Congress would have nearly complete authority over the commencement of war. Reinforcing the same conclusion is the fact that English experience, and particularly the English Whigs to whom Americans paid considerable attention, offered hints about the desirability of legislative supremacy in this area. It remains possible that the President as Commander in Chief was *tacitly* accorded the initiative to meet sudden attacks on the United States. In their public statements, however, contemporaries assigned him the restricted military role of conducting war once it had begun. In any event, the Constitution explicitly authorized the states to act in the face of surprise attack.

The consensus which existed in 1787-88 on the war-making issue did not last, and Hamilton as "Pacificus" began lodging reservations as early as 1793. It is significant, though, that his position appears not to have been an especially persuasive one even to his fellow Federalists,[116] let alone to the Republicans. In 1795, James Kent contended that in the United States "war only can be commenced by an act or resolution of Congress," indicating that he equated "declare" with "commence."[117] The undeclared hostilities with France during John Adams' administration were authorized by Congress,[118] and despite debates over the extent to which specific legislative measures provided a basis in law for action against the French, the notion that authorization must come from Congress was seldom challenged.[119] At one point, when the Republicans in the House of Representatives proposed to modify and weaken legislation authorizing American naval reprisals against the French, an exasperated Federalist protested that preservation of American rights required the legislation to be passed unamended, because "the President has not the power to act in the

116. That is, members of the Federalist Party, not to be confused with the lower case "f" federalists of the ratification controversy in 1787-1788.
117. KENT, *supra* note 87, at 83.
118. See A. DeCONDE, THE QUASI WAR: THE POLITICS AND DIPLOMACY OF THE UNDECLARED WAR WITH FRANCE 1797-1801 *passim* and especially at 89-98 (1966).
119. See, e.g., THE DEBATES AND PROCEEDINGS IN THE CONGRESS OF THE UNITED STATES, 5th Cong., 2d Sess. cols. 1440-1522, 1783, 1798-1812, 1815-35 (1798).

[present] case. Congress only [can] authorize reprisals."[120] Retreating from the position he had earlier taken as "Pacificus," Alexander Hamilton held that the Constitution narrowly constrained the President's actions. Adams might authorize the repelling of actual attacks, but he could not make reprisals without congressional approval.[121]

In two maritime prize cases arising out of the Quasi-War, the Supreme Court of the United States evinced similar views. The seriatim opinions in *Bas v. Tingy* (1800)[122] stressed that whether hostilities were declared or undeclared, they still constituted war—being perfect and general war in the one case, and imperfect and limited war in the other. None of the Justices explicitly stated that only Congress might wage imperfect war, but that conclusion was clearly implicit in their remarks.[123] In *Talbot v. Seeman* (1801), a case involving the salvage rights of Silas Talbot and his officers and crew, John Marshall, the newly appointed Chief Justice, forthrightly stated: "The whole powers of war being, by the Constitution of the United States, vested in congress, the acts of that body alone be resorted to as our guides in the enquiry." He further argued that such powers included the authorization of limited hostilities, which he, too, obviously regarded as war, for he explicitly referred to the recent conflict with France as "war."[124]

Evidence from the years immediately following ratification of the Constitution thus corroborates the conclusion that Americans originally understood Congress to have at least a coordinate, and probably the dominant, role in initiating all but the most obviously defensive wars, whether declared or not. Since that time, and especially during the twentieth century, the presidential role in war-making has nevertheless become dominant. Somewhat in the manner of Teddy Roosevelt and the Panama Canal, while Congress and others have debated, Presi-

---

120. *Id.*, col. 1828 (Representative James A. Bayard).
121. 1 NAVAL DOCUMENTS RELATED TO THE QUASI-WAR BETWEEN THE UNITED STATES AND FRANCE 75-76 (1935) (letter from Hamilton to Sec'y of War J. McHenry, May 17, 1798). *See also id.* at 78 (letter from Sec'y of War J. McHenry to Captain R. Dale, USN, May 22, 1798). On the general conclusions contained in this paragraph, *see* Russell, *supra* note 6, at 65-100 (for the Federalist period 1789-1801) and 102-46 (for the Republican period, 1801-1815).
122. 4 U.S. (4 Dall.) 37 (1800).
123. *See, e.g.*:
Congress is empowered to declare a general war, or congress may wage a limited war; limited in place, in objects, and in time. If a general war is declared, its extent and operations are only restricted and regulated by the *jus belli*, forming a branch of the law of nations; but if a partial [war] is waged, its extent and operation depend on our municipal laws [as passed by Congress].
*Id.* at 43 (Chase, J.).
124. Talbot v. Seeman, 5 U.S. (1 Cranch) 1, 28, 32 (1801). On the conflict's status as war, *see* 1 OP. ATT'Y GEN. 84 (1798) (C. Lee to Sec'y of State).

dents have acted. How long this situation will continue is difficult to predict, though the constitutionality of recent practice is an intriguing question which promises to attract further national attention.[125] Whether the original understanding properly concludes the issue undeniably involves questions quite different from those I have here discussed. Still, paying it some heed is surely consonant with a devotion to constitutionalism.

125.  On April 13, 1972, the Senate passed a bill to regulate undeclared war. *See* S. 2956, 92d Cong., 1st Sess. (1971) ("A bill to make rules governing the use of the Armed Forces of the United States in the absence of a declaration of war by the Congress"). N.Y. Times, Apr. 14, 1972, at 1, col. 6 (city ed.). Though the bill passed 68-16, resistance from both the House and the Executive is likely. *See* Bickel, *The Need for a War-Powers Bill*, New Republic, Jan. 22, 1972, at 17. For earlier bills and resolutions of this sort, see, *e.g.*, S. 731, 92d Cong., 1st Sess. (1971); S. J. Res. 95, 92d Cong., 1st Sess. (1971); and nineteen House bills and resolutions reprinted in *1970 Hearings on Congress, the President, and the War Powers, supra* note 4, at 435-76.

# War-Making by the President

## RAOUL BERGER

### I. Introduction

To a nation wracked by interminable, undeclared war in Vietnam—described by an informed English observer as "the greatest tragedy that has befallen the United States since the Civil War"[1]—the presidential power to commit it to such luckless adventures is of surpassing importance. Thirty-odd years of recurrent international crises, exploding against a background of superpower hostility such as had long been unknown to the American people, have fed swollen executive claims to war-making power, often with the acquiescence if not encouragement of Congress.[2]

It is not my purpose to conduct yet another inquest into the propriety of the presidential steps that led to our involvement in Vietnam, or whether the war received congressional sanction.[3] Instead the focus of discussion will be whether the original constitutional distribution of powers can be restored by statute in order to insure congressional participation in war-making policy. A long overdue step in that direction was recently taken by the Javits-Spong War Powers Bill, approved by a vote of 68 to 16 in the Senate,[4] which seeks to lay down rules governing the use of armed force in the absence of a declaration of war by Congress. Roughly speaking, the Bill would authorize the President in the absence of a declaration of war by Congress only "to repel an armed attack upon the United States" or upon its armed forces "located outside the United States," and to forestall the "direct and imminent threat of such an attack," such use of the armed forces not to extend beyond thirty days without congressional authorization.[5]

---

† A.B. 1932, University of Cincinnati; J.D. 1935, Northwestern University; LL.M. 1938, Harvard University. Charles Warren Senior Fellow in American Legal History, Harvard Law School.

[1] Buchan, *Questions About Vietnam*, in 2 THE VIETNAM WAR AND INTERNATIONAL LAW 35 (R. Falk ed. 1969). Buchan is Director of the Institute for Strategic Studies, London.

[2] *See* text accompanying notes 218-19 *infra*.

[3] *See* Reveley, *Presidential War-Making: Constitutional Prerogative or Usurpation?*, 55 VA. L. REV. 1243 (1969); Rostow, *Great Cases Make Bad Law: The War Powers Act*, 50 TEXAS L. REV. 833 (1972); Wormuth, *The Nixon Theory of the War Powers: A Critique*, 60 CALIF. L. REV. 623 (1972); Wormuth, *The Vietnam War: The President versus the Constitution*, in 2 THE VIETNAM WAR AND INTERNATIONAL LAW 711 (R. Falk ed. 1969). Note, *Congress, the President, and the Power to Commit Forces to Combat*, 81 HARV. L. REV. 1771 (1968) [hereinafter cited as *Power to Commit Forces*].

[4] N.Y. Times, Apr. 14, 1972, at 1, col. 3.

[5] S. 2956, 92d Cong., 2d Sess. §§ 3, 5 (1972).

Secretary of State William Rogers warns that the Bill "would violate the Constitution," that it departs from an allocation of powers which is "basic to our system."[6] Rogers' statement may be heavily discounted as self-serving, just as Justice Jackson dismissed his own "self-serving press statements" as Attorney General when they were paraded before the Court.[7] The case stands differently with Professor Eugene V. Rostow's elaborate attack on the Javits Bill.[8] Although he was one of the executants of the presidential policy, his high repute as a scholar entitles his apologia to careful consideration.

For Professor Rostow, the Javits Bill constitutes a retreat into the "dangerous realm of constitutional myth,"[9] a fundamental "change [in] the constitutional relationship between President and Congress,"[10] a "serious attack on the Constitution"[11] which "would destroy the Presidency" and "abolish the principle of the separation of powers," no less.[12] Congress is portrayed as "drawing all power within its impetuous vortex";[13] but that hardly squares with the fact that the Supreme Court, in rejecting President Truman's seizure of the steel plants in reliance on alleged war powers, "refus[ed]," in the words of Justice Jackson, "further to aggrandize the presidential office . . . at the expense of Congress."[14]

In truth, the Constitution *withheld* from the President the powers claimed for him by Professor Rostow. He makes a mechanical obeisance to "the document, viewed against the background of [the Framers'] words,"[15] but spends precious little time on the governing constitutional provisions and none at all on the explanations of those provisions by the Framers, preferring copious generalities about constitutional purposes. His real reliance is on "182 years of opinion and practice"[16]—the "gloss of life"[17]—whereby successive Presidents have *altered* the original constitutional distribution of powers, reallocating

---

[6] N.Y. Times, Mar. 30, 1972, at 10, col. 1.

[7] Youngstown Sheet & Tube Co. v. Sawyer, 343 U.S. 579, 647 (1952) (concurring opinion).

[8] Rostow, *supra* note 3.

[9] *Id.* 900.

[10] *Id.* 834.

[11] *Id.* 836.

[12] *Id.* 897, 900.

[13] *Id.* 833. *See id.* 835, 840.

[14] Youngstown Sheet & Tube Co. v. Sawyer, 343 U.S. 579, 654 (1952) (concurring opinion).

[15] Rostow, *supra* note 3, at 844. This he does "because the animating principles of their project—democratic responsibility, the theory of checks and balances in the exercise of shared powers, and civilian control of the military—have retained their vitality, and must continue to do so if we hope to survive as a free and democratic society." *Id.*

[16] *Id.* 886.

[17] *Id.* 843.

to the President powers exclusively conferred on Congress. On this, issue must be joined, bearing in mind that Professor Rostow inveighs against the Javits Bill because "it would permit Congress to amend the Constitution without the inconvenience of consulting the people."[18] Amen! No amendment without "consulting the people." But the rule cuts both ways; it is not open to the President to amend the Constitution by *his* "practices."

Professor Rostow recognized that there is a "real crisis of our foreign policy," that

> there is no harmony between [the presidential] pattern of action, and widespread, and now perhaps prevailing views as to what . . . foreign policy ought to be.
> The tension between public opinion and the behavior of government [read President] is much too great for safety. That tension has already destroyed the careers of two Presidents, Truman and Johnson; divided the nation . . . .[19]

A crisis of such dimensions, exhibiting such tensions and divisions, entitles one to question the wisdom of a presidential claim single-handedly to commit the nation to such disastrous policies. But I must eschew analysis in terms of wisdom, a matter endlessly debated, and canvassed afresh by Professor Rostow. Let it be assumed that wisdom counsels solo presidential power to meet terrifying contemporary contingencies,[20] and the core question remains: was such power conferred by the Constitution. "The peculiar circumstances of the moment," said Marshall, "may render a measure more or less wise, but cannot render it more or less constitutional."[21]

The cardinal index of constitutionality is the Constitution itself, not what others have said about it. In the words of the great Erskine, "a statute is ever present to speak for itself";[22] so too, we must look at the Constitution with eyes unclouded by the opinions of others. On so great a constitutional issue, nothing less suffices than the most searching analysis of the immediately relevant text and what the

---

18 *Id.* 835.

19 *Id.* 899. The Korean War, Rostow states, "became unpopular and was a decisive factor both in Truman's decision not to seek a second term and in the elections of 1952." *Id.* 871.

20 "Of course Congress should participate," says Professor Rostow, "in decisions involving major and sustained hostilities, through processes of continuous consultation . . . . That is now the pattern of our politics, and of our constitutional usage." *Id.* 842. It is precisely because there is no such pattern that the Javits Bill went through the Senate. There was no consultation prior to the invasion of Cambodia, note 249 *infra,* or the mining of Haiphong, although the latter might have precipitated a fearful confrontation. The "pattern" was rolling dice out of sight of Congress.

21 JOHN MARSHALL's DEFENSE OF *McCulloch v. Maryland* 190-91 (G. Gunther ed. 1969), discussed in detail at text accompanying notes 150-56 *infra.*

22 Trial of Horne Tooke, 25 How. St. Tr. 1, 268 (1794).

Framers *stated* they meant to accomplish by it. Professor Rostow too quickly cheapens the understanding of the Framers in reliance on Justice Jackson's statement in *Youngstown Sheet & Tube Co. v. Sawyer*[23] that it "must be divined from materials almost as enigmatic as the dreams Joseph was called upon to interpret for Pharaoh."[24] Notwithstanding that rhetorical flourish, Jackson experienced no difficulty in finding the intention clear enough to lead him emphatically to reject inflated presidential claims to war powers.[25] So that the reader may readily determine for himself where the truth lies, I shall set forth the sources. The historical records will appear far removed from the "enigmatic dreams of a Pharaoh," from "constitutional myth."

Preliminarily a few words should be said about the historical background—upon which Professor Rostow lays great stress—from which the Constitution emerged. Among the colonists the prevalent belief was that " 'the executive magistracy' was the natural enemy, the legislative assembly the natural friend of liberty . . . ."[26] This derived first from the fact that the House of Commons had been the cradle of liberty in the seventeenth century struggle against Stuart absolutism,[27] a period that greatly influenced colonial thinking.[28] Then too, colonial assemblies were elected by the colonists themselves whereas governors and judges were placed over them by the Crown.[29] Little wonder that in most of the early state constitutions, the governor's office was "reduced almost to the dimensions of a symbol," with all roots in the royal prerogative cut.[30]

---

[23] 343 U.S. 579, 634 (1952) (concurring opinion).

[24] Rostow, *supra* note 3, at 849.

[25] One after another Jackson dismissed claims based on the executive power, the commander in chief clause, and inherent power. Youngstown Sheet & Tube Co. v. Sawyer, 343 U.S. 579, 640-44, 646-52 (1952) (concurring opinion). Jackson refused to "amend" the work of the Framers. *Id.* at 650.

[26] E. CORWIN, THE PRESIDENT: OFFICE AND POWERS 4 (3d ed. 1948).

[27] G. TREVELYAN, ILLUSTRATED HISTORY OF ENGLAND 391, 401 (1956).

[28] B. BAILYN, THE IDEOLOGICAL ORIGINS OF THE AMERICAN REVOLUTION viii, xi, 34-35, 53 (1967). "The 'founding fathers' owed their mental sustenance much more largely to seventeenth-century England than to the England with which they were themselves contemporary." E. CORWIN, THE TWILIGHT OF THE SUPREME COURT: A HISTORY OF OUR CONSTITUTIONAL THEORY 102 (1934).

[29] 1 J. WILSON, WORKS 292-93 (R. McCloskey ed. 1967). Wilson felt constrained in 1791 to admonish the people that it was "high time" to regard executive officers and judges equally with the legislature as representatives of the people. *Id.* 293.

[30] E. CORWIN, *supra* note 26, at 4-5. For example, the Virginia Constitution of 1776 provided that the Governor shall "exercise the executive powers of government, according to the laws of this Commonwealth and shall not, under any pretence, exercise any power or prerogative, by virtue of any law, statute or custom of England." 2 B. POORE, THE FEDERAL AND STATE CONSTITUTIONS, COLONIAL CHARTERS, AND OTHER ORGANIC LAWS OF THE UNITED STATES 1910-11 (1878). Section 33 of the Maryland Constitution makes similar provision. 1 *id.* 825. Corwin justifiably concludes that under the pre-1787 state constitutions, " 'Executive power' . . . was cut off entirely from the resources of the common law and of English constitutional usage." E. CORWIN, *supra* note 26, at 5. In the Federal Convention James Wilson stated that he "did not consider the Prerogatives

When the colonists assembled in the Continental Congress and adopted the Articles of Confederation, they dispensed with an executive altogether;[31] and in appointing George Washington commander in chief, they made sure, as Professor Rostow remarks, that he was to be "its creature . . . in every respect."[32] Before long the excesses of the new state legislatures led to disenchantment,[33] and the Founders began to think of a genuinely tri-partite structure of government. It was against this background that Madison, in a quotation invoked by Professor Rostow,[34] said that the founders of the several states "seem never for a moment to have turned their eyes from the danger to liberty" from a king to recollect "the danger from legislative usurpations, which, by assembling all power in the same hands, must lead to the same tyranny as is threatened by executive usurpations."[35] This testifies to the need for a strengthened executive coupled with a lively fear of monarchy and of potential executive tyranny.[36] Even so, Madison stated in a subsequent issue of *The Federalist* that "[i]n republican government, the legislative authority necessarily predominates,"[37] as the Constitution clearly designed in the distribution of the war powers.

To say, as does Professor Rostow, that the Framers intended to go beyond the "Executive" of the Continental Congress[38] is to leave open the scope of his function. Here once more the Framers did not leave us in doubt. Roger Sherman "considered the Executive magistracy as nothing more than an institution for carrying the will of the

---

of the British Monarch as a proper guide in defining the Executive powers. Some of these prerogatives were of a Legislative nature. Among others that of war & peace . . . ." 1 RECORDS OF THE FEDERAL CONVENTION OF 1787, at 65-66 (M. Farrand ed. 1911) [hereinafter cited as RECORDS].

[31] Professor Rostow's reference to the "weakness of the Executive under the Articles of Confederation . . . ," Rostow, *supra* note 3, at 844, must therefore be taken to mean the absence of the executive.

[32] Rostow, *supra* note 3, at 840. The instructions given Washington recited that "you are . . . punctually to observe and follow such orders and directions from time to time as you shall receive from this or a future Congress . . . ." *Id.* 840 n.14.

[33] For a collection of authorities, see R. BERGER, CONGRESS V. THE SUPREME COURT 10-11 (1969).

[34] Rostow, *supra* note 3, at 833.

[35] THE FEDERALIST No. 48, at 322 (Mod. Lib. ed. 1937) (J. Madison).

[36] 1 RECORDS, *supra* note 30, at 66, 83, 90, 96, 101, 113, 119, 152, 425; 2 *id.* 35-36, 101, 278, 513, 632, 640. In Virginia Patrick Henry said, "Your President may easily become a king." 3 J. ELLIOT, DEBATES IN THE SEVERAL STATE CONVENTIONS ON THE ADOPTION OF THE FEDERAL CONSTITUTION 58 (2d ed. 1836). *See id.* 60; 4 *id.* 311. *See also* notes 42, 72, 84 *infra*; text accompanying note 52 *infra*.

[37] THE FEDERALIST No. 51, at 338 (Mod. Lib. ed. 1937) (J. Madison). *See also* Madison's explanation of the limited nature of the President's war-making power, notes 75-76 *infra*. Justice Brandeis referred to the deep-seated conviction of the English and American people that they "must look to representative assemblies for the protection of their liberties." Myers v. United States, 272 U.S. 52, 294-95 (1926) (dissenting opinion).

[38] Note 31 *supra*.

Legislature into effect . . . ."[39] Although James Wilson was the "leader of the 'strong executive' party,"[40] the "only powers he conceived strictly executive were those of executing the laws and appointing officers . . . ."[41] Madison emphasized that preliminarily it was essential *"to fix the extent* of the Executive authority . . . as *certain* powers were in their nature executive, and *must be given* to that departmt. . . . ."[42] He added that the executive powers "shd. be confined and defined,"[43] as they were in the subsequent sparse enumeration of executive powers.

The explanation of executive power to the Ratifying Convention reaffirmed these views. The executive powers were "precisely those of the governors," said James Bowdoin in Massachusetts, as did James Iredell in North Carolina.[44] "What are his powers?" said Governor Randolph in Virginia: "To see the laws executed. Every executive in America has that power."[45] In Pennsylvania James Wilson, in order to defend the President against the charge that he "will be the tool of the Senate," pointed first to the fact that he was to be commander in chief, and then added, "[t]here is another power of no small magnitude intrusted to this officer. 'He shall take care that the laws be faithfully executed.' "[46] Iredell likewise stressed that the "office of superintending the execution of the laws . . . is . . . of the utmost importance;" and this was likewise the view expressed in North Carolina by Archibald Maclaine.[47] Charles Pinckney, a Framer, said in South Carolina, "His duties, will be, to attend to the execution of the acts of Congress";[48] and to ward off fears of the danger of the executive. Pinckney stressed that the President cannot "take a single step in his government, without [Senate] advice."[49] Another Framer, William Davie, told the North Carolina convention that "jealousy of executive power which has shown itself so strongly in all American governments, would not admit" of lodging the treaty powers in the President alone.[50]

---

[39] 1 RECORDS, *supra* note 30, at 65.

[40] E. CORWIN, *supra* note 26, at 11.

[41] 1 RECORDS, *supra* note 30, at 66.

[42] *Id.* 66-67 (emphasis added).

[43] King's notes recorded: "Mad: agrees wth. Wilson in his difinition [*sic*] of executive powers . . . [they] do not include the Rights of war & peace & c. but the powers shd. be confined and defined—if large we shall have the Evils of elective Monarchies . . . ." *Id.* 70.

[44] 2 J. ELLIOT, *supra* note 36, at 128; 4 *id.* 107. For the governors' powers, see note 30 *supra*.

[45] 3 J. ELLIOT, *supra* note 36, at 201.

[46] 2 *id.* 512-13 (emphasis in original).

[47] 4 *id.* 106, 136.

[48] 3 RECORDS, *supra* note 30, at 111.

[49] 4 J. ELLIOT, *supra* note 36, at 258.

[50] *Id.* 120. "Fear of a return of Executive authority like that exercised by the Royal

When Professor Rostow relies on *The Federalist* and Madison's notes for a "pattern of shared constitutional authority in this vital area,"[51] he fails to take into account Hamilton's emphasis on how small the presidential share was to be. "Calculating upon the aversion of the people to monarchy," Hamilton wrote, opponents of the Constitution "have endeavored to enlist all their jealousies and apprehensions in opposition to the intended President . . . as the full-grown progeny, of that detested parent."[52] To counter such fears he launched upon a minute analysis of each of the enumerated executive powers; in particular the commander in chief was merely to be the "first General."[53] Nothing was "to be feared" from an executive "with the confined authorities" of the President.[54] After going through the short list he stated, "The *only remaining powers* of the executive are comprehended in giving information to Congress of the state of the Union . . . ."[55]

On the specifics of the commander in chief function, Hamilton took pains to assure the people that the President's authority would be "much inferior" to that of the British King, the bulk of whose powers "would appertain to the legislature."[56] Professor Rostow's statement that the "British monarch was much more in their [the Framers'] minds as a point of departure than the revolutionary commander"[57] is therefore correct, but in a very different sense than he intends—the prerogatives of that monarch were the very thing that the Framers meant at all costs to avoid.[58]

---

Governors or by the King had been ever present in the States from the beginning of the Revolution." C. WARREN, THE MAKING OF THE CONSTITUTION 173 (1947). Warren wrote:
> It is probable that Madison and Randolph in preparing the Virginia Plan had in mind the conception of Executive power which Thomas Jefferson had set forth in his Draft of a Fundamental Constitution for Virginia in 1783, as follows: "By Executive power, we mean no reference to those powers exercised under our former government by the Crown as its prerogative, nor that these shall be the standard of what may or may not be deemed the rightful powers of the Governor. We give them those powers only, which are necessary to execute the laws."

*Id.* 177.

[51] Rostow, *supra* note 3, at 847. For Madison, see text accompanying notes 75-76 *infra*.

[52] THE FEDERALIST No. 67, at 436 (Mod. Lib. ed. 1937) (A. Hamilton).

[53] THE FEDERALIST No. 69, at 448 (Mod. Lib. ed. 1937) (A. Hamilton), quoted at text accompanying note 71 *infra*.

[54] THE FEDERALIST No. 71, at 468 (Mod. Lib. ed. 1937) (A. Hamilton).

[55] THE FEDERALIST No. 77, at 501 (Mod. Lib. ed. 1937) (A. Hamilton) (emphasis added). In the First Congress, Thomas Hartley commented that the President's "powers, taken together, are not very numerous." 1 ANNALS OF CONG. 482 (1789). (2d ed. 1836, print bearing running-title "History of Congress")

[56] *See* text accompanying note 71 *infra*.

[57] Rostow, *supra* note 3, at 841.

[58] See note 30 *supra*. Bagehot said that the Framers "shrank from placing sovereign powers anywhere. They feared it would generate tyranny; George III had been a tyrant to them, and come what might, they would not make a George III." W. BAGEHOT, THE ENGLISH CONSTITUTION 218 (1964). "From the American Revolution we inherited a

## II. The Intention of the Framers

### A. *The Commander in Chief Clause*

The commander in chief as conceived by the Framers bears slight resemblance to the role played by the President today, when, as Justice Jackson said, the clause is invoked for the "power to do anything, anywhere, that can be done with an army or navy."[59] From history the Framers had learned of the dangers of entrusting control of the military establishment to a single man who could commit the nation to war.[60] Let a single quotation suffice. James Wilson, the "most learned and profound legal scholar of his generation," second only to Madison as an architect of the Constitution,[61] who almost single-handedly carried the Constitution through to adoption by the Pennsylvania convention, told that convention that the power to "declare" war was lodged in Congress as a guard against being "hurried" into war, so that no "single man [can] . . . involve us in such distress."[62] It was for this reason that the vast bulk of the war powers was conferred on Congress, leaving to the President a very meager role. Wilson's summary of the constitutional provisions graphically illustrates the glaring disproportion between the allocations to Congress and President:

> The power of declaring war, *and the other powers naturally connected with it*, are vested in congress. To provide and maintain a navy—to make rules for its government—to grant letters of marque and reprisal—to make rules concerning captures—to raise and support armies—to establish rules for their regulation—to provide for organizing . . . the militia, and for calling them forth in the service of the Union—all these are powers naturally connected with the power of declaring war. All these powers, therefore, are vested in Congress.[63]

Congress was also empowered to "provide for the common defense" and to make appropriations for the foregoing purposes. Since all the powers "naturally connected" with that of declaring war are vested in Congress, it follows, so far as war-making goes, that they

---

stubborn distrust of committing power to the executive." J.W. Hurst, The Legitimacy of the Business Corporation 40 (1970).

[59] Youngstown Sheet & Tube Co. v. Sawyer, 343 U.S. 579, 642 (1952) (Jackson, J., concurring).

[60] Text accompanying notes 75-76, 84-85 *infra.*

[61] McCloskey, *Introduction* to J. Wilson, *supra* note 29, at 2.

[62] 2 J. Elliot, *supra* note 36, at 528.

[63] 1 J. Wilson, *supra* note 29, at 433 (emphasis added). The several powers are set out in U.S. Const. art. I, § 8.

are not to be exercised by the President.[64] The President, said Wilson, "is to take care that the laws be faithfully executed; he is commander in chief of the army and navy"; like the Saxon "first executive magistrate . . . he ha[s] authority to lead the army."[65] How narrowly the function was conceived may be gathered from the *instruction* by the Continental Congress to George Washington in 1783 to arrange for the take-over from the British of occupied ports and for the liberation of prisoners.[66]

Virtually every early state constitution made the Governor "captain-general and commander-in-chief" to act under the laws of the State—which is to say, subject to governance by the legislature.[67] In the Convention, the New Jersey Plan proposed by William Paterson provided that the Executive was "to direct all military operations" but not "on any occasion [to] take command of the troops, so as personally to conduct any enterprise as General," that is, in the field.[68] In the plan Hamilton submitted to the Convention, he proposed that the Executive should "have the direction of war when authorized or begun," implying it was not for him to "begin" a war.[69] The words "commander in chief" were adopted without explanation; but it is a fair deduction that Hamilton's explanation in *The Federalist* expressed

---

[64] *See* note 93 *infra.*

[65] 1 J. WILSON, *supra* note 29, at 440. In the Virginia ratification convention George Mason "admitted the propriety of his [the President's] being commander-in-chief, so far as to give orders and have a general superintendency; but he thought it would be dangerous to let him command in person." 3 J. ELLIOT, *supra* note 36, at 496. *See also* the New Jersey Plan, discussed at text accompanying note 67 *infra.*

[66] 24 JOURNALS OF THE CONTINENTAL CONGRESS 1774-1789, at 242-43 (1937). Distrust of executive power, of executive war-making propensities, see text accompanying notes 29-30, 36, 50, 52-56 *supra*, makes it altogether unlikely that the Framers meant to enlarge those powers beyond the conduct of operations once war was commenced by Congress or enemy invasion, as Hamilton confirms. *See* text accompanying notes 69, 71, 144 *infra*, and note 92 *infra.*

[67] Article VII of the Massachusetts Constitution of 1780 provides that the Governor shall be "commander-in-chief of the army and navy" with power to "repel, resist, expel" those who attempt the invasion of the Commonwealth, and entrusts him "with all these and other powers incident to the offices of captain-general and commander-in-chief, and admiral, to be exercised agreeably to the rules and regulations of the constitution and the laws of the land and not otherwise." 1 B. POORE, *supra* note 30, at 965-66. For similar provisions adopted by other states see *id.* 275 (Delaware), and 2 *id.* 1288 (New Hampshire).

Hamilton stated in THE FEDERALIST No. 69, at 449 (Mod. Lib. ed. 1937): "[T]he constitutions of several of the States expressly declare their governors to be commanders-in-chief . . . and it may well be a question, whether those of New Hampshire and Massachusetts in particular, do not, in this instance, confer larger powers upon their respective governors, than could be claimed by a President of the United States."

[68] 1 RECORDS, *supra* note 30, at 244. The Virginia Plan contained no express provision on the subject, incorporating "the Legislative Rights vested in Congress by the Confederation." *Id.* 21. In North Carolina, Robert Miller demanded that "Congress ought to have power to direct the motions of the army," 4 J. ELLIOT, *supra* note 36, at 114.

[69] 1 RECORDS, *supra* note 30, at 292.

the general intention.[70] As commander in chief, said Hamilton, the President's authority would be "much inferior" to that of the British King: "It would amount to nothing more than the supreme command and direction of the military and naval forces, as first General and admiral . . . while that of the British king extends to the *declaring* of war and to the *raising* and *regulating* of fleets and armies,—all which, by the Constitution . . . would appertain to the legislature."[71] Hamilton thus deflated this and other executive functions in order to rebut attacks upon the Constitution by those who, "[c]alculating upon the aversion of the people to monarchy" portrayed the President "as the full-grown progeny of that detested parent."[72]

Corwin commented on Hamilton's explanation of the commander role: "this appears to mean that in any war . . . the President will be top general and top admiral of the forces provided by Congress, so that no one can be put over him or be authorized to give him orders in the direction of the said forces. But otherwise he will have no powers that any high military or naval commander who was not also president might not have."[73] So it appeared to Chief Justice Taney as late as 1850.[74] The severely limited role of the President was a studied response to what Madison called "an axiom that the executive is the department of power most distinguished by its propensity to war: hence it is the practice of all states, in proportion as they are free, to disarm this propensity of its influence."[75] The object, in Wilson's

---

[70] Corwin said of *The Federalist Number 78*: "It cannot be reasonably doubted that Hamilton was here, as at other points, endeavoring to reproduce the matured conclusions of the Convention itself." E. CORWIN, THE DOCTRINE OF JUDICIAL REVIEW 44 (1914). For example, Richard Spaight, a delegate to the Federal Convention, said in the North Carolina ratification convention that he "was surprised that any objection should be made to giving the *command* of the *army* to one man; that it was very well known that the direction of an army could not be properly exercised by a numerous body of men." 4 J. ELLIOT, *supra* note 36, at 114-15 (emphasis added). Lofgren concludes that "the evidence indicates" that the Hamiltonian view with respect to "'the President's authority as commander-in-chief' . . . accorded well with that of his contemporaries in the state debates." Lofgren, *War-Making Under the Constitution: The Original Understanding*, 81 YALE L.J. 672, 687 (1972).

[71] THE FEDERALIST No. 69, at 448 (Mod. Lib. ed. 1937) (A. Hamilton).

[72] THE FEDERALIST No. 67, at 436 (Mod. Lib. ed. 1937) (A. Hamilton). Referring to the proposal to vest appointive power in the President, John Rutledge said in the Federal Convention, "The people will think we are leaning too much towards Monarchy." 1 RECORDS, *supra* note 30, at 119.

[73] E. CORWIN, *supra* note 26, at 276.

[74] Fleming v. Page, 50 U.S. (9 How.) 603, 615 (1850). Until 1850, said Corwin, the commander in chief clause "was still . . . the forgotten clause of the constitution." E. CORWIN, TOTAL WAR AND THE CONSTITUTION 15 (1947). So it appeared to President Buchanan, as is disclosed by his message of December, 1859: "after Congress shall have declared war and provided the force necessary to carry it on, the President, as Commander in Chief . . . can alone employ this force in making war against the enemy." 5 MESSAGES AND PAPERS OF THE PRESIDENTS 1789-1897, at 569 (J. Richardson ed. 1907) [hereinafter cited as MESSAGES]. "Without the authority of Congress," Buchanan continued, "the President can not fire a hostile gun in any case except to repel the attacks of an enemy." *Id.* 570.

[75] 6 J. MADISON, *Letters of Helvidius*, in WRITINGS 138, 174 (G. Hunt ed. 1906).

homelier phrase, was to prevent a "single man" from "hurrying" us into war. "Those who are to *conduct a war*," said Madison, "cannot in the nature of things, be proper or safe judges, whether *a war ought to be commenced, continued or concluded*. They are barred from the latter function by a great principle in free government, analogous to that which separates the sword from the purse, or the power of executing from the power of enacting laws."[76] All appeals to the power of the President as commander in chief must therefore proceed from the incontrovertible fact that the Framers designed the role merely for command of the army as "first General."

B. *"Congress shall have power . . . to declare war."*

Under the Articles of Confederation the Continental Congress had the "sole and exclusive right and power of determining on peace and war."[77] That practice influenced the Framers; thirty-five of the fifty-five Framers had been members of the Continental Congress. No reference was made to the war-making power in either the Virginia or New Jersey Plans; the former endowed Congress with the "Legislative Rights of," the latter with all powers vested in, the Continental Congress.[78] Early in the Convention Madison agreed with Wilson that "executive powers . . . do not include the Rights of war and peace . . . ."[79] The draft submitted by the Committee on Detail provided that the legislature should "make war,"[80] lifting this as well as other powers specifically granted to Congress "bodily from the old Articles of Confederation."[81] It was this provision that became the subject of debate.

Charles Pinckney opposed "vesting this power in the legislature. Its proceedings were too slow";[82] he preferred the Senate, as Hamilton had proposed in his own plan.[83] Pierce Butler, on the other hand, "was for vesting the power in the President"; but Roger Sherman considered that the Committee's provision "stood very well. The Executive shd. be able to repel and not to commence war."[84] Eldridge Gerry was

---

[76] *Id.* 148. See also text accompanying note 138 *infra.*

[77] H. COMMAGER, DOCUMENTS OF AMERICAN HISTORY 113 (7th ed. 1963).

[78] 1 RECORDS, *supra* note 30, at 21, 243.

[79] Note 42 *supra.* Article 26 of the South Carolina Constitution of 1776 carefully spelled out that the governor "and commander-in-chief shall have no power to make war or peace, or enter into any final treaty, without the consent of the general assembly . . . ." 2 B. POORE, *supra* note 30, at 1619. *See also* J. WILSON, *supra* note 29, to the effect that the war power is legislative.

[80] 2 RECORDS, *supra* note 30, at 182.

[81] C. WARREN, THE MAKING OF THE CONSTITUTION 389 (1928).

[82] 2 RECORDS, *supra* note 30, at 318.

[83] 1 *id.* 292.

[84] 2 *id.* 318. Butler later explained to the South Carolina legislature that the grant of the power to "make war" to the President "was objected to, as throwing into his

astonished to hear "a motion to empower the Executive alone to declare war." George Mason also "was agst. giving the power of war to the Executive, because not (safely) to be trusted with it . . . . He was for clogging rather than facilitating war."[85] The fact that no motion was made to substitute the President for Congress and that the power was left in Congress justifies the conclusion that presidential "commencement" of a war or his power "alone to declare a war" found no favor.

Any power to which the President may lay claim, apart from what he enjoys as commander in chief, derives from a joint motion by Madison and Gerry to substitute *declare* for *make* war "leaving to the Executive the power to repel sudden attacks."[86] The textual change from "make" to "declare" was approved; explanation of the change was furnished by Rufus King: " 'make war' might be understood to 'conduct' it [war] which was an executive function,"[87] a function reserved to the commander in chief. But in that role the President was merely to act as "first General" of the army.[88]

The shift from "make" to "declare" has elicited varied explanations;[89] for example, Professor Ratner states that the "declare" clause recognized "the war-making authority of the President, implied by his role as executive and commander-in-chief and by

___

hands the influence of a monarch, having an opportunity of involving his country in a war . . . ." 4 J. ELLIOT, *supra* note 36, at 263.

[85] 2 RECORDS, *supra* note 30, at 318-19.

[86] *Id.* 318. The State Department distorts this interchange: "[I]t was suggested that the Senate might be a better repository. Madison and Gerry then moved to substitute 'to declare war' for 'to make war,' 'leaving to the Executive the power to repel sudden attacks.' It was objected that this might make it too easy for the Executive to involve the nation in war, but the motion carried with but one dissenting vote." OFFICE OF THE LEGAL ADVISOR, U.S. DEP'T OF STATE, THE LEGALITY OF THE UNITED STATES PARTICIPATION IN THE DEFENSE OF VIET NAM, *reprinted in* 75 YALE L.J. 1085, 1101 (1966) [hereinafter cited as LEGAL ADVISOR'S MEMO]. From this one might infer that the Convention intended to "make it too easy for the Executive to involve the nation in war"; but in fact *no* objection was made to the Madison-Gerry motion, which merely gave effect to the Sherman-Mason-Gerry objections to the grant of war-making power to the President, except to "repel sudden attacks." *See* Wormuth, *The Vietnam War: The President versus the Constitution,* in 2 THE VIETNAM WAR AND INTERNATIONAL LAW 711, 713-17 (R. Falk ed. 1969).

[87] 2 RECORDS, *supra* note 30, at 319. Story explains that the role of commander in chief gives the President "command . . . of the public force . . . to resist foreign invasion . . . and the direction of war." 2 J. STORY, COMMENTARIES ON THE CONSTITUTION OF THE UNITED STATES § 1491 (5th ed. 1905).

[88] *Cf.* Ratner, *The Coordinated Warmaking Power—Legislative, Executive and Judicial Roles,* 44 S. CAL. L. REV. 461, 462 (1971). Clinton Rossiter concludes that "the Court has refused to speak about the powers of the President as Commander in Chief in any but the most guarded terms. . . . The breath-taking estimates of their war powers announced and acted upon by Lincoln and Roosevelt have earned no blessing under the hands of the judiciary." C. ROSSITER, THE SUPREME COURT AND THE COMMANDER IN CHIEF 4-5 (1951). Since he wrote, the Court gave such claims a decided setback in Youngstown Sheet & Tube Co. v. Sawyer, 343 U.S. 579 (1952).

[89] *E.g., Power to Commit Forces, supra* note 3, at 1773; S. REP. No. 797, 90th Cong., 1st Sess. 8 (1967).

congressional power to declare, but not make, war."[90] No war-making power was conferred by the commander in chief clause; and Madison and Wilson agreed that "executive powers . . . do not include the rights of war and peace."[91] The grant to Congress of *all* the powers "naturally connected" with the "declare" power (except the command function) excludes any war-making power from the President's "role as executive." Only in a very limited sense—command of the armed forces plus authority to repel sudden attacks—can one accurately refer to a presidential war-making power.[92] Pretty plainly, when Madison and Gerry proposed to *leave* to the President power "to repel sudden attacks" they reflected Sherman's view that the "Executive should be able to repel and not to commence war." This is the true measure of the presidential power. Certainly Gerry did not mean to repudiate his rejection of the proposition that the Executive could "alone declare war," still less propel the nation into undeclared war.[93] It is we who have replaced their blunt realism with semantic speculation.

Viewed against repudiation of royal prerogative, no more can be distilled from the Madison-Gerry remark than a limited *grant* to the President of power to repel attack when, as the very terms "sudden attack" imply, there could be no time to consult with Congress. Despite the fact, therefore, that the replaced "make" is a verbal component of "war-making," the shift to "declare" did not remove the great bulk of the war-making powers from Congress; it merely removed the power to *conduct* a war once declared, as Rufus King explained.[94] If the war-making power did not remain in Congress, the exception for

---

[90] Ratner, *supra* note 88, at 467.

[91] Text accompanying note 79 *supra*.

[92] In the Convention Hamilton stated that the "Executive ought to have but little power." He proposed that the Senate should "have the sole power of declaring war" and that the Executive should "have the direction of war when authorized or begun." 1 RECORDS, *supra* note 30, at 290, 292. Be it remembered that the Massachusetts Constitution, which expressly authorized the commander in chief to "repel, resist, [and] expel" those who attempted invasion of the Commonwealth (thereby implying that this was not an inherent power of the commander), made the exercise of that power subject "to the laws of the land and not otherwise." Note 67 *supra*. And Hamilton explained that the powers of the Massachusetts commander were "larger . . . than could be claimed by the President." *Id.*

[93] In the North Carolina convention, James Iredell stated, "The President has not the power of declaring war by his own authority . . . . Those powers are vested in other hands. The power of declaring war is expressly given to Congress . . . ." 4 J. ELLIOT, *supra* note 36, at 107-08. Charles Pinckney said in South Carolina that "the President's powers did not permit him to declare war." *Id.* 287. These men did not contemplate that he could independently *make* war, leaving to Congress the empty formality of then "declaring" war.

[94] After adoption of the Madison-Gerry motion, Pierce Butler "moved to give the Legislature power of peace, as they were to have that of war." 2 RECORDS, *supra* note 30, at 319. His motion was adopted without objection, suggesting an understanding that the power of making war, except for "conduct" of the war, remained in Congress.

presidential power "to repel sudden attacks" was superfluous.[95] Even the power to repel attacks was to some extent left subject to congressional control for, at a time when standing armies were much feared, the Constitution left it to Congress "[t]o provide for calling forth the militia to . . . repel invasions."[96]

In using "declare war," Professor Rostow argues, the Framers had in mind the sharp distinction drawn by the law of nations between the law of war and law of peace. Under the latter nations enjoyed a right of "self-help," which was "subsumed under the inherent and sovereign right of self-defense." Rostow is critical of Hamilton's suggestion that the President was allocated only the power to exert "self-help in time of peace" on the ground that "[t]he constitutional pattern is, and should be, more complex than any such formula."[97] But where is the evidence that such was the understanding of the Framers? However broad the *national* power of "self-help" may be, the fact, as Justice Frankfurter pointed out, "that power exists in the Government does not vest it in the President."[98] Then too, the very careful distribution of powers by the Framers precludes any inference that they intended to grant to the President any incidents of the "nation's" war power under international law beyond the power to "repel sudden attacks" on the United States.[99] Professor Rostow would substitute

---

[95] Speaking of the need to "provide for the common defence," which by article I, § 8(1) is vested in Congress, Wilson said, "Defence presupposes an attack . . . . We all know . . . the instruments necessary for defence when such an attack is made," and then went on to list the powers conferred upon Congress. 1 J. WILSON, *supra* note 29, at 433. This precludes an inference that the power to "repel sudden attack" was vested in the President ab initio, but rather as a result of ratification of the Madison-Gerry motion. So too, Chancellor R. R. Livingston, in the New York ratification convention, met objections that the Continental Congress did not have "the same powers" as the proposed Congress with the reply, "They have the very same . . . [including] the [exclusive] power of making war." 2 J. ELLIOT, *supra* note 36, at 278.

[96] *Cf.* Statement of Justice Jackson in Youngstown Sheet & Tube Co. v. Sawyer, 343 U.S. 579, 644 (1952) (concurring opinion). Governor Randolph, a Framer, told the Virginia ratification convention that "With respect to a standing army, I believe there was not a member in the federal convention who did not feel indignation at such an institution . . . . In order to . . . exclude the dangers of a standing army, the general defense . . . is left to the militia . . . ." 3 RECORDS, *supra* note 30, at 319. *Cf.* 2 *id.* 330 (statements of L. Martin and E. Gerry). *See also id.* 326 (statement of G. Mason).

[97] Rostow, *supra* note 3, at 850-51.

[98] Youngstown Sheet & Tube Co. v. Sawyer, 343 U.S. 579, 604 (1952) (concurring opinion).

[99] As a delegate to the Federal Convention, Hamilton may be thought to have had a grasp of the Convention's understanding of "international law." In his attack on Jefferson's restrained response to attacks by Tripoli pirates, Hamilton stated, "it belongs to Congress only, *to go to war*. But when a foreign nation declares or openly and avowedly *makes war* upon the United States . . . any declaration on the part of Congress is . . . unnecessary." 8 A. HAMILTON, *Letter No. 1 of "Lucius Crassus,"* in WORKS 249-50 (H. Lodge ed. 1904) (emphasis added).

"What the preponderance of the evidence suggests," states Lofgren, *supra* note 70, at 688, is that the Founders "conceived of the President's war-making role in exceptionally narrow terms." He concludes that "Congress' power 'to declare War' was not understood in a narrow technical sense but rather as meaning the power to commence war, whether declared or not." *Id.* 699.

unsupported speculations for concrete evidence such as Sherman's remark that the Executive should not be able to "commence war," Mason's statement that the Executive was "not safely to be trusted" with the war power, and Wilson's explanation that the power to "declare" war was lodged in Congress to prevent a "single man" from "hurrying" us into war—a "propensity" underscored by Madison.

Professor Alexander Bickel suggests that the " 'sudden attack' concept of the framers . . . denotes a power to act in emergencies in order to guard against the threat of attack, as well as against the attack itself, when the threat arises, for example, in such circumstances as those of the Cuban missile crisis of 1962."[100] Gerry and Madison, however, spoke of a "power to repel sudden attacks," which connotes actual, not threatened attack; and there is reason to believe that a restricted connotation should be given to their remark. Imminent danger of attack had been expressly provided for in the antecedent Articles of Confederation. In conferring the exclusive war power upon the Continental Congress, article IX made an exception for article VI, which provided, "[n]o state shall engage in any war without the consent of the united states in congress assembled, unless such state be actually invaded by enemies, or shall have received certain advice of a resolution being formed by some nation of Indians to invade such state, and the danger is so imminent as not to admit of a delay, till the united states in congress assembled can be consulted . . . ."[101] Thus resistance to invasion was limited to invasion of "such state"; it did not extend to invasion of even a contiguous sister state in the "league of friendship." Georgia was not authorized to resist the invasion of New York, let alone of Canada. And danger of imminent attack permitted reaction only if there was not time for consultation with Congress. We are apt to think that devastating surprise is peculiar to our times, forgetting that the Founders had lived through surprise massacres in frontier forts and settlements and well knew such havoc. It was that experience which led them to leave imminent danger of Indian attacks to the individual threatened state.

A provision similar to the Articles of Confederation exception for state resistance was recommended to the Convention by the Commit-

---

The Lofgren article came to me as this Article was being readied for press; it is solely devoted to the "original intention" and represents the most thoroughgoing discussion of that matter. My conclusions, after having independently gone over much of the same material, coincide with his.

100 S. REP. No. 606, 92d Cong., 2d Sess. 4 (1972). Professor Richard B. Morris also states that "the war-making power of the President was little more than the power to defend against imminent invasion when Congress was not in session." *Id.* 15.

101 H. COMMAGER, *supra* note 77, at 112.

tee of Detail,[102] and was embodied in article I, section 10(3). Thus the Framers well understood the distinction between actual invasion and the imminent threat of invasion, and they expressly empowered a state to meet both. No mention whatsoever was made, however, in any of the conventions of a *presidential* power to react to such imminent danger.[103] The omission is significant against a background of strictly enumerated presidential powers and pervasive jealousy of the Executive.[104]

Asserting "it can scarcely be doubted that the President possesses the authority to take whatever action is necessary to protect the interests of the United States in a threatened emergency," McDougal and Lans cite *Martin v. Mott*[105] for the proposition that "the Supreme Court, in dealing with the powers of the President to call out the militia and employ the armed forces of the United States, concluded that he was empowered to act not only in cases of actual invasion, but also when there was 'imminent danger of invasion.' This latter contingency was held to be a question of fact to be determined by the President."[106] *Mott* presented a challenge by one called into the militia under the Act of 1795 which authorized the President to call out the militia "whenever the United States shall be invaded, or be in imminent danger of invasion."[107] Of course, it could not be left to a soldier to determine whether the emergency existed, and the Court held that the decision "whether the exigency has arisen, belongs exclusively to the President . . . ."[108] This express *statutory* authorization furnishes no

---

[102] The Committee of Detail recommended that no state should, without consent of Congress "engage in any War, unless it shall be actually invaded by Enemies, or the Danger of Invasion be so imminent, as not to admit of a Delay, until the Legislature of the United States can be consulted." 2 RECORDS, *supra* note 30, at 169.

[103] The explanation, in part, may be historical reluctance to permit executive deployment of troops outside the country. In 1701 an act provided that "Englishmen were not to be involved by a foreign king in war for the defence of territory not belonging to the English crown. Henceforth William was scrupulously careful to consult Parliament at every point." C. HILL, THE CENTURY OF REVOLUTION 1603-1714, at 278 (1961). The Massachusetts Constitution of 1780, article VII, provided that the governor should not march inhabitants "out of the limits" of the Commonwealth without their consent or "the consent of the general court [legislature]." 1 B. POORE, *supra* note 30, at 966. Lofgren, *supra* note 70, at 683, states that the presence of the state invasion provision "in the Constitution at least further suggests that Americans of that day need not have envisaged that the President as Commander in Chief would have an especially broad role in repelling sudden attack."

[104] R. BERGER, *supra* note 33, at 260-62.

[105] 25 U.S. (12 Wheat.) 19 (1827).

[106] McDougal & Lans, *Treaties and Congressional-Executive or Presidential Agreements: Interchangeable Instruments of National Policy: II*, 54 YALE L.J. 534, 612-13 (1945).

[107] For Professor Rostow, *Mott* involved "the President's power to call out the militia whenever he deems it desirable to do so." Rostow, *supra* note 3, at 890. The Act conferred no such carte blanche.

[108] 25 U.S. (12 Wheat.) at 30.

foundation for a presidential claim of unlimited *constitutional* power to forestall "imminent danger of invasion."

Expansion of the "sudden attack" remark in the Convention to include "imminent threat of invasion" requires great caution because it opens the door to a whole multitude of other expansive readings of presidential power.[109] To be sure, there must be a means of meeting a Cuban missile crisis, but that means is through congressional authorization, such as the Act of 1839 exemplifies and the War Powers Bill proposes.[110] For Congress, not the President, was given virtually plenary power to deal with all facets of war-making.

This brings us to the question whether the Javits Bill impermissibly delegates to the President authority to use the armed forces "to forestall the direct and imminent threat" of an armed attack on the United States or on its armed forces located abroad.[111] Professor Rostow defends prior delegations chiefly on the basis of *Zemel v. Rusk*,[112] where the Court, citing *United States v. Curtiss-Wright Export Corp.*,[113] stated that "Congress—in giving the Executive authority over matters of foreign affairs—must of necessity paint with a brush broader than that it customarily wields in domestic areas."[114] In opposition, Professor Francis Wormuth makes an extended analysis of the delegation cases and the history of prior attempts to delegate war powers.[115] From the cases he extracts the principle that Congress may determine the general policy to be pursued and then "authorize the President to determine the facts which call the Congressional policy into play."[116] Although he cites the *Zemel v. Rusk* remark that Congress cannot "grant the Executive totally unrestricted freedom of choice,"[117] he recognizes that war cannot be made "perfectly automatic

---

[109] My analysis leads me to dissent from the statement in the War Powers Report, S. REP. No. 606, 92d Cong., 2d Sess. 4 (1972), that the authorizations contained in § 3 of the War Powers Bill to repel attacks on the United States and to forestall imminent danger of such an attack "are recognized to be authority which the President enjoys in his independent Constitutional office as President/Commander-in-Chief."

[110] For the Act of 1839, see text accompanying note 124 *infra*.

[111] S. 2956, 92d Cong., 2d Sess. § 3(1) (1972).

[112] 381 U.S. 1 (1965).

[113] 299 U.S. 304 (1936).

[114] 381 U.S. 1, 17 (1965); Rostow, *supra* note 3, at 888-89. The analogical leap from the relatively innocuous delegation of authority to embargo arms to the belligerents in the Gran Chaco (South America) war—the issue in *Curtiss-Wright*—to the delegation of authority to propel the nation into an international holocaust cannot be lightly made. Wormuth, *supra* note 86, at 789, underlines the quite different considerations that come into play.

[115] Wormuth, *supra* note 86, at 780-99; Wormuth, *The Nixon Theory of the War Power: A Critique*, 60 CALIF. L. REV. 623, 692-97 (1972).

[116] Wormuth, *supra* note 86, at 792.

[117] Wormuth, *The Nixon Theory of the War Power: A Critique*, 60 CALIF. L. REV. 623, 695 (1972).

upon the occurrence of a future event."[118] That is, given a "direct and imminent threat" of attack, the President cannot be left with no choice but to wage war. Wormuth draws the teeth out of this concession, however, by concluding that the decision *for* war must be taken by Congress contemporaneously with the declaration of war,[119] a conclusion which amounts practically to a total ban on delegation in the premises. Generally persuaded by Professor Wormuth's analysis, I find his approach too narrow here. Because, like him, I distrust any doctrine that builds on Justice Sutherland's vulnerable *Curtiss-Wright* opinion,[120] I shall outline at least two considerations which suggest a more flexible approach.

First, having concluded that the plenary war-making power was vested in Congress rather than the President, I would be guided by John Marshall's statement in *McCulloch v. Maryland*:[121]

> It must have been the intention of those who gave these powers, to insure . . . their beneficial execution. This could not be done, by confiding the choice of means to such narrow limits as not to leave it in the power of congress to adopt any which might be appropriate, and which were conducive to the end.[122]

*McCulloch*, to be sure, did not involve a delegation problem, but its principle has wide scope.

Second, the historical course of Congress, charted in part by Professor Wormuth, has not been all one way. It will be recalled that article I, section 8(15), empowers Congress "To provide for calling forth the militia . . . to repel invasion." Instead of providing a detailed expression of policy, Congress was content by the Act of 1795 to authorize the President to call forth the militia "whenever the United States shall be invaded, or be in imminent danger of invasion," a policy no more detailed than the Javits "direct and imminent threat of an attack [on the United States]."[123] It is not a little remarkable that the delegation point was not so much as mentioned in *Martin v. Mott*. A similar course was pursued in the Act of March 3, 1839, which empowered the President "to resist any attempt on the part of Great Britain, to enforce, by arms, her claim to exclusive jurisdiction over" a disputed portion of Maine.[124]

---

[118] Wormuth, *supra* note 86, at 796.

[119] *Id.*

[120] Wormuth, *supra* note 117, at 694. For a discussion of *Curtiss-Wright*, see text accompanying notes 264-86 *infra*.

[121] 17 U.S. (4 Wheat.) 316 (1819).

[122] *Id.* at 415.

[123] S. 2956, 92d Cong., 2d Sess. § 3 (1972).

[124] Act of March 3, 1839, ch. 89, § 1, 5 Stat. 355.

Like Professor Wormuth, I little relish congressional issuance of a blank check to determine policy;[125] and I am aware that on the domestic front it was said in *Panama Refining Co. v. Ryan*[126] that Congress "must establish a criterion to govern the President's course."[127] A criterion, however, can be made only as explicit as the particular circumstances admit. If a tighter standard than that of the Javits Bill can be devised, so much the better; but until then I am satisfied to read the Bill's "forestall" phrase[128] as did Professor Bickel, who instanced before the Senate Foreign Relations Committee a threat like that of the Cuban missile crisis, that is "a reactive, not a self-starting affirmative power."[129] But I would add a provision akin to the early exemption for state action afforded by the Articles of Confederation for resistance when the "danger [of invasion] is so imminent as not to admit of a delay, till the . . . congress assembled can be consulted." Few, if any, recent presidential adventures were launched in circumstances so crucial as to admit of no delay until Congress could be consulted. That circumstances may occur which will render such consultation impossible must be conceded; and it will not do to foreclose *both* Congress and the President from meeting that situation. In fine, the limits on delegation, which some consider a moribund doctrine,[130] must not be so rigorously applied as to deprive Congress as well as the President of power to cope with the fearful exigencies of our contemporary world.[131]

## C. *Rostow's Evocation of the Original Intention*

The Legal Advisor of the State Department had little quarrel with the foregoing reading of the original intention: "In 1787 the world was a far larger place, and the framers probably had in mind attacks upon the United States."[132] Professor Ratner, whom Professor Rostow in-

---

[125] Wormuth, *supra* note 86, at 781; *cf. id.* 789.

[126] 293 U.S. 388 (1935).

[127] *Id.* at 415. *Zemel v. Rusk* also stated that it was not true that "simply because a statute deals with foreign relations, it can grant the Executive totally unrestricted freedom of choice." 381 U.S. at 17.

[128] *See* text accompanying note 111 *supra*.

[129] S. REP. No. 606, 92d Cong., 2d Sess. 4 (1972).

[130] *E.g.*, K. DAVIS, ADMINISTRATIVE LAW TEXT 32 (3d ed. 1972).

[131] When it concerns the powers of the *nation*, as distinguished from those of the *President*, we need to recall Hamilton's words, in *The Federalist Number 23*, respecting the "authorities essential to the common defence": "These powers ought to exist without limitation, *because it is impossible to foresee or define the extent and variety of national exigencies, or the correspondent extent and variety of the means which may be necessary to satisfy them.*" THE FEDERALIST No. 23, at 142 (Mod. Lib. ed. 1939) (A. Hamilton) (emphasis added). Any application of the delegation doctrine that would shackle the *nation* must yield to this necessity.

[132] LEGAL ADVISOR'S MEMO, *supra* note 86, at 1101.

vokes as a Daniel come to judgment,[133] likewise concedes that "[i]n 1787, 'repel sudden attack' probably meant 'resist invasion or rebellion.' "[134] Apparently not entirely satisfied to rely solely on the escape hatch resorted to by others—alteration of the Constitution by presidential practices—Professor Rostow intimates that an expanded presidential war power is immanent in the Constitution,[135] relying on various quotations to create an atmosphere in which any other reading is presumably unthinkable.[136] Coming from so reputable a scholar, they cannot be dismissed out of hand.

The Rostow article begins with several epigraphs that resemble nothing so much as scareheads. One, Madison's "impetuous vortex" of the legislature that threatens to engulf everything in sight, has been shown to be without relevance to our problem.[137] When Madison focussed squarely on the distribution of war powers, he stated:

> Every just view that can be taken of this subject, admonishes the public of the necessity of a rigid adherence to the simple, the received, and the fundamental doctrine of the constitution, that the power to declare war, including *the power of judging the causes of war, is fully and exclusively* vested in the legislature; that the executive has no right, *in any case*, to decide the question, whether there is or is not cause for declaring war; that the right of convening and informing congress, whenever such a question seems to call for a decision, *is all the right* which the constitution has deemed requisite or proper . . . .[138]

What better illustrates the futility of citing generalizations which are well enough in their original context to determine a specific issue, than Madison's own judgment on the President's limited war power, so remote from Professor Rostow's claim that it must be free from the "impetuous vortex" of Congress.

---

[133] Rostow, *supra* note 3, at 857, finds Ratner's study one of the two "most judicious" in the field. I shall have occasion to comment on the core of this "most judicious" piece.

[134] Ratner, *The Coordinated Warmaking Power—Legislative, Executive, and Judicial Roles*, 44 S. CAL. L. REV. 461, 467 (1971), *quoted in* Rostow, *supra* note 3, at 865.

[135] Nevertheless Rostow, *supra* note 3, at 886, is critical of those who "discover the source of their rule in what they regard as the original intent of the men who gave Congress the power 'to declare war,' despite 182 years of opinion and practice to the contrary."

[136] *Id.* 887-92. According to Rostow, *id.* 835, 843, the Javits Bill "would permit a plenipotentiary Congress to dominate the Presidency (and the courts as well) more completely than the House of Commons governs England . . ."; it "seeks to substitute parliamentary government for the tripartite constitution we have so painfully forged."

[137] THE FEDERALIST No. 48, at 322 (Mod. Lib. ed. 1937) (J. Madison), *quoted in* Rostow, *supra* note 3, at 833. *See* text accompanying notes 31-37 *supra*.

[138] 6 J. MADISON, *supra* note 75, at 174 (emphasis partially added). *Cf.* Letter from Alexander Hamilton to Secretary of War James McHenry, May 17, 1798, *reprinted in* 10 A. HAMILTON, WORKS 281 (H. Lodge ed. 1904), *quoted in* note 209 *infra*.

Another Rostow epigraph is Hamilton's statement in *The Federalist Number 23*: "The circumstances that endanger the safety of nations are infinite, and for this reason no constitutional shackles can wisely be imposed on the power to which the care of it is committed."[139] Hamilton was concerned there with the needed surrender by the states to the "federal government" of powers "essential to the common defense," not with a plea that *presidential* war powers must not be shackled.[140] Hamilton's argument for lodging power in the nation rather than the states is not convertible into an argument that power is to be vested in the President rather than in Congress. Well did he know that the presidential powers were indeed limited;[141] and even after he had moved from a narrow[142] to a broader view of the Executive power,[143] he still declared that it is the

> exclusive province of Congress, *when the nation is at peace*, to change that state into a state of war . . . *it belongs to Congress only, to go to war*. But when a foreign nation declares or . . . makes war upon the United States . . . any declaration on the part of Congress is . . . unnecessary.[144]

In short, but for a presidential power to defend against attack upon the United States, "it belongs to Congress only to go to war."[145]

Professor Rostow also paraphrases Chief Justice Marshall's statement that "we should never forget it is a *constitution* we are expounding—a constitution intended to endure for ages to come, and capable of adaptation to the various crises of human affairs."[146] What such

---

[139] Rostow, *supra* note 3, at 833.

[140] *See* note 131 *supra*.

[141] *See* text accompanying notes 52-56, 69-71 *supra*.

[142] *See* note 92 *supra*.

[143] For Hamilton's later expansive reading of executive power in the realm of foreign relations, see E. CORWIN, *supra* note 26, at 217-18. It needs to be viewed in the light of his proposal in the Convention of a permanent body of the "rich and well born" to "check the imprudence of democracy . . . their turbulent and uncontrouling disposition." 1 RECORDS, *supra* note 30, at 290, 299. The patrician Henry Adams stated that "Hamilton considered democracy a fatal curse, and meant to stop its progress." *See* E. SAMUELS, HENRY ADAMS, THE MIDDLE YEARS 58 (1965). He would therefore prefer to concentrate power in the executive and to short-circuit the democratic process which contemplated congressional debate. His views found no favor with the Convention.

[144] 8 A. HAMILTON, *Letter No. 1 of "Lucius Crassus,"* in WORKS 249-50 (H. Lodge ed. 1904) (emphasis partially added). *See also* note 209 *infra*.

[145] Professor Rostow wrings from Wormuth's statement that "When a foreign country attacks the United States . . . the President . . . must . . . wage the war," a concession of broad war powers to the President, "for most Presidential uses of the armed forces" represent resistance to "the hostile act of another state . . . directed *against the security* of the United States." Rostow, *supra* note 3, at 850 n.28 (emphasis added). But it is precisely this difference between an attack on the United States and acts which are deemed by the President to menace "the security of the United States" upon which the whole debate hinges.

[146] Rostow, *supra* note 3, at 844. McDougal and Lans rely on this Marshall statement for an "adaptive or instrumental" theory, which "treats the Constitution as an

"adaptation" has come to mean may be illustrated by the words of the State Department: "In the 20th century the world has grown much smaller. An attack on a country far from our shores can impinge directly on the nation's security . . . . The Constitution leaves to the President the judgment to determine whether the circumstances of a particular armed attack are so urgent and the potential consequences so threatening to the security of the United States that he should act without formally consulting the Congress."[147] That was not the view of the Framers, of Madison and of Hamilton. What portion of the Constitution confers this astonishing power? Because the world is contracting it does not follow that the President's constitutional powers are correspondingly expanding.[148]

Certainly Marshall would have been the last to distil such a proposition from his dictum in *McCulloch v. Maryland*. Too long has the dictum been reiterated without notice of the circumstances in which it was uttered. *McCulloch* presented the question whether Congress had constitutional power to establish the Bank of the United States; the issue turned on whether a bank was a proper *means* for execution of expressly granted federal powers. In granting the powers, said Marshall, the Framers intended to

> insure, their beneficial execution. This could not be done, by confiding the *choice of means* to such narrow limits as not to leave it in the power of congress to adopt any which might be appropriate, and which were conducive to the end. This provision is made in a constitution, intended to endure for ages to come, and consequently, to be adapted to the various

'instrument of government' rather than as a mere 'text for interpretation.' This theory received its classic statement in Chief Justice Marshall's reminder in *McCulloch v. Maryland* . . . ." McDougal & Lans, *Treaties and Congressional-Executive or Presidential Agreements: Interchangeable Instruments of National Policy*, 54 YALE L.J. 181, 213 (1945). Marshall's *McCulloch* dictum had been invoked for the theory of "adaptive interpretation" in 1926 by Corwin in *Judicial Review in Action*, 74 U. PA. L. REV. 639, 658-59 (1926).

[147] LEGAL ADVISOR'S MEMO, *supra* note 86, at 1101.

[148] In *Youngstown*, Justice Jackson said:
The appeal . . . that we declare the existence of inherent powers *ex necessitate* to meet an emergency asks us to do what many think would be wise, although it is something the forefathers omitted. They knew what emergencies were, knew the pressures they engender for authoritative action, knew, too, how they afford a ready pretext for usurpation. . . . Aside from suspension of the privilege of the writ of habeas corpus in time of rebellion or invasion . . . they made no provision for exercise of extraordinary authority because of a crisis. I do not think we rightfully may so amend their work.
343 U.S. at 579, 649-50 (concurring opinion). Emergency powers, Jackson continued, "are consistent with free government only when their control is lodged elsewhere than in the Executive who exercises them. That is the safeguard that would be nullified by our adoption of the 'inherent powers' formula." *Id.* at 652.
The "emergency power" had been strongly advocated by Justice Clark, *id.* at 660-62 (concurring opinion), but Justice Douglas also rejected it, saying the fact that speed was essential "does not mean that the President, rather than the Congress, had the constitutional authority to act." *Id.* at 629.

*crises* of human affairs. To have prescribed the means by which government should, in all future time, execute its powers, would have been . . . [to give the Constitution] the properties of a legal code.[149]

Manifestly this is merely a plea for some freedom in the choice of "means," not for license to create a fresh power at each new crisis. For this we need not rely on inference, because Marshall himself made this plain in a debate with Judge Spencer Roane, the discovery of which we owe to the happy enterprise of Professor Gerald Gunther.[150]

*McCulloch* had immediately come under attack and Marshall leapt to its defense. Speaking directly to the above-quoted passage, he stated,

> it does not contain the most distant allusion to *any extension by construction of the powers of congress.* Its sole object is to remind us that a constitution cannot possibly enumerate the means by which the powers of government are to be carried into execution.[151]

Again and again he repudiated any intention to lay the predicate for such "extension by construction." There is "not a syllable uttered by the court," he said, that "applies to an enlargement of the powers of congress." He rejected any imputation that "those powers ought to be enlarged by construction or otherwise."[152] The Court, he stated, never intimated that construction could extend "the grant beyond the fair and usual import of the words . . . ."[153] Even the means are not to be "strained to comprehend things remote, unlikely or unusual."[154] Translated into terms of the present issue, a grant of power to "repel sudden attacks" on the United States is not to be construed as a presidential power to repel an attack by a foreign nation on Korea.[155]

Over-modestly appraising the impact of his discovery, Professor Gunther states:

> Clearly these essays give cause to be more guarded in invok-

---

[149] 17 U.S. (4 Wheat.) 315, 415-16 (1819) (emphasis partially added), *quoted in* Rostow, *supra* note 3, at 891.

[150] JOHN MARSHALL'S DEFENSE OF *McCulloch v. Maryland* (G. Gunther ed. 1969).

[151] *Id.* 185 (emphasis added).

[152] *Id.* 182, 184.

[153] *Id.* 92; *see id.* 185.

[154] *Id.* 168. "In no single instance does the court admit the unlimited power of congress to adopt any means whatever . . . ." *Id.* 186. Marshall emphasized that "in all the reasoning on the word 'necessary,' the court does not, in a single instance, claim the aid of a 'latitudinous,' or 'liberal' construction . . . ." *Id.* 92.

[155] "It is not pretended," said Marshall, "that this right of selection may be fraudulently used to the destruction of the fair land marks of the constitution." *Id.* 173.

ing *McCulloch* to support views of congressional power now thought necessary. If virtually unlimited discretion is required to meet twentieth century needs, candid argument to that effect, rather than ritual invoking of Marshall's authority, would seem to me more clearly in accord with the Chief Justice's stance.[156]

Enough of such incantations!

Against such misinterpretations of Marshall, there is the pledge of Jefferson, after his election to the presidency, to administer the Constitution "according to the safe and honest meaning contemplated by the plain understanding of the people at the time of its adoption— a meaning to be found in the explanations of those who advocated . . . it."[157] Madison also clung "to the sense in which the Constitution was accepted and ratified by the Nation," adding, "if that be not the guide in expounding it, there can be no security for a consistent and stable government, more than for a faithful exercise of its powers."[158]

Considerations of space and the patience of the reader constrain me to content myself with one last Rostow quotation, Justice Frankfurter's statement in the *Youngstown* case:

> It is an inadmissibly narrow conception of American constitutional law to confine it to the words of the Constitution and to disregard the gloss which life has written on them. In short, a systematic, unbroken, executive practice, long pursued to the knowledge of Congress and never before questioned . . . may be treated as a gloss on the Executive Power vested in the President by § 1 of Art. II.[159]

Apparently Frankfurter was inspired by the Marshall remark in *McCulloch*, for he stated:

> The pole-star for constitutional adjudications is John Marshall's greatest judicial utterance that "it is a *constitution* we are expounding." . . . That requires . . . a spacious view in applying an instrument of government "made for an expanding future". . . .[160]

Marshall, as we have seen, repudiated a "spacious view" of *power* conferred by the Constitution; not for him enlargement of those powers "by construction or otherwise." Moreover, Frankfurter's state-

---

[156] *Id.* 20-21.

[157] 4 J. ELLIOT, *supra* note 36, at 446.

[158] 9 J. MADISON, *supra* note 75, at 191, 372.

[159] Youngstown Sheet & Tube Co. v. Sawyer, 343 U.S. 579, 610-11 (1952) (concurring opinion), *quoted in* Rostow, *supra* note 3, at 843.

[160] Youngstown Sheet & Tube Co. v. Sawyer, 343 U.S. 579, 596 (1952) (concurring opinion).

ment was utterly gratuitous, the sheerest dictum. The setting of the case, in his own words, was that Congress had "frequently—at least 16 times since 1916—specifically provided for executive seizure . . . . In every case it has qualified this grant of power with limitations and safeguards."[161] Congress, he said, had "expressed its will to withhold this power from the President as though it had said so in so many words."[162] Thus the facts at bar were 180 degrees removed from the hypothetical facts to which his dictum was addressed. No more importance should be attached to the Frankfurter dictum, in which no other member of the Court joined, than Marshall attached to his own dictum, uttered on behalf of the entire Court in *Marbury v. Madison*,[163] when it was pressed upon him in *Cohens v. Virginia*.[164] Dicta, Marshall explained, never receive the careful consideration that is given decision of the particular case.[165]

*Youngstown* presented the validity of presidential action in the absence of an express statutory bar; and one may question whether Frankfurter would deny to Congress exercise of power expressly conferred because the President, by a "gloss of life," had reallocated the power to himself. The Marshall who declared in the Roane debate that the Court's exercise of the power of judicial review vested in it by the Constitution "*cannot* be the assertion of a right to *change that instrument*,"[166] would hardly have concurred with Professor Rostow that the President's repeated exercise of power withheld from him and conferred upon Congress constituted a "gloss of life" which converted the usurpation into constitutional dogma.[167] It is time to cry out against the substitution of such glittering generalities for the hard analysis that each specific case demands afresh.

The underlying reality, it may be countered, is that Marshall's acts were at war with his words, that he did in fact change the Constitution. This is to condone a divorce between words and deeds, to take a cynical view of adjudication, reminiscent of the lip service paid by the Renaissance princes to the Holy Church because religion made the masses more docile. Realism, to be sure, calls on us to look

---

161 *Id.* at 597-98.

162 *Id.* at 602.

163 5 U.S. (1 Cranch) 137 (1803).

164 19 U.S. (6 Wheat.) 264, 399-400 (1821).

165 *Id.* at 399-400.

166 JOHN MARSHALL'S DEFENSE OF *McCulloch v. Maryland* 209 (G. Gunther ed. 1969) (emphasis added).

167 To still fears of usurpation, James Iredell, leader in the fight for ratification in North Carolina, and later a Justice of the Supreme Court, said, "If Congress, under pretence of executing one power, should, in fact, usurp another, they will violate the Constitution." 4 J. ELLIOT, *supra* note 36, at 179.

behind what courts say to what they do; but then ordinary honesty requires that the American people be told in plain words, which the man in the street can grasp, that the Court has assumed the function of amending the Constitution. Continued dissimulation on this score is unworthy of bench and bar.

In sum, the transformation of the "repel sudden attacks" exception of Madison and Gerry into an alleged presidential power, without congressional authorization, to commit the armed forces to battle against invasion of Korea or Vietnam can find no warrant either in the constitutional text or in the understanding of the Framers. About this there is virtually no dispute;[168] instead the apologists for the power rest it upon "adaptation by usage."

### III. ADAPTATION BY USAGE

"Adaptation by usage" is a label designed to render palatable the disagreeable claim that the President may by his own practices revise the Constitution, that he may disrupt the constitutional distribution of powers, considered inviolable under the separation of powers. The argument on behalf of presidential "adaptation of the Constitution by usage" was most forcefully made by McDougal and Lans who, impatiently brushing aside the "absolute artifacts of verbal archaeology,"[169] "the idiosyncratic purposes of the Framers,"[170] concluded that "continuance of [a] practice by successive administrations throughout our history makes its contemporary constitutionality unquestionable."[171] In plain words, usurpation of power by the President, if repeated often enough, is legitimated.[172]

We may put to one side the example of the Supreme Court as the allegedly necessary engine for "adaptation" of the Constitution to the needs of a changing society, particularly since the President's single-handed revision of the Constitution is claimed to be immune from

---

[168] *See* text accompanying notes 132-34 *supra.*

[169] McDougal & Lans, *supra* note 146, at 291.

[170] *Id.* 212.

[171] *Id.* 291. *Compare* their comment, "The phrase 'treaty of peace,' when bereft of the reification which makes it some mysterious, special kind of an agreement" excluded from the scope of solo presidential agreements, *id.* 286, *with* events in the Convention. Madison moved to "except treaties of peace" from the two-thirds concurrence provision. Gerry objected that treaties of peace were of special importance; and Hugh Williamson stated, "Treaties of peace should be guarded at least by requiring the same concurrence as in other Treaties." 2 RECORDS, *supra* note 30, at 540-41. The proposed exception was rejected. For the Framers a treaty of peace was unmistakably a "special kind of agreement," for reasons which were not at all "mysterious."

[172] Monaghan, *Presidential War-Making,* 50 B.U.L. REV. 19, 31 (1970): "A practice so deeply embedded in our governmental structure should be treated as decisive of the constitutional issue." "[H]istory has legitimated the practice of presidential war-making." *Id.* 29. For similar views, see Ratner, *supra* note 88, at 467; *cf.* Reveley, *supra* note 3, at 1250-57.

judicial review.[173] So too, the clarification of an ambiguous grant of power to the President by resort to his long continued practice thereunder is to be differentiated. Here we have an attempted take-over by the President of war powers plainly conferred upon Congress alone, and accompanied by an unmistakable intention to withhold them from the President. It therefore constitutes a bare-faced attempt to alter the constitutional distribution of powers, and to violate the separation of powers.[174]

When McDougal and Lans charge those who demur with slavery to "words of the Constitution as timeless absolutes," to "mechanical filiopietistic theory,"[175] they totally misconceive the issue. The issue is not one of words but of *power*: is the President authorized to transfer power conferred upon Congress to himself? Whence comes the mandate to the President to rewrite the Constitution?

"The people," said James Iredell, "have chosen to be governed under such and such principles. They have not chosen to be governed or promised to submit upon any other."[176] Arguing for executive agreements, McDougal and Lans said, "the crucial constitutional fact is that *the people* (Presidents, Supreme Court Justices, Senators, Congressmen *and electorate*) who have lived under the document for 150 years have interpreted it . . . [to] authorize the making of international agreements other than treaties on most of the important problems of peace and war."[177] Now the inescapable fact is that the issue has never really been explained to "the people"; much less has the judgment of "the electorate" ever been solicited.[178] Though sympa-

---

173 For a collection of authorities see Ratner, *supra* note 88, at 482-83.

174 In *Youngstown*, Justice Douglas wrote, "If we sanctioned the present exercise of power by the President, we would be expanding Article II of the Constitution and rewriting it to suit the political conveniences of the present emergency." 343 U.S. at 632 (concurring opinion). *Cf.* notes 93 & 148 *supra*.

175 McDougal & Lans, *supra* note 146, at 212. In their defense of "executive agreements," they further stated, "[w]hether these powers are based on *interpretation* of the language of the Constitution or on *usage* is, strictly, a matter of concern only for rhetoricians . . . ." *Id.* 239 n.104.

176 2 G. McREE, LIFE AND CORRESPONDENCE OF JAMES IREDELL 146 (1857). *See also* Berger, *supra* note 33, at 13-14.

177 McDougal & Lans, *supra* note 146, at 216 (emphasis added). They also state that "In preferring to alter the Constitution by informal adaptation, the *American people* have also been motivated by a wise realization of the inevitable transiency of political arrangements." *Id.* 294 (emphasis added).

178 "The principal enzymes of change have been the emergence of a more democratic philosophy of government, leading to replacement of some of the patrician institutions devised by the statesmen of 1787 . . . ." *Id.* 292. McDougal and Lans were attacking the power of a senate minority to thwart a foreign policy favored by the nation, exemplified by Senate rejection of Wilson's Versailles Treaty. Alas for result-oriented jurisprudence: an even less democratic process has been substituted—executive agreements kept secret from the Senate, foreign policy fashioned by a behind-the-scenes elitist conclave which a recent critic, R. J. Barnet, charges, is not accountable either to the people or to Congress. R. BARNET, ROOTS OF THE WAR (1972). McDougal and Lans have themselves made the fitting comment: "[U]ntil we are furnished with the formula for the selection

thetic to amendment by usage, Reveley sapiently observes that the "general public takes a relatively blackletter view of the Constitution," and that the "subtleties" of adaptation "by usage . . . would probably be lost on the general public."[179] It is therefore idle to impute informal ratification of the presidential power take-over to "the people." The people have been told by the President that he has acted under the Constitution, by which, in their benighted way, they understand textual warrant, not long-continued violation of the Constitution. It is always hazardous to prophesy how the American people would react in any given situation, but in view of the bitter strife over presidential war-making,[180] I venture to think that a nationwide howl of outrage would greet the disclosure that the presidential blood-letting in Vietnam is justified, not by constitutional grants of power to the President, but by a self-serving theory of boot-strap power built upon successive encroachments on exclusive congressional prerogatives.

Professor Ratner tells us that "constitutional policy for ensuing epochs is not congealed in the mold of 1787 referants."[181] Of course not; the Founders provided for change by a process of amendment. That process is cumbersome, and designedly so;[182] but it is a marvelous non-sequitur that in consequence the servants of the people may informally amend the Constitution without consulting them.[183] In-

---

of the elite, we are entitled to doubt that the minority has any unique monopoly of wisdom. Government by a self-designated elite—like that of benevolent despotism or of Plato's philosopher kings—may be a good form of government for some people, but it is not the American way." McDougal & Lans, *supra* note 106, at 577-78.

[179] Reveley, *supra* note 3, at 1255 n.31, 1293.

[180] *See* text accompanying note 19 *supra*.

[181] Ratner, *supra* note 88, at 467.

[182] The Founders fully understood the difficulties of amendment. Thus Patrick Henry argued in the Virginia ratification convention, "[F]our of the smallest states, that do not collectively contain one tenth part of the population . . . may obstruct the most salutary and necessary amendments." 3 J. ELLIOT, *supra* note 36, at 49. But the prevailing view was expressed in the North Carolina convention by James Iredell: the Constitution "can be altered with as much regularity, and as little confusion, as any act of Assembly; not, indeed, quite so easily, which would be extremely impolitic . . . so that alterations can without difficulty be made, agreeable to the general sense of the people." 4 *id.* 177. Charles Jarvis said in Massachusetts, "we shall have in this article an adequate provision for all the purposes of political reformation." 2 *id.* 116.

[183] "When, as has proved to be the case in most of the American states, the process of amendment is a relatively simple political problem, adaptation frequently proceeds by way of formal change; when, as has proved to be the case in the Federal Union, the process of amendment is politically difficult, other modes of change have emerged." McDougal & Lans, *supra* note 146, at 293. Because of the "difficulty of its formal amendment process, alteration by usage has proved to be the principal means of modifying our fundamental law." Reveley, *supra* note 3, at 1252.

In the First Congress, Gerry, one of the Framers, stated, "If it is an omitted case, an attempt in the Legislature to supply the defect, will be in fact an attempt to amend the Constitution. But this can only be done in the way pointed out by the fifth article of that instrument, and an attempt to amend it in any other way may be a high crime or misdemeanor . . . ." The people, he added, have "directed a particular mode of making amendments, which we are not at liberty to depart from . . . . Such a power would render the most important clause in the Constitution nugatory." 1 ANNALS OF CONG.

deed, Professor Rostow upbraids the Senate for attempting by the Javits Bill "to amend the Constitution without . . . consulting the people."[184] It is incongruous to insist that congressional restoration of the "original intention" respecting the constitutional allocation of powers must proceed by amendment while maintaining that the President is free unilaterally to alter the Constitution because, as his school insists, amendment is difficult.

Alexander Hamilton, that daring pioneer advocate of broadly-read presidential powers, writing with respect to the *express* treaty power (as distinguished from a power merely rested on "usage") regarded it as a fundamental maxim that

> a delegated authority [e.g. the President] cannot alter the constituting act, unless so expressly authorized by the constituting power. *An agent cannot new-model his own commission.* A treaty, for example, *cannot transfer* the legislative power to the executive department.[185]

Marshall, as we have seen, disclaimed judicial power to change the Constitution.[186] Now the followers of Hamilton, the citators of Marshall, would claim that the President *can* by his own "usage" "new-model his commission" and "transfer the legislative power to the executive."

To a believer in constitutional government, in the separation of powers[187] as a safeguard against dictatorship, there is no room for a take-over by the President of powers that were denied to him and, as our own times demonstrate, denied with good reason. "Ours is a government of divided authority," declared Justice Black in 1957, "on the assumption that in division there is not only strength but freedom

---

523 (1789). Willard Hurst remarked in our own time that the informal amendment approach "is a way of practically reading Article V out of the Federal Constitution . . . . [The Framers] provided a defined, regular procedure for changing or adapting it." SUPREME COURT AND SUPREME LAW 74 (E. Cahn ed. 1954).

184 Rostow, *supra* note 3, at 835. Secretary of State Rogers likewise asserts that the presidential allocation of powers "should be changed, if at all, only by Constitutional Amendment." N.Y. Times, Mar. 30, 1972, at 10, col. 3.

185 6 A. HAMILTON, *Letters of "Camillus"* in WORKS 166 (H. Lodge ed. 1904) (emphasis added).

186 Notes 151-55, 166 *supra* & accompanying text.

187 The executive branch clings to the separation of powers when it claims a right to withhold information from Congress under the doctrine of "executive privilege." *See Hearings on S. 1125 Before the Subcomm. on Separation of Powers of the Senate Comm. on the Judiciary,* 92d Cong., 1st Sess. 430, 473 (1971) (remarks of Secretary of State William Rogers and Assistant Attorney General William Rehnquist) [hereinafter cited as *Hearings*]. So too, Professor Rostow reminds Congress that it cannot fashion out of the necessary and proper clause "a bootstrap doctrine, empowering Congress to abolish the principle of the separation of powers." Rostow, *supra* note 3, at 897. The historical facts demonstrate that it is the President, rather than the Congress, who seeks to "abolish" the separation of powers, to preempt powers granted exclusively to Congress.

from tyranny."[188] If present exigencies demand a redistribution of powers originally conferred upon Congress—a presidential power to commit the nation to war without congressional consultation or authorization—that decision ought candidly to be submitted to "the people" in the form of a proposed amendment, not masked by euphemisms.[189] For me Washington's advice remains the pole-star:

> The necessity of reciprocal checks in the exercise of political power, by dividing and distributing it into different depositories, and constituting each the Guardian of the Public Weal against invasions by the others, has been evinced . . . . To preserve them must be as necessary as to institute them. If in the opinion of the People, the distribution or modification of the Constitutional powers be in any particular wrong, let it be corrected by an amendment in the way in which the Constitution designates. But let there be no change by usurpation; for though this, in one instance, may be the instrument of good, it is the customary weapon by which free governments are destroyed. The precedent must always greatly overbalance in permanent evil any partial or transient benefit which the use can at any time yield.[190]

## A. *Presidential "Usage"—The "125 Incidents"*

"Since the Constitution was adopted," said the State Department, "there have been at least 125 instances in which the President has ordered the armed forces to take action or maintain positions abroad without obtaining prior Congressional authorization, starting with the 'undeclared war' with France (1798-1800)."[191] Professor Wormuth has located "the first serious discussion of the problem" in 1912, in a monograph by J. Reuben Clark, the Solicitor of the State Depart-

---

[188] Reid v. Covert, 354 U.S. 1, 40 (1957).

[189] Compare Professor Felix Frankfurter's advice to President Franklin D. Roosevelt in 1937: "the Supreme Court for about a quarter of a century has distorted the power of judicial review into a revision of legislative policy, thereby usurping powers belonging to the Congress." And "people have been taught to believe that when the Supreme Court speaks it is not they who speak but the Constitution, whereas, of course, in so many vital cases, it is *they* who speak and *not* the Constitution. And I verily believe that that is what the country needs most to understand." ROOSEVELT AND FRANKFURTER: THEIR CORRESPONDENCE, 1928-1945, at 383-84 (M. Freedman ed. 1967).

[190] 35 G. WASHINGTON, WRITINGS 228-29 (J. Fitzpatrick ed. 1940). The Massachusetts Constitution of 1780, which was drafted by John Adams, provided that the people "have a right to require of their lawgivers and magistrates an exact and constant observance" of the "fundamental principles of the constitution" which are "absolutely necessary to preserve the advantages of liberty and to maintain a free government." 1 B. POORE, *supra* note 30, at 959.

[191] LEGAL ADVISOR'S MEMO, *supra* note 86, at 1101. Wormuth, *supra* note 86, at 718, justly states of the "undeclared war" with France, "This is altogether false. The fact is that President Adams took absolutely no independent action. Congress passed a series of acts [cited by Wormuth] which amounted, so the Supreme Court said, to a declaration of imperfect war; and Adams complied with these statutes." Bas v. Tingy, 4 U.S. (4 Dall.) 36 (1800), amply confirms that Adams acted under congressional authorization.

ment, entitled *The Right to Protect Citizens in Foreign Countries*. There Clark "opined that, with the exception of our political interventions in Cuba and Samoa, all the earlier cases could be regarded as nonpolitical interposition for the protection of citizens. He suggested that they might fall within the President's constitutional power, but this opinion was 'with no thought or pretense of more than a cursory examination. It is entirely possible that a more detailed and careful study would lead to other or modified conclusions.' His tentative argument turned on the fact that the President possessed executive power . . . . Clark made no reference whatever to the commander-in-chief clause."[192]

As late as 1912, therefore, the legal theoretician of the State Department sought refuge in the Constitution rather than appeal to the President's own practices for legitimation of prior presidential nonpolitical interpositions for protection of citizens. From this frail seedling, in the short space of 38 years, grew the present over-weening executive claims. In 1950 the President committed troops to repel the sudden invasion of South Korea. Dean Acheson, then Secretary of State, recommended to the President that he "should not ask for a resolution of approval, but rest on his constitutional authority as Commander in Chief . . . ." Later he wrote, "There has never . . . been any serious doubt . . . of the President's constitutional authority to do what he did. The basis for this conclusion in legal theory and historical precedent," he said, was a State Department memorandum of 1950 which "listed eighty-seven instances in the past century in which [Truman's] predecessors" had exercised "presidential power to send our forces into battle. . . . And thus yet another decision was made."[193] Decisions can be made by executive fiat; but fiat cannot supply constitutional sanction.

The painstaking analysis of the "125 incidents" by Professor Wormuth cuts the ground from under the claims of Acheson and his associates.[194] Under Secretary of State Nicholas Katzenbach himself stated that "most of these [incidents] were relatively minor uses of

---

192 Wormuth, *supra* note 117, at 663.

193 D. ACHESON, PRESENT AT THE CREATION 414-15 (1969). The argument had been made in 1945 by McDougal and Lans, *supra* note 106, at 612: "Now that the technology of war has made it imperative in the interests of national safety that aggressors be met with the threat of overwhelming force before they can commence their own military operations, it can scarcely be doubted that the President possesses the authority to take whatever action is necessary to protect the interests of the United States in a threatened emergency."

194 *See* Wormuth, *supra* note 86. *See also* Wormuth, *supra* note 117, at 652-64. Reveley, *supra* note 3, at 1258, states, "[a]s precedent for Vietnam . . . the majority of the nineteenth century uses of force do not survive close scrutiny."

force."[195] The "vast majority" of such cases, said Edward Corwin, "involved fights with pirates, landings of small naval contingents on barbarous or semi-barbarous coasts [to protect American citizens], the dispatch of small bodies of troops to chase bandits or cattle rustlers across the Mexican border."[196] For one reason or another such cases presented little or no possibility of armed conflict or bloodshed so there was no occasion to approach Congress for authorization to make war;[197] even so, some Presidents did seek such authorization.[198] These incidents are far from "precedents" for sending our troops "into battle."[199]

Even were these incidents to be regarded as equivalent to executive waging of war, the last precedent would stand no better than the first; illegality is not legitimated by repetition.[200] It is one of the ironies of history that such "precedents" should be invoked for vastly greater incursions[201] at a time when "gunboat diplomacy" has been discredited and abandoned.[202] To extrapolate from a practice of landing "six sailors in a long boat to rescue a citizen" to a right to commit the nation to a Vietnam War,[203] which has cost 30 billion dollars a year, engaged upwards of 500,000 men, resulted in some 200,000 wounded and 45,000 dead, is to make a breath-taking analogical leap across a chasm of non-equivalence.[204]

Professor Monaghan criticizes Wormuth's deflation of these "incidents" on which the State Department relies, first on the ground

---

[195] See Mora v. McNamara, 389 U.S. 934, 936 (1967) (Douglas, J., dissenting).

[196] Corwin, *The President's Power* in THE PRESIDENT'S ROLE AND POWERS 361 (D. Haight & L. Johnston eds. 1965). Elsewhere Corwin has written, "The vast proportion of the incidents . . . comprised . . . *efforts to protect definite rights of persons and property* against impending violence, and were defended on that ground *as not amounting to acts of war.*" E. CORWIN, *supra* note 74, at 146. *See also id.* 147-48; Wormuth, *supra* note 86, at 742-43, 746-48.

[197] Reveley, *supra* note 3, at 1258; Wormuth, *supra* note 86, at 742.

[198] Text accompanying notes 209-12, 214 *infra.*

[199] Perhaps President Polk's dispatch of troops into Mexico in 1846 may be deemed an exception, although when hostilities broke out he immediately asked Congress for approval; after bitter debate over his assertions that his acts were "defensive," Congress declared war. *Power to Commit Forces, supra* note 3, at 1780. In 1848, the House of Representatives, by a resolution in which Lincoln joined, condemned Polk's action. Wormuth, *supra* note 86, at 726. *See* text accompanying notes 228-29 *infra.*

[200] Powell v. McCormack, 395 U.S. 486, 546 (1969), reminded us "That an unconstitutional action has been taken before surely does not render that same action any less unconstitutional at a later date."

[201] E. CORWIN, *supra* note 26, at 241, perhaps the most influential 20th century apologist for enlarged presidential powers, states that the President has gathered "to himself powers with respect to war making which ill accord with the specific delegations in the Constitution of the war-declaring power to Congress." *Cf.* note 93 *supra.*

[202] Reveley, *supra* note 3, at 1289.

[203] *Cf.* Wormuth, *supra* note 86, at 762.

[204] Professor Bickel has said that "there comes a point when a difference of degree achieves the magnitude of a difference in kind." S. REP. No. 606, 92d Cong., 2d Sess. 16 (1972).

that "To dismiss American interventions in Latin America as 'minor' amounts to recognition of presidential power to wage war against weak opponents for limited purposes."[205] Consider, for example, the bombardment by an over-zealous navy captain of the "sovereign state of Greytown," Nicaragua, in 1854, in reprisal for some negligible "outrages" by what President Pierce described as a band of outlaws rather than an organized society, and which Secretary of State Marcy wrote was "an embarrassing affair" that could not be repudiated because of domestic political repercussions.[206] Professor Monaghan is welcome to regard this as the "waging of war"; but few would equate it with the presidential commitment of troops to resist the invasion of South Korea.

What if the "incidents" do demonstrate that "with ever-increasing frequency, presidents have employed that amount of force that they deemed necessary to accomplish their political objectives . . . . Whatever the intention of the framers, the military machine has become simply an instrument for the achievement of foreign policy goals, which in turn have become a central responsibility of the presidency."[207] Monaghan's dismissal of "the intention of the framers" vastly simplifies the presidential argument; the Constitution is then merely a scrap of paper to be respected or disregarded at will. On the assumption that it remains, however, a charter of government, the hitching of the "military machine" to the "achievement of foreign policy goals" is a choice example of the tail wagging the dog. By endowing the President with authority to receive ambassadors, and, with Senate consent, to appoint ambassadors and make treaties—such are the slight sources of his claim to be the sole organ of foreign relations —the Framers hardly intended to confer upon him a power unmistakably withheld when the war powers were under consideration, the power singlehandedly to "commence" a war.

Against such dubious precedents there is the testimony of great contemporaries of the Constitution.[208] In 1801, President Jefferson was confronted by Tripoli's declaration of war; when an American naval vessel was attacked it disarmed but released the attacker. Jefferson explained to Congress, "Unauthorized by the Constitution, without the sanction of Congress, to go beyond the line of defense, the vessel, being disabled from committing further hostilities, was liberated with its crew. The Legislature will doubtless consider whether, by

---

205 Monaghan, *supra* note 172, at 27.

206 Wormuth, *supra* note 86, at 743-46.

207 Monaghan, *supra* note 172, at 27.

208 These and other presidential utterances were collected by Putney, *Executive Assumptions of the War Making Power,* 7 NAT'L U.L. REV. 1 (1927).

authorizing measures of offense also, they will place our forces on an equal footing with that of its adversaries."[209] And later, in 1805, when Spain disputed the boundaries of Louisiana, President Jefferson advised Congress that Spain evidenced an "intention to advance on our possessions," adding, "Considering that Congress alone is constitutionally invested with the power of changing our condition from peace to war, I have thought it my duty to await their authority for using force . . . ."[210] "Imminent danger" of invasion did not deter Jefferson from consultation with Congress.

James Madison, the leading architect of the Constitution, who took a very narrow view of the presidential war power,[211] maintained that view after becoming President. In his message of June 1, 1812, he called attention to English outrages on American commerce, and to the failure of American "remonstrances," and then he referred the question whether we should oppose "force to force in defense of [our] national rights" to Congress as a "solemn question which the Constitution wisely confides to the legislative department of the Government."[212]

After adoption of the Monroe Doctrine, Colombia asked for protection against France in 1824. President James Monroe, a participant in the Virginia ratification convention, stated in a letter to Madison that "The Executive has no right to compromit the nation in any question of war"; and his Secretary of State, John Quincy Adams,

---

[209] 1 MESSAGES, *supra* note 74, at 314. In December 1790, Secretary of State Jefferson submitted a report to Congress respecting American seamen captured at Algiers, stating, "it rests with Congress to decide between war, tribute, and ransom, as the means of re-establishing our Mediterranean commerce." 1 AMERICAN STATE PAPERS, FOREIGN RELATIONS 105 (1832). In 1793, Jefferson, then Secretary of State, said of reprisal, "if the case were important and ripe for that step, Congress must be called upon to take it; the right of reprisal being expressly lodged with them by the Constitution, and not with the Executive." Wormuth, *supra* note 86, at 758.

Hamilton, then in private life, attacked Jefferson's Tripoli position on the ground that a declaration of war by a foreign nation unleashes the President's defensive powers so that no congressional declaration of war was required for retention of the Tripolitanian ship and crew. 8 A. HAMILTON, *Letter No. 1 of "Lucius Crassus,"* in WORKS 246-52 (H. Lodge ed. 1904). This was a shift in position apparently dictated by political considerations, if we may credit the explanation by his sympathetic editor, Henry Cabot Lodge, that the letter "really constitutes a defence of the Federalist party and an elaborate and bitter criticism of their opponents." *Id.* 246 n.1. For, when in 1798 the French greatly endangered American shipping, Hamilton wrote Secretary of War James McHenry, "I am not ready to say that he [the President] has any other power than merely to employ ships or convoys, with authority to *repel* force by *force* (but not to capture), and to repress hostilities within our waters . . . . Anything beyond this must fall under the idea of *reprisals,* and requires the sanction of that department which is to declare *or make war.* In so delicate a case, in one which involves so important a consequence as that of war, my opinion is that no doubtful authority ought to be exercised by the President." 10 *id.* 281-82. In 1798 he was therefore in accord with Jefferson's view, reflecting his own earlier narrow view of presidential war powers. *See* text accompanying notes 69, 71, 144 *supra. See also* note 67 *supra* & note 209 *infra.*

[210] 1 MESSAGES, *supra* note 74, at 376-77.

[211] *See* text accompanying notes 26, 27, 62 *supra.*

[212] 2 MESSAGES, *supra* note 74, at 484-85, 489.

replied to Colombia that "by the Constitution . . . the ultimate decision of this question belongs to the Legislative Department."[213]

Few Presidents had a more jealous regard for presidential prerogatives than Andrew Jackson; yet when faced with recognition of Texas he referred the question to Congress, stating, "It will always be consistent with the spirit of the Constitution, and most safe, that it should be exercised, when probably leading to war, with a previous understanding with that body by whom war alone can be declared, and by whom all the provisions for sustaining its perils must be furnished."[214] Can it be doubted that he would have been equally reluctant, without congressional authorization, to send troops into Texas to "defend" it against an attack by Mexico? His view was later reiterated by Secretary of State Daniel Webster when the issue was a possible attack by France on Hawaii: "the war making power . . . rests entirely with Congress . . . no power is given to the Executive to oppose an attack by one independent nation on the possessions of another."[215]

In brief, Jefferson and Madison did not regard attacks on American shipping or commerce on the high seas as dispensing with the constitutional requirement for consultation with Congress. And Monroe, Jackson, J. Q. Adams, and Webster did not view attacks on foreign nations, even though within the American sphere of influence, as a warrant to meet force without congressional authorization. Misguided as is the construction put by the State Department on the actions of Madison, Adams, and Jefferson,[216] the Department yet agrees that "Their views and actions constitute highly persuasive evidence as to the meaning and effect of the Constitution."[217] Their actions were faithful to the intention of the Framers as expressed by the constitutional text and in the records of the Convention; and were that intention in doubt, the actions of these early statesmen provide a contemporaneous construction which carries very great weight in the interpretation of the Constitution.

---

[213] See Wormuth, supra note 86, at 738. Professor Rostow expatiates on Monroe's instructions to General Andrew Jackson "to proceed into Spanish Florida to put down the Seminoles, who were raiding settlements in Georgia from bases in Spanish Florida," on the ground of "Spain's inability to exercise effective control over her territory." Rostow, supra note 3, at 860. But Monroe well knew the distinction between such policing and committing "the nation in any question of war."

[214] 4 MESSAGES, supra note 74, at 1484.

[215] See Wormuth, supra note 86, at 738-39.

[216] LEGAL ADVISOR'S MEMO, supra note 86, at 1106. It is a mark of the State Department Legal Advisor's careless advocacy that he could argue against this background that "James Madison . . . Presidents John Adams, and Jefferson all construed the Constitution, in their official actions during the early years of the Republic, as authorizing the United States to employ its armed forces abroad in hostilities in the absence of any Congressional declaration of war." Id. 1106.

[217] Id.

To the contemporaneous construction by the great statesmen who participated in the formation and adoption of the Constitution, we may add the voice of Chief Justice Marshall, himself a vigorous participant in the Virginia Ratification Convention, who stated in *Talbot v. Seeman*:[218] "The whole powers of war being, by the constitution of the United States, vested in congress, the acts of that body can alone be resorted to as our guides in this inquiry."[219] Not even the crisis of the Civil War led the Court to depart in *The Prize Cases*[220] from the earlier view: "By the Constitution, Congress alone has the power to declare a national or foreign war." The President "has no power to initiate or declare a war either against a foreign nation or a domestic State . . . . If a war be made by invasion of a foreign nation, the President is . . . bound to resist force by force. He does not initiate the war, but is bound to accept the challenge . . . ."[221]

And so we come to Lincoln's "complete transformation in the President's role as Commander-in-Chief," by wedding it, says Corwin, to his duty to execute the laws to derive the "war power."[222] So far as the original meaning and intention are concerned, neither power taken alone conferred a "war-making power," and when nothing is added to nothing the sum remains nothing. In considering Lincoln's acts it needs to be borne in mind that they were triggered by a "sudden attack" on *American soil*, the firing upon Fort Sumter, and this when Congress was not in session,[223] exactly the situation envisioned by the Framers as the sole exception to the exclusivity of congressional war powers.[224] Congress was convened by Lincoln and met in about ten weeks;[225] in the words of Corwin, it accepted "willy-nilly"[226]

---

[218] 5 U.S. (1 Cranch) 1 (1801).

[219] *Id.* at 28.

[220] 67 U.S. (2 Black) 635 (1862).

[221] *Id.* at 668.

[222] E. CORWIN, *supra* note 26, at 275, 277.

[223] *Id.* 277.

[224] The dissenting Justices in *The Prize Cases* admitted that war had been initiated by the South in a "material sense," but maintained that it did not exist in a "legal sense" as "within the meaning of the law of nations" in the absence of a declaration of war by Congress. But the early statutes, which authorized the President to use the military and naval forces to suppress insurrection, would include a blockade as a measure of suppression. Act of Feb. 28, 1795, ch. 36, 1 Stat. 424; Act of Mar. 3, 1807, ch. 39, 2 Stat. 443. Whatever merit the dissenting argument may have is overcome by the fact that the Convention rejected the application of the law of nations to rebellion. 3 RECORDS, *supra* note 30, at 158.

Against this background, McDougal and Lans seem to me mistaken in stating that "the logic of the Civil War *Prize Cases* leads ineluctably to the conclusion that the President may recognize the existence or imminence of a war, which threatens American interests, before there is an actual invasion of our territory . . . ." McDougal & Lans, *supra* note 106, at 613. Lincoln held to the tenet that the Union is indissoluble, that no state can secede. The firing upon Fort Sumter therefore represented an "actual invasion of our territory," and Lincoln was empowered by statute to suppress insurrection.

[225] 7 MESSAGES, *supra* note 74, at 3214-16; E. CORWIN, *supra* note 26, at 277-78.

[226] E. CORWIN, *supra* note 26, at 282.

when it did not expressly ratify the results of Lincoln's actions. It would be pointless to enter upon an examination of Lincoln's acts on the domestic scene, for they do not serve as a "precedent" for presidential resistance to a "sudden attack" on a *foreign* country.[227]

Such conduct had in fact been earlier condemned by Lincoln. When President Polk sent an army into territory disputed with Mexico, which engaged in battle, Congress declared war on Mexico.[228] But in 1848 the House adopted a resolution that the war had been "unconstitutionally begun by the President," and Lincoln, who voted for the resolution along with J. Q. Adams, explained to Herndon:

> Allow the President to invade a neighboring nation whenever he shall deem it necessary to repel an invasion, and you . . . allow him to make war at his pleasure. . . . The provision of the Constitution giving the war-making power to Congress was dictated by the [fact that] Kings had always been involving and impoverishing their people in wars . . . and they resolved so to frame the Constitution that no one man should hold the power of bringing oppression upon us.[229]

That his conduct on the domestic front during the Civil War did not spell repudiation of his 1848 view may be gathered from the fact that in his first annual message, he referred to a prior authorization by Congress to American vessels to "defend themselves against and to capture pirates," and recommended an additional authorization "to recapture any prizes which pirates may make of United States vessels and their cargoes [in the Eastern seas specially]."[230] Clearly this constitutes a disclaimer of power to employ force abroad without the consent of Congress.

It was Congress rather than the reluctant President McKinley which clamored for the Spanish-American War and issued a declaration of war.[231] The nineteenth century, in sum, offers no example of a President who plunged the nation into war in order to repel an attack on some foreign nation.[232] That remained for the twentieth century.

Although World War I proved the truth of Madison's apothegm that "War is . . . the true nurse of executive aggrandizement,"[233] this

---

[227] *Cf. id.,* 279-80.

[228] Wormuth, *supra* note 86, at 726.

[229] *Id.* 727.

[230] 7 MESSAGES, *supra* note 74, at 3245-48.

[231] S. MORISON, THE OXFORD HISTORY OF THE AMERICAN PEOPLE 801 (1965).

[232] Putney, *supra* note 208, at 1-2; *Power to Commit Forces, supra* note 3, at 1790.

[233] 6 J. MADISON, *supra* note 75, at 174.

was again largely on the domestic front, a development traced by Corwin.[234] Reelected in 1916 on the slogan "He kept us out of war," Wilson asked Congress in February, 1917, for authority to arm American merchant ships for their defense. The measure was stalled in the Senate by a filibuster led by Senators Robert LaFollette and George Norris. Wilson then ordered the arming on his own,[235] though he later acknowledged that the action was "practically certain" to draw us into war.[236] Repeated attacks without warning by German submarines together with disclosure of the "Zimmerman note"[237] fueled the rising war fever as Wilson summoned Congress to a special session on April 20. Upon Wilson's request that Congress declare "the recent course of the German Government to be, in fact, nothing less than war . . . ," it declared war.[238] Thus he withstood the temptation "to resist force with force," singlehandedly to commit the nation to war. Much as Wilson expanded the war power for domestic purposes, his conduct gives no comfort to the thesis that invasion of a foreign land affords an excuse for presidential war-making.

Franklin Roosevelt, more far-sighted than the nation, also took measures which might have involved us in World War II; he exchanged fifty destroyers for British bases in the Western Atlantic, and occupied Greenland and Iceland to insure the defense of America.[239] Doubts have been expressed as to the legality of the destroyer deal;[240] but it was soon ratified by Congress. While these measures might have involved the nation in war, they did not commit our troops to battle on foreign soil. In truth, the country, moving slowly from post-World War I isolationism, was sorely divided, and without the Japanese attack on Pearl Harbor, which united the nation, Roosevelt might have had to remain content with measures "short of war."[241]

The historical record therefore confirms the statement by the

---

[234] See E. CORWIN, supra note 26, at 284-87.

[235] S. MORISON, supra note 231, at 855, 859.

[236] 55 CONG. REC. 103 (1917).

[237] See 2 H. CARMAN & H. SYRETT, A HISTORY OF THE AMERICAN PEOPLE 415 (1955). The "Note," sent by the German foreign minister urged Mexico to consider attacking the United States.

[238] S. MORISON, supra note 231, at 859-60; E. CORWIN, THE PRESIDENT'S CONTROL OF FOREIGN RELATIONS 141 (1917).

[239] E. CORWIN, supra note 26, at 288-89; Power to Commit Forces, supra note 3, at 1786.

[240] E. CORWIN, supra note 26, at 289; Kurland, The Impotence of Reticence, 1968 DUKE L.J., 619, 623. But see Youngstown Sheet & Tube Co. v. Sawyer, 343 U.S. 579, 645 n.14 (1952) (Jackson, J., concurring).

[241] S. MORISON, supra note 231, at 991, 995, 997. Justice Frankfurter "said that he had asked Byrnes (then Supreme Court Justice, later economic boss, former senator) if the President had called for a declaration of war the day before Pearl Harbor what the vote would have been. Byrnes estimated that at least two-thirds of Congress would have been in opposition." C. SULZBERGER, A LONG ROW OF CANDLES 200 (1969).

Senate Foreign Relations Committee that "only since 1950 have Presidents regarded themselves as having authority to commit the armed forces to full scale and sustained warfare."[242] In that year President Truman ordered our troops to repel the sudden invasion of South Korea.[243] Acheson's conversion of the "longboat" incidents into "historical precedents" for commitment to full scale warfare[244] exhibits a high order of fantasy, but to elevate it to constitutional doctrine is something else again.

Whether or not the Tonkin Gulf Resolution (1964)[245] authorized President Johnson to commit our armed forces to war in Vietnam, a hotly-debated issue, need not detain us because, like Acheson, Johnson and Under Secretary of State Nicholas Katzenbach claimed plenary power. "[W]e did not think the resolution was necessary to do what we did and what we are doing," the President told the press; "we think we are well within the grounds of our constitutional responsibility."[246] And Katzenbach asserted that the administration could continue to fight the Vietnam War even if Congress repealed the Tonkin resolution.[247] The resolution has since been repealed;[248] and the war goes on and has indeed been extended by the President to Cambodia and Laos.[249]

In summary, the nineteenth century "incidents" mustered by the State Department for a presidential war-making power are wide of the mark;[250] the acts of Wilson and Franklin Roosevelt in the twentieth

---

[242] S. Rep. No. 797, 90th Cong., 1st Sess. 24 (1967). Writing in 1951, Clinton Rossiter said, it is a "canon of our constitutional system that the nation cannot be finally and constitutionally committed to a state of war without the positive approval of both houses of Congress." C. Rossiter, The Supreme Court and the Commander in Chief 66 (1951).

[243] The Senate Foreign Relations Committee observed that "President Truman committed American Armed Forces to Korea in 1950 without Congressional authorization. Congressional leaders and the press were simultaneously informed of the decision but the decision had already been made." S. Rep. No. 797, 90th Cong., 1st Sess. 16 (1967). Dean Acheson stated that Truman consulted with congressional leaders, and that at a second meeting several days later there was a "general chorus of approval." D. Acheson, supra note 193, at 408-09, 413. See also Reveley, supra note 3, at 1263 n.57; J. Robinson, Congress and Foreign Policy Making 48 (1962).

[244] See note 193 supra & accompanying text.

[245] H.R.J. Res. 1145, 88th Cong., 2d Sess., 78 Stat. 384 (1964).

[246] Wormuth, supra note 86, at 711 n.1.

[247] Velvel, The War in Viet Nam: Unconstitutional, Justiciable, and Jurisdictionally Attackable, in 2 The Vietnam War and International Law 651, 654 (R. Falk ed. 1969).

[248] But the repeal did not "direct the termination of Indo-Chinese hostilities, disapprove continuing combat, or correct the President's prior interpretation." Ratner, supra note 88, at 474.

[249] American military forces were committed "to Cambodia in 1970, and to Laos in 1971, without the consent, or even the knowledge of Congress." S. Rep. No. 606, 92d Cong., 2d Sess. 8 (1972).

[250] It needs to be borne in mind that such statements are mere "advocacy" for a predetermined policy, such as led Justice Jackson to dismiss as "self-serving" earlier statements he had made as Attorney General. See note 7 supra & accompanying text.

century were provocative and might have drawn the nation into war, but they were still "short of war"; neither Wilson nor Roosevelt sent combat troops to engage in actual hostilities on foreign soil until Congress declared war. So far as the Korean War is viewed against the over-blown claims of Acheson, it is a "precedent" created by the President only yesterday, and thus is far from "embedded in the Constitution."

The Senate Foreign Relations Committee has handsomely acknowledged that "Congress . . . bears a heavy responsibility for its passive acquiescence in the unwarranted expansion of Presidential power,"[251] that "Congress has acquiesced in, or at the very least has failed to challenge, the transfer of the war power from itself to the executive."[252] Various explanations have been proffered for this inertia,[253] the sufficiency of which need not here come in question. Coke long since said that no "act of parliament by nonuser can be antiquated or lose [its] force . . . ."[254] Even less can Congress, by passivity or otherwise, divest itself of powers conferred upon it by the Constitution and accomplish the transfer of those powers to the President. It is a necessary consequence of the separation of powers that "none of the departments may abdicate its powers to either of the others."[255] Nor can any department, as John Adams was at pains to spell out in the Massachusetts Constitution of 1780, exercise the powers of another.[256] If powers, said Justice Jackson, are "granted, they are not

---

[251] S. Rep. No. 606, 92d Cong., 2d Sess. 18 (1972). Referring to the Middle East debate in 1957, the 1967 senate report on national commitments, S. Rep. No. 797, 90th Cong., 1st Sess. (1967), states, "Senator Fulbright, whose view has changed with time and experience, thought at the time that the President had power as Commander in Chief to use the armed forces to defend the 'vital interests' of the country . . ." *Id.* 18. The report concludes: "The Gulf of Tonkin resolution represents the extreme point in the process of constitutional erosion." *Id.* 20.

[252] S. Rep. No. 797, 90th Cong., 1st Sess. 14 (1967).

[253] *Id.* 14, 20-21; S. Rep. No. 606, 92d Cong., 2d Sess. 10-11 (1972). Reveley, *supra* note 3, at 1263, 1265-71; Wormuth, *supra* note 86, at 806.

[254] 1 E. Coke, Commentary on Littleton § 81b (1832).

[255] *See* Panama Refining Co. v. Ryan, 293 U.S. 388, 421 (1935); *cf.* E. Corwin, *supra* note 26, at 9.

[256] The Massachusetts Constitution of 1780 provides: "In the government of this commonwealth, the legislative department shall never exercise the executive and judicial powers . . . the executive shall never exercise the legislative and judicial powers . . . the judicial shall never exercise the legislative and executive powers . . . to the end it may be a government of laws, and not of men." 1 B. Poore, *supra* note 30, at 960. The New Hampshire Constitution of 1784 is similar, 2 *id.* 1283.

Charles Pinckney submitted to the Convention that the President "cannot be cloathed with those executive authorities the Chief Magistrate of a Government often possesses, because they are vested in the Legislature and cannot be used or delegated by them in any but the specified mode." 3 Records, *supra* note 30, at 111. In the Jay Treaty debate, Jonathan Havens "laid it down as an incontrovertible maxim, that neither of the branches of the Government could, rightly or constitutionally, divest itself of any powers . . . by a neglect to exercise those powers that were granted to it by the Constitution . . . ." 5 Annals of Cong. 486 (1797). *See also id.* 447 (remarks of John Nicholas).

Madison regarded the separation of powers as "a fundamental principle of free

lost by being allowed to lie dormant, any more than non-existent powers can be prescripted by unchallenged exercise."[257]

On the foregoing analysis, the sole presidential "war-making" powers conferred by the Framers are to serve as commander in chief of the armed forces and to repel sudden attacks on American soil.

### IV.  "INHERENT" POWER AND United States v. Curtiss-Wright Export Corp.

Before considering how far these two presidential functions are exclusive and beyond congressional control, it is necessary to examine the oft-invoked doctrine of "inherent" power, of which United States v. Curtiss-Wright Export Corp.[258] was the finest flowering. In a recent Yale memorandum,[259] the writers, after setting forth Justice Jackson's categorization of exclusive presidential power, exclusive congressional power, and a "twilight area" in which either branch can act,[260] assert that in the latter area "there is a residuum of power over and above those specifically enumerated in the constitution."[261]

Preliminarily it needs to be noted that Justice Jackson's remarks were uttered in the context of action on the *domestic* scene—President Truman's seizure of strike-bound steel plants during the Korean War—that Jackson none too obliquely cast doubt upon the legitimacy of Truman's commitment of troops to Korea,[262] and that he made no

government." 2 RECORDS, *supra* note 30, at 56. In 1796 President Washington, speaking to the demand of the House for information about the Jay Treaty, said, "it is essential to the due administration of the Government, that the boundaries fixed by the Constitution between the different departments should be preserved . . . ." 5 ANNALS OF CONG. 761-62 (1797). No incident is more frequently cited by the executive branch for the separation of powers when the issue is executive privilege than this Jay incident.

257 United States v. Morton Salt Co., 338 U.S. 632, 647 (1950).

258 299 U.S. 304 (1936), *cited in* United States v. Pink, 315 U.S. 203, 229 (1942). *See* E. CORWIN, *supra* note 26, at 210; McDougal & Lans, *supra* note 146, at 255-58. As late as 1929, Willoughby wrote, "There can be no question as to the constitutional unsoundness, as well as of the revolutionary character of the theory" of inherent powers. 1 W. WILLOUGHBY, THE CONSTITUTIONAL LAW OF THE UNITED STATES 92 (2d ed. 1929).

259 The memorandum, entitled *Indochina: The Constitution Crisis*, is reprinted in two parts at 116 CONG. REC. S7117-22 (daily ed. May 13, 1970) (Part I), and *id.* S7528-31 (daily ed. May 20, 1970) (Part II) [hereinafter cited as YALE MEMO]. The memorandum was prepared for filing with the Senate by a group of Yale Law School students under the aegis of several eminent professors and former high government officers.

260 Youngstown Sheet & Tube Co. v. Sawyer, 343 U.S. 579, 634 (1952) (concurring opinion).

261 YALE MEMO, *supra* note 259, at S7528-29. The plenary grant to Congress and the severely limited grant of war power to the President leave little "twilight" zone in this area.

262 When the government argued in *Youngstown*, 343 U.S. at 632, that the President "had invested himself with 'war powers'" by sending troops to Korea "by an exercise of the President's constitutional powers," Justice Jackson said, "How widely this doctrine . . . departs from the early view of presidential power is shown by a comparison" with Jefferson's message to Congress respecting the Tripoli pirates (note 209 *supra*) 343 U.S. at

reference to a "residuum" of extraconstitutional power, but rather rejected what may be regarded as its equivalent—a claim to "inherent" power.[263]

Reliance for that "residuum" is placed by the Yale memorandum on dicta in the *Curtiss-Wright* case,[264] itself dismissed by Jackson because it "involved, not the question of the President's power to act without congressional authority, but the question of his right to act . . . in accord with an Act of Congress."[265] Justice Sutherland, it is true, threw off a dictum that in foreign affairs there are supraconstitutional powers outside the sphere of "enumerated" powers on the theory that

> since the states severally never possessed international powers, such powers could not have been carved from the mass of state powers but obviously were transmitted to the United States from some other source . . . the powers of external sovereignty passed from the Crown not to the colonies severally, but to the colonies in their collective and corporate capacity as the United States. . . . Sovereignty is never held in suspense. When, therefore, the external sovereignty of Great Britain in respect of the colonies ceased, it immediately passed to the Union. See *Penhallow v. Doane*, 3 Dall. 54, 80-81.[266]

Sutherland did violence to the historical facts.[267] To the minds of the colonists, "thirteen sovereignties," as Chief Justice John Jay[268] said in 1793, "were considered as emerged from the principles of the Revolution."[269] For this we need go no further than the Articles of

---

642 n.10. Professor Rostow repeatedly cites this Jackson opinion but takes no account of Jackson's rejection of inflated executive claims.

Prior to *Youngstown*, Clinton Rossiter had noted, "The breath-taking estimates of their war powers announced and acted upon by Lincoln and Roosevelt have earned no blessing under the hands of the judiciary." C. ROSSITER, THE SUPREME COURT AND THE COMMANDER IN CHIEF 5 (1951). The Court, he said, "has refused to speak about the powers of the President as commander-in-chief in any but the most guarded terms," or "to approve a challenged presidential or military order solely on authority of the commander-in-chief clause if it can find a more specific and less controversial basis," such as "any evidence of congressional approval." *Id.* 4, 6.

263 *See* note 148 *supra.* "The United States is entirely a creature of the Constitution. Its power and authority have no other source." Reid v. Covert, 354 U.S. 1, 5-6 (1957).

264 YALE MEMO, *supra* note 259, at S7529; United States v. Curtiss-Wright Export Corp., 299 U.S. 304, 315-16 n.2 (1936).

265 Youngstown Sheet & Tube Co. v. Sawyer, 343 U.S. 579, 635-36 n.2 (1952). For a trenchant critique of the *Curtiss-Wright* dictum, see Kurland, *supra* note 240, at 622-23.

266 United States v. Curtiss-Wright Export Corp., 299 U.S. 304, 316-17 (1936).

267 Although they rely heavily on *Curtiss-Wright*, McDougal and Lans concede that Sutherland's analysis "unquestionably involves certain metaphorical elements and considerable differences of opinion about historical facts." McDougal & Lans, *supra* note 106, at 257-58. The Framers, as we shall see, would have no part of such metaphors. The issue is not, as McDougal and Lans suggest, merely a "quarrel about the naming of powers," *id.* 258, but a claim to powers not granted under a system of enumerated powers.

268 Jay had served as Secretary of Foreign Affairs to the Continental Congress.

269 Chisholm v. Georgia, 2 U.S. (2 Dall.) 419, 470 (1793). The Massachusetts Con-

Confederation, agreed to by the Continental Congress on November 15, 1777, signed by all but Maryland in 1778 and 1779, and ratified March 1, 1781.[270] Article II recited, "Each State retains its sovereignty, freedom and independence, and every power . . . which is not . . . expressly delegated to the United States, in Congress assembled."[271] Article III provided, "The said states hereby severally enter into a firm league of friendship with each other for their common defense . . . ."[272] They entered into a "league"; they did not purport to create a "corporate" or "sovereign" body. Article IX declared that "The United States, in Congress assembled, shall have the sole and exclusive right and power of determining on peace and war . . . [and] entering into treaties and alliances."[273] This express grant of war and treaty powers undermines Justice Sutherland's central premise that these powers were derived from "some other source" than the several states. If the fledgling Continental Congress possessed "inherent" war and treaty powers from the outset, the express grant was superfluous.

Nor did the Framers share Justice Sutherland's views on sovereignty. More pragmatic than he, they spoke, not in terms of sovereignty, but of power; and they were quite clear that the *people*, not even the cherished states, were sovereign. Power flowed from them, not from the Crown to fill a vacuum. Hear James Iredell in North Carolina: "It is necessary to particularize the power intended *to be given* . . . as having *no existence* before . . . ."[274] The people, stated Madison in the Convention, "were in fact, the fountain of all power";[275] a part they conferred upon the individual states. In the clause "We, the people of the United States . . . do ordain and establish this Constitution," said Chief Justice Jay, "we see the people acting as sovereign of the whole country."[276] "Sovereignty" was taken by the people to themselves.

Justice Sutherland's citation of *Penhallow v. Doane* referred

---

stitution of 1780 provided, "The people of this commonwealth have the sole and exclusive right of governing themselves as a free, sovereign, and independent State, and do, and forever hereafter shall, exercise and enjoy every power, jurisdiction, and right which is not, . . . by them expressly delegated to the United States . . . ." 1 B. POORE, *supra* note 30, at 958.

[270] H. COMMAGER, *supra* note 77, at 111.

[271] *Id.*

[272] *Id.*

[273] *Id.* 113.

[274] 4 J. ELLIOT, *supra* note 36, at 179 (emphasis added).

[275] 2 RECORDS, *supra* note 30, at 476. For similar remarks by Mason, Iredell, Wilson and others, see R. BERGER, *supra* note 33, at 173 n.99, 174-75. With justice, therefore, did Professor Kurland dismiss Justice Sutherland's "discovery" that "the presidential power over foreign affairs derived not at all from the Constitution but rather from the Crown of England." Kurland, *supra* note 240, at 622. *See also* note 295 *infra*.

[276] Chisholm v. Georgia, 2 U.S. (2 Dall.) 419, 470 (1793).

solely to the opinion of Justice William Paterson,[277] ignoring the contrary majority opinions of Justices Iredell and Cushing. The case arose on a state of facts that antedated the adoption of the Articles of Confederation; and Paterson stated that the Continental Congress exercised the "rights and powers of war and peace" that "states individually did not." This does not tell the whole story. For example, Congress resolved on November 4, 1775, "That the town of Charleston ought to be defended against attempts that may be made to take possession thereof by the enemies of America, and that the convention or council of safety of the colony of South Carolina, ought to pursue such measures, as to them shall seem most efficacious for the purpose, and that they proceed immediately to erect such fortifications and batteries in or near Charleston, as will best conduce to promote its security, the expence to be paid by the said Colony."[278] Other testimony that the war-making power was thought to reside in each of the colonies is furnished by the July 12, 1776, draft of the Articles of Confederation: "The said Colonies unite themselves . . . and hereby severally enter into a firm League of Friendship . . . binding the said Colonies to assist one another against all Force offered to or attack made upon them . . . ."[279] Indeed, as Justice Chase was to remark in a cognate case, the very fact of delegation of war power by the states to the Congress demonstrates that the states must have "rightfully possessed" it.[280] In course of time the states did not "individually" exercise the power of war; but that did not spring from absence of original power but from a voluntary surrender expressed both in the article IX delegation and in article XIII of the 1776 draft Articles: "No Colony . . . shall engage in any War without the previous Consent of the United States assembled," a provision that was preserved in article VI of the Articles as adopted.[281]

Justice James Iredell, whose opinion in *Penhallow* went unnoticed by Sutherland, understood all this full well. Each province, he pointed out, had comprised "a body politic," in no wise connected with the others "than as being subject to the same common sovereign."[282] "If Congress," he continued, "previous to the articles of confederation,

---

277 3 U.S. (3 Dall.) 54, 80-81 (1793).

278 3 JOURNALS OF THE CONTINENTAL CONGRESS 1774-1789, at 326 (1937).

279 5 *id.* 546.

280 "Virginia had a right, as a sovereign and independent nation, to confiscate any British property within its territory, unless she had before delegated that power to Congress . . . . [I]f she had parted with such power, it must be conceded, that she once rightfully possessed it." Ware v. Hylton, 3 U.S. (3 Dall.) 192, 231 (1796).

281 3 JOURNALS OF THE CONTINENTAL CONGRESS 1774-1789, at 549 (1937); H. COMMAGER, *supra* note 77, at 112.

282 3 U.S. (3 Dall.) at 90.

possessed any authority, it was an authority derived from the people of each province . . . ."[283] "[T]his authority was conveyed by each body politic separately, and not by all the people in the several . . . states, jointly . . . ."[284] And he concluded that the war-making authority "was not possessed by congress, unless given by all the states."[285] In this view he was joined by Justice William Cushing;[286] and both are abundantly confirmed by the specific grants of war and treaty powers to the Congress in the Articles of Confederation.

Reliance for "inherent" war and treaty powers that antedate the Articles of Confederation also has been placed upon some remarks of Justice Chase[287] in *Ware v. Hylton*:[288] "The powers of Congress originated from necessity . . . ; they were revolutionary in their very nature . . . . It was absolutely and indispensably necessary that Congress should possess the power of *conducting* the war against *Great Britain*, and therefore if not expressly given by all (as it was by some [who had ratified in 1778]) of the States . . . Congress did rightfully possess *such* power."[289] A simpler and more prosaic explanation is at hand. Sitting and working together, the delegates from the thirteen states, who as early as July, 1776, proposed in the draft Articles of Confederation to reduce to writing the necessary delegation by the states to Congress and who agreed to the Articles of Confederation in November, 1777, presumably were agreed that the conduct of the war required centralization and thus authorized the necessary "confederated" acts pending formal adoption of the proposed Articles. Roughly that view was taken by Iredell, one of the great Founders who led the struggle for adoption of the Constitution in North Carolina.

The invocation of the treaty with France signed by Benjamin Franklin and his fellow commissioners in February, 1778, and ratified by Congress in May, little advances the argument for "inherent" national power.[290] Franklin and the other commissioners had proceeded to France under express instructions to enter into a treaty with the King of France, carrying with them "letters of credence" (September, 1776), running *not* from the Congress but from "the *delegates*

---

283 *Id.* at 92.

284 *Id.* at 94.

285 *Id.* at 95.

286 *Id.* at 116. Cushing stated, "I have no doubt of the sovereignty of the states, saving the powers delegated to congress . . . to carry on, unitedly,. the common defense in the open war." *Id.* at 117.

287 McDougal & Lans, *supra* note 106, at 258.

288 3 U.S. (3 Dall.) 199 (1796).

289 *Id.* at 232.

290 McDougal & Lans, *supra* note 106, at 258; 11 JOURNALS OF THE CONTINENTAL CONGRESS 1774-1789, at 421, 444, 457 (1937).

of the United States of New Hampshire, Massachusetts Bay" and each of the other enumerated states.[291] Doubtless the delegates from the several states believed themselves authorized to send Franklin in search of an alliance, so that again we have a power delegated by the states. The resulting treaty, it bears emphasis, was concluded with "the thirteen United States of North America, viz. New Hampshire, Massachusetts Bay" and so forth,[292] scarcely testimony that France deemed it was concluding an alliance with a "sovereign" nation. But give the "revolutionary central government" its widest scope and the question remains: what relevance do deeds resulting from "revolutionary necessity" in the absence of an existing structure have to a subsequent written document, such as the Articles of Confederation, which carefully enumerates the powers granted and reserves all powers not "expressly delegated"? John Jay wrote of the cognate treaty making power in *The Federalist Number 64*, that it "should not be *delegated* but . . . with such precautions, as will afford the highest security . . . ."[293]

Study of the constitutional records convinces that the Framers jealously insisted on a federal government of enumerated, strictly limited powers.[294] Avowal of a supraconstitutional "residuum" of powers not granted expressly or by necessary implication[295] would have affrighted them and barred adoption of the Constitution.[296] We

---

[291] 5 JOURNALS OF THE CONTINENTAL CONGRESS 1774-1789, at 827, 833 (1937) (emphasis added). McDougal and Lans say that "these early Congresses . . . although controlling foreign policy, essentially functioned as councils of ambassadorial delegates from a group of federated states . . . ," the very point I have been making. McDougal & Lans, *supra* note 106, at 537. But this statement is at war with Sutherland's dictum that the states never had external "sovereignty."

[292] 11 JOURNALS OF THE CONTINENTAL CONGRESS 1774-1789, at 421 (1937). Rufus King's remarks in the Convention exhibit ignorance of the background: "The States were not 'sovereigns' in the sense contended for by some. They did not possess the peculiar features of sovereignty. They could not make war, nor peace, nor alliances nor treaties." 1 RECORDS, *supra* note 30, at 323.

[293] THE FEDERALIST No. 64, at 417 (Mod. Lib. ed. 1939) (John Jay) (emphasis added).

[294] For example, in the Virginia Ratification Convention, Governor Edmund Randolph, defending the Constitution against powerful onslaughts, said that the powers of government "are enumerated. Is it not, then, fairly deductible, that it has no power but what is expressly given it?—for if its powers were to be general, an enumeration would be needless." 3 J. ELLIOT, *supra* note 36, at 464. *See* text accompanying notes 42, 274 *supra*. Other authorities are collected in Berger, *supra* note 33, at 13-14, 377 n.52.

[295] In his 1791 lectures, James Wilson, then a Justice of the Supreme Court, referred to the executive powers granted by the Constitution and to the presidential veto as "a guard to protect his powers against their encroachment. Such powers and such a guard he ought to possess: but a just distribution of the powers of government requires that *he should possess no more*." 1 J. WILSON, *supra* note 29, at 319 (emphasis added).

Justice Sutherland's easy assumption of supraconstitutional foreign powers contradicts Madison's statement that "The powers delegated by the proposed Constitution are few and defined. . . . [They] will be exercised principally on external objects, as war, peace, negotiation, and foreign commerce." THE FEDERALIST No. 45, at 303 (Mod. Lib. ed. 1937).

[296] As Alexander White of Virginia stated in the First Congress, after insisting that

have the testimony of James Wilson that *all* the "powers naturally connected" with that of declaring war were conferred on the Congress.[297] And John Quincy Adams, after serving as Secretary of State and as President, stated, "in the authority given to Congress by the Constitution . . . to declare war, all the powers incidental to war are, by necessary implication, conferred upon the Government of the United States." The "war power," he continued, "is strictly constitutional."[298] To invoke an extraconstitutional "residuum" of war powers can only deepen the "twilight" gloom.[299]

## V. Exclusive Presidential Power Over War-Making

The statement in the Yale memorandum that there is an "exclusive" war-making zone where the President "is authorized to act even against the express will of Congress,"[300] requires a caveat insofar as it is rested on the schema set forth by Justice Jackson in *Youngstown.* Jackson preferred three categories for presidential activities. First, when "the President acts pursuant to an express or implied authorization of Congress, his authority is at its maximum, for it includes all that he possesses in his own right plus all that Congress can delegate." The steel seizure, he said, "is eliminated from the first" category "for

---

the federal government must adhere to the limits described in the Constitution: "This was the ground on which the friends of the Government supported the Constitution . . . it could not have been supported on any other. If this principle had not been successfully maintained by its advocates in the convention of the State from which I came, the Constitution would never have been ratified." 1 ANNALS OF CONG. 515 (1789). *Cf.* R. BERGER, *supra* note 33, at 13-16.

297 Text accompanying note 63 *supra.*

298 12 CONG. DEB. 4037-38 (1836). In Reid v. Covert, 354 U.S. 1, 69 (1957) (concurring opinion), Justice Harlan wrote: "Chief Justice Marshall, in *McCulloch v. Maryland,* . . . has taught us that the Necessary and Proper Clause is to be read with *all* the powers of Congress, so that 'where the law is not prohibited, and is really calculated to effect any of the objects entrusted to the government'" the Court will not "'inquire into the degree of its necessity . . . .'" So read, the war powers are little short of plenary.

299 It has been said that the "executive power clause is capable of indefinite expansion," that a construction thereof "as a broad grant of residual power to the executive was given the imprimatur of judicial approval in Myers v. United States [272 U.S. 52 (1926)]." McDougal & Lans, *supra* note 146, at 252, 260. The argument, it is true, had been advanced by Chief Justice Taft, over the vigorous dissent of Justices Holmes and Brandeis, whose views were later espoused by Justices Black, Douglas, Frankfurter, and Jackson in Youngstown Sheet & Tube Co. v. Sawyer, 343 U.S. 579 (1952). *See* text accompanying notes 39-58 *supra; cf.* notes 256 (statement of C. Pinckney), 294, 295 *supra. See generally* Berger, *Executive Privilege v. Congressional Inquiry,* 12 U.C.L.A.L. REV. 1043, 1074-76 (1965).

Justice Jackson brushed aside the claim of residual power with the query, why did the Framers expressly empower the President to "require the Opinion, in writing" of each department head, a trifling power that "would seem inherent in the executive if anything is." 343 U.S. at 640-41 (Jackson, J., concurring). Taft's view is squarely contrary to the design of the Framers to create a government of "enumerated" powers, an executive of "defined" and limited functions, and to preclude utterly any "inherent" executive prerogative.

300 YALE MEMO, *supra* note 259, at S7529.

it is conceded that no Congressional authorization exists for this seizure."[301]

His second category "is a zone of twilight in which he [the President] may have concurrent authority, or in which its distribution is uncertain." Here again presidential authority is subject to that of Congress. The steel seizure, said Jackson, "seems clearly eliminated from that class because Congress . . . has covered [the field] by three statutory policies inconsistent with this seizure."[302] Given concurrent powers, as Chief Justice Marshall held in an early war-powers case,[303] a congressional statute must prevail.

There remains the third category: "When the President takes measures incompatible with the expressed or implied will of Congress, his power is at its lowest ebb, for then he can rely only upon his own constitutional powers minus any constitutional powers of Congress over the matter."[304] Judicial caution is required in such cases lest "by disabling the Congress from acting upon the subject . . . the equilibrium established by our constitutional system" be disturbed.[305] Jackson stressed that where the Court can sustain the President only by holding that his actions were "within his domain and beyond control by Congress," the President's position was "most vulnerable to attack and in the least favorable of possible constitutional postures."[306] Jackson went on to reject the argument that Truman's commitment of troops to Korea vested him with power to seize the nation's steel mills.[307] He could find no such power under the "executive power," the "commander-in-chief power," or in an "inherent power" (presumably drawn out of the "residuum") which he preemptorily rejected.[308]

If, following Jackson's analysis, we are to speak of an "exclusive" presidential power "beyond control by Congress," we should keep in mind Jackson's warning that such claims are the most difficult to sustain. Where they are raised the "presidential power [is] most vulnerable to attack and in the least favorable of possible constitutional postures."[309]

---

[301] 343 U.S. at 635, 638 (Jackson, J., concurring).

[302] *Id.* at 637, 639. So far as Jackson's "concurrent authority" or "uncertain distribution" tests go, there is next to no "twilight" zone in the area of war powers. Congress cannot encroach on the President's command of the armed forces, that is, it cannot conduct a campaign. *But see* note 310 *infra* & accompanying text. The Framers left little doubt about the restricted nature of the presidential power "to repel sudden attacks."

[303] Little v. Barreme, 6 U.S. (2 Cranch) 170, 177-78 (1804).

[304] 343 U.S. at 637 (Jackson, J., concurring).

[305] *Id.* at 637.

[306] *Id.* at 640.

[307] *Id.* at 642; *see* note 61 *supra*.

[308] 343 U.S. at 641-52 (Jackson, J., concurring).

[309] Professor Rostow sets forth the three Jackson classifications in extenso, and

Is the role of commander in chief altogether beyond the control of Congress? This can be confidently affirmed of one set of circumstances only: once war is commenced, Congress cannot conduct a campaign; it cannot "deprive the President of command of the army and navy." But in the words of Justice Jackson, "only Congress can provide him an army or navy to command."[310] What it gives it can take away, in whole or in part.[311]

Presidential peace-time deployment of the armed forces in troubled areas sharply focuses the problem. Testifying in 1951 on behalf of President Truman's plan to station six divisions of American soldiers in Europe, Secretary of State Acheson asserted:

> Not only has the President the authority to use the Armed Forces in carrying out the broad foreign policy of the United States and implementing treaties, but it is equally clear that this authority may not be interfered with by Congress in the exercise of powers which it has under the Constitution.[312]

Acheson spoke *ex cathedra,* disdaining the citation of authority. His claim will not withstand scrutiny. Deployment of the armed forces in "hot-spots" may invite or provoke attack, dangerously risk American involvement in war,[313] and present Congress with a *fait accompli.*

---

considers that the history of our foreign affairs "matches the classification." Rostow, *supra* note 3, at 862-63. Some match! More and more the President has sought to exercise monopolistic control of military and foreign affairs, from which, by executive agreements, by resort to claims of executive privilege, and the like, Congress is virtually excluded. How does this "match" the exceedingly narrow role assigned by Jackson to exclusive presidential power?

[310] 343 U.S. at 644 (Jackson, J., concurring). Another limitation, as Madison observed, is that although the President can command, the appointment of officers requires Senate consent. 3 J. ELLIOT, *supra* note 36, at 394. By its power to make rules for the "Government and Regulation of land and naval Forces," Congress, said Justice Jackson "may to some unknown extent impinge upon even command functions." 343 U.S. at 644. "Presidential power, even in the exercise of the commander-in-chief power, is not autonomous . . . ." Moore, *The National Executive and the Use of the Armed Forces Abroad,* in 2 THE VIETNAM WAR AND INTERNATIONAL LAW 808, 813 (R. Falk ed. 1969).

[311] *Cf.* United States v. Hudson & Goodwin, 11 U.S. (7 Cranch) 32, 33 (1812): "the power which congress possesses to create Courts of inferior jurisdiction, necessarily implies the power to limit the jurisdiction of those Courts to particular objects . . . ." *See also* Sheldon v. Sill, 49 U.S. (8 How.) 441, 448-49 (1850).

[312] S. REP. No. 606, 92d Cong., 2d Sess. 17, 19 (1972). Resort to presidential power over foreign policy cannot supply any *military* power which the commander in chief lacks.

My criticism of Acheson's claim is not meant to be a covert attack on the *policy* of stationing troops in Europe, but on the presidential claim to be the sole arbiter of that policy.

[313] For example, Corwin reports that on November 28, 1941, the President and his "War Cabinet" "discussed the question: 'How shall we maneuver them [the Japanese] into the position of firing the first shot . . . .'" E. CORWIN, *supra* note 74, at 32.

Reveley, *supra* note 3, at 1262, states that Wilson and "especially Roosevelt, were forced to resort to deception and flagrant disregard of Congress in military deployment decisions because they were unable to rally congressional backing for action essential

It is Congress that is to "provide for the common Defense,"[314] which implies the right to decide what is requisite thereto. Congress also is "to raise and support armies," and by necessary implication it can withhold or withdraw that support.[315] In determining the size of the army it will "support" it is entitled to weigh priorities: shall troops be stationed in Germany or deployed in Cambodia? Indeed the constitutional mandate that "no appropriation" for support of the armies "shall be for a longer term than two years" implies that it is for Congress to decide at any point whether further appropriations should be made and in what amounts.[316] The duty of Congress, in Hamilton's words, "to deliberate upon the propriety of keeping a military force on foot,"[317] surely comprehends the right to insist that a portion of the military forces should not be kept "on foot" in Vietnam or Europe.[318]

With the power of appropriation goes the right to specify how

---

to national security." This substitutes a "Great White Father" for constitutional process. See also Power to Commit Forces, supra note 3, at 1785-87, 1796, 1798.

[314] U.S. Const. art. I, § 8(1).

[315] Id. § 8(12); see note 311 supra. In 1697, the Commons voted to disband the army notwithstanding that adherents of the King urged that the nation was still unsettled, and that there were fears of King James. 5 W. Cobbett, Parliamentary History of England 1167 (1809). The Commons voted in 1698-1699 to reduce the army. Id. 1191.

[316] U.S. Const. art I, § 8(12). When Gerry expressed fear about the absence of restrictions on the numbers of a peace-time army, Hugh Williamson "reminded him of Mr. Mason's motion for limiting the appropriation of revenue as the best guard in this case." 2 Records, supra note 30, at 327, 330. In the early days the President was compelled to come to Congress for authorizations to employ troops abroad because he had to obtain funds to raise and support troops. Only when Congress supplied a standing army was he enabled to escape from this necessity. See note 96 supra.

[317] The Federalist No. 26, at 163 (Mod. Lib. ed. 1937). The Congress "will be obliged, by this provision, once at least in every two years, to deliberate upon the propriety of keeping a military force on foot; to come to a new resolution on the point . . . . They are not at liberty to vest in the executive department permanent funds for the support of an army, if they were even incautious enough to be willing to repose in it so improper a confidence." Id.

[318] In his testimony before the Senate Foreign Relations Committee, Professor Alexander Bickel stated, "Congress can govern absolutely, absolutely, the deployment of our forces outside our borders and . . . Congress should undertake to review and to revise present dispositions." S. Rep. No. 606, 92d Cong., 2d Sess. 29 (1972). I would dissent from the proposition that "[t]o require congressional approval for every decision to deploy American troops is hardly either desirable or constitutionally required." Power to Commit Forces, supra note 3, at 1798. The congressional power is plenary, subject to no exceptions. It may be, as a practical matter, that Congress should leave the President free to make some peace-time deployments that cannot possibly lead to involvement in war; but that is a matter of accommodation by Congress, not "inherent" presidential power. In any event, the authors of the Note on presidential power to commit forces, id., conclude that "there will be some situations, such as the rushing of troops to Lebanon . . . which, although not involving immediate commitment to combat, so clearly entail the possibility of conflict that prior approval should be sought . . . . [I]nstead of assuming that the President may deploy American forces as he sees fit and only in the exceptional case need he seek congressional approval, the presumption should be that congressional collaboration is the general rule wherever the use of the military is involved, with presidential initiative being reserved for the exceptional case." What these authors, and Moore, supra note 310, at 814, regard merely as the part of wisdom, seems to me to lie within the constitutional power of Congress to require.

appropriated moneys shall be spent. This is not a mere matter of logic but of established parliamentary practice. After 1665, states Hallam, it became "an undisputed principle" that moneys "granted by Parliament, are only to be expended for particular objects specified by itself . . . ."[319] The Framers were quite familiar with parliamentary practice;[320] and we may be sure that in reposing in Congress the power of raising revenues and of making and reviewing appropriations for support of the armies they conferred the concomitant right to "specify" the "particular objects upon which its appropriations are to be expended."[321] So an early Congress read its constitutional powers in enacting a statute that all "sums appropriated by law for each branch of expenditure in the several departments shall be solely applied to the objects for which they are respectively appropriated."[322] The 1971 Act which prohibits use of appropriated funds "to finance the introduction of United States ground combat troops into Cambodia" is in this tradition.[323] If we may safely infer that the long-established parliamentary practice was adopted by the Founders, such statutes do not

---

[319] 2 H. HALLAM, CONSTITUTIONAL HISTORY OF ENGLAND 357 (1884). In 1624 "The king consented that the supplies granted should be used solely for purposes designated and spent under the direction of officers accountable to the house of commons." Turner, *Parliament and Foreign Affairs 1603-1760*, 34 ENG. HIST. REV. 172, 174 (1919). In 1701 the Act of Settlement, 12 & 13 Will. 3, c. 9, § 27, provided that appropriations were to be applied "to the several Uses and Purposes by this act directed and intended as aforesaid, and to no other Use, Intent or Purpose whatsoever." For an earlier example (1697), see 5 W. COBETT, *supra* note 315, at 1168. In 1711 the Commons complained to Queen Anne that the armed "service has been enlarged, and the charge of it increased beyond the bounds prescribed . . . a dangerous invasion of the rights of parliament. The Commons must ever assert it as their sole and undoubted privilege, to grant money and to adjust and limit the proportions of it." 6 *id.* 1027. Queen Anne replied that she would "give the necessary directions to redress the Grievances you complain of." *Id.* 1031. In 1697 the Commons resolved to disband the army notwithstanding opposition by royal adherents. 5 *id.* 1167. The principle remains vital in England. I. JENNINGS, PARLIAMENT 292, 338 (2d ed. 1957). Sir Edward Seymour was impeached for having applied appropriated funds to public purposes other than those specified. 8 How. St. Tr. 127-31 (1680). The misapplication of public moneys issued to the Earl of Ranelagh, Paymaster General of the Army, "to be applied to the use of the army and forces only, and to no other use or purpose whatsoever" was branded a "high crime and misdemeanor," and he was expelled from the Commons. 6 W. COBETT, *supra* note 315, at 97, 127.

[320] On a related point, Mason said in the Convention, "He considered the caution observed in Great Britain on this point as the paladium of the public liberty." 2 RECORDS, *supra* note 30, at 327. Madison referred to British appropriation practices in THE FEDERALIST No. 41, at 265 (Mod. Lib. ed. 1937). Madison, John Marshall and others assured the Virginia convention that the provision for jury trial carried with it all its attributes under English practice, including specifically, the right to challenge jurors. 3 J. ELLIOT, *supra* note 36, at 531, 546, 558-59, 573.

[321] For English use of appropriations to reduce the armed forces, see Coolidge & Sharrow, *The War-Making Powers: The Intentions of the Framers in the Light of Parliamentary History*, 50 B.U.L. REV. 5, 7 (1970).

[322] Act of March 3, 1809, ch. 28, 2 Stat. 535. The foregoing history refutes the executive argument that Congress' attempt "to command the expenditure of moneys that it appropriated for the construction" of the B-70 super-planes "would be a violation of the separation of powers, the invasion of presidential prerogative under the Constitution!" Kurland, *supra* note 240, at 630. *See also* note 324 *infra*.

[323] Special Foreign Assistance Act of 1971, Pub. L. No. 91-652, § 7, 84 Stat. 1942.

constitute an invasion of the President's powers as commander in chief.[324]

There remains the congressional power "To make Rules for Government and the Regulation of the land and naval forces."[325] This was added from the existing Articles of Confederation; but the Framers omitted the phrase that followed—"and directing their operations"[326] —having in mind that the President would be commander in chief who, in the words of the New Jersey Plan, would "direct all military operations."[327] Thus the Framers separated the presidential direction of "military operations" in time of war from the congressional power to make rules "for the government and regulation of the armed forces," a plenary power enjoyed by the Continental Congress. The word "government" connotes a power to control, to administer the government of the armed forces; the word "regulate" connotes a power to dispose, order, or govern. Such powers manifestly embrace congressional restraint upon deployment of the armed forces. Since the Constitution places no limits on the power to support and to govern the armed forces and to make or withhold appropriations therefor, arguments addressed to the impracticability of regulating all deployments go to the wisdom of the exercise, not the existence, of the congressional power.

The commander in chief clause empowers the President to conduct a campaign once a war is initiated by Congress or by foreign invasion of American soil, not to create incidents which embroil the nation in war. No "first General" may provoke, extend, or persist in a war against the will of Congress.[328] The duty of the President is to "take care that the laws be faithfully executed," and nothing in the Constitution absolves him from that duty in the role of commander in chief. Indeed the early state constitutions were careful to spell out that the executive was subject to the laws in his capacity of commander in chief.[329] In fine, the constitutional distribution of powers refutes Acheson's assumption that the President may deploy the armed forces as

---

[324] *Cf.* Justice Jackson's statement: "Congress alone controls the raising of revenues and their appropriation and may determine in what manner and by what means they shall be spent for military and naval procurement." Youngstown Sheet & Tube Co. v. Sawyer, 343 U.S. 579, 643 (1952) (Jackson, J., concurring).

[325] U.S. CONST. art. I, § 8(14).

[326] 2 RECORDS, *supra* note 30, at 330; H. COMMAGER, *supra* note 77, at 114.

[327] 1 RECORDS, *supra* note 30, at 244.

[328] Consider also General Douglas MacArthur's crossing of the Yalu River, which drew powerful Chinese forces into the Korean War, and contributed to his removal by President Truman. D. ACHESON, *supra* note 243, at 462-66. As "first General," the President must be equally responsible to Congress for expanding a war upon Korea to one on China.

[329] Note 67 *supra*.

he sees fit in disregard of congressional will. This is the logic of Jefferson's statement that "We have already given in example one effectual check to the Dog of war by transferring the power of letting him loose from the Executive to the Legislative body, from those who are to spend to those who are to pay."[330]

Against this background, I submit, the constitutionality of the proposed War Powers Bill is unassailable. In limiting the President's use of the armed forces "to repel an armed attack upon the United States," section 3 of the Bill is declaratory of the Madison-Gerry "sudden attacks" remark in the Convention, upon which any claim to presidential power, apart from the "first General's" direction of the military forces, ultimately rests.[331] The section 3 authorization to repel an attack on the armed forces "located outside the United States," and "to forestall the direct and imminent threat of such an attack," goes beyond the Madison-Gerry remark; but it lies within the power of Congress, and it enables the President to meet modern exigencies.

I would add a requirement that congressional authorization be had for deployment of the armed forces outside the United States, recognizing that matters of practical convenience may be left to the legislative draftsmen. My concern herein has not been with the sufficiency or wisdom of the Javits Bill, but with whether Congress is prevented by the Constitution from enacting a bill which would draw back unto itself powers conferred upon it by the Constitution and preempted by the President without constitutional warrant. Only if the "intention of the Framers" counts for little,[332] is it possible to argue on the basis of the "125 incidents" that "a practice so deeply embedded in our constitutional structure should be treated as decisive of the constitutional issue."[333]

---

[330] 15 THE PAPERS OF THOMAS JEFFERSON 397 (J. P. Boyd ed. 1955), *quoted in* S. REP. No. 797, 90th Cong., 1st Sess. 8 (1967).

[331] Text accompanying notes 77-99 *supra*.

[332] *Cf.* text accompanying note 207 *supra*.

[333] Monaghan, *supra* note 172, at 31. Monaghan questions the constitutionality of a requirement that "the president obtain authorization from Congress before making any (major?) commitment of the armed forces to hostilities" on the ground that "it is too uncertain in what it demands." "What," he asks, "precisely is the President to ask of Congress?" *Id.* 29. Let him ask, as a succession of early Presidents did, an authorization for a given "commitment of the armed forces to hostilities" and leave it to Congress to determine whether the authorization should take the form of a statute, a resolution, a declaration of war, or any other form deemed by it appropriate. The Act of March 21, 1839, ch. 89, § 1, 5 Stat. 355, may serve as a guide; it authorized the President to resist any attempt by Great Britain "to enforce, by arms, her claims to exclusive jurisdiction over that part of Maine which is in dispute between the United States and Great Britain." If Congress "is too divided to act clearly," the President will not obtain his authorization. Monaghan, *supra* note 172, at 29. He should not be permitted to commit a divided nation to war or to the grave risk of war. Even the strong-willed Franklin Roosevelt had to wait for Pearl Harbor.

Who would maintain that the President, by proclamation, can revise the Constitution in particulars he considers sadly wanting? Why should his progressive revision by actions rather than by writing be entitled to more respect? The fact that Congress countenanced the encroachments cannot lift them to the plane of constitutional dogma any more than the President and Congress can revise the Constitution by mutual consent without submitting an amendment to the people. At bottom the President lays claim "to set aside, not a particular clause of the Constitution, but its most fundamental characteristic, its division of powers between Congress and the President, and thereby gather into his own hands the combined power of both."[334] It cannot be that a statute which seeks to give effect to the original intention of the Framers, aptly expressed in the text of the Constitution, is unconstitutional.[335]

## V. Conclusion

Surveying the labors of the Framers some forty years later, Joseph Story said:

> [T]he power of declaring war is . . . so critical and calamitous, that it requires the utmost deliberation, and the successive review of all the councils of the nation . . . . The representatives of the people are to lay the taxes to support a war [and to draft men for combat], and therefore have a right to be consulted, as to its propriety and necessity.[336]

For this reason the Constitution conferred virtually all of the war-making powers upon the Congress, leaving to the President only the power "to repel sudden attacks" on the United States. They meant, in the words of James Wilson, to put it beyond the power of a single man to hurry us into war. Their wisdom is confirmed by recent events: the mounting frightfulness of war, its staggering costs in blood, money, disruption of the national and international economies, the wounds it inflicts on the national psyche—alienation of the young, desertion, draft evasion—all cry out for consultation before plunging into war.[337]

---

Monaghan also questions the "textual basis" of an authorization that falls short of a declaration of war. *Id.* 30. A power to "declare" war surely comprehends authorization of steps short of war; the greater embraces the lesser, the more so as all power "naturally connected" with the power of declaring war is vested in Congress. Congress is authorized to wage both "perfect" and "imperfect" war. Bas v. Tingy, 4 U.S. (4 Dall.) 37, 40-42 (1800). *See also* Lofgren, *supra* note 70, at 699.

[334] E. Corwin, *supra* note 74, at 65.

[335] "In my considered judgment," said Professor Richard B. Morris, the "bill sets the constitutional balance true." Morris, *The Power to Make Wars*, N.Y. Times, Apr. 13, 1972, at 43, col. 6.

[336] J. Story, *supra* note 87, at § 1171.

[337] The "executive, by acquiring the authority to commit the country to war, now

Some have referred to Congress' occasional lack of wisdom,[338] but that lack cannot justify a presidential take-over of power confided to Congress. Courts, for example, cannot overturn legislation merely because it is unwise; the choice of options is for the grantee of the power. Then too, lack of wisdom may also be exhibited by the President, as the Vietnam conflict shows. Arthur Schlesinger, who sat close to the throne while some of the fateful commitments were being made, stated that "in retrospect, Viet Nam is a triumph of the politics of inadvertence";[339] and if we are to credit General de Gaulle, a triumph of wrongheadedness.[340] Perhaps the decisions would not have been better had they been debated in Congress, but, as George Reedy, former special assistant and then Press Secretary to President Lyndon Johnson, remarked, they could not have "been much worse."[341] Since

exercises something approaching absolute power over the life or death of every living American—to say nothing of millions of other people all over the world. . . . Plenary powers in the hands of any man or group threaten all other men with tyranny or disaster." S. REP. No. 797, 90th Cong., 1st Sess. 26-27 (1967). Even those who take a broad view of presidential powers conclude on practical grounds that "Congress must be given an opportunity to say whether it finds the potential gains from the use of force worth the potential losses." Reveley, *supra* note 3, at 1288, 1299-301; Moore, *supra* note 310, at 814.

In the course of a tremendous effort on behalf of "executive agreements," McDougal and Lans conclude that "surely the history of the United States affords every reason to believe that powers given to permit rapid action in an emergency will be used as sparingly as possible. Except in case of imperative self-defense, it is to be assumed that no President will commit the use of American troops without prior consultation of Congress. If direct action by the President will sometimes be necessary, it is again to be assumed that, as soon as possible, the situation will be explained to Congress and its views sought." McDougal & Lans, *supra* note 106, at 615. In connection with these words consider the presidential commitment of troops in Cambodia and Laos after repeal of the Gulf of Tonkin Resolution. Note 249 *supra*.

[338] Reveley, *supra* note 3, at 1293; Monaghan, *supra* note 172, at 25 n.33. Former Ambassador John Kenneth Galbraith stated, "Over the last half-decade Fulbright, Morse, Gruening, Kennedy, Cooper, Church, Hatfield and McGovern have surely been more sensible than the senior officials of the Department of State. On the average I think we are safer if we keep foreign policy under the influence of men who must be re-elected." Galbraith, *Book Review*, N.Y. Times, Oct. 8, 1972, § 6 (Book Reviews), at 1, 12.

[339] Buchan, *supra* note 1, at 38.

[340] Consider President Kennedy's disregard of the informed advice of President Charles de Gaulle. On the occasion of his visit to France in May, 1961, Kennedy *"made no secret of the fact that the United States was planning to intervene* [in Indochina]." De Gaulle records that he told Kennedy "he was taking the wrong road" that would lead to "an endless entanglement . . . . We French have had experience of it. . . . You Americans . . . want to . . . revive a war which we brought to an end. I predict that you will sink step by step into a bottomless military and political quagmire . . . ." C. DE GAULLE, MEMOIRS OF HOPE, RENEWAL AND ENDEAVOR, *reprinted in* N.Y. Times, Mar. 15, 1972, at 47, col. 5. Buchan observed of our Vietnam involvement "one cannot fail to be impressed by the slapdash manner in which decisions of profound importance were taken." Buchan, *supra* note 1, at 38.

The wage-control powers presently being exercised by the President derive from a statutory grant which he did not want. *Hearings, supra* note 187, at 519.

The National Commitments Report, S. REP. No. 797, 90th Cong., 1st Sess. (1972), states that, "Congress, it seems clear, was deficient in vision during the 1920's and 1930's, but so were Presidents Harding, Coolidge and Hoover and—prior to 1938—Roosevelt. Just as no one has a monopoly on vision, no one has a monopoly on myopia either." *Id.* 14.

[341] *Hearings, supra* note 187, at 460, 464. *See also* R. DAHL, CONGRESS AND FOREIGN POLICY 245 (1950) (assessment of Roosevelt's World War II policy).

a nation of many millions cannot be convened in a town meeting, the great arena of public debate is necessarily the Congress.[342] Debate may bring into the open risks that executive advisers have overlooked; it may deflate the supposed advantages of a recommended course of action; it substitutes the experience of the many for that of the one; and above all it may serve to secure the consent of the people.

"[W]ithin the executive branch," states Reedy, "there exists a virtual horror of public debate on issues," compounded by the complacent assumption that the executive branch "have some sort of a truth that comes out of their technical expertise and that this truth . . . is not something to be debated."[343] But executive decision itself suffers from a deep-seated malady; as Reedy points out, it lacks the benefit of "adversary discussion of issues"; the "so-called debates are really monologues in which one man is getting reflections of what he sends out."[344] That courtiers are apt to reflect the desires of the monarch needs little documentation.[345]

---

[342] *Hearings, supra* note 187, at 462. "Congressional inquiry, discussion and debate ought to serve a second function: facilitating a rational decision by the electorate *outside* the Congress." R. DAHL, *supra* note 341, at 125.

[343] *Hearings, supra* note 187, at 455, 459. The philosopher Charles Frankel, who served as an Assistant Secretary of State, shed his outsider's respect for governmental expertise: "often the government does know something that people on the outside don't, but its something that isn't so . . . . After a while I came to suspect that I might not be dealing with hard facts but rather with a world created out of hunch, hope, and collective illusion." *Id.* 480. Military reports of constant progress in Vietnam illustrate the point. As Professor Dahl said, "The more closely debate moves toward broad and basic policy, the more competent is the legislative decision likely to be, and correspondingly less competent is the expert." R. DAHL, *supra* note 341, at 244.

In the executive branch there is also an ill-concealed contempt for Congress. "People like Mr. Acheson," stated Senator Fulbright, who had occasion as a member of the Foreign Relations Committee to know at first hand, "make no bones about it. They just say they [Senators] are boobs and ought to have nothing to do with foreign policy . . . ." *Hearings, supra* note 187, at 468. Acheson himself referred to the "anguishing hours" he spent in the Senate to "suffer fools gladly." D. ACHESON, *supra* note 193, at 101. When we reflect that Truman, Kennedy, Johnson, and Nixon came to the Presidency from the Senate, we may ask by what miracle "boobs" became demi-gods.

W. W. Rostow states, "In the period 1961-69 I had the privilege of observing the process of Congressional consultation with the President [Kennedy and Johnson] on many occasions . . . . I emerged with great respect for members of Congress and have heard them make wise and helpful observations, both critical of the President's course and supportive." *Hearings, supra* note 187, at 535.

[344] *Hearings, supra* note 187, at 465-66. Reedy states of some meetings of the Cabinet and of the National Security Council that "everyone [was] trying desperately to determine just what it is that the President wants to do." *Id.* 466. Former Attorney General Ramsey Clark stated that "he had been wrong not to speak out against the Vietnam war when he was . . . Attorney General in President Johnson's cabinet while the war was expanding," and is quoted as saying, "There is too much tendency in the executive branch not to argue with policy." N.Y. Times, Aug. 16, 1972, at 7, col. 1. Of course, there is the occasional maverick, like Under Secretary of State George Ball, who persisted in opposition to Vietnam escalation in the face of an inner-circle consensus.

[345] Senator Charles Mathias said, "The more a President sits surrounded only by his own views and those of his personal advisers, the more he lives in a house of mirrors, in which all views and ideas tend to reflect and reinforce his own." *Hearings, supra* note 187, at 17.

Even worse is a situation such as that of President Eisenhower. Ambassador Douglas Dillon, according to C. SULZBERGER, *supra* note 241, at 1018, said that "Eisenhower never

Of course public criticism is painful; but official pain is out-weighed by public benefit. A seasoned observer, Sir Ivor Jennings, stated, "Negotiations with foreign powers are difficult to conduct when a lynx-eyed Opposition sits suspiciously on the watch. We might have a better foreign policy if we had no Parliament: but we might have a worse . . . . We are a free people because we can criticize freely . . . ."[346] It is quite likely, as Reedy concludes, that the present division in our country, the loss of confidence in the government, results in large part from the fact that the Vietnam commitments were made without consultation with the people.[347]

Whatever the merits of debate, this is a requirement of our democratic system. Those who are to bleed and die have a right to be consulted, to have the issues debated by their elected representatives.[348] Unlike the totalitarian nations, we have not placed our faith in a "Fuehrer," a "Big Brother"; a benign dictatorship is not for us.[349] It is for that reason that there is an "American propensity to substitute 'for . . . the question of the beneficial *use* of the powers of government . . . the question of their *existence*.' "[350] Events since 1936, when Corwin penned the quoted words, have demonstrated still again that "use" of power may be not only "beneficial" but "malign, fearsome, hateful and dangerous."[351]

It was because the Framers were alive to the insatiable maw of power that they contrived the separation of powers.[352] It remains a bulwark against oppression, not a hollow shibboleth.[353] "With all its

---

reads the newspapers and therefore doesn't know what goes on, and the apparatus around him sees that he doesn't know what goes on. The President's information nowadays is limited to what he is allowed to see by his entourage."

[346] I. JENNINGS, THE BRITISH CONSTITUTION 82 (3d ed. 1950).

[347] *Hearings, supra* note 187, at 455-56. "In the conduct of foreign relations, unity is one of the most important assets leadership can possess, disagreement one of the greatest liabilities." R. DAHL, *supra* note 341, at 221, 262. In addition to the examples cited by Dahl, there is the current divisiveness over Vietnam, which toppled one President, and has strewn boulders in the path of another, in no little part because the people were not really consulted.

[348] Senator Fulbright stated, "the Congressman or Senator has to respond to the wishes . . . of his electorate. This anchor in reality is the elected Representative's one indispensable credential for participation in the policymaking process." *Hearings, supra* note 187, at 23.

[349] *Cf.* Kurland, *The Impotence of Reticence*, 1968 DUKE L.J. 619, 625-28. *See generally* McDougal & Lans, *supra* notes 106 & 146.

[350] Monaghan, *supra* note 172, at 19.

[351] Jaffe, *The Right of Judicial Review*, 71 HARV. L. REV. 401, 404 (1958).

[352] B. BAILYN, THE IDEOLOGICAL ORIGINS OF THE AMERICAN REVOLUTION 56-57 (1967); R. BERGER, *supra* note 33, at 9. Attorney General Rogers stated in 1958 that "The doctrine of the separation of powers was thus the very foundation stone of the Federal Government . . . the basic guarantee of the liberties of the people." *See Hearings, supra* note 187, at 562.

[353] Justice Black stated in Reid v. Covert, 354 U.S. 1, 40 (1957), "Ours is a government of divided authority on the assumption that in division there is not only strength but freedom from tyranny."

defects, delays and inconveniences," said Justice Jackson, "men have discovered no technique for long preserving free government except that the Executive be under the law, and that the law be made by parliamentary deliberations."[354] That is what the Framers provided in distributing the war-powers, and to that scheme we must return.

---

[354] Youngstown Sheet & Tube Co. v. Sawyer, 343 U.S. 579, 655 (1952) (Jackson, J., concurring).

# The War-Making Powers: A Constitutional Flaw?

## DON WALLACE, JR.[†]

As the Vietnam War became more controversial, and as American emotions about it mounted, its legality was increasingly questioned.[1] The entry of United States troops into Cambodia in May 1970 elicited great emotion and much dispute.[2] Notwithstanding such controversy, the essential issue raised by Vietnam and Cambodia is not the

---

[†] Professor of Law, Georgetown University; Director, Institute for International & Foreign Trade Law. B.A. 1953, Yale University; LL.B. 1957, Harvard University.

[1] *Compare* U.S. Dep't of State, *The Legality of U.S. Participation in the Defense of Viet-Nam,* 112 CONG. REC. 11,202 (1966), *with* Lawyer's Comm. on American Policy Towards Vietnam, *American Policy Vis-à-Vis Vietnam in Light of Our Constitution, the United Nations Charter, the 1954 Geneva Accords, and the Southeast Asia Collective Defense Treaty,* 112 CONG. REC. 2666 (1966).

[2] *See* Memorandum, The Congressional and Executive Roles in Warmaking: An Analytical Framework, *reprinted in* 116 CONG. REC. 16,478 (1970); Memorandum, Indochina: The Constitutional Crisis (pts. 1 & 2), *reprinted in* 116 CONG. REC. 15,410, 16,352 (1970). These two memoranda, prepared by a number of scholars and attorneys with the assistance of Yale Law School students, provide an excellent discussion of the war power and of legislative actions taken to justify our posture in Southeast Asia. A similar memorandum prepared at the Harvard Law School discusses in particular the efforts of Senators John Cooper and Frank Church (*see* note 149 *infra*). Legal Memorandum on the Amendment To End the War, *reprinted in* 116 CONG. REC. 16,120 (1970).

Former Secretary of State Dean Rusk presided over a meeting of the American Society of International Law in Washington on June 16, 1970, at which opposing ideas on the nature of the Cambodian action were expressed. On one hand, William D. Rogers, a Washington attorney, stated:

> This was war. It is the Congress's responsibility to declare it so.
> Ultimately, to explain the dispatch of impressive United States ground forces into Cambodia as just another tactical field decision is to expand the scope of the President's unilateral authority by a quantum jump. . . .
> Such an escalation of the Presidency's powers is not only inconsistent with the intent of the Founders; it is also bad policy and bad politics.

Rogers, *The Constitutionality of the Cambodian Incursion,* 65 AM. J. INT'L L. 26, 36 (1971) (footnote omitted). In response, William H. Rehnquist, then Assistant Attorney General for the Office of Legal Counsel of the Department of Justice, stated:

> The President's determination to authorize incursion into these Cambodian border areas is precisely the sort of tactical decision traditionally confided to the Commander-in-Chief in the conduct of armed conflict. . . . It is a decision made during the course of an armed conflict already commenced as to how that conflict shall be conducted, rather than a determination that some new and previously unauthorized military venture shall be taken.

STAFF OF SENATE COMM. ON FOREIGN RELATIONS, 91ST CONG., 2D SESS., DOCUMENTS RELATING TO THE WAR POWER OF CONGRESS, THE PRESIDENT'S AUTHORITY AS COMMANDER-IN-CHIEF AND THE WAR IN INDOCHINA 182 (Comm. Print 1970) (statement of W. H. Rehnquist).

President Nixon's decision to mine Haiphong harbor and North Vietnamese coastal waters also engendered controversy. *See* N.Y. Times, May 14, 1972, § 4, at 1, col. 3.

legality of American actions per se. In fact, courts have declared our participation in Vietnam to be congressionally authorized and hence legal,[3] and have declared the Cambodian invasion to be "tactical" and hence within the commander-in-chief's constitutional powers.[4] Rather, Vietnam raises once again a persisting constitutional question:[5] does the Constitution make proper provision for the making of war by the United States? The question arises because of that singular and unprecedented American institution, the separation of powers between the Executive, Congress, and the courts in our system of federal government.

To be sure, the question can be answered in more or less conventional constitutional terms, that is, in terms of who has the power to initiate, conduct, and terminate wars. But a closer examination reveals that what is involved is no ordinary legal or constitutional issue. War is an aspect of a nation's international relations and must therefore be seen from the perspective of the international as well as the domestic order. However, to the extent that there is domestic controversy about a war—as there most visibly has been about Vietnam—the issue should be seen primarily as one of domestic American politics rather than law. Profound questions about the soundness of our Vietnam war policy have given rise to a passionate debate on American foreign policy in general and indeed on our proper "role" in the world. One should be aware that this controversy has taken place within a specific domestic institutional setting. This domestic setting includes not only the sometimes shifting division of external and war powers between the President and Congress[6] (which is the focus of this article), but also phenomena such as the general historical relationship between the

---

[3] *E.g.*, Orlando v. Laird, 443 F.2d 1039 (2d Cir.), *cert. denied*, 404 U.S. 869 (1971). *See also* Atlee v. Laird, Civil No. 71-2324 (E.D. Pa., filed Sept. 24, 1971).

[4] *See* Mottola v. Nixon, 318 F. Supp. 538 (N.D. Cal. 1970). Courts have also indicated that they were not prepared to consider the allegation that the Vietnam War violated international law. *E.g.*, United States v. Mitchell, 369 F.2d 323 (2d Cir.), *cert. denied*, 386 U.S. 972 (1967).

[5] Compare the celebrated debate between James Madison (writing as Pacificus) and Alexander Hamilton (writing as Helvidius) on the related subject of the power of President Washington to declare our neutrality in the war between Britain and France in 1793. *See* E. CORWIN, THE PRESIDENT'S CONTROL OF FOREIGN RELATIONS 7-32 (1917).

[6] In the words of former Undersecretary of State George W. Ball,
[I]t was inevitable that effective distribution of powers would be subject to periodic tidal flows, with authority shifting from one branch to the other and then back again, reflecting changes in the objective situation faced by the nation, the differing personalities of the individuals from time to time dominating each branch, and fluctuations in the mood of the country.
Nowhere has this been more conspicuously the case than in our external relations . . . .
*Round table: The Role of Congress in the Making of Foreign Policy*, PROC. AM. SOC'Y INT'L L., 65TH ANNUAL MEETING, April 29-May 1, 1971, at 173-74.

President and Congress,[7] the role of political parties,[8] the scope of government powers generally, and more short-term phenomena such as bipartisanship in foreign policy.[9]

## I

### THE NATURE OF THE ISSUE: MORE POLITICAL THAN LEGAL

The constitutional debate over Vietnam is the result of a fierce political disagreement over the soundness of our performance on the international stage. Paradoxically the constitutional dispute over the allocation of the war powers between the Executive and Congress, although provoked by disagreement over the soundness of our policy, centers largely on the issue of the democratic responsibility of the policy maker.[10] The question becomes whether the President has undemocratically usurped from Congress, alleged to be the most popular branch of government, the power to make war—both in Vietnam and generally.

One of the major themes of this article is that many critics of Vietnam have misconceived the nature of the constitutional issue presented by the war. Their desire to obtain injunctions against the President, to obtain writs of habeas corpus,[11] or to get laws passed[12] has largely been misplaced. Three variables usually not present in legal or constitutional problems have given rise to misunderstanding: the reality of the international system, the flawed character of the separation of powers in the foreign affairs area, and the almost total refusal of the judiciary to become involved. I shall analyze these three factors before proceeding to the *lege lata*—the actual law—of the war powers.

### A. *The Reality of the International System*

An obvious truth, not always remembered,[13] is that the international order is very different from the domestic order. Whereas the do-

---

7 Very significant, for our purposes, was the emergence under Andrew Jackson of a presidency which no longer looked to the Congress for its lead. In the words of Professor Robert Dahl, "[W]ith Jackson a new type of president appeared, the plebiscitary, mass-based executive, operating with his own 'mandate' and often fighting fierce battles with the Congress." R. DAHL, CONGRESS AND FOREIGN POLICY 170 (1950) [hereinafter cited as DAHL].

8 *Id.* at 185-204.

9 *Id.* at 210-11.

10 *Id.* at 99-102.

11 *See* text accompanying notes 210-13 *infra*.

12 *See* text accompanying notes 179-209 *infra*.

13 *See generally* Ratner, *The Coordinated Warmaking Power—Legislative, Executive, and Judicial Roles*, 44 S. CAL. L. REV. 461 (1971); Tigar, *Judicial Power, the "Political Question" Doctrine, and Foreign Relations*, 17 U.C.L.A.L. REV. 1135 (1970).

mestic order is in large part subject to the rule of law, the international order more closely resembles a jungle.[14] Instability of relations among individual nation states is a prominent feature of the international order. More significant, for present purposes, is the view of the situation from the perspective of any individual nation state. Although many governments including, one hopes, that of the United States, have the power largely to control their domestic affairs,[15] they cannot always unilaterally control their foreign affairs; there will often be activities of

---

[14] John Locke's statement on the distinction between the domestic order and the international order remains classic: "[F]or though in a commonwealth the members of it are . . . governed by the laws of the society, yet in reference to the rest of mankind they make one body, which is . . . still in the state of nature." J. LOCKE, THE SECOND TREATISE OF GOVERNMENT 74 (J. Gough ed. 1966). Professor Raymond Aron has stated this concept in more modern terms:

> [S]o long as humanity has not achieved unification into a universal state, an *essential* difference will exist between internal politics and foreign politics. The former tends to reserve the monopoly on violence to those wielding legitimate authority, the latter accepts the plurality of centers of armed force. Politics, insofar as it concerns the internal organization of collectivities, has for its immanent goal the subordination of men to the rule of law. Politics, insofar as it concerns relations among states, seems to signify—in both ideal and objective terms—simply the survival of states confronting the potential threat created by the existence of other states. Hence the common opposition in classical philosophy: the art of politics teaches men to live in peace within collectivities, while it teaches collectivities to live in either peace or war. States have not emerged, in their mutual relations, from the *state of nature*.

R. ARON, PEACE AND WAR: A THEORY OF INTERNATIONAL RELATIONS 6-7 (1966) (emphasis in original) [hereinafter cited as ARON].

Former Judge of the International Court of Justice Charles de Visscher has stated that the "instability [of social relations], exceptional in the internal order, is the more or less general condition of the international order, dominated and constantly troubled . . . by the factor of force." C. DE VISSCHER, THEORY AND REALITY IN PUBLIC INTERNATIONAL LAW 135 (1957). Judge de Visscher acknowledges that the international order consists of and is defined by nation states, even though he seeks a new international order based on a humane concern for individuals. As to the sometimes seemingly irrational and bloody-minded behavior of nation states, no one has spoken more eloquently than Rinehold Niebuhr.

> [M]ost learned men would not be rational enough to penetrate and transform the unconscious and sub-rational sources of parochial loyalties, which determine the limits of community and which prompt inhuman brutalities to other human beings, who do not share the same marks of race, language, religion, or culture.

R. NIEBUHR, MAN'S NATURE AND HIS COMMUNITIES 93 (1965).

The difference between the international and domestic orders is thought to lead to a distinction between the foreign and domestic powers of our federal government as regards both their origin and nature. *See* United States v. Curtiss-Wright Export Corp., 299 U.S. 304 (1936). *But see* Penhallow v. Doane, 3 U.S. (3 Dall.) 54 (1795).

[15] To be sure, control is not perfect. The division between federal and state governments in the United States creates many difficulties. So too one has only to think of racial issues to appreciate the difficulties in managing some domestic affairs and the social costs that can be involved in domestic control. Additionally, in an increasingly interdependent world the line between the foreign and domestic affairs of a particular nation state may become blurred. Nonetheless the basic generalization remains true.

other nation states over which they do not have control. This is one fact which the events of the last few years have brought home to us. The United States cannot make law for other countries; rather we act, they react, and we act again. The consequences of our actions cannot be certain; like those of all nation states, our actions involve a search for advantage. They are subject to risks and, as Professor Raymond Aron makes clear, they always take place in the "shadow of war."[16] In a country's external dealings foreign policy and war constitute a continuum. In the words of Karl von Clausewitz, "[W]ar is not merely a political act but a real political instrument, a continuation of political intercourse, a carrying out of the same by other means."[17] Diplomacy and strategy (the conduct of military operations as a whole) "are complementary aspects of the . . . art of conducting relations with other states."[18]

It is clear that today's international realities put a great and continuing pressure on all nation states, including the United States, and that this pressure is felt equally by our Executive, Congress, and courts.[19] Professor Aron has put well the impact of nuclear weapons, wars of liberation, and wars of escalation: "The weapons of mass destruction, the techniques of subversion, the ubiquity of military force because of aviation and electronics, introduce new human and material factors which render the lessons of the past equivocal at best."[20]

Just as the nature of international struggle has changed dramatically so has the role of the United States in the international order. Since 1787 the United States has moved from the sheltered margin of a European power system to the very center of a global power system.

> After this century's Second World War, the United States, which throughout its history had dreamed of standing aloof from the affairs of the Old World, found itself responsible for the peace, the prosperity, and the very existence of half the planet. GIs were garrisoned in Tokyo and Seoul in the Orient, in Berlin in Europe.[21]

---

16 ARON 6-8.

17 K. VON CLAUSEWITZ, ON WAR 16 (1943). See ARON 23.

18 ARON 24.

19 See, e.g., New York Times Co. v. United States, 403 U.S. 713 (1971) (per curiam) (pressure on the courts); R. KENNEDY, THIRTEEN DAYS: A MEMOIR OF THE CUBAN MISSILE CRISIS (1969) (pressure on the Executive); Fulbright, American Foreign Policy in the 20th Century Under an 18th-Century Constitution, 47 CORNELL L.Q. 1 (1961) (pressure on Congress). The fact is that if the founding fathers in 1787 anticipated our foreign and war affairs decisions taking place in a situation without emergency, then reality has belied their anticipation. See text accompanying note 123 infra.

20 ARON 2.

21 Id. 1. Thus we have moved from a state of "no foreign entanglements" and virtually no standing army to membership in the United Nations and a leading role in a

As the United States has moved to the center of the international power system, the significance of hostilities in which it engages has changed. Much of the debate over Vietnam concerns the question whether the magnitude of the conflict makes necessary a formal declaration of war. But the magnitude of hostilities is not the only dimension to the problem; the centrality of the United States in the international system and the centrality of particular hostilities to the interests of the United States are other factors which must be considered. Vietnam, and to a lesser extent Korea before it, have made a coherent foreign policy in America more difficult.[22] It is too early to know how long this state of affairs will continue.

## B.   *The Reality of Separation of Powers: Some Possible Flaws*

American lawyers sometimes forget what students of government have frequently noted—that separation of governmental powers is in many ways an obsolete system. Professor Samuel Huntington has compared it to the government of Tudor England.[23] Montesquieu, whose paeans to the separation of powers probably exercised some influence on Jefferson, Madison, and other founding fathers, was describing a

---

complex system of alliances, and from a disinclination to become involved in the wars of England and France in the 1790's to our involvement in World War I, our leadership in World War II, and our major role in the cold war. I do not believe that the events in Vietnam and recent efforts to redefine the United States's role, as exemplified by the so-called "Nixon Doctrine," substantially negate Aron's characterization. *See* note 294 *infra*.

22 *The Economist* has stated the matter well:

The way in which the democracies appear to sidle up to the question of war . . . is largely a result of the problem their governments have with one fairly small, but important, section of their population. The name this section of the population gives to itself is the liberal intelligentsia. . . . [I]t has one over-riding characteristic when it applies itself to the problems of international politics. Its emotions understand the misery of war, but it does not possess a matching intellectual grasp of the way cause and effect continuously operate among the powers of the world. Its feelings are international, but its reasoning remains parochial. Because it is so nice itself, it is unwilling to look too closely into the minds of the adversaries its country has to deal with.

THE ECONOMIST, June 26, 1971, at 16. *See Hearings on Executive Privilege: The Withholding of Information by the Executive Before the Subcomm. on Separation of Powers of the Senate Comm. on the Judiciary*, 92d Cong., 1st Sess., at 454, 460 (1971) (statement of G. Reedy, Fellow, Woodrow Wilson International Center for Scholars).

23 In his words:

[T]he principal elements of the English sixteenth-century constitution were exported to the new world, took root there, and were given new life precisely at the time that they were being abandoned in the home country. They were essentially Tudor and hence significantly medieval in character.

S. HUNTINGTON, POLITICAL ORDER IN CHANGING SOCIETIES 96 (1968). The Tudor system continued into Stuart times and began to change substantially only in the eighteenth century with the emergence of cabinet government. *See generally id.* at 119; text accompanying note 269 *infra*.

system which never existed in England in the form he described and whose apogee had in any event passed.[24] The United Kingdom had moved on to a system of cabinet government resting on the confidence of Parliament. This governmental system, which has been described as a fusion of executive and legislature, is generally considered more modern and mature.[25] It permits a "political" balance between executive and legislature with respect to both the power to declare war and the power to command the armed forces.

By "politics" I mean that "complicated interweaving" of a society's perceptions of reality, its preferences, and its actions.[26] In Professor Robert Dahl's terms, an effective political process permits a society to pursue "rationality," that is, soundness in its policies, to achieve "agreement" about those policies, and to do so through political institutions which are "responsible" in that they take account of and ultimately respond to the wishes of society.[27] I shall try to show that political balance is substantially lacking in the American scheme with respect to certain war decisions.[28]

The American Executive possesses great initiative with respect to foreign and war policy; its responses to the realities of the international order often confront Congress with what might be called *faits accomplis*. Indeed the initiative and momentum of executive action is so great

---

24 *See* L. FISHER, PRESIDENT AND CONGRESS: POWER AND POLICY 3-5, 248-51, (1972). Professor Fisher quotes Holmes as saying of Montesquieu, "His England—the England of the threefold division of power into legislative, executive and judicial—was a fiction invented by him . . . ." *Id.* at 248.

25 *See* DAHL 169.

26 [T]he selection of a policy must be a complicated interweaving of interpretations about reality, the preferences relevant to dealing with that reality, and the ways of mediating between those preferences and reality; hence, competent or "correct" judgment in the policy area requires a special kind of skill. This is the political skill.

*Id.* at 104. Compare the remarks of George Reedy:

[H]olding a nation together is a very difficult art. It is really the art of politics. I have never despised the word "politics" and I am very unhappy that in the English language, at least as spoken in America, it has become a pejorative word, because I think it is one of the necessary professions.

I do not think any sort of decent orderly structure is possible without it. And the art of holding a country together in a democracy is the art of politics and that is the art of convincing everybody that he has had his say.

*Hearings on Executive Privilege, supra* note 22, at 469.

27 *See* DAHL 4-5.

28 A lack of political balance is not exclusively a characteristic of the war powers. The allocation and balance of the diplomatic and other foreign policy powers is not wholly clear. *See generally* E. CORWIN, THE PRESIDENT: OFFICE AND POWERS 1787-1957 (4th rev. ed. 1957) [hereinafter cited as CORWIN]; Wallace, *The President's Exclusive Foreign Affairs Powers over Foreign Aid* (pts. 1 & 2), 1970 DUKE L.J. 293, 453 (1970) [hereinafter cited as Wallace].

that the Executive may be able to ignore congressional restraints.[29] In the United Kingdom, Parliament can at least in theory bring an executive down in this situation by a vote of no confidence. Congress, to be sure, has the power of impeachment, but history has shown that this power is practically unusable.[30] Congress also has the power, as does the British Parliament, to withhold appropriations entirely. But this too is a difficult power to manage,[31] although there have been several attempts at improvisation in this country.[32] The answer of the founding fathers to the problem of executive initiative was to add the innovation that Congress alone has the power to declare war. It is the thesis of this article that this device does not constitute a realistic or effective check on the Executive. If so, this failure would demonstrate a basic flaw in the constitutional scheme of foreign affairs powers.[33]

I suggest that there may be a second flaw in the scheme, namely, the failure of the Constitution to reflect in domestic power arrange-

---

[29] See notes 166-71 and accompanying text *infra*.

[30] CORWIN 291-92.

[31] See generally R. FENNO, THE POWER OF THE PURSE (1966). Congressman Paul Findley has said,

I am very concerned about the long-term effect of the nuclear proliferation treaty, and at one point I attempted to use the power of the purse in the House to shut off the salaries of any State Department personnel who might use their official time to advance that treaty.

. . . I must add my amendment did not get very far. The House is reluctant to use the power of the purse in specific matters like this.

*Hearings on S. Res. 151 Relating to United States Commitment to Foreign Powers Before the Senate Comm. on Foreign Relations*, 90th Cong., 1st Sess. 235-36 (1967) (remarks of Congressman P. Findley).

The British system, of course, has not relied solely on the power of the purse to check its executive. In the cabinet system based on the confidence of Parliament there is a fusion of legislature and executive and therefore a mutual, political check. *See* note 269 and accompanying text *infra*.

[32] See notes 153-73 and accompanying text *infra*.

[33] Senator Gale McGee seemed to be getting at this point in his testimony before the Senate Foreign Relations Committee when he questioned whether the hearings were not "missing the point, if we are not addressing ourselves to the wrong question. Maybe we ought to enlarge the constitutional process." *Hearings on War Powers Legislation, S. 731, S.J. Res. 18 and S.J. Res. 59 Before the Senate Comm. on Foreign Relations*, 92d Cong., 1st Sess., at 579 (1971) (remarks of Senator G. McGee) [hereinafter cited as *War Powers Hearings*].

There has certainly been a demonstrable shift in the treaty power—the other major innovation of 1787 with respect to foreign affairs. *See* Wallace 300-02. Thus while it was initially thought that the Senate would act as a council to the President in the negotiation and conclusion of treaties, it is now the practice for the President to negotiate treaties and for the Senate either to withhold or to give its consent with or without reservations. Moreover, the use of the treaty power itself has become secondary to executive agreements both of the congressional variety pursuant to congressional authorization or ratification and of the presidential variety pursuant to the President's own asserted powers. *See id.* at 302.

ments the continuum between a nation's foreign policy and war policy.[34] The great bulk of foreign policy powers have fallen to the President, yet the power to declare war was assigned to Congress. Was it not inevitable that as the Executive responded to the continuum of external pressures it would assume the war power so as to permit the United States to respond soundly and reasonably to an indivisible international reality? In point of fact the reality of foreign and war policy making in the United States is very different from the image conjured up by the phrase "separation of powers." It appears that what we have is an executive-bureaucratic policy-making model[35] with Congress merely forming a part of the setting in which policy is made.[36] In making policy, decision makers usually seek the consensus of interested constituencies[37]— and Congress has become one of those constituencies.[38]

If all this is so, then the problem is a deep constitutional one, and both the various attempts to stop the war in court and to pass laws to stop it, and the attendant scholarship, may be superficial and irrelevant. This article seeks to make clear that this is largely the case.

C.  *The Absence of Substantial Judicial Control and Its Consequences*

The basic absence of judicial control over the war powers is possibly the most difficult point of all for lawyers to grasp, accustomed as they are to handling constitutional as well as other disputes largely through court adjudication.[39] The Supreme Court and other courts of the federal and state systems have on the whole refused to adjudicate war power issues.[40] War power issues are essentially and inherently political and not legal. The reluctance of the courts to adjudicate these issues has made them even less "legal" in the sense that they have not

---

34 *See* text accompanying note 22 *supra.* Professor Alfred Kelly has remarked that our "constitutional system . . . isolated war as a legal abnormality." *War Powers Hearings* 87 (statement of A. Kelly).

35 *See generally* B. SAPIN, THE MAKING OF UNITED STATES FOREIGN POLICY 49-53 (1966); Hilsman, *Congressional-Executive Relations and the Foreign Policy Consensus,* 52 AM. POL. SCI. REV. 725 (1958); Hilsman, *The Foreign Policy Consensus: An Interim Research Report,* 3 CONFLICT RESOLUTION 361 (1959).

36 B. SAPIN, *supra* note 35, at 34-64.

37 Hilsman, 52 AM. POL. SCI. REV., *supra* note 35, at 727.

38 *Id.* at 742. The worldwide decline of the power of legislatures relative to that of executives has been noted. *See* R. DAHL, PLURALIST DEMOCRACY IN THE UNITED STATES: CONFLICT AND CONSENT 139-42 (1967). Compare the assumption of James Madison and other founding fathers that it was Congress, rather than the Executive, whose powers might wax. L. FISHER, *supra* note 24, at 18-27.

39 *See generally* G. Christie, A Theory of Judicial Review of Legislation, Dec. 11, 1970 (unpublished paper on file at the *Cornell Law Review*).

40 *See* Henkin, *Constitutional Issues in Foreign Policy,* 23 J. INT'L AFF. 222 (1969); Wallace 485-87; notes 211-62 and accompanying text *infra.*

been subject to principled decision. On the other hand, they indisputably arise out of the Constitution and involve the allocation of governmental power and authority; in this sense they undoubtedly constitute normative and constitutional questions.

There are great gaps in the Constitution as written. The function of the commander-in-chief is undefined and its relationship to the requirement that Congress declare war is unstated. The President's exclusive power to conduct foreign affairs, recognized by the courts,[41] is nowhere expressly stated. Because the courts have not often spoken, the allocation of powers between Executive and Congress[42] has been left largely to the "verdicts of history."[43] These verdicts have been rendered with respect to matters on which the constitutional fathers were either silent in 1787[44] or wrong,[45] and with respect to matters to which international relations or the position of the United States in the international order have required a new approach.[46] Indeed, there are areas

---

[41] The Supreme Court has recognized the President as "the sole organ of the federal government in the field of international relations." United States v. Curtiss-Wright Export Corp., 299 U.S. 304, 320 (1936).

[42] In the absence of a political balance, the ambiguities in the allocation of foreign affairs powers have given rise to great contrasts. Thus Professor Dahl points out that during the 1930's when Congress was seeking to hobble the President with neutrality legislation, there was not the slightest political control on the President in formulating United States policy towards Japan. The attack on Pearl Harbor, of course, reduced neutrality legislation to a nullity. DAHL 172-73.

[43] See Wallace 295 n.10; cf. Henkin, supra note 40, at 221-23. Justice Felix Frankfurter in his concurring opinion in Youngstown spoke of congressional acquiescence in a pattern of executive action giving rise to a constitutional norm. Youngstown Sheet & Tube Co. v. Sawyer, 343 U.S. 579, 610-11 (1952) (concurring opinion). Presumably, such acquiescence is one way that a verdict of history may be rendered. However, in Youngstown the Court found presidential power (to seize property during peacetime) to be lacking. This suggests the possibility that the verdicts of history can be judicially undone.

One should guard against taking too seriously precedents from prior low or high tides which may not be relevant to the level of the tide today. Examples of "tidal" shifts might include the neutrality legislation of the 1930's in reaction to President Wilson's interventionism and the current congressional efforts in reaction to Vietnam. See notes 149-51 and accompanying text infra.

[44] The Constitution does not define the scope of the commander-in-chief power; the Constitution does not by its terms indicate that the President may repulse a sudden attack on the continental United States (see notes 92-100 and accompanying text infra); and the Constitution nowhere speaks of the executive branch as the sole organ of foreign affairs (see note 41 and accompanying text supra). Moreover, the Constitution nowhere speaks of judicial review.

[45] In a number of instances the power allocated by the Constitution has in fact been reallocated. The evolution of the treaty powers is a possible example. See note 33 supra. In several instances power allocated to Congress has also been exercised independently by the Executive. See note 79 infra (commerce power); notes 79 & 80 infra (envoys); note 83 infra (calling up of troops).

[46] The treaty power is certainly one example. See note 33 supra.

in which there is yet no verdict of history.[47] Even when a matter involving the allocation of foreign affairs powers is litigated, it is upon individual initiative, since our system does not provide for suits by the Attorney General seeking a declaration of government power or an advisory opinion. As a consequence, even when a court speaks on great issues of separation of powers, it often does so in dicta in cases primarily involving individual rights.[48]

Some citizens and public officials have been much disturbed by the apparent growth in the President's war powers. Although they frequently have been strong advocates of the expansion of federal power under the commerce clause and the expansion of individual rights under the Bill of Rights, they continue to revert to the "understandings" of 1787 to argue for limiting the scope of the President's power in foreign and war affairs.[49] Possibly what they find objectionable is the unlitigated and unadjudicated growth of the President's power. This growth is, however, a product of a "liberal construction" of the Constitution, a construction by executive and legislative practice and assertion rather than by principled judicial decision.[50] It is a construction now so strong, however, that it may permit a President to ignore legislation[51] without serious objection from the courts.

There is one final observation about the courts. Alexis de Tocqueville's comment that "[s]carcely any political question arises in the United States which is not resolved, sooner or later, into a judicial

---

47 For example, may a declaration of war be revoked by Congress? *See* text accompanying notes 173-75 *infra*.

48 *E.g., Ex parte* Milligan, 71 U.S. (4 Wall.) 2, 139 (1866) (power and duty of the President as commander-in-chief to command American forces and conduct campaigns) (dictum); *Prize Cases*, 67 U.S. (2 Black) 635, 641 (1863) (power of the President to "recognize" a state of war) (dictum).

49 An example of "1787-ism" is the frequent citation to a passage by Hamilton, who was certainly no enemy of executive power, which reads:

[T]he President is to be Commander in Chief of the army and navy of the United States. In this respect his authority would be nominally the same with that of the King of Great-Britain, but in substance much inferior to it. It would amount to nothing more than the supreme command and direction of the military and naval forces, as first General and Admiral of the confederacy; while that of the British King extends to the *declaring* of war and to the *raising* and *regulating* of fleets and armies; all which by the Constitution under consideration would appertain to the Legislature.

THE FEDERALIST No. 69, at 465 (J. Cooke ed. 1961) (A. Hamilton) (emphasis in original).

50 This phenomenon is not without precedent. Thus Andrew Jackson asserted in 1832, with respect to the National Bank, that the President's authority was coequal with an independent of Congress and the Court. *See* CORWIN 21.

51 *See* notes 166-70 and accompanying text *infra*. A comparable development is exemplified by statements in presidential signing messages that certain provisions of the approved legislation are unconstitutional and will be ignored; this in effect is a presidential "item veto." *See* note 205 *infra*.

question,"[52] is well known. The instinct of lawyers to resort to an injunction or a writ of habeas corpus with regard to our actions in Cambodia and Vietnam thus was predictable. Former Secretary of State Dean Acheson, shortly before he died, stated of deTocqueville's dictum that "this is true, and it has been a disaster."[53] While this is certainly an overstatement, it does put deTocqueville's dictum into perspective. My guess, however, is that in the foreign affairs and war area the "political question" will not become a "judicial question."

## II

### THE WAR POWERS: *De Lege Lata*

### A.  *The Analytic Scheme*

I have elsewhere elaborated an analytic scheme in the diplomatic area;[54] with some modifications the same analytic scheme can also be applied in the war area. One must, however, take care to distinguish myth from reality. This article focuses on the constitutional development with respect to the war powers as it has actually taken place to date; it is not therefore principally concerned with the allocation of powers in the document of 1787. The analytic scheme is essentially this: there are some areas in which the President has no power under the

---

[52] A. DE TOCQUEVILLE, DEMOCRACY IN AMERICA 106 (A. Hacker ed. 1964). Compare Justice Frankfurter's reference to the hunting blood in the general public:

> So-called constitutional questions seem to exercise a mesmeric influence over the popular mind. This eagerness to settle—preferably forever—a specific problem on the basis of the broadest possible constitutional pronouncements may not unfairly be called one of our minor national traits. An English observer of our scene has acutely described it: "At first sound of a new argument over the United States Constitution and its interpretation the hearts of Americans leap with a fearful joy. The blood stirs powerfully in their veins and a new lustre brightens their eyes. Like King Harry's men before Harfleur, they stand like greyhounds in the slips, straining upon the start."

Youngstown Sheet & Tube Co. v. Sawyer, 343 U.S. 579, 594 (1952) (concurring opinion), *quoting* THE ECONOMIST, May 10, 1952, at 370.

[53] *Hearings on Executive Privilege, supra* note 22, at 266.

[54] Wallace 309-10. As I have elsewhere noted (*id.* at 296, 305 n.89), the allocation of powers in the domestic area is substantially different from that in the foreign affairs area: almost all domestic substantive powers that the President has—for example, program powers in the areas of commerce, health, housing, and so forth—are in fact delegated to him by Congress. The President does have certain independent and indeed exclusive substantive domestic powers, such as the pardon power. He also has been recognized to have or to have asserted certain administrative executive powers: the power to appoint and remove executive officers, the power of executive privilege, the power to resist committee vetoes, and the power of unitary management. *See* notes 57-60 and accompanying text *infra*. *See also* Grundstein, *Presidential Power, Administration and Administrative Law*, 18 GEO. WASH. L. REV. 285, 287 (1950). On the other hand, Congress has a certain power over administrative detail. Wallace 307-08.

Constitution and can only act if Congress delegates power to him;[55] there are other areas in which the President has independent constitutional powers.[56] These powers are of two classes, (1) substantive and (2) executive or procedural; the former class includes the diplomatic and commander-in-chief powers; the latter includes executive privilege,[57] the power to resist committee vetoes,[58] the removal and appointment powers,[59] and the attendant unitary management power.[60] Some of these independent powers of the President are exclusive, that is, the Constitution not only gives them to the President but Congress may not take them away.[61] I have elsewhere suggested that in the diplomatic and foreign assistance areas these exclusive executive powers pertain to what I call "core areas" of decision.[62] The exact definition and current content of the independent and exclusive powers is extremely difficult to ascertain.[63] Apart from the difficulty of detailing the actual decisions that the President is able to make pursuant to these powers, there is the conceptual problem of relating these powers to what are undoubtedly independent powers given by the Constitution to Congress—for example the power to declare war and the appropriations power.[64] Thus courts have suggested on a few occasions that certain independent

---

[55] This, of course, brings into focus one of the basic questions with respect to Vietnam. Did the President have the power to do what he did absent congressional delegation? As will be seen, at least one court has answered that Congress did in fact delegate power. Orlando v. Laird, 443 F.2d 1039 (2d Cir.), cert. denied, 404 U.S. 869 (1971); see text accompanying note 138 infra. On the other hand, the Executive seems to have taken the position that it had power without any delegation. See note 116 and accompanying text infra.

[56] I take the position that all federal executive (as well as congressional and judicial) power derives from the Constitution and that there are no powers "inherent" in the Executive which in some way antedate the Constitution. See Wallace 296-98. But see United States v. Curtiss-Wright Export Corp., 299 U.S. 304, 318 (1936); Penhallow v. Doane, 3 U.S. (3 Dall.) 4, 91 (1795).

[57] Wallace 296-302, 314.

[58] Id. at 473-75. See note 51 supra.

[59] The appointment power is shared with the Senate in important instances. See U.S. Const. art. II, § 2.

[60] See Grundstein, supra note 54, at 287.

[61] See generally Wallace 314-28.

[62] Id. at 314-21.

[63] See text accompanying notes 145-47. Again, one can think of this definitional uncertainty as raising the Vietnam issue in another form. Does the admittedly exclusive commander-in-chief power, which is thought of as the power to conduct or wage war, include the power to initiate war in some circumstances? The Executive sometimes seems to have taken this view.

[64] U.S. Const. art. I, § 8. As a variant of the appropriations power, Congress is also given the power to raise and support the Army and the Navy (id.) and the power to regulate the Army and the Navy (id.), which is the basis of its power to regulate the administrative detail of the military. See notes 81 & 85 infra.

powers of the President may be exercised only as long as Congress has not legislated either against the President directly or at least in a manner affecting presidential power.[65] However, the courts have never indicated in any kind of systematic fashion the powers to which this approach will be applied; as a practical matter, it is not at all clear which independent executive powers will be considered exclusive and which will not.

There is another aspect to the scheme: there is a spectrum of devices of congressional control, from inquiries and advice to purportedly rigid legislation, which can take a variety of forms, including explicit directions, conditioned appropriations, and specific line item appropriations.[66] Just as the Supreme Court has not defined the outer limits of the independent and exclusive executive powers, so it has not addressed itself to the permissibility of these various devices of congressional control. For example, it is possible that certain independent powers of the President might be exclusive of certain varieties of congressional control but not of others. None of these matters has been explored.

The above scheme is itself—as an analytic framework or model—incomplete; this is because the substantive constitutional law of war and foreign policy powers is also incomplete, since the intervention of the courts is sporadic at best. The upshot is that the *lege lata* of the war powers—as of the foreign affairs powers—is inchoate. Much of it comprises "verdicts of history," and history may not be repeated as tides shift in underlying political institutions.[67] Given the realities of the international order and the possible flaws in the separation of powers, is there any rational explanation for the above constitutional scheme? I have elsewhere suggested that there are a number of factors which a court or scholars would consider in determining whether the President had certain independent powers or exclusive powers in the foreign affairs area. Briefly these factors are external necessity, executive efficiency and expertise, individual rights, democratic control, and congressional expertise.[68] These factors are subject to further refinement and adjustment in the war area.[69] Of course they are of a variety typically considered by courts, and even though the law has not developed by judicial decision in this area, they might be kept in mind. They

[65] *See, e.g.,* Youngstown Sheet & Tube Co. v. Sawyer, 343 U.S. 579 (1952). Little v. Barreme, 6 U.S. (2 Cranch) 465 (1804), is often cited in this connection. *See also* New York Times Co. v. United States, 403 U.S. 713 (1971) (per curiam).

[66] *But see* notes 158-61 and accompanying text *infra.*

[67] *See* note 6 *supra.*

[68] Wallace 454-68.

[69] *Id.* at 466.

might help to delineate the outer limits not only of independent powers, but exclusive powers as well; the factors pointing to independent executive power where present with greater intensity might indicate exclusive power. Interestingly, the actual patterns of congressional and executive participation in war-related foreign affairs decisions, although largely unadjudicated, reflect the factors that I have mentioned.

## B. *Pre-war Powers*

Before analyzing the war powers, I shall deal briefly with those foreign policy and other powers which relate primarily to the "pre-war" period. I have indicated that foreign policy and war are on a continuum. In this sense, foreign policy can be thought of as pre- or post-war policy.[70] Indeed, the separation of pre-war from war policy may be artificial and a root cause of our difficulty.

Professor Edward Corwin has stated that the Constitution constitutes an invitation to the Executive and Congress to struggle for primacy in the formulation of foreign policy.[71] Corwin has also pointed out that the Executive has won the lion's share of the power in this area.[72] Most importantly, given the allocation of constitutional powers and the nature of the international order, the primacy of the Executive is inevitable.[73] A moment's reflection will bear this out. The executive department is on the job full time, scanning the world and gathering information about it;[74] the President receives the advice of a special assistant for national security affairs, the State Department, the Defense Department, the CIA, and supporting agencies and interagency committees;[75] and he constantly confers with foreign leaders,[76] making policy statements and commitments. It is the President who decides whether or not to negotiate with foreign governments, whether or not to recognize or to have diplomatic relations with them, how to interpret and carry out treaties, and to what degree to participate in such international agencies as the United Nations. In another dimension, it is

---

[70] Professor Aron has pointed out that in a successfully conducted war, foreign policy continues throughout the war. He suggests that President Franklin Roosevelt sometimes forgot this during World War II. ARON 23-27, 36-40, 70.

[71] CORWIN 208.

[72] *Id.*

[73] *Id.* at 200-01.

[74] Wallace 458.

[75] *See* B. SAPIN, *supra* note 35, at 83-90; Cooper, *The CIA and Decision-Making*, 50 FOREIGN AFFAIRS 223 (1972); Destler, *Can One Man Do?*, FOREIGN POLICY, WINTER 1971-72, No. 5, at 28; Halperin, *The President and the Military*, 50 FOREIGN AFFAIRS 310 (1972); Leacacos, *Kissinger's Apparat*, FOREIGN POLICY, Winter 1971-72, No. 5, at 3.

[76] For example, President Nixon has recently met with Messrs. Pompidou, Trudeau, Heath, Brandt, Sato, Mao, Chou, and Brezhnev.

the President who takes the initiative with Congress with respect to the level of military forces and weapons systems. The President dispatches troops abroad,[77] as well as ships and planes, and decides upon their maneuvers in peacetime.[78]

It is recognized that the President has the independent and indeed exclusive power to recognize foreign governments and states, to commence and sever diplomatic relations, to decide whether or not to negotiate international agreements, and to assert claims of nationals against foreign governments in international courts or arbitral commissions.[79] These are the so-called diplomatic powers of the President.[80]

The problems of force levels,[81] weapons systems, peacetime deploy-

---

[77] See text accompanying note 83 infra.

[78] One need only think of such episodes as the Pueblo incident, the flight of U-2 reconnaissance aircraft over Russia and Cuba, and the dispatch of naval forces to the Bay of Bengal in December, 1971.

[79] Wallace 297-300. The President may also have certain independent powers in the foreign commerce area (id. at 313), and arguably in other areas such as foreign assistance both economic and military, clandestine operations, intelligence gathering, and information and cultural exchange. See id. at 471 n.309; cf. Hearings on Separation of Powers Before the Subcomm. on Separation of Powers of the Senate Comm. on the Judiciary, 90th Cong., 1st Sess. 44 (1967) (statement of Senator J. W. Fulbright).

[80] Wallace 314-21. The President is the sole organ of the government for foreign affairs (see note 41 supra), and thus possesses the diplomatic functions I have just outlined. In addition, the President shares with the Senate the power to make treaties and has the duty to see that laws including treaties and other "international obligations" are enforced. See In re Neagle, 135 U.S. 1, 63-65 (1890). A difficult problem arises under treaties, such as those forming NATO and SEATO, which provide that the United States will respond to aggression in a manner consistent with our "constitutional processes." See note 101 infra.

[81] Congress is given the power to raise taxes for the "common Defence" and to appropriate funds for the same. Similarly, it is given the power to raise and support the Army and the Navy. U.S. CONST. art. I, § 8. Congress also has the power to regulate the Army and the Navy. Id. The Supreme Court has recognized the power of Congress to specify certain items of military pay. United States v. Symonds, 120 U.S. 46 (1887).

Congressional power may, however, interfere with executive unitary management. See Rogers, Congress, the President, and the War Powers, 59 CALIF. L. REV. 1194 (1971); Wallace 314-21. Professor Corwin has declared that Congress's rider to the Army Appropriations Act of 1867, ch. 170, § 2, 15 Stat. 485, by which Congress attempted to transfer part of President Andrew Johnson's commander-in-chief powers to General Grant, was "unquestionably unconstitutional." CORWIN 463 n.89. In a similar congressional action, an 1860 appropriations bill designated one Captain Meigs to supervise certain military construction. President James Buchanan asserted that such action would be construed only as a congressional preference since the designation would otherwise constitute an unconstitutional interference with the commander-in-chief powers—presumably the unitary management aspect. Id. at 402 n.64. In this connection one might also consider executive resistance to attempted congressional vetoes—for example, with respect to the location of domestic military bases. See H.R. 3096, 82d Cong., 1st Sess. (1951); Ginnane, The Control of Federal Administration by Congressional Resolutions and Committees, 66 HARV. L. REV. 569, 603 (1953).

In Swaim v. United States, 28 Ct. Cl. 173, 221 (1893), aff'd, 165 U.S. 553 (1897), the

ment of troops, and the related control of the overall military budget are more difficult.[82] As a practical matter power over the sinews of war is of course as crucial to the war power as foreign policy decisions. The issue of the peacetime deployment of troops overseas is unresolved. Does this power fall within the commander-in-chief function? The President has often behaved as if it does.[83] Justice Robert Jackson suggested that Congress, pursuant to its power to raise and support the Army and Navy, controls the procurement of weapons.[84] On the other hand, the President has taken great initiative with respect to selection of weapons systems, and certain episodes suggest that the President and Congress consider this an area of at least independent if not exclusive executive power.[85]

---

Court of Claims stated, "[Although] Congress may increase the Army, or reduce the Army, or abolish it altogether . . . so long as we have a military force Congress can not take away from the President the supreme command." Or, as Justice Jackson put it in *Youngstown*, the President's position as commander-in-chief is "something more than an empty title." 343 U.S. at 641 (concurring opinion).

[82] *The Federalist* makes clear that one of the principal purposes of the two-year limit on appropriations for the military and the grant of power to Congress to raise and support armies was to prevent the establishment of a standing peacetime army, an abuse of the British colonial governments. THE FEDERALIST Nos. 24-28 (A. Hamilton). The cold war finds us in a very different situation, however, and Congress regularly authorizes and appropriates funds for the military services. Although it has sometimes been suggested that Congress has an obligation to appropriate funds for essential purposes—for example the maintenance of the State Department, the White House, and possibly the military service —I have indicated elsewhere that I do not believe this to be the case. Wallace 302-05. The Constitution provides that no funds may be appropriated except by law. U.S. CONST. art. I, § 9. Nowhere in the Constitution is it suggested that the Congress is under an obligation to pass appropriations bills, and, as a practical matter, the Supreme Court could never so require.

[83] President Franklin D. Roosevelt dispatched troops to Greenland and Iceland in 1940 in the face of a provision in the Selective Training and Service Act of 1940, ch. 720, § 3(e), 54 Stat. 885, that no troops could be sent outside the Western Hemisphere. *See* note 167 *infra*. Former Secretary of State Elihu Root stated in 1912 that he believed it was within the power of the President to commit troops anywhere in the world and that a proposed provision in an appropriations bill barring such deployment was unconstitutional. *See* Nobleman, *Financial Aspects of Congressional Participation in Foreign Relations*, 289 ANNALS 145, 154 (1953). *See also* C. BERDAHL, WAR POWERS OF THE EXECUTIVE IN THE UNITED STATES 34 (1920).

[84] "Congress alone controls the raising of revenues and their appropriation and may determine in what manner and by what means they shall be spent for military and naval procurement." Youngstown Sheet & Tube Co. v. Sawyer, 343 U.S. 579, 643 (1952) (concurring opinion).

[85] For example, President John F. Kennedy in 1962 indicated he would not develop the RS-70 manned bomber although Congress might direct him to do so. Wallace 322. Congressman Perkins Bass, suggesting that the President asserts an exclusive power in this area, stated: "It is inconceivable to me that Congress should tell a Commander in Chief what weapons system to develop any more than it should attempt to tell a general in the field which weapons to fire." 108 CONG. REC. 4719 (1962). *But see* Stassen, *Separation*

It has been suggested that the President, in the exercise of the above-mentioned powers, can in effect "provoke" war by the dispatch of troops, the enforcement or denunciation of a treaty, or the severance of diplomatic relations. Of course, Congress can also be provocative. One need only recall the activities of Senator Joseph McCarthy in the 1950's, various reductions in the amount of and restrictions on the foreign aid program, the creation and cutting of sugar quotas,[86] as well as the comments of individual Senators or Congressmen to imagine the possible responses of adversely affected nations.[87] In a sense, the neutrality legislation which sought to hobble the President in the late 1930's might be seen as provocation if one believes that appeasement can provoke aggression.[88]

Although congressional participation in a range of foreign affairs activities exists, especially with respect to appropriations, the role of the Executive is clearly predominant. Although one authority has spoken of a broad foreign affairs power in Congress,[89] it is misleading to think of this area merely as one of divided or unclear distribution of powers.[90]

## C. The War Powers: The Power To Initiate, Conduct, and Terminate War

### 1. Initiation of War

The decision to initiate a war or lesser hostilities is an intensely political decision made in response to international events. How have we got into our wars? There is, plainly, no single pattern of starting or resisting all wars; we have found ourselves in different positions in different eras. The magnitude of hostilities has also varied, as has their significance. We probably sought some wars, for example, by our actions

---

of Powers and the Uncommon Defense: The Case Against Appropriations, 57 GEO. L.J. 1159, 1176-95 (1969).

86 The cutting of sugar quotas seems especially provocative. Cf. South Puerto Rico Sugar Co. Trading Corp. v. United States, 334 F.2d 622 (Ct. Cl. 1964), cert. denied, 379 U.S. 964 (1965).

87 Many congressional and senatorial remarks can only be described as provocative. Consider, for example, the remarks of Senators Bourke Hickenlooper, Jack Miller, and Wayne Morse when Argentina attempted to invalidate certain contracts with foreign oil companies in 1961. 109 CONG. REC. 21,758-64 (1963).

88 See note 42 supra.

89 See Henkin, The Treaty Makers and the Law Makers: The Law of the Land and Foreign Relations, 107 U. PA. L. REV. 903 (1959).

90 Cf. Youngstown Sheet & Tube Co. v. Sawyer, 343 U.S. 579, 634-38 (1952) (concurring opinion).

in Florida in 1819, Polk's initiatives in Mexico in 1846, and congressional pressure with respect to Cuba in 1898.[91] But from 1914 to 1917 we avoided involvement in World War I, and from 1939 to 1941 in World War II. Since World War II we have acted in Korea and in other areas of conflict.

a. *The President's Power To Repulse Sudden Attacks.* The Executive has often initiated American participation in hostilities without explicit congressional authorization;[92] to be sure, many of these episodes have involved relatively minor use of force. Although the Constitution nowhere authorizes this initiative on its face, the history of the 1787 Convention makes clear that the President was expected to repulse a sudden attack on the United States. What might be termed the independent presidential "sudden repulse" power seems to have broadened considerably over the years by usage, so as to be no longer limited to situations involving a sudden attack on United States territory.[93] Thus Presidents have used military force to repulse attacks on our citizens and their property abroad,[94] on our diplomats,[95] and on our troops.

---

[91] *See* C. BERDAHL, *supra* note 83, at 45-46, 70-74, 91-92; *cf.* Wallace 298.

[92] U.S. Dep't of State, *supra* note 1, at 11,206; Rogers, *supra* note 81, at 1198-1203.

[93] Spong, *Can Balance Be Restored in the Constitutional War Powers of the President and Congress?*, 6 RICHMOND L. REV. 1, 17-18 (1971) [hereinafter cited as Spong]. Interestingly, there was no suggestion in 1787 that the President would have to request Congress to ratify his repulse of a sudden attack as soon as possible after he acted; perhaps it was assumed that he would do so. *Id.* at 4. The Constitution gives the states the power to repulse sudden attacks without congressional authorization. U.S. CONST. art. I, § 10. Congress passed statutes in 1795 and 1807 giving the President a comparable power to resist rebellion without congressional authorization. Act of Feb. 28, 1795, ch. 36, § 2, 1 Stat. 424; Act of March 3, 1807, ch. 39, 2 Stat. 443; *see Prize Cases*, 67 U.S. (2 Black) 635, 668 (1863); *cf.* Burmah Oil Co. v. Lord Advocate, 1965 A. C. 75, 100 (1964), quoting a 1703 English statute:

> [N]o person being King or Queen of Scotland and England shall have the sole power of making war . . . without consent of Parliament: . . . this shall no wise be understood to impede the Sovereign of this Kingdom to call forth, command and employ the subjects thereof to suppress any insurrection within the Kingdom, or repell any invasion from abroad, according to former laws.

Presumably, the President could have resisted the attack on Pearl Harbor without congressional authorization under the sudden repulse theory.

The growth of an independent sudden repulse power in the President is analogous to the emergence of presidential power with respect to foreign commerce and captures, in that these matters were originally thought to be assigned by the Constitution to Congress. U.S. CONST. art. I, § 8. For a discussion of the President's independent commerce power, see Feller, *The International Antidumping Code—The Confrontation and Accommodation of Independent Executive and Legislative Powers in the Regulation of Foreign Commerce*, 5 J. INT'L L. & ECON. 121 (1971).

[94] Protection of citizens was the nominal justification for our intervention in the Dominican Republic in 1965 (Spong 15), although later phases of the intervention were justified as coming under the auspices of the Organization of American States. *See* note 107 and accompanying text *infra.*

[95] *E.g.*, President McKinley sent troops to China in 1900 to help suppress the Boxer

This power has been acknowledged by the courts.[96] Presumably, the President would consider himself empowered to order resistance to an attack on our ships and planes.[97] In fact, it has been suggested that this sudden repulse power goes even further and permits presidential use of force to protect undefined national security interests. I find the latter assertion difficult to reconcile with any notion of control over presidential power.[98]

An interesting "expansion" of the sudden repulse power may have taken place at the time of the Cuban missile crisis. Neither Russia nor Cuba was in a position to attack the United States, since there were no warheads in the intermediate range missiles installed in Cuba at that time.[99] Thus it appears that the President acted solely to preserve the balance of power in the Western Hemisphere[100] or perhaps in the world.

The post-World War II period has seen a special change in presidential activity, largely because of the network of treaties into which we have entered,[101] including the United Nations Charter, the agreements

---

Rebellion, in part to protect American and third country diplomats. See S. Morison, The Oxford History of the American People 807 (1965).

[96] E.g., Durand v. Hollins, 8 F. Cas. 111 (No. 4186) (C.C.S.D.N.Y. 1860). In the Slaughter-House Cases, 3 U.S. (16 Wall.) 36 (1873), the Court stated that "another privilege of a citizen of the United States is to demand the care and protection of the Federal government over his life, liberty, and property when on the high seas or within the jurisdiction of a foreign government." Id. at 79. See United States ex rel. Keefe v. Dulles, 22 F.2d 390 (D.C. Cir. 1954).

[97] Consider, for example, President Jefferson's defense of United States merchantmen against the Barbary pirates in 1801. Spong 3. If action had been taken with respect to the Pueblo it might have fallen in this category.

[98] Senator Spong suggests that the Supreme Court has in effect recognized this extension of the sudden repulse power in In re Neagle, 135 U.S. 1, 64-65 (1890), where the Court acknowledged the President's power to carry out not only domestic laws but the obligations generated by international relations. Spong 14. This strikes me as troublesome; even if Senator Spong is right, must there not be some limit on the scope and magnitude of the President's power under this rubric?

[99] R. Kennedy, supra note 19, at 29.

[100] Id. at 166.

[101] The extent to which such treaties enhance the President's powers is dependent, at least in part, on the meaning of the phrase "constitutional processes," which first appeared in the ratification provision of the NATO treaty. North Atlantic Treaty, April 4, 1949, art. 11, 63 Stat. 2246 (1949), T.I.A.S. No. 1964. Professor Dahl suggests that Congress sought to create ambiguity as to the nature of the Executive's powers. Dahl 256-57. Presumably, Congress thought it had preserved its power to declare war; possibly the Executive thought it could act under a treaty either as commander-in-chief or as enforcer of our legal obligations. The fact of the matter is that the phrase "constitutional processes" in a treaty begs the question if we do not know what the Constitution provides with respect to the carrying out of treaties, and we do not. Professor Leonard Ratner has suggested that in effect the phrase permits the President to do that which he could do in the absence of a treaty. Ratner believes that that includes the power to station troops abroad but not

establishing NATO[102] and SEATO,[103] the Rio Pact,[104] and others. Thus the President acted in Korea pursuant to recommendations of the Security Council and General Assembly of the United Nations,[105] without express initial congressional authorization.[106] So too the President's action in the Dominican Republic in 1965 was ultimately rationalized as action under the charter of the Organization of American States and the Rio Pact.[107] Even Vietnam has from time to time been asserted to be justified by our "commitment" under SEATO.[108] In all these cases, the President has argued[109] that he was carrying out his duty to see that laws—which include treaties and other international law obligations—were faithfully enforced.

Congressional resolutions authorizing the President in advance of hostilities to use force if necessary have been another post-World War II feature encouraging presidential activity. Professor Dahl in 1950 predicted that such resolutions would be necessary if the United States were to be in a position to move quickly to resist Soviet expansion and pressure.[110] The Tonkin Gulf Resolution[111] is only the most recent of such resolutions; others have concerned the Middle East, cited at the

---

the power to commit them to combat (except presumably in a "sudden repulse" situation). Ratner, *supra* note 13, at 476.

Article 5 of the treaty provides that "an armed attack against one [party] . . . shall be considered an attack against them all." North Atlantic Treaty, April 14, 1949, art. 5, 63 Stat. 2244 (1949), T.I.A.S. No. 1964. This formula does not appear in any other defense treaty. Is it possible that this international obligation, which is to be sure, somewhat qualified by the remainder of the treaty, enlarges the President's powers in some way, notwithstanding the later reference in article 11 to "constitutional processes"? This question remains unanswered.

102 North Atlantic Treaty, April 4, 1949, 63 Stat. 2244 (1949), T.I.A.S. No. 1964.

103 Southeast Asia Collective Defense Treaty, Sept. 8, 1954, [1955] 1 U.S.T. 81, T.I.A.S. No. 3170.

104 Rio de Janeiro Pact, Sept. 2, 1947, 62 Stat. 1681 (1948), T.I.A.S. No. 1838.

105 Professor Fisher suggests that President Truman in fact acted on his own authority and not in response to the recommendations of the United Nations. L. FISHER, *supra* note 24, at 194-95.

106 It has been reported that the Republican and Democratic senatorial leadership advised President Truman not to seek congressional support. D. ACHESON, PRESENT AT THE CREATION: MY YEARS IN THE STATE DEPARTMENT 414 (1969). Justice Jackson, concurring in *Youngstown*, noted but did not question the presence of United States troops in Korea. 343 U.S. at 642. To be sure, in Korea as in Vietnam the Congress eventually participated extensively through appropriations, selective service legislation, and other legislation. See generally Orlando v. Laird, 443 F.2d 1039 (2d Cir.), *cert. denied*, 404 U.S. 869 (1971).

107 See A. CHAYES, T. ERLICH, & A. LOWENFELD, INTERNATIONAL LEGAL PROCESS 1179-82 (1969).

108 *E.g.*, U.S. Dep't of State, *supra* note 1, at 11,204-05.

109 See id. at 11,206-07.

110 DAHL 251-52, 260.

111 More accurately known as the Southeast Asia Resolution, 78 Stat. 384.

time of the landing of marines in Lebanon in 1958,[112] Formosa,[113] and Cuba.[114] The constitutional significance of these resolutions is not clear. Some of them, in their wording, in effect acknowledge that the President has the power to which they refer.[115] President Nixon, in agreeing to the repeal of the Tonkin Gulf Resolution, indicated that the resolution conferred no power which he did not already have.[116] Do such congressional resolutions constitute part of a "verdict of history" on the expanded power of the Executive? The answer to this question depends in part on the status of the remaining unrepealed resolutions.[117] Certainly, further resolutions might not be welcomed by Congress today.[118]

---

112 22 U.S.C. §§ 1961-65 (1970).

113 69 Stat. 7.

114 76 Stat. 697.

115 For example: "[I]f the President determines the necessity thereof, the United States is prepared to use armed forces . . . ." 22 U.S.C. § 1962 (1970). *See* Note, *Congress, the President, and the Power To Commit Forces to Combat*, 81 HARV. L. REV. 1771, 1802-03 (1968); note 118 *infra*.

116 President Nixon signed the repeal, included as a rider to the Foreign Military Sales Act of 1971, § 12, 84 Stat. 2055. The President's position, stated at the time of his signature, was that he did not need the authority of the resolution to "wind down" the war, since that power was contained within his commander-in-chief power. *See* N.Y. Times, Jan. 1, 1971, at 1, col. 8. However, the authority for the start of the war is thus left uncertain. In many ways, the repeal of the Tonkin Gulf Resolution is a paradox. Senator Spong has stated that the repeal has left a vacuum. Spong 24.

117 There were suggestions in Congress at the time Communist China took the Chinese seat at the United Nations that the Formosa resolution be repealed. *See* S.J. Res. 48, 92d Cong., 1st Sess. (1971).

118 *See* Spong 19. These resolutions have also been attacked as an improper grant or delegation of power to the President—in those cases where they are worded as giving power. *See, e.g.,* 22 U.S.C. §§ 1961-65 (1970) (the Formosa resolution). I feel that this argument is a nonissue. One may, I suppose, consider such resolutions to be a partial exercise of the declaration of war power. Certainly the Tonkin Gulf Resolution by its terms seemed to give the President all the power he required in Vietnam. The Resolution provided in relevant part

[t]hat the Congress approves and supports the determination of the President, as Commander in Chief, to take all necessary measures to repel any armed attack against the forces of the United States and to prevent further aggression. . . . Consonant with the Constitution of the United States . . . the United States is, therefore, prepared, as the President determines, to take all necessary steps, including the use of armed force, to assist any member or protocol state . . . requesting assistance in the defense of its freedom.

Joint Resolution of Aug. 10, 1964, Pub. L. No. 88-408, 78 Stat. 384 (1964).

It has been suggested that this resolution was obtained by fraud. *See* A. AUSTIN, THE PRESIDENT'S WAR 153-60 (1971). In this connection it is interesting to note several colloquies at the time of the introduction of the resolution by Senator Fulbright. Senator Daniel Brewster asked whether the resolution would authorize sending a large American army to Vietnam. Fulbright replied: "It would authorize whatever the Commander in Chief feels is necessary . . . . Whether or not that should ever be done is a matter of wisdom un-

It is, of course, this post-World War II development which is at the heart of the current controversy over the independent power of the Executive to initiate hostilities. What is the constitutional significance of these post-World War II events? The Executive has never stated clearly whether its currently asserted powers are merely an extension of the commander-in-chief power or whether they are based on other executive powers.[119] Neither the Executive nor post-World War II events has made clear whether this executive power is limited to military engagements of some maximum size. The finding of the Second Circuit in *Orlando v. Laird*[120] that congressional appropriations legislation, selective service legislation, and other Vietnam-related legislation constitute congressional authorization and ratification of the war[121] may conceivably have rendered moot the narrow legal question of whether the President could have acted in Vietnam under an independent sudden repulse power. However, the congressional acts the court saw as constituting ratification are inevitable during any prolonged hostilities and possibly whenever Congress is confronted with an executive *fait accompli*.

b. *Declarations of War*. The requirement that Congress declare war has been called one of the great innovations of the Constitution.[122]

---

der the circumstances that exist at the particular time it is contemplated." 110 Cong. Rec. 18,403 (1964). Similarly Senator Gaylord Nelson asked:

> Am I to understand that . . . we are saying to the executive branch: ". . . [W]e agree now, in advance, that you may land as many divisions as deemed necessary, and engage in a direct military assault on North Vietnam if it becomes the judgment of . . . the Commander in Chief, that this is the only way to prevent further aggression [against South Vietnam]"?

*Id.* at 18,406. Fulbright replied:

> If the situation should deteriorate to such an extent that the only way to save it from going completely under to the Communists would be action such as the Senator suggests, then that would be a grave decision on the part of our country.
> . . .
> I personally feel it would be very unwise under any circumstances to put a large land army on the Asian Continent.

*Id.* It is also interesting to note that a similar charge of fraud was raised in 1798 against legislation authorizing the President to use force against France, in lieu of a declaration of war which Congress was unwilling to give. *See* C. Berdahl, *supra* note 83, at 82.

119 *See generally* U.S. Dep't of State, *supra* note 1, at 11,206-07.

120 443 F.2d 1039 (2nd Cir.), *cert. denied*, 404 U.S. 869 (1971).

121 *Id.* at 1043.

122 The democratic rationale of this congressional power was well stated by President Lincoln in these words:

> Kings had always been involving and impoverishing their people in wars . . . .
> This, our Convention understood to be the most oppressive of all Kingly oppressions; and they resolved to so frame the Constitution that *no one man* should hold the power of bringing this oppression upon us.

1 The Collected Works of Abraham Lincoln 451-52 (R. Bosler ed. 1953) (emphasis in

It is my thesis that it may never have been a practicable requirement and that if viable in 1787, when the United States was distant from the center of the European system, it it not viable in 1972, when we have moved to the center of the international system and order.[123] We continue to give ritual obeisance to the necessity of a declaration of war,[124] even while recognizing that the President has often involved the United States in hostilities without such a declaration.[125] Some have suggested that the declaration of war may only be required for hostilities above a certain magnitude.[126] But even this approach appears highly unrealistic. There has not been a declaration of war anywhere in the world since 1945,[127] and many have categorized the declaration of war as obsolete.[128] This aversion to formal declarations of war has been attributed to the proscription of the use of force in article 2(4) of the United Nations Charter and to the impropriety of a formal declaration in the cold war age of nuclear weapons.[129] In any event, the aversion to formal declarations of war is an international fact of life, one which has undermined and indeed eliminated the formal role assigned to Congress by the Con-

---

original). The grant to Congress of the power to declare war was not without early critics; John Quincy Adams called it the "great error" of the Constitution. C. BERDAHL, *supra* note 83, at 46 n.12, 79.

[123] In 1787 the line between peace and war seemed clear, and a declaration of war was seen as marking the "disruption" of peace and the descent into war. *See* L. FISHER, *supra* note 24, at 194. Professor Dahl has referred to the "relative stability of power relations vis-à-vis the United States in the nineteenth century." DAHL 254. In the cold war era the declaration of war appears outmoded. *See* notes 127-32 and accompanying text *infra*.

[124] Thus the Hatfield-McGovern amendment to the Military Procurements Act of 1971, 84 Stat. 905, as first introduced, began "[u]nless there has been a declaration of war by the Congress." Amend. No. 605 to H.R. 17123, 91st Cong., 2d Sess., 116 CONG. REC. 13,547 (1970). The Massachusetts statute which was the subject of Massachusetts v. Laird, 400 U.S. 886 (1970), referred to the necessity of a "declaration of war" before citizens of that state could be drafted. It is interesting that a number of courts have found for such purposes as military liability insurance that the term "war" as used in various statutes does not apply to Vietnam because of the absence of a formal "declaration of war." *See* United States v. Averette, 19 U.S.C.M.A. 363, 41 C.M.R. 363 (1970).

[125] *See* note 92 and accompanying text *supra*.

[126] Note, *supra* note 115, at 1795.

[127] N.Y. Times, May 19, 1966, at 11, col. 2.

[128] Senator Javits has stated, "In this thermonuclear age, it may well be unlikely that we will be faced again with 'declared wars.'" *War Powers Hearings* 136. Undersecretary of State Nicholas Katzenbach in 1967 stated:

I do not think the declaration of war as such is better, considering the consequences a declaration of war has. I would say almost flatly it has nothing in the way of international law consequences today. It is a term that is in effect outmoded in international law unless it is used to denote some sort of aggression one is performing when one declares war.

*Hearings on S. Res. 151, supra* note 31, at 161-62.

[129] Note, *supra* note 115, at 1772-73.

stitution with respect to declarations of war.[130] It is indeed possible that the declaration of war, even as contemplated by the Constitution, is functionally of use today only in circumstances which would also permit the President to use his sudden repulse power—especially as that power has been enlarged through usage. In other words, it can be maintained that the declaration of war power is limited to "defensive" wars,[131] which are just the kind of situations in which the President asserts the right to act pursuant to his own independent power.[132]

The most important point about declarations of war is that even when used they have largely been procured from Congress at the instance of the Executive; scholarship seems to have established this,[133] and one need only consider America's major wars to appreciate the essential truth of the statement.[134] If the President did not request a

---

[130] Of course, congressional action short of a formal declaration of war occurred as early as 1798 when the Congress passed legislation authorizing presidential use of force against France. Act of May 28, 1798, ch. 48, 2 Stat. 561. Congress was unwilling to pass a formal declaration of war at the time. See Bas v. Tingy, 4 U.S. (4 Dall.) 37 (1800); note 118 and accompanying text *supra*; note 139 and accompanying text *infra*.

[131] Professor Aron has pointed out that it is very difficult to distinguish a "defensive" war from an "offensive" war and that one must view war as part of the foreign policy continuum. ARON 82-88. He suggests that it is possible for a country to conduct an "offensive" foreign policy which may put it into a "defensive" position vis-à-vis the war which the foreign policy has forced. *Id.* at 85.

[132] The Supreme Court, in Fleming v. Page, 50 U.S. (9 How.) 603, 614 (1850), suggested that the United States under its Constitution can only engage in defensive wars:

> [T]he genius and character of our institutions are peaceful, and the power to declare war was not conferred upon Congress for the purposes of aggression or aggrandizement, but to enable the general government to vindicate by arms, if it should become necessary, its own rights and the rights of its citizens.

If this is so, and if it can be maintained that all such defensive wars fall within the sudden repulse power of the President, the question as to what kinds of wars can only be authorized by Congress is answered—in fact, none. Offensive wars it cannot authorize, defensive wars it need not authorize. *Cf.* U.N. CHARTER art. 2, para. 4 (proscribing use of force in international conflict); *id.* art. 51 (preserving the inherent right of individual and collective self-defense of member states). These Charter provisions also seem to proscribe offensive war.

Alexander Hamilton suggested that when another nation commenced war on the United States, there was nothing left for Congress to do as we were "already at war" and "any declaration . . . is nugatory." 7 WORKS OF ALEXANDER HAMILTON 203 (H. Lodge ed. 1886). The Supreme Court stated in the *Prize Cases*, 67 U.S. (2 Black) 635, 668 (1863), that the President "does not initiate the war, but is bound to accept the challenge without waiting for any special legislative authority."

[133] *See, e.g.*, Garner, *Executive Discretion in the Conduct of Foreign Relations*, 31 AM. J. INT'L L. 289, 292 & n.9 (1937).

[134] The Spanish-American War might be thought of as an exception. Congress sought to force President McKinley to favor Cuba and to oppose Spain. The President did not, however, seek the declaration of war until he was ready to do so. *See War Powers Hearings* 298. Once sought by the President, declarations of war have always been voted overwhelmingly. *See generally* C. BERDAHL, *supra* note 83, at 93.

particular declaration of war, he might veto it or refuse to comply with it as commander-in-chief.[135] Of course the President may also so conduct the foreign affairs of the country as to make a war a great likelihood.

I suggest that just as there has been a great practical shift in the relative power of the Executive and Congress with respect to the treaty power,[136] so there has been a great shift with respect to the formal power to declare war from the situation originally contemplated in the Constitution. It is unrealistic not to recognize this fact. Of course Congress may exercise influence on war policy through appropriations votes, selective service legislation, veterans' benefits legislation, and so forth.[137] But the fact remains that the great purpose of democratic control sought to be served by a congressional declaration of war can easily be emasculated. Moreover, the declaration of war device is inherently unsuited to situations such as that in Vietnam of gradually escalating engagement, which may begin at a level well within the President's sudden repulse power—at least as that power has been expanded by usage and the emergence of our treaty network. By the time such a conflict becomes a major hostility, in terms of its significance both in the domestic and international orders, the possibility of an express prior congressional authorization has been precluded.

### 2. Conduct of War

The decision to initiate war or lesser hostilities is analytically distinguishable from the conduct of war. There has been so much dispute about the propriety of the initiation of fighting in Vietnam that the distinction between initiation and conduct has not always been made.

---

[135] Compare this with the proposition that the President need not undertake the negotiation of a treaty or other agreement, notwithstanding congressional direction, if he does not choose to do so. See Wallace 317. Nor need he implement a treaty although consented to by the Senate. Id.

[136] See note 33 supra.

[137] See Orlando v. Laird, 443 F.2d 1039 (2d Cir.), cert. denied, 404 U.S. 869 (1971); Bas v. Tingy, 4 U.S. (4 Dall.) 37 (1800). The result in Orlando, although resting largely on the political question doctrine (notes 228-29 infra), unfortunately also seemed to establish that through measures which Congress cannot easily avoid, such as appropriations, extensions of selective service legislation, and the like, Congress will be considered to have given assent to a war. Senator Thomas Eagleton, in a resolution which he proposed (S.J. Res. 59, 92d Cong., 1st Sess. (1971)) suggested that any such congressional action will not amount to an exercise of the declaration of war power unless Congress explicitly states this to be the case. Were such a resolution passed, however, I do not believe that a court would be precluded from finding that other legislation amounted to such a declaration, along the lines of Orlando. The Supreme Court has indicated it would permit such ratification in other contexts. See Greene v. McElroy, 360 U.S. 474, 506 (1959) (dictum); Ex parte Endo, 323 U.S. 283, 303 n.24 (1944) (dictum).

Now that courts have in fact found the initiation of the War to be at least impliedly authorized by Congress,[138] the focus has shifted from the initiation to the conduct of the War.

The conduct of war is normally thought to be the exclusive province of the President as commander-in-chief, but there remain a number of problems. For one thing, the conduct of foreign policy continues during the conduct of war and may be inseparable from it.[139] For another, there is the suggestion that the commander-in-chief power is not limited to the conduct of campaigns and the management of operations, but may have within it the power to initiate hostilities by means of the sudden repulse power[140] and certainly to broaden the scope of previously initiated hostilities.[141] Even if we limit the commander-in-chief function exclusively to that of the conduct or waging of war, there are problems of definition. Certainly the function must include tactics and military strategy.[142] It has normally been thought that the commander-in-chief controls the movement of troops within a theater of operations; that he controls the use of weapons, including bombing; and that he controls the timing of various military movements, the level of fighting, and the use of espionage and other devices. The Executive also determines whether to establish second fronts.[143] For example, in Korea the President made the decision not to cross the Yalu; in World War II the President determined second fronts, as well as global strategy and the policy of unconditional surrender.[144] As a practical matter, the Presi-

---

138 See cases cited in notes 3-4 supra.

139 See text accompanying note 17 supra. Even during the height of a war when a nation's emotions are most strongly engaged and when the conduct of a nation state seems to take on an aspect of animal force, an intelligent government will be fitting war tactics and strategy into its foreign policy and looking towards post-war foreign policy. See note 70 supra.

140 See notes 92-100 and accompanying text supra.

141 On the question whether the Cambodian invasion represented a tactical maneuver within the commander-in-chief's power to conduct war or the initiation of a new war, see note 2 supra; note 143 infra.

142 See ARON 36-40, where the author considers the range of military tactics and strategies. Senator William Fulbright has sought to distinguish "detail" and "policy" in foreign policy, arguing that control over the latter lies with Congress. Hearings on Separation of Powers, supra note 79, at 43-44. I have elsewhere demonstrated that a good deal of control over the formulation of foreign policy in fact has come to reside exclusively in the President. Wallace 320-21.

143 The court in Mottola v. Nixon, 318 F. Supp. 538, 540, (N.D. Cal. 1970), indicated that Cambodia was a "necessary incidental, tactical incursion." In some ways, including its length and apparent purpose, the invasion seems more "tactical" than the strategic second fronts of World War II. See Moore, Legal Dimensions of the Decision To Intercede in Cambodia, 65 AM. J. INT'L L. 38, 63 (1971). Any attempt, however, to draw fine distinctions between "tactics" and "strategy" in the military sphere seems somewhat futile.

144 See ARON 27.

dent also makes decisions with respect to the production of weapons and the raising of troops during a war.

There are few statements by the courts as to the exact extent of even the basic, war-conducting area of the commander-in-chief power. In *United States v. Sweeny*,[145] the Supreme Court stated that the purpose of the commander-in-chief clause "is evidently to vest in the President the supreme command over all the military forces,—such supreme and undivided command as would be necessary to the prosecution of a successful war."[146] Although the exact scope of the President's independent commander-in-chief power is thus somewhat ill-defined, the Court has made clear that at least the core of such power, however defined, is exclusive and not subject to congressional control. On another occasion the Supreme Court stated,

> Congress has the power not only to raise and support and govern armies but to declare war. It has, therefore, the power to provide by law for carrying on war. This power necessarily extends to all legislation essential to the prosecution of war with vigor and success, except such as interferes with the command of the forces and the conduct of campaigns. That power and duty belong to the President as commander-in-chief. Both these powers are derived from the Constitution, but neither is defined by that instrument. Their extent must be determined by their nature, and by the principles of our institutions.[147]

As in foreign affairs, so in the "command of the forces and the conduct of campaigns" the country must speak with one voice.[148]

---

[145] 157 U.S. 281 (1895).

[146] *Id.* at 284. *See also* note 49 *supra*.

[147] *Ex parte* Milligan, 71 U.S. (4 Wall.) 2, 139 (1866) (concurring opinion). *See* Swaim v. United States, 28 Ct. Cl. 173, 221 (1893), *aff'd*, 165 U.S. 553 (1897).
Senator William Borah once stated,
Undoubtedly the Congress may refuse to appropriate and undoubtedly the Congress may say that an appropriation is for a specific purpose. In that respect the President will undoubtedly be bound by it. But the Congress could not, through the power of appropriation, in my judgment, infringe upon the right of the President to command whatever army he might find. . . .
*Quoted in* CORWIN 403 n.64. On another occasion, when Congress voted legislation requiring President Theodore Roosevelt to maintain marines on all ships equal to at least 8% of each ship's complement (Act of March 3, 1909, ch. 255, 35 Stat. 773), Senator Borah was even more explicit:
Congress has not the power to say that an army shall be at a particular place at a particular time or shall maneuver in a particular instance. That belongs exclusively to the Commander in Chief of the Army. The dividing line is between the question of raising, supporting, and regulating an army, and commanding it. It is difficult to define, for the reason that it is difficult to tell where the dividing line is. But when it is ascertained, there is no question about the constitutional provision covering it.
43 CONG. REC. 2452 (1909).

[148] *See* Baker v. Carr, 369 U.S. 186, 211 (1962).

This principle has recently been tested by the attempt of Congress to control the "conduct" of the war in Vietnam, or more accurately in Indochina, through such efforts as the Cooper-Church[149] amendments restricting military activity in Laos, Thailand, and Cambodia, and the successful Mansfield[150] and unsuccessful Hatfield-McGovern amend-

---

[149] The Cooper-Church amendment to the Department of Defense Appropriations Act of 1970, § 643, 83 Stat. 469, reads as follows: "[N]one of the funds appropriated by this Act shall be used to finance the introduction of American ground combat troops into Laos or Thailand." The Cooper-Church amendment to the Special Foreign Assistance Act of 1971, § 7, 84 Stat. 1942, provides:

(a) In line with the expressed intention of the President of the United States, none of the funds authorized or appropriated pursuant to this or any other Act may be used to finance the introduction of United States ground combat troops into Cambodia, or to provide United States advisers to or for Cambodian military forces in Cambodia.

(b) Military and economic assistance provided by the United States to Cambodia and authorized or appropriated pursuant to this or any other Act shall not be construed as a commitment by the United States to Cambodia for its defense.

Some months after the enactment of the latter Cooper-Church amendment there was a good deal of dispute as to whether or not its terms had been violated when American planes engaged in close air support were alleged to have touched Cambodian ground. The Executive maintained the aircraft were involved in rescue operations; some Congressmen maintained they were involved in ground combat. After this incident, Senator John Stennis indicated that there might have to be a revision of the Cooper-Church amendment to permit certain additional activities in Cambodia. N.Y. Times, Jan. 28, 1971, at 1, col. 8. One can only wonder about the wisdom and propriety of legislation which requires congressional consideration of such "tactical" detail.

The original amendment to § 47 of the Foreign Military Sales Act—Amendment of 1971 (84 Stat. 2053) proposed by Senators Cooper and Church, as reported out of the Senate Foreign Relations Committee, passed in somewhat modified form by the Senate, but rejected by the House, had read:

[U]nless specifically authorized by law hereafter enacted, no funds authorized or appropriated pursuant to this Act or any other law may be expended for the purpose of—

1) retaining United States forces in Cambodia;

2) paying the compensation or allowances of, or otherwise supporting, directly or indirectly, any United States personnel in Cambodia who furnish military instruction to Cambodian forces or engage in any combat activity in support of Cambodian forces;

3) entering into or carrying out any contract or agreement to provide military instruction in Cambodia, or to provide persons to engage in any combat activity in support of Cambodian forces; or

4) conducting any combat activity in the air above Cambodia in support of Cambodian forces.

Amend. to H.R. 15628, 91st Cong., 2d Sess. § 47, 116 CONG. REC. 15,400 (1970).

[150] The Mansfield amendment provides:

It is hereby declared to be the policy of the United States to terminate at the earliest practicable date all military operations of the United States in Indochina, and to provide for the prompt and orderly withdrawal of all United States military forces at a date certain, subject to the release of all American prisoners of war held by the Government of North Vietnam and forces allied with such Government and an accounting for all Americans missing in action who have been held by or known to such Government or such forces. The Congress hereby urges and requests the President to implement the above-expressed policy by initiating immediately the following actions:

ments.[151] It is not the purpose of this article to consider the wisdom of such provisions, although as binding legal strictures their wisdom does seem questionable. Rather, I shall address myself to the constitutionality of such provisions. My position is that they constitute an improper congressional encroachment on the exclusive powers of the President as commander-in-chief and are thus unconstitutional.[152]

Presumably, such legislation is based either on the congressional power over appropriations[153] or on Congress's power to declare war.[154] I have elsewhere explored the power of Congress to condition appropriations.[155] I do not believe that merely because restrictive legislation may also be based on the declaration of war power the analytic framework need be changed.

As then Congressman Martin Van Buren noted with respect to the diplomatic power, Congress could not give directions to the President with respect to that portion of the diplomatic power which was exclusively his. In a well-known statement, Daniel Webster added that what

---

(1) Establishing a final date for the withdrawal from Indochina of all military forces of the United States contingent upon the release of all American prisoners of war held by the Government of North Vietnam and forces allied with such Government and an accounting for all Americans missing in action who have been held by or known to such Government or such forces.

(2) Negotiate with the Government of North Vietnam for an immediate cease-fire by all parties to the hostilities in Indochina.

(3) Negotiate with the Government of North Vietnam for an agreement which would provide for a series of phased and rapid withdrawals of United States military forces from Indochina in exchange for a corresponding series of phased releases of American prisoners of war, and for the release of any remaining American prisoners of war concurrently with the withdrawal of all remaining military forces of the United States by not later than the date established by the President pursuant to paragraph (1) hereof or by such earlier date as may be agreed upon by the negotiating parties.

Military Procurement Authorization Act of 1972, § 601(a), 85 Stat. 430.

[151] Amend. No. 862 to H.R. 17123, 91st Cong., 2d Sess., 116 CONG. REC. 30,080 (1970); Amend. No. 605 to H.R. 17123, 91st Cong., 2d Sess., 116 CONG. REC. 13,547 (1970); *see* note 124 *supra;* note 172 *infra.* The recent Case-Church "amendment" to the Foreign Relations Authorization Bill (S. 3526, 92d Cong., 2d Sess. § 701 (1972)) represents a similar effort.

[152] Congressional activity runs the gamut from inquiry and investigation, advice and resolutions to rigid, mandatory legislation. The scope of permissible congressional conditions and pressures is considered at notes 158-71 and accompanying text *infra. See also* Wallace 302-09.

[153] The appropriations power has not been greatly litigated or adjudicated. *See* Wallace 302-05. It is to be distinguished from the taxing power, to which it is of course related. *See* U.S. CONST. art. I, § 8. Congress may entirely withhold or deny appropriations; it may vote them on a fiscal year basis (indeed the Constitution requires that appropriations for the military be voted for only two years (U.S. CONST. art. 1, § 8)); and it can reduce appropriations and thus legitimately pressure the Executive. *But see* note 147 *supra.*

[154] The question might be raised in terms of whether Congress can revoke a declaration of war or revoke its support of an undeclared war. *See* notes 172-78 and accompanying text *infra.* There is no authority on this subject.

[155] Wallace 302-08.

Congress could not do directly, it could not do indirectly by conditioning appropriations to be available only if the President complied with congressional directions.[156] This is what Congress has sought to do with respect to the commander-in-chief powers by its legislative riders regarding action in Laos, Thailand, and Cambodia.[157] There has been some judicial recognition of the impermissibility of congressional interference in matters of exclusive presidential power.[158] Additionally,

[156] 9 ABRIDGEMENT OF THE DEBATES OF CONGRESS 94 (T. Benton comp. 1858).

[157] See notes 149-52 and accompanying text supra.

[158] Thus, in Lovett v. United States, Judge Madden stated: "Section 304 is asserted by the plaintiffs to be unconstitutional because . . . it purports to remove the plaintiffs from executive offices, and no power of removal resides in the legislative branch of the Government, except, by impeachment . . . ." 66 F. Supp. 142, 151 (Ct. Cl. 1945) (concurring opinion), aff'd, 328 U.S. 303 (1946). He later concluded: "I do not think, therefore, that the power of the purse may be constitutionally exercised to produce . . . a trespass upon the constitutional functions of another branch of the Government." Id. at 152. Justice Frankfurter, concurring in the opinion of the Supreme Court in Lovett, spoke of the "grave constitutional" issue that would be raised by an attempted invasion of the removal power by the refusal to appropriate funds for the salaries of certain government employees. 328 U.S. at 328-29.

The Supreme Court in Butler v. United States, 297 U.S. 1, 74 (1936), stated in a slightly different context, "An affirmance of the authority of Congress . . . to condition the expenditure of an [educational] appropriation [on the assumption of a contractual obligation to submit to federal regulation] would tend to nullify all constitutional limitations upon legislative power." James Madison's view is also interesting:

The legislative department derives superiority in our government from other circumstances. Its constitutional powers being at once more extensive and less susceptible of precise limits, it can with the greater facility, mask under complicated and indirect measures, the encroachments which it makes on the co-ordinate departments. It is not unfrequently a question of real-nicety in legislative bodies, whether the operation of a particular measure, will, or will not extend beyond the legislative sphere.

THE FEDERALIST No. 48, at 334 (J. Cooke ed. 1961) (J. Madison).

Congressman James Mann once stated that it would be appropriate to "limit appropriations . . . [so that] no money shall be given in this bill except to red-headed men." N.Y. Times, March 23, 1922, at 17, col. 2. Would such a restriction be the equivalent of withholding all appropriations, or would it be an unconstitutional condition on approved appropriations? Should an attempt be made to plumb congressional intention, much as the intention of a private testator or settlor is examined, to determine whether Congress would or would not have intended the appropriation to fail if the condition were struck? I doubt that a court would take such an approach. I have urged elsewhere a simpler approach: any condition or line item or other legislative provision putting "pressure" on what are otherwise the exclusive powers of the President should be struck. Wallace 314-28.

The following hypothetical examples demonstrate how sophisticated legislative provisions can become. (1) Congress votes money to the State Department for its general operations. In a separate bill it provides that the President may not maintain diplomatic relations with Soviet Russia or have an embassy in Moscow. Presumably this would be unconstitutional. (2) Congress in the appropriations bill provides that none of the appropriation may be spent if an embassy is maintained in Moscow. Presumably the Executive would maintain this was an unconstitutional condition. (3) Congress provides money for the State Department but provides that none of it may be spent in Moscow. (4) Line item

commentators have alleged the impropriety of imposing conditions of conduct, in appropriations measures or otherwise, upon benefits for individuals such as government contracts, licenses, and grants when a constitutional provision would be violated if such conduct were expressly ordered.[159] However, the President has commander-in-chief powers by virtue of the Constitution; they are not granted to him by Congress as is the case with governmental benefits.[160]

---

by line item, Congress votes specific amounts of money for embassies all over the world, but votes no money for a Moscow embassy. All four of these approaches would achieve the congressional purpose of preventing diplomatic relations with Moscow; however, an attack on the constitutionality of the congressional action would be vastly more difficult if approach (4) rather than approach (1) were taken. Compare Congressman John McCormack's attempt in 1940 to abolish the embassy in Moscow. Nobleman, *supra* note 83, at 157.

Direct instructions to the President, such as those hypothesized in (1) above, have largely been resisted by the Executive. For example President Kennedy resisted, and the House eventually scuttled, a proposal to direct the President to develop the RS-70. *See* note 85 *supra*. President Truman stated that he would treat a congressional directive that he make a particular loan to Spain as no more than an authorization. Nobleman, *supra* note 83, at 161.

[159] *See, e.g.*, Note, *Unconstitutional Conditions*, 73 HARV. L. REV. 1595, 1596-98 (1960).

Former Attorney General Herbert Brownell, Jr. had this to say about an attempt to condition an appropriation: "If the practice of attaching invalid conditions to legislative enactments were permissible, it is evident that the constitutional system of the separability of the branches of Government would be placed in the gravest jeopardy." 41 OP. ATT'Y GEN. 233 (1955).

Concerning an attempt by Congress to withhold certain funds from the Executive unless it disclosed certain information, Senator A. Willis Robertson once stated:

> If the President, in keeping with the well established principle under the Constitution of the right of the President to handle foreign policy, decides that the disclosure of some phase of foreign policy would be against the public interest, he can so certify, and the Congress will not be able to get the information.

HOUSE COMM. ON GOV'T OPERATIONS, AVAILABILITY OF INFORMATION FROM FEDERAL DEPARTMENTS AND AGENCIES, H.R. REP. No. 818, 87th Cong., 1st Sess. 165 (1961).

[160] *Cf.* notes 55-62 and accompanying text *supra*. A condition on an independent presidential power is, of course, a more serious matter than a condition on a power delegated to the President by Congress. Even with respect to delegated powers, however, the Executive has resisted congressional restrictions. It has done so with respect to executive secrecy. "To admit that . . . what Congress creates it may control—would be to emasculate the separation of powers." Younger, *Congressional Investigations and Executive Secrecy: A Study in the Separation of Powers*, 20 U. PITT. L. REV. 755, 771 (1959). President Woodrow Wilson resisted an attempt at a committee veto with respect to delegated domestic powers with the following words:

> The Congress has the power and the right to grant or deny an appropriation, or to enact or refuse to enact a law; but once an appropriation is made or a law is passed, the appropriation should be administered or the law executed by the executive branch of the Government. In no other way can the Government be efficiently managed or responsibility definitely fixed. The Congress has the right to confer upon its committees full authority for purposes of investigation and the accumulation of information for its guidance, but I do not concede the right, and certainly not the wisdom, of the Congress of endowing a committee of either House or a joint Committee of both Houses with Power to prescribe regulations under which executive departments may operate.

Of course, there remains an unanswered question: just what are the exclusive executive powers which cannot be subjected to congressional conditions?[161] Putting to one side this question, which the courts have not answered, the fact is that the impropriety of congressional restrictions seems to be borne out by the verdict of history.[162] Many efforts to restrict the President's diplomatic and commander-in-chief powers have been beaten back in Congress.[163] Moreover, Congress, confronted with presidential resistance to proposed restrictive legislation, has frequently responded with ambiguous legislation, "sense of Congress" or "sense of Senate" resolutions,[164] or mere resolutions of advice.[165] In other cases, for example with respect to the conduct of foreign negotiations,[166] the stationing of troops abroad,[167] the exchange of used destroyers for bases,[168] and the assertion of claims of United States

---

*Quoted in Hearings on Separation of Powers, supra* note 79, at 203 (statement of F. Wozencraft, Assistant United States Attorney General). *See also* Ginnane, *supra* note 81, at 569.

[161] *See* notes 142-48 and accompanying text *supra.*

[162] *Cf.* text accompanying notes 42-47 *supra.*

[163] *See* Wallace 322-26.

[164] Thus the 1967 resolution introduced by Senator Fullbright stated

[t]hat it is the sense of the Senate that a national commitment by the United States to a foreign power necessarily and exclusively results from affirmative action taken by the executive and legislative branches cf the United States Government through means of a treaty, convention, or other legislative instrumentality specifically intended to give effect to such a commitment.

S. Res. 151, 90th Cong., 1st Sess. (1967). *See Hearings on S. Res. 151 Relating to United States Commitments to Foreign Powers Before the Senate Comm. on Foreign Relations,* 90th Cong., 1st Sess. (1967). The resolution which emerged from these hearings, S. Res. 187, 90th Cong., 1st Sess. (1967), expressed a similar sentiment.

[165] *E.g.,* Foreign Assistance and Related Agencies Appropriations Act of 1969, § 105, 82 Stat. 1139 (recommending that Communist China not be admitted to the United Nations).

[166] A law enacted in 1913 provides that the President shall attend no international conference without specific congressional authorization. Act of March 4, 1913, § 1, 22 U.S.C. § 262 (1970). However, Presidents have participated in hundreds of conferences, including Versailles, without such authorization. Nobleman, *supra* note 83, at 155 states:

This provision appears clearly to be an unconstitutional interference with the President's prerogatives. Since the United States participates in approximately three hundred international conferences each year, it is difficult to determine the extent to which attention has been paid to the act in recent years. In any event, it appears that when the Congress appropriates funds each fiscal year to enable United States participation in international organizations, either by way of regular annual appropriations for contributions and administrative expenses or for the international contingencies fund of the Department of State, implied consent is given.

[167] The Selective Service Act of 1940 provided, "Persons inducted into the land forces of the United States under this Act shall not be employed beyond the limits of the Western Hemisphere except in the Territories and possessions of the United States, including the Philippine Islands." Act of Sept. 16, 1940, ch. 720, § 3(e), 54 Stat. 885. The President stationed troops in Greenland and Iceland in 1940, in the latter case maintaining that they were not "beyond the limits of the Western Hemisphere." *See* note 83 *supra.*

[168] *E.g.,* Act of June 28, 1940, ch. 440, § 14(a), 54 Stat. 681 (1940), provided that no

nationals wronged by a foreign government,[169] the President has in fact ignored restrictive legislation. To this extent he may be illustrating Alexander Hamilton's observation, made in another context, that laws which do not fit the necessities of society will be flouted.[170] Professor Myres McDougal long ago anticipated this possibility:

> Moreover, if the subject . . . is a matter within the President's special constitutional competence—related, for example, to the recognition of a foreign government or to an exercise of his authority as Commander-in-Chief—a realistic application of the separation of powers doctrine might in some situations appropriately permit the President to disregard the statute as an unconstitutional invasion of his own power.[171]

## 3. Termination of War

Congressional attempts[172] to restrict the war in Indochina can be considered a further effort to control the President's conduct of the war or can be thought of as an attempt to revoke a "declaration of war."[173] Not only have there been no adjudicated cases on the validity of such congressional action, but there have been almost no historical episodes which might serve as precedent.[174] A revocation of a declaration of war

---

military property of the United States could be disposed of without a certification by the Chief of Naval Operations or the Chief of Staff of the Army. The President exchanged overaged destroyers for British bases without such approval. See 39 Op. Att'y Gen. 484 (1940). So too, the President sent armed convoys to Britain in the face of neutrality legislation prior to World War II.

[169] The President seems to have ignored the strictures of the Hickenlooper Amendment (Foreign Assistance Act of 1961, § 620(e), 22 U.S.C. § 2370(e)(1) (1970)) in continuing to provide assistance to Peru, notwithstanding Peru's seizure of private American property without compensation. See Wallace 294.

[170] The Federalist No. 25, at 163 (J. Cooke ed. 1961) (A. Hamilton).

[171] McDougal & Lans, Treaties and Congressional-Executive or Presidential Agreements: Interchangeable Instruments of National Policy: I, 54 Yale L.J. 181, 317 (1945) (footnote omitted).

[172] See notes 149-51 and accompanying text supra. Such attempts appear to be based on the appropriations power. The unsuccessful Hatfield-McGovern amendment of August 26, 1970, to the Military Procurements Act of 1971 (84 Stat. 905) provided that "[a]fter April 30, 1971, funds . . . hereafter appropriated may be expended . . . only to accomplish . . . [inter alia] the orderly termination of military operations there [in and over Indochina] and the safe and systematic withdrawal of remaining armed forces by December 31, 1971." Amend. No. 862 to H.R. 17123, 91st Cong., 2d Sess., 116 Cong. Rec. 30,080 (1970).

[173] See note 154 and accompanying text infra.

[174] Presumably, a war should be ended when the political purposes for which it was entered have been achieved, have become impossible of attainment, or have become no longer worth their cost. The consequences of war are often quite different from those initially anticipated. There is no international law on termination of war.

The history of the 1787 Convention indicates that whereas it was intended that Congress would commence wars by declaring them, the President and Senate would end

is conceivable;[175] certainly the significance of a nation's wars and international conduct, the notion that war is a continuation of foreign policy,[176] and the recognition of the President's exclusive diplomatic and tactical-strategic military powers are components of this question. In practice, of course, it is the President who ends most wars and hostilities by concluding armistices under his diplomatic and commander-in-chief powers.[177] In short, the power of Congress to end hostilities—except of course through its theoretical power to stop all appropriations—is not clear.[178]

# III

## *De Lege Ferenda*—SOLUTION BY LEGISLATION OR LITIGATION?

The preponderance of power over foreign affairs and war has devolved on the President under our separation of powers system, and existing law reflects this fact. I have noted certain legislative efforts by Congress to change this situation. I shall now examine some addi-

---

them through the treaty power. *See* C. BERDAHL, *supra* note 83, at 228. President Wilson actually vetoed as unconstitutional a joint resolution of Congress purporting to terminate hostilities in 1920, indicating that formal termination could only be accomplished through the treaty power; President Harding, however, later requested such a resolution from Congress. *Id.* at 230 n.28. *See also* Corwin, *The Power of Congress To Declare Peace,* 18 MICH. L. REV. 661 (1920). The actual fighting in most American wars has been ended by the President pursuant to the armistice power. *See* note 177 and accompanying text *infra.* Of course, a historical pattern does not mean that Congress may not also enjoy this power.

A seventeenth-century English episode has been cited as a possible precedent for the Hatfield-McGovern or Mansfield type amendment. *See* Memorandum, Indochina: The Constitutional Crisis, *supra* note 2, at 15,414 n.60; Legal Memorandum on the Amendment To End the War, *supra* note 2, at 16,121. An appropriation of the House of Commons in 1678 directed that certain troops be brought from Flanders and be "disbanded and discharged on or before 26 August 1678." J. KENYON, THE STUART CONSTITUTION 396 (1966). However, Parliament was "induced to vote money for [this] . . . disbandment" by the King. Parliament added the quoted provision, not with the view of influencing war policy, but rather so that the King would not apply the money to other purposes. *See id.* at 389. Moreover, the provision was thought to constitute a clear infringement of the King's prerogative of peace and war. In one respect the episode may be relevant: the relationship between the seventeenth-century English King and Parliament may be more akin to that of President and Congress today than would the relationship between executive and Parliament in England today. *See* note 23 *supra.*

175 Henkin, *supra* note 40, at 216.

176 ARON 7; *see* notes 16 & 17 and accompanying text *supra.*

177 *See* Mathews, *The Constitutional Power of the President To Conclude International Agreements,* 64 YALE L.J. 345, 352-54 (1955).

178 Other "end the war" efforts, outside the halls of Congress, have had a legal aspect. *See* New York Times Co. v. United States, 403 U.S. 713 (1971) (per curiam) (pressure on the Executive through distribution of classified government documents protected under the first amendment).

tional proposed congressional responses and shall also review efforts to correct the present "imbalance" of war powers through litigation. I think it will appear that neither legislation nor litigation is a sufficient answer to the fundamental problem.

## A.  Correction by Legislation

I have noted efforts by Congress through the Cooper-Church and Mansfield amendments and the unsuccessful Hatfield-McGovern amendments to use the power of the purse to curb the President's conduct of war. These efforts were addressed to the Vietnam War and were designed to bring about an early end to that war.[179] A bill introduced by Senator Jacob Javits,[180] passed by the Senate and currently pending in the House of Representatives, addresses future presidential conduct and seeks to elaborate Congress's power to declare war. In essence it provides that in the absence of a declaration of war the President may use his sudden repulse power only in specified situations—when United States territory or the armed forces are under attack or in imminent danger of attack, when United States nationals abroad need protection, or when there is specific statutory authorization.[181] The bill further provides that Congress, within thirty days of

---

[179] See notes 149-51 & 172 supra. There of course have been many other resolutions over the last few years addressed to Vietnam and wars generally. E.g., S. Res. 271, 91st Cong., 1st Sess. (1969); see Spong 18-20. There have also been a number of resolutions addressed to foreign policy generally. See notes 285-91 and accompanying text infra. Congressional efforts have had two objectives: (1) to establish substantive policy, especially with regard to the Vietnam War (the Mansfield riders fall in this category); and (2) to shift the balance of foreign affairs power between Congress and the Executive on an institutional basis (see notes 266-71 infra). One reporter has suggested that the high tide of both these developments may have been reached some months ago. Finney, Congress Leaders Break Deadlock over Aid Funds, N.Y. Times, Dec. 11, 1971, at 18, col. 4. But see notes 2 & 151 supra.

[180] S. 2956, 92d Cong., 1st Sess. (1971); see S. REP. No. 606, 92d Cong., 2d Sess. (1972) (report of the Senate Foreign Relations Committee); War Powers Hearings (hearings on S. 2956 and its predecessors). S. 2956 passed the Senate by a vote 68 to 16. 118 CONG. REC. S 6101 (daily ed. April 13, 1972).

[181] The Javits bill provides in relevant part:

In the absence of a declaration of war by the Congress, the Armed Forces of the United States may be introduced in hostilities, or in situations where imminent involvement in hostilities is clearly indicated by the circumstances, only—

(1) to repel an armed attack upon the United States, its territories and possessions; to take necessary and appropriate retaliatory actions in the event of such an attack; and to forestall the direct and imminent threat of such an attack;

(2) to repel an armed attack against the Armed Forces of the United States located outside of the United States, its territories and possessions, and to forestall the direct and imminent threat of such an attack;

(3) to protect while evacuating citizens and nationals of the United States, as rapidly as possible, from (A) any situation on the high seas involving a

the initiation of hostilities, must approve even authorized uses of force by specific legislation; otherwise such force must end.[182] One section of the bill provides that authority to introduce United States forces in hostilities "shall not be inferred . . . from any provision . . . contained in any appropriation Act, unless such provision specifically authorizes

direct and imminent threat to the lives of such citizens and nationals, or (B) any country in which such citizens and nationals are present with the express or tacit consent of the government of such country and are being subjected to a direct and imminent threat to their lives, either sponsored by such government or beyond the power of such government to control; but the President shall make every effort to terminate such a threat without using the Armed Forces of the United States, and shall, where possible, obtain the consent of the government of such country before using the Armed Forces of the United States to protect citizens and nationals of the United States being evacuated from such country; or

(4) pursuant to specific statutory authorization, but authority to introduce the Armed Forces of the United States in hostilities or in any such situation shall not be inferred (A) from any provision of law hereafter enacted, including any provision contained in any appropriation Act, unless such provision specifically authorizes the introduction of such Armed Forces in hostilities or in such situation and specifically exempts the introduction of such Armed Forces from compliance with the provisions of this Act, or (B) from any treaty hereafter ratified unless such treaty is implemented by legislation specifically authorizing the introduction of the Armed Forces of the United States in hostilities or in such situation and specifically exempting the introduction of such Armed Forces from compliance with the provisions of this Act. Specific statutory authorization is required for the assignment of members of the Armed Forces of the United States to command, coordinate, participate in the movement of, or accompany the regular or irregular military forces of any foreign country or government when such Armed Forces are engaged, or there exists an imminent threat that such forces will become engaged, in hostilities. No treaty in force at the time of the enactment of this Act shall be construed as specific statutory authorization for, or a specific exemption permitting, the introduction of the Armed Forces of the United States in hostilities or in any such situation, within the meaning of this clause (4); and no provision of law in force at the time of the enactment of this Act shall be so construed unless such provision specifically authorizes the introduction of such Armed Forces in hostilities or in any such situation.

S. 2956, 92d Cong., 2d Sess. § 3 (1972), *amending* S. 2956, 92d Cong., 1st Sess. § 3 (1971).

For some possible problems raised by the treatment of treaties in subsection (4), **see** note 188 *infra*.

182 The use of the Armed Forces of the United States in hostilities, or in any situation where imminent involvement in hostilities is clearly indicated by the circumstances, under any of the conditions described in section 3 of this Act shall not be sustained beyond thirty days from the date of the introduction of such Armed Forces in hostilities or in any such situation unless (1) the President determines and certifies to the Congress in writing that unavoidable military necessity respecting the safety of Armed Forces of the United States engaged pursuant to section 3(1) or 3(2) of this Act requires the continued use of such Armed Forces in the course of bringing about a prompt disengagement from such hostilities; or (2) Congress is physically unable to meet as a result of an armed attack upon the United States; or (3) the continued use of such Armed Forces in such hostilities or in such situation has been authorized in specific legislation enacted for that purpose by the Congress and pursuant to the provisions thereof.

S. 2956, 92d Cong., 2d Sess. § 5 (1972), *amending* S. 2956, 92d Cong., 1st Sess. § 5 (1971).

. . . [such] introduction."[183] This is an attempt to avoid the situation, possibly inevitable in any long hostility, that congressional consent will be inferred from congressional support.[184] Another section requires the President promptly to report hostilities involving United States forces to Congress.[185]

I shall only address a few general problems raised by the Javits bill. The bill, which authorizes unilateral executive action only in "hostilities" or situations of "imminent involvement in hostilities," does not define the word "hostilities." The difficulties encountered by the United Nations in attempting for the last twenty years to define "aggression" and the difficulty in applying the Geneva conventions on land warfare[186] to various occupation situations may suggest some of the definitional problems in this area. Possibly this is why Javits's bill does not define the term. Unquestionably this definitional uncertainty will give rise to disputes. Executive actions such as the dispatch of an aircraft carrier to the Bay of Bengal during the recent Indo-Pakistani war, the dispatch of ships to the area of the *Pueblo*, and even the mobilization of troops during the Berlin crisis of 1961, illustrate the problem of defining with precision those executive actions that would be considered a response to "hostilities."

The proposed legislation also seems to be based on what I believe to be a false notion: that there are emergency situations in which the President may act alone, readily distinguishable from nonemergency situations in which he may not. The assumption that nonemergency hostilities permit congressional participation is, of course, the principal notion behind the grant to Congress in 1787 of the power to declare war.[187] But must not the President be able to threaten to use force even in "nonemergency situations" if subsequent emergencies are to be avoided? The danger is that Congress, by failing to recognize the continuum of emergency and nonemergency situations and by limiting the

---

[183] *Id.* § 3(4).

[184] *See* notes 3 & 120-21 and accompanying text *supra*.

[185] The introduction of the Armed Forces of the United States . . . under any of the conditions described in section 3 . . . shall be reported promptly in writing by the President to the Speaker of the House of Representatives and the President of the Senate, together with a full account of the circumstances . . . , the estimated scope . . . , and the consistency of the introduction of such forces . . . with the provisions of section 3 of this Act.

S. 2956, 92d Cong., 2d Sess. § 4 (1972), *amending* S. 2956, 92d Cong., 1st Sess. § 4 (1971).

[186] *See* ARON 121-24.

[187] If the intent of the Founding Fathers is to be fulfilled and the public's expectations of what the Constitution requires are to be realized, there should be congressional participation in decisions committing the nation to hostilities other than of an emergency nature.

Spong 18.

President's discretion to emergency situations only, will in effect create such situations by prohibiting executive action at earlier times. For example, would proponents of the Javits bill consider the 1962 Cuban missile crisis a nonemergency situation? The answer to this question is not clear. It has been pointed out that the attempt to specify the situations in which the President may act will certainly result in action being prohibited in some situations in which it should not be. In those cases the President will either be powerless or he will simply stretch the language of restrictive legislation to exclude such situations.[188]

With regard to the requirement of congressional ratification of unilateral executive action within thirty days, it has been noted that of the 192 times the United States has committed armed forces abroad, in ninety-three cases actions lasting more than thirty days have resulted.[189] In addition, a principal purpose in permitting the President to repulse sudden attacks should be to enable him to threaten to do so. How credible will this threat be to other nations if it is known that the use of force must cease within thirty days, absent congressional ratification? To be sure, an aggressor cannot be certain what Congress will do; however, the belief that Congress may bar prolonged use of force may enter into its calculations, even if that belief later proves to be inaccurate.

Senator William Spong, one of the co-sponsors of the Javits bill, has called such legislation an attempt to seek an interpretation of the war powers of the Constitution.[190] Certainly Congress has the right to legislate with respect to its powers, in this case its power to declare war. If Congress is within its powers in the Javits bill, one can only speak of the lack of wisdom in the effort.[191] But one may also question the con-

---

188 *See War Powers Hearings* 470-71 (statement of J. Moore, Professor of Law).
    I cannot imagine that any President, who wanted to do something, could not do it within the framework of the restrictions which have been proposed tonight [the Javits proposal], though it might be a little more tortured and a little less fair to the American people.
*Round Table, supra* note 6, at 176 (remarks of G. Ball, member of the New York Bar).
    The Javits bill (S. 2956, 92d Cong., 1st Sess. § 4 (1971)) explicitly states that no existing treaty can be deemed to authorize the use of force in hostilities or in a situation of imminent threat of hostilities. What does this do to our possible NATO obligations? *See* note 101 *supra.* Does the Javits bill in effect constitute an authorization for breaches of treaties? *Cf.* United Nations Participation Act of 1945, § 6, 22 U.S.C. § 287d (1970).
189 Emerson, *War Powers Legislation,* 74 W. VA. L. REV. 53, 70-71 (1971).
190 Spong 21.
191 Referring to earlier English experience, Lord Reid remarked,
    The reason for leaving the waging of war to the King (or now the executive) is obvious. A schoolboy's knowledge of history is ample to disclose some of the disasters which have been due to parliamentary or other outside attempts at control.
Burmah Oil Co. v. Lord Advocate, [1965] A.C. 75, 100 (1964).

stitutionality of the effort. To the extent that the Javits bill seeks to control the independent sudden repulse power of the President, it raises the question whether the sudden repulse power is exclusive to the Executive.[192]

Another form of legislation, complementary to the Javits approach, has also been proposed. It would provide that when Congress authorizes hostilities, as for example through a formal declaration of war, it could specify their duration, the geographic area in which American action was authorized, and possibly even the magnitude of the force that might be used.[193] Thus the Senate Foreign Relations Committee has suggested that any future resolution of the Tonkin Gulf variety should make clear that it "authorizes" or "empowers" the President rather than that it merely supports him or recognizes his power; and it should state "as explicitly as possible under the circumstances the kind of military action that is being authorized and the place and purpose of its use . . . and . . . a time limit on the resolution."[194] The constitutionality of such an approach is far from clear. Congress in the exercise of its independent power to declare war may authorize a special or limited war,[195] but it may not, under the aegis of this power, be able either to inhibit the President's sudden repulse power or to control his independent commander-in-chief power.[196]

Certain general observations about these various legislative attempts to control the President are in order. Congress should of course participate in foreign policy and war decisions; the impropriety, however, of specific rigid legislation with respect to foreign affairs has often been marked.[197] A nation's decisions in the foreign sphere and with

---

[192] See notes 92-98 and accompanying text *supra*.

[193] Merlo Pusey has proposed machinery of this kind. M. PUSEY, THE WAY WE GO TO WAR 177-78 (1969). It has been suggested that congressional participation may be required if a war is above a certain magnitude. See Note, *supra* note 115, at 1775. It has also been suggested that Congress can impose "reasonable conditions" on the President's war power. Memorandum, Indochina: The Constitutional Crisis, *supra* note 2, at 15,411-12. It is interesting to note how broad the operative provisions of our declarations of war have been. For example:

> [T]he President is hereby authorized and directed to employ the entire naval and military forces of the United States and the resources of the Government to carry on war against the Imperial Government of Japan; and, to bring the conflict to a successful termination, all of the resources of the country are hereby pledged by the Congress of the United States.

Declaration of War on Japan, Dec. 8, 1941, 55 Stat. 795.

[194] SENATE COMM. ON FOREIGN RELATIONS, NATIONAL COMMITMENTS, S. REP. No. 129, 91ST CONG., 1ST SESS. 33 (1969).

[195] See Bas v. Tingy, 4 U.S. (4 Dall.) 37 (1800).

[196] Cf. notes 175-78 and accompanying text *supra*.

[197] Many authors have spoken against rigid legislation with respect to foreign affairs.

respect to war involve a constant assessment of risk and advantage, an extremely fine calculation.[198] Because legislation cannot always antici-pate all variables and because it is not easy to change rigid legislation, it is quite possible that the President would, in what he deems to be the national interest, ignore legislation restricting his alternatives in the foreign affairs field.[199] For Congress knowingly to pass legislation which it may reasonably suppose the President will ignore is, it seems to me, most unwise.[200] Senators and Congressmen should not create a situation in which the law will be flouted.[201]

There is, to be sure, another rationale for this sort of legislation: not rigidly to proscribe executive actions, but rather only to put pres-sure on the Executive. This would be the case not only if the President were prohibited from acting, but also were he only told that there would be a penalty on his action, such as the loss of appropriations for another purpose.[202] Any congressional effort to infringe upon the Ex-ecutive's exclusive powers, either directly or indirectly, however, seems objectionable.[203]

There is a third significance to such legislation. Proposed legisla-tion may be used not as a specific proscription or as specific pressure but rather only as a political signal. The attempts to enact the Hatfield-McGovern and Mansfield amendments may perhaps be understood in this sense. It can be assumed that the President will look carefully at the closeness of the votes and at the tightness and pattern of various provi-sions. Arguably such efforts at legislation represent a rough substitute for a vote of no confidence. There are several difficulties with this argu-ment, however. Are such efforts really effective? Have they actually changed the President's course in Cambodia or Vietnam?[204] Does the use of laws solely as a political signal not contribute to a certain cyni-cism about the law?[205] It could be argued that although the President

---

*E.g.*, J. BRYCE, THE AMERICAN COMMONWEALTH 244 (3d ed. 1906); G. KENNAN, MEMOIRS: 1925-1950, at 409 (1967).

[198] *See Hearings on Administration of National Security Before the Subcomm. on National Security Staffing and Operations of the Senate Comm. on Government Operations,* 88th Cong., 2d Sess., pt. 1, at 86 (1965).

[199] *See* notes 166-71 and accompanying text *supra.*

[200] *But see* Spong 28-31.

[201] *See* note 170 and accompanying text *supra.*

[202] *See* Wallace 472.

[203] *See id.* 477. Provisions creating such pressure may in fact be deemed unconstitu-tional conditions. *See* notes 157-60 and accompanying text *supra.*

[204] When President Nixon announced, on January 25, 1972, that he would accept a "date certain" for withdrawal from Vietnam if certain conditions were accepted by North Vietnam and the Viet Cong, Senator Mansfield was reported to be pleased. N.Y. Times, Jan. 27, 1972, at 1, col. 6.

[205] Consider President Nixon's statement on the occasion of his signing the Military

might not feel specifically bound by all of the Javits bill, he would accept the legislation as a political signal and would therefore seek ways to consult more closely with Congress with respect to the use of armed forces abroad.[206] Certainly the object is admirable. But is this not an abuse of legislation?[207]

This is not the place to review at great length the relative competence of Congress and the Executive. Even after the Vietnam War, I think it clear that most people would still conclude, however reluctantly, that the Executive is the most capable of the three branches with respect to the conduct of foreign and therefore war affairs.[208] Congress of course must have a role in the basic policy making of the country. It might be argued that wars, or at least some of them, are expressions of more basic streams of policy but are not themselves basic.[209] In any event, the inherent deficiencies of Congress as a sole or ultimate policy maker in the foreign affairs field, and the inherent problems of rigid, restrictive legislation seem to make such legislation an unacceptable device in the formulation of foreign and war policy.

## B. *Attempts at Litigation*

The desire to litigate the legality of the Vietnam War has been widespread.[210] The effort to litigate may be in part owing to the general

---

Procurement Authorization Act of 1972, 85 Stat. 423, which contained the Mansfield amendment, § 601, 85 Stat. 430: "I wish to emphasize that § 601 of this Act—the so-called 'Mansfield Amendment'—does not represent the policies of this administration . . . . [I]t is without binding force or effect." 7 WEEKLY COMP. PRES. DOCS. 1531 (Nov. 22, 1971). This statement elicited a full page advertisement in the *New York Times* headed, "We are suing Nixon." N.Y. Times, Nov. 21, 1971, § 4, at 5. The advertisement says, in part, "Then on November 17, Nixon announced that he will disregard the Mansfield Amendment, which he has signed, and which is now law." *Id.* The advertisement quotes Senator Church as saying, "[T]he Mansfield Amendment is now part of the law and, as such, is not subject to dismissal by the President." *Id.* It concludes by saying, "Nixon is fond of talking about law and order. Well, the law exists. Now we need a court order to get him to obey it." *Id; see* Gravel v. Nixon, Civil No. 945-72 (D.D.C., filed May 11, 1972).

[206] *See* S. REP. No. 606, *supra* note 180, at 30 (remarks of Senator J. S. Cooper).

[207] *See* text accompanying notes 199-201 *supra*.

[208] Most citizens perceive [the President] to be uniquely mandated to act in foreign and military policy, areas in which they are apt to feel insufficiently well-informed and in which they are inclined to doubt the judgment of legislators as well.

Legere, *Defense Spending: A Presidential Perspective*, FOREIGN POLICY, Spring 1972, No. 6, at 84, 88.

[209] Professor Dahl and others point out that if we are to have a healthy democracy, the public and its representatives in Congress must participate in some way in the making of basic and broad policy. DAHL 82. Nelson Polsby has suggested that the Vietnam War does not represent such basic policy, but is rather a "mere" episode in our basic policy of containment. *See generally* N. POLSBY, THE CITIZEN'S CHOICE, HUMPHREY OR NIXON (1968). By any criterion, however, the decision whether to continue with the Vietnam War has become a basic policy issue.

[210] *See* G. GUNTHER & N. DOWLING, CASES AND MATERIAL ON INDIVIDUAL RIGHTS IN

"social activism" recently evident in the legal profession and to the belief that the courts can solve our "social" problems,[211] among which the
frustrations generated by the Vietnam War certainly can be counted. On
the other hand, deTocqueville's famous dictum that political questions
in the United States are usually resolved into judicial questions[212] suggests that such litigation was inevitable. Indeed there seems to be a
tendency in our society to examine all problems, even philosophical
ones, in a legal light.[213] The efforts of lawyers to litigate the issues of the
War have largely been frustrated, however, and it appears that they will
continue to be.

The courts are extremely reluctant to involve themselves in problems of the international order, preferring to leave such problems to the
"political departments" of government.[214] Notwithstanding occasional
remarks to the contrary,[215] this reluctance seems to preclude consideration of the extent of executive power or indeed of the relationship of
executive to congressional power in the foreign affairs area.[216] The Supreme Court has used various devices to avoid adjudication of foreign
affairs issues, for example, the standing doctrine, the denial of certiorari,

---

CONSTITUTIONAL LAW 601 (1970); DaCosta v. Nixon, Civil No. 72C626 (E.D.N.Y., filed May
11, 1972); Gravel v. Nixon, Civil No. 945-72 (D.D.C., filed May 11, 1972).

211 See Barron, *The Ambiguity of Judicial Review: A Response to Professor Bickel,*
1970 DUKE L.J. 591. This activism, which extends to questions involving the poor, the
environment, civil rights, prison reform, consumers' rights, and so forth, may have
received some of its impetus from the relative success of the desegregation and reapportionment cases.

212 A. DE TOCQUEVILLE, *supra* note 52, at 106. Of course such resolution may take
time. For example, it took the Supreme Court 137 years to address certain questions concerning the removal power, first raised in the "great debate" of 1789. *See* Myers v. United
States, 272 U.S. 52 (1926).

213 This tendency is exemplified, it seems to me, in the area of the first amendment.
Certainly the question of free speech is a profound problem of political philosophy. *See*
J. S. MILL, ON LIBERTY AND CONSIDERATIONS ON REPRESENTATIVE GOVERNMENT 13-48 (R.
McCallum ed. 1948). Because of our written Constitution and judicial review these profound
questions have become substantially involved with law and the courts. I do not think it is
an exaggeration to say that many Americans today focus on the outer limits of the legality
or constitutionality of speech rather than on the philosophy underlying freedom of
speech. I believe this possibly unintended side effect of the "legalization" of philosophic
issues to be unfortunate. It is compatible, however, with an often noted American
tendency to prefer rules to ambiguity and norms to politics and judgment.

214 *E.g.,* Oetjen v. Central Leather Co., 246 U.S. 297 (1918) (recognition of legitimate
government of Mexico).

215 Baker v. Carr, 369 U.S. 186, 211-213 (1962).

216 The Supreme Court has, however, concerned itself with separation of powers in
certain areas. *E.g.,* Youngstown Sheet & Tube Co. v. Sawyer, 343 U.S. 579 (1952) (power to
seize domestic property during war is a legislative rather than executive power); Myers v.
United States, 272 U.S. 52 (1926) (removal power resides in Executive, not Congress); United
States v. Klein, 80 U.S. (13 Wall.) 128 (1871) (power to grant pardons resides in Executive,
not Congress).

and the political question doctrine. Overriding all of these devices—and in this respect the approach of the Court is quite different from that in domestic cases—is the substantial Supreme Court deference to the Executive, a deference which may often be indistinguishable from the judicial view that, on the merits, many war and other foreign policy decisions are committed to the Executive and are therefore not examinable by the judicial branch. In other words, the Court is extremely reluctant to adjudicate the merits of war and foreign policy cases.[217]

The matter of standing may be disposed of briefly. As the Supreme Court pointed out in *Flast v. Cohen*,[218] this is a shifting area. One requirement for standing to exist is that there must be a "nexus" between the plaintiff who asserts standing and a right guaranteed to him by statute or by the Constitution.[219] Federal courts have continued to refuse standing to raise war power issues to inductees[220] and to persons merely asserting the status of citizen or taxpayer;[221] however, soldiers on the verge of dispatch to Vietnam have, at least implicitly, been given standing to raise war power issues—albeit in cases ultimately unsuccessful on the merits.[222] Although *Flast* is not as clear on the matter as it might be,[223] the Supreme Court's later language in *Association of Data Processing Service Organizations, Inc. v. Camp*[224] suggests that there can be no standing if there is no substantive right with respect to

---

[217] The Court's deference takes many forms. *E.g.*, Banco Nacional de Cuba v. Sabbatino, 376 U.S. 398 (1964) (act of state doctrine); *Ex parte* Peru, 318 U.S. 578 (1943) (sovereign immunity doctrine); United States v. Pink, 315 U.S. 203 (1942) (power to recognize a foreign government); United States v. Belmont, 301 U.S. 324 (1937) (executive agreements); Foster v. Neilson, 27 U.S. (2 Pet.) 253 (1829) (executive interpretation of treaties).

[218] 392 U.S. 83 (1968).

[219] *Id.* at 102.

[220] *E.g.*, United States v. Mitchell, 369 F.2d 323 (2d Cir. 1966), *cert. denied*, 386 U.S. 972 (1967); *cf.* United States v. Bolton, 192 F.2d 805 (2d Cir. 1951) (Korean War).

[221] *E.g.*, Velvel v. Nixon, 415 F.2d 236 (10th Cir. 1969), *cert. denied*, 396 U.S. 1042 (1970).

[222] Orlando v. Laird, 443 F.2d 1039 (2d Cir.), *cert. denied*, 404 U.S. 869 (1971) (authority of executive branch to wage war in Vietnam implied from congressional acquiescence); Luftig v. McNamara, 373 F.2d 664 (D.C. Cir.), *cert. denied*, 387 U.S. 945 (1967) (injunction preventing member of armed services from being sent to Vietnam denied); Mottola v. Nixon, 318 F. Supp. 538 (N.D. Cal. 1970) (court rejected plaintiff's attempt to classify himself as about to be dispatched to Cambodia specifically, rather than Indochina generally).

[223] Although indicating that standing is part of the issue of justiciability, the Court in *Flast* suggests that it is to be determined separately from other aspects of justiciability, such as the political question doctrine. 392 U.S. at 95.

[224] 397 U.S. 150, 153 (1970): "The question of standing . . . concerns . . . the question whether the interest sought to be protected by the complainant is arguably within the zone of interests to be protected or regulated by the statute or constitutional guarantee in question."

which the individual litigant can demonstrate some nexus.[225] On the one occasion the Supreme Court spoke to the matter of standing with respect to war issues, it appeared to indicate—albeit in dicta and before the later convolutions of *Flast*—that a private litigant had neither a recognized substantive interest nor the required nexus. In *Johnson v. Eisentrager*[226] the Court stated,

> Certainly it is not the function of the Judiciary to entertain private litigation—even by a citizen—which challenges the legality, the wisdom, or the propriety of the Commander-in-Chief in sending our armed forces abroad or to any particular region.[227]

The main bulwark erected by the Court to avoid a decision on the merits appears to be the political question doctrine.[228] The political question doctrine is an exceedingly complicated subject,[229] and one cannot begin to understand its operation unless one appreciates that in the area of foreign affairs and war it is merely one expression of an overriding Supreme Court attitude of noninterference with regard to the functioning of government in the international order.[230] The Court recognizes that the requirements of international affairs make it largely inappropriate for it to become involved.[231] Notwithstanding the sug-

---

[225] *Cf.* Reservists Comm. To Stop the War v. Laird, 323 F. Supp. 833 (D.D.C. 1971).

[226] 339 U.S. 763 (1950).

[227] *Id.* at 789.

[228] The Supreme Court has in fact usually resorted to a denial of certiorari without giving reasons. *E.g.*, Luftig v. McNamara, 373 F.2d 664 (D.C. Cir.), *cert. denied*, 387 U.S. 945 (1967). Dissenting justices, however, have often suggested the political question doctrine to be the Court's real reason. *See, e.g.*, Mora v. McNamara, 389 U.S. 934, 934 (1967); United States v. Mitchell, 386 U.S. 972, 972 (1967).

[229] *See generally* Michelman, *The Supreme Court, 1968 Term*, 83 HARV. L. REV. 7, 63-71 (1969); Scharpf, *Judicial Review and the Political Question: A Functional Analysis*, 75 YALE L.J. 517 (1966); Tigar, *supra* note 13.

Professor Alexander Bickel, who has addressed the issues involved in the political question doctrine in two books, *The Least Dangerous Branch* and *Politics and the Warren Court*, takes the position that the Supreme Court need not articulate when and why it will invoke the various devices of judicial self-restraint available, including the political question doctrine. A. BICKEL, THE LEAST DANGEROUS BRANCH (1962); A. BICKEL, POLITICS AND THE WARREN COURT (1965). Others think that the Court should articulate the basis of the application of the political question doctrine, much as if it were a principled rule of law. *E.g.*, Hughes, *Civil Disobedience and the Political Question Doctrine*, 43 N.Y.U.L. REV. 1, 14-15 (1968).

[230] *See* United States v. Curtiss-Wright Export Corp., 299 U.S. 304, 319 (1936).

[231] The cases are legion. *E.g.*, Chicago & S. Air Lines, Inc. v. Waterman S.S. Corp., 333 U.S. 103 (1948); Oetjen v. Central Leather Co., 246 U.S. 297 (1918); Foster v. Nielsen, 27 U.S. (2 Pet.) 253 (1829).

Justice Jackson expressed a comparable sentiment, concurring in *Youngstown*:

I should indulge the widest latitude of interpretation to sustain [the President's] exclusive function to command the instruments of national force, at least when turned against the outside world for the security of our society. But, when it is

gestion in *Baker v. Carr* that not all matters of foreign affairs come within the political question doctrine,[232] and indeed that questions of separation of powers belong pre-eminently to the Court,[233] the record clearly indicates that the Court will not consider foreign affairs questions, or that if it does so, it will usually uphold decisions of other branches of government.[234] In any event, the crux is this: there are certain matters and decisions committed to the political departments. Such matters, as the Court stated in *Marbury v. Madison*,[235] are not "examinable by courts."[236] *Marbury* itself suggested that one such area was foreign affairs.[237]

Of course, if an area of political decision is not examinable by courts, then a fortiori a court cannot recognize and create individual rights with respect to such decisions. This is the answer to the suggestion of commentators such as Professor Leonard Ratner that the Vietnam dispatchee has a "life-expectancy interest," a right which the courts

---

turned inward, not because of rebellion but because of a lawful economic struggle between industry and labor, it should have no such indulgence.

Youngstown Sheet & Tube Co. v. Sawyer, 343 U.S. 579, 645 (1952) (concurring opinion); *cf.* United States v. Debs, 249 U.S. 211 (1919). *See also* United States v. Curtiss-Wright Export Corp., 299 U.S. 304, 322 (1936).

In *In re Neagle*, Justice Lamar went so far as to suggest that the "balance" inherent in separation of powers may not be applicable in the area of foreign affairs: "[T]o foreign nations . . . the internal adjustment of federal power, with its complex system of checks and balances, [is] unknown, and the only authority those nations are permitted to deal with is the authority of the nation as a unit." 135 U.S. 1, 85 (1890) (dissenting opinion).

232 369 U.S. 186, 211 (1962); *cf.* note 216 *supra*.

233 369 U.S. at 210-214.

234 *See* cases cited in note 217 *supra*. The Court's sentiments are well reflected in its dictum in Chicago & S. Air Lines, Inc. v. Waterman S.S. Corp., 333 U.S. 103, 111 (1948):

The President, both as Commander-in-Chief and as the Nation's organ for foreign affairs, has available intelligence services whose reports are not and ought not to be published to the world. It would be intolerable that courts, without the relevant information, should review and perhaps nullify actions of the Executive taken on information properly held secret. Nor can courts sit *in camera* in order to be taken into executive confidences. But even if courts could require full disclosure, the very nature of executive decisions as to foreign policy is political, not judicial. Such decisions are wholly confided by our Constitution to the political departments of the government, Executive and Legislative. They are delicate, complex, and involve large elements of prophecy. They are and should be undertaken only by those directly responsible to the people whose welfare they advance or imperil. They are decisions of a kind for which the Judiciary has neither aptitude, facilities nor responsibility and which has long been held to belong in the domain of political power not subject to judicial intrusion or inquiry.

235 5 U.S. (1 Cranch) 137 (1803).

236 *Id.* at 166. Compare Professor Abram Chayes's interesting observation that the immunity from judicial scrutiny of executive-legislative relations and activity in the foreign affairs area resembles the immunity of nation states from international judicial scrutiny. Chayes, *A Common Lawyer Looks at International Law*, 78 HARV. L. REV. 1396, 1410 (1965).

237 5 U.S. (1 Cranch) at 164-66.

may protect against the government.[238] The fact of the matter is that no such right is recognized. If there is no such right then the application of the political question doctrine or a decision on the merits yields the same result. Before passing to the merits, however, let me suggest a further point. When the Supreme Court pursuant to the political question doctrine refuses to examine separation of powers in the foreign affairs area, notwithstanding its suggestion in *Baker v. Carr* that it has the power to do so[239] and notwithstanding that it has passed on separation of powers problems in other areas,[240] it may be acknowledging that separation of powers is not a wholly viable device in the foreign affairs area.[241] This is of course speculative. My principal point is only that the Court is basically committed to the idea that powers in this area are given to the political branches and that therefore it will not become involved.

The Court has not extensively addressed the merits of cases involving foreign affairs issues. Additionally, there would appear to be somewhat of a theoretical impasse when the merits of foreign affairs cases are approached, an impasse which extends far beyond Vietnam dispatch cases or the propriety of the initiation of the war.[242] Although this is not the place to explore this theoretical impasse in detail, it may be noted that the Court appears not to have developed any general analytical framework by which to weigh and evaluate the assertion of individual claims on the one hand and the foreign policy or national security of the government on the other. For example, there is no theoretical framework similar to either the "preferred position" of freedom of speech under the first amendment,[243] the "compelling state interest" required to validate an "invidious classification" or infringe-

---

238 Ratner, *supra* note 13, at 489.

239 369 U.S. at 210-14.

240 *See* cases cited in note 216 *supra*.

241 In *Orlando v. Laird* the Second Circuit indicated that once a minimum mutual participation by the Executive and Congress in hostilities had occurred, it was a political question as to what degrees of congressional participation would be necessary for differing degrees of hostilities. 443 F.2d 1039, 1043 (2d Cir. 1971). In a sense the court decided that the matter was beyond its competence—even in the face of an elaborate demonstration by the plaintiff that judicially manageable standards existed. *Id.* at 1041.

242 This impasse is discernible in a wide variety of cases. *E.g.*, Derecktor v. United States, 128 F. Supp. 136 (Ct. Cl.), *appeal dismissed per stipulation*, 350 U.S. 802 (1955) (contract rights and foreign policy); Duncan v. Kahanamoku, 327 U.S. 304 (1946) (application for writ of habeas corpus during war for military court convictions of civilians for nonmilitary offenses in Hawaii); Korematsu v. United States, 323 U.S. 214 (1944) (Japanese-American citizen convicted for remaining in a "military area" contrary to wartime Civilian Exclusion Order); *Ex parte* Quirin, 317 U.S. 1 (1942) (petition for habeas corpus upon imprisonment for espionage during war).

243 *See, e.g.*, Kovacs v. Cooper, 336 U.S. 77 (1949).

ment upon a "fundamental interest,"[244] or the required "rational basis" of exercises of the police power.[245]

When the Court feels compelled to address the merits of claims, it inevitably leans towards the Executive or Congress and away from the individual. It seems fairly clear that neither the individual soldier, nor the individual citizen, nor anyone else has a legally enforceable right to question whether a President's decision to dispatch troops is made pursuant to congressional authority or not.[246] The President's decision is political in the *Marbury* sense of not being "examinable by courts."[247] One can say broadly that the Court will be very slow to examine the executive use of force when that force is directed outward;[248] the Court will rather say that it is committed to the Executive. This would very clearly appear to be the implication of decisions or dicta in a number of celebrated cases: *United States v. Curtiss-Wright Export Corp.*,[249] *Chicago & Southern Air Lines, Inc. v. Waterman Steamship Co.*,[250] *Korematsu v. United States*,[251] and *Youngtown Sheet & Tube Co. v. Sawyer*.[252]

To be sure, many foreign affairs questions are unlitigated and we have only fragmentary historical precedent; but I believe that future decisions will not be inconsistent with those to date.[253] I think the Supreme Court appreciates that it is an institution of dissimilar competence from the Executive and Congress.[254] On the one hand, the Executive has certain characteristics and resources which the Court could never obtain or develop, including access to information, full time specialization in foreign affairs, substantial expertise, and a political mandate.[255]

---

[244] *See, e.g.,* Shapiro v. Thompson, 394 U.S. 618 (1969).

[245] *See, e.g.,* Nashville, C. & St. L. Ry. v. Walters, 294 U.S. 405 (1935).

[246] *Cf.* Johnson v. Eisentager, 339 U.S. 763 (1950).

[247] *See* note 213 and accompanying text *supra. See also* Shachtman v. Dulles, 225 F.2d 938 (D.C. Cir. 1955).

[248] *See* Youngstown Sheet & Tube Co. v. Sawyer, 343 U.S. 579, 645 (1952) (concurring opinion).

[249] 299 U.S. 304 (1936).

[250] 333 U.S. 103 (1948).

[251] 319 U.S. 432 (1943).

[252] 343 U.S. 579, 645 (1952) (concurring opinion).

[253] If the holding of Orlando v. Laird, 443 F.2d 1039 (2d Cir. 1970), *cert. denied,* 404 U.S. 869 (1971), that a sufficient exercise of the congressional declaration of war power had been manifested through appropriations, selective service legislation, and the like, and that a prior express exercise of the declaration of war power was not required under the Constitution, were to be adopted and embraced by Congress, the original constitutional intention might well be thwarted and the path of future verdicts of history shifted considerably. *See* note 137 *supra.*

[254] *See* Banco Nacional de Cuba v. Sabbatino, 376 U.S. 398, 431-33 (1964).

[255] *See* notes 208 & 209 and accompanying text *supra.*

On the other hand, there are inherent Supreme Court deficiencies with regard to international issues: its capacity to find facts is limited by the adversary process[256] and its members are uncomfortable with the frequent requirement of keeping facts having to do with national security secret.[257]

Because the Court has largely stayed out of the foreign affairs area, it has not had to delineate the limits of possible judicial remedies; the difficulty of formulating remedies in this area is of course a classic ingredient of the political question doctrine.[258] But there is a more profound fact: the point might be reached when the Executive would ignore the Court. I have argued that the Executive might ignore Congress if it tried to restrict the exercise of his commander-in-chief powers;[259] if the Executive were to ignore the Court it would not be acting entirely without precedent.[260] Moreover, as Professor Alexander Bickel has suggested,[261] the Court does not have the political or democratic base or mandate to justify its involvement in this area. In short, just as rigid legislation is not appropriate to decisions in the foreign affairs area, so principled decision—the great hallmark of the judicial role—is not appropriate. The instability and fluid nature of the international order is simply different in kind from the nature of the domestic order.[262]

---

[256] See Chicago & S. Air Lines, Inc. v. Waterman S.S. Corp., 333 U.S. 103, 114 (1948).

[257] United States v. Reynolds, 345 U.S. 1, 7-8 (1953); Chicago & S. Air Lines, Inc. v. Waterman S.S. Corp., 333 U.S. 103, 111 (1948); United States v. Curtiss-Wright Export Corp., 299 U.S. 103, 111 (1936).

[258] See Baker v. Carr, 369 U.S. 186, 211-14 (1962).

Certain limits on remedies against the President are more formal than real. Thus although the President himself cannot be subject to a mandatory injunction (Mississippi v. Johnson, 71 U.S. (4 Wall.) 475 (1866)), cabinet officers can be given directions by the Court (Youngstown Sheet & Tube Co. v. Sawyer, 343 U.S. 579 (1952)). Cf. Kendall v. United States, 37 U.S. (12 Pet.) 524 (1838) (cabinet officer directed to carry out ministerial duty to pay funds).

[259] See notes 166-71 and accompanying text supra.

[260] In Ex parte Merryman, F. Cas. 144 (No. 9487) (C.C.D. Md. 1861), Justice Roger Taney, on circuit, ordered a writ of habeas corpus to issue to General George Cadwalader. When the general failed to comply with the writ, Justice Taney observed that he had done his duty and that the matter now lay with General Cadwalader's superior, President Lincoln—who also did not comply. CORWIN 144-45; cf. Duncan v. Kahanamoku, 327 U.S. 304 (1946). More recently, the President has undercut contrary court rulings by proposing a busing moratorium. For the President's statement, see Educational Opportunity and Busing, 8 WEEKLY COMP. PRES. DOCS. 590 (March 20, 1972).

[261] A. BICKEL, THE LEAST DANGEROUS BRANCH 184-86 (1962).

[262] Foreign affairs matters are political rather than justiciable in both the domestic and international sense. As Judge de Visscher has pointed out, the instability of the international order limits the subjection of nation states to international law; the international order remains largely a function of the power relations among nation states. C. DE VISSCHER, supra note 14, at 135-36. Conditions in the international order are simply less

## IV

### CAN OUR POLITICAL INSTITUTIONS BE ADJUSTED? PROPOSED AND UNPROPOSED SOLUTIONS

It can be argued that there have been two failings with respect to our involvement in Vietnam: the policy pursued has been irrational, and the manner in which we entered and persisted in the war was not sufficiently democratic in that Congress was deprived of its power to declare war.[263] This article has been addressed to the second failing. Is there anything that can be done to prevent failings of the second type, recognizing that but for the first the second would not be nearly so urgent? In other words, can we adjust our political institutions so as to ensure a more meaningful foreign and war policy role for Congress?

I have sought to demonstrate that the origin of the constitutional problem lies in the system of separation of powers created in 1787 and in its subsequent (I would submit inevitable) development, which has revealed the absence of suitable political mechanisms to ensure democratic responsibility with respect to war and foreign policy decisions. Neither the legislative approach of the Cooper-Church amendments[264] based on the appropriations power, nor that of the Javits bill[265] based on the declaration of war power, nor litigation is a sufficient solution. I shall now examine other solutions that have been proposed and some that have not.

### A. A New System?

One proposed solution would be a substantial overhaul of the present system. Essentially, the "replacers" would substitute the British

---

static than those in the domestic order. The facts upon which a judicial decree could be formulated might be radically different several days following the decision; one need only think of the progress of the Arab-Israeli War in 1967 or the recent Indian-Pakistani War for evidence of this fact. The courts neither have access to, nor can they effectively handle, a sufficient range of facts about the international order. *See* text accompanying notes 255-56 *supra.*

I do not suggest that there will be no adjudication with respect to foreign affairs. Of course there will continue to be cases involving conflict of laws, enforcement of foreign judgments, and foreign evidence. *See* Tigar, *supra* note 13, at 1152-58. And there will continue to be cases involving the interpretation and application of treaties, sovereign immunity, and the act of state doctrine. And although there will also continue to be cases involving martial law, military justice, espionage, and wartime seizure of property, none of these issues should be confused with the central issue of the nation's response by war to the pressures of the international order; this issue the courts will not adjudicate.

[263] *See* DAHL 4.

[264] *See* note 149 *supra.*

[265] *See* notes 180-92 and accompanying text *supra.*

ministerial system[266] for our own. Given the historical reluctance of Americans to tamper with the basic constitutional scheme[267] and the perceived quality of the system's domestic performance, such a change seems highly unlikely. A second faction, the "improvers," presents a variation on this theme. Basically, their idea is to associate more closely the Executive and Congress through participation by senior members of Congress in an executive-congressional cabinet. The purposes of this plan are several: (1) to put members of the Congress on career paths leading to the Executive;[268] (2) to develop a greater sense of executive responsibility to Congress; and (3) to give the Executive greater access to the thinking of members of Congress.

I am skeptical of these proposals. The ministerial or cabinet system, based on the confidence of Parliament, represents a fusion of the executive and legislature with many subtle cross-controls and balances which are not present in our system.[269] Although not all of these cross-controls work today in the way they have in the past, their presence leads to an entirely different system of political balance.[270] Additionally, our Constitution would appear to bar members of Congress from serving in the executive department, and to change the rule would presumably require a constitutional amendment.[271]

It is true that the British scheme avoids some of our most serious problems; that the top members of the executive department come from the legislature tends to assure a shared administrative and foreign experience. "Improvers" such as Professor Dahl would seek to achieve this shared experience as well as the creation of more responsible—that is to say disciplined—political parties.[272] All this is interesting but in my opinion unlikely to occur.

---

266 *See generally* DAHL 169. Presumably, the American innovation of Supreme Court judicial review, not present in the United Kingdom, would be retained.

267 Consider, for example, recent discussion over a proposed six-year presidential term. *See* Schlesinger, *The Presidency Under Glass*, N.Y. Times, Jan. 4, 1972, at 33, col. 4.

268 Congress does not at present often constitute a career path to high executive office in the field of foreign affairs. *See* Wallace 460.

269 These cross-controls and balances include the power of the executive to pick ministers from the legislature, the power of party discipline, and the power of Parliament to vote no confidence in the executive. *See generally* K. BRADSHAW & D. PRING, PARLIAMENT AND CONGRESS (1971).

270 *See* notes 23-25 and accompanying text *supra.*

271 U.S. CONST. art. I, § 6 provides in pertinent part, "[N]o Person holding any Office under the United States shall be a Member of either House during his Continuance in Office." Dahl calls this provision a "blunder." DAHL 173.

272 *See* DAHL 226-38.

## B. *Improvement of the Executive*

A second proposed solution focuses on the American Executive. Basically, the idea is to improve the efficiency of the Executive and consequently the rationality of its foreign policy, thus in effect avoiding the "problem" of democratic responsibility which inheres in the legislative process.[273] Some would center even greater power in the White House, or indeed think this is inevitable;[274] others seek an improved State Department restored to greater power, and a generally improved bureaucracy.[275]

## C. *Increases in Congressional Power*

Many now seem to believe that the Executive's "failure" to get more explicit congressional authorization for Vietnam was in reality a failure of Congress to assert itself.[276] More recently there have been a considerable number of proposals and initiatives to increase the power of Congress and to improve its operations. In the face of the troubled international order and the phenomenon of legislative decline relative to the executive throughout the world,[277] it is not clear what the effect of these proposals will be. The proposed modifications have taken several forms. The most basic suggests a revision of the seniority system and new methods of selection of leadership and committee chairmen.[278] Although some energy has recently been put into this proposal, its ultimate prospects are problematical.[279] Another proposal seeks to strengthen the hand of Congress by replacing the present foreign affairs and armed services committees and related appropriations committees with a new committee structure which would act somewhat as a "foreign affairs" directorate for Congress.[280] Related proposals speak in terms of

---

[273] *See* Fulbright, *American Foreign Policy in the 20th Century Under an 18th-Century Constitution*, 47 CORNELL L.Q. 1 (1961).

[274] Destler, *supra* note 75, at 31-32.

[275] *See generally* Cooper, *supra* note 75; Destler, *supra* note 75; Halperin, *supra* note 75.

[276] *See, e.g., War Powers Hearings* 706 (remarks of Senator J. Stennis).

[277] Note 38 *supra.*

[278] *See* 116 CONG. REC. 29,780-95 (1970) (remarks of Senator Packwood).

[279] In fact, however, some changes have recently been made: a rule has been adopted that a Congressman may hold only one committee or subcommittee chairmanship. Legislative Reorganization Act of 1970, § 132(d), 84 Stat. 1140 (amend. to Senate R. 6, ¶ 25). The effect of this provision, however, may be merely to endear more Congressmen to the seniority system by making their committee positions irreplaceable.

[280] Senator Hubert Humphrey has proposed a Joint Congressional Committee on National Security. S. 2290, 92d Cong., 1st Sess. (1971). *See* 117 CONG. REC. S 11,088 (daily ed. July 15, 1971) (remarks of Senator Humphrey).

improvement of the congressional staff[281] and of Congress's general information gathering facilities.[282] The thrust of some of these proposals would seem to be the creation of a congressional leviathan to counter the executive leviathan. My feeling is that this is not the proper develop-ment of the separation of powers system and would certainly not facilitate the conduct of foreign affairs.

Another set of proposals focuses on better use by Congress of its present facilities. Congress might investigate problems more vigorously, using the subpoena power if necessary.[283] Of course the congressional investigation of national security functions presents serious problems. A related device would be a requirement of greater reporting to Congress by the Executive, including reports with respect to the transport of troops abroad.[284] Senator Clifford Case has suggested that all international agreements—whether in the form of treaties or executive agreements—be submitted to the Senate for its information.[285] So that the Senate may give its advice and consent, Senator William Fulbright would also have the Executive use treaties more frequently than executive agreements[286] and have the President submit to the Senate the names not only of proposed ambassadors but of all foreign envoys.[287] Fulbright has in fact succeeded in having the State Department's annual budget made subject to review by both appropriations and foreign

---

281 The total congressional staff is already very large, amounting in 1970 to 11,687 employees, of which a significant number are professionals. 116 CONG. REC. S 17,131 (daily ed. Oct. 5, 1970). In recent years Senators have employed personal foreign affairs advisers.

282 It is thought that additional general staff, systems analysts, and computers might enable Congress to review the Pentagon budget in a more meaningful way.

283 The investigative power of Congress is only as effective as its subpoena power, and that power has occasionally been stymied by the invocation of executive privilege. See N.Y. Times, April 16, 1972, § 4, at 6, col. 4.

284 The Javits bill contains a provision of this kind. S. 2956, 92d Cong., 1st Sess. § 4 (1971). Of course the Executive will be reluctant to disclose all details of a foreign affairs or military matter to the entire Congress; therefore, such executive reports might necessarily be quite general, and might exclude many of the factors on the basis of which fine calculations as to foreign or war policy are made. See DAHL 171-72.

285 N.Y. Times, Dec. 3, 1970, at 15, col. 1. This proposal was submitted to the Senate in February, 1971 as a resolution, S. Res. 36, 92d Cong., 1st Sess. Cf. N.Y. Times, Dec. 8, 1971, at 14, col. 4.

286 For example, Senator Fulbright has suggested that any guarantees to Israel take the form of a treaty rather than an executive agreement. See Fulbright, Old Myths and New Realities—II: The Middle East, 116 CONG. REC. 29,796 (1970). S. 3475, 92d Cong., 2d Sess. (1972), introduced by Senator Sam Ervin, which would require all executive agreements to be submitted to Congress and be subject to disapproval by concurrent resolution within 60 days of submission, might meet both Senator Fulbright's proposal and Senator Case's proposal (note 285 and accompanying text supra).

287 115 CONG. REC. 16,080 (1969) (remarks of Senator Fulbright).

affairs committees of both houses.[288] In addition, Senate Resolution 151 of 1967[289] states it to be the "sense" of the Senate[290] that all "national commitments" require congressional participation.[291] I have already considered the effort to pass the Hatfield-McGovern and Case-Church amendments, the status of the Javits bill, and the actual passage of the Cooper-Church and Mansfield amendments.

What are the prospects for these proposals? It is agreed that the appropriations power is the bulwark and the heart of congressional power.[292] No doubt many of the proposals are aimed towards facilitating a more efficient exercise of that power by Congress. Basically, congressional power can be exercised through withholding or reducing of appropriations, and legislative efforts such as those by Senators Case, Cooper, Church, Hatfield, McGovern, and Mansfield. The former require great congressional will and expertise, and involve the possible creation of a competing leviathan. The latter to some extent involve measures which in my opinion are constitutionally impermissible under a proper understanding and working of our delicate system of separation of powers.[293] On the other hand, the adroit use of some or all of these devices, if truly reflective of a new congressional will to influence the Executive, may have some effect despite executive resistance.

## D. America's Place in the International System

Before examining some other developments which might affect the working of our constitutional system, we might pause briefly to look at the international system. What are the prospects for the international order to change so radically as to alter significantly the nature of the external problems confronting the United States? Here one must be skeptical. One must remember that the international order is exceedingly

---

[288] Foreign Assistance Act of 1971, §§ 407(a)-(b), 86 Stat. 35.

[289] S. Res. 151, 90th Cong., 1st Sess. (1967).

[290] A "sense of the Senate" resolution may be intended as no more than "advice" or indeed as a political show. Presumably S. Res. 151 is intended as something more.

[291] In fact executive "commitments" are still common. President Nixon, for example, recently assured Chancellor Willy Brandt of West Germany that "American commitments in Europe will remain unchanged, and that, in particular, no reductions in American troops stationed in Europe will be made." THE ECONOMIST, Jan. 1, 1972, at 28.

[292] The orchestration of the appropriations power either to withhold or to reduce funds will be difficult. To some it may seem a war on the war power.

[293] See Massachusetts v. Mellon, 262 U.S. 447, 488 (1923):

To the legislative department has been committed the duty of making laws; to the executive the duty of executing them; and to the judiciary the duty of interpreting and applying them in cases properly brought before the courts. The general rule is that neither department may invade the province of the other and neither may control, direct or restrain the action of the other.

complex, and the expected move to multi-polarity from present bi-polarity will not make it less complex. In any case a multi-polar international order will still be composed of nation states; one will still have to think about the relations among the United States, Russia, and China; among the United States, Europe, and Latin America; between Russia and Europe; between India and Pakistan, Israel and the Arab nations, and so forth. To be sure the American role in the world could be significantly changed under the "Nixon doctrine."[294] My own belief is that American dependence on foreign economic resources, the foreign activity of United States investors and traders,[295] and our general concern with world affairs will mean a continual, substantial international involvement. One question, however, will probably remain unresolved —whether the United States can eschew idealism for realism in foreign affairs.[296]

## E. A Balance Between Rationality and Responsibility: Cooperation Between the Executive and Congress

The domestic cousin to a more realistic attitude towards foreign affairs is a more cooperative attitude in both executive and legislative branches towards the separation of powers. Although I reject the overall approach of the Javits bill, it is possible that some portions of it, such as the reporting requirement and the direction that the President come to Congress with a strong justification for participation in any substantial hostility, combined with a more adroit use of the appropriations power by Congress, might exert pressure on the Executive to increase

---

[294] The "Nixon Doctrine" represents the attempt of the Nixon administration to redefine the American foreign policy role without destroying "confidence abroad." The President detailed the three elements of the "new partnership" as follows:

First, *the United States will keep all of its treaty commitments.* . . .

Second, *we shall provide a shield if a nuclear power threatens the freedom of a nation allied with us or of a nation whose survival we consider vital to our security.* . . .

Third, *in cases involving other types of aggression we shall furnish military and economic assistance when requested in accordance with our treaty commitments. But we shall look to the nation directly threatened to assume the primary responsibility of providing the manpower for its defense.*

*United States Foreign Policy for the 1970's: Building for Peace,* 7 WEEKLY COMP. PRES. DOCS. 305, 309 (Feb. 25, 1971) (emphasis in original).

[295] The current problems of international trade and investment are discussed in Javits & Freeman, *Two Responses to Senator Hartke,* N.Y. Times, March 5, 1972, § 3, at 16, col. 3.

[296] Our tendency towards idealism in foreign affairs, exemplified by the foreign policy of Woodrow Wilson, has often been pointed out, as has the necessity for realism. *See generally* G. KENNAN, REALITIES OF AMERICAN FOREIGN POLICY (1954). Are we on the verge of finally achieving such realism? Some hope that the Vietnam experience will produce this result. *E.g.,* Shannon, *America Comes of Age,* N.Y. Times, Jan. 3, 1972, at 27, col. 1.

congressional participation. The President might reexamine, for example, the constitutional implications of the extensive power of a "national security adviser" such as Henry Kissinger, or he might seek to increase consultation with Senators or Congressmen, either as individuals or as representatives of Congress. Of course a great deal depends on personalities: Dean Acheson and Arthur Vandenberg, for example, cooperated because both were strong and both insisted on cooperation.[297]

There is also a somewhat more metaphysical point. Americans —especially lawyers—are accustomed to think in terms of external checks and balances, of the adversary system, of economic competition, of the marketplace of ideas, and of similar mechanisms and notions. Much of this may be rooted in our peculiar form of democracy; the objective, whether it be truth, a low price, or consensus, is thought best achieved through a process in which ideas and practices freely conflict. This approach has served America reasonably well. On the other hand it may, in itself, no longer be sufficient. We may increasingly have to look to the Greek notion of *sophrosyne,* or moderation. We may have to learn, as a habit, to strike internal balances—in this case between executive perceptions and congressional preference—to achieve rationality and responsibility.[298] Quite frankly I believe Congress will have to continue to give quite a lot to the Executive. But if important officials in the executive branch and important members of Congress can acquire or strengthen an attitude of cooperation, a good deal may be accomplished.[299]

We thus seem to return to the usual adjuration for the necessity of cooperation between the Executive and Congress if our system is to work. Let me pose some questions without answering them. How might greater cooperation work, or have worked, in the following situations?

---

[297] D. ACHESON, *supra* note 106, at 71-72; A. VANDENBERG, THE PRIVATE PAPERS OF SENATOR VANDENBERG 72 (1952).

[298] Senator Stennis has stated:

The most important balance to be restored is the balance in the minds of the Nation's citizens, both those who are inclined to surrender their own responsibilities of decision to the executive, as many in the Congress have too often done, and those who believe that no cause is worth fighting for.

*War Powers Hearings* 707.

[299] Senator Ervin has said:

We must be ever mindful of the necessity for cooperation between the Congress and the Executive if the Government is to operate efficiently. That pressing requirement makes it mandatory that we seek and find an amicable settlement of the problems involved in the invocation of executive privilege to prevent Congress and the American people from knowing the details of executive actions.

*Hearings on Executive Privilege, supra* note 22, at 7.

## 1. *World Wars I and II*

What should a President do with respect to a succession of events such as those preceding both World Wars? Is consultation on each event realistic?[300]

## 2. *The Cuban Missile Crisis*

Senator Fulbright actually participated in the executive decisions. Did he represent the Senate or only himself? Would it have been feasible for the full Congress to have been involved in decisions on such fast moving events? To what extent could Fulbright and his colleagues have sounded out Congress and obtained a true reading of congressional sentiment? To what extent would the Executive have adhered to that sentiment? To what extent did Congress have relevant information which would lead the Executive to respect its opinion?[301]

## 3. *Vietnam*

President Johnson obtained the Tonkin Gulf Resolution from Congress in 1964. Should he have gone back to Congress, say in 1967, for reaffirmation of his authority? Should he have submitted the decision to escalate the conflict to Congress for its affirmative approval? The Javits bill would not appear to require such reaffirmation, but under that bill there would theoretically have been proper and fully informed congressional authorization at the beginning of hostilities. Can Congress, realistically, be consulted at various stages of an escalating war?[302]

---

[300] Can another Versailles be avoided? The President has since World War II invited senatorial observers to important treaty negotiations, and this practice should of course be continued. Thus the President invited Senators to participate in the drafting of the United Nations Charter in San Francisco in 1945. *See* Wallace 318 n.175. Congress, possibly because the power to regulate foreign commerce is assigned to it by the Constitution, has provided for congressional participation in trade negotiation delegations. *See generally* A. CHAYES, T. ERLICH, & A. LOWENFELD, *supra* note 107, at 307. No congressional participation was invited at the recent Strategic Arms Limitations Talks (SALT).

[301] Presidents Eisenhower and Kennedy apparently consulted frequently with members of the Senate Foreign Relations Committee on major foreign policy initiatives. So too, President Truman consulted with congressional leadership over Korea. *See* note 106 *supra.*

[302] Von Clausewitz, prior to the existence of nuclear weapons and theories of limited war, was of the opinion that all wars tend to escalate: "War is an act of force, and to the application of that force there is no limit. Each of the adversaries forces the hand of the other, and a reciprocal action results which in theory can have no limit." K. VON CLAUSEWITZ, *supra* note 17, at 5.

## 4. Cambodia

Was the incursion a second front or more akin to a new war? If it is seen as part of the larger Vietnam War, was the lack of consultation proper under the Executive's commander-in-chief power? On the other hand, since the problems in Cambodia did not evolve with the urgency of the Cuban missile crisis, would not congressional consultation have been appropriate?

## CONCLUSION

What is likely to happen as a result of the Vietnam experience? Will we change our ways or will new external pressures merely lead to a further development of virtual executive monopoly over foreign policy initiative? Personalities may be crucial; a congressional leadership sufficiently able and determined effectively to assert its authority while cooperating with the Executive, and a President equally able and willing to cooperate, can provide a satisfactory solution.

# The Indochina War Cases in the United States Court of Appeals for the Second Circuit

## SCOTT J. WENNER

### INTRODUCTION

Between the years 1970–1973, a series of cases involving the Indochina War arose in the U.S. Court of Appeals for the Second Circuit. Each raised constitutional issues regarding the allocation of the war-making power between Congress and the President in the context of a war that was alleged by plaintiffs to be unconstitutional. The Second Circuit developed a principle governing the role of the judiciary in connection with the war-making power. As will be explained in this note, the judiciary was held to have some power to check the executive in its war-making activities, but this power was in fact very limited and largely ineffectual.

The Congressional war-making power is derived from explicit constitutional provisions. Article I, Section 8, clause 11 of the U.S. Constitution states that "The Congress shall have Power . . . To declare War."[1] It is also stated in clause 12 that "Congress shall have Power . . . To raise and support Armies."[2] In contrast to this explicit delegation to Congress of the power to declare war, the war-making powers of the President are derived by inference from his role as Commander-in-Chief of the Army and Navy of the U.S. and of the militia when called into the actual service of the United States.[3]

Since the days of Alexander Hamilton who construed war-making as an executive function[4] and James Madison who read the Constitution as giving Congress pre-eminence in this area,[5] the debate over the sparsely worded war powers provisions of the Constitution has raged. And, since the occurrence of the wars in Korea and Indochina, both formally undeclared, interest in the issue has been intensified.[6]

---

1. U.S. Const., art. I, § 8, cl. 11.

2. Id., cl. 12.

3. Id., art II, § 2.

4. 4 The Works of Alexander Hamilton 437–44 (H. Lodge, ed., 1904) .

5. 6 The Writings of James Madison 138–88 (G. Hunt, ed., 1906) .

6. For a comprehensive and recent treatment of the question of the original meaning of the war powers clauses of the constitution, see Lofgren, Warmaking Under the Constitution: The Original Understanding, 81 Yale L.J 672 (1972) .

This note will deal with the issue of the constitutional allocation of war-making powers[7] as it arose in the Indochina War cases
in the Second Circuit. While no attempt will be made to analyze the
issues contained herein from an international law perspective, the
manner in which the United States can, under its domestic law, be
committed to war is a subject of great importance in the field of international relations.[8]

## INDOCHINA WAR CASES IN THE SECOND CIRCUIT

### A. *Berk v. Laird*

After he was ordered to report to Fort Dix for dispatch to
Vietnam, PFC Malcolm A. Berk, an enlistee in the U.S. Army,
commenced an action against the Secretary of Defense and his commanding officers declaring that his military superiors were without
authority to order him to Vietnam or Cambodia.[9] He sought to enjoin the named defendants from issuing said orders on the grounds
that they had exceeded their constitutional authority, as Congress
had not authorized the war. The district court[10] denied Berk's application for a preliminary injunction, and the Second Circuit affirmed and remanded the case for a hearing on Berk's application
for a permanent injunction, holding, *inter alia,* that his claim that
orders to fight must be authorized by a mutual legislative-executive
action was justiciable.[11] The court stated that "[s]ince orders to

On this point, see also 2 M. Farrand, The Records of the Federal Convention 318
(M. Farrand, ed., 1911) ; Donahoe & Smelser, The Congressional Power to Raise
Armies: The Constitutional and Ratifying Conventions, 1787–88, 33 Rev. of Pol.
202 (1971) ; Hearings on War Powers Legislation Before the Subcommittee on
National Security Policy and Scientific Developments of the House Committee on
Foreign Affairs, 91st Cong. 2nd Sess. (1970) , and 92d Cong. 1st Sess. (1971) ; Note,
Congress, the President, and the Power to Commit Forces to Combat, 81 Harv.
Law Rev. 1771 (1968) .

7. Note that Congress is given the power to declare war; the use of the
phrase "make war" is nowhere found in the Constitution. Much of the confusion
on the question of the proper allocation of the war powers turns on the
difference between these two phrases. See 2 M. Farrand, supra note 6 at 318 for
the debate in the Constitutional convention over the defeated resolution to
substitute the word "make" for "declare." See also Lofgren, supra note 6 at
675–78.

8. For such examination, see Richard A. Falk, The Cambodian Operation
and International Law, 65 Am.J. Int'l. L at 1 (1971) ; Symposium on U.S. Action
in Cambodia: Cambodian Actions and International Law, 65 Am.J. Int'l L at 1
(1971) .

9. 429 F.2d 302 (2d Cir. 1970) [*hereinafter* cited as Berk].

10. 317 F. Supp. 1013 (E.D.N.Y. 1970) .

11. Berk, supra note 9, at 305. The Court directed that PFC Berk be afforded

fight must be issued in accordance with proper authorization from both branches under some circumstances, executive officers are under a threshold constitutional duty [which] can be judicially identified, and its breach judicially determined."[12] The court reasoned that since the duty of the executive to get congressional authorization can be measured by the courts, the question of whether the executive branch has complied with this duty is not a political question.

It should be noted that the political question doctrine has been the major obstacle to plaintiffs in the Indochina War cases.[13] Applying the principles set forth in *Baker v. Carr*,[14] the court in each case tried to identify a "judicially manageable standard"[15] for resolving the issues presented.[16] As will be discussed later in this note, such questions as the degree of the participation of Congress in the prosecution of the war,[17] the question of whether a war has been escalated[18] and the question of whether a war has ended [19] and a new one begun[20] were all recently characterized by the Second Cir-

---

an opportunity to suggest a method for resolving the question of what degree joint legislative-executive action would be sufficient to authorize the military activity in question.

12. Id., at 302 citing Baker v. Carr, 369 U.S. 186, 198 (1966).

13. Scholars have written extensively about the political question doctrine. See, e.g., Tigar, Judicial Power, The "Political Question Doctrine," and Foreign Relations, 17 U.C.L.A. L. Rev. 1135 (1970); Note, The Supreme Court, 1968 Term, 83 Harv. L. Rev. 7, 62–77 (1969); Wechsler, Toward Neutral Principles of Constitutional Law, 73 Harv. L. Rev. 1 (1959); Bickel, The Least Dangerous Branch (1962); and Scharpf, Judicial Review and the Political Question: A Functional Analysis, 75 Yale L.J. 517 (1966).

14. See supra note 12.

15. Baker v. Carr, 369 U.S. 186, 217.

16. Id. The other five criteria for an issue to be considered a political question are:

    1. A textually demonstrable constitutional commitment of the issue to a coordinate political department.
    2. Some possibility of deciding the question without an initial policy determination of a kind clearly for non-judicial discretion.
    3. Some possibility of a court's undertaking independent resolution without expressing a lack of the respect due coordinate branches of government.
    4. Unusual need for unquestioned adherance to political decisions already made.
    5. Potential of embarrassment from multifarious prouncements by various departments on one question.

17. Orlando v. Laird, 443 F2d 1039, cert. denied, 404 U.S. 869 (1971), [*hereinafter cited as* Orlando.]

18. Da Costa v. Laird, 471 F.2d 1146 (2d Cir. 1973), [*hereinafter* cited as Da Costa III].

19. Ludecke v. Watkins, 335 U.S. 160, 169 (1947).

20. Holtzman v. Schlesinger, 484 F.2d 1307 (2d Cir. 1973).

cuit as being political questions. The common thread running through each was the lack of judicial competence to deal with the political, miliary and diplomatic issues presented, and thus, the lack of a "judicially manageable standard."

In *Berk,* the court took one step towards an examination of the constitutionality of plaintiffs' orders for combat by holding that the question of whether there was mutual participation by the legislative and the executive branch *was* justiciable.[21] However, the court warned that even if the claim possesses this general preliminary attribute of justiciability, it still may not be decided if it involves a political question,[22] "lack[ing] . . . judicially discoverable and manageable standards for resolving it."[23] And, "if the issue involved in this case is political, Congress and the executive will decide whether there has been a usurpation of authority by the latter, through political means."[24] The court further warned that even if Berk were able to show that his claim does not raise an unmanageable political question, he would be required to show the district court on remand that Congressional debates and actions, from the Tonkin Gulf resolution,[25] through appropriations acts and other support of the Vietnam action, fall short of whatever explicit standards of authorization he propounds.[26]

Thus, the import of *Berk* lies only partially in the court's pronouncement that the power of Congress to declare war, enumerated in Article I, Section 8 of the Constitution, contains a discoverable standard calling for *some* mutual participation by Congress. The court left open the question as to what joint legislative-executive action would be sufficient to authorize military acts of war. While Congress has the power to declare war, it is clear that the power does not mandate a formal declaration whenever Congress intends to authorize the conduct of war by the President.[27] Therefore, it

---

21. Berk, supra note 9, at 305.

22. Id.

23. Baker v. Carr, supra note 15.

24. Berk, supra note 9, at 305.

25. Tonkin Gulf Resolution, Pub. L. 88–408, 78 Stat. 384, (1964), which read in pertinent part:

> The Congress approves and supports the determination of the President, as Commander-in-Chief, to take all necessary measures to repel any armed attack against the forces of the United States and to prevent further aggression.
> "Sec. 2 . . . The United States is . . . prepared, as the President determines, to take all necessary steps, including the use of armed force, to assist any member or protocol state of the Southeast Asian Collective Defense Treaty requesting assistance in defense of its freedom.

26. Berk, supra note 9, at 306.

27. Cf. Greene v. McElroy, 360 U.S. 474 (1959), where it was held that

became crucial for plaintiffs to formulate a judicially manageable standard to measure the sufficiency of Congressional action in authorizing war.[28] The alternative for plaintiffs was to suffer defeat on the basis of the political question doctrine.[29]

## B. *Orlando v. Laird*

The *Orlando*[30] decision demonstrates that the holding in *Berk* on the "first level" of the political question issue, that there must be *some* form of authorization by Congress, was not a major victory for plaintiffs in the Indochina War cases. Plaintiff, Salvatore Orlando, was an army enlistee in Vietnam, seeking to enjoin the Secretary of Defense and his commanding officers from enforcing deployment orders on the ground that the executive officers exceeded their constitutional authority by ordering military personnel to participate in a war not properly authorized by Congress.[31]

The court cited *Berk* to the effect that the constitutional delegation of the power to declare war to Congress contains a discoverable and manageable standard, imposing on the Congress a duty of mutual participation in the prosecution of a war and allowing judicial scrutiny of that duty.[32] The court then proceeded to set down the appropriate test of mutual participation, stating that "the test is whether there is *any* action by the Congress sufficient to authorize or ratify the military activity in question."[33]

In the instant case, the court considered the test to be satisfied by several acts of Congressional participation. The first was the Tonkin Gulf resolution,[34] which was "expressed in broad language which clearly showed the state of mind of the Congress and its in-

---

Congressional ratification can be inferred from acts such as appropriation for a function expressly delegated to the Executive branch.

> [However,] such [congressional] decisions cannot be assumed by acquiescence or non-action . . . because explicit action, especially in area of doubtful constitutionality, requires careful and purposeful consideration by those responsible for enacting and implementing our law, at 507.

28. See Orlando, supra note 17.

29. On remand, the district court denied the requested injunction, and held Berk's deployment orders valid, for the reason that no manageable standard for measuring the sufficiency of the means by which Congress authorized the Indochina War were presented by plaintiff. Berk v. Laird, 317 F. Supp. 715, 730 (E.D.N.Y., 1970) aff'd sub nom, Orlando v. Laird, 443 F.2d 1039, cert. denied, 404 U.S. 869 (1971).

30. See supra note 17.

31. On appeal, Orlando was joined with the appeal of the District Court's decision in the remand of Berk.

32. Orlando, supra note 17.

33. Id.

34. See supra note 25.

tent to fully implement and support the . . . actions taken by and planned to be taken by the President 'to prevent further aggression.' "[35] And, although the resolution was repealed in 1970,[36] there were further Congressional actions that fulfilled the test of mutual participation. Examples cited by the court were the affirmative acts of appropriating billions of dollars to carry out military operations in Southeast Asia[37] and extending the Military Selective Service Act with full knowledge that persons conscripted thereunder had been and would continue to be sent to Vietnam.[38]

After noting that the framer's intent to vest the war power in Congress is in no way defeated by permitting an inference of authorization from legislative action furnishing the manpower and materials of war for the military operation in Southeast Asia, the court stated:

> The choice, for example, between an explicit declaration on the one hand, and a resolution and war implementing legislation on the other, as the medium for expression of Congressional consent involves the 'exercise of a discretion demonstrably committed to the legislature,'[39] and therefore invokes the political question doctrine.[40]

The court added that such choice involves an area of decision-making best left to the processes of reciprocal action and mutual influence between the President and Congress, as it involves policies governing the United States and other parts of the world. Questions of such complexity as deployment of troops need flexibility, such as the option *not* to declare war formally, as was the case in the collaborative policy of the executive and the legislature in Vietnam.[41] The court summarized its holding by stating that:

> [b]eyond determining that there has been *some* mutual participation between the Congress and the President, with action by the Congress sufficient to authorize or ratify the military activity at issue, it is clear that the constitutional propriety of the means by which Congress has chosen to ratify and approve the

---

35. Orlando, supra note 17.

36. Pub. L. 91–672, § 12, 84 Stat. 2053, 2055.

37. See note 93 and note 95 infra, for examples of such appropriations acts.

38. See H.R. Rep. No. 267, 90th Cong. 1st Sess. 38, 41 (1967) ,

39. Citing Baker v. Carr, supra note 15, at 211.

40. Orlando, supra note 17, at 1043.

41. Id.

protracted military operation in Southeast Asia is a political question. The form which Congressional authorization should take is one of policy, committed to the discretion of the Congress and outside the power and competency of the judiciary because there are no intelligible and objectively manageable standards by which to judge such actions.[42]

Thus, as became clear in *Orlando,* there were two stages at which plaintiff was confronted with the political question obstacle: First, the plaintiff had to convince the court that the question of the necessity for Congressional authorization of the war was justiciable. Secondly, plaintiff had to formulate a test for the sufficiency of Congressional participation which could avoid application of the political question doctrine. While *Berk* enabled plaintiffs to hurdle the first legal obstacle, *Orlando* demonstrated that the second level of inquiry presented plaintiffs with a nearly insurmountable obstacle.

## C. *DaCosta I*

In *Da Costa I,*[43] plaintiff, a draftee, received orders to report to Vietnam and brought an action to challenge the orders on the grounds of lack of authority to issue them. His major contention was that Congressional repeal of the Gulf of Tonkin Resolution[44] removed one of two grounds upon which the court in *Orlando*[45] had based its conclusion that there was legislative conduct equivalent to a declaration of war.[46]

The Court stated that "there was sufficient legislative action in extending the Selective Service Act and in appropriating billions of dollars to carry on military and naval operations in Vietnam to ratify and approve the measures taken by the executive, even in the absence of the Gulf of Tonkin Resolution."[47] Noting that Congress continued to support the steps taken by the Executive to achieve an

---

42. Id. In so stating, the court relied on Baker v. Carr at 217, supra note 15, and Powell v. McCormack, 395 U.S. 486, 518–49 (1969). This latter case held that the question of whether Congress overstepped its constitutional bounds is *not* a political question. (The issue was whether Congress had the power to deny a duly elected Representative his seat in Congress.)

43. DaCosta v. Laird, 448 F.2d 1368 (2d Cir. 1971), cert. denied, 405 U.S. 979 (1972), [*hereinafter* cited as Da Costa I].

44. See supra note 25.

45. See supra note 17, at 1043.

46. The other support was appropriations, selective service acts, and other related legislation.

47. DaCosta I, supra note 43, at 1369.

orderly deceleration and termination of the conflict, the court added that "[i]f the Executive were now escalating the prolonged struggle instead of decreasing it, additional supporting action by the Legislative Branch over what is presently afforded, might well be required."[48]

However, the important point was that even in the absence of the Gulf of Tonkin Resolution, mutual participation between the branches was found. Thus, the court held that:

[a]s the constitutional propriety of the means by which the executive and the legislative branches engaged in mutual participation in prosecuting the military operations in Southeast Asia is, as we held in *Orlando,* a political question, so the constitutional propriety of the method and means by which they mutually participate in winding down the conflict and disengaging the nation from it, is also a political question outside the power and competency of the judiciary.[49]

The argument is made by some that continuing appropriations alone should not be held sufficient to authorize military action by the Executive Branch, either in the context of escalating a conflict or of winding one down.[50] The argument has its greatest force in the latter situation, where certain Congressional actions indicate withdrawal from a prior position of support and authorization. It is argued that in most of these cases, the President has presented Congress with a *fait accompli,* and Congress has little choice but to ratify the actions of the executive.[51]

As the War Powers Act[52] and the Cambodia bombing cut-off

---

48. Id. at 1370. The court also noted that the conference committee recommending the repeal amendment in 1970, stated as its reason that

[r]ecent legislative and executive statements make the 1964 resolution unnecessary for the prosecution of U.S. foreign policy. Cong. Rep. No. 1805, 91st Cong., 2nd Sess., U.S. Code Cong. and Ad. News, at 6069 (1970) ." 448 F.2d at 1369.

49. Id. at 1370.

50. See Note, "Congress, the President and the Power to Commit Forces to Combat," supra note 6. A. D'Amato & R. O'Neill, The Judiciary and Vietnam, 75–84 (1972).

51. The fact that in an undeclared war, appropriations are asked for after the fact should militate against treating this Congressional action as a blanket authorization "since such appropriations must generally come after the hostilities have already begun, [and] the effective choice remaining to Congress is likely to be severely limited." Note, Congress, the President and the Power to Commit Forces to Combat, supra, note 6.

52. Pub. L. 93–148; 87 Stat. 554 (1973) .

date[53] indicate, there is much that Congress could have done, through political means, to have ended its authorization, had it so chosen. The simplest way would have been to appropriate no money at all. However, affirmative action by Congress in the form of legislation would be subject to the Presidential veto.[54]

However, since there were political alternatives available to resolve this problem, the Court recognized the situation as being inappropriate for judicial action. The fact that decisions of a nature particularly beyond the competence of the judiciary were in issue, reinforced the position of the court that it was dealing with a political question.[55]

### D. Da Costa III

In *Da Costa III*,[56] plaintiff, the same party as in *Da Costa I*,[57] sued to enjoin the Secretaries of Defense, Army, Navy and Air Force, and the chief of military forces in Vietnam, from implementing the directive of the President, announced May 8, 1972, ordering the mining of the ports and harbors of North Vietnam, and the continuation of air and naval strikes against military targets in North Vietnam.[58] The plaintiff characterized these actions as a massive unilateral Executive escalation of the war in violation of the Mansfield Amendment and requiring Article I Section 8 authorization. Since the court in *Da Costa I* had suggested by way of dictum that escalation might require fresh authorization, the plaintiff hoped the *Da Costa III* court would follow this line of reasoning.

Contrasting this case with *Orlando*,[59] where the court "acting within its powers and duties [was] obliged to rule on the legality of the war in Vietnam,"[60] the Court stated that *Da Costa III* presented a non-justiciable controversy. "Here, appellant invites us to ex-

---

53. Second Supplemental Appropriation Act of 1973, Pub. L. 93–50, 87 Stat. 99, § 307 (1973); and Joint Resolution, Making Continuing Appropriations For the Fiscal Year 1974, Pub. L. 93–52, 87 Stat. 130, § 108 (1973), signed by the President on July 1, 1973, ordered an end to the bombing of Cambodia on August 15, 1973.

54. See discussion of veto power, infra, text at 152–3.

55. In support of the position that questions of war and peace are political issues, to be decided by the political branches using their political powers and influence, see Wallace, The Warmaking Powers: A Constitutional Flaw?, 57 Cornell L. Rev. 719 (1972).

56. DaCosta III, supra note 18.

57. See supra note 43.

58. DaCosta III, supra note 18.

59. See supra note 17.

60. DaCosta III, supra note 56, at 1147.

tend the reach of judicial inquiry into the domain of tactical and
strategic military decisions ordered by the President in his capacity
as Commander-in-Chief."[61] This, the court argued, presented a political question.[62]

This case also differed from the previous cases in that the order challenged was not an order for plaintiff to report to combat.
*Berk*[63] and *Orlando*[64] held that a soldier with orders to report for
duty in a war zone has standing to challenge the constitutionality of
the war. However, the court noted that the constitutionality of the
war was not before the court in the instant case. Rather the issue
was the more limited one of whether within the context of a lawful
war, the President's order to mine North Vietnam's harbors was
properly authorized. As the court in *Pietsch v. President of the
United States*[65] held that a citizen taxpayer does not have standing
to challenge the constitutionality of the Vietnam War, the court
found it difficult to perceive how a citizen taxpayer would have
standing to challenge specific military orders issued in furtherance
of the war effort.[66] However, since the Supreme Court, in *Sierra
Club v. Morton*,[67] held that the question of standing necessarily involves an analysis of "whether a party has a sufficient stake in an
otherwise justiciable controversy to obtain judicial resolution of that
controversy,"[68] the court in *Da Costa III* stated that

---

61. Id.

62. Id. The court further undertook a full examination of the political
question doctrine at 1152–1154.

> Some are of the view that the court must decide all cases which are
> properly before it, and that discretion in the exercise of jurisdiction is
> forbidden by the Constitution. The only circumstance in which a court
> may decline to hear a matter is when constitutional jurisdictional requi-
> sites have not been met, or when the Constitution has committed to
> another agency of government the autonomous determination of the
> issue raised . . . Others view application of the political question doc-
> trine as a matter of judicial discretion, not of Constitutional compulsion,
> and argue that there are matters so controversial and inappropriate for
> judicial resolution that courts follow a wiser course by
> abstaining . . . This approach, as Baker v. Carr [supra note 15] and
> Powell v. McCormack [supra note 45] attest, has not been favored by the
> Supreme Court. Still others . . . seek to establish categories of cases or
> concerns which have previously invoked application of the political
> question doctrine, and indicate that when the objective achieved by a
> court in refraining from deciding a case is important, the political
> question doctrine will be a means of achieving that doctrine.

63. See supra note 9.

64. See supra note 17.

65. 434 F.2d 861 (2d. Cir., 1970), cert. denied, 403 U.S. 920 (1971).

66. DaCosta III, supra note 56, at 1151–2.

67. 405 U.S. 727 (1972).

68. Id. at 731–2 (emphasis added)

"the standing of a party need not come into question if a court determines that for other reasons the issue raised before the bench is non-justiciable. We are of the view that the issue raised in these proceedings is a political question which the court is without power to hear. Thus, the non-justiciable nature of the dispute not merely obviates, but logically precludes resolution of the question of plaintiffs standing to sue."[69]

Thus the court did not squarely answer the important question of standing.[70]

Judge Kaufman's decision was based solely on the political question doctrine. Once initial Congressional authorization for the commitment of American forces to combat in Vietnam was found in the passage of military appropriation bills,[71] the question of whether military tactics designed to protect the lives of American troops in the field fell within the original Congressional grant of authority was deemed to constitute a non-justiciable political question. The Judge noted however, that the judiciary continued to recognize a threshold obligation to determine whether, within the meaning of Berk[72] and Orlando,[73] sufficient Congressional authorization existed for the commitment of American forces to combat.

### E. Holtzman v. Schlesinger

As a result of a suit[74] brought by Congresswoman Elizabeth Holtzman and three U.S. servicemen, Judge Orrin G. Judd of the U.S. District Court, Eastern District of New York, issued an injunction on July 23, 1973,[75] prohibiting the Secretary of Defense from ordering American bombing of Cambodia. The order was temporarily stayed, pending consideration of the case by the Second Circuit Court of Appeals, which granted a government petition for a stay until the issue could be heard by a panel of that court.[76] In a frenetic thirteen-day period following the stay order of the Court of Appeals until the hearing scheduled for August 13, 1973, Supreme Court Justice Marshall denied plaintiffs application to vacate the

---

69. DaCosta III, supra note 18 at 1152.

70. The court relied instead on Sierra Club v. Morton, supra note 67.

71. Infra note 93.

72. See supra note 9.

73. See supra note 17.

74. 484 F.2d 1307 (2d Cir. 1973), [hereinafter cited as Holtzman].

75. Holtzman v. Schlesinger, 361 F. Supp. 553 (E.D.N.Y. 1973), cert. denied, _____ U.S. _____, 1974, [hereinafter cited as Holtzman].

76. Pursuant to a court order of July 27, 1973.

stay,[77] the Second Circuit granted plaintiffs motion to accelerate the appeal to August 8, 1973,[78] Mr. Justice Douglas ordered vacation of the stay,[79] and Mr. Justice Marshall, after polling the other members of the Supreme Court, overruled the order of Mr. Justice Douglas.[80] The appeal was heard on August 8, 1973.[81]

An examination of both the District Court and Appellate decisions illuminates the issues involved in this and the prior cases.

## 1. DISTRICT COURT

This action[82] was brought by Congresswoman Elizabeth Holtzman (D-N.Y.) and three[83] members of the U.S. Air Force for both declaratory and injunctive relief against the Secretary of Defense, James R. Schlesinger in the U.S. District Court, Eastern District of New York.

Plaintiff Holtzman's initial memorandum of law alleged that

Congress, the branch explicitly designated by Article I, Section 8, Clause 11 of the Constitution to be the ultimate arbiter of war and peace, has been totally ignored by the Executive's unilateral decision to commit American Forces to combat [in Cambodia after the U.S. withdrawal date of April 1, 1973.] The plaintiff herein . . . has been prevented from carrying out her responsibilities under Article I, Section 8 by the failure of the Executive to consult with Congress concerning the commitment of American forces to combat in Cambodia.[84]

The District Court in an unexpected opinion granted the injunction and preliminary judgment prayed for pursuant to a stay. After tracing both legislative and executive declarations and actions dating from the initial Cambodian invasion on April 30, 1970,[85] Judge Judd examined the law as developed in the previous Second Circuit Indochina cases. Citing *Da Costa III*, *Orlando* and *Berk*, he

---

77. 414 U.S. 1316 (1973).
78. Motion by Plaintiffs, August 8, 1973.
79. 414 U.S 1316 (1973), on plaintiffs motion of August 2, 1973.
80. 414 U.S. 1321 (1973).
81. The decision was handed down that afternoon.
82. See supra note 75.
83. Later joined by a fourth serviceman.
84. Plaintiff's Memorandum of Law, pp. 3–4.
85. See note 93, note 95, and notes 167–170, infra.

noted that if plaintiffs can show that there are manageable standards, the issue of the constitutional balance between the legislative
and executive in the declaration, authorization and conduct of a
war presents a justiciable issue and is not a political question.[86]

Judge Judd then tried to distinguish the instant case from *Da
Costa III*. He argued that if the Cambodian bombing after April 1,
1973 could be severed from the Vietnam War—i.e., that if the
Vietnam War, as a Congressionally authorized conflict, were over
as of the removal date of all American ground forces and repatriation of all prisoners of war—a manageable standard might be available in *Holtzman* that was not discernable in *Da Costa III*. He stated:
"The manageable standard that this court must apply is the existence of Congressional authority for the present bombing activities
over Cambodia now that the American forces have withdrawn and
the prisoners of war have been repatriated . . .".[88] "To be entitled
to relief, plaintiffs must show, under this standard and the test of
'continuing mutual participation' set forth in *Orlando,* either that
Congress has not participated with the Executive in the authorization of the hostilities in Cambodia, or that Congress has terminated
any such authorization."[89]

Judge Judd then examined the "extent of Congressional authorization of Cambodian hostilities"[90] to determine whether the
above mentioned test had been met. First, he noted that Cambodia
was not mentioned in any of the appropriations bills noted in
*Berk*[91] as indications of Congressional ratification of the Vietnam
War.[92] Furthermore, since 1970, all appropriations bills had contained the Fulbright Proviso[93] "forbidding military support to the

---

86. Holtzman, supra note 75, at 561.

87. Id. at 562.

88. Id.

89. Id.

90. Id.

91. See supra note 9.

92. Cf. 1964 Appropriations Bill for the Department of Defense, Pub. L. 89–18,
79 Stat. 109, referring to "military activities in Southeast Asia." But see also the
Department of Defense Appropriations Act for 1968, Pub. L. 90–96, 81 Stat. 231,
§ 639 (a) , making appropriations available to support only (a) Vietnamese and
other free world forces in Vietnam, and (b) local forces in Thailand, and for
related costs.

93. The Fulbright Proviso, adopted by Congress in the summer of 1970, and
inserted in the War Forces Military Procurement Act of 1971, became law with
the President's approval on October 7, 1970. Repeated in every subsequent
military appropriation and authorization act, the proviso reads:

> nothing [herein] shall be construed as authorizing the use of any such
> funds to support Vietnamese or other free world forces in actions de-
> signed to provide military support and assistance to the Government of

government of Cambodia, except in support of actions to insure the safe withdrawal of American forces or to aid in the release of prisoners of war."[94] In November 1971 the Mansfield Amendment[95] became law, expressing as its policy, "to terminate at the earliest practicable date all military operations of the United States in Indochina." This amendment too was included in all subsequent military appropriations and authorization acts. Judge Judd pointed to other bills, acts and reports of Congress which denied any commitment to a U.S. defense of Cambodia.[96]

From the Congressional Acts and statements of policy referred to above, Judge Judd concluded that "Congress did not acquiesce in the Presidential statements that the Indochina war was all of one piece, but rather gave only limited authorization for continued hostilities in Cambodia."[97] Applying the principles of the law of agency, the court stated: "it is the usual rule that the principal (Congress) may limit the duration of any authorization which it gives the agent (the Executive)."[98] The resort by Judge Judd to the Second Restatement of Agency was perhaps an oversight, as in its scope note, the Restatement's applicability to public officers is

---

Cambodia or Laos: *Provided* That nothing contained in this section shall be construed to prohibit support of actions required to insure the safe and orderly withdrawal or disengagement of United States forces from Southeast Asia, or to aid in the release of Americans held as prisoners of war."

Pub.L. 91–441, 84 Stat. 905 § 502; Pub.L. 91–668, 84 Stat. 2020 § 838(a); Pub.L. 92–156, 85 Stat. 423, § 501; Pub.L. 92–204, 85 Stat. 716 § 738(a); Pub.L. 92–436, 86 Stat. 734, § 601 (b); Pub.L. 92–570, 86 Stat. 1184, § 737.

94. Holtzman, supra note 75, at 562–63.

95. This amendment was part of the Appropriations Authorization-Military Procurement Act of 1972, stating:

Sec. 601.(a) It is hereby declared to be the policy of the United States to terminate at the earliest practicable date all military operations of the United States in Indochina, and to provide for the prompt and orderly withdrawal of all United States military forces at a date certain, subject to the release of all American prisoners of war held by the Government of North Vietnam and forces allied with such government, and an accounting for all Americans missing in Action who have been held by or known to such government or such forces.

The amendment requested the President to establish a final withdrawal date contingent on release of United States prisoners of war, to negotiate for a ceasefire, and to negotiate for phased withdrawals. See Appropriations Authorization-Military Procurement Act of 1972, Pub.L. 92–156, 85 Stat. 423; Military Procurement Act, 1973, Pub.L. 92–436, 86 Stat. 734; Department of Defense Appropriation Act, 1973, Pub.L. 92–570, 86 Stat. 1184.

96. Cf. Department of Defense Appropriation Act of 1972, Pub.L. 92–204, § 738(a). 85 Stat. 716, 734 (1971) and other appropriation acts cited supra note 93.

97. Holtzman, supra note 75, at 563.

98. Id. citing Restatement of Agency 2d, § 38, (1958).

disclaimed.[99] Nevertheless, authorization by Congress cannot be understood to last in perpetuity once given. Certainly Congress should have the right to withdraw its authorization should it so desire, and in fact, such right exists.

Judge Judd construed the removal of American forces and prisoners of war from Vietnam to be a "basic change" in the situation, a factor which he believed must be considered in determining the scope and duration of any Congressional authorization. Attempting to avoid the holding in *Da Costa III*[100] on the non-justiciability of the question of escalation, he stated that the post-April first bombing of Cambodia is not the sort of tactical decision traditionally confided to the Commander-in-Chief in the conduct of an armed conflict. Furthermore, he argued, Congressional action never included authorization to bomb Cambodia. And "non-action by Congress does not constitute an implied grant of power."[101] The question was thus narrowed by Judge Judd to "whether Congress has authorized bombing in Cambodia after the withdrawal of American troops from Vietnam and the release of the prisoners of war."[102]

On June 29, 1973, provisions were adopted by both Houses of Congress and signed by the President on July 1, 1973 forbidding any expenditure of funds in connection with hostilities over Cambodia after August 15, 1973.[103] It was Judge Judd's interpretation that these provisos did not grant authority to bomb Cambodia *until* the August 15th cut-off date.[104] His reasoning stems from the Senate debate on the provisions[105] which is quoted in his opinion, but which omits a crucial colloquy between Senator Fulbright and Senator Eagleton that renders the debate unclear and of questionable worth as support for the court's position.[106]

---

99. Restatement of Agency, 2d, supra note 98 at 2.

100. See supra note 18 which spoke of the mining of North Vietnamese harbors and intensification of bombing as a tactical decision.

101. Holtzman, supra note 75 at 564.

102. Id.

103. Pub.L. 93–50, Second Supplemental Appropriations Act of 1973, 87 Stat. 99, § 307, and Pub.L. 93–52, Joint Resolution Making Continuing Appropriations for the Fiscal Year 1974, 87 Stat. 130, § 108.

104. Holtzman, supra note 75 at 566.

105. Citing 119 Cong. Rec., S. 12560, 12562 (daily ed., June 29, 1973).

106. See Transcript, Holtzman v. Schlesinger, August 8, 1973, pp. 872–88. It should be noted that the quote in Judge Judd's opinion, at 564, is identical to the quote presented to him in the plaintiff's brief, omitting this crucial colloquy. The omitted colloquy reads:

> Mr. Eagleton: In the light of the legislative history meaning . . . the statement of [former] Secretary of Defense, [Elliott] Richardson that we

The import of the portions of the debate quoted in Judge Judd's opinion was that by passing the provisos, Congress was not sanctioning the bombing of Cambodia up to the cut-off date.[107] In cognizance of the "ratification by appropriation" rule that the courts apply,[108] Judge Judd pointed out that in the case of the provisos of July 1, 1973, there was a clear and definite intent *not* to authorize the Cambodia bombing. The cut-off date was not included in order to allow money to be spent on bombing Cambodia up to that date. Rather, the intent was to include it as a compromise in order to avoid a Presidential veto.[109]

It may be a fair inference that those who voted against the compromise provisos did so to avoid the appearance of authorizing the bombing until August 15th.[110] In any event, the confusion surrounding this point on the floor of the Senate is in sharp contrast to the presumption of clarity in which the district court opinion indulges.

The closing point in Judge Judd's decision is that the consequence of holding that Congress must override a presidential veto in order to terminate hostilities which it has not authorized would be to allow the President to conduct a war with a vote of only one-third plus one of either house. This he would not allow.[111] This point has also been made by a recent commentator[112] and can be easily answered. Authorization of war can only be by affirmative[113] Congressional action, such as appropriation.[114] Thus if Congress takes no action at all, i.e., appropriates nothing, there is nothing to veto. Furthermore, just as Congress has a constitutional duty in the area of war, the President has a constitutional power to veto acts of Congress.[115] It is illogical to call the exercise of a constitutional

---

will continue the bombing unless the funds are cut off, will we with the adoption of this resolution permit the bombing of Cambodia for the next 45 days? That is the question I pose to the Senator from Arkansas. Mr. Fulbright: Until August 15th."
119 Cong. Rec. S12562 (daily ed. June 29, 1973)
Senator Eagleton then voted against the bill.

107. See supra note 105.

108. Greene v. McElroy, supra note 27.

109. Holtzman, supra note 75 at 565.

110. Note the fact that Senator Eagleton voted against the compromise bill after his colloquy with Senator Fulbright, supra n. 106; Representative Holzman herself voted against the compromise provisos.

111. Holtzman, supra note 75 at 565.

112. Note, 15 Harv. Int'l L. J. 143, 153 (1974).

113. Greene v. McElroy, supra note 27.

114. Id. See also Orlando, supra note 17.

115. U.S. Const., art I, § 7, cl. 2.

power, used for its constitutional purpose (i.e., to veto acts of Congress) unconstitutional.

Notably, the ever present issue of standing was nowhere mentioned in the decision of the District Court in *Holtzman*. Although this issue was argued vigorously in the briefs of both plaintiffs and defendants, it was inexplicably ignored by Judge Judd. Not so, however, in the decision of the Second Circuit Court of Appeals.[116]

## 2. DECISION OF THE COURT OF APPEALS

Pursuant to the stay of judgment issued by the District Court and the furious activities surrounding the stay described *supra*,[117] the court heard argument on the case on the morning of August 8, 1973 and decided the case that afternoon.[118]

As preceived by the court, Mulligan, J., its responsibility was "to determine the legality of the challenged action and the threshold question is whether under the 'political question' doctrine we should decline even to do that."[119] Citing its decision in *Orlando*,[120] the court began its analysis by stating that the question of "whether or not Congress was required to take some action to authorize the Indochina War was justiciable under *Baker v. Carr*."[121] However, judicial inquiry is limited to whether *some* action by Congress was taken. The constitutional propriety of the means by which Congress has chosen to ratify the military actions is a political question,[122] as is the question of the method in which Congress chooses to participate in winding down the conflict.[123]

Then citing *Da Costa III*,[124] the court noted that the question of the legality of escalation of the war due to lack of Congressional authorization was also a political question. This is because judges

---

116. Holtzman, supra note 74.

117. See text supra at 147–8.

118. Holtzman, supra note 74, at 1308. The Court stated:

> The argument of this appeal was heard on August 8th, and to further speed any further appellate review, this court filed its judgment in the late afternoon of that day, reversing the judgment below, and dismissing the complaint.

119. Holtzman, supra note 74, at 1309.

120. See supra note 17, at 1043.

121. Holtzman, supra note 74, at 1309.

122. Id., relying on Orlando, supra note 17, at 1043.

123. Id., relying on DaCosta I, supra note 47.

124. Id. at 1310.

cannot reasonably determine whether a specific military operation constitutes an escalation or is merely a new tactical approach within a continuing strategic plan. The court "fail[ed] to see how the present challenge involving the bombing in Cambodia is in any significant manner distinguishable from the situation discussed by Judge Kaufman in *Da Costa [III]*. . . ."[125] This is in sharp contrast to the finding by Judge Judd of "a basic change in the situation which must be considered in determining the duration of prior Congressional authorization."[126] Judge Judd had further found such action a tactical decision not traditionally confided in the commander-in-chief.

The appellate court stated that the issues presented in the case are "questions of fact involving military and diplomatic expertise not vested in the judiciary which makes the issue political . . . we are not privy to the information . . . [and] we are hardly competent to evaluate it."[127] The court stated that if it was not capable of judging the significance of bombing North Vietnam's harbors in *Da Costa III*, it certainly could not determine in the instant case that the bombing of Cambodia was a "basic change"[128] in the war, requiring further authorization from Congress. Stressing the disparate opinions of the Executive and Legislative branches on the issue of the purpose and necessity of the bombing of Cambodia,[129] the court held in strong language that "the sharing of Presidential and Congressional responsibility particularly at this juncture is a bluntly political and *not* a judicial question."[130]

In answer to the finding of the court below that the Mansfield Amendment[131] removed Congressional authorization once all American prisoners of war and ground troops were removed from Vietnam, the court stated that it had no way of knowing whether the Cambodian bombing furthered or hindered the goals of the Mansfield Amendment.[132] The court found this especially true as the Amendment urged the President to negotiate for an immediate ceasefire for all parties engaged in the conflict in *Indo-China*, and the court could not tell whether bombing was in furtherance of this

---

125. Id.

126. Id.

127. Id.

128. Id.

129. Cf. Holtzman, supra note 74, at 1310–11, fn. 1 (Affadavit of Secretary of State William P. Rogers) .

130. Id. at 1311.

131. See supra note 95.

132. The Court noted that this was precisely the holding of DaCosta III, supra note 18, at 1153.

goal. The return of the troops was only part of the data needed to determine whether a basic change had occurred and the goals of the Mansfield Amendment had been met. The other data needed was military and diplomatic in nature, and thus outside the competence of the judiciary.[133]

Since the argument that continuing Congressional approval was necessary was based on a determination that the Cambodian bombing constituted a "basic change" in the war not within the tactical discretion of the President, a determination the Court found to be a political question, there was no necessity for the court to dwell at length upon Congressional participation,[134] as did both the court below and the plaintiffs. In dictum however, the court stated that the July 1st compromise measure[135] constituted Congressional approval of the Cambodian bombing,[136] despite conclusions to the contrary drawn by the Court below and the plaintiff on the basis of their analysis of the legislative history.[137] The court pointed out that "since the statute is not ambiguous, resort to legislative history is unjustified."[138] Furthermore, resort to legislative materials is not permissible where they are contradictory or ambiguous,[139] and a fair reading of the Congressional Record of June 29, 1973[140] establishes that this was the case.

Ambiguity as to the effect of the compromise measure is apparent in the portion of the Senate debate omitted by the lower court. Senator Eagleton, suspecting that it might constitue authorization to bomb up to August 15, asked whether by adoption of this measure, the Senate would be permitting the bombing of Cambodia until that date. Senator Fulbright responded in the affirmative, despite the fact that most of the Senate apparently had intended the measure to serve as a cut-off date, and not as an authorization to bomb.[141] In fact, Congresswoman Holtzman, who argued in the plaintiff's brief that the language clearly did not authorize bombing until August 15, voted against the measure in the House because she apparently believed it might be construed as authorization.[142]

---

133. Holtzman, supra note 74, at 1312.

134. Id. at 1313.

135. Pub.L. 93–50; Pub.L. 93–52, supra note 103.

136. Holtzman, supra note 74, at 1313.

137. Id. at 1314. See also supra note 105.

138. Id., relying on Schwegmann v. Calvert Distillers Corp., 341 U.S. 384, 395–96 (1951).

139. Citing NLRB v. Plasterers Local 79, 404 U.S. 116, 129, n. 24 (1971).

140. See supra note 105.

141. Holtzman, supra note 74, at 1314.

142. Id.

The court found nothing unconstitutional in the use of the veto power by the President[143] to bring about a political compromise between the Executive and Legislative Branches. The plaintiffs asserted that the veto power[144] cannot be employed to modify or nullify a substantive power constitutionally delegated to Congress, such as the power to declare war. However, the court responded by noting that this proposition, as the plaintiffs attempted to apply it in this case, was unsupported in law.[145]

Although the court considered an examination of the standing issue to be unnecessary in view of the political question holding, it nevertheless stated that none of the parties' plaintiffs had standing.[146] Under *Berk*,[147] a serviceman under orders to fight in the combat to which he objects has standing to challenge those orders. But in this case, none of the servicemen were under such orders, having been relieved of combat duties. Plaintiffs raised the point that as soon as they announced their intention to challenge the legality of their orders, they were immediately removed from flight duty under the Air Force Human Reliability Program. But for their participation as plaintiffs in this action, the Air Force officers would have been actively engaged in the bombing of Cambodia at the time of this action.[148] The issue thus presented was whether the Air Force could moot a challenge to the legality of its combat orders in this manner, thereby rendering it virtually impossible for any court to exercise judicial review of the legality of combat operations.[149] The court addressed this issue by referring to the "cognizable danger of recurrent violation" doctrine of *United States v. W. T. Grant Co.*[150] The court felt that in view of the termination of the air strikes on August 15, 1973,[151] a mere week after the decision, there was little danger that the servicemen plaintiffs would be sent back on bombing missions. The doctrine would require a much more cognizable danger in order to give the servicemen plaintiffs standing.[152]

As for Representative Holtzman, the court found no adequate

---

143. Holtzman, supra note 74, at 1314.

144. U.S. Const., art. I, § 7, cl. 2.

145. Holtzman, supra note 74, at 1315.

146. Id. at 1315.

147. Id.

148. Plaintiff's brief at 44. Under ordinary practice the Air Force officers would have continued to bomb Cambodia until mid-June. They then would have been returned to combat over Cambodia in mid-July, and would have remained on duty through August 15, 1973.

149. Id. at 45.

150. 345 U.S. 629, 633 (1953).

151. As per Pub.L. 93–50 and Pub.L. 93–52, supra note 103.

152. Holtzman, supra note 74, at 1316.

support for her standing claim. First, it noted that she had neither been denied the right to vote nor the right to speak. Secondly, the fact that her vote was ineffective was due to the votes of her colleagues. Her powerlessness was thus not due to any action of the defendants.[153]

The point was made by the plaintiff-appellees that a clear majority of Representative Holtzman's colleagues voted to terminate the bombing immediately. Their votes, so the argument states, were not ineffective because of contrary votes of their colleagues, but because of the President's power to veto.[154] The challenge, then, was to the constitutional validity of a threatened veto of a measure to cut off war funds passed by Congress, which according to the Constitution has the sole right to declare war.[155] However, as the court pointed out, it *was* the votes of the Congresswoman's colleagues that would have prevented a veto from being overridden. The President does have a constitutional power to veto legislation passed by Congress,[156] and since, as discussed earlier, the bill involved was an appropriations-type measure and not a declaration of war,[157] there could have been no valid constitutional objection to an exercise of the President's veto in this situation.

Thus, *Holtzman* reaffirmed the two-step analysis of *Berk* and *Orlando*, holding that the threshold issue of the necessity for Congressional participation was justiciable, but that the sufficiency of the methods by which Congress chooses to authorize a war is a political question. Furthermore, while *Da Costa I* suggested that escalation must be accompanied by fresh Congressional authorization, or is at least susceptable to Congressional disapproval, the court as demonstrated in *Holtzman* will not decide whether a particular act or chain of events constitutes escalation. Such a question is to be answered by military tacticians and foreign policy experts or by Congress itself.

This has led to a somewhat anomalous situation. On the one hand, the court has intimated that escalation must be authorized by Congress (hence, this narrow issue is *not* a political question), yet the court will not resolve the issue of whether escalation has actually occurred.

153. Id.

154. Plaintiff's Brief at 26–36.

155. Note, however, that Congress was not given the power by the Constitution to declare *peace;* a resolution to explicitly give Congress the power to make peace was submitted to the Constitutional Convention by Pierce Butler and was rejected. Farrand, supra note 6.

156. U.S. Const., Art. I, § 7.

157. The question of whether a President can veto a declaration of war has been an issue of debate by those claiming usurpation by the Executive of Congressional power.

However, this is consistent with the court's prior reasoning in the area of war. Political alternatives do exist for Congress if it determines that there has been escalation without authorization—withholding of appropriations and impeachment are two such alternatives. The court reasoned that as long as the single, loosely interpreted requirement of Article I, Section 8 is met, Congress has absolute power to prevent escalation of war. This being the case, there is no reason for the court to rush in where Congress fears to tread, even though the latter has the means to correct the situation. The problem is a political power struggle between the executive and the legislative branches.

Thus, Judge Judd attempted to squeeze past the holding in *Da Costa III* that escalation must be authorized, but paid no heed to the further holding that the court is not competent to determine whether that escalation has occurred. His belief that a "basic change," measurable by the court, occurred once the U.S. forces were out of Indochina was not unreasonable, yet he failed to acknowledge the possibility that the bombing might have been a tactical decision, military or diplomatic in nature. It is this contingency that the *Da Costa III* court was guarding against, and this was ignored by Judge Judd. How rigid the *Da Costa III* rule is could only be tested by an executive act of "escalation" that is enormous in its magnitude, such as the bombing of factories in Peking to prevent the manufacture of war material to be sent to Hanoi. There have been cases where prior "political" issues, such as racial discrimination [Brown v. Board of Education][158] and legislative apportionment [Baker v. Carr][159] have finally been resolved by the judiciary but only when political inaction had caused a near crisis, and political action did not appear to be a realistic possibility. As the bombing of Peking without advance authorization by Congress could cause such a crisis, perhaps the court might change its rule regarding the political nature of escalation. More realistically, the court would find a basic change and thus a manageable standard that could label the act unconstitutional for lack of advance Congressional authorization.

## DISSENT

Judge Oakes, dissenting,[160] felt that under the theory of *Da Costa III*[161] a justiciable issue was presented. He found a manage-

---

158. 347 U.S. 483 (1954).
159. See supra note 12.
160. 484 F.2d at 1315.
161. See supra note 18.

able standard in the radical change in the war operations. The justiciable issue he found was "whether there is any Constitutional authorization for the employment of United States armed forces over Cambodia, now that the war in Vietnam has come to an end."[162]

Granting that Congress can ratify acts of the Executive Branch through appropriations, the thrust of Judge Oakes' dissent is that Congress did not ratify the continued bombing of Cambodia after the end of U.S. ground presence in Vietnam. Alleging that at the time it was voting appropriations in aid of the war in Vietnam, Congress was not given facts pertaining to the bombing of Cambodia,[163] and was not aware of these covert bombings until July of 1973,[164] he stated that in combination with the Mansfield Amendment,[165] this does "not in my mind amount to an appropriations carte blanche to the military to carry on bombing in Cambodia. . . ."[166]

The fact is that on several occasions, the Congress was put on notice of U.S. air operations in Cambodia. On June 30, 1970 the President stated that "The following will be the guidelines for our policy in Cambodia:

> 3. We will conduct—with the approval of the Cambodian Government—air interdiction missions against the enemy efforts to move supplies and personnel through Cambodia toward South Vietnam and to re-establish base areas relevant to the war in Vietnam . . .[167]

On February 25, 1971 in a statement to Congress, the President described his policy in Cambodia, which then included

> Air missions against enemy supplies and personnel that pose a potential threat to South Vietnam or seek to establish base areas relevant to Vietnam.[168]

Other evidences of Congressional knowledge of bombing activities are a 1972 Senate staff report setting forth aerial sortie in-

---

162. Holtzman, supra note 74 at 1315.

163. Id., citing Baker v. Carr, supra note 15; Coleman v. Miller, 307 U.S. 433, 437–46 (1939); Berk v. Laird, supra note 9; U.S. v. W. T. Grant Co., supra note 138 at 632.

164. Id., citing New York Times, July 17, 1973 at 1; July 18 at 1; July 22, Sec. E at 3; July 24 at 1, July 25 at 1; July 29 at 1; August 8 at 6; August 9 at 7.

165. See supra note 95.

166. Holtzman, supra note 74 at 1316.

167. 6 Weekly Compilation of Presidential Documents, 843,855 (1970).

168. 7 Weekly Compliation of Presidential Documents, 305,332 (1971).

formation as to Cambodia for fiscal 1970 and 1971;[169] and a House Armed Services Committee Print[170] in which the Defense Department provided classified information as to U.S. aerial sorties flown over Laos and Cambodia. The latter material was made available for examination by any member of Congress. Furthermore, on June 19, 1973 the Department of Defense submitted to the Senate Armed Services Committee a monthly statistical summary of U.S. bombing operations in Southeast Asia from January 1965 through March 1973.[171]

In short, in view of the dates as to the aerial operations in all phases of this war set forth, it is hard to see how Judge Oakes can maintain that Congress did not acquiesce in the bombing of Cambodia

Judge Oakes' final point is to register agreement with Judge Judd that the July 1 compromise did not recognize legality or past authorization of the bombing in Cambodia. This conclusion is based in part on his earlier finding of lack of authorization in past appropriation bills[172] and in part on his view that the compromise did not constitute authorization to continue bombing until August 15th.[173]

## CONCLUSION

*Holtzman* represents the logical capstone to the line of cases beginning with *Berk*,[174] and progressing stepwise through *Orlando*,[175] *Da Costa I*[176] and *Da Costa III*.[177] After *Berk*, each of these cases in turn applied and built on the principles of the cases decided before. In light of the four prior Second Circuit cases mentioned, it is difficult to see how the Court of Appeals could have decided differently in *Holtzman* and still have adhered to the doctrine of *stare decisis*.

Apart from considerations of logic and judicial precedent, was

---

169. Staff of Subcommittee on U.S. Security Agreements and Commitments Abroad, Senate Committee on Foreign Relations, Thailand, Laos and Cambodia, 92d Cong., 2d Sess. 34–36 (May 1972, Comm. Print.)

170. Full Committee Hearing and Consideration of H. Res. 918, House Armed Services Committee, Print No. 92–44, (1972).

171. See Exhibit J to Affadavit of James D. Porter, Jr., Appendix for Defendants-Appellees, Vol. II, P.A–587.

172. Holtzman, supra note 74 at 1315.

173. Id.

174. See supra note 9.

175. See supra note 17.

176. See supra note 43.

177. See supra note 18.

the court correct in holding as it did in *Holtzman et al*? The plaintiffs in *Holtzman*, as well as some commentators have tried to analogize the President's war powers in the Indochina war cases to the
holding in *Youngstown Sheet and Tube Co. v. Sawyer*,[178] citing
the latter as authority for the proposition that there are limits to the
President's independent constitutional authority under the war
power. It is important to note the major difference between the situation in *Youngstown*,[179] and that of the Vietnam War cases. The
issue in *Youngstown* was not the President's authority to conduct
hostilities, but rather the scope of his authority over a clearly domestic matter—labor-management relations. Furthermore, Congress had enacted a number of laws concerning domestic labor disputes and in so doing, explicitly withheld the power of seizure from
the President.[180]

In the Vietnam War cases, authority was granted to the President through appropriations for the conduct of the war in Vietnam
and less clearly, for the bombing of Cambodia. More importantly
however, the Vietnam War cases involved foreign policy and war.
By their nature, courts are not equipped to pass judgment in this
area where military tactics and secret diplomacy require a degree of
highly specialized expertise that is possessed by members and staff
of the Executive and Legislative branches, but is lacking in the judiciary.

Thus, while the judiciary will examine substantive limits on Presidential power in the relatively open domestic area (i.e.,
*Youngstown*), courts realize that beyond examination of the formal
requirement of *some* mutual participation, issues of war and peace
must be resolved outside the courtroom by the political branches of
government.[181] This is what the court has been saying in these cases. Each branch has sufficient constitutional power in this area, and
beyond a superficial examination to see if the powers of one branch
have been abused, the court will not become involved in such political questions. In conclusion, this line of cases in the Second Circuit
represent a judicial 'slap on the wrist' of the United States Congress
which was possessed of the power to end the war at any time, but
placidly deferred to the Executive.

Scott J. Wenner

---

178. 343 U.S. 579 (1952).

179. Id.

180. See William P. Rogers, Congress, The President and the War Powers, 59
Calif. L. Rev. 1194, 1205–8 (1971).

181. For a probing study on this point, written prior to Holtzman and
DaCosta III, see Wallace, supra note 55.

# Department of State Gives Views on Proposed War Powers Legislation

## CHARLES N. BROWER

I appreciate the opportunity to testify before this subcommittee on the subject of proposed war powers legislation. I am particularly pleased to be able to testify on what I consider a unique occasion; namely, the first time in the long history of deliberations on war powers legislation that we can consider these proposed bills free from the distraction of major American involvement in hostilities overseas and divorced from the special political pressures of an election year. The stunning foreign policy successes which President Nixon has achieved in his first term, precisely through the judicious exercise of his constitutional authority, must also be considered in these deliberations. Hopefully, the perspective can now be more broad.

The changes in the public environment are particularly significant since war powers legislation has undoubtedly had its genesis in disenchantment with the protracted hostilities in which the United States became engaged during the last decade. Blaming those events on the Presidents who were in office during that time, the proponents of the more restrictive forms of war powers legislation seek to avoid similar policies in the future by diminishing the fundamental authority of the

¹ Made before the Subcommittee on National Security Policy and Scientific Developments of the House Committee on Foreign Affairs on Mar. 13. The complete transcript of the hearings will be published by the committee and will be available from the Superintendent of Documents, U.S. Government Printing Office, Washington, D.C. 20402.

Presidency, now and forever. Many such advocates do concede, albeit reluctantly, that Congress itself played a role in past policies, but argue that Congress was led to act unwisely because it was supplied inadequate information and therefore was unable to exercise its responsibilities competently.

This view of history, which I personally reject, is worth noting because the conclusions drawn from it by advocates of restrictive war powers legislation are not logically consistent with this view. These advocates have sought to place arbitrarily defined legal obstacles in the way of expeditious executive branch action, while ignoring what from their point of view should be the real source of concern; namely, a need for Congress to have more complete and timely information, to be capable of better analysis, and to maintain a more thorough exchange of ideas in the development of particular foreign policies.

It is, I would suggest, only through availability and knowledgeable use of adequate information, on a timely basis and with the best possible analysis of what that information means, that the executive branch or the Congress can exercise its respective constitutional responsibilities in the foreign policy field to the best of its ability. Imperfect performance by one branch of government cannot be remedied by attempts to undercut or diminish the fundamental constitutional authority of another branch. Because the war powers are distributed between the Congress and the executive, those two branches must cooperate closely in order for either to exercise its powers effectively, each making the particular contribution assigned it by the Constitution. Performance is more likely to be enhanced by the increased and improved flow of information to and between those bodies in an effective and timely manner.

The negative approach to war powers legislation, namely, the interposition of arbitrary legal obstacles hindering the exercise of executive responsibilities, has an additional serious fault. Proponents of such legislation overlook the fact that it is impossible for Congress to tie the hands of the executive branch without itself suffering a similar limitation of its freedom to act. Every proposed reduction of Presidential authority in this area effects a comparable diminution of congressional freedom. If, for example, the President's exercise of certain powers were restricted to a period of 30 days, as a practical matter the President would also become the beneficiary of a 30-day blank check endorsed by the Congress. If congressional debate were required in all cases immediately upon the submission of a report from the President or at predetermined intervals which might have no relevance to the course of events, Congress would also lose its flexibility to adjust its own schedule of activities to the uneven pace of unforeseen events. These are but two examples; yet they are illustrative of the fact that in declaring the executive branch incompetent to act except in prescribed circumstances, Congress would also be inhibiting its own ability to act except in a precisely delineated fashion.

The correct balance between the Congress and the executive in the exercise of war powers is struck by each branch exercising the powers assigned to it in the most informed, and hence the most responsible way; that balance cannot be established or maintained—indeed, it could well be destroyed—by legislative attempts to alter the basic scheme which the drafters of the Constitution so carefully established. What is needed, I submit, are processes designed to increase the

likelihood that our government, including both the executive branch and the Congress, will be able to exercise its responsibilities on the basis of maximum information, rather than as a result of sterile confrontation. The answer to dissatisfaction with a particular foreign policy is not to be found in alteration of constitutional authority. It is rather to be found through enhancement of our respective abilities, exercised within that authority, to formulate wise foreign policies for the future. From this point of departure, I would like to address the three bills on which you have requested our comments.

### Specification of Executive Powers

The first bill is S. 440, which would allow the President to employ the armed forces in hostilities or situations where imminent involvement in hostilities is indicated by the circumstances in only four categories of situations absent a declaration of war. In each of those four situations the President would be barred from continuing to use those troops beyond 30 days without the affirmative consent of Congress unless Congress were physically unable to meet as a result of an armed attack on the United States or unless it were necessary to use troops to protect their own prompt disengagement.

The Department of State continues to believe strongly that it would be unwise and unconstitutional for the Congress to adopt this bill. S. 440 seeks by statute to redefine specifically and restrictively the constitutional allocation of the war powers. The drafters of the Constitution, however, recognized the extreme difficulty of anticipating all circumstances which might in the future call for the use of the armed forces. As Alexander Hamilton said, writing in "The Federalist":

. . . it is impossible to foresee or define the extent and variety of national exigencies, or the correspondent extent and variety of the means which may be necessary to satisfy them.

This difficulty was underscored by the repeated amendments to the same bill as it was being debated last year in the Senate. The Founding Fathers wisely avoided a precise definition of the interface between congressional and executive authority, establishing instead a general structure of shared powers requiring the cooperation of both branches, predicated on the assumption that the form of that cooperation would remain, within certain limits, sufficiently flexible to accommodate many different kinds of circumstances. S. 440 would change that scheme by imposing technical legal prerequisites to action and in so doing would insure that every important national security debate following emergency action by the President would, instead of being argued entirely on the merits, be obscured by procedural arguments as to whether or not the President had acted in accordance with this new legislation. The scheme envisaged in S. 440 is a significant departure from that established in the Constitution and hence could legitimately be effected only by a constitutional amendment even if it were desirable.

Contrary to the apparent assertion of section 2 of this bill, nothing in the "necessary and proper" clause of article 1, section 8, of the Constitution gives Congress this power. As Alexander Hamilton also made clear in "The Federalist," the "necessary and proper" clause was intended principally to guard against an excessively narrow construction of the authority of the Union vis-a-vis State authority. There has never been a judicial decision which has held that the "necessary and proper" clause was intended to limit the principle of separation of powers. In fact, the case of *Myers* v. *United States* (272 U.S. 52 (1926)), in which the Supreme Court held that Congress did not have the power to condition the President's removal power on the concurrence of the Senate, indicates that the separation of powers is not limited by Congress' power under the "necessary and proper" clause. While this provision gives Congress the authority to implement both congressional and executive powers, it does not empower Congress to change the balance

between those powers by defining and limiting the President's authority.

S. 440 noticeably omits Presidential authority to deploy armed forces abroad as an instrument of foreign policy in the absence of an actual attack or imminent threat of attack on American territory or forces. Yet this historic Presidential prerogative for nearly 200 years has been essential to resist aggression and to protect American security interests. As Secretary Rogers has said: [2]

. . . such a restriction could seriously limit the ability of the President to make a demonstration of force to back up the exercise of our rights and responsibilities in Berlin or to deploy elements of the 6th Fleet in the Mediterranean in connection with the Middle East situation.

Elimination of this weapon from the Presidential arsenal could very seriously undermine our security posture and likewise cannot be properly achieved except by constitutional amendment.

S. 440 also purports to restrict the authority of the President to defend the United States itself against an actual armed attack by limiting to 30 days his right to use the armed forces in such hostilities unless Congress specifically authorizes a continuation or is physically unable to meet as a result of the attack. The defense of the United States against armed attack, however, is a core area of Presidential authority; Congress cannot affect the President's constitutional authority in this area. Even the States have constitutional authority to provide for their own defense when invaded or in imminent danger of invasion (article I, section 10). Surely the President can have no less authority or responsibility for defense than the States, particularly inasmuch as the Federal Government has an unlimited constitutional obligation to defend the States (article IV, section 4) and the President as Chief Executive (article II, section 1) and Commander in Chief (article II, section 2) has the responsibility

---

[2] For a statement by Secretary Rogers made before the Senate Committee on Foreign Relations on May 14, 1971, see BULLETIN of June 7, 1971, p. 721.

and the authority to provide that defense. Surely the Congress cannot by legislation reduce these constitutionally prescribed rights and obligations.

Since Congress already has the authority to conduct at any time the same kinds of review that S. 440 proposes to mandate within 30 days, it is difficult to see what advantages Congress gains by legislating an arbitrary deadline. Congress can in any particular case undertake its consideration in a manner and within a period of time appropriate to the circumstances. An arbitrarily fixed time limitation on Presidential authority contributes nothing to the right of Congress to exercise its constitutional authority and at the same time could seriously impede action or undermine negotiations in the future in a manner not desired by either the President or the Congress at that time. To seek to terminate Presidential authority if, for whatever reason, the Congress does not expressly affirm an action within an arbitrary time limit is neither helpful to the interests of either branch nor a constructive contribution to the development of a wise foreign policy.

### Termination by Either House

The second bill to which I have been asked to address myself, H.R. 317, avoids some of the serious problems of S. 440. It does not propose to specify the constitutional powers of the President. Neither does it propose a fixed and arbitrary time limitation for congressional action in response to Presidential initiatives. It would call for prompt reports from the President to the Congress whenever the armed forces are used in hostilities absent specific congressional authorization or a declaration of war.

We question the necessity, and even the advisability, of requiring, as H.R. 317 would, that the Congress be convened if not in session at the time the President submits such a report. It is certainly conceivable that the formality and attention given to a special session of the Congress could negate the advantages of quiet diplomacy in the case of an understated show of strength. A decision to convene Congress constitutionally lies within the discretion of the President and should depend on the circumstances prevailing at the time.

Section 4 of H.R. 317, entitled "Termination of Authority," presents difficulty in two respects. This section proposes that the authority of the President to deploy the armed forces or to direct or authorize them to engage in hostile action, absent specific congressional authorization or a declaration of war, is terminated if either House of the Congress adopts a resolution disapproving continuation of an action the President has taken. First, the proscription of Presidential action would seem far too broadly drawn for both constitutional and policy reasons. Although within its constitutional authority Congress clearly can decide, for example, whether or not to appropriate funds to support policies or programs of which it disapproves, it is extremely doubtful, as I mentioned earlier, that Congress could terminate Presidential authority to deploy forces as the President saw fit; for example, to protect the United States against an armed attack.

A second difficulty with section 4 of H.R. 317 is that it purports to terminate the authority of the President upon the passage of a resolution by either House of Congress. This must be considered an unworkable standard for a number of reasons. We are dealing here with a division of power between the Congress and the executive, not between the Senate or the House and the executive. When one branch purports to impose legally binding restrictions on the exercise of the authority of the other, it clearly must be acting with its own full authority. The Congress clearly has authority to approve or not to approve funds for use by the executive branch. Such a decision governs to some extent the activities of the executive and clearly depends on the consent of both Houses of the Congress. A law which states that the same effect can be accomplished by the passage of a simple resolution by only one House of Congress is constitutionally defective. It impairs the constitutional authority of Congress itself as well as that of the executive. Furthermore, what is the true position of Congress if, for example, one House passes a resolution supporting the President's action and the other a resolution calling for its termination? It is clear that in matters of such significance the Congress must speak with one voice to have legal force.

## Need To Increase Communications

Let me now turn to the third measure I have been asked to discuss. H.J. Res. 2, introduced by you, Mr. Chairman [Representative Clement J. Zablocki], for yourself and others, is primarily oriented toward increasing the flow of information on which Congress can base its decisions in exercising its constitutional responsibilities. As I have discussed at some length, it is this general approach, rather than that of attempting to change the underlying authority of either branch, that we strongly feel is the more constructive and positive way to proceed. I would like to mention that we have the greatest respect and appreciation for your efforts, Mr. Chairman, over the past several years to conduct a balanced, responsible, and searching investigation into the issues raised by war powers legislation.

Unlike the Zablocki bill passed last year by the House of Representatives, however, H.J. Res. 2 includes provisions in section 3 which could be read as limiting the fundamental authority of the President to introduce the armed forces into hostilities or situations where imminent involvement in hostilities is clearly indicated. As I have discussed earlier, this type of provision leads us into very difficult constitutional and general policy problems and does not, in my view, take us very far along the road to developing responsible and forward-looking foreign policies in the future. I do note that H.J. Res. 2 does not impose any artificial deadline for congressional response to a Presidential initiative, although of course it maintains the option for such a response at any time.

In addition, section 6, which provides that Congress should meet after the President has committed armed forces as described in section 5 in order to decide whether to authorize such use of the armed forces or the expenditure of funds for that action, seems to imply that the President may not have authority to act in the first place. It is clear from what I have already said, however, that the President possesses broad constitutional authority to commit military forces in cases contemplated by section 5. Finally, as I have indicated, I do not think it necessarily appropriate that Congress be mandatorily convened as required by section 6, upon the receipt of every report rendered pursuant to section 5.

It is my hope, Mr. Chairman, that Congress will reject the highly restrictive approach to war powers legislation, which is unsound, and concentrate instead on enhancing its own ability to participate in the development of future foreign policies with the executive branch, as the drafters of the Constitution intended. To help move us toward that goal, I would like to repeat for your serious consideration several proposals which the Secretary of State made to the Congress in his war powers testimony of May 14, 1971. We are prepared to explore with you ways of reinforcing the information capability of Congress on issues involving war and peace. For example, we would be prepared to have each geographic Assistant Secretary provide on a regular basis full briefings on developments in his respective area. Such briefings would help the Congress to stay abreast of developing crisis situations as well as to build up a deeper background of information in many areas.

There is, as we have noted many times, the need to be able to act speedily and sometimes without prior publicity in crisis situations. We should concentrate on efforts to find better institutional methods to keep these requirements from becoming an obstacle to the exercise by Congress of its full and proper role, rather than on counterproductive efforts to impede the executive in exercising its role. We have heard a number of suggestions concerning the possibility of establishing a joint congressional committee which could act as a consultative body with the President in times of emergencies, and as Secretary Rogers indicated, if there is interest in this idea in the Congress we would be willing to discuss this possibility with you to determine how best we might cooperate.

We must both retain flexibility, for we are living in a dynamic world; and we must both work together, for the decisions we make in this area are frequently momentous and profound. Let us join together to improve the quality and facility of our decisions, rather than inhibit our capacity to make them.

# Great Cases Make Bad Law: The War Powers Act

## EUGENE V. ROSTOW

*Great cases like hard cases make bad law. For great cases are
called great, not by reason of their real importance in shaping
the law of the future, but because of some accident of immediate overwhelming interest which appeals to the feelings and
distorts the judgment. These immediate interests exercise a
kind of hydraulic pressure which makes what previously was
clear seem doubtful, and before which even well settled principles of law will bend.*

> HOLMES, J., dissenting in *Northern
> Securities Co. v. United States,* 193
> U.S. 197, 400-01 (1904).

*The circumstances that endanger the safety of nations are
infinite, and for this reason no constitutional shackles can
wisely be imposed on the power to which the care of it is
committed.*

> Alexander Hamilton, THE FEDER-
> ALIST No. 23

*The legislative department is everywhere extending the sphere
of its activity, and drawing all power into its impetuous vortex
. . . it is against the enterprising ambition of this department
that the people ought to indulge all their jealousy and exhaust
all their precautions.*

> James Madison, THE FEDERALIST
> No. 48

## I. INTRODUCTION

Responding to the bitterness and tragedy of Vietnam, a group of
Senators led by Jacob K. Javits of New York proposes fundamentally to

---

* Sterling Professor of Law and Public Affairs at Yale University. This article is based
on the author's Leon Green Address, delivered at the Fiftieth Anniversary Dinner of the
TEXAS LAW REVIEW, March 11, 1972. It is a pleasure to note my admiration for Dean
Green, and my enthusiasm for his distinguished service to the law, and to our law schools.

change the constitutional relationship between President and Congress in the field of foreign affairs.[1] They assert that the underlying cause of the Vietnam tragedy is a modern and most unconstitutional excess of presidential power—a shift in the rightful balance of authority between the two branches caused by presidential "usurpations" at least since the time of McKinley, and especially those they claim Lyndon B. Johnson made with regard to Vietnam.

Ignoring their own repeated votes for Vietnam, these Senators say, "We live in an age of undeclared war, which has meant Presidential war. Prolonged engagement in undeclared, Presidential war has created a most dangerous imbalance in our Constitutional system of checks and balances."[2] Although Senator John Sherman Cooper has rightly criticized their theory as a rewriting of history, without factual foundation,[3] these men have offered a Bill which in their view would correct nearly two hundred years of error, strip the Presidency of many of its most essential powers, and restore what they fondly imagine was the constitutional model of 1789.

This contention, which is the major premise of the Senate Foreign Relations Committee Report on the Javits Bill, confuses two concepts, one of international law, the second of American constitutional law. "Undeclared" (or "limited" or "imperfect") war is a category of public international law, used to denote hostilities on a considerable scale conducted in time of "peace" rather than of "war," so far as international

---

The present version of the address draws on passages from PEACE IN THE BALANCE: THE FUTURE OF AMERICAN FOREIGN POLICY, to be published during 1972 by Simon & Schuster, Inc., of New York.

[1] SENATE COMM. ON FOREIGN RELATIONS, WAR POWERS, S. REP. No. 92-606, 92d Cong., 2d Sess. (1972), to accompany S. 2956, 92d Cong., 2d Sess. (1972) [hereinafter cited as WAR POWERS]; War Powers Legislation, Hearings on S. 731, S.J. Res. 18, and S.J. Res. 59 Before the Senate Comm. on Foreign Relations, 92d Cong., 1st Sess. (1972) [hereinafter cited as 1971 Hearings]. See also SENATE COMM. ON FOREIGN RELATIONS, 91ST CONG., 2D SESS., DOCUMENTS RELATING TO THE WAR POWER OF CONGRESS, THE PRESIDENT'S AUTHORITY AS COMMANDER-IN-CHIEF AND THE WAR IN INDOCHINA (Comm. Print 1970) [hereinafter cited as DOCUMENTS]; Congress, the President, and the War Powers, Hearings Before the Subcomm. on National Security Policy and Scientific Developments of the House Comm. on Foreign Affairs, 91st Cong., 2d Sess. (1970) [hereinafter cited as 1970 Hearings].

[2] WAR POWERS, supra note 1, at 3.

[3] In a statement of individual views, Senator Cooper remarks:

I do not concur in one underlying theme of the Committee's report—which was never discussed in Committee and never voted on—that the Executive has taken from the Congress its powers. The record, if studied, discloses that the Congress, particularly since World War II, has not only acceded to but has supported Executive resolutions requesting Congressional authority to use the armed forces of the United States, if necessary, in hostilities.

These are settled facts of history. We can change our course but we cannot revise and rewrite history.

Id. at 32.

law is concerned. "Presidential" war, as the Committee uses the phrase, obviously refers to hostilities undertaken by the United States, and authorized by the President alone. The United States, like most other nations during the last two and a half centuries, has rarely chosen to invoke the international law of war by solemnly "declaring" that a state of war exists, signalling maximum hostility, and implying the invasion or even the destruction of an enemy state. But a considerable number of our many "limited" or "undeclared" wars, like Vietnam itself, have been authorized by Congress as well as the President through procedures which have been approved in usage and in Supreme Court opinions since the first years of the nation under the Constitution of 1789. Such hostilities cannot therefore be described as "Presidential."

The Javits Bill rests on heady new perspectives the Senate Foreign Relations Committee has discovered in the necessary and proper clause.[4] Its doctrine would permit a plenipotentiary Congress to dominate the Presidency (and the courts as well) more completely than the House of Commons governs England; that is, it would permit Congress to amend the Constitution without the inconvenience of consulting the people.

The battle cry of "constitutional usurpation" quickens the blood of every Congressman, and indeed of every American.[5] Accustomed as we are to treat nearly all questions of policy as questions of constitutional law, we find it easy to conclude that whatever we dislike intensely must also, and therefore, be unconstitutional as well. It is as natural for us to preach a return to the true orthodoxy of the Founding Fathers as it is for devout Moslems to make a pilgrimage to Mecca.

Holmes once remarked that great cases, like hard cases, make bad law. The Javits Bill confirms Holmes' quip more vividly than any proposal since that of the Bricker Amendment, which was in part a response to the Korean War. We should find safer outlets than the Javits Bill for the hydraulic pressure of our present discontents about Vietnam.

---

[4] Members of Congress have themselves perhaps underestimated the authority vested in them by the "necessary and proper" clause of Article I, Section 8, of the Constitution. That clause entrusts the Congress to make all laws "necessary and proper for carrying into execution" not only its own powers but "all other powers vested by this Constitution in the Government of the United States, or in any department or office thereof." Strictly interpreted, the "necessary and proper" clause entrusts the Congress not only to "carry into execution" its own constitutional war power, but also, should it be thought necessary, to define and codify the powers of the government as a whole, including those of the President as its principal officer.
*Id.* at 16. *See* discussion pp. 896-97 *infra.*

[5] Youngstown Sheet & Tube Co. v. Sawyer, 343 U.S. 579, 594 (1952), (Frankfurter, J., concurring).

We wisely refrained from curbing the powers of the Supreme Court even after the catastrophic error of *Dred Scott*. The same calm prudence should guide our course now, with respect to the Presidency.

The Javits Bill rests on a premise of constitutional law and constitutional history which is in error. Its passage would be a constitutional disaster, depriving the government of the powers it needs most to safeguard the nation in a dangerous and unstable world. Even if a President were to ignore such a statute, assuming that it passed over his veto, on the ground that it is unconstitutional, the passage of the Bill would create uncertainties, and envenom politics, in ways which would themselves be dangerous, both at home and abroad. It would tend to convert every crisis of foreign policy into a crisis of will, of pride, and of precedence between Congress and the President, making the policy process even more athletic than it is today.

The Javits Bill is a more serious attack on the Constitution and the security of the nation than one or another of the Bricker Amendments, which were nearly recommended by the Congress in the middle fifties. Those Amendments dealt only with the legal effect of treaties as internal law. They would have required affirmative action by Congress before treaties become operative as the supreme law of the land.[6]

The Javits Bill is more ambitious. It would allow the President, as the constitutional head of state, commander-in-chief, and representative of the nation in the conduct of foreign affairs, to use the armed forces of the United States in five and only five classes of cases: pursuant (1) to a declaration of war, or (2) to a specific statutory authorization of undeclared war passed after the passage of the Javits Bill itself, and specifically exempting a proposed use of force from its provisions, or like legislation in force at the time of the enactment of the Javits Bill, if it is sufficiently "specific";[7] absent such Congressional mandates, the

---

6 Association of the Bar of the City of New York, *Report on the 1957 Bricker Amendment*, 12 THE RECORD 320 (1957); Bricker & Webb, *Treaty Law v. Domestic Constitutional Law*, 29 NOTRE DAME LAW. 529 (1954); Hatch, Finch & Ober, *The Treaty Power and the Constitution: The Case for Amendment*, 40 A.B.A.J. 207 (1954); MacChesney, *The Fallacies in the Case for the Bricker Amendment*, 29 NOTRE DAME LAW. 551 (1954); MacChesney, McDougal, Mathews, Oliver & Ribble, *The Treaty Power and the Constitution: The Case Against Amendment*, 40 A.B.A.J. 203 (1954).

7 S. 2956, 92d Cong., 2d Sess. § 3 (1972):
In the absence of a declaration of war by the Congress, the Armed Forces of the United States may be introduced in hostilities, or in situations where imminent involvement in hostilities is clearly indicated by the circumstances, only . . . (4) pursuant to specific statutory authorization, but authority to introduce the Armed Forces of the United States in hostilities or in any such situation shall not be inferred (A) from any provision of law hereafter enacted, including any provision contained in any appropriation Act, unless such provision specifically authorizes the introduction of such Armed Forces in hostilities or in such situation and specifically exempts the introduction of such Armed Forces from compli-

Bill would permit the use of the armed forces of the United States by the President only (3) to *repel* an armed attack on the United States, or (4) on the armed forces of the United States located outside of the United States; to *forestall* the direct and imminent threat of such an armed attack; to *retaliate* against armed attacks on the United States (not, however, against armed attacks on the armed forces of the United States located outside of the United States); or (5) to protect American citizens abroad being evacuated from a situation of direct and imminent threat to their lives. And in all hostilities except those authorized by a declaration of war—that is—those of "specific" advance statutory authorization of undeclared war; the evacuation of citizens in danger; and of armed attack on the United States or on its forces—the President could not use force for more than thirty days unless Congress ratified his course within that period or had exempted the particular use of force from the Javits Act in advance. The Bill would also require the President to report in writing to both Houses of Congress regarding the introduction of the armed forces "in hostilities, or in any situation where imminent involvement in hostilities is clearly indicated by the circumstances,"[8] and provides that within thirty days Congress could overrule even a President's decision to use force in conformity with the Bill by an act or joint resolution.

The Javits Bill would annul the military provisions of all outstanding treaties, and probably of other legislative commitments dealing with the use of force as well, including the authority specified in the Middle Eastern Resolution and other Resolutions of similar import.[9] We should

---

ance with the provisions of this Act, or (B) from any treaty hereafter ratified unless such treaty is implemented by legislation specifically authorizing the introduction of the Armed Forces of the United States in hostilities or in such situation and specifically exempting the introduction of such Armed Forces from compliance with the provisions of this Act. Specific statutory authorization is required for the assignment of members of the Armed Forces of the United States to command, coordinate, participate in the movement of, or accompany the regular or irregular military forces of any foreign country or government when such Armed Forces are engaged, or there exists an imminent threat that such forces will become engaged, in hostilities. No treaty in force at the time of the enactment of this Act shall be construed as specific statutory authorization for, or a specific exemption permitting, the introduction of the Armed Forces of the United States in hostilities or in any such situation, within the meaning of this clause (4); and no provision of law in force at the time of the enactment of this Act shall be so construed unless such provision specifically authorizes the introduction of such Armed Forces in hostilities or in any such situation.

How one Congress could constitutionally bind its successors in this way passes my understanding. The problem is hardly comparable to the provisions of § 12 of the Administrative Procedure Act, providing guidelines to the courts in interpreting subsequent statutes as repeals by implication. 60 Stat. 244, (1946), 5 U.S.C. § 559 (1970); Rusk v. Cort, 369 U.S. 367 (1962).

[8] S. 2956, 92d Cong., 2d Sess. § 4 (1972).

[9] Middle East Resolution, Pub. L. No. 85-7, 71 Stat. 5 (1957), *as amended*, Pub. L.

become the only nation in the world unable to make credible treaties or other security commitments. If the Javits Bill should become law, there would be a difficult and dangerous hiatus, maximizing uncertainty, until new treaties could be negotiated, and new legislation confirming them be considered and passed. With respect to the use of the armed forces by the President acting without prior authorization from Congress, the Bill would abolish at least half the categories in a pattern of practice which extends in an unbroken line of more than 150 instances to the Presidency of George Washington; equally, it would put the Presidency in the straitjacket of a rigid code, and prevent new categories of action from emerging, in response to the necessities of a tense and unstable world. Under the Javits Bill, no President could make a credible threat to use force as an instrument of deterrent diplomacy, even to head off explosive confrontations. And, on those occasions when the Bill would authorize the President to move quickly, the reporting requirements could well of themselves blow every secret diplomatic brush into a major crisis.

The Javits Bill is full of paradox. While its nominal motivation is to assure the nation that a pacific Congress will staunchly keep jingo Presidents from engaging in limited wars like that in Vietnam, the Bill would not have prevented the campaign in Vietnam if it had been enacted thirty years ago. Our participation in Vietnam was specifically authorized by President Eisenhower's SEATO Treaty, and by several

---

No. 87-195, 75 Stat. 424 (1961); Formosa Resolution, ch. 4, 69 Stat. 7 (1955); Berlin Resolution, H.R. Con. Res. 570, 87th Cong., 2d Sess., 118 CONG. REC. 22637 (1962); Cuba Resolution, Pub. L. No. 87-733, 76 Stat. 697 (1962); The United Nations Participation Act of 1945, ch. 583, 59 Stat. 619 (1949), as amended, ch. 660, 63 Stat. 734 (1949), Pub. L. No. 86-707, 74 Stat. 797 (1960), Pub. L. No. 89-206, 79 Stat. 841 (1965).

The last clause of § 3(4) of the Javits Bill, quoted in note 7 supra, is ambiguous on this point. Nor is it clarified in the Senate Report on the Bill, WAR POWERS, supra note 1. The important question remains whether the language of outstanding statutes and Joint and Concurrent Resolutions should be regarded as "specific" enough to survive the passage of the Bill, in view of the first sentence of § 3(4), and the flat statement that "no treaty in force at the time of the enactment of this Act shall be construed as specific statutory authorization for, or a specific exemption permitting, the introduction" of the armed forces in hostilities.

The Middle East Resolution, for example, provides that the United States regards as vital to the national interest and world peace the preservation of the independence and integrity of the nations of the Middle East. To this end, if the President determines the necessity thereof, the United States is prepared to use armed forces to assist any such nation or group of such nations requesting assistance against armed aggression from any country controlled by international communism: Provided, That such employment shall be consonant with the treaty obligations of the United States and with the Constitution of the United States. Pub. L. No. 85-7, § 2, 71 Stat. 5 (1957).

In view of the policies of strict construction and Congressional control embodied in the Javits Bill, would this language be construed to authorize Presidential action to assist Jordan, for example, against an attack from (or by) Syria?

other laws, including the Tonkin Gulf Resolution, which authorized the use of armed force by the President to carry out that Treaty.[10] The procedures used to bring Congress and the Presidency together behind the campaign in Vietnam fully comply with the substantive standards of the Javits Bill. In the case of Korea, the Javits Bill would have prevented President Truman from taking any action whatsoever before obtaining a Congressional Resolution, despite the risks of delay, since the North Korean attack was not directed against the territory or the armed forces of the United States. Such a Resolution could surely have been obtained at the time, although the President and the Congressional leaders thought it unwise and unnecessary to do so.[11]

If the Javits Bill had been on the books, it would have prevented President Kennedy from resolving the Cuban Missile Crisis as he did, by the skillful and minimal deployment of our armed forces as an instrument of diplomatic deterrence and persuasion, in the interest of protecting vital national interests without precipitating nuclear war, or any other kind of war. In its Report, the Senate Foreign Relations Committee, relying on testimony by Professor Bickel, asserts that the Cuban Missile Crisis could have been treated under Section 3(1) of the Javits Bill as a case of forestalling "the direct and imminent threat" of armed attack on the United States. The United States government, however, has made no such claim, even under the "inherent" right of self-defense provision of Article 51 of the United Nations Charter, far broader than the Javits Bill in its reach. Indeed, the notion that the Soviet Union in 1962 was about to launch nuclear missiles against the United States from Cuba, knowing that it would have received a nuclear attack in response, is incredible. The Cuban Missile Crisis, real as it was, must be seen as part of the push and pull of Soviet-American diplomacy, in the context of the Berlin and Laos crises of the period, President Kennedy's Vienna meeting with Khrushchev, the Bay of Pigs fiasco, and other factors.[12]

---

[10] *See* discussion pp. 872-885 *infra.*

[11] *See* discussion pp. 867-870 *infra.*

[12] R. KENNEDY, THIRTEEN DAYS 31-33, 111-19, *Afterword* by R. Neustadt & G. Allison, 138-39 (1969); KHRUSHCHEV REMEMBERS ch. 20 (S. Talbott ed. 1971); WAR POWERS, *supra* note 1, at 4; Chayes, *Law and the Quarantine of Cuba*, 41 FOR. AFF. 550 (1963) (expressly refusing to rest the American legal case on "self-defense," even in the ample perspective of Article 51). The most penetrating analysis of the crisis is A. WOHLSTETTER & R. WOHLSTETTER, CONTROLLING THE RISKS IN CUBA (1965). *See also* INTERNATIONAL LAW AND POLITICAL CRISIS (L. Sheinman & D. Wilkinson eds. 1968); MacChesney, *Some Comments on the "Quarantine" of Cuba*, 57 AM. J. INT'L L. 592 (1963); McDougal, *The Soviet-Cuban Quarantine and Self-Defense*, 57 AM. J. INT'L L. 597 (1963).

In the Cuban case, Congress had passed a Resolution less than a month before the Missile Crisis of 1962, authorizing the President to use force if necessary to prevent "the

Under the Javits Bill, President Johnson could not have employed the implicit threat of force to keep the Soviets out of the Six Day War in 1967,[13] and President Nixon could not have used the same method to avert a general war in the Middle East in September, 1970, or to confine and contain the India-Pakistan War of 1972. Nor could earlier Presidents have used or threatened to use the nation's armed forces to persuade France to leave Mexico in 1865-66, to avoid war with Spain or Britain over Florida, or to send Commodore Perry on his fateful voyage to Japan.

As Senator Javits has said with admirable candor, the purpose of his Bill is to reduce the elective Presidency, which the Founding Fathers were at pains to establish as a third autonomous and coequal branch of the government, to the humble posture of George Washington during the Revolution, when he functioned as commander-in-chief, appointed by the Continental Congress, and its creature, or the creature of its committees, in every respect.[14] I should have supposed that if anything *is* clear about the intent of the Founding Fathers, it is that one of the major goals of the Philadelphia Convention was to remedy what was

---

Marxist-Leninist regime in Cuba" from extending its activities by force or the threat of force to any part of the hemisphere. The Resolution also announced our determination to prevent in Cuba the creation or use of an externally supported military capability endangering the security of the United States. That clause of the Resolution, unlike clause (a), did not mention the use of arms. *See* Cuban Resolution, note 9 *supra*. Mr. Chayes believes, however, that the Resolution was "one of the bases" of the President's authority to do what he did. *1970 Hearings, supra* note 1, at 138. It would seem a better reading of the Cuban Resolution, in light of the restrictive policy of the Javits Bill, to interpret it as contemplating what President Johnson did in the Dominican Republic, but not what President Kennedy did before and during the Missile Crisis.

13 L. JOHNSON, THE VANTAGE POINT 301-03 (1971).

14 "The Case for War Powers Legislation," Address to the American Bar Association Standing Comm. on World Order under Law, Hearing on War Powers of the President and Congress, Feb. 5, 1972, at 4-5.

Because this important speech is not yet readily available in libraries, it may be convenient to quote its extraordinary conclusion in full:

Clearly, the drafters of the Constitution had in mind the experience of the Continental Congress with George Washington when they designated the President as "Commander-in-Chief" in Article II Section 2. Thus, the "legislative history" of the Constitutional concept of a Commander-in-Chief was the relationship of George Washington as colonial Commander-in-Chief to the Continental Congress.

That relationship is clearly defined in the Commission as Commander-in-Chief which was given to Washington on June 19, 1775.

I would like to quote the final clause of this Commander-in-Chief's Commission, because it establishes the relationship of the Congress to the Commander-in-Chief in unmistakable terms:

"AND you are to regulate your conduct in every respect by the rules and discipline of war (as herewith given you) and punctually to observe and follow such orders and directions from time to time as you shall receive from this or a future Congress of the said United Colonies or a committee of Congress for that purpose appointed."

This historical background clarifies, and gives added meaning to, those phrases in the Constitution concerning the war powers which are the subject of such contemporary controversy.

perceived as a critical weakness of the Articles of Confederation, namely, the absence of a strong and independent executive. The British monarch was much more in their minds as a point of departure than the revolutionary commander.

A wistful and nostalgic chord runs through the testimony and the speeches which favor the Javits Bill. The Founding Fathers, the distinguished and appealing proponents of the Bill say, wanted to make it hard to go to war, and easy to make peace. They wanted America to remain aloof from the quarrels of a naughty world, to eschew the pride and arrogance of power, and to use force only when openly attacked. Let us return to the wisdom of the patriarchs and prophets, these leaders tell us, and require Congress itself—or perhaps even the people through a referendum—to authorize every use of the sword. Thus they would wrap a foreign policy of nearly pacifist isolationism in the priestly mantle of constitutional command.[15]

The Bill's supporters dismiss the fact that the men who made the Constitution had quite another view of its imperatives when they became Presidents, Senators, Congressmen, and Secretaries of State. The words and conduct of the Founding Fathers in office hardly support the simplified and unworldly models we are asked to accept as embodiments of the only True Faith. Nor did the policies the Founding Fathers adopted when they became officials always shine with the innocence of Professor Commager's spirit. Above all, the essence of the Constitution was to build a framework which could last for ages. To suppose that the Constitution binds the nation forever to a particular foreign policy, or even a particular theory for foreign policy, is a fantasy, entirely alien to the chilly realism of No. 23 of *The Federalist*, and of *McCulloch v. Maryland*. The makers of the Constitution built in anticipation of changes in world politics that could not be anticipated in 1787. They wished to endow their successors with the full freedom of democratic responsibility to choose the foreign policy they found best suited to the politics and military technology of the period in which they lived. If the Constitution does not enact the Social Statics of Herbert Spencer, it surely does not enact the foreign policy of William E. Borah or J. William Fulbright. Constitutionally, the United States is as free to follow McKinley's example in making its foreign policy as that of Cleveland.

The constitution of the United States is a process—a process of

---

[15] *1971 Hearings, supra* note 1, at 8-74 (testimony of Professor H. S. Commager), 75-85 (testimony of Professor R. B. Morris).

tension, conducted in a matrix of custom, and guided by certain standards, habits, and rules. Justice Brandeis once said that

> [t]he doctrine of the separation of powers was adopted by the Convention of 1787, not to promote efficiency but to preclude the exercise of arbitrary power. The purpose was, not to avoid friction, but, by means of the inevitable friction incident to the distribution of the governmental powers among three departments, to save the people from autocracy.[16]

The same theme runs through the Federalist papers.

In the contest for preeminence between President and Congress which constitutes one phase of Justice Brandeis' vision, the Javits Bill is nearly alone. Congress has made no bid for supremacy so bold, and so foreign to the American Constitution, since the impeachment of Andrew Johnson. The Bill would not restore the constitutional balance of 1787; it would profoundly alter that balance with regard to the conduct of foreign relations, as it has evolved in nearly two hundred years of testing experience.

I reach this conclusion not as an advocate of increased presidential power, but as a defender of the constitutional pattern of enforced cooperation between President and Congress we have inherited, for all the friction it inevitably generates. I disagree with the arguments for enlarged presidential power put forth in recent years by McGeorge Bundy, James McGregor Burns, and Senator Fulbright.[17] No President, and no Congress, can develop or carry out a foreign policy unless in fact they work together. Of course Congress should participate, and participate as early as possible, in decisions involving major and sustained hostilities, through processes of continuous consultation, and, where desirable and feasible, through formal legislative actions approving declared or undeclared war. That is now the pattern of our politics, and of our constitutional usage. The respective powers of each branch are indispensable if the making and execution of foreign policy are to remain under effective democratic control. Our practice is strenuous, and hardly conducive to a quiet, easy life, either for Presidents or for members of Congress. A quiet life for public officials is not, however, the most important goal of our constitutional arrangements and practices. There is no safe way to codify those arrangements and practices,

---

16 Myers v. United States, 272 U.S. 52, 293 (1926) (Brandeis, J., dissenting).
17 M. BUNDY, THE STRENGTH OF GOVERNMENT (1968); J. BURNS, PRESIDENTIAL GOVERNMENT (1965); R. NEUSTADT, PRESIDENTIAL POWER; THE POLITICS OF LEADERSHIP (1968); 1970 Hearings, supra note 1, at 81 (testimony of Dr. Burns); Fulbright, American Foreign Policy in the 20th Century Under an 18th-Century Constitution, 47 CORNELL L.Q. 1 (1961).

especially with regard to the use of nuclear weapons, in ways which could meet all the contingencies likely to arise. It is striking that Senator Fulbright was alone on the Senate Foreign Relations Committee in urging a congressional vote before the President could legally use the nuclear weapon.[18]

Gouverneur Morris remarked that "no constitution is the same on paper and in life."[19] Justice Frankfurter carried the thought further, writing about the relation between President and Congress in regard to the war power:

> [T]he content of the three authorities of government is not to be derived from an abstract analysis. The areas are partly interacting, not wholly disjointed. The Constitution is a framework for government. Therefore the way the framework has consistently operated fairly establishes that it has operated according to its true nature. Deeply embedded traditional ways of conducting government cannot supplant the Constitution or legislation, but they give meaning to the words of a text or supply them. It is an inadmissibly narrow conception of American constitutional law to confine it to the words of the Constitution and to disregard the gloss which life has written upon them. In short, a systematic, unbroken, executive practice, long pursued to the knowledge of the Congress and never before questioned, engaged in by Presidents who have also sworn to uphold the Constitution, making as it were such exercise of power part of the structure of our government, may be treated as a gloss on executive Power vested in the President by § 1 of Art. II.[20]

The Javits Bill repudiates that history root and branch, and seeks to substitute parliamentary government for the tripartite constitution we have so painfully forged.

## II. THE BACKGROUND OF CONSTITUTIONAL USAGE

The most serious illusion of legal positivism is the notion that "the original intention" of those who drafted and voted for a law is thereafter knowable, save as a guideline of broad purpose or principle. The debates of judges and scholars about the legitimacy of *Marbury v.*

---

18 WAR POWERS, *supra* note 1, at 26. Even Justice Goldberg, who vigorously urges a return to the "very plain language" of the Constitution, exempts the nuclear problem from his recommendations, *1971 Hearings, supra* note 1, at 770-71.

19 1 S. MORISON, OXFORD HISTORY OF THE UNITED STATES 103 (1st ed. 1927).

20 Youngstown Sheet & Tube Co. v. Sawyer, 343 U.S. 579, 610-11 (1952) (Frankfurter, J., concurring).

*Madison*, the scope of the commerce power, or the true import of the Fourteenth Amendment are evidence enough of the limited value of such inquests as a guide to later decisions. It is psychologically impossible for a man of the twentieth century, however learned and sensitive, to perceive the world as the men of 1787 did. There is no way for him to reproduce the structure and climate of their universe —to understand as they did the relation of the several parts to each other and the weight which various fears, concerns and ambitions had in their minds.[21] The most important words John Marshall ever wrote were that we should never forget it is a *constitution* we are expounding—a constitution intended to endure for ages to come, and capable of adaptation to the various crises of human affairs—but a *constitution* nonetheless, assuring continuity as well as flexibility, boundaries of power, coupled with a wide freedom of democratic choice.[22]

How did the Founding Fathers intend to allocate the power to use the armed forces between the President and the Congress? I do not start here because I believe that we can conjure up from their few spare words on the subject a sacred norm of Arcadian purity to which at all costs we must "return," a tight model, capable, like a magical computer or coin machine, of providing clear solutions for every contingency likely to arise. The astute men who drafted the Constitution and started it on its way had a much deeper and more realistic sense of the relationship between law and life than that. Nonetheless, it is right as well as customary to start with the document, viewed against the background of their words and their experience, because the animating principles of their project—democratic responsibility, the theory of checks and balances in the exercise of shared powers, and civilian control of the military—have retained their vitality, and must continue to do so if we hope to survive as a free and democratic society.

In the perspective of political theory, the Presidency is one of the two great inventions of the Constitution, the other being judicial review. The weakness of the Executive under the Articles of Confederation was one of the major reasons for convening the Constitutional Convention of

---

21 In 1857, W. H. Trescot, in his DIPLOMATIC HISTORY OF THE ADMINISTRATION OF WASHINGTON AND ADAMS, 1789-1801, at 7-8, remarked that

> [i]t would be almost as easy for a man in the vigorous and varied activity of his matured life to realize faithfully to himself the uncertainty and weakness of his infancy, as for a citizen of the United States at the present day to reproduce the condition of his country at the date of that treaty which secured its independence —the weakness of its institutions, its economic life, and its internal and external situation.

*See also id.* at 97.

22 E. ROSTOW, THE SOVEREIGN PREROGATIVE: THE SUPREME COURT AND THE QUEST FOR LAW 121-24 (1962).

1787. Problems of security and of diplomacy were among the dominant preoccupations of the men who met at Philadelphia, and first among their arguments for Union. The nation was surrounded by British, French and Spanish territories, to say nothing of hostile Indian tribes. The Founding Fathers were mortally afraid the United States might be dismembered as a pawn in the Great Game of European power politics. Their Revolution had succeeded because they had the help of France. They knew that France had not assisted the American revolutionaries because the Bourbon King was a secret republican at heart, or a believer in the right of revolution. They feared a turn of the wheel of European politics which might undo all that had been achieved, despite their military alliance with France. Hence their concern with the Presidency and with the establishment of clearly national authority over defense and foreign relations in the new constitution. Of the 85 Federalist papers, 26 are devoted to one or another aspect of the problem.[23]

---

[23] The basic idea which governed the drafting of the provisions of the Constitution dealing with the safety of the nation was classically stated by Hamilton in No. 23 of THE FEDERALIST:

The principal purposes to be answered by union are these—the common defence of the members; the preservation of the public peace, as well against internal convulsions as external attacks; the regulation of commerce with other nations and between the States; the superintendence of our intercourse, political and commercial, with foreign countries.

The authorities essential to the common defence are these: to raise armies; to build and equip fleets; to prescribe rules for the government of both; to direct their operations; to provide for their support. These powers ought to exist without limitation, *because it is impossible to foresee or define the extent and variety of national exigencies, or the correspondent extent and variety of the means which may be necessary to satisfy them.* The circumstances that endanger the safety of nations are infinite, and for this reason no constitutional shackles can wisely be imposed on the power to which the care of it is committed. This power ought to be co-extensive with all the possible combinations of such circumstances; and ought to be under the direction of the same councils which are appointed to preside over the common defence.

This is one of those truths which, to a correct and unprejudiced mind, carries its own evidence along with it; and may be obscured, but cannot be made plainer by argument or reasoning. It rests upon axioms as simple as they are universal; the *means* ought to be proportioned to the *end;* the persons, from whose agency the attainment of any *end* is expected, ought to possess the *means* by which it is to be attained.

Whether there ought to be a federal government intrusted with the care of the common defence, is a question in the first instance, open for discussion; but the moment it is decided in the affirmative, it will follow, that that government ought to be clothed with all the powers requisite to complete execution of its trust. And unless it can be shown that the circumstances which may affect the public safety are reducible within certain determinate limits; unless the contrary of this position can be fairly and rationally disputed, it must be admitted, as a necessary consequence, that there can be no limitation of that authority which is to provide for the defence and protection of the community, in any matter essential to its efficacy—that is, in any matter essential to the *formation, direction,* or *support* of the NATIONAL FORCES.

THE FEDERALIST 142-43 (Modern Library ed. 1937). Hamilton's views on the President's independent role in assuring the security of the nation were developed later in a number of papers. *See, e.g.,* those collected by Professor R. B. Morris in ALEXANDER HAMILTON AND

The Presidency which emerged from the deliberations at Philadelphia as the repository of "the executive power" of the United States was a remarkable office. Its essence was that the incumbents be endowed with ample authority to discharge the executive task, both at home and abroad, but not enough to become tyrants or kings. As Clinton Rossiter concludes:

> Considering the spirit of the age, which was still proudly and loudly Whiggish, the proposed Presidency was an office of unusual vigor and independence. As Hamilton was soon to point out in *The Federalist*, it joined energy, unity, duration, competent powers, and "an adequate provision for its support" with "a due dependence on the people" and "a due responsibility." The President had a source of election legally separated if not totally divorced from the legislature, a fixed term and untrammeled reeligibility, a fixed compensation (which could be "neither increased nor diminished" while he was in office), immunity from collective advice he had not sought (whether tendered by the Court, the heads of executive departments, or a council of revision), and broad constitutional powers of his own. It would be his first task to run the new government: to be its administrative chief, to appoint and supervise the heads of departments and their principal aides, and to "take care" that the laws were "faithfully executed." He was to lead the government in its foreign relations, peaceful and hostile, and he was, it would appear, to be ceremonial head of state, a "republican monarch" with the prerogative of mercy. Despite the allegiance of the Convention to the principle of the separation of powers, it had by no means cut him off from the two houses of Congress. To them he could tender information and advice; over their labors he held a qualified but effective veto; at his request they were bound to convene "on extraordinary occasions." He was, in short, to be a strong, dignified, largely nonpolitical chief of state and government.[24]

THE FOUNDING OF THE NATION 209, 526-27 (1957); IV WORKS OF ALEXANDER HAMILTON 227-489, esp. 432-44 (2d ed. H. Lodge 1903).

24 C. ROSSITER, 1787: THE GRAND CONVENTION 221-22 (1966).

Rossiter adds that the framers had in mind not an abstraction as President, but George Washington.

> Washington was not a candidate for this or any other office on earth, but when Dr. Franklin predicted on June 4 that "the first man put at the helm will be a good one," . . . every delegate knew perfectly well who that first good man would be. We cannot measure even crudely the influence of the commanding presence of the most famous and trusted of Americans, yet we may be sure that it was sizable, that it pointed (as we know from Washington's recorded votes) toward unity, strength, and independence in the executive, and that the doubts of some old fashioned Whigs were soothed, if never entirely laid to rest, by the expectation that he would be chosen as first occupant of the proposed Presidency, and chosen and chosen again until claimed by the grave. The powers of the President "are full great," Pierce Butler wrote the following year to a relative in England,

In the field of foreign affairs, Congress too was given far-ranging responsibility. While foreign affairs are not mentioned as such in the Constitution, it is apparent from *The Federalist* (for example, Nos. 64 and 69) that the conduct of diplomatic relations is an exclusively executive function, with the Senate sharing in the process of making treaties, and Congress as a whole entrusted with the legislative dimensions of the problem of making foreign policy. Among the legislative powers bearing on the making and conduct of foreign policy, Article I Section 8 mentions the power to appropriate moneys in providing for the common defense and general welfare; to define and punish piracies and felonies committed on the high seas and offenses against the Law of Nations; to declare war, grant letters of Marque and Reprisal, and make rules concerning captures on land and water; to raise and support armies, subject to the important proviso that no appropriation of money to that use shall be for a longer term than two years; to provide and maintain a Navy; to make rules for the government and regulation of the land and naval forces; to provide for calling forth the militia to execute the laws of the union, suppress insurrections and repel invasions; and to provide for organizing, arming and disciplining the militia, subject to a reservation of authority in the states.

What emerges from the text, and from the discussions available in *The Federalist*, in Farrand, in Madison's notes, and in other contemporaneous sources, is a pattern of shared constitutional authority in this vital area, evoking the memory of tyrannies ancient and modern much in the minds of the Founding Fathers. It is not an hermetic separation of powers, but a scheme of divided power—what Hamilton called an intermixture of powers, the only effective way to prevent a monopoly of power in any one branch of government.

Of this problem, Madison said:

> One of the principal objections inculcated by the more respectable adversaries to the Constitution, is its supposed violation of the political maxim, that the legislative, executive, and judiciary departments ought to be separate and distinct.
>
> . . . .
>
> The accumulation of all powers, legislative, executive, and judiciary, in the same hands, whether of one, a few, or many, and whether hereditary, self-appointed, or elective, may justly be

---

and greater than I was disposed to make them. Nor, entre nous, do I believe they would have been so great had not many of the members cast their eyes towards General Washington as President; and shaped their ideas of powers to be given a President, by their opinions of his virtue.

*Id.*

pronounced the very definition of tyranny. . . . [T]he charge
cannot be supported, and the . . . maxim on which it relies
has been totally misconceived and misapplied.[25]

---

25 THE FEDERALIST No. 47, at 312-13 (Modern Library ed. 1937). Referring to
Montesquieu's famous analysis of the British constitution, and of British experience,
Madison continued:

From these facts, by which Montesquieu was guided, it may clearly be
inferred that, in saying "There can be no liberty where the legislative and
executive powers are united in the same person, or body of magistrates," or, "if
the power of judging be not separated from the legislative and executive powers,"
he did not mean that these departments ought to have no *partial agency* in, or no
*control* over, the acts of each other. His meaning, as his own words import, and
still more conclusively as illustrated by the example in his eye, can amount to
no more than this, that where the *whole* power of one department is exercised
by the same hands which possess the *whole* power of another department, the
fundamental principles of a free constitution are subverted. . . . This, however is
not among the vices of that constitution. The magistrate in whom the whole
executive power resides cannot of himself make a law, though he can put a negative on every law; nor administer justice in person, though he has the appointment
of those who do administer it. The judges can exercise no executive prerogative,
though they are shoots from the executive stock; nor any legislative function,
though they may be advised with by the legislative councils. The entire legislature
can perform no judiciary act, though by the joint act of two of its branches the
judges may be removed from their offices, and though one of its branches is
possessed of the judicial power in the last resort. The entire legislature, again, can
exercise no executive prerogative, though one of its branches constitutes the
supreme executive magistracy, and another, on the impeachment of a third, can
try and condemn all the subordinate officers in the executive department.
*Id.* at 314-15. In another of the Federalist Papers, Madison added:

[U]nless these departments be so far connected and blended as to give to
each a constitutional control over the others, the degree of separation which the
maxim requires, as essential to a free government, can never in practice be duly
maintained.

It is agreed on all sides, that the powers properly belonging to one of the
departments ought not to be directly and completely administered by either of
the other departments. It is equally evident, that none of them ought to possess,
directly or indirectly, an overruling influence over the others, in the administration
of their respective powers. It will not be denied, that power is of an encroaching
nature, and that it ought to be effectually restrained from passing the limits
assigned to it. After discriminating, therefore, in theory, the several classes of
power, as they may in their nature be legislative, executive, or judiciary, the
next and most difficult task is to provide some practical security for each, against
the invasion of the others. What this security ought to be, is the great problem
to be solved.

Will it be sufficient to mark, with precision, the boundaries of these departments, in the constitution of the government, and to trust to these parchment
barriers against the encroaching spirit of power? This is the security which appears
to have been principally relied on by the compilers of most of the American
constitutions. But experience assures us, that the efficacy of the provision has been
greatly overrated; and that some more adequate defence is indispensably necessary
for the more feeble, against the more powerful, members of the government. The
legislative department is everywhere extending the sphere of its activity, and
drawing all power into its impetuous vortex.

The founders of our republics have so much merit for the wisdom which they
have displayed, that no task can be less pleasing than that of pointing out the
errors into which they have fallen. A respect for truth, however, obliges us to
remark, that they seem never for a moment to have turned their eyes from the
danger to liberty from the overgrown and all-grasping prerogative of an hereditary
magistrate, supported and fortified by an hereditary branch of the legislative
authority. They seem never to have recollected the danger from legislative usurpations, which, by assembling all power in the same hands, must lead to the same
tyranny as is threatened by executive usurpations.

In what is probably his finest opinion, Justice Jackson commented on the exercise of their war powers by President and Congress in these terms:

> Just what our forefathers did envision, or would have envisioned had they foreseen modern conditions, must be divined from materials almost as enigmatic as the dreams Joseph was called upon to interpret for Pharaoh. A century and a half of partisan debate and scholarly speculation yields no net result but only supplies more or less apt quotations from respected sources on each side of any question. They largely cancel each other. And court decisions are indecisive because of the judicial practice of dealing with the largest questions in the most narrow way.
>
> The actual art of governing under our Constitution does not and cannot conform to judicial definitions of the power of any of its branches based on isolated clauses or even single Articles torn from context. While the Constitution diffuses power the better to secure liberty, it also contemplates that practice will integrate the dispersed powers into a workable government. It enjoins upon its branches separateness but interdependence, autonomy but reciprocity.[26]

The early years of the nation under the new constitution were a period of acute turbulence which tested the parchment rules of the document in the crucible of intense and sustained experience. The respective authority of Congress and the President with regard to the use

---

... [I]n a representative republic, where the executive magistracy is carefully limited, both in the extent and the duration of its power; and where the legislative power is exercised by an assembly, which is inspired, by a supposed influence over the people, with an intrepid confidence in its own strength; which is sufficiently numerous to feel all the passions which actuate a multitude, yet not so numerous as to be incapable of pursuing the objects of its passions, by means which reason prescribes; it is against the enterprising ambition of this department that the people ought to indulge all their jealousy and exhaust all their precautions.

The legislative department derives a superiority in our governments from other circumstances. Its constitutional powers being at once more extensive, and less susceptible of precise limits, it can, with the greater facility, mask, under complicated and indirect measures, the encroachments which it makes on the coördinate departments. It is not unfrequently a question of real nicety in legislative bodies, whether the operation of a particular measure will, or will not, extend beyond the legislative sphere. On the other side, the executive power being restrained within a narrower compass, and being more simple in its nature, and the judiciary being described by landmarks still less uncertain, projects of usurpation by either of these departments would immediately betray and defeat themselves. Nor is this all: the legislative department alone has access to the pockets of the people, and has in some constitutions full discretion, and in all a prevailing influence, over the pecuniary rewards of those who fill the other departments, a dependence, is thus created in the latter, which gives still greater facility to encroachments of the former.

THE FEDERALIST No. 48, at 321-23 (Modern Library ed. 1937).

26 Youngstown Sheet & Tube Co. v. Sawyer, 343 U.S. 579, 634-35 (1952) (Jackson, J., concurring).

of the armed forces was a matter of active controversy. Several issues of principle were settled not only by the pattern of practice, but by decisions of the Supreme Court as well. The system of ideas that emerged from this period has special weight, since it was produced by the generation of men who had drafted and enacted the Constitution, and launched it on its course. The rules they established have dominated constitutional usage and doctrine ever since.

Among these rules, several are of particular importance to the theory of the Javits Bill. As Hamilton had anticipated, "the actual conduct of foreign negotiations, the preparatory plans of finance, the application and disbursements of the public moneys in conformity to the general appropriations of the legislature, the arrangement of the army and navy, the direction of the operations of war,—these, and other matters of a like nature" were accepted as normal prerogatives of the Presidency.[27] At the other end of the spectrum, it was equally clear that only the Congress can "declare war," appropriate funds, and prescribe rules for governing the armed forces and for calling the militia into national service.

With regard to the actual employment of the armed forces, it is apparent that the term "declare war" in the Constitution referred to the classifications of the law of nations, which makes a sharp distinction between the law of war and the law of peace.[28] The law of nations was

---

[27] THE FEDERALIST No. 72, at 468-69 (Modern Library ed. 1937).

[28] *See, e.g.,* J. BRIERLY, THE LAW OF NATIONS (6th ed. H. Waldock 1963); C. HYDE, INTERNATIONAL LAW (2d rev. ed. 1945); M. McDOUGAL & F. FELICIANO, LAW AND MINIMUM WORLD PUBLIC ORDER, 5-11, 138-43 (1961); L. OPPENHEIM, INTERNATIONAL LAW (8th ed. H. Lauterpacht 1955).

With regard to the construction of the phrase "declare war" in the Constitution, see L. KOTZSCH, THE CONCEPT OF WAR IN CONTEMPORARY HISTORY AND INTERNATIONAL LAW 62 (1956); *1971 Hearings, supra* note 1, at 462-64 (testimony of J. N. Moore); Potter, *The Power of the President of the United States to Utilize its Armed Forces Abroad,* 48 AM. J. INT'L LAW 458 (1954). *See also* Miller v. The Ship Resolution, 2 U.S. (2 Dall.) 19, 21-23 (1781).

Professor Wormuth recognizes that the language of Article I § 8 of the Constitution is addressed to the categories of the law of nations, but claims that under Article I Congress has the complete and exclusive right to initiate all forms of hostility recognized under international law, including, *e.g.,* reprisals. *The Vietnam War: The President versus the Constitution,* Occasional Paper No. 1, Center for the Study of Democratic Institutions (1968), reprinted in 2 THE VIETNAM WAR AND INTERNATIONAL LAW 711, 717-18 (R. Falk ed. 1969) [hereinafter cited as FALK]. This is surely going too far. Professor Wormuth, accepting the Hamiltonian view, acknowledges that the "Constitution recognizes that the power to initiate wars is lodged in two places: in Congress, and in a foreign enemy . . . . When a foreign country attacks the United States, war exists and the President as Commander-in-Chief may and must make—that is, wage—the war." Thus he concedes most of the case he opposes, for most Presidential uses of the armed forces rest on the President's judgment that he is resisting, forestalling, or retaliating against the hostile act of another state, illegal under international law, and directed against the security of the United States. *See, e.g.,* The Prize Cases, 67 U.S. (2 Black) 635, 668, 671 (1863); Durand v. Hollins, 8 F. Cas. 111, 112 (No. 4186) (C.C.S.D.N.Y. 1860); Note, 81 HARV. L. REV. 1771 (1968).

an intimate familiar to the men of the revolutionary generation in America. So far as international law is concerned, nations were then, and are now, free to use force in time of peace by way of self-help against acts or policies of other nations which they deem contrary to international law, and which have remained unredressed after a demand for amends. Different words are used to describe various categories of self-help: retorsion; reprisal; pacific embargoes or blockades; limited intervention to protect nationals; humanitarian intervention to restore order in situations of massacre, natural disaster, or extreme civil disturbance; and others. They are all subsumed under the inherent and sovereign right of self-defense, which has been reenacted in Article 51 of the Charter of the United Nations.[29] In the period before the United Nations, international law also accepted as legal other uses of force which now would be regarded as violating Article 2(4) of the Charter.

It is tempting, but would be incorrect, to suggest, as Hamilton did, that the constitutional allocation of power between President and Congress with respect to the use of the armed forces corresponds to the categories of international law, with the President authorized to use the armed forces as head of state and commander-in-chief in those situations in which international law would acknowledge the use of armed force as permissible self-help in time of peace, while only Congress could move the nation into the juridical world of a state of war, within the meaning of international law. The constitutional pattern is, and should be, more complex than any such formula.

In the formative years of the Republic, Presidents and Congress alike found that the exigencies of diplomacy in a world at war required many uses and threats to use military power which defied simplified classification. When in office, Jefferson, Madison, and Hamilton all discovered that they could not quite live according to the brave rules they had pronounced as theorists of the Constitution. Then, and since, the invocation of force as a tool of national policy ranged from the purely Presidential to the full declaration of war, the latter as rare in the eighteenth century and the early days of the nation as it has been in this century.

In Washington's first administration, Congress passed broad legislation under its power to provide for calling forth the militia to execute the laws of the union, suppress insurrections and repel invasions. These

---

29 D. BOWETT, SELF-DEFENSE IN INTERNATIONAL LAW (1958); F. KALSHOVEN, BELLIGERENT REPRISALS (1971); M. McDOUGAL & F. FELICIANO, *supra* note 28, ch. 3; A. ROSS, THE UNITED NATIONS: PEACE AND PROGRESS ch. 4 (1966); Bowett, *Reprisals Involving Recourse to Armed Force*, 66 AM. J. INT'L LAW 1 (1972) (collecting literature).

early statutes and their application have been little altered by the passage of time, save in their steady enlargement of the President's prerogative. As standing delegations of emergency power, they bespeak the ultimate right of self-preservation which every nation possesses because it is a nation. Jefferson, Fillmore, and Pierce employed the power broadly. Lincoln relied on it during his first anxious months of resisting the Rebellion.[30] Hayes and Cleveland used force in situations of domestic turbulence almost without reference to the militia statutes,[31] exercising inherent Presidential power unaided by legislation, and the Supreme Court upheld what Cleveland did in ringing terms.[32] Truman, Kennedy, and Eisenhower invoked these and cognate statutes during various crises at home and abroad.[33]

In view of current controversies about the constitutionality of congressional "delegations" to the President of the power to use the armed forces, the text of the first militia statute, that of 1789, is significant:

> That for the purpose of protecting the inhabitants of the frontiers of the United States from the hostile incursions of Indians, the President is hereby authorized to call into service from time to time, such part of the militia of the states respectively, as he may judge necessary for the purpose aforesaid.[34]

It was essential for the President to be able to use the militia, since the small Regular Army of the day was fully employed in manning the seacoast and frontier fortifications.[35] Without further action by the Congress, President Washington relied on this statute to call up some militia and undertake military operations against Indian incursions in disputed territory, and beyond.[36]

Under comparably broad legislation authorizing the President to call out the militia in order to enforce the laws of the United States,

---

30 E. CORWIN, THE PRESIDENT: OFFICE AND POWERS 130-33 (4th rev. ed. 1957). The evolution of these statutes can be traced in 10 U.S.C. §§ 331-34, and 3500 (1970).

31 E. CORWIN, *supra* note 30, at 134-35.

32 *In re* Debs, 158 U.S. 564 (1895).

33 Act of June 30, 1950, ch. 445, § 21, 64 Stat. 318, *as amended*, Act of June 15, 1951, ch. 138, § 21, 65 Stat. 87 (Truman during the Korean War, 16 Fed. Reg. 6659 (1951)); 10 U.S.C. §§ 332-34 (1970) (Eisenhower during the desegregation of the Arkansas schools, 22 Fed. Reg. 7628 (1957)); 27 Fed. Reg. 9681, 9693 (1962) (Kennedy during disturbances in Mississippi); 28 Fed. Reg. 5707, 5709, 9861, 9863 (1963) (Kennedy during disturbances in Alabama); Act of Aug. 1, 1961, Pub. L. No. 87-117, § 2, 75 Stat. 242 (Kennedy during the 1961 Berlin crisis, 26 Fed. Reg. 6448 (1961)); Joint Resolution of Oct. 3, 1962, Act of Oct. 3, 1962, Pub. L. No. 87-736, § 2, 76 Stat. 710 (Kennedy during the Cuban Missile Crisis, 27 Fed. Reg. 10403 (1962)).

34 Act of Sept. 29, 1789, ch. 25, § 5, 1 Stat. 95, 96.

35 E. CORWIN, *supra* note 30, at 131.

36 C. BERDHAL, WAR POWERS OF THE EXECUTIVE IN THE UNITED STATES 61-63 (1921); H. WARD, THE DEPARTMENT OF WAR, 1781-1795 (1962); 31 WRITINGS OF WASHINGTON 268 (1939).

President Washington put down the Whiskey Rebellion in Pennsylvania.[37] In that famous and colorful instance of riotous resistance to the revenue laws of the United States in the Western counties of Pennsylvania, President Washington dispatched commissioners of conciliation to negotiate a peaceful and agreed submission of the resisters to "the general will"[38] on the basis of an offer of amnesty. When their mission failed, he led a force of 12,000 to 13,000 men, drawn from the militias of New Jersey, Maryland, Virginia, and Pennsylvania, to see to it that the laws of the United States be faithfully executed. The procedures of Article IV, Section 4, of the Constitution—requiring an application of the state legislature, or the governor, when the legislature cannot be convened, before the national force is used to put down domestic violence—were ignored. Indeed Governor Mifflin of Pennsylvania urged that the use of force be delayed until it could be more conclusively demonstrated that judicial enforcement of the laws in the normal course was impossible.[39]

In *Martin v. Mott*, a case testing the legality of a fine imposed by court-martial against a member of the New York militia who refused to obey an order to rendezvous and enter the national service, the Supreme Court upheld the constitutionality of such statutes. Writing for the Court, Justice Story said:

> In pursuance of this authority, the act of 1795 has provided, "that whenever the United States shall be invaded, or be in imminent danger of invasion from any foreign nation or Indian tribe, it shall be lawful for the President of the United States to call forth such number of the militia of the State or States most convenient to the place of danger, or scene of action, as he may judge necessary to repel such invasion, and to issue his order for that purpose to such officer or officers of the militia as he shall think proper." And like provisions are

---

[37] Act of May 2, 1792, ch. 28, 1 Stat. 264, Section 2 provides:
That whenever the laws of the United States shall be opposed, or the execution thereof obstructed, in any State, by combinations too powerful to be suppressed by the ordinary course of judicial proceedings, or by the powers vested in the Marshals by this act, the same being notified to the President of the United States, by an Associate Justice or the District Judge, it shall be lawful for the President of the United States to call forth the militia of such State to suppress such combinations, and to cause the laws to be duly executed.
The statute provided also, in a provision subsequently dropped, that the President could use the militia in any given case for this purpose until the expiration of thirty days after the commencement of the ensuing session of Congress. See generally L. BALDWIN, WHISKEY REBELS (rev. ed. 1965).
[38] UNITED STATES SENATE, THE PROCEEDINGS OF EXECUTIVE OF THE UNITED STATES RESPECTING THE INSURGENTS, 1794 at 18 (Published by order of the Secretary of the Senate, Philadelphia 1795).
[39] *Id.* at 58-59.

made for the other cases stated in the constitution. It has not been denied here, that the act of 1795 is within the constitutional authority of Congress, or that Congress may not lawfully provide for cases of imminent danger of invasion, as well as for cases where an invasion has actually taken place. In our opinion there is no ground for a doubt on this point, even if it had been relied on, for the power to provide for repelling invasions includes the power to provide against the attempt and danger of invasion, as the necessary and proper means to effectuate the object. One of the best means to repel invasion is to provide the requisite force for action before the invader himself has reached the soil.

The power thus confided by Congress to the President, is, doubtless, of a very high and delicate nature. A free people are naturally jealous of the exercise of military power; and the power to call the militia into actual service is certainly felt to be one of no ordinary magnitude. But it is not a power which can be executed without a correspondent responsibility. It is, in its terms, a limited power, confined to cases of actual invasion, or of imminent danger of invasion. If it be a limited power, the question arises, by whom is the exigency to be judged of and decided? Is the President the sole and exclusive judge whether the exigency has arisen, or is it to be considered as an open question, upon which every officer to whom the orders of the President are addressed, may decide for himself, and equally open to be contested by every militiaman who shall refuse to obey the orders of the President? We are all of opinion, that the authority to decide whether the exigency has arisen, belongs exclusively to the President, and that his decision is conclusive upon all other persons. We think that this construction necessarily results from the nature of the power itself, and from the manifest object contemplated by the act of Congress. The power itself is to be exercised upon sudden emergencies, upon great occasions of state, and under circumstances which may be vital to the existence of the Union. A prompt and unhesitating obedience to orders is indispensable to the complete attainment of the object. The service is a military service, and the command of a military nature; and in such cases, every delay, and every obstacle to an efficient and immediate compliance, necessarily tend to jeopard the public interests. While subordinate officers or soldiers are pausing to consider whether they ought to obey, or are scrupulously weighing the evidence of the facts upon which the commander in chief exercises the right to demand their services, the hostile enterprise may be accomplished without the means of resistance. . . . The power itself is confided to the Executive of the Union, to him who is, by the constitution, "the commander in chief of the militia, when called into the actual service of the United States," whose duty it is to "take care that the laws be faithfully executed," and whose responsibility for an honest discharge of his official obligations is secured by the highest sanctions. He is necessarily constituted the judge of the existence of the exigency in the first instance, and is bound to act according to his belief of the facts. If he does so act, and decides to call forth the militia, his orders for this purpose are in strict conformity with the provisions of the law; and it would seem to follow as a necessary consequence, that every act done by a subordinate officer, in obedience to such orders, is equally justifiable. . . . It is no answer that such a power may be abused, for there is no power which is not susceptible of abuse. The remedy for this, as well as for all other official misconduct, if it should occur, is to be found in the constitution itself. In a free government, the danger must be remote, since in addition to the high qualities which the Executive must be presumed to possess, of public virtue, and honest devotion to the public interests, the frequency of elections, and the watchfulness of the representatives of the nation, carry with them all the checks which can be useful to guard against usurpation or wanton tyranny.[40]

Similarly, early Presidents used their inherent power to deploy the armed forces, without Congressional authorization, to precipitate confrontations with the "piratical" forces of North African states, and, with and without legislation, to combat them as well.[41]

The most notable episode of the period dealing with the distinction between hostilities pursuant to a declaration of war and those the nation could constitutionally undertake in times of peace was the limited war with France, "John Adams' undeclared war," which arose out of French raids on American shipping and the strains and tensions of the Napoleonic Wars.[42] The restraint and prudence of President Adams and of Talleyrand, opposing the forces in both countries pressing for general war, was one of the important factors preventing the full involvement of the United States in the convulsions of the European war. The domestic political controversies swirling about the episode produced the abrogation of the alliance between France and the United States, made John Adams a one-term President, destroyed the Feder-

---

40 Martin v. Mott, 25 U.S. (12 Wheat.) 19, 29-32 (1827). *See* Stewart v. Kahn, 11 Wall. 493, 506 (1870); C. ROSSITER, THE SUPREME COURT AND THE COMMANDER IN CHIEF 11-17 (1951).
41 J. ROGERS, WORLD POLICING AND THE CONSTITUTION 46-47 (America Looks Ahead No. 11, 1945); *1971 Hearings, supra* note 1, at 20 (testimony of Prof. Commager), 352-60 (testimony of Senator Goldwater), 299.
42 A. DECONDE, THE QUASI-WAR 8-10 (1966).

alist Party, and led to the election of Jefferson, and ultimately to the Louisiana Purchase.[43]

Although there were many who advocated a declaration of war against France, the President's resistance brought Congress to the compromise of a series of acts authorizing limited maritime warfare with France.[44] Those statutes did not declare that a state of war existed, in the sense of international law. Such declarations have far-reaching consequences, both in international and domestic law, authorizing many classes of activities otherwise illegal or of doubtful legality, from censorship and blockade to the internment of enemy aliens. They have far-reaching political consequences as well.

The legality of these decisions by the Congress and the President came before the courts in a series of cases concerned with captures at sea and the disposition of prize money. A number of the cases reached the Supreme Court, which decided that the provision of the Constitution regarding declarations of war was not exclusive, but that Congress could authorize hostilities in more restricted ways if it wished to do so. "Congress is empowered to declare a general war," Justice Chase said,

> or congress may wage a limited war; limited in place, in objects, and in time. If a general war is declared, its extent and operations are only restricted and regulated by the *jus belli*, forming a part of the law of nations; but if a partial war is waged, its extent and operation depend on our municipal laws.[45]

The hostilities with France, the Justice declared, were "a limited, partial war," in which Congress had not made France our general enemy: "but this only proves the circumspection and prudence of the legislature."[46] In *Talbot v. Seeman*, a later case dealing with the same subject, Chief Justice Marshall noted with approval that neither side had ventured to claim that hostilities could be authorized only by a declaration of war.[47]

In these early cases the court also sharply defended the civil control

---

[43] *Id.* at 336-38.

[44] Act of May 28, 1798, ch. 48, 1 Stat. 561; Act of June 25, 1798, ch. 60, 1 Stat. 572; Act of July 9, 1798, ch. 68, 1 Stat. 578; Act of March 3, 1799, ch. 45, 1 Stat. 743.

[45] Bas v. Tingy, 4 U.S. (4 Dall.) 37, 43 (1800).

[46] *Id.* at 43-45.

[47] 5 U.S. (1 Cranch) 1, 28-29 (1801). This is the foundation for Undersecretary of State Katzenbach's unassailable judgment that the Tonkin Gulf Resolution was "the functional equivalent" of a declaration of war, so far as the Constitution is concerned, although of course its effects on international politics, and in international law, are quite different. *U.S. Commitments to Foreign Powers, Hearings on S. Res. 151 Before the Senate Committee on Foreign Relations*, 90th Cong., 1st Sess. 71-110, esp. at 82 (1967).

of the military, and held an officer liable, despite authorization from the President, when the President had empowered him to commit an act not covered by the statute authorizing captures at sea.[48]

The constitutional boundaries sketched by this early experience have remained the guidelines of practice ever since. This is not the occasion for yet another full-scale review of the historical exercise of the power to make war by the President, with and without the support of legislation. There are now several compilations of that experience,[49] and a number of scholars have drawn a variety of conclusions from their study of the entrails.[50] Of these studies, I find Professor Moore's and Professor Ratner's the most judicious, but they all deserve examination, in the perspective of Justice Jackson's comment about Pharaoh's dream.

For present purposes, however, I should refer to one of the most important of these affairs, the handling of problems relating to Florida by President Monroe and his astute Secretary of State, John Quincy Adams. No case in the long history of the debate better illustrates the interplay of Presidential and Congressional authority with regard to the use of force, and the relationship between diplomacy and military power. The credentials of Monroe and Adams as exemplars of constitutional propriety in the exercise of their functions are beyond reproach. Their practice can safely be taken, with *Talbot v. Seeman*, as a benchmark of orthodoxy in applying the principles of 1787 to the complexity of the real world.

The decay of the Spanish Empire in America was the dominant foreign policy problem of Monroe's administration.[51] In one dimension, it led to his promulgation of the Monroe Doctrine, in another, to the Transcontinental Treaty of 1819 with Spain, through which Florida was annexed, the disputes over Louisiana resolved, and the western

---

[48] Little v. Barreme, 6 U.S. (2 Cranch) 170 (1804) (per Marshall, C. J.).

[49] J. ROGERS, *supra* note 41; *1971 Hearings, supra* note 1, at 298-316, 359-79.

[50] 1 FALK, *supra* note 28; 2 FALK, *supra* note 28, at 597-836; *1971 Hearings, supra* note 1; *1970 Hearings, supra* note 1. *See also* R. HULL & J. NOVOGROD, LAW AND VIETNAM (1968); R. FALK, THE SIX LEGAL DIMENSIONS OF THE VIETNAM WAR (Research Monograph No. 34, Princeton University Center for International Studies, 1968), reprinted in 2 FALK, *supra* note 28, at 216; Moore & Underwood, *The Lawfulness of United States Assistance to the Republic of Viet-Nam*, 112 CONG. REC. 15519-67 (1966), reprinted in 5 DUQ. L. REV. 235 (1967); Jones, *The President, Congress, and Foreign Relations*, 29 CALIF. L. REV. 565 (1941); Mathews, *The Constitutional Power of the President to Conclude International Agreements*, 64 YALE L.J. 345 (1955); Ratner, *The Coordinated Warmaking Power—Legislative, Executive, and Judicial Roles*, 44 S. CAL. L. REV. 461 (1971); Reveley, *Presidential Warmaking: Constitutional Prerogative or Usurpation?*, 55 VA. L. REV. 1243 (1969).

[51] H. AMMON, JAMES MONROE, THE QUEST FOR NATIONAL IDENTITY ch. 23-24 (1971); S. BEMIS, JOHN QUINCY ADAMS AND THE FOUNDATIONS OF AMERICAN FOREIGN POLICY ch. 15-19 (1949); P. BROOKS, DIPLOMACY AND THE BORDERLANDS, THE ADAMS—ONIS TREATY OF 1819 (1939); J. LOGAN, NO TRANSFER, AN AMERICAN SECURITY PRINCIPLE (1961); B. PERKINS, CASTLEREAGH AND ADAMS (1964).

boundaries of the United States fixed, so far as Spanish claims were concerned.

Monroe's overriding goal was what came to be called the Transcontinental Treaty, and the avoidance of political or military friction that might hinder the negotiations, or precipitate war either with Spain or with Great Britain, Spain's ally in the Napoleonic Wars just concluded at Vienna.

In order to move Spain to accept the path of negotiation, Monroe used both carrots and sticks. With regard to the revolutions in Latin America, he pursued a course of neutrality, despite the overwhelming popular sympathy in the United States for the revolutionaries. He carefully refrained from recognizing the new national regimes in any way until the Treaty was ratified by Spain in 1821, and sought to curb the procurement of supplies and other assistance for the revolutionaries in the United States. In Florida he employed military force twice to convince Spain that her control over Florida had in fact vanished, and that the transfer of the territory to the United States had become inevitable. In a situation of complex rivalry involving Spain, France, and Great Britain, force was used sparingly, and under close restraint, but it was used effectively by the President alone as a tool of his diplomacy.

Amelia Island—Spanish territory in the mouth of St. Mary's River—had been seized from Spain by a Scots adventurer named Gregor McGregor and a Venezuelan patriot named Louis Aury on the pretext of using it as a base for help to Venezuelan revolutionaries. Under their control, Amelia Island was an active base for privateering against Spanish shipping, and also became a haven for smugglers, slave traders, and pirates. A similar establishment had taken over Galveztown.

Monroe sent an expedition to Amelia Island in 1817, clearing out the occupants, and holding the territory without annexing it.[52] He buttressed his authority by referring to a Resolution and Act passed at a secret session of Congress on January 15, 1811, and withheld from publication until April 29, 1818. This legislation, too, constitutes a remarkable example of what some would regard as Congressional "delegation" of legislative power to the executive; I should prefer to regard it as an instance of cooperation between Congress and the Presidency, and the practical pooling of their powers. The Resolution provided:

Taking into view the peculiar situation of Spain, and of

[52] H. Ammon, *supra* note 51, at 412-18, 427-30; S. Bemis, *supra* note 51, at 305-08.

her American provinces; and considering the influence which the destiny of the territory adjoining the southern border of the United States may have upon their security, tranquillity, and commerce: Therefore,

*Resolved by the Senate and House of Representatives of the United States of America, in Congress assembled,* That the United States, under the peculiar circumstances of the existing crisis, cannot, without serious inquietude, see any part of the said territory pass into the hands of any foreign power; and that a due regard to their own safety compels them to provide, under certain contingencies, for the temporary occupation of the said territory; they, at the same time, declare that the said territory shall, in their hands, remain subject to future negotiation.

The statute specified:

*Be it enacted by the Senate and House of Representatives of the United States of America, in Congress assembled,* That the President of the United States be, and he is hereby, authorized, to take possession of, and occupy, all or any part of the territory lying east of the river Perdido, and south of the state of Georgia and the Mississippi territory, in case an arrangement has been, or shall be, made with the local authority of the said territory, for delivering up the possession of the same, or any part thereof, to the United States, or in the event of an attempt to occupy the said territory, or any part thereof, by any foreign government; and he may, for the purpose of taking possession, and occupying the territory aforesaid, and in order to maintain therein the authority of the United States, employ any part of the army and navy of the United States which he may deem necessary.[53]

The United States had occupied West Florida (as far east as the Pearl River) under this authority on the eve of the War of 1812. The international repercussions of this event were so ominous that Monroe, as Madison's Secretary of State, disavowed responsibility.[54] At that point, of course, the inflammatory statute had not been published.

Although it is difficult to suppose that McGregor's regime constituted a "foreign power" or a "foreign government" within the intendment of Congress—indeed the United States had been assured by Great Britain that it would not take over any Spanish Colonies[55]—President Monroe reported to Congress on January 13, 1818:

---

[53] 3 Stat. 471 (1818).
[54] *See* S. BEMIS, *supra* note 51, at 314.
[55] *Id.* at 304.

The path of duty was plain from the commencement, but it was painful to enter upon it while the obligation could be resisted. The law of 1811, lately published, and which it is therefore proper now to mention, was considered applicable to the case from the moment that the proclamation of the chief of the enterprise was seen, and its obligation was daily increased by other considerations of high importance already mentioned, which were deemed sufficiently strong in themselves to dictate the course which has been pursued.[56]

The President carefully put the justification for his action on another ground as well—Spain's inability to exercise effective control over her territory, to prevent its use for purposes hostile to the interests of the United States.

For these injuries, especially those proceeding from Amelia Island, Spain would be responsible if it was not manifest that, though committed in the latter instance through her territory, she was utterly unable to prevent them. Her territory, however, ought not to be made instrumental, through her inability to defend it, to purposes so injurious to the United States. To a country over which she fails to maintain her authority, and which she permits to be converted to the annoyance of her neighbors, her jurisdiction for the time necessarily ceases to exist. The territory of Spain will nevertheless be respected so far as it may de done consistently with the essential interests and safety of the United States.[57]

During the same year as the Amelia Island expedition, Monroe ordered General Andrew Jackson to proceed into Spanish Florida to put down the Seminoles, who were raiding settlements in Georgia from bases in Spanish Florida, with some encouragement and technical assistance from English advisers who may or may not have represented the British government.[58] The President justified his course—without benefit of any statute—under the international law allowing reprisals by way of self-defense in time of peace.

We have seen with regret that her Government has altogether failed to fulfill this obligation, nor are we aware that it made any effort to that effect. When we consider her utter inability

---

[56] 2 J. RICHARDSON, MESSAGES AND PAPERS OF THE PRESIDENTS 24 (1898).

[57] Id. at 24-25.

[58] H. AMMON, supra note 51, at 414-30, 567-69; S. BEMIS, supra note 51, at 313-16, 326, 339. The episode gave rise to a bitter and unresolved controversy about whether Jackson had exceeded his orders, and whether Monroe's disavowal of Jackson's action was an aspect of his own diplomatic tactics. Bemis comments that "Monroe had done this sort of thing more than once before." Id. at 314.

to check, even in the slightest degree, the movements of this tribe by her very small and incompetent force in Florida, we are not disposed to ascribe the failure to any other cause. The inability, however, of Spain to maintain her authority over the territory and Indians within her limits, and in consequence to fulfill the treaty, ought not to expose the United States to other and greater injuries. When the authority of Spain ceases to exist there, the United States have a right to pursue their enemy on a principle of self-defense. In this instance the right is more complete and obvious because we shall perform only what Spain was bound to have performed herself. To the high obligations and privileges of this great and sacred right of self-defense will the movement of our troops be strictly confined.[59]

Monroe was fortunate in that Castlereagh was still British Minister of Foreign Affairs during the second round of the Florida affair. Under Castlereagh, British policy was "to appease controversy and to secure if possible for all states a long interval of repose."[60] Castlereagh had a quite special sense as well of the overriding long-term importance of Anglo-American friendship and collaboration, a subject to which he devoted imaginative attention.[61] Despite the hypersensitive feelings of popular animosity on both sides of the ocean which plagued Anglo-American relations then and for a long time thereafter, Castlereagh was able to pass off Andrew Jackson's invasion of Florida lightly, although Jackson had hanged two Englishmen for inciting the Indians to attack. Sir Charles Webster concludes that "in the delicate question of the Floridas . . . the indefensible conduct of Andrew Jackson in 1819 produced a situation which, in the hands of a diplomatist less zealous in the cause of peace than Castlereagh, would undoubtedly have resulted in war."[62] Our Ambassador in London, Richard Rush, believed that "had the English Cabinet felt and acted otherwise than it did, such was the temper of Parliament and such the feeling of the country [that] *war might have been produced by holding up a finger.*"[63]

Assisted by Castlereagh's forbearance, Monroe's plan had its in-

---

[59] 2 J. RICHARDSON, *supra* note 56, at 31-32.

[60] 2 C. WEBSTER, THE FOREIGN POLICY OF CASTLEREAGH 449 (2d ed. 1934, reprinted 1963).

[61] *Id.* at 437 ("Certainly no other British statesman did more to lay the foundation of the hundred years peace which few in either country at that time expected and certainly many did not desire."). For example, appreciating the depth of anti-British feeling in the United States, and the general American habit of "contentious discussion", as well as Adams' proclivities in that direction, Castlereagh instructed his Ambassadors in Washington to do as much business as possible with the American government through conversations, rather than notes. *Id.* at 438-39. *See* B. PERKINS, *supra* note 51, at 283-98.

[62] C. WEBSTER, *supra* note 60, at 447-48.

[63] *Id.* at 450.

tended result. Spain decided to negotiate, in the hope of avoiding American recognition of the new regimes in South America.[64]

The President's careful course was complicated by the ambitions of several aspirants to the Presidency, including John C. Calhoun, William H. Crawford, and Henry Clay. Clay denounced the invasion of Florida as an act of war by the President in violation of the Constitution,[65] and excoriated Andrew Jackson, whom he rightly viewed as a rival for the Presidency.[66] In the end, however, constitutional attacks in Congress on the President's authority with regard to recognition, the power to deal with territorial claims and annexations by treaty, and the hostilities in Florida were all beaten down.

The earlier history of our foreign affairs is replete with many episodes of comparable import. Without attempting to encapsulate that experience into a formula, it can be said, I believe, that its diversity reflects reasons inherent in the nature of the problem and of our polity. It matches the classification presented by Justice Jackson in his concurring opinion in the *Youngstown Sheet and Tube Co.* case:

> Presidential powers are not fixed but fluctuate, depending upon their disjunction or conjunction with those of Congress. We may well begin by a somewhat over-simplified grouping of practical situations in which a President may doubt, or others may challenge, his powers, and by distinguishing roughly the legal consequences of this factor of relativity.
> 1. When the President acts pursuant to an express or implied authorization of Congress, his authority is at its maximum, for it includes all that he possesses in his own right plus all that Congress can delegate. In these circumstances, and in these only, may he be said (for what it may be worth) to personify the federal sovereignty. If his act is held unconstitutional under these circumstances, it usually means that the Federal Government as an undivided whole lacks power. A seizure executed by the President pursuant to an Act of Congress would be supported by the strongest of presumptions and the widest latitude of judicial interpretation, and the burden of persuasion would rest heavily upon any who might attack it.
> 2. When the President acts in absence of either a congressional grant or denial of authority, he can only rely upon his own independent powers, but there is a zone of twilight in which he and Congress may have concurrent authority, or in

---

64 S. BEMIS, *supra* note 51, at 308.
65 *Id.* at 315.
66 H. AMMON, *supra* note 51, at 422; S. BEMIS, *supra* note 51, at 315.

which its distribution is uncertain. Therefore, congressional inertia, indifference or quiescence may sometimes, at least as a practical matter, enable, if not invite, measures on independent presidential responsibility. In this area, any actual test of power is likely to depend on the imperatives of events and contemporary imponderables rather than on abstract theories of law.

3. When the President takes measures incompatible with the expressed or implied will of Congress, his power is at its lowest ebb, for then he can rely only upon his own constitutional powers minus any constitutional powers of Congress over the matter. Courts can sustain exclusive presidential control in such a case only by disabling the Congress from acting upon the subject. Presidential claim to a power at once so conclusive and preclusive must be scrutinized with caution, for what is at stake is the equilibrium established by our constitutional system.[67]

The United States has used its armed forces abroad more than 150 times since 1789, and on many more occasions the President has threatened to use force. A declaration of "solemn war," fully invoking the international law of war, has been issued on only five occasions. Some of the remaining uses of force or the threat of force were undertaken pursuant to Congressional authority, although the experts debate about how many were actually responsive to prior Congressional action. In the rest, including some costly and extended campaigns, the President acted, formally at least, on his own constitutional authority.

A number of lists have been compiled, reaching different conclusions as to the number of episodes of hostilities in time of peace actually authorized in any meaningful sense by statute.[68] Naturally, any President will seek to invoke a statute as partial justification for his use of armed force, as Monroe did in 1818. But in many of these cases, the statute was in fact only vaguely and imperfectly linked to the event. Professor James Grafton Rogers, in his pioneer study of the subject, reached the conclusion that there were "only a dozen or two" instances of undeclared war possibly authorized by legislation.[69] In the most recent compilation of this kind, Senator Goldwater lists 153 military actions taken by the United States abroad without a declaration of war, of which he claims 63 were "arguably" initiated under prior legislative authority, 34 under a treaty, 26 under legislation, and, in the

---

67 343 U.S. 579, 635-38 (1952).
68 *See* note 50 *supra*.
69 J. ROGERS, *supra* note 41, at 79.

case of Samoa in 1888-89 and 1899, Lebanon in 1958, and Vietnam, both under a treaty and under legislation implementing it.[70] Arguably, one could count the Cuban Missile Crisis of 1962 in this final category as well, although it is more realistic to classify that incident as an example of a use of force by the President alone.[71]

These lists include major events: Commodore Perry's expedition to Japan and those which followed it; the array of 50,000 troops in Texas during 1865 and 1866 to support our diplomatic suggestion that France withdraw from Mexico; the participation of American forces in the hostilities following the Boxer Rebellion in China in 1900-01; the suppression of revolt in the Philippines between 1899 and 1901; the hostilities with Mexico, between 1914 and 1917; the deployments and uses of force by Wilson and Franklin Roosevelt before both World Wars; and the occupations of Haiti, the Dominican Republic, and Nicaragua, to note only the more conspicuous.

This brief evocation of history suggests two conclusions.

First, the pattern against which the Javits Bill protests is old, familiar, and rooted in the nature of things. There is nothing constitutionally illegitimate or even dubious about "undeclared" wars. We and other nations fought them frequently in the eighteenth and nineteenth centuries, as well as in the twentieth. The charge that the practice is an unconstitutional invention of this century, or of Presidents McKinley, Wilson, Franklin Roosevelt, Truman, Kennedy, and Johnson is a myth.

In the development of the foreign relations power of the United States, and of the respective roles of President and of Congress in making foreign policy, and carrying it out, it is clear that certain functions are exclusively those of the President: for example, the power to negotiate with foreign nations; the power to recognize foreign governments; and the power to deploy troops, to command them in hostilities, and to conclude an armistice. Certain authority is shared between Congress and the President; for instance, the power to issue a declaration of neutrality. President Washington proclaimed our neutrality in 1793, after a considerable constitutional debate over his authority to do so in the absence of legislation on the subject. But a confirmatory statute was passed the next year. Congress has passed other neutrality statutes from time to time, and no President has claimed that they were unconstitutional. Only Congress can declare that a "formal" or "solemn" state of war exists; provide for calling up the militia; make rules concerning

---

70 *1971 Hearings, supra* note 1, at 359-79.
71 *See* p. 839 & note 12 *supra*.

captures on land and water, and for the government and regulation of the armed forces; and appropriate funds for the armed forces.

Congress has the last word on matters of peace and war, but the President's authority goes far beyond that to repel sudden attacks, the example Madison gave to illustrate the desirability of changing the language in Article I Section 8 from "make war" to "declare war." As Professor Ratner says:

> But preeminent war-peace authority is not necessarily exclusive war-peace authority, although that congruence has been suggested by some executive and judicial statements. The ultimate decider should not always be the initial decider. Congressional action takes time. Invariably, the President confronts the problem first; may he as commander-in-chief order American forces to fight without waiting for congressional authorization?
>
> The Constitutional Convention suggested the answer by approving the motion of Madison and Gerry to amend the congressional power by "insert[ing] 'declare,' striking out 'make' war; leaving to the Executive the power to repel sudden attacks"—though the explanatory clause was not included in the constitutional text nor given the scrutiny of proposed inclusion. That clause thus recognized, but did not authoritatively delineate, the war-making authority of the President, implied by his role as executive and commander-in-chief and by congressional power to declare, but not make, war.
>
> In 1787, "repel sudden attack" probably meant "resist invasion or rebellion." But constitutional policy for ensuing epochs is not congealed in the mold of 1787 referants. Such policy is derived from the long-range goals that underlie the constitutional language as illuminated by the Convention proceedings, from the implications of the language disclosed by resolution of subsequent problems, and from its function in the context of altered social needs. Aggression beyond the seas could not threaten Americans in the eighteenth century as it can in the twentieth. Underlying the constitutional language and the explanatory clause is a long-range purpose that authorizes the President to protect Americans from external force in an emergency.

Listing eight categories of purely Presidential use of force in time of peace under circumstances recognized as legitimate by international law, Ratner concludes:

> The amorphous distinction between offense and defense does not effectively delineate the scope of the President's emergency war power. In a world where increasingly mobile weapons enhance the advantage of military initiative, the

distinction turns, for the most part, on an appraisal of motives and intentions. With his heavy load of responsibility, the President may sometimes conclude that offense is the best defense. As the foregoing examples indicate, presidentially-authorized hostilities are always ostensibly "defensive." And, though his characterization may be debatable, the President must necessarily be accorded a broad discretion.[72]

As to sustained hostilities in the absence of a declaration of war, the pattern of constitutional practice offers no sharp and formal lines. There are instances of Congressional action to authorize undeclared wars, and instances in which, nominally at least, Congress was silent. The practice, however, does justify a second general conclusion: It is an illusion to suppose, in the nature of our political system, that the formal silence of Congress on some of these occasions when force was used extensively represents a genuine opposition between Congress and the Presidency. The power of the United States to employ force or to carry on any other sustained policy can be exercised in fact only when Congress and the President cooperate, however unwillingly. The silences and the tacit arrangements of American politics are often more important than its nominal dispositions and documents.

In the closing days of his second Administration, for example, Cleveland, repudiated by his party, was functioning as a lame-duck President, waiting to transfer his office to McKinley. Congress, meanwhile, exercised by the revolution in Cuba and no doubt emboldened by the inherent weakness of the President's position, took a number of initiatives.

The Senate Foreign Relations Committee let it be known that it was proposing to report out the Cameron Resolution, which purported to recognize the independence of the Republic of Cuba. Cleveland's redoubtable Secretary of State, Richard Olney, commented:

> It is, perhaps, my duty to point out that the resolution, if passed by the Senate, can probably be regarded only as an expression of opinion by the eminent gentlemen who voted for it in the Senate, and if passed by the House of Representatives, can only be regarded as another expression of opinion by the eminent gentlemen who vote for it in the House.
>
> The power to recognize the so-called Republic of Cuba as an independent state rests exclusively with the Executive.
>
> A resolution on the subject by the Senate or by the House, by both bodies or by one, whether concurrent or joint, is

---

72 Ratner, *supra* note 50, at 466-69.

inoperative as legislation, and is important only as advice of great weight voluntarily tendered to the Executive regarding the manner in which he shall exercise his constitutional functions.

The operation and effect of the proposed resolution, therefore, even if passed by both houses of Congress by a two-thirds vote, are perfectly plain. It may raise expectations in some quarters which can never be realized. It may inflame popular passions, both in this country and elsewhere; may thus put in peril the lives and property of American citizens who are resident and traveling abroad, and will certainly obstruct and perhaps defeat the best efforts of this Government to afford such citizens due protection.

But except in these ways, and unless the advice embodied in the resolution shall lead the Executive to revise conclusions already reached and officially declared, the resolution will be without effect and will leave unaltered the attitude of this Government toward the two contending parties in Cuba.[73]

The Cameron Resolution was reported out of Committee, but never put to a vote.

In the same period, a number of Congressional leaders called on President Cleveland to discuss an "important matter." They said,

"We have about decided to declare war against Spain over the Cuban question. Conditions are intolerable."

Mr. Cleveland drew himself up and said, "There will be no war with Spain over Cuba while I am President."

One of the members flushed up and said angrily, "Mr. President, you seem to forget that the Constitution of the United States gives Congress the right to declare war."

He answered, "Yes, but it also makes me Commander-in-Chief, and I will not mobilize the army. I happen to know that we can buy the Island of Cuba from Spain for $100,000,000, and a war will cost vastly more than that and will entail another long list of pensioners. It would be an outrage to declare war."[74]

The project died.

On the other side of the coin, the formal arrangements for carrying on the Korean War give a misleading impression. When South Korea was invaded in 1950, President Truman met several times with the Congressional leadership, as is customary, to consult with them about policy. As Dean Acheson reports the meeting of June 30:

---

[73] H. JAMES, RICHARD OLNEY AND HIS PUBLIC SERVICE 168-69 (1923).
[74] 2 R. MCELROY, GROVER CLEVELAND, THE MAN AND THE STATESMAN 249-50 (1923).

At eleven o'clock I returned to the White House for a meeting with congressional leaders, taking Foster Dulles, just back from Tokyo, with me. The congressional group was perhaps twice as large as the one at the Tuesday meeting. The President reported the situation in Korea, reviewed the actions previously taken by the United Nations Security Council and the United States Government, and the orders he had issued that morning. A general chorus of approval was interrupted by, I think, Senator Kenneth Wherry questioning the legal authority of the executive to take this action. Senator Alexander Smith suggested a congressional resolution approving the President's action. The President said that he would consider Smith's suggestion and asked me to prepare a recommendation. The meeting ended with Representative Dewey Short stating that Congress was practically unanimous in its appreciation of the President's leadership. Short was a Republican from the President's home state of Missouri and ranking minority member of the Armed Services Committee.[75]

After this meeting, according to Dean Acheson's recollection, Senator Taft, the Republican leader in the Senate, offered to support any Resolution the President should propose to put Congress firmly on record behind his actions, and those of the Security Council.[76]

A draft Resolution was prepared. Senator Smith asked for a delay while he took care of some urgent political problems in New Jersey. Acheson's account continues:

My recommendation was that the President make a full report on the Korean situation to a joint session of Congress. This would, of course, be largely formal but would bring the whole story together in one official narrative and meet the objection of some members that information had come to them only through the leaders and the press. I also recommended that the President should not ask for a resolution of approval, but rest on his constitutional authority as Commander-in-chief of the armed forces. However, we had drafted a resolution commending the action taken by the United States that would be acceptable if proposed by members of Congress.

In the ensuing discussion it appeared that the two houses of Congress had just recessed for a week and the President was unwilling to call them back. Senator Lucas, General Bradley, and Secretary Johnson were opposed to both recommendations: to the report because it would come too long after the events to stand by itself and had better accompany a request

75 D. Acheson, Present at the Creation 413 (1969).
76 Conversations of author with Dean Acheson, 1953, 1967.

for money and necessary powers; and to the resolution because the vast majority in Congress were satisfied and the irreconcilable minority could not be won over. They could, however, keep debating and delaying a resolution so as to dilute much of its public effect. The others were divided. My sympathies lay with the Lucas-Bradley view. So apparently did the President's, for he put off a decision until the "Big Four" (the presiding officers and majority leaders of both houses) would be back after the recess. By then we were pretty well won over to Senator Lucas' view.

There has never, I believe, been any serious doubt—in the sense of nonpolitically inspired doubt—of the President's constitutional authority to do what he did. The basis for this conclusion in legal theory and historical precedent was fully set out in the State Department's memorandum of July 3, 1950, extensively published. . . . But the wisdom of the decision not to ask for congressional approval has been doubted. To have obtained congressional approval, it has been argued, would have obviated later criticism of "Truman's war." In my opinion, it would have changed pejorative phrases, but little else. Congressional approval did not soften or divert the antiwar critics of Presidents Lincoln, Wilson, and Roosevelt. What inspired the later criticism of the Korean war was the long, hard struggle, casualties, cost, frustration of a limited and apparently inconclusive war, and—most of all—the determination of the opposition to end seemingly interminable Democratic rule.

Nevertheless, it is said, congressional approval would have done no harm. True, approval would have done none, but the process of gaining it might well have done a great deal. July—and especially the first part of it—was a time of anguishing anxiety. As American troops were committed to battle, they and their Korean allies under brutal punishment staggered back down the peninsula until they maintained only a precarious hold on the coastal perimeter around Pusan. An incredulous country and world held its breath and read the mounting casualties suffered by these gallant troops, most of them without combat experience. In the confusion of the retreat even their divisional commander, Major General William F. Dean, was captured. Congressional hearings on a resolution of approval at such a time, opening the possibility of endless criticism, would hardly be calculated to support the shaken morale of the troops or the unity that, for the moment, prevailed at home. The harm it could do seemed to me far to outweigh the little good that might ultimately accrue.

The President agreed, moved also, I think, by another passionately held conviction. His great office was to him a sacred and temporary trust, which he was determined to pass on unimpaired by the slightest loss of power or prestige. This attitude would incline him strongly against any attempt to divert criticism from himself by action that might establish a precedent in derogation of presidential power to send our forces into battle. The memorandum that we prepared listed eighty-seven instances in the past century in which his predecessors had done this. And thus yet another decision was made.[77]

This experience did not prevent Senator Taft, at a later date, from attacking the constitutionality of Truman's decision to fight in Korea under his authority as President to ensure that the treaties of the United States be faithfully executed as the supreme law of the land.[78]

## III. THE IMMEDIATE CONTEXT OF THE JAVITS BILL

The modern controversies over the division of constitutional authority between Congress and the President with respect to military operations have a special intensity, which reflects the scale of American involvement in world politics since 1940, and the shock and controversy resulting from Korea and Vietnam.

Of course the nation faces foreign policy problems today altogether different from those it faced in 1800, or even in 1900. Between 1815 and 1914, we lived safely within a system of general peace maintained by the Concert of Europe. Our diplomacy, while active, was peripheral to the overriding problem of maintaining the balance of power which allowed the entire world to enjoy an extraordinary century without large scale war. That system broke down in 1914, and collapsed finally in 1945, imposing on the United States for the first time direct responsibility for protecting its primal security as a nation by direct and continuous involvement in world politics.

It does not follow that we live in a world where Presidential primacy in the making of American foreign policy is inevitable, or desirable. All but a few believe that under the Constitution Congress should play an active, responsible, and indeed the ultimate role in making foreign policy. Certainly I am no friend of unlimited Presidential discretion to decide when the nation should go to war.

---

77 D. ACHESON, *supra* note 75, at 414-15. *See also* 2 H. TRUMAN, MEMOIRS, YEARS OF TRIAL AND HOPE 331-48, 409-10, 420-26, 478 (1956).
78 Taft, *The Place of the President and Congress in Foreign Policy,* in A FOREIGN POLICY FOR AMERICANS ch. 2 (1951), reprinted in *1970 Hearings, supra* note 1, at 557.

The circumstances of modern world politics, however, require Presidents to act quickly, and often alone. They continue to face the delicate problems of diplomatic judgment which John Adams confronted in seeking to protect American shipping without full scale war with France; which Madison and Monroe faced in trying to solve the problem of Florida without precipitating war with Spain or England; which Cleveland met in seeking to avoid war with Spain over Cuba; and comparable dilemmas which have plagued nearly all our Presidents.

That fact does not preclude the possibility of effective cooperation between Congress and the President. Congress should be able to act effectively both before and after moments of crisis or potential crisis. It may join the President in seeking to deter crises by publicly defining national policy in advance, through the sanctioning of treaties or other legislative declarations. Equally, Congress may participate formally in policymaking after the event through legislative authorization of sustained combat, either by means of a declaration of war, or through legislative action having more limited legal and political consequences. Either of these devices, or both in combination, should be available in situations where cooperation between the two branches is indicated at many points along an arc ranging from pure diplomacy at one end to a declaration of war at the other.

The constitutional storm which has given rise to the Javits Bill began shortly after the Korean War. As noted earlier, the United States acted formally in Korea under the United Nations Charter, viewed as a Treaty of the United States, and under the President's inherent constitutional powers in carrying out that Treaty obligation, without benefit of a formal, direct vote by Congress.

The legal posture of American intervention in Korea aroused genuine constitutional concern.[79] There was anxiety at the apparent authority of the Security Council, an international body sitting in New York, to take a vote that would bind the United States to go to war —concern about sovereignty, and concern, too, about the seemingly unlimited powers of the President in relation to those of the Congress. There was, of course, repeated Congressional support for various aspects of the Korean War and for the war itself through appropriations statutes and otherwise. But the war became unpopular and was a decisive factor both in Truman's decision not to seek a second term and in the elections of 1952.

---

[79] See pp. 867-870 & note 77 *supra*.

Although Senator Bricker's proposals for a constitutional amendment failed, President Eisenhower responded to the outcry by developing the practice of making many treaties embodying national security commitments, and obtaining Congressional Resolutions authorizing him to employ the armed forces in the Mediterranean, and the Formosa Straits, a practice pursued thereafter with regard to Berlin, Cuba, and Vietnam.[80] These formal modes of cooperation between Congress and the Presidency constitute the immediate legal context of our involvement in Vietnam, and of the debates which have resulted in the Javits Bill.

From the point of view of the constitutional argument over the respective war powers of the President and Congress, our engagement in Vietnam rests first on the South East Asia Collective Defense Treaty, generally known as SEATO. The Treaty was negotiated and ratified shortly after the Geneva Conference of 1954, as part of a general strategy of containing the consequences of French defeat in Indo-China, and limiting the outward thrust of Communist bids for power in Malaysia, the Philippines, and Korea, as well as in Indo-China.[81] Under that Treaty, the United States, Australia, France, New Zealand, Pakistan, the Philippines, Thailand, and the United Kingdom became guarantors against direct and indirect aggression not only for the three non-communist successor states of French Indo-China, but for South East Asia as a whole.

In the preamble to the Treaty, the signatories declared their sense of unity publicly and formally, as notice to "any potential aggressor" in the area. In Article II, they undertook, "separately and jointly," to "maintain and develop their individual and collective capacity to resist armed attack and to prevent and counter subversive activities

---

80 See note 9 supra. President Johnson has said,
I was determined, from the time I became President, to seek the fullest support of Congress for any major action that I took, whether in foreign affairs or in the domestic field. I believed that President Truman's one mistake in courageously going to the defense of South Korea in 1950 had been his failure to ask Congress for an expression of its backing. He could have had it easily, and it would have strengthened his hand. I had made up my mind not to repeat that error, but always to follow the advice I myself had given President Eisenhower.
L. JOHNSON, supra note 13, at 115 (1971).
In the event, of course, Dean Acheson's judgment, pp. 868-870 supra turned out to rest on a more realistic appreciation of human fallibility. "Johnson's War" joined "Truman's War" and "John Adams' Undeclared War" in the demonology of American politics. In 1964 and 1965, Johnson often said that he knew that if he wanted Congress with him at the landing, it should be with him at the take-off. He remarked later that he had not counted on the availability of parachutes.
81 Southeast Asia Collective Defense Treaty, Sept. 8, 1954, [1955] 1 U.S.T. 81, T.I.A.S. No. 3170. See C. COOPER, THE LOST CRUSADE: AMERICA IN VIETNAM (1970); R. RANDLE, GENEVA 1954 (1969).

directed from without against their territorial integrity and political stability." The first paragraph of Article IV provides that *"each* party recognizes that aggression by means of armed attack in the treaty area against any of the Parties" (or against states or territories designated in the protocol to the Treaty, which lists Laos, Cambodia, and what is now South Vietnam, if they choose to be protected) "would endanger its own peace and safety, and agrees that *it will* in that event act to meet the common danger in accordance with its constitutional processes" (italics added). In contrast to the individual and categorical obligation of paragraph 1, paragraph 2 provides that if threats or problems other than armed attacks arise, "the Parties shall consult immediately in order to agree on the measures which should be taken for the common defense."[82]

While SEATO has had a checkered history as an international organization, the Treaty did put the United States squarely into the Southeast Asian picture. As Chester Cooper points out, "it was a commitment, albeit one considerably less robust than was originally conceived, to involve the United States in the security and economic development of the countries in that area—a part of the world which until 1954 had been pretty much left to the British and the French."[83]

The United States government has based its policy in Vietnam on the SEATO Treaty, as well as on South Vietnam's inherent right of self-defense, and our right under the U.N. Charter to assist South Vietnam in that defense.[84] For example, President Eisenhower noted in

---

[82] For the formal relation between SEATO and the Geneva arrangements see R. RANDLE, *supra* note 81, at 539-41.

[83] C. COOPER, *supra* note 81, at 114.

[84] In the perspective of international law, two related arguments are raised against the American course in Vietnam:—(1) the Vietnamese war is a civil war, internal to the conceptual state, or nation, of "Vietnam"; and (2) the North Vietnamese attack on South Vietnam is justified because no referendum on unifying North and South Vietnam was held in 1956, as contemplated by the Declaration issued at the end of the Geneva Conference in 1954.

The war in Vietnam is not a civil war, but an international war. Two Vietnamese states emerged from the Geneva Conference, and the years of fighting which preceded it. It was clearly understood at Geneva that Vietnam, like Germany and Korea, was a nation divided against its will by the circumstances of the Cold War, and that its reunification, like that of Germany and Korea, would have to come through political agreement, not war.

C. COOPER, *supra* note 81, at 98, 100; R. RANDLE, *supra* note 81, at 429, 444-46. North and South Vietnam are political entities—two states within a single nation, to borrow Chancellor Brandt's phrase—entitled to all the normal rights of states, and entitled also to the protection of the United Nations Charter.

This protection was not suspended by the unsigned Declaration issued at the end of the Geneva Conference—a document that had even nominal support only from four of the nine participants in the Conference. That document cannot authorize North Vietnam to attack South Vietnam, or, if one prefers, to assist revolutionaries within South Vietnam, because no referendum on the possible unification of the two states was held in 1956. South Vietnam did not accept the Declaration of Geneva, and the United States formally

a formal statement in 1957 that South Vietnam is covered by the Treaty, and said "that aggression or subversion threatening the political independence of the Republic of Vietnam would be considered as endangering peace and stability" within the meaning of that document.[85] The theme has been sounded in official speeches and statements ever since. Both Congress and four Presidents have repeatedly concluded that North Vietnam's participation in the war against South Vietnam constitutes "armed attack" within the meaning of Article IV of the Treaty.

The commitment of SEATO was later reiterated, so far as the United States is concerned, in the Tonkin Gulf Resolution, passed in 1964. That Resolution, which has since become a matter of considerable controversy, says:

> The United States regards as vital to its national interest and to world peace the maintenance of international peace and security in southeast asia. Consonant with the Constitution of the United States and the Charter of the United Nations and in accordance with its obligations under the Southeast Asia Collective Defense Treaty, the United States is, therefore, prepared, as the President determines, to take all necessary steps, including the use of armed force, to assist any member of protocol state of the Southeast Asia Collective Defense Treaty requesting assistance in defense of its freedom.[86]

The Resolution stated the full support and approval of Congress for the President to take all necessary measures to protect our own forces, "and to prevent further aggression."

In a colloquy with Senator Cooper, Senator Fulbright explained that the passage of this Resolution fulfilled the provision of the SEATO Treaty requiring each nation to carry out its obligations under the

refused to adhere to it. In any event, the failure to hold such elections, or otherwise to unify the two halves of a divided country by political means, could hardly justify its unification by force, even where unification has been promised by the Great Powers, as is the case for Korea and Germany as well as Vietnam. This is precisely what the Security Council decided in 1950 when it held that North Korea had violated the Charter by attacking South Korea; that South Korea was therefore justified in exercising its inherent rights of self-defense assured by Article 51 of the Charter; and that other nations were allowed—indeed required—to assist South Korea collectively in that defense. *See* E. ROSTOW, PEACE IN THE BALANCE ch. 5 (1972, in press); E. ROSTOW, LAW, POWER AND THE PURSUIT OF PEACE 60-67 (1968). For further examination of the justification for American policy in Vietnam as a matter of international law, see J. MOORE, LAW AND INDOCHINA WAR (1972); and materials cited in notes 28 & 50 *supra*.

85 Foreign Policy and Foreign Aid, 36 DEP'T STATE BULL. 851, 852 (1957). *See also* Address by President Eisenhower, The Importance of Understanding, 40 DEP'T STATE BULL. 579-83 (1959); SENATE COMM. ON FOREIGN RELATIONS, BACKGROUND INFORMATION RELATING TO SOUTHEAST ASIA AND VIETNAM, 91st Cong., 2d Sess. 184-91, 208-14, 218-35 (Comm. Print 6th rev. ed. 1970).

86 H.R.J. Res. of Aug. 10, 1964, Pub. L. No. 88-408, § 2, 78 Stat. 384. Section 3 of the Resolution provides that it may be terminated by concurrent resolution of the Congress.

Treaty through its own constitutional processes. That exchange is so central to the present debate as to require its full reproduction here:

MR. COOPER. I ask these questions for two reasons: One is to get the opinion of the chairman of the Foreign Relations Committee and of the chairman of the Armed Services Committee as to the extent of the powers that are given to the President under the resolution. The second is to distinguish between a situation in which we act in defense of our own forces, in which without question we would risk war, and the commitment to defend South Vietnam.

My first question goes to the first section of the resolution —the operative part which, as the chairman has said, applies to any armed attack or any aggression directed against the forces of the United States.

MR. FULBRIGHT. That is correct.

MR. COOPER. In that case, of course, we confirm the power that the President now has to defend our forces against an immediate attack.

MR. FULBRIGHT. The Senator is a very distinguished lawyer, and I therefore hesitate to engage in a discussion with him on the separation of powers and the powers of the President. We are not giving to the President any powers he has under the Constitution as Commander in Chief. We are in effect approving of his use of the powers that he has. That is the way I feel about it.

MR. COOPER. I understand that, too. In the first section we are confirming the powers.

MR. FULBRIGHT. We are approving them. I do not know that we give him anything that he does not already have. Perhaps we are quibbling over words.

MR. COOPER. We support and approve his judgment.

MR. RUSSELL. Approve and support.

MR. FULBRIGHT. Approve and support the use he has made of his powers.

MR. COOPER. The second section of the resolution goes, as the Senator said, to steps the President might take concerning the parties to the Southeast Asia Collective Defense Treaty and the countries under the protocol—which are, of course, Laos, Cambodia, and South Vietnam. The Senator will remember that the SEATO Treaty, in article IV, provides that in the event an armed attack is made upon a party to the Southeast Asia Collective Defense Treaty, or upon one of the protocol states such as South Vietnam, the parties to the treaty, one of whom is the United States, would then take such action as might be appropriate, after resorting to their constitutional processes. I assume that would mean, in the case of the United

States, that Congress would be asked to grant the authority to act.

Does the Senator consider that in enacting this resolution we are satisfying that requirement of article IV of the Southeast Asia Collective Defense Treaty? In other words, are we now giving the President advance authority to take whatever action he may deem necessary respecting South Vietnam and its defense, or with respect to the defense of any other country included in the treaty?

MR. FULBRIGHT. I think that is correct.

MR. COOPER. Then, looking ahead, if the President decided that it was necessary to use such force as could lead into war, we will give that authority by this resolution?

MR. FULBRIGHT. That is the way I would interpret it. If a situation later developed in which we thought the approval should be withdrawn, it could be withdrawn by concurrent resolution. That is the reason for the third section.

MR. COOPER. I ask these questions—

MR. FULBRIGHT. The Senator is properly asking these questions.

MR. COOPER. I ask these questions because it is well for the country and all of us to know what is being undertaken.

Following up the question I have just asked and the Senator's answer, I present two situations that might arise.

Under the first section of the joint resolution, the President is supported and approved in action he may take "to repel any armed attack against the forces of the United States and to prevent further aggression."

It has been reported that we have already sent our planes against certain ports in North Vietnam. I am sure that the reason is "to repel armed attack and to prevent further aggression" against U.S. forces.

Under section 2, are we now providing the President, if he determines it necessary, the authority to attack cities and ports in North Vietnam, not primarily to prevent an attack upon our forces but, as he might see fit, to prevent any further aggression against South Vietnam?

MR. FULBRIGHT. One of the reasons for the procedure provided in this joint resolution, and also in the Formosa and Middle East instances, is in response, let us say, to the new developments in the field of warfare. In the old days, when war usually resulted from a formal declaration of war—and that is what the Founding Fathers contemplated when they included that provision in the Constitution—there was time in which to act. Things moved slowly, and things could be seen developing. Congress could participate in that way.

Under modern conditions of warfare—and I have tried to

describe them, including the way the Second World War developed—it is necessary to anticipate what may occur. Things move so rapidly that this is the way in which we must respond to the new developments. That is why this provision is necessary or important. Does the Senator agree with me that this is so?

MR. COOPER. Yes, warfare today is different. Time is of the essence. But the power provided the President in section 2 is great.

MR. FULBRIGHT. This provision is intended to give clearance to the President to use his discretion. We all hope and believe that the President will not use this discretion arbitrarily or irresponsibly. We know that he is accustomed to consulting with the Joint Chiefs of Staff and with congressional leaders. But he does not have to do that.

MR. COOPER. I understand, and believe that the President will use this vast power with judgment.

MR. FULBRIGHT. He intends to do it, and he has done it.

MR. COOPER. I do not wish to take more time now, because the distinguished Senator from Georgia wishes to speak, and I want to hear him.

MR. FULBRIGHT. I have no doubt that the President will consult with Congress in case a major change in present policy becomes necessary.

MR. COOPER. I will speak further later in the day. I wish to say this now: I know it is understood and agreed that in the defense of our own ships and forces any action we might take to repel attacks could lead to war, if the Vietnamese or the Chinese Communists continued to engage in attacks against our forces. I hope they will be deterred by the prompt action of the President.

We accept this first duty of security and honor. But I would feel untrue to my own convictions if I did not say that a different situation obtains with respect to South Vietnam. I know that a progression of events for 10 years has carried us to this crisis. Ten years have passed and perhaps the events are inevitable now, no one can tell. But as long as there is hope and the possibility of avoiding with honor a war in southeast Asia—a conflagration which, I must say, could lead into war with Communist China, and perhaps to a third world war with consequences one can scarcely contemplate today—I hope the President will use this power wisely with respect to our commitments in South Vietnam, and that he will use all other honorable means which may be available, such as consultations in the United Nations, and even with the Geneva powers.

We have confidence in the President and in his good judgment. But I believe we have the obligation of understanding fully that there is a distinction between defending our own forces, and taking offensive measures in South Vietnam which could lead progressively to a third world war.

MR. FULBRIGHT. The question concerns the kind of actions taken in this instance. I think the President took action that is designed to accomplish the objective the Senator from Kentucky has stated. That is what I have tried to make clear. I join in the Senator's hope that all-out war can be avoided.[87]

Whether Congressional action of this kind is necessary under the American Constitution, or whether the President can properly act alone in carrying out Treaty obligations, as President Truman did in Korea, remains a matter for debate. As Senator Cooper writes in his candid and thoughtful statement of Individual Views with respect to the Javits Bill:

> I consider it important that the words "constitutional processes" used in existing and in any future bilateral or multilateral defense treaties to which the United States may become a party, be interpreted in S. 2956 to affirmatively require that the engagement of United States forces in hostilities beyond the emergency authority of the Executive shall not be undertaken without the approval of the Congress. This is the purpose of the first amendment which I have discussed above in this statement.
>
> Existing post-World War II defense treaties are under attack today, and I think it proper to recall the background and events under which they were entered into following World War II, and to state that at the time they had practically unanimous support of the Congress, the news media, and the people.
>
> The collapse of Nazi Germany brought the Soviet armies into Eastern Europe at the close of World War II. The Communist coup in Czechoslovakia in 1948, the fall of Nationalist China, the attack upon South Korea and the possibility of a thrust from Communist China toward Southeast Asia, caused great concern in the United States, Europe and Southeast Asian countries as to their security and led to the negotiation of the treaties. There were 8 of these treaties and they included 43 nations. Among them are NATO, SEATO, ANZUS, Inter-American, and bilateral treaties with Japan, Korea, the Philippines and Nationalist China.
>
> While these treaties differ in certain respects—particularly NATO, which recites that an attack upon a vast area defined by the treaty shall be considered an attack upon all the parties—they are similar in substance. Typical is the language

---

[87] 110 CONG. REC. 18409-10 (1964).

of the SEATO Treaty, which provides in Article I, Section 1, that:

> Each Party recognizes that aggression by means of armed attack in the treaty area against any of the Parties . . . would endanger its own peace and safety, and agrees that it will in that event act to meet the common danger in accordance with its constitutional process.

The term "constitutional processes" is not defined in the treaties. And the reports of the committees and the debates in the Congress on its meaning show disagreement, without definition. It was not settled whether the requirement of "constitutional processes" meant that the President, acting as Commander-in-Chief, could commit the forces of the United States to the military assistance of another treaty party, or meant that the President should consult with the Congress to determine jointly whether the commitment of military forces was essential to the security of the United States as well as that of other parties to the treaty and that the Executive would not commit our forces until the Congress had given its approval, either by a declaration of war or by a joint resolution.

During the Senate's consideration of the Korean Defense treaty in 1954, several Senators, including myself, but particularly Senator John Stennis and former Senator Watkins of Utah, insisted that the proper interpretation of the term "constitutional processes" as used in that treaty required the authorization of the Congress. There was no authoritative answer. I support such an interpretation.

The record of the hearing before the Senate Foreign Relations Committee and the debates in the Senate disclose that all of these treaties were approved by the Senate Foreign Relations Committee and the Senate with little opposition and without precisely determining the interpretation of "constitutional processes" and the commitment of the United States. Resolutions approved by Congress—some implementing certain of these treaties—uniformly provided to the Executive broad powers to involve the armed forces of the United States in hostilities, whether in the administrations of Presidents Truman, Eisenhower, Kennedy or Johnson. President Eisenhower was particularly insistent upon Congressional approval for military movements that might have involved the United States in a war. He was supported by Secretary of State John Foster Dulles who stated, in response to Committee inquiries, that the Executive would seek approval by the Congress for any such involvement. No involvement in war occurred during the Administration of President Eisenhower.

In fact, reservations offered in Committee and on the Senate floor during the consideration of several of these treaties, and amendments offered to Executive resolutions—Formosa, Middle East, Berlin, Cuba and Tonkin Gulf—to prohibit the use of the armed forces of the United States without Congressional approval were consistently opposed and rejected in the Foreign Relations Committee and in the Senate.

I present these facts because I do not concur in one underlying theme of the Committee's report—which was never discussed in Committee and never voted on—that the Executive has taken from the Congress its powers. The record, if studied, discloses that the Congress, particularly since World War II, has not only acceded to but has supported Executive resolutions requesting Congressional authority to use the armed forces of the United States, if necessary, in hostilities.

These are settled facts of history. We can change our course but we cannot revise and rewrite history.[88]

Naturally, in facing an issue of this kind, both Presidents and members of Congress will be sensitive to their prerogatives. No President will, or should, acquiesce in a diminution of the historical powers of his office. And Congress can be expected to insist, as best it can, on the claims which Senator Cooper puts forward. Thus far we have been able to devise forms of language which accommodate these conflicting principles in a pattern of cooperative action involving both Congress and the Presidency. For every participant, however proud, thoroughly understands, as Justice Jackson said, that the United States speaks with a stronger voice when the President and Congress act together.

Thus the Senate's action in consenting to the SEATO Treaty, and Congress' action in passing the Tonkin Gulf Resolution and several similar statutes, meant that in Vietnam Congress and the Presidency had acted together, both in giving solemn advance notice of American policy towards Vietnam, and in reaffirming that policy after hostilities began. So far as the constitutional proprieties are concerned, the American involvement in Vietnam occurred through a procedure which is a model for democratic decisionmaking. There is therefore no basis for the charge that the American course of action in Vietnam violates the

---

88 WAR POWERS, *supra* note 1, at 30-32. The unsettled state of doctrine analyzed by Senator Cooper permitted some to indulge in a meaningless gesture of protest against the war in Vietnam by voting for the repeal of the Tonkin Gulf Resolution, while leaving the SEATO Treaty untouched. By accepting Truman's view of the matter—for the moment, at least—they could enjoy the best of both worlds. S. Con. Res. 64, 91st Cong., 2d Sess., 116 CONG. REC. 23496, 23710-46, 23965 (1970); SENATE COMM. ON FOREIGN RELATIONS, TERMINATION OF SOUTH EAST ASIA RESOLUTION, S. REP. No. 91-872, 91st Cong., 2d Sess. 13 (1970).

internal law of the United States, or arrogates power to the President at the expense of Congress. In this regard, the constitutional practice with regard to Vietnam was more punctilious and complete in pooling Congressional and Presidential power than that used in Korea.[89]

### A.  Sauve Qui Peut—*by Parachute:* Exorcising the Tonkin Gulf Resolution

Many attempts have been made to avoid the force of these facts in support of the claim that the actions of the United States in Vietnam are unconstitutional.

We can put to one side the erroneous view that Congress can authorize sustained hostilities only by "declaring" war. While this position has no support in constitutional history, it is surprisingly widespread in public opinion, and strongly colors popular, and even professional attitudes towards "undeclared" war.

A more serious basis for the charge of unconstitutionality with regard to Vietnam is the argument (a) that the constitutional processes of the United States require action by Congress as well as by the President before the obligation of the SEATO Treaty could be translated into action; and (b) that the Tonkin Gulf Resolution and other legislation of like effect can be ignored as public acts of the United States because Congress did not intend to authorize what was done, or was insufficiently informed, or acted hastily in passing these resolutions, or was deceived by the Executive Branch.

The first part of this contention is settled by Senator Cooper's analysis, quoted above. In passing the Tonkin Gulf Resolution, Congress was explicitly aware that it was closing the constitutional gap arguably left open by the procedure adopted in the Korean case, in

---

[89] Professor Bickel has suggested elsewhere that President Truman's action in Korea had another constitutional base, the President's power to repel sudden attacks, which might distinguish Korea from Vietnam.

I would add about Korea that it was a massive attack by organized armies across a previously established border. We had troops with a full-scale establishment in Japan, right across the ditch. Thus, the surmise that this was a venture which threatened the safety of an established American military presence seemed plausible.

*The Power to Make War: A Debate Between Alexander M. Bickel and Eugene V. Rostow,* 18 YALE L. REP. 3, 6 (1971-72). *See also 1971 Hearings, supra* note 1, at 552. This argument contradicts Professor Bickel's testimony before the Senate Foreign Relations Committee, and the theory and language of the Javits Bill, which would admit a Presidential power to repel sudden attacks only against the territory or armed forces of the United States, not those of the South Korea. *Id.* at 553, 558-59, 566, 572, 574. In any event, Professor Bickel's new contention surely proves too much. In 1968, it would have authorized the President to use force in Czechoslovakia, a country separated from the NATO military establishment in Germany by a land boundary—not even a "ditch."

which, nominally at least, the President acted alone in carrying out the United Nations Charter, viewed as a Treaty of the United States. Whether Congressional action was or was not constitutionally necessary to authorize the use of American military power in carrying out the commitments of the United States under the SEATO Treaty, it was made available, so that under either theory—that of President Truman or that of Senators Cooper and Stennis—the full array of American constitutional authority was formally deployed behind the campaign in Vietnam.

In his attacks on the constitutionality of the Vietnam War, Professor Velvel accepts this critical fact. He writes,

> As the text of the Resolution illustrates, any reasonable man must concede that, if one considers only the language of the Resolution and totally ignores the congressional intent expressed in its ample legislative history, its language is broad enough to authorize the President, in his sole discretion, to fight a large scale land, sea and air war on the continent of Asia.[90]

Like several other scholars, however, Professor Velvel contends that even where legislation is unambiguous, it is permissible, indeed necessary, to refer to its legislative history to determine its true scope. Selectively culling over the messages and debates of the time, and the explanatory comments made later by Senators who came to regret their vote, Velvel urges that the Resolution be given a narrower reading, as authorizing the President only to respond to the immediate attack which precipitated the Resolution.

This argument cannot survive a reasonably dispassionate reading of the debates in the House and Senate. Many were troubled. A few were opposed. All hoped another Korea could be avoided. But all who spoke knew exactly what they were authorizing, or opposing. As Senator Javits said, "We who support the joint resolution do so with full knowledge of its seriousness and with the understanding that we are voting [for] a resolution which means life or the loss of it for who knows how many hundreds or thousands . . . ."[91] "Who knows how

---

90 Velvel, *The War in Vietnam: Unconstitutional, Justiciable, and Jurisdictionally Attackable*, 16 KANSAS L. REV. 449, 473 (1968), reprinted in 2 FALK, *supra* note 28, at 651, 675. Wormuth, *supra* note 28, at 781, recognizes the Resolution as a "blank check," but argues principally that it is void as an impermissible delegation of legislative power. *See id.* at 781-99. The problem of delegation is discussed at pp. 885-892 *infra*.

91 110 CONG. REC. 18418 (1964). *See also id.* at 18406, 18410, 18419.

Professor Velvel's treatment of the debate on the Tonkin Gulf Resolution, and other Congressional votes in support of the Vietnam policy, is extraordinarily selective. For

many hundreds or thousands" of casualties is hardly a phrase to be applied to a limited reprisal for an attack on two naval vessels.

But Professor Velvel's argument for treating the Tonkin Gulf Resolution as a nullity is inadmissible for a more fundamental reason, even without invoking Justice Jackson's sardonic comment that some would look to the text of a statute only when its legislative history is ambiguous.

The Congress which passed the Tonkin Gulf Resolution and similar legislative declarations lived in the shadow of the long, bitter, and frustrating campaign of Korea. Of course neither the President nor any member of the Congress wanted to repeat that experience if it could possibly be avoided. Of course they hoped that a firm manifestation of American will would persuade the North Vietnamese government and those who supported it to accept the repeated offers of negotiation and

---

example, he refers to an exchange between Senator Brewster and Senator Fulbright in these terms:

> At 112 [110] Congressional Record 18403 Senator Brewster said that he "would look with great dismay on the landing of large land armies on the continent of Asia." He therefore asked Senator Fulbright if the Resolution would approve "the landing of large American armies in Vietnam or China." Senator Fulbright replied, "There is nothing in the resolution, as I read it, that contemplates it. I agree with the Senator that that is the last thing we would want to do." Senator Fulbright, speaking for the Senate Foreign Relations Committee, continued by stating that everyone he had heard agreed that the United States must not become involved in an Asian land war and that the purpose of the Resolution was to deter the North Vietnamese from spreading the war. Senator Fulbright admitted that the *language* of the Resolution would not prevent the President from escalating the war, but he clearly indicated that this was not the congressional *intent*. The intent did not contemplate vast escalation, but deterrence of it.

Velvel, *supra* note 90, at 473-74, in 2 FALK, *supra* note 28, at 651, 675-76.

What Senator Fulbright said, in his exchange with Senator Brewster about the use of the armed forces on the continent of Asia, is this:

> There is nothing in the Resolution that, as I read it, contemplates it. I agree with the Senator that that is the last thing we would want to do. However, the language of the resolution would not prevent it. *It would authorize whatever the Commander in Chief feels is necessary. It does not restrain the Executive from doing it. Whether or not that should ever be done is a matter of wisdom under the circumstances that exist at the particular time it is contemplated. . . .*

110 CONG. REC. 18403 (1964) (emphasis added).

When President Johnson made his decision to send troops to Vietnam on a large scale in the spring of 1965, he sought and obtained another vote from Congress, through an appropriation bill accompanied by a message which said:

> This is not a routine appropriation. For each member of Congress who supports this request is also voting to persist in our effort to halt Communist aggression in South Vietnam. Each is saying that the Congress and the President stand united before the world in joint determination that the independence of South Vietnam shall be preserved and Communist attack will not succeed.

Message of May 4, 1965, in SENATE COMMITTEE ON FOREIGN RELATIONS, BACKGROUND INFORMATION RELATING TO SOUTHEAST ASIA AND VIETNAM, 89th Cong., 1st Sess. 219 (Comm. Print rev. ed. 1965).

The Committee Reports and debates associated with this appropriation make it clear that the vote was indeed a reiteration and reaffirmation of the policy and of its implementation. Comparable debates, and votes, occurred in 1966 as well. These materials are magisterially reviewed in Moore & Underwood, *supra* note 50, at 15553-67.

compromise which the United States put forward, notably that contained in President Johnson's Baltimore speech of April 7, 1965.[92] But these men knew too that of all human enterprises, recourse to military power is the least susceptible to easy prediction or control. It is always replete with nasty surprises, disappointments, and setbacks, campaigns that could not possibly have been anticipated when the initial decision to use force was undertaken. They knew too that solemn and public declarations of this order are addressed not only to the American people, but to those of the world at large, friendly and unfriendly governments alike, who are required to rely on what Congress does, not on the private fears and reservations of some of the men who voted for a text which said what it said.

Nor can the argument of deception be given any weight in evaluating the legal effect of legislation. Astute and worldly men who spoke and voted for SEATO, the Tonkin Gulf Resolution, and other legislative steps into the Vietnam War now claim that they were brainwashed, and that we should therefore treat public acts of the United States as if they never happened. Washington is a living society, not a series of closed enclaves labelled "legislative" and "executive." The atmosphere of that society consists of far more than formal messages and texts, testimony and votes. Congressmen and Senators live in a maze of information, rumor, speculation, and gossip, the product of continuous processes of consultation, leakage, and seepage between the executive and the legislative branches at all levels, as well as the table talk of journalists, ambassadors, and other regular and occasional members of the community—consultants, members of advisory committees, and so on. The key Congressmen and Senators responsible for the passage of the Tonkin Gulf and other Vietnam Resolutions knew what the executive branch knew when they voted. For some of these men to claim now that they were brainwashed is not only unseemly, but incredible.

As the basis for an argument that would justify the courts or anyone else in ignoring these Resolutions, the claim ranks with the historic efforts to treat the fourteenth amendment as a nullity because it was ratified by a number of state legislatures which met in the coercive presence of an army of occupation, and in some instances were elected by dubious and indeed fraudulent procedures. Many of these contentions are true, but a public act of the United States stands on its own

---

92 1 PUBLIC PAPERS OF THE PRESIDENTS: LYNDON B. JOHNSON 394, 396 (1966).

foundations, officially and legally, and cannot be collaterally attacked on such grounds.

## B. Undue Delegation of Legislative Authority

Professors Velvel, Wormuth, and Bickel advance another contention in their effort to exorcise the Tonkin Gulf Resolution and other legislation supporting the war in Vietnam. To them, the cycle of Presidential, Senatorial, and Congressional decisions with regard to Vietnam, regularly renewed over a period of more than sixteen years, is insufficient to satisfy what they regard as the unambiguous requirements of constitutional orthodoxy. Through a process of reasoning worthy of Justice Black in his most fundamentalist moments, they argue that, save for minor exceptions, hostilities can be authorized only by Congressional action *at the time they begin,* and then by delegations narrowly limited in scope. In their opinion, neither a treaty nor a congressional resolution can authorize a President to use force *in advance of the event.* Such provisions, they argue, unconstitutionally delegate legislative power to the President, because they are not suitably limited to the circumstances of the event which gave rise to the resolution— in the case of the Tonkin Gulf Resolution, the attack on American naval vessels in the Gulf of Tonkin.[93]

The Javits Bill does not accept this theory. Indeed, to Professors Velvel, Wormuth and Bickel, the Javits Bill is as unconstitutional as the Tonkin Gulf Resolution itself.[94] For the Javits Bill concedes that an explicit and advance Congressional authorization of the President's use of force is constitutionally proper, provided it is voted after the passage of the Javits Bill and explicitly exempts the authorization from its restrictions or, if voted before the passage of the Javits Bill, is sufficiently "specific." As a practical matter, the sponsors of the Javits Bill could hardly embrace the Velvel-Wormuth-Bickel theory of delegation. If congressional resolutions or other acts, like those for Formosa, United Nations participation, the Middle East, Berlin, and the expansion of Castro's power, were nullities whose operative provisions had to be repeated every time a President wanted to put them into action, it would be impossible for Congress and the President to cooperate at all

---

[93] Velvel, *supra* note 90, at 478, in 2 FALK, *supra* note 28, at 651, 680; Wormuth, *supra* note 28, at 780-99; *1971 Hearings, supra* note 1, at 549, 554-55, 560-63 (testimony of Alexander M. Bickel). "[T]he real answer to the Tonkin Gulf resolution is that if it authorized anything, beyond an immediate reaction, beyond its own factual context, it was an unconstitutionally broad delegation." *Id.* at 563.

[94] *See* testimony cited in note 93 *supra.*

in planning and formulating foreign policy in a way that would be credible.

Velvel, Wormuth, and Bickel discover the source of their rule in what they regard as the original intent of the men who gave Congress the power "to declare war," despite 182 years of opinion and practice to the contrary. The principle of full legislative control of the military power, they argue, precludes much Presidential discretion, and requires Congressional action only at the ritual moment, and then only in terms addressed to defined circumstances. Advance approval for the use of force they regard as a transfer to the President of a power Congress cannot yield even for a moment, even though it retains full authority to change the course of the nation thereafter by repealing, modifying, or reversing its policy, and the President's.

These scholars do not of course claim that Congressional support for the use of force by the President can be given only through a document labelled a "Declaration of War." Nor do they quite deny that the President has some inherent and independent power to use the force of the nation in aid of his conduct of foreign relations, as commander-in-chief of the armed forces, and as chief executive, charged with ensuring that the laws and treaties of the United States be faithfully executed. Without clarifying their views on these questions, however, and above all without considering the constitutional propriety of the Korean War, Wormuth and Bickel in particular conclude that the Tonkin Gulf Resolution, explicitly passed to reinforce and reiterate the policies of the SEATO Treaty, should be regarded as violating the principle they propose.

Actually, the Tonkin Gulf Resolution would appear to be beyond censure even under Bickel's extraordinary rule, since there had been some use of force by the United States in Vietnam, and Congress knew more was being considered at the time the Resolution was passed. Furthermore, the Tonkin Gulf Resolution would seem to contain suitably practical and defined standards to channel and confine the President's authority: it was addressed to what Congress and the President had found to be an "armed attack" by North Vietnam on South Vietnam within the meaning of the SEATO Treaty; and it could be terminated by Congress through a concurrent resolution, that is, without risk of veto. It is hard to conceive of a more precise or controlled "delegation" than one to help defeat a particular attack by one named state against another, pursuant to a policy already embodied in a Treaty.

More broadly, however, the Velvel-Wormuth-Bickel delegation

argument falls before a series of Supreme Court decisions going back at least to *Martin v. Mott*,[95] upholding standing delegations of discretion to the President in areas close to those of his independent constitutional responsibilities, and in areas of purely Congressional concern as well.

In advancing the argument that the Tonkin Gulf Resolution constitutes an unconstitutional delegation of Congress' power to declare war—which is assumed to include an equally unique power to authorize undeclared war—the commentators, especially Professor Bickel, place some reliance on *Kent v. Dulles*.[96] That important case considered the legality of denying a passport to Rockwell Kent on the ground that he was a member of the Communist Party. The basic statute on the subject goes back to 1856, and provides that "the Secretary of State may grant and issue passports . . . under such rules as the President shall designate and prescribe for and on behalf of the United States, and no other person shall grant, issue or verify such passports." In modern times the passport has become an important facility of international travel, and indeed a 1952 statute purports to make it unlawful for a citizen to depart from or enter the United States without a valid passport.

The Supreme Court upheld Kent's right to a passport, in an opinion which did not reach the question of constitutionality. Starting with the premise that the right to travel was an aspect of liberty protected by the Fifth Amendment, the court hesitated to infer from a pattern of longstanding administrative practice, which it found ambiguous at best, a Congressional purpose to authorize so drastic a curtailment of the liberty of the citizen. Interpreting the statute to avoid constitutional doubts, the court concluded that it should not construe Congressional silence to permit the Secretary to deny passports to individuals on the basis of their political opinions or associations. "If we were dealing with political questions entrusted to the Chief Executive by the Constitution," the Court said, "we would have a different case."[97] *Kent v. Dulles*, the court wrote, was concerned only with the personal right of the citizen to travel:

> If that 'liberty' is to be regulated, it must be pursuant to the law-making functions of the Congress. . . . And if that power is delegated, the standards must be adequate to pass scrutiny by the accepted tests. . . . Where activities or enjoyment, natural and often necessary to the well-being of an American citizen,

---

[95] 25 U.S. (12 Wheat.) 19 (1827).
[96] 357 U.S. 116 (1958). *See 1971 Hearings, supra* note 1, at 555.
[97] 357 U.S. 116, 129 (1958).

such as travel, are involved, we will construe narrowly all delegated powers that curtail or dilute them. . . . We hesitate to
find in this broad generalized power an authority to trench so
heavily on the rights of the citizen. . . . We only conclude that
§ 1185 and § 211a do not delegate to the Secretary the kind of
authority exercised here.[98]

The limits of *Kent v. Dulles* were explored in *Zemel v. Rusk,*[99]
considering the same statute, in the context of the same argument that
Congress had acquiesced through silence in a long-standing pattern of
administrative practice in construing and applying the passport act.
*Zemel* dealt with the Secretary of State's refusal to validate a citizen's
passport for travel to Cuba during 1962, a tense period in Cuban-Ameri-
can relations culminating in the Cuban Missile Crisis. In 1961 the Department of State had issued regulations requiring passports for travel
to Cuba, and the specific endorsement of such passports by the Department before a citizen could travel to Cuba. Mr. Zemel said the purpose
of his trip was "to satisfy my curiosity about the state of affairs in Cuba
and to make me a better informed citizen."[100]
Reviewing the history of periodic restraints of travel to areas of
war, pestilence, famine, or disorder since 1915—that is, both before and
since the reenactment of the statute of 1856 in 1926—the Court upheld
the Department's position. The issue of statutory construction in *Kent,*
the court said, was "whether a citizen could be denied a passport because of his beliefs or associations."[101] In *Zemel,* however, the issue before the court, as a question of both statutory interpretation and
constitutional law, was whether the Secretary could refuse to validate
a citizen's passport for travel to Cuba "because of foreign policy considerations affecting all citizens."[102]
The Court concluded that the history of the problem justified the
inference that the statute did delegate to the President an unreviewable
discretion to restrict travel to areas where for reasons of foreign policy,[103] and indeed for weighty considerations of national security,[104] unlimited travel by citizens could "directly and materially interfere with
the safety and welfare of the area or the Nation as a whole."[105]

---

98 *Id.*
99 381 U.S. 1 (1965).
100 *Id.* at 4.
101 *Id.* at 13.
102 *Id.*
103 *Id.* at 15.
104 *Id.* at 16.
105 *Id.* at 15-16.

In *Zemel*, unlike *Kent*, the Court was therefore required to pass on the constitutional validity of such a delegation of legislative authority. It said:

> Finally, appellant challenges the 1926 Act on the ground that it does not contain sufficiently definite standards for the formulation of travel controls by the Executive. It is important to bear in mind, in appraising this argument, that because of the changeable and explosive nature of contemporary international relations, and the fact that the Executive is immediately privy to information which cannot be swiftly presented to, evaluated by, and acted upon by the legislature, Congress—in giving the Executive authority over matters of foreign affairs—must of necessity paint with a brush broader than that it customarily wields in domestic areas.
>
> > "Practically every volume of the United States Statutes contains one or more acts or joint resolutions of Congress authorizing action by the President in respect of subjects affecting foreign relations, which either leave the exercise of the power to his unrestricted judgment, or provide a standard far more general than that which has always been considered requisite with regard to domestic affairs." *United States* v. *Curtiss-Wright Corp.*, 299 U.S. 304, 324.
>
> This does not mean that simply because a statute deals with foreign relations, it can grant the Executive totally unrestricted freedom of choice. However, the 1926 Act contains no such grant. We have held, *Kent* v. *Dulles, supra,* and reaffirm today, that the 1926 Act must take its content from history: it authorizes only those passport refusals and restrictions "which it could fairly be argued were adopted by Congress in light of prior administrative practice." *Kent* v. *Dulles, supra,* at 128. So limited, the Act does not constitute an invalid delegation.[106]

Thus, *Kent* and *Zemel* together would seem to confirm, not to challenge, the constitutional validity of the Tonkin Gulf Resolution.

The Courts have upheld other broad delegations of discretion to the President, including many in areas which are purely legislative in character and have no roots in one or another of the inherent powers of the Presidency: in the field of tariffs and of responsibility for banking, to take only two examples.[107] The distinction in *Zemel* between delega-

---

106 *Id.* at 17-18.

107 19 U.S.C. §§ 181, 1336-38 (1970) (tariff statutes delegating to the President power over rates and duties); 12 U.S.C. §§ 95-95a (1970) (President's emergency powers over banks).

tions in the field of domestic and of foreign affairs is frequently made, and certainly the conduct of foreign affairs requires the flexibility of broad discretion. Still, it is hard to imagine a "delegation" more complete than that of *Martin v. Mott*, for example, involving the President's power to call out the militia whenever he deems it desirable to do so. Generally speaking, the reasonableness of a delegation should be considered in relation to the nature of the problem Congress was trying to resolve, and its freedom within broad limits to select means which might conceivably contribute to the end it sought to achieve.[108]

No standard even reasonably close to the precedents and their reasoning provides support for the argument that the Tonkin Gulf Resolution can be treated as a nullity because it constitutes an unconstitutional delegation of legislative power. This cannot be the basis for Senator Fulbright's position that the war in Vietnam is "unconstitutional,"[109] since the Javits Bill, which he supports, contemplates the possibility that Congress and the President might well decide to use advance statutory authorizations for the use of armed force by the President.[110]

The argument of undue delegation fails for a deeper reason. It is at war with the "nature of things," those stubborn exigencies of the external world that Montesquieu rightly saw as the true source of law, the nature of things in the late eighteenth century and the nature of things now. The necessities of circumstance in dealing with the hurly-burly of the real world have produced a quite different pattern of practice since 1789, not less democratic than the model in the minds of Professors Bickel, Wormuth, and Velvel, but far more flexible, resourceful, and effective. To treat Resolutions like the Tonkin Gulf Resolutions as nullities would make it nearly impossible to associate Congress with the President in the articulation of an effective deterrent diplomacy. Such a rule would make foreign affairs even more exclusively the province of the President than is the case today.

In Marshall's classic words, echoing those of Hamilton in No. 23

---

*See also* Comment, *Federal Taxation and Economic Stability*, 57 YALE L.J. 1229, 1248-55 (1948).

108 E. CORWIN, THE PRESIDENT: OFFICE AND POWERS 369-73 (1940) (a compilation of the discretionary powers of the President in 1940). *See also* E. CORWIN, *supra* note 30, at 119-30; K. DAVIS, ADMINISTRATIVE LAW TREATISE § 2.00 (1970 Supp.); Jaffe, *An Essay on Delegation of Legislative Power*, 47 COLUM. L. REV. 359, 561 (1947).

109 WAR POWERS, *supra* note 1, at 27; Fulbright, *Congress, the President and the War Power*, 25 ARK. L. REV. 71, 72 (1971). *See also* testimony of Alexander Bickel in *1971 Hearings, supra* note 1, at 566-77, 579.

110 S. 2956, 92d Cong., 2d Sess. § 3(4) (1972).

of *The Federalist*, the first rule in interpreting "those great powers on which the welfare of a nation essentially depends" is that

> [i]t must have been the intention of those who gave these powers, to insure, as far as human prudence could insure, their beneficial execution. This could not be done by confiding the choice of means to such narrow limits as not to leave it in the power of Congress to adopt any which might be appropriate, and which were conducive to the end. This provision is made in a constitution intended to endure for ages to come, and, consequently, to be adapted to the various *crises* of human affairs. To have prescribed the means by which government should, in all future time, execute its powers, would have been to change, entirely, the character of the instrument, and give it the properties of a legal code. It would have been an unwise attempt to provide, by immutable rules, for exigencies which, if foreseen at all, must have been seen dimly, and which can best be provided for as they occur. To have declared that the best means shall not be used, but those alone without which the power given would be nugatory, would have been to deprive the legislature of the capacity to avail itself of experience, to exercise its reason, and to accommodate its legislation to circumstances. . . .[111]

Marshall had noted previously that

> [t]he power being given, it is the interest of the nation to facilitate its execution. It can never be their interest, and cannot be presumed to have been their intention, to clog and embarrass its execution by withholding the most appropriate means.[112]

What Marshall wrote about the power of Congress to charter a bank in *McCulloch* v. *Maryland* applies even more emphatically to the respective roles of the President and Congress in exercising the great powers of the nation abroad, powers whose constitutional contours derive as much from international law and international life as from the deliberately few words of the document of 1787.

The American nation which entered the family of nations in 1776 was endowed in its external relations with all the attributes of sovereignty. The written constitution which went into effect in 1789 must be read, Justice Frankfurter has said, to recognize in the national gov-

---

111 McCulloch v. Maryland, 17 U.S. (4 Wheat.) 316, 415-16 (1819.)
112 *Id.* at 408.

ernment "the powers indispensable to its functioning effectively in the company of sovereign nations."[113]

The delegation theory of Professors Velvel, Wormuth, and Bickel would deny the President and the Congress the most ordinary and elementary tools for protecting the nation in a time of international turbulence. Under their rule, we should be the only nation on earth incapable of making a credible military treaty. Their rule would make it impossible firmly to delineate American interests in advance, and thus to deter and contain processes of expansion which Congress and the President deem threatening to national security. It would emasculate both Congress and the Presidency, and deprive even treaties like NATO of their weight and credibility.

The Constitution, Justice Goldberg once said, is not "a suicide pact."[114] The war power, the Supreme Court has remarked, is the power to wage war successfully. So too, the power of the President and of the Congress over foreign relations is the power to wage peace successfully. There is nothing in the history of the war power and the foreign relations power, since President Washington's first term, to suggest that the United States may not seek to avert the danger of war by giving potential enemies of the nation a credible and effective warning in advance. *McCulloch v. Maryland* teaches that those who oppose the presumptive constitutional validity of the means Congress and the President together select as appropriate to protect the security of the nation face a nearly insuperable burden of proof.[115]

## C. The Political Question Doctrine

It is sometimes claimed that the "political question" doctrine makes it impossible to reach final decisions—that is, "final" decisions by courts—on the constitutionality of procedures like those used by Presidents and Congress in Korea and Vietnam. This contention misconceives the political question doctrine. It is not, as some contend, a flexible and amorphous idea used by the Courts to avoid questions they do not wish to decide, although judges sometimes use it for this purpose. As Marshall made clear in *Marbury v. Madison*,[116] the doctrine is something quite different: that courts cannot and should not pass on the

---

113 Perez v. Brownell, 356 U.S. 44, 57 (1958).
114 Aptheker v. Secretary of State, 378 U.S. 500, 509 (1964).
115 17 U.S. (4 Wheat.) 316, 409-11 (1918).
116 5 U.S. (1 Cranch) 137 (1803).

propriety of decisions entrusted by the Constitution or the laws to the discretion of another branch of government.[117]

In *Marbury's* case, no court could have questioned the propriety of the President's decision to nominate Marbury rather than John Doe or Richard Roe; the Senate's vote in its absolute discretion to advise his appointment, and consent to it; or the President's final decision, having received a favorable vote from the Senate, to sign Marbury's commission, and have it sealed. The question became justiciable, the Court said, only because the political discretion of the President and the Senate was exhausted when the seal was affixed. At that moment, and not before, Marbury acquired a vested legal right, a property interest, in the office.

The question whether Marbury's right to the judgeship should be protected in court, the Court said, "far from being an intrusion into the secrets of the cabinet, . . . respects a paper, which, according to law, is upon record, and to a copy of which the law gives a right, on the payment of ten cents."[118]

Like nearly all the intervening cases, *Powell v. McCormack*[119] rests upon the same simple principle. The Court did not attempt to control the political decision of Congress to exclude Adam Clayton Powell, duly elected to membership in Congress. It carefully ruled, however, that while under the Constitution each House was indeed "the Judge of the Elections, Returns and Qualifications of its own members," the discretion of Congress over the admission of members could rest only on the grounds specified in the constitution—age, citizenship, residence, and election. Since it was conceded in this case that Powell met these

---

117 The intimate political relation, subsisting between the president of the United States and the heads of departments, necessarily renders any legal investigation of the acts of one of those high officers peculiarly irksome, as well as delicate; and excites some hesitation with respect to the propriety of entering into such investigation. Impressions are often received without much reflection or examination, and it is not wonderful that in such a case as this, the assertion, by an individual, of his legal claims in a court of justice; to which claims it is the duty of that court to attend; should at first view be considered by some, as an attempt to intrude into the cabinet, and to intermeddle with the prerogatives of the executive.

It is scarcely necessary for the court to disclaim all pretensions to such a jurisdiction. An extravagance, so absurd and excessive, could not have been entertained for a moment. The province of the court is, solely, to decide on the rights of individuals, not to enquire how the executive, or executive officers, perform duties in which they have a discretion. Questions, in their nature political, or which are, by the constitution and the laws, submitted to the executive, can never be made in this court.

*Id.* at 169-70.
118 *Id.* at 170.
119 395 U.S. 486 (1969).

constitutional qualifications, which were unalterable by the legislature, it followed that the vote excluding him was invalid.[120] The Court took exactly the same position in *Roudebush v. Hartke*: "Which candidate is entitled to be seated in the Senate is, to be sure, a nonjusticiable political question."[121]

By now many lower courts, faced with the complaint of young men about to be drafted into the armed forces, have passed upon the constitutionality of the war in Vietnam. Such plaintiffs surely have standing to raise the question, in the sense of a direct personal interest in the outcome of the litigation; the possibility that they may be killed or maimed in the course of military operations represents the most direct and most personal of all interests. I can imagine no civil right more profound, and more to be respected, than the right of a conscript to be assured that the war he is required to fight has been constitutionally authorized. All the courts which have passed upon the question have given these plaintiffs the answer Justice Story gave to the militiamen in *Martin v. Mott*: that whether the United States acts or does not act under a treaty; whether it decides to help or not to help a friendly government in measures of self-defense against a rebellion aided or instigated and organized from abroad; whether the President and Congress "declare" war, or choose the course of limited war—all are matters peculiarly within the discretion entrusted to the President, or to Congress, or to both, under our constitution and laws and, therefore "political" questions within the meaning of *Marbury v. Madison*.[122] When Courts decide that the way in which the political arms of the government exercise such discretion is a "political question," they are not *abstaining* from a decision on its legality; on the contrary, they are deciding that the choices made were within the zone of discretion entrusted to the political branches of the government, and are therefore legal.

I should be the last to urge, as some have done, that the courts should refrain from decisions of this kind on the ground that it may be

---

120 *Id.* at 518-22, 548-49.

121 92 S. Ct. 804, 807 (1972). *See* Dionisopoulos, *A Commentary on the Constitutional Issues in* Powell *and Related Cases,* 17 J. PUB. L. 103 (1968); Henkin, *Viet-Nam in the Courts of the United States: "Political Questions,"* 63 AM. J. INT'L L. 284 (1969); Scharpf, *Judicial Review and the Political Question: A Functional Analysis,* 75 YALE L.J. 517 (1966); Schwartz & McCormack, *The Justiciability of Legal Objections to the American Military Effort in Vietnam,* 46 TEXAS L. REV. 1033 (1968).

122 *See, e.g.,* Orlando v. Laird, 317 F. Supp. 1013 (E.D.N.Y. 1970), *aff'd,* 443 F.2d 1039 (2d Cir.), *cert. denied,* 404 U.S. 869 (1971); United States v. Sisson, 294 F. Supp. 511, 515, 520 (D. Mass. 1968), 297 F. Supp. 902 (D. Mass. 1969), *appeal dismissed for lack of jurisdiction,* 399 U.S. 267 (1970).

impractical and undesirable to have the courts pass on such difficult and sensitive problems.[123] On the contrary, I believe that many exercises of the military power do produce justiciable controversies, and that in such cases the courts should review the exercise of the war power by political authority to make sure it is kept within constitutional limits. I believe our national debate about Vietnam might well have been less confused and less poisonous if the Supreme Court, in a great opinion, had said what the lower courts have all said—and what I think any judge under the pressure of responsibility would necessarily conclude—that there is no constitutional basis for challenging the legality of the war in Vietnam. Men can reasonably debate whether the United States should have made the commitment of the SEATO Treaty, or honored its commitment when the Treaty was breached. They can argue about the strategy and tactics of the combat and diplomacy of the war in Indo-China. Equally, with Senator Cooper they can question whether a vote of Congress was necessary, in addition to a Treaty, to authorize the President to use the national force on a large scale in Vietnam. But when President and Congress pool all the war powers they possess, jointly and separately, what is there left to debate? It is difficult, at least for me, to discover any plausible basis for contending that the Vietnam War is unconstitutional, or even constitutionally doubtful.

## D. *"Necessary and Proper"*

In the tense and cautious diplomacy of our present relations with the Soviet Union, as they have developed over the last twenty-five years, the authority of the President to set clear and silent limits in advance is perhaps the most important of all the powers in our constitutional armory to prevent confrontations that could carry nuclear implications. No shots have been fired between the armed forces of the United States and those of the Soviet Union; and the inhibition against firing the first shot has been an immensely powerful factor of restraint in the conduct of the cold war. The basic rule of cold war diplomacy, thus far, has been that the Soviet Union does not use force to challenge our presence, or what we clearly and privately inform them are our state interests, and

---

[123] *See* Rostow, *The Japanese American Cases—A Disaster*, 54 YALE L.J. 489 (1945), reprinted in E. ROSTOW, THE SOVEREIGN PREROGATIVE 193 (1962); H. WECHSLER, PRINCIPLES, POLITICS, AND FUNDAMENTAL LAW 11-13 (1961). *Cf.* A. BICKEL, THE LEAST DANGEROUS BRANCH 69-70 (1962); T. TAYLOR, NUREMBERG AND VIETNAM: AN AMERICAN TRAGEDY 109-13, 116-21 (1970). The limits of presidential power in war have never been better analyzed than by Justice Curtis in his pamphlet Executive Power (1862), reprinted in II B. CURTIS, A MEMOIR OF BENJAMIN ROBBINS CURTIS, L.L.D. 306 (1879).

that we likewise do not use force to oppose hers. We did not intervene in East Germany, Hungary, or Czechoslovakia. They did not use their own force to oppose our actions in Berlin, in Yugoslavia, in Greece, in Korea, and in Vietnam. In resisting the Berlin Blockade, President Truman carefully chose the air lift, a method of action that would have required the Soviets to fire the first shot. President Kennedy sought to accomplish the same end in his handling of the Cuban Missile Crisis, cautiously choosing a limited naval blockade rather than air strike or invasion, the latter strongly urged upon him by Senator Fulbright and others.[124]

The nature of the problem requires promptness of action, great flexibility in the choice of means, and freedom to shift, from hour to hour, in response to the exigencies of the diplomatic situation. It puts a decisive premium on establishing a deterrent presence, or a credible deterrent threat, before irrevocable steps have been taken, or decisions made.

The Javits Bill purports to abolish this power—essential to diplomacy, and to the process of avoiding war. It is a power which nearly every President has used, at least since 1794, when President Washington sent troops to drive Indians—perhaps supported by the British—from Western territories in dispute. And it is the diplomatic power the President needs most under the circumstances of modern life—the power to make a credible threat to use force in order to prevent a confrontation which might escalate.

I believe that an attempt by Congress to deprive the President of power so crucial to his duties as organ of the nation in the conduct of foreign relations is unconstitutional. It is as unconstitutional as a Presidential assumption of power deemed legislative, or as Congressional invasions of the President's much mooted power to remove subordinate officials of the Executive branch, or his pardoning power, or of the authority of the courts under Article III.[125]

The Senate Foreign Relations Committee claims to have discovered new potentialities in the necessary and proper clause authorizing Congress to control the way in which "any Department or officer thereof"

---

124 R. KENNEDY, *supra* note 12, at 32, 119.
125 *See, e.g.,* Wiener v. United States, 357 U.S. 349 (1958); Reid v. Covert, 354 U.S. 1 (1957); Myers v. United States, 272 U.S. 52 (1926); Muskrat v. United States, 219 U.S. 346 (1911); United States v. Klein, 80 U.S. (13 Wall.) 128, 147-48 (1871); Ex Parte Yerger, 75 U.S. (8 Wall.) 85 (1869); Ex Parte Garland, 71 U.S. (4 Wall.) 333, 380 (1867); Marbury v. Madison, 5 U.S. (1 Cranch) 137 (1803); E. CORWIN, THE PRESIDENT'S REMOVAL POWER UNDER THE CONSTITUTION (1927). This argument was the heart of the impeachment proceedings against President Andrew Johnson. See B. CURTIS, *supra* note 123, at 343.

exercises its functions. But the necessary and proper clause, impressive as it is, cannot be the source of a bootstrap doctrine, empowering Congress to abolish the principle of the separation of powers. Every piece of legislation has as its tacit predicate a Congressional finding that the statute or resolution is, in the view of Congress, "necessary and proper for carrying into Execution" one or another of the powers allocated to it in Article I, Section 8. Congress has been talking the prose (or poetry) of the necessary and proper clause since 1789.

## IV. CONCLUSION

The Javits Bill and similar proposals represent the passionate conviction that the campaigns in Korea and Vietnam were a mistake. Many proponents of the Bill also contend that Korea and Vietnam were "Presidential" wars, and could have been avoided if only Congress had not been stripped of its rightful powers by the usurpations of overweening modern Presidents. We are therefore in the midst of a constitutional crisis, they tell us, a crisis which can be cured, and equilibrium in the constitutional order restored, only by the passage of a statute like the Javits Bill. Men like Senator Cooper and Senator Stennis, of course, do not accept this step in the argument. They know that Korea and Vietnam did not come about because the Presidency had arrogated Congress' powers over foreign policy; Congress fully supported those efforts when they were undertaken. But Senators Cooper and Stennis support the Javits Bill for another reason: they are trying to take advantage of the present state of opinion about Korea and Vietnam to establish certain Congressional prerogatives they have long urged in the perpetual conflict between Congress and the Presidency over their respective roles in making foreign policy. Their effort is addressed to the constitutional practice of Korea, not Vietnam. It represents Bricker's thesis that treaties are not self-executing, but require Congressional action before they become law.

The nation *is* in the midst of an important foreign policy crisis. It is not a constitutional crisis requiring a redefinition of the relationship between the President and the Congress, but an intellectual and moral crisis caused by a growing tension between what we do and what we think. The ideas that for twenty-five years have shaped American foreign policy, and the foreign policy of our Allies—the visions which dominated the minds of the delegates who met at San Francisco in 1945 to write the Charter of the United Nations—have suddenly lost their power to command. When the delegates met at San Francisco in 1945, they saw Haile Selassie standing sadly before them, as he had stood in the Palace of the League of Nations ten years before, asking in vain for help against Mussolini's aggression. With equal shame they remembered China, which had also met silence when it besought the League to stop Japan. If the world had acted promptly, and in concert, would Japan have conquered Manchuria, and gone on to wage general war against China, and then against others? Would Italy have attacked harmless Ethiopia? Would Germany and Italy have made war against Spain, by sending arms and men to support Franco's revolution? Would the Rhineland have been occupied, Austria and Czechoslovakia invaded? In short, could the drive towards war have been stopped earlier, before its momentum became irresistible?

To the men of 1945, the answer to these questions was self-evident. World War II could have been prevented, they believed, if Britain, France, and the United States had acted against aggression, firmly, boldly, and above all in good time.

Today there is an outcry against these ideas. Something is wrong with the notion of small wars to prevent big ones, men say, if it produces consequences as ghastly as the campaigns in Korea and Vietnam. There must be a "new" foreign policy that could liberate us from the burdens we have had to bear since 1945.

This demand is the most conspicuous theme of a bellicose literature about how to achieve peace. It is conventional to describe that literature as a "Great Debate." Like many features of the conventional wisdom, the phrase is misleading. There is disagreement to spare in these books and articles, but little or no debate. Few of the protagonists read what their opponents write, or listen to what they say. Generally speaking, arguments are answered by epithets. The devotees of geopolitics, brooding about nuclear deterrence, dismiss their critics as amateurs, demagogues, journalists, dupes, or worse. Their critics return the compliment. Why should they waste time considering the ideas of fascists, war criminals, revisionists (or other lackeys of monopoly capitalism), or burnt-out cases whose minds were paralyzed in cold war postures twenty years ago?

In contemplating our national priorities, I can think of nothing we need more urgently than a genuine debate about what foreign policy is for. Until we come much closer to agreement on this central question, we shall have little opportunity to deal with the others.

Since 1945, there has been acute dissonance in the nation between what we thought and what we did in the name of foreign policy. While neither the United States nor any other nation has ever dared contemplate the full-throated enforcement of the United Nations Charter —in Eastern Europe, for example—American policy has nonetheless been strongly influenced by the experience of the thirties, and by the ideas of the Charter. President Truman regarded the Korean War as atonement for the League's failure in Ethiopia. His point was underscored by the presence of Ethiopian troops in Korea. And the memory of Munich, and of President Wilson, is a living part of American consciousness.

Truman's view has not, of course, been universally accepted. The United States has offered many explanations for its foreign policy since the Truman Doctrine was announced in 1947: as the "containment" of "Communism," or of the Soviet Union, China, and Cuba; as the protection of "free nations" or of "the free world"; as the manifest destiny of a Great Power; or as the application of the oldest and most nearly instinctive policy in all politics—that of the balance of power.

Public opinion has not yet crystallized around any one of these competing principles as the proper compass for our foreign policy. Since 1945, the American government under five Presidents has felt compelled to act in a certain pattern, from Iran, Greece, and Turkey, to Berlin, Korea, the Middle East and Vietnam. But there is no harmony between this pattern of action, and widespread, and now perhaps prevailing views as to what American and Allied foreign policy ought to be.

The tension between public opinion and the behavior of government is much too great for safety. That tension has already destroyed the careers of two Presidents, Truman and Johnson; divided the nation; split the Democratic Party; and perhaps weakened the Presidency as well. It could have even more serious consequences, for it has given rise to uncertainty all over the world as to what the United States will do to protect its own security, and the security of nations it has undertaken to defend. Uncertainty of this order invites miscalculation, the kind of miscalculation which had led to so many catastrophes already during this brutal and tragic century. It is hardly hyperbole to conclude that the nation must reexamine its foreign policy before its foreign policy destroys the nation.

The real crisis of our foreign policy can be resolved only through a disciplined and scrupulous examination of what the nation must do, given the condition of world politics, to preserve the possibility of surviving as a democracy at home. That process will be difficult at best.

The relevant Congressional Committees, and Congress as a whole, should be leading the nation in a courteous and sustained debate, through which we could hope to achieve a new consensus about foreign policy, as vital, and creative, as that which sustained the line of policy which started with the Truman Doctrine, the Marshall Plan, NATO and its progeny, and the Point Four Program.

Instead, the Senate Foreign Relations Committee has chosen to escape from the demanding but manageable task of reality by retreating into the insoluble and dangerous realm of constitutional myth. No one could possibly write the statute the Javits Bill purports to be—a codification of what the Founding Fathers prudently left uncodified, the respective powers of Congress and the President in relation to the use of the national force. As George Ball pointed out in his persuasive testimony opposing the Javits Bill, the Bill

> represents an attempt to do what the Founding Fathers felt they were not wise enough to do: to give precision and automatic operation to the kind of legislative-executive collaboration which they deemed essential to prevent the unrestricted use of American forces by the Executive acting in the pattern of monarch, while at the same time assuring him sufficient flexibility to defend the country against any threats that might suddenly appear.[126]

In this time of trouble, almost as threatening to the nation as the Great European Wars of 1789-1815, we should not be diverted from the compelling task of rethinking foreign policy into a ritual purge of evil spirits, and an emasculation of the Presidency we have never needed more. The Javits Bill would turn the clock back to the Articles of Confederation, and destroy the Presidency which it was one of the chief aims of the men of Annapolis and Philadelphia to create.

---

126 *1971 Hearings, supra* note 1, at 621.

# VI. DOCUMENTARY APPENDIX 1
## SETTLEMENT OF THE INDOCHINA WAR
### Part A. Vietnam

# Texts of (Paris) Agreement and Protocols on Ending the War and Restoring Peace in Vietnam

**Text of Agreement**

White House press release dated January 24

### AGREEMENT ON ENDING THE WAR AND RESTORING PEACE IN VIETNAM

The Parties participating in the Paris Conference on Vietnam,

With a view to ending the war and restoring peace in Vietnam on the basis of respect for the Vietnamese people's fundamental national rights and the South Vietnamese people's right to self-determination, and to contributing to the consolidation of peace in Asia and the world,

Have agreed on the following provisions and undertake to respect and to implement them:

## Chapter I
### THE VIETNAMESE PEOPLE'S FUNDAMENTAL NATIONAL RIGHTS

#### Article 1

The United States and all other countries respect the independence, sovereignty, unity, and territorial integrity of Vietnam as recognized by the 1954 Geneva Agreements on Vietnam.

## Chapter II
### CESSATION OF HOSTILITIES—WITHDRAWAL OF TROOPS

#### Article 2

A cease-fire shall be observed throughout South Vietnam as of 2400 hours G.M.T., on January 27, 1973.

At the same hour, the United States will stop all its military activities against the territory of the Democratic Republic of Vietnam by ground, air and naval forces, wherever they may be based, and end the mining of the territorial waters, ports, harbors, and waterways of the Democratic Republic of Vietnam. The United States will remove, permanently deactivate or destroy all the mines in the territorial waters, ports, harbors, and waterways of North Vietnam as soon as this Agreement goes into effect.

The complete cessation of hostilities mentioned in this Article shall be durable and without limit of time.

#### Article 3

The parties undertake to maintain the cease-fire and to ensure a lasting and stable peace.

As soon as the cease-fire goes into effect:

(a) The United States forces and those of the other foreign countries allied with the United States and the Republic of Vietnam shall remain in-place pending the implementation of the plan of troop withdrawal. The Four-Party Joint Military Commission described in Article 16 shall determine the modalities.

(b) The armed forces of the two South Vietnamese parties shall remain in-place. The Two-Party Joint Military Commission described in Article 17 shall determine the areas controlled by each party and the modalities of stationing.

(c) The regular forces of all services and arms and the irregular forces of the parties in South Vietnam shall stop all offensive activities against each other and shall strictly abide by the following stipulations:

—All acts of force on the ground, in the air, and on the sea shall be prohibited;

—All hostile acts, terrorism and reprisals by both sides will be banned.

#### Article 4

The United States will not continue its military involvement or intervene in the internal affairs of South Vietnam.

#### Article 5

Within sixty days of the signing of this Agreement, there will be a total withdrawal from South Vietnam of troops, military advisers, and military personnel, including technical military personnel and military personnel associated with the pacification program, armaments, munitions, and war material of the United States and those of the other foreign countries mentioned in Article 3 (a). Advisers from the above-mentioned countries to all paramilitary organizations and the police force will also be withdrawn within the same period of time.

#### Article 6

The dismantlement of all military bases in South Vietnam of the United States and of the other foreign countries mentioned in Article 3 (a) shall be completed within sixty days of the signing of this Agreement.

#### Article 7

From the enforcement of the cease-fire to the formation of the government provided for in Articles 9 (b) and 14 of this Agreement, the two South Vietnamese parties shall not accept the introduction of troops, military advisers, and military personnel including technical military personnel, armaments, munitions, and war material into South Vietnam.

The two South Vietnamese parties shall be permitted to make periodic replacement of armaments, munitions and war material which have been destroyed, damaged, worn out or used up after the cease-fire, on the basis of piece-for-piece, of the same characteristics and properties, under the supervision of the Joint Military Commission of the two South Vietnamese parties and of the International Commission of Control and Supervision.

## Chapter III
### THE RETURN OF CAPTURED MILITARY PERSONNEL AND FOREIGN CIVILIANS, AND CAPTURED AND DETAINED VIETNAMESE CIVILIAN PERSONNEL

#### Article 8

(a) The return of captured military personnel and foreign civilians of the parties shall be carried out simultaneously with and completed not later than the same day as the troop withdrawal mentioned in Article 5. The parties shall exchange complete lists of the above-mentioned captured military personnel and foreign civilians on the day of the signing of this Agreement.

(b) The parties shall help each other to get information about those military personnel and foreign civilians of the parties missing in action, to determine the location and take care of the graves of the dead so as to facilitate the exhumation and repatriation of the remains, and to take any such other measures as may be required to get information about those still considered missing in action.

(c) The question of the return of Vietnamese civilian personnel captured and detained in South Vietnam will be resolved by the two South Vietnamese parties on the basis of the principles of Article 21 (b) of the Agreement on the Cessation of Hostilities in Vietnam of July 20, 1954. The two South Vietnamese parties will do so in a spirit of national reconciliation and concord, with a view to ending hatred and enmity, in order to ease suffering and to reunite families. The two South Vietnamese parties will do their utmost to resolve this question within ninety days after the cease-fire comes into effect.

## Chapter IV
### THE EXERCISE OF THE SOUTH VIETNAMESE PEOPLE'S RIGHT TO SELF-DETERMINATION

### Article 9

The Government of the United States of America and the Government of the Democratic Republic of Vietnam undertake to respect the following principles for the exercise of the South Vietnamese people's right to self-determination:

(a) The South Vietnamese people's right to self-determination is sacred, inalienable, and shall be respected by all countries.

(b) The South Vietnamese people shall decide themselves the political future of South Vietnam through genuinely free and democratic general elections under international supervision.

(c) Foreign countries shall not impose any political tendency or personality on the South Vietnamese people.

### Article 10

The two South Vietnamese parties undertake to respect the cease-fire and maintain peace in South Vietnam, settle all matters of contention through negotiations, and avoid all armed conflict.

### Article 11

Immediately after the cease-fire, the two South Vietnamese parties will:

—achieve national reconciliation and concord, end hatred and enmity, prohibit all acts of reprisal and discrimination against individuals or organizations that have collaborated with one side or the other;

—ensure the democratic liberties of the people: personal freedom, freedom of speech, freedom of the press, freedom of meeting, freedom of organization, freedom of political activities, freedom of belief, freedom of movement, freedom of residence, freedom of work, right to property ownership, and right to free enterprise.

### Article 12

(a) Immediately after the cease-fire, the two South Vietnamese parties shall hold consultations in a spirit of national reconciliation and concord, mutual respect, and mutual non-elimination to set up a National Council of National Reconciliation and Concord of three equal segments. The Council shall operate on the principle of unanimity. After the National Council of National Reconciliation and Concord has assumed its functions, the two South Vietnamese parties will consult about the formation of councils at lower levels. The two South Vietnamese parties shall sign an agreement on the internal matters of South Vietnam as soon as possible and do their utmost to accomplish this within ninety days after the cease-fire comes into effect, in keeping with the South Vietnamese people's aspirations for peace, independence and

democracy.

(b) The National Council of National Reconciliation and Concord shall have the task of promoting the two South Vietnamese parties' implementation of this Agreement, achievement of national reconciliation and concord and ensurance of democratic liberties. The National Council of National Reconciliation and Concord will organize the free and democratic general elections provided for in Article 9 (b) and decide the procedures and modalities of these general elections. The institutions for which the general elections are to be held will be agreed upon through consultations between the two South Vietnamese parties. The National Council of National Reconciliation and Concord will also decide the procedures and modalities of such local elections as the two South Vietnamese parties agree upon.

### Article 13

The question of Vietnamese armed forces in South Vietnam shall be settled by the two South Vietnamese parties in a spirit of national reconciliation and concord, equality and mutual respect, without foreign interference, in accordance with the postwar situation. Among the questions to be discussed by the two South Vietnamese parties are steps to reduce their military effectives and to demobilize the troops being reduced. The two South Vietnamese parties will accomplish this as soon as possible.

### Article 14

South Vietnam will pursue a foreign policy of peace and independence. It will be prepared to establish relations with all countries irrespective of their political and social systems on the basis of mutual respect for independence and sovereignty and accept economic and technical aid from any country with no political conditions attached. The acceptance of military aid by South Vietnam in the future shall come under the authority of the government set up after the general elections in South Vietnam provided for in Article 9 (b).

## Chapter V
### THE REUNIFICATION OF VIETNAM AND THE RELATIONSHIP BETWEEN NORTH AND SOUTH VIETNAM

### Article 15

The reunification of Vietnam shall be carried out step by step through peaceful means on the basis of discussions and agreements between North and South Vietnam, without coercion or annexation by either party, and without foreign interference. The time for reunification will be agreed upon by North and South Vietnam.

Pending reunification:

(a) The military demarcation line between the two zones at the 17th parallel is only provisional and not a political or territorial boundary, as provided for in paragraph 6 of the Final Declaration of the 1954 Geneva Conference.

(b) North and South Vietnam shall respect the Demilitarized Zone on either side of the Provisional Military Demarcation Line.

(c) North and South Vietnam shall promptly start negotiations with a view to reestablishing normal relations in various fields. Among the questions to be negotiated are the modalities of civilian movement across the Provisional Military Demarcation Line.

(d) North and South Vietnam shall not join any military alliance or military bloc and shall not allow foreign powers to maintain military bases, troops, military advisers, and military personnel on their respective territories, as stipulated in the 1954 Geneva Agreements on Vietnam.

## Chapter VI

THE JOINT MILITARY COMMISSIONS, THE INTERNATIONAL COMMISSION OF CONTROL AND SUPERVISION, THE INTERNATIONAL CONFERENCE

### Article 16

(a) The Parties participating in the Paris Conference on Vietnam shall immediately designate representatives to form a Four-Party Joint Military Commission with the task of ensuring joint action by the parties in implementing the following provisions of this Agreement:

—The first paragraph of Article 2, regarding the enforcement of the cease-fire throughout South Vietnam;

—Article 3 (a), regarding the cease-fire by U.S. forces and those of the other foreign countries referred to in that Article;

—Article 3 (c), regarding the cease-fire between all parties in South Vietnam;

—Article 5, regarding the withdrawal from South Vietnam of U.S. troops and those of the other foreign countries mentioned in Article 3 (a);

—Article 6, regarding the dismantlement of military bases in South Vietnam of the United States and those of the other foreign countries mentioned in Article 3 (a);

—Article 8 (a), regarding the return of captured military personnel and foreign civilians of the parties;

—Article 8 (b), regarding the mutual assistance of the parties in getting information about those military personnel and foreign civilians of the parties missing in action.

(b) The Four-Party Joint Military Commission shall operate in accordance with the principle of consultations and unanimity. Disagreements shall be referred to the International Commission of Control and Supervision.

(c) The Four-Party Joint Military Commission shall begin operating immediately after the signing of this Agreement and end its activities in sixty days, after the completion of the withdrawal of U.S. troops and those of the other foreign countries mentioned in Article 3 (a) and the completion of the return of captured military personnel and foreign civilians of the parties.

(d) The four parties shall agree immediately on the organization, the working procedure, means of activity, and expenditures of the Four-Party Joint Military Commission.

### Article 17

(a) The two South Vietnamese parties shall immediately designate representatives to form a Two-Party Joint Military Commission with the task of ensuring joint action by the two South Vietnamese

parties in implementing the following provisions of this Agreement:

—The first paragraph of Article 2, regarding the enforcement of the cease-fire throughout South Vietnam, when the Four-Party Joint Military Commission has ended its activities;

—Article 3 (b), regarding the cease-fire between the two South Vietnamese parties;

—Article 3 (c), regarding the cease-fire between all parties in South Vietnam, when the Four-Party Joint Military Commission has ended its activities;

—Article 7, regarding the prohibition of the introduction of troops into South Vietnam and all other provisions of this article;

—Article 8 (c), regarding the question of the return of Vietnamese civilian personnel captured and detained in South Vietnam;

—Article 13, regarding the reduction of the military effectives of the two South Vietnamese parties and the demobilization of the troops being reduced.

(b) Disagreements shall be referred to the International Commission of Control and Supervision.

(c) After the signing of this Agreement, the Two-Party Joint Military Commission shall agree immediately on the measures and organization aimed at enforcing the cease-fire and preserving peace in South Vietnam.

### Article 18

(a) After the signing of this Agreement, an International Commission of Control and Supervision shall be established immediately.

(b) Until the International Conference provided for in Article 19 makes definitive arrangements, the International Commission of Control and Supervision will report to the four parties on matters concerning the control and supervision of the implementation of the following provisions of this Agreement:

—The first paragraph of Article 2, regarding the enforcement of the cease-fire throughout South Vietnam;

—Article 3 (a), regarding the cease-fire by U.S. forces and those of the other foreign countries referred to in that Article;

—Article 3 (c), regarding the cease-fire between all the parties in South Vietnam;

—Article 5, regarding the withdrawal from Vietnam of U.S. troops and those of the other foreign countries mentioned in Article 3 (a);

—Article 6, regarding the dismantlement of military bases in South Vietnam of the United States and those of the other foreign countries mentioned in Article 3 (a);

—Article 8 (a), regarding the return of captured military personnel and foreign civilians of the parties.

The International Commission of Control and Supervision shall form control teams for carrying out its tasks. The four parties shall agree immediately on the location and operation of these teams. The parties will facilitate their operation.

(c) Until the International Conference makes definitive arrangements, the International Commission of Control and Supervision will report to the two South Vietnamese parties on matters concerning the control and supervision of the implementation of the following provisions of this Agreement:

—The first paragraph of Article 2, regarding the enforcement of the cease-fire throuhout South Vietnam, when the Four-Party Joint Military Commission has ended its activities;

—Article 3 (b), regarding the cease-fire between the two South Vietnamese parties;

—Article 3 (c), regarding the cease-fire between all parties in South Vietnam, when the Four-Party Joint Military Commission has ended its activities;

—Article 7, regarding the prohibition of the introduction of troops into South Vietnam and all other provisions of this Article;

—Article 8 (c), regarding the question of the return of Vietnamese civilian personnel captured and detained in South Vietnam;

—Article 9 (b), regarding the free and democratic general elections in South Vietnam;

—Article 13, regarding the reduction of the military effectives of the two South Vietnamese parties and the demobilization of the troops being reduced.

The International Commission of Control and Supervision shall form control teams for carrying out its tasks. The two South Vietnamese parties shall agree immediately on the location and operation of these teams. The two South Vietnamese parties will facilitate their operation.

(d) The International Commission of Control and Supervision shall be composed of representatives of four countries: Canada, Hungary, Indonesia and Poland. The chairmanship of this Commission will rotate among the members for specific periods to be determined by the Commission.

(e) The International Commission of Control and Supervision shall carry out its tasks in accordance with the principle of respect for the sovereignty of South Vietnam.

(f) The International Commission of Control and Supervision shall operate in accordance with the principle of consultations and unanimity.

(g) The International Commission of Control and Supervision shall begin operating when a cease-fire comes into force in Vietnam. As regards the provisions in Article 18 (b) concerning the four parties, the International Commission of Control and Supervision shall end its activities when the Commission's tasks of control and supervision regarding these provisions have been fulfilled. As regards the provisions in Article 18 (c) concerning the two South Vietnamese parties, the International Commission of Control and Supervision shall end

its activities on the request of the government formed after the general elections in South Vietnam provided for in Article 9 (b).

(h) The four parties shall agree immediately on the organization, means of activity, and expenditures of the International Commission of Control and Supervision. The relationship between the International Commission and the International Conference will be agreed upon by the International Commission and the International Conference.

### Article 19

The parties agree on the convening of an International Conference within thirty days of the signing of this Agreement to acknowledge the signed agreements; to guarantee the ending of the war, the maintenance of peace in Vietnam, the respect of the Vietnamese people's fundamental national rights, and the South Vietnamese people's right to self-determination; and to contribute to and guarantee peace in Indochina.

The United States and the Democratic Republic of Vietnam, on behalf of the parties participating in the Paris Conference on Vietnam, will propose to the following parties that they participate in this International Conference: the People's Republic of China, the Republic of France, the Union of Soviet Socialist Republics, the United Kingdom, the four countries of the International Commission of Control and Supervision, and the Secretary General of the United Nations, together with the parties participating in the Paris Conference on Vietnam.

### Chapter VII

#### REGARDING CAMBODIA AND LAOS

#### Article 20

(a) The parties participating in the Paris Conference on Vietnam shall strictly respect the 1954 Geneva Agreements on Cambodia and the 1962 Geneva Agreements on Laos, which recognized the Cambodian and the Lao peoples' fundamental national rights, i.e., the independence, sovereignty, unity, and territorial integrity of these countries. The parties shall respect the neutrality of Cambodia and Laos.

The parties participating in the Paris Conference on Vietnam undertake to refrain from using the territory of Cambodia and the territory of Laos to encroach on the sovereignty and security of one another and of other countries.

(b) Foreign countries shall put an end to all military activities in Cambodia and Laos, totally withdraw from and refrain from reintroducing into these two countries troops, military advisers and military personnel, armaments, munitions and war material.

(c) The internal affairs of Cambodia and Laos shall be settled by the people of each of these countries without foreign interference.

(d) The problems existing between the Indochinese countries shall be settled by the Indochinese parties on the basis of respect for each other's independence, sovereignty, and territorial integrity, and non-interference in each other's internal affairs.

## Chapter VIII

### THE RELATIONSHIP BETWEEN THE UNITED STATES AND THE DEMOCRATIC REPUBLIC OF VIETNAM

#### Article 21

The United States anticipates that this Agreement will usher in an era of reconciliation with the Democratic Republic of Vietnam as with all the peoples of Indochina. In pursuance of its traditional policy, the United States will contribute to healing the wounds of war and to postwar reconstruction of the Democratic Republic of Vietnam and throughout Indochina.

#### Article 22

The ending of the war, the restoration of peace in Vietnam, and the strict implementation of this Agreement will create conditions for establishing a new, equal and mutually beneficial relationship between the United States and the Democratic Republic of Vietnam on the basis of respect for each other's independence and sovereignty, and non-interference in each other's internal affairs. At the same time this will ensure stable peace in Vietnam and contribute to the preservation of lasting peace in Indochina and Southeast Asia.

## Chapter IX

### OTHER PROVISIONS

#### Article 23

This Agreement shall enter into force upon signature by plenipotentiary representatives of the parties participating in the Paris Conference on Vietnam. All the parties concerned shall strictly implement this Agreement and its Protocols.

DONE in Paris this twenty-seventh day of January, One Thousand Nine Hundred and Seventy-Three, in Vietnamese and English. The Vietnamese and English texts are official and equally authentic.

[Separate Numbered Page]

For the Government of the United States of America

WILLIAM P. ROGERS
*Secretary of State*

For the Government of the Republic of Vietnam

TRAN VAN LAM
*Minister for Foreign Affairs*

[Separate Numbered Page]

For the Government of the Democratic Republic of Vietnam

NGUYEN DUY TRINH
*Minister for Foreign Affairs*

For the Provisional Revolutionary Government of the Republic of South Vietnam

NGUYEN THI BINH
*Minister for Foreign Affairs*

## AGREEMENT ON ENDING THE WAR AND RESTORING PEACE IN VIETNAM

The Government of the United States of America, with the concurrence of the Government of the Republic of Vietnam,

The Government of the Democratic Republic of Vietnam, with the concurrence of the Provisional Revolutionary Government of the Republic of South Vietnam,

With a view to ending the war and restoring peace in Vietnam on the basis of respect for the Vietnamese people's fundamental national rights and the South Vietnamese people's right to self-determination, and to contributing to the consolidation of peace in Asia and the world,

Have agreed on the following provisions and undertake to respect and to implement them:

[Text of Agreement Chapters I–VIII Same As Above]

### Chapter IX

#### OTHER PROVISIONS

#### Article 23

The Paris Agreement on Ending the War and Restoring Peace in Vietnam shall enter into force upon signature of this document by the Secretary of State of the Government of the United States of America and the Minister for Foreign Affairs of the Government of the Democratic Republic of Vietnam, and upon signature of a document in the same terms by the Secretary of State of the Government of the United States of America, the Minister for Foreign Affairs of the Government of the Republic of Vietnam, the Minister for Foreign Affairs of the Government of the Democratic Republic of Vietnam, and the Minister for Foreign Affairs of the Provisional Revolutionary Government of the Republic of South Vietnam. The Agreement and the protocols to it shall be strictly implemented by all the parties concerned.

DONE in Paris this twenty-seventh day of January, One Thousand Nine Hundred and Seventy-Three, in Vietnamese and English. The Vietnamese and English texts are official and equally authentic.

For the Government of the United States of America

WILLIAM P. ROGERS
*Secretary of State*

For the Government of the Democratic Republic of Vietnam

NGUYEN DUY TRINH
*Minister for Foreign Affairs*

### Protocol on Prisoners and Detainees

White House press release dated January 24

PROTOCOL TO THE AGREEMENT ON ENDING THE WAR AND RESTORING PEACE IN VIETNAM CONCERNING THE RETURN OF CAPTURED MILITARY PERSONNEL AND FOREIGN CIVILIANS AND CAPTURED AND DETAINED VIETNAMESE CIVILIAN PERSONNEL.

The Parties participating in the Paris Conference on Vietnam,

In implementation of Article 8 of the Agreement on Ending the War and Restoring Peace in Vietnam signed on this date providing for the return of captured military personnel and foreign civilians, and captured and detained Vietnamese civilian personnel,

Have agreed as follows:

### THE RETURN OF CAPTURED MILITARY PERSONNEL AND FOREIGN CIVILIANS

#### Article 1

The parties signatory to the Agreement shall return the captured military personnel of the parties mentioned in Article 8 (a) of the Agreement as follows:

—all captured military personnel of the United States and those of the other foreign countries mentioned in Article 3 (a) of the Agreement shall be returned to United States authorities;

—all captured Vietnamese military personnel, whether belonging to regular or irregular armed forces, shall be returned to the two South Vietnamese parties; they shall be returned to that South Vietnamese party under whose command they served.

#### Article 2

All captured civilians who are nationals of the United States or of any other foreign countries mentioned in Article 3 (a) of the Agreement shall be returned to United States authorities. All other captured foreign civilians shall be returned to the authorities of their country of nationality by any one of the parties willing and able to do so.

#### Article 3

The parties shall today exchange complete lists of captured persons mentioned in Articles 1 and 2 of this Protocol.

#### Article 4

(a) The return of all captured persons mentioned in Articles 1 and 2 of this Protocol shall be completed within sixty days of the signing of the Agreement at a rate no slower than the rate of withdrawal from South Vietnam of United States forces and those of the other foreign countries mentioned in Article 5 of the Agreement.

(b) Persons who are seriously ill, wounded or maimed, old persons and women shall be returned first. The remainder shall be returned either by returning all from one detention place after another or in order of their dates of capture, beginning with those who have been held the longest.

#### Article 5

The return and reception of the persons mentioned in Articles 1 and 2 of this Protocol shall be carried out at places convenient to the concerned parties. Places of return shall be agreed upon by the Four-Party Joint Military Commission. The parties shall ensure the safety of personnel engaged in the return and reception of those persons.

#### Article 6

Each party shall return all captured persons mentioned in Articles 1 and 2 of this Protocol without delay and shall facilitate their return and reception. The detaining parties shall not deny or delay their return for any reason, including the fact that captured persons may, on any grounds, have been prosecuted or sentenced.

### THE RETURN OF CAPTURED AND DETAINED VIETNAMESE CIVILIAN PERSONNEL

#### Article 7

(a) The question of the return of Vietnamese civilian personnel captured and detained in South Vietnam will be resolved by the two South Vietnamese parties on the basis of the principles of Article 21 (b) of the Agreement on the Cessation of Hostilities in Vietnam of July 20, 1954, which reads as follows:

"The term 'civilian internees' is understood to mean all persons who, having in any way contributed to the political and armed struggle between the two parties, have been arrested for that reason and have been kept in detention by either party during the period of hostilities."

(b) The two South Vietnamese parties will do so in a spirit of national reconciliation and concord with a view to ending hatred and enmity in order to ease suffering and to reunite families. The two South Vietnamese parties will do their utmost to resolve this question within ninety days after the cease-fire comes into effect.

(c) Within fifteen days after the cease-fire comes into effect, the two South Vietnamese parties shall exchange lists of the Vietnamese civilian personnel captured and detained by each party and lists of the places at which they are held.

### TREATMENT OF CAPTURED PERSONS DURING DETENTION

#### Article 8

(a) All captured military personnel of the parties and captured foreign civilians of the parties shall be treated humanely at all times, and in accordance with international practice.

They shall be protected against all violence to life and person, in particular against murder in any form, mutilation, torture and cruel treatment, and outrages upon personal dignity. These persons shall not be forced to join the armed forces of the detaining party.

They shall be given adequate food, clothing, shelter, and the medical attention required for their state of health. They shall be allowed to exchange post cards and letters with their families and receive parcels.

(b) All Vietnamese civilian personnel captured and detained in South Vietnam shall be treated humanely at all times, and in accordance with international practice.

They shall be protected against all violence to life and person, in particular against murder in any form, mutilation, torture and cruel treatment, and outrages against personal dignity. The detaining parties shall not deny or delay their return for any reason, including the fact that captured persons may, on any grounds, have been prosecuted or sentenced. These persons shall not be forced to join the armed forces of the detaining party.

They shall be given adequate food, clothing, shelter, and the medical attention required for their state of health. They shall be allowed to exchange post cards and letters with their families and receive parcels.

### Article 9

(a) To contribute to improving the living conditions of the captured military personnel of the parties and foreign civilians of the parties, the parties shall, within fifteen days after the cease-fire comes into effect, agree upon the designation of two or more national Red Cross societies to visit all places where captured military personnel and foreign civilians are held.

(b) To contribute to improving the living conditions of the captured and detained Vietnamese civilian personnel, the two South Vietnamese parties shall, within fifteen days after the cease-fire comes into effect, agree upon the designation of two or more national Red Cross societies to visit all places where the captured and detained Vietnamese civilian personnel are held.

### WITH REGARD TO DEAD AND MISSING PERSONS

### Article 10

(a) The Four-Party Joint Military Commission shall ensure joint action by the parties in implementing Article 8 (b) of the Agreement. When the Four-Party Joint Military Commission has ended its activities, a Four-Party Joint Military team shall be maintained to carry on this task.

(b) With regard to Vietnamese civilian personnel dead or missing in South Vietnam, the two South Vietnamese parties shall help each other to obtain information about missing persons, determine the location and take care of the graves of the dead, in a spirit of national reconciliation and concord, in keeping with the people's aspirations.

### OTHER PROVISIONS

### Article 11

(a) The Four-Party and Two-Party Joint Military Commissions will have the responsibility of determining immediately the modalities of implementing the provisions of this Protocol consistent with their respective responsibilities under Articles 16 (a) and 17 (a) of the Agreement. In case the Joint Military Commissions, when carrying out their tasks, cannot reach agreement on a matter pertaining to the return of captured personnel they shall refer to the International Commission for its assistance.

(b) The Four-Party Joint Military Commission shall form, in addition to the teams established by the Protocol concerning the cease-fire in South Vietnam and the Joint Military Commissions, a sub-commission on captured persons and, as required, joint military teams on captured persons to assist the Commission in its tasks.

(c) From the time the cease-fire comes into force to the time when the Two-Party Joint Military Commission becomes operational, the two South Vietnamese parties' delegations to the Four-Party Joint Military Commission shall form a provisional sub-commission and provisional joint military teams to carry out its tasks concerning captured and detained Vietnamese civilian personnel.

(d) The Four-Party Joint Military Commission shall send joint military teams to observe the return of the persons mentioned in Articles 1 and 2 of this Protocol at each place in Vietnam where such persons are being returned, and at the last detention places from which these persons will be taken to the places of return. The Two-Party Joint Military Commission shall send joint military teams to observe the return of Vietnamese civilian personnel captured and detained at each place in South Vietnam where such persons are being returned, and at the last detention places from which these persons will be taken to the places of return.

### Article 12

In implementation of Articles 18 (b) and 18 (c) of the Agreement, the International Commission of Control and Supervision shall have the responsibility to control and supervise the observance of Articles 1 through 7 of this Protocol through observation of the return of captured military personnel, foreign civilians and captured and detained Vietnamese civilian personnel at each place in Vietnam where these persons are being returned, and at the last detention places from which these persons will be taken to the places of return, the examination of lists, and the investigation of violations of the provisions of the above-mentioned Articles.

### Article 13

Within five days after signature of this Protocol, each party shall publish the text of the Protocol and communicate it to all the captured persons covered by the Protocol and being detained by that party.

### Article 14

This Protocol shall come into force upon signature by plenipotentiary representatives of all the parties participating in the Paris Conference on Vietnam. It shall be strictly implemented by all the parties concerned.

DONE in Paris this twenty-seventh day of January, One Thousand Nine Hundred and Seventy-Three, in Vietnamese and English. The Vietnamese and English texts are official and equally authentic.

| For the Government of the United States of America | For the Government of the Republic of Vietnam |
| --- | --- |
| WILLIAM P. ROGERS<br>*Secretary of State* | TRAN VAN LAM<br>*Minister for Foreign Affairs* |

| For the Government of the Democratic Republic of Vietnam | For the Provisional Revolutionary Government of the Republic of South Vietnam |
| --- | --- |
| NGUYEN DUY TRINH<br>*Minister for Foreign Affairs* | NGUYEN THI BINH<br>*Minister for Foreign Affairs* |

PROTOCOL TO THE AGREEMENT ON ENDING THE WAR AND RESTORING PEACE IN VIETNAM CONCERNING THE RETURN OF CAPTURED MILITARY PERSONNEL AND FOREIGN CIVILIANS AND CAPTURED AND DETAINED VIETNAMESE CIVILIAN PERSONNEL

The Government of the United States of America, with the concurrence of the Government of the Republic of Vietnam,

The Government of the Democratic Republic of Vietnam, with the concurrence of the Provisional Revolutionary Government of the Republic of South Vietnam,

In implementation of Article 8 of the Agreement on Ending the War and Restoring Peace in Vietnam signed on this date providing for the return of captured military personnel and foreign civilians, and captured and detained Vietnamese civilian personnel,

Have agreed as follows:

[Text of Protocol Articles 1–13 same as above]

*Article 14*

The Protocol to the Paris Agreement on Ending the War and Restoring Peace in Vietnam concerning the Return of Captured Military Personnel and Foreign Civilians and Captured and Detained Vietnamese Civilian Personnel shall enter into force upon signature of this document by the Secretary of State of the Government of the United States of America and the Minister for Foreign Affairs of the Government of the Democratic Republic of Vietnam, and upon signature of a document in the same terms by the Secretary of State of the Government of the United States of America, the Minister for Foreign Affairs of the Government of the Republic of Vietnam, the Minister for Foreign Affairs of the Government of the Democratic Republic of Vietnam, and the Minister for Foreign Affairs of the Provisional Revolutionary Government of the Republic of South Vietnam. The Protocol shall be strictly implemented by all the parties concerned.

DONE in Paris this twenty-seventh day of January, One Thousand Nine Hundred and Seventy-Three, in Vietnamese and English. The Vietnamese and English texts are official and equally authentic.

| For the Government of the United States of America | For the Government of the Democratic Republic of Vietnam |
| --- | --- |
| WILLIAM P. ROGERS<br>*Secretary of State* | NGUYEN DUY TRINH<br>*Minister for Foreign Affairs* |

### Protocol on the International Commission of Control and Supervision

White House press release dated January 24

PROTOCOL TO THE AGREEMENT ON ENDING THE WAR AND RESTORING PEACE IN VIETNAM CONCERNING THE INTERNATIONAL COMMISSION OF CONTROL AND SUPERVISION

The parties participating in the Paris Conference on Vietnam,

In implementation of Article 18 of the Agreement on Ending the War and Restoring Peace in Vietnam signed on this date providing for the formation of the International Commission of Control and Supervision,

Have agreed as follows:

*Article 1*

The implementation of the Agreement is the responsibility of the parties signatory to the Agreement.

The functions of the International Commission are to control and supervise the implementation of the provisions mentioned in Article 18 of the Agreement. In carrying out these functions, the International Commission shall:

(a) Follow the implementation of the above-mentioned provisions of the Agreement through communication with the parties and on-the-spot observation at the places where this is required;

(b) Investigate violations of the provisions which fall under the control and supervision of the Commission;

(c) When necessary, cooperate with the Joint Military Commissions in deterring and detecting violations of the above-mentioned provisions.

*Article 2*

The International Commission shall investigate violations of the provisions described in Article 18 of the Agreement on the request of the Four-Party Joint Military Commission, or of the Two-Party Joint Military Commission, or of any party, or, with respect to Article 9 (b) of the Agreement on general elections, of the National Council of National Reconciliation and Concord, or in any case where the International Commission has other adequate grounds for considering that there has been a violation of those provisions. It is understood that, in carrying out this task, the International Commission shall function with the concerned parties' assistance and cooperation as required.

### Article 3

(a) When the International Commission finds that there is a serious violation in the implementation of the Agreement or a threat to peace against which the Commission can find no appropriate measure, the Commission shall report this to the four parties to the Agreement so that they can hold consultations to find a solution.

(b) In accordance with Article 18 (f) of the Agreement, the International Commission's reports shall be made with the unanimous agreement of the representatives of all the four members. In case no unanimity is reached, the Commission shall forward the different views to the four parties in accordance with Article 18 (b) of the Agreement, or to the two South Vietnamese parties in accordance with Article 18 (c) of the Agreement, but these shall not be considered as reports of the Commission.

### Article 4

(a) The headquarters of the International Commission shall be at Saigon.

(b) There shall be seven regional teams located in the regions shown on the annexed map and based at the following places:

| Regions | Places |
|---------|--------|
| I | Hue |
| II | Danang |
| III | Pleiku |
| IV | Phan Thiet |
| V | Bien Hoa |
| VI | My Tho |
| VII | Can Tho |

The International Commission shall designate three teams for the region of Saigon-Gia Dinh.

(c) There shall be twenty-six teams operating in the areas shown on the annexed map and based at the following places in South Vietnam:

*Region I*
Quang Tri
Phu Bai

*Region II*
Hoi An
Tam Ky
Chu Lai

*Region III*
Kontum
Hau Bon
Phu Cat
Tuy An
Ninh Hoa
Ban Me Thuot

*Region IV*
Da Lat

Bao Loc
Phan Rang

*Region V*
An Loc
Xuan Loc
Ben Cat
Cu Chi
Tan An

*Region VI*
Moc Hoa
Giong Trom

*Region VII*
Tri Ton
Vinh Long
Vi Thanh
Khanh Hung
Quan Long

(d) There shall be twelve teams located as shown on the annexed map and based at the following places:

Gio Linh (to cover the area south of the Provisional Military Demarcation Line)
Lao Bao
Ben Het
Duc Co
Chu Lai
Qui Nhon
Nha Trang
Vung Tau
Xa Mat
Bien Hoa Airfield
Hong Ngu
Can Tho

(e) There shall be seven teams, six of which shall be available for assignment to the points of entry which are not listed in paragraph (d) above and which the two South Vietnamese parties choose as points for legitimate entry to South Vietnam for replacement of armaments, munitions, and war material permitted by Article 7 of the Agreement. Any team or teams not needed for the above-mentioned assignment shall be available for other tasks, in keeping with the Commission's responsibility for control and supervision.

(f) There shall be seven teams to control and supervise the return of captured and detained personnel of the parties.

### Article 5

(a) To carry out its tasks concerning the return of the captured military personnel and foreign civilians of the parties as stipulated by Article 8 (a) of the Agreement, the International Commission shall, during the time of such return, send one control and supervision team to each place in Vietnam where the captured persons are being returned, and to the last detention places from which these persons will be taken to the places of return.

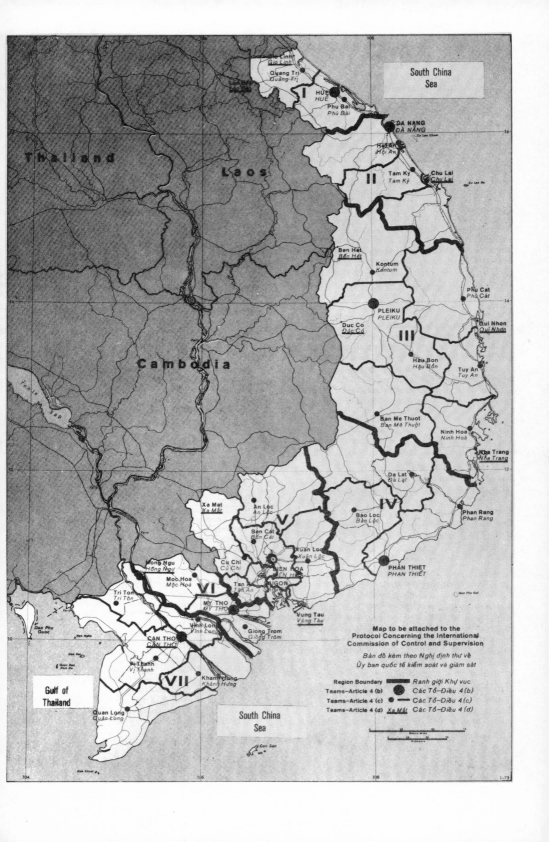

South China
Sea

Thailand

L a o s

C a m b o d i a

Gulf of
Thailand

South China
Sea

Cio Linh
Gio Linh
Quang Tri
Quảng Trị

I

HUE
HUẾ
Phu Bai
Phú Bài

DA NANG
ĐÀ NẴNG
Cu Lao Cham

Hoi An
Hội An

II

Tam Ky
Tam Kỳ

Chu Lai
Chu Lai

Cu Lao Re

Ben Het
Bến Hét

Kontum
Kontum

Phu Cat
Phú Cát

Duc Co
Đức Cơ

PLEIKU
PLEIKU

III

Qui Nhon
Qui Nhơn

Hau Bon
Hậu Bổn

Tuy An
Tuy An

Ban Me Thuot
Ban Mê Thuột

Ninh Hoa
Ninh Hoà

Nha Trang
Nha Trang

Da Lat
Đà Lạt

Xa Mat
Xa Mất

An Loc
An Lộc

V

IV

Bao Loc
Bảo Lộc

Phan Rang
Phan Rang

Ben Cat
Bến Cát

Cu Chi
Củ Chi

Xuan Loc
Xuân Lộc

Hong Ngu
Hồng Ngự

Moc Hoa
Mộc Hoá

VI

Tan An
Tân An

BIEN HOA
BIÊN HOÀ

SAIGON

PHAN THIET
PHAN THIẾT

Dao Phu Qui

Tri Ton
Tri Tôn

MY THO
MỸ THO

Vung Tau
Vũng Tàu

Vinh Long
Vĩnh Long

Giong Trom
Giồng Trôm

Dao Phu
Quoc

CAN THO
CẦN THƠ

Hon Nghe

Vi Thanh
Vị Thanh

Quan Dao
Nam Du

Hon Rai

VII

Khanh Hung
Khánh Hưng

Map to be attached to the
Protocol Concerning the International
Commission of Control and Supervision

Bản đồ kèm theo Nghị định thư về
Ủy ban quốc tế kiểm soát và giám sát

Quan Long
Quản Long

Con Son

Hon Khoai Đ.

Region Boundary        Ranh giới Khu vực
Teams–Article 4 (b)    Các Tổ–Điều 4 (b)
Teams–Article 4 (c)    Các Tổ–Điều 4 (c)
Teams–Article 4 (d)  Xa Mất  Các Tổ–Điều 4 (d)

Statute Miles

Kilometers

1–73

(b) To carry out its tasks concerning the return of the Vietnamese civilian personnel captured and detained in South Vietnam mentioned in Article 8 (c) of the Agreement, the International Commission shall, during the time of such return, send one control and supervision team to each place in South Vietnam where the above-mentioned captured and detained persons are being returned, and to the last detention places from which these persons shall be taken to the places of return.

### Article 6

To carry out its tasks regarding Article 9 (b) of the Agreement on the free and democratic general elections in South Vietnam, the International Commission shall organize additional teams, when necessary. The International Commission shall discuss this question in advance with the National Council of National Reconciliation and Concord. If additional teams are necessary for this purpose, they shall be formed thirty days before the general elections.

### Article 7

The International Commission shall continually keep under review its size, and shall reduce the number of its teams, its representatives or other personnel, or both, when those teams, representatives or personnel have accomplished the tasks assigned to them and are not required for other tasks. At the same time, the expenditures of the International Commission shall be reduced correspondingly.

### Article 8

Each member of the International Commission shall make available at all times the following numbers of qualified personnel:

(a) One senior representative and twenty-six others for the headquarters staff.

(b) Five for each of the seven regional teams.

(c) Two for each of the other international control teams, except for the teams at Gio Linh and Vung Tau, each of which shall have three.

(d) One hundred sixteen for the purpose of providing support to the Commission Headquarters and its teams.

### Article 9

(a) The International Commission, and each of its teams, shall act as a single body comprising representatives of all four members.

(b) Each member has the responsibility to ensure the presence of its representatives at all levels of the International Commission. In case a representative is absent, the member concerned shall immediately designate a replacement.

### Article 10

(a) The parties shall afford full cooperation, assistance, and protection to the International Commission.

(b) The parties shall at all times maintain regular and continuous liaison with the International Commission. During the existence of the Four-Party Joint Military Commission, the delegations of the parties to that Commission shall also perform liaison functions with the International Commission. After the Four-Party Joint Military Commission has ended its activities, such liaison shall be maintained through the Two-Party Joint Military Commission, liaison missions, or other adequate means.

(c) The International Commission and the Joint Military Commissions shall closely cooperate with and assist each other in carrying out their respective functions.

(d) Wherever a team is stationed or operating, the concerned party shall designate a liaison officer to the team to cooperate with and assist it in carrying out without hindrance its task of control and supervision. When a team is carrying out an investigation, a liaison officer from each concerned party shall have the opportunity to accompany it, provided the investigation is not thereby delayed.

(e) Each party shall give the International Commission reasonable advance notice of all proposed actions concerning those provisions of the Agreement that are to be controlled and supervised by the International Commission.

(f) The International Commission, including its teams, is allowed such movement for observation as is reasonably required for the proper exercise of its functions as stipulated in the Agreement. In carrying out these functions, the International Commission, including its teams, shall enjoy all necessary assistance and cooperation from the parties concerned.

### Article 11

In supervising the holding of the free and democratic general elections described in Articles 9 (b) and 12 (b) of the Agreement in accordance with modalities to be agreed upon between the National Council of National Reconciliation and Concord and the International Commission, the latter shall receive full cooperation and assistance from the National Council.

### Article 12

The International Commission and its personnel who have the nationality of a member state shall, while carrying out their tasks, enjoy privileges and immunities equivalent to those accorded diplomatic missions and diplomatic agents.

### Article 13

The International Commission may use the means of communication and transport necessary to perform its functions. Each South Vietnamese party shall make available for rent to the International Commission appropriate office and accommodation facilities and shall assist it in obtaining such facilities. The International Commission may receive from the parties, on mutually agreeable terms, the necessary means of communication and transport and may purchase from any source necessary equipment and services not obtained from the parties. The International Commission shall possess these means.

### Article 14

The expenses for the activities of the International Commission shall be borne by the parties and the members of the International Commission in accordance with the provisions of this Article:

(a) Each member country of the International Commission shall pay the salaries and allowances of its personnel.

(b) All other expenses incurred by the International Commission shall be met from a fund to which each of the four parties shall contribute twenty-three percent (23%) and to which each member of the International Commission shall contribute two percent (2%).

(c) Within thirty days of the date of entry into force of this Protocol, each of the four parties shall provide the International Commission with an initial sum equivalent to four million, five hundred thousand (4,500,000) French francs in convertible currency, which sum shall be credited against the amounts due from that party under the first budget.

(d) The International Commission shall prepare its own budgets. After the International Commission approves a budget, it shall transmit it to all parties signatory to the Agreement for their approval. Only after the budgets have been approved by the four parties to the Agreement shall they be obliged to make their contributions. However, in case the parties to the Agreement do not agree on a new budget, the International Commission shall temporarily base its expenditures on the previous budget, except for the extraordinary, one-time expenditures for installation or for the acquisition of equipment, and the parties shall continue to make their contributions on that basis until a new budget is approved.

### Article 15

(a) The headquarters shall be operational and in place within twenty-four hours after the cease-fire.

(b) The regional teams shall be operational and in place, and three teams for supervision and control of the return of the captured and detained personnel shall be operational and ready for dispatch within forty-eight hours after the cease-fire.

(c) Other teams shall be operational and in place within fifteen to thirty days after the cease-fire.

### Article 16

Meetings shall be convened at the call of the Chairman. The International Commission shall adopt other working procedures appropriate for the effective discharge of its functions and consistent with respect for the sovereignty of South Vietnam.

### Article 17

The Members of the International Commission may accept the obligations of this Protocol by sending notes of acceptance to the four parties signatory to the Agreement. Should a member of the International Commission decide to withdraw from the International Commission, it may do so by giving three months notice by means of notes to the four parties to the Agreement, in which case those four parties shall consult among themselves for the purpose of agreeing upon a replacement member.

### Article 18

This Protocol shall enter into force upon signature by plenipotentiary representatives of all the parties participating in the Paris Conference on Vietnam. It shall be strictly implemented by all the parties concerned.

DONE in Paris this twenty-seventh day of January, One Thousand Nine Hundred and Seventy-Three, in Vietnamese and English. The Vietnamese and English texts are official and equally authentic.

[Separate Numbered Page]

For the Government of the United States of America

WILLIAM P. ROGERS
*Secretary of State*

For the Government of the Republic of Vietnam

TRAN VAN LAM
*Minister for Foreign Affairs*

[Separate Numbered Page]

For the Government of the Democratic Republic of Vietnam

NGUYEN DUY TRINH
*Minister for Foreign Affairs*

For the Provisional Revolutionary Government of the Republic of South Vietnam

NGUYEN THI BINH
*Minister for Foreign Affairs*

PROTOCOL TO THE AGREEMENT ON ENDING THE WAR AND RESTORING PEACE IN VIETNAM CONCERNING THE INTERNATIONAL COMMISSION OF CONTROL AND SUPERVISION

The Government of the United States of America, with the concurrence of the Government of the Republic of Vietnam,

The Government of the Democratic Republic of Vietnam, with the concurrence of the Provisional Revolutionary Government of the Republic of South Vietnam,

In implementation of Article 18 of the Agreement on Ending the War and Restoring Peace in Vietnam signed on this date providing for the formation of the International Commission of Control and Supervision,

Have agreed as follows:

[Text of Protocol Articles 1–17 same as above.]

*Article 18*

The Protocol to the Paris Agreement on Ending the War and Restoring Peace in Vietnam concerning the International Commission of Control and Supervision shall enter into force upon signature of this document by the Secretary of State of the Government of the United States of America and the Minister for Foreign Affairs of the Government of the Democratic Republic of Vietnam, and upon signature of a document in the same terms by the Secretary of State of the Government of the United States of America, the Minister for Foreign Affairs of the Government of the Republic of Vietnam, the Minister for Foreign Affairs of the Government of the Democratic Republic of Vietnam, and the Minister for Foreign Affairs of the Provisional Revolutionary Government of the Republic of South Vietnam. The Protocol shall be strictly implemented by all the parties concerned.

DONE in Paris this twenty-seventh day of January, One Thousand Nine Hundred and Seventy-Three, in Vietnamese and English. The Vietnamese and English texts are official and equally authentic.

| For the Government of the United States of America | For the Government of the Democratic Republic of Vietnam |
| --- | --- |
| WILLIAM P. ROGERS<br>*Secretary of State* | NGUYEN DUY TRINH<br>*Minister for Foreign Affairs* |

## Protocol on the Cease-Fire in South Viet-Nam and the Joint Military Commissions

White House press release dated January 24

PROTOCOL TO THE AGREEMENT ON ENDING THE WAR AND RESTORING PEACE IN VIETNAM CONCERNING THE CEASE-FIRE IN SOUTH VIETNAM AND THE JOINT MILITARY COMMISSIONS

The parties participating in the Paris Conference on Vietnam,

In implementation of the first paragraph of Article 2, Article 3, Article 5, Article 6, Article 16 and Article 17 of the Agreement on Ending the War and Restoring Peace in Vietnam signed on this date which provide for the cease-fire in South Vietnam and the establishment of a Four-Party Joint Military Commission and a Two-Party Joint Military Commission,

Have agreed as follows:

CEASE-FIRE IN SOUTH VIETNAM

*Article 1*

The High Commands of the parties in South Vietnam shall issue prompt and timely orders to all regular and irregular armed forces and the armed police under their command to completely end hostilities throughout South Vietnam, at the exact time stipulated in Article 2 of the Agreement and ensure that these armed forces and armed police comply with these orders and respect the cease-fire.

*Article 2*

(a) As soon as the cease-fire comes into force and until regulations are issued by the Joint Military Commissions, all ground, river, sea and air combat forces of the parties in South Vietnam shall remain in place; that is, in order to ensure a stable cease-fire, there shall be no major redeployments or movements that would extend each party's area of control or would result in contact between opposing armed forces and clashes which might take place.

(b) All regular and irregular armed forces and the armed police of the parties in South Vietnam shall observe the prohibition of the following acts:

(1) Armed patrols into areas controlled by opposing armed forces and flights by bomber and fighter aircraft of all types, except for unarmed flights for proficiency training and maintenance;

(2) Armed attacks against any person, either military or civilian, by any means whatsoever, including the use of small arms, mortars, artillery, bombing and strafing by airplanes and any other type of weapon or explosive device;

(3) All combat operations on the ground, on rivers, on the sea and in the air;

(4) All hostile acts, terrorism or reprisals; and

(5) All acts endangering lives or public or private property.

*Article 3*

(a) The above-mentioned prohibitions shall not hamper or restrict:

(1) Civilian supply, freedom of movement, freedom to work, and freedom of the people to engage in trade, and civilian communication and transportation between and among all areas in South Vietnam;

(2) The use by each party in areas under its control of military support elements, such as engineer and transportation units, in repair and construction of public facilities and the transportation and supplying of the population;

(3) Normal military proficiency training conducted by the parties in the areas under their respective control with due regard for public safety.

(b) The Joint Military Commissions shall immediately agree on corridors, routes, and other regulations governing the movement of military transport aircraft, military transport vehicles, and military transport vessels of all types of one party going through areas under the control of other parties.

*Article 4*

In order to avert conflict and ensure normal conditions for those armed forces which are in direct contact, and pending regulation by the Joint Military Commissions, the commanders of the opposing armed forces at those places of direct contact shall meet as soon as the cease-fire comes into force with a view to reaching an agreement on temporary measures to avert conflict and to ensure supply and medical care for these armed forces.

### Article 5

(a) Within fifteen days after the cease-fire comes into effect, each party shall do its utmost to complete the removal or deactivation of all demolition objects, mine-fields, traps, obstacles or other dangerous objects placed previously, so as not to hamper the population's movement and work, in the first place on waterways, roads and railroads in South Vietnam. Those mines which cannot be removed or deactivated within that time shall be clearly marked and must be removed or deactivated as soon as possible.

(b) Emplacement of mines is prohibited, except as a defensive measure around the edges of military installations in places where they do not hamper the population's movement and work, and movement on waterways, roads and railroads. Mines and other obstacles already in place at the edges of military installations may remain in place if they are in places where they do not hamper the population's movement and work, and movement on waterways, roads and railroads.

### Article 6

Civilian police and civilian security personnel of the parties in South Vietnam, who are responsible for the maintenance of law and order, shall strictly respect the prohibitions set forth in Article 2 of this Protocol. As required by their responsibilities, normally they shall be authorized to carry pistols, but when required by unusual circumstances, they shall be allowed to carry other small individual arms.

### Article 7

(a) The entry into South Vietnam of replacement armaments, munitions, and war material permitted under Article 7 of the Agreement shall take place under the supervision and control of the Two-Party Joint Military Commission and of the International Commission of Control and Supervision and through such points of entry only as are designated by the two South Vietnamese parties. The two South Vietnamese parties shall agree on these points of entry within fifteen days after the entry into force of the cease-fire. The two South Vietnamese parties may select as many as six points of entry which are not included in the list of places where teams of the International Commission of Control and Supervision are to be based contained in Article 4 (d) of the Protocol concerning the International Commission. At the same time, the two South Vietnamese parties may also select points of entry from the list of places set forth in Article 4 (d) of that Protocol.

(b) Each of the designated points of entry shall be available only for that South Vietnamese party which is in control of that point. The two South Vietnamese parties shall have an equal number of points of entry.

### Article 8

(a) In implementation of Article 5 of the Agreement, the United States and the other foreign countries referred to in Article 5 of the Agreement shall take with them all their armaments, munitions, and war material. Transfers of such items which would leave them in South Vietnam shall not be made subsequent to the entry into force of the Agreement except for transfers of communications, transport, and other non-combat material to the Four-Party Joint Military Commission or the International Commission of Control and Supervision.

(b) Within five days after the entry into force of the cease-fire, the United States shall inform the Four-Party Joint Military Commission and the International Commission of Control and Supervision of the general plans for timing of complete troop withdrawals which shall take place in four phases of fifteen days each. It is anticipated that the numbers of troops withdrawn in each phase are not likely to be widely different, although it is not feasible to ensure equal numbers. The approximate numbers to be withdrawn in each phase shall be given to the Four-Party Joint Military Commission and the International Commission of Control and Supervision sufficiently in advance of actual withdrawals so that they can properly carry out their tasks in relation thereto.

### Article 9

(a) In implementation of Article 6 of the Agreement, the United States and the other foreign countries referred to in that Article shall dismantle and remove from South Vietnam or destroy all military bases in South Vietnam of the United States and of the other foreign countries referred to in that Article, including weapons, mines, and other military equipment at these bases, for the purpose of making them unusable for military purposes.

(b) The United States shall supply the Four-Party Joint Military Commission and the International Commission of Control and Supervision with necessary information on plans for base dismantlement so that those Commissions can properly carry out their tasks in relation thereto.

### THE JOINT MILITARY COMMISSIONS

### Article 10

(a) The implementation of the Agreement is the responsibility of the parties signatory to the Agreement.

The Four-Party Joint Military Commission has the task of ensuring joint action by the parties in implementing the Agreement by serving as a channel of communication among the parties, by drawing up plans and fixing the modalities to carry out, coordinate, follow and inspect the implementation of the provisions mentioned in Article 16 of the Agreement, and by negotiating and settling all matters concerning the implementation of those provisions.

(b) The concrete tasks of the Four-Party Joint Military Commission are:

(1) To coordinate, follow and inspect the implementation of the above-mentioned provisions of the Agreement by the four parties;

(2) To deter and detect violations, to deal with cases of violation, and to settle conflicts and matters of contention between the parties relating to the above-mentioned provisions;

(3) To dispatch without delay one or more joint teams, as required by specific cases, to any part of South Vietnam, to investigate alleged violations of the Agreement and to assist the parties in finding measures to prevent recurrence of similar cases;

(4) To engage in observation at the places where this is necessary in the exercise of its functions;

(5) To perform such additional tasks as it may, by unanimous decision, determine.

### Article 11

(a) There shall be a Central Joint Military Commission located in Saigon. Each party shall designate immediately a military delegation of fifty-nine persons to represent it on the Central Commission. The senior officer designated by each party shall be a general officer, or equivalent.

(b) There shall be seven Regional Joint Military Commissions located in the regions shown on the annexed map and based at the following places:

| Regions | Places |
|---------|--------|
| I | Hue |
| II | Danang |
| III | Pleiku |
| IV | Phan Thiet |
| V | Bien Hoa |
| VI | My Tho |
| VII | Can Tho |

Each party shall designate a military delegation of sixteen persons to represent it on each Regional Commission. The senior officer designated by each party shall be an officer from the rank of Lieutenant Colonel to Colonel, or equivalent.

(c) There shall be a joint military team operating in each of the areas shown on the annexed map and based at each of the following places in South Vietnam:

*Region I*
Quang Tri
Phu Bai

*Region II*
Hoi An
Tam Ky
Chu Lai

*Region III*
Kontum
Hau Bon
Phu Cat
Tuy An
Ninh Hoa
Ban Me Thuot

*Region IV*
Da Lat
Bao Loc
Phan Rang

*Region V*
An Loc
Xuan Loc
Ben Cat
Cu Chi
Tan An

*Region VI*
Moc Hoa
Giong Trom

*Region VII*
Tri Ton
Vinh Long
Vi Thanh
Khanh Hung
Quan Long

Each party shall provide four qualified persons for each joint military team. The senior person designated by each party shall be an officer from the rank of Major to Lieutenant Colonel, or equivalent.

(d) The Regional Joint Military Commissions shall assist the Central Joint Military Commission in performing its tasks and shall supervise the operations of the joint military teams. The region of Saigon-Gia Dinh is placed under the responsibility of the Central Commission which shall designate joint military teams to operate in this region.

(e) Each party shall be authorized to provide support and guard personnel for its delegations to the Central Joint Military Commission and Regional Joint Military Commissions, and for its members of the joint military teams. The total number of support and guard personnel for each party shall not exceed five hundred and fifty.

(f) The Central Joint Military Commission may establish such joint sub-commissions, joint staffs and joint military teams as circumstances may require. The Central Commission shall determine the numbers of personnel required for any additional sub-commissions, staffs or teams it establishes, provided that each party shall designate one-fourth of the number of personnel required and that the total number of personnel for the Four-Party Joint Military Commission, to include its staffs, teams, and support personnel, shall not exceed three thousand three hundred.

(g) The delegations of the two South Vietnamese

South China
Sea

Thailand

Laos

Quang Tri
Quảng Trị

I

HUE
HUẾ

Phu Bai
Phú Bài

DA NANG
ĐÀ NẴNG

HOI AN
Hội An

II

Tam Ky
Tam Kỳ

Chu Lai
Chu Lai

Kontum
Kontum

Phu Cat
Phú Cát

PLEIKU
PLEIKU

III

Hau Bon
Hậu Bốn

Tuy An
Tuy An

Cambodia

Ban Me Thuot
Ban Mê Thuột

Ninh Hoa
Ninh Hoà

Tonle Sap

Da Lat
Đà Lạt

An Loc
An Lộc

V

Bao Loc
Bảo Lộc

IV

Phan Rang
Phan Rang

Ben Cat
Bến Cát

Cu Chi
Củ Chi

Xuan Loc
Xuân Lộc

PHAN THIET
PHAN THIẾT

Moc Hoa
Mộc Hoá

BIEN HOA
BIÊN HOÀ

SAIGON

Tri Ton
Tri Tôn

VI

Tan An
Tân An

MY THO
MỸ THO

Vinh Long
Vĩnh Long

Giong Trom
Giồng Trôm

Dao Phu Quoc

CAN THO
CẦN THƠ

Gulf of
Thailand

Vi Thanh
Vị Thanh

VII

Khanh Hung
Khánh Hưng

Quan Long
Quản Long

South China
Sea

Con Son

Map to be attached to the
Protocol Concerning the Cease-fire in
South Vietnam and the
Joint Military Commissions

Bản đồ kèm theo Nghị định thư
về ngừng bắn ở Miền Nam Việt-Nam
và các Ban liên hợp quân sự

Region Boundary ▬▬▬ Ranh giới Khu vực
Teams–Article 11 (b) ● Các Tổ–Điều 11 (b)
Teams–Article 11 (c) ● Các Tổ–Điều 11 (c)

parties may, by agreement, establish provisional sub-commissions and joint military teams to carry out the tasks specifically assigned to them by Article 17 of the Agreement. With respect to Article 7 of the Agreement, the two South Vietnamese parties' delegations to the Four-Party Joint Military Commission shall establish joint military teams at the points of entry into South Vietnam used for replacement of armaments, munitions and war material which are designated in accordance with Article 7 of this Protocol. From the time the cease-fire comes into force to the time when the Two-Party Joint Military Commission becomes operational, the two South Vietnamese parties' delegations to the Four-Party Joint Military Commission shall form a provisional sub-commission and provisional joint military teams to carry out its tasks concerning captured and detained Vietnamese civilian personnel. Where necessary for the above purposes, the two South Vietnamese parties may agree to assign personnel additional to those assigned to the two South Vietnamese delegations to the Four-Party Joint Military Commission.

## Article 12

(a) In accordance with Article 17 of the Agreement which stipulates that the two South Vietnamese parties shall immediately designate their respective representatives to form the Two-Party Joint Military Commission, twenty-four hours after the cease-fire comes into force, the two designated South Vietnamese parties' delegations to the Two-Party Joint Military Commission shall meet in Saigon so as to reach an agreement as soon as possible on organization and operation of the Two-Party Joint Military Commission, as well as the measures and organization aimed at enforcing the cease-fire and preserving peace in South Vietnam.

(b) From the time the cease-fire comes into force to the time when the Two-Party Joint Military Commission becomes operational, the two South Vietnamese parties' delegations to the Four-Party Joint Military Commission at all levels shall simultaneously assume the tasks of the Two-Party Joint Military Commission at all levels, in addition to their functions as delegations to the Four-Party Joint Military Commission.

(c) If, at the time the Four-Party Joint Military Commission ceases its operation in accordance with Article 16 of the Agreement, agreement has not been reached on organization of the Two-Party Joint Military Commission, the delegations of the two South Vietnamese parties serving with the Four-Party Joint Military Commission at all levels shall continue temporarily to work together as a provisional two-party joint military commission and to assume the tasks of the Two-Party Joint Military Commission at all levels until the Two-Party Joint Military Commission becomes operational.

## Article 13

In application of the principle of unanimity, the Joint Military Commissions shall have no chairmen, and meetings shall be convened at the request of any representative. The Joint Military Commissions shall adopt working procedures appropriate for the effective discharge of their functions and responsibilities.

## Article 14

The Joint Military Commissions and the International Commission of Control and Supervision shall closely cooperate with and assist each other in carrying out their respective functions. Each Joint Military Commission shall inform the International Commission about the implementation of those provisions of the Agreement for which that Joint Military Commission has responsibility and which are within the competence of the International Commission. Each Joint Military Commission may request the International Commission to carry out specific observation activities.

## Article 15

The Central Four-Party Joint Military Commission shall begin operating twenty-four hours after the cease-fire comes into force. The Regional Four-Party Joint Military Commissions shall begin operating forty-eight hours after the cease-fire comes into force. The joint military teams based at the places listed in Article 11 (c) of this Protocol shall begin operating no later than fifteen days after the cease-fire comes into force. The delegations of the two South Vietnamese parties shall simultaneously begin to assume the tasks of the Two-Party Joint Military Commission as provided in Article 12 of this Protocol.

## Article 16

(a) The parties shall provide full protection and all necessary assistance and cooperation to the Joint Military Commissions at all levels, in the discharge of their tasks.

(b) The Joint Military Commissions and their personnel, while carrying out their tasks, shall enjoy privileges and immunities equivalent to those accorded diplomatic missions and diplomatic agents.

(c) The personnel of the Joint Military Commissions may carry pistols and wear special insignia decided upon by each Central Joint Military Commission. The personnel of each party while guarding Commission installations or equipment may be authorized to carry other individual small arms, as determined by each Central Joint Military Commission.

## Article 17

(a) The delegation of each party to the Four-

Party Joint Military Commission and the Two-Party Joint Military Commission shall have its own offices, communication, logistics and transportation means, including aircraft when necessary.

(b) Each party, in its areas of control shall provide appropriate office and accommodation facilities to the Four-Party Joint Military Commission and the Two-Party Joint Military Commission at all levels.

(c) The parties shall endeavor to provide to the Four-Party Joint Military Commission and the Two-Party Joint Military Commission, by means of loan, lease, or gift, the common means of operation, including equipment for communication, supply, and transport, including aircraft when necessary. The Joint Military Commissions may purchase from any source necessary facilities, equipment, and services which are not supplied by the parties. The Joint Military Commissions shall possess and use these facilities and this equipment.

(d) The facilities and the equipment for common use mentioned above shall be returned to the parties when the Joint Military Commissions have ended their activities.

### Article 18

The common expenses of the Four-Party Joint Military Commission shall be borne equally by the four parties, and the common expenses of the Two-Party Joint Military Commission in South Vietnam shall be borne equally by these two parties.

### Article 19

This Protocol shall enter into force upon signature by plenipotentiary representatives of all the parties participating in the Paris Conference on Vietnam. It shall be strictly implemented by all the parties concerned.

DONE in Paris this twenty-seventh day of January, One Thousand Nine Hundred and Seventy-Three, in Vietnamese and English. The Vietnamese and English texts are official and equally authentic.

[Separate Numbered Page]

For the Government of the United States of America

For the Government of the Republic of Vietnam

WILLIAM P. ROGERS
*Secretary of State*

TRAN VAN LAM
*Minister for Foreign Affairs*

[Separate Numbered Page]

For the Government of the Democratic Republic of Vietnam

For the Provisional Revolutionary Government of the Republic of South Vietnam

NGUYEN DUY TRINH
*Minister for Foreign Affairs*

NGUYEN THI BINH
*Minister for Foreign Affairs*

PROTOCOL TO THE AGREEMENT ON ENDING THE WAR AND RESTORING PEACE IN VIETNAM CONCERNING THE CEASE-FIRE IN SOUTH VIETNAM AND THE JOINT MILITARY COMMISSIONS

The Government of the United States of America, with the concurrence of the Government of the Republic of Vietnam,

The Government of the Democratic Republic of Vietnam, with the concurrence of the Provisional Revolutionary Government of the Republic of South Vietnam,

In implementation of the first paragraph of Article 2, Article 3, Article 5, Article 6, Article 16 and Article 17 of the Agreement on Ending the War and Restoring Peace in Vietnam signed on this date which provide for the cease-fire in South Vietnam and the establishment of a Four-Party Joint Military Commission and a Two-Party Joint Military Commission,

Have agreed as follows:

[Text of Protocol Articles 1–18 same as above]

### Article 19

The Protocol to the Paris Agreement on Ending the War and Restoring Peace in Vietnam concerning the Cease-fire in South Vietnam and the Joint Military Commissions shall enter into force upon signature of this document by the Secretary of State of the Government of the United States of America and the Minister for Foreign Affairs of the Government of the Democratic Republic of Vietnam, and upon signature of a document in the same terms by the Secretary of State of the Government of the United States of America, the Minister for Foreign Affairs of the Government of the Republic of Vietnam, the Minister for Foreign Affairs of the Government of the Democratic Republic of Vietnam, and the Minister for Foreign Affairs of the Provisional Revolutionary Government of the Republic of South Vietnam. The Protocol shall be strictly implemented by all the parties concerned.

DONE in Paris this twenty-seventh day of January, One Thousand Nine Hundred and Seventy-Three, in Vietnamese and English. The Vietnamese and English texts are official and equally authentic.

For the Government of the United States of America

For the Government of the Democratic Republic of Vietnam

WILLIAM P. ROGERS
*Secretary of State*

NGUYEN DUY TRINH
*Minister for Foreign Affairs*

## Protocol on Mine Clearing in North Viet-Nam

White House press release dated January 24

PROTOCOL TO THE AGREEMENT ON ENDING THE WAR AND RESTORING PEACE IN VIETNAM CONCERNING

THE REMOVAL, PERMANENT DEACTIVATION, OR DE-
STRUCTION OF MINES IN THE TERRITORIAL WATERS,
PORTS, HARBORS, AND WATERWAYS OF THE DEMO-
CRATIC REPUBLIC OF VIETNAM

The Government of the United States of America,
The Government of the Democratic Republic of
Vietnam,
In implementation of the second paragraph of
Article 2 of the Agreement on Ending the War and
Restoring Peace in Vietnam signed on this date,
Have agreed as follows:

## Article 1

The United States shall clear all the mines it
has placed in the territorial waters, ports, harbors,
and waterways of the Democratic Republic of Vietnam. This mine clearing operation shall be accomplished by rendering the mines harmless through
removal, permanent deactivation, or destruction.

## Article 2

With a view to ensuring lasting safety for the
movement of people and watercraft and the protection of important installations, mines shall, on
the request of the Democratic Republic of Vietnam,
be removed or destroyed in the indicated areas; and
whenever their removal or destruction is impossible,
mines shall be permanently deactivated and their
emplacement clearly marked.

## Article 3

The mine clearing operation shall begin at twenty-
four hundred (2400) hours GMT on January 27,
1973. The representatives of the two parties shall
consult immediately on relevant factors and agree
upon the earliest possible target date for the completion of the work.

## Article 4

The mine clearing operation shall be conducted
in accordance with priorities and timing agreed
upon by the two parties. For this purpose, representatives of the two parties shall meet at an early
date to reach agreement on a program and a plan
of implementation. To this end:

(a) The United States shall provide its plan for
mine clearing operations, including maps of the
minefields and information concerning the types,
numbers and properties of the mines;

(b) The Democratic Republic of Vietnam shall
provide all available maps and hydrographic charts
and indicate the mined places and all other potential

hazards to the mine clearing operations that the
Democratic Republic of Vietnam is aware of;

(c) The two parties shall agree on the timing of
implementation of each segment of the plan and
provide timely notice to the public at least forty-
eight hours in advance of the beginning of mine
clearing operations for that segment.

## Article 5

The United States shall be responsible for the
mine clearance on inland waterways of the Democratic Republic of Vietnam. The Democratic Republic of Vietnam shall, to the full extent of its
capabilities, actively participate in the mine clearance with the means of surveying, removal and
destruction and technical advice supplied by the
United States.

## Article 6

With a view to ensuring the safe movement of
people and watercraft on waterways and at sea,
the United States shall in the mine clearing process
supply timely information about the progress of
mine clearing in each area, and about the remaining mines to be destroyed. The United States shall
issue a communique when the operations have been
concluded.

## Article 7

In conducting mine clearing operations, the U.S.
personnel engaged in these operations shall respect
the sovereignty of the Democratic Republic of Vietnam and shall engage in no activities inconsistent
with the Agreement on Ending the War and Restoring Peace in Vietnam and this Protocol. The
U.S. personnel engaged in the mine clearing operations shall be immune from the jurisdiction of the
Democratic Republic of Vietnam for the duration
of the mine clearing operations.

The Democratic Republic of Vietnam shall ensure
the safety of the U.S. personnel for the duration of
their mine clearing activities on the territory of the
Democratic Republic of Vietnam, and shall provide
this personnel with all possible assistance and the
means needed in the Democratic Republic of Vietnam that have been agreed upon by the two parties.

## Article 8

This Protocol to the Paris Agreement on Ending
the War and Restoring Peace in Vietnam shall enter into force upon signature by the Secretary of
State of the Government of the United States of
America and the Minister for Foreign Affairs of
the Government of the Democratic Republic of

Vietnam. It shall be strictly implemented by the two parties.

DONE in Paris this twenty-seventh day of January, One Thousand Nine Hundred and Seventy-Three, in Vietnamese and English. The Vietnamese and English texts are official and equally authentic.

For the Government of the United States of America

WILLIAM P. ROGERS
*Secretary of State*

For the Government of the Democratic Republic of Vietnam

NGUYEN DUY TRINH
*Minister for Foreign Affairs*

# Transcript of Le Duc Tho's News Conference in Paris on Vietnam Accord

PARIS, Jan. 24 [Reuters]—Following, in unofficial translation from the French, is a transcript of Le Duc Tho's news conference today:

Dear friends, the struggle of the Vietnamese people for independence and liberty has lasted nearly 30 years. In particular, the resistance in the last 13 years with its many trials was the most difficult in the history of our people's struggle against foreign invasion over several centuries.

It is also the most murderous war in the history of the movement of national liberation of the oppressed peoples throughout the world.

Finally, this war has deeply stirred the conscience of mankind.

The negotiations between our Government and the Government of the United States of America for a peaceful settlement of the Vietnamese problem have lasted nearly five years and have gone through many particularly difficult and tense moments.

But we have overcome all obstacles and we have at last reached the agreement on ending the war and restoring peace in Vietnam.

This agreement will be officially signed in Paris in a few days.

The just cause triumphs over the evil cause. The will to live in freedom triumphs over cruelty.

The conclusion of such an agreement represents a very big victory for the Vietnamese people. It is the crowning of a valiant struggle waged in unity by the army and the people of Vietnam on all fronts, at the price of countless sacrifices and privations.

## A Very Big Victory

It is a very big victory for the figting solidarity of the peoples of the three countries of Indochina who have always fought side by side against the common enemy for independence and liberty.

It is a very great victory for the Socialist countries, the oppressed peoples and all the peace-loving and justice-loving peoples throughout the world, including the American people, who have demonstrated their solidarity and given devoted assistance to the just struggle of our people.

The return of peace in Vietnam will be greeted with immense joy by our people. At the same time, it will answer the hope which has so long been harbored by the American people and the peace-loving peoples in the world.

With the return of peace, the struggle of the Vietnamese people enters a new period. Our people, lifting high the banner of peace and of national concord, is decided to strictly apply clauses of the agreement maintaining peace, independence and democracy and heading toward the peaceful reunification of its country.

It will also have to rebuild its war-devastated country and consolidate and develop its friendly relations with all the peoples of the world, including the American people.

## Big Tasks Lie Ahead

Heavy tasks still await us in this new period. But the Vietnamese in the North as in the South, at home as abroad, rich in their traditions of unity and perseverance in struggle, following a just policy, strengthened by the close solidarity of the peoples of Laos and Cambodia and bene-fiting from strong aid from the Socialist countries and all the peace-loving countries of the world, will be able to smooth out all difficulties and victoriously accomplish their tasks.

At a time when peace is dawning on our country, in the name of the Government and people of Vietnam we wish to address our warm thanks to the Socialist countries, to the governments of many countries and to the peoples of the entire world for the sympathy they have shown toward the just struggle of the Vietnamese people and for the active help given in all fields.

In the past years, how many fighters for peace in many countries have known repression and prison, and certainly even sacrificed their lives in the fight they carried out to support the resistance of the Vietnamese people. These noble internationalist feelings and these sublime sacrifices occupy forever a place in our hearts.

The signature of the "Agreement for the Cessation of War and the Re-establishment of Peace in Vietnam" is only a first victory, because the task of strictly applying the agreement is important.

## Application of Agreement

Anxious to maintain peace, independence and democracy and heading toward reunification of the country, the Vietnamese people will act in a unified manner to insure the correct and serious application of the clauses of the agreement which will be signed in a few days, and at the same time it will show vigilance towards reactionaries who try to sabotage the agreement.

But we must say that the situation in our country and

in the world is developing in an extremely favorable way for the cause of the Vietnamese people.

We have the conviction that the dark designs of the reactionary forces in the country and abroad to obstruct the application of the agreement, or to sabotage it, can only fail.

The Vietnamese people has, therefore, every reason to believe in the victorious accomplishment of its tasks in the new period. No reactionary force will be able to slow down the march forward of the Vietnamese people.

I have finished my statement and I now reserve 20 minutes for questions and replies.

## Questions and Answers

Q. I have two questions to put. First, what role did international solidarity in the struggle of the Vietnamese people play in the success of the negotiations? Second, do you think that the Vietnam war will be the last war in the world?

A. The victory of the Vietnamese people is due, above all, to the Vietnamese people's own efforts in its resistance for independence and true freedom. But this victory cannot be separated from the powerful and vigorous help brought by the Socialist countries, by the working class of the whole world and by the oppressed peoples in the whole world.

I will now reply to your second question. I am a Communist, and according to Marxist-Leninist theories so long as imperialism persists in the world there will still be wars.

Q. Where will the scheduled international conference take place? Have the Americans dropped their objections to your proposals to hold it in Paris?

A. As regards the international conference and the location of the conference, the American side and our side are in the process of discussing this question and we have not yet reached a final decision.

Q. Is the January agreement different from the October agreement?

A. Basically, as regards the agreement we reached in the month of October, 1972, and the agreement we reached in the month of January, 1973, the contents are the same.

You can make the comparison in comparing the texts of the agreement of the month of October, 1972, and the agreement of the month of January, 1973.

### 'No More Problems'

Q. Aside from the conference site, after the signature of the agreements, are there other subjects for discussion between you and the United States?

My second question is, I note a difference between the résumé of the agreements of October and those you have shown us and the fact that you talk of negotiations between the concerned South Vietnamese parties. Is there a date fixed for this?

A. After the end of the negotiations, the completion of the agreement and the annex protocols between the American side and our side there are no more problems to be solved. Everything has been completed. That is to say the only thing we will have to discuss will be the site of the conference of international guarantees.

But according to the agreement, the guarantees conference will be called one month after the signature of the agreement. We still have time to solve this question.

After the start of the ceasefire, the South Vietnamese sides will immediately meet to settle the internal questions of South Vietnam. Naturally the two South Vietnamese sides will meet and fix the first dates for the start of their work.

Q. Aside from the four protocols you have just handed to us, are there other protocols which have not been published and are there other tacit annex agreements which have not been published?

A. There is one agreement and four protocols—all the documents which have just been distributed to the press —And these are complete documents covering everything which was negotiated between the two sides.

### 'What Will Happen?'

Q. You said earlier that the agreement would be initialed by the P.R.G. as a government. President Thieu as well as Mr. Tran Van Lam said yesterday that they would refuse to sign a document on which they found the signature of the P.R.G. as a government. What will happen exactly?

A. The situation in South Vietnam can be characterized in the following manner: There is the existence of two administrations, two armies, two controlled zones and three political forces. No one can deny this truth. Those who deny this truth pass themselves off as blind men. Anyway this truth is well reflected by the agreement which will be signed between the Government of the Democratic Republic of Vietnam and the United States and in the document which will be signed by the four sides at the Paris conference, by the four foreign affairs ministers, on January 27.

Q. Last night President Nixon said the United States continued to admit the Saigon Government as the only true Government of South Vietnam. Does the Government of the DRVN agree with this point of view and if not what will it do?

A. As I answered earlier, the situation in Vietnam is characterized by the existence of two administrations, of two armies of two differently controlled zones and of three public forces, and this idea is well reflected in the clauses of the agreement and in the course of the negotiations.

You can refer back to the document, the document signed by the two sides, the document signed by the four sides, that is, by the DRVN, the Provisional Revolutionary Government, the Government of the United States, the Government of the Republic of Vietnam, and you will see that this idea is well represented in this agreement.

This idea comes out well in the first paragraph of the agreement on the end of the war and in Article 23 of the agreement—the agreement signed by the Democratic Republic of Vietnam and the United States of America, the bipartite agreement.

And, besides, you will have the chance of attending in a few days the official signature of the agreement by the four foreign ministers and naturally this will be an event which will concretize this situation existing in South Vietnam.

### On Hanoi's Troops

Q. [in English]. On the status of North Vietnamese troops in South Vietnam—?

A. [Translated into English by interpreter]. Regarding the question of the so-called North Vietnamese forces in South Vietnam, we have been discussing this question for over five years now, and during the scores of private meetings between Dr. Kissinger, Minister Thuy and myself we repeatedly discussed this question.

We have completely re-jected the allegation about the so-called North Vietnamese forces in South Vietnam. We have completely rejected this question because, politically speaking, as well as legally speaking, this allegation has no point—is pointless.

And finally, the United States side dropped completely this proposal of theirs. Therefore in the agreement you can find no word, not a single word implying the presence of the so-called North Vietnamese troops.

Q. The negotiations have been held in France. What do you think of the role of France?

A. The negotiations have lasted for nearly five years and during this period of time I can say that the French Government has made an appreciable contribution.

### Reunification Situation

Q. (In English, on whether the reunification situation in Vietnam could be compared with that in Germany or Korea.)

A. [Translated by interpreter into English.] The conditions in Vietnam are quite different from those in Korea and Germany.

Moreover, the 1954 Geneva agreement recognized the independence, the sovereignty, the unity and territorial integrity of Vietnam and stipulated that the 17th Parallel is only a provisional military demarcation line.

It can in no way be interpreted as a political or territorial boundary.

Moreover, the Geneva agreement of 1954 provided that general elections should be, would be, organized with a view to reunifying the country.

But these provisions have not been implemented over the past years.

As to the historical causes of this nonimplementation of the general agreement which

we repeatedly expounded to you, I think it is unnecessary to repeat here.

Now in the current agreement, there is an explicit provision that the United States, as are other countries, should respect the independence, sovereignty, the unity and the territorial integrity of Vietnam.

The current agreement also stipulates that the 17th Parallel is only a provisional military demarcation line. It is not a political or territorial boundary.

Therefore, it is also stipulated in the agreement that the two zones of Vietnam should consult each other as soon as possible to reunify the country.

Therefore, undoubtedly our people, the Vietnamese people, will advance to the reunification of the country. There is the necessary advance of history. No force can prevent this advance. Moreover, in the agreement there are explicit provisions in this connection.

### On Elections in South

Q. [in English.] Despite your hopes, do you really believe that the Thieu Government will allow free and democratic elections in the South? Can the Thieu regime allow the possibility of a Communist Government?

A. [Translated by interpreter into English.] Undoubtedly, as I said, the Vietnamese people will advance to reunification of the country. But under what regime the country will be reunited? It depends on the decision of the people in North and South Vietnam.

Q. [On possibility of disagreement between Saigon and the Provisional Revolutionary Government in consultations on setting up National Council of Reconciliation and Concord.]

A. We are firmly convinced

that the will for peace, reconciliation and national concord will triumph in South Vietnam. This is why, if there are difficulties, it will always be possible to settle the question of forming a National Council of Reconciliation and Concord.

Q. If, as you have just said, the agreement which you have signed and the December agreement are more or less the same, then why the breakdown in December and why the American bombings?

A. It must be said that, at the time, the negotiations were in the process of developing and I had returned home to report to my Government. The first waves of bombings took place a few hours after my arrival in Hanoi.

And it must be said that these bombings failed completely.

As regards the reaction in the world from the peoples, the organizations, the governments, I believe that you journalists were certainly aware of this reaction.

And naturally these bombings in no way helped the negotiations. On the contrary, they contributed to delay the negotiations. Besides, I already had the oppohtunity of discussing this subject with you the last time.

But in the end, our side and the American side reached agreement. It is a **very great victory for our people.**

### Vietnamese-American Ties

Q. (On future relations between the United States, and North Vietnam and on the October draft agreement.)

A. On this subject, Article 22 states that the cessation of the war, the re-establishment of peace in Vietnam as well as the strict application of the present accord will create conditions for the establishment between the Democratic Republic of Vietnam and the United States of new relations of equality and mutual advantage on the basis of mutual respect, independence, sovereignty and reciprocal noninterference in the internal affairs of each country.

As far as the draft project of October is concerned, we have already given extracts of its main points.

Q. What will be the fate of Saigon's political prisoners?

A. The fate of Saigon's political prisoners is clearly dealt with in Article 8(c) of the agreement. It is certain that the sides should free all political prisoners.

Q. Could you indicate the zones controlled by the Saigon Government and the P.R.G., and the number of residents in them?

A. When the cease-fire becomes effective, there will be very clearly indications on this question of the zones controlled by the two parties.

Q. What is the number of inhabitants of the zones?

A. It is difficult to establish the population in one zone or the other now. There will have to be a control after the cease-fire.

Naturally, one must beware of hazardous forecasts, for example, that such and such a population in such and such a zone follows such and such party, etc. It is difficult to evaluate the exact figure of the population behind such and such a party in a mechanical fashion.

### U.S. Aid for Reconstruction

Q. Can you tell us categorically if there are any additional secret understandings or agreements in addition to the published accords and protocols, and if the answer is yes, can you tell us what general subjects might be covered by these additional agreements?

A. (translated into English by interpreter.) The answer to this question has been given.

Q. (on what specific agreements have been reached concerning the amount and form of United States aid for the reconstruction of Vietnam.)

A. (translated into English by interpreter.) The question has been discussed with the U.S. side and it will continue to be discussed with the U.S. side. The United States cannot avoid responsibility for contributing to the healing of the war wounds after so many years of war.

Q. Where will the South Vietnamese parties meet, in Paris or in South Vietnam itself? And, secondly, what provisions have been made for bringing about a cease-fire in Laos and Cambodia?

A. After the cease-fire comes into effect, the two sides of Vietnamese parties will meet to discuss procedural questions and to determine the place of their next meeting. The negotiations between the D.R.V. and the U.S. deal with the question of peace in Vietnam.

As to the question of peace in Laos and Cambodia, it falls within the competence and the sovereignty of the peoples of Laos and Cambodia. As to the international guarantee conference, its aim is to guarantee peace in Vietnam and not for Indochina.

### Signing by the Parties

Q. (on whether meetings between South Vietnamese sides will be based on equality of the two sides and on the procedure for signing the agreement and protocols.)

A. The two South Vietnamese sides will meet on a basis of equality, of mutual respect and reciprocal nonelimination.

The four ministers of foreign affairs will sign the agreement and three protocols, and the two sides—the Democratic Republic of Vietnam and the United States of America—will sign four protocols, the fourth protocol being a protocol which concerns the U.S.A. and the D.R.V.N. only since it is a protocol dealing with minesweeping in North Vietnam.

Q. (on the agreement on the National Council of Reconciliation and Concord.)

A. In the end, we reached an agreement not to use the term "structure of power" or "administrative structure" but to call it directly the National Council of Reconciliation and National Concord, for the importance of the body lies in its way of proceeding in its work. The council has three equal components, therefore the unanimity principle is indispensable so as not to allow one party to eliminate or bring pressure to bear on another party; therefore, the principle does not at all weaken the power of this council. On the contrary, this principle responds to the very nature of the council.

### The 60-Day Period

Q. (concerns the immediate events expected to take place in Vietnam within 60 days.)

A. [translated into English by interpreter.] The 60-day period is determined for the complete withdrawal from South Vietnam of United States forces and of those countries allied with the United States. This is also the trial period for the dismantling of U.S. military bases in South Vietnam, and this is also the trial period for the total release of captured military personnel of the parties. All these things can be done within 60 days.

Q. (On the third force.)

A. The two South Vietnamese parties will start consultation to fix the composition of the National Council of Concord.

Q. Have the four countries of the International Control Commission agreed to participate?

A. (Translated into English by interpreter.) They have accepted to be members of the I.C.C., and the commission begins operating immediately after the cease-fire comes into effect.

Q. Have Canada, Poland, Hungary and Indonesia agreed to participate in that commission? A. They have.

Q. (On possible difficulties of talks in October being due to controversy over number of members of the International Control Commission.)

A. As far as the October difficulties are concerned, there were several reasons, not only the reason concerning the International Commission. Concerning the number of personnel of the International Commission, we have arrived at an agreement—1,160.

### Vietcong in the South

Q. (on contacts between Vietcong and Saigon.)

A. At present, Madame Binh is in Paris. Naturally we await the signature by the four foreign ministers. Naturally after the re-establishment of peace the parties will enter into consultation and there will not be any difficulties about movement.

Q. Has the Provisional Revolutionary Government established a capital in South Vietnam?

A. (translated into English by interpreter.) After the restoration of peace, of course the P.R.G. will have its government machinery and mechanisms and its location in South Vietnam. You will know about that. The reason why we cannot tell you the location of the P.R.G. before is because if it is known then the U.S. will bomb it.

Q. How many U.S. Military personnel will be based in North Vietnam to supervise the mining operations in the rivers and estuaries?

A. (translated into English by interpreter.) We have come to an agreement on the removal of mines. The U.S. will play the principal role in this removal of mines and we are now discussing such questions with the United States.

Q. How many will be based in North Vietnam?

A. (translated into English by interpreter.) We have not decided on that question. This question, technical questions, are being discussed now. But in any case, there will be a number of Americans admitted to cooperate with us on the removal of the mines.

Mr. Tho: Thank you to you all. During our long resistance and during the long years of negotiations our journalist friends have closely followed the situation, and I can say you have contributed in part to the re-establishment of peace in Vietnam.

In the name of the Government and the people of Vietnam, I wish to thank you. I have accomplished my task and I will be returning very soon to my country. I wish to take the opportunity to say goodbye and thank you, and since the Vietnamese Tet is close, I wish you a good Vietnamese New Year.

An Interview With

LY VAN SAU

Of the Provisional Revolutionary Government

Paris, January 31, 1973


You know that the Agreement has been signed. Officially the
cease-fire has been in force since the 28th, but the news still
talks of combat in many places. What does this show? It shows
that although our government, our army, observes the cease-fire,
the Saigon government is violating the Agreement because it
finds itself in a situation which is not favorable for them
and they want to change the reality of South Vietnam. It is
a reality that the popular forces are everywhere and that the
population of South Vietnam is filled with enthusiasm by the
Peace Agreement and turn their eyes toward the Provisional
Revolutionary Government (PRG). One has only to look at the
actions of Thieu before and after the signing of the Agreement
to understand what the maneuvers are, now, of the Americans.

For one thing we speak of the cessation of the war and the
re-establishing of peace, but Thieu speaks only of a "truce"
and Thieu puts his troops in a permanent state of alert,
suppresses all passes, all permissions to go home, and even
orders his troops to carry out operations to "prevent the
forces of the Liberation Army to control the terrain."

For another thing, Thieu has given orders to shoot down on
the spot anyone who has the PRG flag, who hails the Agreement,
and who welcomes the Vietcong.

Then, too, we speak of "national concord" and "national
reconciliation". Thieu speaks of killing every last Communist.

We see here, in other words, two completely different attitudes.
While the PRG and the people rejoice in the victory we have
achieved -- a great victory (you know that the PRG, in its
statement published the 28th, thanked the American people, all
the progressive people in the United States, for their support),
so while we are rejoicing in this, the attitude of Thieu is
an attitude of anger and hate, of despair. And this fact in
itself shows that the Accord is a good Accord -- that this
Accord is favorable for the Vietnamese people and unfavorable
for the enemies of the Vietnamese people. I said yesterday
to our friends that just the fact that the United States of
America has had to sign an Accord with the Vietnamese is
already a great victory. You know that at the time of Geneva
they refused to sign. But now it isn't simply one signature,
but more than 140 signatures that the delegates put on the
Accords and the protocols, which fix point by point the
modalities and the implementations.

Secondly, the United States has had to recognize the fundamental
national rights of the Vietnamese people. We could perhaps
say that these are just words. But no, this is very important
because this hasn't been at all easy. You know at the time
of the October Agreement that Point #1 stated that the United
States recognized the independence, soverignty, territorial
integrity, unity of our country, and agreed to respect the
Accords of Geneva. After the about face, Kissinger wanted
to eliminate this point. He said the President didn't want
this point because it was implying that until now the United
States has been violating these rights, which is why they now
have to recognize and respect them. He even thought to eliminate this point altogether or put it further down in a less
conspicuous place. A very long argument ensued among the

deputies, and finally we found the formula which is the
following: "The United States and all countries respect the
independence, etc. ..." (Much laughter)

We also spoke of the principle of respect for the self-determination of the population of South Vietnam and the democratic
process which allows this self determination to be implemented.

The American demand for the withdrawal of North Vietnamese
troops was not accepted, nowhere, which shows that the
Vietnamese people are one and have the right to defend their
country wherever it is being invaded.

The recognition of the PRG is also a fact of the Agreement
because the PRG is a signator as an equal party, as a foreign
minister, and in the Agreement their are many mentions of
two South Vietnamese parties. That is to say the PRG and
Saigon.

So the Agreement, like the protocols, is a very important
document. It creates a new basis for the establishment of
a new period in South Vietnam. And in all this there is the
dynamic of peace, of national concord, which is the most
legitimate aspiration of the Vietnamese people.

In the Saigon administration there are still very reactionary
forces, of which Nguyen Van Thieu is the chief, who have until
now become rich with the war and wanted the war to continue.
But as Madame Binh said yesterday, in following this policy
Thieu and the reactionary forces will be even more isolated
and in conflict with the people, even the people within their
own ranks.

You know that the news from South Vietnam is still infrequent,
but already we know that in several cities and villages the
inhabitants have raised the flag of the PRG. For example,
Da Lat is a large city. According to Western sources, half
the population of the city has planted the flag in front of
their houses and demonstrated. And the news sources say that
the PRG flag is flying at Binh Chanh, which is some twenty
kilometers from Saigon on Route Four. And the news is that
all the routes surrounding Saigon are controlled by the PRG:
National Route #1, #13, #4, #15. That is to say all the exits
from Saigon are PRG controlled. According to the newspaper
Le Monde of yesterday (January 30, 1973), Saigon is lacking
vegetables and foodstuffs, and the prices are skyrocketing
and that the Saigon administration is in the process of
establishing a system of rationing.

All this means that first of all the military position of
the revolutionary forces is excellent. Secondly, that the
political situation is also excellent and that the Peace
Agreement, with its circulation of democratic freedoms and
everything else, opens the possibility of a new form of
struggle.

Naturally we must be very vigilant. And we are always
vigilant. But it is necessary to be ready to denounce the
violations of the Accord, ready to repulse an enemy attack,
to defend the liberated zones, to defend the PRG. But we
are sure the aspirations for peace, for national concord,
will in the end triumph over the reactionary forces.

The Accord was signed barely a few days ago. It needs time
for it to be implemented. It has been a very long war. We
think the coming days, that is to say the approach of Tet,
will witness important events. The people for the first time
can celebrate Tet in time of peace.

World opinion, as in the United States, is still skeptical.
We know they have every reason to be skeptical because the
situation is still very difficult.  But on our side we are
determined to implement the Agreement, and have it implemented.
Because it is an Agreement which has been realized thanks to
our efforts and is an Agreement which is favorable to us.

The Vietnamese people who knew how to begin the war have also
known how to terminate the war in a favorable and intelligent
manner, opening for us an era of peace but also of struggle
under new conditions.

As we have said, the struggle is not yet over.  It continues
in another form.  And in this struggle it is certain that
we still have need of our American friends and we think it
is a duty of all the pacifists and revolutionaries in the
United States to not let the American people forget Vietnam.
Vietnam as an unhappy experience of aggression.  Vietnam as
a crime committed against the Vietnamese people.  Vietnam
as the awakening of conscience in the United States.  And
Vietnam as friendship between our two people.

For us, this war is the greatest lesson of our history.  But
also the greatest experience we have achieved in our long
struggle for national independence.  We think that for you
others, the war has also, despite all its suffering and misery,
been a unique experience in your history, which shows that
American imperialism isn't as strong as one thought, and that
the American people have many friends among the Vietnamese
people.  There is one thing very strange perhaps to consider
and to see:  There exists no ill feelings between our people.
Between the French and the Germans, after the war, for example,
there was great hate.  But do you see anything between our
people?  Not at all.

Before, in your country, people said, "Remember Pearl Harbor."
Now, I say, "Remember Vietnam.  For always."  Remember Vietnam
for what it means, for our people and for your people.  For
the revolutionary movement in the United States.  For the solidarity of the world's people.  One cannot forget the crimes
which have been perpetrated against Vietnam, and it is a great
duty of the revolutionary movement of the United States to
educate the young generation on the basis of the experience
in Vietnam, and to maintain the links of friendship, of solidarity between ourselves, between you and the Vietnamese
people.  And to continue the best way possible to make known
to the Vietnamese people that there are two Americas:  the
America of Calley, and the America of Jane Fonda.

# Dr. Kissinger's News Conference, January 24, 1973

Ladies and gentlemen: The President last evening presented the outlines of the agreement, and by common agreement between us and the North Vietnamese we have today released the texts. And I am here to explain, to go over briefly, what these texts contain and how we got there, what we have tried to achieve in recent months, and where we expect to go from here.

Let me begin by going through the agreement, which you have read.

The agreement, as you know, is in nine chapters. The first affirms the independence, sovereignty, unity, and territorial integrity, as recognized by the 1954 Geneva agreements on Viet-Nam, agreements which established two zones divided by a military demarcation line.

Chapter II deals with the cease-fire. The cease-fire will go into effect at 7 o'clock, Washington time, on Saturday night. The principal provisions of chapter II deal with permitted acts during the cease-fire and with what the obligations of the various parties are with respect to the cease-fire.

Chapter II also deals with the withdrawal of American and all other foreign forces from Viet-Nam within a period of 60 days. And it specifies the forces that have to be withdrawn. These are, in effect, all military personnel and all civilian personnel dealing with combat operations. We are permitted to retain economic advisers, and civilian technicians serving in certain of the military branches.

Chapter II further deals with the provisions for resupply and for the introduction of outside forces. There is a flat prohibition against the introduction of any military

force into South Viet-Nam from outside of South Viet-Nam, which is to say that whatever forces may be in South Viet-Nam from outside South Viet-Nam, specifically North Vietnamese forces, cannot receive reinforcements, replacements, or any other form of augmentation by any means whatsoever. With respect to military equipment, both sides are permitted to replace all existing military equipment on a one-to-one basis under international supervision and control.

There will be established, as I will explain when I discuss the protocols, for each side three legitimate points of entry through which all replacement equipment has to move. These legitimate points of entry will be under international supervision.

## Release of Prisoners

Chapter III deals with the return of captured military personnel and foreign civilians, as well as with the question of civilian detainees within South Viet-Nam.

This, as you know, throughout the negotiations presented enormous difficulties for us. We insisted throughout that the question of American prisoners of war and of American civilians captured throughout Indochina should be separated from the issue of Vietnamese civilian personnel detained, partly because of the enormous difficulty of classifying the Vietnamese civilian personnel by categories of who was detained for reasons of the civil war and who was detained for criminal activities, and secondly, because it was foreseeable that negotiations about the release of civilian detainees would be complex and difficult and because we did not want to have the issue of American personnel mixed up with the issues of civilian personnel in South Viet-Nam.

This turned out to be one of the thorniest issues, that was settled at some point and kept reappearing throughout the negotiations. It was one of the difficulties we had during the December negotiations.

As you can see from the agreement, the return of American military personnel and captured civilians is separated in terms of obligation, and in terms of the time frame, from the return of Vietnamese civilian personnel.

The return of American personnel and the accounting of missing in action is unconditional and will take place within the same time frame as the American withdrawal.

The issue of Vietnamese civilian personnel will be negotiated between the two Vietnamese parties over a period of three months, and as the agreement says, they will do their utmost to resolve this question within the three-month period.

So I repeat, the issue is separated, both in terms of obligation and in terms of the relevant time frame, from the return of American prisoners, which is unconditional.

We expect that American prisoners will be released at intervals of two weeks or 15 days in roughly equal installments. We have been told that no American prisoners are held in Cambodia. American prisoners held in Laos and North Viet-Nam will be returned to us in Hanoi. They will be received by American medical evacuation teams and flown on American airplanes from Hanoi to places of our own choice, probably Vientiane.

There will be international supervision of both this provision and of the provision for the missing in action. And all American prisoners will, of course, be released, within 60 days of the signing of the agreement. The signing will take place on January 27 in two installments, the significance of which I will explain to you when I have run through the provisions of the agreement and the associated protocols.

### Self-Determination for South Viet-Nam

Chapter IV of the agreement deals with the right of the South Vietnamese people to self-determination. Its first provision contains a joint statement by the United States and North Viet-Nam in which those two countries jointly recognize the South Vietnamese people's right to self-determination, in which those two countries jointly affirm that the South Vietnamese people shall decide for themselves the political system that they shall choose and jointly affirm that no foreign country shall impose any political tendency on the South Vietnamese people.

The other principal provisions of the agreement are that in implementing the South Vietnamese people's right to self-determination, the two South Vietnamese parties will decide, will agree among each other, on free elections, for offices to be decided by the two parties, at a time to be decided by the two parties. These elections will be supervised and organized first by an institution which has the title of National Council for National Reconciliation and Concord, whose members will be equally appointed by the two sides, which will operate on the principle of unanimity, and which will come into being after negotiation between the two parties, who are obligated by this agreement to do their utmost to bring this institution into being within 90 days.

Leaving aside the technical jargon, the significance of this part of the agreement is that the United States has consistently maintained that we would not impose any political solution on the people of South Viet-Nam. The United States has consistently maintained that we would not impose a coalition government or a disguised coalition government on the people of South Viet-Nam.

If you examine the provisions of this chapter, you will see, first, that the existing government in Saigon can remain in office; secondly, that the political future of South Viet-Nam depends on agreement between the South Vietnamese parties, and not on an agreement that the United States has imposed on these parties; thirdly, that the nature of this political evolution, the timing of this political evolution, is left to the South Vietnamese parties, and that the organ that is created to see to it that the elections that are organized will be conducted properly is one in which each of the South Vietnamese parties has a veto.

The other significant provision of this agreement is the requirement that the South Vietnamese parties will bring about a reduction of their armed forces and that the forces being reduced will be demobilized.

### The Issue of the Demilitarized Zone

The next chapter deals with the reunification of Viet-Nam and the relationship between North and South Viet-Nam. In the many negotiations that I have conducted over recent weeks, not the least arduous was the negotiation conducted with the ladies and gentlemen of the press, who constantly raised issues with respect to sovereignty, the existence of South Viet-Nam as a political entity, and other matters of this kind.

I will return to this issue at the end when I sum up the agreement, but it is obvious that there is no dispute in the agreement between the parties that there is an entity called South Viet-Nam and that the future unity of Viet-Nam, as it comes about, will be decided by negotiation between North and South Viet-Nam; that it will not be achieved by military force; indeed, that the use of military force with respect to bringing about unification, or any other form of coercion, is impermissible according to the terms of this agreement.

Secondly, there are specific provisions in this chapter with respect to the demilitarized zone (DMZ). There is a repetition of the agreement of 1954 which makes the demarcation line along the 17th parallel provisional, which means pending reunification. There is a specific provision that both North and South Viet-Nam shall respect the demilitarized zone on either side of the provisional military demarcation line, and there is another provision that indicates that among the subjects that can be negotiated will be modalities of civilian movement across the demarcation line, which makes it clear that military movement across the demilitarized zone is in all circumstances prohibited.

Now, this may be an appropriate point to explain what our position has been with respect to the DMZ. There has been a great deal of discussion about the issue of sovereignty and about the issue of legitimacy—which is to say, which government is in control of South Viet-Nam—and finally, about why we laid such great stress on the issue of the demilitarized zone.

We had to place stress on the issue of the demilitarized zone because the provisions of the agreement with respect to infiltration, with respect to replacement, with respect to any of the military provisions, would have made no sense whatsoever if there was not some demarcation line that defined where South Viet-Nam began. If we had accepted the proposition that would have in effect eroded the demilitarized zone, then the provisions of the agreement with respect to restrictions about the introduction of men and materiel into South Viet-Nam would have been unilateral restrictions applying only to the United States and only to our allies. Therefore, if there was to be any meaning to the separation of military and political issues, if there was to be any permanence to the military provisions that had been negotiated, then it was essential that there was a definition of where the obligations of this agreement began. As you can see from the text of the agreement, the principles that we defended were essentially achieved.

Chapter VI deals with the international machinery, and we will discuss that when I talk about the associated protocols of the agreement.

### Laos and Cambodia

Chapter VII deals with Laos and Cambodia. Now, the problem of Laos and Cambodia has two parts. One part concerns those obligations which can be undertaken by the parties signing the agreement—that is to say, the three Vietnamese parties and the United States—those measures that they can take which affect the situation in Laos and Cambodia. A second part of the situation in Laos has to concern the nature of the civil conflict that is taking place within Laos and Cambodia and the solution of which, of course, must involve as well the two Laotian parties and the innumerable Cambodian factions.

Let me talk about the provisions of the agreement with respect to Laos and Cambodia and our firm expectations as to the future in Laos and Cambodia.

The provisions of the agreement with respect to Laos and Cambodia reaffirm, as an obligation to all the parties, the provisions of the 1954 agreement on Cambodia and of the 1962 agreement on Laos, which affirm the neutrality and right to self-determination of those two countries. They are therefore consistent with our basic position with respect also to South Viet-Nam.

In terms of the immediate conflict, the provisions of the agreement specifically prohibit the use of Laos and Cambodia for military and any other operations against any of the signatories of the Paris agreement or against any other country. In other words, there is a flat prohibition against the use of base areas in Laos and Cambodia.

There is a flat prohibition against the use of Laos and Cambodia for infiltration into Viet-Nam or, for that matter, into any other country.

Finally, there is a requirement that all foreign troops be withdrawn from Laos and Cambodia, and it is clearly understood that North Vietnamese troops are considered foreign with respect to Laos and Cambodia.

Now, as to the conflict within these countries which could not be formally settled in an agreement which is not signed by the parties of that conflict, let me make this statement, without elaborating it: It is our firm expectation that within a short period of time there will be a formal cease-fire in Laos which in turn will lead to a withdrawal of all foreign forces from Laos and, of course, to the end of the use of Laos as a corridor of infiltration.

Secondly, the situation in Cambodia, as those of you who have studied it will know, is somewhat more complex because there are several parties headquartered in different countries. Therefore, we can say about Cambodia that it is our expectation that a de facto cease-fire will come into being over a period of time relevant to the execution of this agreement.

Our side will take the appropriate measures to indicate that it will not attempt to change the situation by force. We have reason to believe that our position is clearly understood by all concerned parties, and I will not go beyond this in my statement.

## Relationship of the U.S. to North Viet-Nam

Chapter VIII deals with the relationship between the United States and the Democratic Republic of Viet-Nam.

As I have said in my briefings on October 26 and on December 16 and as the President affirmed on many occasions, the last time in his speech last evening, the United States is seeking a peace that heals.[2] We have had many armistices in Indochina. We want a peace that will last.

And therefore it is our firm intention in our relationship to the Democratic Republic of Viet-Nam to move from hostility to normalization, and from normalization to conciliation and cooperation. And we believe that under conditions of peace we can contribute throughout Indochina to a realization of the humane aspirations of all the people of Indochina. And we will, in that spirit, perform our traditional role of helping people realize these aspirations in peace.

Chapter IX of the agreement is the usual implementing provision.

So much for the agreement.

## Provisions of Protocols to the Agreement

Now let me say a word about the protocols. There are four protocols or implementing instruments to the agreement: on the return of American prisoners, on the implementation and institution of an International Control Commission, on the regulations with respect to the cease-fire and the implementation and institution of a Joint Military Commission among the concerned parties, and a

---

[2] For Dr. Kissinger's news conferences of Oct. 26 and Dec. 16, 1972, see BULLETIN of Nov. 13, 1972, p. 549, and Jan. 8, 1973, p. 33.

protocol about the deactivation and removal of mines.

I have given you the relevant provisions of the protocol concerning the return of prisoners. They will be returned at periodic intervals in Hanoi to American authorities and not to American private groups. They will be picked up by American airplanes, except for prisoners held in the southern part of South Viet-Nam, which will be released at designated points in the South, again to American authorities.

We will receive on Saturday, the day of the signing of the agreement, a list of all American prisoners held throughout Indochina. And both parties—that is to say, all parties—have an obligation to assist each other in obtaining information about the prisoners, missing in action, and about the location of graves of American personnel throughout Indochina.

The International Commission has the right to visit the last place of detention of the prisoners, as well as the place from which they are released.

Now to the International Control Commission. You will remember that one of the reasons for the impasse in December was the difficulty of agreeing with the North Vietnamese about the size of the International Commission, its function, or the location of its teams.

On this occasion, there is no point in rehashing all the differences. It is, however, useful to point out that at that time the proposal of the North Vietnamese was that the International Control Commission have a membership of 250, no organic logistics or communication, dependent entirely for its authority to move on the party it was supposed to be investigating; and over half of its personnel were supposed to be located in Saigon, which is not the place where most of the infiltration that we were concerned with was likely to take place.

We have distributed to you an outline of the basic structure of this Commission.[3] Briefly stated, its total number is 1,160,

---

[3] Not printed here.

drawn from Canada, Hungary, Indonesia, and Poland. It has a headquarters in Saigon. It has seven regional teams, 26 teams based in localities throughout Viet-Nam which were chosen either because forces were in contact there or because we estimated that these were the areas where the violations of the cease-fire were most probable.

There are 12 teams at border-crossing points. There are seven teams that are set aside for points of entry, which have yet to be chosen, for the replacement of military equipment. That is for article 7 of the agreement. There will be three on each side, and there will be no legitimate point of entry into South Viet-Nam other than those three points. The other border and coastal teams are there simply to make certain that no other entry occurs, and any other entry is by definition illegal. There has to be no other demonstration except the fact that it occurred.

This leaves one team free for use, in particular, at the discretion of the Commission. And of course the seven teams that are being used for the return of the prisoners can be used at the discretion of the Commission after the prisoners are returned.

There is one reinforced team located at the demilitarized zone, and its responsibility extends along the entire demilitarized zone. It is in fact a team and a half. It is 50 percent larger than a normal border team and it represents one of the many compromises that were made, between our insistence on two teams and their insistence on one team. By a brilliant stroke, we settled on a team and a half. [Laughter.]

With respect to the operation of the International Commission, it is supposed to operate on the principle of unanimity, which is to say that its reports, if they are Commission reports, have to have the approval of all four members. However, each member is permitted to submit his own opinion, so that as a practical matter any member of the Commission can make a finding of a violation and submit a report, in the first instance to the parties.

The International Commission will report for the time being to the four parties to the agreement. An international conference will take place, we expect, at the foreign ministers level within a month of signing the agreement.

That international conference will establish a relationship between the International Commission and itself, or any other international body that is mutually agreed upon, so that the International Commission is not only reporting to the parties that it is investigating. But for the time being, until the international conference has met, there was no other practical group to which the International Commission could report.

In addition to this international group, there are two other institutions that are supposed to supervise the cease-fire. There is, first of all, an institution called the Four-Party Joint Military Commission, which is composed of ourselves and the three Vietnamese parties, which is located in the same place as the International Commission, charged with roughly the same functions, but as a practical matter, it is supposed to conduct the preliminary investigations, its disagreements are automatically referred to the International Commission, and moreover, any party can request the International Commission to conduct an investigation regardless of what the Four-Party Commission does and regardless of whether the Four-Party Commission has completed its investigation or not.

After the United States has completed its withdrawal, the Four-Party Military Commission will be transformed into a Two-Party Commission composed of the two South Vietnamese parties. The total number of supervisory personnel, therefore, will be in the neighborhood of 4,500 during the period that the Four-Party Commission is in existence, and in the neighborhood of about 3,000 after the Four-Party Commission ceases operating and the Two-Party Commission comes into being.

Finally, there is a protocol concerning the removal and deactivation of mines, which is self-explanatory and simply explains—

discusses the relationship between our efforts and the efforts of the DRV concerning the removal and deactivation of mines, which is one of the obligations we have undertaken in the agreement.

### Procedure for Signing Documents

Now let me point out one other problem. On Saturday, January 27, the Secretary of State, on behalf of the United States, will sign the agreement bringing the cease-fire and all the other provisions of the agreement and the protocols into force. He will sign in the morning a document involving four parties, and in the afternoon a document between us and the Democratic Republic of Viet-Nam. These documents are identical, except that the preamble differs in both cases.

The reason for this somewhat convoluted procedure is that while the agreement provides that the two South Vietnamese parties should settle their disputes in an atmosphere of national reconciliation and concord, I think it is safe to say that they have not yet quite reached that point, indeed, that they have not yet been prepared to recognize each other's existence.

This being the case, it was necessary to devise one document in which neither of the South Vietnamese parties was mentioned by name, and therefore no other party could be mentioned by name, on the principle of equality. So the four-party document, the document that will have four signatures, can be read with great care and you will not know until you get to the signature page whom exactly it applies to. It refers only to the parties participating in the Paris Conference, which are, of course, well known to the parties participating in the Paris Conference. [Laughter.]

It will be signed on two separate pages. The United States and the GVN are signing on one page, and the Democratic Republic of Viet-Nam and its ally are signing on a separate page. And this procedure has aged us all by several years. [Laughter.]

Then there is another document, which will

be signed by the Secretary of State and the Foreign Minister of the Democratic Republic of Viet-Nam in the afternoon. That document, in its operative provisions, is word for word the same as the document which will be signed in the morning and which contains the obligations to which the two South Vietnamese parties are obligated.

It differs from that document only in the preamble and in its concluding paragraph. In the preamble it says the United States, with the concurrence of the Government of the Republic of Viet-Nam, and the DRV, with the concurrence of the Provisional Revolutionary Government, and the rest is the same, and then the concluding paragraph has the same adaptation. That document, of course, is not signed by either Saigon or its opponent, and therefore their obligations are derived from the four-party document.

I do not want to take any time in going into the abstruse legalisms. I simply wanted to explain to you why there were two different signature ceremonies and why, when we handed out the text of the agreement, we appended to the document which contains the legal obligations which apply to everybody—namely, the four parties—why we appended another section that contained a different preamble and a different implementing paragraph which is going to be signed by the Secretary of State and the Foreign Minister of the Democratic Republic of Viet-Nam.

This will be true with respect to the agreement and three of the protocols. The fourth protocol, regarding the removal of mines, applies only to the United States and the Democratic Republic of Viet-Nam, and therefore we are in the happy position of having to sign only one document.

### Negotiating Process and Achievements

Now then, let me summarize for you how we got to this point and some of the aspects of the agreement that we consider significant, and then I will answer your questions.

As you know, when I met with this group on December 16, we had to report that the negotiations in Paris seemed to have reached a stalemate. We had not agreed at that time, although we didn't say so, on the—we could not find a formula to take into account the conflicting views with respect to signing. There were disagreements with respect to the DMZ and with the associated aspects of what identity South Viet-Nam was to have in the agreement.

There was a total deadlock with respect to the protocols, which I summed up in the December 16 press conference. The North Vietnamese approach to international control and ours were so totally at variance that it seemed impossible at that point to come to any satisfactory conclusion. And there began to be even some concern that the separation which we thought we had achieved in October between the release of our prisoners and the question of civilian prisoners in South Viet-Nam was breaking down.

When we reassembled on January 8, we did not do so in the most cordial atmosphere that I remember. However, by the morning of January 9 it became apparent that both sides were determined to make a serious effort to break the deadlock in negotiations. And we adopted a mode of procedure by which issues in the agreement and issues of principle with respect to the protocols were discussed at meetings between Special Advisor Le Duc Tho and myself while concurrently an American team headed by Ambassador Sullivan [William H. Sullivan, Deputy Assistant Secretary of State for East Asian and Pacific Affairs] and a Vietnamese team headed by Vice Minister Thach [Nguyen Co Thach, Vice Minister for Foreign Affairs] would work on the implementation of the principles as they applied to the protocols.

For example, the Special Advisor and I might agree on the principle of border control posts and their number, but then the problem of how to locate them, according to what criteria, and with what mode of operation presented enormous difficulties.

Let me on this occasion also point out that these negotiations required the closest cooperation throughout our government, be-

tween the White House and the State
Department, between all the elements of our
team, and that therefore the usual speculation of who did what to whom is really extraordinarily misplaced.

Without a cooperative effort by everybody,
we could not have achieved what we have
presented last night and this morning.

The Special Advisor and I then spent the
week first on working out the unresolved
issues in the agreement and then the unresolved issues with respect to the protocols
and, finally, the surrounding circumstances
of schedules and procedures.

Ambassador Sullivan remained behind to
draft the implementing provisions of the
agreements that had been achieved during
the week. The Special Advisor and I remained in close contact.

So by the time we met again yesterday,
the issues that remained were very few, indeed, were settled relatively rapidly. And I
may on this occasion also point out that
while the North Vietnamese are the most
difficult people to negotiate with that I have
ever encountered when they do not want to
settle, they are also the most effective that I
have dealt with when they finally decide to
settle—so that we have gone through peaks
and valleys in these negotiations of extraordinary intensity.

Now then, let me sum up where this agreement has left us—first with respect to what
we said we would try to achieve, then with
respect to some of its significance, and finally,
with respect to the future.

First, when I met this group on October
26 and delivered myself of some epigram-
matic phrases, we obviously did not want to
give a complete checklist and we did not want
to release the agreement as it then stood,
because it did not seem to us desirable to
provide a checklist against which both sides
would then have to measure success and
failure in terms of their prestige.

At that time, too, we did not say that it
had always been foreseen that there would be
another three or four days of negotiation
after this tentative agreement had been
reached. The reason why we asked for an-

other negotiation was because it seemed to
us at that point that for a variety of reasons,
which I explained then and again on December 16, those issues could not be settled
within the time frame that the North Vietnamese expected.

It is now a matter of history, and it is
therefore not essential to go into a debate of
on what we based this judgment. But that
was the reason why the agreement was not
signed on October 31, and not any of the
speculations that have been so much in print
and on television.

Now, what did we say on October 26 we
wanted to achieve? We said, first of all, that
we wanted to make sure that the control
machinery would be in place at the time of
the cease-fire. We did this because we had
information that there were plans by the
other side to mount a major offensive to
coincide with the signing of the cease-fire
agreement.

This objective has been achieved by the
fact that the protocols will be signed on the
same day as the agreement, by the fact that
the International Control Commission and
the Four-Party Military Commission will
meet within 24 hours of the agreement going
into effect, or no later than Monday morning,
Saigon time, that the regional teams of the
International Control Commission will be in
place 48 hours thereafter, and that all other
teams will be in place within 15 and a maximum of 30 days after that.

Second, we said that we wanted to com-
press the time interval between the cease-
fires we expected in Laos and Cambodia and
the cease-fire in Viet-Nam.

For reasons which I have explained to you,
we cannot be as specific about the cease-
fires in Laos and Cambodia as we can about
the agreements that are being signed on
Saturday, but we can say with confidence
that the formal cease-fire in Laos will go
into effect in a considerably shorter period
of time than was envisaged in October, and
since the cease-fire in Cambodia depends to
some extent on developments in Laos, we
expect the same to be true there.

We said that certain linguistic ambiguities should be removed. The linguistic ambiguit'es were produced by the somewhat extraordinary negotiating procedure whereby a change in the English text did not always produce a correlative change in the Vietnamese text. All the linguistic ambiguities to which we referred in October have in fact been removed. At that time I mentioned only one, and therefore I am free to recall it.

I pointed out that the U.S. position had consistently been a rejection of the imposition of a coalition government on the people of South Viet-Nam. I said then that the National Council of Reconciliation was not a coalition government, nor was it conceived as a coalition government.

The Vietnamese language text, however, permitted an interpretation of the words "administrative structure" as applied to the National Council of Reconciliation which would have lent itself to the interpretation that it came close or was identical with a coalition government.

You will find that in the text of this agreement the words "administrative structure" no longer exist and therefore this particular —shall we say—ambiguity has been removed.

I pointed out in October that we had to find a procedure for signing which would be acceptable to all the parties for whom obligations were involved. This has been achieved.

I pointed out on October 26 that we would seek greater precision with respect to certain obligations particularly, without spelling them out, as they applied to the demilitarized zone and to the obligations with respect to Laos and Cambodia. That, too, has been achieved.

And I pointed out in December that we were looking for some means, some expression, which would make clear that the two parts of Viet-Nam would live in peace with each other and that neither side would impose its solution on the other by force.

This is now explicitly provided, and we have achieved formulations in which in a number of the paragraphs, such as article 14, 18(e), and 20, there are specific references to the sovereignty of South Viet-Nam.

There are specific references, moreover, to the same thing in article 6 and article 11 of the ICCS [International Commission of Control and Supervision] protocol. There are specific references to the right of the South Vietnamese people to self-determination.

And therefore we believe that we have achieved the substantial adaptations that we asked for on October 26. We did not increase our demands after October 26, and we substantially achieved the clarifications which we sought.

Now then, it is obvious that a war that has lasted for 10 years will have many elements that cannot be completely satisfactory to all the parties concerned. And in the two periods where the North Vietnamese were working with dedication and seriousness on a conclusion, the period in October and the period after we resumed talks on January 8, it was always clear that a lasting peace could come about only if neither side sought to achieve everything that it had wanted; indeed, that stability depended on the relative satisfaction and therefore on the relative dissatisfaction of all of the parties concerned. And therefore it is also clear that whether this agreement brings a lasting peace or not depends not only on its provisions but also on the spirit in which it is implemented.

It will be our challenge in the future to move the controversies that could not be stilled by any one document from the level of military conflict to the level of positive human aspirations, and to absorb the enormous talents and dedication of the people of Indochina in tasks of construction, rather than in tasks of destruction.

We will make a major effort to move to create a framework where we hope in a short time the animosities and the hatred and the suffering of this period will be seen as aspects of the past and where the debates concern differences of opinion as to how to achieve positive goals.

Of course the hatreds will not rapidly disappear, and of course people who have fought for 25 years will not easily give up their objectives, but also people who have suffered for 25 years may at last come to know that they can achieve their real satisfaction by other and less brutal means.

The President said yesterday that we have to remain vigilant, and so we shall, but we shall also dedicate ourselves to positive efforts. And as for us at home, it should be clear by now that no one in this war has had a monopoly of anguish and that no one in these debates has had a monopoly of moral insight. And now that at last we have achieved an agreement in which the United States did not prescribe the political future to its allies, an agreement which should preserve the dignity and the self-respect of all of the parties, together with healing the wounds in Indochina we can begin to heal the wounds in America.

I will be glad to answer any questions.

*Q. Dr. Kissinger, what, if any, supervision do you envisage over the Ho Chi Minh Trail by an international agency?*

*Dr. Kissinger:* We expect that the International Control Commission that exists in Laos will be reinstituted. We have also provided for the establishment of border teams, as you can see from the maps, at all the terminal points of the Ho Chi Minh Trail into South Viet-Nam. And therefore, we believe that there will be international supervision of the provisions, both within Laos and within South Viet-Nam.

Marvin [Marvin Kalb, CBS News].

*Q. Dr. Kissinger, one of the major problems has been the continued presence of North Vietnamese troops in the South. Could you tell us, first, so far as you know, how many of these troops are there in the South now, and do you have any understanding or assurance that these troops will be withdrawn?*

*Dr. Kissinger:* Our estimate of the number of North Vietnamese troops in the South is approximately 145,000. Now, I want to say a number of things with respect to this.

First, nothing in the agreement establishes the right of North Vietnamese troops to be in the South.

Secondly, the North Vietnamese have never claimed that they have a right to have troops in the South, and while opinions may differ about the exact accuracy of that statement, from a legal point of view it is important because it maintains the distinction that we, too, maintain.

Thirdly, if this agreement is implemented, the North Vietnamese troops in the South should, over a period of time, be subject to considerable reduction. First, there is a flat prohibition against the introduction of any outside forces for any reason whatsoever, so that the normal attrition of personnel cannot be made up by the reinfiltration of outside forces. I am talking now about the provisions of the agreement. Secondly, there is a flat prohibition against the presence of foreign forces in Laos and Cambodia and therefore a flat prohibition against the use of the normal infiltration corridors. Thirdly, as the agreement makes clear, military movement of any kind across the demilitarized zone is prohibited, both in the clause requiring respect for the demilitarized zone, which by definition excludes military personnel, and second, in the clause that says only modalities of civilian movement can be discussed, not of any other movement between North and South Viet-Nam. Fourth, there is a provision requiring the reduction and demobilization of forces on both sides, the major part of which on the South Vietnamese (Communist) side is believed, by all knowledgeable observers, to have arrived from outside of South Viet-Nam.

Therefore it is our judgment that there is no way that North Viet-Nam can live up to that agreement without there being a reduction of the North Vietnamese forces in South Viet-Nam, without this being explicitly stated.

Of course, it is not inconceivable that the agreement will not in all respects be lived up to. In that case, adding another clause that will not be lived up to, specifically requiring it, would not change the situation.

It is our judgment and our expectation—it is our expectation that the agreement will be lived up to, and therefore we believe that the problem of these forces will be taken care of by the evolution of events in South Viet-Nam.

Peter [Peter Lisagor, Chicago Daily News].

*Q. Dr. Kissinger, can I try to get a clarification of just that point? Several times, I think, you have said it is understood that North Vietnamese troops in Laos and Cambodia are considered foreign troops.*

*Dr. Kissinger:* That is right.

*Q. Are they so considered?*

*Dr. Kissinger:* I said it once, Peter.

*Q. You said it in answer to Marvin's question, but is it so considered in South Viet-Nam? Is North Viet-Nam a foreign entity in South Viet-Nam according to this agreement?*

*Dr. Kissinger:* This is one of the points on which the bitterest feeling rages and with which it is best not to deal in a formal and legalistic manner.

As I have pointed out, in this agreement there are repeated references to the identity of South Viet-Nam, to the fact that the South Vietnamese people's right of self-determination is recognized both by the DRV and by the United States, to the fact that North and South Viet-Nam shall settle their disputes peacefully and through negotiation, and other provisions of a similar kind.

Therefore it is clear there is no legal way by which North Viet-Nam can use military force against South Viet-Nam.

Now, whether that is due to the fact that there are two zones temporarily divided by a **p**rovisional demarcation line or because North Viet-Nam is a foreign country with relation to South Viet-Nam—that is an issue which we have avoided making explicit in the agreement and in which ambiguity has its merits. From the point of view of the international position and from the point of view of the obligations of the agreement, there is no legal way by which North Viet-Nam can use military force vis-a-vis South Viet-Nam to achieve its objectives.

*Q. Dr. Kissinger, on that subject, by what means was the United States able to con-*

*vince President Thieu to accept the presence of North Vietnamese troops in South Viet-Nam?*

*Dr. Kissinger:* First of all, it is not easy to achieve through negotiations what has not been achieved on the battlefield, and if you look at the settlements that have been made in the postwar period, the lines of demarcation have almost always followed the lines of actual control.

Secondly, we have taken the position throughout that the agreement cannot be analyzed in terms of any one of its provisions, but it has to be seen in its totality and in terms of the evolution that it starts.

Thirdly, we have not asked President Thieu, nor has he accepted, the presence of North Vietnamese troops in South Viet-Nam as a legal right, nor do we accept that as a legal right.

We have, since October 1970, proposed a cease-fire-in-place. A cease-fire-in-place always has to be between the forces that exist. The alternative of continued war also would have maintained the forces in the country.

Under these conditions, they are cut off from the possibility of renewed infiltration. They are prevented from undertaking military action. Their resupply is severely restricted.

And President Thieu, after examining the totality of the agreement, came to the conclusion that it achieved the essential objectives of South Viet-Nam, of permitting his people to bring about self-determination and of not posing a security risk that he could not handle with the forces that we have equipped and trained.

Mr. Horner [Garnett D. Horner, Washington Star-News].

*Q. Because of a news report from Paris this morning that actually there were some 15 or 20 protocols, of which only four are being made public, were there any secret protocols agreed to?*

*Dr. Kissinger:* The only protocols that exist are the protocols that have been made public.

*Q. What about understandings?*

*Dr. Kissinger:* There are, with respect to certain phrases, read into the record certain statements as to what they mean, but these have been explained in these briefings and made clear.

There are no secret understandings.

*Q. Dr. Kissinger, it has been widely speculated that the 12-day saturation bombing of the North was the key to achieving the agreement that you found acceptable. Was it, and if not, what was?*

*Dr. Kissinger:* I was asked in October whether the bombing or mining of May 8 brought about the breakthrough in October, and I said then that I did not want to speculate on North Vietnamese motives. I have too much trouble analyzing our own.

I will give the same answer to your question, but I will say that there was a deadlock which was described in the middle of December, and there was a rapid movement when negotiations resumed on the technical level on January 3 (January 2) and on the substantive level on January 8. These facts have to be analyzed by each person for himself.

I want to make one point with respect to the question about understandings. It is obvious that when I speak with some confidence about certain developments that happen with respect to Laos and other places, that this must be based on exchanges that have taken place, but for obvious reasons I cannot go further into them.

The formal obligations of the parties have all been revealed, and there are no secret formal obligations.

*Q. Dr. Kissinger, the dollar amount put on the amount to which the United States is committed in rebuilding—this construction you referred to in North Viet-Nam or reparations or whatever it is to be—is there any dollar amount suggested?*

*Dr. Kissinger:* We will discuss the issue of economic reconstruction of all of Indochina, including North Viet-Nam, only after the signature of the agreements and after the implementation is well advanced. And the definition of any particular sum will have to await the discussions which will take place after the agreements are in force.

*Q. Dr. Kissinger, is there any understanding with the Soviet Union or with Communist China that they will take part in an international conference or will help toward the preservation of this framework of the agreement?*

*Dr. Kissinger:* Formal invitations to the international conference have not yet been extended. But we expect both the Soviet Union and the People's Republic of China to participate in the international conference which will take place within 30 days of the signature of the agreement.

We have reason to believe that both of these countries will participate in this conference.

Now, with respect to their willingness to help this agreement become viable, it is, of course, clear that peace in Indochina requires the self-restraint of all of the major countries and especially of those countries which on all sides have supplied the wherewithal for this conflict.

We, on our part, are prepared to exercise such restraint; we believe that the other countries, the Soviet Union and the People's Republic of China, can make a very major contribution to peace in Indochina by exercising similar restraint.

*Q. If a peace treaty is violated and if the ICC proves ineffective, will the United States ever again send troops into Viet-Nam?*

*Dr. Kissinger:* I don't want to speculate on hypothetical situations that we don't expect to arise.

*Q. Dr. Kissinger, what agreement or understanding is there on the role that will be played by the so-called neutralist or third-force groups in Viet-Nam in the National Council of Reconciliation?*

*Dr. Kissinger:* We have taken the position throughout that the future political evolution of South Viet-Nam should be left, to the greatest extent possible, to the South Vietnamese themselves and should not be predetermined by the United States.

Therefore, there is no understanding in any detail on the role of any particular force in South Viet-Nam. The United States has always taken the view that it favored free elections, but on the whole, the essence of this agreement is to leave the political evolution of South Viet-Nam to negotiation among the various South Vietnamese parties or factions.

*Q. Dr. Kissinger, about a year ago, President Nixon outlined a peace proposal which included a provision for President Thieu to resign prior to elections. Is there any similar provision in this agreement?*

*Dr. Kissinger:* That proposal was in a somewhat different context. In any event, there is no such provision in this agreement and this, again, is a matter that will have to be decided by the Vietnamese parties within the context of whatever negotiation they have, but there is no requirement of any kind like this in the agreement.

*Q. Dr. Kissinger, when do you expect the first American planes to arrive in Hanoi to pick up the prisoners?*

*Dr. Kissinger:* Our expectation is that the withdrawals, as well as the release of prisoners, will take place in roughly equal increments of 15 days over the 60-day period, so within 15 days of January 27. That is the outside time. It could be faster.

*Q. I wanted to know the earliest time.*

*Dr. Kissinger:* I can't give any earlier time than within 15 days.

*Q. Dr. Kissinger, you have addressed yourself to this general area before, but the question keeps coming up. Would you just review for us briefly how you feel that the agreement that you have reached differs from one that could have been reached, say, four years ago?*

*Dr. Kissinger:* Four years ago the North Vietnamese totally refused to separate political and military issues. Four years ago the North Vietnamese insisted that as a condition to negotiations the existing governmental structure in South Viet-Nam would have to be disbanded, and only after this governmental structure had been disbanded and a different one had been installed would they even discuss, much less implement, any of the other provisions of the agreement.

Therefore, until October 8 of this year, all of the various schemes that were constantly being discussed foundered on the one root factor of the situation—that the North Vietnamese, until October 8 of this year, demanded that a political victory be handed to them as a precondition for a discussion of all military questions. But in that case, all military questions would have become totally irrelevant because there was no longer the political structure to which they could apply.

It was not until October 8 this year that the North Vietnamese ever agreed to separate these two aspects of the problem, and as soon as this was done, we moved rapidly.

Then, there was the second phase, which I have described, which included the changes that were made between October and January, which produced this agreement.

*Q. Dr. Kissinger, earlier you said that as of December 16 there were various disagreements which you then listed, and the first one was the question of the demilitarized zone and associated aspects over what identity South Viet-Nam should have under the agreement. Can you elaborate on this, and most particularly, can you elaborate on it from the standpoint of whether you are referring here to President Thieu's objections?*

*Dr. Kissinger:* I have made clear what exactly was involved. We have here several separate issues. One, is there such a thing as a South Viet-Nam, even temporarily, until unification? Secondly, who is the legitimate ruler of South Viet-Nam? This is what the civil war has been all about. Thirdly, what is the demarcation line that separates North Viet-Nam from South Viet-Nam?

Now, we believe that the agreement defines adequately the demarcation line. It defines adequately what the identity is to which we refer. It leaves open to negotiation among the parties the political evolution of South Viet-Nam and therefore the definition of what ultimately will be considered by all South Vietnamese the legitimate ruler.

The President made clear yesterday that as far as the United States is concerned, we recognize President Thieu. This is a situation that has existed in other countries. And these were the three principal issues involved, of which two have international significance and were settled within the agreement, and the third has significance in terms of the political evolution of South Viet-Nam, and that has been left to the self-determination of the South Vietnamese people.

As to the question of President Thieu's objections, comments, and so forth, we said on October 26 that obviously in a war fought in South Viet-Nam, in a war that has had hundreds of thousands of casualties of South Vietnamese, enormous devastation within South Viet-Nam, it stands to reason that the views of our allies will have to be considered. There is nothing wrong or immoral for them to have such views.

Secondly, their perception of the risks has to be different from our perception of the risks. We are 12,000 miles away. If we make a mistake in our assessment of the situation, it will be painful. If they make a mistake in the assessment of the situation, it can be fatal. And therefore, they have had a somewhat less flexible attitude. Where we in some respects have at some points been content with more ambiguous formulations, they were not.

Nevertheless, it is also obvious to any reader of the Saigon press and of their official communications that we did not accept all of their comments and that we carried out precisely what the President had said and what was said at the various press conferences in which I presented the U.S. Government view; namely, that we would make the final determination as to when the American participation in the war should end.

Those parts of their comments that we thought were reasonable we made our own; those that we did not, we did not. And once we had achieved an agreement with the North Vietnamese that we considered fair and just and honorable, we presented it with great energy and conviction in Saigon.

*Q. This is what I am asking you, doctor. You say you made some of his points your points. What did he get in January that he didn't have in October?*

*Dr. Kissinger:* I do not want to discuss what he got. I pointed out the list of objectives we set ourselves in October and what was achieved. I pointed out the changes that were achieved between October and January. We believe them to be substantial, and I do not want to make a checklist of saying which originated in Saigon or which originated in Washington.

*Q. Dr. Kissinger, did you personally feel strengthened in the negotiations as a result of the saturation bombing?*

*Dr. Kissinger:* The term "saturation bombing" has certain connotations. We carried out what was considered to be necessary at the time in order to make clear that the United States could not stand for an indefinite delay in the negotiations.

My role in the negotiations was to present the American point of view. I can only say that we resumed the negotiations on January 8 and the breakthrough occurred on January 9, and I will let those facts speak for themselves.

*Q. Dr. Kissinger, what is now the extent and the nature of the American commitment to South Viet-Nam?*

*Dr. Kissinger:* The United States, as the President said, will continue economic aid to South Viet-Nam. It will continue that military aid which is permitted by the agreement. The United States is prepared to gear that military aid to the actions of other countries and not to treat it as an end in itself.

And the United States expects all countries to live up to the provisions of the agreement.

*Q. Dr. Kissinger, you say, "The two South Vietnamese parties shall be permitted to make periodic replacements of armaments, munitions and war materials which have been destroyed." Why do we have to put any more materials in there? Why should they be in there, and will these materials come from the United States or what countries?*

*Dr. Kissinger:* Let's separate two things: what is permitted by the agreement and what we shall do. What is permitted by the agreement is that military equipment that, as you read, is destroyed, worn out, used up, or damaged can be replaced.

The reason for that provision is that if for any reason the war should start at any level, it would be an unfair restriction on our South Vietnamese allies to prohibit them from replacing their weapons if their enemies are able to do so.

The degree, therefore, to which these weapons have to be replaced will depend on the degree to which there is military activity. If there is no military activity in South Viet-Nam, then the number of weapons that are destroyed, damaged, or worn out will of course be substantially less than in other circumstances.

Secondly, what will be the U.S. position? This depends on the overall situation. If there is no military activity, if other countries do not introduce massive military equipment into Viet-Nam, we do not consider it an end in itself to give military aid. But we believe that it would be unfair and wrong for one country to be armed by its allies while the other one has no right to do so. This is what will govern our actions.

*Q. Dr. Kissinger, what is the plan for the rather sizable U.S. military force offshore in warships off South Viet-Nam and also B–52 bases in Thailand? Will these forces be reduced, and is there an understanding with the North Vietnamese that you have not mentioned to us here that would reduce those forces?*

*Dr. Kissinger:* There is no restriction on American military forces that is not mentioned in the agreement. One would expect, as time goes on, that the deployment of our naval forces will take account of the new situation.

As you know, we have kept many of our forces on station for longer than the normal period of time, and we have had more carriers in the area than before, but this is not required by the agreement and this is simply a projection of what might happen.

The same is true with respect to Thailand. There are no restrictions on our forces in Thailand. It has always been part of the Nixon doctrine that the deployment of our forces would be related to the degree of the danger and has not an abstract quality of its own.

So that as a general rule one can say that in the initial phases of the agreement, before one knows how it will be implemented, the deployment will be more geared to the war situation, and as the agreement is being implemented, the conditions of peace will have a major impact on it. But this is simply a projection of our normal policy and is not an outgrowth required by the agreement.

*The press: Thank you, Dr. Kissinger.*

# Act of the International Conference on Viet Nam, Signed at Paris March 2, 1973

The Government of the United States of America;
The Government of the French Republic;
The Provisional Revolutionary Government of the Republic of South Viet-Nam;
The Government of the Hungarian People's Republic;
The Government of the Republic of Indonesia;
The Government of the Polish People's Republic;
The Government of the Democratic Republic of Viet-Nam;
The Government of the United Kingdom of Great Britain and Northern Ireland;
The Government of the Republic of Viet-Nam;
The Government of the Union of Soviet Socialist Republics;
The Government of Canada; and
The Government of the People's Republic of China;
In the presence of the Secretary-General of the United Nations;

With a view to acknowledging the signed Agreements; guaranteeing the ending of the war, the maintenance of peace in Viet-Nam, the respect of the Vietnamese people's fundamental national rights, and the South Vietnamese people's right to self-determination; and contributing to and guaranteeing peace in Indochina; [1]

Have agreed on the following provisions, and undertake to respect and implement them;

## ARTICLE 1

The Parties to this Act solemnly acknowledge, express their approval of, and support the Paris Agreement on Ending the War and Restoring Peace in Viet-Nam signed in Paris on January 27, 1973, and the four Protocols to the Agreement signed on the same date (hereinafter referred to respectively as the Agreement and the Protocols).

## ARTICLE 2

The Agreement responds to the aspirations and fundamental national rights of the Vietnamese people, *i.e.*, the independence, sovereignty, unity, and territorial integrity of Viet-Nam, to the right of the South Vietnamese people to self-determination, and to the earnest desire for peace shared by all countries in the world. The Agreement constitutes a major contribution to peace, self-determination, national independence, and the improvement of relations among countries. The Agreement and the Protocols should be strictly respected and scrupulously implemented.

---

* Entered into force March 2, 1973. TIAS 7568; 12 ILM 392 (1973).

1 TIAS 7542; 24 UST; 12 ILM 48 (1973); 67 AJIL 389 (1973).

## ARTICLE 3

The Parties to this Act solemnly acknowledge the commitments by the parties to the Agreement and the Protocols to strictly respect and scrupulously implement the Agreement and the Protocols.

## ARTICLE 4

The Parties to this Act solemnly recognize and strictly respect the fundamental national rights of the Vietnamese people, *i.e.*, the independence, sovereignty, unity, and territorial integrity of Viet-Nam, as well as the right of the South Vietnamese people to self-determination. The Parties to this Act shall strictly respect the Agreement and the Protocols by refraining from any action at variance with their provisions.

## ARTICLE 5

For the sake of a durable peace in Viet-Nam, the Parties to this Act call on all countries to strictly respect the fundamental national rights of the Vietnamese people, *i.e.*, the independence, sovereignty, unity, and territorial integrity of Viet-Nam and the right of the South Vietnamese people to self-determination and to strictly respect the Agreement and the Protocols by refraining from any action at variance with their provisions.

## ARTICLE 6

(a) The four parties to the Agreement or the two South Vietnamese parties may, either individually or through joint action, inform the other Parties to this Act about the implementation of the Agreement and the Protocols. Since the reports and views submitted by the International Commission of Control and Supervision concerning the control and supervision of the implementation of those provisions of the Agreement and the Protocols which are within the tasks of the Commission will be sent to either the four parties signatory to the Agreement or to the two South Vietnamese parties, those parties shall be responsible, either individually or through joint action, for forwarding them promptly to the other Parties to this Act.

(b) The four parties to the Agreement or the two South Vietnamese parties shall also, either individually or through joint action, forward this information and these reports and views to the other participant in the International Conference on Viet-Nam for his information.

## ARTICLE 7

(a) In the event of a violation of the Agreement or the Protocols which threatens the peace, the independence, sovereignty, unity, or territorial integrity of Viet-Nam, or the right of the South Vietnamese people to self-determination, the parties signatory to the Agreement and the Protocols shall, either individually or jointly, consult with the other Parties to this Act with a view to determining necessary remedial measures.

(b) The International Conference on Viet-Nam shall be reconvened upon a joint request by the Government of the United States of America and the Government of the Democratic Republic of Viet-Nam on behalf of the parties signatory to the Agreement or upon a request by six or more of the Parties to this Act.

## ARTICLE 8

With a view to contributing to and guaranteeing peace in Indochina, the Parties to this Act acknowledge the commitment of the parties to the Agreement to respect the independence, sovereignty, unity, territorial integrity, and neutrality of Cambodia and Laos as stipulated in the Agreement, agree also to respect them and to refrain from any action at variance with them, and call on other countries to do the same.

## ARTICLE 9

This Act shall enter into force upon signature by plenipotentiary representatives of all twelve Parties and shall be strictly implemented by all the Parties. Signature of this Act does not constitute recognition of any Party in any case in which it has not previously been accorded.

DONE in twelve copies in Paris this second day of March, One Thousand Nine Hundred and Seventy-Three, in English, French, Russian, Vietnamese, and Chinese. All texts are equally authentic.

# Four-Party Joint Communique, Signed at Paris on Implementation of Viet Nam Agreement, June 13, 1973

## TEXTS OF JOINT COMMUNIQUES

### Four-Party Joint Communique

JOINT COMMUNIQUE

The Parties signatory to the Paris Agreement on Ending the War and Restoring Peace in Viet-Nam, signed on January 27, 1973,

Considering that strict respect and scrupulous implementation of all provisions of the Agreement and its Protocols by all the parties signatory to them are necessary to ensure the peace in Viet-Nam and contribute to the cause of peace in Indochina and Southeast Asia,

Have agreed on the following points (in the sequence of the relevant articles in the Agreement):

1. In conformity with Article 2 of the Agreement, the United States shall cease immediately, completely, and indefinitely aerial reconnaissance over the territory of the Democratic Republic of Viet-Nam.

2. In conformity with Article 2 of the Agreement and with the Protocol on Mine Clearance:

(a) The United States shall resume mine clearance operations within five days from the date of signature of this Joint Communique and shall successfully complete those operations within thirty days thereafter.

(b) The United States shall supply to the Democratic Republic of Viet-Nam means which are agreed to be adequate and sufficient for sweeping mines in rivers.

(c) The United States shall announce when the mine clearance in each main channel is completed and issue a final announcement when all the operations are completed.

3. In implementation of Article 2 of the Agreement, at 1200 hours, G.M.T., June 14, 1973, the High Commands of the two South Vietnamese parties shall issue identical orders to all regular and irregular armed forces and the armed police under their command, to strictly observe the cease-fire throughout South Viet-Nam beginning at 0400 hours, G.M.T., June 15, 1973, and scrupulously implement the Agreement and its Protocols.

4. The two South Vietnamese parties shall strictly implement Articles 2 and 3 of the Protocol on the Cease-Fire in South Viet-Nam which read as follows:

*"Article 2*

(a) As soon as the cease-fire comes into force and until regulations are issued by the Joint Military Commissions, all ground, river, sea and air combat forces of the parties in South Viet-Nam shall remain in place; that is, in order to ensure a stable cease-fire, there shall be no major redeployments or movements that would extend each party's area of control or would result in contact between opposing armed forces and clashes which might take place.

(b) All regular and irregular armed forces and the armed police of the parties in South Viet-Nam shall observe the prohibition of the following acts:

(1) Armed patrols into areas controlled by opposing armed forces and flights by bomber and fighter aircraft of all types, except for unarmed flights for proficiency training and maintenance;

(2) Armed attacks against any person, either military or civilian, by any means whatsoever, including the use of small arms, mortars, artillery, bombing and strafing by airplanes and any other type of weapon or explosive device;

(3) All combat operations on the ground, on rivers, on the sea and in the air;

(4) All hostile acts, terrorism or reprisals; and

(5) All acts endangering lives or public or private property.

*Article 3*

(a) The above-mentioned prohibitions shall not hamper or restrict:

(1) Civilian supply, freedom of movement, freedom to work, and freedom of the people to engage in trade, and civilian communication and transportation between and among all areas in South Viet-Nam;

(2) The use by each party in areas under its control of military support elements, such as engineer and transportation units, in repair

and construction of public facilities and the transportation and supplying of the population;

(3) Normal military proficiency training conducted by the parties in the areas under their respective control with due regard for public safety.

(b) The Joint Military Commissions shall immediately agree on corridors, routes, and other regulations governing the movement of military transport aircraft, military transport vehicles, and military transport vessels of all types of one party going through areas under the control of other parties."

5. The Two-Party Joint Military Commission shall immediately carry out its task pursuant to Article 3(b) of the Agreement to determine the areas controlled by each of the two South Vietnamese parties and the modalities of stationing. This task shall be completed as soon as possible. The Commission shall also immediately discuss the movements necessary to accomplish a return of the armed forces of the two South Vietnamese parties to the positions they occupied at the time the cease-fire entered into force on January 28, 1973.

6. Twenty-four hours after the cease-fire referred to in paragraph 3 enters into force, the commanders of the opposing armed forces at those places of direct contact shall meet to carry out the provisions of Article 4 of the Protocol on the Cease-Fire in South Viet-Nam with a view to reaching an agreement on temporary measures to avert conflict and to ensure supply and medical care for these armed forces.

7. In conformity with Article 7 of the Agreement:

(a) The two South Vietnamese parties shall not accept the introduction of troops, military advisers, and military personnel, including technical military personnel, into South Viet-Nam.

(b) The two South Vietnamese parties shall not accept the introduction of armaments, munitions, and war material into South Viet-Nam. However, the two South Vietnamese parties are permitted to make periodic replacement of armaments, munitions, and war material, as authorized by Article 7 of the Agreement, through designated points of entry and subject to supervision by the Two-Party Joint Military Commission and the International Commission of Control and Supervision.

In conformity with Article 15(b) of the Agreement regarding the respect of the Demilitarized Zone, military equipment may transit the Demilitarized Zone only if introduced into South Viet-Nam as replacements pursuant to Article 7 of the Agreement and through a designated point of entry.

(c) Twenty-four hours after the entry into force of the cease-fire referred to in paragraph 3, the Two-Party Joint Military Commission shall discuss the modalities for the supervision of the replacements of armaments, munitions, and war material permitted by Article 7 of the Agreement at the three

points of entry already agreed upon for each party. Within fifteen days of the entry into force of the cease-fire referred to in paragraph 3, the two South Vietnamese parties shall also designate by agreement three additional points of entry for each party in the area controlled by that party.

8. In conformity with Article 8 of the Agreement:

(a) Any captured personnel covered by Article 8(a) of the Agreement who have not yet been returned shall be returned without delay, and in any event within no more than thirty days from the date of signature of this Joint Communique.

(b) All the provisions of the Agreement and the Protocol on the Return of Captured Personnel shall be scrupulously implemented. All Vietnamese civilian personnel covered by Article 8(c) of the Agreement and Article 7 of the Protocol on the Return of Captured Personnel shall be returned as soon as possible. The two South Vietnamese parties shall do their utmost to accomplish this within forty-five days from the date of signature of this Joint Communique.

(c) In conformity with Article 8 of the Protocol on the Return of Captured Personnel, all captured and detained personnel covered by that Protocol shall be treated humanely at all times. The two South Vietnamese parties shall immediately implement Article 9 of that Protocol and, within fifteen days from the date of signature of this Joint Communique, allow National Red Cross Societies they have agreed upon to visit all places where these personnel are held.

(d) The two South Vietnamese parties shall cooperate in obtaining information about missing persons and in determining the location of and in taking care of the graves of the dead.

(e) In conformity with Article 8(b) of the Agreement, the parties shall help each other to get information about those military personnel and foreign civilians of the parties missing in action, to determine the location and take care of the graves of the dead so as to facilitate the exhumation and repatriation of the remains, and to take any such other measures as may be required to get information about those still considered missing in action. For this purpose, frequent and regular liaison flights shall be made between Saigon and Hanoi.

9. The two South Vietnamese parties shall implement Article 11 of the Agreement, which reads as follows:

"Immediately after the cease-fire, the two South Vietnamese parties will:

—achieve national reconciliation and concord, end hatred and enmity, prohibit all acts of reprisal and discrimination against individuals or organizations that have collaborated with one side or the other;

—ensure the democratic liberties of the people: personal freedom, freedom of speech, freedom of the press, freedom of meeting, freedom of organization, freedom of political activities, freedom of belief, freedom of movement, freedom of residence, freedom of work, right to property ownership and right to free enterprise."

10. Consistent with the principles for the exercise of the South Vietnamese people's right to self-determination stated in Chapter IV of the Agreement:

(a) The South Vietnamese people shall decide themselves the political future of South Viet-Nam through genuinely free and democratic general elections under international supervision.

(b) The National Council of National Reconciliation and Concord consisting of three equal segments shall be formed as soon as possible, in conformity with Article 12 of the Agreement.

The two South Vietnamese parties shall sign an agreement on the internal matters of South Viet-Nam as soon as possible, and shall do their utmost to accomplish this within forty-five days from the date of signature of this Joint Communique.

(c) The two South Vietnamese parties shall agree through consultations on the institutions for which the free and democratic general elections provided for in Article 9(b) of the Agreement will be held.

(d) The two South Vietnamese parties shall implement Article 13 of the Agreement, which reads as follows:

"The question of Vietnamese armed forces in South Viet-Nam shall be settled by the two South Vietnamese parties in a spirit of national reconciliation and concord, equality and mutual respect, without foreign interference, in accordance with the postwar situation. Among the questions to be discussed by the two South Vietnamese parties are steps to reduce their military effectives and to demobilize the troops being reduced. The two South Vietnamese parties will accomplish this as soon as possible."

11. In implementation of Article 17 of the Agreement:

(a) All the provisions of Articles 16 and 17 of the Protocol on the Cease-Fire in South Viet-Nam shall immediately be implemented with respect to the Two-Party Joint Military Commission. That Commission shall also immediately be accorded the eleven points of privileges and immunities agreed upon by the Four-Party Joint Military Commission. Frequent and regular liaison flights shall be made between Saigon and the headquarters of the Regional Two-Party Joint Military Commissions and other places in South Viet-Nam as required for the operations of the Two-Party Joint Military Commission. Frequent and regular liaison flights shall also be made between Saigon and Loc Ninh.

(b) The headquarters of the Central Two-Party Joint Military Commission shall be located in Saigon proper or at a place agreed upon by the two South Vietnamese parties where an area controlled by one of them adjoins an area controlled by the other. The locations of the headquarters of the Regional Two-Party Joint Military Commissions and of the teams of the Two-Party Joint Military Commission shall be determined by that Commission within fifteen days after the entry into force of the cease-fire referred to in paragraph 3. These locations may be changed at any time as determined by the Commission. The locations, except for teams at the points of entry, shall be selected from among those towns specified in Article 11(b) and (c) of the Protocol on the Cease-Fire in South Viet-Nam and those places where an area controlled by one South Vietnamese party adjoins an area controlled by the other, or at any other place agreed upon by the Commission.

(c) Once the privileges and immunities mentioned in paragraph 11(a) are accorded by both South Vietnamese parties, the Two-Party Joint Military Commission shall be fully staffed and its regional commissions and teams fully deployed within fifteen days after their locations have been determined.

(d) The Two-Party Joint Military Commission and the International Commission of Control and Supervision shall closely cooperate with and assist each other in carrying out their respective functions.

12. In conformity with Article 18 of the Agreement and Article 10 of the Protocol on the International Commission of Control and Supervision, the International Commission, including its teams, is allowed such movement for observation as is reasonably required for the proper exercise of its functions as stipulated in the Agreement. In carrying out these functions, the International Commission, including its teams, shall enjoy all necessary assistance and cooperation from the parties concerned. The two South Vietnamese parties shall issue the necessary instructions to their personnel and take all other necessary measures to ensure the safety of such movement.

13. Article 20 of the Agreement, regarding Cambodia and Laos, shall be scrupulously implemented.

14. In conformity with Article 21 of the Agreement, the United States-Democratic Republic of Viet-Nam Joint Economic Commission shall resume its meetings four days from the date of signature of this Joint Communique and shall complete the first phase of its work within fifteen days thereafter.

Affirming that the parties concerned shall strictly respect and scrupulously implement all the provisions of the Paris Agreement, its Protocols, and this Joint Communique, the undersigned representatives of the parties signatory to the Paris Agreement have decided to issue this Joint Communique to record and publish the points on which they have agreed.

Signed in Paris, June 13, 1973.

For the Government of the United States of America:

HENRY A. KISSINGER
*Assistant to the President of the United States of America*

For the Government of the Republic of Viet-Nam:

NGUYEN LUU VIEN
*Representative of the Government of the Republic of Viet-Nam*

For the Government of the Democratic Republic of Viet-Nam:

LE DUC THO
*Representative of the Government of the Democratic Republic of Viet-Nam*

For the Provisional Revolutionary Government of the Republic of South Viet-Nam:

NGUYEN VAN HIEU
*Minister of State of the Provisional Revolutionary Government of the Republic of South Viet-Nam*

## Two-Party Joint Communique

### JOINT COMMUNIQUE

From May 17 to May 23, from June 6 to June 9, and on June 12 and June 13, 1973, Dr. Henry A. Kissinger, on behalf of the Government of the United States of America, and Mr. Le Duc Tho, on behalf of the Government of the Democratic Republic of Viet-Nam, reviewed the implementation of the Paris Agreement on Ending the War and Restoring Peace in Viet-Nam and its Protocols and discussed urgent measures to ensure the correct and strict implementation of the Agreement and its Protocols.

The Government of the United States of America, with the concurrence of the Government of the Republic of Viet-Nam,

The Government of the Democratic Republic of Viet-Nam, with the concurrence of the Provisional Revolutionary Government of the Republic of South Viet-Nam,

Considering that strict respect and scrupulous implementation of all provisions of the Paris Agreement and its Protocols by all the parties signatory to them are necessary to ensure the peace in Viet-Nam and contribute to the cause of peace in Indochina and Southeast Asia,

Have agreed on the following points (in the sequence of the relevant articles in the Agreement):

[Texts of paragraphs 1–14 as above]

Affirming that the parties concerned shall strictly respect and scrupulously implement all the provisions of the Paris Agreement, its Protocols, this Joint Communique, and a Joint Communique in the same terms signed by representatives of the Government of the United States of America, the Government of the Republic of Viet-Nam, the Government of the Democratic Republic of Viet-Nam, and the Provisional Revolutionary Government of the Republic of South Viet-Nam, the representative of the United States of America, Dr. Henry A. Kissinger, and the representative of the Democratic Republic of Viet-Nam, Mr. Le Duc Tho, have decided to issue this Joint Communique to record and publish the points on which they have agreed.

Signed in Paris, June 13, 1973.

For the Government of the United States of America:

HENRY A. KISSINGER
*Assistant to the President of the United States of America*

For the Government of the Democratic Republic of Viet-Nam:

LE DUC THO
*Representative of the Government of the Democratic Republic of Viet-Nam*

# VI. DOCUMENTARY APPENDIX 1
# SETTLEMENT OF THE INDOCHINA WAR
## Part B. Laos

# Lao Government of Vientiane-Lao Patriotic Forces: Agreement on Cease-Fire in Laos*

## [Done at Vientiane, February 21, 1973]

*Unofficial Translation of Laos Cease-Fire Agreement*

In response to the supreme desires of His Majesty the King and the earnest aspirations of the people of all races throughout the country, who desire to see a rapid end to the war, the re-establishment and maintenance of peace in a lasting way, to build Laos into a peaceful, independent, neutral, democratic, unified and prosperous country in order to contribute positively to the consolidation of peace in Indochina and in Southeast Asia, on the basis of the Geneva Accords of 1962 and of the present realities in Laos, the party of the Government of Vientiane and the party of the Patriotic Forces are unanimously agreed on the following:

### *Chapter I—General Principles*

ARTICLE 1

A. The desire of the Lao people is to preserve and to rigorously apply its national, fundamental, sacred and inviolable rights such as: independence, sovereignty, unity and the territorial integrity of Laos.

B. The Declaration of Neutrality of Laos of July 9, 1962 and the Geneva Accords of 1962 on Laos are the correct bases for the foreign policy of peace, independence, neutrality of the Kingdom of Laos; the interested Lao parties, the United States of America, Thailand and other foreign countries must respect them and strictly apply them. The foreign affairs of Laos must be run by the Lao themselves, without interference by foreign nations.

C. Within the noble aim of re-establishing peace, consolidating independence, achieving national concord and the unification of the Motherland, from the fact that within the present realities in Laos there exists two zones, separately controlled by the two parties, the internal problems of Laos must be resolved in the spirit of national concord in accordance with the principles of equality between the parties and of mutual respect in order that one of the parties may not constrain and annex the other.

D. In order to preserve the independence and national sovereignty,

---

* Reproduced from an unofficial English translation provided by the U.S. Department of State.

to achieve national concord and the unification of the Motherland, it is necessary to rigorously carry out the democratic liberties of the people which include: individual liberty, freedom of thought, freedom of expression, freedom of the press, freedom of assembly, freedom to form political parties and organizations, the freedom to appear as candidates in elections and the freedom to elect, freedom of movement, freedom of residence, freedom of business and the right of private property; it is necessary to abolish all laws, regulations and organizations which are contrary to said freedoms.

## Chapter II—Military Provisions

ARTICLE 2

As of 1200 hours (Vientiane time) on February 22, 1973, there will be applied a cease-fire in place, total and simultaneous over all Lao territory, which will include the following measures:

A. Foreign countries will completely and definitively end their bombing on all Lao territories, ending all their intervention and aggressions against Laos and ending all types of military activities on their part in Laos.

B. The armed forces of foreign nations end completely and definitively all their military activities in Laos.

C. The armed forces of all Lao parties end definitively all their military activities which constitute hostilities on land and in the air.

ARTICLE 3: AS SOON AS THE CEASE-FIRE ENTERS INTO EFFECT:

A. There are absolutely forbidden all activities involving attacks, encroachments, menace or military violations on land or in the air by one of the parties against the zone temporarily under the control of the opposing party.

B. Absolutely forbidden are all hostile military actions, including the activities of bandits, commandos and all armed activities and those of espionage on land and in the air; in the event that one of the parties wishes to resupply in food those dependent on it by passing through the zone controlled by the other party, the mixed commission for the execution of the Accord will discuss this and will decide unanimously the precise modalities of this resupply.

C. Absolutely forbidden are all operations involving mop-up, terror, repression, assassination and attacks on the lives and goods of the population and all acts of reprisal and of discrimination towards people who have collaborated with the opposing party during the war; to aid refugees who have been obliged to leave their villages of origin during the war and to return there freely in order to earn their living according to their desires.

D. There is forbidden the entry into Laos of all types of military personnel, of all categories of regular and irregular troops as well as of all types of armament and military materiel from foreign countries, with the exception of those stipulated in the Geneva Accords of 1954 and 1962. In the case where it becomes necessary to replace damaged and used arms and military materiel, the two parties will discuss it and will reach a joint decision.

ARTICLE 4

Within 60 days from the date of the formation of the Provisional Government of National Union and of the National Political Consultative Council, there must be completely achieved the withdrawal from Laos of military personnel, regular and irregular foreign troops and the dismantling of military and paramilitary organizations of foreign countries.

The "special forces" organized, armed, trained and commanded by foreigners must be liquidated as well as all the bases, installations and positions of these special forces.

ARTICLE 5

Each of the two Lao parties will turn over to the other party all persons, without distinction of nationality, who have been captured and imprisoned for having collaborated with the opposing party during the war.

This exchange will be carried out in accordance with arrangements decided by the two parties together, and at the latest within the 60 days from the date of the formation of the Provisional Government of National Union and of the National Political Consultative Council.

After the final turning over of captured persons, each party has the obligation of researching and furnishing to the other party information on persons who disappeared during the war.

### Chapter III—Political Clauses

ARTICLE 6

General elections will be undertaken in accordance with principles of true liberty and democracy in order to establish the National Assembly and the definitive Government of National Union, true representative of the people of all races of all Laos. The method and date of general elections will be fixed by the two parties acting jointly.

During the period during which general elections will not have been carried out, the two parties will form a new Provisional Government of National Union and a National Political Consultative Council at the latest within the 30 days of the date of the signature of the present Accord in order to carry out the signed Accords and to carry on the affairs of the country.

## ARTICLE 7

The new Provisional Government of National Union will include representatives of the party of the Government of Vientiane and of the party of the Patriotic Forces in equal number and of two persons who are for peace, independence, neutrality, democracy; these two persons will be chosen by the two parties acting in common accord; the future Prime Minister will not be included within the equal numbers of the representatives of the parties. The Provisional Government of National Union will be formed in accordance with a special procedure by the direct investiture of His Majesty the King; it will function in accordance with the principle of unanimity between the two parties, and has the duty of carrying out the signed Accords and the political program adopted by the two parties in common accord, notably achieving the cease-fire, maintaining the cease-fire, preserving a lasting peace, applying throughout democratic liberties of the people, carrying out a foreign policy of peace, independence and neutrality, coordinating the plan for economic construction, cultural development, receiving and dividing aid granted to Laos by different countries.

## ARTICLE 8

The National Political Consultative Council, the Organization of National Concord, is composed of representatives of the party of the Government of Vientiane and of the party of the Patriotic Forces in equal numbers and of a certain number of personalities who are for peace, independence, neutrality and democracy, a number to be determined in common by the two parties; it functions in accordance with the principle of unanimity between the two parties and has as its task:

—to discuss the large problems dealing with the internal and external policies of the country and to present opinions concerning these problems to the Provisional Government of National Union.

—to activate and assist the Provisional Government of National

Union and to inspire and assist the two parties in application of the signed Accords in order to achieve national unity.

—to examine and to adopt together the laws and regulations concerning the general elections and to collaborate with the Provisional Government of National Union in the organization of the general elections in order to install the National Assembly and the definitive Government of National Union.

The procedure for installing the National Political Consultative Council is as follows: The two parties are to discuss it in detail and take an agreed decision on this subject, then transmit this decision to the Provisional Government of National Union which will submit it to His Majesty the King for investiture. The same procedure will be followed for the dissolution of the National Political Consultative Council.

ARTICLE 9

The two parties have agreed to neutralize the city of Luang Prabang and the capital, Vientiane, and to seek by all means to assure the security and the functioning of the Provisional Government of National Union and of the National Political Consultative Council, to prevent any sabotage or pressure by all forces, internal or external.

ARTICLE 10

A. While awaiting the election of the National Assembly and the establishment of the definitive Government of National Union, within the spirit of Article 6 of the second part of the agreed communique of Zurich dated 22 June 1961, each party will maintain the zone provisionally under its control and will carry out the political program of the Provisional Government of National Union, a program adopted jointly by the two parties.

B. The two parties will initiate the carrying out of normal relations between the two governments, create favorable conditions which permit the people to move about, to seek the means of livelihood, to visit each other, to carry out economic, cultural and other exchanges with a view to consolidating national union in order to rapidly fulfill the unification of the country.

C. The two parties take note of the declaration of the Government of the United States of America according to which the United States of America will bring their contribution to the healing of the wounds of war and to the postwar task of reconstruction in Indochina. The

Government of National Union will discuss with the Government of the United States of America concerning this contribution as it concerns Laos.

## Chapter IV

*Concerning the Joint Commission for the Carrying Out of the Agreements and Concerning the International Commission for Control and Supervision*

ARTICLE 11

For the execution of the present Agreement, responsibility falls principally on the two parties concerned in Laos. The two parties will establish immediately a Joint Commission for the Carrying Out of the Accords with representatives in equal numbers. The Commission for the Carrying Out of the Accords will enter immediately into action as soon as the cease-fire takes effect.

The Commission for the Carrying Out of the Accords will function in accordance with the principle of discussion and of unanimous decision.

ARTICLE 12

The ICCS established in accordance with the Geneva Accords of 1962 on Laos, made up of Indian, Polish and Canadian delegates with the Indian delegate as President, will carry out its activities in accordance with the tasks, powers and work principles as stipulated in the Protocol of said Geneva Accords.

## Chapter V—Other Provisions

ARTICLE 13

The Party of the Government of Vientiane and the Party of the Patriotic Forces undertake to carry out the present Accord and to carry on the negotiations in order to achieve all the clauses already agreed on and to resolve the problems concerning the two parties in a spirit of equality and mutual respect in order to end the war, restore and preserve the peace in a firm and durable manner, in order to achieve national unity and national unification, in order to build a Laos into a peaceful, independent, neutral, democratic, unified and prosperous nation.

ARTICLE 14

The present Accord entered into force from the date of its signing.

DONE at Vientiane, 21 February 1973, in Lao and in five copies, one of which will be transmitted to His Majesty the King, one to be kept by each Party, and one each to be kept in the Archives of the Provisional Government and the National Political Consultative Council.

| | |
|---|---|
| The Representative of the Party of the Government of Vientiane | The Representative of the Party of the Patriotic Forces |
| Phagna Pheng Phongsavan Representative Extraordinary and Plenipotentiary of the Government of Vientiane | Phagna Phoumi Vongvichit Representative Extraordinary and Plenipotentiary of the Patriotic Forces |

# VI. DOCUMENTARY APPENDIX 1
## SETTLEMENT OF THE INDOCHINA WAR
### Part C. Cambodia

# Public Law 93-50

# Second Supplemental Appropriation Act, 1973

SEC. 307. None of the funds herein appropriated under this Act may be expended to support directly or indirectly combat activities in or over Cambodia, Laos, North Vietnam and South Vietnam or off the shores of Cambodia, Laos, North Vietnam and South Vietnam by United States forces, and after August 15, 1973, no other funds heretofore appropriated under any other Act may be expended for such purpose.

Approved July 1, 1973.

## Presidential Letter Concerning End to American Bombing in Cambodia*

### THE WHITE HOUSE

### TEXT OF A LETTER FROM THE PRESIDENT TO SPEAKER CARL ALBERT AND SENATOR MIKE MANSFIELD

August 3, 1973

Dear Mr. Speaker:

By legislative action the Congress has required an end to American bombing in Cambodia on August 15th. The wording of the Cambodia rider is unmistakable; its intent is clear. The Congress has expressed its will in the form of law and the Administration will obey that law.

I cannot do so, however, without stating my grave personal reservations concerning the dangerous potential consequences of this measure. I would be remiss in my constitutional responsibilities if I did not warn of the hazards that lie in the path chosen by Congress.

Since entering office in January of 1969, I have worked ceaselessly to secure an honorable peace in Southeast Asia. Thanks to the support of the American people and the gallantry of our fighting men and allies, a ceasefire agreement in Vietnam and a political settlement in Laos have already been achieved. The attainment of a settlement in Cambodia has

* Reproduced from the White House press release of August 3, 1973.

been the unremitting effort of this Administration, and we have had every confidence of being able to achieve that goal. With the passage of the Congressional act, the incentive to negotiate a settlement in Cambodia has been undermined, and August 15 will accelerate this process.

This abandonment of a friend will have a profound impact in other countries, such as Thailand, which have relied on the constancy and determination of the United States, and I want the Congress to be fully aware of the consequences of its action. For my part, I assure America's allies that this Administration will do everything permitted by Congressional action to achieve a lasting peace in Indochina. In particular, I want the brave and beleaguered Cambodian people to know that the end to the bombing in Cambodia does not signal an abdication of America's determination to work for a lasting peace in Indochina. We will continue to provide all possible support permitted under the law. We will continue to work for a durable peace with all the legal means at our disposal.

I can only hope that the North Vietnamese will not draw the erroneous conclusion from this Congressional action that they are free to launch a military offensive in other areas in Indochina. North Vietnam would be making a very dangerous error if it mistook the cessation of bombing in Cambodia for an invitation to fresh aggression or further violations of the Paris Agreements. The American people would respond to such aggression with appropriate action.

I have sent an identical letter to the Majority Leader of the Senate.

Sincerely,
RICHARD NIXON

# VII. DOCUMENTARY APPENDIX 2

## SOME PRINCIPAL DECISIONS BY UNITED STATES COURTS

## AND LEGISLATIVE ACTION BY THE UNITED STATES CONGRESS ON INDOCHINA-RELATED ISSUES

### Part A. Judicial Appendix

# Holtzman v. Schlesinger

Elizabeth HOLTZMAN, Individually and in her capacity as a member of the United States House of Representatives, et al., Plaintiffs,

v.

James R. SCHLESINGER, Individually and as Secretary of Defense, et al., Defendants.

No. 73–C–537.

United States District Court,
E. D. New York.

July 25, 1973.

———◆———

Neuborne & Friedman, New York City by Burt Neuborne, Leon Friedman, New York City, of counsel, for plaintiffs.

Robert A. Morse, U. S. Atty., E. D. N. Y., by James D. Porter, Jr., Brooklyn, N. Y., Cyril Hyman, Asst. U. S. Attys., New York City, of counsel, for defendants.

Earle K. Moore, New York City, for Council for Christian Social Action of the United Church of Christ, and others, amici curiae.

Rabinowitz, Boudin & Standard, New York City, for Congressman Parren J. Mitchell and others, amici curiae by Michael Krinsky and Eric Lieberman, New York City, of counsel.

## MEMORANDUM AND ORDER

JUDD, District Judge.

Plaintiffs seek a determination that the President of the United States and the military personnel under his direction and control may not engage in intensive combat operations in Cambodia and elsewhere in Indochina in the absence of Congressional authorization required under Article I, § 8, Clause 11 of the Constitution. The case is before the court on plaintiffs' motion for summary judgment for lack of genuine issues of material fact. Additionally, plaintiffs seek declaratory and/or injunctive relief.

Plaintiffs have also moved to add as plaintiff another Air Force officer on active duty, Captain Donald Dawson, and to stay the defendants from ordering him to engage in bombing missions over Cambodia.

### Posture of the Case

At an earlier stage this court denied defendants' motion to dismiss the complaint, and overruled the contentions that Congresswoman Holtzman lacked standing to challenge the military activities in question and that the controversy presented a nonjusticiable political question.

Both sides were given an opportunity to submit any additional papers that would bear on the appropriateness of summary judgment.

### Facts

Review of the facts may begin with 1970, since the earlier phases of hostilities in Indochina have been summarized in an earlier case.

This court held in September 1970 in Berk v. Laird, 317 F.Supp. 715 (E.D.N. Y.1970), aff'd sub nom., Orlando v. Laird, 443 F.2d 1039 (2d Cir. 1971), that Congress had authorized hostilities in Vietnam to that date through a series of appropriation acts.

## Hostilities in Cambodia

In response to Presidential pronouncements concerning the necessity of military action in Cambodia, there was a series of Congressional responses seeking in the main to limit such military action, and culminating in two laws enacted on July 1, 1973 which directed that no funds might be expended for Cambodian combat activities after August 15, 1973.

On April 30, 1970, the President stated in an address to the nation that "North Vietnam has occupied military sanctuaries all along the Cambodian frontier with South Vietnam," that Cambodia had therefore called on the United States for assistance, and that attacks were therefore being launched "to clean out major enemy sanctuaries on the Cambodian-Vietnam border." The Situation in Southeast Asia, 6 Presidential Documents 596, 597, 598.

On June 30, 1970, a report by the President on the Cambodian operation, released at San Clemente, California, stated that all American troops had withdrawn from Cambodia, but that the United States would continue to conduct air interdiction missions to prevent supplies and personnel being moved through Cambodia toward South Vietnam, and that "We do this to protect our forces in South Vietnam." The President also stated that one of the reasons for attacking the enemy's "sanctuaries" in Cambodia was that this would "enhance the prospects of a negotiated peace." The Cambodian Operation, 6 Presidential Documents 843, 850, 852.

The so-called Fulbright proviso, limiting military support to Cambodia except to the extent necessary to insure the safe withdrawal of United States forces from Southeast Asia and the release of American prisoners of war, was adopted by the Congress during the summer of 1970 and inserted in the War Forces-Military Procurement Act of 1971 and became law with the President's approval on October 7, 1970. This proviso, which was repeated in every subsequent military appropriation and authorization act, reads as follows:

. . . nothing [herein] shall be construed as authorizing the use of any such funds to support Vietnamese or other free world forces in actions designed to provide military support and assistance to the Government of Cambodia or Laos: *Provided further,* That nothing contained in this section shall be construed to prohibit support of actions required to insure the safe and orderly withdrawal or disengagement of U.S. Forces from Southeast Asia, or to aid in the release of Americans held as prisoners of war.

P.L. 91–441, 84 Stat. 905; P.L. 91–668, 84 Stat. 2020; P.L. 92–156, 85 Stat. 423; P.L. 92–204, 85 Stat. 716; P.L. 92–436, 86 Stat. 734; P.L. 92–570, 86 Stat. 1184.

On the evening of the same day the Fulbright proviso became law, October 7, 1970, the President addressed the nation by radio and television and stated that the North Vietnamese were carrying on aggression in Laos and Cambodia as well as in Vietnam and that "The war in Indochina has been proved to be of one piece; it cannot be cured by treating only one of its areas of outbreak." The New Initiative for Peace in Southeast Asia, 6 Presidential Documents 1349, 1350.

The Special Foreign Assistance Act of 1971 (P.L. 91–652, 84 Stat. 1942), approved January 1, 1971, provided:

Sec. 7. (a) In line with the expressed intention of the President of the United States, none of the funds authorized or appropriated pursuant to this or any other Act may be used to finance the introduction of United States ground combat troops into Cambodia, or to provide United States advisers to or for Cambodian military forces in Cambodia.

(b) Military and economic assistance provided by the United States to Cambodia and authorized or appropriated pursuant to this or any other Act shall not be construed as a commitment by the United States to Cambodia for its defense.

On February 25, 1971, the President submitted a foreign policy report to Congress, saying again that the war in Indochina was "of one piece," that because of North Vietnamese infiltration in Cambodia "We faced the prospect of one large enemy base camp 600 miles along South Vietnam's flank;" and that our policy for Cambodia included "air missions against enemy supplies and personnel that pose a potential threat to South Vietnam or seek to establish base areas relevant to Vietnam." United States Foreign Policy for the 1970's: Building for Peace, 7 Presidential Documents 305, 328, 332.

On November 17, 1971, the so-called Mansfield amendment became law by action of Congress with the President's approval, and expressed the United States policy "to terminate at the earliest practicable date all military operations of the United States in Indochina." The pertinent portions of this amendment, which was part of the Appropriations Authorizations-Military Procurement Act, 1972, state:

Sec. 601. (a) It is hereby declared to be the policy of the United States to terminate at the earliest practicable date all military operations of the United States in Indochina, and to provide for the prompt and orderly withdrawal of all United States military forces at a date certain, subject to the release of all American prisoners of war held by the Government of North Vietnam and forces allied with such Government and an accounting for all Americans missing in action who have been held by or known to

such Government or such forces. The Congress hereby urges and requests the President to implement the above-expressed policy by initiating immediately the following actions:

(1) Establishing a final date for the withdrawal from Indochina of all military forces of the United States contingent upon the release of all American prisoners of war held by the Government of North Vietnam and forces allied with such Government and an accounting for all Americans missing in action who have been held by or known to such Government or such forces.

(2) Negotiate with the Government of North Vietnam for an immediate cease-fire by all parties to the hostilities in Indochina.

(3) Negotiate with the Government of North Vietnam for an agreement which would provide for a series of phased and rapid withdrawals of United States military forces from Indochina in exchange for a corresponding series of phased releases of American prisoners of war, and for the release of any remaining American prisoners of war concurrently with the withdrawal of all remaining military forces of the United States by not later than the date established by the President pursuant to paragraph (1) hereof or by such earlier date as may be agreed upon by the negotiating parties.

In the Defense Appropriation Act of 1972 (P.L. 92–204), approved December 18, 1971, Congress specified:

Sec. 738(a) Not to exceed $2,500,000,-000 of the appropriations available to the Department of Defense during the current fiscal year shall be available for their stated purposes to support; (1) Vietnamese and other free world forces in support of Vietnamese forces (2) local forces in Laos and Thailand; and for related costs, on such terms and conditions as the Secretary of Defense may determine: . . . Provided further, that nothing in clause (1) of the first sentence of this subsection shall be construed as authorizing the use of any such funds to support Vietnamese or other free world forces in actions designed to provide military support and assistance to the Government of Cambodia or Laos: Provided further that nothing contained in this section shall be construed to prohibit support of actions required to insure the safe and orderly withdrawal or disengagement of U.S. Forces from Southeast Asia, or to aid in the release of Americans held as prisoners of war.

This language was continued in all subsequent military authorization or appropriations acts. See Appropriations Authorization-Military Procurement Act, 1972, P.L. 92–156, 85 Stat. 423, November 17, 1971, Sec. 501; Military Procurement Act, 1973, P.L. 92–436, 86 Stat. 734, September 26, 1972, Sec. 601; Department of Defense Appropriation Act, 1973, P.L. 92–570, 86 Stat. 1184, October 26, 1972, Sec. 737.

In the Foreign Assistance Act, 1971, approved on February 7, 1972, the Congress expressly stated that limited foreign aid to Cambodia "shall not be construed as a commitment by the United States to Cambodia for its defense." P.L. 92–226, 22 U.S.C. § 2415(g). The Act recognized the existence of bombing in Cambodia, in language which both sides cite. The pertinent provisions of the Act read as follows:

Sec. 655. Limitations Upon Assistance to or for Cambodia.—(a) Notwithstanding any other provision of law, no funds authorized to be appropriated by this or any other law may be obligated in any amount in excess of $341,000,000 for the purpose of carrying out directly or indirectly any economic or military assistance, or any operation, project, or program of any kind, or for providing any goods, supplies, materials, equipment, services, personnel, or advisers in, to, for, or on behalf of Cambodia during the fiscal year ending June 30, 1972.

. . . . . .

(c) No funds may be obligated for any of the purposes described in subsection (a) of this section in, to, for, or on behalf of Cambodia in any fiscal year beginning after June 30, 1972, unless such funds have been specifically authorized by law enacted after the date of enactment of this section. In no case shall funds in any amount in excess of the amount specifically authorized by law for any fiscal year be obligated for any such purpose during such fiscal year.

(d) The provisions of subsections (a) and (c) of this section shall not apply with respect to the obligation of funds to carry out combat air operations over Cambodia.

(e) After the date of enactment of this section, whenever any request is made to the Congress for the appropriation of funds for use in, for, or on behalf of Cambodia for any fiscal year, the President shall furnish a written report to the Congress explaining the purpose for which such funds are to be used in such fiscal year.

. . . . . .

Sec. 656. Limitations on United States Personnel and Personnel Assisted by United States in Cambodia. —The total number of civilian officers and employees of executive agencies of the United States Government who are citizens of the United States and of members of the Armed Forces of the United States (*excluding such members while actually engaged in air operations in or over Cambodia which originate outside Cambodia*) present in Cambodia at any one time shall not exceed two hundred. The United States shall not, at any time, pay in whole or in part, directly or indirectly, the compensation or allowances of more than eighty-five individuals in Cambodia who are citizens of countries other than Cambodia or the United States. For purposes of this section, "executive agency of the United States Government" means any agency, department, board, wholly or partly owned corporation, instrumentality, commission, or establishment within the executive branch of the United States Government. (Emphasis added).

On February 9, 1972, the President stated to Congress that North Vietnam continued to threaten the legitimate governments in Laos and Cambodia "in order to further its attacks on South Vietnam," and stated that "In Cambodia, operations are at the request of the Government and serve to relieve enemy pressures against Cambodia as well as South Vietnam." United States Foreign Policy for the 1970's: The Emerging Structure of Peace, 8 Presidential Documents 235, 343–45.

On April 18, 1972, testimony before the House of Representatives Committee on Armed Services stated that a significant portion of the Navy and Air Force incremental war costs of $2,023,000,000 for fiscal 1972 "could be attributed to operations in Laos and Cambodia." Cong.Rec. 9173. Some information presented at that time was classified and made available for inspection only by members of Congress.

### Events in 1973

On January 27, 1973, the parties participating in the Paris Conference on Vietnam signed an Agreement on Ending the War and Restoring Peace in Vietnam, which stated in Article 20(a):

. . . The parties participating in the Paris Conference on Vietnam undertake to refrain from using the territory of Cambodia and the territory of Laos to encroach on the sovereignty and security of one another and of other countries.

The affidavit of the Assistant United States Attorney opposing the motion for summary judgment asserts that after January 27, 1973, despite a unilateral cessation of hostilities by the governments of Cambodia and the United States, "the North Vietnamese launched

a general offensive in Cambodia, continuing the combat there. The military response of the United States continued."

In fact, there is evidence that air operations over Cambodia since January 27, 1973 have escalated sharply. A report on United States Air Operations in Cambodia prepared for the Subcommittee on United States Security Agreements and Commitments Abroad (April 1973—G.P.O.), states on page 7 that in the period February 16 through February 28, 1973, an average of twenty-three tactical air sorties a day and five B-52 sorties were flown in Cambodia. In the following two-week period, March 1– March 15, an average of fifty-eight tactical and gunship sorties and twenty B-52 sorties were flown. Between March 16–March 31, an average of 184 tactical sorties and fifty-eight B-52 sorties were flown. A statistical summary submitted by the Department of Defense to the Senate Armed Services Committee on June 19, 1973 shows that in the period October 30, 1972–January 27, 1973, 936 combat sorties were flown over Cambodia and that in the period January 27, 1973–April 30, 1973, 12,136 sorties were flown.

The last American combat troops were withdrawn from South Vietnam on March 28, 1973 and the last known American prisoners of war were released on April 1, 1973.

Secretary of State Rogers on April 3, 1973, submitted a statement on "Presidential Authority to Continue U.S. Air Combat Operations in Cambodia" to the Senate Committee on Foreign Relations at hearings concerning the Department of State Appropriations Authorization for fiscal 1974. The statement asserted its view that

the conflicts in Laos and Cambodia are closely related to the conflict in Vietnam and, in fact, are so inter-related as to be considered parts of a single conflict.

Hearings on S. 1248 and H.R. 5610, 93d Cong. 1st Sess. p. 452. It was further stated that the presence of North Vietnamese troops in Laos and Cambodia threatened the right of self-determination of the South Vietnamese people, which was guaranteed by the Paris Agreement, and that air strikes in Cambodia were not for the defense of Cambodia as such, but to enforce compliance with the Vietnam (cease-fire) Agreement. *Id.* 453.

*Congressional Moves After the Repatriation of American Prisoners of War*

The Defense Department sought authority in May 1973 to transfer $500 million to cover existing shortages of men and material. About $175 million was earmarked for Cambodian bombing operations. See 119 Cong.Rec. H 3449 (daily ed. May 8, 1973). On May 10, 1973, the House voted down the transfer authority by a vote of 219–188. 119 Cong.Rec. H 3561, 3592–93 (daily ed. May 10, 1973).

Immediately thereafter the House adopted the Long Amendment to the Second Supplemental Appropriations Bill H.R. 7447, which explicitly forbade the use of Defense Department funds for the Cambodian bombing. The amendment read:

> None of the funds herein appropriated to the Department of Defense under this Act shall be expended to support directly or indirectly combat activities in, over, or from off the shores of Cambodia by United States Forces.

119 Cong.Rec. H 3593 (daily ed. May 10, 1973). The Long Amendment passed by a vote of 224–172. *Ibid.* at H 3598.

Thereafter the Senate adopted a broader amendment to H.R. 7447, barring the use of any and all funds theretofore appropriated for the Defense Department for the bombing of Cambodia. It was introduced by Senator Eagleton on May 29, 1973:

> Sec. 305. None of the funds herein appropriated under this Act or heretofore appropriated under any other Act may be expended to support directly or indirectly combat activities in, over

or from off the shores of Cambodia, or in or over Laos by United States forces.

119 Cong.Rec. S 9827 (daily ed. May 29, 1973). The Eagleton amendment was adopted by a vote of 63–19 on May 31, 1973. 119 Cong.Rec. S 10128 (daily ed. May 31, 1973).

Since the Eagleton amendment was more inclusive than the Long amendment, the measure went to a conference committee of the two houses. On June 25, 1973, the House receded and accepted the broader Eagleton amendment by a vote of 235 to 172. 119 Cong.Rec. H 5268 (daily ed. June 25, 1973). The House refused to adopt a proposed amendment to delay the effect of the Eagleton amendment. The vote was 204 to 204. *Ibid.* H 5274.

Thereafter on June 26, 1973, the Senate agreed to the conference report on H.R. 7447 containing the Eagleton amendment. The vote was 81 to 11. 119 Cong.Rec. S 12057 (daily ed. June 26, 1973). The bill was then sent to the President.

The President vetoed H.R. 7447 on June 27, 1973. The House voted 241 to 173 to override the veto—a majority of sixty-eight votes but short of the required two-thirds vote. 119 Cong.Rec. H 5487 (daily ed. June 27, 1973).

On the same day, the Senate voted to attach the Eagleton amendment to H.R. 8410, a bill to continue the existing increase in public debt through November 30, 1973. The amendment read as follows:

> Sec. 501. No funds heretofore or hereafter appropriated under any Act of Congress may be obligated or expended to support directly or indirectly combat activities in, over, or from off the shores of Cambodia or in or over Laos by United States forces.

119 Cong.Rec. S 12171 (daily ed. June 27, 1973). The amendment was adopted by a vote of 67 to 29. *Ibid.* at S 12173. Thereafter the debt limit bill with the Eagleton amendment was passed by a vote of 72 to 19. *Ibid.* at S 12220.

On June 26, 1973 the House also adopted two amendments to the Continuing Appropriations Resolution (H.J.Res. 636), barring funds for Cambodian bombing. Congressman Long introduced the following amendment:

None of the funds under this joint resolution heretofore appropriated may be expended to support directly or indirectly combat activities in or over Cambodia or Laos or off the shores of Cambodia or Laos by United States forces.

Cong.Rec. H 5363 (daily ed. June 26, 1973). It passed by a vote of 218 to 194. *Ibid.* at H 5371. Congressman Addabbo introduced a similar amendment.

Sec. 108. None of the funds under this Joint Resolution may be expended to support directly or indirectly combat activities in or over Cambodia, Laos, Vietnam and South Vietnam or off the shores of Cambodia, Laos, North Vietnam and South Vietnam by United States forces without the express consent of Congress.

It passed by a vote of 240 to 172. *Ibid.* at H 5373.

Faced with the dilemma of the President set upon vetoing any bill containing riders cutting off funds for Cambodian military operations and the urgency of providing funds for the operation of the federal government, Senator Fulbright on June 29, 1973, after conferences with White House representatives, introduced the following amendment to the Continuing Appropriations Resolution (H.J. Res. 636):

Sec. 109. Notwithstanding any other provision of law, on or after August 15, 1973, no funds herein, heretofore or hereafter appropriated may be obligated or expended to finance the involvement of United States military forces in hostilities in or over or from off the shores of North Vietnam, South Vietnam, Laos, or Cambodia.

119 Cong.Rec. S 12560 (daily ed. June 29, 1973). The Senate voted to adopt the Fulbright amendment 64 to 26. *Ibid.* S 12580. The Senate then voted to de-

lete the earlier Eagleton amendment from the Continuing Appropriations Resolution. *Ibid.* S 12581.

The House refused to pass S 109 as worded and in conference S 108 was adopted. 119 Cong.Rec.No. 104 (daily ed. June 30, 1973). The Conference Report was approved by the House on June 30. *Ibid.* at H 5781. H.J.Res. 636, the Joint Resolution Continuing Appropriations for Fiscal 1974, Public Law 93–52, was signed into law by the President on July 1 and provided:

Sec. 108. Notwithstanding any other provision of law, on or after August 15, 1973, no funds herein or heretofore appropriated may be obligated or expended to finance directly or indirectly combat activities by United States military forces in or over or from off the shores of North Vietnam, South Vietnam, Laos or Cambodia.

On July 1, the President also signed into law H.R. 9055, the Second Supplemental Appropriations Act, 1973, Public Law 93–50. The Act includes the following provision:

Sec. 307. None of the funds herein appropriated under this Act may be expended to support directly or indirectly combat activities in or over Cambodia, Laos, North Vietnam and South Vietnam by United States forces, *and after August 15, 1973, no other funds heretofore appropriated, under any other Act may be expended for such purpose.* (Emphasis added).

### Other Facts

The defendants do not disagree with plaintiffs' contention that all ground combat troops were withdrawn from Indochina on March 28, 1973. There is reference in the papers to a few members of the armed forces stationed as guards to the Embassy in Saigon, but no assertion that they are there to continue the Vietnam war.

The complete repatriation of all known American prisoners of war is established by testimony before Congress quoted in plaintiffs' papers. Frank A. Sieverts, Special Assistant to the Deputy Secretary of State for Prisoner of War/Missing in Action Matters, in testimony before the National Security Policy and Scientific Developments Subcommittee of the House Committee on Foreign Affairs, May 31, 1973, stated:

It should be noted that there is no indication from these debriefings [of returning POW's] that any American personnel continue to be held in Indochina. All American prisoners known to any of our returned POW's have either been released or been listed by the communist authorities as having died in captivity. Returnees with whom I have talked, including those who appeared before this Subcommittee May 23, are clear in their belief that no U.S. prisoners continue to be held.

Defendants assert that the complete repatriation of prisoners of war is not an undisputed fact, but they have presented no evidence that there are any such prisoners remaining in North Vietnam or anywhere in Indochina. There remain, however, over 1,250 members of the armed forces listed as missing in action, who have not been located or officially declared to have died.

Plaintiffs and the *amici* assert that continuing hostilities in Cambodia do not represent activities of North Vietnamese troops, but a civil war between Khmer insurgents and the official government of Cambodia.

Plaintiffs and the *amici* also assert that continued U.S. bombing in Cambodia is causing the death and maiming of many civilians.

Defendants stated on oral argument that if summary judgment is denied, they would propose to offer testimony from Secretary of State Rogers, Secretary of Defense Schlesinger, and Dr. Kissinger concerning the necessity for the air operations and the importance of continuing bombing in Cambodia because of continuing confidential negotiations for a Cambodian cease-fire. No other

offer of proof has been made on behalf of the defendants.

On July 23, 1973, the government informed the court that statistical data reflecting bombing activities in Cambodia between March 1969 and April 1970 had been "declassified" and were published in revised Table concerning fighter-bomber munitions and B-52 munitions in the Congressional Record for July 18, 1973. Defendants do not contend, however, that these facts were known to Congress before July 1, 1973. The court does not find that these facts are relevant to the issues dealt with herein.

### Discussion

1. *Legal Standards*

The Court of Appeals of this circuit has spoken several times concerning earlier aspects of the Vietnam hostilities.

[1] The teaching of DaCosta v. Laird, 471 F.2d 1146 (2d Cir. 1973), Orlando v. Laird, 443 F.2d 1039 (2d Cir. 1971), and Berk v. Laird, 429 F.2d 302 (2d Cir. 1970), is that the question of the balance of constitutional authority to declare war, as between the executive and legislative branches, is not a political question and hence presents a justiciable issue, if plaintiffs can succeed in showing that there are manageable standards to resolve the controversy.

The Court of Appeals in Berk v. Laird, *supra*, 429 F.2d at 305, stated that there might be manageable standards to determine whether "prolonged foreign military activities without any significant congressional authorization" might violate

a discoverable standard calling for *some* mutual participation by Congress in accordance with Article I, section 8. (Emphasis from the original).

This court on remand found that Congress in appropriations bills from 1965 through 1969 had shown "its continued support of the Vietnam action" and that Congress' choice of appropriations bills rather than a formal declaration of war to effectuate its intent involved a political question which did not prevent the finding that the fighting in Vietnam was authorized by Congress and that such fighting was not a usurpation of power by either of the Presidents who had been in office after 1964. Berk v. Laird, *supra*, 317 F.Supp. at 726, 728–731.

[2] Nevertheless, appropriations bills do not necessarily indicate an open-ended approval of all military operations which may be conducted. See Mitchell v. Laird, 476 F.2d 533, 538 (D. C. Cir. 1973); Note, Congress, The President and the Power to Commit Forces to Combat, 81 Harv.L.Rev. 1171, 1802 (1968).

In affirming this court's *Berk* decision and Judge Dooling's similar *Orlando* decision, the Court of Appeals stated the test of whether there were manageable standards for adjudication as being "whether there is any action by the Congress sufficient to authorize or ratify the military activity in question." Orlando v. Laird, *supra*, 443 F.2d at 1042. It found that there was evidence of "an abundance of *continuing* mutual participation in the prosecution of the war." 443 F.2d at 1042. (Emphasis added).

More recently in DaCosta v. Laird, *supra*, 471 F.2d at 1151, the Court of Appeals dealt with the question "whether within the context of a lawful war, the President's order to mine the harbors of North Vietnam was properly authorized." It held in that instance (at p. 1155) that judges could not determine "whether a specific military operation constitutes an 'escalation' of the war or is merely a new tactical approach within a continuing strategic plan." However, it added (at p. 1156):

> In so stating, however, we specifically do not pass on the point urged by appellant whether a radical change in the character of war operations—as by an intentional policy of indiscriminate bombing of civilians without any military objective—might be sufficiently measurable judicially to warrant a court's consideration, i.e.,

might contain a standard which we seek in this record and do not find.

The court finds no evidence of intentional bombing of civilians, but the mining of North Vietnam harbors was a part of the war in Vietnam. If bombing in Cambodia is not part of the war in Vietnam, there may be a standard available here which the Court of Appeals did not find in *DaCosta*.

Therefore the manageable standard which this court must apply is the existence of Congressional authority for the present bombing activities over Cambodia, now that American forces have been withdrawn and prisoners of war have been repatriated. In order to be entitled to relief, plaintiffs must show, under this standard, and the test of "continuing mutual participation" set forth in *Orlando*, either that Congress has not participated with the executive in the authorization of the hostilities in Cambodia or that Congress has terminated any such authorization.

2. *The Extent of Congressional Authorization of Cambodian Hostilities*

Cambodia was not mentioned in any of the appropriations bills referred to in *Berk*. The 1964 appropriations bill for the Department of Defense (P.L. 89–18, 79 Stat. 109) referred to "military activities in Southeast Asia." See 317 F. Supp. at 724. But the Department of Defense Appropriations Act for 1968 (P.L. 90–96, 81 Stat. 231, 248, § 639(a)) made appropriations available to support only

> (1) Vietnamese and other free world forces in Vietnam, (2) local forces in Laos and Thailand; and for related costs;

and subsequent authorization and appropriations bills used similar language. See 317 F.Supp. at 726–27.

Ever since the hostilities in Cambodia were announced by the President in April 1970, the appropriations bills have all contained the Fulbright proviso forbidding military support to the government of Cambodia, except in support of actions to insure the safe withdrawal of American forces or to aid in the release of prisoners of war. *Supra,* p. 555.

The Mansfield amendment referred also to the desirability of an accounting for all Americans missing in action, but this was only in relation to the establishment of a final date for withdrawal of United States military forces from Indochina. *Supra,* pp. 555–556. No Congressional purpose or authorization has been shown for the bombing of Cambodia in aid of persons missing in action, after all known prisoners of war have been released. Other actions by Congress specifically denied any commitment by the United States to Cambodia in its defense (*supra,* pp. 555–556), and the Defense Appropriation Act for 1972, approved a month after the Mansfield amendment, referred only to the withdrawal of United States forces and the release of prisoners of war. *Supra,* pp. 556–557.

The defendants point to the language in the Foreign Assistance Act of 1971, Section 655(d), excluding members of the armed forces engaged in air operations over Cambodia from the limitation on United States personnel in Cambodia, as an authorization for continued bombing. However, the Senate report concerning this bill indicates that the authorization was intended to be correlative with the Fulbright proviso, for it stated (Sen.Rep.No. 92–431, Nov. 8, 1971):

> Section 655 specifically excepts all combat air operations over Cambodia from this ceiling. This exception covers all United States and South Vietnamese combat air operations as well as combat air operations by other countries which involve the expenditure of U.S. funds. This exception is included because of the view of some Committee members that monetary limitations on air operations in Cambodia might jeopardize the continuing withdrawal of U.S. forces from Vietnam.

U.S.Code Cong. & Admin.News, 1972, p. 1897.

Any inference flowing from the negatively phrased exception in Section 656 of the same act would be too indirect a route for Congress to express its will to continue a bombing operation which it had repeatedly questioned. The court does not find such authorization in the Foreign Assistance Act.

The documents described in the statement of facts indicate that Congress did not acquiesce in the Presidential statements that the Indochina war was all of one piece, but rather gave only limited authorization for continued hostilities in Cambodia.

[3] Applying principles of the law of agency, as this court did in the *Berk* case, 317 F.Supp. at 728, it is the usual rule that the principal (Congress) may limit the duration of any authorization which it gives to the agent (the Executive). Section 38 of the Agency Restatement of the Law, Second (1958) states:

> § 38. Interpretation as to Duration of Authority
>
> Authority exists only during the period in which, from the manifestations of the principal and the happening of events of which the agent has notice, the agent reasonably believes that the principal desires him to act.

In considering the continued bombing of Cambodia, the removal of American forces and prisoners of war from Vietnam represents a basic change in the situation, which must be considered in determining the scope and duration of any Congressional authorization. The bombing of Cambodia in July 1973 is not "the sort of tactical decision traditionally confided to the Commander-in-Chief in the conduct of armed conflict," as once described by then Assistant Attorney General Rehnquist. Rehnquist, The Constitutional Issues, Administrative Position in 3 Falk, The Vietnam

War and International Law, 163, 173 (1972).

[4] The Congressional action before and after the beginning of hostilities in Cambodia does not include authorization to bomb Cambodia in order to achieve a Cambodian cease-fire or even to protect the Vietnamese cease-fire as urged by defendants. The extent of the power granted by Congress depends on the language used by Congress, not on the President's statements to Congress.

[5, 6] An emergency does not create power unless Congress has granted it. Youngstown Sheet & Tube Co. v. Sawyer, 343 U.S. 579, 629, 72 S.Ct. 863, 886, 96 L.Ed. 1153 (1952). The Constitution provides (Article II, Section 3) that the President shall recommend to the Congress "such Measures as he shall deem necessary and expedient," and that "he shall take Care that the Laws be faithfully executed." Non-action by Congress does not constitute an implied grant of power. Greene v. McElroy, 360 U.S. 474, 79 S.Ct. 1400, 3 L.Ed.2d 1377 (1959).

The question here is not the one posed by the government, whether aerial action in Cambodia is the termination of a continuing war or the initiation of a new and distinct war; but whether Congress has authorized bombing in Cambodia after the withdrawal of American troops from Vietnam and the release of prisoners of war.

3. *The Effect of the July 1, 1973 Proviso*

Authority to bomb Cambodia was not granted by the provisions adopted by both Houses of Congress on June 29, 1973 and signed by the President on July 1, 1973, forbidding any expenditure of funds in connection with hostilities over Cambodia after August 15, 1973. This is made clear by the statements of Senator Fulbright and others during the debate in the Senate, where Senator Fulbright stated:

The acceptance of an August 15 cut off date should in no way be inter-

preted as recognition by the committee of the President's authority to engage U.S. forces in hostilities until that date. The view of most members of the committee has been and continues to be that the President does not have such authority in the absence of specific congressional approval.

119 Cong.Rec. S 12560 (daily ed. June 29, 1973).

He reiterated this point in colloquy with Senator Eagleton:

MR. EAGLETON: I want to inquire as to what this resolution includes. What does it prevent within the next 45 days? Does it permit continued bombing between now and August 15?

MR. FULBRIGHT: As I have said, I do not regard him as having the right to do this. He has the power to do it. And unless we have something like this, the only sanction we have here is to impeach him. And I do not think that is practical. I do not recommend it. I know of no other alternative.

MR. EAGLETON: Would it permit the bombing of North and South Vietnam until August 15?

MR. FULBRIGHT: I do not think it is legal or constitutional. But whether it is right to do it or not, he has done it. He has the power to do it because under our system there is not any easy way to stop him.

I do not want my statement to be taken to mean that I approve of it or think that it is constitutional or legal for him to do it. He can do it. He has done it. Do I make myself clear?

MR. EAGLETON: In a way yes, and in a way no. If we adopt this resolution, the President will continue to bomb Cambodia. That means quite simply that we will sanction it, does it not?

MR. FULBRIGHT: We do not sanction it. It does not mean that we approve of the bombing. This is the best way to stop it. I have never approved of it. And I do not wish my answer to indicate that I approve of the bombing, because I do not.

MR. EAGLETON: But the President will exercise a power to bomb in Indochina within the next 45 days, is that correct? A power that will now be sanctioned by our action?

MR. FULBRIGHT: The President has the power to do a lot of things of which I do not approve.

MR. EAGLETON: He will exercise that power, and whether he exercises that power wisely we know that within the next 45 days he will exercise a right to bomb Cambodia—a right given him by the Congress of the United States.

MR. FULBRIGHT: I do not consider that he has the right to do it.

119 Cong.Rec. S 12562 (daily ed. June 29, 1973).

This is not a situation where the views of a few members of Congress, holding attitudes antithetical to the majority, are being proffered to defeat what Congress had intended to be a grant of authority. There is no indication of a contrary majority sentiment. Majorities in both Houses had previously made plain that they were opposed to any continuation of bombing in Cambodia, and they included an August 15 cutoff date merely in order to avoid the veto which had met their earlier efforts.

[7, 8] The defendants urge that Congress' will as expressed through bills which were not enacted cannot be used as a factor in interpreting the July 1 legislation. But this contention misconstrues the basic issue. The question is not whether Congress has affirmatively acted to disavow participation, but whether Congress has acted to authorize the continuation of hostilities in Cambodia. While Congress can exercise its war-making power through measures other than an express declaration of war, courts should not easily infer the exercise of such a grave responsibility. Legislative history as evidenced through bills that were vetoed is relevant to a judicial inquiry of whether or not Congress intended to participate in the military campaign under challenge.

It cannot be the rule that the President needs a vote of only one-third plus one of either House in order to conduct a war, but this would be the consequence of holding that Congress must override a Presidential veto in order to terminate hostilities which it has not authorized.

In order to avoid a constitutional crisis that would have resulted in a temporary shutdown of vital federal activities (including issuance of monthly Social Security checks), due to lack of funds for the new fiscal year, Congress agreed to hold off any action affirmatively cutting off funds for military purposes until August 15, 1973.

This does not reach the question whether such activities had previously been authorized.

The period from now until August 15 is relatively short, the court necessarily having taken several weeks in studying the matter and preparing this memorandum. However, the court cannot say that the Cambodian and American lives which may be lost during the next three weeks are so unimportant that it should defer action in this case still further.

There are no disputed issues of material fact. The issues relate to the interpretation of Congressional acts.

[9] Even if part of the fighting in Cambodia is being conducted by North Vietnamese troops rather than by Khmer insurgents, the court has found that there is no Congressional authorization to fight in Cambodia after the withdrawal of American troops and the release of American prisoners of war. Even though the executive and the military may consider Cambodian bombing

an effective means of enforcing paragraph 20 of the Paris Agreement of January 27, 1973, it does not appear that Congress has given its authority for such acts.

There is no indication that any of the classified information mentioned by the government will affect the interpretation of the Congressional acts or that the testimony of the officials suggested as witnesses will do so. The reasons which may have led the executive to continue bombing in Cambodia are not decisive, in the absence of continuing authority from Congress to do so.

There is nothing in the case of Gilligan v. Morgan, —— U.S. ——, 93 S.Ct. 2440, 37 L.Ed.2d 407 (1973) cited to the court during the typing of the opinion, which is contrary to what has been written above. The Supreme Court in *Gilligan* held that it would be inappropriate for a judge to evaluate the appropriateness of the "training, weaponing and orders" of the Ohio National Guard and establish standards to control the actions of the National Guard. Pp. ——, ——, 93 S.Ct. 2440. What is involved in this case is not the training or tactics of American forces, but whether Congress has authorized the Cambodian bombing. That question is capable of judicial resolution, under the cases cited above, by applying traditional processes of statutory construction.

The court will therefore permit the addition of Captain Donald E. Dawson as plaintiff, and will grant summary judgment for declaratory and equitable relief as set forth in the accompanying judgment, but will postpone the effective date of the injunction until Friday in order to permit the defendants to apply for a stay from the Court of Appeals.

It is ordered that Captain Donald E. Dawson be added as a plaintiff, that plaintiffs have leave to file and serve a second amended complaint in the form proposed, and that the caption be amended accordingly.

# Holtzman v. Schlesinger

Elizabeth **HOLTZMAN**, Individually and
in her capacity as a member of the
United States House of Representatives, et al., Plaintiffs-Appellees,

v.

James R. **SCHLESINGER**, Individually
and as Secretary of Defense, et al.,
Defendants-Appellants.

No. 1132, Docket 73–2094.

United States Court of Appeals,
Second Circuit.

Argued Aug. 8, 1973.

Decided Aug. 8, 1973.

Burt Neuborne, New York City (Leon
Friedman, American Civil Liberties Union, New York City, Norman Siegel and
Paul G. Chevigny, New York Civil Liberties Union, New York City, of counsel), for plaintiffs-appellees.

James Dunlop Porter, Jr., Asst. U. S.
Atty., Chief, Civil Div., Brooklyn, N. Y.
(Robert A. Morse, U. S. Atty., E.D.N.
Y.), for defendants-appellants.

Eric M. Lieberman, New York City
(Michael Krinsky, New York City, of
counsel), for Parren J. Mitchell, and
others, as amici curiae.

Joseph F. McDonald, New York City, for The Lawyers Committee to End the War and Certain Individuals as amici curiae.

Before MULLIGAN, OAKES and TIMBERS, Circuit Judges.

MULLIGAN, Circuit Judge:

This is an appeal from a judgment of the United States District Court, Eastern District of New York, Hon. Orrin G. Judd, District Judge, dated July 25, 1973, 361 F.Supp. 553, granting plaintiffs' motion for summary judgment and providing both declaratory and injunctive relief. The judgment declared that "there is no existing Congressional authority to order military forces into combat in Cambodia or to release bombs over Cambodia, and that military activities in Cambodia by American armed forces are unauthorized and unlawful . . . .." The order further enjoined and restrained the named defendants and their officers, agents, servants, employees and attorneys "from participating in any way in military activities in or over Cambodia or releasing any bombs which may fall in Cambodia." The effective date of the injunction was postponed until 4:00 o'clock on July 27, 1973 to provide the defendants with an opportunity to apply to this court for a stay pending appeal. A panel of this court heard oral argument on the stay on the morning of July 27, 1973 and unanimously granted defendants' motion for a stay, setting the time for argument of the appeal on August 13, 1973 which was the first day of sitting of the next panel of this court. The parties were given leave to move for further expedition of the appeal. Plaintiffs then made application to Mr. Justice Marshall of the Supreme Court, Circuit Justice for the Second Circuit, for a vacatur of the stay. Mr. Justice Marshall denied the application to vacate the stay on August 1, 1973 writing an opinion in which he noted that either side could further advance the date of the argument before this court, —— U.S. ——, 94 S.Ct. 1, 38 L.Ed.2d 18. On the motion of plaintiffs, not opposed by defendants, this court on August 1st further accelerated argument of the appeal to August 8, 1973. On August 2, 1973, plaintiffs made application to Mr. Justice Douglas to vacate the stay and on August 4, 1973 he issued an opinion and order vacating the stay entered by this court. —— U.S. ——, 94 S.Ct. 8, 38 L.Ed.2d 28. Later in the afternoon of August 4, 1973, Mr. Justice Marshall reinstated the stay announcing that he had polled the other members of the Supreme Court and that they were unanimous in overruling the order of Mr. Justice Douglas. —— U.S. ——, 94 S.Ct. 11, 38 L.Ed.2d 33. On August 3, 1973, after a hearing before Mr. Justice Douglas, plaintiffs petitioned this court for an *en banc* hearing of this appeal. By order dated August 6th this motion was denied by the unanimous vote of the five active judges of this court who could be readily contacted. In view of the admonition of Mr. Justice Marshall that it is in the public interest that the issues herein be resolved as expeditiously as possible, the convening of this court *en banc* could only have delayed a hearing on the merits.

The argument of this appeal was heard on August 8th and to further speed any further appellate review this court filed its judgment in the late afternoon of that day, reversing the judgment below and dismissing the complaint. Judge Oakes dissented. We announced that opinions would promptly follow so that if the Supreme Court did entertain an appeal it might have the benefit of the views of the panel. Even though the exigencies of time preclude the articulation of the majority view as elaborately or completely as might otherwise be appropriate in a case of this significance, it nonetheless represents our considered and deliberate opinion.

I

[1] At the outset, as the parties agreed below and on the argument on appeal, we should emphasize that we are

not deciding the wisdom, the propriety or the morality of the war in Indo-China and particularly the on-going bombing in Cambodia. This is the responsibility of the Executive and the Legislative branches of the government. The role of the Judiciary is to determine the legality of the challenged action and the threshold question is whether under the "political question" doctrine we should decline even to do that. Ever since Marbury v. Madison, 5 U.S. (1 Cranch) 137, 2 L.Ed. 60 (1803) the federal courts have declined to judge some actions of the Executive and some interaction between the Executive and Legislative branches where it is deemed inappropriate that the judiciary intrude. It is not possible or even necessary to define the metes and bounds of that doctrine here. The most authoritative discussion of the subject is found in Mr. Justice Brennan's opinion in Baker v. Carr, 369 U.S. 186, 82 S.Ct. 691, 7 L.Ed. 2d 663 (1962) which elaborated criteria that have since guided this court in determining whether a question involving the separation of powers is justiciable or is a political question beyond our purview. In Orlando v. Laird, 443 F.2d 1039 (2d Cir.), cert. denied, 404 U.S. 869, 92 S.Ct. 94, 30 L.Ed.2d 113 (1971), this court held that the question of whether or not Congress was required to take some action to authorize the Indo-China war was justiciable under Baker v. Carr, *supra*, since there was present a judicially discoverable and manageable issue. See Coleman v. Miller, 307 U.S. 433, 454–455, 59 S.Ct. 972, 83 L.Ed. 1385 (1939). On the basis of evidence produced at the hearings in the district court, this court found Congressional authorization in support of the military operations in Southeast Asia from the beginning, relying on the Tonkin Gulf Resolution of August 10, 1964, plus continuing appropriation bills providing billions of dollars in support of military operations as well as the extension of the Military Selective Service Act. We were careful to note:

Beyond determining that there has been *some* mutual participation between Congress and the President, which unquestionably exists here, with action by the Congress sufficient to authorize or ratify the military activity at issue, it is clear that the constitutional propriety of the means by which Congress has chosen to ratify and approve the protracted military operations in Southeast Asia is a political question. Id., 443 F.2d at 1043 (emphasis in original).

It is significant that the court noted that the Tonkin Gulf Resolution of August 10, 1964 had since been repealed on December 31, 1970.

In Da Costa v. Laird, 448 F.2d 1368 (2d Cir. 1971), cert. denied, 405 U.S. 979, 92 S.Ct. 1193, 31 L.Ed.2d 255 (1972), this court specifically rejected the contention that the repeal by Congress of the Tonkin Gulf Resolution removed the Congressional authorization previously found sufficient in *Orlando*. We noted:

As the constitutional propriety of the means by which the Executive and the Legislative branches engaged in mutual participation in prosecuting the military operations in Southeast Asia, is, as we held in *Orlando*, a political question, so the constitutional propriety of the method and means by which they mutually participate in winding down the conflict and in disengaging the nation from it, is also a political question and outside of the power and competency of the judiciary. Id. at 1370.

The most recent holding of this court now pertinent is Da Costa v. Laird, 471 F.2d 1146 (1973) where an inductee urged that the President's unilateral decision to mine the harbors of North Vietnam and to bomb targets in that country constituted an escalation of the war, which was illegal in the absence of additional Congressional authorization. Judge Kaufman found that this was a political question which was non-justiciable, recognizing that the court was incapable of assessing the facts. He stated in part:

> Judges, deficient in military knowledge, lacking vital information upon which to assess the nature of battlefield decisions, and sitting thousands of miles from the field of action, cannot reasonably or appropriately determine whether a specific military operation constitutes an "escalation" of the war or is merely a new tactical approach within a continuing strategic plan. What if, for example, the war "de-escalates" so that it is waged as it was prior to the mining of North Vietnam's harbors, and then "escalates" again? Are the courts required to oversee the conduct of the war on a daily basis, away from the scene of action? In this instance, it was the President's view that the mining of North Vietnam's harbors was necessary to preserve the lives of American soliders (*sic*) in South Vietnam and to bring the war to a close. History will tell whether or not that assessment was correct, but without the benefit of such extended hindsight we are powerless to know.

We fail to see how the present challenge involving the bombing in Cambodia is in any significant manner distinguishable from the situation discussed by Judge Kaufman in Da Costa v. Laird. Judge Judd found that the continuing bombing of Cambodia, after the removal of American forces and prisoners of war from Vietnam, represents "a basic change in the situation: which must be considered in determining the duration of prior Congressional authorization." He further found such action a tactical decision not traditionally confided to the Commander-in-Chief. These are precisely the questions of fact involving military and diplomatic expertise not vested in the judiciary, which make the issue political and thus beyond the competence of that court or this court to determine. We are not privy to the information supplied to the Executive by his professional military and diplomatic advisers and even if we were, we are hardly competent to evaluate it. If we were incompetent to judge the significance of the mining and bombing of North Vietnam's harbors and territories, we fail to see our competence to determine that the bombing of Cambodia is a "basic change" in the situation and that it is not a "tactical decision" within the competence of the President. It is true that we have repatriated American troops and have returned American ground forces in Vietnam but we have also negotiated a cease fire and have entered into the Paris Accords which mandated a cease fire in Cambodia and Laos. The President has announced that the bombing of Cambodia will terminate on August 15, 1973 and Secretary of State Rogers has submitted an affidavit to this court[1] providing the justification for

---

1. Affidavit of William P. Rogers
Washington,
District of Columbia, *ss.*
William P. Rogers, being duly sworn, deposes and says as follows:

1. In my capacity as Secretary of State of the United States of America, I have knowledge of and responsibility for the conduct of the foreign relations of the United States, including relations with the Government of Cambodia.

2. It is my understanding that on July 25, 1973, the United States District Court for the Eastern District of New York in the case of Holtzman et al v. Schlesinger et al, ordered the cessation of further military activities by United States armed forces in Cambodia and that this order was stayed by the United States Court of Appeals for the Second Circuit. It is my judgment, that if that stay were not continued, the District Court's order would cause irreparable harm to the United States, to the conduct of our foreign relations, and to the protection of United States nationals in Cambodia.

3. In the conduct of United States relations with Cambodia, the American Ambassador in Phnom Penh has communicated to the Cambodian Government the fact of the enactment on July 1, 1973 of Public Law 93–50 (87 Stat. 99) and Public Law 93–52 (87 Stat. 130). Our Ambassador has further informed the Cambodian Government that the United States Government interprets the aforesaid public laws as requiring a cessation of all combat activities in Cam-

our military presence and action until that time. The situation fluctuates daily and we cannot ascertain at any fixed time either the military or diplomatic status. We are in no position to determine whether the Cambodian insurgents are patriots or whether in fact they are inspired and manned by North Vietnam Communists. While we as men may well agonize and bewail the horror of this or any war, the sharing of Presidential and Congressional responsibility particularly at this juncture is a bluntly political and not a judicial question.

We think the comments of Judge Wyzanski writing for a unanimous Court

of Appeals panel in the District of Columbia are particularly apt here:

Whether President Nixon did so proceed [to end the war] is a question which at this stage in history a court is incompetent to answer. A court cannot procure the relevant evidence: some is in the hands of foreign governments, some is privileged. Even if the necessary facts were to be laid before it, a court would not substitute its judgment for that of the President, who has an unusually wide measure of discretion in this area, and who should not be judicially condemned except in a case of clear abuse

---

bodia by the armed forces of the United States on and after August 15, 1973.

4. In consequence of the enactment of the aforesaid public laws, intensive planning has been undertaken within the United States Government and between representatives of the American and Cambodian Governments. As a result, plans have been developed which include:

(i) emergency increases in the levels of the Cambodian armed forces;

(ii) accelerated deliveries and distribution during the first two weeks in August of military equipment, especially aircraft and related spare parts, pursuant to the United States Military Assistance Program;

(iii) accelerated deliveries and distribution during this same period of food stuffs, medical supplies and other items for humanitarian relief of the Cambodian population.

(iv) redeployment of Cambodian armed forces, and in some cases civilians whom those forces are protecting, from exposed positions to positions where they can defend themselves and be resupplied in the absence of United States combat air support on and after August 15, 1973.

5. All of the above-described plans are for the purpose of improving the Government of Cambodia's self-defense capability through assistance programs approved by the Congress and the President. All of these plans have been premised upon an assumption of continued United States combat air support for the Cambodian armed forces through August 14, 1973. On the basis of the information available to me, it is my judgment that the absence of such air support prior to that date would permit hostile military forces to disrupt those plans and would expose United States military and civilian personnel who are responsible for their implementation, to grave risk of personal injury or death.

6. Moreover, in view of this close cooperation and planning between the United States and the Cambodian Government, and considerable reliance placed by the Cambodian Government on this agreed timing, any premature and unilateral cessation of needed air support by the United States would be seen by the Government of Cambodia and by many other governments as a breach of faith by the United States and would seriously undermine the credibility of the United States and impair the conduct of our foreign relations.

7. Quite apart from the question of timing, the order of the District Court, in enjoining "military activities" might well be construed more broadly than the prohibitions against "combat activities" contained in the above-mentioned public laws and thereby could be deemed to preclude such activities as the use of United States armed forces to evacuate United States diplomatic personnel and other United States nationals from Cambodia should this be required at any future time, even after United States combat activities in Cambodia have ceased.

8. The specific consequences as described herein of a failure to stay the District Court's order would constitute irreparable harm to the conduct of the foreign relations of the United States by imperiling the ability of the Government of Cambodia to prepare for assuming full responsibility for its defense, by imperiling the safety of United States nationals in Cambodia, and by undermining the credibility of the United States. In a broader sense, the efforts of the United States to achieve a stable peace in Indochina would be undermined and the ceasefire agreements presently in effect in Viet-Nam and Laos would be gravely jeopardized.

/s/ William P. Rogers

amounting to bad faith. Otherwise a court would be ignoring the delicacies of diplomatic negotiation, the inevitable bargaining for the best solution of an international conflict, and the scope which in foreign affairs must be allowed to the President if this country is to play a responsible role in the council of the nations. Mitchell v. Laird, 476 F.2d 533, 538 (1973).

The court below and our dissenting Brother assume that since American ground forces and prisoners have been removed and accounted for, Congressional authorization has ceased to be determined by virtue of the so-called Mansfield Amendment, P.L. 92–156, 85 Stat. 430, § 601. The fallacy of this position is that we have no way of knowing whether the Cambodian bombing furthers or hinders the goals of the Mansfield Amendment. That is precisely the holding of Da Costa v. Laird, *supra*, 471 F.2d at 1157. Moreover, although § 601(a)(1) of the Amendment urges the

President to remove all military forces contingent upon release of American prisoners, it also in § 601(a)(2) urges him to negotiate for an immediate cease fire by all parties in the hostilities in *Indo-China*. (Emphasis added). In our view, the return and repatriation of American troops only represents the beginning and not the end of the inquiry as to whether such a basic change has occurred that the Executive at this stage is suddenly bereft of power and authority. That inquiry involves diplomatic and military intelligence which is totally absent in the record before us, and its digestion in any event is beyond judicial management. The strictures of the political question doctrine cannot be avoided by resort to the law of agency as the court did below, finding the Congress the principal and the President an agent or servant.[2] Judicial *ipse dixits* cannot provide any proper basis particularly for the injunctive relief granted here which is unprecedented in American Jurisprudence.[3]

---

**2.** The resort of the court below to the Second Restatement of Agency § 38, promulgated by the American Law Institute, is indeed inapposite. Aside from its introductory Scope Note (p. 2) which disclaims the Restatement's applicability to public officers, the denomination of the Congress as the Principal and the President as the Agent in the conduct of hostilities is overly simplistic. It ignores the President's role as Commander-in-Chief, and his primacy in foreign relations, particularly in achieving the peace. See Wallace, The War Making Powers: A Constitutional Flaw? 57 Cornell L.Rev. 719, 744 (1972). It is perhaps significant that the Constitutional Convention explicitly rejected a proposal that the Constitution provide the Congress with the power to declare peace as well as war, and carefully noted that the conduct of war "was an Executive function." 2 M. Farrand, Records of the Federal Convention of 1787, at 313, 319 & n.* (rev. ed. 1937).

**3.** To date no other federal court has attempted to halt American involvement in hostilities in Southeast Asia. Our own court as well as the First Circuit has concluded that the war-implementing legislation passed by Congress was sufficient authorization. Da Costa v. Laird, 448 F.2d 1368 (2d Cir. 1971), cert. denied, 405 U.S. 979,

92 S.Ct. 1193, 31 L.Ed.2d 255 (1972); Orlando v. Laird, 443 F.2d 1039 (2d Cir.), cert. denied, 404 U.S. 869, 92 S.Ct. 94, 30 L.Ed.2d 113 (1971), aff'g 317 F.Supp. 1013 (E.D.N.Y.1970) and Berk v. Laird, 317 F. Supp. 715 (E.D.N.Y.1970) (Judd, J.); Massachusetts v. Laird, 451 F.2d 26 (1st Cir.), aff'g 327 F.Supp. 378 (D.Mass.1971). Numerous courts have dismissed suits challenging American involvement on the ground that a "political question" was involved. Mitchell v. Laird, 476 F.2d 533 (D.C.Cir. 1973); Da Costa v. Laird, 471 F.2d 1146 (2d Cir. 1973); Mora v. McNamara, 128 U.S.App.D.C. 297, 387 F.2d 862, cert. denied, 389 U.S. 934, 88 S.Ct. 282, 19 L.Ed.2d 287 (1967); Luftig v. McNamara, 126 U.S. App.D.C. 4, 373 F.2d 664, cert. denied, 387 U.S. 945, 87 S.Ct. 2078, 18 L.Ed.2d 1332 (1967) (cf. Mitchell v. Laird, *supra*); Drinan v. Nixon, 364 F.Supp. 854 (D.Mass. 1973); Mitchell v. Richardson, Civ.No. 939–73 (D.D.C., July 23, 1973), notice of appeal filed, Aug. 1, 1973; Gravel v. Laird, 347 F.Supp. 7 (D.D.C.1972); Atlee v. Laird, 347 F.Supp. 689 (E.D.Pa.1972), aff'd without opinion, 411 U.S. 911, 93 S.Ct. 1545, 36 L.Ed.2d 304 (1973); Massachusetts v. Laird, 327 F.Supp. 378 (D.Mass.), aff'd on other grounds, 451 F.2d 26 (1st Cir. 1971) (but cf. Mitchell v. Laird, *supra*); Davi v. Laird, 318 F.Supp. 478 (W.

## II

Since the argument that continuing Congressional approval was necessary, was predicated upon a determination that the Cambodian bombing constituted a basic change in the war not within the tactical discretion of the President and since that is a determination we have found to be a political question, we have not found it necessary to dwell at length upon Congressional participation. We see no need to address ourselves to the Fulbright provisos discussed in Judge Oakes' opinion since they predate the Paris Accord which places the military stance in Cambodia in such focus that we cannot judge their present efficacy or applicability. In any event we agree with his conclusion that they do not affect American forces which is the issue here. We cannot resist however commenting that the most recent expression of Congressional approval by appropriation, the Joint Resolution Continuing Appropriations for Fiscal 1974 (P.L. 93–52), enacted into law July 1, 1973, contains the following provision:

Sec. 108. Notwithstanding any other provision of law, on or after August 15, 1973, no funds herein or heretofore appropriated may be obligated or expended to finance directly or indirectly combat activities by United States military forces in or over or from off the shores of North Vietnam, South Vietnam, Laos or Cambodia.

[2] Assuming arguendo that the military and diplomatic issues were manageable and that we were obliged to find some participation by Congress, we cannot see how this provision does not support the proposition that the Congress has approved the Cambodian bombing. The statute is facially clear but its applicability is contested by plaintiffs on several grounds which were essentially adopted by the court below. The argument is made that the Congress didn't really mean what it said because it was coerced by the President who had vetoed Congressional Bills which would have immediately cut off Cambodian funds. Not being able to muster sufficient strength to overcome the veto, the argument runs, the Congress was forced willy nilly to enact the appropriation legislation. Resort is made to the floor debate which it is argued bolsters the view that individual legislators expressed personal disapproval of the bombing and did not interpret the appropriation as an approval to bomb but simply a recognition that it gave the President the power to bomb. It is further urged that since the Constitution entrusts the power to declare war to a majority of the Congress, the veto exercised makes it possible for the President to thwart the will of Congress by holding one-third

D.Va.1970). One might also include cases such as Sarnoff v. Connally, 457 F.2d 809 (9th Cir.), cert. denied, 409 U.S. 929, 93 S. Ct. 227, 34 L.Ed.2d 186 (1972), and Head v. Nixon, 342 F.Supp. 521 (E.D.La.), aff'd, 468 F.2d 951 (5th Cir. 1972), where the courts dismissed claims that Congressional appropriations were an unconstitutional delegation of the war-making powers, as involving political questions. See also Atlee v. Laird, *supra*. Other suits challenging the legality of the war have been dismissed on other grounds. Mottola v. Nixon, 464 F.2d 178 (9th Cir. 1972), rev'g 318 F.Supp. 538 (N.D.Cal.1970) (standing); Pietsch v. President of the United States, 434 F.2d 861 (2d Cir. 1970), cert. denied, 403 U.S. 920, 91 S.Ct. 2236, 29 L.Ed.2d 698 (1971) (standing); Velvel v. Nixon, 415 F.2d 236 (10th Cir. 1969), cert. denied, 396 U.S. 1042, 90 S.Ct. 684, 24 L.Ed.2d 686 (1970),

aff'g 287 F.Supp. 846 (D.Kan.1968) (standing); Campen v. Nixon, 56 F.R.D. 404 (N. D.Cal.1972) (standing); Gravel v. Laird, *supra* (political question, standing and sovereign immunity); Da Costa v. Nixon, 55 F.R.D. 145 (E.D.N.Y.), aff'd without opinion, 456 F.2d 1335 (2 Cir. 1972).

We find particularly persuasive the scholarly opinion of Judge Adams of the Third Circuit in Atlee v. Laird, *supra*, the only case involving the Southeast Asia conflict which the Supreme Court has affirmed. In all other cases where review was sought, certiorari has been denied as this note documents. In Massachusetts v. Laird, 400 U.S. 886, 91 S.Ct. 128, 27 L.Ed.2d 130 (1970), the Supreme Court denied the Commonwealth of Massachusetts leave to file an original bill of complaint seeking an adjudication of the constitutionality of the United States role in the Indo-China war.

plus one of the members of either House. We find none of these arguments persuasive.

[3] 1) Since the statute is not ambiguous, resort to legislative history is unjustified. See Mr. Justice Jackson's opinion in Schwegmann v. Calvert Distillers Corp., 341 U.S. 384, 395–396, 71 S.Ct. 745, 95 L.Ed. 1035 (1951).

[4] 2) Resort to legislative materials is not permissible where they are contradictory or ambiguous. NLRB v. Plasterers' Local, etc., 79, 404 U.S. 116, 129 n. 24, 92 S.Ct. 360, 30 L.Ed.2d 312 (1971). A fair reading of the Congressional Record for June 29, 1973 establishes this proposition. Members of Congress Drinan and the plaintiff Holtzman here for example both voted against the measure because it would authorize the bombing until August 15, 1973.

While the court below relied on the colloquy between Senators Eagleton and Fulbright, it inadvertently omitted the following:

> Mr. Eagleton. In the light of the legislative history, meaning the statement of former Secretary of Defense Richardson that we will continue the bombing unless the funds are cut off, will we with the adoption of this resolution permit the bombing of Cambodia for the next 45 days? This is the question I pose to the Senator from Arkansas.
>
> Mr. Fulbright. *Until August 15.*
>
> Mr. Eagleton. Would it permit the bombing of Laos?
>
> Mr. Fulbright. It would not prevent it.

119 Cong.Rec. S 12562 (daily ed. June 29, 1973) [Emphasis added].

In sum, even if the legislative history were considered it is at best ambiguous and does not clearly support the theory that the Congress did not mean what it said.

3) We cannot agree that the Congress was "coerced" by the President's veto. There was unquestionably a Congressional impasse resulting from the desire of a majority of Congress to stop bombing immediately and the desire of the President that his discretion be unfettered by an arbitrarily selected date. Instead of an acute constitutional confrontation, as Senator Javits noted an "agreement" was reached. (119 Cong. Rec. S 12561 (daily ed. June 29, 1973)). This version of the situation is also the conclusion of Judge Tauro in his opinion of August 8, 1973 (Drinan v. Nixon, 364 F.Supp. 854 (D.Mass.)) which exhaustively studies the record.

4) While the Constitution vests the war declaring authority in the Congress, the Founding Fathers also conferred the veto power upon the President. (Art. I, § 7, cl. 2). The suggestion that the veto power is impotent with respect to an authority vested solely in Congress by the Constitution is unsupported by any citation of authority and is hardly persuasive. It of course assumes here that the Cambodian bombing constitutes a new war requiring a new declaration and that it is not part of the extrication of a long suffering nation from an Indo-China war lasting for several years. This again in our view is the nucleus of the issue and we have no way of resolving that question particularly here on a motion for summary judgment.[4]

---

4. The dissenting opinion of Judge Oakes, finding no Congressional authorization by appropriation by reason of the secret bombings of Cambodia in 1969 and 1970 as reported in the *New York Times* (which is not in the Record before us any more than the Pentagon Papers were before this court in Da Costa v. Laird, *supra*, 448 F.2d at 1370) if anything emphasizes the inability of the judiciary to make reasoned judgments with manageable or discoverable information in foreign relations particularly in time of war. Secrecy in diplomacy and in military strategy during hostilities has been customary since at least the time of the Trojan War. The relationship of the alleged misfeasance here committed and the action of Congress is again a political question. Its propriety in any event is beyond the scope of appropriate judicial scrutiny. See *Proverbs* 20, v. 18 "Designs are strengthened by counsels: and wars are to be managed by governments."

## III

[5, 6] We finally note, although again not necessary in view of our holding in Part I, our disagreement with our colleague Judge Oakes that any of the parties plaintiff have standing. We have held that mere taxpayer status does not confer standing to litigate the constitutionality of the Indo-China war. Pietsch v. President of the United States, 434 F.2d 861 (2d Cir. 1970), cert. denied, 403 U.S. 920, 91 S.Ct. 2236, 29 L.Ed.2d 698 (1971); see Velvel v. Nixon, 415 F.2d 236 (10th Cir. 1969), cert. denied, 396 U.S. 1042, 90 S.Ct. 684, 24 L.Ed.2d 686 (1970). See also Mottola v. Nixon, 464 F.2d 178 (9th Cir. 1972). In Berk v. Laird, 429 F.2d 302, 306 (2d Cir. 1970), we held that a serviceman does have standing if he is under orders to fight in the combat to which he objects. Here none of the servicemen plaintiffs are presently under orders to fight in Cambodia. They have been relieved of any such military obligation and indeed one has been separated from the service. Their present status in our view moots the appeal as to them and we cannot agree that their status is preserved because of the "cognizable danger of recurrent violation" doctrine of United States v. W. T. Grant Co., 345 U.S. 629, 633, 73 S.Ct. 894, 97 L.Ed. 1303 (1953). In view of the termination of the air strikes on August 15, 1973 and their present status, we can perceive of nothing more than the merest possibility that such eventuality will occur. United States v. W. T. Grant Co., supra, requires more than this. See Atherton Mills v. Johnston, 259 U.S. 13, 42 S.Ct. 422, 66 L.Ed. 814 (1922). Neither do we see any adequate support for the standing of Representative Holtzman. She has not been denied any right to vote on Cambodia by any action of the defendants. She has fully participated in the Congressional debates which have transpired since her election to the Congress. The fact that her vote was ineffective was due to the contrary votes of her colleagues and not the defendants herein. The claim that the establishment of illegality here would be relevant in possible impeachment proceedings against the President would in effect be asking the judiciary for an advisory opinion which is precisely and historically what the "case and controversy" conditions set forth in Article III, Section 2 of the Constitution forbid. See Correspondence of the Justices (1793), reprinted in part in H. Hart & H. Wechsler, The Federal Courts and the Federal System 64–66 (2d ed. P. Bator et al. 1973). The judgment sought could hardly have any subsequent binding effect on those who have the responsibility for such a measure. Its effect on the named defendants would be clearly academic and moot since they have no interest in controverting it.

The judgment is reversed and the case is remanded with instructions to dismiss the complaint. The mandate shall issue forthwith.

OAKES, Circuit Judge (dissenting):

I believe there is standing for Congresswoman Holtzman under Baker v. Carr, 369 U.S. 186, 207–208, 82 S.Ct. 691, 7 L.Ed.2d 663 (1962) and Coleman v. Miller, 307 U.S. 433, 437–446, 59 S.Ct. 972, 83 L.Ed. 1385 (1939). I believe there is standing for the airmen-appellees under Berk v. Laird, 429 F.2d 302 (2d Cir. 1970) and Massachusetts v. Laird, 451 F.2d 26, 29 (1st Cir. 1971) which has not been mooted by their return to the United States. United States v. W. T. Grant Co., 345 U.S. 629, 632, 73 S.Ct. 894, 97 L.Ed. 1303 (1953).

I believe there is justiciability under Da Costa v. Laird, 471 F.2d 1146, 1156 (2d Cir. 1973), (Da Costa III) where the question "whether a radical change in the character of war operations . . . might be sufficiently measurable judicially to warrant a court's consideration . . . ." was expressly reserved. There is here "a manageable standard" under Da Costa III and Youngstown Sheet & Tube Co. v. Sawyer, 343 U.S. 579, 72 S.Ct. 863, 96 L.Ed. 1153 (1952), since there has been such a "radical change in the character of war operations." The Defense Department is continuing to bomb in Cambodia despite the cease-fire in Vietnam and despite the return of our prisoners of war from North Vietnam. The justiciable question then is whether there is any Constitutional authorization for the employment of United States armed forces over Cambodia, now that the war in Vietnam has come to an end. There is no question under the law of this Circuit, Orlando v. Laird, 443 F.2d 1039, 1042 (2d Cir.) cert. denied, 404 U.S. 869, 92 S.Ct. 94, 30 L.Ed.2d 113 (1971), that the Executive lacks unilateral power to commit American forces to combat absent a "belligerent attack" or "a grave emergency." See Mitchell v. Laird, 476 F.2d 533 (D.C.Cir. 1973).

Has Congress ratified or authorized the bombing in Cambodia by appropriations acts or otherwise? Congress can confer power on the Executive by way of an appropriations act. Fleming v. Mohawk Wrecking & Lumber Co., 331 U.S. 111, 116, 67 S.Ct. 1129, 91 L.Ed. 1375 (1947) (creation of new agency by Executive Order ratified by appropriation). And this Circuit has expressly held that congressional authorization for the war in Vietnam may be found in appropriations acts. Da Costa v. Laird, 448 F.2d 1368, 1370 (2d Cir. 1971), cert. denied, 405 U.S. 979, 92 S.Ct. 1193, 31 L.Ed.2d 255 (1972) (*Da Costa II*). Orlando v. Laird, *supra*, 443 F.2d at 1042.

I do not, moreover, agree with appellees' argument that the Fulbright "proviso" adopted in all of the recent appropriations bills and limiting the use of Defense Department funds to support "Vietnamese or other free world forces in actions designed to provide military support and assistance to the government of Cambodia or Laos," limited all prior authorizations to expenditures for United States forces in Cambodia only in aid in the release of Americans held as prisoners of war. *E. g.*, Armed Forces Military Procurement Act of 1971, Pub.L.No.91–441, § 502(a)(1), 84 Stat. 905 (1970). The language of the

appropriations acts seems to me to differentiate between "other free world forces" and "Armed Forces of the United States," *e. g., id.* § 502(a)(2). The legislative history indicates also that there is a difference between "other free world forces" and "United States armed forces." Even though the Fulbright proviso did not provide any *affirmative* grant of authority to the President to use "Armed Forces of the United States" in Cambodia, 119 Cong.Rec. S 7385–87 (daily ed. Apr. 13, 1973), Senator Fulbright himself considered the proviso operative only in respect to "South Vietnamese or other *foreign* military operations in support of the Cambodian or Laotian Governments." *Id.* at S. 7385 (emphasis supplied).

Thus an argument could be made that congressional authorization of appropriations with knowledge of our "presence" in Cambodia was ratification. But for authorization on the part of Congress by way of an appropriation to be effective, the congressional action must be based on a knowledge of the facts. Greene v. McElroy, 360 U.S. 474, 506–507, 79 S.Ct. 1400, 3 L.Ed.2d 1377 (1959) (appropriation to Defense Department for security program did not ratify procedure denying right of an individual to confront witnesses). I am aware of only one instance in which it has previously been argued that a war was illegal as a result of Congress being misinformed as to the underlying facts surrounding American participation in that war. While the argument was unique and unsuccessful to boot, however, time has vindicated it, I believe. Furthermore, it was advanced by one whose views are worth consideration, even if they were expressed in "dissent," so to speak. I refer of course to Abraham Lincoln and his argument as a lone Congressman on January 12, 1848, in opposition to our "incursion" into Mexico and what later was called the Mexican War. *See* Cong. Globe, 30th Cong. 1st Sess. 93 et seq. (Appendix 1848).

And here, incredibly enough, it appears that neither the American people nor the Congress, at the time it was voting appropriations in aid of the war in Vietnam, were given the facts pertaining to our bombing in Cambodia. Recent disclosures have indicated that Air Force B–52 bombers were secretly attacking Cambodia in 1969, 1970 and even later while the United States was publicly proclaiming respect for Cambodian neutrality. *See* N.Y.Times July 17, 1973, at 1; July 18, 1973, at 1, July 22, 1973, Sec. E, at 3; July 24, 1973, at 1; July 25, 1973, at 1; July 29, 1973, at 1; Aug. 8, 1973, at 6; Aug. 9, 1973, at 7.

The government argues that these secret bombings occurred in 1969 and 1970, and ended when our activities in Cambodia became open subsequently. But the Congress whose ratification by way of appropriations acts is contended for here did not become aware of these covert bombings until July of 1973. And meanwhile the Congress had declared in the so-called Mansfield Amendment that it was "the policy of the United States to terminate at the earliest practicable date all military operations of the United States in Indochina . . . ." Appropriations Authorization-Miltary Procurement Act of 1972, Pub.L.No.92–156, § 601, 85 Stat. 423 (92nd Cong., 1st Sess. 1971).

The combination of concealment of the facts from Congress together with the enactment of a policy of "earliest practicable" withdrawal do not amount in my mind to an appropriations carte blanche to the military to carry on bombing in Cambodia after the cease-fire, withdrawal of our troops from Vietnam, and return of our prisoners of war from North Vietnam.

We come then to the effect of the legislation, following upon a presidential veto of an immediate prohibition against the use of funds to bomb in Cambodia, adopted as a compromise this July 1st: the Continuing Appropriations Act for Fiscal Year 1974, Pub.L.No.93–52, 93rd Cong. 2nd Sess. (July 1, 1973) which expressly provided that ". . . on or after August 15, 1973, no funds herein

or heretofore appropriated may be obligated or expended to finance directly or indirectly combat activities by United States military forces in or over or from off the shores of North Vietnam, South Vietnam, Laos or Cambodia." § 108. In colloquy between Senators Eagleton and Fulbright, inadvertently omitted in the briefs of appellees and the opinion of the lower court, the former inquired whether "the adoption of this resolution [would] permit the bombing of Cambodia" and Senator Fulbright replied, "Until August 15". 119 Cong.Rec. S 12562 (daily ed. June 29, 1973). Again, in the same colloquy Senator Fulbright, conceding "Presidential power", said that "The President has the power to do a lot of things of which I do not approve," after being asked by Senator Eagleton whether under the resolution the President's "power to bomb in Indochina . . . will now be sanctioned by our action." *Id.* In neither case, however, is there recognition of *legality* or *past authorization.* Senator Fulbright had previously stated, as Judge Judd recognized, that "The acceptance of an August 15 cut off date should in no way be interpreted as recognition by the committee of the President's authority to engage U.S. forces in hostilities until that date. The view of most members of the committee has been and continues to be that the President does not have such authority in the absence of specific congressional approval." 119 Cong.Rec. S 12560 (daily ed. June 29, 1973).

It can be argued that Congress could, if it had so desired, cut off the funds for bombing Cambodia immediately by overriding the Presidential veto. This was indeed championed by those voting against the ultimate compromise Resolution. But it does not follow that those who voted in favor of the Resolution were thereby putting the Congressional stamp of approval on the bombing continuation. While the Resolution constituted a recognition that Executive *power* was being exercised, it did not constitute a concession that such exercise was rightful, lawful or constitutional.

It may be that those voting for the Resolution thought that in some way previous appropriations acts or the omission expressly to prohibit a continuation of bombing after the cease-fire and return of our prisoners of war amounted to an authorization, which could only be limited by affirmative congressional action. But as I have previously suggested I cannot find any express congressional authorization for such a continuation of the Cambodian bombing, nor do I think that authorization can be implied from prior appropriations acts. This being true, affirmative action on the part of Congress was not necessary as a matter of constitutional law. An agreement by the Executive to some cut off date was essential, however, because the *legality* of bombing continuation might not be tested or testable for months to come, by the very nature of the judicial process. Therefore, Congress as I see it, took the only practical way out. It acknowledged the reality of the Executive's exercise of power even while it disputed the Executive's authority for that exercise. It agreed to a final cut-off date as the best practical result but never conceded the legality or constitutionality of interim exercise.

Thus the Resolution of July 1, 1973 cannot be the basis for legalization of otherwise unlawful Executive action. We are talking here about the separate branches of government, and in doing so we must distinguish between the exercise of power on the one hand and authorization for such exercise on the other. That the Executive Branch had the power to bomb in Cambodia, there can be no doubt; it did so, and indeed is continuing to do so. Whether it had the constitutional authority for its action is another question.

If we return to fundamentals, as I think we must in the case of any conflict of view between the other two Branches of Government, it will be recalled that the Founding Fathers deliberately eschewed the example of the British Monarchy in which was lodged the authority to declare war and to raise and regulate fleets and armies. *See* The Federalist No. 69 (A. Hamilton). Rather, these powers were deliberately given to the Legislative Branch of the new American Republic in Article I, section 8 of the Constitution. *See* 7 Works of Alexander Hamilton 81 (J. Hamilton ed. 1851), cited in Note, Congress, The President, and The Power to Commit Forces to Combat, 81 Harv.L.Rev. 1771, 1773, n. 14 (1968). I fail to see, and the Government in its able presentation has failed to point out, where the Congress ever authorized the continuation of bombing in Cambodia after the cease-fire in Vietnam, the withdrawal of our forces there, and the return of our prisoners of war to our shores. Accordingly, I must dissent, and although on a somewhat different analysis would affirm the judgment below.

# Mottola v. Nixon

**Gary F. MOTTOLA et al., Plaintiffs,**

**v.**

**Richard M. NIXON, President of the United States, and Melvin Laird, Secretary of Defense of the United States, Defendants.**

### No. C 70 943.

United States District Court,
N. D. California.
Sept. 10, 1970.

Gary Mottola and Roy Godfrey Olson in pro. per.

James L. Browning, U. S. Atty., and Brian Denton, Asst. U. S. Atty., San Francisco, Cal., for defendants.

## MEMORANDUM OF DECISION

SWEIGERT, District Judge.

This suit is brought by four plaintiffs, three of them being members of the United States Military Reserves and one being a registrant eligible for draft under the Selective Service Act, against the President of the United States and his Secretary of Defense to obtain a judgment (1) enjoining defendants from ordering United States military personnel to conduct military operations in Cambodia, and (2) declaring that these four plaintiffs have the right to refuse to participate in what they claim to be an illegal, unconstitutional war.

The case is now before the court on plaintiffs' motion for a preliminary injunction and on defendants' counter motion to dismiss the suit upon the grounds of lack of jurisdiction of the subject matter, specifically on the grounds of (1) non-justiciable political question; (2) lack of plaintiffs' standing to raise the question, and (3) sovereign immunity from suit.

Although the complaint is directed in terms only at the Cambodian military operation, that issue necessarily involves the constitutionality of the whole Vietnam war. This is so because, if our South Vietnam presence and operation are lawful, then, certainly, any necessary incidental, tactical incursion ordered by the Commander in Chief against dangerous, threatening enemy strongholds across the Cambodian border to protect our South Vietnam forces from attack would likewise be lawful; if, on the other hand, the Vietnam operation, itself, is unlawful then all its actions, including its Cambodian operation, would be unlawful.[1]

It must be borne in mind that the issue here is, not whether our involvement in Vietnam has been necessary, wise or moral. That is a subject beyond the province of any court. Only the branches of our government constitutionally vested with the power to make such a judgment—the Congress, the President, or both, can decide whether the Vietnam war has been in the national interest and, if so, when and on what conditions it should be continued or terminated.

The only issue now before this court is the different, narrow, legal question whether, regardless of the necessity, wisdom or morality of the war, it is being waged by and under the authority of the branch of our government in which such power is constitutionally vested.

Plaintiffs contend that it is not being waged in compliance with constitutional processes because it has never been declared by the Congress as provided by Article I, Section 8(11) of the Constitution.

## THE CONSTITUTION, THE INDISPUTABLE FACTS AND THE ISSUE

That Article provides that "Congress shall have power * * * to declare war * * *."

The court can take judicial notice of the fact that the armed forces of the United States are now committed and have been for nearly five years, committed to a full scale war in Vietnam; that this war has never been declared by the Congress and that the President of the United States, through the incumbent and his predecessor in office, has continued, nevertheless, to conduct the war without receiving or even requesting a congressional declaration.

[1] The question arises: How can a situation like this continue in what plaintiffs contend is plain disregard of the Constitution, Article I, Section 8(11)? [2]

---

1. We do not regard the issue as moot merely because the plaintiffs are mainly concerned about Cambodia. Withdrawal of American armed forces from Cambodia subsequent to the filing of this action would not preclude the reasonable probability of a further Cambodian operation so long as the Vietnam operation continues and for the same or similar reason that triggered and justified the first Cambodian operation.

2. It is unnecessary to long dwell on the purpose and importance of Article I, Section 8(11). An early draft of the Constitution gave Congress the power to "make" war rather than "declare" war. The change from "make" to "declare" was intended, not to shift from Congress to the President the general power to initiate and engage the country in war, but only to make clear that the President would have the power to repel sudden attacks and to manage, as Commander in Chief of the armed forces, any war declared by the Congress. See for references to the purposes of the Constitutional Convention "The Congress, The President, and the Power to Commit Forces to Combat," 81 Harv.L.Rev., pp. 1771, 1772, 1773, et seq.; also Velvel, L.R., "The War in Vietnam," 16 Kansas Law Review, pp. 449, 451; also E. Corwin, "The President: Office & Powers," (4th Ed.1964); also National Commitments Senate Report (S.Rep. No. 797, 90th Cong. (1st Sess.1967) 26–27.

Justice Story in his "Commentaries on the Constitution of the United States" (2d Ed. 1851), pp. 89–90, describes the power of declaring war as "the highest sovereign prerogative" which is in its nature and effects "so critical and calamitous, that it requires the utmost delibera-

It has been claimed that, notwithstanding Article I, Section 8(11) of the Constitution, the President, exercising his general executive powers and acting in his role as Commander in Chief of the armed forces under Article II, Sections 1(1) and 2(1) of the Constitution, can lawfully commit the nation and its armed forces to such a war as now exists in Vietnam and continue that war in his discretion without receiving or even requesting a congressional declaration. Many reasons have been put forward to support this claim.

### The "Repel Attack" Argument.

[2]  For example, it has been argued that the President must be in a position to repel attack upon the nation or its armed forces in emergencies when there is no time to consult the Congress.  This is an obviously correct qualification of Article I, Section 8, vesting in the Congress the power to declare war—a qualification that finds support in the debates of the Constitutional Convention and one that must be part of any reasonable interpretation of the power of Congress to declare war, i. e., the President has power under Article II, acting in his role as Chief Executive and as Commander in Chief of the armed forces, to repel on his own initiative any attack upon the United States or upon

its armed forces or its citizens wherever they may be.

The question remains, however, whether the President may otherwise initiate or continue a war operation, such as the Vietnam operation has now become, without requesting as soon as reasonably possible, and receiving, a congressional declaration of war, or an equally explicit congressional authorization, either general or limited, but in any event phrased to indicate a congressional intent to consent, pursuant to its prerogative under Article I, Section 8(11), to the initiation or continuance of the war.

Most commentators and some courts concede [3] that the Vietnam operation has now obviously gone far beyond mere emergency repulsion of any 1964 Tonquin Gulf attack upon our armed forces and that it is obviously a "war" within the meaning of Article I, Section 8(11); that it has come to involve not only defensive, but also offensive military operations of great magnitude, and that it has continued over a period more than sufficiently long to permit and to require exercise by the Congress of its power and responsibility under Article I, Section 8(11).

### The Historic Precedents Argument.

[3]  It has also been argued that President Lincoln in the Civil War [4] and

---

tion and the successive review of all councils of the nation. * * * *" * * * "the cooperation of all the branches of the legislative power ought, upon principle, to be required in this highest act of legislation. * * * *"

President Lincoln pointed out that the reason for the provision of the Constitution giving the war power to Congress was that the Constitutional Convention understood that the most oppressive of all kingly oppressions stemmed from the power to lead their people into wars and that the Convention "resolved to so frame the Constitution that no one man should hold the power of bringing this oppression upon us."  (as quoted in E. Corwin, supra, p. 45).

The National Commitments Report of the United States Senate Report (S.Rep. No. 797, 90th Cong., 1st Sess. (1967) at

26–27, states: "The concentration in the hands of the President of virtually unlimited authority over matters of law and peace has all but removed the limits to executive power in the most important single area of our national life.  Until they are restored the American people will be threatened with tyranny or disaster."

3.  See Harvard Law Review, pp. 1771, 1803 (1968) supra; 16 Kansas Law Review, pp. 450, 453 (1968), supra; Orlando v. Laird, 317 F.Supp. 1013 (E.D. N.Y.1970) infra.

4.  Lincoln's war action was taken, not against a foreign country, but against domestic, civil insurrection designed to destroy the Union; presidential action was not only clearly authorized by preexisting statutes, but also was explicitly

President Truman during the Korean War took large scale, long sustained military action without a congressional declaration of war and that in numerous other, lesser instances, presidents have ordered the armed forces into warlike presence abroad without any such declaration. This is true but, even if we assume that those precedents are fairly comparable with the Vietnam war, the fact that constitutional processes may not have been observed in the past would be no legal excuse if the Vietnam war is otherwise constitutionally unauthorized as contended by plaintiffs in this case—a principle recognized by the Supreme Court in Youngstown Sheet & Tube Co. v. Sawyer, 343 U.S. 579, 587, 72 S.Ct. 863, 96 L.Ed. 1153 (1951).[5]

*The Treaty Obligations Argument.*

[4] It has also been argued that the President can commit the nation to war if necessary to carry out the obligations of the United States under the various mutual defense treaties into which the United States has entered with almost 50 nations, including the so-called SEATO treaty which provides that armed attack against one of the parties poses a danger to all the parties and that each will act to meet the danger. These treaties provide, however, that the obligation of each party is subject to its own "constitutional processes" which, in the case of the United States, includes the provision of Article I, Section 8(11) that the power to declare war lies, not in the President, but in the Congress.

*The Foreign Policy Argument.*

It has also been argued that the President must have power to commit the nation to war whenever necessary to strengthen or enforce the foreign policy for which the President, through his State Department, is responsible. It should be noted, however, that the presidential power over foreign policy is by no means unlimited; it is dependent on congressional or senatorial cooperation in many respects including, specifically, dependence upon the Congress when it comes to a declaration of war.

*The "Outmoded" Argument.*

It has also been argued that declarations of war are outmoded, even dangerous, in the nuclear age because such formal declarations may trigger the treaty obligations of nations aligned against the United States and, further, the nation must often be careful to make clear that its warlike operations have only limited objectives lest other nations be mislead to overreaction.

On the contrary, however, it is argued that other nations are more concerned with this nation's actual military moves than with its internal, formal constitutional processes and, further, that in any event, the congressional power to declare war necessarily includes the exercise, if prudently preferable, of the lesser power to limit any declaration of war to stated objectives or to a stated scale or to a stated time according to the particular circumstances. As stated in the early case of Bas v. Tingy, 4 U.S. (4 Dall.)

---

ratified for further assurance by congressional resolution. See The Prize Cases, 67 U.S. (2 Black) 635, 17 L.Ed. 459 (1862).

5. In *Youngstown*, the court annulling President Truman's seizure of strike-bound steel mills as a war measure to prevent disaster in our Korean War effort, said: "It is said that other Presidents without congressional authority have taken possession of private business enterprises in order to settle labor disputes. But even if this be true, Congress has not thereby lost its exclusive consti-

tutional authority to make laws necessary and proper to carry out the powers vested by the Constitution 'in the Government of the United States, or in any Department or Officer thereof.' The Founders of this Nation entrusted the law making power to the Congress alone in both good and bad times. It would do no good to recall the historical events, the fears of power and the hopes for freedom that lay behind their choice. Such a review would but confirm our holding that this seizure order cannot stand."

36, 43, 1 L.Ed. 731, "Congress is empowered to declare a general war or Congress may wage a limited war—limited in place, in objects or in time."

It will be noted that none of the foregoing arguments make any pretense that Article I, Section 8(11) has been complied with in the case of Vietnam; they merely purport to explain why, for various reasons of expediency, the Constitution has *not* been complied with. They are, therefore, of doubtful relevance in a court whose duty it is to see that the Constitution *is* complied with.

There are, however, two further arguments which must be separately considered because they do imply that in the case of Vietnam the provision of Article I, Section 8(11) for a congressional declaration of war has been met—at least in substance and effect.

### *The Implied Ratification Argument.*

First, it is argued that the Congress, by continuing supportive war-related legislation and by continuing supportive appropriations of huge amounts of money for the maintenance of the armed forces, must be deemed to have ratified the President's conduct of the war and that this ratification is in effect a compliance with Article I, Section 8(11).

The response to this claim has been first, that Congress faced with a Presidential fait accompli, has acted at great disadvantage in making these appropriations for the armed forces under strong pressure to provide for and protect men already involved in battle, and second, that for this very reason supportive legislation and appropriations of this kind are insufficient to constitute the explicit ratification necessary to validate otherwise unauthorized executive action—a principle that has been recognized by the Supreme Court in Greene v. McElroy, 360 U.S. 474, 507, 79 S.Ct. 1400, 3 L.Ed.2d 1377 (1959).[6]

### *The Gulf of Tonquin Resolution Argument.*

It is also argued that the Gulf of Tonquin Resolution passed by the Congress in 1964 in response to a reported North Vietnam attack on two American destroyers, constitutes the functional

---

6. In *Greene*, the court, dealing with the question whether certain administrative security clearance programs of the Department of Defense had been impliedly authorized or at least ratified by the Congress, held that they had not been impliedly authorized, also held that they could not be deemed to have been impliedly ratified by continued congressional appropriation of funds to finance the programs.

Responding to the argument that, although Congress had not enacted specific legislation relating to clearance procedures, it had acquiesced in the programs and had ratified them by specifically appropriating funds to finance them, the court said (pp. 506–507, 79 S.Ct. pp. 1418–1419): "If acquiescence or implied ratification were enough to show delegation of authority to take actions within the area of questionable constitutionality, we might agree with respondents that delegation has been shown here. * * * (but) * * * We deal here with substantial restraints on employment opportunities of numerous persons imposed in a manner which is in conflict with our long-accepted notions of fair procedures. Before we are asked to judge whether, in the context of security clearance cases, a person may be deprived of the right to follow his chosen profession without full hearings * * * it must be made clear that the President or Congress, within their respective constitutional powers, *specifically* has decided that the imposed procedures are necessary and warranted and has authorized their use. * * * *Such decisions cannot be assumed by acquiescence or nonaction.* * * * They must be made explicitly not only to assure that individuals are not deprived of cherished rights under procedures not actually authorized * * * but also because *explicit action, especially in areas of doubtful constitutionality*, requires careful and purposeful consideration by those responsible for enacting and implementing our laws. *Without explicit action by lawmakers, decisions of great constitutional import and effect would be relegated by default to administrators who, under our system of government, are not endowed with authority to decide them.*" (all emphasis added).

equivalent of a Congressional declaration of war.[7]

It will be noted, however, that the first part of the Resolution, an expression of approval and support for the President's determination "to repel attack against the forces of the United States," falls far short of a declaration of war, or even of implied authorization for the kind of all out, full scale war subsequently launched by the President in Vietnam.

It is contended, however, that the second and third parts of the Resolution, expressing the preparedness of the United States, as the President may determine, to render assistance, including the use of armed force, to any member of SEATO requesting assistance, is in substance and effect the "functional equivalent" of a congressional declaration of war.

Against this claim, however, it is argued that the Gulf of Tonquin Resolution, considered in the light of its legislative history, the circumstances of its enactment and its careful avoidance of any reference to a declaration of war, was never intended by Congress to authorize the large scale, long sustained all-out war subsequently launched by the President; that on the contrary, the intent of the Congress, based on well understood presidential assurances that no wider war was being sought and that American boys would not do the fighting that Asian boys should do for themselves and that the Congress would be further consulted, was merely to support the President during a reported emergency in his announced determination to repel any attack upon American ships or personnel in Vietnam. (See the legislative debate leading to the passage of the Tonquin Resolution and the subsequent testimony at the National Commitments Hearings—as summarized in 16 Kansas Law Review 449 at p. 472).

It is contended, therefore, that at best the Gulf of Tonquin Resolution is vague as to whether it was ever intended by Congress as an exercise of its constitutional power under Article I, Section 8(11) and that in any event it is ambiguous with respect to the function it was supposed to serve and the extent to which congressional authorization of war, if such ever was its intent, was being expressed. See 81 Harv.L.Rev. 1771, 1802, 1805.

This seems to be recognized by the United States Senate whose National Commitment Hearings held in 1967 culminated in a Senate Resolution (S.Res. 187 (1967)) to the effect that "under any circumstances *arising in the future*" any commitment of our armed forces to hostility on foreign territory should "result from a decision made in accordance with constitutional processes which, in addition to appropriate executive action, require affirmative action by Congress specifically intended to give rise to such a commitment." (emphasis added).

7. The Resolution recites the attack by the Communist regime in Vietnam against United States naval vessels in international waters as part of a campaign of aggression by North Vietnam against its neighbors and the nations, including the United States, joined with them in collective defense of their freedom. The document then resolves, first, that the Congress "approves and supports the determination of the President, as Commander in Chief to take all necessary measures—to repel any armed attack against the forces of the United States and to prevent further aggression and, second, that the United States, regarding the maintenance of peace and security in Southeast Asia as vital to its national interests, is prepared, consonant with the Constitution of the United States and the Charter of the United Nations and in accordance with its obligations under the Southeast Asia Collective Defense Treaty and as the President determines, "to take all necessary steps, including the use of armed force, to assist any member or protocol state of the Southeast Asia Collective Defense Treaty requesting assistance in defense of its freedom," and, third, that "this Resolution shall expire when the President shall determine that the peace and security of the area is reasonably assured by international conditions created by the action of the United Nations or otherwise, except that it may be terminated earlier by the Congress."

The implication is clear that in the senatorial opinion "constitutional processes" had not been followed in the case of the Vietnam war but that such a departure from constitutional processes should never again be tolerated "in the future."

In fact, the Senate has within the last several months repealed the Tonquin Gulf Resolution and, apparently, regards it so lightly that it preferred outright repeal rather than termination under Section 3 of the Resolution.

Further, the administration has disclaimed exclusive reliance upon this ambiguous and, therefore, controversial Tonquin Gulf Resolution, preferring to rest its Vietnam war power on what it claims to be the President's general executive and Commander in Chief powers under Article II and taking the position that the President could have initiated and can continue the Vietnam war in his own sound discretion even if the Gulf of Tonquin Resolution had never been passed by the Congress—a claim that is difficult to maintain against rulings of the Supreme Court and other lower federal courts in cases to be hereinafter discussed. (See Youngstown Sheet & Tube Co. v. Sawyer, *supra*; Berk v. Laird, *infra*; Orlando v. Laird, *infra*; United States v. Sisson, *infra*.)

It is also argued that, even if the Gulf of Tonquin Resolution could be construed as congressional compliance with Article I, Section 8(11), authorizing the President, upon receiving a request from any SEATO nation, to forthwith launch an all out Asian war in his complete discretion, without further authorization from Congress, then the Resolution would be a flagrantly invalid delegation and surrender by Congress to the President of its expressly vested constitutional power and responsibility for the declaration of war.

[5] It is true, as pointed out in United States v. Curtiss Wright, 299 U. S. 304, 315, 320, 324–329, 57 S.Ct. 216, 81 L.Ed. 255, that the President has delicate, plenary and exclusive power as the sole organ of the federal government in

318 F.Supp.—35

the field of international relations—"a power which does not" (ordinarily "require as a basis for its exercise an act of Congress" (page 320, 57 S.Ct. page 221); that, therefore, congressional legislation, which is to be made effective through negotiation and inquiry within the international field must often accord to the President a degree of discretion and freedom from statutory restriction which would not be admissible were domestic affairs alone involved (p. 320, 57 S.Ct. 216); that in such situations the Congress may either leave the exercise of a power to the President's unrestricted judgment or provide standards far more general than has always been considered requisite for domestic affairs (p. 324, 57 S.Ct. 216) and that such a broad delegation of congressional power to the President is not unconstitutional (p. 322, 57 S.Ct. 216).

It can be argued, however, that such a broad delegation is permissible only when, as indicated in United States v. Curtiss Wright, *supra*, the subject matter of the delegated power is one "which does not require as a basis for its exercise an act of Congress"—and that, therefore, the Congress, whatever other powers it may so wholly delegate to the President, can *not* do so with respect to the power to declare, initiate or continue a war—since the power to declare war *does* require an act of Congress—a declaration of war—under the express provisions of Article I, Section 8(11).

## THE ISSUE AND THE COURTS

It is apparent from the foregoing discussion of the issue that the constitutional question whether the President can initiate and wage a foreign war without requesting and receiving as soon as possible a congressional declaration of war or an equally explicit congressional authorization, either general or limited, under Article I, Section 8(11), is unsettled and in great controversy.

The question naturally arises: Why has this question not been settled one way or the other, or even considered, by the Supreme Court of the United States?

This is not due to any lack of cases seeking to present the issue. But, thus far (with a few recent exceptions to be later discussed) the lower federal courts —the Federal District Courts and Courts of Appeal have avoided ruling on the issue by disposing of these cases on technical, jurisdictional, procedural grounds, e. g., upon the ground that the issue is "political" in nature and, therefore, beyond the jurisdiction of the courts to decide [8] or that the suit presenting the question was an "unconsented" suit against the sovereign United States and, therefore, unmaintainable [9] or that the particular plaintiff presenting the question had no "standing" to raise it.[10]

[6] In all these cases the Supreme Court has denied petitions seeking its review of the questions involved.[11] Since mere refusal by the Supreme Court to accept and review may not be considered as determinative, one way or the other, of the issues presented, the serious questions raised by these cases remain undecided by the Supreme Court.

*Standing.*

[7] As far as the threshold question of "standing" is concerned, the Supreme Court in June, 1968, handed down its decision in Flast v. Cohen, 392 U.S. 83, 88 S.Ct. 1942, 20 L.Ed.2d 947 (1968), greatly broadening the earlier "standing" rule of Frothingham v. Mellon, 262 U.S. 447, 43 S.Ct. 597, 67 L.Ed. 1078 (1923) under which a plaintiff, to have standing, must have suffered some direct injury which is neither indefinite nor shared in common with people generally.

In *Flast* the court, after pointing out that the reason for the standing doctrine is merely to make sure that cases presented to the courts will involve well defined and truly adversary disputes rather than mere general, hypothetical or collusive suits, goes on to hold that the new test for standing is simply whether the plaintiff has alleged such a personal stake in the outcome of the controversy as to assure that concrete adverseness upon which the courts depend for illumination of difficult constitutional questions; that even an ordinary taxpayer will be deemed to have sufficient personal stake in the controversy if he is challenging the exercise of congressional power under the taxing and spending clause of Article I, Section 8 of the Constitution and if he can show that the challenged enactment exceeds some specific constitutional limitation imposed upon the exercise of that congressional

8. E. G. Luftig v. McNamara, 252 F.Supp. 819 (D.D.C.1966); (aff'd 126 U.S.App. D.C. 4, 373 F.2d 664 (1967); (cert. den. 387 U.S. 945, 87 S.Ct. 2078, 18 L.Ed. 2d 1332 (1967); Mora v. McNamara, 128 U.S.App.D.C. 297, 387 F.2d 862 (1967); (cert. den. 389 U.S. 934, 88 S.Ct. 282, 19 L.Ed.2d 287 (1967); Holmes v. United States, 387 F.2d 781 (7th Cir. 1967); (cert. den. 391 U.S. 936, 88 S.Ct. 1835, 20 L.Ed.2d 856 (1968); Velvel v. Nixon, 287 F.Supp. 846 (D.Kan.1968) (affirmed 415 F.2d 236 (10th Cir. 1969); (cert. den. 396 U.S. 1042, 90 S.Ct. 684, 24 L.Ed.2d 686 (1970); see also United States v. Sisson, 294 F.Supp. 511 (D. Mass.1968).

9. E. G. Luftig v. McNamara, supra; Velvel v. Nixon, supra.

10. Velvel v. Nixon, supra; see also Kalish v. United States, 411 F.2d 606 (9th Cir.

1969); (cert. den. 396 U.S. 835, 90 S.Ct. 93, 24 L.Ed.2d 86 (1969); Ashton v. United States, 404 F.2d 95, 97 (8th Cir. 1968); (cert. den. 394 U.S. 960, 89 S.Ct. 1308, 22 L.Ed.2d 561 (1969); United States v. Bolton, 192 F.2d 805, 806 (2d Cir. 1951).

11. In Holmes v. United States, 391 U.S. 936, 88 S.Ct. 1835, 20 L.Ed.2d 856 (1968), Justice Douglas, dissenting from the Supreme Court's refusal to grant review, recognized as "weighty" the argument that what has transpired in Vietnam is unconstitutional absent a declaration of war, also weighty the argument that the Tonkin Gulf Resolution is no constitutional substitute for a declaration of war; also weighty the argument that the making of appropriations is not an adequate substitute and that executive warmaking is illegal.

power—not simply that the enactment is beyond the general congressional power.

Although the court in *Flast* was dealing with a taxpayer's challenge to the congressional power, the rationale of the decision is equally, if not for stronger reason, applicable to a challenge by a member of the armed forces reserves, (such as are three of the plaintiffs herein) to the power of the President, as Commander in Chief of the armed forces to order him into the Vietnam conflict absent a congressional declaration of war—a challenge which, within the meaning of *Flast* rests, not merely on the ground that the President has exceeded his general executive powers (as in Kalish v. United States, supra, see footnote 10), but on the ground, within the meaning of *Flast*, that the President has acted in violation of a specific limitation upon his powers—the provision of Article I, Section 8(11) vesting in Congress the power to declare war.

In the very recent case of Berk v. Laird, 429 F.2d 302 (2d Cir. 1970), wherein an enlisted army private challenged the legality of an order requiring him to report for duty in the South Vietnam war area on the ground the war had never been declared by Congress, the Court of Appeals rejected this "no standing" defense, stating that, although alleged illegality of the Vietnam war may not be raised as a defense to prosecution for refusal of a draft registrant to submit to induction (citing United States v. Mitchell, 369 F.2d 323 (2d Cir. 1967), cert. den. 386 U.S. 972, 87 S.Ct. 1162, 18 L.Ed.2d 132 (1967); see also Ashton v. United States, 404 F. 2d 95, 97 (8th Cir. 1968)), any question of illegality of an order sending men to fight in a foreign undeclared war may be raised by some to whom such an or-

der has been directed. The court then proceeded to dispose of the case on other grounds which we will presently discuss.

Similarly, in Orlando v. Laird, 317 F. Supp. 1013 (E.D.N.Y.1970) the court, following *Berk, supra,* recognized standing of a serviceman who was under orders to report for Vietnam war duty, to challenge the constitutionality of the undeclared war and proceeded to dispose of the case on other grounds presently to be discussed.

In Holmes v. United States, 391 U.S. 936, 88 S.Ct. 1835, 20 L.Ed.2d 856 (1968) (denying certiorari in 387 F.2d 1010 (7th Cir. 1967)), wherein the issue was, not the legality of a military order requiring a serviceman to go to Vietnam, but only the legality of a compulsory selective service law absent a congressional declaration of war, Justice Douglas dissented, voting to grant certiorari, even under those circumstances, and Justice Stewart, explaining his concurrence, stated that if the former had been the issue, he would have voted to grant certiorari.

Earlier, in United States v. Sisson, 294 F.Supp. 511 (D.Mass.1968) the court had gone so far as to recognize, as Justice Douglas was willing to recognize, "standing," even though the plaintiff was, not a service man, but only a civilian draft registrant who had refused induction into the armed forces.

It is not necessary in the pending case to go that far because here three of the plaintiffs herein, i. e., Mottola, Schwartz and Gross are enlisted men in the armed forces reserves who, although not yet called up on orders to report to the Vietnam war area, as in *Berk* and *Orlando, supra,* are, as members of the reserves, ever vulnerable and subject to such orders.[12]

---

12. To argue that these three members of our armed forces reserves should have to wait until they are actually called and ordered to service in the Vietnam war before acquiring "standing" to raise the question of the validity of such an order, is such a thin, unworthy distinction that we decline to recognize it as ground

for refusing "standing." To say that these three plaintiffs must wait until they are called up, perhaps suddenly, and ordered to the Vietnam area, perhaps quickly, and then file a court suit for a declaration of their legal rights, perhaps with too little time to properly do so, borders, we think, on the absurd. So far

[8] On the other hand, plaintiff Olsen is only a registrant eligible for draft under the Selective Service Act and may be denied standing. A compulsory draft system without a war declaration would not necessarily be illegal. (See United States v. Mitchell, *supra*). Undoubtedly, Congress has the power to provide armed forces through compulsory draft or otherwise, even in peacetime as a preparation for the eventuality of war. To allow standing for such a plaintiff would lead to a flood of similar, fruitless challenges by Selective Service registrants.

For these reasons we conclude that the government's motion to dismiss on the ground of "no standing" should be denied as to plaintiffs Mottola, Schwartz and Gross, but granted as to plaintiff Olsen.

### Sovereign Immunity.

[9] This threshold defense of sovereign immunity is often, and in many cases mistakenly, used by the government to prevent court rulings on the constitutionality of challenged executive action. We believe that the cases which have avoided decision of the Vietnam war power issue on this ground, have misplaced their reliance on the doctrine. The proper place of the sovereign immunity doctrine is noted in *Berk, supra*, which rejected that defense, citing Washington v. Udall, 417 F.2d 1310 (9th Cir. 1969), and held that sovereign immunity is no bar to an action challenging the Vietnam war power of the President since the essence of the challenge is that the executive, although purporting to act in the name of the sovereign, has really exceeded its constitutional authority and that in such a case the requested relief does not require affirmative governmental action but only that the executive cease its allegedly unauthorized

and, therefore, improper continuance of the war without either a general or limited declaration of war by Congress.

For this reason we conclude that the government's motion in this case to dismiss on the ground of sovereign immunity should be denied.

### Political Question or Decision on the Merits.

[10] Turning now to the argument that the issue is "political" in nature and, therefore, non-justiciable, it would seem that such a means of avoiding the main issue comes strangely from a judiciary whose Supreme Court has decided such cases as Youngstown Sheet & Tube Co. v. Sawyer, 343 U.S. 579, 72 S.Ct. 863, 96 L.Ed. 1153 (1952); Baker v. Carr, 369 U.S. 186, 82 S.Ct. 691, 7 L. Ed.2d 663 (1962) and Powell v. McCormack, 395 U.S. 486, 89 S.Ct. 1944, 23 L.Ed.2d 491 (1969).

In *Youngstown*, as already noted, President Truman, claiming to be acting under his executive and Commander in Chief powers, as set forth in Article II of the Constitution during a national emergency declared by him, had ordered seizure of the strikebound steel mills as a war measure necessary in connection with our Korean war operation in order to prevent a work stoppage that would, according to the executive order "immediately jeopardize and imperil our national defense and the defense of those joined with us in resisting aggression, and would add to the continuing danger to our soldiers, sailors, and airmen engaged in combat in the field."

The steel companies did not present any challenge concerning the constitutionality of the Korean war, itself, (admittedly an undeclared war). That ultimate question was, therefore, never reached by the court. The steel companies, however, did challenge the constitu-

---

as "concrete adverseness" and adequate presentation of the legal issues in this case are concerned, we see no difficulty. These three enlistees have a real, and not too remote, stake in the outcome, perhaps their lives, and, further, it appears

that they are not only reserve enlistees but also law students with unique access to the law literature and to professional counseling. On the other side, the United States Attorney is well able to represent the defendants.

tionality of the President's incidental seizure of their property in his role as Commander in Chief of the armed forces.

The Supreme Court found no "political question" difficulty [13] and proceeded forthwith to rule on the merits. The court, interpreting the Constitution concerning the President's executive and Commander in Chief powers, nullified the seizure and affirmed, not merely declaratory but injunctive relief against the President's Secretary of Commerce, saying (343 U.S. p. 587, 72 S.Ct. pp. 866–867):

"It is clear that if the President had authority to issue the order he did, it must be found in some provisions of the Constitution. And it is not claimed that express constitutional language grants this power to the President. The contention is that presidential power should be implied from the aggregate of his powers under the Constitution. Particular reliance is placed on provisions in Article II which say that 'the executive Power shall be vested in a President * * *'; that 'he shall take

Care that the Laws be faithfully executed'; and that he 'shall be Commander in Chief of the Army and Navy of the United States.' The order cannot properly be sustained as an exercise of the President's military power as Commander in Chief of the Armed Forces. The Government attempts to do so by citing a number of cases upholding broad powers in military commanders engaged in day-to-day fighting in a theater of war. Such cases need not concern us here. Even though 'theater of war' be an expanding concept, we cannot with faithfulness to our constitutional system hold that the Commander in Chief of the Armed Forces has the ultimate power as such to take possession of private property in order to keep labor disputes from stopping production. This is a job for the Nation's lawmakers, not for its military authorities." [14]

Notably, the court in *Youngstown* ruled out implied Commander in Chief powers even though in that case there was no express constitutional provision covering the subject matter there in-

---

13. Justice Frankfurter concurred in *Youngstown* notwithstanding what he described as the unpleasant judicial duty to find that the President had exceeded his powers, adding, at page 596, 72 S.Ct. p. 890, "To deny inquiry into the President's power in a case like this, because of the damage to the public interest to be feared from upsetting its exercise by him, would in effect always preclude inquiry into challenged power, which presumably only avowed great public interest brings into action. And so, with the utmost unwillingness, with every desire to avoid judicial inquiry into the powers and duties of the other two branches of the government, I cannot escape consideration of the legality of Executive Order No. 10340."

Justice Clark, concurring, quoted Justice Story concerning the propriety of a ruling on the merits, saying: "As Justice Story once said: 'For the executive department of the government, this court entertain the most entire respect; and admidst the multiplicity of cares in that department, it may, without any violation of decorum, be presumed, that

sometimes there may be an inaccurate construction of a law. It is our duty to expound the laws as we find them in the records of state; and we cannot, when called upon by the citizens of the country, refuse our opinion, however it may differ from that of very great authorities.' "

14. In *Youngstown*, Justice Clark, notwithstanding his emphasis upon the point that the Constitution grants to the President extensive authority in times of grave and imperative national emergency, concurred (p. 660, 72 S.Ct. p. 884) on the ground that in his view the Congress had in various pieces of legislation provided other means for dealing with producers who failed to supply defense material, adding, "Where Congress has laid down specific procedures to deal with the type of crisis confronting the President, he must follow those procedures in meeting the crisis,"—a statement which we believe to be even more strongly applicable where, not merely the Congress but the Constitution, itself, lays down in Article I, Section 8(11) the specific procedure for committing the nation to war.

volved—the power to seize private property as a war measure. In our pending case there is an express constitutional provision concerning the subject matter —the provision of Article I, Section 8(11) that the power to declare war (and thus to commit, not only property, but also human life to war) is vested, not in the Commander in Chief, but in the Congress—a stronger reason for excluding any implied presidential power to the contrary.

It seems to this court that to strike down as unconstitutional a President's wartime seizure of a few private steel mills but to shy away on "political question" grounds from interfering with a presidential war, itself, would be to strain at a gnat and swallow a camel.

In Baker v. Carr, the question was whether the State of Tennessee, having exercised its power to determine the qualifications of its voters and regulate its elections—powers reserved to the states by Article I, Sections 2 and 4 of the Constitution subject only to congressional supervision under Section 4, could be required by the judiciary to reapportion legislative districts which the state had allegedly apportioned for election of members to its State General Assembly without regard to population. Plaintiffs claimed that this had debased their votes and that it amounted to a deprival of equal protection of the law. The court, after an extensive review of the political question doctrine [15] held that the question before it was not a political question and that the court could and did order reapportionment.

In Kansas Law Review, 449 at pp. 479–485, the author of an article on this subject makes a detailed analysis of these Baker v. Carr tests (see footnote 15), as applied to the Vietnam situation and comes pursuasively to the conclusion that none of them is sufficient to justify judicial avoidance of responsibility for deciding the legal, constitutional question raised by Article I, Section 8(11) of the Constitution.

In Powell v. McCormack, 395 U.S. 486 at pp. 518, 522, 548–549, 89 S.Ct. 1944, 23 L.Ed.2d 491 (1969), the Supreme Court found no "political question" difficulty when it held that the House of Representatives, although expressly vested by the Constitution, Article I, Section 5(1) (2), with the power to judge the qualifications of its own members, had exceeded its constitutional power when it excluded the duly elected petitioner for reasons other than the qualifications specified in Article I, Section 2(2), holding that the question of the constitutional power of the House, and the question whether such power had been exceeded, is a justiciable matter of constitutional interpretation and the responsibility of the court as ultimate interpreter of the Constitution; further, that none of the formulations of the political question doctrine, as stated in Baker v. Carr, barred adjudication of the issue.[16]

---

15. In Baker v. Carr, the court concluded (369 U.S. p. 217, 82 S.Ct. 691) that the political question doctrine assumes at least one of the following: (1) a textually demonstrable constitutional commitment of the issue to a coordinate political department, (2) a lack of judicially discoverable and manageable standards for resolving the issue, (3) the impossibility of deciding without an initial policy determination of a kind clearly for nonjudicial discretion, (4) the impossibility of a court's undertaking independent resolution without expressing lack of the respect due coordinate branches of government, (5) an unusual need for unquestioning adherence to a political decision already made, (6) the potentiality of embarrassment from multifarious pronounce-

ments by various departments on one question.

16. On this subject of "political question" the court in *Powell* said (pp. 548–549, 89 S.Ct. p. 1978): "Respondents' alternate contention is that the case presents a political question because judicial resolution of petitioners' claim would produce a 'potentially embarrassing confrontation between coordinate branches' of the Federal Government. But, as our interpretation of Art. I, § 5, discloses, a determination of petitioner Powell's right to sit would require no more than an interpretation of the Constitution. Such a determination falls within the traditional role accorded courts to interpret the law, and does not involve a 'lack of the respect due

In view of the foregoing three decisions of the Supreme Court, *Youngstown, Baker* and *Powell,*—all of which found no "political question" obstacle in situations essentially similar to the plain constitutional interpretation issue here presented, it is not surprising that some lower courts have come recently to reject the "political question" doctrine as an excuse for summarily refusing to decide the Vietnam constitutional war power issue on the merits—the Second Circuit Court of Appeal in Berk v. Laird, 429 F.2d 302 (1970), already cited supra, and the District Court for the Eastern District of New York in Orlando v. Laird, 317 F.Supp. 1013 (1970), already cited supra.

In *Berk,* the trial court had raised no political question difficulty but had denied preliminary injunction on grounds that such an injunction against ordering the serviceman plaintiff to Vietnam would invite a flood of similar applications and, further, that plaintiff had not made a prima facie showing on the merits. The Court of Appeals affirmed the denial of preliminary injunction relief but, notably, remanded the case for further proceedings with directions, not to dismiss, but to give the plaintiff an opportunity to show whether the issue of the constitutionality of the war was really a political issue.[17]

Shortly following *Berk* came *Orlando, supra,* wherein the District Court, considering the challenge by a serviceman of an order requiring Vietnam service, expressly held that the question whether the decision to commit the nation to war in Vietnam has been made by the properly authorized branch of the federal government, is *not* a "political question" but, rather, a purely justiciable question, pointing out the distinction between such a justiciable question, on the one hand, and the different, truly political nature of an administrative decision once made by the branch of government to which the decisional power is constitutionally committed.

In both *Berk* and *Orlando, supra,* the courts dealt with the central constitutional issue involved. In *Berk* the Court of Appeals directed that, if the trial court should find that the issue was not really "political," it should then proceed to determine on the merits whether con-

---

[a] coordinate [branch] of government,' nor does it involve an 'initial policy determination of a kind clearly for nonjudicial discretion.' Baker v. Carr, 369 U.S. 186, at 217, [82 S.Ct. 691, 7 L.Ed. 2d 663]. Our system of government requires that federal courts on occasion interpret the Constitution in a manner at variance with the construction given the document by another branch. The alleged conflict that such an adjudication may cause cannot justify the courts' avoiding their constitutional responsibility. See United States v. Brown, 381 U.S. 437, 462, [85 S.Ct. 1707, 14 L.Ed.2d 484] (1965); Youngstown Sheet & Tube Co. v. Sawyer, 343 U.S. 579, 613–614, [72 S.Ct. 863, 96 L.Ed. 1153] (1952) (Frankfurter, J., concurring); Myers v. United States, 272 U.S. 52, 293, [47 S.Ct. 21, 71 L.Ed. 160] (1926) (Brandeis, J., dissenting). Nor does any of the other formulations of a political question 'inextricable from the case at bar.' Baker v. Carr, *supra,* [369 U.S.] at 217, [82 S. Ct. 691]. Petitioners seek a determination that the House was without power to exclude Powell from the 90th Con-

gress, which, we have seen, requires an interpretation of the Constitution—determination for which clearly there are 'judicially * * * manageable standards.' Finally, a judicial resolution of petitioners' claim will not result in 'multifarious pronouncements by various departments on one question.' For, as we noted in Baker v. Carr, *supra,* at 211, [82 S.Ct. 691], it is the responsibility of this court to act as the ultimate interpreter of the Constitution. Marbury v. Madison, (1 Cranch) 137, [2 L.Ed. 60] (1803). Thus, we conclude that petitioners' claim is not barred by the political question doctrine, and, having determined that the claim is otherwise generally justiciable, we hold that the case is justiciable."

17. It is true that the Court in *Berk,* although declining to decide the point, expresses some concern about plaintiff's ability to suggest a "judicially discoverable standard" for resolving the question of what joint legislative action would be sufficient to authorize various levels of military action.

gressional concern with the Vietnam war has been such as to constitute the congressional approval required by Article I, Section 8(11) of the Constitution.

In *Orlando,* the court, having held the issue before it to be justiciable, proceeded on the merits to first decide the legal phase of the issue, i. e., the meaning of Article I, Section 811), the congressional declaration of law clause, considered in relation to the powers of the President under Article II.

The Constitution was interpreted by the court to mean that: "The systematic vesting of control over the means and the determination of the occasions of belligerency in the Congress makes inevitable that no combat activity of magnitude in ,size and duration can continue without affirmative and systematic legislative support. That Vietnam long ago attained that magnitude is history."

The court then went on to hold, however, that the degree and kind of congressional concern with the Vietnam war, specifically congressional implementation of the war by huge annual military appropriations, amendments to the Selective Service Act and provision of veterans' benefits [18] have in fact been such as to amount to "the reality of the collaborative action of the executive and the legislative branches required by the Constitution"—as interpreted by that court.[19]

Earlier (1968) in *Sisson, supra,* a district court had similarly proceeded on the merits to interpret Article I, Section 8(11) of the Constitution, holding in substance and effect that, although its declaration of war provision is important, it is not the only way in which the nation can be committed to such a war as exists in Vietnam; that this can be accomplished by joint, cooperative action of the President and the Congress short of a declaration of war; that the declaration of war provision of Article I, Section 8(11) is not exclusive of other means of authorizing such a commitment; that under the doctrine of implied powers, McCulloch v. Maryland, 17 U.S. (4 Wheat) 316, 4 L.Ed. 579, the national government has implied powers beyond those expressly set forth in the Constitution; specifically, that commitment on the nation to war can be made either (1) by an unlimited declaration of war, or (2) by a limited undeclared war approved by the President and the Congress, i. e., the President not acting alone but with congressional cooperation in the form of supportive legislation, appropriations and resolutions such as the Gulf of Tonquin Resolution.[20]

Then, having interpreted the Constitution as permitting implied congressional approval of war by the supportive legislative and appropriations route—as well as by declaration of war—the court, either inadvertently or deliberately, omitted to find on the factual issue thus presented, i. e., whether the kind and degree of congressional action in the Vietnam situation has or has not been sufficient to amount to the cooperative joint congressional action required by that method of committing the nation to war.

18. Notably, the court did not consider the Gulf of Tonquin Resolution as any significant contribution to what the court finds to be the collaborative action of the Congress, conceding that "The place of the controversial Tonkin Gulf Resolution in the whole of Congressional action is unclear; its importance lay in its practical effect on the presidential initiative rather than its constitutional meaning, but it has not the compelling significance of the steady legislative support of the prosecution of the war."

19. It is difficult to reconcile this rationale of implied ratification by appropriations,

etc., with the rationale of the Supreme Court in Greene v. McElroy, 360 U.S. 474, 507, 79 S.Ct. 1400, 3 L.Ed.2d 1377, supra, on the same subject.

20. It is difficult to reconcile this district court rationale of an implied power of the congressional branch to validate a presidential war by various means other than an explicit declaration of war under Article I, Section 8(11) with the rationale of the Supreme Court in *Youngstown, supra,* to the effect that no such implication would be drawn with respect to the power of the executive branch under Article II.

Instead, the court, apparently assuming that implied congressional ratification could be found from its appropriations [21] moved directly to the conclusion that the choice of one of these two permissible methods of approving war is a "political question" beyond the province or capacity of the court and wholly within the province of the coordinate governmental branches involved—the Congress and the President.

## CONCLUSIONS

In summary, after years of litigation in the federal courts, only one court, the Massachusetts District Court in Orlando v. Laird, *supra*, has been able (with an assist from *Berk* and with some suggestions out of *Sisson*) to completely extricate itself from the three-fold obstacle course of "no standing", "sovereign immunity" and "political question" and emerge with what is at least, whether right or wrong, a decision on the *merits*.[22]

Whether the ultimate decision on the merits reached by the court in Orlando v. Laird, *supra*, should be followed by this court is a matter that cannot be decided at this juncture of the pending case because, although defendants have appeared herein and have moved to dismiss upon the three grounds above discussed, they have not yet filed responsive pleadings or motions directed to the merits of the central question here presented.

The reasoned conclusion reached in *Orlando* on this central issue is, of course, entitled to respect and careful consideration. On the other hand, a strong case can be made for the proposition that compliance with the Constitution of the United States and its plain provision that the power to declare war lies, not in the President, but in the Congress, should be made to rest upon

something better than the ambivalences of congressional inaction or mere defense legislation, appropriations and questionable resolutions; that such compliance calls for nothing less than what the Constitution plainly says—a declaration of war by the Congress or at least an equally explicit congressional expression, either general or limited, but in any event such as to clearly indicate a congressional intent to meet its responsibilities under Article I, Section 8(11) by consenting to (or refusing to consent to), the initiation or continuance of war by the President; that unless the President receives, upon his request or otherwise, such a declaratory consent, either general or limited, as soon as reasonably possible, any undeclared war becomes a usurpation by the President or an abdication by the Congress—or, perhaps, both.

It is argued that, unless the courts so interpret the Constitution, Article I, Section 8(11) will be so devitalized as to remain subject to evasion, as it has been evaded in some past wars and up to now in the Vietnam war, and the American people will be thus deprived of an opportunity to reliably judge the Congress, the President, or both, in terms of the constitutionality of their conduct.

Indeed, it has already been charged that the failure of the courts to decide the constitutional question one way or the other, has contributed to the controversy and the consequent unprecedented disunity of our country on the Vietnam war issue (see Hughes, 43 N.Y. Law Review (1968), cited in the *Douglas* dissent in Holmes v. United States, 391 U. S. 936, 88 S.Ct. 1835, 20 L.Ed.2d 856).

Whatever the ultimate decision on the merits of the constitutional question may be, we are of the opinion that the courts, eschewing indecision, inaction or avoidance on such grounds as "no stand-

---

21. It is also difficult to reconcile this rationale of implied ratification by appropriations with the rationale of the Supreme Court in Greene v. McElroy, 360 U.S. 474, 507, 79 S.Ct. 1400, 3 L.Ed.2d 1377, *supra*, on the same subject.

22. We agree with *Orlando* insofar as it rejects these jurisdictional and procedural grounds for denying a judicial ruling on the merits.

ing," "sovereign immunity" and "political question," should discharge their traditional responsibility for interpreting the Constitution of the United States.

The Supreme Court has demonstrated its resourcefulness in finding ways and means of eliminating or minimizing undesirable, practical consequences that might otherwise follow major decisions charting new requirements in the field of constitutional law. For example, in Powell v. McCormack, *supra*, the court, annulling the exclusion action of the House of Representatives, held (395 U.S. pp. 517–518, 89 S.Ct. 1944, 23 L.Ed.2d 491) that coercive, injunctive relief need not be granted when deemed inappropriate under circumstances, indicating that a simple declaratory decree resolving the constitutional question would be preferable. The Supreme Court has also used the device of non-retroactivity with respect to the past and the device of deliberate or reasonable speed with respect to the future. In any event, the Supreme Court would not be called upon to decide what to do about the Vienam war—only to decide the legal question: By whose authority—the President, the Congress or both, can the Vietnam war be continued (or discontinued) and how must that authorization be expressed to comply with the plain, but very solemn and tremendously important provisions of Article I, Section 8(11).

Upon the foregoing considerations, this court has made its order, filed herewith, designed to further, so far as a District Court can appropriately do so, an ultimate ruling in our Ninth Circuit and, hopefully, by the Supreme Court, upon all the important issues here considered.

It is ordered as follows:

(1) Defendants' motion to dismiss on the grounds of (1) no standing, (2) sovereign immunity, and (3) nonjusticiable political question, is hereby denied as to plaintiffs Mottola, Schwartz and Gross —but granted as to plaintiff Olson on the ground of no standing.

(2) Defendants, having appeared herein, shall file their responsive pleadings within fifteen (15) days from expiration of defendants' statutory time to plead—whichever is later.

[11] (3) That injunctive relief from this court, either preliminary or final, as prayed by plaintiffs, would be inappropriate and plaintiffs' motion for a preliminary injunction herein is, therefore, denied—without prejudice, however, to plaintiffs' prayer for a declaratory judgment of this court concerning the legal rights of the three plaintiffs herein (Mottola, Schwartz and Gross).

[12] (4) That, insofar as these named plaintiffs claim to represent and sue in behalf of other citizens of the United States, such representative and class action status is hereby disallowed.

(5) All further proceedings in this case shall be under a rule that, in the event declaratory judgment is ever rendered in favor of plaintiffs, the effect of any such judgment will be stayed pending any appeal by defendants.

# Orlando v. Laird

**Salvatore ORLANDO, Plaintiff-Appellant,**

**v.**

**Melvin LAIRD, individually and as Secretary of Defense of the United States; and Stanley R. Resor, individually and as Secretary of the Army of the United States, Defendants-Appellees.**

**Malcolm A. BERK, Plaintiff-Appellant,**

**v.**

**Melvin LAIRD, individually, and as Secretary of Defense of the United States, Stanley R. Resor, individually, and as Secretary of the Army of the United States, and Col. T. F. Spencer, individually, and as Chief of Staff, United States Army Engineers Center, Fort Belvoir, Defendants-Appellees.**

Nos. 477, 478, Dockets 35270, 35535.

United States Court of Appeals,
Second Circuit.

Argued March 3, 1971.

Decided April 20, 1971.

Leon Friedman, New York Civil Liberties Union, New York City (Burt Neuborne, Kunstler, Kunstler & Hyman, Norman Dorsen and Kay Ellen Hayes, New York City, on the brief), for plaintiff-appellant Salvatore Orlando.

Norman Dorsen, New York City (Leon Friedman, Burt Neuborne, New York Civil Liberties Union, Theodore C. Sorensen, Kay Ellen Hayes, and Marc Luxemberg, New York City, on the brief), for plaintiff-appellant Malcolm A. Berk.

Edward R. Neaher, U. S. Atty., E. D. New York (Robert A. Morse, Chief Asst. U. S. Atty., David G. Trager, Edward R. Korman, and James D. Porter, Jr., Asst. U. S. Attys., E. D. New York, on the brief), for defendants-appellees.

Before LUMBARD, Chief Judge, and KAUFMAN and ANDERSON, Circuit Judges.

ANDERSON, Circuit Judge:

Shortly after receiving orders to report for transfer to Vietnam, Pfc. Malcolm A. Berk and Sp. E5 Salvatore Orlando, enlistees in the United States Army, commenced separate actions in June, 1970, seeking to enjoin the Secretary of Defense, the Secretary of the Army and the commanding officers, who signed their deployment orders, from enforcing them. The plaintiffs-appellants contended that these executive officers exceeded their constitutional authority by ordering them to participate in a war not properly authorized by Congress.

In Orlando's case the district court held in abeyance his motion for a preliminary injunction pending disposition in this court of Berk's expedited appeal from a denial of the same preliminary relief. On June 19, 1970 we affirmed the denial of a preliminary injunction in Berk v. Laird, 429 F.2d 302 (2 Cir. 1970), but held that Berk's claim that orders to fight must be authorized by joint executive-legislative action was justiciable. The case was remanded for a hearing on his application for a permanent injunction. We held that the war declaring power of Congress, enumerated in Article I, section 8, of the Constitution, contains a "discoverable standard calling for *some* mutual participation by Congress," and directed that Berk be given an opportunity "to provide a method for resolving the question of when specified joint legislative-executive action is sufficient to authorize various levels of military activity," and thereby escape application of the political question doctrine to his claim that congressional participation has been in this instance, insufficient.

After a hearing on June 23, 1970, Judge Dooling in the district court denied Orlando's motion for a preliminary injunction on the ground that his deployment orders were constitutionally authorized, because Congress, by "appropriating the nation's treasure and conscripting its manpower," had "furnished forth the sinew of war" and because "the reality of the collaborative action of the executive and the legislative required by the Constitution has been present from the earliest stages." Orlando v. Laird, 317 F.Supp. 1013, 1019 (E.D.N.Y.1970).

On remand of Berk's action, Judge Judd of the district court granted the appellees' motion for summary judgment. Finding that there had been joint action by the President and Congress, he ruled that the method of congressional collaboration was a political question. Berk v. Laird, 317 F.Supp. 715, 728 (E.D.N.Y.1970).

The appellants contend that the respective rulings of the district court that congressional authorization could be expressed through appropriations and other supporting legislation misconstrue the war declaring clause, and alternatively, that congressional enactments relating to Vietnam were incorrectly interpreted.

It is the appellants' position that the sufficiency of congressional authorization is a matter within judicial competence because that question can be resolved by "judicially discoverable and manageable standards" dictated by the congressional power "to declare War." See Baker v. Carr, 369 U.S. 186, 217, 82 S.Ct. 691, 7 L.Ed.2d 663 (1962); Powell v. McCormack, 395 U.S. 486, 89 S.Ct. 1944, 23 L.Ed.2d 491 (1969). They interpret the constitutional provision to require an express and explicit congressional authorization of the Vietnam hostilities though not necessarily in the words, "We declare that the United States of America is at war with North Vietnam." In support of this construction they point out that the original intent of the clause was to place responsibility for the initiation of war upon the body most responsive to popular will and argue that historical developments have not altered the need for significant congressional participation in such commitments of national resources. They further assert that, without a requirement of express and explicit congressional authorization, developments committing the nation to war, as a *fait accompli,* became the inevitable adjuncts of presidential direction of foreign policy, and, because military appropriations and other war-implementing enactments lack an explicit authorization of particular hostilities, they cannot, as a matter of law, be considered sufficient.

Alternatively, appellants would have this court find that, because the President requested accelerating defense appropriations and extensions of the conscription laws after the war was well under way, Congress was, in effect, placed in a strait jacket and could not freely decide whether or not to enact this legislation, but rather was compelled to do so. For this reason appellants claim that such enactments cannot, as a factual matter, be considered sufficient congressional approval or ratification.

The Government on the other hand takes the position that the suits concern a non-justiciable political question; that the military action in South Vietnam was authorized by Congress in the "Joint Resolution to Promote the Maintenance of Internal Peace and Security in Southeast Asia"[1] (the Tonkin Gulf Resolution) considered in connection with the Seato Treaty; and that the military action was authorized and ratified by congressional appropriations expressly designated for use in support of the military operations in Vietnam.

---

1. The two district judges differed over the significance of the Tonkin Gulf Resolution, Pub.Law 88–408, 78 Stat. 384, August 10, 1964, in the context of the entire course of the congressional action which related to Vietnam. Judge Judd relied in part on the Resolution as supplying the requisite congressional authorization; Judge Dooling found that its importance lay in its practical effect on the presidential initiative rather than its constitutional meaning.

Although the Senate repealed the Resolution on June 24, 1970, it remained in effect at the time appellants' deployment orders issued. Cong.Record S. 9670 (June 24, 1970); *see* Foreign Military Sales Act of 1971 § 12, P.L. 91–672 (January 12, 1971). The repeal was based on the proposition that the Resolution was no longer necessary and amounted to no more than a gesture on the part of the Congress at the time the executive had taken substantial steps to unwind the conflict, when the principal issue was the speed of deceleration and termination of the war.

[1, 2] We held in the first *Berk* opinion that the constitutional delegation of the war-declaring power to the Congress contains a discoverable and manageable standard imposing on the Congress a duty of mutual participation in the prosecution of war. Judicial scrutiny of that duty, therefore, is not foreclosed by the political question doctrine. Baker v. Carr, *supra;* Powell v. McCormack, *supra.* As we see it, the test is whether there is any action by the Congress sufficient to authorize or ratify the military activity in question. The evidentiary materials produced at the hearings in the district court clearly disclose that this test is satisfied.

The Congress and the Executive have taken mutual and joint action in the prosecution and support of military operations in Southeast Asia from the beginning of those operations. The Tonkin Gulf Resolution, enacted August 10, 1964 (repealed December 31, 1970) was passed at the request of President Johnson and, though occasioned by specific

naval incidents in the Gulf of Tonkin, was expressed in broad language which clearly showed the state of mind of the Congress and its intention fully to implement and support the military and naval actions taken by and planned to be taken by the President at that time in Southeast Asia, and as might be required in the future "to prevent further aggression." Congress has ratified the executive's initiatives by appropriating billions of dollars to carry out military operations in Southeast Asia[2] and by extending the Military Selective Service Act with full knowledge that persons conscripted under that Act had been, and would continue to be, sent to Vietnam. Moreover, it specifically conscripted manpower to fill "the substantial induction calls necessitated by the current Vietnam buildup."[3]

There is, therefore, no lack of clear evidence to support a conclusion that there was an abundance of continuing mutual participation in the prosecution of the war. Both branches collaborated

---

2. In response to the demands of the military operations the executive during the 1960s ordered more and more men and material into the war zone; and congressional appropriations have been commensurate with each new level of fighting. Until 1965, defense appropriations had not earmarked funds for Vietnam. In May of that year President Johnson asked Congress for an emergency supplemental appropriation "to provide our forces [then numbering 35,000] with the best and most modern supplies and equipment." 111 Cong.Rec. 9283 (May 4, 1965). Congress appropriated $700 million for use "upon determination by the President that such action is necessary in connection with military activities in Southeast Asia." Pub.L. 89–18, 79 Stat. 109 (1965). Appropriation acts in each subsequent year explicitly authorized expenditures for men and material sent to Vietnam. The 1967 appropriations act, for example, declared Congress' "firm intention to provide all necessary support for members of the Armed Forces of the United States fighting in Vietnam" and supported "the efforts being made by the President of the United States * * * to prevent an expansion of the war in Vietnam and to bring that conflict to an end through a negotiated settlement

* * *." Pub.L. 90–5, 81 Stat. 5 (1967).

The district court opinion in Berk v. Laird, 317 F.Supp. 715 (E.D.N.Y.1970), sets out relevant portions of each of these military appropriation acts and discusses their legislative history.

3. In H.Rep.No.267, 90th Cong., 1st Sess. 38 (1967), in addition to extending the conscription mechanism, Congress continued a suspension of the permanent ceiling on the active duty strength of the Armed Forces, fixed at 2 million men, and replaced it with a secondary ceiling of 5 million. The House Report recommending extension of the draft concluded that the permanent manpower limitations "are much lower than the currently required strength." The Report referred to President Johnson's selective service message which said, " * * * that without the draft we cannot realistically expect to meet our present commitments or the requirements we can now foresee and that volunteers alone could be expected to man a force of little more than 2.0 million. The present number of personnel on active duty is about 3.3 million and it is scheduled to reach almost 3.5 million by June, 1968 if the present conflict is not concluded by then." H.Rep.No.267, 90th Cong., 1st Sess. 38, 41 (1967).

in the endeavor, and neither could long maintain such a war without the concurrence and cooperation of the other.

[3] Although appellants do not contend that Congress can exercise its war-declaring power only through a formal declaration, they argue that congressional authorization cannot, as a matter of law, be inferred from military appropriations or other war-implementing legislation that does not contain an express and explicit authorization for the making of war by the President. Putting aside for a moment the explicit authorization of the Tonkin Gulf Resolution, we disagree with appellants' interpretation of the declaration clause for neither the language nor the purpose underlying that provision prohibits an inference of the fact of authorization from such legislative action as we have in this instance. The framers' intent to vest the war power in Congress is in no way defeated by permitting an inference of authorization from legislative action furnishing the manpower and materials of war for the protracted military operation in Southeast Asia.

The choice, for example, between an explicit declaration on the one hand and a resolution and war-implementing legislation, on the other, as the medium for expression of congressional consent involves "the exercise of a discretion demonstrably committed to the * * * legislature," Baker v. Carr, *supra* 9 at 211, 82 S.Ct. at 707, and therefore, invokes the political question doctrine.

Such a choice involves an important area of decision making in which, through mutual influence and reciprocal action between the President and the Congress, policies governing the relationship between this country and other parts of the world are formulated in the best interests of the United States. If there can be nothing more than minor military operations conducted under any circumstances, short of an express and explicit declaration of war by Congress, then extended military operations could not be conducted even though both the Congress and the President were agreed that they were necessary and were also agreed that a formal declaration of war would place the nation in a posture in its international relations which would be against its best interests. For the judicial branch to enunciate and enforce such a standard would be not only extremely unwise but also would constitute a deep invasion of the political question domain. As the Government says, " * * * decisions regarding the form and substance of congressional enactments authorizing hostilities are determined by highly complex considerations of diplomacy, foreign policy and military strategy inappropriate to judicial inquiry." It would, indeed, destroy the flexibility of action which the executive and legislative branches must have in dealing with other sovereigns. What has been said and done by both the President and the Congress in their collaborative conduct of the military operations in Vietnam implies a consensus on the advisability of *not* making a formal declaration of war because it would be contrary to the interests of the United States to do so. The making of a policy decision of that kind is clearly within the constitutional domain of those two branches and is just as clearly not within the competency or power of the judiciary.

[4] Beyond determining that there has been *some* mutual participation between the Congress and the President, which unquestionably exists here, with action by the Congress sufficient to authorize or ratify the military activity at issue, it is clear that the constitutional propriety of the means by which Congress has chosen to ratify and approve the protracted military operations in Southeast Asia is a political question. The form which congressional authorization should take is one of policy, committed to the discretion of the Congress and outside the power and competency of the judiciary, because there are no intelligible and objectively manageable standards by which to judge such ac-

tions. Baker v. Carr, *supra,* 369 U.S. at 217, 82 S.Ct. 691; Powell v. McCormack, *supra,* 395 U.S. at 518, 89 S.Ct. 1944.

The judgments of the district court are affirmed.

IRVING R. KAUFMAN, Circuit Judge (concurring):

In light of the adoption by Congress of the Tonkin Gulf Resolution, and the clear evidence of continuing and distinctly expressed participation by the legislative branch in the prosecution of the war, I agree that the judgments below must be affirmed.

# Commonwealth of Massachusetts v. Laird

COMMONWEALTH OF MASSACHU-
SETTS et al., Plaintiffs, Appellants,

v.

Melvin R. LAIRD, etc., Defendant,
Appellee.

No. 71–1177.

United States Court of Appeals,
First Circuit.

Oct. 21, 1971.

Robert J. Condlin, Asst. Atty. Gen.,
with whom Robert H. Quinn, Atty. Gen.,
Walter H. Mayo, III, and Daniel J. John-
edis, Asst. Atty. Gen., were on brief, for
appellants.

William A. Brown, Asst. U. S. Atty.,
with whom Herbert F. Travers, Jr., U. S.
Atty., and James N. Gabriel, Asst. U. S.
Atty., were on brief, for appellee.

David L. Norvell, Atty. Gen., State of
New Mexico, on brief pro se, amicus
curiae.

Before ALDRICH, Chief Judge, Mc-
ENTEE and COFFIN, Circuit Judges.

COFFIN, Circuit Judge.

The question sought to be raised in
this action is whether the United States
involvement in Vietnam is unconstitutional, a war not having been declared or
ratified by the Congress. Plaintiffs seek
a declaration of unconstitutionality and
an injunction against the Secretary of
Defense barring further orders to duty
in Southeast Asia of Massachusetts inhabitants if within ninety days of a decree the Congress has not declared war
or otherwise authorized United States
participation.

The individual plaintiffs are residents
of Massachusetts and members of the
United States forces who are either serving in Southeast Asia or are subject to
such service. They allege that their
forced service in an undeclared war is a
deprivation of liberty in violation of the
due process clause of the Fifth Amendment. The Commonwealth of Massachusetts is a plaintiff pursuant to an act of
its legislature proscribing military service by its inhabitants in the conduct of
extra-territorial non-emergency armed
hostilities in the absence of a Congressional declaration of war and directing
its Attorney General to bring an action
in the Supreme Court or, in the event of
a final determination that such action is
not one of which that Court has original
jurisdiction,[1] an action in an inferior
federal court to defend the rights of its
inhabitants and of the Commonwealth.
M.G.L.A. c. 33 app., § 26–1.

The complaint, alleging active engagement by the United States in Indochina
in armed hostilities "for the last six
years," traces the familiar and unhappy
history of escalation since 1950: assistance to the French, the first American
casualties in 1959, the accumulation of
23,000 "military advisors" by 1964, the
Gulf of Tonkin Resolution in the same
year, and the subsequent exponential increase in air strike sorties, troops, casualties, and expenditures. The complaint
repeatedly alleges the absence of a Congressional declaration of war or ratification. The Commonwealth alleges damage
both as a sovereign state and as *parens
patriae,* citing the deaths and injuries of
its inhabitants, consequential loss of
their prospective civic and tax contributions, increased claims of dependents, additional burdens on its economy, disadvantage to its absentee voters, mass demonstrations, and damage to its public's
morale. It also asserts its interest in
"maintaining the integrity of the Constitution" which is allegedly impaired in
that "one branch, the executive, has exercised war-making powers, which the
Commonwealth and its sister states had
agreed would be exercised only by Congress."

The district court dismissed the complaint, relying on the alternate grounds
that the controversy was not justiciable
and that, if justiciable, continual Congressional legislation in support of the
Vietnam war implied sufficient authorization. 327 F.Supp. 378 (D.Mass.1971).

[1–3]  As to threshold matters, we reject respondent's claim that subject matter jurisdiction is lacking. As we understand the argument, it is partly a restatement of arguments against justiciability.

---

1. The Supreme Court denied leave to file
a similar complaint, Justice Douglas contending in dissent that Massachusetts
had standing and that the matter was
justiciable. Massachusetts v. Laird, 400
U.S. 886, 91 S.Ct. 128, 27 L.Ed.2d 130
(1970). Since the disposition does not
purport to decide the case, it technically
does not qualify as a "final determination" as required by the Massachusetts
statute. We do not deem this fact relevant to the proceedings before us.

What remains is the contention that, since the substantiality of plaintiffs' constitutional claims is challenged, there is lack of subject matter jurisdiction, citing Powell v. McCormack, 395 U.S. 486, 514 n. 37, 89 S.Ct. 1944, 23 L.Ed.2d 491 (1969). No such doctrine can be drawn from *Powell*; the contrary was made clear in Baker v. Carr, 369 U.S. 186, 199, 82 S.Ct. 691, 7 L.Ed.2d 663 (1962), i. e., that only if a claim is absolutely devoid of merit or frivolous could dismissal for lack of jurisdiction be justified. Nor do we find any merit in the claim that the individual plaintiffs, particularly those serving in Southeast Asia, lack standing. Berk v. Laird, 429 F.2d 302 (2d Cir. 1970).

We do not see, however, that Massachusetts achieves any special status as a protector of the rights of its citizens, solely as United States citizens, and not as a sovereign with unique interests. South Carolina v. Katzenbach, 383 U.S. 301, 86 S.Ct. 803, 15 L.Ed.2d 769 (1966).

*See also*, Note, The Supreme Court as Arbitrator in the Conflict Between Presidential and Congressional War-Making Powers, 50 B.U.L.Rev. 78, 79 n. 9 (Special Issue 1970). The traditional rationale is that the federal government is "the ultimate *parens patriae* of every American citizen," 383 U.S. at 324, 86 S. Ct. at 816. This admittedly seems inappropriate in a suit challenging the constitutionality of a war waged by the putative *parens*. Suffice it to say that some of the plaintiffs are properly before us.

While the challenge to the constitutionality of our participation in the Vietnam war is a large question, so also is the question whether such an issue is given to the courts to decide, under the circumstances of this case. The Supreme Court has thus far not ruled on the latter issue in this context. Other federal courts have differed in their rationales.[2] Scholars have probed "the political question" and have found it just as much an impenetrable thicket as have the courts.[3]

2. The spectrum of analysis is indicated by the positions taken vis-a-vis the "political question" in the following cases: Luftig v. McNamara, 126 U.S.App.D.C. 4, 373 F.2d 664, 666, cert. denied, 387 U.S. 945, 87 S.Ct. 207, 18 L.Ed.2d 1332 (1967)—"plainly the exclusive province of Congress and the Executive"; United States v. Sisson, 294 F.Supp. 511 (D.Mass. 1968)—evidence, policy considerations, and constitutional principles beyond normal judicial expertise; Velvel v. Johnson, 287 F.Supp. 846 (D.Kan. 1968)—activities of government "under the direction of the President, fall within the political question", 287 F.Supp. at 850; also, committed to both branches, id. at 852; also, "decisions of basic national policy, as of foreign policy, present no judicially cognizable issue", id. at 853; Davi v. Laird, 318 F.Supp. 478 (W.D.Va.1970), "clearly demonstrat[e] constitutional commitment * * * to the legislative branch", id. at 482, and to the other "political branches", id. at 484; Berk v. Laird [I], 317 F.Supp. 715 (E.D.N.Y. 1970) (unreported)—issue committed to Commander-in-Chief; Berk v. Laird [II], 429 F.2d 302 (2d Cir. 1970)—orders to fight are generally justiciable, the judicially discoverable standard being some mutual participation of Congress and the executive, but would be political question

if standards lacking to judge adequacy of participation; Berk v. Laird [III], 317 F.Supp. 715 (E.D.N.Y.1970)—"Congressional authorization here is sufficiently 'explicit' to satisfy constitutional requirements", id. at 730, but method of authorization is a political question; Orlando v. Laird [I], 317 F.Supp. 1013 (E.D.N.Y.1970)—"reality of the collaborative action * * * required by the Constitution has been present", id. at 1019; Orlando v. Laird [II], 443 F.2d 1039 (2d Cir. April 20, 1971), cert. denied, October 12, 1971, 92 S.Ct. 94 —standard is some mutual participation, sufficiency of participation is not foreclosed by political question doctrine, but choice in form between a Congressional declaration and war-supporting legislation is a political question, courts having no standards by which to judge. *Contra* Mottola v. Nixon, 318 F.Supp. 538 (N.D. Cal.1970)—this is an issue of "plain constitutional interpretation", id. at 551, from which courts ought not "shy away on 'political question' grounds", id. at 550.

3. For overview, see Note, The Supreme Court as Arbitrator in the Conflict Between Presidential and Congressional War-Making Powers, 50 B.U.L.Rev. 78, 83–84 (Special Issue 1970). For analysis

In our own search for a principled resolution of the question of the appropriateness of our deciding the merits, we seek first to understand the theory of the complaint, then to identify the appropriate legal standard, and finally to apply that standard to the issue raised.

[4]  The Massachusetts statute, pursuant to which plaintiffs bring this action, is based on the simple proposition that participation by the United States in hostilities other than an emergency is unconstitutional unless "initially authorized or subsequently ratified by a congressional declaration of war according to the constitutionally established procedures in Article 1, Section 8 [Clause 11th], of the Constitution." [4] M.G.L.A. c. 33 app., § 26–1. The complaint expands this theory by recognizing that constitutionality could be achieved by a "constitutional equivalent" for a declaration of war or by specific ratification of executive actions.

In any event, despite some language charging the executive with exercising the "war-making powers" of Congress, the thrust of the complaint is not that the executive has usurped a power—the power to declare war—given to Congress. There is no claim that the executive has made any declaration. The charge is, rather, that since hostilities have long since transcended a response to an emergency, both Congress and the executive have acted unconstitutionally in sustaining the hostilities without a Congressional declaration of war. In effect the relief sought by the complaint is to order the executive to "get out or get a declaration from Congress."

[5]  Plaintiffs have understandably devoted considerable attention to the criteria of justiciability catalogued in Baker v. Carr, 369 U.S. 186, 82 S.Ct. 691 (1962).[5]  In assessing what have been termed the "prudential" and "functional" factors,[6] they assert that there are judicially discoverable standards for determining whether hostilities in Vietnam require a declaration of war; that no nonjudicial policy determination is required—only a determination of authority; that no lack of respect to coordinate branches will be shown, but, rather, respect for the Constitution; that circumstances do not require unquestioning adherence to a political decision already made; and that, with a court acting as final arbiter, there is no risk of embarrassment from multifarious pronouncements.

We are not so sanguine that these factors can be so easily disposed of.  Per-

---

in terms of "classical", "prudential", and "functional" views, see Scharpf, Judicial Review and the Political Question: A Functional Analysis, 75 Yale L.J. 517 (1966). For an exposition of the "classical" view, see Wechsler, Toward Neutral Principles of Constitutional Law, 73 Harv.L.Rev. 1 (1959) and for critical comment on Powell v. McCormack, 395 U.S. 486, 89 S.Ct. 1944 (1969), see Note, The Supreme Court, 1968 Term, 83 Harv. L.Rev. 1, 62–77 (1969). See generally, Monaghan, Presidential War-Making, 50 B.U.L.Rev. 19 (Special Issue 1970); Note, Congress, The President, and The Power to Commit Forces to Combat, 81 Harv.L.Rev. 1771 (1968); Velvel, Undeclared War and Civil Disobedience (1970).

4.  "The Congress shall have Power * * * to declare War, grant Letters of Marque and Reprisal, and make Rules concerning Captures on Land and Water . . . . "

5.  Those factors were "a textually demonstrable constitutional commitment of the issue to a coordinate political department; or a lack of judicially discoverable and manageable standards for resolving it; or the impossibility of deciding without an initial policy determination of a kind clearly for nonjudicial discretion; or the impossibility of a court's undertaking independent resolution without expressing lack of the respect due coordinate branches of government; or an unusual need for unquestioning adherence to a political decision already made; or the potentiality of embarrassment from multifarious pronouncements by various departments on one question." 369 U.S. at 217, 82 S.Ct. at 710.

6.  See Scharpf, n. 3, supra.

haps they impose no insuperable obstacle to principled decision in the case of long-continued, large-scale hostilities. But, once given the principle that a plaintiff may challenge the constitutionality of undeclared military operations, a court must be prepared to adjudicate whether actions are justified as emergency ones needing no declaration, or have gone beyond this bound. In the latter event the court must adjudicate whether Congress has expressly or impliedly ratified them. Workable standards, fact finding, the prospect of conflicting inferior court decisions, and other factors might well give pause to the most intrepid court.

We do not, however, rely on these factors. Partly we feel that to base abstinence on such pragmatic, if realistic, considerations is not desirable unless so clearly dictated by circumstances that it cannot be mistaken as abdication. Moreover, on a question so dominant in the minds of so many, we deem it important to rule as a matter of constitutional interpretation if at all possible. Finally, and of course most pertinently, we derive recent guidance from the Supreme Court's approach in Powell v. McCormack, 395 U.S. 486, 89 S.Ct. 1944 (1969), giving dominant consideration to the first decisional factor listed in Baker v. Carr, *supra*. This is the inquiry "whether there is a 'textually demonstrable constitutional commitment of the issue to a coordinate political department' of government and what is the scope of such commitment." 395 U.S. at 521, 89 S.Ct. at 1964.

To this critical factor of textual commitment, plaintiffs devoted one paragraph of their lengthy brief. They construed the issue as "judicial assessment of executive action in Vietnam against a constitutional standard." So phrased, the issue is of course, by definition, com-

mitted to the judiciary. Were the issue to be so defined, the Court in Powell v. McCormack, *supra*, would have spared itself much difficulty by stating simply that the issue was "judicial assessment of the action of the House in expelling a member against a constitutional standard." [7] In short, to any issue of challenged authority could be affixed the phrase "judicial assessment", and, by the affixing, the criterion of textual commitment eradicated. While the Court in *Powell* finally was able to pose the issue before it in substantially similar terms, it was only after a very lengthy discussion concluding that there had been no textual commitment of the unlimited power of expulsion to the House, and that none of the other factors of nonjusticiability listed in Baker v. Carr, *supra*, applied.

These observations do not spare us the task of trying to identify the scope of the power which has been committed to a coordinate branch in this case. The complaint at one point alleges that the executive has usurped the war-making power of Congress but more generally alleges that the executive errs only in proceeding to make war without Congressional declaration or ratification. This very ambiguity underscores the fact that the war power of the country is an amalgam of powers, some distinct and others less sharply limned. In certain respects, the executive and the Congress may act independently. The Congress may without executive cooperation declare war, thus triggering treaty obligations and domestic emergency powers. The executive may without Congressional participation repel attack,[8] perhaps catapulting the country into a major conflict. But beyond these independent powers, each of which has its own rationale, the Constitutional scheme envisages the joint participation of the Congress and

---

7. Similarly, the plaintiffs' theory does not account for the failure of the Court in Luther v. Borden, 48 U.S. (7 How.) 1, 12 L.Ed. 581 (1849) to pose the issue as "judicial assessment, against a constitutional standard, of failure of Con-

gress to guarantee a republican form of government."

8. 2 Farrand, The Records of the Federal Convention of 1787, 318 (1911).

the executive in determining the scale and duration of hostilities. To Congress is granted the power to appropriate funds for sustaining armies. Article I, Section 8, Clause 12th. An analogous power given to the President is his power as Commander-in-Chief to station forces abroad. Article II, Section 2. Johnson v. Eisentrager, 339 U.S. 763, 70 S.Ct. 936, 94 L.Ed. 1255 (1950). Congress has the power to concur in or to counter the President's actions by its exclusive authority to appropriate monies in support of an army, navy and air force, Article I, Section 8, Clause 12th,[9] and by granting letters of marque and reprisal. Article I, Section 8, Clause 11th.

While the fact of shared war-making powers is clearly established by the Constitution, however, and some of its elements are indicated, a number of relevant specifics are missing. The Constitution does not contain an explicit provision to indicate whether these interdependent powers can properly be employed to sustain hostilities in the absence of a Congressional declaration of war. Hence this case.

The brief debate of the Founding Fathers sheds no light on this.[10] All we can observe, after almost two centuries,

is that the extreme supporters of each branch lost; Congress did not receive the power to "make war"; the executive was given the power to repel attacks and conduct operations; the Congress was given the power to "declare" war—and nothing was said about undeclared hostilities.

Under these circumstances, what can we say was "textually committed" to the Congress or to the executive? Strictly speaking, we lack the text. Yet if "[d]eciding whether a matter has in any measure been committed by the Constitution to another branch of government, or whether the action of that branch exceeds whatever authority has been committed, is itself a delicate exercise in constitutional interpretation", Baker v. Carr, *supra*, 369 U.S. at 211, 82 S.Ct. at 706, surely our task is more than parsing. We must have some license to construe the sense of the Constitutional framework, wholly apart from any doctrine of implied powers inherent in sovereignty, *cf.* United States v. Curtiss-Wright Export Corp., 299 U.S. 304, 315–318, 57 S. Ct. 216, 81 L.Ed. 255 (1936).

We observe, first, that the Founders' silence on the subject of hostilities beyond repelling attack and without a dec-

---

9. *See also* Note, The Appropriations Power as a Tool of Congressional Foreign Policy Making, 50 B.U.L.Rev. 34 (Special Issue 1970).

10. It was, from the skeletal report in Farrand [(2 Farrand, 318–319)], less than encyclopedic in its coverage. The sequence of deliberations was as follows: (1) the draft constitutional provision, allowing the Congress "to make war" was moved; (2) Pinkney opposed, saying the Senate was better suited for expedition and wisdom than both houses jointly; (3) Butler, for the same reasons, thought the power should be in the President; (4) then Madison and Gerry moved to change "make" to "declare", "leaving to the Executive the power to repel sudden attacks"; (5) Sharman [sic] thought the existing wording "stood very well" permitting the executive "to repel and not to commence war" and feeling that "declare" would "narrow" the power

given to Congress; (6) Gerry interjected that he "never expected to hear in a republic a motion to empower the Executive alone to declare war"; (7) Elseworth [sic] said it should be more easy to get out of war than into it—but added that war "is a simple and overt declaration. peace attended with intricate & secret negotiations"; (8) Mason was against giving the power of war to the Executive or to the Senate; he was "for clogging rather than facilitating war; but for facilitating peace". 2 Farrand 318–319. The Journal records a first vote of 5 to 4 against changing "make" to "declare" and a second vote of 8 to 1 for making the change. 2 Farrand 313. One member was persuaded to vote for the change by the argument that "make" might be understood to mean "conduct", which was an executive function. Butler then moved to give Congress the power "to make peace"; this failed 10–0. 2 Farrand 319.

laration of war was not because the phenomenon was unknown. In The Federalist No. 25, Hamilton, in opposing a proposed prohibition on raising armies in time of peace, described the effect of such a prohibition in these words: "As the ceremony of a formal denunciation of war has of late fallen into disuse, the presence of an enemy within our territories must be waited for, as the legal warrant to the government to begin its levies of men. * * *" The Federalist No. 25, at 156 (Mod. Lib. ed.) (Hamilton).

Secondly, we note that the Congressional power to declare war implies a negative: no one else has that power. But is the more general negative implied —that Congress has no power to support a state of belligerency beyond repelling attack and short of a declared war? The drafters of the Constitution, who were not inept, did not say, "power to commence war". Nor did they say, "No war shall be engaged in without a declaration by Congress unless the country is 'actually invaded, or in such imminent Danger as will not admit of delay.'" (Language from Article I, Section 10, proscribing states from engaging in war.) Nor did they resort to other uses of the negative as they so often did elsewhere. See, e. g., Article I, Section 9. And the "declare" power was not, like the "judge" power of the House of Representatives, Article I, Section 5, in a context limited by another specific provision, such as that specifying the three qualifications of a Representative. See Powell v. McCormack, supra.

Finally, we give some significance to the fact that in the same "power to declare war clause", Article I, Section 8, Clause 11th, there is the power to grant letters of marque and reprisal. Were this a power attendant to and dependent upon a declared war, there would be no reason to specify it separately. Indeed, it was first broached by Gerry as a matter not included in the "declare" power. 2 Farrand 326. Nevertheless, this is a power to be invoked only against an enemy. It is clear that there can be an "enemy", even though our country is not in a declared war. Bas v. Tingy, 4 U.S. (4 Dall.) 37, 1 L.Ed. 731 (1800).[11] The hostilities against France in 1799 were obviously not confined to repelling attack. This was an authorized but undeclared state of warfare. See also, Prize Cases (The Amy Warwick), 67 U. S. (2 Black) 635, 17 L.Ed. 459 (1862).

As to the power to conduct undeclared hostilities beyond emergency defense, then, we are inclined to believe that the Constitution, in giving some essential powers to Congress and others to the executive, committed the matter to both branches, whose joint concord precludes the judiciary from measuring a specific executive action against any specific clause in isolation. Cf. Oetjen v. Central Leather Co., 246 U.S. 297, 302, 38 S.Ct. 309, 62 L.Ed. 726 (1918).[12] In arriving at this conclusion we are aware that while we have addressed the problem of justiciability in the light of the textual commitment criterion, we have also addressed the merits of the constitutional issue. We think, however, that this is

---

11. Justice Washington stated that "If [a war] be declared in form, it is called solemn, and is of the perfect kind. * * *" but that "hostilities may subsist between two nations, more confined in its nature and extent being limited to places, persons and things; and this is more properly termed imperfect war. * * *" 4 U.S. (4 Dall.) at 40.

12. "The conduct of the foreign relations of our government is committed by the Constitution to the executive and legislative— 'the political'—departments of the government, and the propriety of what may be done in the exercise of this political power is not subject to judicial inquiry or decision." 246 U.S. at 302, 38 S.Ct. at 311. Cf. Hamilton v. Dillin, 88 U.S. (21 Wall.) 73, 22 L.Ed. 528 (1874). "[W]hatever view may be taken as to the precise boundary between the legislative and executive powers in reference to [trade with the Confederacy during wartime] there is no doubt that a concurrence of both affords ample foundation for any regulations on the subject." 88 U.S. (21 Wall.) at 88.

451 F.2d—3

inherent when the constitutional issue is posed in terms of scope of authority.

In the circumstance where powers are interrelated, Mr. Justice Jackson has said that:

"When the President acts in absence of either a congressional grant or denial of authority, he can only rely upon his own independent powers, but there is a zone of twilight in which he and Congress may have concurrent authority, or in which its distribution is uncertain. Therefore, congressional inertia, indifference or quiescence may sometimes, at least as a practical matter, enable, if not invite, measures on independent presidential responsibility. In this area, any actual test of power is likely to depend on the imperatives of events and contemporary imponderables rather than on abstract theories of law." Youngstown Sheet & Tube Co. v. Sawyer, 343 U.S. 579, 637, 72 S.Ct. 863, 871, 96 L.Ed. 1153 (1952) (concurring opinion).

We need not go so far as to say that in a situation of shared powers, the executive acting and the Congress silent, no constitutional issue arises. Here the complaint itself alleges the escalation of expenditures supporting United States efforts in Vietnam from $1.7 billion in 1965 to over $30 billion annually today, and a total expenditure over the past decade of $110 billion. Whether or not such appropriating and other actions of the Congress during the past six years can be said to amount to an "equivalent" of a declaration, or express or implied ratification is an issue we do not reach. At the very least, the complaint reveals a prolonged period of Congressional support of executive activities.

The question remains to be asked: when the executive and Congress disagree not as to the advisability of fighting a war but as to the appropriate level of fighting, how shall the Constitution be served? When the executive takes a strong hand, Congress has no lack of corrective power. Congress has the power to tax, to appropriate, to impound, to override a veto. The executive has only the inherent power to propose and to implement, and the formal power to veto. The objective of the drafters of the Constitution was to give each branch "constitutional arms for its own defense". The Federalist No. 23, at 476 (Mod. Lib. ed.) (Hamilton). But the advantage was given the Congress, Hamilton noting the "superior weight and influence of the legislative body in a free government, and the hazard to the Executive in a trial of strength with that body." Id. at 478.

[6, 7]  All we hold here is that in a situation of prolonged but undeclared hostilities, where the executive continues to act not only in the absence of any conflicting Congressional claim of authority but with steady Congressional support, the Constitution has not been breached. The war in Vietnam is a product of the jointly supportive actions of the two branches to whom the congeries of the war powers have been committed. Because the branches are not in opposition, there is no necessity of determining boundaries. Should either branch be opposed to the continuance of hostilities, however, and present the issue in clear terms, a court might well take a different view. This question we do not face. Nor does the prospect that such a question might be posed indicate a different answer in the present case.

Affirmed.

November 9, 1970 400 U. S.

No. 42, Orig. MASSACHUSETTS *v.* LAIRD, SECRETARY OF DEFENSE. Motion of Constitutional Lawyers' Committee on Undeclared War for leave to file supplemental brief as *amicus curiae* granted. Motion of John M. Wells et al. for leave to file a brief as *amici curiae,* to participate in oral argument, or alternative motion to be named as parties plaintiff, denied. Motion for leave to file bill of complaint denied. MR. JUSTICE HARLAN and MR. JUSTICE STEWART dissent. They would set the latter motion for argument on questions of standing and justiciability.

MR. JUSTICE DOUGLAS, dissenting.

This motion was filed by the Commonwealth of Massachusetts against the Secretary of Defense, a citizen of another State. It is brought pursuant to a mandate contained in an act of the Massachusetts Legislature. 1970 Laws, c. 174. Massachusetts seeks to obtain an adjudication of the constitutionality of the United States' participation in the Indochina war. It requests that the United States' participation be declared "unconstitutional in that it was not initially authorized or subsequently ratified by Congressional declaration"; it asks that the Secretary of Defense be enjoined "from carrying out, issuing or causing to be issued any further orders which would increase the present level of United States troops in Indochina"; and it asks that, if appropriate congressional action is not forthcoming within 90 days of this Court's decree, the Secretary of Defense be enjoined "from carrying out, issuing, or causing to be issued any further orders directing any inhabitant of the Commonwealth of Massachusetts to Indochina for the purpose of participating in combat or supporting combat troops in the Vietnam war." Today this Court denies leave to file the complaint. I dissent.

The threshold issues for granting leave to file a complaint in this case are standing and justiciability. I believe that Massachusetts has standing and the controversy is justiciable. At the very least, however, it is apparent that the issues are not so clearly foreclosed as to justify a summary denial of leave to file.

## STANDING

In *Massachusetts* v. *Mellon,* 262 U. S. 447 (hereafter *Mellon*), the Court held that a State lacked standing to challenge, as *parens patriae,* a federal grant-in-aid program under which the Federal Government was allegedly usurping powers reserved to the States. It was said in *Mellon:*

> "[T]he citizens of Massachusetts are also citizens of the United States. It cannot be conceded that a State, as *parens patriae,* may institute judicial proceedings to protect citizens of the United States from the operation of the statutes thereof. While the State, under some circumstances, may sue in that capacity for the protection of its citizens (*Missouri* v. *Illinois,* 180 U. S. 208, 241), it is no part of its duty or power to enforce their rights in respect of their relations with the Federal Government. In that field it is the United States, and not the State, which represents them as *parens patriae,* when such representation becomes appropriate; and to the former, and not to the latter, they must look for such protective measures as flow from that status." *Id.,* at 485–486.

The Solicitor General argues that *Mellon* stands as a bar to this suit.

Yet the ruling of the Court in that case is not dispositive of this one. The opinion states: "We need not go so far as to say that a State may never intervene by suit to protect its citizens against any form of enforcement of unconstitutional acts of Congress; but we are clear that the right to do so does not arise here." *Id.*, at 485. Thus the case did not announce a *per se* rule to bar all suits against the Federal Government as *parens patriae,* and a closer look at the bases of the opinion is necessary to determine the limits on its applicability.

*Mellon* relates to an Act of Congress signed by the Executive, a distinction noted in other original actions. In *Georgia* v. *Pennsylvania R. Co.,* 324 U. S. 439, we stated, "[t]his is not a suit like those in *Massachusetts* v. *Mellon,* and *Florida* v. *Mellon, supra,* [273 U. S. 12] where a State sought to protect her citizens from the operation of federal statutes." *Id.*, at 446–447.

Massachusetts attacks no federal statute. In fact, the basis of Massachusetts' complaint is the absence of congressional action.

It is said that the Federal Government "represents" the citizens. Here the complaint is that only one representative of the people, the Executive, has acted and the other representatives of the citizens have not acted, although, it is argued, the Constitution provides that they must act before an overseas "war" can be conducted.

There was a companion case to *Mellon* in which the Court held that a taxpayer lacked standing to challenge the same federal spending statute. *Frothingham* v. *Mellon,* 262 U. S. 447 (hereafter *Frothingham*). Two years ago we reconsidered *Frothingham* and found at least part of the ruling could not stand the test of time. Concurring in the result, I stated:

> "*Frothingham,* decided in 1923, was in the heyday of substantive due process, when courts were sitting in judgment on the wisdom or reasonableness of legislation. The claim in *Frothingham* was that a

federal regulatory Act dealing with maternity deprived the plaintiff of property without due process of law. When the Court used substantive due process to determine the wisdom or reasonableness of legislation, it was indeed transforming itself into the Council of Revision which was rejected by the Constitutional Convention. It was that judicial attitude, not the theory of standing to sue rejected in *Frothingham*, that involved 'important hazards for the continued effectiveness of the federal judiciary,' to borrow a phrase from my Brother HARLAN. A contrary result in *Frothingham* in that setting might well have accentuated an ominous trend to judicial supremacy." *Flast* v. *Cohen*, 392 U. S. 83, 107.

In *Flast* we held that a taxpayer had standing to challenge a federal spending program, if he showed that Congress breached a specific limitation on its taxing and spending power. As MR. JUSTICE STEWART stated in his concurring opinion, "[t]he present case is thus readily distinguishable from *Frothingham* v. *Mellon*, 262 U. S. 447, where the taxpayer did not rely on an explicit constitutional prohibition but instead questioned the scope of the powers delegated to the national legislature by Article I of the Constitution." 392 U. S., at 114.

The erosion of *Frothingham* does not, of course, necessarily mean that the authority of *Mellon* has been affected. But if the current debate over *Frothingham* "suggests that we should undertake a fresh examination of the limitations upon standing to sue," 392 U. S., at 94, then surely the erosion of *Frothingham* suggests it is time to re-examine its companion case.

*Mellon*, too, has been eroded by time. In the spring of 1963 the Governor of Alabama moved for leave to file a complaint to prevent the President from using troops in Birmingham during civil rights marches there. Under the Solicitor General's reading of *Mellon* Alabama would have lacked standing to challenge such an exercise of presidential authority. The Court denied Alabama relief, not because of *Mellon,* but because:

> "In essence the papers show no more than that the President has made ready to exercise the authority conferred upon him by 10 U. S. C. § 333 by alerting and stationing military personnel in the Birmingham area. Such purely preparatory measures and their alleged adverse general effects upon the plaintiffs afford no basis for the granting of any relief."

*Alabama* v. *United States,* 373 U. S. 545.

In *South Carolina* v. *Katzenbach,* 383 U. S. 301, *Mellon* was further weakened. In that case we denied standing to South Carolina to assert claims under the Bill of Attainder Clause of Art. I and the principle of separation of powers which were regarded "only as protections for individual persons and private groups, those who are peculiarly vulnerable to nonjudicial determinations of guilt." 383 U. S., at 324. Yet we went on to allow South Carolina to challenge the Voting Rights Act of 1965 as beyond congressional power under the Fifteenth Amendment.

The main interest of South Carolina was in the continuing operation of its election laws. Massachusetts' claim to standing in this case is certainly as strong as South Carolina's was in the *Katzenbach* case.

Massachusetts complains, as *parens patriae,* that its citizens are drafted and sent to fight in an unconstitutional overseas war. Their lives are in jeopardy. Their liberty is impaired.

Furthermore, the basis on which *Flast* distinguished *Frothingham* is also present here. The allegation in both *Mellon* and *Frothingham* was that Congress had exceeded the general powers delegated to it by Art. I, § 8, and invaded the reserved powers of the States under the Tenth Amendment. The claim was not specific; but, as *Flast* held, if a taxpayer can allege spending violates a *specific constitutional limitation,* then he has standing. Here Massachusetts points to a specific provision of the Constitution. Congress by Art. I, § 8, has the power "To declare War." Does not that make this case comparable to *Flast?*

It has been settled, at least since 1901, that "if the health and comfort of the inhabitants of a State are threatened, the State is the proper party to represent and defend them," *Missouri* v. *Illinois,* 180 U. S. 208, 241, in an original action in this Court. And see *Georgia* v. *Tennessee Copper Co.,* 206 U. S. 230, 237–238; *Pennsylvania* v. *West Virginia,* 262 U. S. 553, 591–592; *North Dakota* v. *Minnesota,* 263 U. S. 365, 372–376; *Georgia* v. *Pennsylvania R. Co.,* 324 U. S. 439, 450–451. Those cases involved injury to inhabitants of one State by water or air pollution of another State, by interference with navigation, by economic losses caused by an out-of-state agency, and the like. The harm to citizens of Massachusetts suffered by being drafted for a war are certainly of no less a magnitude. Massachusetts would clearly seem to have standing as *parens patriae* to represent, as alleged in its complaint, its male citizens being drafted for overseas combat in Indochina.

## JUSTICIABILITY

A question that is "political" is opposed to one that is "justiciable." In reviewing the dimensions of the "political" question we said in *Baker* v. *Carr,* 369 U. S. 186, 217:

"Prominent on the surface of any case held to involve a political question is found a textually demonstrable constitutional commitment of the issue to a coordinate political department; or a lack of judicially discoverable and manageable standards for resolving it; or the impossibility of deciding without an initial policy determination of a kind clearly for nonjudicial discretion; or the impossibility of a court's undertaking independent resolution without expressing lack of the respect due coordinate branches of government; or an unusual need for unquestioning adherence to a political decision already made; or the potentiality of embarrassment from multifarious pronouncements by various departments on one question."

1. *A textually demonstrable constitutional commitment of the issue to a coordinate political department.* At issue here is the phrase in Art. I, § 8, cl. 11: "To declare War." Congress definitely has that power. The Solicitor General argues that only Congress can determine whether it has declared war. He states, " 'To declare War' includes a power to determine, free of judicial interference, the form which its authorization of hostilities will take." This may be correct. But, as we stated in *Powell* v. *McCormack,* 395 U. S. 486, the question of a textually demonstrable commitment and "what is the *scope* of such commitment are questions [this Court] must resolve for the first time in this case." *Id.,* at 521 (emphasis added). It may well be that it is for Congress, and Congress alone, to determine the form of its authorization, but if that is the case we should make that determination only after full briefs on the merits and oral argument.

2. *A lack of judicially discoverable and manageable standards for resolving the issue.* The standards that are applicable are not elusive. The case is not one where

the Executive is repelling a sudden attack.[1] The present Indochina "war" has gone on for six years. The question is whether the Gulf of Tonkin Resolution was a declaration of war or whether other Acts of Congress were its equivalent.

3. *The impossibility of deciding without an initial policy determination of a kind clearly for nonjudicial discretion.* In *Ex parte Milligan*, 4 Wall. 2, 139 (concurring opinion), it was stated that "neither can the President, in war more than in peace, intrude upon the proper authority of Congress . . . ."[2] The issue in this case is not whether we ought to fight a war in Indochina, but whether the Executive can authorize it without congressional authorization. This is not a case where we would have to determine the wisdom of any policy.

4. *The impossibility of a court's undertaking independent resolution without expressing lack of respect due coordinate branches of government.* The Solicitor General argues that it would show disrespect of the Executive to go behind his statements and determine his au-

---

[1] An early draft of the Constitution vested in Congress the power to "make" war rather than the power to "declare" war. The change from "make" to "declare" was intended to authorize the President the power to repel sudden attacks and to manage, as Commander in Chief, any war declared by Congress. The change was not intended to give the President power to initiate hostilities and commit troops in war at his own will. The Framers were afraid of unlimited executive power and "resolved to so frame the Constitution that no one man should hold the power of bringing this oppression upon us." A. Lincoln as quoted in E. Corwin, The President: Office & Powers, 1787–1957, p. 451 (4th ed. 1957). See generally Note, Congress, the President, and the Power to Commit Forces to Combat, 81 Harv. L. Rev. 1771 (1968).

[2] The majority in *Milligan* stated: "The Constitution of the United States is a law for rulers and people, equally in war and in peace, and covers with the shield of its protection all classes of men, at all times, and under all circumstances." 4 Wall., at 120–121.

thority to act in these circumstances.   Both *Powell* and
the *Steel Seizure Case* (*Youngstown Sheet & Tube* v.
*Sawyer,* 343 U. S. 579), however, demonstrate that the
duty of this Court is to interpret the Constitution, and in
the latter case we did go behind an executive order to
determine his authority.   As Mr. Justice Frankfurter
stated in the *Steel Seizure Case:*

> "To deny inquiry into the President's power in a
> case like this, because of the damage to the public
> interest to be feared from upsetting its exercise
> by him, would in effect always preclude inquiry
> into challenged power, which presumably only
> avowed great public interest brings into action.   And
> so, with the utmost unwillingness, with every desire
> to avoid judicial inquiry into the powers and duties
> of the other two branches of the government, I can-
> not escape consideration of the legality of Execu-
> tive Order No. 10340.

.                .              .              .

> "Marshall's admonition that 'it is *a constitution*
> we are expounding' [*McCulloch* v. *Maryland,* 4
> Wheat. 316, 407] is especially relevant when the
> Court is required to give legal sanctions to an under-
> lying principle of the Constitution—that of separa-
> tion of powers."   343 U. S., at 596–597 (concurring
> opinion).

It is far more important to be respectful to the Constitution than to a coordinate branch of government.[3]
   5. *An unusual need for unquestioning adherence to a
political decision already made.*   This test is essentially

---

[3] "When all is said and done, one is inclined to think that a rigid
constitutional frame is on the whole preferable even if it serves
no better purpose than to embarrass an overactive Executive."
G. Hausner, Individual Rights in the Courts of Israel, International Lawyers' Convention in Israel 201, 228 (1958).

a reference to a commitment of a problem and its solution to a coordinate branch of government[4]—a matter not involved here.

---

[4] The classic political questions case is *Luther* v. *Borden*, 7 How. 1, growing out of the Dorr Rebellion in Rhode Island. That State had been unaffected by the constitutional changes during the Revolutionary War and when Connecticut acquired a new constitution in 1818, Rhode Island was the only State which retained its original colonial charter as fundamental law. The charter government was malapportioned and required ownership of $134 of real property for voting purposes.

From the early 1820's on there was agitation for a new constitution in Rhode Island. Finally one constitution put to the "voters" was passed. A "people's" convention on November 18, 1841, put forth a new constitution with a Bill of Rights, better apportionment, and white manhood suffrage. Under the voting requirements established by that constitution, all white adult males were allowed to vote for or against the "people's" constitution. A majority of the voters ratified the constitution. Following the ratification, elections were held. Rhode Island then had two governments, one under the "people's" constitution, the other under the original charter. The "people's" government had a quick legislative session and did not attempt to change either the judiciary or the administrative officers of the State. On June 26, 1842, the charter governor finally proclaimed martial law to establish his authority. *Luther* v. *Borden* arose out of Borden's attempt pursuant to instructions to arrest Luther. Luther brought action in the federal courts for trespass and Borden defended his actions as taken under martial law, lawfully proclaimed. Judge Story refused to give Luther's requested jury instructions, that the "people's" constitution was in full force in June 1842 because "a majority of the free white male citizens of Rhode Island, of twenty-one years and upwards, had a right to reassume the powers of government and establish a written constitution; and that, having so exercised such right, the pre-existing charter government became null and void." The case then went to the Supreme Court and, faced with the question of which of the two governments was the lawful one, the Court held that determination was a political question, not for judicial determination—that the political question was for Rhode Island

6. *The potentiality of embarrassment from multifarious pronouncements by various departments of government on one question.* Once again this relates back to whether the problem and its solution are committed to a given branch of government.

We have never ruled, I believe, that when the Federal Government takes a person by the neck and submits him to punishment, imprisonment, taxation, or to some ordeal, the complaining person may not be heard in court. The rationale in cases such as the present is that government cannot take life, liberty, or property of the individual and escape adjudication by the courts of the legality of its action.

That is the heart of this case. It does not concern the wisdom of fighting in Southeast Asia. Likewise no question of whether the conflict is either just or necessary is present. We are asked instead whether the Executive has power, absent a congressional declaration of war, to commit Massachusetts citizens to armed hostilities on foreign soil. Another way of putting the question is whether under our Constitution presidential wars are permissible. Should that question be answered in the negative we would then have to determine whether Congress has declared war. That question which Massachusetts presents is in my view justiciable.

---

to resolve or for Congress under Art. IV, § 4, of the Constitution, 7 How., at 38–43.

Dorr, who had been the governor under the "people's" constitution, was tried and convicted of treason against the State in early 1844. In January he was offered a legislative pardon if he would take an oath affirming support for the government in power. He refused since he believed the "people's" constitution was still binding. In June 1845, he was unconditionally pardoned under a new governor. Finally, in February 1854, the legislature reversed and annulled Dorr's conviction. For a history of the Dorr Rebellion, see A. Mowry, The Dorr War (1970).

It is said that "the notion has persisted, despite the results in *Baker v. Carr* and *Powell v. McCormack,* [395 U. S. 486] . . . that there is a means for the Court to avoid deciding any case or issue upon the basis of a broad, highly general, and almost entirely discretionary principle of nondecision." Tigar, Judicial Power, The "Political Question Doctrine," and Foreign Relations, 17 U. C. L. A. L. Rev. 1135, 1163 (1970). Yet no such discretionary principle, if germane to our problem, is applicable here.

"The war power of the United States, like its other powers . . . is subject to applicable constitutional limitations." *Hamilton v. Kentucky Distilleries & Warehouse Co.,* 251 U. S. 146, 156. No less than the war power—the greatest leveler of them all—is the power of the Commander in Chief subject to constitutional limitations. That was the crux of the *Steel Seizure Case.* Concurring in the judgment in that case, Mr. Justice Clark stated: "I conclude that where Congress has laid down specific procedures to deal with the type of crisis confronting the President, he must follow those procedures in meeting the crisis . . . . I cannot sustain the seizure in question because . . . Congress had [*sic*] prescribed methods to be followed by the President . . . ." 343 U. S., at 662. If the President must follow procedures prescribed by Congress, it follows *a fortiori* that he must follow procedures prescribed by the Constitution.

This Court has previously faced issues of presidential war making. The legality of Lincoln's blockade was considered in the *Prize Cases,* 2 Black 635, and although the Court narrowly split in supporting the President's position, the split was on the merits, not on whether the claim was justiciable. And even though that war was the Civil War and not one involving an overseas expedition, the decision was 5 to 4.

In the *Steel Seizure Case* members of this Court wrote seven opinions and each reached the merits of the Executive's seizure. In that case, as here, the issue related to the President's powers as Commander in Chief and the fact that all nine Justices decided the case on the merits and construed the powers of a coordinate branch at a time of extreme emergency should be instructive. In that case we said:

> "It is clear that if the President had authority to issue the order he did, it must be found in some provision of the Constitution. And it is not claimed that express constitutional language grants this power to the President. The contention is that presidential power should be implied from the aggregate of his powers under the Constitution. Particular reliance is placed on provisions in Article II which say that 'The executive Power shall be vested in a President . . .'; that 'he shall take Care that the Laws be faithfully executed'; and that he 'shall be Commander in Chief of the Army and Navy of the United States.'

> "The order cannot properly be sustained as an exercise of the President's military power as Commander in Chief of the Armed Forces. The Government attempts to do so by citing a number of cases upholding broad powers in military commanders engaged in day-to-day fighting in a theater of war. Such cases need not concern us here. Even though 'theater of war' be an expanding concept, we cannot with faithfulness to our constitutional system hold that the Commander in Chief of the Armed Forces has the ultimate power as such to take possession of private property in order to keep labor disputes from stopping production. This is a job for the Nation's lawmakers, not for its military authorities." 343 U. S., at 587.

If we determine that the Indochina conflict is unconstitutional because it lacks a congressional declaration of war, the Chief Executive is free to seek one, as was President Truman free to seek congressional approval after our *Steel Seizure* decision.

There is, of course, a difference between this case and the *Prize Cases* and the *Steel Seizure Case*. In those cases a private party was asserting a wrong to him: his *property* was being taken and he demanded a determination of the legality of the taking. Here the *lives* and *liberties* of Massachusetts citizens are in jeopardy. Certainly the Constitution gives no greater protection to *property* than to *life* and *liberty*. It might be argued that the authority in the *Steel Seizure Case* was not textually apparent in the Constitution, while the power of the Commander in Chief to commit troops is obvious and therefore a different determination on justiciability is needed. The *Prize Cases*, however, involved Lincoln's exercise of power in ordering a blockade by virtue of his powers as the Commander in Chief.

Since private parties—represented by Massachusetts as *parens patriae*—are involved in this case, the teaching of the *Prize Cases* and the *Steel Seizure Case* is that their claims are justiciable.

The Solicitor General urges that no effective remedy can be formulated. He correctly points out enforcing or supervising injunctive relief would involve immense complexities and difficulties. But there is no requirement that we issue an injunction. Massachusetts seeks declaratory relief as well as injunctive relief. In *Baker v. Carr* we stated that we must determine whether "the duty asserted can be judicially identified and its breach judicially determined, and whether protection for the right asserted can be judicially molded." 369 U. S., at 198. The Declaratory Judgment Act, 28 U. S. C. § 2201, provides that "any court of the United States . . .

may declare the rights . . . of any interested party . . . whether or not further relief is or could be sought." It may well be that even declaratory relief would be inappropriate respecting many of the numerous issues involved if the Court held that the war were unconstitutional. I restrict this opinion to the question of the propriety of a declaratory judgment that no Massachusetts man can be taken against his will and made to serve in the war. *Powell* involved just one man while this case involves large numbers of men. But that goes only to the mechanical task of making any remedy granted available to all members of a large class.

Today we deny a hearing to a State which attempts to determine whether it is constitutional to require its citizens to fight in a foreign war absent a congressional declaration of war. Three years ago we refused to hear a case involving draftees who sought to prevent their shipment overseas. *Mora* v. *McNamara,* 128 U. S. App. D. C. 297, 387 F. 2d 862, cert. denied, 389 U. S. 934 (1967). The question of an unconstitutional war is neither academic nor "political." This case has raised the question in an adversary setting. It should be settled here and now.

I would set the motion for leave to file down for argument and decide the merits only after full argument.

# VII. DOCUMENTARY APPENDIX 2

## SOME PRINCIPAL DECISIONS BY UNITED STATES COURTS

## AND LEGISLATIVE ACTION BY THE UNITED STATES CONGRESS ON INDOCHINA-RELATED ISSUES

### Part B. Legislative Action

# Special Foreign Assistance Act of 1971

Sec. 7. (a) In line with the expressed intention of the President of the United States, none of the funds authorized or appropriated pursuant to this or any other Act may be used to finance the introduction of United States ground combat troops into Cambodia, or to provide United States advisers to or for Cambodian military forces in Cambodia.

(b) Military and economic assistance provided by the United States to Cambodia and authorized or appropriated pursuant to this or any other Act shall not be construed as a commitment by the United States to Cambodia for its defense.

Sec. 8. The Foreign Assistance Act of 1961 is amended by adding at the end thereof the following new section:

"Sec. 652. Limitation Upon Additional Assistance to Cambodia.—The President shall not exercise any special authority granted to him under sections 506(a), 610(a), and 614(a) of this Act for the purpose of providing additional assistance to Cambodia, unless the President, at least thirty days prior to the date he intends to exercise any such authority on behalf of Cambodia (or ten days prior to such date if the President certifies in writing that an emergency exists requiring immediate assistance to Cambodia), notifies the Speaker of the House of Representatives and the Committee on Foreign Relations of the Senate in writing of each such intended exercise, the section of this Act under which such authority is to be exercised, and the justification for, and the extent of, the exercise of such authority.".

**Approved January 5, 1971.**

## President Nixon's Veto of War Powers Measure Overridden by the Congress

*Following are texts of a message from President Nixon to the House of Representatives dated October 24 and a White House statement issued November 7, when the House and Senate voted to override the President's veto of House Joint Resolution 542.*

### MESSAGE FROM PRESIDENT NIXON, OCTOBER 24

Weekly Compilation of Presidential Documents dated October 29

*To the House of Representatives:*

I hereby return without my approval House Joint Resolution 542—the War Powers Resolution. While I am in accord with the desire of the Congress to assert its proper role in the conduct of our foreign affairs, the restrictions which this resolution would impose upon the authority of the President are both unconstitutional and dangerous to the best interests of our Nation.

The proper roles of the Congress and the Executive in the conduct of foreign affairs have been debated since the founding of our country. Only recently, however, has there been a serious challenge to the wisdom of the Founding Fathers in choosing not to draw a precise and detailed line of demarcation between the foreign policy powers of the two branches.

The Founding Fathers understood the impossibility of foreseeing every contingency that might arise in this complex area. They acknowledged the need for flexibility in responding to changing circumstances. They recognized that foreign policy decisions must be made through close cooperation between the two branches and not through rigidly codified procedures.

These principles remain as valid today as they were when our Constitution was written. Yet House Joint Resolution 542 would violate those principles by defining the President's powers in ways which would strictly limit his constitutional authority.

### CLEARLY UNCONSTITUTIONAL

House Joint Resolution 542 would attempt to take away, by a mere legislative act, authorities which the President has properly exercised under the Constitution for almost 200 years. One of its provisions would automatically cut off certain authorities after sixty days unless the Congress extended them. Another would allow the Congress to eliminate certain authorities merely by the passage of a concurrent resolution—an action which does not normally have the force of law, since it denies the President his constitutional role in approving legislation.

I believe that both these provisions are unconstitutional. The only way in which the constitutional powers of a branch of the Government can be altered is by amending the Constitution—and any attempt to make such alterations by legislation alone is clearly without force.

### UNDERMINING OUR FOREIGN POLICY

While I firmly believe that a veto of House Joint Resolution 542 is warranted solely on constitutional grounds, I am also deeply disturbed by the practical consequences of this resolution. For it would seriously undermine this Nation's ability to act decisively and convincingly in times of international crisis. As a result, the confidence of our allies in our ability to assist them could be diminished and the respect of our adversaries for our deterrent posture could decline. A permanent and substantial element of unpredictability would be injected into the world's assessment of American behavior, further increasing the likelihood of miscalculation and war.

If this resolution had been in operation, America's effective response to a variety of challenges in recent years would have been vastly complicated or even made impossible. We may well have been unable to respond in the way we did during the Berlin crisis of 1961, the Cuban missile crisis of 1962, the Congo rescue operation in 1964, and the Jordanian crisis of 1970—to mention just a few examples. In addition, our recent actions to bring about a peaceful settlement of the hostilities in the Middle East would have been seriously impaired if this resolution had been in force.

While all the specific consequences of House Joint Resolution 542 cannot yet be predicted, it is clear that it would undercut the ability of the United States to act as an effective influence for peace. For example, the provision automatically cutting off certain authorities after 60 days unless they are extended by the Congress could work to prolong or intensify a crisis. Until the Congress suspended the deadline, there would be at least a chance of United States withdrawal and an adversary would be tempted therefore to postpone serious negotiations until the 60 days were up. Only after the Congress acted would there be a strong incentive for an adversary to negotiate. In addition, the very existence of a deadline could lead to an escalation of hostilities in order to achieve certain objectives before the 60 days expired.

The measure would jeopardize our role as a force for peace in other ways as well. It would, for example, strike from the President's hand a wide range of important peacekeeping tools by eliminating his ability to exercise quiet diplomacy backed by subtle shifts in our military deployments. It would also cast into doubt authorities which Pres-

idents have used to undertake certain humanitarian relief missions in conflict areas, to protect fishing boats from seizure, to deal with ship or aircraft hijackings, and to respond to threats of attack. Not the least of the adverse consequences of this resolution would be the prohibition contained in section 8 against fulfilling our obligations under the NATO treaty as ratified by the Senate. Finally, since the bill is somewhat vague as to when the 60 day rule would apply, it could lead to extreme confusion and dangerous disagreements concerning the prerogatives of the two branches, seriously damaging our ability to respond to international crises.

### FAILURE TO REQUIRE POSITIVE CONGRESSIONAL ACTION

I am particularly disturbed by the fact that certain of the President's constitutional powers as Commander in Chief of the Armed Forces would terminate automatically under this resolution 60 days after they were invoked. No overt Congressional action would be required to cut off these powers—they would disappear automatically unless the Congress extended them. In effect, the Congress is here attempting to increase its policy-making role through a provision which requires it to take absolutely no action at all.

In my view, the proper way for the Congress to make known its will on such foreign policy questions is through a positive action, with full debate on the merits of the issue and with each member taking the responsibility of casting a yes or no vote after considering those merits. The authorization and appropriations process represents one of the ways in which such influence can be exercised. I do not, however, believe that the Congress can responsibly contribute its considered, collective judgment on such grave questions without full debate and without a yes or no vote. Yet this is precisely what the joint resolution would allow. It would give every future Congress the ability to handcuff every future President merely by doing nothing and sitting still.

In my view, one cannot become a responsible partner unless one is prepared to take responsible action.

### STRENGTHENING COOPERATION BETWEEN THE CONGRESS AND THE EXECUTIVE BRANCHES

The responsible and effective exercise of the war powers requires the fullest cooperation between the Congress and the Executive and the prudent fulfillment by each branch of its constitutional responsibilities. House Joint Resolution 542 includes certain constructive measures which would foster this process by enhancing the flow of information from the executive branch to the Congress. Section 3, for example, calls for consultations with the Congress before and during the involvement of United States forces in hostilities abroad. This provision is consistent with the desire of this Administration for regularized consultations with the Congress in an even wider range of circumstances.

I believe that full and cooperative participation in foreign policy matters by both the executive and the legislative branches could be enhanced by a careful and dispassionate study of their constitutional roles. Helpful proposals for such a study have already been made in the Congress. I would welcome the establishment of a non-partisan commission on the constitutional roles of the Congress and the President in the conduct of foreign affairs. This commission could make a thorough review of the principal constitutional issues in Executive-Congressional relations, including the war powers, the international agreement powers, and the question of Executive privilege, and then submit its recommendations to the President and the Congress. The members of such a commission could be drawn from both parties—and could represent many perspectives including those of the Congress, the executive branch, the legal profession, and the academic community.

This Administration is dedicated to strengthening cooperation between the Congress and the President in the conduct of foreign affairs and to preserving the constitutional prerogatives of both branches of our Government. I know that the Congress shares that goal. A commission on the constitutional roles of the Congress and the President would provide a useful opportunity for both branches to work together toward that common objective.

RICHARD NIXON.

THE WHITE HOUSE, *October 24, 1973.*

# WHITE HOUSE STATEMENT, NOVEMBER 7

Weekly Compilation of Presidential Documents dated November 12

The President is extremely disappointed with the House vote to override his veto of House Joint Resolution 542.

He feels the action seriously undermines this Nation's ability to act decisively and convincingly in times of international crisis.

The confidence of our allies in our ability to assist them will be diminished by the House's action. Our potential adversaries may be encouraged to engage in future acts of international mischief because of this blow to our deterrent posture.

# UNITED STATES: WAR POWERS RESOLUTION *

Public Law 93-148
93rd Congress, H. J. Res. 542
November 7, 1973

## JOINT RESOLUTION

Concerning the war powers of Congress and the President.

*Resolved by the Senate and House of Representatives of the United States of America in Congress assembled,*

### SHORT TITLE

SECTION 1. This joint resolution may be cited as the "War Powers Resolution."

### PURPOSE AND POLICY

SEC. 2. (a) It is the purpose of this joint resolution to fulfill the intent of the framers of the Constitution of the United States and insure that the collective judgment of both the Congress and the President will apply to the introduction of United States Armed Forces into hostilities, or into situations where imminent involvement in hostilities is clearly indicated by the circumstances, and to the continued use of such forces in hostilities or in such situations.

(b) Under article I, section 8, of the Constitution, it is specifically provided that the Congress shall have the power to make all laws necessary and proper for carrying into execution, not only its own powers but also all other powers vested by the Constitution in the Government of the United States, or in any department or officer thereof.

(c) The constitutional powers of the President as Commander-in-Chief to introduce United States Armed Forces into hostilities, or into situations where imminent involvement in hostilities is clearly indicated by the circumstances, are exercised only pursuant to (1) a declaration of war, (2) specific statutory authorization, or (3) a national emergency created by attack upon the United States, its territories or possessions, or its armed forces.

### CONSULTATION

SEC. 3. The President in every possible instance shall consult with Congress before introducing United States Armed Forces into hostilities

* The Resolution (H.J. Res. 542) was vetoed by the President on October 24, 1973. On November 7, the veto was overridden in the House by a vote of 284 to 135, and in the Senate by 75 to 18. For further comment, *see Contemporary Practice* section *supra* p. 324.

or into situations where imminent involvement in hostilities is clearly indicated by the circumstances, and after every such introduction shall consult regularly with the Congress until United States Armed Forces are no longer engaged in hostilities or have been removed from such situations.

## REPORTING

SEC. 4. (a) In the absence of a declaration of war, in any case in which United States Armed Forces are introduced—

(1) into hostilities or into situations where imminent involvement in hostilities is clearly indicated by the circumstances;

(2) into the territory, airspace or waters of a foreign nation, while equipped for combat, except for deployments which relate solely to supply, replacement, repair, or training of such forces; or

(3) in numbers which substantially enlarge United States Armed Forces equipped for combat already located in a foreign nation;

the President shall submit within 48 hours to the Speaker of the House of Representatives and to the President pro tempore of the Senate a report, in writing, setting forth—

(A) the circumstances necessitating the introduction of United States Armed Forces;

(B) the constitutional and legislative authority under which such introduction took place; and

(C) the estimated scope and duration of the hostilities or involvement.

(b) The President shall provide such other information as the Congress may request in the fulfillment of its constitutional responsibilities with respect to committing the Nation to war and to the use of United States Armed Forces abroad.

(c) Whenever United States Armed Forces are introduced into hostilities or into any situation described in subsection (a) of this section, the President shall, so long as such armed forces continue to be engaged in such hostilities or situation, report to the Congress periodically on the status of such hostilities or situation as well as on the scope and duration of such hostilities or situation, but in no event shall he report to the Congress less often than once every six months.

## CONGRESSIONAL ACTION

SEC. 5. (a) Each report submitted pursuant to section 4(a)(1) shall be transmitted to the Speaker of the House of Representatives and to the President pro tempore of the Senate on the same calendar day. Each report so transmitted shall be referred to the Committee on Foreign Affairs of the House of Representatives and to the Committee on Foreign Relations of the Senate for appropriate action. If, when the report is transmitted, the Congress has adjourned sine die or has adjourned for any period in excess of three calendar days, the Speaker of the House of Representatives and the President pro tempore of the Senate, if they deem it advisable (or if petitioned by at least 30 percent of the membership of their respective Houses) shall jointly request the President to convene

Congress in order that it may consider the report and take appropriate action pursuant to this section.

(b) Within sixty calendar days after a report is submitted or is required to be submitted pursuant to section 4(a)(1), whichever is earlier, the President shall terminate any use of United States Armed Forces with respect to which such report was submitted (or required to be submitted), unless the Congress (1) has declared war or has enacted a specific authorization for such use of United States Armed Forces, (2) has extended by law such sixty-day period, or (3) is physically unable to meet as a result of an armed attack upon the United States. Such sixty-day period shall be extended for not more than an additional thirty days if the President determines and certifies to the Congress in writing that unavoidable military necessity respecting the safety of United States Armed Forces requires the continued use of such armed forces in the course of bringing about a prompt removal of such forces.

(c) Notwithstanding subsection (b), at any time that United States Armed Forces are engaged in hostilities outside the territory of the United States, its possessions and territories without a declaration of war or specific statutory authorization, such forces shall be removed by the President if the Congress so directs by concurrent resolution.

CONGRESSIONAL PRIORITY PROCEDURES FOR JOINT RESOLUTION OR BILL

SEC. 6. (a) Any joint resolution or bill introduced pursuant to section 5(b) at least thirty calendar days before the expiration of the sixty-day period specified in such section shall be referred to the Committee on Foreign Affairs of the House of Representatives or the Committee on Foreign Relations of the Senate, as the case may be, and such committee shall report one such joint resolution or bill, together with its recommendations, not later than twenty-four calendar days before the expiration of the sixty-day period specified in such section, unless such House shall otherwise determine by the yeas and nays.

(b) Any joint resolution or bill so reported shall become the pending business of the House in question (in the case of the Senate the time for debate shall be equally divided between the proponents and the opponents), and shall be voted on within three calendar days thereafter, unless such House shall otherwise determine by yeas and nays.

(c) Such a joint resolution or bill passed by one House shall be referred to the committee of the other House named in subsection (a) and shall be reported out not later than fourteen calendar days before the expiration of the sixty-day period specified in section 5(b). The joint resolution or bill so reported shall become the pending business of the House in question and shall be voted on within three calendar days after it has been reported, unless such House shall otherwise determine by yeas and nays.

(d) In the case of any disagreement between the two Houses of Congress with respect to a joint resolution or bill passed by both Houses, conferees shall be promptly appointed and the committee of conference shall make and file a report with respect to such resolution or bill not later than four calendar days before the expiration of the sixty-day period specified in section 5(b). In the event the conferees are unable to agree within 48 hours, they shall report back to their respective Houses in disagreement. Notwithstanding any rule in either House concerning the printing of conference reports in the Record or concerning any delay in the consideration of such reports, such report shall be acted on by both Houses not later than the expiration of such sixty-day period.

SEC. 7. (a) Any concurrent resolution introduced pursuant to section 5(c) shall be referred to the Committee on Foreign Affairs of the House of Representatives or the Committee on Foreign Relations of the Senate, as the case may be, and one such concurrent resolution shall be reported out by such committee together with its recommendations within fifteen calendar days, unless such House shall otherwise determine by the yeas and nays.

(b) Any concurrent resolution so reported shall become the pending business of the House in question (in the case of the Senate the time for debate shall be equally divided between the proponents and the opponents) and shall be voted on within three calendar days thereafter, unless such House shall otherwise determine by yeas and nays.

(c) Such a concurrent resolution passed by one House shall be referred to the committee of the other House named in subsection (a) and shall be reported out by such committee together with its recommendations within fifteen calendar days and shall thereupon become the pending business of such House and shall be voted upon within three calendar days, unless such House shall otherwise determine by yeas and nays.

(d) In the case of any disagreement between the two Houses of Congress with respect to a concurrent resolution passed by both Houses, conferees shall be promptly appointed and the committee of conference shall make and file a report with respect to such concurrent resolution within six calendar days after the legislation is referred to the committee of conference. Notwithstanding any rule in either House concerning the printing of conference reports in the Record or concerning any delay in the consideration of such reports, such report shall be acted on by both Houses not later than six calendar days after the conference report is filed. In the event the conferees are unable to agree within 48 hours, they shall report back to their respective Houses in disagreement.

INTERPRETATION OF JOINT RESOLUTION

SEC. 8. (a) Authority to introduce United States Armed Forces into hostilities or into situations wherein involvement in hostilities is clearly indicated by the circumstances shall not be inferred—

(1) from any provision of law (whether or not in effect before the date of the enactment of this joint resolution), including any provision contained in any appropriation Act, unless such provision specifically authorizes the introduction of United States Armed Forces into hostilities or into such situations and states that it is intended to constitute specific statutory authorization within the meaning of this joint resolution; or

(2) from any treaty heretofore or hereafter ratified unless such treaty is implemented by legislation specifically authorizing the introduction of United States Armed Forces into hostilities or into such situations and stating that it is intended to constitute specific statutory authorization within the meaning of this joint resolution.

(b) Nothing in this joint resolution shall be construed to require any further specific statutory authorization to permit members of United States Armed Forces to participate jointly with members of the armed forces of one or more foreign countries in the headquarters operations of high-level military commands which were established prior to the date of enactment of this joint resolution and pursuant to the United Nations Charter or any treaty ratified by the United States prior to such date.

(c) For purposes of this joint resolution, the term "introduction of United States Armed Forces" includes the assignment of members of such armed forces to command, coordinate, participate in the movement of, or accompany the regular or irregular military forces of any foreign country or government when such military forces are engaged, or there exists an imminent threat that such forces will become engaged, in hostilities.

(d) Nothing in this joint resolution—

  (1) is intended to alter the constitutional authority of the Congress or of the President, or the provisions of existing treaties; or

  (2) shall be construed as granting any authority to the President with respect to the introduction of United States Armed Forces into hostilities or into situations wherein involvement in hostilities is clearly indicated by the circumstances which authority he would not have had in the absence of this joint resolution.

SEPARABILITY CLAUSE

SEC. 9. If any provision of this joint resolution or the application thereof to any person or circumstance is held invalid, the remainder of the joint resolution and the application of such provision to any other person or circumstance shall not be affected thereby.

EFFECTIVE DATE

SEC. 10. This joint resolution shall take effect on the date of its enactment.

# Department of Defense Appropriation Authorization Act

## TITLE VIII—GENERAL PROVISIONS

SEC. 801. Subsection (a)(1) of section 401 of Public Law 89–367, approved March 15, 1966 (80 Stat. 37), as amended, is hereby amended to read as follows:

"(a)(1) Not to exceed $1,126,000,000 of the funds authorized for appropriation for the use of the Armed Forces of the United States under this or any other Act are authorized to be made available for their stated purposes to support: (A) Vietnamese and other free world forces in support of Vietnamese forces, (B) local forces in Laos; and for related costs, during the fiscal year 1974 on such terms and conditions as the Secretary of Defense may determine. None of the funds appropriated to or for the use of the Armed Forces of the United States may be used for the purpose of paying any overseas allowance, per diem allowance, or any other addition to the regular base pay of any person serving with the free world forces in South Vietnam if the amount of such payment would be greater than the amount of special pay authorized to be paid, for an equivalent period of service, to members of the Armed Forces of the United States (under section 310 of title 37, United States Code) serving in Vietnam or in any other hostile fire area, except for continuation of payments of such additions to regular base pay provided in agreements executed prior to July 1, 1970. Nothing in clause (A) of the first sentence of this paragraph shall be construed as authorizing the use of any such funds to support Vietnamese or other free world forces in actions designed to provide military support and assistance to the Government of Cambodia or Laos: *Provided*, That nothing contained in this section shall be construed to prohibit support of actions required to insure the safe and orderly withdrawal or disengagement of United States forces from Southeast Asia, or to aid in the release of Americans held as prisoners of war."

SEC. 805. Notwithstanding any other provision of law, no funds authorized to be appropriated by this or any other Act may be obligated or expended for the purpose of carrying out directly or indirectly any economic or military assistance for or on behalf of North Vietnam unless specifically authorized by Act of Congress enacted after the date of the enactment of this Act.

SEC. 806. Notwithstanding any other provision of law, upon enactment of this Act, no funds heretofore or hereafter appropriated may be obligated or expended to finance the involvement of United States military forces in hostilities in or over or from off the shores of North Vietnam, South Vietnam, Laos, or Cambodia, unless specifically authorized hereafter by the Congress.

# Foreign Assistance Act of 1973

"Sec. 112. Prohibiting Police Training.—(a) No part of any appropriation made available to carry out this Act shall be used to conduct any police training or related program in a foreign country.

"(b) Subsection (a) of this section shall not apply—

"(1) with respect to assistance rendered under section 515(c) of the Omnibus Crime Control and Safe Streets Act of 1968, as amended, or with respect to any authority of the Drug Enforcement Administration or the Federal Bureau of Investigation which relates to crimes of the nature which are unlawful under the laws of the United States; or

"(2) to any contract entered into prior to the date of enactment of this section with any person, organization, or agency of the United States Government to provide personnel to conduct, or assist in conducting, any such program.

Notwithstanding paragraph (2), subsection (a) shall apply to any renewal or extension of any contract referred to in such paragraph entered into on or after such date of enactment.

(6) Section 513 is amended—

(A) by striking out "Thailand.—" in the section heading and inserting in lieu thereof "Thailand and Laos.—(a)"; and

(B) by adding at the end thereof the following new subsection:

"(b) After June 30, 1974, no military assistance shall be furnished by the United States to Laos directly or through any other foreign country unless that assistance is authorized under this Act or the Foreign Military Sales Act."

(c) Section 655(c) shall not apply to assistance authorized to be furnished under any provision of law for fiscal year 1974.

Sec. 24. The Foreign Assistance Act of 1961 is amended by adding at the end thereof the following new part:

## "PART V

"Sec. 801. General Authority.—The President is authorized to furnish, on such terms and conditions as he may determine, assistance for relief and reconstruction of South Vietnam, Cambodia, and Laos, including especially humanitarian assistance to refugees, civilian war casualties, and other persons disadvantaged by hostilities or conditions related to those hostilities in South Vietnam, Cambodia, and Laos. No assistance shall be furnished under this section to South Vietnam unless the President receives assurances satisfactory to him that no assistance furnished under this part, and no local currencies generated as a result of assistance furnished under this part, will be used for support of police, or prison construction and administration, within South Vietnam.

"Sec. 802. Authorization.—There are authorized to be appropriated to the President to carry out the purposes of this chapter, in addition to funds otherwise available for such purposes, for the fiscal year 1974 not to exceed $504,000,000, which amount is authorized to remain available until expended.

"Sec. 803. Assistance to South Vietnamese Children.—(a) It is the sense of the Congress that inadequate provision has been made (1) for the establishment, expansion, and improvement of day care centers, orphanages, hostels, school feeding programs, health and welfare programs, and training related to these programs which are designed for the benefit of South Vietnamese children, disadvantaged by hostilties in Vietnam or conditions related to those hostilities, and (2) for the adoption by United States citizens of South Vietnamese children who are orphaned or abandoned, or whose parents or sole surviving parent, as the case may be, has irrevocably relinquished all parental rights, particularly children fathered by United States citizens.

"(b) The President is, therefore, authorized to provide assistance, on terms and conditions he considers appropriate, for the purposes described in clauses (1) and (2) of subsection (a) of this section. Of the funds appropriated pursuant to section 802 for fiscal year 1974, $5,000,000, or its equivalent in local currency, shall be available until expended solely to carry out this section. Not more than 10 per centum of the funds made available to carry out this section may be expended for the purposes referred to in clause (2) of subsection (a). Assistance provided under this section shall be furnished, to the maximum extent practicable. under the auspices of and by international agencies or private voluntary agencies.

"SEC. 804. CENTER FOR PLASTIC AND RECONSTRUCTIVE SURGERY IN SAIGON.—Of the funds appropriated pursuant to section 802 for the fiscal year 1974, not less than $712,000 shall be available solely for furnishing assistance to the Center for Plastic and Reconstructive Surgery in Saigon.

"SEC. 805. AUTHORITY.—All references to part I, whether heretofore or hereafter enacted, shall be deemed to be references also to this part unless otherwise specifically provided. The authorities available to administer part I of this Act shall be available to administer programs authorized in this part."

## TERMINATION OF INDOCHINA WAR

SEC. 30. No funds authorized or appropriated under this or any other law may be expended to finance military or paramilitary operations by the United States in or over Vietnam, Laos, or Cambodia.

## LIMITATION ON USE OF FUNDS

SEC. 31. No funds authorized or appropriated under any provision of law shall be made available for the purpose of financing directly or indirectly any military or paramilitary combat operations by foreign forces in Laos, Cambodia, North Vietnam, South Vietnam, or Thailand unless (1) such operations are conducted by the forces of that government receiving such funds within the borders of that country, or (2) specifically authorized by law enacted after the date of enactment of this Act.

## POLITICAL PRISONERS

SEC. 32. It is the sense of Congress that the President should deny any economic or military assistance to the government of any foreign country which practices the internment or imprisonment of that country's citizens for political purposes.

## PRISONERS OF WAR AND INDIVIDUALS MISSING IN ACTION

SEC. 34. (a) The Congress declares that—

(1) the families of those one thousand three hundred individuals missing in action during the Indochina conflict have suffered extraordinary torment in ascertaining the full and complete information about their loved ones who are formally classified as missing in action;

(2) United States involvement in the Indochina conflict has

come to a negotiated end with the signing of the Vietnam Agreement in Paris on January 27, 1973, and section 307 of the Second Supplemental Appropriations Act, 1973, requires that "None of the funds herein appropriated under this Act may be expended to support directly or indirectly combat activities in or over Cambodia, Laos, North Vietnam, and South Vietnam or off the shores of Cambodia, Laos, North Vietnam and South Vietnam by United States forces, and after August 15, 1973, no other funds heretofore appropriated under any other Act may be expended for such purpose.";

(3) the question of the return of prisoners of war and accounting for individuals missing in action and dead in Laos is covered by article 18 of the Protocol signed by representatives of the Lao Patriotic Front (Pathet Lao) and the Royal Laotian Government in Vientiane on September 14, 1973 (which implements article 5 of the Agreement signed by the Pathet Lao and that government in Vientiane on February 21, 1973, requiring the release of all prisoners "regardless of nationality" captured and held in Laos), and paragraph C of such article 18 provides that, within "15 to 30 days" from the date of the signing of the Protocol, each side is to report the number of those prisoners and individuals still held, with an indication of their nationality and status, together with a list of names and any who died in captivity; and

(4) few of the United States men lost in Laos during the military engagements in Indochina have been returned, and with knowledge about many of these men not yet being fully disclosed, and the North Vietnam cease-fire provisions calling for inspection of crash and grave sites and for other forms of cooperation have not been fully complied with.

(b) It is, therefore, the sense of the Congress that—

(1) the provisions for the release of prisoners and an accounting of individuals missing and dead, as provided for in article 18 of the Protocol signed on September 14, 1973, by the Pathet Lao and the Royal Laotian Government, be adhered to in spirit and in deed; and

(2) the faithful compliance with the spirit of the Laotian Agreement and Protocol on the question of individuals missing in action will encourage all parties in Indochina to cooperate in providing complete information on all nationals of any nation who may be captured or missing at any place in Indochina.

#### PROHIBITION ON ASSISTANCE TO NORTH VIETNAM

SEC. 37. Notwithstanding any other provision of law, no funds authorized by this Act shall be expended to aid or assist in the reconstruction of the Democratic Republic of Vietnam (North Vietnam), unless by an Act of Congress assistance to North Vietnam is specifically authorized.

# Foreign Assistance and Related Programs Appropriation Act

SEC. 109. None of the funds appropriated or made available pursuant to this Act for carrying out the Foreign Assistance Act of 1961, as amended, may be used to finance the procurement of iron and steel products for use in Vietnam containing any component acquired by the producer of the commodity, in the form in which imported into the country of production, from sources other than the United States.

SEC. 110. None of the funds contained in title I of this Act may be used to carry out the provisions of sections 209(d) and 251(h) of the Foreign Assistance Act of 1961, as amended.

SEC. 111. None of the funds appropriated or made available pursuant to this Act shall be used to provide assistance to the Democratic Republic of Vietnam (North Vietnam).

SEC. 112. None of the funds appropriated or made available pursuant to this Act, and no local currencies generated as a result of assistance furnished under this Act, may be used for the support of police, or prison construction and administration within South Vietnam, for training, including computer training, of South Vietnamese with respect to police, criminal, or prison matters, or for computers or computer parts for use for South Vietnam with respect to police, criminal, or prison matters.

SEC. 604. None of the funds contained in this Act shall be used to furnish petroleum fuels produced in the continental United States to Southeast Asia for use by non-United States nationals.

# VIII. SPECIAL SUPPLEMENT: WAR ENDS

## WAR ENDS IN INDOCHINA

Editorial Note

In the Spring of 1975 all combat activities in Indochina came to an end. The negotiated peace has held up in Laos, although control over the apparatus of government has been gradually shifting to the Pathet Lao, especially after the fall of South Vietnam. In Cambodia peace was restored by the military victory of the Khymer Rouge, culminating in surrender by the Phom Phenh government headed by Premier Long Boret on April 16, 1975.

In South Vietnam, a series of dramatic military reversals by the Saigon government led to the resignation of President Nguyen Van Thieu and his replacement by his Vice President, Tran Van Huong, who lasted in office for one week. On April 28, General Duong Van Minh ("Big Minh") became President and two days later signed an instrument of surrender, giving formal authority to govern all of South Vietnam over to the Provisional Revolutionary Government of South Vietnam. The military forces of North Vietnam played a leading role in achieving the military victory and it remains as yet unclear as to whether independent political leadership from the Provisional Revolutionary Government will emerge in South Vietnam.

The question of greatest interest to international lawyers concerns the collapse of the Paris Agreement of 1973 which had been negotiated at such great length and which had been hailed as such a significant breakthrough for peace that Henry Kissinger and the Le Duc Tho, the chief negotiators, were jointly awarded a Nobel Peace Prize. It is of great practical consequence to interpret the failure of the Paris Agreements accurately. Such an interpretation will undoubtedly influence the reliance of the American government (and other governments) on negotiated settlements of armed conflicts, especially with Communist powers. In this special supplement we concentrate on the issue of why the Paris Agreement collapsed, presenting the official explanation of American leaders, President Thieu's resignation speech, the letters President Nixon sent to Thieu shortly before the Paris signing, and a sampling of commentaries by scholarly experts.

Other important legal issues remain:

--do any provisions of the Paris Agreement survive to define future relations between the United States and North Vietnam (e. g. reconstruction aid as promised in Art. 21)?;

--was the removal of Vietnamese orphan children from South Vietnam to the United States accomplished in accord with international law?

--was the removal of South Vietnamese officials, including those accused of war crimes, an instance of "humanitarian intervention" that is consistent with modern international law?

A lingering issue in Vietnam is, of course, the reunification of the country. It seems clear that reunification will occur, but the pace, the modality, and the diplomatic consequences remain uncertain. These aspects of future developments may determine whether Vietnam participates in international institutions as one country or as two. A related question is whether the United States will extend diplomatic recognition to the new government in South Vietnam and enter into normal diplomatic relations with North Vietnam.

## U.S. Protests North Viet-Nam's Violations of Peace Accords

*Following is the text of a note transmitted to U.S. missions on January 11 for delivery to non-Vietnamese participants in the International Conference on Viet-Nam and to members of the International Commission of Control and Supervision (ICCS).*[1]

Press release 12 dated January 13

The Department of State of the United States of America presents its compliments to [recipient of this note] and has the honor to refer to the Agreement on Ending the War and Restoring Peace in Viet-Nam signed at Paris January 27, 1973, and to the Act of the International Conference on Viet-Nam signed at Paris March 2, 1973.

When the Agreement was concluded nearly two years ago, our hope was that it would provide a framework under which the Vietnamese people could make their own political choices and resolve their own problems in an atmosphere of peace. Unfortunately this hope, which was clearly shared by the Republic of Viet-Nam and the South Vietnamese people, has been frustrated by the persistent refusal of the Democratic Republic of Viet-Nam to abide by the Agreement's most fundamental provisions. Specifically, in flagrant violation of the Agreement, the North Vietnamese and "Provisional Revolutionary Government" authorities have:

—built up the North Vietnamese mainforce army in the South through the illegal infiltration of over 160,000 troops;

—tripled the strength of their armor in the South by sending in over 400 new vehicles, as well as greatly increased their artillery and anti-aircraft weaponry;

—improved their military logistics system running through Laos, Cambodia and the Demilitarized Zone as well as within South Viet-Nam, and expanded their armament stockpiles;

—refused to deploy the teams which under the Agreement were to oversee the cease-fire;

—refused to pay their prescribed share of the expenses of the International Commission of Control and Supervision;

—failed to honor their commitment to cooperate in resolving the status of American and other personnel missing in action, even breaking off all discussions on this matter by refusing for the past seven months to meet with U.S. and Republic of Viet-Nam representatives in the Four-Party Joint Military Team;

—broken off all negotiations with the Republic of Viet-Nam including the political negotiations in Paris and the Two Party Joint Military Commission talks in Saigon, answering the Republic of Viet-Nam's repeated calls for unconditional resumption of the negotiations with demands for the overthrow of the government as a pre-condition for any renewed talks; and

—gradually increased their military pressure, over-running several areas, including 11 district towns, which were clearly and unequivocally held by the Republic of Viet-Nam at the time of the cease-fire. Their latest and most serious escalation of the fighting began in early December with offensives in the southern half of South Viet-Nam which have brought the level of casualties and destruction back up to what it was before the Agreement. These attacks—which included for the first time since the massive North Vietnamese 1972 offensive the over-running of a province capital (Song Be in Phuoc Long Province)—appear to reflect a decision by Hanoi to seek once again to impose a military solution in Viet-Nam. Coming just before the second anniversary of the Agreement, this dramatically belies Hanoi's claims that it is the United States and the Republic of Viet-Nam who are violating the Agreement and standing in the way of peace.

The United States deplores the Democratic Republic of Viet-Nam's turning from the path of negotiation to that of war, not

---

[1] Union of Soviet Socialist Republics, People's Republic of China, United Kingdom, France, Hungary, Poland, Indonesia, Iran, and U.N. Secretary General Kurt Waldheim.

only because it is a grave violation of a solemn international agreement, but also because of the cruel price it is imposing on the people of South Viet-Nam. The Democratic Republic of Viet-Nam must accept the full consequences of its actions. We are deeply concerned about the threat posed to international peace and security, to the political stability of Southeast Asia, to the progress which has been made in removing Viet-Nam as a major issue of great-power contention, and to the hopes of mankind for the building of structures of peace and the strengthening of mechanisms to avert war. We therefore reiterate our strong support for the Republic of Viet-Nam's call to the Hanoi-"Provisional Revolutionary Government" side to reopen the talks in Paris and Saigon which are mandated by the Agreement. We also urge that the [addressee] call upon the Democratic Republic of Viet-Nam to halt its military offensive and join the Republic of Viet-Nam in re-establishing stability and seeking a political solution.

JANUARY 11, 1975.

## Department Discusses Goal of Military Assistance to Viet-Nam and Cambodia

*Statement by Philip C. Habib*
*Assistant Secretary for East Asian and Pacific Affairs* [1]

I welcome the opportunity to appear before you today. The House Foreign Affairs Committee has been a thoughtful and constructive participant in the evolution of U.S. policy toward East Asia, and it is appropriate that early consideration of the new and difficult situations in Viet-Nam and Cambodia should take place here. In the interim since this hearing was originally scheduled, I visited Indochina briefly, accompanying a congressional delegation. I found the experience illuminating, as I believe did your colleagues, and I will draw on my observations there in my testimony today. My opening remarks will be relatively brief so that most of our time can be devoted to your questions.

Two years ago in Paris we concluded an agreement which we hoped would end the war in Viet-Nam and pave the way for settlements of the conflicts in Laos and Cambodia. We felt the Paris agreement was fair to both sides. From the standpoint of the United States, the agreement in large measure met what had been our purpose throughout the long period of our involvement in Viet-Nam. It established a formula through which the people of South Viet-Nam could

determine their political future, without outside interference. U.S. forces were withdrawn and our prisoners released. The Government of South Viet-Nam was left intact, and the agreement permitted the provision of necessary military and economic assistance to that government.

The war has not ended in Indochina; peace has not been restored. Only in Laos have the contending parties moved from military confrontation toward a political solution. In Cambodia, the conflict is unabated In Viet-Nam, after a brief period of relative quiescence, warfare is again intensive and the structure established by the Paris agreement for working toward a political settlement is not functioning. This is deeply disappointing, but it is not surprising. The Paris agreement contained no automatic self-enforcing mechanisms. Although instruments were established which could have been effective in restricting subsequent military action, the viability of those instruments—and of the agreement itself—depended ultimately on the voluntary adherence of the signatories. Such adherence has been conspicuously lacking in Hanoi's approach.

The Communist record in the last two years, in sharp contrast to that of the GVN [Government of Viet-Nam] and the United States, is one of massive and systematic violations of the agreement's most fundamental provisions. Hanoi has sent nearly 200,000

[1] Made before the Special Subcommittee on Investigations of the House Committee on Foreign Affairs on Mar. 6. The complete transcript of the hearings will be published by the committee and will be available from the Superintendent of Documents, U.S. Government Printing Office, Washington, D.C. 20402.

additional troops into South Viet-Nam although the introduction of any new forces was expressly prohibited by the agreement. Amply supplied by the Soviet Union and the People's Republic of China, Hanoi has tripled the strength of its armor in the South, sending in more than 400 new armored vehicles, and has greatly increased its artillery and antiaircraft weaponry. The agreement, of course, permitted only a one-for-one replacement of weapons and material. Hanoi has improved and expanded its logistic system in the South and, drawing on Soviet and Chinese support, has built up its armament stockpiles—within the borders of South Viet-Nam—to levels exceeding even those which existed just prior to the Easter offensive of 1972.

Hanoi has employed a rich variety of tactics to undermine the mechanisms established by the agreement for the purpose of monitoring the cease-fire. It has, for example, refused to deploy the jointly manned military teams which were to oversee the cease-fire. It has also refused to pay its share of the support costs for the International Commission of Control and Supervision, has not allowed the ICCS to station teams in areas its forces control, and has prevented, by delay and obfuscation, any effective investigation of cease-fire violations.

Hanoi has been similarly obstructive on the political front, breaking off all political (and military) negotiations with the GVN, which were a cornerstone of the agreement. The South Vietnamese Government has repeatedly called for negotiations to be resumed. Hanoi's response—reminiscent of its position prior to the fall of 1972—has been to demand the overthrow of President Thieu as a precondition to any talks. As you all know, Hanoi has also failed to cooperate with us and the GVN in helping to resolve the status of American and other personnel who are missing in action.

Finally, Hanoi has applied gradually increasing military pressure, seizing territory clearly held by the GVN when the agreement was signed. More recently, beginning last December 5, Hanoi embarked on a major new offensive. Since that date it has over-run six district towns and one provincial capital and now threatens additional administrative and population centers.

Through its massive infiltration of men and equipment since the cease-fire was signed, Hanoi obviously has the ability to conduct even more widespread and intensive actions. Through its systematic sabotage of the mechanisms set up by the agreement to monitor violations of the cease-fire and from the evidence of the past two months, it is also clear that Hanoi intends to step up its attacks. The aim of this new offensive clearly is to force additional political concessions from the GVN and to dictate a political solution on Hanoi's terms or, if South Viet-Nam proves unable to resist, to achieve outright military victory. In either case the Paris agreement, and the progress toward peace which it represented, is gravely threatened.

The South Vietnamese have fought well, indeed valiantly, against difficult odds. The GVN still controls most of the territory it held in January 1973, which of course includes the vast majority of the South Vietnamese people, and it has done this without direct U.S. military involvement and despite sharply declining levels of U.S. assistance. But the current North Vietnamese offensive poses new dangers. Present levels of U.S. military aid to South Viet-Nam are clearly inadequate to meet them. We are unable to replace, on the one-for-one basis permitted by the agreement, the consumables essential for South Viet-Nam's defense effort—ammunition, fuel, spare parts, and medical supplies. We are unable to provide any replacement of major equipment losses—tanks, trucks, planes, or artillery pieces. Thus, South Viet-Nam's stockpiles are being drawn down at a dangerous rate; and its ability to successfully withstand further large-scale North Vietnamese attacks is being eroded. South Viet-Nam is even now faced with a harsh choice: to husband its diminishing resources and face additional battlefield losses or to use supplies at a rate sufficient to stem the tide—and risk running out at an early date.

It is for these reasons that the President has requested urgent congressional approval of a $300 million supplemental appropriation for military assistance for Viet-Nam. This additional amount is the absolute minimum required, and it is needed now.

The Paris agreement also contained provisions relating to Laos and Cambodia. The signatories were enjoined to respect the sovereignty and territorial integrity of those countries and to refrain from using their territory for military purposes. South Viet-Nam and the United States have abided by these strictures. Hanoi has not. North Viet-Nam continues to use the territory of Laos to send forces and war material to South Viet-Nam and continues to station troops in remote areas of that country. Nevertheless the contending Laotian parties were able to establish a cease-fire—which is only infrequently broken—and to form a Provisional Government of National Union.

As a result of these encouraging developments, our military presence in Laos has been withdrawn (except of course for the normal Defense attache office as part of our diplomatic establishment) and we have been able to reduce our military assistance to an enormous degree. For example, during the last fiscal year of widespread combat, fiscal year 1973, U.S. military aid amounted to $360 million. For fiscal year 1975, the figure is $30 million.

Unfortunately, a similar evolution has not occurred in Cambodia. North Viet-Nam continues to use the territory of Cambodia to support its military operations in South Viet-Nam and in addition gives material assistance and advice in the military operations of Cambodian Communist forces. We do not contend that Hanoi is the sole motive force for the Cambodian insurgency. However, in its support and encouragement of that conflict as well as in its own flagrant abuse of Cambodian territory, Hanoi bears a large measure of responsibility for the continuation of the fighting there. That fighting has recently intensified. Since January 1, Communist forces have stepped up their attacks in the area near Phnom Penh. At the same time they have increased their pressure along the Mekong River between Phnom Penh and the South Vietnamese border, the capital's main supply route. Cambodian forces have fought well, but they are stretched thin in attempting to combat this two-pronged offensive. And despite stringent economies their supplies of ammunition and fuel are dangerously low.

The intensified Communist attacks have taken a heavy human toll, evident in even a short visit to that country. Casualties are running at more than 1,000 a day for both sides—killed, wounded, and missing—and the stricken economic life of Cambodia is further weakened. At least 60,000 new refugees have been created, posing additional strain on the resources and the administrative capacity of the government.

The Cambodian Government does not seek an end to the conflict through conclusive military victory. Nor, however, does it wish it to end in military victory by Communist forces. The only logical and fair solution is one involving negotiations and a compromise settlement. To this end we welcomed the resolution, sponsored by Cambodia's neighbors and adopted by the last U.N. General Assembly, calling for early negotiations. The Cambodian Government has repeatedly expressed its readiness to negotiate, without preconditions and with any interlocutor the other side may choose. We fully support that position and have pledged to do our utmost to facilitate such talks.

As you are aware, we have recently documented the efforts the United States has already made to promote a negotiated settlement in Cambodia—in 1973–74 and as recently as February of this year.[2] Those efforts, which included attempts to establish direct contact with the Communists and Sihanouk, have thus far been futile. The Cambodian Communists have been adamantly opposed to a negotiated settlement, and we believe their attitude is unlikely to change unless and until they conclude that military victory is not possible. The first imperative, therefore, and the aim of our military assist-

---

[2] See p. 401.

ance program in Cambodia is to maintain a military balance and thereby to promote negotiations.

Restrictions on our military and economic aid contained in the Foreign Assistance Act of 1974 make it impossible to accomplish that goal. Both the $200 million ceiling on military assistance and the $75 million drawdown authorized from Department of Defense stocks have been largely exhausted as a result of significantly intensified Communist offensive actions. In addition, Cambodia also faces a serious impending food shortage. Therefore, to meet the minimum requirements for the survival of the Khmer Republic, the President has asked the Congress to provide on an urgent basis an additional $222 million in military aid for Cambodia and to eliminate the $200 million ceiling. He has also asked that the $377 million ceiling on overall assistance be removed, or at least that Public Law 480 food be exempted from the ceiling.

In Viet-Nam we seek to restore the rough military balance, now threatened by North Vietnamese action, which permitted the progress toward peace represented by the Paris agreement and without which further progress toward a lasting political solution is unlikely to be found. Despite Hanoi's flagrant violation of the Paris agreement, we believe it remains a potentially workable framework for an overall settlement and it must be preserved. By redressing the deteriorating military situation in South Viet-Nam our hope is that the momentum can once again be shifted from warfare toward negotiations among the Vietnamese parties. In Cambodia also, only by maintaining the defensive capability of government forces can conditions be established which will permit negotiations to take place.

For neither Viet-Nam nor Cambodia is the provision of additional aid the harbinger of a new and open-ended commitment for the United States. Our record in Indochina supports rather than contradicts that assertion. We worked successfully with the South Vietnamese in reducing and eventually eliminating our own direct military role, and

subsequently with both the South Vietnamese and Cambodian Governments in achieving maximum economies and maximum impact from our aid. Those efforts will continue.

In previous testimony before this and other committees of the Congress in behalf of assistance for Indochina, I and other Administration witnesses have attempted to relate our policies and our programs there to the broader purposes of the United States in the world. For despite the agony of this nation's experience in Indochina and the substantial reappraisal which has taken place concerning our proper role there, Indochina remains relevant to those broader foreign policy concerns. We no longer see the security of the United States as directly, immediately at issue. Nonetheless it remains true that failure to sustain our purposes in Indochina would have a corrosive effect on our ability to conduct effective diplomacy worldwide. Our readiness to see through to an orderly conclusion the obligations we undertook in Indochina cannot fail to influence other nations' estimates of our stamina and our determination. Thus we cannot isolate the situation in Indochina from our other and broader interests in this increasingly interdependent world. To now weaken in our resolve would have consequences inimical to those interests.

Finally, we cannot ignore another aspect of our policy toward Indochina. In entering into the Paris agreement, we in effect told South Viet-Nam that we would no longer defend that country with U.S. forces but that we would give it the means to defend itself. The South Vietnamese have carried on impressively, as have our friends in Cambodia, in the face of extreme difficulty. I do not believe that we can walk away. Measured against the sacrifices which we, and the people of Indochina, have already offered, the amounts which are now being requested are not large. Nor, even in this time of economic constraint, are they beyond our ability to provide. They are, however, vital to the restoration of conditions which can lead to lasting peace in Indochina.

"Policy in Seven Points Promulgated and Applied by Provisional Revolutionary Government of South Vietnam," text of statement, April 2, 1975. *

1.

Policy with regard to efforts of the entire population to unite to block forced enrollment and forced displacing and regrouping of the population, the sabotaging of the Paris accord and the continuation of the neo-colonialist war undertaken by the United States and the administration of Saigon.

A. All Vietnamese have the duty and the honor of uniting to block by their struggle forced displacement and regrouping of the population. They are determined to protect the young and to prevent the enemy from pushing them along the path of crime upon their compatriots and their country.

B. The revolutionary authority will do all it can to help those who oppose forced enrollment, displacement and regrouping of the population. Youths who seek to escape forced enrollment and Saigon soldiers who desert will be actively protected and aided for the defense of their lives as well as the protection of their belongings. If they wish to enter the zone controlled by the revolutionary authority, they will be helped to find means of existence.

C. Those who help the young, or counsel the soldiers, officers and civil servants of Saigon to act in the interest of the people and of the country or in favor of the application of the Paris accord, will be honorably cited by the revolutionary authority. Those who merit it will be recompensed.

2.

Policy with regard to families that have members in the Saigon military or administrative apparatus.

A. Families with members in the military and administrative apparatus of the Saigon Government, families of orphans and widows who

*Reprinted from New York Times, April 3, 1975, p. 17.

have been the victims of the American puppet neocolonialist regime of op-pression, if they have done nothing against the revolutionary cause, will have the same rights and the same duties as other citizens. The revolu-tionary government welcomes any Vietnamese family that manifests a spirit of solidarity in the fight for peace, independence, democratic liberties and national concord.

B.   Those who contributed to the revolutionary cause or who have members of their families who have participated in the revolutionary strug-gle, even if they have other members of their families in the military or administrative apparatus of the Saigon administration, will be considered revolutionary families.

C.   Those who have not had the occasion to contribute to the national cause but who now seek to encourage members of their families to fight for the application of the Paris agreement, against the American aggressors and against the bellicose clique in the Saigon army and administration will be ac-claimed and their names cited by the revolutionary authority. Those who have encouraged members of their families to contribute to the revolutionary cause will be recompensed. If they participate in uprisings, they will be recognized as families having acquired merit in the revolutionary cause.

3.

Policy with regard to those who were forced to participate in the "popular self-defense forces," the militia or other paramilitary organiza-tions.

A.   If they have done nothing against the population they will have the same rights and the same duties as the other citizens.

B.  Individuals and units having struggled to refuse participation in military training, guard duty, patrols, ambushes, operations, opposing the transfer of men from one kind of armed forces to another, to the enrollment of the young or coercion exerted by extortionists, or who have protected and helped youngsters in evading forced enrollment or soldiers after they de-serted, or who helped inhabitants to move freely so as to find work or to return to their place of origin,  or who participated in the people's fight against the enemy will receive an honorable citation by the people and by the revolutionary authority.

C.   Individuals and units that brought their arms to the revolutionary authority or participated in uprisings with a view to destroying the Saigon apparatus of coercion or the concentration camps, or were opposing the forced regroupings of the population, or sought to annihilate military posts or to liberate villages will receive compensation depending on their actions.

D.   Those who wish to devote themselves to revolutionary tasks or enroll in the revolutionary armed forces will be well received.

4.

Policy with regard to soldiers manning military posts or in militia units, "civil guards" or regular troops, or belonging to the different armed branches and police of Saigon.

A.   Individuals and garrisons that took part in the struggle against the draconian regime imposed upon soldiers and their families, against forced enrollment and the transfer of soldiers from one category of troops to another, who have demanded demobilization or left their units to go home, and who oppose the operations of encroaching or illegal implanting of military posts, to forced displacement and regrouping of the population, police operations and repression, and who join the struggle of the population and who have taken part in it, will be favorably welcomed and aided by the population and the revolutionary authority.

B.   Individuals, garrisons and units that have revolted and handed over their posts and their weapons or brought their weapons and their documents to the revolutionary authority, who have taken part in people's uprisings to eliminate the torturers, wipe out their posts, their bases, their depots or other points of departure for criminal operations contrary to the Paris accord and who contribute to the liberation of villages will be recognized as insurgent soldiers or insurgent units. The same will be true of individuals or units that mutiny at the front to join the People's Armed Forces of Liberation to help punish those who violate the Paris accord. The insurgent units will be recompensed in accordance with their actions.

Those who are wounded during these actions will benefit from the same advantages as injured revolutionary combatants. If they are killed in the course of these actions they will be recognized as "killed on mission."

### 5.

Policy with regard to the members of the Saigon army and administration now finding themselves in the areas under the control of the revolutionary power:

A. The soldiers, officers, policemen, wounded and war invalids, former soldiers, officials of the Saigon administration, having left the ranks of the Saigon army and administration and gone to the areas controlled by the revolutionary authority, if they do nothing against the revolution and against the people and respect the laws promulgated by the revolutionary power will receive help in their search for a means of existence. Those among them who wish to work the land can receive land in accordance with the agricultural policy in force. Those who wish to return to their places of origin will be helped to do so. Those who wish to accomplish a task where they now are will receive encouragement and employment according to their competence.

B. In the newly liberated areas those among them who chose voluntarily to stay on and present themselves to the revolutionary authority in accordance with the dispositions made will receive help. Those that have contributed to the defense of public property, given their arms and documents, helped to unmask those who stirred up trouble, disclosed the existence of underground passageways or of secret stocks of the enemy or have called on others to present themselves to the authorities will receive citations according to their actions. Those who wish to contribute to the edification of the new regime or put themselves at the service of the people and the homeland will be given appropriate tasks.

### 6.

Policy with regard to officers, general officers and high civil servants of the Saigon administration in South Vietnam or abroad.

A. The revolutionary authority favorably salutes all those who are really in favor of peace, independence and democracy and national concord and who wish to work together for a strict application of the Paris accord, without distinction as to their past, their opinions or their position.

B. The officers and general officers belonging to tendencies and organization of the political third force will be treated in the same fashion as other members of this force by the revolutionary authority.

C. As to officers and general officers whose units revolt or mutiny under their command to join the revolutionary ranks, they will be recognized as insurgent officers. They retain their rank, will receive important assignments and will be cited. Those who lead particularly meritorious actions will receive promotions.

D. Those who must, because of their actions in favor of the national cause, make their way to the liberated zone, alone or with their families, will be granted all facilities and will have all their belongings safeguarded. Those who send their families into the liberated zone with their capital and their means of production to take part in economic activities will be helped by the revolutionary authority.

### 7.

Policy toward soldiers and officers who have been captured or who surrender, and toward criminals who have really repented.

A. The population and revolutionary authority accord humane treatment to prisoners of war and humane treatment to those who have surrendered. Those who wish to earn their livings honestly among their families or to devote themselves to revolutionary tasks will be aided.

B. Those who have committed crimes but who have really repented will benefit from the clemency of the population and of the revolutionary authority. Those who have carried out positive actions will be rewarded according to their actions.

## U.S. Calls on North Viet-Nam To End Military Offensive

*Following are texts of a note delivered by U.S. Missions on April 10 to non-Vietnamese participants in the International Conference on Viet-Nam and members of the International Commission of Control and Supervision (ICCS) and of a note delivered to the Embassy of the Democratic Republic of Viet-Nam at Paris by the U.S. Embassy on April 11.*

### NOTE TO NON-VIETNAMESE PARTICIPANTS IN CONFERENCE AND MEMBERS OF ICCS

Press release 193 dated April 11

The Department of State of the United States of America presents its compliments to [the Ministry of Foreign Affairs/Ministry of External Affairs of the Union of Soviet Socialist Republics, People's Republic of China, Great Britain, France, Hungary, Poland, Indonesia, Iran, and Secretary General of the U.N. Kurt Waldheim] and has the honor to refer to the Agreement on Ending the War and Restoring Peace in Viet-Nam signed at Paris January 27, 1973; to the Act of the International Conference on Viet-Nam signed at Paris March 2, 1973; and to the Department's Diplomatic Note of January 11, 1975, on the situation in Viet-Nam.

More than two years ago, the signatories of the Paris Agreement accepted a solemn obligation to end the fighting in Viet-Nam and to shift the conflict there from the battlefield to the negotiating table. All nations and peoples who love peace had the right to expect from that Agreement that the South Vietnamese people would be able to peacefully determine their own future and their own political institutions after the Paris Agreement was signed. The parties to the International Conference on Viet-Nam undertook a responsibility to support and uphold the settlement which the Agreement embodied.

The Democratic Republic of Viet-Nam has undertaken a massive, all-out offensive against South Viet-Nam in total contempt of the Paris Agreement. Their forces, which were built up over the past two years in violation of the Agreement, are more numerous and better equipped with modern weaponry than ever before during the course of the war. A human flight of historic proportions has taken place before the advancing North Vietnamese armies, and untold misery has been inflicted on the land which has already seen more than its share of misery.

We believe the suffering of the South Vietnamese people must be ended. It must be ended now. We therefore call upon the [addressee] to join the Government of the United States of America in calling upon Hanoi to cease its military operations immediately and to honor the terms of the Paris Agreement. The United States is requesting all the parties to the Act of the International Conference to meet their obligations to use their influence to halt the fighting and enforce the Paris Agreement.

The United States Government looks forward to prompt and constructive responses to this Note from all the parties.

### NOTE TO NORTH VIET-NAM

Press release 193A dated April 11

The Department of State of the United States of America presents its compliments to the Ministry of Foreign Affairs of the Democratic Republic of Viet-Nam and has the honor to refer to the Agreement on Ending the War and Restoring Peace in Viet-Nam signed at Paris January 27, 1973; and to the Act of the International Conference on Viet-Nam signed at Paris March 2, 1973.

More than two years ago, the Democratic Republic of Viet-Nam, as a signatory of the Paris Agreement and the Act of the International Conference on Viet-Nam, accepted a solemn obligation to end the fighting in Viet-Nam and to shift the conflict there from the battlefield to the negotiating table. All nations and peoples who love peace hoped and expected from these Agreements that the South Vietnamese people would be able to peacefully determine their own future. Tragically, these hopes and expectations have been shattered by the Democratic Republic of Viet-Nam's total violation of these Accords.

The Democratic Republic of Viet-Nam has now undertaken a massive, all-out offensive against South Viet-Nam in total contempt of these Agreements. DRV forces in South Viet-Nam, which have been built up over the past two years in contravention of the Paris Agreement, are more numerous and better equipped than ever before during the course of the entire war. This North Vietnamese invasion has produced a human flight of refugees which is of historic proportions. By this calculated use of immense force North Viet-Nam has inflicted untold misery on a land which has already seen its share of misery.

We believe the suffering of the South Vietnamese people must be ended and must be ended now. We therefore advise the Government of the Democratic Republic of Viet-Nam to cease immediately its military offensive against South Viet-Nam and to honor the terms of the Paris Agreement. If the DRV does not reverse its present military course, it should have no doubt that it will be held responsible for the consequences.

*Q. Mr. President, how and why did the United States miscalculate the intentions of the will of the South Vietnamese to resist?*

*President Ford:* I don't believe that we miscalculated the will of the South Vietnamese to carry on their fight for their own freedom.

There were several situations that developed that I think got beyond the control of the Vietnamese people. The unilateral military decision to withdraw created a chaotic situation in Viet-Nam that appears to have brought about tremendous disorganization.

I believe that the will of the South Vietnamese people to fight for their freedom is best evidenced by the fact that they are fleeing from the North Vietnamese, and that clearly is an indication they don't want to live under the kind of government that exists in North Viet-Nam.

The will of the South Vietnamese people, I think, still exists. They want freedom under a different kind of government than has existed in North Viet-Nam. The problem is how to organize that will under the traumatic experiences of the present.

*Q. Mr. President, what is your response to the South Vietnamese Ambassador to Washington's statement that we had not lived up to the Paris peace accords and that the Communists are safer allies?*

*President Ford:* I won't comment on his statement. I will say this: that the North Vietnamese repeatedly and in massive efforts violated the Paris peace accords. They sent North Vietnamese regular forces into South Viet-Nam in massive numbers— I think around 150,000 to 175,000 well-trained North Vietnamese regular forces— in violation of the Paris peace accords, moved into South Viet-Nam. We have objected to that violation.

I still believe that the United States, in this case and in other cases, is a reliable ally. And although I am saddened by the events that we have read about and seen, it is a tragedy unbelievable in its ramifications.

I must say that I am frustrated by the action of the Congress in not responding to some of the requests for both economic and humanitarian and military assistance in South Viet-Nam. And I am frustrated by the limitations that were placed on the Chief Executive over the last two years.

But let me add very strongly: I am convinced that this country is going to continue its leadership. We will stand by our allies, and I specifically warn any adversaries they should not, under any circumstances, feel that the tragedy of Viet-Nam is an indication that the American people have lost their will or their desire to stand up for freedom anyplace in the world.

# U.S. Foreign Policy: Finding Strength Through Adversity

*Following is an address by Secretary Kissinger made before the American Society of Newspaper Editors at Washington on April 17, together with the transcript of a question-and-answer session after the address.*

## ADDRESS BY SECRETARY KISSINGER

Press release 204 dated April 17; as prepared for delivery

I am here to sound a note of hope about the future of our foreign policy despite the fact that we are now going through a period of adversity.

A nation facing setbacks can submerge itself in acrimony, looking for scapegoats rather than lessons. It can ignore or gloss over its difficulties and fatuously proceed as if nothing serious had happened.

Or it can examine its situation dispassionately, draw appropriate conclusions, and chart its future with realism and hope.

President Ford has chosen this latter course. A week ago he called upon Congress and the American people to turn this time of difficulty into a demonstration of spirit— to prove once again our devotion and our courage and to put these into the service of building a better world.

For the entire postwar period our strength and our leadership have been essential in preserving peace and promoting progress. If either falters, major shifts in political alignments will occur all around the world. The result will be new dangers for America's security and economic well-being. The Middle East war and oil embargo of 1973 demonstrated how distant events can threaten world peace and global prosperity simultaneously. A reduction of American influence in key areas can have disastrous consequences.

How other nations perceive us is thus a matter of major consequence. Every day I see reports from our embassies relaying anguished questions raised by our friends. What do events in Indochina, the southern flank of NATO, and the Middle East signify for America's competence—constancy— credibility—coherence? How will Americans react? What are the implications for future American policy? We can be certain that potential adversaries are asking themselves the same questions—not with sympathy, but to estimate their opportunities.

It is fashionable to maintain that pointing to dangers produces a self-fulfilling prophecy, that the prediction of consequences brings them about. Unfortunately, life is not that simple. We cannot achieve credibility by rhetoric; we cannot manufacture coherence by proclamation; and we cannot change facts by not talking about them.

We can do little about the world's judgment of our past actions. But we have it within our power to take charge of our future: if the United States responds to adversity with dignity, if we make clear to the world that we continue to hold a coherent perception of a constructive international role and mean to implement it, we can usher in a new era of creativity and accomplishment. We intend to do just that.

I know that it is not easy for a people that faces major domestic difficulties to gear itself up for new international efforts. But our economic future is bound up with the rest of the world—and with international developments in energy, trade, and economic policy. Our economic health depends on the preservation of American leadership abroad.

This country has no choice. We must,

for our own sake, play a major role in world affairs. We have strong assets: a sound foreign policy design, major international achievements in recent years, and the enormous capacities of an industrious and gifted people. We have the resources, and the will, to turn adversity into opportunity.

### Indochina

Let me start with our most tragic and immediate problem.

I can add nothing to the President's request for military and humanitarian assistance for the anguished people of South Viet-Nam. I support this appeal and have testified at length to that effect before congressional committees over the past several days.

The time will come when it will be clear that no President could do less than to ask aid for those whom we encouraged to defend their independence and at whose side we fought for over a decade. Then Americans will be glad that they had a President who refused to abandon those who desperately sought help in an hour of travail.

In Indochina our nation undertook a major enterprise for almost 15 years. We invested enormous prestige; tens of thousands died, and many more were wounded, imprisoned, and lost; we spent over $150 billion; and our domestic fabric was severely strained. Whether or not this enterprise was well conceived does not now change the nature of our problem. When such an effort founders, it is an event of profound significance—for ourselves and for others.

I, for one, do not believe that it was ignoble to have sought to preserve the independence of a small and brave people. Only a very idealistic nation could have persevered in the face of so much discouragement.

But where so many think that the war was a dreadful mistake, where thousands grieve for those they loved and others sorrow over their country's setback, there has been sufficient heartache for all to share.

The Viet-Nam debate has now run its course. The time has come for restraint and compassion. The Administration has made its case. Let all now abide by the verdict of the Congress—without recrimination or vindictiveness.

### The Design

Let us therefore look to the future. We start with a sound foreign policy structure.

We are convinced that a continuing strong American role is indispensable to global stability and progress. Therefore the central thrust of our foreign policy has been to adjust our role in the world and the conceptions, methods, and commitments which define it to the conditions of a new era—including an America fatigued by Indochina.

The postwar order of international relations ended with the last decade. No sudden upheaval marked the passage of that era, but the cumulative change by the end of the 1960's was profound. Gone was the rigid bipolar confrontation of the cold war. In its place was a more fluid and complex world —with many centers of power, more subtle dangers, and new hopeful opportunities. Western Europe and Japan were stronger and more self-confident; our alliances needed to be adjusted toward a more equal partnership. The Communist world had fragmented over doctrine and national interests; there were promising prospects for more stable relations based on restraint and negotiation. And many of our friends in other parts of the globe were now better prepared to shoulder responsibility for their security and wellbeing, but they needed our assistance during the period of transition.

At home, the American people and Congress were weary from two decades of global exertion and years of domestic turmoil. They were not prepared for confrontation unless all avenues toward peace had been explored.

The challenge for our foreign policy has been to define an effective but more balanced U.S. role in the world, reducing excessive commitments without swinging toward precipitate and dangerous withdrawal.

We have come a long way.

Our major allies in the Atlantic world and Japan have grown in strength politically and economically; our alliances are firm anchors of world security and prosperity. They are the basis for close cooperation on a range of unprecedented new problems, from détente to energy.

We have launched a hopeful new dialogue with Latin America.

We are looking to a new era of relations with Africa.

We have taken historic steps to stabilize and improve our relations with our major adversaries. We have reduced tensions, deepened dialogue, and reached a number of major agreements.

We have begun the process of controlling the rival strategic arms programs which, unconstrained, threaten global security. When the Vladivostok agreement is completed, a ceiling will have been placed for the first time on the level of strategic arsenals of the superpowers.

We have helped to ease longstanding political conflicts in such sensitive areas as Berlin and the Middle East.

And we have taken the major initiatives to mobilize the international response to new global challenges such as energy, food, the environment, and the law of the sea.

In all these areas the American role has frequently been decisive. The design still stands; our responsibilities remain. There is every prospect for major progress. There is every reason for confidence.

### The Domestic Dimension

If this be true, what then is the cause of our problem? Why the setbacks? Why the signs of impasse between the executive and the Congress? What must we do to pull ourselves together?

Setbacks are bound to occur in a world which no nation alone can dominate or control. The peculiar aspect of many of our problems is that they are of our own making. Domestic division has either compounded or caused difficulties from the southern flank of NATO to the Pacific, from the eastern Mediterranean to relations between the superpowers.

Paradoxically, herein resides a cause for optimism. For to the extent that the causes of our difficulties are within ourselves, so are the remedies.

The American people expect an effective foreign policy which preserves the peace and furthers our national interests. They want their leaders to shape the future, not just manage the present. This requires boldness, direction, nuance, and—above all—confidence between the public and the government and between the executive and the legislative branches of the government. But precisely this mutual confidence has been eroding over the past decade.

There are many causes for this state of affairs. Some afflict democracies everywhere; some are unique to America's tradition and recent history. Modern democracies are besieged by social, economic, and political challenges that cut across national boundaries and lie at the margin of governments' ability to control. The energies of leaders are too often consumed by the management of bureaucracy, which turns questions of public purpose into issues for institutional bargaining. Instant communications force the pace of events and of expectations. Persuasion, the essential method of democracy, becomes extraordinarily difficult in an era where issues are complex and outcomes uncertain. A premium is placed on simplification—an invitation to demagogues. Too often, the result is a disaffection that simultaneously debunks government and drains it of the very confidence that a democracy needs to act with conviction.

All of this has compounded the complex problem of executive-legislative relations. In every country, the authority of the modern state seems frustratingly impersonal or remote from those whose lives it increasingly affects; in nearly every democracy, executive authority is challenged by legislators who themselves find it difficult to affect policy except piecemeal or negatively. Issues become so technical that legislative oversight becomes increasingly difficult just as the issues become increasingly vital. The very essence of problem-solving on domestic issues—accommodation of special interests—robs foreign policy of consistency and focus when applied to our dealings with other nations.

Statesmen must act, even when premises cannot be proved; they must decide, even when intangibles will determine the outcome. Yet predictions are impossible to prove; consequences avoided are never evident. Skepticism and suspicion thus become a way of life and infect the atmosphere of executive-legislative debate; reasoned arguments are overwhelmed by a series of confrontations on peripheral issues.

America faces as well the problem of its new generation. The gulf between their historical experience and ours is enormous. They have been traumatized by Viet-Nam as we were by Munich. Their nightmare is foreign commitment as ours was abdication from international responsibility. It is possible that both generations learned their lessons too well. The young take for granted the great postwar achievements in restoring Europe, building peacetime alliances, and maintaining global prosperity. An impersonal, technological, bureaucratized world provides them too few incentives for dedication and idealism.

Let us remember that America's commitment to international involvement has always been ambivalent—even while our doubts were being temporarily submerged by the exertions of World War II and the postwar era. The roots of isolationism, nourished by geography and history, go deep in the American tradition. The reluctance to be involved in foreign conflicts, the belief that we somehow defile ourselves if we engage in "power politics" and balances of power, the sense that foreign policy is a form of Old World imperialism, the notion that weapons are the causes of conflict, the belief that humanitarian assistance and participation in the economic order are an adequate substitute for political engagement—all these were familiar characteristics of the American isolationism of the twenties and thirties. We took our power for granted, attributed our successes to virtue, and blamed our failures on the evil of others. We disparaged means. In our foreign involvement we have oscillated between exuberance and exhaustion, be-

tween crusading and retreats into self-doubt.

Following the Second World War a broad spectrum of civic leaders, professional groups, educators, businessmen, clergy, the media, congressional and national leaders of both parties led American public opinion to a new internationalist consensus. Taught by them and experience of the war, the nation understood that we best secured our domestic tranquillity and prosperity by enlightened participation and leadership in world affairs. Assistance to friends and allies was not a price to be paid, but a service to be rendered to international stability and therefore to our self-interest.

But in the last decade, as a consequence of Indochina and other frustrations of global engagement, some of our earlier impulses have reasserted themselves. Leadership opinion has, to an alarming degree, turned sharply against many of the internationalist premises of the postwar period. We now hear, and have for several years, that suffering is prolonged by American involvement, that injustice is perpetuated by American inaction, that defense spending is wasteful at best and produces conflict at worse, that American intelligence activities are immoral, that the necessary confidentiality of diplomacy is a plot to deceive the public, that flexibility is cynical and amoral—and that tranquillity is somehow to be brought about by an abstract purity of motive for which history offers no example.

This has a profound—and inevitable—impact on the national mood and on the national consensus regarding foreign policy. In the nation with the highest standard of living and one of the richest cultures in the world, in the nation that is certainly the most secure in the world, in the nation which has come closest of all to the ideals of civil liberty and pluralist democracy, we find a deep and chronic self-doubt, especially in the large urban centers and among presumptive leaders.

Will the American people support a responsible and active American foreign policy in these conditions? I deeply believe that they will—if their leaders, in and out of government, give them a sense that they have something to be proud of and something important to accomplish.

When one ventures away from Washington into the heart of America, one is struck by the confidence, the buoyancy, and the lack of any corrosive cynicism. We who sit at what my friend Stewart Alsop, a great journalist, once called "the center" tend to dwell too much on our problems; we dissect in overly exquisite detail our difficulties and our disputes.

I find it remarkable that two-thirds of the Americans interviewed in a nationwide poll in December, at a time of severe recession, still thought an active role in the world served their country's interests better than withdrawal. Even as other nations are closely watching the way we act in Washington, I suspect they marvel at the resiliency of our people and our institutions.

There is a great reservoir of confidence within America. We have the values, the means, and we bear the responsibility to strive for a safer and better world. And there is a great reservoir of confidence around the globe in this country's values and strength.

### Where Do We Go From Here?

So, let us learn the right lessons from today's trials.

We shall have to pay the price for our setbacks in Indochina by increasing our exertions. We no longer have the margin of safety. In the era of American predominance, America's preferences held great sway. We could overwhelm our problems with our resources. We had little need to resort to the style of nations conducting foreign policy with limited means: patience, subtlety, flexibility. Today, disarray, abdication of responsibility, or shortsightedness exact a price that may prove beyond our means.

We are still the largest single factor in international affairs, but we are one nation among many. The weight of our influence now depends crucially on our purposefulness, our perseverance, our creativity, our power, and our perceived reliability. We shall have to work harder to establish the coherence and constancy of our policy—and we shall.

We must give up the illusion that foreign policy can choose between morality and pragmatism. America cannot be true to itself unless it upholds humane values and the dignity of the individual. But equally it cannot realize its values unless it is secure. No nation has a monopoly of justice or virtue, and none has the capacity to enforce its own conceptions globally. In the nuclear age especially, diplomacy—like democracy—often involves the compromise of clashing principles. I need not remind you that there are some 140 nations in the world, of which only a bare handful subscribe to our values.

Abstract moralism can easily turn into retreat from painful choices or endless interference in the domestic affairs of others; strict pragmatism, on the other hand, robs policy of vision and heart. Principles without security spell impotence; security without principles means irrelevance. The American people must never forget that our strength gives force to our principles and our principles give purpose to our strength.

Let us understand, too, the nature of our commitments. We have an obligation of steadfastness simply by virtue of our position as a great power upon which many others depend. Thus our actions and policies over time embody their own commitment whether or not they are enshrined in legal documents. Indeed, our actions and the perception of them by other countries may represent our most important commitments.

At the same time, diplomacy must be permitted a degree of confidentiality, or most serious exchange with other governments is destroyed. To focus the national debate on so-called secret agreements which no party has ever sought to implement and whose alleged subject matter has been prohibited by law for two years is to indulge what Mencken called the "national appetite for bogus revelation." It goes without saying that a commitment involving national action must be known to the Congress or it is meaningless.

One lesson we must surely learn from Viet-Nam is that new commitments of our nation's honor and prestige must be carefully weighed. As Walter Lippmann observed, "In foreign relations, as in all other relations, a policy has been formed only when commitments and power have been brought into balance." But after our recent experiences we have a special obligation to make certain that commitments we have made will be rigorously kept and that this is understood by all concerned. Let no ally doubt our steadfastness. Let no nation ever believe again that it can tear up with impunity a solemn agreement signed with the United States.

We must continue our policy of seeking to ease tensions. But we shall insist that the easing of tensions cannot occur selectively. We shall not forget who supplied the arms which North Viet-Nam used to make a mockery of its signature on the Paris accords.

Nor can we overlook the melancholy fact that not one of the other signatories of the Paris accords has responded to our repeated requests that they at least point out North Viet-Nam's flagrant violations of these agreements. Such silence can only undermine any meaningful standards of international responsibility.

At home, a great responsibility rests upon all of us in Washington.

Comity between the executive and legislative branches is the only possible basis for national action. The decade-long struggle in this country over executive dominance in foreign affairs is over. The recognition that the Congress is a coequal branch of government is the dominant fact of national politics today.

The executive accepts that the Congress must have both the sense and the reality of participation; foreign policy must be a shared enterprise. The question is whether the Congress will go beyond the setting of guidelines to the conduct of tactics; whether it will deprive the executive of discretion and authority in the conduct of diplomacy while at the same time remaining institutionally incapable of formulating or carrying out a clear national policy of its own.

The effective performance of our constitutional system has always rested on the restrained exercise of the powers and rights conferred by it. At this moment in our history there is a grave national imperative for a spirit of cooperation and humility between the two branches of our government.

Cooperation must be a two-way street. Just as the executive has an obligation to re-examine and then to explain its policies, so the Congress should reconsider the actions which have paralyzed our policies in the eastern Mediterranean, weakened our hand in relations with the U.S.S.R., and inhibited our dialogue in this hemisphere. Foreign policy must have continuity. If it becomes partisan, paralysis results. Problems are passed on to the future under progressively worse conditions.

When other countries look to the United States, they see one nation. When they look to Washington, they see one government. They judge us as a unit—not as a series of unrelated or uncoordinated institutions. If we cannot agree among ourselves, there is little hope that we can negotiate effectively with those abroad.

So one of the most important lessons to be drawn from recent events is the need to restore the civility of our domestic discourse. Over the years of the Viet-Nam debate rational dialogue has yielded to emotion, sweeping far beyond the issues involved. Not only judgments but motives have been called into question. Not only policy but character has been attacked. What began as consensus progressively deteriorated into poisonous contention.

Leaders in government must do their share. The Administration, following the President's example, will strive for moderation and mutual respect in the national dialogue. We know that if we ask for public confidence we must keep faith with the people.

Debate is the essence of democracy. But it can elevate the nation only if conducted with restraint.

The American people yearn for an end to the bitterness and divisiveness of the past decade. Our domestic stability requires it. Our international responsibilities impose it.

You, in this audience, are today in a unique position to contribute to the healing of the nation.

## The Coming Agenda

Ralph Waldo Emerson once said "No great man ever complains a want of opportunity." Neither does a great nation.

Our resources are vast; our leadership is essential; our opportunities are unprecedented and insistent.

The challenges of the coming decades will dwarf today's disputes. A new world order is taking shape around us. It will engulf us or isolate us if we do not act boldly. We cannot consume ourselves in self-destruction. We have great responsibilities:

—We must maintain the vigor of the great democratic alliances. They can provide the anchor of shared values and purposes as we grapple with a radically new agenda.

—We must overcome the current economic and energy crisis. A domestic energy program is thus an urgent national priority. Looking ahead, we envisage a fundamentally reformed international economic system, a Bretton Woods for the 1980's and beyond.

—We must stand up for what we believe in international forums, including the United Nations, and resist the politics of resentment, of confrontation, and stale ideology. International collaboration has a more vital role now than ever, but so has mutual respect among nations.

—We must meet our continuing responsibility for peace in many regions of the world, especially where we uniquely have the confidence of both sides and where failure could spell disaster beyond the confines of the region, as in the Middle East. We will not be pushed by threats of war or economic pressure into giving up vital interests. But equally, we will not, in the President's words, "accept stagnation or stalemate with all its attendant risks to peace and prosperity." [1]

—We must stop the spiral, and the spread, of nuclear weapons. We can then move on to a more ambitious agenda: mutual reductions in strategic arms, control of other weaponry, military restraint in other environments.

—We must overcome two scourges of mankind: famine and the vagaries of nature. We reaffirm the food program announced at the World Food Conference last November. Our fundamental challenge is to help others feed themselves so that no child goes to bed hungry in the year 2000.

—We must continue to reduce conflict and tensions with our adversaries. Over time, we hope that vigilance and conciliation will lead to more positive relationships and ultimately a true global community.

—We must insure that the oceans and space become areas of cooperation rather than conflict. We can then leave to future generations vast economic and technological resources to enrich life on this earth.

Our nation is uniquely endowed to play a creative and decisive role in the new order which is taking form around us. In an era of turbulence, uncertainty, and conflict, the world still looks to us for a protecting hand, a mediating influence, a path to follow. It sees in us, most of all, a tradition and vision of hope. Just as America has symbolized for generations man's conquest of nature, so too has America—with its banner of progress and freedom—symbolized man's mastery over his own future.

For the better part of two centuries our forefathers, citizens of a small and relatively weak country, met adversity with courage and imagination. In the course of their struggle they built the freest, richest, and most powerful nation the world has ever known. As we, their heirs, take America into its third century, as we take up the unprecedented agenda of the modern world, we are determined to rediscover the belief in ourselves that characterized the most creative periods in our country.

We have come of age, and we shall do our duty.

---

[1] For President Ford's address before a joint session of the Congress on Apr. 10, see BULLETIN of Apr. 28, 1975, p. 529.

Excerpts from Nguyen Van Thieu's Resignation Address as President of Republic of Vietnam, April 21, 1975[*]

I argued with the Americans. I told them. "You are selling out South Vietnam to the Communists." But the American officials said, "We demand you sign this agreement."

I rejected that plan. I said we would not go along with it. I do not go along with any agreement with the Communists in any form whatsoever. The North Vietnamese will not agree to our Constitution, our laws, in reaching a solution on what is to be done here in South Vietnam.

This has been shown. Russians, Chinese, Americans, even Kissinger, have not been able to work it out.

If only the American Government gives us support, we can hold off the North Vietnamese Communists and there is nothing to worry about.

President Nixon told me that all accords are only pieces of paper, with no value unless they are implemented. What was important, he said, was not that he had signed the accord but that the United States would always stand ready to help South Vietnam in case the Communists violated the accord.

I asked that the United States should be ready to come back in force to help directly, not just Vietnamization, in case the Communists renewed their aggression against South Vietnam.

The most important question in my view at that time was direct United States intervention. So I won a solid pledge from our great ally, leader of the free world, that when and if North Vietnam renewed its aggression against South Vietnam, the United States would actively and strongly intervene.

As far as economic assistance goes, particularly Vietnamization of the economy, many foreigners caused great difficulty in our internal situation. We have not seen the Communists helping the people of South Vietnam either. The Communists want nothing else but to dominate us. This is the fifth time the Communists have tried to take over our country. They were not successful.

[*]Reprinted from New York Times, April 22, 1975, p. 14

If soldiers at outposts are overrun, where do they go? They have no place. We have no place to run if we give up the Republic of Vietnam.

To fight against the rebels we have to have ammunition, the wherewithal to fight. The other side gets it from the Communists. The Communists bring down more people, more tanks, more guns, and they would like to overrun us.

If the United States had intervened as it should have we would not be losing province capitals, district capitals, and we would not be faced with losing the national capital. Maybe we could have worked out something with the Communists.

We lost tanks. We lost artillery. The United States, when this happened, should have reacted.

Let me ask you: When the Americans saw the loss of those vehicles and weapons, why did you not come and replace them? When you saw our people being lost, why did you not come in and help our people? You signed the Paris agreement, which said you would do this.

Now I have told you the situation and how the allies have treated us. I am hiding nothing.

Now we are going to regroup and we are going to retain III Corps and IV Corps, even though others made stupid mistakes in I Corps and II Corps. Do not lay down your arms. Keep your arms. If you make the mistake of abandoning outposts and laying down your arms, we are going to lose everything.

In front of the National Assembly I announce my resignation as President.

I accept all responsibility for what has happened in South Vietnam during my terms as President, whether it was good or bad.

My flesh is worthless. The important thing is you, the soldier, and you, the people. I do not know when I can live with you again, but I am looking forward to that time.

You must remember that in 1968 the American pressure was not small. They wanted us to bring the so-called liberation forces into power.

I fought against it. Anyone who wants to know what kind of person I am, who wants to know about the power of the regime, should ask the American Government about what happened in 1968.

I told you in those days that if you listened to these political schemes of the Americans you would be lost. Now you are going to find out what I meant in those days in 1968.

I put out the plan that there was only one solution.

I was given an alternative solution. The alternative solution was that I could take an airplane out of Vietnam on Oct. 26, 1972. I was told I could leave the country. I also was told my life was threatened by Vietnamese. I was not worried about the threats. I was worried about safeguarding the independence of South Vietnam.

If you give us the same aid as the other side gives North Vietnam we would win.

If the Americans do not want to support us any more, let them go, get out! Let them forget their humanitarian promises!

No matter what we cannot accept, we are adults. We are going to continue to be insulted because Americans will not help us.

The Americans promised us--we trusted them. But you have not given us the aid you promised us. With that aid which you promised us, I would not be afraid of the Communists.

My resignation will let the United States give you aid and open the way to negotiations.

Inaugural Address of Duong Van Minh as President of Republic of Vietnam, April 28, 1975[*]

You must have realized that the situation, militarily and in all respects is very critical. We have seen for a long time now that the use of force is not a good solution.

For many years, we have talked among ourselves, and we have reached the conclusion to seek mutual understanding among the people. We intend no revenge on anyone, and there is no reason why we cannot have reconciliation among brothers in the same house.

All the tragic things we have heard about, occurring minute by minute, second by second, in our country, we have been paying for with our blood. I am distressed by all this.

I accept the responsibility now for myself: I feel a responsibility to seek a ceasefire, and to reopen negotiations and bring peace on the basis of the Paris agreement.

That is the single objective for the present. I also believe that peace for the nation must be based on mutual understanding. That is a basic trait of the Vietnamese.

With that spirit, with all of our will and sense of responsibility, I accept the task of being President of the Republic of Vietnam.

Lawyer Nguyen Van Huyen is Vice President. He has agreed to help me in the negotiations.

I also want to inform you, ladies and gentlemen, that Vu Van Mau will assume the function of Premier. He has agreed to accept this role.

Now I would like to address the nation.

Fellow citizens, in the past days a situation so urgent and critical has arisen that many religious groups and generals have asked me to become President.

The mission assigned to me is clear: to attempt to bring peace, the sooner the better, and to negotiate a political solution for South Vietnam

[*]Reprinted from New York Times, April 29, 1975, p. 14.

based on the Paris agreement; to put an end to the war and re-establish peace.

The Administration under me will be composed of elements of all parties, to bring unification to our country. I strongly believe I can form such an idealistic Administration and Cabinet in a short time.

Faced with the current situation, I have only one hope. That is to bring a mutual understanding among the people. Such an understanding can be realized only when all elements of the political parties accept the policy.

The coming days will be very difficult. I cannot promise you much.

One of the primary policies is to free all political prisoners and put an end to discrimination against the press.

The success of this Administration will depend on calm and support among the people. I call upon all political parties and religious sects to forget about the hatred and suspicion they have for each other, and to unite for national strength.

I will welcome any initiative and suggestion for peace and I am willing to cooperate with people of goodwill.

Fellow soldiers, I have spend most of my life in the armed forces. I know more than anyone else, I understand the hardships you have suffered in the last few weeks.

Today an old page of history will be turned. You have a new duty: This is to defend the territory that is left and to defend peace. Keep your spirit high, your ranks intact, and your positions firm to accomplish that duty.

When the cease-fire order is given, your mission will be rigorously to execute that order in accordance with the clauses of the Paris agreement and maintain order and security in your areas.

You will not abandon your arms nor your ranks, and in any circum-stances, you will strictly obey your officers. All undisciplined action will be immediately punished.

Now a few words to our friends of the other side, the Provisional Revolutionary Government of South Vietnam.

We sincerely want reconciliation. You know that. Reconciliation requires that each element of the nation respect the other's right to live.

That is the spirit of the Paris agreement.

Let us sit together and negotiate and work out a solution. I propose we stop all aggression against each other. I hope you will approve my suggestion.

To friendly nations, I say the Administration of South Vietnam wishes to maintain good relations and will welcome any help. We sincerely call on all the world's people to come to our aid to recover peace.

Fellow citizens, in past days you have wondered why so many people have quietly left the country. I want to tell you, dear citizens, that this is our beloved land. Please be courageous and stay here and accept the fate of God.

Please remain, and stay together. Rebuild South Vietnam. Build an independent South Vietnam, democratic and prosperous, so Vietnamese will live with Vietnamese in brotherhood.

Thank you very much.

President Ford's Statement on Vietnam, April 29, 1975 [*]

During the past week, I had ordered the reduction of American personnel in the United States Mission in Saigon to levels that could be quickly evacuated during emergency, while enabling that mission to continue to fulfill its duties.

During the day on Monday, Washington time, the airport at Saigon came under persistent rocket as well as artillery fire and was effectively closed. The military situation in the area deteriorated rapidly.

I therefore ordered the evacuation of all American personnel remaining in South Vietnam.

The evacuation has been completed. I commend the personnel of the armed forces who accomplished it, as well as Ambassador Graham Martin and the staff of his mission who served so well under difficult conditions.

This action closes a chapter in the American experience. I ask all Americans to close ranks, to avoid recrimination about the past, to look ahead to the many goals we share and to work together on the great tasks that remain to be accomplished.

[*] Reprinted from New York Times, April 30, 1975, p. 16.

Texts of letters sent by President Richard M. Nixon to President Nguyen Van Thieu, November 14, 1972 and January 5, 1973 released April 30, 1975 by Nguyen Tien Hung, former Minister of Planning, Republic of Vietnam [*]

First Letter

November 14, 1972

Dear Mr. President:

I was pleased to learn from General Haig that you held useful and con-structive discussions with him in Saigon in preparation for Dr. Kissinger's forthcoming meeting with North Vietnam's negotiators in Paris.

After studying your letter of November 11 with great care I have con-cluded that we have made substantial progress towards reaching a common un-derstanding on many of the important issues before us. You can be sure that we will pursue the proposed changes in the draft agreement that General Haig discussed with you with the utmost firmness and that, as these discussions proceed, we shall keep you fully informed through your Ambassador to the Paris conference on Vietnam who will be briefed daily by Dr. Kissinger.

I understand from your letter and from General Haig's personal report that your principal remaining concern with respect to the draft agreement is the status of North Vietnamese forces now in South Vietnam. As General Haig explained to you, it is our intention to deal with this problem first by seeking to insert a reference to respect for the demilitarized zone in the pro-posed agreement and, second, by proposing a clause which provides for the reduction and demobilization of forces on both sides in South Vietnam on a one-to-one basis and to have demobilized personnel return to their homes.

Upon reviewing this proposed language, it is my conviction that such a provision can go a long way toward dealing with your concern with respect to North Vietnamese forces. General Haig tells me, however, that you are also seriously concerned about the timing and verification of such reductions. In light of this, I have asked Dr. Kissinger to convey to you, through Ambas-sador Bunker, some additional clauses we would propose adding to the agreement dealing with each of these points. In addition, I have asked that

*Reprinted from New York Times, May 1, 1975, p. 16.

Dr. Kissinger send you the other technical and less important substantive changes which General Haig did not have the opportunity to discuss with you because they had not yet been fully developed in Washington. With these proposed modifications, I think you will agree that we have done everything we can to improve the existing draft while remaining within its general framework.

You also raise in your letter the question of participation by other Asian countries in the international conference. As you know, the presently contemplated composition are the permanent members of the United Nations Security Council, the members of the I.C.C.S., the parties to the Paris conference on Vietnam, and the Secretary General of the United Nations. We seriously considered Cambodian and Loatian participation but decided that these would be unnecessary complications with respect to representation. We do not, however, exclude the possibility of delegations from these countries participating in an observer status at the invitation of the conference.

As for Japan, this question was raised earlier in our negotiations with Hanoi and set aside because of their strenuous objections to any Japanese role in guaranteeing the settlement and also because it inevitably raises the possibility of Indian participation. I have, however, asked that Dr. Kissinger raise this matter again in Paris and he will inform your representative what progress we make on this. What we must recognize as a practical matter is that participation of Japan is very likely to lead to the participation of India. We would appreciate hearing your preference on whether it is better to include both countries or neither of them.

Finally, in respect to the composition of the I.C.C.S. I must say in all candor that I do not share your view that its contemplated membership is unbalanced. I am hopeful that it will prove to be a useful mechanism in detecting and reporting violations of the agreement. In any event, what we both must recognize is that the supervisory mechanism in no measure as important as our own firm determination to see to it that the agreement works and our vigilance with respect to the prospect of its violation.

I will not repeat here all that I said to you in my letter of Nov. 8, but I do wish to reaffirm its essential content and stress again my determination

to work toward an early agreement along the lines of the schedule which
General Haig explained to you. I must explain in all frankness that while
we will do our very best to secure the changes in the agreement which General
Haig discussed with you and those additional ones which Ambassador Bunker
will bring you, we cannot expect to secure them all. For example, it is unrealistic to assume that we will be able to secure the absolute assurances
which you would hope to have on the troop issue.

But far more important than what we say in the agreement on this issue
is what we do in the event the enemy renews its aggression. You have my
absolute assurance that if Hanoi fails to abide by the terms of this agreement
it is my intention to take swift and severe retaliatory action.

I believe the existing agreement to be an essentially sound one which
should become even more so if we succeed in obtaining some of the changes
we have discussed. Our best assurance of success is to move into this new
situation with confidence and cooperation.

With this attitude and the inherent strength of your government and
army on the ground in South Vietnam, I am confident this agreement will be a
successful one.

If, on the other hand, we are unable to agree on the course that I have
outlined, it is difficult for me to see how we will be able to continue our common effort towards securing a just and honorable peace. As General Haig told
you I would with great reluctance be forced to consider other alternatives. For
this reason, it is essential that we have your agreement as we proceed into
our next meeting with Hanoi's negotiators. And I strongly urge you and your
advisers to work promptly with Ambassador Bunker and our mission in Saigon
on the many practical problems which will face us in implementing the agreement. I cannot overemphasize the urgency of the task at hand nor my unalterable determination to proceed along the course which we have outlined.

Above all we must bear in mind what will really maintain the agreement.
It is not any particulr clause in the agreement but our joint willingness to maintain its clauses. I repeat my personal assurances to you that the United States
will react very strongly and rapidly to any violation of the agreement. But in
order to do this effectively it is essential that I have public support and that

your government does not emerge as the obstacle to a peace which American public opinion now universally desires. It is for this reason that I am pressing for the acceptance of an agreement which I am convinced is honorable and fair and which can be made essentially secure by our joint determination.

Mrs. Nixon joins me in extending our warmest personal regards to Madame Thieu and to you. We look forward to seeing you again at our home in California once the just peace we have both fought for so long is finally achieved.

Sincerely,

Richard Nixon

His Excellency
Nguyen Van Thieu
President of the Republic of Vietnam
Saigon.

## Second Letter

January 5, 1973

Dear Mr. President:

This will acknowledge your letter of December 20, 1972.

There is nothing substantial that I can add to my many previous messages, including my December 17 letter; which clearly stated my opinions and intentions. With respect to the question of North Vietnamese troops, we will again present your views to the Communists as we have done vigorously at every other opportunity in the negotiations. The result is certain to be once more the rejection of our position. We have explained to you repeatedly why we believe the problem of North Vietnamese troops is manageable under the agreement, and I see no reason to repeat all the arguments.

We will proceed next week in Paris along the lines that General Haig explained to you. Accordingly, if the North Vietnamese meet our concerns on the two outstanding substantive issues in the agreement, concerning the DMZ and the method of signing and if we can arrange acceptable supervisory machinery, we will proceed to conclude the settlement. The gravest consequence would then ensue if your government chose to reject the agreement and split off from the United States. As I said in my December 17 letter, "I am convinced that your refusal to join us would be an invitation to disaster--to the loss of all that we together have fought for over the past decade. It would be inexcusable above all because we will have lost a just and honorable alternative."

As we enter this new round of talks, I hope that our countries will now show a united front. It is imperative for our common objectives that your government take no further actions that complicate our task and would make more difficult the acceptance of the settlement by all parties. We will keep you informed of the negotiations in Paris through daily briefings of Ambassador Lam.

I can only repeat what I have so often said: The best guarantee for the survival of South Vietnam is the unity of our two countries which would be gravely jeopardized if you persist in your present course. The actions of our Congress since its return have clearly borne out the many warnings we have made.

Should you decide, as I trust you will, to go with us, you have my assurance of continued assistance in the post-settlement period and that we will respond with full force should the settlement be violated by North Vietnam. So once more I conclude with an appeal to you to close ranks with us.

Sincerely,

Richard Nixon

His Excellency
Nguyen Van Thieu
President of the Republic of Vietnam
Saigon

President Ford's Proclamation specifying end of the "Vietnam Era" for purposes of qualifying for veterans benefits, May 7, 1975.[*]

The Congress has provided that entitlement to certain veterans benefits be limited to persons serving in the armed forces during the period, beginning August 5, 1964, referred to as the Vietnam era. The President is authorized to determine the last day on which a person must have entered the active military, naval, or air service of the United States in order for such service to qualify as service during that period.

The signing of the cease-fire agreements and implementing protocols on January 27, 1973, between the United States of America and the Republic of Vietnam, on the one hand, and the Democratic Republic of Vietnam and the Provisional Revolutionary Government of the Republic of South Vietnam on the other hand, has terminated active participation by the armed forces of the United States in the Vietnam conflict.

NOW, THEREFORE, I Gerald R. Ford, President of the United States of America, by virtue of the authority vested in me by Section 101 (29) of Title 38 of United States Code, do hereby proclaim, for the purposes of said Section 101 (29), that May 7, 1975, is designated as the last day of the "Vietnam era."

IN WITNESS WHEREOF, I have hereunto set my hand this seventh day of May in the year of our Lord nineteen hundred seventy-five, and of the independence of the United States of America the one hundred and ninety-ninth.

[*]Reprinted from New York Times, May 8, 1975, p. 14.

# Vietnam: The Final Reckoning

## *Robert W. Tucker*

A T LAST, the final reckoning in Vietnam is at hand. Barring some unforeseen and unexpected reversal, the last act in what has seemed a never-ending drama has begun. How should we behave in the concluding phase of a conflict whose outcome we have for so long sought to influence? How should we act toward those we chose to support and whose destiny we presumed to guide? However one answers these questions, their importance is apparent. For what we ultimately learn, if anything, from this our first defeat in war will depend in large measure upon our collective memory of Vietnam. In turn, this memory will surely be affected by how we behave in the moment of defeat.

It may be argued that these are questions which should have been asked long ago, that at the very least they should have been asked in January 1973 when American military forces withdrew from Vietnam in accordance with the cease-fire agreements. In fact, they were only seldom raised. To be sure, many have asked how the war, and continued American support of South Vietnam, might be ended. But few have permitted themselves the assumption that these questions would one day have to be raised and answered in the circumstances we now face. The unwelcome truth is that most of us have been loath to confront the issues we have now been forced to confront. The sudden and dramatic turn in the course of the war has brought us to the full accounting we have so long sought to avoid making and one we have been encouraged to avoid making by those bearing official responsibility for American policy. If there is a pervasive air of unease over Vietnam today, it must be largely attributed to the realization that this dreaded accounting can no longer be put off.

At the same time, it is necessary to stress that this accounting is of a special sort and, as such, not to be equated simply, or perhaps even primarily, with conventional diplomatic-strategic calcu-

ROBERT W. TUCKER, whose article, "Oil: The Issue of American Intervention," in our January issue has provoked worldwide discussion, is professor of international relations at John Hopkins and the author of several books on world affairs and American foreign policy. He wishes to thank his colleague, Professor Piero Gleijeses, for invaluable help in preparing this article.

lations. It is not President Ford's falling dominoes and the presumably vital American security interests thereby jeopardized that have given rise to the unease. Nor is it Secretary Kissinger's strictures on the indivisibility of peace and the effects on American global interests in abandoning an ally (South Vietnam) in its moment of extremity. These arguments, invoked from the outset of the American involvement in Vietnam, are still not without *some* effect. But the effect appears rather minimal, and this quite apart from whatever intrinsic merit the arguments might have. Indeed, it may well be that the world of the middle 1970's gives a considerably greater plausibility to such arguments than did the world of the early-to-middle 1960's. Certainly, the American position in the world today is not one that will bear favorable comparison with the American position of a decade ago. These considerations apart, the point remains that the altogether familiar arguments of the administration in response to the recent events in Vietnam are markedly less persuasive than they were in earlier years, and even in the earlier years of American involvement in the war their persuasiveness was limited. The currents of public opinion, and of a substantial portion of elite opinion as well, are running in directions other than those set out by the President and his Secretary of State in defining American security interests both in, and affected by, Indochina.

Nor does it seem plausible that the unease over the impending dénouement in Vietnam is a response to expected recriminations—already surfaced by leading administration figures—over "who lost Vietnam." If anything, these recriminations are likely to still much of the unease that does clearly exist by submerging it in domestic political considerations. There is little the Ford administration can reasonably expect to gain by assigning the loss of Vietnam to the Democratically-controlled Congress accused of having been niggardly in the amount of support it was prepared to give South Vietnam, though there is a good deal the administration could quite possibly lose. This is so if only for the reason that the administration must contend with something approaching the status of a law of politics: responsibility for what happens at a given time falls upon those who currently hold power. To escape the operation of this law, however cruel and unjust it may in practice occasionally prove, the present power holders must make a persuasive demonstration that Vietnam might—even would—have been saved had it not been for a recalcitrant and penurious Congress. Given the difficulties of such demonstration, the prospects that it might succeed cannot be rated very bright. Clearly, it will take a good deal more in the way of "proof" than merely to argue that Vietnam would have been saved had Congress only complied with whatsoever requests for aid were made by the executive.

More generally, the circumstances of 1975 simply do not favor in the case of Vietnam even a mini-repetition of the earlier Republican "loss-of-China" gambit. It is not only that in the present case a Republican administration will have presided over the "loss," but that it will have done so in a period when détente with the Soviet Union (and, in lesser degree, with China) has been the great desideratum of policy. How is one to explain simply and persuasively to the great public that those who have been so instrumental in bringing about the loss by presumably being more generous with their ally than we have been with ours, are nevertheless the states with which we must continue to seek closer and more understanding relationships? The initiated may find little trouble in grasping these subtleties of statecraft, though in the case of the Soviet Union even many of the initiated are evidently beginning to experience some difficulty. It seems doubtful, though, that the public will be able to follow this logic.

Yet the charge against Congress of "losing Vietnam" may still elicit a strong public response simply by virtue of the blood and treasure the American people have sacrificed in Vietnam. To invoke this particular logic, to tell the people that its sacrifice has been in vain because in the end this sacrifice was willfully betrayed by those who refused to comply with the administration's requests, would be reckless and irresponsible in the extreme. It would recall a dark and shameful chapter in our history and, in doing so, it would put an even more miserable end to an involvement that has been marked throughout by little else than misery. Despite the occasional intimation that charges reminiscent of McCarthyism may yet be raised, it is difficult to believe we have in recent recriminations more than misguided, though understandable, efforts to prod a Congress no longer willing passively to accept either the judgments or the requests of the executive branch on Indochina—and, for that matter, on foreign policy generally.

## II

THE question persists: Why the unease in watching the dénouement in Vietnam?* Why do I feel uneasy in observing a tragedy the last act of which can come as no surprise? Clearly, it is not because of any regret over a position of opposition taken and held for more than a decade. In retrospect, there is no apparent reason for altering that position today. I remain persuaded that the American involvement in Vietnam represented, more than anything else, the triumph of an expansionist and imperial interest which, by the 1960's, had submerged the narrower and more conventional security interest the policy of containment initially expressed. Without question, the involvement in Vietnam was also a legacy of the classic cold war, of the momentum generated by the cold war, and of the habits of thought and action the years of intense conflict had encouraged. Yet the greatest legacy of the classic cold war was the gradual submission of the narrower interest that containment initially expressed in the larger interest of maintaining under American leadership a stable and congenial global order. Vietnam was perceived as a threat to this larger interest, and it was the preservation of this larger interest—an imperial interest —that must ultimately explain Vietnam. In the purpose of maintaining a particular vision of world order, in the equation of this order with American security, in the hubris of those who led the nation into war, and in the reluctance to withdraw from a conflict that could not be "won" without resort to odious measures, Vietnam affords a classic case of an imperial war.

Thus the United States involvement in Vietnam was not primarily due to intellectual error, as the prevailing liberal orthodoxy on the war would have it. Nor can it be adequately explained either in terms of an ideological obsession pursued for its own sake or, with more plausibility, in terms of the domestic constraints of anti-Communism. These and similar explanations of the policy that led to Vietnam give to this policy a quality of disinterestedness it did not possess and a quality of innocence it did not have. That policy was not the work of incompetent ideologues who were blind to political realities and oblivious to age-old considerations of interest. It was the work of men who, though they obviously made mistakes, wished to preserve America's global preponderance, and who not unreasonably saw in Vietnam a threat to the nation's preeminent

---

* It is perhaps well to emphasize that "unease" is used here in a sense to be distinguished from the unease that arises simply from witnessing death and destruction (and, in this instance, the sense of shame among many South Vietnamese that an ordeal many bore with so much courage and dignity has been mocked by the behavior of an army in defeat). We all feel uneasy in the face of the suffering of others, quite apart from whether or not we have had any role in, or relationship to, that suffering. In the case of Vietnam, however, the particular unease experienced today stems in large part from the role we have played in the war and the nagging doubts almost all must feel about that role. Then, too, unease might in part stem from the self-deceptions that have been entertained almost to the very end.

position. In the manner of all imperial visions, the vision of a preponderant America was solidly rooted in the will to exercise dominion over others, however benign the intent of those who entertained the vision. That this will was commonly cloaked in such disarming terms as "liberal internationalism" does not alter the reality. The policy of intervention—of liberal intervention—that culminated in Vietnam was the expected response of an imperial power with a vital interest in maintaining an order that, quite apart from the material benefits it conferred, had become synonymous with the nation's vision of its role in history.

Yet even for one who opposed this vision and the results to which it finally led in Vietnam, there is something awesome and disquieting in the swiftness with which so many have apparently abandoned it in the conviction that we have entered a new period of world history. It may of course be argued that the vision has not in fact been abandoned, only the methods by which it was formerly sustained. But given the world in which foreign policy must still be conducted, the abandonment of these methods is very likely to leave the vision little more than an empty shell. Indeed, the abandonment of these methods may well result in jeopardizing narrower and more traditional security interests. In any event, it is in the excess of Vietnam that we may find a root cause—perhaps *the* root cause—of an outlook today that promises to be as indiscriminate in its anti-interventionism as was the interventionism of only yesterday. If some of the now visible consequences of this sudden change are to be deplored, this consideration cannot alter the judgment rendered on our involvement in Vietnam. On the contrary, it can only strengthen the judgment made on the intrinsic folly of that involvement.

### III

WE come closer to answering the question of why the sense of unease over Vietnam once it is acknowledged that we never honestly faced the issue of how we were to disengage entirely from an enterprise—and this regardless of the consequences—which, even though we should never have undertaken it, we nevertheless did undertake. To have faced up to this issue necessarily meant facing up to its probable consequences—indeed, to its almost certain consequences—and this we could not bring ourselves to do. At least, this is true for almost all of those who, however opposed to American involvement in Vietnam, have not been sympathetic to the cause of the other side in the conflict. A very small minority apart, then, the rest of us have sought, whether consciously or unconsciously, varying ways to escape from confronting the issue we now find we can no longer avoid.

Although few were ever seriously persuaded that Vietnamization would really work, many nevertheless managed to find comfort in the promise that it might do so. Even so, the seductive promise of Vietnamization itself necessarily implied the indefinite continuance of American aid to South Vietnam, both economic and military, or at least so long as the war continued and the North continued to receive help from its allies. To agree to the one—Vietnamization—while denying the other—aid for an indefinite period—was either obtuse or insincere, provided that the South Vietnamese government and army made reasonably effective use of such aid. Moreover, experience had amply demonstrated that "reasonably effective use" in the South Vietnamese context could only be realistically interpreted with some looseness, unless it too was to prove no more than a deceptive—or self-deceptive—formula.

The premise underlying Vietnamization, and thus the implicit obligation to continue aid support, was not the representative character of the South Vietnamese government. On this all-important point, there has been, and remains even today, much confusion. It is true that, during the years Vietnamization was pushed as a way to disengage from direct participation in the conflict, many argued that such assistance as we might later provide would never be effectively used in the absence of a more representative government. Whether subsequent events have confirmed this long-held view must at least remain unclear in one respect, since we have no way of knowing whether a more representative government would in fact have made better use of the aid South Vietnam was given in the period following the American withdrawal. The contrary position is not self-evident, despite the tendency of its proponents to assume that it is. There have been governments before which, while broadly representative, have nevertheless shown themselves incompetent to conduct a war effectively. Moreover, in the case of South Vietnam a government more representative than the Thieu government—though a government that excluded the Vietcong—would still be one that represented disparate political factions which have always been largely devoid of any real popular support. After so many years of discussion and debate, we still do not have a plausible, let alone a persuasive, picture of the kind of government that would have elicited such support in South Vietnam. It is, after all, quite possible that none would have done so.

At any rate, this much at least is clear: if the strategy of disengaging from direct involvement in the war did not mean the abandonment of the South, it implied the commitment in principle to continued economic and military aid after disengagement was completed. It is disingenuous to argue today, though many do, that this strategy implied no commitment of aid, certainly no commitment of military aid, and that if such commitment was undertaken it was done in secret. The argument is disingenuous because the strategy of disengagement was largely based upon just such a commitment, and this was generally understood and accepted at the time. Nor is it relevant, in contending the contrary, to point to the instrument that completed and formalized American disengagement, the January 1973 Vietnam cease-fire agreement.* For that instrument did not have as its purpose the specification of commitments undertaken by the United States toward its ally, and it is captious to pretend otherwise.

It is for these reasons that it is difficult to gainsay the position of the Secretary of State in urging a review of the "public debate during the period that these [1973] agreements were negotiated to see what the imperatives were of the administration in negotiating these settlements" (although it is rather startling to find the Secretary making so ardent an appeal to a process he discouraged at the time). "There was never any proposition," Mr. Kissinger went on to insist at his March 26 news conference, "that the United States would withdraw and cut off aid, and these agreements were negotiated on the assumption that the United States would continue economic and military aid to South Vietnam."

The record broadly supports these assertions. Although in the press conferences and other public statements made at the time by Nixon administration officials in explaining the agreements the military aid question was played down, it was nevertheless answered in a manner that was clear enough given the circumstances. Thus Kissinger himself declared in a news conference immediately following the conclusion of the Paris accords that the United States would continue to provide South Vietnam with "that military aid which is permitted by the agreement" (that is, to replace used-up equipment on a one-for-one basis with identical equipment) and went on to state: "The United States is prepared to gear that military aid to the action of other countries and not to treat it as an end in itself. . . ." Similar statements were made in subsequent official explanations of the cease-fire agreement. When Thieu visited President Nixon in early April 1973, the joint communiqué issued at the end of the talks reaffirmed, though in guarded terms, what was by then a well-understood position. And in considering the administration's aid requests for Vietnam in the spring of 1973, Congress not only proved quite uncritical in its examination of the requests but appeared to take for granted a continuing commitment to military aid.

It is necessary to review these events, since

---

* The "Agreement on Ending the War and Restoring Peace in Vietnam" was concluded in Paris on January 23, 1973, the parties to it being the United States, North Vietnam, South Vietnam, and the Provisional Revolutionary Government of South Vietnam (PRG). It was attended by various protocols, thus giving rise to such varying descriptions as the cease-fire agreement(s), the Paris accords, etc., and subsequently transmitted to Congress in the form of an executive agreement.

---

memories are often quite short, even over issues that once aroused deep passions. The view that the American government, with the knowledge of Congress and the public, undertook no commitment to the government of South Vietnam in the course of disengaging from active participation in the war, may be true in the narrow legalistic sense, but it is only in this sense that it is true. The commitment the American government did evidently undertake was not unconditional. Few, if any, such commitments between states are. It was conditioned on the performance of the South Vietnamese and, of course, on the behavior of the North. But a commitment there was, and it is not only misleading but somehow demeaning to attempt to deny this today.

## IV

IN SOME MEASURE, the argument that has gone on over whether we have had a commitment to aid South Vietnam may be seen as one manifestation of the temptation to believe that we were deceived throughout the course of the war by whichever administration was in power—though above all by the Nixon administration. And where we were not deceived, it is tempting to believe that our will, however inarticulately it might have been expressed, was simply ignored by those who bore official responsibility for conducting Vietnam policy. It is tempting to believe this—indeed, the temptation verges on a compulsion—since it relieves us of a responsibility that, for good reason, we do not wish to bear. In fact, the deception of the public and the ignoring of its will do not contrast so markedly with a number of other chapters in post-World War II foreign policy. Moreover, it is often forgotten how frequently in the course of the war deceptions were exposed and secret undertakings uncovered. This is true even of the Nixon years when secrecy and deception, particularly with respect to Vietnam, were carried to yet new extremes. Prior to Watergate, however, they did not represent a political liability for Mr. Nixon. Quite the contrary: if anything, the Nixon Vietnam policy, despite its manner of execution, ultimately turned out to be a factor contributing to his 1972 victory.

Nor is this all. The public will—one uses that shadowy concept with diffidence, though use it we must—was not subverted in the case of Vietnam, not even by Richard Nixon. It may fairly be charged that Nixon exploited this will for his own purposes. But if he did so successfully, it was because this will remained profoundly ambivalent toward the war. Though clearly desiring to get out of the conflict from 1968 on, the public never accepted the stark prospect of defeat. Nor, for that matter, did a majority of the foreign-policy elites, and this despite their opposition to the war. Nixon instinctively recognized this ambivalence, and it dictated his Vietnamese strategy throughout. By changing the costs of the war to the nation,* while effectively exploiting public unwillingness to accept undisguised defeat, the President was able to marshal broad domestic support in 1972 for measures that carried the war as never before to North Vietnam. The relative absence of opposition to the war in the last six months of direct American involvement indicated that public —and also, in substantial measure, elite—disaffection with the war had been largely a function of costs (and, of course, the absence of definitive results). This may be a depressing conclusion to reach, but it is one that is difficult to avoid.

The 1973 cease-fire agreement preserved virtually intact the belief that if we had not won the war, we also had not lost it, that we had not been defeated. This being achieved, the public could readily endorse, and was only too willing to endorse, Nixon's "peace with honor." The President and his principal national-security assistant, for their part, were almost as eager as the public to achieve American disengagement. In addition to its role as the most troublesome of domestic issues, continued American involvement in the war was seen as a constant threat to further progress in détente with the great Communist powers. The Paris accords, particularly coming in the aftermath of the last and greatest display of American air power, satisfied Nixon's and Kissinger's dual requirement that American withdrawal not be seen by the public as a defeat, thereby not jeopardizing the domestic support needed for "larger policies," and by allies and adversaries as an erosion of the nation's prestige and credibility.

I T MAY BE no more than poetic justice that the man who negotiated the Paris cease-fire accords has recently suffered so much criticism for efforts that were almost universally acclaimed at the time. But if Henry Kissinger merits condemnation for what is rapidly becoming in the eyes of growing legions of critics a veritable catalogue of sins, it is difficult to see why the Paris accords should be counted among these sins. Admittedly, the Nobel Peace Prize appeared at the time, and appears even more so today, a rather excessive appraisal of the Kissinger handiwork. But the present condemnation of that handiwork seems only slightly less excessive. For even if it is true, and it is true, that the Paris accords amounted to a delayed and ultimately miserable death sentence for South Vietnam, this condemns the Kissinger efforts only if it is plausible to argue

* To this nation, and not to the Vietnamese, South or North. The key was the reduction of American casualties and the build-up of American firepower. In 1972, the virtual disappearance of what had once been a strong anti-war movement testified to the effectiveness of the Nixon strategy. Elite groups were almost as vulnerable to the strategy as the general public, though they indignantly denied being so. Yet the record is clear that it was American casualties— and, of course, the draft—which above all supported the anti-war movement.

that the results could have been otherwise and better.

No doubt, the results could have been otherwise and better had more favorable terms for the South been extracted from Hanoi. But more favorable terms could only have meant, in the main, the complete withdrawal from the South of the North's forces (together with some mechanism for enforcing the withdrawal), and on this critical issue Hanoi had remained intractable for years. There is no evidence we have that Hanoi might have been induced to alter its position on this issue, short of an American threat literally to destroy the North. Save for a handful of unreconstructed hawks on the war, nearly everyone else drew back in horror at the very suggestion. Indeed, the terms that Kissinger did finally get, though legitimizing the North's presence in the South, might (no more is claimed) still have given the South an indefinite lease on life had they been accompanied by the meaningful prospect that the American bombers would return should the North again initiate large-scale military action. Kissinger evidently wanted to retain that option—he strongly hinted so publicly at the time—but he was effectively deprived of it only months later by a President in decline and a Congress that forbade American military forces from engaging in hostile acts in or over Indochina. Once it was made clear that the bombers would not return, there remained no effective means of protecting the South, whether from its own misdeeds or from its endemic vulnerability to large-scale attacks by Hanoi's forces, and it is difficult to fault Kissinger's plaintive comment to this effect in his March 26 news conference.

It has been argued that better terms for South Vietnam might have been gained had the United States agreed to Hanoi's longstanding demand for an unconditional American withdrawal and Thieu's removal. But these terms would have been tantamount to American acknowledgment of an undisguised defeat and, for this reason alone, were out of the question. Even so, it obviously does not follow that if these demands had been accepted, Hanoi would then have been willing to withdraw its forces from South Vietnam. At least, this does not follow in the absence of a government in Saigon that at the least included, if it was not dominated by, the Vietcong. With or without Thieu, Hanoi gave every indication that its forces were in the South to stay.

There remains the view that even given the terms of the Paris accords the results for South Vietnam could have been otherwise and better had Saigon and the United States made a sincere attempt to abide by the terms of the cease-fire. Moreover, this argument runs, had the provisions of the cease-fire agreement been carried out by Saigon and this government, there would have been no need to send additional military aid—or, alternatively, even if the need still had arisen, it might well have been kept to very modest proportions.

Clearly, what is implied here is an overall judgment on the nature of the Paris accords, and it is a judgment to the effect that the accords provided a reasonable chance for achieving a tolerable peace between the South and North. Those who take this view do not deny that, in the best of circumstances, difficulties would have remained in implementing the accords, given the suspicion and hatred that persisted and the many imprecisions and deliberate ambiguities that characterized many provisions of the accords. Even so, it is contended that whatever hope there was for a tolerable peace was dashed by our behavior and the behavior of our ally.

The detailing of this behavior has been made on innumerable occasions and requires only the barest summary. Saigon, with our encouragement, hardly waited until the ink of the agreement was dry before initiating what amounted to offensive actions. Thieu almost immediately reneged on his pledge to release political prisoners, as he did with respect to the obligations entailed in setting up a National Council of National Reconciliation and Concord. The mechanism for broadening political activity in the South was thus subverted while the provisions for organizing free elections under international supervision were simply ignored. On the American side, a series of commitments, some public though others secret, presumably went unfulfilled. Among the latter are included the promise to withdraw all American civilians in the South who were engaged in the support of Saigon's armed forces and the undertaking to cease American air reconnaissance over North Vietnam.*

One might counter this indictment with the numerous violations of the Paris accords charged to the North Vietnamese and Vietcong, violations also alleged to have begun in the months immediately following conclusion of the accords. Would any useful purpose be served by doing so, and by entering into a detailed examination of the order and magnitude of the violations undertaken by the two sides in order to assess relative responsibility for the breakdown of the cease-fire agreement? It would not seem so. Even a casual rereading of the Paris accords only serves to reinforce the conclusion, apparent at the time they were negotiated, that their almost incredible ambiguities meant either that their successful implementation required maximum efforts toward mutual understanding and good will, or that their purpose was simply to provide the means for America's military disengagement while leaving the situation otherwise essentially unchanged. Since the former interpretation is either merely tendentious or absurd, or perhaps both, we are left with the

* These and other secret commitments are discussed by Tad Szulc, "Beyond the Vietnam Cease-Fire Agreement," *Foreign Policy* (Summer 1974), pp. 21-69.

latter interpretation. This being so, it is a largely useless exercise to ask who undermined the agreement. The agreement was made to be undermined; its provisions seemed almost designed to invite evasion and subversion.

The American negotiators may still be judged adversely for having concluded the cease-fire agreement. But fairness requires recognition that the alternatives were either roughly the kind of agreement that was concluded or no agreement at all. Whereas the former alternative permitted military disengagement and the return of American war prisoners, the latter alternative promised —at best—military disengagement. There was of course a third alternative that would have obtained military disengagement and the return of the prisoners of war. This was the acknowledgment of defeat and, as a consequence of such admission, the abandonment of an ally. It was not only the Nixon administration that was completely unwilling to contemplate this third alternative. So was the nation, though in lesser degree. In light of what we now know, it is easy and fashionable to say that the third alternative would have represented the course of wisdom. For it is only by the barest of subterfuges that we may now continue to pretend that we were not defeated in Vietnam. Pride often counts for more than wisdom, however, and particularly in the case of powerful nations. And even were it not for pride, there was always the question of what to do with those whose destiny we sought to determine, however misguidedly, and whom, though their destiny is no longer within our reach (if, indeed, it ever really was), we cannot with honor simply cast aside.

## V

THERE is an almost instinctively negative reaction to once again raising the matter of honor in relation to Vietnam. The reaction is surely understandable, even if misplaced. Abused and perverted on so many occasions during the past decade in relation to the war, the American involvement in Vietnam has almost succeeded in giving honor a bad name. Are we to conclude from this experience, however, that there is no such thing as honor or that honor can have no relevance to the manner in which as a nation we behave toward others? Apparently not, for it is the most extreme opponents of the war who have themselves been most insistent on seeing Vietnam as raising above all a moral issue and therefore, by implication, a matter of honor. Whether morality, and honor, occupy so exalted a position in the affairs of nations is a question that need not be entered into here. It is sufficient to insist that honor does enter into such affairs and that nations may dishonor, and have dishonored, themselves.

There can be no objection, then, to raising the matter of honor at this late date and to ask what remaining obligations, if any, we have that have grown out of our role in the Vietnamese conflict. It is no criticism of the Secretary of State that he has seen fit to ask this question and to answer it. Mr. Kissinger believes that in the "moment of extremity" of an ally the test of our character as a people is whether we are willing to stand by a commitment earlier made and to continue aid to that ally. This is, to him, "an elementary question of what kind of a people we are . . . a fundamental question of how we are viewed by all other people, and it has nothing to do with the question of whether we should ever have gotten involved there [Indochina] in the first place." To desert one's ally even when the latter's cause has become extreme is to dishonor oneself. And so it is, provided the commitment itself was an honorable one and the recipient has fulfilled the conditions implied by the commitment. To argue that even a dishonorable commitment, once made, can only be abandoned at the cost of honor itself is simply perverse. To insist that the recipient of a commitment deserves one's continued loyalty even if he has failed to fulfill the conditions of the commitment is unreasonable.

Whether the commitment made to South Vietnam is judged more than a mistake is a question that need not be argued here. What is of relevance is whether· the South Vietnamese government made reasonably effective use of such aid as was given it. For if it did not do so, the further question whether it was given "adequate" aid need not even be considered. Did our ally fulfill the elementary condition implied by the commitment? There is very little evidence to support the view that it did, and a great deal of evidence to support the view that it did not. By almost any reasonable standard of effectiveness of performance, and even assuming for the sake of argument the existence of certain shortages due to the alleged penury of the aid-giver, the indispensable condition of continued moral obligation simply was not met. What follows from this is not that one may view with indifference the plight of those remnants of an armed force which do remain willing and able to fight. There is, in fact, no generally satisfactory answer that can be given in such extreme and agonizing situations, save to say —and it is concededly not much—that such answer must be determined by practical as well as humanitarian criteria. On the major issue, however, the response seems quite clear: there remains no obligation to be violated.

These considerations have taken administration arguments, particularly those of Mr. Kissinger, at face value. But this surely cannot be the end of the matter. We are entitled to ask, why the extraordinary sensitivity shown, not merely over keeping commitments—this is altogether expected—but over the moral necessity of doing so? While the Secretary may not be altogether insensitive to moral issues in statecraft, as his critics so regularly

depict him as being, no one can accuse him of ever having been obsessed with such issues. Clearly, he is obsessed with issues of credibility and prestige, and while the importance of these issues may be granted, they are not synonymous with moral issues. The suspicion accordingly must arise that the Secretary has sought to use the moral on behalf of the strategic, that he has been looking at strategic interests and presenting them in moral terms.

I F THERE is nothing heinous in this, it is also not particularly admirable, above all in the present agony of South Vietnam. Moral sensitivity, one would have thought, might well have been directed in other and rather obvious directions, while strategic interests were being displayed for what they are. One such direction moral sensitivity can take is toward those South Vietnamese whose lives may be placed in jeopardy under a Communist, or Communist-dominated, regime if only because of past associations with the Americans. No one knows how many such persons may fall into this, and still other, categories, but it would be rash to assume the number is small.

Those who have for so long pressed the specter of a "blood bath" cannot in good conscience remain silent today toward the one measure that could remove their fear. The responsibility for granting asylum must be seen as a kind of litmus-paper test of the sense of obligation we feel, if not toward all those who will be placed in danger for whatever reason in a new regime, then at least toward those who have compromised themselves through past association with us. If the question of numbers is raised, it is well to recall that we took in 600,000 refugees from Cuba during the years following Castro's accession to power. Yet in the majority of cases, there was no physical danger posed to the Cuban emigrés and little obligation on our part by virtue of our own actions, as there is in Vietnam.

Nor is it only a matter of simple moral obligation that is involved in the case of Vietnam; it is also a test of the racism with which we have been taxed by others, and particularly in our attitudes and actions toward Asians. A refusal to make every effort to take in those Vietnamese who wish to leave and whose position has been compromised by us will confirm, as perhaps nothing else could, the charge we have so indignantly denied throughout the war.

Beyond this, if we are so concerned with our image of ourselves in defeat, as well we should be, we cannot avoid facing the issue of American economic aid to a South Vietnam we no longer influence. It is now known that in March 1973, the United States and North Vietnam came close to an agreement on American aid to the North for reconstruction. The agreement proved abortive because of the Nixon administration's ire over

Communist truce violations and public indignation, reflected in Congress, over Hanoi's treatment of American prisoners of war, then being released. If aid for reconstruction was nevertheless justified in principle in the case of the North in 1973, then there is surely as strong a case to be made today for aiding the South, or, for that matter, the whole of Vietnam. To be militarily frustrated, and eventually defeated, by so small a state is humiliating, and nothing we say can deny this. Even so, generosity in defeat is not demeaning and certainly not for a great power. There is no reason why we cannot be as generous in defeat today as we have been in victory in the past.

## VI

THESE observations are not intended to convey the impression that the final reckoning in Vietnam must be seen only in moral terms. Although the moral dimension of any accounting we are to make is important, the strategic dimension obviously cannot be neglected. What I have objected to is a view that misreads, if it does not pervert, the nature of the moral obligation that emerged from our commitment to South Vietnam, and that does so out of concern for strategic interests. Moreover, considering the immediate area to which this view has been applied, one must amend the preceding sentence to read that a mistaken strategic interest is equated with a spurious moral obligation. Applied elsewhere, to areas of real interest and to conditions altogether different from those that prevailed in Vietnam, the effects of this argument could prove to be devastating.

It is the tone as much as the substance of administration reactions to what has happened in Vietnam that are disturbing. While many have in retrospect unfairly criticized the 1973 Paris accords, the principal architect of those accords also insists upon finding a meaning in them they did not have. The apparent intent is to relieve himself of any responsibility for recent events in Vietnam. Yet there is the more ominous suggestion in the Kissinger reaction that what might now happen elsewhere (the Middle East?) must be seen as a result of the nation's failure to have appreciated its interests in and to have stood by its commitments to South Vietnam. One can only trust that this is little more than a passing mood, a short-lived reaction to a failure that can no longer be obscured. If it is more than that, if it is indicative of a more persistent attitude that finds increasing expression in American policy, then the prospect beckons of a determination by our policy-makers to create their own dominoes.

# The Sulking Giant

## by Stanley Hoffmann

At the time of the 1973 "peace" agreements, commentators liked to discuss the "lessons of Vietnam." Today, when one reads many of the statements provoked by the latest, if not the last, inevitable act of the tragedy, and especially the President's remarks, one cannot help feeling that those who had the most to learn have been taught nothing at all. They still believe that all it would have taken for "our side" to win was more American will, guts, power. Had we kept our "commitment," the good guys would have prevailed. And so, once more, self-denunciation substitutes for self-criticism, and the very people who warned us most solemnly about the peril of a right-wing backlash should we "bug out," are now busy trying to provoke it.

At the cost, therefore, of repeating oneself, one must once again go back to the roots of our mistake. The first one was the belief that in the battle between an opponent with a formidable will, the advantage of geography, patience and available supplies, and a "friend" who showed neither ability nor determination to turn his people into a national community, American power could redress the balance. All it could do was delay the outcome. The 1973 agreements seemed like a triumph for Kissinger's 1968 scheme: it was a military truce between us and Hanoi, leaving political issues to Hanoi and Saigon. But it can now be seen for what it was: a screen behind which we got out, inevitably leaving Hanoi in place. What half a million American troops and our air power had only slowed down could not be contained forever by mere American military aid. The equation has not changed in 12 or 15 years.

A different outcome would have required either the physical annihilation of North Vietnam, obliterated from the air or occupied on the ground—but we never wanted to incur the costs and risks of such an operation, precisely because our interests were limited—or else, the establishment in South Vietnam of a genuine nation. But the very forces on which we relied and which we maintained in power were the least capable of such a feat. In their absence our proclamation of support to a "nation fighting for its freedom" became an exercise in self-deception and ventriloquy. We kept projecting on South Vietnam a pattern that had been genuine in Europe and in Korea. There were, indeed, groups and people fighting for freedom from communism, but there never was a general will or a national regime. Having, in effect, given up trying to create one, yet not having given up the hope of "holding" South Vietnam militarily, we have merely held back the flood

at a terrifying human cost. We have combined the ineffective and the destructive, the futile and the corrupt. As Elliot Richardson has suggested in an interview in Boston, surely the same result could have been achieved sooner at less cost. We are the last who should speak of a bloodbath. Rarely has there been such an example of a moral disaster resulting from radically flawed political premises.

There was no elegant way of climbing out of the wreckage. Once the original mistake had been made, the more men and money we threw into the inferno, the more we made sure that the end would be dreadful for us, and even more so for those with whom we shared the illusion of ultimate salvation. To stop all aid while they keep fighting is indeed a callous act. But to keep feeding the flames, while pretending at this late stage that our supplies might "stabilize" the situation long enough to provide for the negotiated political settlement which we never sought to achieve in the days when Thieu seemed in firm control is equally callous. When we decided to maintain by all means short of the risk of a general war the cliques and factions that relied on us, we made sure that we would have only a choice between ignominious endings. But, as one of the most pro-American French journalists has put it, once one has made a mistake, one does not have to persevere in it forever in order to protect one's good word.

At least there was no need to make the end even worse by proclaiming what could be called a self-domino theory. There was no need to weaken our own credibility by asserting that our failure to do the impossible in Vietnam affected our capability to do the possible and the necessary elsewhere. However, that we would indulge in such absurd and self-destructive rhetoric was implicit in our second original mistake. We saw in Hanoi an arm of "international communism," one head of a single if multiheaded hydra. We had to prove that the "free world" would not yield any more, and we believed that the only way to cope with the hydra was to do battle. Today we have reached accommodation with several Communist powers: not only Yugoslavia or Rumania, but China. We realize that Communist diversity means at least varying degrees of hostility between them and us, and chances of tension among them. However we have not lost our instinctive tendency to oversimplify and overdramatize unfavorable trends. We may have become more sophisticated about "Asian communism" (although the hand-wringing of those who view with alarm the tendency of

Stanley Hoffmann, author of Gulliver's Troubles, is a professor of government at Harvard.

Thailand or the Philippines to question the value of US bases shows that in many minds the confusion between the necessary global balance of military might and universal military containment persists). But when a "threat" appears elsewhere, we are still prone to see dominoes falling, and prompt at imagining violent replies. Thus many officials fear the "domino" effect of Portugal, even though the events in Portugal are clearly hurting Communists in Spain, Italy and France.

In this respect Vietnam should teach us an important lesson. On the one hand Hanoi is one of several among the poorest nations in the world that have tried or will, try to create a collectivist society, based on principles that are repugnant to us, yet likely to produce greater welfare and security for its people than any local alternative ever offered, at a cost in freedom that affects a small elite. On the other hand many states, whatever their regimes and societies, are now beginning to challenge the international economic order that was established by the non-Communist industrial powers after World War II and benefited them more than it has served the rest of the world. We have to learn, first, that we shall not be able to cope with such changes and demands by force and subversion; secondly, that whether we face a common front of enemies or not depends largely on our own response. To declare our hostility at the outset, to act as "the United States in opposition" (to use Prof. Moynihan's expression), is a recipe for disaster, for this would contribute to turning a rhetorical common front into an effective one, and strain relations with our own allies. Thirdly, we will have to realize that among those who challenge the past economic order there are many of our own best political and economic clients, and among those whose social model is most shocking to us there are not only Communists but other kinds of leftists as well.

In other words our failure in Vietnam should force us to face seriously at last what is perhaps the most difficult proposition for Americans to accept: that even though much of the world admires our technology, envies our standard of living, or respects our might, the American model cannot be easily exported and is not relevant to huge parts of mankind. To see in other nations' efforts at shaping their own societies or a new international economic order a declaration of war *on us* would be both the apex of egocentrism and diplomatic suicide.

We must pursue accommodation. This means, of course, neither selling out the security of our threatened friends, whether in Israel or in Western Europe, nor ceasing to defend our own economic interests. But it does mean giving up our flattering self-image as a desired model, and our deep conviction that the methods that have made America great—the free market, the giant corporation, aggressive individualism, the two-party system—are ideal for all mankind. If we keep seeing ourselves as universal, we shall end up isolated. Whenever we find ourselves, or think we find ourselves faced with a hostile world, we either want to repudiate the world altogether, or to react with force—two forms of vain impatience with uncertainty and the frustrations of involvement. If instead we see ourselves as we are, the strongest military and economic power in a world of growing diversity and rising demands for broader participation, our chances of waging a wise diplomacy will be preserved, our chances for negotiating mutually beneficial deals will be enhanced.

This is no longer a world that one nation can control, or in which one nation alone can direct the traffic and trace the roads. At present the least we can say is that we are too deeply mired in the past to have begun to envisage the future. It is not surprising that reactions in Congress are often confused and contradictory. Rather than denouncing Congress and haranguing the public in indignant tones, the administration ought to try to create a consensus around a new and sensible policy. But is it capable of reeducating itself, of repudiating what is obsolete, of reintroducing candor and trust around what is necessary? And if not, who is there in the opposition willing and able to do the job?

# VIETNAM: THE FINAL DECEPTIONS

**RICHARD A. FALK**

After fifteen years of continuous American involvement in the war for control of Southern Vietnam, one's first impulse is to breathe a sigh of relief that this ugliest chapter in American history is at last at an end. There is a further impulse to join the Administration in its plea that we forgo recriminations by leaving the task of assessing our experience in Vietnam to historians and, instead, marshal the energies of America to meet the mounting challenges both at home and abroad that threaten soon to engulf this nation in economic, political and ecological woes.

And yet it seems too soon to give way to these impulses. For one thing, there is still much important unfinished business left over from the war:

—The extension of an unconditional amnesty to those young Americans who are still suffering for their acts of opposition to the war (i.e., draft resisters, deserters, recipients of less than honorable discharges).

—The extension of large-scale humanitarian and reconstruction aid to all of Indochina through the medium of international institutions and private relief agencies.

—The improvement of facilities for all those Americans wounded in body or mind by the experience of combat, as well as an absolute national commitment to find secure and appropriate jobs for every veteran of Vietnam.

In my view, a serious commitment to this three-part program by our national political leadership could help clear the domestic atmosphere and, perhaps, restore the national confidence required to face the tasks of the future.

Unfortunately, our present leadership does not yet appear inclined to move in this direction. The spirit of reconciliation requires more than amnesia. It requires a vision that transcends the controversies of the past, coupled with integrity about acknowledging how and why the war ended as it did. President Ford and Secretary Kissinger have, up to this very hour, dealt falsely with the last stage of the war in Vietnam. The American people have once again been misled, as they have been on so many other occasions in the past decade and a half. The collapse of Saigon is alternatively blamed on North Vietnamese violations of the Paris agreements, on Soviet and Chinese military aid to North Vietnam in excess of what we gave to South Vietnam and on a Congress that failed to send Saigon what it needed to survive militarily. These assorted accusations convey a set of almost totally false impressions.

The most important distortion is the charge, made repeatedly by Ford and Kissinger, that the Paris agreements collapsed because of actions by the other side. The liberal press has largely supported the Administration's contentions. The issue as to who is responsible for violating the Paris agreements is not a merely academic matter; it influences the public mood in America, and indirectly bears on such questions as reconstruction aid, amnesty and

*Richard Falk, Albert G. Milbank professor of international law and practice, Princeton University, is editor of* The Vietnam War and International Law *(in three volumes), issued by Princeton University Press.*

postwar diplomatic relations between the United States and Indochina. As long as it remains credible to blame the other side for resuming warfare after the negotiated cease-fire in 1973, it is plausible to remain self-righteous about the American role in the final phase of the war and to maintain a hostile and aloof posture toward the new governments in Indochina. Therefore, it is crucial to correct the false account that has so far been impressed on the public mind by the distortions of our official institutions.

The Paris agreements had two parts: the first, an agreement that the United States would stop bombing and mining Vietnam in exchange for the release of American POWs held by Hanoi; the second, a bargain to establish a cease-fire in South Vietnam in exchange for a political process that gave some promise of settling the struggle to control South Vietnam. I believe that up to October 1972 Kissinger was sincere in negotiating this bargain, but that he underestimated Nguyen Van Thieu's opposition to the second part of the bargain as well as the leverage that Thieu could exert in Washington by simply withholding his signature. Because the North Vietnamese were determined to link both sections of the agreement, Thieu's refusal to sign meant that the first part, the part Washington cared about, would not be carried out. How, then, were Kissinger and Nixon to get Thieu to sign the Paris agreement despite his implacable and ill-disguised opposition to its explicit terms? Virtually all subsequent events flowed from this central dilemma.

The answer to this key question can be formulated along these lines: in the weeks after October 1972 Kissinger and Nixon entered into a parallel set of secret understandings with Thieu that nullified the obligations stipulated by the public agreement on the table at Paris. These secret understandings appear to have included the following elements:

—Carpet bombing of the Hanoi-Haiphong area in December 1972.

—Massive military aid to Saigon just before and after signing the Paris agreement.

—Assurances that Washington would not press Saigon to carry out its obligations under part two of the Paris bargain, namely, to release political prisoners [Art. 8(c)], establish political freedoms [Art. 11], create a tripartite National Council of Concord and Reconciliation [Art. 12(a)] and organize general elections to select a permanent government for South Vietnam [Art. 9(b) and 12(b)].

—A pledge that the United States would reintervene directly in the event of a North Vietnamese offensive (this pledge is substantiated by the Nixon-Thieu correspondence).

—Assurances that after the Paris signing the Provisional Revolutionary Government of South Vietnam (PRG) would again be treated by Washington as the "Vietcong" and that Saigon would again be regarded as the sole legitimate government of South Vietnam.

The reintervention pledge made to Thieu was, perhaps, the most flagrant undertaking by the United States in violation of the Paris agreement. In Article 4 the United States had accepted a unilateral commitment formulated as follows: "The United States will not continue its military involvement or intervene in the internal affairs of South Vietnam." It is significant that the terms of Article 4 were neither reciprocal nor conditional. North Vietnam accepted no comparable obligation toward South Vietnam, nor was the American pledge conditioned on North Vietnamese compliance. Yet, anticipating a violation of the Paris agreement, Nixon gave official assurances to Thieu. In his letter of November 14, 1972 he writes: "You have my absolute assurance that if Hanoi fails to abide by the terms of this agreement it is my intention to take swift and severe retaliatory action." And then again in Nixon's letter of January 5, 1973: ". . . we will respond with full force should the settlement be violated by North Vietnam."

Such secret assurances in the form of letters between heads of state constitute an "Executive agreement" binding on the government. The fact that this secret agreement with Saigon contravenes the public agreement previously negotiated with the North Vietnamese is decisive on the issue of bad faith in Washington. President Ford's claim of "Executive privilege" as the basis for withholding the full exchange between Thieu and Nixon demonstrates that the ghost of Watergate still stalks the land. But even within its own terms Nixon's published letters projected into the future the kind of unilateralism that had led us into Vietnam in the first place. Even if there had been no absolute nonintervention pledge written into the Paris agreement, the terms of Nixon's reintervention pledge was premised on violations by North Vietnam. But who was to decide what constitutes a violation, or the identity of the violator? Clearly, Nixon had in mind any effective use of military power by the other side. But suppose, as was the case, that Saigon resumed the war first and the other side reacted? Or suppose, again as actually happened, that the other side reluctantly abandoned the cease-fire when it became clear that the political provisions of the agreement had been totally repudiated by Saigon with the acquiescence of Washington? In such a situation, it is self-serving in the extreme to regard North Vietnam as the violator of the Paris agreement, but that is precisely the interpretation our leaders have been disseminating in recent weeks.

An impartial judgment as to who is responsible for the breakdown of the Paris agreements is not likely to be made at an official level. The ten governments that guaranteed the agreements would find it "academic" to pass judgment at this point, and would undoubtedly be unable, for political reasons, to reach an agreement among themselves. Given the delicacy of his role, the Secretary-General of the United Nations, in whose presence the Act of Guaranty was made at Paris on March 2, 1973, would be unwilling to assess legal responsibility, however clear the legal situation. Nevertheless, the conclusions seem self-evident—before the Paris agreements took effect, Washington reached an understanding with Saigon that was incompatible with the express undertakings and which assured Saigon that it would be protected by the military might of the United States even if South Vietnam defied the political bargain.

The North Vietnamese and the PRG saw the Paris agreements as a great step toward victory because they felt sure that they would prevail in the anticipated political competition. Correspondents visiting PRG territory after January 1973 reported that the Paris agreements were venerated second only to Ho Chi Minh. PRG and North Vietnamese forces held back during most of 1973 and even

accepted losses of territory when, after the Paris signing, Saigon launched a land, sea and air offensive that recaptured as many as 400 hamlets held by the PRG. What the North Vietnamese did do, recalling their bitter experience with the 1954 Geneva accords, was strengthen their logistical capacity to revive the war in the South, should Saigon continue to repudiate the political bargain and the United States do nothing to insure its implementation. In 1975, shortly after the so-called "decent interval," the North Vietnamese-PRG launched their offensive. The results exceeded all expectations when the North's concerted drive overran the Saigon military establishment, despite the latter's military edge, total control of the air and relatively short supply lines. Due to corruption and weak morale, the Saigon military—with a few exceptions—had neither the will nor the capability to resist. To say that the North Vietnamese were violating the Paris agreements is almost beside the point. Given Saigon's refusal to carry out the political bargain, on what basis could the cease-fire rest, short of an absurd expectation that Hanoi and the PRG would make a unilateral renunciation of force, while Saigon went on with the war and political repression? In truth, because of Congressional action, probably combined with Executive ambivalence, the Administration failed to carry out either the *open* agreement it had signed in Paris, or the *secret* understandings negotiated with Thieu. In effect, once American POWs were safely home, our policy was basically that of disappointing the reasonable expectations held by both our adversaries in Hanoi and our "friends" in Saigon, thus demonstrating our pervasive indifference to the well-being of Vietnam.

On the relative amount of military aid given to both sides, figures are hard to get, but according to the Senate Foreign Relations Committee, basing its sources on the "U.S. intelligence community," the combined Chinese-Soviet military aid to North Vietnam was $300 million in 1973 and $400 million in 1974. In contrast, the United States gave South Vietnam $2.2 billion worth of military aid for fiscal year 1973, $937 million for fiscal year 1974, $700 million for fiscal year 1975. And this does not include the value of the aid given around the time of the Paris signing.

Concerning Congressional reluctance during the last weeks of conflict to authorize military assistance to Saigon requested by the Administration, there seems no serious reason to believe that an additional few hundred million dollars would have made any difference. Without the actual presence of the American military machine, Saigon, on its own, had never stopped an offensive by the other side.

This review of the facts enables us now to interpret the ending of the war in Vietnam. There seems little doubt that the North Vietnamese scored an epic victory, surely the greatest triumph by an underdog in modern warfare. This triumph should be understood mainly as a heroic phase of the anti-colonial movement: Vietnam, finally, belongs to the Vietnamese. What will happen next is still uncertain, but it is hard to imagine that even "worst case" possibilities could approach the agony of these last fifteen years.

It is not too late for Americans to learn why we should have never helped the French in the early 1950s and why we could never make a positive contribution by bringing our military power to bear on Indochina. It is disappointing that our leaders and media are so slow to draw these conclusions. And it is discouraging that not even our students are moved to celebrate the coming of peace to Vietnam.

Struggle against official American policies toward the Third World is still needed. Disclosures of the CIA role in "destabilizing" Allende's government in Chile or of official Washington opposition to moderate socialism in Portugal suggest that the men who brought us Vietnam have, at most, merely changed their tactics. Our policy makers seem no less counterrevolutionary in 1975 than they did in 1960, and so we can expect a host of efforts around the world to do quietly and effectively what we did so clumsily and unsuccessfully in Vietnam. In high Washington circles, there is even present a sly admiration for "the Prague model," i.e., the brutally effective Soviet intervention of 1968 in Czechoslovakia. Only if American public opinion is informed and vigilant can we reorient our foreign policy toward the sort of values we proclaim for our own society.                                                                                    □

# Civil War Panel

RICHARD J. BARNET, Director, Institute for Policy Studies

THOMAS EHRLICH, Associate Professor of Law, Stanford Law School

RICHARD A. FALK, Chairman, Civil War Panel; Milbank Professor of International Law and Practice, Princeton University

TOM J. FARER, Professor of Law, Rutgers Law School

G. W. HAIGHT, Member of New York Bar

ELIOT D. HAWKINS, Member of New York Bar

BRUNSON MacCHESNEY, Professor of Law, Northwestern University; former President of the American Society of International Law

JOHN NORTON MOORE, Professor of Law, University of Virginia School of Law; Chairman, National Security Council Interagency Task Force on the Law of the Sea

STEPHEN SCHWEBEL, Executive Director of the American Society of International Law and Professor of International Law at the School of Advanced International Studies, The Johns Hopkins University; former Assistant Legal Adviser of the Department of State

LOUIS B. SOHN, Bemis Professor of International Law, Harvard University.

JOHN R. STEVENSON, Legal Adviser, United States Department of State; former President of the American Society of International Law

HOWARD J. TAUBENFELD, Professor of Law, Southern Methodist University

BURNS H. WESTON, Associate Professor of Law, University of Iowa

# Contributors

RAOUL BERGER, Professor of Law, Harvard University

CHARLES N. BROWER, Acting Legal Adviser, U.S. Department of State

ABRAM CHAYES, Professor of Law, Harvard University

HAMILTON DESAUSSURE, Associate Professor of Law, University of Akron

RICHARD A. FALK, Milbank Professor of International Law and Practice, Princeton University

TOM J. FARER, Professor of Law, Rutgers Law School, Camden, New Jersey

EDWIN BROWN FIRMAGE, Associate Professor of Law, University of Utah

ROBERT G. GARD, JR., Brigadier General, GS, U.S. Army

L. C. GREEN, University Professor, University of Alberta

STANLEY HOFFMAN, Professor of Government, Harvard University

T. ISRAEL, Research Scholar, Jawaharlal Nehru University, New Delhi, India

MICHAEL KREPON, Legislative Assistant to Congressman Floyd V. Hicks

HOWARD S. LEVIE, Professor of Law, St. Louis University

CHARLES A. LOFGREN, Professor of History, Claremont Men's College

DONALD W. MCNEMAR, Assistant Professor of Government, Dartmouth College

JOHN NORTON MOORE, Professor of Law, University of Virginia School of Law; Chairman, National Security Council Interagency Task Force on the Law of the Sea

JORDAN J. PAUST, Associate Professor of Law, University of Houston

PERRY L. PICKERT, Fletcher School of Law and Diplomacy

M. S. RAJAN, Professor of International Organization, Jawaharlal Nehru University, New Delhi, India

EUGENE V. ROSTOW, Sterling Professor of Law and Public Affairs, Yale University

WALDEMAR A. SOLF, Acting Chief, International Affairs Division, Office of the Judge Advocate General, Department of the Army

PHILIPPA STRUM, Associate Professor of Political Science, Brooklyn College of the City University of New York

TELFORD TAYLOR, Professor of Law, Columbia University Law School

ROBERT W. TUCKER, Professor of Political Science, The Johns Hopkins University

TRAN VAN DINH, Institute of Pan-African Studies, Temple University

DON WALLACE, JR., Professor of Law, Georgetown University

SCOTT J. WENNER, New York University School of Law

ARTHUR H. WESTING, Professor of Biology, Windham College

# Permissions*

JOHN NORTON MOORE, "Law and National Security." Reprinted by permission of the author and publisher from *Foreign Affairs*, 51, 1973, 408-421

EDWIN BROWN FIRMAGE, "Law and the Indochina War." Reprinted by permission of the author and publisher from *Utah Law Review*, 1, 1974, 1-24

M. S. RAJAN and T. ISRAEL, "The United Nations and the Conflict in Vietnam." Reprinted by permission of the authors and publisher from *International Studies*, 12, 1973, 511-540

JOHN NORTON MOORE, "Ratification of the Geneva Protocol on Gas and Bacterial Warfare." Reprinted by permission of the author and publisher from *University of Virginia Law Review*, 58, 1972, 420-509

MICHAEL KREPON, "Weapons Potentially Inhumane." Reprinted by permission of the author and publisher from *Foreign Affairs*, 52, 1974, 595-611

ARTHUR H. WESTING, "Proscription of Ecocide." Reprinted by permission of the author and publisher from *Bulletin of the Atomic Scientists*, 30, 1974, 24-27

RICHARD A. FALK, "Environmental Warfare and Ecocide." Reprinted by permission of the author and publisher from *Bulletin of Peace Proposals*, 173, 1973, 1-17

HAMILTON DESAUSSURE, "The Laws of Air Warfare: Are There Any?" Reprinted by permission of the author and publisher from *International Lawyer*, 5, 1971, 527-548

RICHARD A. FALK, "International Law Aspects of Repatriation of Prisoners of War during Hostilities." Reprinted by permission of the author and publisher from *American Journal of International Law*, 67, 1973, 465-478

HOWARD S. LEVIE, "International Law Aspects of Repatriation of Prisoners of War during Hostilities." Reprinted by permission of the

* Permissions are listed to correspond to the sequence of materials included in this volume.

author and publisher from *American Journal of International Law*, 67, 1973, 693-710

RICHARD A. FALK, "Correspondence." Reprinted by permission of the author and publisher from *American Journal of International Law*, 68, 1974, 104-106

TOM J. FARER, ROBERT G. GARD, JR., TELFORD TAYLOR, "Vietnam and The Nuremberg Principles." Reprinted by permission of the authors and publisher from *Rutgers-Camden Law Journal*, 5, 1973, 1-58

WALDEMAR A. SOLF, "A Response to Telford Taylor's 'Nuremberg and Vietnam: An American Tragedy.' " Reprinted by permission of the author and publisher from *Akron Law Review*, 5, 1972, 43-68

JORDAN J. PAUST, "After My Lai." Reprinted by permission of the author and publisher from *Texas Law Review*, 50, 1971, 6-34

RICHARD A. FALK and EUGENE V. ROSTOW, "The Justness of the Peace." Reprinted by permission of the authors and publisher from *American Journal of International Law*, 67, 1973, 258-271

TRAN VAN DINH, "Vietnam 1974." Reprinted by permission of the author and publisher from *Pacific Community*, 5, 1974, 435-444

PHILIPPA STRUM, "The Supreme Court and the Vietnamese War." Printed by permission of the author and the American Political Science Association

CHARLES A. LOFGREN, "War-Making Under the Constitution." Reprinted by permission of the author and publisher from *Yale Law Journal*, 81, 1972, 672-702

RAOUL BERGER, "War-making By the President." Reprinted by permission of the author and publisher from *University of Pennsylvania Law Review*, 121, 1971, 29-86

DON WALLACE, JR. "The War-Making Powers." Reprinted by permission of the author and publisher from *Cornell Law Review*, 57, 1972, 719-776

SCOTT J. WENNER, "The Indochina War Cases in the United States Court of Appeals for the Second Circuit." Reprinted by permission of the author and publisher from *New York University Journal of International Law and Politics*, 7, 1974, 137-161

EUGENE V. ROSTOW, "Great Cases Make Bad Law." Reprinted by permission of the author and publisher from *Texas Law Review*, 50, 1972, 833-900

ROBERT W. TUCKER, "Vietnam: The Final Reckoning." Reprinted by permission of the author and publisher from *Commentary*, May 17, 1975, 27-34

STANLEY HOFFMAN, "The Sulking Giant." Reprinted by permission of the author and publisher from *The New Republic*, May 3, 1975, 15-17

RICHARD A. FALK, "Vietnam: The Final Deceptions." Reprinted by permission of the author and publisher from *The Nation*, May 17, 1975, 582-584

# Index